GLOBAL MARKETING MANAGEMENT

GLOBAL MARKETING MANAGEMENT

SECOND EDITION

Masaaki Kotabe
Temple University

Kristiaan Helsen
Hong Kong University of Science and Technology

JOHN WILEY & SONS, INC.

NEW YORK / CHICHESTER / WEINHEIM
BRISBANE / SINGAPORE / TORONTO

ACQUISITIONS EDITOR   Jeff Marshall
MARKETING MANAGER   Jessica Garcia
PRODUCTION EDITOR   Robin Factor/Ken Santor
COVER DESIGNER   Joyce Thomas
PHOTO EDITOR   Hilary Newman
PHOTO RESEARCHER   Elyse Rieder
ILLUSTRATION COORDINATOR   Sandra Rigby
COVER PHOTO: © William Whitehurst/The Stock Market

This book was set in Times Roman by Progressive Information Technologies and printed and bound by R.R. Donnelley/Willard. The cover was printed by Phoenix Color Corporation.

This book is printed on acid-free paper.∞

The paper in this book was manufactured by a mill whose forest management programs include sustained yield harvesting of its timberlands. Sustained yield harvesting principles ensure that the numbers of trees cut each year does not exceed the amount of new growth.

Library of Congress Cataloging in Publication Data:
Kotabe, Masaaki.
   Global marketing management/Masaaki Kotabe, Kristiaan Helsen.—2nd ed.
      p. cm.
   Includes bibliographical references and index.
   ISBN 0-471-37289-7 (cloth: alk. paper)
      1. Export marketing—Management. 2. International business enterprises—Management.
   I. Helsen, Kristiaan. II. Title.
   HF1416 .K68 2000
   658.8'48—dc21   00-043585

L.C. Call no.   Dewey Classification No.   L.C. Card No.
ISBN 0-471-37289-7

Printed in the United States of America

10 9 8 7 6 5 4 3 2 1

ABOUT THE AUTHORS

Masaaki "Mike" Kotabe holds the Washburn Chair of International Business and Marketing, and is Director of Research at the Institute of Global Management Studies at the Fox School of Business and Management at Temple University. Prior to joining Temple University in 1998, he was Ambassador Edward Clark Centennial Endowed Fellow and Professor of Marketing and International Business at the University of Texas at Austin. Dr. Kotabe also served as the Vice President of the Academy of International Business in the 1997–98 period. He received his Ph.D. in Marketing and International Business at Michigan State University. Dr. Kotabe teaches international marketing, global sourcing strategy (R&D, manufacturing, and marketing interfaces), and Japanese business practices at the undergraduate and MBA levels and theories of international business at the Ph.D. level. He has lectured widely at various business schools around the world, including Austria, Germany, Finland, Brazil, Colombia, Mexico, Japan, Korea, Indonesia, and Turkey. For his research, he has worked closely with leading companies such as AT&T, NEC, Nissan, Philips, Sony, and Ito-Yokado (parent of 7-Eleven stores). Dr. Kotabe currently serves as advisor to the United Nations' and World Trade Organization's Executive Forum on National Export Strategies.

Dr. Kotabe has written many scholarly publications. His research work has appeared in such journals as the *Journal of International Business Studies, Journal of Marketing, Strategic Management Journal,* and *Academy of Management Journal.* His books include *Global Sourcing Strategy: R&D, Manufacturing, Marketing Interfaces* (1992), *Japanese Distribution System* (1993), *Anticompetitive Practices in Japan* (1996), *MERCOSUR and Beyond* (1997), *Trends in International Business: Critical Perspectives* (1998), and *Marketing Management* (2001).

He is the Associate Editor of the *Journal of International Business Studies.* He serves on the editorial boards of the *Journal of Marketing,* the *Journal of International Marketing,* the *Journal of World Business,* the *Journal of Business Research,* the *Latin American Economic Abstracts,* and the *Thunderbird International Business Review.* He also serves as an Advisor to the Institute of Industrial Policy Studies (IPS) *National Competitiveness Report.*

In a recent issue of *Journal of Teaching in International Business* in 1997, Dr. Kotabe was ranked the most prolific international marketing researcher in the world in the last ten years. He has been recently elected a Fellow of the Academy of International Business for his lifetime contribution to international business research and education. He is also an elected member of the New York Academy of Sciences.

Kristiaan Helsen has been an Associate Professor of Marketing at the Hong Kong University of Science and Technology (HKUST) since 1995. Prior to joining HKUST, he was on the faculty of the University of Chicago for five years. He has lectured at Nijenrode University (Netherlands), Purdue University, the Catholic University of Lisbon, and CEIBS (Shanghai). Dr. Helsen received his Ph.D. in Marketing at the Wharton School of the University of Pennsylvania.

His research areas include promotional strategy, competitive strategy, and hazard rate modeling. His articles have appeared in journals such as *Marketing Science*, *Journal of Marketing*, *Journal of Marketing Research*, and *European Journal of Operations Research*, among others. Dr. Helsen is on the editorial boards of the *International Journal of Research in Marketing* and the *Journal of Marketing*.

PREFACE

THREE FUNDAMENTAL ISSUES ADDRESSED ◆ ◆ ◆ ◆ ◆ ◆
IN THE SECOND EDITION

We received quite a few letters and e-mails from instructors around the world who used our first edition of *Global Marketing Management*, with three questions. The *first* inquiry is when the book would be translated into such languages as Chinese, Spanish, and Portuguese, among other languages. The Chinese translation was published in late 1998. The Portuguese version came out in October 1999. Japanese and Spanish translations are also well under way. Our book has become truly global as it is read not only in the English-speaking regions of the world but also in countries where instruction is in various other languages.

The *second* inquiry is whether we could upload on our textbook website our views on the recent Asian financial crisis and marketing under the euro, a new currency, in the European Union. Up until the mid-1990s, we were pretty certain that the Asian economy would grow at a fairly fast pace, as it had done in the last 30 years. However, to everyone's surprise, the Asian economic miracle was brought to a screeching halt by the region's financial crisis toward the end of 1998. The ramifications of the Asian financial crisis are not limited to Asian countries and their trading partners. Another epoch-making event was the introduction of a common European currency, known as the euro, on January 1, 1999. Many pundits expected a gradual evolutionary development toward the unification of the European Union. To address these issues, we added an update to our book in 1999. Now in this second edition, we have fully incorporated the issues on marketing implications of the Asian financial crisis and marketing in Euro-Land.

The *third* inquiry is more or less the question that many instructors started asking themselves: How does the revolutionary growth of the Internet and electronic commerce (e-commerce) affect the way we do business internationally? This is a new phenomenon that we need to have a careful look at. Everyone seems to believe that business transactions will be faster and more global early on. And it is generally true. However, the more deeply we have examined this issue, the more convinced we have become that certain things will not change, or could even become more local as a result of the globalization that the Internet and e-commerce bestows on us. For example, many more peoples around the world are trying to emphasize cultural and ethnic differences—as well as accept those differences—than ever before. Just think about how many new countries are being born around the world as well as regional unifications taking place at the same time. Another example is that while e-commerce promotion on the Internet goes global, product delivery may need to be fairly local in order to address local competition and exchange rate fluctuations as well as the complexities of international physical distribution (export declarations, tariffs, and non-tariff barriers). In this second edition, we have incorporated issues surrounding the Internet and e-commerce in all the chapters where they are relevant.

Indeed, the changes we observed in the last few years of the 1990s are more than extraordinary. In our preface to the first edition of this book, we began by stating:

> "Markets have become truly global. If you stand still in your domestic market, you will likely be trampled by competitors from around the world. As one globe-trotting executive put it, 'If you don't act right now, somebody else will always do it for you at your expense . . . and quickly.' This book is designed to portray this competitive urgency and present how executives should design and execute marketing strategies to optimize their market performance on a global basis."

We practiced what we stated. It was a lot of work. But it was well worth the effort to hear so many favorable comments that satisfied readers expressed to us.

In the second edition of our book, we emphasize the enormous changes that have taken, and are taking, place as we speak. We incorporated an entirely new chapter (Chapter 19) that looks at the interface between the Internet and international marketing. We have added many examples that have occurred in the last few short, but epoch-making, years. However, we do not sacrifice logical depth in favor of brand-new examples.

We strongly believe that case studies provide students not only with lively discussions of what goes on with many companies but also with in-depth understanding of many marketing-related concepts and tools as used by those companies. In this revision, we added many new cases as well as kept several cases from the first edition voted as *favorites* by our textbook users and their students. We have a total of 23 cases to go with this edition. The cases represent many products and services and many regions and countries as well as many nationalities. Ten of them are included in the book itself, and the rest are placed on the textbook website for easy download.

Many users of the first edition commented that while our book is academically rigorous and conceptually sound, it is full of lively examples that students can easily identify with in order to drive important points across. We combine the academic rigor and relevance (and fun of reading) of materials to meet both undergraduate and MBA educational requirements. We keep this tradition in our second edition.

◆ ◆ ◆ ◆ ◆ ◆ OUR PEDAGOGICAL ORIENTATION

Marketing in the global arena is indeed a very dynamic discipline. Today, there are many international or global marketing management books vying for their respective niches in the market. It is a mature market. As you will learn in our book, in a mature market, firms tend to focus closely—or maybe, too closely—on immediate product features for sources of differentiation and may inadvertently ignore the fundamental changes that may be re-shaping the industry. Often, those fundamental changes come from outside the industry. The same logic applies to the textbook market. Whether existing textbooks are titled international marketing or global marketing, they continue to be bound by the traditional bilateral (inter-national) view of competition. While any new textbook has to embrace the traditional coverage of existing textbooks, we intend to emphasize the multilateral (global) nature of marketing throughout our book.

We have seen textbooks replacing the word, "international," with "global." Such a change amounts to a repackaging of an existing product we often see in a mature product market, and it does not necessarily make a textbook globally oriented. We need some paradigm shift to accomplish the task of adding truly global dimensions and realities to a textbook. You might ask, "What fundamental changes are needed for a paradigm shift?" and then, "Why do we need fundamental changes to begin with?"

Our answer is straightforward. Our ultimate objective is to help you prepare for the 21st Century and become an effective manager overseeing global marketing activities in an increasingly competitive environment. You may or may not choose marketing for your career. If you pursue a marketing career, what you will learn in our book will not only have direct relevance but also help you understand how you, as a marketing manager, can affect other business functions for effective corporate performance on a global basis. If you choose other functional areas of business for your career, then our book will help you understand how you could work effectively with marketing people for the same corporate goal.

We believe that our pedagogical orientation not only embraces the existing stock of useful marketing knowledge and methods but also sets itself apart from the competition in a number of fundamental ways, as follows:

Global Orientation

As we indicated at the outset, the term, "global," epitomizes the competitive pressure and market opportunities from around the world and the firm's need to optimize its market performance on a global basis. Whether a company operates domestically or across national boundaries, it can no longer avoid the competitive pressure and market opportunities. For optimal market performance, the firm should also be ready and willing to take advantage of resources on a global basis, and at the same time respond to different needs and wants of consumers. In a way, global marketing is a constant struggle with economies of scale and scope, needs of the firm, and its responsiveness and sensitivity to different market conditions. While some people call it a "glocal" orientation, we stay with the term, "global," to emphasize marketing flexibility on a global basis.

Let us take a look at a hypothetical U.S. company exporting finished products to Western Europe and Japan. Traditionally, this export phenomenon has been treated as a bilateral business transaction between a U.S. company and foreign customers. However, in reality, to the executives of the U.S. company, this export transaction may be nothing more than the last phase of the company's activities they manage. Indeed, this company procures certain components from Japan and Mexico, other components from Malaysia, and also from its domestic sources in the United States, and assembles a finished product in its Singapore plant for export to Western Europe and Japan as well as back to the United States. Indeed, a Japanese supplier of critical components is a joint venture majority-owned by this American company, while a Mexican supplier has a licensing agreement with the U.S. company that provides most of the technical know-how. A domestic supplier in the

United States is in fact a subsidiary of a German company. In other words, this particular export transaction by the U.S. company involves a joint venture, a licensing agreement, subsidiary operation, local assembly, and R&D, all managed directly or indirectly by the U.S. company. And add the realities of market complexities. Think about how these arrangements could affect the company's decisions over product policy, pricing, promotion, and distribution channels.

Many existing textbooks have focused on each of these value-adding activities as if they could be investigated independently. Obviously, in reality, they are not independent of each other, and cannot be. We emphasize this multilateral realism by examining these value-adding activities as holistically as possible.

Interdisciplinary Perspective

To complement our global orientation, we will offer an interdisciplinary perspective in all relevant chapters. We are of the strong belief that you cannot become a seasoned marketing practitioner without an understanding of how other functional areas interface with marketing. The reverse is also true for non-marketing managers. Some of the exemplary areas in which such a broad understanding of the interface issues are needed are product innovation, designing for manufacturability, product/components standardization, and product positioning. In particular, Japanese competition has made us aware of the importance of these issues, and leading-edge business schools are increasingly adopting such an integrated approach to business education. Our book strongly reflects this state-of-the-art orientation.

Proactive Orientation

Market orientation is a fundamental philosophy of marketing. It is an organizational culture that puts customers' interest first in order to develop a long-term profitable enterprise. In essence, market orientation symbolizes the market-driven firm that is willing to constantly update its strategies using signals from the marketplace. Thus, marketing managers take market cues from the expressed needs and wants of customers. Consequently, the dominant orientation is that of a firm reacting to forces in the marketplace in order to differentiate itself from its competitors. This reactive "outside-in" perspective is reflected in the typical marketing manager's reliance on marketing intelligence, forecasting, and market research.

While not denying this traditional market orientation, we also believe that marketing managers should adopt an "inside-out" perspective and capabilities to shape or drive markets. This aspect of the link between strategic planning and marketing implementation has not been sufficiently treated in existing textbooks. For example, recent trends in technology licensing indicate that it is increasingly used as a conscious, proactive component of a firm's global product strategy. We believe that it is important for marketers to influence those actions of the firm which are some distance away from the customer in the value chain, because such actions have considerable influence on the size of the market and customer choice in intermediate and end product markets.

Cultural Sensitivity. A book could not be written devoid of its authors' background, expertise, and experiences. Our book represents an amalgam of our truly diverse backgrounds, expertise, and experiences across the North and South Americas, Asia, and Western and Eastern Europe. Given our upbringing and work experience in Japan and Western Europe, respectively, as well as our educational background in the United States, we have been sensitive not only to cultural differences and diversities but also to similarities.

Realistically speaking, there are more similarities than differences across many countries. In many cases, most of us tend to focus too much on cultural differences rather than similarities; or else, completely ignore differences or similarities. If you look only at cultural differences, you will be led to believe that country markets are uniquely different, thus requiring marketing strategy adaptations. If, on the other hand, you do not care about, or care to know about, cultural differences, you may be extending a culture-blind, ethnocentric view of the world. Either way, you may not benefit from the economies of scale and scope accruing from exploiting cultural similarities—and differences.

Over the years, two fundamental counteracting forces have shaped the nature of marketing in the international arena. The same counteracting forces have been revisited by many authors in such terms as "standardization vs. adaptation" (1960s), "globalization vs. localization" (1970s), "global integration vs. local responsiveness" (1980s), and most recently, "scale vs. sensitivity" (1990s). Terms have changed, but the quintessence of the strategic dilemma that multinational firms face today has not changed and will probably remain unchanged for years to come. However, they are no longer an either/or issue. Forward-looking, proactive firms have the ability and willingness to accomplish both tasks simultaneously. As we explain later in the text, Honda, for example, developed its Accord car to satisfy the universal customer needs for reliability, drivability, and comfort, but marketed it as a family sedan in Japan, as a commuter car in the United States, and as an inexpensive sports car in Germany, thereby addressing cultural differences in the way people of different nationalities perceive and drive what is essentially the same car.

With our emphasis on global and proactive orientations, however, we will share with you how to hone your expertise to be both culturally sensitive and able to see how to benefit from cultural similarities and differences.

We strongly believe that theory is useful to the extent it helps practices. And there are many useful theories in international marketing practices. Some of the practical theories are a logical extension of generic marketing theories you may have encountered in a marketing course. Others are, however, very much unique to the international environment.

Research Orientation

Many people believe—rather erroneously—that international or global marketing is just a logical extension of domestic marketing, and that if you have taken a generic marketing course, you would not need to learn anything international. The international arena is just like a Pandora's box. Once you move into the international arena, there are many more facts, concepts, and frameworks you need to learn than you ever thought of in order to become a seasoned marketing manager working globally. To assist you in acquiring this new knowledge, various theories provide you with the conceptual tools which enable you to abstract, analyze, understand, predict phenomena, and formulate effective decisions. Theories also provide you with an effective means to convey your logic to your peers and bosses with a strong, convincing power.

We also apply those theories in our own extensive international work, advising corporate executives, helping them design effective global strategies, and teaching our students at various business schools around the world. Our role as educators is to convey sometimes complex theories in everyday languages. Our effort is reflected well in our textbook. This leads to our next orientation.

Practical Orientation

Not only is this book designed to be user-friendly, but also it emphasizes practice. We believe in experiential learning and practical applications. Rote learning of facts, concepts, and theories is not sufficient. A good marketing manager should be able to put these to practice. We use many examples and anecdotes as well as our own observations and experiences to vividly portray practical applications. This book also contains real-life, lively cases so that you can further apply your newly acquired knowledge to practice, and experience for yourself what it takes to be an effective international marketing manager.

Therefore, this book has been written for both upper-level undergraduate and MBA students who wish to learn practical applications of marketing and related logic and subsequently work internationally. Although we overview foundation materials in this book, we expect that students have completed a basic marketing course.

Internet Implications

As we stated earlier, we extensively address the implications of the Internet and e-commerce in global marketing activities. E-commerce is very promising, but various environmental differences–particularly cultural and legal as well as consumer needs differences–are bound to prevent it from becoming an instantaneous free-wheeling tool for global marketing. What we need to learn is how to manage *online scale and scope economies* and *offline sensitivities to different market requirements*. We try our best to make you become Internet-savvy: these issues are addressed in all the chapters where relevant. In particular, Chapter 19 provides an in-depth analysis of global marketing issues in the age of the Internet. We admit that there are many more unknowns than knowns about the impact of the Internet on global marketing activities. That is why we point out areas in which the Internet is likely to affect the way we do business and have you think seriously about the imminent managerial issues that you will have to be dealing with upon graduation. Chapter 19 serves not as an epilogue to the second edition but as a prologue to your exciting career ahead of you.

Not only is this book designed to be user-friendly, but also it emphasizes practice. We believe in Instructor Support Materials. To accomplish our stated goals and orientations, we have made a major effort to provide the instructor and the student with practical theories and their explanations using examples, anecdotes, and cases to maximize the student's learning experience. Some of the specific teaching features are:

- **Global Perspectives**, which appear in every chapter, to bring concrete examples from the global marketing environment into the classroom. They are designed to highlight some of the hottest global topics that students should be aware of and may actually act on in their career. The instructor can use these inserts to exemplify theory or use them as mini-cases for class discussion.

- **Cases** that are designed to challenge students with real and current business problems and issues. They require in-depth analysis and discussion of various topics covered in the chapters and help students experience how the knowledge they have gained can be applied in real-life situations. There are a total of 23 cases covering various aspects of marketing situations as well as products, regions, and nationalities of firms. Ten of them are included in the text and the rest are placed on the textbook website for easy download.

- **Video Cases** provide contemporary, yet fundamental, business problems and issues facing the international marketing managers today. These Video Cases may be used effectively as lively "short cases" or "vignettes" for class discussions.

- **Maps** which provide economic geography of the world. Students should be knowledgeable about where various economic resources are available and how they shape the nature of trade and investment and thus the nature of global competition. Global marketing could not be appreciated devoid of understanding economic geography.

- **Review Questions** which help students test themselves with, and summarize, the facts, concepts, theories, and other chapter materials in their own words. We strongly believe that by doing so, students will gain an active working knowledge, rather than passive knowledge by rote learning.

- **Discussion Questions** which help students apply the specific knowledge they learned in each chapter to actual business situations. They are designed to serve as mini-cases. Most of the issues presented in these questions are acute problems facing multinational marketing managers and have been adopted from recent issues of leading business newspapers and magazines.

- **Information Sources for Global Marketing Management** are available on the Web at http://www.wiley.com/college/kotabe. This comprehensive list of sources includes not only published information compiled by various international agencies, governments, and corporations, but also various useful Web sites for accessing international business information on the Internet. A brief description is also provided about the types of information available from each information source.

- **The Instructor's Manual** that is designed provides major assistance to the instructor while allowing flexibility in the course scheduling and teaching emphasis. The materials in the manual include the following:
    a) Teaching Plans: Alternative teaching plans and syllabi are included to accommodate the instructor's preferred course structure and teaching schedules. Alternative teaching schedules are developed for the course to be taught in a semester format, on a quarter basis, or as an executive seminar.
    b) Discussion Guidelines: For each chapter, specific teaching objectives and guidelines are developed to help stimulate classroom discussion.
    c) Exercises Using Various Web Sites on the Internet: The explosion of information available on the Internet has changed the milieu for intelligence gathering for business decision making forever. Students need to be well versed in this new information technology. We strongly believe that actual hands-on use of Web site materials on the Internet for solving business problems will provide students with a systematic opportunity to learn how to find and how to use available information for competitive advantage.
    d) Test Bank: A test bank consists of short essay questions and multiple choice questions. This test bank is also computerized and available to adopters on IBM compatible computer diskettes.
    e) Power Point Slides: Available on the Web to assist the instructor in preparing presentation materials.
    f) Video Materials: As indicated earlier, videos provide for students' visualization of critical issues discussed in the cases as well as in the text itself.
    g) Home Page on the Web: Make sure to visit our Website **http://www.wiley.com/college/kotabe/** for useful instructional information.

Finally, we are delighted to share our teaching experience with you through this book. Our teaching experience is an amalgam of our own learning and knowledge gained through our continued discussion with our colleagues, our students, and our executive friends. We would also like to learn from you, the instructor and the students, who use our book. Not only do we wish that you can learn from our book but we also believe that there are many more things that we can learn from you. We welcome your sincere comments and questions. Our contact addresses are as follows:

Masaaki Kotabe
Ph. (215) 204-7704
e-mail: mkotabe@sbm.temple.edu

Kristiaan Helsen
Ph. (852) 2358-7720
e-mail: mkhel@ust.hk

ACKNOWLEDGMENTS

This book would not have ever materialized without guidance, assistance, and encouragement of many of our mentors, colleagues, students, and executives we have worked with and learned from over the years. We are truly indebted to each one of them. We also thank the many reviewers for their constructive comments and suggestions which helped us improve our argument and clarity and raise the quality of our book.

Preet S. Aulakh
Temple University

John R. Brooks
Houston Baptist University

Wendy Bryce
Western Washington University

Helen M. Caldwell
Providence College

Branko Cavarkapa
Eastern Connecticut State University

Peggy Cunningham
Queen's University, Kingston, Ontario

John Deighton
Harvard University

K. C. Dhawan
Concordia University, Montreal, Quebec

Sevging Eroglu
Georgia State University

P. Everett Ferguson
Iona College

James W. Gentry
University of Nebraska-Lincoln

Andrew C. Gross
Cleveland State University

Braxton Hinchly
University of Massachusetts-Lowell

Richard T. Hise
Texas A&M University

Alfred C. Holden
Fordham University

Lenard Huff
University of Hawaii

Dipak Jain
Northwestern University

Ann T. Kuzma
Mankato State University

D. Maheswaran
New York University

Dr. Carlos Ruy Martinez
Instituto Tecnologico y de Estudios Superiores de Monterrey

Martin Meyers
University of Wisconsin-Stevens Point

Chip Miller
Pacific Lutheran University

Janet Murray
City University of Hong Kong

Sukgoo Pak
University of Nebraska-Omaha

Thomas Ponzurick
West Virginia University

Daniel Rajaratnam
Baylor University

C. P. Rao
Old Dominion University

Thomas M. Rogers
University of Arkansas

Sunanda Sangwan
Aston University, Birmingham, UK

Carol K. Scarborough
Rutgers University

T. N. Somasundaram
University of San Diego

Scott Swan
College of William and Mary

Peter K. Tat
The University of Memphis

Janice E. Taylor
Miami University

Hildy Teegen
George Washington University

Kathy Frazier Winsted
Pace University, Pleasantville

Van R. Wood
Virginia Commonwealth University

The first co-author would like to extend thanks to his colleagues at Temple University and the University of Texas at Austin. In particular, Dean Moshe Porat at the Fox School of Business and Management at Temple is acknowledged for emphasizing international business education and research as the school's primary focus of excellence, providing enormous opportunities for this co-author to meet with leading practitioners/executives of international business and discuss those emerging issues that are shaping and reshaping the way business is conducted around the world. A good deal of credit also goes to Christine A. DeLalio (World Game Institute, Philadelphia) for having educated me with so many fascinating business examples from around the world throughout the revision process. At the University of Texas at Austin, Kate Gillespie kept this co-author informed of regional marketing issues, particularly, in emerging markets. Tomasz Lenartowicz provided "insider" insights into Latin American issues. Special thanks also go to several of the first co-author's past and current doctoral students. Aldor Lanctot (now with Dell Computer) and Arvind Sahay (now with London Business School) helped us with ever-changing technology and competitive issues in global marketing. Preet Aulakh (now with Temple University) provided intellectual insight, in particular, in the area of transaction cost argument and distribution channel management. Brad McBride (now with Instituto Tecnológico Autónomo de México) offered his expertise in managing in developing countries. Jaishanker Ganesh (now with his own consulting company) provided a critical review of marketing standardization/adaptation debate. Janet Y. Murray of City University of Hong Kong and Cleveland State University kindly volunteered to provide many valuable comments about factual and statistical details that eluded us.

The first co-author was traveling extensively throughout the revision process in 1998–2000. He would like to acknowledge Heikki Topi (Helsinki School of Economics and Business Administration, Helsinki, Finland), Jaime Ferrerosa (Pontificia Universidad Javeriana, Cali, Colombia); David McClain (University of Hawaii at Manoa), John Le Bourgeois (Temple University Japan, Tokyo, Japan); Esra Gencturk and Aysegül Özsomer (Koç University, Istanbul, Turkey); and Dong-Sung Cho (Seoul National University, Seoul, Korea) for providing him with their insight into recent developments in their respective regional economies. Maria Cecilia Coutinho de Arruda (Fundação Getúlio Vargas, São Paulo, Brazil) deserves a special credit for keeping me up-to-date with the market and financial environments of countries in the Southern Common Market (MERCOSUR) as well as for working on a Portuguese translation of our book. Another credit goes to Stephen Holden of Bond University, Australia for being extremely helpful in offering Australian perspectives.

The second co-author would like to extend his thanks to MBA students at the University of Chicago, Nijenrode University, Hong Kong University of Science and Technology, and MIM students at Thammassat University (Bangkok). Particularly Joe Giblin and Vincent Chan (Baxter) for assisting with two of the case studies and Wiebeke Vuursteen (now with Nestlé), Edmund Wong and Philip Cheung (now with IBM) for their help with some of the exhibits. He also acknowledges the valuable comments on Chapter 14 from Chris Beaumont and John Mackay, both with McCann-Erickson, Japan. Thanks are also due to the Executive MBA students at Purdue's AT&T/Lucent Technology program. A word of gratitude for their feedback and encouragement is given to two colleagues who spent their sabbatical at HKUST: Jerry Albaum (University of Oregon) and Al Shocker (University of Minnesota).

We would also like to thank some of the day-to-day "warriors" in the global marketing arena for sharing their insights and experiences with us, in particular: Doug Barrie (Wrigley Company), Mark Boersma (Blistex), Keith Alm (formerly Sara Lee), F.J. Thompson (Heineken), Monika Sturm (Siemens Hong Kong), Bill Hicks and Jim Austin (Baxter Healthcare), and Olivia Kan (formerly PepsiCo China).

A very special word of appreciation goes to the staff of John Wiley & Sons, Inc., particularly Brent Gordon and Jeff Marshall for their continued enthusiasm and support throughout the course of this project.

Finally and most importantly, we are deeply grateful to you, the professors, students, and professionals for using this book. We stand by our book, and sincerely hope that our book adds to your knowledge and expertise. We would also like to continuously improve our product in the future.

As we indicated in the Preface, we would like to hear from you as you are our valued customers. Thank you!

CONTENTS

GLOBALIZATION IMPERATIVE

1

CHAPTER OVERVIEW

1. WHY GLOBAL MARKETING IS IMPERATIVE
2. GLOBALIZATION OF MARKETS AND COMPETITION
3. EVOLUTION OF GLOBAL MARKETING
4. APPENDIX: THEORIES OF INTERNATIONAL TRADE AND THE MULTINATIONAL ENTERPRISE

Marketing products and services around the world, transcending national and political boundaries, is a fascinating phenomenon. The phenomenon, however, is not entirely new. Products have been traded across borders throughout recorded civilization, extending back beyond the Silk Road that once connected East with West from Xian to Rome. What is relatively new about the phenomenon, beginning with large U.S. companies in the 1950s and 1960s and with European and Japanese companies in the 1970s and 1980s, is the large number of companies with interrelated production and sales operations located around the world. The emergence of competitive European and Asian companies has given the role of global competition a touch of extra urgency and significance that you see almost daily in print media such as *The New York Times*, *Newsweek*, and *Fortune*, as well as TV media such as ABC, NBC, and CNN.

In this chapter, we will introduce you to the complex and constantly evolving realities of global marketing. The objective is to make you think beyond exporting and importing. As you will learn shortly, despite wide media attention, exporting and importing are a relatively small portion of what constitutes international business. We are not saying, however, that exporting and importing are not important. Total world trade volume in goods and services amounted to $6.5 trillion in 1998.[1]

---

[1]http://www.wto.org/wto/intltrad/internat.htm, accessed May 9, 2000.

The contractionary forces of the Asian financial crisis and falling commodity prices were, however, attenuated by the robustness of continued economic growth in the United States and strengthened demand in Western Europe. The world's five largest exporting countries are the United States ($700 billion), Germany ($560 billion), Japan ($390 billion), France ($320 billion), and Britain ($260 billion), collectively accounting for 42 percent of global trade.[2]

Large economies and large trading partners were located mostly in the **Triad Regions** of the world (North America, Western Europe, and Japan, collectively producing more than 80 percent of world GDP with 20 percent of the world's population) throughout much of the twentieth century.[3] However, in the next ten to twenty years, the greatest commercial opportunities are expected to be found increasingly in ten **big emerging markets** (BEMs)—the Chinese Economic Area (CEA: including China, Hong Kong region, and Taiwan), India, South Korea, Mexico, Brazil, Argentina, South Africa, Poland, Turkey, and the Association of Southeast Asian Nations (ASEAN: including Indonesia, Brunei, Malaysia, Singapore, Thailand, the Philippines, and Vietnam). An increasing number of competitors are also expected to originate from those emerging economies.

◆ ◆ ◆ ◆ ◆ ◆ WHY GLOBAL MAKETING IS IMPERATIVE

We frequently hear terms such as global markets, global competition, global technology, and global competitiveness. In the past, we heard similar words with *international* or *multinational* instead of *global* attached to them. Are these terms just fashionable concepts of the time without deep meanings? Or has something inherently changed?

First and fundamentally, domestic-market saturation in the industrialized parts of the world forced many companies to look for marketing opportunities beyond their national boundaries. The economic and population growths in developing countries also gave those companies an additional incentive to venture abroad. Now companies from emerging economies, such as Korea's Samsung and Hyundai and Mexico's Cemex and Grupo Modelo, have made inroads into the developed markets around the world.

Second, we believe something profound has indeed happened in our view of competition around the world. About twenty years ago, the world's greatest automobile manufacturers were General Motors, Ford, and Chrysler. Today, companies like Toyota, Honda, BMW, and DaimlerChrysler (a recent merger of Daimler-Benz and Chrysler), among others, stand out as competitive nameplates in the automobile market. Similarly, *personal computer* was almost synonymous with IBM, which dominated the PC business worldwide. Today, the computer market is crowded with Dell and Compaq from the United States, Toshiba and NEC from Japan, Acer from Taiwan, and so on. Color TVs were invented in the United States, but today it is almost impossible to find a color TV made by U.S. companies. Instead, foreign brands such as Sony, Panasonic, and Magnavox are in most homes in the United

---

[2]"A Survey of World Trade," *Economist* (October 3, 1998), pp. 1–38.
[3]Lowell Bryan, *Race for the World: Strategies to Build A Great Global Firm*, Boston, MA: Harvard Business School Press, 1999.

States. Even RCA and Zenith televisions are made overseas. Nike is a U.S. company with a truly all-American shoe brand, but its shoes are all made in foreign countries and exported to the United States. Burger King and Pillsbury (known for its Häagen-Dazs ice cream brand) are two American institutions owned and managed across the Atlantic Ocean by Diageo, a newly created company as a result of the merger of Britain's Grand Metropolitan PLC and Guinness PLC.

Third, another profound change in the last decade is the proliferation of the Internet and electronic commerce, or **e-commerce**. Who could have anticipated the success of Cisco, Qwest, Lucent, Netscape, AOL, Yahoo, Nokia, Ariba, Exodus, and Softbank? The Internet opened the gates for companies to sell direct-to-consumers easily across national boundaries. Many argue that e-commerce is less intimate than face-to-face retail, but it could actually provide more targeted demographic and psychographic information. Manufacturers that traditionally sell through the retail channel may benefit the most from e-commerce. Furthermore, customer information no longer is held hostage by the retail channel. Most important, the data allow for the development of relevant marketing messages aimed at important customers and loyal relationships on a global basis.[4] However, as presented in Global Perspective 1–1, the proliferation of e-commerce does not necessarily mean that global marketing activities are going culture- and human contact-free. Learning foreign languages could remain as important as ever.

An examination of the top one hundred largest companies in the world also vividly illustrates the profound changes in competitive milieu that we have seen in the past thirty years (see Exhibit 1–1). Of the top hundred largest industrial companies in the world, sixty-four were from the United States in 1970; in 1980 the number declined to forty-five companies. The latest figure came down to twenty-four in 1997 (not shown) and went back up to thirty-five in 1999. The number of Japanese companies in the top hundred has increased from eight in 1970 to twenty-four in 1999, almost a threefold increase. A similar increase has also been observed with French companies, from three in 1970 to ten in 1997. The relative decline in the number of U.S. companies in the top is reflected in the banking, insurance, and other services sectors, as well as in the manufacturing sectors. The current world economy has changed drastically from what it was merely a decade ago.

The changes observed in the past thirty years simply reflect that companies from other parts of the world have grown in size relative to those of the United States. In other words, today's environment is characterized by much more competition from around the world than in the past. As a result, many U.S. executives are feeling much more competitive urgency in product development, materials procurement, manufacturing, and marketing around the world. It does not necessarily mean that U.S. companies have lost their competitiveness, however. The robust economy in the United States since the late 1990s has fueled a strong comeback for many U.S. companies. On the other hand, many Asian, including Japanese, companies are still struggling with a deep recession wrought by the Asian financial crisis (see Chapter 3 for details).

The same competitive pressure equally applies to executives of foreign companies. For example, due to cost pressures in its home country, Hoechst, a German chemicals giant with annual revenues larger than those of Dow Chemical and

---

[4]Andrew Degenholtz, "E-Commerce Fueling the Flame for New Product Development," *Marketing News* (March 29, 1999), p. 18.

◆ ◆

$\mathcal{G}$LOBAL PERSPECTIVE 1–1

THE INTERNET WORLD AND CULTURAL AND HUMAN ASPECTS OF GLOBAL MARKETING

Would a typical mid-sized manufacturer in, for example, Taiwan, China, or Thailand enter into a strategic business relationship with companies and people that they only encounter through computerized interactions? The short answer is yes; they will enter into such relationships. However, we qualify our positive reply by adding that the initial courtship ritual must continue to have personal face-to-face, one-to-one, or what we feel is becoming a new "screen-to-screen" relationship dimension, just as with traditional business model.

However, after the initial mating ritual, you can and already do see tremendous transactional business-to-business activity in these countries. There is nothing to say that e-commerce can or should replace the human element in relationship building. In fact, e-commerce is a new form of personalized relationship building engaged in by even the highest context cultures. For example, eBay and other online auction companies have made electronic relationship and trust building the foundation of a successful business. Even in the eastern cultures, we see numerous gambling sites springing up where the only aspects of the relationship are related to anonymous e-commerce.

Creating the right Web site is the first critical step in developing the personal international business relationship. The ability to "connect" will be stilted unless the Web site makes the first connection based on sensitivity to the cross-cultural aspects of interface design, human factors, navigation currency, time and date conventions, localization, internationalization, and so on.

In the information technology sector one can look at Dell and Gateway, which both do very strong business in the Asia/Pacific region. The networking company, Cisco Systems, serves as an example of the morphing of electronic and personal relationships. Although it has done a tremendous job of building global relationships and partnerships on an in-country face-to-face level, almost 90 percent of its business (i.e., sales transactions) is conducted over the Web.

Has the Web replaced the need for the personal business courtship? Absolutely not. Has it added a new element to the same relationship after the bonds are formed? Most definitely. Will there be new electronic forms of relationship building that replace the old model of face-to-face in a karaoke bar? Yes, it is happening already. You could start with video/teleconferences in the boardroom on down to Microsoft NetMeeting using a mini-cam on the desktop.

Just think, one decade ago very few of us would hardly dream that most Web-enabled adolescents communicate more on AOL Instant Messenger than they do over the phone or in person. In ten years technology will give us HDTV screen quality with real-time audio and video bandwidth. This surely will not completely replace face-to-face interaction among global sellers and buyers. But it will certainly offer a viable substitute for those who grew up chatting online.

Source: Frank Cutitta, GINLIST@LIST.MSU.EDU, April 17, 1999.

Union Carbide combined, is de-Germanizing its operations by reducing its German work force to only 30 percent of its worldwide total, down from 70 percent three years earlier. It is beefing up its U.S. operations from less than 6 percent of its annual revenues to 40 percent by the year 2000.[5] As Mark Twain once wrote, "if you stand still, you could get run over." This analogy holds true in describing such competitive pressure in this era of global competition.

But competition is not the only force shaping global business today. Particularly in the past several years, many political and economic events have affected the nature of global business. The demise of the Soviet Union, the establishment of the

---

[5]Greg Steinmetz and Matt Marshall, "How a Chemicals Giant Goes About Becoming a Lot Less German," *Wall Street Journal* (February 18, 1997), pp. A1, A18; and www.hoechst.com, accessed August 30, 1999.

EXHIBIT 1-1
CHANGE IN THE WORLD'S 100 LARGEST
COMPANIES AND THEIR NATIONALITIES

Country	1970	1980	1990	1999*
United States	64	45	33	35
Japan	8	8	16	24
Germany	8	13	12	13
France	3	12	10	10
Switzerland	2	3	3	5
Netherlands	4	5	3	5
Britain	9	7	8	5
Italy	3	4	4	3
Belgium	0	1	1	1
Venezuela	0	1	1	0
China	0	0	0	1
South Korea	0	0	2	0
Spain	0	0	2	0
Sweden	0	0	2	0
Brazil	0	1	1	0
Mexico	0	1	1	0
Austria	0	0	1	0
Finland	0	0	1	0
South Africa	0	0	1	0
Canada	0	2	0	0
Australia	1	0	0	0
Total	102	103	102	102**

Source: Fortune, various issues up to 2000.

*Fortune 500 criteria changed to include services firms (including retailing and trading)
**Includes joint nationality of firms (joint nationality has been counted for both the countries), so the total may exceed 100.

European Union and the North American Free Trade Agreement, deregulation, and privatization of state-owned industries have also changed the market environments around the world. Furthermore, the emerging markets of Eastern Europe and the rapidly re-emerging markets of Southeast Asia contribute to an international climate.

The fluid nature of global markets and competition makes the study of global marketing not only interesting but also challenging and rewarding. The term *global* epitomizes both the competitive pressure and the expanding market opportunities all over the world. It does not mean, however, that all companies have to operate globally, as do IBM, Sony, Phillips, and ABB (Asea Brown Boveri), for example. Whether a company operates domestically or across national boundaries, it can no longer avoid competitive pressure from around the world. Competitive pressure also comes from competitors at home. When Weyerhaeuser, a forest products company headquartered in Seattle, Washington, began exporting newspaper rolls to Japan, it had to meet the exacting quality standard that Japanese newspaper publishers demanded—and it did. As a result, this Seattle company now boasts the best newspaper rolls, and it outperforms other domestic companies in the U.S. market as well. Even smaller firms could benefit from exacting foreign market

Globe-trotting companies are vying for customers' "mind share" in many parts of the world such as in Piccadilly Circus, London, England.

requirements. When Weaver Popcorn Co. of Van Buren, Indiana, started to export popcorn to Japan, Japanese distributors demanded better quality and less imperfections. This led to improvements in Weaver's processing equipment and product, which helped its domestic as well as international sales.[6] Therefore, even purely domestic companies that have never sold anything abroad cannot be shielded from international competitive pressure. The point is that when we come across the term *global*, we should be aware of both this intense competitive pressure and expanding market opportunities on a global basis.

◆ ◆ ◆ ◆ ◆ ◆ GLOBALIZATION OF MARKETS AND COMPETITION

When a country's per capita income is less than $10,000, much of the income is spent on food and other necessity items, and very little disposable income remains. However, once per capita income reaches $20,000 or so, the disposable portion of income increases dramatically because the part of the income spent on necessities does not rise nearly as fast as income increases. As a result, people around the world with per capita income of $20,000 and above have considerable purchasing power. With this level of purchasing power, people, irrespective of their nationality, tend to enjoy similar educational levels, academic and cultural backgrounds, lifestyles, and access to information. As these cultural and social dimensions begin to resemble each other in many countries, people's desire for material possessions, ways of spending leisure time, and aspirations for the future become increasingly similar. Even deeply rooted cultures have begun to converge.[7] As a result, you might find joggers wearing Nike shoes (an American product made in China) and listening to

---

[6]Doug LeDuc, "Overseas Markets Spur Growth for Van Buren, Ind.-Based Popcorn Maker," *The News-Sentinel* (April 19, 1999).

[7]For an excellent story about global cultural convergence, read "Global Culture" and "A World Together," *National Geographic*, 196 (August 1999), pp. 2–33.

Rammstein (a German rock group) or Madonna (an American pop singer) on a Sony Walkman (a Japanese product) in almost any city on Earth. Similarly, Yuppies (young, urban professionals) in Paris, Hong Kong, Osaka, and Chicago share a common lifestyle. They drive a BMW (a German car) to the office, listen to Emma Shapplin's Carmine Meo (a foreign CD purchased while on an overseas business trip), and use a Toshiba notebook computer (a Japanese product) at work. They call their colleagues with a Nokia cellular phone (a Finnish product), sign important documents with an exquisite Parker Pen (made by an ex-British, currently U.S.-headquartered company), and have a nice seafood buffet at Mövenpick (a Swiss restaurant chain) on a Friday. In the evenings, these people spend their spare time browsing around various Web sites using LookSmart search engine (an Australian Internet startup, now headquartered in San Francisco) on America Online (an American Internet provider) to do some "virtual" window shopping. The convergence of consumer needs in many parts of the world translates into tremendous business opportunities for companies willing to risk venturing abroad.

The United States, which enjoys one of the highest per-capita income levels in the world, has long been the most important single market for both foreign and domestic companies. As a result of its insatiable demand for foreign products, the United States has been running a trade deficit since 1973—for more than twenty-five years (more on this in Chapter 2). In the popular press, the trade deficits have often been portrayed as a declining competitiveness of the United States. This assumes—rather erroneously—that U.S. companies engaged only in exports and imports and that international trade takes place between independent buyers and sellers across national boundaries. In order to appreciate the complexities of global competition, the nature of international trade and international business have to be clarified first, followed by a discussion of who manages international trade.

International Trade versus International Business

Here we have to understand the distinction between international trade and international business. Indeed, **international trade** consists of exports and imports, say, between the United States and the rest of the world. If U.S. imports exceed U.S. exports, then the nation would register a trade deficit. If the opposite were the case, then the United States would register a trade surplus. On the other hand, **international business** is a broader concept and includes international trade and foreign production. U.S. companies typically market their products in three ways. First, they can export their products from the United States, which is recorded as a U.S. export. Second, they can invest in their foreign production on their own and manufacture those products abroad for sale there. This transaction does not show up as a U.S. export, however. And third, they can contract out manufacturing in whole or part to a company in a foreign country, either by way of licensing or joint venture agreement. Of course, not all companies engage in all three forms of international transaction. Nonetheless, foreign manufacture on their own or on a contractual basis is a viable alternative means to exporting products abroad. Although it is not widely known, foreign production constitutes a much larger portion of international business than international trade.

The extensive international penetration of U.S. and other companies has been referred to as *global reach*.[8] Since the mid-1960s, U.S.-owned subsidiaries located around the world have produced and sold three times the value of all U.S. exports.

---

[8] Richard J. Barnet and R. E. Muller, *Global Reach: The Power of the Multinational Corporations* (New York: Simon and Schuster, 1974).

A Global Reach: Executives increasingly use a global map to visualize their strategy.

This 3:1 ratio of foreign manufacture to international trade has remained largely unchanged, and it becomes much more conspicuous if we look at U.S. business with the European Union, where U.S.-owned subsidiaries sold more than six times the total U.S. exports in 1990. Similarly, European-owned subsidiaries operating in the United States sold five times as much as U.S. imports from Europe.[9] This suggests that experienced companies tend to manufacture overseas much more than they export. On the other hand, Japanese companies have not expanded their foreign manufacturing activities until recently. According to one estimate, more than 90 percent of all the cases of Japanese foreign direct investment have taken place since 1985.[10] Despite their relative inexperience in international expansion, Japanese subsidiaries registered two and a half times as much foreign sales as all Japanese exports worldwide by 1990.[11]

Who Manages International Trade?

As just discussed, international trade and foreign production are increasingly managed on a global basis. Furthermore, international trade and foreign production are also intertwined in a complex manner. Think about Honda Motors, a Japanese automobile manufacturer. Honda initially exported its Accords and Civics to the United States in the 1970s. By the mid-1980s, the Japanese company had begun manufacturing those cars in Marysville, Ohio. Now the company exports U.S.-made Accord models to Japan and elsewhere, and boasts that it is the largest exporter of U.S.-made automobiles in the United States. Similarly, Texas Instruments has a large semiconductor manufacturing plant in Japan, not only marketing its semiconductor chips in Japan but also exporting them from Japan to the United States and elsewhere. In

[9]Dennis J. Encarnation, "Transforming Trade and Investment, American, European, and Japanese Multinationals Across the Triad," a paper presented at the Academy of International Business Annual Meetings, November 22, 1992.

[10]Masaaki Kotabe, "The Promotional Roles of the State Government and Japanese Manufacturing Direct Investment in the United States," *Journal of Business Research*, 27 (June 1993), pp. 131–46.

[11]Dennis J. Encarnation, "Transforming Trade and Investment, American, European, and Japanese Multinationals Across the Triad," a paper presented at the Academy of International Business Annual Meetings, November 22, 1992.

addition to traditional exporting from their home base, those companies manufacture their products in various foreign countries, both for local sale and for further exporting to the rest of the world, including their respective home countries. In other words, multinational corporations (MNCs) are increasingly managing the international trade flow within themselves. This phenomenon is called **intra-firm trade**.

Intra-firm trade makes trade statistics more complex to interpret, since part of the international flow of products and components is taking place between affiliated companies within the same corporate system, transcending national boundaries. The most recent United Nations official report shows that in 1999, 34 percent of world trade was intra-firm trade between MNCs and their foreign affiliates and between those affiliates. An additional 33.3 percent of world trade was exports by those MNCs and their affiliates. In other words, two-thirds of world trade was managed one way or another by multinational companies.[12] These trade ratios have been fairly stable over time.[13]

Although few statistics are available, service industries are going through the same evolution as manufacturing industries. Indeed, some similarities exist in intra-firm trade of services. In 1998, $1.3 trillion worth of commercial services was trade globally. Among the top global service exporters and importers, the United States was ranked the largest exporter, providing nearly $300 billion of services to the rest of the world in 1998. The United States was also the top importer of services, receiving $191 billion worth of services.[14] Today, approximately 16 percent of the total value of U.S. exports and imports of services were conducted across national boundaries on an intra-firm basis.[15] Government deregulation and technological advancement have facilitated the tradability of some services globally and economically.

EVOLUTION OF GLOBAL MARKETING ◆ ◆ ◆ ◆ ◆ ◆

Marketing is essentially a creative corporate activity involving the planning and execution of the conception, pricing, promotion, and distribution of ideas, products, and services in an exchange that not only *satisfies* customers' current needs but also

What Is Marketing?

---

[12]Khalil Hamdani, "The Role of Foreign Direct Investment in Export Strategy," presented at 1999 Executive Forum on National Export Strategies, International Trade Centre, the United Nations, September 26–28, 1999.

[13]United Nations Center on Transnational Corporations, *Transnational Corporations in World Development: Trends and Perspectives*, New York: United Nations, 1988; Organization for Economic Cooperation and Development, *Intra-Firm Trade*, Paris, OECD, 1993; Stefan H. Robock, "U.S. Multinationals: Intra-Firm Trade, Overseas Sourcing and the U.S. Trade Balance," a paper presented at the 1999 Academy of International Business-Southeast Conference, June 4–5, 1999.

[14]*Statistical Abstract of the United States 1998*, Washington, D.C.: Bureau of Statistics, 1999.

[15]Masaaki Kotabe, Janet Y. Murray, and Rajshekhar G. Javalgi, "Global Sourcing of Services and Market Performance: An Empirical Investigation," *Journal of International Marketing*, 6 (4), (1998), pp. 10–31; and Janet Y. Murray and Masaaki Kotabe, "Sourcing Strategies of U.S. Service Companies: A Modified Transaction-Cost Analysis," *Strategic Management Journal*, forthcoming in 1999.

anticipates and *creates* their future needs at a profit.[16] Marketing is not only much broader than selling, it also encompasses the entire company's *market orientation* toward customer satisfaction in a competitive environment. In other words, marketing strategy requires close attention to both customers and competitors.[17] Quite often marketers have focused excessively on satisfying customer needs while ignoring competitors. In the process, competitors have outmaneuvered them in the marketplace with better, less-expensive products. It is widely believed that in many cases, U.S. companies have won the battle of discovering and filling customer needs initially, only to be defeated in the competitive war by losing the markets they pioneered to European and Japanese competitors.[18]

It is increasingly difficult for companies to avoid the effect of world competition and converging world markets. As a result, an increasing number of companies are drawn into marketing activities outside their home country. However, as previously indicated, companies approach marketing around the world very differently. For example, Michael Dell established Dell Computer because he saw a burgeoning market potential for IBM-compatible personal computers in the United States. After his immediate success at home, he realized a future growth potential would exist in foreign markets. Then his company began exporting Dell PCs to Europe and Japan. In a way, this was a predictable pattern of foreign expansion. On the other hand, not all companies go through this predictable pattern. Think about a notebook-size Macintosh computer called the PowerBook 100 that Apple Computer introduced in 1991. In 1989, Apple enlisted Sony, the Japanese consumer-electronics giant, to design and manufacture this notebook computer for both the U.S. and Japanese markets.[19] Sony has world-class expertise in miniaturization and has been a supplier of disk drives, monitors, and power supplies to Apple for various Macintosh models. In an industry such as personal computers, where technology changes quickly and products become obsolete in a short period of time, a window of business opportunity is naturally limited. Therefore, Apple's motivation was to introduce the notebook computer on the markets around the world as soon as it could before competition picked up.

Companies generally develop different marketing strategies depending on the degree of experience and the nature of operations in international markets. Companies tend to evolve over time, accumulating international business experience

---

[16]This definition is modified from the American Marketing Association's definition of marketing, and is strongly influenced by Drucker's conception of two entrepreneurial functions—marketing and innovation—that constitute business. Recent thinking about marketing also suggests the task of the marketer is not only to satisfy the current needs and wants of customers, but also to innovate on products and services, anticipating and even creating their future needs and wants. See Peter F. Drucker, *The Practice of Management* (New York: Harper & Brothers, 1954), pp. 37–39; and also Frederick E. Webster, Jr., "The Changing Role of Marketing in the Corporation," *Journal of Marketing*, 56 (October 1992), pp. 1–16.

[17]Aysegül Özsomer and Bernard Simonin, "Antecedents and Conseqeunces of Market Orientation in a Subsidiary Context, *Enhancing Knowledge Development in Marketing*, 1999 American Marketing Association Educators' Proceedings, Summer 1999, p. 68.

[18]Robert M. Peterson, Clay Dibrell, and Timothy L. Pett, "Whose Market Orientation is Longest: A Study of Japan, Europe, and the United States," *Enhancing Knowledge Development in Marketing*, 1999 American Marketing Association Educators' Proceedings, Summer 1999, p. 69.

[19]"Apple's Japanese Ally," *Fortune* (November 4, 1991), pp. 151–52.

and learning the advantages and disadvantages associated with complexities of manufacturing and marketing around the world.[20] As a result, many researchers have adopted an evolutionary perspective of internationalization of the company just like the evolution of the species over time. In the following pages we will formally define and explain five stages characterizing the evolution of global marketing. Of course, not all companies go through the complete evolution from a purely domestic marketing stage to a purely global marketing stage. An actual evolution depends also on the economic, cultural, political, and legal environments of various country markets in which the company operates, as well as on the nature of the company's offerings. A key point here is that many companies are constantly under competitive pressure to move forward both *reactively* (responding to the changes in the market and competitive environments) and *proactively* (anticipating the change). Remember, "If you don't do it, somebody else will."

Therefore, knowing the dynamics of the evolutionary development of international marketing involvement is important for two reasons. First, it helps in the understanding of how companies learn and acquire international experience and how they use it for gaining competitive advantage over time. This may help an executive to be better prepared for the likely change needed in the company's marketing strategy. Second, with this knowledge, a company may be able to compete more effectively by predicting its competitors' likely marketing strategy in advance.

Domestic Marketing

As shown in Exhibit 1–2, there are five identifiable stages in the evolution of marketing across national boundaries.[21] The first stage is **domestic marketing**. Before entry into international markets, many companies focus solely on their domestic market. Their marketing strategy is developed based on information about domestic customer needs and wants, industry trends, economic, technological, and political environments at home. When those companies consider competition, they essentially look at domestic competition. Today, it is highly conceivable that domestic competition is made up of both domestic competitors and foreign competitors marketing their products in the home market. Domestic marketers tend to be *ethnocentric* and pay little attention to changes taking place in the global marketplace, such as changing lifestyles and market segments, emerging competition, and better products that have yet to arrive in their domestic market. *Ethnocentrism* is defined here as a predisposition of a firm to be predominantly concerned with its viability worldwide and legitimacy only in its home country[22]—that is, where all strategic actions of a company are tailored to domestic responses under similar situations. As a result, they may be vulnerable to the sudden changes forced on them from foreign competition. U.S. automobile and consumer electronics manufacturers suffered from this ethnocentrism in the 1960s and 1970s as a result of their neglect of imminent competition from Japanese low-cost manufacturers.

---

[20]William H. Davidson, *Experience Effects in International Investment and Technology Transfer* (Ann Arbor, Mich.: UMI Research Press, 1980).

[21]This section draws from Balaj S. Chakravarthy and Howard V. Perlmutter, "Strategic Planning for a Global Business," *Columbia Journal of World Business* (Summer 1985), pp. 3–10; Susan P. Douglas and C. Samuel Craig, "Evolution of Global Marketing Strategy: Scale, Scope and Synergy," *Columbia Journal of World Business* 24 (Fall 1989), pp. 47–59.

[22]Chakravarthy and Perlmutter, pp. 3–10.

EXHIBIT 1–2
EVOLUTION OF GLOBAL MARKETING

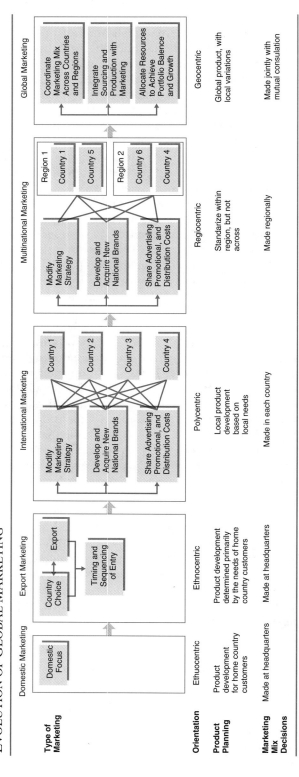

Type of Marketing	Domestic Marketing	Export Marketing	International Marketing	Multinational Marketing	Global Marketing
	Domestic Focus	Country Choice ⇄ Export; Timing and Sequencing of Entry	Modify Marketing Strategy; Develop and Acquire New National Brands; Share Advertising Promotional, and Distribution Costs; Country 1, Country 2, Country 3, Country 4	Modify Marketing Strategy; Develop and Acquire New National Brands; Share Advertising Promotional, and Distribution Costs; Region 1 (Country 1, Country 5); Region 2 (Country 6, Country 4)	Coordinate Marketing Mix Across Countries and Regions; Integrate Sourcing and Production with Marketing; Allocate Resources to Achieve Portfolio Balance and Growth
Orientation	Ethuocentric	Ethnocentric	Polycentric	Regiocentric	Geocentric
Product Planning	Product development for home country customers	Product development determined primarily by the needs of home country customers	Local product development based on local needs	Standarize within region, but not across	Global product, with local variations
Marketing Mix Decisions	Made at headquarters	Made at headquarters	Made in each country	Made regionally	Made jointly with mutual consulation

Source: Adapted from Susan P. Douglas and C. Samuel Craig, "Evolution of Global Marketing Strategy: Scale, Scope and Synergy," *Columbia Journal of World Business,* 24 (Fall 1985): 50; and Balai S. Chakravarthy and Howard V. Perlmutter, "Strategic Planning for a Global Business," *Columbia Journal of World Business,* 20 (Summer 1985): 6.

The second stage is **export marketing**. Usually, initial export marketing begins with unsolicited orders from foreign customers. When a company receives an order from abroad, it may fill it reluctantly initially, but it gradually learns the benefit of marketing overseas. In general, in the early stage of export marketing involvement, the internationalization process is a consequence of incremental adjustments to the changing conditions of the company and its environment, rather than a result of its deliberate strategy. Such a pattern is due to the consequence of greater uncertainty in international business, higher costs of information, and the lack of technical knowledge about international marketing activities. At this early export marketing stage, exporters tend to engage in *indirect exporting* by relying on export management companies or trading companies to handle their export business.

Some companies progress to a more involved stage of internationalization by *direct exporting*, once three internal conditions are satisfied. First, the management of the company obtains favorable expectations of the attractiveness of exporting based on experience. Second, the company has access to key resources necessary for undertaking additional export-related tasks. Such availability of physical, financial, and managerial resources is closely associated with firm size. Particularly, small companies may have few trained managers, and little time for long-term planning as they are preoccupied with day-to-day operational problems, and consequently find it difficult to become involved in exporting. Third, management is willing to commit adequate resources to export activities.[23] The company's long-term commitment to export marketing depends on how successful management is in overcoming various barriers encountered in international marketing activities. An experienced export marketer has to deal with difficulties in maintaining and expanding export involvement. These difficulties include import/export restrictions, cost and availability of shipping, exchange rate fluctuations, collection of money, and development of distribution channels, among others. Overall, favorable experience appears to be a key component in getting companies involved in managing exports directly without relying on specialized outside export handlers. To a large degree an appropriate measure of favorableness for many companies consists of profits. An increase in profits due to a certain activity is likely to increase the company's interest in such activity.[24]

External pressures also prod companies into export marketing activities. Saturated domestic markets may make it difficult for a company to maintain sales volume in an increasingly competitive domestic market; it will become much more serious when foreign competitors begin marketing products in the domestic market. Export marketers begin paying attention to technological and other changes in the global marketplace that domestic marketers tend to ignore. However, export marketers still tend to take an ethnocentric approach to foreign markets as being an extension of their domestic market—they export products developed primarily for home country customers with limited adaptation to foreign customers' needs.

Export Marketing

[23]S. Tamer Cavusgil, "On the Internationalization Process of Firms," *European Research*, 8 (November 1980), pp. 273–79.

[24]Masaaki Kotabe and Michael R. Czinkota, "State Government Promotion of Manufacturing Exports: A Gap Analysis," *Journal of International Business Studies*, 23 (Fourth Quarter 1992), pp. 637–58.

International Marketing

Once export marketing becomes an integral part of the company's marketing activity, it will begin to seek new directions for growth and expansion. We call this stage **international marketing**. A unique feature of international marketing is its *polycentric* orientation with emphasis on product and promotional adaptation in foreign markets, whenever necessary.[25] Polycentric orientation refers to a predisposition of a firm to the existence of significant local cultural differences across markets, necessitating the operation in each country being viewed independently (i.e., all strategic decisions are thus tailored to suit the cultures of the concerned country). As the company's market share in a number of countries reaches a certain point, it becomes important for the company to defend its position through local competition. Because of local competitors' proximity to, and familiarity of, local customers, they tend to have an inherent "insider" advantage over foreign competition. To strengthen its competitive position, the international marketer begins to adapt products and promotion, if necessary, to meet the needs and wants of local customers in two alternative ways. First, the company may allocate a certain portion of its manufacturing capacity to its export business. Second, because of transportation costs, tariffs, and other regulations, and availability of human and capital resources in the foreign markets, the company may even begin manufacturing locally. BMW has been exporting its cars to the United States for many years. It decided to build a manufacturing plant in South Carolina in order to be more adaptive to the changing customer needs in this important market and to take advantage of rather inexpensive resources as a result of the dollar depreciation against the German mark.

If international marketing is taken to the extreme, a company may establish an independent foreign subsidiary in each and every foreign market and have each of the subsidiaries operate independently of each other without any measurable headquarters control. This special case of international marketing is known as **multidomestic marketing**. Product development, manufacturing, and marketing are all executed by each subsidiary for its own local market. As a result, different product lines, product positioning, and pricing may be observed across those subsidiaries. Few economies-of-scale benefits can be obtained. However, multidomestic marketing is useful when customer needs are so different across different national markets that no common product or promotional strategy can be developed. One example is the luxury clothing brand Burberry's, which for many years offered different product lines and pricing in various countries. Although it mostly marketed expensive raincoats and scarves in the United States, Burberry also carried men's suits in Italy, watches in Switzerland, and biscuits in Britain.[26]

Multinational Marketing

Now the company markets its products in many countries around the world—this is **multinational marketing**. Management of the company comes to realize the benefit of economies of scale in product development, manufacturing, and marketing by consolidating some of its activities on a regional basis. This *regiocentric* approach suggests that product planning may be standardized within a region (e.g., a

---

[25]Warren J. Keegan, "Multinational Product Planning: Strategic Alternatives," *Journal of Marketing*, 33 (January 1969): pp. 58–62.

[26]Lauren Goldstein, "Dressing Up an Old Brand," *Fortune*, (November 9, 1998), pp. 154–56.

group of contiguous and similar countries), such as Western Europe, but not across regions. Products may be manufactured regionally as well. Similarly, advertising, promotional, and distribution costs may also be shared by subsidiaries in the region. In order for the company to develop its regional image in the marketplace, it may develop and acquire new regional brands to beef up its regional operations. General Motors has a regional subsidiary, Opel (headquartered in Germany), to market both GM and Opel cars with a strong European distinction.

Global Marketing

The international (country-by-country) or multinational (region-by-region) orientation, while enabling the consolidation of operations within countries or regions, will tend to result in market fragmentation worldwide, nonetheless. Operational fragmentation leads to higher costs. As many Japanese companies entered the world markets as low-cost manufacturers of reliable products in the 1970s, well-established U.S. and European MNCs were made acutely aware of the vulnerability of being high-cost manufacturers. Levitt, an arduous globalization proponent, argues:

> Gone are accustomed differences in national or regional preference. Gone are the days when a company could sell last year's models—or lesser versions of advanced products—in the less developed world. . . . The multinational and the global corporation are not the same thing. The multinational corporation operates in a number of countries, and adjusts its products and practices in each—at high relative costs. The global corporation operates with resolute constancy—at low relative cost—as if the entire world (or major regions of it) were a single entity; it sells the same things in the same way everywhere.[27]

Global marketing refers to marketing activities by companies that emphasize the following:

1. Reduction of cost inefficiencies and duplication of efforts among their national and regional subsidiaries
2. Opportunities for the transfer of products, brands, and other ideas across subsidiaries
3. Emergence of global customers
4. Improved linkages among national marketing infrastructures leading to the development of a global marketing infrastructure[28]

Although Levitt's view is somewhat extreme, many researchers agree that global marketing does not necessarily mean standardization of products, promotion, pricing, and distribution worldwide, but rather, it is a company's proactive willingness to adopt a global perspective instead of a country-by-country or region-by-region perspective in developing a marketing strategy. Although not all companies adopt global marketing, an increasing number of companies are proactively trying to find commonality in their marketing strategy among national subsidiaries (see Global Perspective 1–2). For example, Black & Decker, a U.S. hand-tool manufacturer, adopted a global perspective by standardizing and streamlining components

---

[27]Theodore Levitt, "The Globalization of Markets," *Harvard Business Review*, 61 (May–June 1983), pp. 92–102.
[28]Douglas and Craig, 1989.

◆ ◆

𝒢LOBAL PERSPECTIVE 1–2

GLOBALIZING THE BUSINESS TERMS BEFORE GLOBALIZING THE FIRM

International was the first word that William Hudson, president and CEO of AMP Inc., Harrisburg, Pennsylvania, told his corporate colleagues to cut from their business vocabularies. Why? The term creates a "Chinese wall" that divides a globalizing company into "domestic" and "international" sides, he explained to A. T. Kearney Inc. officers meeting in Chicago. "It's almost as if you don't jump over that wall" to work or team together, he said.

Another banished word: *subsidiary*. It conveys "a parent/child relationship," said Mr. Hudson. Headquarters tends to lord its power over foreign and domestic operations and "make them feel like inferior souls." Revising the business lexicon is not easy, Mr. Hudson readily admitted. "Every now and then [one of the words] shows up on a . . . slide when somebody makes a presentation. And I've got to put up my hand and say: 'Erase that word.'"

Source: *Industry Week* (June 7, 1993), pp. 51–53.

such as motors and rotors while maintaining a wide range of product lines, and created a universal image for its products. In this case, it was not standardization of products per se but rather, the company's effort at standardizing key components and product design for manufacturability in manufacturing industry and core and supplementary services in service industry to achieve global leadership in cost and value.

The Impact of Economic Geography and Climate on Global Marketing

Global marketing does not necessarily mean that products can be developed anywhere on a global basis. The economic geography, climate, and culture, among other things, affect how companies develop certain products and how consumers want them. First, the availability of resources is a major determinant of industry location. The U.S. automobile industry was born at the dawn of the twentieth century as a result of Henry Ford having decided to locate his steel-making foundry in Detroit, located midway between sources of iron ore in the Mesabi range in Minnesota and sources of bituminous coal in Pennsylvania. Similarly, in the last quarter of the twentieth century, Silicon Valley in and around Palo Alto, California, and Silicon Hill in Austin, Texas, emerged as high-tech meccas as a result of abundant skilled human resources (thanks to leading universities in the areas), aided by warm, carefree environments—a coveted atmosphere conducive to creative thinking. For the same reason, Bangalore in India has emerged as an important location for software development. Brazil boasts that more than half of the automobiles on the road run on 100 percent pure alcohol, thanks to an abundant supply of ethanol produced from subsidized sugarcane. Even bananas are produced in abundance in Iceland, thanks to nature-provided geothermal energy tapped in greenhouses.[29] Since Germans consume the largest amount of bananas, about 33 lbs. (or 15 kg) on a per capita basis, in the European Union, Iceland could become an exporter of bananas to Germany![30]

Obviously, the availability of both natural and human resources is important in primarily determining industry location because those resources, if unavailable,

---

[29]"About Iceland," http://www.lysator.liu.se/nordic/scnfaq5.html, accessed April 8, 1999.

[30]Paul Sutton, "The Banana Regime of the European Union, the Caribbean, and Latin America," *Journal of Interamerican Studies and World Affairs*, 39 (Summer 1997), pp. 5–36.

could become a bottleneck. It is to be stressed that consumer needs are equally important as a determinant of industry location.[31] As the Icelandic banana example shows, the fact that Germans consume a large amount of bananas gives Icelandic growers a logistical advantage. Ask yourself why cellular phones have been most widely adopted in Finland, and fax machines and bubble-jet printers in Japan. In Finland and other Scandinavian countries, it snows heavily in winter but it is very damp snow, owing to the warm Gulf Stream moderating what could otherwise be a frigid climate. The damp snow frequently cuts off powerlines. Thus, Scandinavians always wished for mobile means of communication such as CB radio and cellular phones. Companies such as Nokia in Finland and Ericsson in Sweden have become world-class suppliers of cellular technology. Similarly, Japanese consumers always wanted machines that could easily produce and reproduce complex characters in their language. Thus, Japanese companies such as Canon, Epson (a subsidiary of Seiko Watch), and Fujitsu have emerged as the major producers of fax and bubble-jet printers in the world. Indeed, as the old proverb says, "Necessity is the mother of invention."

The point is that what companies can offer competitively may be determined either by the availability of natural and human resources or by the unique consumer needs in different countries or regions or by both. Global marketers are willing to exploit their local advantages for global business opportunities. Ask yourself another question about an emerging societal need around the world: environmental protection. Where are formidable competitors likely to originate in the near future? We think it is Germany. Germans have long been concerned about their environmental quality, represented by the cleanliness of the Rhine River. When the Rhine got polluted by phosphorus—a major whitening agent in laundry detergent—the German government banned its use first in the world. Now German companies are keen on developing products that are fully recyclable. Naturally, marketing executives need to have acute understanding of not only the availability of various resources but also emerging consumer and societal needs on a global basis.

The Impact of the Internet on Global Marketing

The Internet adds a new dimension to global marketing. The Internet and e-commerce have changed the paradigm, as now any company with a Web site can market globally. No longer a novelty, shopping on the Internet is projected to grow into a $31 billion market by year 2002.[32] Consumers can not only order books and CDs, but virtually "try on" clothes at the Gap's Web site, and "sit" inside the latest-model car from BMW, Ford, Mercedes-Benz, and GM at any of these auto-makers' sites.[33]

Many MNCs are realizing the huge potential of the Internet in terms of global marketing and e-commerce. Some established companies almost missed this potential and are now playing catch-up to upstarts. For example, Toys "R" Us is investing $80 million into its online retailing services in its quest to become the number-one toy retailer on the Internet. Included in the investment is the creation of a separate business unit solely for e-commerce, and the purchase of a $30 million, 500,000-

[31]Michael E. Porter, *The Competitive Advantage of Nations* (New York: Free Press, 1990).
[32]"Intel is Eyeing E-Commernce," *Business Week* (May 3, 1999), p. 52.
[33]"Commerce—No Longer a Novelty, Internet Shopping Takes Off," *Fortune* (December 7, 1998), pp. 245–46.

square-foot warehouse to handle only products sold online. Toys "R" Us was forced to recognize the strategic importance of e-commerce when an upstart, eToys, began selling toys only online, and started cutting into Toys "R" Us's profits. A similar example is that of Compaq's inability to catch up to Dell computer's success online.[34]

The message about e-commerce is simple: "Don't wait," says one e-commerce executive. A well-known British retailer, Liberty, recently launched its own e-commerce site in hopes of gaining first-mover advantages by building a monopolistic position on the market over other entrenched British retailers, such as Harrods and Selfridges, who have yet to offer online services.[35] Besides first-mover advantages, e-commerce retailers gain substantial cost savings by selling virtually, and providing customer service through the Web rather than the telephone. "Electronic selling and purchasing are going to be the default method of doing business, not the special case," says Stu Feldman, director of the IBM Institute for Advanced Commerce. "And 'going to be' is a matter of months, not decades."[36]

So far we have focused on complex realities of international trade and investment that have characterized our global economy in the past twenty years. Some vital statistics have been provided. The more statistics we see, the more befuddled we become by the sheer complexities of our global economy. It even seems as though there were not a modicum of orderliness in our global economy, it being just like a jungle. Naturally, we wish the world were much simpler. In reality, it is becoming ever more complex. Luckily enough, however, economists and business researchers have tried over the years to explain the ever-increasing complexities of the global economy in simpler terms. A simplified yet logical view of the world is called a theory. Indeed, there are many different ways—theories—of looking at international trade and investment taking place in the world. For those of you interested in understanding some orderliness in the complex world of international trade and investment, we encourage you to read the appendix to this chapter. Some theoretical understanding will not only help you appreciate the competitive world in which we live, but also help you make better strategy decisions for a company you may join shortly or a company you may own.

SUMMARY ◆

World trade has grown from $200 billion to more than $5 trillion in the last twenty-five years. Although world trade volume is significant in and of itself, international business is much more than trade statistics show. Companies from Western Europe, the United States, and Japan collectively produce probably more than three times as much in their foreign markets as they export. And about a third of their exports and imports are transacted on an intra-firm basis between their parent companies and their affiliated companies abroad or between the affiliated companies themselves.

What this all means is that it is almost impossible for domestic company executives to consider their domestic markets and domestic competition alone. If they fail to look beyond their national boundaries, they may unknowingly lose marketing opportunities to competitors that do. Worse yet, foreign competitors will encroach on their hard-earned market position at home so fast that it may be too late for them to re-

---

[34]Clinton Wilder and Gregory Dalton, "E-Commerce Dividends" *Information Week* (May 3, 1999), p. 18.

[35]"Liberty Fashions E-Commerce Site for Gifts," *Precision Marketing* (May 3, 1999), p. 2.

[36]Clinton Wilder and Gregory Dalton, "E-Commerce Dividends" *Information Week* (May 3, 1999), p. 18.

spond. International markets are so intertwined that separating international from domestic business may be a futile mental exercise.

Historically, international expansion has always been a strategy consideration after domestic marketing, and has therefore been reactionary to such things as a decline in domestic sales and increased domestic competition. Global marketing is a proactive response to the intertwined nature of business opportunities and competition that know no political boundaries. However, global marketing does not necessarily mean that companies should market the same product in the same way around the world as world markets are con-

verging. To the extent feasible, they probably should. Nonetheless, global marketing is a company's willingness to adopt a global perspective instead of a country-by-country or region-by-region perspective in developing a marketing strategy for growth and profit.

What companies can offer competitively may be determined either by the availability of natural and human resources or by the unique consumer needs in different countries or regions or by both. Global marketers should be willing to exploit their local advantages for global marketing opportunities. The proliferation of e-commerce on the Internet accelerates such global marketing opportunities.

KEY TERMS ◆

big emerging markets (BEMs)	export marketing	international marketing	multidomestic marketing
domestic marketing	global marketing	international trade	multinational marketing
electronic commerce (E-commerce)	international business	intra-firm trade	

REVIEW QUESTIONS ◆

1. Discuss the reasons why international business is much more complex today than it was twenty years ago.

2. What is the nature of global competition?

3. Does international trade accurately reflect the nature of global competition?

4. Why are consumption patterns similar across industrialized countries despite cultural differences?

5. How is global marketing different from international marketing?

6. Why do you think a company should or should not market the same product in the same way around the world?

7. What is proactive standardization?

8. How is the Internet reshaping the nature of global marketing?

DISCUSSION QUESTIONS ◆ ◆ ◆ ◆ ◆ ◆ ◆ ◆ ◆ ◆ ◆ ◆ ◆ ◆ ◆ ◆ ◆ ◆ ◆

1. The United States and Japan, the two largest economies in the world, are also the largest importers and exporters of goods and services. However, imports and exports put together comprise only 20 to 30 percent of their GNPs. This percentage has not changed much over the last three decades for both of these countries. Does this imply that the corporations and the media may be overemphasizing globalization? Discuss why you agree or do not agree with the last statement.

2. Merchandise trade today accounts for less than 2 percent of all the foreign exchange transactions around the world. Can one deduce that merchandise plays an insignificant role in today's economies? Why or why not?

3. A major cereal manufacturer produces and markets standardized breakfast cereals to countries around the world. Minor modifications in attributes such as sweetness of the product are made to cater to local needs. However, the core products and brands are standardized. The company entered the Chinese market a few years back and was extremely satisfied with the results. The company's sales continue to grow at a rate of around 50 percent a year in China. Encouraged by its marketing success in China and other Asian countries, and based on the market reforms taking place, the company started operations in India by manufacturing and marketing its products. Initial response to the product

was extremely encouraging, and within one year the company was thinking in terms of rapidly expanding its production capacity. However, after a year, sales tapered off and started to fall. Detailed consumer research seemed to suggest that while the upper-middle social class, especially families where both spouses were working, to whom this product was targeted, adopted the cereals as an alternative meal (i.e., breakfast) for a short time, they eventually returned to the traditional Indian breakfast. The CEOs of some other firms in the food industry in India are quoted as saying that non–Indian snack products and restaurant business are the areas where MNCs can hope for success. Trying to replace a full meal with a non–Indian product has less of a chance of succeeding. You are a senior executive in the international division of this food MNC with experience of operating in various countries in a product management function. The CEO plans to send you to India on a fact-finding mission to determine answers to these specific questions. What, in your opinion, would be the answers to these questions:

a. Was entering the market with a standardized product a mistake?

b. Was it a problem of the product, or the way it was positioned?

c. Given the advantages to be gained through leveraging of brand equity and product knowledge on a global basis, and the disadvantages of differing local tastes, what would be your strategy for entering new markets?

4. Globalization involves the organizationwide development of a global perspective. This global perspective requires globally thinking managers. Although the benefits of globalization have received widespread attention, the difficulties in developing managers who think globally has received scant attention. Some senior managers consider this to be a significant stumbling block in the globalization efforts of companies. Do you agree with their concerns? Would the lack of truly globally thinking managers cause problems for implementing a global strategy? And how does the proliferation of e-commerce affect the way these managers conduct business?

FURTHER READING

Bartlett, Christopher A., and Sumantra Ghoshal. "What Is a Global Manager?" *Harvard Business Review* (September–October 1992): 124–32.

Bartlett, Christopher, and Sumantra Ghoshal. "Tap Your Subsidiaries for Global Reach." *Harvard Business Review* (November–December 1986): 87–94.

Bryan, Lowell L., Jeremy Oppenheim, Wilheim Rall, and Jane Fraser. *Race for the World: Strategies to Build a Great Global Firm*. Cambridge, MA: Harvard Business School Press, 1999.

Clark, Ian. *Globalization and Fragmentation: International Relations in the Twentieth Century*. Oxford: Oxford University Press, 1997.

Craig, C. Samuel, and Susan P. Douglas. "Configural Advantage in Global Markets." *Journal of International Marketing*, 8(1)(2000): 6–26.

Fleenor, Debra. "The Coming and Going of the Global Corporation." *Columbia Journal of World Business*, 28 (Winter 1993): 6–16.

Royal, Weld. "Global Reach." *Industry Week* (April 5, 1999): 84–94.

Speier, Cheri, Michael G. Harvey, and Johathan Palmer. "Virtual Management of Global Marketing Relationships." *Journal of World Business*, 33 (Fall 1998): 263–76.

Yip, George S. *Total Global Strategy*. Englewood Cliffs, NJ: Prentice-Hall, 1992.

Zahra, Shaker A. "The Changing Rules of Global Competitiveness in the 21st Century." *Academy of Management Executive*, 13 (February 1999): 36–42.

APPENDIX

THEORIES OF INTERNATIONAL TRADE AND THE MULTINATIONAL ENTERPRISE

Theories are a simplification of complex realities in one way or another. A few important theories will be explained here. Each of the theories provides a number of fundamental principles, with which you can not only appreciate why international trade and investment occur but also prepare for the next impending change you will probably see in a not-so-distant future. These theories are arranged chronologically so that you can better understand what aspect of the ever-increasing complexities of international business each theory was designed to explain.

Comparative Advantage Theory. At the aggregate level, countries trade with each other for fundamentally the same reasons that individuals exchange products and services for mutual benefit. By doing so, we all benefit collectively. Comparative advantage theory is an arithmetic demonstration that was made by the English economist David Ricardo almost 180 years ago: A country can gain from engaging in trade even if it has an absolute advantage or disadvantage. In other words, even if the United States is more efficient in the production of everything than China, both countries will benefit from trade between them by specializing in what each country can produce relatively more efficiently.

Let us demonstrate comparative advantage theory in its simplest form: The world is made up of two countries (the United States and China) and two products (personal computers and desks). We assume that there is only one PC model and only one type of desk. We further assume that labor is the only input to produce both products. Transportation costs are also assumed to be zero. The production conditions and consumption pattern in the two countries before and after trade are presented in Exhibit 1–3. As shown, U.S. labor is assumed to be more productive absolutely in the production of both personal computers (PC) and desks than Chinese labor.

Intuitively, you might argue that since the United States is more productive in both products, U.S. companies will export both PCs and desks to China, and Chinese companies cannot compete with U.S. companies in either product category. Furthermore, you might argue that as China cannot sell anything to the United States, China cannot pay for imports from the United States. Therefore, these two countries cannot engage in trade. This is essentially the **absolute advantage** argument. Is this argument true? The answer is no.

If you closely look at labor productivity of the two industries, you see that the United States can produce PCs more efficiently than desks compared to the situation in China. The United States has a three-to-one advantage in PCs, but only a two-to-one advantage in desks over China. In other words, the United States can produce three PCs instead of a desk (or as few as one-third of a desk per PC), while China can produce two PCs for a desk (or as many as a half desk per PC). Relatively speaking, the United States is comparatively more efficient in making PCs (at a rate of three PCs per desk) than China (at a rate of two PCs per desk). However, China is comparatively more efficient in making desks

(at a rate of half a desk per PC) than the United States (at a rate of one-third of a desk per PC). Therefore, we say that the United States has a **comparative advantage** in making PCs, while China has a comparative advantage in making desks.

Comparative advantage theory suggests that the United States should specialize in production of PCs, while China should specialize in production of desks. As shown in Exhibit 1–3, the United States produced and consumed 100 PCs and 20 desks, and China produced and consumed 40 PCs and 30 desks. As a whole, the world (the United States and China combined) produced and consumed 140 PCs and 50 desks. Now as a result of specialization, the United States concentrates all its labor resources on PC production, while China allocates all labor resources to desk production. The United States can produce 60 more PCs by giving up on 20 desks it used to produce (at a rate of three PCs per desk), resulting in a total production of 160 PCs and no desks. Similarly, China can produce 20 more desks by moving its labor from PC production to desk production (at a rate of half a desk per PC), with a total production of 50 desks and no PCs. Now the world as a whole produces 160 PCs and 50 desks.

Before trade occurs, U.S. consumers are willing to exchange as many as three PCs for each desk, while Chinese consumers are willing to exchange as few as two PCs for each desk, given their labor productivity, respectively. Therefore, the price of a desk acceptable to both U.S. and Chinese consumers should be somewhere between two and three PCs. Let us assume that the mutually acceptable price, or **commodity terms of trade** (a price of one good in terms of another), is 2.5 PCs per desk. Now let the United States and China engage in trade at the commodity terms of trade of 2.5 PCs per desk. To simplify our argument, further assume that the United States and China consume the same number of desks after trade as they did before trade, that is, 20 desks and 30 desks, respectively. In other words, the United States has to import 20 desks from China in exchange for 50 PCs (20 desks × 2.5 is the price of the desks in terms of PCs), which are exported to China from the United States. As a result of trade, the United States consumes 110 PCs and 20 desks, while China consumes 50 PCs and 30 desks. Given the same amount of labor resources, both countries respectively consume 10 more PCs while consuming the same number of desks. Obviously, specialization and trade have benefited both countries.

In reality, we rarely exchange one product for another. We use foreign exchange instead. Let us assume that the price of a desk is $900 in the United States and 2,000 yuan in China. Based on the labor productivity in the two countries, the price of a PC should be $300 (at a rate of a third of a desk per PC) in the United States and 1,000 yuan (at a rate of half a desk per PC) in China. As

EXHIBIT 1–3
COMPARATIVE ADVANTAGE AT WORK

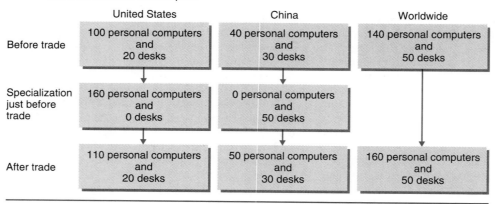

1. One Person-Day Productivity

United States	China
6 personal computers or 2 desks	2 personal computers or 1 desks

2. Production and Consumption

	United States	China	Worldwide
Before trade	100 personal computers and 20 desks	40 personal computers and 30 desks	140 personal computers and 50 desks
Specialization just before trade	160 personal computers and 0 desks	0 personal computers and 50 desks	
After trade	110 personal computers and 20 desks	50 personal computers and 30 desks	160 personal computers and 50 desks

we indicated earlier, U.S. consumers are willing to exchange as many as three PCs for each desk worth $900 in the United States. Three PCs in China are worth 3,000 yuan. Therefore, U.S. consumers are willing to pay as much as 3,000 yuan to import a $900 desk from China. Similarly, Chinese consumers are willing to import a minimum of two PCs (worth 2,000 yuan in China) for each desk they produce (worth $900 in the United States). Therefore, the mutually acceptable exchange rate should be:

$$2,000 \text{ yuan} \leq \$900 \leq 3,000 \text{ yuan},$$

$$\text{or } 2.22 \text{ yuan} \leq \$1 \leq 3.33 \text{ yuan}.$$

An actual exchange rate will be affected also by consumer demands and money supply situations in the two countries. Nonetheless, it is clear that exchange rates are primarily determined by international trade.

From this simple exercise, we can make a few general statements or **principles of international trade**.

Principle 1: Countries benefit from international trade.

Principle 2: International trade increases worldwide production by specialization.

Principle 3: Exchange rates are determined primarily by traded goods.

By now you might have wondered why U.S. workers are more productive than Chinese workers. So far, we have assumed that labor is the only input in economic production. In reality, we do not produce anything with manual labor alone. We use machinery, computers, and other capital equipment (capital, for short) to help us produce efficiently. In other words, our implicit assumption was that the United States has more abundant capital relative to labor than China does. Naturally, the more capital we have relative to our labor stock, the less expensive a unit of capital should be relative to a unit of labor. The less expensive a unit of capital relative to a unit of labor, the more capital we tend to use and specialize in industry that requires a large amount of capital. In other words, the capital–labor endowment ratio affects what type of industry a country tends to specialize in. In general, a capital-abundant country (e.g., the United States) tends to specialize in capital-intensive industry and export capital-intensive products (personal computers), and import labor-intensive products (desks). Conversely, a labor-abundant country (China) tends to specialize in labor-intensive industry and export labor-intensive products (desks), and import capital-intensive products (personal computers). This refined argument is known as **factor endowment theory** of comparative advantage.

The factor endowment theory can be generalized a bit further. For example, the United States is not only capital-abundant but also abundant with a highly educated (i.e., skilled) labor force. Therefore, it is easy to predict that the United States has comparative advantage in skill-intensive industries such as computers and biotechnology and exports a lot of computers and genetically engineered ethical drugs around the world, and imports manual-labor-intensive products such as textiles and shoes from labor-abundant countries such as China and Brazil. Global Perspective 1–3 clearly shows that labor productivity alone shows a very erroneous impression of industry competitiveness.

Now you might have begun wondering how comparative advantage arguments will help businesspeople in the real world. Suppose that you work as a strategic planner for Nike. Shoe manufacturing is extremely labor-intensive, while shoe designing is becoming increasingly hi-tech (i.e., skill-intensive). The United States is a relatively skill-abundant and labor-scarce country. Therefore, the country has a comparative advantage in skill-intensive operations but has a comparative disadvantage in labor-intensive operations. There are two ways to use your knowledge of comparative advantage arguments. First, it is easy to predict where competition comes from. Companies from countries like China and Brazil will have a comparative advantage in shoe manufacturing over Nike in the United States. Second, you can advise Nike to establish shoe manufacturing plants in labor-abundant countries instead of in the labor-scarce United States. As we said earlier, shoe designing has become increasingly hi-tech, involving computer-aided designing and development of light, shock-absorbent material, which requires an extremely high level of expertise. Therefore, based on the comparative advantage argument, you suggest that product designing and development be done in the United States, where required expertise is relatively abundant. Indeed, that is what Nike does as a result of global competitive pressure, and has exploited various countries' comparative advantage to its advantage (no pun intended). Nike has product designing and development and special material development conducted in the United States and has manufacturing operations in labor-abundant countries like China and Brazil.

The comparative advantage theory is useful in explaining inter-industry trade, say computers and desks, between countries that have very different factor endowments. It suggests efficient allocation of limited resources across national boundaries by specialization and trade, but hardly explains business competition, because computer manufacturers and desk manufacturers do not compete directly. Further, it fails to explain the expansion of trade among the industrialized countries with similar factor endowments. Trade among the twenty or so industrialized countries now constitutes almost 60 percent of world trade, and much of it is intra-industry in nature. In other words, similar products are differentiated either physically or

GLOBAL PERSPECTIVE 1–3
PROMISING SOURCES OF THE COUNTRY'S COMPETITIVE ADVANTAGE

It is correct to say, "The best way to improve living standards is to encourage investment in sophisticated industries like computers and aerospace." Is it correct to say, "The best way to improve living standards is to encourage investment in industries that provide high value added per worker"? The real high-value industries in the United States are extremely capital-intensive sectors like cigarettes and oil refining. High-tech sectors that everyone imagines are the keys to the future, like aircraft and electronics, are only average in their value added per worker, but are extremely skill-intensive industries. Look at these statistics:

Value Added Per Worker	Thousands
Cigarettes	$823
Petroleum Refining	$270
Automobiles	$112
Tires and Inner Tubes	$101
Aerospace	$86
Electronics	$74
All Manufacturing	$73

Adapted from Paul Krugman, "Competitiveness: Does it Matter?" Fortune (March 7, 1994), pp. 109–15.

only in the customers' minds and traded across countries. Thus, BMW exports its sports cars to Japan, while Honda exports its competing models to Germany. BMW and Honda compete directly within the same automobile industry. This type of intra-industry competition cannot be explained by comparative advantage theory.

International Product Cycle Theory.

When business practitioners think of competition, they usually refer to intra-industry competition. Why and how does competition tend to evolve over time and across national boundaries in the same industry? Then, how does a company develop its marketing strategy in the presence of competitors at home and abroad? **International product cycle theory** addresses all these questions.

Several speculations have been made.[37] First, a large domestic market such as the United States makes it possible for U.S. companies to enjoy **economies of scale** in mass production and mass marketing, enabling them to become lower-cost producers than their competition in foreign countries. Therefore, those low-cost producers can market their products in foreign markets and still remain profitable. In addition, an **economies of scope** argument augments an economies of scale argument. Companies from a small country can still enjoy economies of scale in production and marketing by extending their business scope beyond their national boundary. For example, Nestlé, a Swiss food company, can enjoy economies of scale by considering European, U.S., and Japanese markets together as its primary market. Second, technological innovation can provide an innovative company a competitive advantage, or **technological gap**, over its competitors both at home and abroad. Until competitors learn about and imitate the innovation, the original innovator company enjoys a temporary monopoly power around the world. Therefore, it is technological innovators that tend to market new products abroad. Third, it is generally the per-capita income level that determines consumers' **preference similarity**, or consumption patterns, irrespective of nationality. Preference similarity explains why intra-industry trade has grown tremendously among the industrialized countries with similar income levels.

Combining these forces with the earlier comparative advantage theory, international product cycle theory was developed in the 1960s and 1970s to explain a realistic, dynamic change in international competition over time and place.[38] This comprehensive theory describes the relationship between trade and investment over the product life cycle.

One of the key underlying assumptions in the international product cycle theory is that "Necessity is the mother of invention." In the United States, where personal incomes and labor costs were the highest in the world, particularly in the 1960s and 1970s, consumers desired products that would save their labor and time and satisfy materialistic needs. Historically, U.S. companies developed and introduced many products that were labor- and time-saving or responded to high-income consumer needs, including dishwashers, microwave ovens, automatic washers and dryers, personal computers, and so on. Similarly, companies in Western Europe tend to innovate on material- and capital-saving products and processes to meet their local consumers' needs and lifestyle orientation. Small and no-frill automobiles and recyclable products are such examples. Japanese companies stress products that conserve not only material and capital but also space to address their local consumers' acute concern about space limitation. Therefore, Japanese companies excel in developing and marketing small energy-efficient products of all kinds.[39]

International product cycle theory suggests that new products are developed primarily to address the needs of the local consumers, only to be demanded by foreign consumers who have similar needs with a similar purchasing power. As the nature of new products and their manufacturing processes becomes widely disseminated over time, the products eventually become mass-produced standard products around the world. At that point, the products' cost competitiveness becomes a determinant of success and failure in global competition. Your knowledge of comparative advantage theory helps your company identify where strong low-cost competitors tend to appear and how the company should plan production locations.

As presented in Exhibit 1–4, the pattern of evolution of the production and marketing process explained

---

[37]Mordechai E. Kreinin, *International Economics: A Policy Approach*, 5th ed. (New York: Harcourt Brace Jovanovich, 1987), pp. 276–78.

[38]See, for example, Raymond Vernon, "International Investment and International Trade in the Product Cycle," *Quarterly Journal of Economics*, 80 (May 1966), pp. 190–207; "The Location of Economic Activity," *Economic*

Analysis and the Multinational Enterprise, John H. Dunning, ed. (London: George Allen and Unwin, 1974), pp. 89–114; and "The Product Cycle Hypothesis in a New International Environment," *Oxford Bulletin of Economics and Statistics*, 41 (November 1979), pp. 255–67.

[39]Vernon, 1979.

EXHIBIT 1–4
INTERNATIONAL PRODUCT CYCLE

	Introductory	*Growth*	*Maturity*	*Decline*
Demand structure	-Nature of demand not well understood -Consumers willing to pay premium price for a new product	-Price competition begins -Product standard emerging	-Competition based on price and product differentiation	-Mostly price competition
Production	-Short runs, rapidly changing techniques -Dependent on skilled labor	-Mass production	-Long runs with stable techniques -Capital intensive	-Long runs with stable techniques -Lowest cost production needed either by capital intensive production or by massive use of inexpensive labor
Innovator company marketing strategy	-Sales mostly to home-country (e.g., U.S.) consumers -Some exported to other developed countries (e.g., Europe and Japan)	-Increased exports to the other developed countries (e.g., Europe and Japan)	-Innovator company (e.g., U.S.) begins production in Europe and Japan to protect its foreign market from local competition	-Innovator company (U.S.) may begin production in developing countries
International competition	-A few competitors at home (e.g., U.S.)	-Competitors in developed countries (e.g., Europe and Japan) begin production for their domestic markets -They also begin exporting to the United States	-European and Japanese companies increase exports to the United States -They begin exporting to developing countries	-European and Japanese competitors may begin production in developing countries -Competitors from developing countries also begin exporting to the world

Source: Expanded on Louis T. Wells, Jr, "International Trade The Product Life Cycle Approach," In Reed Moyer, ed., International Business: Issues and Concepts (New York: John Wiley, 1984), pp. 5–22.

in the international product cycle consists of four stages: introduction, growth, maturity, and decline. Let us explain the international product cycle from a U.S. point of view. Remember, however, that different kinds of product innovations also occur in countries (mostly developed) other than the United States. If so, a similar evolutionary pattern of development will begin from those other industrialized countries.

In the *introductory stage*, a U.S. company innovates on a new product to meet domestic consumers' needs in the U.S. market. A few other U.S. companies may introduce the same product. At this stage, competition is mostly domestic among U.S. companies. Some of those companies may begin exporting the product to a few

European countries and Japan where they can find willing buyers similar to U.S. consumers. Product standards are not likely to be established yet. As a result, competing product models or specifications may exist on the market. Prices tend to be high. In the *growth stage*, product standards emerge and mass production becomes feasible. Lower production prices spawn price competition. U.S. companies increase exports to Europe and Japan as those foreign markets expand. However, European and Japanese companies also begin producing the product in their own local markets and even begin exporting it to the United States. In the *maturity stage*, many U.S. and foreign companies vie for market share in the international markets. They try to lower prices and differentiate their products to outbid their competition. U.S. companies that have carved out market share in Europe and Japan by exporting decide to make a direct investment in production in those markets to protect their market position there. U.S. and foreign companies also begin to export to developing countries, because more consumers in those developing countries can afford the product as its price falls. Then, in the *decline stage,* companies in the developing countries also begin producing the product and marketing it in the rest of the world. U.S., European, and Japanese companies may also begin locating their manufacturing plants in those developing countries to take advantage of inexpensive labor. The United States eventually begins to import what was once a U.S. innovation.

The international product cycle argument holds true as long as we can assume that innovator companies are not informed about conditions in foreign markets, whether in other industrialized countries or in the developing world. As we amply indicated in Chapter 1, such an assumption has become very "iffy". Nor can it be safely assumed that U.S. companies are exposed to a very different home environment from European and Japanese companies. Indeed, the differences among the industrialized countries are reduced to trivial dimensions. Seeking to exploit global scale economies, an increasing number of companies are likely to establish various plants in both developed countries and developing countries, and to crosshaul between plants for the manufacture of final products. As an explanation of international business behavior, international product cycle theory has limited explanatory power. It does describe the initial international expansion (exporting followed by direct investment) of many companies, but the mature globe-trotting companies of today have succeeded in developing a number of other strategies for surviving in global competition.

Internalization/Transaction Cost Theory.

Now that many companies have established plants in various countries, they have to manage their corporate activities across national boundaries. Those companies are conventionally called multinational companies. It is inherently much more complex and difficult to manage corporate activities and market products across national boundaries, rather than from a domestic base. Then why do those multinational companies invest in foreign manufacturing and marketing operations instead of just ex-

porting from their home base? International product cycle theory explains that companies invest abroad reactively once their foreign market positions are threatened by local competitors. Thus, the primary objective of foreign direct investment for the exporting companies is to keep their market positions from being eroded. Are there any proactive reasons for companies to invest overseas?

To address this issue, a new strand of theory has been developed. It is known as **internalization** or **transaction cost theory**. Any company has some proprietary expertise that makes it different from its competitors. Without such expertise no company can sustain its competitive advantage. Such expertise may be reflected in a new product, unique product design, efficient production technique, or even brand image itself. As in the international product cycle argument, a company's expertise may eventually become common knowledge as a result of competitors copying it or reverse-engineering its product. Therefore, it is sometimes to an innovator company's advantage to keep its expertise to itself as long as possible in order to maximize the economic value of the expertise. A company's unique expertise is just like any information. Once information is let out, it becomes a "public good"—and free.

In other words, the MNC can be considered an organization that uses its internal market to produce and distribute products in an efficient manner in situations where the true value of its expertise cannot be assessed in ordinary external business transactions. Generating expertise or knowledge requires the company to invest in research and development. In most circumstances, it is necessary for the company to overcome this appropriability problem by the creation of a monopolistic internal market (i.e., internalization) when the knowledge advantage can be developed and explored in an optimal manner on a global basis.[40] The motive to internalize knowledge is generally strong when the company needs to invest in business assets (e.g., manufacturing and marketing infrastructure) that have few alternative uses, uses those assets frequently, and faces uncertainty in negotiating, monitoring, and enforcing a contract. Such a situation suggests a high level of transaction costs due to specific assets and contractual uncertainty involved.[41]

The company's expertise can be channeled through three routes to garner competitive advantage: appropriability regime, dominant design, and manufacturing/mar-

[40]Alan M. Rugman, ed., *New Theories of the Multinational Enterprise* (London: Croom Helm, 1982).

[41]Oliver E. Williamson, "The Economics of Organization: The Transaction Cost Approach," *American Journal of Sociology*, 87 (1981), pp. 548–77.

keting ability.[42] **Appropriability regime** refers to aspects of the commercial environment that govern a company's ability to retain its technological advantage. It depends on the efficacy of legal mechanisms of protection, such as patents, copyrights, and trade secrets. However, in today's highly competitive market, legal means of protecting proprietary technology have become ineffective as new product innovations are relatively easily reverse-engineered, improved upon, and invented around by competitors without violating patents and other proprietary protections bestowed on them. It is widely recognized that the most effective ways of securing maximum returns from a new product innovation are through lead time and moving fast down the experience curve (i.e., quickly resorting to mass production).[43] Obviously, the value of owning technology has lessened drastically in recent years because the inventor company's temporary monopoly over its technology has shortened.

Dominant design is a narrow class of product designs that begins to emerge as a "standard" design. A company that has won a dominant design status has an absolute competitive advantage over its competition. In an early stage of product development, many competing product designs exist. After considerable trial and error in the marketplace, a product standard tends to emerge. A good case example is Sony's Betamax format and Matsushita's VHS format for VCRs. The Betamax format was technologically superior with better picture quality than the VHS format, but could not play as long to record movies as the VHS. Although the Sony system was introduced slightly earlier than the Matsushita system, the tape's capability to record movies turned out to be fatal to Sony as the VHS tape was increasingly used for rental home movies and home recording of movies. Thus, the VHS emerged as the worldwide standard for videocassette recording.

Was it simply the act of the "invisible hand" in the marketplace? The answer is clearly no. Matsushita actively licensed its VHS technology to Sanyo, Sharp, and Toshiba for production and supplied VHS-format videocassette recorders to RCA, Magnavox, and GTE Sylvania for resale under their respective brand names.[44]

When Philips introduced a cassette tape recorder earlier, a similar active licensing strategy had been employed for a quick adoption as a dominant standard around the world. Despite various government hurdles to stall the Japanese domination of emerging HDTV technology, Sony is currently trying to make its format a standard by working its way into Hollywood movie studios. It is clear that a wide adoption of a new product around the world, whether autonomous or deliberated, seems to guarantee it a dominant design status.

Manufacturing and marketing ability is in almost all cases required for successful commercialization of a product innovation. The issue here is to what extent this ability is specialized to the development and commercialization of a new product. Indeed, many successful companies have highly committed their productive assets to closely related areas without diversifying into unrelated businesses. This commitment is crucial. Take semiconductor production, for example. A director at SEMATECH (a U.S. government–industry semiconductor manufacturing technology consortium established in Austin, Texas, to regain U.S. competitive edge in semiconductor manufacturing equipment from Japanese competition) admits that despite and because of a rapid technological turnover, any serious company wishing to compete on a state-of-the-art computer chip with the Japanese will have to invest a minimum of a billion dollars in a semiconductor manufacturing equipment and facility. General Motors has invested more than $5 billion for its Saturn project to compete with the Japanese in small car production and marketing. A massive retooling is also necessary for any significant upgrade in both industries. Furthermore, the software side of the manufacturing ability may be even more difficult to match, as it involves such specialized operational aspects as JIT (just-in-time) manufacturing management, quality control, and components-sourcing relationships. Irrespective of nationality, MNCs that are successful in global markets tend to excel not only in product innovative ability but also in manufacturing and marketing competencies.[45] It is clear that innova-

[42]David J. Teece, "Capturing Value from Technological Innovation: Integration, Strategic Partnering, and Licensing Decisions," in Bruce R. Guile and Harvey Brooks, eds., *Technology and Global Industry: Companies and Nations in the World Economy* (Washington, D.C.: National Academy Press), pp. 65–95.

[43]Richard C. Levin, Alvin K. Klevorick, Richard R. Nelson, and Sidney G. Winter, "Appropriating the Returns from Industrial Research and Development," *Brookings Papers on Economic Activity*, 3 (1987), pp. 783–831.

[44]Richard S. Rosenbloom and Michael A. Cusumano, "Technological Pioneering and Competitive Advantage: The Birth of VCR Industry," *California Management Review*, 29 (Summer 1987), pp. 51–76.

[45]Masaaki Kotabe, "Corporate Product Policy and Innovative Behavior of European and Japanese Multinationals: An Empirical Investigation," *Journal of Marketing*, 54 (April 1990), pp. 19–33.

tive companies committed to manufacturing and marketing excellence will likely remain strong competitors in industry.

These three sources of competitive advantage are not independent of each other. Given the relative ease of learning about competitors' proprietary knowledge without violating patents and other legal protections, many companies resort to mass production and mass marketing to drive down the cost along the experience curve. To do so requires enormous investment in manufacturing capacity. As a result, the efficacy of appropriability regime is highly dependent on investment in manufacturing and marketing ability. Similarly, a wide acceptance of a product is most likely necessary for the product to become a dominant design in the world for a next generation of the product. Thus, mass production and marketing on a global scale is likely to be a necessary, if not suf-ficient, condition for a company to attain a dominant design status for its product.

It is apparent that patents, copyrights, and trade secrets are not necessarily optimal means of garnering competitive advantage unless they are strongly backed by strengths in innovative manufacturing and marketing on a global basis. Likewise, companies strong in manufacturing without innovative products also suffer from competitive disadvantage. In other words, it takes such an enormous investment to develop new products and to penetrate new markets that few companies can go it alone anymore. Thus, to compete with integrated global competitors, an increasing number of companies have entered into strategic alliances so as to complement their competitive weaknesses with their partner's competitive strengths.

SUMMARY ✦

Three theories that cast some insight into the workings of international business have been reviewed. These theories supplement each other. Comparative advantage theory is useful when we think broadly about the nature of industrial development and international trade around the world. International product cycle theory helps explain why and how a company initially extends its market horizons abroad and how foreign competitors shape global competition over time and place. Internalization or trans-action cost theory provides some answers to how to manage multinational operations in a very competitive world.

There are other theories to supplement our understanding of international business. However, they are beyond the scope of this textbook and are probably unnecessary. Now you can appreciate how international business has expanded in scope over time. With understanding of these theories, we hope you can better understand the rest of the book.

KEY TERMS ✦

absolute advantage	factor endowment theory	economies of scale	preference similarity
comparative advantage	international product cycle theory	economies of scope	internalization theory
commodity terms of trade		technological gap	transaction cost theory

GLOBAL ECONOMIC ENVIRONMENT

2

CHAPTER OVERVIEW

1. INTERTWINED WORLD ECONOMY

2. COUNTRY COMPETITIVENESS

3. EVOLUTION OF COOPERATIVE GLOBAL TRADE AGREEMENTS

4. U.S. POSITION IN FOREIGN DIRECT INVESTMENT AND TRADE

5. INFORMATION TECHNOLOGY AND THE CHANGING
   NATURE OF COMPETITION

6. REGIONAL ECONOMIC ARRANGEMENTS

7. MULTINATIONAL CORPORATIONS

At no other time in economic history have countries been more economically interdependent. Although the second half of the twentieth century saw the highest ever sustained growth rates in **gross domestic product** (GDP) in history, the growth in international flows in goods and services (called international trade) has consistently surpassed the growth rate of the world economy. Simultaneously, the growth in international financial flows—which includes foreign direct investment, portfolio investment, and trading in currencies—has achieved a life of its own. The annual trade in goods and services amounted to almost $11 trillion in 1998.[1] Daily international financial flows now exceed $1 trillion. Thanks to trade liberalization heralded by the General Agreement on Tariffs and Trade (GATT) and the World

---

[1]*World Trade Growth Slower In 1998 After Unusually Strong Growth In 1997*, World Trade Organization, Press Release, April 16, 1999, http://www.wto.org/wto/intltrad/internat.htm, Accessed May 10, 2000.

Trade Organization (WTO), the GATT's successor, the barriers to international trade and financial flows keep getting lower. While global GDP has grown fivefold since 1950, global trade has expanded seventeenfold during the same period.[2] On the average of fortynine countries, exports as a share of GDP also increased to approximately 24 percent in 1998 from 17 percent a decade earlier.[3] Expanding world markets are a key driving force for the twenty-first century economy. Although the severe slump in Asia in the late 1990s points out the vulnerabilities to the global marketplace, the long-term trends of fast-rising trade and rising world incomes remain in place.

Short of war, an epidemic, or market-closing, inward-turning policies, most countries in the twenty-first century are likely to keep pursuing globalization. According to forecasts by Standard & Poor's DRI, world exports of goods and services will reach $11.4 trillion by 2005, or 28 percent of world GDP, nearly double this year's projected $6.5 trillion, or 24.3 percent of world GDP.[4] World trade's share of GDP in 1980 was no more than 9 percent. As a consequence, even a firm that is operating in only one domestic market is not immune to the influence of economic activities external to that market. The net result of these factors has been the increased interdependence of countries and economies, increased competitiveness, and the concomitant need for firms to keep a constant watch on the international economic environment.

◆ ◆ ◆ ◆ ◆ ◆ INTERTWINED WORLD ECONOMY

Despite the increasingly intertwined world economy, the United States is still relatively more insulated from the global economy than other nations. In a $7.4 trillion economy in 1998, a trade deficit of $247 billion is about 3.3 percent of the GDP. Foreigners owned only 6 percent of the stocks and 14 percent of the bonds in 1995, and despite a surge in overseas investing by Americans, more than 95 percent of the stocks and 97 percent of the bonds owned by Americans were still U.S. stocks and bonds in 1995.[5] About 90 percent of what Americans consume is produced in America (measured as the ratio of the country's imports to its GDP)—which implies that in the absence of a chain reaction from abroad, the United States is relatively more insulated from external shocks than, say, Britain and Taiwan. The imports/GDP ratios for Britain and Taiwan are 24 percent and 43 percent, respectively. Nonetheless, the U.S. economy, too, is getting increasingly intertwined with the rest of the world economy. The dollar value of international trade in goods and services in 1998 for the United States was $2.56 trillion.[6] Most of the trade in goods was with a few major trading partners, as shown in Exhibit 2–1.

---

[2]"World Trade: Time for Another Round," *Economist* (October 3, 1998), p. 3.

[3]"The 21st Century Economy," *Business Week* (August 31, 1998), pp. 66–67.

[4]"Two Steps Forward, One Step Back: Asian Crisis or No, Globalization Is on the Rise— Promising Both Greater Opportunities and Higher Risks," *Business Week* (August 31, 1998), p. 116.

[5]"Global Mythmaking," *Newsweek* (May 8, 1995), p. 55.

[6]*Statistical Abstract of the United States* (Washington, D.C.: U.S. Census Bureau, 1999), p. 790.

EXHIBIT 2–1
TOP PURCHASERS OF U.S. EXPORTS AND SUPPLIERS OF U.S. GENERAL IMPORTS, 1998

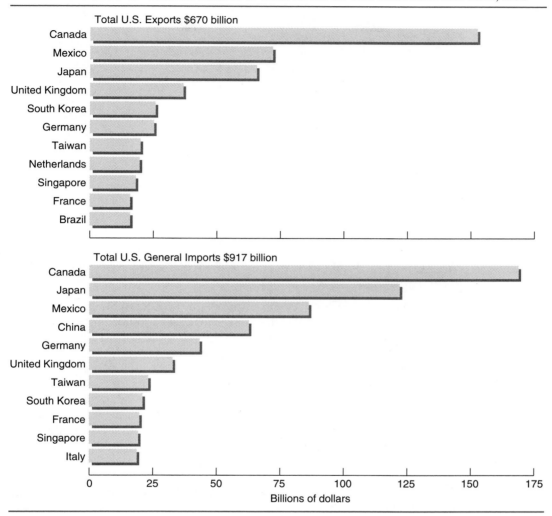

Source: U.S. Census Bureau, *Statistical Abstract of the United States 1999*, 1999.

Over the next two decades, however, the markets that hold the greatest potential for dramatic increases in U.S. exports are not the traditional trading partners in Europe and Japan, which now account for the overwhelming bulk of the international trade of the United States. But, as introduced in Chapter 1, they will be major emerging economies, known as **big emerging markets** (BEMs).[7] Already, there are signs that in the future the biggest trade headache for the United States may

[7]BEMs include the Chinese Economic Area (CEA: including China, Hong Kong region, and Taiwan), India, South Korea, Mexico, Brazil, Argentina, South Africa, Poland, Turkey, and the Association of Southeast Asian Nations (ASEAN: including Indonesia, Brunei, Malaysia, Singapore, Thailand, the Philippines, and Vietnam).

"The repairs will take awhile. We need a part from Mexico, a part from Brazil and one from Taiwan."

Even a simple "domestic" job involves inputs from various countries in an intertwined world.

not be Japan, but China.[8] China's trade surplus with the United States in 1997 was $50 billion; with current trends it will surpass Japan's $56 billion surplus with the United States, which is on its way down.

The importance of international trade and investment cannot be overemphasized for any country. In general, the larger the country's domestic economy, the less dependent it tends to be on exports and imports relative to its GDP. For the United States (GDP = $7.4 trillion in 1998), international trade in goods and services (sum of exports and imports) has risen from 10 percent of the GDP in 1970 to about 20 percent in 1998. For Japan (GDP = $5.2 trillion), international trade forms a little over 14 percent. For Germany (GDP = $2.4 trillion), trade forms about 40 percent of the GDP, for Taiwan (GDP = $0.3 trillion), trade is as high as 82 percent.[9] These trade statistics are relative to the country's GDP. In absolute dollar terms, however, a small relative trade percentage of a large economy still translates into large volumes of trade (See Exhibit 2–2). As shown in the last column for exports and imports in Exhibit 2–2, the per-capita amount of exports and imports is another important statistic for marketing purposes as it represents, on average, how much involved or dependent each individual is on international trade. For instance, individuals (consumers and companies) in the United States and Japan tend to be able to find domestic sources for their needs, since their economies are diversified and extremely large. The U.S. per-capita value of exports and imports is $3,320 and $4,090, respectively. For Japan, it is very similar—$3,560 and $6,650, respectively. On the other hand, individuals in smaller and rich economies tend to rely more heavily on international trade, as illustrated by the Netherlands, with per-capita exports and imports of $15,670 and $7,820, respectively, and by Hong Kong with per-capita exports and imports of a whopping $31,080 and $31,530,

[8]"The New Trade Superpower," *Business Week* (October 16, 1995), pp. 56–57.
[9]*Japan 1998: An International Comparison*, Tokyo: Keizai Koho Center, 1998.

EXHIBIT 2–2

LEADING EXPORTERS AND IMPORTERS IN WORLD TRADE IN MERCHANDISE AND SERVICES, 1998 (IN $ BILLION)

Rank	Exporters	Value	Value per capita	Rank	Importers	Value	Value per capita
1	United States	911.6	3,320	1	United States	1,106.1	4,090
2	Germany	615.4	7,500	2	Germany	588.4	7,170
3	Japan	448.0	3,560	3	United Kingdom	392.2	6,650
4	France	385.6	6.560	4	Japan	390.0	3,100
5	United Kingdom	372.2	6,310	5	France	350.0	5,950
6	Italy	311.0	5,480	6	Italy	283.3	4,990
7	The Netherlands	246.5	15,670	7	Canada	239.8	7,820
8	Canada	243.1	7,930	8	The Netherlands	228.9	14,550
9	Hong Kong, China	208.3	31,080	9	Hong Kong, China	211.4	31,530
	Domestic exports	24.3	–		*Retained imports*[a]	38.9	–
10	China	206.8	170	10	Belgium-Luxembourg	192.4	17,443

[a]Retained imports are defined as imports less re-exports.

Source: Computed from *Statistical Abstract of the United States 1998* (Washington, D.C.: Census Bureau, 1998); and *World Trade Growth Slower In 1998 After Unusually Strong Growth In 1997,* World Trade Organization, Press Release, April 16, 1999.

respectively. Although China's overall exports and imports amounted to $206.8 billion and $168.8 billion (not shown in Exhibit 2–2), respectively, the per-capita exports and imports amounted to only $170 and $136 in 1998. One implication of these figures is that the higher the per-capita trade, the more closely intertwined is that country's economy with the rest of the world. Intertwining of economies by the process of specialization due to international trade leads to job creation in both the exporting country and the importing country.

However, beyond the simple figure of trade as a rising percentage of a nation's GDP lies the more interesting question of what rising trade does to the economy of a nation. A nation that is a successful trader—i.e., it makes goods and services that other nations buy and it buys goods and services from other nations—displays a natural inclination to be competitive in the world market. The threat of a possible foreign competitor is a powerful incentive for firms and nations to invest in technology and markets in order to remain competitive. Also, apart from trade flows, foreign direct investment, portfolio investment, and daily financial flows in the international money markets profoundly influence the economies of countries that may be seemingly completely separate.

Foreign direct investment—which means investment in manufacturing and service facilities in a foreign country with an intention to engage actively in managing them—is another facet of the increasing integration of national economies. Between 1990 and 1997, the value of international trade grew by just under 60 percent in dollar terms, whereas foreign direct investment nearly doubled over the same period. Most of this investment went from one developed country to another, but a growing share is now going to developing countries, mainly in Asia. The overall annual world inflow of foreign direct investment reached $400 billion in 1997.

Foreign Direct Investment

Flows to developing countries amounted to $149 billion, representing 37 percent of all global foreign direct investment, in 1997 compared with $34 billion, or 17 percent of all foreign direct investment in 1990.[10]

In the past, foreign direct investment was considered as an alternative to exports in order to avoid tariff barriers. However, these days, foreign direct investment and international trade have become complementary.[11] For example, Dell Computer uses a factory in Ireland to supply personal computers in Europe instead of exporting from Austin, Texas. Similarly, Honda, a Japanese automaker with a major factory in Marysville, Ohio, is the largest exporter of automobiles from the United States. As firms invest in manufacturing and distribution facilities outside their home countries to expand into new markets around the world, they have added to the stock of foreign direct investment.

The increase in foreign direct investment is also promoted by efforts by many national governments to woo multinationals and by the leverage that the governments of large potential markets such as China and India have in granting access to multinationals. Sometimes trade friction can also promote foreign direct investment. Investment in the United States by Japanese companies is, to an extent, a function of the trade imbalances between the two nations and by the consequent pressure applied by the U.S. government on Japan to do something to reduce the bilateral trade deficit. Since most of the U.S. trade deficit with Japan is attributed to Japanese cars exported from Japan, Japanese automakers (e.g., Honda, Toyota, Nissan, and Mitsubishi) have set up production facilities in the United States. In 1986, Japanese automakers exported 3.43 million cars from Japan and assembled only 0.62 million cars in the United States. By 1992, the number of exported cars equaled the number of U.S.-built Japanese cars, at 1.7 million cars each. Since then, Japanese automakers have manufactured more cars in the United States than exported from Japan. In 1997, they produced 2.31 million cars in the United States and imported 1.27 million cars from Japan. During the 1986–97 period, Japanese automakers also increased their purchases of U.S.-made components tenfold, from $2.5 billion in 1986 to $25.0 billion in 1997.[12] This localization strategy reduces Japanese automakers' vulnerability to retaliation by the United States under the Super 301 laws of the Omnibus Trade and Competitiveness Act of 1988.

Portfolio Investment

An additional facet to the rising integration of economies has to do with **portfolio investment** (or **indirect investment**) in foreign countries and with money flows in the international financial markets. Portfolio investment refers to investments in foreign countries that are withdrawable at short notice, such as investment in foreign stocks and bonds. In the international financial markets, the borders between nations have, for all practical purposes, disappeared.[13] The enormous quantities of money that get traded on a daily basis have assumed a life of their own. When trading in foreign currencies began, it was as an adjunct transaction to an international

[10]*World Investment Report 1998*, Geneva: UNCTAD, 1999, http://www.un.org/publications.

[11]"Trade by Any Other Name," *Economist* (October 3, 1998), pp. 10–14.

[12]"The Role the Japanese Auto Industry Played in the United States and the Challenges the Global Auto Industry Will Face," *JAMA Forum*, 17 (December 1998), pp. 3–18.

[13]Kenichi Ohmae, *The Borderless World* (New York: Harper Collins Books, 1990).

trade transaction in goods and services—banks and firms bought and sold currencies to complete the export or import transaction or to hedge the exposure to fluctuations in the exchange rates in the currencies of interest in the trade transaction. However, in today's international financial markets, traders trade currencies most of the time without an underlying trade transaction. They trade on the accounts of the banks and financial institutions they work for, mostly on the basis of daily news on inflation rates, interest rates, political events, stock and bond market movements, commodity supplies and demand, and so on. As mentioned earlier, the weekly volume of international trade in currencies exceeds the annual value of the trade in goods and services.

The effect of this proverbial tail wagging the dog is that all nations with even partially convertible currencies are exposed to the fluctuations in the currency markets. A rise in the value of the local currency due to these daily flows vis-à-vis other currencies makes exports more expensive (at least in the short run) and can add to the trade deficit or reduce the trade surplus. A rising currency value will also deter foreign investment in the country and will encourage outflow of investment.[14] It may also encourage a decrease in the interest rates in the country if the central bank of that country wants to maintain the currency exchange rate, and a decrease in the interest rate will spur local investment. An interesting example is the Mexican meltdown in early 1995 and the massive devaluation of the peso, which was exacerbated by the withdrawal of money by foreign investors. More recently, the massive depreciation of many Asian currencies in the 1997–99 period, known as the Asian financial crisis, is also an instance of the influence of these short-term movements of money.[15] Implications of the Asian financial crisis are explained in detail in Chapter 3. Unfortunately, the influences of these short-term money flows are nowadays far more powerful determinants of exchange rates than an investment by a Japanese or German automaker.

Another example is provided by Brazil, which was a largely protected market until 1995. Liberalization is on the way as a result of the formation in 1994 of the Southern Common Market (Mercado Común del Sur, or MERCOSUR), consisting of Brazil, Argentina, Uruguay, and Paraguay, and Chile and Bolivia as associate members.[16] Since the debt crisis of 1982, Brazil had suffered a chronic hyperinflation that ruined its economy and competitiveness. Brazil's new currency, the *real* (pronounced *re äl'*), was launched in 1994 both as the instrument and as the symbol of a huge effort for Brazil to catch up with the developed world. Financial markets had first attacked the Brazilian real in March 1995, in the wake of Mexico's peso devaluation. Brazil responded by adopting a pegged exchange rate, under which the real devalued by 7.5 percent a year against the U.S. dollar. Then, the Asian financial crisis and the crash of many Asian currencies (as much as 75 percent in the case of Indonesian currency in a matter of a few months) in 1998 reverberated again in Brazil and Mexico as well, because portfolio investors started viewing all emerging markets with a jaundiced eye. The Brazilian real was under pressure through

[14]"Hot Money," *Business Week* (March 20, 1995), pp. 46–50.

[15]Masaaki Kotabe, "The Four Faces of the Asian Financial Crisis: How to Cope with the Southeast Asia Problem, the Japan Problem, the Korea Problem, and the China Problem," *Journal of International Management*, 4(1) (1998), 1S-6S.

[16]Masaaki Kotabe and Maria Cecilia Coutinho de Arruda, "South America's Free Trade Gambit," *Marketing Management*, 7 (Spring 1998), pp. 38–46.

much of 1998, falling from R1/US$ in July 1994 to R1.80/US$ in August 1999—80 percent depreciation since its introduction. The central bank had to sell dollars and buy real to shore up the value of the real. This led to a credit crunch, causing a slowdown in export growth.[17] There were adverse effects on the Indian stock markets as well. The point is that, at least in the short run, these daily international flows of money have dealt a blow to the notion of economic independence and nationalism.

◆ ◆ ◆ ◆ ◆ ◆ COUNTRY COMPETITIVENESS

Country competitiveness refers to the productiveness of a country, which is represented by its firms' domestic and international productive capacity. Human, natural, and capital resources of a country primarily shape the nature of corporate productive capacity in the world, and thus the nature of international business. As explained in the Appendix to Chapter 1, a country's relative endowment in those resources shape its competitiveness.

Changing Country Competitiveness

Country competitiveness is not a fixed thing. The dominant feature of the global economy is the rapid change in the relative status of various countries' economic output. In 1830, China and India alone accounted for about 60 percent of the manufactured output of the world. Since then, the share of the world manufacturing output produced by the twenty or so countries that are today known as the rich industrial economies moved from about 30 percent in 1830 to almost 80 percent by 1913.[18] In the 1980s, the U.S. economy was characterized as "floundering" or even "declining," and many pundits predicted that Asia, led by Japan, would become the leading regional economy in the twenty-first century. Then the 1998–99 Asian financial crisis changed the economic milieu of the world (to be explained in detail in Chapter 3); now, the U.S. economy has been growing at a faster rate than any other developed countries. In recent years, the United States and Western European economies have become the twin drivers of the world economy, fueled by increased trade and investment as a result of continued deregulation, improved technology, and cross-Atlantic mergers, among other things.[19] Obviously, a decade is a long time in today's world economy, and indeed, no single country has sustained its economic performance indefinitely. U.S., European, and Japanese economies, *on the average*, enjoyed similar economic growth rates over the last fifteen years.[20]

Human Resources and Technology

Although wholesale generalizations should not be made, the role of human skill resources has become increasingly important as a primary determinant of industry and country competitiveness as the level of technology has advanced. As shown in

[17]"Brazil: The Devaluing of a Presidency," *Economist* (March 27, 1999), pp. 3–5.

[18]Paul Bairoch, "International Industrialization Levels from 1750 to 1980," *Journal of European Economic History*, 11 (1982), pp. 36–54.

[19]Joan Warner, Pete Engardino, and Thane Peterson, "The Atlantic Century?" *Business Week* (February 8, 1999), pp. 64–67.

[20]"Desperately Seeking a Perfect Model," *Economist* (April 10, 1999), pp. 67–69.

EXHIBIT 2–3
COUNTRY COMPETITIVENESS REPORT

Human Resources			Natural Resources			Capital Resources		
Country	Score	Rank	Country	Score	Rank	Country	Score	Rank
Japan	73.2	1	Russia	74.1	1	France	97.3	1
United States	73.0	2	Australia	69.1	2	Japan	96.9	2
Indonesia	72.1	3	Canada	62.8	3	Luxembourg	96.4	3
Thailand	70.9	4	Iceland	60.3	4	Singapore	96.3	4
Singapore	70.7	5	Austria	53.7	5	United Kingdom	96.2	5
Taiwan	69.0	6	Norway	53.1	6	Norway	96.0	6
Korea	67.9	7	France	48.6	7	Denmark	95.8	7
Hong Kong	67.7	8	United States	48.5	8	The Netherlands	95.6	8
Malaysia	66.5	9	Spain	47.5	9	United States	95.6	9
Austria	65.7	10	Italy	47.5	10	Hong Kong	95.4	10

Source: 1999 IPS National Competitiveness Report, The Institute of Industrial Policy Studies, http://www.ips.or.kr/ 1999ncrdownload.htm, 1999.

Exhibit 2–3, the Institute of Industrial Policy Studies' 1999 country competitiveness report[21] placed Asian Tigers (Singapore, Taiwan, Korea, and Hong Kong) and Indonesia, Thailand, and Malaysia among the world's top ten economies (along with Japan, the United States, and Austria) in terms of human resources. A word of caution is in order when we use any aggregate reports. Although the rankings for human and natural resources may not vary much from year to year, the ranking for capital resources could change drastically from year to year due to their fluid nature. Once all these resources are combined, we could expect a very complex nature of country competitiveness in the short run, as evidenced by the financial crisis in Asia and Latin America.

Human resources are crucial particularly for a country's long-term economic vitality. Although many of those Asian countries are still reeling from the financial crisis, their fundamental long-term corporate strengths, which have been slowed down or stymied by their huge financial burden, seem to be intact or even improved over the years.

This prognosis—seemingly contradictory to the current situation—is further supported by a recent research report published in 1999 by U.S. Council on Competitiveness,[22] which concluded that U.S. technological competitiveness had peaked in 1985 and that the United States might be living off historical assets that are not being renewed. Another conclusion was that although the United States and Switzerland have been the most innovative in the last three decades, other OECD nations have been catching up. Further conclusions: that Japan has dramatically improved its innovative capacity since the early 1970s with little sign of weakening despite its economic slowdown in the 1990s; that Denmark, Finland, and Sweden have made major gains in innovative capacity since the mid-1980s; and that Singapore, Taiwan, South Korea, Israel, and Ireland have upgraded their innovative

[21]*1999 IPS National Competitiveness Report,* The Institute of Industrial Policy Studies, http://www.ips.or.kr, 1999.
[22]Michael E. Porter and Scott Stern, *The Challenge to America's Prosperity: Findings from the Innovation Index* (Washington, D.C.: Council on Competitiveness, 1999).

EXHIBIT 2–4
CHANGE IN COUNTRY INNOVATIVENESS: A KEY TO A COUNTRY'S LONG-TERM COMPETITIVENESS

Rank	1980	1986	1993	1995	1999	2005 (expected)
1	Switzerland	Switzerland	Switzerland	U.S.A.	Japan	Japan
2	U.S.A.	U.S.A.	Japan	Switzerland	Switzerland	Finland
3	Germany	Japan	U.S.A.	Japan	U.S.A.	Switzerland
4	Japan	Germany	Germany	Sweden	Sweden	Denmark
5	Sweden	Sweden	Sweden	Germany	Germany	Sweden
6	Canada	Canada	Denmark	Finland	Finland	U.S.A.
7	France	Finland	France	Denmark	Denmark	Germany
8	The Netherlands	The Netherlands	Canada	France	France	France
9	Finland	Norway	Finland	Canada	Norway	Norway
10	U.K.	France	Australia	Norway	Canada	Canada
11	Norway	Denmark	The Netherlands	The Netherlands	Australia	Australia
12	Denmark	U.K.	Norway	Australia	The Netherlands	Austria
13	Austria	Australia	U.K.	Austria	Austria	The Netherlands
14	Australia	Austria	Austria	U.K.	U.K.	U.K.
15	Italy	Italy	New Zealand	New Zealand	New Zealand	New Zealand
16	New Zealand	New Zealand	Italy	Italy	Italy	Spain
17	Spain	Spain	Spain	Spain	Spain	Italy

Source: Michael E. Porter and Scott Stern, *The Challenge to America's Prosperity: Findings from the Innovation Index* (Washington, D.C.: Council on Competitiveness, 1999), pp. 34–35.

capacity over the past decade, becoming new centers of innovative activity.[23] See Exhibit 2–4 showing the change in the innovative capability of leading countries over the years.

One major lesson here is that we should not be misled by mass media coverage of the current economic situations of various countries. Although mass media coverage is factual and near-term focused, it may inadvertently cloud our strategic thinking. In other words, the current stellar performance of the U.S. economy should not erroneously lull us into believing that U.S. companies are invincible in the global economy.[24] Despite the Asian financial crisis, executives of U.S. and European companies should not ignore either the potential competitive threat re-emerging from their Asian competitors or their marketing opportunities in Asia and the rest of the world.

◆ ◆ ◆ ◆ ◆ ◆ **EVOLUTION OF COOPERATIVE GLOBAL TRADE AGREEMENTS**

General Agreements on Tariffs and Trade

In the aftermath of World War II, the then-big powers negotiated the setting up of an **International Trade Organization (ITO)**, with the objective of ensuring free trade among nations through negotiated lowering of trade barriers. ITO would

---

[23]Ibid., p. 7.
[24]Paul Krugman, "America the Boastful," *Foreign Affairs* 77 (May/June 1998), pp. 32–45.

have been an international organization operating under the umbrella of the United Nations with statutory powers to enforce agreements. However, when the U.S. government announced, in 1950, that it would not seek congressional approval, ITO was effectively dead. Instead, to keep the momentum of increasing trade through the lowering of trade barriers alive, the signatories to ITO agreed to operate under the informal aegis of the **General Agreements on Tariffs and Trade (GATT)**. GATT provided a forum for multilateral discussion among countries to reduce trade barriers. Nations met periodically to review the status of world trade and to negotiate mutually agreeable reductions in trade barriers.

The main operating principle of GATT was the concept of **most favored nations (MFN)**. The MFN status meant that any country that was a member state to a GATT agreement and that extended a reduction in tariff to another nation must automatically extend the same benefit to all members of GATT. However, there was no enforcement mechanism, and over time many countries negotiated bilateral agreements, especially for agricultural products, steel, textiles, and automobiles. As Global Perspective 2–1 shows, the United States also frequently violated the GATT principles and resorted to unilateral trade sanctions against foreign trading partners.

GATT was successful in lowering trade barriers to a substantial extent (e.g., developed countries' average tariffs on manufactured goods from around 40 percent down to a mere 4 percent during its existence from 1948 to 1994). However, some major shortcomings limited its potential and effectiveness. The initial rounds of GATT concentrated only on lowering tariff barriers. As trade in services expanded faster than the trade in goods and GATT concentrated on merchandise trade, more and more international trade came to be outside the purview of GATT. Second, GATT tended to concentrate mostly on tariffs, and many nations used nontariff barriers, such as quota and onerous customs procedure, to get around the spirit of GATT when they could not increase tariffs. Finally, as developed nations moved from manufacturing-based economies to services- and knowledge-based economies, they felt the need to bring intellectual property within the purview of international agreement, because that was where the competitive advantage lay for firms in the developed nations.

World Trade Organization

The eighth and last round of GATT talks—called the **Uruguay Round**—lasted from 1986 to 1994 and was successful in bringing many agricultural products and textiles under the purview of GATT. The Uruguay Round created an environment in which a global body of customs and trade law is developing. In particular, the Uruguay Round ensured the ultimate harmonization of the overall customs process and the fundamental determinations that are made for all goods crossing an international border: admissibility, classification, and valuation.[25] It also included provisions for trade in intellectual property for the first time and provided for many services. Most important, perhaps, it set up an international body called the **World Trade Organization (WTO)**, which took effect on January 1, 1995. At the

[25]Paulsen K. Vandevert, "The Uruguay Round and the World Trade Organization: A New Era Dawns in the Private Law of International Customs and Trade," *Case Western Reserve Journal of International Law*, 31 (Winter 1999), pp. 107–38.

❖ ❖

*G*LOBAL PERSPECTIVE 2–1

TRADE BARRIERS AND POLITICS

The United States thinks of itself as a leading exponent of free trade and frequently brings actions against other nations as unfair trade partners. Section 301 of the Omnibus Trade and Competitiveness Act empowers the federal government to investigate and retaliate against specific foreign trade barriers judged to be unfair by the United States and to impose up to 100 percent tariffs on exports to the United States from guilty nations unless they satisfy U.S. criteria for fairness. But critics say that the United States is sometimes hypocritical in such actions, because it is guilty of the very acts of which it is accusing other nations. A Japanese government study alleges that the United States engages in unfair trade practices in ten of the twelve policy areas looked at in the study. This Japanese study suggests that the U.S. quotas on imports have high tariffs and abuse anti-dumping measures.

The United States launched a Section 301 investigation of Japanese citrus quotas. "The removal of Japan's unfair trade barriers could cut the prices of oranges for Japanese consumers by up to a third, according to the U.S. trade representative." Coincidentally, the United States had a 40 percent tariff on Brazilian orange juice imports when the investigation was initiated. The United States used Section 301 against Korea for its beef import quotas, even though the U.S. has beef import quotas that cost U.S. consumers up $870 million in higher prices.

Sources: Abstracted from James Bovard, "A U.S. History of Trade Hypocrisy," *Wall Street Journal* (March 8, 1994), p. A10; "The Great Trade Violator?" *World Press Review* (August 1994), p. 41; Robert S. Greenberger, "Washington Will Boycott WTO Panel," *Wall Street Journal* (February 21, 1997), p. A2; and Michael R. Czinkota and Masaaki Kotabe, "A Marketing Perspective of the U.S. International Trade Commission's Antidumping Actions: An Empirical Inquiry," *Journal of World Business*, 32 (Spring 1997).

Another case was brought against Brazil, Korea, and Taiwan for trade barriers on footwear, even though the United States, at the time of the bringing of the case, had tariffs as high as 67 percent on footwear imports. Many Section 301 complaints have involved agricultural export subsidies, including European Union poultry export subsidies, EU wheat and wheat export subsidies, and Taiwan rice export subsidies. However, in recent years, the United States has provided export subsidies of 111 percent for poultry, 78 percent for wheat flour, 94 percent for wheat, and more than 100 percent for rice.

So, is the United States as guilty as the rest or not? Examining 310 cases filed with the U.S. International Trade Commission (ITC), one recent study has shown unequivocally that the ITC tends to support with an antidumping charge not only those fragmented industries with a declining market, but also more concentrated industries with a stable or even growing market. This finding indicates that for large U.S. firms, antidumping regulations may even be useful as a strategic competitive tool. In other words, like any other country, the U.S. tries to protect what it perceives to be its trade interests—and some of these interests are often driven by local political considerations. The advent of the World Trade Organization (WTO) and the establishment of procedures for hearing and adjudicating complaints will hopefully lead to a reduction in unilateral actions by all countries—including the United States. This means that local political interests will be less able to determine trade policies—which, in a sense, is an infringement of national sovereignty. Infringement of national sovereignty has long been a reason for opposition against lowering trade barriers and forming organizations like WTO in the United States.

At the time of writing this book, the United States is contemplating a boycott of a WTO's panel requested by the European Union to review the legality of certain U.S. trade sanctions against Cuba.

time of writing this chapter, the WTO had 135 member countries, with Estonia having become the newest member on May 21, 1999. Many newly created countries from Eastern Europe and the ex-Soviet Union, as well as developing countries that have realized the benefits of multilateral free trade, have requested to join the WTO, and their applications are currently being considered by accession working parties: Albania, Algeria, Andorra, Armenia, Azerbaijan, Belarus, Cambodia,

People's Republic of China,[26] Croatia, Georgia, Jordan, Kazakhstan, Lao People's Democratic Republic, Lebanon, Lithuania, Former Yugoslav Republic of Macedonia, Moldova, Nepal, Sultanate of Oman, Russian Federation, Samoa, Saudi Arabia, Seychelles, Sudan, Chinese Taipei, Tonga, Ukraine, Uzbekistan, Vanuatu, and Vietnam.[27]

WTO has statutory powers to adjudicate trade disputes among nations. The agreement provides for setting up a permanent international organization (i.e., the World Trade Organization or WTO) headed by a director-general to oversee the smooth functioning of the multilateral trade accords agreed upon under the Uruguay Round. The WTO is the new legal and institutional foundation for a multilateral trading system. It provides the contractual obligations determining how governments frame and implement domestic trade legislation and regulations. Moreover, it is the platform on which trade relations among countries evolve through collective debate, negotiation, and adjudication.

One of the objectives of the developed nations in the Uruguay Round was to get developing nations (primarily Brazil, China, and India) to agree to accept intellectual property rights for product patents in pharmaceuticals, chemicals, and food products. By and large, developing nations have tended not to grant product patents for pharmaceuticals, chemicals, and food products—only process patents have been granted. Thus, many international pharmaceutical firms have complained that the drugs that they produce at a great cost get reproduced at a lower cost by a different process in developing nations like India and China. The justification that the developing nations have given is that if they did not do so, life-saving drugs would be priced out of reach of all but the very rich. As a result of the Uruguay Round, developing nations have agreed to phase in product patents in these areas by the year 2005.[28] Partly as a quid pro quo to this agreement, the developed nations have given concessions in other areas, such as the agreement to phase out over ten years beginning in 1995 the Multi-Fibre Agreement, which restricted textile exports from the developing countries.[29] Developing country exporters will still face one old problem—add value and the tariff goes up—that is, manufactured goods face a higher tariff than agricultural goods. Exhibit 2–5 gives an idea of the scope of the Uruguay Round of GATT that is manifested through WTO.

Incidentally, the WTO is not simply an extension of GATT. GATT was a multilateral agreement with no institutional foundations. The WTO is a permanent institution with its own secretariat. The GATT was applied on a provisional basis in strict legal terms. WTO commitments are full and permanent and legally binding

---

[26]"The United States and China came to mutually agreed-upon terms for China's participation in the WTO on November 15, 1999. Now that the European Union signed a landmark trade pact with China on May 19, 2000, China's entry to the WTO has moved an inch closer to reality (at the time of this writing). The WTO sets global trade rules and China has been seeking entry for more than a decade by agreeing to reduce trade barriers that have propped up large parts of its state-owned industry. China, the seventh largest economy in the world with a population of 1.2 billion people, promises to offer major business opportunities to foreign companies by opening its markets, including telecommunications industry."

[27]World Trade Organization Press Release, "Estonia to Become 135th Member of WTO," May 21, 1999, www.wto.org/new/pressest.htm, accessed June 24, 1999.

[28]"The Uruguay Round: Winners and Winners," *World Bank Policy Research Bulletin*, 6 (January–February 1997), pp. 2–3.

[29]"Textile–Back in the Mainstream," www.wto.org/about/test0.htm, accessed June 30, 1999.

EXHIBIT 2–5

AGENDA FOR WTO: A SUMMARY OF THE FINAL ACT OF THE URUGUAY ROUND OF GATT

- Agreement Establishing the WTO (World Trade Organization)
- General Agreement on Tariffs and Trade 1994
- Uruguay Round Protocol GATT 1994
- Agreement on Agriculture
- Agreement on Sanitary and Phytosanitary Measures
- Decision on Measures Concerning the Possible Negative Effects of the Reform Program on Least-Developed and Net Food-Importing Developing Countries
- Agreement on Textiles and Clothing
- Agreement on Technical Barriers to Trade
- Agreement on Trade-Related Investment Measures
- Agreement on Implementation of Article VI (Anti-Dumping)
- Agreement on Implementation of Article VII (Customs Valuation)
- Agreement on Preshipment Inspection
- Agreement on Rules of Origin
- Agreement on Import Licensing Procedures
- Agreement on Subsidies and Countervailing Measures
- Agreement on Safeguards
- General Agreement on Trade in Services
- Agreement on Trade-Related Aspects of Intellectual Property Rights, Including Trade in Counterfeit Goods
- Understanding on Rules and Procedures Governing the Settlement of Disputes
- Decision of Achieving Greater Coherence in Global Economic Policy Making

Source: World Trade Organization, http://www.wto.org/legal/ursum_wp.htm, accessed on May 10, 2000.

under international law. Although GATT was restricted to trade in merchandise goods, WTO includes trade in services and trade-related aspects of intellectual property. It is to be noted that GATT lives on within WTO. The Uruguay Round resulting in GATT, 1994, is an integral part of WTO.

The WTO dispute settlement mechanism is faster, more automatic, and therefore much less susceptible to blockages than the old GATT system. Once a country indicates to WTO that it has a complaint about the trade practices of another country, an automatic schedule kicks in. The two countries have three months for mutual "consultations" to iron out their differences. If the disputants cannot come to a mutually satisfactory settlement, then the dispute is referred to the Dispute Settlement Mechanism of WTO, under which a decision has to be rendered within six months of the setting up of the panel to resolve the dispute. The decision of the panel is supposed to be legally binding. However, Global Perspective 2–2 provides as an example a banana import dispute against the European Union brought by the United States and four Latin American banana-producing countries that is currently testing the binding authority, and thus viability, of WTO as the global regulatory body of international commerce.

GLOBAL PERSPECTIVE 2–2

WTO ALREADY UNDER PRESSURE OVER BANANAS

In April 1996, the European Union (EU) blocked immediate creation of a dispute panel in the World Trade Organization (WTO) over its controversial banana-import regime. The panel had been requested by the United States and four Latin American banana-producer countries—Guatemala, Honduras, Ecuador, and Mexico. EU told the WTO Dispute Settlement Body (DSB) that consultations to try to find a solution had not yet been exhausted and could not yet agree on formation of a panel, the sources said. But under DSB rules, the EU was not able to block a decision at the May 8, 1996, meeting of the body, so a panel—which had six months to make its findings known—was automatically created.

The five countries argued that the EU banana import regime introduced in July 1993 violated WTO open trade rules because it discriminates in favor of producers from the African, Caribbean, and Pacific (ACP) countries. Two panels set up under the WTO's predecessor, the General Agreement on Tariffs and Trade (GATT), found against Brussels. But under GATT's looser rules, the EU was able to block adoption of the findings by the old trade watchdog. Under the WTO, the EU could appeal against a finding that went against it, but if it lost it would then be ordered to either bring the banana regime into line with the rules or pay compensation to the five. Although not a producer, the United States joined the dispute with the four Latin American states because it argued the EU banana-trade licensing system discriminated against firms outside the Union, including major U.S. companies. The United States contends that U.S. banana companies, such as Chiquita, are losing $520 million annually in lost sales to Europe because of its trade barriers that favor bananas imported from former European colonies in the Caribbean and Africa.

The dispute pits the interest of Caribbean and African banana growers against those of Ecuador, Mexico, Guatemala, Honduras, and Panama. Caribbean bananas have an 8 percent share of the EU market. Latin American bananas have more than a 60 percent share, despite the European quota. In countries such as St. Lucia, St. Vincent and the Grenadines and Dominica, where bananas account for more than half of their exports, the crop is a vital source of employment. The U.S. sanctions will force a majority of meager-income workers in those ex-European colonies out of jobs.

The United States has threatened retaliatory tariffs of 100 percent on hundreds of millions of dollars in European imports, effectively doubling their price, to compensate U.S. banana companies for their lost sales to Europe. A trade war waged by the U.S. government could make such seemingly unrelated items as Scottish cashmere sweaters, Pecorino cheese (but only the soft kind), German coffee makers, and French handbags scarce on American store shelves. The United States specifically exempted products from Denmark and the Netherlands from the sanctions list because they were the only countries that voted against the banana rules.

The confrontation is still escalating. The WTO has recently ruled in favor of the United States to slap on sanctions valued at $300 million to punish the EU's recalcitrance. However, EU Trade Minister Leon Brittan counterargued that the United States decided to defy the WTO system by introducing a form of sanctions that has no WTO authorization. He claims that what the United States has done is unacceptable and unlawful. Is the WTO an open battleground for trade disputes or a trade dispute adjudicating organization? Indeed, there is no easy end in sight.

Sources : "U.S. Threatens Tariffs on European Luxury Items," CNN Interactive, www.cnn.com; December 22, 1998; "Trade Fight Spills Over into Handbags, Coffee Makers," CNN Interactive, www.cnn.com, March 3, 1999; and "EU, U.S. Squabble Over Agenda for WTO's Millennium Round," Wall Street Journal Interactive, interactive.wsj.com, October 25, 1999.

Finally, although WTO is a global institutional proponent of free trade, it is not without critics. In December 1999, WTO launched what would have become the beginning of a ninth round of negotiations inaugurated in Seattle, the United States. However, it was only to be greeted by jeers and riots triggered by labor unions, environmentalists, and other onlookers who were opposed to free trade for various reasons.

Although WTO is a global institutional proponent of free trade, it is not without critics. In December 1999, WTO launched what would have become the beginning of a ninth round of negotiations inaugurated in Seattle, United States. However, it was only to be greeted by jeers and riots triggered by labor unions, environmentalists, and other on-lookers who were opposed to free trade for various reasons.

Financial Services in WTO/GATT. Key developed powers and emerging and ex-communist economies, brushing aside a U.S. refusal to join them in a wide-ranging pact opening up global trade in financial services, agreed to a pact that went into effect in July 1996. The accord, signed in July 1995, was approved by twenty-nine members of the World Trade Organization (WTO), the new global commerce watchdog. Some of its provisions were applied in many countries immediately. But the deal—covering the booming multibillion-dollar trade in banking, insurance, and securities—involves a total of forty-three countries, as the European Union, its main promoter, speaks in the WTO for all its fifteen member states. Additionally, under most-favored-nation (MFN) rules, it will be extended to about fifty more current and pending WTO members with commitments in the sector—ironically, including the United States, which argues that the pact does not go far enough.[30]

Among major backers of the deal (apart from the EU) were Japan, Canada, and Australia from the established economies; India, Malaysia, South Korea, Indonesia, and Singapore in Asia; and Brazil, Chile, and Venezuela in Latin America. For the average person using banks, buying insurance, and selling shares, a WTO spokesman said, "it will mean more providers to choose from, which means more competition, and that should mean a better deal for consumers." For the finance industry in industrialized countries, it will bring guaranteed access—although at varying levels—to the fiercely protected domestic markets of the emerging and transition economies, including Poland and Hungary. India, for example, has pledged to allow up to 49 percent of foreign equity in stockbroker firms and permit opening of eight instead of five foreign banks or branches a year. Cash-dispensing machines will no longer be counted as branches. By the end of 1999, India had committed to the WTO to improve its patent laws, protect its indigenous plant life, reduce further its restrictions on foreign investment, and remove import restrictions on 2,714 tariff levels.[31] Brazil agreed to allow a wider foreign role in the privatization of state-owned banks, while South Korea agreed to raise the limit on foreign investment in domestic companies from 10 to 15 percent.

---

[30]"Financial Services Trade Pact Agreed: U.S. Stands Aside," *Reuters* (July 28, 1995).

[31]N. Vasuki Rao, "India Opposed to Broad WTO Agenda," *Journal of Commerce* (April 30, 1999), 3A.

It is the first major deal under the WTO to absorb the old GATT, and the first big international trade accord since World War II that left out the United States. Washington, under pressure from Congress and parts of the U.S. financial service industry, argued that opening offers from developing countries were not enough to justify it throwing wide its domestic market to all other WTO members.

But the EU, which says its companies in the sector will now have access to 90 percent of all world financial business because it already has a bilateral deal with the United States, insisted the package was a good interim deal that could be improved later. Today's achievement should be considered as a key step forward, but by no means the end of the process. The twenty-nine WTO members who joined the accord were those that delivered market-opening offers made in the GATT's seven-year Uruguay Round negotiations. The U.S. government said that it would continue talking about a full global pact it could join. But trade diplomats say they doubt this will come for some time—perhaps not until after the year 2000, when all WTO service accords are up for review.

WTO and E-Commerce.   Due to an explosive use of the Internet, a global effort to regulate international e-commerce has become increasingly necessary (See Chapter 19 for the impact of the Internet on various marketing activities). Nua Internet Survey results show that 171 million people around the world used the Internet in 1999—an increase of 48 million users, or a 33 percent increase, in one year alone from 1998.[32] To address this issue, the WTO's Work Program on Electronic Commerce is in the process of trying to define the trade-related aspects of electronic commerce—e-commerce—that would fall under the parameters of WTO mandates. The Work Program submitted a report to the organization's general council on March 31, 1999, in which it sought to define such services as intellectual barriers to trade in the context of electronic commerce. Probably the best thing the WTO can do to assist the development of e-commerce in global trade is to meet its stated goal of assisting in the creation of an environment in which e-commerce can flourish. According to WTO documents, such an environment requires liberalized market policies and predictable trade regimes that encourage the massive investments in technology that is required for electronic commerce to work.

The United States is taking the lead in bringing e-commerce-related issues to the table. A U.S. document presented to the Work Program's general meeting on March 22, 1999, clearly outlined both the issues raised by the introduction of e-commerce in international trade and the importance of e-commerce to the global economy. The United States also proposed that the WTO examine services that might emerge as more viable in terms of international trade through e-commerce. For example, with widespread use of the Internet, has the notion of retailing across borders—previously inhibited by different time zones and the high cost of international communications—become commercially viable? Also, now that networked appliances increasingly are used, will remote monitoring, testing, and diagnostics of such devices become increasingly important? Much has yet to be clarified and resolved. The WTO Work Program on Electronic Commerce is in the process of defining the trade-related aspects of electronic commerce that would fall under the

---

[32]*Nua Internet Surveys*, Nua, Ltd., http://www.nua.ie/index.html, accessed March 1, 2000.

parameters of WTO mandates. The Work Program submitted a report to the organization's General Council on March 31, 1999, in which it sought to define such services as intellectual barriers to trade in the context of e-commerce. Probably the best thing the WTO can do to assist the development of e-commerce in global trade is to meet its stated goal of assisting in the creation of an environment in which e-commerce can flourish.[33]

◆ ◆ ◆ ◆ ◆ ◆ **U.S. POSITION IN FOREIGN DIRECT INVESTMENT AND TRADE**

U.S. Direct Investment Overseas

The United States has been a significant overseas investor since 1945. The first wave of major investment was part of the Marshall Plan in the 1950s to revitalize the European industries that had been devastated by World War II. The Marshall Plan was not entirely an altruistic gesture. The exigencies of the Cold War required that Western Europe be an economically and militarily strong region. The destruction caused by World War II meant that left to their own resources, the countries of Western Europe would have taken a long time to recover and may have proven to be tempting targets for a communist takeover—a prospect that was to be avoided at all costs. Also, a vibrant Europe would be an attractive market for American goods and services.

U.S. direct investment abroad continued to grow over the years, with a spurt in the early 1980s. The rise in foreign direct investment was partly due to the massive appreciation of the dollar in the early 1980s. In the late 1980s, the dollar depreciated in value by as much as 50 percent compared to its peak in 1985. The depreciation of the dollar was responsible for a fall in foreign direct investment outflow from the United States and a rise in foreign direct investment inflow into the United States in the 1980s. However, in the 1990s, when globalization had become imminent, both U.S. direct investment abroad and foreign direct investment in the United States picked up speed. Part of the increase in two-way direct investment flows is attributed to many mergers and acquisitions across the Atlantic (See Exhibit 2–6).

Most U.S. investment abroad has been concentrated in Europe in general and in Britain in particular. In the 1990s, however, U.S. direct investment started flowing in increasing amounts into Asian countries, especially into the countries that have been classified as the emerging markets. U.S. firms invested $115 billion overseas in 1998. In the twentieth century, the United States was at the forefront of investing in other countries, much like Britain was in the nineteenth century. From 1990 to 1997, U.S. firms' direct investment position abroad increased 145 percent in market value—from $732 billion in 1990 to $1.79 trillion in 1997. Similarly, foreign firms' direct investment position in the United States increased 200 percent in market value—from $540 billion to $1.62 trillion during the same period.[34]

---

[33]David Biederman, "E-Commerce and World Trade," *Traffic World*, 258 (April 26, 1999), p. 22.

[34]Computed from information in *Statistical Abstract of the United States 1998* (Washington, D.C.: U.S. Census Bureau, July 1999).

EXHIBIT 2–6

U.S. DIRECT INVESTMENT ABROAD AND FOREIGN DIRECT INVESTMENT IN
THE UNITED STATES 1985–1998

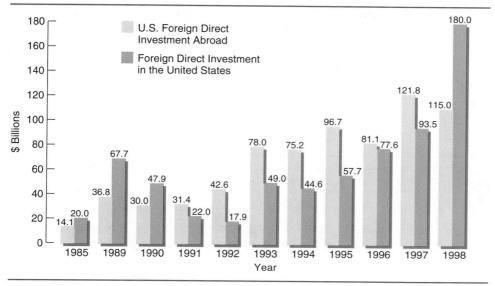

Source: *Statistical Abstract of the United States 1998* (Washington, D.C.: U.S. Census Bureau, July 1999);
and Sylvia E. Bargas and Rosaria Troia, "Direct Investment Positions for 1998: County and Industry
Detail," *Survey of Current Business* (July 1999), pp. 48–59.

Foreign Direct Investment in the United States

Foreign direct investment in the United States, on the other hand, historically remained at more modest levels in the twentieth century before commencing a sharp climb in the 1980s. Exhibit 2–7 shows the cumulative stock of foreign direct investment from the seven largest investors in the United States from 1986 through 1998. Foreign investment in the United States surged in the late 1980s, in part because the dollar fell against the Japanese yen and German mark, making it attractive for investors with stronger currencies to buy U.S. assets at bargain-basement prices. (This was the same period in which the United States ran its largest trade deficits.) As stated earlier, the 1990s was marked by the globalization movement, which encouraged foreign companies to increase their direct investment in the United States. Firms based in Britain and the Netherlands have traditionally been the largest investors in the United States, though in the last decade, Japanese firms have increased their direct investment position rapidly and now collectively occupy the second largest investment position in the United States.

The United States has a unique relationship with Canada due to their cultural and geographical proximity. Although U.S. investment in Canada has been growing, Canadian investment in the United States has outperformed. The pattern of the last ten years for foreign investing has been North American integration. In 1967, U.S. foreign direct investment in Canada was eight times the amount of Canadian foreign direct investment in the United States. Ten years later it had fallen to five times. By 1995, U.S. foreign direct investment was less than one and a half times Canadian foreign direct investment in the United States. That year the total U.S. foreign direct investment in Canada was $113 billion, while Canadian

EXHIBIT 2-7

FOREIGN DIRECT INVESTMENT STOCK IN THE UNITED STATES FOR SEVEN LARGEST COUNTRIES, 1987–1998 ($ BILLIONS AT YEAR-END—HISTORICAL VALUE)

	1987	*1988*	*1989*	*1990*	*1991*	*1992*	*1993*	*1994*	*1995*	*1996*	*1997*	*1998*
United Kingdom	75.5	95.7	105.5	108.8	100.4	90.4	102.3	113.5	117.4	121.3	129.6	151.3
Japan	34.4	51.1	67.3	83.5	95.1	99.6	99.2	103.1	108.8	114.5	123.5	132.6
Netherlands	46.6	48.1	56.3	64.3	63.1	69.2	72.2	70.6	72.5	74.3	84.9	96.9
Canada	24.7	26.6	30.4	29.5	36.8	37.8	40.1	43.2	49.0	54.8	64.0	74.8
Germany	21.9	25.3	29.0	27.3	28.6	29.2	34.8	39.6	49.8	59.9	69.7	95.0
France	10.1	13.2	16.8	19.6	24.2	23.8	n.a.	n.a.	n.a.	41.1	47.1	62.2
Switzerland	13.8	14.4	18.8	17.5	19.2	19.6	19.6	25.3	27.9	30.4	38.6	54.0

Source: Statistical Abstracts of the United States (Washington, D.C.: Bureau of Statistics, Treasury Department, various issues up to 1999) for 1987-1998 data; and *Survey of Current Business*, International Data, July 1999, p. D-55, for 1999 data.

foreign direct investment in the United States was $76 billion. Canadians now hold more in U.S. stocks than Americans hold in Canadian stocks.[35]

Balance of Payments Position

As far as the balance of payments position is concerned, the United States has run a persistent deficit on the current account since the first oil shock in 1973. The United States has huge trade deficits in some major industries such as automobile, consumer electronics, and petroleum, but has trade surpluses in such industries as aircraft and agriculture. All combined, however, the deficit on the overall merchandise trade account seems to keep rising with time—and the media exacerbate matters by focusing only on the merchandise trade account, when the fact is that the United States has been running a persistent surplus on the services trade account during the same period. The fact that by a historical quirk of convention merchandise trade data are accumulated by the U.S. Department of Commerce on a monthly basis, while the services trade data are available only on a quarterly basis, also tends to highlight the merchandise trade deficit.

In the context of trade deficits, there is increasing concern that the conventional measures of the deficit may not accurately reflect a country's transactions with the rest of the world. For example, when a wholly owned subsidiary of Texas Instruments in Japan sells microprocessors to a firm in Malaysia, should it show up as an export from Japan to Malaysia or as an American export to Malaysia? Under current accounting rules, this transaction shows as a Japanese export to Malaysia. America's National Academy of Sciences (NAS) has suggested measuring trade entirely on the basis of ownership. It defines exports as the sum of three numbers: cross-border sales to foreigners; net sales to foreigners by subsidiaries abroad; and sales by U.S. firms to U.S. subsidiaries of foreign firms. The NAS's approach would result in the United States showing a whopping trade surplus of $164 billion for 1991,[36] while the official

---

[35] "U.S.-Canada Foreign Investment," *Statistics Canada* (1999).

[36] "Grossly Distorted Picture," *Economist* (February 5, 1994), p. 71; and William G. Shepherd and Dexter Hutchins, "There's No Trade Deficit, Sam!" *Financial World* (February 23, 1988), pp. 28–32.

EXHIBIT 2–8

U.S. BALANCE OF GOODS, SERVICES, AND INCOME 1974–1998

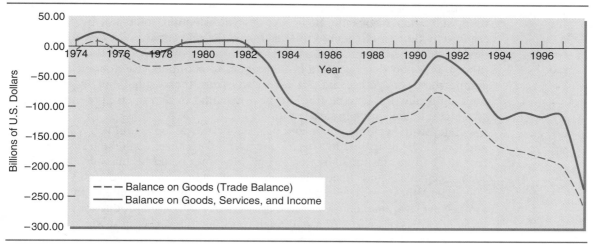

Source: Compiled from *Statistical Abstract of the United States* (Washinton, D.C.: U.S. Census Bureau), various issues.

U.S. trade deficit was reported at $74 billion for that year—a difference of $238 billion! Although the NAS has not since reported its version of trade statistics, the conventional trade statistics (i.e., difference in dollar value between exports and imports) obviously fails to capture the extent of a country's transaction with the rest of the world. As multinationals spread throughout the world and a substantial proportion of international trade consists of intra-firm transfer, this question will assume increasing importance. Exhibit 2–8 presents the data for the balance of payments in goods (trade balance) and the balance of payments in goods and services (including investment income), based on the current conventional method of accounting for international trade transactions. Note that while the trade deficit remains substantial, it has declined substantially as a percentage of the sum of imports and exports and as a percentage of the U.S. GDP since peaking in 1987.

INFORMATION TECHNOLOGY AND THE CHANGING NATURE OF COMPETITION

◆ ◆ ◆ ◆ ◆ ◆

As the nature of value-adding activities in developed nations shifts more and more to information creation, manipulation, and analysis, the developed nations have started taking an increased interest in protecting intellectual property. Imagine a farmer in the nineteenth century headed into the twentieth century. The intrinsic value of food will not go away in the new century, but as food becomes cheaper and cheaper to produce, the share of the economy devoted to agriculture will shrink (in the United States, agriculture contributes less than 3 percent to the GDP) and so will the margins for the farmer. It would be advisable to move into manufacturing, or at least into food processing, to maintain margins.

An analogous situation faces a content maker for **information-related products** such as software, music, movies, newspapers, magazines, and education as we move into the twenty-first century. For thousands of years, content had been manifested physically—first in people who knew how to do things; then in books, sheet music, records, newspapers, loose-leaf binders, and catalogs; and most recently in tapes, discs, and other electronic media. At first, information could not be "copied": it could only be reimplemented or transferred. People could build new machines or devices that were copies of or improvements on the original; people could tell each other things and share wisdom or techniques to act upon. (Reimplementation was cumbersome and re-use did not take away from the original, but the process of building a new implementation—a new machine or a trained apprentice—took considerable time and physical resources.)

Later, with symbols, paper, and printing presses, people could copy knowledge, and it could be distributed in "fixed" media; performances could be transcribed and recreated from musical scores or scripts. Machines could be mass-produced. With such mechanical and electronic media, intellectual value could easily be reproduced, and the need (or demand from creators) to protect intellectual property arose. New laws enabled owners and creators to control the production and distribution of copies of their works. Although reproduction was easy, it was still mostly a manufacturing process, not something an individual could do easily. It took time and money. Physical implementation contributed a substantial portion of the cost.

Value of Intellectual Property in the Information Age

However, with the advent of the information age, firms are faced with a new situation; not only is it easy for individuals to make duplicates of many works or to re-use their content in new works, but the physical manifestation of content is almost irrelevant. Over the Internet, any piece of electronically represented intellectual property can be almost instantly copied anywhere in the world. Since more and more of value creation in the developed nations is coming from the development and sale of such information-based intellectual property, it is no surprise that developed nations are highly interested in putting strong international intellectual property laws in place. The U.S. insistence on the inclusion of provisions relating to intellectual property in GATT and WTO is a direct consequence. **Trade Related Aspects of Intellectual Property Rights (TRIPS) Agreement**, concluded as part of the GATT Uruguay Round, mandates that each member country accord to the nationals of other member countries the same treatment as its nationals with regard to intellectual property protection. Technology-based protection of electronic information through hardware, software, or a combination thereof in the form of encryption and digital signatures has been suggested as the means of circumventing the problem of unauthorized copying.[37]

Controlling copies (once created by the author or by a third party), however, becomes a complex challenge. A firm can either control something very tightly, limiting distribution to a small, trusted group, or it can rest assured that eventually its product will find its way to a large nonpaying audience—if anyone cares to have it in the first place. But creators of content on the Internet still face the eternal problem: the value of their work generally will not receive recognition without wide distribution. Only by attracting broad attention can an artist or creator hope to attract high payment for copies. Thus, on the Internet, the creators give first performances or books

[37]Ravi Kalaktota and Andrew B. Whinston, *Frontiers of Electronic Commerce* (Reading, Mass.: Addison Wesley, 1996). See Chapter 15.

(or whatever) away widely in hopes of recouping with subsequent works. But that breadth of distribution lessens the creator's control of who gets copies and what they do with them. In principle, it should be possible to control and charge for such widely disseminated works, but it will become more and more difficult. People want to pay only for what is perceived as scarce—a personal performance or a custom application, or some tangible manifestation that cannot easily be reproduced (by nature or by fiat; that is why the art world has numbered lithographs, for example).

The trick may be to control not the copies of the firm's information product but instead a relationship with the customers—subscriptions or membership. And that is often what the customers want, because they see it as an assurance of a continuing supply of reliable, timely content. Thus, the role of marketing may be expected to assume increasing importance. A firm can, of course, charge a small amount for mass copies. Metering schemes will allow vendors to charge—in fractions of a penny, if desired—according to usage or users rather than copies. However, it will not much change the overall approaching-zero trend of content pricing. At best, it will make it much easier to charge those low prices.

E-commerce creates other hurdles for content creators. One is the rise of a truly efficient market for information. Content used to be unfungible: It was difficult to replace one item with another. But most information is not unique, though its creators like to believe so. There are now specs for content such as stock prices, search criteria, movie ratings, and classifications. In the world of software, for instance, it is becoming easier to define and create products equivalent to a standard. Unknown vendors who can guarantee functionality will squeeze the prices of the market leaders. Of course the leaders (such as Microsoft) can use almost-free content to sell ancillary products or upgrades, because they are the leaders and because they have reinvested in loyal distribution channels. The content is advertising for the dealers who resell, as well as for the vendors who create. This transformation in the form of value creation and ease of dissemination implies a jump in economic integration as nations become part of an international electronic commerce network. Not only money but also products and services will flow faster.

The other consequence of fungible content, information products, and electronic networks is an additional assault on the power of national governments to regulate international commerce (See Global Perspective 2–3). Ford uses a product design process whereby designers at Dearborn, Michigan, pass on their day's work in an electronic form to an office in Japan, who then pass the baton along to designers in Britain, who pass it back to Dearborn the next day. When the information represented in the design crosses borders, how do the governments of the United States, Japan, and Britain treat this information? How will such exchanges be regulated? Less-open societies like China and Singapore, recognizing the power of electronic networks, are already attempting to regulate the infrastructure of and access to the electronic network.

The similar problem applies to electronic commerce. Countries' regulators have not kept pace with the rapid proliferation of International e-commerce led by Internet and e-commerce providers in the United States such as America Online (AOL), Yahoo, and Amazon.com, as well as by traditional marketers that have gone into e-commerce, such as Dell Computer, Victoria's Secret, and Nokia. In terms of e-commerce, how do countries control online purchases and sales? If one looks at Europe, each country has different tax laws and Internet regulations, as

Proliferation of E-commerce and Regulations

◆ ◆

ℊLOBAL PERSPECTIVE 2–3

THE REAL TRUTH ABOUT THE ECONOMY

Because the economies of the developed nations are becoming information intensive—are becoming knowledge economies—the data regarding these economies are coming under increasing scrutiny. The methods of collating data relating to economies were developed in a time when today's developed economies were primarily producers of agricultural and manufactured goods—when the service and information sector of the economy was very small.

For example, business investment in equipment, after adjusting for depreciation, is fully 30 percent higher than the government statistics because the data capture only a fraction of the money that firms spend on software, employee skill upgrades, and telecommunication equipment. Estimates of inflation may also be overstated because they do not take into account the pro-ductivity gains that firms have brought about over the last decade.

From a trade perspective this has two implications. Wrong inflation estimates misstate the value of the dollar in the international money markets because markets take into account the rate of inflation. Additionally, the government no longer classifies exports and imports by whether they are for final sales or for assembly purposes. So it is not clear whether semiconductor chips shipped to South Korea will be plugged into a VCR for sale in Eugene, Oregon, or in Pusan, Korea. This makes it much more difficult to trace net imports and exports.

Furthermore, trade statistics shape the economic climate in which policy decisions are made. In the debate over the 1988 Omnibus Trade Law, which provided U.S. firms with a weapon to defend themselves against foreign competition, the then-available data suggested a trade deficit of $171 billion. Later revisions and the inclusion of trade in services reduced the deficit to $151 billion.

Adapted from "The Real Truth About the Economy," *Business Week* (November 7, 1994), p. 110.

---

well as consumer protection laws. In addition, import and export formalities still apply to goods bought electronically. How to monitor e-commerce transactions remains a problem for most national governments.[38]

One such example is illustrated by the launch of Viagra by Pfizer in 1998. The company celebrated the most successful drug launch in history with the introduction of Viagra, the first pill that allows effective oral treatment for men who suffer from erectile dysfunction (impotence). Since that time the name Pfizer has become a synonym for Viagra and vice versa, due to a media hype that arose after this launch of the first of so-called *lifestyle drugs* to treat undesired symptoms that suppress quality of life. The Internet attracted the portion of patients who are not willing to talk about their problem even to their doctors. The Internet quickly filled up with "virtual" pharmacies that promised to supply Viagra via a mouse click. Internet pharmacies sometimes try to conceal their location, set up in offshore places, and sell their items in a gray area of doing business. Customers who are not willing to disclose their erectile dysfunction can easily order Viagra without consulting their physicians, but they run the risk of becoming fraud victims. Internet pharmacies that are selling genuine Viagra pills have found a way to get around prescription requirements in the following way: An online-consultation form can be filled out in a few minutes (at a consultation fee of $65–$75). The pharmacy's physician then will issue the prescription based on the information "honestly" given by the

---

[38]Marcia Macleod: "Analysis; European E-Commerce Stands Divided," *Network News* (April 28, 1999), p. 14.

candidate.[39] This procedure allows the customer to retain a high degree of anonymity, while the pharmacy fulfills the obligation to distribute Viagra only after a physician's consultation.

Pfizer and counterfeiting experts have warned the public not to buy from Internet pharmacies.[40] In reputable pharmacies cases of fraud usually do not occur, but there are many fraudulent Web sites that will exploit the patient's unwillingness to talk about impotence. The Federal Trade Commission (FTC) is in charge of cases where entities are trying to mislead potential customers and commit fraud. The FTC sent out some warnings about products that claim to be related to Viagra, and no prescription is necessary. The warnings advise people to check credentials of suppliers. Fraud on the Internet has been found in reports where businesses that were set up to sell counterfeiting pills managed to get about 150,000 customers a year. One owner of these enterprises advertised pills under names similar to Viagra, like Viagrae. Pfizer sued, and the FTC was able to find that this name was only one small part in a larger fraud to distribute large amounts of phony pills.[41]

REGIONAL ECONOMIC ARRANGEMENTS   ◆ ◆ ◆ ◆ ◆ ◆ ◆

An evolving trend in international economic activity is the formation of multinational trading blocs. These blocs take the form of a group of contiguous countries that decide to have common trading policies for the rest of the world in terms of tariffs and market access but have preferential treatment for one another. Organizational form varies among market regions, but the universal reason for the formation of such groups is to ensure the economic growth and benefit of the participating countries. Regional cooperative agreements have proliferated since the end of World War II. Among the more well-known ones existing today are the European Union and the North American Free Trade Agreement. Some of the lesser-known ones include the MERCOSUR (Southern Cone Free Trade Area) and the Andean Group in South America, the Gulf Cooperation Council in the Arabian Gulf region (GCC), the South Asian Agreement for Regional Cooperation in South Asia (SAARC) and the Association of South East Asian Nations (ASEAN). The existence and growing influence of these multinational groupings imply that nations need to become part of such groups to remain globally competitive. To an extent, the regional groupings reflect the countervailing force to the increasing integration of the global economy—it is an effort by governments to control the pace of the integration.

Market groups take many forms, depending on the degree of cooperation and inter-relationships, which lead to different levels of integration among the participating countries. There are five levels of formal cooperation among member

---

[39]See, e.g., www.qualitymed.com, www.medservices.com, or www.MDHealthline.com.

[40]"Black Market Filled Phony Viagra Tablets," article at www.cafecrowd.com, accessed August 10, 1999.

[41]See "FTC: Watch for Viagra Knock-Offs," at www.msnbc.com/news/2090, accessed August 10, 1999.

countries of these regional groupings, ranging from a free trade area to the ultimate level of integration—political union.

Before the formation of a regional group of nations for freer trade, some governments agree to participate jointly in projects that create economic infrastructure (such as dams, pipelines, roads) and that decrease the levels of barriers from a level of little or no trade to substantial trade. Each country may make a commitment to financing part of the project, such as India and Nepal did for a hydroelectric dam on the Gandak River. Alternatively, they may share expertise on rural development and poverty alleviation programs, may lower trade barriers in selected goods such as in SAARC, which comprises India, Pakistan, Sri Lanka, Bangladesh, Nepal, Maldives, and Bhutan. This type of loose cooperation is considered a precursor to a more formal trade agreement.

Free Trade Area. A **free trade area** has a higher level of integration than a loosely formed regional cooperation and is a formal agreement among two or more countries to reduce or eliminate customs duties and nontariff trade barriers among partner countries. However, member countries are free to maintain individual tariff schedules for countries that do not belong to the free trade group. One fundamental problem with this arrangement is that a free trade area can be circumvented by nonmember countries that can export to the nation having the lowest external tariff in a free trade area, and then transport the goods to the destination country in the free trade area without paying the higher tariff that would be applicable if it had gone directly to the destination country. In order to stem foreign companies from benefiting from this tariff-avoiding method of exporting, *local content laws* are usually introduced. Local content laws require that in order for a product to be considered domestic, thus not subject to import duties, a certain percentage or more of the value of the product should be sourced locally within the free trade area. Thus, local content laws are designed to encourage foreign exporters to set up their manufacturing locations in the free trade area.

The North American Free Trade Agreement (NAFTA) is the free trade agreement among Canada, the United States, and Mexico. It provides for elimination of all tariffs on industrial products traded between Canada, Mexico, and the United States within a period of ten years from the date of implementation of the NAFTA agreement—January 1, 1994. NAFTA was preceded by the free trade agreement between Canada and the United States, which went into effect in 1989. The United States has a free trade area agreement with Israel as well. Mexico is also negotiating with the European Union about a creation of a trans-Atlantic free trade area without U.S. involvement.[42] Likewise, Canada signed a trade deal with the Andean Group in 1999 as a forerunner to a possible free trade agreement.[43]

Another free trade group is the European Free Trade Association (EFTA) comprising Iceland, Liechtenstein, Norway, and Switzerland. Although Austria, Finland, Sweden, and Switzerland used to be EFTA member countries, Austria, Finland, and Sweden recently joined the European Union and Switzerland has applied to become a member. It appears that some, if not all of, the remaining EFTA members may gradually merge into the European Union (which we discuss later). MERCO-

---

[42]Brandon Mitchener, "Mexican, EU Negotiators Set to Start Round 2 of Talks on Free Trade Zone," *Wall Street Journal* (January 18, 1999), p. A14.

[43]"Canada Signs Andean Deal despite Rights Concerns," CNN Interactive, www.cnn.com, June 1, 1999.

SUR is a free trade area consisting of Brazil, Argentina, Uruguay, and Paraguay, with an automatic schedule for the lowering of internal trade barriers and the ultimate goal of the creation of a customs union.[44] Chile and Bolivia also became associate members in 1996 and 1997, respectively.

It is to be noted that a free trade area is not necessarily free of trade barriers, even among its member countries. Although it is a treaty by which to attempt to develop freer trade among the member countries, trade disputes and restrictions frequently occur, nonetheless (see Global Perspective 2–4).

Customs Union

The inherent weakness of the free trade area concept may lead to its gradual disappearance in the future—though it may continue to be an attractive stepping stone to a higher level of integration. When members of a free trade area add common external tariffs to the provisions of the free trade agreement, then the free trade area becomes a **customs union**.

$\mathcal{G}$LOBAL PERSPECTIVE 2–4

NAFTA PROMISING FREER TRADE MAY END UP LESS FREE

"Whenever the rules do not favor the United States, there is a tendency to bend them," decried Raymond Chrétien, Canada's ambassador to the United States, implying that U.S. politics, particularly in an election year, tend to turn protectionist. Despite $1 billion in trade every day between Canada and the United States, the United States has caused many trade disputes with Canada involving softwood lumber, wheat, dairy products, poultry, and Pacific salmon over the years.

The most recent example involves the U.S. decision to effectively reduce tomato imports from Mexico. Under NAFTA, tomatoes from Mexico are subject to quarterly seasonal quotas. Thus, Mexican growers can make up a temporary slowdown in exports during the remaining part of the quarter. During 1995, there was a 129 percent surge in the volume of tomato exports from Mexico, leading to the U.S. changing the quota rules from a seasonal quota to a weekly quota. Under this unilateral action, if the quota for the week is missed then it is lost for the year—effectively reducing the actual level of exports from the stated quota levels.

The immediate cause for the unilateral action by the United States appears to be the deleterious effect that the rise in the tomato exports is having on the tomato growers in Florida. Under pressure from the Florida tomato growers, the U.S. administration proposed the weekly quota. Under the spirit and letter of NAFTA, the proposal goes against the free trade principle and indeed leads to less free trade. However, also under the provisions of NAFTA, Mexico has to first go through a consultative process that can last ninety days. If the dispute cannot be resolved by consultation, then the dispute resolution mechanism (patterned after GATT rules) kicks into effect—but this can take another nine months. In effect, by the time the seasonal quota was reinstated in December 1996, the U.S. presidential election was over. After presidential elections are over, there is less pressure on Washington to accede to the tomato growers of Florida.

Sources: "Dealing with Uncle Sam: Our Ambassador Learns 'Realism'," Canada Newscan (May 10, 1996), p. 4; "U.S., Mexico Hope to Solve NAFTA Tomato Dispute," Austin American Statesman (January 21, 1996), p. H4.

---

[44]Maria Cecilia Coutinho de Arruda and Masaaki Kotabe, "MERCOSUR: An Emergent Market in South America," in Masaaki Kotabe, *MERCOSUR and Beyond: The Imminent Emergence of the South American Markets* (Austin, TX: The University of Texas at Austin, 1997).

Therefore, members of a customs union not only have reduced or eliminated tariffs among themselves, but also they have a common external tariff of countries that are not members of the customs union. This prevents nonmember countries from exporting to member countries that have low external tariffs with the goal of sending the exports to a country that has a higher external tariff through the first country that has a low external tariff. The ASEAN (Indonesia, Brunei, Malaysia, Singapore, Thailand, the Philippines, and Vietnam) is a good example of a currently functional customs union with the goal of a common market. The Treaty of Rome of 1958, which formed the European Economic Community, created a customs union between West Germany, France, Italy, Belgium, the Netherlands, and Luxembourg.

Common Market

As cooperation increases among the countries of a customs union, they can form a **common market**. A common market eliminates all tariffs and other barriers to trade among members of the common market, adopts a common set of external tariffs on nonmembers, and removes all restrictions on the flow of capital and labor among member nations. The 1958 Treaty of Rome that created the European Economic Community had the ultimate goal of creating a common market—a goal that was substantially achieved by the early 1990s in Western Europe. German banks can now open branches in Italy, and Portuguese workers can live and work in Luxembourg. Similarly, South American countries, led by the MERCOSUR and the Andean Group, are actively seeking to create a common market of more than 300 million consumers by 2005.[45]

Monetary Union

The **Maastricht Treaty**, which succeeded the Treaty of Rome and called for the creation of a union (and hence the change in name to European Union),[46] has accomplished the creation of a **monetary union** and has an ultimate goal of creating a political union, where the member countries switch over to a common currency and a common central bank. A monetary union represents the fourth level of integration with a single common currency among politically independent countries. In strict technical terms, a monetary union does not require the existence of a common market or a customs union, a free trade area, or a regional cooperation for development. However, it is the logical next step to a common market, because it requires the next higher level of cooperation among member nations. As per the Maastricht Treaty, those European Union (EU) member countries, except Britain, Greece, Denmark, and Sweden, adopted a common currency, the euro, effective on January 1, 1999 (See Chapter 3 for details).

Political Union

The culmination of the process of integration is the creation of a **political union**, which can be another name for a nation when such a union truly achieves the levels of integration described here on a voluntary basis. The ultimate stated goal of

---

[45]"Andean Countries Vow to Form Common Market by 2005," CNN Interactive, www.cnn.com, accessed May 27, 1999.

[46]The European Union consists of fifteen countries with different voting rights for most economic issues: Germany, France, Italy, the United Kingdom (10 votes each); Spain (8 votes); Belgium, Greece, the Netherlands, and Portugal (5 votes each); Austria and Sweden (4 votes each); Ireland, Denmark, and Finland (3 votes each); and Luxembourg (2 votes).

❖ ❖

*G*LOBAL PERSPECTIVE 2–5

CROSSING NATIONAL BORDERS IS EASIER THAN EVER IN THE EUROPEAN UNION

It is easy to caricaturize the European Union: fifteen countries squabbling over subsidies, 18,000 Brussels bureaucrats quarreling over perks, and 567 Strasbourg parliamentarians moaning over their relative lack of power. Whatever the latent truth of this caricature, it is also true that no country wants to leave the EU; and plenty are queuing to join, attracted by its economic mass and its implicit promise of security. Monet's dream of modernizing and uniting Western Europe and then drawing in Eastern Europe is alive and well.

The three main institutions of the EU are the Commission, the Council of Ministers, and the European Parliament. The Commission is a body of permanent civil servants and government appointees that administers EU business and proposes and drafts legislation. The Council of Ministers attended by the appropriate government ministers from the member coun-

tries is the EU's legislature, and it deliberates in secret. The European Parliament—the only body that is directly elected by the EU citizens—has few of the powers of a national parliament like that of the U.S. Congress or the German Bundestag. This structure, designed for the initial six members, is now creaking with fifteen members, and will need to be changed to accommodate new members.

The single market has moved forward in many areas. Since January 1, 1993, Spanish drivers who once needed to fill out seventy forms to cross a border have been able to truck oranges to Holland unhindered by customs officers and border police; German banks can now open branches in Italy; Greek students can attend Danish universities by right; and labor can move across borders in the EU. The Schegen Agreement eliminated the need for passports among all EU countries except Britain. The next step is the monetary union, although it is unlikely that all EU members will be able to join it simultaneously. A political union is still distant, due to strong nationalism in many EU nations.

Sources: "Survey of the European Union," *Economist* (October 22, 1994); "Who Will Join the EU Next?" *Economist* (October 2, 1999), p. 54.

---

the Maastricht Treaty is a political union. Currently, France and Britain remain the principal opponents of ceding any part of the sovereignty of the nation-state to any envisaged political union.[47] Even the leading proponents of European integration—Germany and France—have reservations about a common defense and foreign policy (See Global Perspective 2–5).

Sometimes, countries come together in a loose political union for historical reasons, as in the British Commonwealth comprising nations that were part of the British Empire. Members received preferential tariffs in the early days, but when Britain joined the European Union this preferential treatment was lost. The group exists as a forum for discussion and common historical ties.

MULTINATIONAL CORPORATIONS   ❖ ❖ ❖ ❖ ❖ ❖

Although no steadfast definition of **multinational corporations (MNCs)** exists, the U.S. government defines the multinational corporation for statistical purposes as a company that owns or controls 10 percent or more of the voting securities, or the equivalent, of at least one foreign business enterprise. Many large multinationals have many subsidiaries and affiliates in many parts of the world. In the early 1970s,

---

[47]"Survey of the European Union," *Economist* (October 22, 1994).

Howard Perlmutter, a professor at the Wharton School in Philadelphia, predicted that by 1985 around 80 percent of the noncommunist world's productive assets would be controlled by just 200 to 300 companies. There are now 40,000 MNCs with 250,000 affiliates in foreign countries. Two-thirds of world trade in goods and services is controlled by multinational companies. One third of multinational companies' trade is accounted for by intra-firm activities between the multinational parent company and its affiliates or among those affiliates. The one hundred largest multinationals accounts for one-sixth of the world's stock of foreign investment.[48] The UNCTAD report indicates that those hundred largest multinationals alone account for more than $2 trillion in sales around the world and employ six million people.[49] The forces of economies of scale, lowering trade and investment barriers, the need to be close to markets, internalization of operations within the boundaries of one firm, and the diffusion of technology will continue to increase the size and influence of multinationals.

The sovereignty of nations will perhaps continue to weaken due to multinationals and the increasing integration of economies. Some developing countries harbor negative feelings about the sense of domination by large multinationals, but the threat to sovereignty may not assume the proportions alluded to by some researchers.[50] Although established multinationals' sheer size may appear hegemonic and have some monopolistic power in smaller economies, they have yet to solve the problems associated with their large size. Current trends indicate that beyond a certain size, firms tend to become complacent and slow, and they falter against competition. They are no longer able to remain focused on their businesses and lack the drive, motivation, and a can-do attitude that permeates smaller firms. Those firms that do focus on their core businesses shed unrelated businesses. Just recently, Novartis, the Swiss pharmaceutical group, sold off its Swedish Wasa biscuits and crackers subsidiary to the Italian food company, Barilla, in order to concentrate on its health science products.[51] Thus, the nation-state, while considerably weaker than its nineteenth century counterpart, is likely to remain alive and well.

International firms are more international than before. In 1970, of the 7,000 multinationals identified by the United Nations, more than half were from two countries: the United States and Britain. By 1995, less than half of the 36,000 multinationals identified by the United Nations were from four countries: the United States, Japan, Germany, and Switzerland. Britain was seventh. Currency movements, capital surpluses, faster growth rates, and falling trade and investment barriers have all helped multinationals from other countries join the cross-border fray. In today's world it is not unusual for a startup firm to be multinational at its inception.[52] It is now easier than ever for small firms to be in international business

---

[48]"TNCs Stride the World," Corporate Watch, http://www.corpwatch.org/corner/glob/guardian, listed March 1, 1999.

[49]*World Investment Report 1998*, Geneva: UNCTAD, 1999, http://www.un.org/publications.

[50]Raymond Vernon, *Sovereignty At Bay* (New York: Basic Books, 1971).

[51]Paul Betts, "Barilla Pays SFr475m for Wasa Biscuits," *Financial Times* (April 27, 1999), p. 33.

[52]Benjamin M. Oviatt and Patricia P. McDougall, "Toward a Theory of International New Ventures," *Journal of International Business Studies*, 25(1) (1994), pp. 45–64.

through exports and imports and through e-commerce. A survey of companies with fewer than 500 employees by Arthur Andersen & Co. and National Small Business United, a trade group, found that exporters averaged $3.1 million in revenue, compared with $2.1 million for all companies in the survey in 1996, and also reported that exporters' profits increased 4.4 percent while the overall average was 2.6 percent. Exporters are also more technology-savvy: 92 percent have computers (vs. 79 percent overall) and 70 percent use the Internet (vs. 44 percent overall).[53]

SUMMARY ◆

The world economy is getting increasingly intertwined, and virtually no country that has a steadily rising standard of living is independent of the economic events in the rest of the world. It is almost as if participation in the international economy is a *sine quo non* of economic growth and prosperity—a country has to participate in the world economy in order to grow and prosper—but participation is not without its risks. Events outside one country can have detrimental effect on the economic health of that country. The Asian financial crisis that started in 1997 with a precipitous depreciation of Thailand's baht, Indonesia's rupiah, Malaysia's ringgit, and Korea's won, among others, is an example of a situation where withdrawal of funds by portfolio investors caused a severe economic crisis. In effect, participating in the international economy imposes its own discipline on a nation, independent of the policies of the government of that nation. This is not to suggest that countries should stay outside the international economic system because of the risks. Those countries that have elected to stay outside the international economic system—autarkies like Burma and North Korea—continue to fall farther behind the rest of the world in terms of living standards and prosperity.

Various forces are responsible for the increased integration. Growth in international trade continuously outpaces the rise in national outputs. Transportation and communications are becoming faster, cheaper, and more widely accessible. The nature of value-adding activities is changing in the advanced countries from manufacturing to services and information manipulation. Such changes are a result of and are a force behind the rapid advancement in telecommunications and computers. Even developing nations, regardless of their political colors, have realized the importance of telecommunications and electronic commerce and are attempting to improve their infrastructure. The capital markets of the world are already integrated for all practical purposes, and this integration affects exchange rates, interest rates, investments, employment, and growth across the world. Multinational corporations have truly become the global operations in name and spirit that they were envisaged to be. Even smaller companies are leapfrogging the gradual expansion pattern of traditional multinational companies by adopting e-commerce that has no national boundaries. In short, to repeat an old maxim, the world is becoming a global village. When Karl Marx said in 1848 that the world was becoming a smaller place, he could not have imagined how small it truly has become.

KEY TERMS ◆

balance of payments
common market
country competitiveness
customs union
foreign direct investment
free trade area
General Agreements on

Tariffs and Trade (GATT)
gross domestic product (GDP)
information-related products
Maastricht Treaty

monetary union
most favored nation (MFN)
multinational corporation (MNC)
political union
portfolio (indirect) investment

Trade Related Aspects of Intellectual Property Rights (TRIPS) Agreement
Uruguay Round
World Trade Organization (WTO)

---

[53]"Export Energy," *Business Week*, November 17, 1997, at http://www.businessweek.com/1997/46/b3553019.htm, accessed July 29, 1999.

READINGS QUESTIONS ◆ ◆ ◆ ◆ ◆ ◆ ◆ ◆ ◆ ◆ ◆ ◆ ◆ ◆ ◆ ◆ ◆ ◆ ◆

1. What are some of the visible signs that reflect the current increased economic interdependence among countries? What are some reasons for this growth in interdependence and for the rise in global integration?

2. What is GATT, and what is its role in international transactions?

3. How is the WTO different from GATT? What functions is WTO expected to perform?

4. In what ways have the U.S. foreign direct investment and trade patterns changed over the past decade?

5. Cooperative interrelationships between countries (regional groupings) can be classified into five broad categories. What are these categories, and how do they differ from each other?

6. Do current measures of balance of payments accurately reflect a country's transactions with the rest of the world? What are the concerns?

7. What challenges do the content creators and information providers face due to the advent and popularity of the electronic media? Are there current mechanisms to protect their rights? What are the macroeconomic implications for industrialized countries?

8. What are some of the forces influencing the increase in size of multinational corporations? Are there any forces that are influencing them to downsize?

DISCUSSION QUESTIONS ◆ ◆ ◆ ◆ ◆ ◆ ◆ ◆ ◆ ◆ ◆ ◆ ◆ ◆ ◆ ◆ ◆ ◆

1. A justification of developing countries against product patents for pharmaceutical products has been that if they were enforced, life-saving drugs would be out of reach for all but the very rich. A similar argument is being used in a populist move in the U.S. Senate for reducing the patent lives of innovative drugs, in a bid to reduce health care costs. Some senators and pharmaceutical industry leaders claim that this move would discourage medical innovation and slow down the development of drugs for the cure of such diseases as AIDS and cancer, and thereby increase the costs of taking care of current and future patients. How would you react to the arguments and counterarguments for reducing patent lives, and what would be your stance on this issue? In your opinion, what would be the international repercussions if this bill were to pass? How do you think other developed and developing countries would react?

2. In 1990, Robert Reich, a Harvard professor (and ex-Labor Secretary in the Clinton administration) stated that multinational corporations (MNCs) have become so internationally oriented that what is good for U.S. multinationals may no longer be good for the United States. Therefore, the U.S. government should not treat U.S. MNCs any differently from foreign corporations' subsidiaries in the United States. Laura Tyson, then a professor at the University of California, Berkeley (and the chairperson of the Council of Economic Advisers in the Clinton administration), countered this by stating that U.S. MNCs still remained overwhelmingly American in terms of their highest-value production, and that economic and national security considerations required U.S. policy makers to differentiate between U.S.- and foreign-owned corporations. Whom would you agree with, and why? According to the International Automobile Manufacturers Association, foreign-owned auto plants in the United States contributed to 500,000 jobs and U.S. $10 billion in investments. Would this information influence your previous answer? How?

3. Information technology is having significant effects on the globalization activities of corporations. Texas Instruments is now developing sophisticated chips in India. Motorola has set up programming and equipment design centers in China, India, Singapore, Hong Kong, Taiwan, and Australia. Similarly, a large number of U.S. and European corporations are looking at ways to transfer activities such as preparing tax returns, account statements, insurance claims, and other information processing work to Asia. Although until now it was only blue-collar employees in the industrialized countries who faced the threat of competition from low-wage countries (which could be countered to some extent through direct and indirect trade barriers), this new trend in movement of white-collar tasks may be a cause for concern to industrialized countries, as the sophistication of these tasks increases. This movement of white-collar jobs could be a cause for social concern in the near future. Do you foresee social pressures in developed countries having the potential of reversing the trend of movement of white-collar tasks to developing countries? Given the intangibility of information, are there any effective ways of controlling the movement of information across borders?

4. The effects of the formation of regional trade blocs on international trade could be interpreted in two ways. One way is to view regional blocs as one step forward in

the process of ensuring completely free trade between countries on a global basis. On the other hand, the formation of regional blocs could be seen as a step backward toward an era of greater protectionism and greater trade tensions between the regions. Which view would you agree with, and why?

5. Electronic commerce (e-commerce) blurs the distinction between a good and a service. Under WTO, goods tend to be subject to tariffs; services are not, but trade in services is limited by restrictions on "national treatment" or quantitative controls on access to foreign markets. For example, a compact disc sent from one country to another is clearly a good, and will be subject to an import tariff as it crosses the national border. But if the music on the disc is sent electronically from a computer in one country to another on the Internet, will it be a good or a service? Customized data and software, which can be put on CD, are usually treated as services. What kind of confusion would you expect with WTO overseeing increased transaction on the Internet?

FURTHER READING

Anderson, Kym. "The WTO Agenda for the New Millennium," *Economic Record*; 75 (March 1999): 77–88.

"A Survey of World Trade," *Economist*, Special Section (October 3, 1998).

Blecker, Robert A. *U.S. Trade Policy & Global Growth: New Directions in the International Economy.* Armonk, NY, 1996.

Bovard, James. "U.S. Trade Laws Harm U.S. Industries." *Regulation* 16 (4) (1993): 47–53.

Jacquemin, Alexis, and Lucio R. Pench, ed. *Europe Competing in the Global Economy.* Lyme, NH: Edward Elgar, 1997.

Kotler, Philip, Somkid Jatusripitak, and Suvit Maesincee. *The Marketing of Nations: A Strategic Approach to Building National Wealth.* New York: Free Press, 1997.

Panagariya, Arvind. "The Regionalism Debate: An Overview." *World Economy*, 22 (June 1999): 477–511.

Park, Seung Ho. "The Interfirm Collaboration in Global Competition." *Multinational Business Review*, 4 (1) (1996): 94–106.

Porter, Michael, and Scott Stern. *The Challenge to America's Prosperity: Findings from the Innovation Index.* Washington, DC: Council on Competitiveness, 1999.

Springer, Reiner, and Michael R. Czinkota. "Marketing's Contribution to the Transformation of Central and Eastern Europe." *Thunderbird International Business Review*, 41 (January/February 1999): 29–48.

FINANCIAL
ENVIRONMENT

CHAPTER OVERVIEW

1. HISTORICAL ROLE OF THE U.S. DOLLAR

2. DEVELOPMENT OF THE CURRENT INTERNATIONAL
   MONETARY SYSTEM

3. FIXED VERSUS FLOATING EXCHANGE RATES

4. FOREIGN EXCHANGE AND FOREIGN EXCHANGE RATES

5. BALANCE OF PAYMENTS

6. THE ASIAN FINANCIAL CRISIS

7. MARKETING IN EURO-LAND

When international transactions occur, foreign exchange is the monetary mechanism allowing the transfer of funds from one nation to another. The existing international monetary system always affects companies as well as individuals whenever they buy or sell products and services traded across national boundaries. For example, the low value of the Canadian dollar in comparison to the U.S. dollar in recent years has severely affected such Canadian national companies as Canadian Airlines, which collect revenue mostly in Canadian dollars, but must pay for equipment, fuel, and aircraft in U.S. dollars.[1] Similarly, when the Japanese yen is high relative to the dollar, many PC makers in the United States have to deal with an increase in costs of LCD monitors they purchase from Japanese manufacturers, who control about 90 percent of the LCD market in the world. On the other hand, a depreciated dollar

---

[1]Scott Morrison, "Losses from Canadian Airlines Highlight Crisis," Financial Times (May 5, 1999), p. 32.

also enables those PC makers to export more PCs abroad, as the U.S.-made PCs become less expensive in terms of foreign currencies. It is obvious that the current international monetary system has a profound impact not only on individuals and companies but also on the U.S. balance of payments at the aggregate level.

This chapter examines international trade in monetary terms. In fact, the international monetary system has changed dramatically over the years. Given the drastic realignment in recent years of the exchange rates of major currencies, including the U.S. dollar, Japanese yen, and German mark, the current international monetary system may well be in for a major change. The adoption of the euro as a common currency in the European Union in 1999 is just one example of the many changes to come. Although international marketers have to operate in a currently existing international monetary system for international transactions and settlements, they should understand how the scope and nature of the system has changed and how it has worked over time. Forward-looking international marketers need to be aware of the dynamics of the international monetary system.

The 1990s—particularly, the second half of the decade—proved to be one of the most turbulent periods in recent history. The seemingly unstoppable rapid economic growth of Asia came to a screeching halt in 1997, and the introduction of the euro in the European Union in 1999 has drastically changed the European economic environment. These events profoundly affect international marketing practices. We are convinced that these epoch-making events need your special attention and that your understanding of them will allow you to become seasoned marketing decision makers in crucial areas such as product development, brand management, and pricing, among others, when developing marketing strategy on a global basis. It is another way to tell you that you have to be up to the minute with everchanging events that could affect your understanding of the class material, let alone your future career. In this chapter, we also provide a special detailed examination of the implications of the Asian financial crisis and marketing in the Euro-Land.

HISTORICAL ROLE OF THE U.S. DOLLAR   ◆ ◆ ◆ ◆ ◆ ◆

Each country has its own currency through which it expresses the value of its products. An international monetary system is necessary because each country has a different monetary unit or currency that serves as a medium of exchange and store of value. The absence of a universal currency means that we must have a system that allows for the transfer of purchasing power between countries with different national currencies. For international trade settlements, the various currencies of the world must be exchanged from one to another. This is accomplished through foreign exchange markets.

Periodically, a country must review the status of its economic relations with the rest of the world in terms of its exports and imports, its exchange of various kinds of services, and its purchase and sale of different types of capital assets and other international payments, receipts, and transfers. In the post–World War II period, a number of institutions came into existence to monitor and assist countries as necessary in keeping their international financial commitments. This new system of international monetary relations promoted increased international trade through the 1950s and 1960s. The United States agreed to exchange the dollar at $35 per ounce of gold. With the value of the dollar stabilized, countries could deal in dollars without being constrained by currency fluctuations. Thus, the dollar became the common denominator in world trade. In the early 1970s, however, a weakening U.S. dollar caused the existing system to show strains and eventually break down. The U.S. dollar standard was dropped; the dollar was no longer the anchor.

Because of the weakened dollar and other issues, the monetary stability of the world was unsettled throughout the 1970s and into the early 1980s. As the 1980s advanced, however, the U.S. economy stabilized and the value of the dollar against other currencies climbed to an all-time high. This caused U.S. exports to become costlier, and foreign imports to become cheaper, resulting in an adverse trade balance. In the fall of 1985, leading industrialized countries joined the U.S. effort to intervene in the foreign exchange markets to decrease the value of the dollar. The dollar fell and remained weak in the remaining years of the 1980s and 1990s. Despite the boom in the U.S. economy, the persistent U.S. trade deficits suggest that the dollar is more likely to depreciate than appreciate in the future.

DEVELOPMENT OF TODAY'S INTERNATIONAL MONETARY SYSTEM

The Bretton Woods Conference

Post–World War II developments had long-range effects on international financial arrangements, the role of gold, and the problems of adjustment of balance of payments disequilibria. Following World War II, there was a strong desire to adhere to goals that would bring economic prosperity and hopefully a long-term peace to the world. The negotiations to establish the postwar international monetary system took place at the resort of Bretton Woods in New Hampshire in 1944. The negotiators at the **Bretton Woods Conference** recommended the following:[2]

1. Each nation should be at liberty to use macroeconomic policies for full employment.
2. Free floating exchange rates could not work. Their ineffectiveness had been demonstrated in the interwar years. The extremes of both permanently fixed and floating rates should be avoided.
3. A monetary system was needed that would recognize that exchange rates were both a national and international concern.

In order to avoid both the rigidity of a fixed exchange rate system and at the same time the chaos of freely floating exchange rates, the Bretton Woods Agreement provided for an adjustable peg. Under this system, currencies were to establish par values in terms of gold, but there was to be little, if any, convertibility of the currencies for gold. Each government was responsible for monitoring its own currency to see that it did not float beyond 1 percent above or below its established par value. As a nation's currency attained or approached either limit, its central bank intervened in the world financial markets to prevent the rate from passing the limit.

Under this system, a country experiencing a balance-of-payments deficit would normally experience devaluation pressure on its current value. The country's

[2]Carlo Cottarelli and Curzio Giannini, *Credibility Without Rules?: Monetary Framework in the Post-Bretton Woods Era* (Washington, D.C.: International Monetary Fund, 1997).

authorities would defend its currency by using its foreign currency reserves, primarily U.S. dollars, to purchase its own currency on the open market to push its value back up to its par value. A country experiencing a balance-of-payments surplus would do the opposite and sell its currency on the open market. An institution called the **International Monetary Fund (IMF)** was established at Bretton Woods to oversee the newly agreed-upon monetary system. If a country experienced a fundamental or long-term disequilibrium in its balance of payments, it could alter its peg by up to 10 percent from its initial par value without approval from the International Monetary Fund. Adjustment beyond 10 percent required IMF approval.

In the 1960s, the United States began to experience sequential balance-of-payments deficits, resulting in downward pressure on the dollar. Since the U.S. government was obligated to maintain the dollar at its par value, it had to spend much of its gold and foreign currency reserves in order to purchase dollars on the world financial markets. In addition, the U.S. dollar was the reserve currency, convertible to gold under the Bretton Woods Agreement; the U.S. Treasury was obligated to convert dollars to gold upon demand by foreign central banks.

Furthermore, many central banks engaged in massive dollar purchases on the foreign exchange markets to counteract the downward pressure on the dollar and related upward pressure on their own currencies. The continued defense of the dollar left central banks around the world with massive quantities of dollars. These countries, knowing that the dollars they held were in fact convertible to gold with the U.S. Treasury, attempted to hold back, demanding gold in exchange. However, it became clear by 1971 that the dollar was quite overvalued, and devaluation of the dollar versus gold was inevitable. Central banks increasingly presented U.S. dollar balances to the U.S. Treasury for conversion to gold, and gold flowed out of the U.S. vaults at an alarming rate.

This situation led President Richard Nixon to suspend the convertibility of the dollar to gold on August 15, 1971. This effectively ended the exchange rate regime begun at Bretton Woods more than twenty-five years earlier.

The International Monetary Fund (IMF) oversees the international monetary system. The IMF was a specialized agency within the United Nations, established to promote international monetary cooperation and to facilitate the expansion of trade, and, in turn, to contribute to increased employment and improved economic conditions in all member countries.

Its purposes are defined in the following terms.[3]

The International Monetary Fund

1. To promote international monetary cooperation through a permanent institution, providing the machinery for consultations and collaboration on international monetary problems

2. To facilitate the expansion and balanced growth of international trade, and to contribute thereby to the promotion and maintenance of high levels of employment and real income, and to the development of the productive resources of all members as primary objectives of economic policy

---

[3]International Monetary Fund, *The Role and Function of the International Monetary Fund* (Washington, D.C.: International Monetary Fund, 1985).

3. To promote exchange stability, to maintain orderly exchange arrangements among members, and to avoid competitive exchange depreciation

4. To assist in the establishment of a multilateral system of payments in respect to current transactions between members and in the elimination of foreign exchange restrictions that hamper the growth of world trade

5. To give confidence to members by making the general resources of the fund temporarily available to them under adequate safeguards, thus providing them with the opportunity to correct maladjustments in their balance of payments without resorting to measures destructive of national or international prosperity

6. In accordance with the above, to shorten the duration and lessen the degree of disequilibrium in the international balance of payments to members

Today there are more than 150 members of the IMF. Its accomplishments include sustaining a rapidly increasing volume of trade and investment and displaying flexibility in adapting to changes in international commerce. To an extent, the IMF served as an international central bank to help countries during periods of temporary balance of payments difficulties, by protecting their rates of exchange. This helped countries avoid the placement of foreign exchange controls and other trade barriers.

As time passed, it became evident that the IMF's resources for providing short-term accommodation to countries in monetary difficulties were not sufficient. To resolve the situation, and to reduce upward pressure on the U.S. dollar by countries holding dollar reserves, the fund created special drawing rights in 1969. **Special drawing rights (SDRs)** are special account entries on the IMF books designed to provide additional liquidity to support growing world trade. The value of SDRs is determined by a weighted average of a basket of four currencies: the U.S. dollar, the Japanese yen, the European Union's euro, and the British pound. Although SDRs are a form of fiat money and not convertible to gold, their gold value is guaranteed, which helps to ensure their acceptability.

Participant nations may use SDRs as a source of currency in a spot transaction, as a loan for clearing a financial obligation, as security for a loan, as a swap against a currency, or in a forward exchange operation. A nation with a balance-of-payments problem may use its SDRs to obtain usable currency from another nation designated by the fund. By providing a mechanism for international monetary cooperation, working to reduce restrictions to trade and investment flows, and helping members with their short-term balance-of-payments difficulties, the IMF makes a significant and unique contribution to economic stability and improved living standards throughout the world.

Most recently, during the 1997–98 Asian financial crisis, the IMF provided more than $110 billion in bailout packages to Thailand, Indonesia, and South Korea. The IMF nearly depleted its own reserves. The issue to be resolved is not if the IMF has done a good job in stabilizing the world economy in general, and in handling more recent financial crises that engulfed East Asia in particular, but if the IMF could have done a better job with the surveillance functions mandated in the IMF Article of Agreement, alleviating the need for additional resources by the IMF.[4]

---

[4]Chong-Soo Pyun, "Roles of the IMF in the Asian Financial Turmoil," *Multinational Business Review*, 7 (Fall 1999), pp. 68–72.

Various foreign currencies and gold coins, nuggets, and bars as a means to measure and store economic value.

The International Bank for Reconstruction and Development

Another creation of the Bretton Woods Agreement was the International Bank for Reconstruction and Development, known as the **World Bank**. Although the International Monetary Fund was created to aid countries in financing their balance-of-payments difficulties and maintaining a relatively stable currency, the World Bank was initially intended to finance postwar reconstruction and development and later to finance development infrastructure in the developing world. More recently, the World Bank has begun to participate actively with the IMF to resolve debt problems of the developing world, and it may also play a major role in bringing a market economy to the former members of the Eastern bloc.

Fixed versus Floating Exchange Rates

Since the 1970s all major nations have had floating currencies. An IMF meeting in Jamaica in 1976 reached consensus on amendments to the IMF Articles of Agreement that accepted floating rates as the basis for the international monetary system. The amended agreement recognized that real rate stability can only be achieved through stability in underlying economic and financial conditions. Exchange rate stability cannot be imposed by adoption of pegged exchange rates and official intervention in the foreign exchange markets.

There are two kinds of currency floats, and these are referred to as free or managed, or as clean or dirty. The **free (clean) float** is the closest approximation to perfect competition, because there is no government intervention and because billions of units of currency are being traded by buyers and sellers. Buyers and sellers may change sides on short notice as information, rumors, or moods change, or as their clients' needs differ.

A **managed float** allows for a limited amount of government intervention to soften sudden swings in the value of a currency. If a nation's currency enters into a rapid ascent or decline, that nation's central bank may wish to sell or buy that currency on the open market in a countervailing movement to offset the prevailing market tendency. This is for the purpose of maintaining an orderly, less-volatile foreign exchange market.

In March 1973, the major currencies began to float in the foreign exchange markets. The advocates for floating exchange regime argued that it would end balance of payments disequilibria because the value of each currency would float up or down to a point where supply equaled demand. It has not worked that way, at least in part due to the reluctance of governments to permit extreme changes in the value of their currencies. Governments have intervened in the currency markets to moderate or prevent value changes. In reality, however, the supposed benefits of floating exchange rates have not been borne to date. For example:

1. Floating exchange rates were supposed to facilitate balance of payments adjustments. However, not only have imbalances not disappeared, they have become worse, as attested to by the recent Asian and Latin American financial crises.

2. Currency speculation was expected to be curtailed. But speculation has since been greater than ever. Similarly, short-term speculations worsened the Asian and Latin financial crises.

3. Market forces, left to their own devices, were expected to determine the correct foreign exchange rate balance. But imbalances have become greater than ever, as have fluctuations in rates.

4. Autonomy in economic and monetary policy was hoped to be preserved, allowing each country free choice of its monetary policy and rate of inflation. But this has also not materialized.

As a result, international marketers have had to cope with the ever-fluctuating exchange rates (see Exhibit 3–1). Even a small fluctuation in exchange rates cannot be ignored, since it has an enormous impact on a company's operating profit. For example, a one-yen rise against the dollar cuts Honda's annual operating profit by a whopping 8 to 9 billion yen (or some $80 million to $90 million).[5]

Currency Blocs   While currencies of most countries float in value against one another, those of many developing countries are pegged (or fixed) to one of the major currencies or to a basket of major currencies such as the U.S. dollar, SDRs, or some specially chosen currency mix. In general, developing countries that depend on their trading relationships with a major country, such as the United States, for economic growth tend to use the currency of the principal country.

Today, the global economy is increasingly dominated by three major currency blocs. The U.S. dollar, the Japanese yen, and the EU's euro each represent their "sphere of influence" on the currencies of other countries in their respective regions (i.e., North and South America, East Asia, and Europe, respectively).[6] Although the U.S. dollar has lost some of its role as the international transaction currency, it remains a currency of choice that many Latin American companies use for operating purposes. The Japanese yen has increasingly be-

---

[5]Mitsuo Suzuki, "Honda's Profits Plunge but It Sees Good Year Ahead," *The Reuter European Business Report* (May 20, 1994).

[6]David K. Eiteman, Arthur I. Stonehill, and Michael H. Moffett, *Multinational Business Finance*, 8th ed. (Reading, Mass.: Addison-Wesley, 1997).

EXHIBIT 3–1
FOREIGN EXCHANGE RATE FLUCTUATIONS OVER THE PAST 30 YEARS
(FOREIGN CURRENCY UNITS/U.S. DOLLAR)

Year	Japanese Yen	Deutsche Mark	British Pound	French Franc	Swiss Franc
1970	358	3.65	0.42	5.55	4.32
1971	315	3.27	0.39	5.12	3.92
1972	302	3.20	0.43	5.12	3.77
1973	280	2.70	0.43	4.71	3.24
1974	301	2.41	0.43	4.44	2.54
1975	305	2.62	0.49	4.49	2.62
1976	293	2.36	0.59	4.97	2.45
1977	240	2.11	0.52	4.71	2.00
1978	195	1.83	0.49	4.18	1.62
1979	240	1.73	0.45	4.02	1.58
1980	203	1.96	0.42	4.55	1.76
1981	220	2.25	0.52	5.75	1.80
1982	235	2.39	0.62	6.73	1.99
1983	232	2.72	0.69	8.35	2.18
1984	251	3.15	0.86	9.59	2.59
1985	201	2.46	0.69	7.56	2.08
1986	159	1.94	0.68	6.46	1.62
1987	123	1.58	0.53	5.34	1.28
1988	126	1.78	0.55	6.06	1.50
1989	143	1.70	0.62	5.79	1.55
1990	134	1.49	0.52	5.13	1.30
1991	125	1.52	0.53	5.18	1.36
1992	125	1.61	0.66	5.51	1.46
1993	112	1.73	0.68	5.90	1.48
1994	100	1.55	0.64	5.35	1.31
1995	103	1.43	0.65	4.90	1.15
1996	94	1.50	0.64	5.12	1.24
1997	121	1.73	0.64	5.84	1.45
1998	139	1.82	0.60	6.10	1.53
1999	102	1.93	0.62	6.46	1.58

Sources: International Monetary Fund, *Balance of Payments Statistics Yearbook* (Washington, D.C.: U.S. Government Printing Office), and Federal Reserve Board, *Federal Reserve Bulletin* (Washington, D.C.: U.S. Government Printing Office, various issues). The rates on December 23, 1999 are shown for 1999.

come a regional transaction currency in Asia. In other words, U.S. companies will find it easier to do business with companies in Latin America as business planning as well as transactions are increasingly conducted in dollar denominations. On the other hand, those U.S. companies will increasingly have to accept yen-denominated business transactions in Asia and euro-denominated transactions in Europe, thus being susceptible to exchange rate fluctuations. Considering increased trade volumes with Asian and European countries as well as with Latin American countries, it has become all the more important for U.S. marketing executives to understand the dynamic forces that affect exchange rates and to predict the exchange rate fluctuations.

◆ ◆ ◆ ◆ ◆ ◆ FOREIGN EXCHANGE AND FOREIGN EXCHANGE RATES

Foreign exchange, as the term implies, refers to the exchange of one country's money for that of another country. When international transactions occur, foreign exchange is the monetary mechanism allowing the transfer of funds from one nation to another. In this section, we explore what factors influence the exchange rates over time and how the exchange rates are determined.

Purchasing Power Parity

One of the most fundamental determinants of the exchange rate is **purchasing power parity (PPP)**, whereby the exchange rate between the currencies of two countries makes the purchasing power of both currencies equal. In other words, the value of a currency is determined by what it can buy.

The following formula represents the relationship between inflation rates and the exchange rate:

$$R_t = R_0 \times \frac{(1 + Infl_{\text{Brt}})}{(1 + Infl_{\text{US}})}$$

where

    R = the exchange rate quoted in £/$
    Infl = inflation rate
    t = time period

For example, if British inflation were 2 percent a year and U.S. inflation were 5 percent a year, the value of the dollar would be expected to fall by the difference of 3 percent, so that the real prices of goods in the two countries would remain fairly similar. If the current exchange rate (R_0) is 0.616 British pounds to the dollar (£0.616/$), then

$$R_t = 0.616 \times \frac{(1 + .02)}{(1 + .05)} = £\,0.598/\$.$$

In other words, the dollar is expected to depreciate from £0.616/$ to £0.598/$ in a year. The U.S. dollar will be able to buy slightly fewer pounds.

In fact, the *Economist* publishes a PPP study every year based on McDonald's Big Mac hamburger, sold all over the world. It is known as the Big Mac Index, and it shows whether currencies are at their "correct" exchange rate. Look at the recent Big Mac Index to see how actual exchange rates deviate from the Big Mac Index (see Exhibit 3–2). If the dollar is undervalued relative to a foreign currency (i.e., the foreign currency is overvalued relative to the dollar), people using that foreign currency will find it cheaper to buy goods from the United States. Conversely, people living in the United States will find it more expensive to import goods from a country with an overvalued currency.

Forecasting Exchange Rate Fluctuation

Actual exchange rates can be very different from the expected rates. Those deviations are not necessarily a random variation. As summarized in Exhibit 3–3, many interrelated factors influence the value of a floating currency. In particu-

Exhibit 3–2
The Big Mac Index

	Big Mac prices		Implied PPP* of the dollar	Actual $ exchange rate 3/30/99	Local currency under (−)/over(+) valuation,[†] %
	In local currency	In dollars			
United States[‡]	$2.43	2.43	—	—	—
Argentina	Peso 2.50	2.50	1.03	1.00	+3
Australia	A $2.65	1.66	1.09	1.59	−32
Brazil	Real 2.95	1.71	1.21	1.73	−30
Britain	£1.90	3.07	1.28[††]	1.61[††]	+26
Canada	C$2.99	1.98	1.23	1.51	−19
Chile	Peso 1,250	2.60	518	484	+7
China	Yuan 9.90	1.20	4.07	8.28	−51
Denmark	DKr 25.75	3.58	10.19	6.91	+47
Euro area	2.52	2.71	0.97[§]	1.08[§]	+11
France	FFr 8.50	2.87	7.20	6.10	+18
Germany	DM 4.95	2.72	2.04	1.82	+12
Italy	Lire 4,500	2.50	1,852	1,799	+3
Netherlands	F 15.45	2.66	2.24	2.05	+10
Spain	Pta 375	2.43	154	155	0
Hong Kong	HK $10.2	1.32	4.20	7.75	−46
Hungary	Forint 299	1.26	123	237	−48
Indonesia	Rupiah 14,500	1.66	5,967	8,725	−32
Israel	Shekel 13.9	3.44	5.72	4.04	+42
Japan	¥294	2.44	121	120	0
Malaysia	M $4.52	1.19	1.86	3.80	−51
Mexico	Peso 19.9	2.09	8.19	9.54	−14
New Zealand	NZ $3.40	1.82	1.40	1.87	−25
Poland	Zloty 5.50	1.39	2.26	3.98	−43
Russia	Rouble 33.5	1.35	13.79	24.7	−44
Singapore	S $3.20	1.85	1.32	1.73	−24
South Africa	Rand 8.60	1.38	3.54	6.22	−43
South Korea	Won 3,000	2.46	1,235	1,218	+1
Sweden	SKr 24.0	2.88	9.88	8.32	+19
Switzerland	SFr 5.90	3.97	2.43	1.48	+64
Taiwan	NT $70.0	2.11	28.8	33.2	−13
Thailand	Baht 52.0	1.38	21.4	37.6	−43

*Purchasing-power parity: local price divided by price in the United States.

[†]Against the U.S. dollar

[‡]Average of New York, Chicago, San Francisco, and Atlanta

[††]U.S. Dollars per pound

[§]U.S. Dollars per euro

Source: McDonald's. "Big MacCurrencies," *Economist* (April 3, 1999), p. 66.

lar, the nation's inflation rate relative to its trading partners, its balance of payments situation, and world political events are the three most fundamental factors.

Although accurately predicting the actual exchange rate fluctuations is not possible and it is not related directly to marketing executives' jobs, seasoned

EXHIBIT 3–3
FACTORS INFLUENCING FOREIGN EXCHANGE RATES

Macroeconomic Factors

1. **Relative inflation:** A country suffering relatively higher inflation rates than other major trading partners will cause depreciation of its currency.

2. **Balance of payments:** Improvement (deterioration) in the balance of payments for goods and services is an early sign of a currency appreciation (depreciation).

3. **Foreign exchange reserves:** A government may intervene in the foreign exchange markets to either push up or push down the value of its currency. The central bank can support (depreciate) the domestic currency by selling its foreign currency reserves to buy its own currency (selling its domestic currency to buy foreign currency).

4. **Economic growth:** If the domestic economy is growing fast relative to major trading partners, the country's imports tends to rise faster than exports, resulting in deterioration of the trade balance and thus depreciation of its currency. However, if the domestic economic growth attracts a large amount of investment from abroad, it could offset the negative trade effect, thus potentially resulting in appreciation of the domestic currency.

5. **Government spending:** An increase in government spending, particularly if financed through deficit spending, causes increased inflationary pressures on the economy. Inflation leads to domestic currency depreciation (as in 1).

6. **Money supply growth:** Many countries' central banks attempt to stave off recession by increasing money supply to lower domestic interest rates for increased consumption and investment. Increase in money supply usually leads to higher inflation rates and subsequently currency depreciation.

7. **Interest rate policy:** As in 6, the central bank may also control its discount rate (interest rate charged to banks) to raise domestic lending rates so as to control inflation. Higher interest rates discourage economic activity and tend to reduce inflation and also attract investment from abroad. Reduced inflation and increased investment from abroad both lead to currency appreciation.

Political Factors

1. **Exchange rate control:** Some governments have an explicit control on the exchange rate. The official rate for domestic currency is artificially overvalued, thereby discouraging foreign companies from exporting to such a country. However, as long as there is a genuine domestic demand for imported products, the black market tends to appear for foreign currency. Black market exchange rates for a domestic currency tend to be much lower than the government-imposed artificial rate. Thus, a wide spread between the official exchange rate and the black market rate indicates potential pressures leading to domestic currency devaluation.

2. **Election year or leadership change:** Expectations about imminent government policy change influence exchange rates. In general, pro-business government policy tends to lead to domestic currency appreciation as foreign companies are willing to accept that currency for business transactions.

Random Factors

Unexpected and/or unpredicted events in a country, such as assassination of political figures and sudden stock market crash, can cause its currency to depreciate for fear of uncertainty. Similarly, events such as sudden discovery of huge oil reserves and gold mines tend to push up the currency value.

Source: David K. Eiteman, Arthur I. Stonehill, and Michael H. Moffett, *Multinational Business Finance*, 8th ed. (see Exhibit 6–5). ©1997 by Addison-Wesley Publishing Company, Inc. Reprinted by permission of Addison-Wesley Longman, Inc.

marketers can benefit from the knowledge. Exchange rate fluctuations have an enormous direct impact on the bottom line for the company—profitability.

Coping with Exchange Rate Fluctuations

When the fast-food operator KFC opens new restaurants in Mexico, for example, it often imports some of the kitchen equipment, including fryers, roasters, stainless steel counters, and other items for its stores from U.S. suppliers.

In order to pay for these imports, the Mexican subsidiary of KFC must purchase U.S. dollars with Mexican pesos through its bank in Mexico City. This is necessary because Mexican pesos are not readily accepted currency in the United States. Most likely, KFC–Mexico will pay for the imported merchandise via a bank cashier's check from its local bank in Mexico City, denominated in U.S. dollars. If the exchange rate on the date of purchase is 9.41 Mexican pesos per U.S. dollar and its debt is $10,000 dollars, then KFC–Mexico must pay 94,100 pesos, plus a commission to the bank, for the dollars it sends to the U.S. supplier. The bank in Mexico acquires the dollars on the open foreign exchange market or through other banks for the purpose of satisfying the foreign exchange needs of its customers.

This is the case when currency is freely convertible with minimal government foreign exchange controls, as is currently true in Mexico. However, this is not always the case. Governments have often limited the amount of domestic currency that can leave a country, in order to avoid capital flight and decapitalization. One example of this was South Africa in the 1980s, where it was illegal to buy foreign currency or take domestic currency out of the country without government approval. If a company in South Africa required foreign manufactured goods, it had to solicit authorization for the purchase of foreign exchange through the national treasury in order to make payment.

Even more rigid exchange controls existed in the former Soviet Union and other Eastern bloc countries prior to the fall of communism, where trade in foreign currency was a crime meriting harsh punishment. The problem with such tight exchange controls is that often they promote a black market in unauthorized trade in the controlled currency. In such cases, the official rate of exchange for a currency will tend to be overvalued, or in other words, possessing an officially stated value that does not reflect its true worth. The black market will more likely reflect its true worth on the street.

Another issue affecting foreign exchange concerns fluctuation in the rates of exchange, whereby currencies either appreciate or depreciate with respect to one another. Since the 1970s most of the world's currencies have been on a floating system, often fluctuating with wide variations. For example, in 1976, the Mexican peso traded at an exchange rate of 12.5 per dollar, but in 1987 it had fallen to 2,300 pesos per dollar.

This peso devaluation reflected much greater inflation in Mexico compared to the United States; the fear of political/financial instability in Mexico prompted Mexican residents to buy dollars for security. By 1993, the exchange rate had fallen to 3,200 pesos per dollar, and the Mexican government dropped three zeroes off the currency, creating a new peso (nuevo peso) worth 3.2 pesos per dollar. This rate climbed again with the devaluation that began in December 1994, to the 9 pesos-per-dollar range by 1999. On the other hand, in the early 1980s, the Japanese yen traded at approximately 250 yen per dollar, but by 1994 had appreciated to 97 yen per dollar, before losing value slightly to approximately 110 yen per dollar in early 2000. This long-term devaluation of the dollar against the yen reflected continuing U.S. trade deficits with Japan, as well as a higher level of inflation in the United States relative to Japan.

Many countries attempt to maintain a lower value for their currency in order to encourage exports. The reason for this is that if the dollar devalues against the Japanese yen, for example, U.S. manufactured goods should become cheaper to the Japanese consumers, who find that their supply of yen suddenly purchases a greater quantity of dollars. The devaluation of a currency should then help to reduce a nation's deficit with its trading partners, in the absence of other countervailing factors.

Directly related to the issue of floating currency is the concept of transaction gain or loss on the import or export of merchandise. Returning to the example of KFC–Mexico's import of $10,000 in kitchen equipment, if that company ordered the equipment in late 1998 (when the exchange rate was 8 pesos per dollar) for payment in April 1999 (when the exchange rate had fallen to 9 pesos per dollar), it would incur a foreign exchange transaction loss. This is because the company would have to buy dollars for payment in the month of December at a devalued rate, thus paying more pesos for every dollar purchased. Only if it had the foresight (or good luck) to buy the dollars in late 1998 at the more favorable rate could it avoid this foreign exchange loss. A more detailed illustration follows:

Cost of imported equipment in pesos at exchange rate in effect at order date (8 pesos per dollar)	80,000 pesos
Cost of imported equipment in pesos at exchange rate in effect at payment date (9 pesos per dollar)	90,000 pesos
Foreign exchange loss in pesos	10,000 pesos

Conversely, if the peso were to *revalue* (or appreciate) prior to the payment date, KFC–Mexico would have a transaction gain in foreign exchange.

Spot versus Forward Foreign Exchange

If payment on a transaction is to be made immediately, the purchaser has no choice other than to buy foreign exchange on the spot (or current) market, for immediate delivery. However, if payment is to be made at some future date, as was the case in the KFC–Mexico example, the purchaser has the option of buying foreign exchange on the *spot market* or on the *forward market*, for delivery at some future date. The advantage of the forward market is that the buyer can lock in an exchange rate and avoid the risk of currency fluctuations; this is called **hedging**, or protecting oneself against potential loss.

The sound management of foreign exchange in an environment of volatile floating rates requires an astute corporate treasurer and effective coordination with the purchasing or marketing functions of the business.[7] If they see their national currency or the currency of one of their subsidiaries declining, they may purchase a stronger foreign currency as a reserve for future use. Often, if the

---

[7]Raj Aggarwal and Luc A. Soenen, "Managing Persistent Real Changes in Currency Values: The Role of Multinational Operating Strategies," *Columbia Journal of World Business* (Fall 1989), pp. 60–67.

corporation's money managers are savvy enough, significant income can be generated through foreign exchange transactions beyond that of normal company operations.[8] However, in recent years, many companies seem to be reducing hedging because exchange rate fluctuations have become so erratic and unpredictable. According to a survey conducted by the University of Pennsylvania's Wharton School and Canadian Imperial Bank of Commerce, only one-third of large U.S. companies engage in some kind of foreign-currency hedging.[9]

For example, Merck, a pharmaceutical giant, hedges some of its foreign cash flows using one- to five-year options to sell the currencies for dollars at fixed rates. Merck argues that it can protect adverse currency moves by exercising its options or enjoy favorable moves by not exercising them. But many well-established companies see no strong need to hedge for protection against currency risk. The reason is that fluctuations in the underlying business can spoil the hedge's effectiveness. For companies with a strong belief in hedging, the sustained rise in the dollar over the past several years proved a serious test. Coca-Cola hopes to limit the negative impact of unfavorable currency swings on earnings to 3 percent annually over the long term. However, Coca-Cola's profits from foreign sales were knocked off by 10 percent due to the stronger dollar in 1998. Eastman Kodak used to use aggressive hedging strategy, but abandoned such practice recently, as it realized that hedging was not necessary since the ups and downs of currencies would even out in the long run.[10]

Forward currency markets exist for the strongest currencies, including the EU's euro, the British pound, Canadian dollar, German mark, Japanese yen, Swiss franc, and U.S. dollar. The terms of purchase are usually for delivery of the foreign currency in either thirty, sixty, or ninety days from the date of purchase. These aforementioned currencies are often called *hard currencies*, because they are the world's strongest and represent the world's leading economies.

Forward currency markets do not exist for the traditionally weaker currencies such as the Mexican peso or the Indian rupee, because there is no worldwide demand for such a market; nearly all international transactions are expressed in terms of a hard currency. Exhibit 3–4 illustrates the daily quotes for foreign exchange on the spot and forward markets. In the second column, the foreign currency is expressed in terms of how many dollars it takes to buy one unit of foreign currency. The third column indicates the inverse, or how many units of a foreign currency it would take to purchase one dollar. For example, on March 1, 2000, one Japanese yen was worth $0.009330; or more conventionally, the value of the yen was expressed as 107.18 yen per dollar. Similarly, on the same day, one euro was worth $0.9728; or conversely, one U.S. dollar could buy 1.0280 euro.

---

[8]Ike Mathur, "Managing Foreign Exchange Risk Profitably," *Columbia Journal of World Business* (Winter 1982), pp. 23–30.

[9]Peter Coy, De'Ann Weimer, and Amy Barrett, "Perils of the Hedge Highwire," *Business Week* (October 26, 1998), p. 74.

[10]Ibid.

EXHIBIT 3–4
EXCHANGE RATES (WEDNESDAY, MARCH 1, 2000)

The New York foreign exchange mid-range rates apply to trading among banks in amounts of $1 million and more, as quoted at 4 P.M. Eastern time by Reuters and other sources. Retail transactions provide fewer units of foreign currency per dollar. Rates for the eleven euro currency countries are derived from the latest dollar–euro rate using the exchange ratios set January 1, 1999.

Country	U.S.$ equivalent	Currency per U.S.$
Argentina (peso)	1.0002	0.9998
Australia (dollar)	0.6050	1.6530
Austria (schilling)	0.0707	14.145
Bahrain (dinar)	2.6525	0.3770
Belgium (franc)	0.0241	41.468
Brazil (real)	0.5675	1.7620
Britain (pound)	1.5865	0.6303
1-month forward	1.5864	0.6304
3-months forward	1.5864	0.6304
6-months forward	1.5870	0.6301
Canada (dollar)	0.6902	1.4489
1-month forward	0.6907	1.4478
3-months forward	0.6917	1.4458
6-months forward	0.6933	1.4424
Chile (peso)	0.001986	503.45
China (renminbi)	0.1208	8.2786
Colombia (peso)	0.0005126	1951.00
Czech. Rep. (koruna)	0.02720	36.765
Denmark (krone)	0.1306	7.6557
Ecuador (sucre) *Float*	0.00004	24997.50
Finland (markka)	0.1636	6.1120
France (franc)	0.1483	6.7430
1-month forward	0.1486	6.7291
3-months forward	0.1492	6.7004
6-months forward	0.1502	6.6584
Germany (mark)	0.4974	2.0105
1-month forward	0.4984	2.0064
3-months forward	0.5006	1.9978
6-months forward	0.5037	1.9853
Greece (drachma)	0.002915	343.05
Hong Kong (dollar)	0.1285	7.7823
Hungary (forint)	0.003794	263.57
India (rupee)	0.02292	43.625
Indonesia (rupiah)	0.0001358	7365.00
Ireland (punt)	1.2352	0.8096
Israel (shekel)	0.2482	4.0285
Italy (lira)	0.0005024	1990.41
Japan (yen)	0.009330	107.18
1-month forward	0.009377	106.65
3-months forward	0.009475	105.54
6-months forward	0.009628	103.87
Jordan (dinar)	1.4085	0.7100
Kuwait (dinar)	3.2595	0.3068

Country	U.S.$ equivalent	Currency per U.S.$
Lebanon (pound)	0.0006634	1507.50
Malaysia (ringgit-b)	0.2632	3.8000
Malta (lira)	2.3781	0.4205
Mexico (peso) *Float*	0.1070	9.3500
Netherland (guilder)	0.4414	2.2653
New Zealand (dollar)	0.4865	2.0555
Norway (krone)	0.1205	8.2972
Pakistan (rupee)	0.01923	52.000
Peru (new Sol)	0.2935	3.4070
Philippines (peso)	0.02436	41.050
Poland (Zloty)	0.2434	4.1080
Portugal (escudo)	0.004852	206.09
Russia (ruble) [a]	0.03493	28.630
Saudi Arabia (riyal)	0.2666	3.7506
Singapore (dollar)	0.5827	1.7162
Slovak Rep. (koruna)	0.02327	42.979
South Africa (rand)	0.1576	6.3450
South Korea (won)	0.0008865	1128.00
Spain (peseta)	0.005847	171.04
Sweden (krona)	0.1152	8.6837
Switzerland (franc)	0.6055	1.6515
1-month forward	0.6075	1.6461
3-months forward	0.6113	1.6358
6-months forward	0.6168	1.6213
Taiwan (dollar)	0.03260	30.675
Thailand (baht)	0.02630	38.025
Turkey (lira)	0.00000174	573275.00
United Arab (dirham)	0.2723	3.6729
Uruguay (new peso)		
Financial	0.08505	11.758
Venezuela (bolivar)	0.001509	662.51
SDR	1.3392	0.7467
Euro	0.9728	1.0280

Special drawing rights (SDR) are based on exchange rates for the U. S., German, British, French, and Japanese currencies.

a-Russian Central Bank rate. Trading band lowered on 8/17/98.
b-Government rate.
d-Floating rate. n.a.-Not available.

Source: Wall Street Journal (March 1, 2000).

Exchange Rate Pass-Through

The dramatic swings in the value of the dollar since the early 1980s have made it clear that foreign companies charge different prices in the United States than in other markets.[11] When the dollar appreciated against the Japanese yen and the German mark in the 1980s, Japanese cars were priced fairly low in the United

---

[11]Terry Clark, Masaaki Kotabe, and Dan Rajaratnam, "Exchange Rate Pass-Through and International Pricing Strategy: A Conceptual Framework and Research Propositions," *Journal of International Business Studies*, 30 (Second Quarter 1999), pp. 249–68.

States, justified by the cheaper yen, while German cars became far more expensive in the United States than in Europe. In the 1990s, when the dollar began depreciating against the yen and the mark, Japanese and German automakers had to increase their dollar prices in the United States. Japanese automakers did not raise their prices nearly as much as German competitors. Obviously, they "price to market."[12] As a result, Japanese car makers did not lose as much U.S. market share as did German car makers.

One of the success factors for many Japanese companies in the U.S. markets seems to be in the way they used dollar-yen exchange rates to their advantage, known as the **target exchange rate**. Japanese companies, in particular, are known to employ a very unfavorable target exchange rate (i.e., hypothetically appreciated yen environment) for their costing strategy to make sure they will not be adversely affected should the yen appreciate. Therefore, despite close to a twofold appreciation of the yen vis-à-vis the dollar from 240 yen/$ in to 110 yen/$ in a decade, the dollar prices of Japanese products have not increased nearly as much. The extent to which a foreign company changes dollar prices of its products in the U.S. market as a result of exchange rate fluctuations is called **exchange rate pass-through**. Although accurately estimating the average increase in dollar prices of Japanese products is almost impossible, our estimate suggests about 30 percent price increase, or pass-through, over the same period. If this estimate is accurate, Japanese companies must have somehow absorbed more than 70 percent of the price increase. This cost absorption could result from smaller profit margins and cost reductions as well as effective use of the unfavorable target exchange rate for planning purposes. According to Morgan Stanley Japan Ltd.'s estimate,[13] Toyota could break even at an unheard-of 52 yen to the dollar. In other words, as long as the Japanese currency does not appreciate all the way to 52 yen to the dollar, Toyota is expected to earn windfall operating profits.

The emergence of the Internet as a global purchasing tool also brings a whole new aspect to the concept of pass-through, particularly at the retail setting. Now that retailers can sell to the world through one Web site, it is increasingly difficult for them to set different prices for each country. One can already see this with software purchased and downloaded over the Net. Consumers in England will not pay 150 pounds for a software program that they know sells for $150 in the United States. Online commerce will limit price flexibility in foreign markets.

This pass-through issue will be elaborated on in Chapter 13 when we discuss global pricing issues.

◆ ◆ ◆ ◆ ◆ ◆   BALANCE OF PAYMENTS

The balance of payments of a nation summarizes all the transactions that have taken place between its residents and the residents of other countries over a specified time period, usually a month, quarter, or year. The transactions contain three categories: current account, capital account, and official reserves. There is also an

---

[12]"Pricing Paradox: Consumers Still Find Imported Bargains Despite Weak Dollar," *Wall Street Journal* (October 7, 1992), p. A6.

[13]Valerie Reitman, "Toyota Names a Chief Likely to Shake Up Global Auto Business," *Wall Street Journal* (August 11, 1995), pp. A1, A5.

extra category for statistical discrepancy. Exhibit 3–5 shows the balance of payments for the United States (the historical trend of the U.S. balance of payments position is presented earlier in Exhibit 2–8 in Chapter 2).

The balance of payments record is made on the basis of rules of credits (transaction that result in an inflow of money) and debits (i.e., transactions that result in an outflow of money), similar to those in business accounting. Exports, like sales, are outflows of goods, and are entered as credits to merchandise trade. Imports, or inflows of goods, are represented by debits to the same account. These exports and imports are most likely offset by an opposite entry to the capital account, reflecting the receipt of cash or the outflow of cash for payment.

When a German tourist visits the United States and spends money on meals and lodging, it is a credit to the U.S. trade in services balance reflecting the rendering of a service to a foreign resident. On the other hand, this transaction would represent a debit to the trade in services account of Germany, reflecting the receipt of a service from a foreign resident by a resident of Germany. If the foreign resident's payment is made in cash, the credit to trade in services is offset by a debit (inflow) to short-term capital. On the other hand, if a foreign resident purchases land in the United States, paying cash, this is represented on the United States' balance of payments as a debit to short-term capital (representing the inflow of payment for the land) and a credit to long-term capital (representing the outflow of ownership of real estate).

This is based on the principle of double-entry accounting, so theoretically every debit must be offset by a credit to some other account within the balance of payments statement. In other words, the balance of payments statement must always balance, because total debits must equal total credits. A deficit (debit balance) in one account will then be offset by a surplus (credit balance) in another account. If the statement does not balance, an entry must be made as a statistical discrepancy. But in reality, there is no national accountant making accounting entries for every international transaction. In the United States, the Department of Commerce, which prepares the balance of payments statement, must gather information from a variety of sources, including banks and other business entities concerning the inflow and outflow of goods, services, gifts, and capital items. Since the information will come from a number of different sources, it is near certain that the statement will not balance like a balance sheet of a corporation, where double entries are made by corporate accountants for each transaction. Therefore, the statistical discrepancy category will reflect a significant dollar volume.

The balance of payments on goods (**trade balance**, for short) shows trade in currently produced goods. Trade balance is the most frequently used indicator of the health of a country's international trade position. The balance of payments on current account (**current account balance**) shows trade in currently produced goods and services, as well as unilateral transfers including private gifts and foreign aid. The goods or merchandise account deals with tangibles such as autos, grain, machinery, or equipment that can be seen and felt, as well as exported and imported. The services account deals with intangibles that are sold or bought internationally. Examples include dividends or interest on foreign investments, royalties on trademarks or patents abroad, food or lodging (travel expenses), and transportation. Unilateral transfers are transactions with no quid pro quo; some of these transfers are made by private individuals and institutions and some by government. These gifts are sometimes for charitable, missionary, or educational purposes, and other times they consist of funds wired home by migrant workers to their families

EXHIBIT 3–5
U.S. BALANCE OF PAYMENTS, 1980–1998. (IN $ MILLIONS. MINUS SIGN (−) INDICATES DEBITS)

Type of transaction	1980	1985	1990	1991	1992	1993	1994	1995	1996	1997	1998
Exports of goods and services and income receipts	344,440	387,806	708,135	729,513	748,431	776,404	868,041	1,005,715	1,074,425	1,197,206	1,192,231
Exports of goods and services	271,834	289,070	536,058	579,956	615,909	641,783	702,073	793,482	849,806	938,543	933,907
Goods, balance of payments basis	224,250	215,915	389,307	416,913	440,352	456,832	502,398	575,845	612,057	679,715	670,246
Services	47,584	73,155	146,751	163,043	175,557	184,951	199,675	217,637	237,749	258,828	263,661
Income receipts	72,606	98,736	172,078	149,558	132,523	134,621	165,968	212,233	224,619	258,663	258,324
Income receipts on U.S.-owned assets abroad	72,606	98,736	170,906	148,268	131,098	133,187	164,425	210,472	222,863	256,861	256,467
Compensation of employees	(NA)	(NA)	1,172	1,290	1,425	1,434	1,543	1,761	1,756	1,802	1,857
Imports of goods and services and income payments	−333,774	−484,106	−759,646	−735,048	−763,187	−823,167	−950,529	−1,083,844	−1,161,533	−1,298,705	−1,368,718
Imports of goods and services	−291,241	−410,950	−615,996	−609,440	−652,934	−711,722	−800,468	−891,021	−954,124	−1,043,273	−1,098,189
Goods, balance of payments basis	−249,750	−338,088	−498,337	−490,981	−536,458	−589,441	−668,590	−749,574	−803,327	−876,366	−917,178
Services	−41,491	−72,862	−117,659	−118,459	−116,476	−122,281	−131,878	−141,447	−150,797	−166,907	−181,011
Income payments	−42,532	−73,156	−143,649	−125,608	−110,253	−111,445	−150,061	−192,823	−207,409	−255,432	−270,529
Income payments on foreign-owned assets in the U.S.	−42,532	−73,156	−140,185	−121,582	−105,501	−106,313	−144,109	−186,560	−201,109	−248,676	−263,423
Compensation of employees	(NA)	(NA)	−3,464	−4,026	−4,752	−5,132	−5,952	−6,263	−6,300	−6,756	−7,106
Unilateral current transfers, net	−8,349	−22,762	−27,821	9,819	−35,873	−38,522	−39,192	−35,437	−42,187	−41,966	−44,075
U.S. assets abroad, net (increase/financial outflow (−))	−85,815	−44,946	−81,570	−64,732	−74,877	−201,014	−176,586	−330,675	−380,762	−465,296	−292,818
U.S. official reserve assets, net	−7,003	−3,858	−2,158	5,763	3,901	−1,379	5,346	−9,742	6,668	−1,010	−6,784
U.S. Govt. assets, other than official reserve assets, net	−5,162	−2,821	2,317	2,924	−1,667	−351	−390	−984	−989	68	−429
U.S. private assets, net	−73,651	−38,268	−81,729	−73,419	−77,111	−199,284	−181,542	−319,949	−386,441	−464,354	−285,605
Direct investments abroad	−19,222	−19,121	−37,519	−38,233	−48,733	−84,412	−80,697	−99,481	−92,694	−109,955	−132,829
Foreign securities	−3,568	−7,481	−28,765	−45,673	−49,166	−146,253	−60,309	−100,074	−115,859	−89,174	−102,817

Item										
U.S. claims on unaffiliated foreigners reported by U.S. nonbanking concerns	−4,023	−10,342	−27,824	11,097	−387	766	−36,336	−45,286	−86,333	−120,403	−25,041
U.S. claims reported by U.S. banks, n.i.e.	−46,838	−1,323	12,379	−610	21,175	30,615	−4,200	−75,108	−91,555	−144,822	−24,918
Foreign assets in the U.S., net (increase/financial inflow (+))	62,612	146,452	142,028	111,332	171,815	283,230	307,306	467,552	574,847	751,661	502,637
Foreign official assets in the U.S., net	15,497	−1,119	33,910	17,389	40,477	71,753	39,583	109,880	127,390	18,119	−21,684
Other foreign assets in the U.S., net	47,115	147,570	108,118	93,944	131,338	211,477	267,723	357,672	447,457	733,542	524,321
Direct investments in U.S.	16,918	20,079	48,951	23,695	20,975	52,552	47,438	59,644	88,977	109,264	193,375
U.S. Treasury securities	2,645	20,433	−2,534	18,826	37,131	24,381	34,274	99,548	154,996	146,433	46,155
U.S. securities other than U.S. Treasury securities	5,457	50,962	1,592	35,144	30,043	80,092	56,971	96,367	130,240	196,258	218,026
U.S. currency flows	4,500	5,200	18,800	15,400	13,400	18,900	23,400	12,300	17,362	24,782	16,622
U.S. liabilities to unaffiliated foreigners reported by U.S. nonbanking concerns	6,852	9,851	45,133	−3,115	13,573	10,489	1,302	59,637	39,404	107,779	9,412
U.S. liabilities reported by U.S. banks, n.i.e.	10,743	41,045	−3,824	3,994	16,216	25,063	104,338	30,176	16,478	149,026	40,731
Statistical discrepancy (sum of above items with sign reversed)	20,886	17,242	25,454	−46,405	−46,921	3,157	−8,571	−23,683	−65,462	−143,192	10,126
Balance on goods (Trade balance)	−25,500	−122,173	−109,030	−74,068	−96,106	−132,609	−166,192	−173,729	−191,270	−196,651	−246,932
Balance on services	6,093	294	29,091	44,584	59,081	62,669	67,797	76,190	86,952	91,921	82,650
Balance on income	30,073	25,580	28,429	23,950	22,269	23,176	15,907	19,410	17,210	3,231	−12,205
Balance on current account	2,317	−119,062	−79,332	4,284	−50,629	−85,286	−121,680	−113,566	−129,295	−143,465	−220,562

NA Not available.

Source: Statistical Abstract of the United States 1999, Washington D.C.: Census Bureau, 1999.

in their country of origin. The largest unilateral transfers are aid, either in money or in the form of goods and services, from developed to developing countries.

The balance of payments on capital account (*capital account*, for short) summarizes financial transactions and is divided into two sections, short- and long-term capital accounts. Long-term capital includes any financial asset maturing in a period exceeding one year, including equities. Subaccounts under long-term capital are direct investment and portfolio investment.

Direct investments are those investments in enterprises or properties that are effectively controlled by residents of another country. Whenever 10 percent or more of the voting shares in a U.S. company are held by foreign investors, the company is classified as a U.S. affiliate of a foreign company and therefore a foreign direct investment.[14] Similarly, if U.S. investors hold 10 percent or more of the voting shares of a foreign company, the entity is considered a foreign affiliate of a U.S. company.

Portfolio investment includes all long-term investments that do not give the investors effective control over the investment. Such transactions typically involve the purchase of stocks or bonds of foreign investors for investment. These shares are normally bought for investment, not control, purposes.

Short-term capital includes only those items maturing in less than one year, including cash. The official reserves account registers the movement of funds to or from central banks.

A key point to remember here is that the deficit or surplus is calculated based not on the aggregate of all transactions in the balance of payments, but on the net balance for certain selected categories.

There are three particularly important balances to identify on the balance of payments statement of a country, including the balance of the merchandise trade account, the current account (including merchandise trade, trade in services, and unilateral transfers) and the basic balance (the current account and long-term capital). Everyone knows about the U.S. deficit in merchandise trade, but what is less commonly known is that the U.S. regularly runs a surplus in trade in services. This surplus offsets a large part of the deficit in the merchandise account (see Global Perspective 3–1).

Many observers have commented that in the 1980s the United States was able to continue its import binge via the sale of long-term investments, including real estate and ownership in companies. This belief was heightened by the high-profile sale of such U.S. landmarks as Chrysler and Columbia Records to foreign investors. These foreigners invested in U.S. capital assets, paying in cash that was then recycled in payment for merchandise imports by U.S. residents. The criticism was made that the U.S. was selling off capital assets for short-term merchandise imports like a wealthy heir who sells off the family jewels to finance a profligate lifestyle. Meanwhile, others viewed the increase in foreign investment in the United States as proof of the nation's vitality and long-term attractiveness to investors.

The Internal and External Adjustments

According to the theory of international trade and balance of payments, a surplus or deficit in a country's basic balance should be self-correcting to some extent. This self-correction is accomplished through the internal and external market

---

[14]Department of Commerce, *U.S. Direct Investment Abroad* (Washington, D.C.: Bureau of Economic Analysis, 1996).

❖ ❖

$\mathcal{G}$LOBAL PERSPECTIVE 3–1

BALANCE OF PAYMENTS AND COMPETITIVENESS OF A NATION

The information age characterizes the world we live in today, but some people do not seem to recognize it.

Each time the U.S. trade statistics are reported, we hear the dismal news of a trade deficit of almost $262 billion in 1998, despite a U.S. export boom. But when it comes to U.S. balance of payments, many people do not look beyond the "trade" statistics.

When we say trade statistics, we talk about exports and imports of goods. Trade of services is not included. When the United States incurred a $247 billion trade deficit in goods in 1998, its trade deficit was partly—albeit weakly—offset by a $83 billion trade surplus in services. Such services—the hallmark of the information age—include telecommunications, education, financial services, and a host of other intangibles.

These and other services did not only have one good year. Around the world, service companies are expanding rapidly, ringing up sales at a fast pace. Indeed, worldwide, services now account for more than $1.3 trillion in international trade.[15]

Why, then, don't we notice this important development? It is primarily because many of us are still measuring our economic performance based on the facts of an earlier era, which meant apples, steel, sneakers, and the like—tangible merchandise and nothing else. Many just do not realize a new day has dawned—one in which advertising exports can mean as much as auto exports.

Take the Department of Commerce, which collects U.S. trade data. The department keeps track of more than 10,000 different kinds of tangible goods. But when it comes to services, the agency collects trade data for only a few service categories. Services excluded from Department of Commerce data, or addressed only partially, include such significant ones as public relations, management consulting, legal services, and many financial and information-related services. While accurate estimates are difficult, it is believed that exports of services would be 70 percent higher than reported in Department of Commerce trade data.

What is wrong with underplaying the importance of services? First, it misleads the public about the nation's true competitiveness. Second, it induces government officials to develop trade policy on mistaken premises. Third, and worst of all, the growth of services could be thwarted because many nontariff barriers to trade in services—such as discriminatory licensing and certification rules, and bans of the use of internationally known company names—do not get as much policy attention as tariffs on goods and thus could harm U.S. service companies trying to sell various services abroad.

There is also a word of caution. The increased importance of services in the U.S. balance of payments does not necessarily mean that the United States can ignore manufacturing businesses. First, exports of services have been historically too small to offset the staggering deficits in goods. Second, if the United States loses mastery and control of manufacturing, the high-paying and thus important service jobs that are directly linked to manufacturing—such as product designing, engineering, accounting, financing and insurance, and transportation—may also wither away. Manufacturing and those services are tightly linked and may not be separable.

Source: Based on Daniel J. Connors, Jr. and Douglas S. Heller, "The Good Word in Trade is 'Services'," *New York Times* (September 19, 1993), p. B1; Stephen S. Cohen and John Zysman, *Manufacturing Matters: The Myth of the Post-Industrial Economy* (New York: Basic Books, 1987); and trade figures adapted from the International Monetary Fund, *Balance of Payments Statistics Yearbook 1998;* and *World Trade Growth Slower In 1998 After Unusually Strong Growth In 1997,* World Trade Organization, Press Release, April 16, 1999, http://www.wto.org/wto/intltrad/internat.htm, accessed on May 1, 2000.

adjustments. The market adjustment mechanisms bring a nation's deficit or surplus within the basic balance back into equilibrium. This is a natural event where the economy of a nation corrects its prior excesses by moving back toward the middle.[16]

---

[15]*World Trade Growth Slower In 1998 After Unusually Strong Growth In 1997,* World Trade Organization, Press Release, April 16, 1999, http://www.wto.org/wto/intltrad/internat.htm, accessed on May 1, 2000.

[16]Franklin R. Root, *International Trade and Investment* (Cincinnati, Ohio: South-Western Publishing Co., 1993).

The **internal market adjustment** refers to the movement of prices and incomes in a country. The following is a hypothetical example of such an adjustment process in the case of a current account surplus country, such as Japan.

1. As Japan continues to export more than it imports, resulting in a surplus in the current account, its internal money supply grows, the result of receiving payment from foreigners for their purchases of goods, services, and investments originating in Japan. The payments are made to Japanese residents and may be deposited in banks either in Japan or abroad, either in yen or foreign currency. But wherever and however payment is made, it becomes an asset of a Japanese resident.

2. As Japan's money supply increases, domestic residents of Japan spend more, because they have more money available to spend. Japan's money supply is increasing because foreigners are buying Japanese goods in greater quantities than Japanese are buying foreign goods.

3. As local residents in Japan spend more (i.e., have greater demand for products and services), domestic prices rise. In other words, inflation occurs.

4. As domestic prices increase, Japanese residents find that foreign goods are relatively cheaper.

5. Because the Japanese find foreign goods cheaper, they import more goods from abroad. This begins to reduce Japan's current account surplus and bring it back into balance.

The **external market adjustment** concerns exchange rates or a nation's currency and its value with respect to the currencies of other nations. The following is a hypothetical description of the application of the external adjustment to a surplus nation, in this case again, Japan:

1. Japan exports more than it imports, resulting in a surplus in its current account. So, foreigners must pay Japanese residents for the goods they purchase from Japan. Payment will likely be made in Japanese yen.

2. Because Japanese residents export more than they import, there is more demand for yen by foreigners than demand for dollars by Japanese residents. This excess in relative demand for yen causes it to appreciate in value with respect to other currencies. Remember, it appreciates because foreigners must pay Japanese suppliers for their goods and services.

3. The appreciated yen causes Japanese goods, services, and investments to be more expensive to foreign residents who convert prices quoted in yen to their local currencies.

4. All other things being equal, this should cause foreigners to buy fewer Japanese goods and thus shrink Japan's trade surplus.

However, other factors, such as a country's taste for foreign goods and general habits of consumption, must be taken into account, as well as the quality and reputation of a country's manufactured goods. Many other factors beyond domestic prices and foreign exchange values affect Japan's trade balance with the United States, and these have become a topic of serious discussion between the governments of these two nations.

THE ASIAN FINANCIAL CRISIS[17]   ◆ ◆ ◆ ◆ ◆ ◆

The Asian financial crisis in the latter half of the 1990s escalated into the biggest threat to global prosperity since the oil crisis of the 1970s. The region's once booming economies are still fragile, liquidity problems are hurting regional trade, and losses from Asian investments are eroding profits for many Japanese companies. Similarly, among Western companies, quite a few U.S. companies that have large investments in Asia are reporting less-than-expected earnings. Some feared that the Asian crisis would wash ashore to the seemingly unrelated regions of the world, including the United States and Europe.[18] For example, the unsettling ups and downs of the Dow Jones Industrial Average reflect the precarious nature of U.S. investments in Asia. Economists blamed Asia for nipping the world's economic growth by one percentage point in 1998–99.

The U.S. trade deficit consistently deteriorated from $96 billion in 1992 to $247 billion in 1998 (latest year when official statistics were available at the time of this writing) and continues to do so. Since about 80 percent of the U.S. trade deficit is with Japan and other Asian countries, the Asian crisis has the potential to worsen U.S. trade deficits, dampen corporate profits, weaken the U.S. stock market, and reduce consumer confidence.[19] European companies could not operate unscathed, as they are heavily dependent on the U.S. market for their livelihood as well. It now appears that the optimists' hope that the surge in U.S. production, employment, and exports would offset Asia's problems could be well founded. If a second round of major currency depreciation were to occur in Asian countries, however, Latin American countries could be forced to devalue their currencies.[20]

The Asian financial crisis and its ramifications could not only have far-reaching economic consequences but also force many companies to adopt new business views and practices for competing around the world at the dawn of the new century (See Global Perspective 3–2).

Although there is some commonality across the recent financial problems facing Asian countries, how they could affect businesses and consumers varies from country to country. Therefore, the Asian financial crisis can be better understood if its causal sequence is separated from reasons for various Asian countries' structural strengths and weaknesses. We see four discrete scenarios unique to Southeast Asia, Japan, Korea, and China, respectively. A clearer understanding of the Asian crisis helps U.S. and other foreign companies develop an Asian strategy better suited to the climate and environment of the time.

Chronologically speaking, China's devaluation of its currency, yuan, from 5.7 yuan/$ to 8.7 yuan/$ in 1994, triggered the Asian financial crisis. The mechanism of how the Asian financial crisis occurred is summarized in Exhibit 3–6. The currency

The Nature of the Asian Financial Crisis

[17]This section builds on Masaaki Kotabe, "The Four Faces of the Asian Financial Crisis: How to Cope with the Southeast Asia Problem, the Japan Problem, the Korea Problem, and the China Problem," *Journal of International Management*, 4 (1) (1998), pp. 1S-6S.
[18]"Europeans, Despite Big Stakes Involved, Follow U.S. Lead in Asia Financial Crisis," *Wall Street Journal* (January 16, 1998), p. A11.
[19]See World Trade Organization, Press Release, April 16, 1999, http://www.wto.org/wto/ intl-trad/internat.htm, accessed on May 1, 2000.
[20]"Latin America and the Market," *Economist* (November 21, 1998), pp. 23–25.

$\mathcal{G}$LOBAL PERSPECTIVE 3–2

THE ASIAN FINANCIAL CRISIS'S RIPPLE EFFECT BEING FELT IN LATIN AMERICA AND OTHER PARTS OF THE WORLD

What started out as an initial adjustment in the exchange rates of the Southeast Asian countries became a case of contagion that affected all the financial markets around the globe. In the process, they pushed down stock prices and pushed up interest rates in emerging markets including Brazil, Venezuela, and Russia. In the world in which markets are increasingly globalized and there is a high degree of freedom of capital movements, liquidity (i.e., short-term capital flow) has become of paramount importance. Indeed, short-term capital flow at the whim of speculative investors can move money around the world very fast, ending up affecting the economic fundamentals of various countries.

In the past, economic fundamentals—trade balance, interest rates, inflation rates, and domestic income level—were chiefly responsible for exchange rate fluctuations. But, today, a sudden short-term capital flight out of a country could wreck its economy instantaneously, as it did in Asia.

Take a look at Brazil, for example. Brazil is the largest economy in Latin America. In the last decade, South American countries, under the leadership of Brazil and Argentina, have been experimenting with regional free trading blocs, with seemingly promising results. Although dampened recently by the repercussion of the Asian financial crisis, economic liberalization in South America in the 1990s unleashed a fast growth in exports and imports, and was expected to make a significant contribution to overall GNP growth in the region.

Then, suddenly, Brazil faced the dire consequences of frightened speculative investors pulling their money out of the country. More than $30 billion fled the country in two months in 1998 alone. Interest rates went up to 40

to 50 percent to stem the outflow of money. The government announced a tax hike and cut spending to slash a fiscal deficit. Consequently, Brazil's domestic economic activities came to a sudden halt. For example, Brazil's car industry, which was bursting with new plants and increased production until 1997, is now grappling with layoffs and temporary plant closedowns.

Although Brazil was worst hit, the same financial difficulties are plaguing much of Latin America. Mexico's peso recently lost some 20 percent of its value in 1998. Many Mexican companies are scaling back investment as their profits fall. Argentina and Chile have stopped growing altogether.

Economists are debating whether governments should control short-term capital flows. The Asian, and now international, financial crisis, precipitated by the short-term capital flows, has led to a perception that the financial system has put capitalism itself at risk. Free-market economists largely reject the idea of capital controls, seeing it as a form of protectionism. But the case for free capital flows and the case for free trade are not identical. Free trade and free capital flows have striking differences. Free trade represents real wealth-creating corporate activities to meet consumer needs around the world, while short-term capital flow more often than not represents the whim of speculative investors who move capital around the world irrespective of the market need for capital. We are not sure when government policy makers will come to terms with these realities.

In the meantime, how could business executives plan for those inevitable uncertainties? There is no easy answer for it. One thing seems to be certain. In the remaining chapters, we should keep a close eye on those economic fundamentals described earlier for clues. The only thing that has changed dramatically is the enormity of speed at which speculative investors force economic corrections on the economy, and worse yet, their tendency to overshoot the corrections, wrecking what could otherwise be a smoothly adjusting economic system.

Sources: "As Currency Crisis Spreads, Need of a Cure Grows More Pressing," *Wall Street Journal* (August 24, 1998), pp. A1, A6; "Latin America and the Market," *Economist* (November 21, 1998), pp. 23–25; Masaaki Kotabe and Maria Cecilia Coutinho de Arruda, "South America's Free Trade Gambit," *Marketing Management*, 7 (Spring 1998), pp. 38–46; and Jagdish Bhagwati, "Yes to Free Trade, Maybe to Capital Controls," *Wall Street Journal* (November 16, 1998), p. A. 38.

EXHIBIT 3–6
MECHANISM OF THE ASIAN FINANCIAL CRISIS

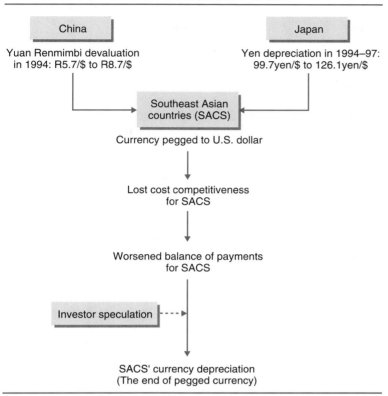

devaluation made China's exports cheaper in Southeast Asia, where most currencies were virtually pegged to the U.S. dollar. According to Lawrence Klein, a Nobel laureate in economics, the Southeast Asian countries' strict tie to the U.S. dollar cost them between 10 and 20 percent of export loss spread over three or four years.[21]

Separately, Japan's post-bubble recession also caused its currency to depreciate from 99.7 yen/$ in 1994 to 126.1 yen/$ in 1997, resulting in a two-pronged problem for Southeast Asian countries. First, recession-stricken Japan reduced imports from its Asian neighbors; second, the depreciated yen helped Japanese companies increase their exports to the rest of Asia. Consequently, Southeast Asian countries' trade deficits with China and Japan increased abruptly in a relatively short period. Southeast Asian countries' trade deficits were paid for by their heavy borrowing from abroad, leaving their financial systems vulnerable and making it impossible to maintain their currency exchange rates vis-à-vis the U.S. dollar. The end result was the sudden currency depreciation by the end of 1997. For example, Thailand lost almost 60 percent of its baht's purchasing power in dollar terms in 1997. The Malaysian ringgit lost some 40 percent of its value in the same period. The Korean won was similarly hit toward the end of 1997; it depreciated 50 percent against the

[21]"Panel Discussion One: An Overview of the Crisis," *Journal of International Management*, Supplement, 4 (1) (1998), pp. 7S–17S.

U.S. dollar in less than two months. The worst case was Indonesia, whose rupiah lost a whopping 80 percent of its value in the last quarter of 1997. In a way, it would amount to a U.S. dollar bill becoming worth only 20 cents in three months! How could this unconscionable incident happen?

This financial crisis was further complicated not only by various structural problems unique to different Asian countries but also by their fundamental competitive strengths now shrouded in the shadow of the financial crisis itself. One could argue that the recent events show that there is no basis for the "Asian model" and that the crisis marks the end of the competitive threat from Asian companies.[22] To the contrary, another would argue that while the U.S. economy is currently in a period of robust growth, nothing fundamental has changed over the years. Indeed, Paul Krugman, a well-known international trade economist, maintains that the U.S. economy was lucky enough to be in a cyclical upswing in the late 1990s while it was in a cyclical trough in the late 1980s, when the end of the American century was widely believed.[23] The turnaround of the U.S. economy in a decade suggests that Asian countries are not standing still, either.

First, we briefly summarize likely scenarios for each of the four regions/countries that will shape the Asian economies for the next decade and into the twenty-first century. The summary is also presented in Exhibit 3–7. Second, we offer likely changes in perspectives in marketing practices and strategy development.

The Southeast Asian Countries Scenario. Thailand, which had borrowed money heavily from abroad, was the first to be hit hard during the Asian financial crisis. Foreign investors pulled their money out of the country in the second half of 1997. Investors and companies in neighboring countries including the Philippines, Malaysia, and Indonesia realized that these economies shared all or some of Thailand's problems with heavy foreign debt and wobbly banks. The same "bank-on-the-run" phenomenon ensued with their currencies.

Relying heavily on inexpensive international credit line, many manufacturing companies in these Southeast Asian countries expanded their production by increasing the use of unskilled and semiskilled labor. The shortage of skilled labor will further thwart those companies' productivity improvement. Given the abundance of unskilled and semiskilled labor, they are likely to increase labor-intensive exports as a primary way out of the recession.

The Japan Scenario. Then came Japan's financial problem, not led by foreign debt but rather by internal debt exposed by the burst of its asset-inflated bubble economy. Despite its internal debt problem, Japan remains the largest creditor nation in the world—a very different situation from the rest of Asia. Nevertheless, Japan's financial problem exposed its wobbly financial system. Like the U.S. savings-and-loan crisis of the 1980s, Japanese banks are struggling to get a mountain of bad loans off their books.[24]

Until Japan's internal debt situation improves, Japanese companies' technological and marketing prowess, once touted to be invincible, will remain checked by low

---

[22]Pam Woodall, "Survey: East Asian Economies: Six Deadly Sins," *Economist*, Special Issue (March 7, 1998), pp. S12-S14.

[23]Paul Krugman, "America the Boastful," *Foreign Affairs*, 77 (May/June 1998), pp. 32–45.

[24]Raj Aggarwal, ed., *Restructuring Japanese Business for Growth: Strategy, Finance, Management, and Marketing Perspectives* (Norwell, MA: Kluwer Academic Publishers, 2000).

EXHIBIT 3–7
THE STRUCTURE OF ASIAN ECONOMIES AND CORPORATE STRATEGY OF ASIAN FIRMS

Country	Developed	Newly Industrialized	Newly Industrialized	Emerging	Communo-Capitalistic
	Japan	*Korea*	*Taiwan* *Singapore* *Hong Kong*	*Thailand* *Indonesia* *Malaysia* *Philippines*	*China*
Trade Balance	Surplus	Deficit; expected to turn surplus	Some surplus	Deficit until late 1990s; now in surplus	Surplus
Debt Obligation	Heavy internal debt	Heavy foreign debt	Low foreign debt	Heavy foreign debt	Low foreign debt
Currency	Likely to appreciate	Likely to appreciate somewhat	Relatively stable	Likely to appreciate	Possible devaluation
Highlights of Technical Resources	Increased R&D despite recession	Chaebols' dominance in skilled labor and capital	Highly skilled labor	Increased use of temporary unskilled/semi-skilled workers	Classic labor-intensive operations and some high-tech ventures
Competitive Position	Formidable on technology side; but checked by low investment	Reeling from careless foreign investment and low ROI	Increasingly competent and technology intensive	Decline in labor skills	Formidable low-cost producers
Strategy	Increased technology transfer; local procurement and production	Retreating from foreign expansion; operational consolidation	Increased domestic sales and exports	Try to export their way out of recession	Export-driven and mass production

Note: Shaded areas represent the structural problems facing the four key Asian economies into the next millennium.

Source: Adapted and updated from Masaaki Kotabe, "The Four Faces of the Asian Financial Crisis: How to Cope with the Southeast Asia Problem, the Japan Problem, the Korea Problem, and the China Problem," *Journal of International Management*, 4 (1) (1998), pp. 1S–6S.

investment at home. However, while struggling in the post-bubble economy, many Japanese companies have accelerated their move toward their Pacific Rim global sourcing (i.e., product development and procurement) platform for marketing around the world (see Chapter 10 for details). It is based on Japan's regional ties with the rest of Asia, Australia, and increasingly other parts of the Pacific Rim. Japanese companies' global sourcing platform builds on their famed target costing, target exchange rate, new product development style, and *keiretsu* (inter-firm alliances).[25]

Japanese companies may have slowed the pace of their onslaught on the U.S. market but have begun their geographical diversification into the emerging parts of the world market. As a result, U.S. and European companies are bound to face increasingly formidable Japanese competition around the world.

The Korea Scenario. Korea is geographically too close to the rest of Asia to go unnoticed for different reasons. Korean conglomerates, known as *chaebols*, led by Samsung, Hyundai, and Daewoo, had borrowed heavily abroad to invest in their rapid and sometimes careless foreign expansion. Most of their foreign direct investment has gone into mature industries characterized by overcapacity, such as the automobile and semiconductor businesses. Similarly, investors started parting with the Korean currency, causing it to depreciate.

Korean companies are reeling both from heavy foreign debt and from lackluster corporate performance. The five largest *chaebols* that employ only 2.7 percent of the nation's labor force shoulder as much as 30 percent of the nation's debt.[26] Worse yet, given their investment in mature industries, poor corporate performance may linger on for several years. As a result, Korean companies may retreat from aggressive foreign expansion and try to consolidate their operations by selling some of their underperforming units.

The China Scenario. As stated earlier, the devaluation of Chinese yuan is generally considered to have caused the beginning of the Asian financial crisis, resulting in a disastrous competitive depreciation of the currencies of Thailand, the Philippines, Malaysia, Indonesia, and Korea. However, now that other Asian currencies have depreciated—some even much more than China's, Chinese products have lost their cost-competitiveness vis-à-vis those from the Southeast Asian countries in the markets around the world.

China keeps its foreign exchange controls, making its yuan nonconvertible. The black market rate of the yuan has already been pushed down to 9.0 yuan/$ in Beijing and Shanghai, as opposed to the official rate of 8.3 yuan/$.[27] Although the Chinese government has promised to defend its currency at all costs, there is some concern that China might devalue the yuan in an attempt to boost its enfeebled exports.

If the yuan did get devalued, Chinese companies would regain their status as export-driven, low-cost, mass producers for the world market. Unfortunately, such government action might cause another round of competitive currency depreciation in Asia, further reducing the purchasing power of many Asian economies and even causing political instability in the region.

---

[25]Masaaki Kotabe, "Efficiency vs. Effectiveness Orientation of Global Sourcing Strategy: A Comparison of U.S. and Japanese Multinational Companies," *Academy of Management Executive*, 12 (November 1998), pp. 107–19.

[26]"The Chaebols that Ate Korea," *Economist* (November 14, 1998), pp. 67–68.

[27]"Can Beijing Hang Tough?" *Business Week* (February 8, 1999), p. 36.

So far, Singapore, Hong Kong, and Taiwan have escaped from the full brunt of the Asian financial crisis. Singapore reported a 6 percent growth for the second quarter of 1998, but analysts consider it artificial because the first quarter was unusually depressed. In 1998, Hong Kong's economy reported the first negative economic growth in thirteen years, contracting 2 percent in the first quarter of the year. Taiwan expects that the regional crisis will keep its growth rate lower for 2000 and beyond than prior to the crisis.[28] However, overall, Asia's developing economies, including Singapore, South Korea, and Hong Kong, are expected to increase by 4.4 percent in 1999, and a more robust economic recovery is expected during 2000 and beyond.[29]

The Asian financial crisis has to be placed in a proper perspective: The "economic miracles" of the East and Southeast Asian countries have already shifted the pendulum of international trade from cross-Atlantic to cross-Pacific in the last decade. Companies from the United States and Japan, in particular, have been helping shape the nature of the cross-Pacific bilateral and multilateral trade and investment. Today, as a result, North America's trade with these five Asian countries alone exceeds its trade with the European community by upwards of 20 percent. The trend seems irreversible. Although the recent stock market turmoil and the subsequent depreciation of the foreign exchange rates of many Asian countries may have set back their economic progress temporarily, the fundamental economic forces are likely to remain intact.

The Asian Financial Crisis in Perspective

However, in order for these countries to sustain their strong economic performance, the importance of several necessary conditions needs to be stressed. Those include strong financial institutions—commercial and investment banks and stock exchanges; transparency in the way the institutions do business; financial reporting systems that are consistent with free markets where capital and goods flow competitively; and supply of a managerial pool to shepherd these economies through very difficult transitional periods. While the Asian countries remain strong and attractive with respect to their "economic" fundamentals, recent events have demonstrated that the institutional environment of the countries need reforms.

Reeling from the initial shock of Asia's financial crisis, marketing executives have begun to cope with the realities of marketing their products in a completely changed world—from the world that was once believed to keep growing with ever-increasing prosperity to a world that has decimated the burgeoning middle class by snapping up more than 50 percent of the consumers' spending power. Marketers are facing two dire consequences of the crisis: namely, declining markets and increased competition from existing competitors. Their major task is to figure out how to keep current customers and gain new ones and maintain profitability in the long run.

Responses to the Asian Financial Crisis

Although Asia's current recession caused by its financial crisis is a serious one, every other country or region has also experienced economic slumps over the

---

[28]"Changes of Direction, for Better or Worse," *Asia Week* (October 9, 1998), p. 12.
[29]Paul Miller, "Asian Crisis Control," *Catalog Age* (July 1999), p. 41.

years. Recession is usually defined as an economic situation in which the country's GDP has shrunk for two consecutive quarters. Based on this definition, the United States has experienced twenty-eight recessions since 1894, approximately once every four to five years.[30] First, we examine how consumers react to an economic slump. Second, we show different ways in which competing companies cope with the recession and the changed consumer needs.

Consumer Response to the Recession. Personal experiences show that we tend to become more selective in choosing products and we stay away from impulse buying in a recessionary period. In other words, consumers begin to spend their money more wisely and emphasize value for the money. We may consume less of some products but we may even consume more of certain other products. General changes in the consumption pattern in an economic downturn are summarized in Exhibit 3-8.

Although a recession alters the mood of a country, it does not necessarily affect consumption of all products in the same way. If you travel to any major city in Asia, such as Kuala Lumpur in Malaysia, you will hardly notice any change in shopping behavior at first glance. Finding a parking spot at One Utama, a large shopping mall on the outskirts of Kuala Lumpur, is as difficult now as it was two years ago. Young Malaysian couples shop for groceries and kitchenware, while moviegoers flock to a cinema multiplex showing *The Sixth Sense.* The coffee houses such as Starbucks are as successful as ever, teeming with trendy customers, and high-tech aficionados are trying out the latest PalmPilots. In sharp contrast, if you visit the huge, upscale Meladas Casa Mobili store, you will see few middle-class families buying its exquisite Italian furniture there.[31] Indeed, the most susceptible to a recessionary downturn usually are big-ticket items, such as cars, home furnishings, large appliances, travel, and convenience foods. Those relatively unaffected are alcohol, tobacco, small appliances, packaged goods, and computer items.[32]

Corporate Response to the Recession. Different companies reacted differently to Asia's recession, based on their different corporate objectives. In general, there are short-term and long-term orientations in crisis management. Short-term orientation dictates that the corporate goal is to maximize year-to-year profit (or minimize loss), whereas long-term orientation tolerates some short-term loss for the benefit of future gains. Although any definitive value judgment should not be made of the two different orientations, short-term orientation tends to serve stockholders' speculative needs, while long-term orientation tends to cater to customer needs. A short-term oriented solution is to pull out of the market, at least temporarily, as long as the markets remain in a recession. Long-term oriented solutions are to modify marketing strategies in various ways to address the consumer needs completely changed during the recession.

- *Pull-out.* Pulling out of the market is an easy way out, at least financially, in the short run. Immediately after Indonesia's rupiah depreciated by almost 80 percent in a couple of months, J.C. Penney and Wal-Mart had no second thoughts

---

[30]James Chadwick, "Communicating through Tough Times in Asia," *Economic Bulletin* (August 1998), pp. 25–29.

[31]"Asia's Sinking Middle Class," *Far Eastern Economic Review* (April 9, 1998), pp. 10–15.

[32]James Chadwick, p. 26.

EXHIBIT 3–8
CHANGES IN THE CONSUMPTION PATTERN DURING A RECESSION

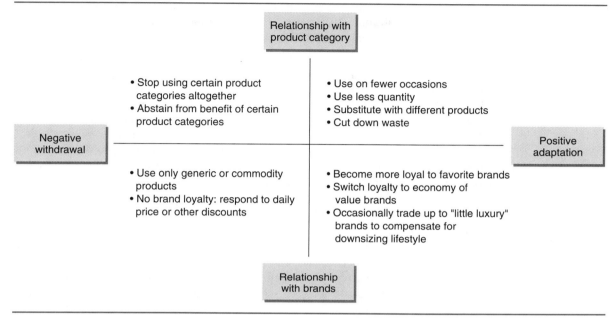

Source: James Chadwick, "Communicating through Tough Times," *Economic Bulletin* (August 1998), p. 27.

but simply left the Indonesian market. Similarly, Daihatsu, a small Japanese automobile manufacturer, decided to pull out of Thailand. While pull-out strategy may be the least painful option in the short run, it could cause some irreparable consequences in the long run, and particularly so in many Asian countries where long-term, trustworthy, and loyal relationships are a vital part of doing business and short-term financial sacrifices are revered as an honorable act. A better strategy would be to cut the planned production volume and maintain corporate presence on the market, as General Motors did in Thailand.[33]

- *Emphasize a product's value.* Weary consumers become wiser consumers. In a prosperous time, middle-class consumers may have resorted to some impulse buying and conspicuous consumption. During the current recession, they want to maintain their current lifestyle and standard of living. However, they want to feel vindicated that the product or service they purchase is worth the money they pay for it. Marketers must develop a promotion that emphasizes the value contained in the product. For example, Procter & Gamble's Pantene shampoo line, which sells for $2.20 to $7.30, is one of the most expensive shampoos available in Hong Kong. Its advertising campaign promotes Pantene's extra moisturizers and other high-tech ingredients to tell clearly the benefits of Pantene over other less-expensive brands.[34]

[33]"Asia's Sinking Middle Class," *Far Eastern Economic Review* (April 9, 1998), p. 12.
[34]"Multinationals Press On in Asia despite Perils of Unstable Economies," *Asian Wall Street Journal* (September 4–5, 1998), p. 12.

Another way to add value is to enhance the perceived quality image of a product. For example, in Thailand, there is an advertising campaign for a relatively cheap Clan MacGregor scotch whiskey made locally under license emphasizes the product value: "Even if you have to buy something cheap, you are getting something of real value." This is stated in reference to three times more expensive imported Johnnie Walker Black Label whiskey. This ad helps enhance Clan MacGregor's quality image in the minds of consumers.[35]

- *Change the product mix.* If a company has a wide array of product lines, it can shift the product mix by pushing relatively inexpensive product lines while deemphasizing expensive lines. This strategy is suited to ride over a slump by generating sufficient cash flow not only to cover the fixed costs of business operations but also to maintain the corporate presence on the market. Particularly in Asia, the company's dedication to the market as perceived by local customers will win many favorable points in the long run. For example, Burberry's, a British fashion retailer, has replaced its expensive jackets in window displays with relatively inexpensive T-shirts, stressing that everyone can still afford some luxury, even in hard times.[36]

- *Repackage the goods.* As stated earlier, middle-class consumers want to maintain their lifestyle and quality of life as much as possible. It means that they will keep buying what they have been buying but consume less. Companies like Unilever are repackaging their products to suit consumers' declining purchasing power. Unilever has reduced the size of its Magnum brand ice cream packs and made them cheaper, offers giveaways on its Lux soaps (buy six, get one free), and markets its detergents in smaller and cheaper refillable packs.[37]

- *Maintain stricter inventory.* Japanese companies have long taught us that their just-in-time inventory management practices not only reduce unnecessary inventory but also improve their product assortment by selling only what customers want at the moment. Even if companies are not practicing just-in-time inventory management, it would make a lot of sense to keep inventory low. Essentially, inventory is a tied-up capital of unsold merchandise that can be costly to the company. For example, the Kuala Lumpur store of Swedish furniture retailer Ikea has not restocked certain slow-selling items.[38]

- *Look outside the region for expansion opportunities.* Asia's recession is still a regional problem, although there is some risk that it will bring down the rest of the world with it to cause a global economic crisis. Nevertheless, market opportunities can be found outside the recession-stricken part of Asia. This strategy is not only a part of geographical diversification to spread out the market risk but also an effective way to take advantage of cheaper Asian currencies, which translate to lower prices in other foreign countries. For instance, Esprit, the Hong Kong–based retailer, is now marketing very aggressively in Europe. Despite the Asian slump, its revenues increased 52 percent during fiscal 1998 with most of the gain coming from the European market.[39] Hewlett-Packard and Dell

---

[35]"Asia's Sinking Middle Class," p. 12.

[36]Ibid., p. 13.

[37]Ibid., p. 12.

[38]Ibid., p. 13.

[39]"With Asia in Collapse, Esprit Pushes Aggressively into Europe," *Asian Wall Street Journal* (January 4, 1999), p. 2.

Computer, among others, depend heavily on now less-expensive components made in Asia, and so have begun to trim the prices of their products.[40]

- *Increase advertising in the region.* It sounds somewhat antithetical to the strategy already stated. However, there is also a strong incentive to introduce new products now. It is a buyer's market for advertising space. Television stations are maintaining advertising rates but giving bonus airtime, effectively cutting advertising costs. As a result, Unilever can better afford to reach the large middle-class market segment in Hong Kong that its SunSilk shampoo targets. American Express is launching the Platinum card for the first time in Malaysia, and it is targeted at the highest-income consumers whose wealth has been cushioned by investment overseas.[41]

Historical evidence also suggests that it is usually a mistake to cut advertising budgets during a recession.[42] For example, Oxy, a South Korean household products manufacturer, like many other hard-hit companies, slashed its advertising budget by a third, while its competitors halted their advertising completely. Before the slump, Oxy had commanded an 81 percent of the closet dehumidifier

❖ ◆ ❖ ◆ ❖ ◆ ❖ ◆ ❖ ◆ ❖ ◆ ❖ ◆ ❖ ◆ ❖ ◆ ❖ ◆ ❖ ◆ ❖

VIDEO CASE

HOW WOULD THE ASIAN FINANCIAL CRISIS AFFECT THE WAY MULTINATIONAL COMPANIES DEVELOP THEIR GLOBAL STRATEGY?

The Asian financial crisis in the latter half of the 1990s started in a relatively small country, Thailand, but engendered repercussions on a global scale. It is a clear signal as to how globally intertwined the world has become today. It also shows how volatile exchange rates have become. However, as shown in the table, while the currencies of many Southeast Asian countries depreciated drastically against the U.S. dollar, their purchasing power in those countries did not decline nearly as much. Some U.S. companies pulled out of Southeast Asia as they could not pay for components imported from home as well as from countries such as Japan. On the other hand, other companies, particularly European and Japanese, managed to keep operating as they were not as badly affected by the depreciated local currencies as U.S. companies were. How could this be? Can you draw some interesting implications on the changes occurring in the meaning of "global strategy"?

Shrinking GDP (in U.S.$ billion)			
	1996	*1998**	*1998 at PPP***
China	839	1,063	4,730
Hong Kong	154	188	190
Indonesia	226	51	1,020
Malaysia	92	71	240
Philippines	84	68	240
South Korea	485	272	660
Singapore	94	92	90
Taiwan	272	269	450
Thailand	186	97	530
Total	2,432	2,172	8,150

*Using exchange rate on February 4, 1998
**Purchasing power parity

Source: The Economist, February 7, 1998, p. 71.

---

[40]"Asia Crisis May Benefit U.S. Companies," *New York Times on the Web* (January 19, 1998), at www.nytimes.com.

[41]"Multinationals Press On in Asia Despite Perils of Unstable Economies," p. 12.

[42]James Chadwick, "Communicating Through Tough Times in Asia," pp. 26–28.

market with its Thirsty Hippo model. Now instead of losing sales, Oxy boosted its market share to 94 percent at the expense of its rivals.[43]

- *Increase local procurement.* Many foreign companies operating in Asian countries tend to procure certain crucial components and equipment from their parent companies. When Asian currencies depreciated precipitously, those foreign companies were faced with those imported components and equipment whose prices had gone up enormously in local currencies. Companies that have localized procurement do not have to be affected easily by fluctuating exchange rates. As a result, many companies are scurrying to speed steps toward making their operations in Asian countries more local. Japanese companies seem to be one step ahead of U.S. and European competitors in this localization strategy. Since the yen's sharp appreciation in the mid-1980s, Japanese manufacturers have moved to build an international production system less vulnerable to currency fluctuations by investing in local procurement.[44]

♦ ♦ ♦ ♦ ♦ ♦ MARKETING IN EURO-LAND

Those of you who have traversed Europe may remember the financial strains of exchanging one European currency for another one. Very soon, when the **euro** (see Exhibit 3–9 for some spelling rules) replaces the German mark, the Dutch guilder and scores of other currencies, this hassle will become a thing of the past. The creation of the euro has been described as "the most far-reaching development in Europe since the fall of the Berlin Wall."[45] Yet, the jury is still out on the impact of the euro. While some of the benefits of the euro to firms and consumers are clear, many questions are still left unanswered. Only the future will tell whether the euro will indeed deliver the promises that its creators envisioned.

In what follows we will first discuss what the euro is all about. We will then give a brief historical sketch. The second part focuses on the strategic and managerial marketing implications of the euro. We then highlight the key issues that firms doing business in the euro-zone will need to tackle.

What Is the Euro? The European Union consists of fifteen countries. Of those fifteen nations, eleven countries (Exhibit 3–10) form the *euro-zone*. Britain, Denmark, and Sweden, although qualified, declined to join the euro-zone, while Greece did not meet necessary criteria for participation. Their economies represent a combined 28 percent of world's gross domestic product[46] and 20 percent of overall international trade, with

---

[43]Karene Witcher, "Marketing Strategies Help Asian Firms Beat a Downturn," *Asian Wall Street Journal* (December 7, 1998), p. 9.

[44]"Manufacturers Reshape Asian Strategies," *Nikkei Weekly* (January 12, 1998), pp. 1, 5.

[45]"The Long and Arduous ascent of Euro-Man," *Financial Times* (December 15, 1998), p. 4.

[46]"Business Performance Will Need Sharper Edge," *Financial Times* (November 5, 1998), p. VIII.

EXHIBIT 3–9
THE EURO—OFFICIAL SPELLING RULES

One indication of the confusion surrounding the euro is the spelling of the word *euro*. Here are the "official" rules:

Question 1: Uppercase or lowercase?

Answer: Lowercase. In English but also in almost all other official EU languages, the spelling should always be lowercase—that is, euro and not Euro. One notable exception is Denmark—one of the four euro-out countries—where it is spelled Euro.

Question 2: Plural: euros or euro?

Answer: Just euro. This rule sounds puzzling but that is the official plural form in English (and also in Dutch and Italian, for example). Some of the EU languages (e.g., French, Spanish) add an 's'.

Source: The European Union's Server at http://www.europa.eu.int

EXHIBIT 3–10
EURO-ZONE COUNTRIES

EXHIBIT 3–11

THE EURO CURRENCY

The structure on the euro bank notes does not represent any existing monuments. The front side of each bill depicts images of windows and gateways while the reverse side features a bridge, a metaphor for communication within and outside Europe. The eight euro coins will carry a common European face on one side and an individual design for each member country on the other.

The official rates for the euro as of January 1, 1999, were as follows.

1 euro equaled	40.340 Belgian francs
	1.956 German marks
	166.386 Spanish pesetas
	6.560 French francs
	0.788 Irish punt
	1,936.27 Italian lire
	40.340 Luxembourg francs
	2.204 Dutch guilders
	13.760 Austrian schillings
	200.482 Portuguese escudos
	5.946 Finnish markka

Source: "Europe Launches Single Currency: The Euro," CNN Interactive, http://www.cnn.com/WORLD/europe/9812/31/euro.01/, December 31, 1998.

a population of roughly 300 million people. Each of these countries has committed itself to adopt a single currency, the euro. As of January 1, 1999, the local currency of each of these countries was linked to the euro at a permanently fixed conversion rate. For all intents and purposes, local currencies within the euro-zone are now simply subdivisions of the euro—somewhat like one cent relates to one dollar—until July 1, 2002, when they will cease to exist. The euro bank notes and coins are listed in Exhibit 3–11.

Historical Background

On January 1, 1999, the eleven countries listed in Exhibit 3–11 of the euro-zone embarked on a venture that created the world's second largest economic zone, after the United States. The seeds for the euro were laid almost exactly three decades ago. In 1969, Pierre Werner, a former prime minister of Luxembourg, was asked to chair a think-tank on how European monetary union (EMU) could be achieved by 1980. The Werner report published in October 1970 outlined a three-phase plan that was very similar to the blueprint ultimately adopted in the Maastricht Treaty, signed on February 7, 1992. Just like the Maastricht treaty, the plan envisioned the replacement of local currencies by a single currency. However, EMU was put on hold following the monetary chaos created by the first oil crisis of 1973. The next step on the path to monetary union was the creation of the European monetary system (EMS) in the late 1970s. Except for the United Kingdom, all member states of the European Union joined the Exchange Rate Mechanism (ERM). The ERM determined bilateral currency exchange rates. Currencies of the then-nine member states could still fluctuate, but movements were limited to a margin of 2.25 percent. The EMS also led to the European currency unit (ecu)—in some sense, the predecessor of the euro. Note that this newly bred currency never became a physical currency.

EXHIBIT 3–12
TIMELINE OF CHANGEOVER TO EURO

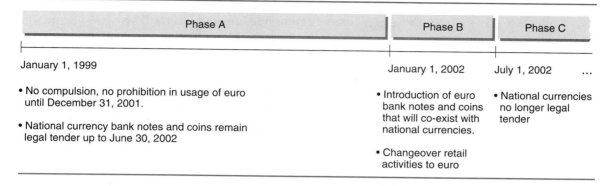

The foundations for monetary union were laid at the Madrid summit in 1989 when the EU member states undertook steps that would lead to free movement of capital. The Maastricht Treaty signed shortly afterward spelled out the guidelines toward EMU. Monetary union was to be capped by the launch of a single currency by 1999. This treaty also set norms in terms of government deficits, government debt, and inflation that applicants had to meet in order to qualify for EMU membership. All applicants, with the exception of Greece, met the norms, though in some cases (e.g., Belgium, Italy) the rules were bent rather liberally. These eleven countries forming the euro-zone surrendered their right to issue their own money, starting January 1999. Monetary policy for this group of countries is now run by the European Central Bank headquartered in Frankfurt, Germany. Three of the EU member states, namely the United Kingdom (not surprisingly), Sweden, and Denmark decided to opt out and sit on the fence. Stocks, bonds, and government debt are now denominated in euro. Companies can use the euro for their transactions and accounting procedures. Until 2002, the euro will be in a "twilight zone"—something that exists as a virtual currency but is not yet physically there. The Big Bang in the euro-zone will occur in the year 2002. That is when the euro becomes a physical reality. By then, euro coins and notes must be in circulation in all EMU member states. During the first half of 2002, local currencies and the euro will co-exist. After July 1, 2002, the euro will replace local currencies, which will then no longer be accepted as legal tender. The timeline in Exhibit 3–12 summarizes the key events.

Ramifications of the Euro for Marketers

Will the euro be the final stage leading to a "United States of Europe"? What opportunities does the euro create for firms operating in the euro-zone? What are the possible threats? Answers to these and many other euro-related questions are murky at best. What is clear is that the switch to the euro will have a wide-ranging impact on companies doing business in the euro-zone. There will be gains but also plenty of pain. Massive investments in computer infrastructure and logistical expenses are needed to put in place the change-over. For example, Allianz, the German insurance group, is spending $124 million in euro-related data processing and devoting the equivalent of 342 years' worth of extra manpower into its euro-changeover enterprise. DaimlerChrysler is pumping $120 million into its euro-conversion projects.[47] A consensus estimate is that the euro-switch will cost companies around $65 billion.[48] On top of these upfront investments, there is also the cost of lost revenues from price harmonization within the euro-zone. Apart from these immediate bottom-line effects, EMU will also have a strategic impact on companies' operations. For marketers, the key challenges include the following:

- **Price transparency.** Drug prices currently vary as much as 250 percent within Europe. German cars in Italy can cost up to 30 percent less than in their home market.[49] Conventional wisdom says that prices will slide down to the same level throughout the euro-zone. The reason for that is that the single currency makes markets more transparent for consumers and corporate purchase departments. Once retailers in different euro-zone member states display their prices in euro, price differentials will become clear to the consumer. Customers can then easily compare prices of goods across countries. Savvy shoppers will bargain-hunt cross-border or search the Internet for the best deal. Significant price gaps will also open up arbitrage opportunities, leading to parallel imports from low-priced to high-priced markets. Ultimately, manufacturers will be forced to make their prices more uniform. Although the logic of this argument sounds strong, there is some skepticism about whether the greater transparency achieved via the euro will really push prices downward. For one thing, one could argue that anyone capable of browsing the Internet or handling a pocket calculator already enjoys the benefits of full price transparency. Hence, whether a single currency will enlighten shoppers a great deal is debatable. For many goods and services, cross-border transaction costs (e.g., shipping bulky goods), cost differentials (e.g., labor, energy), standard differences (e.g., televisions in France), and different tax regimes will still justify significant price gaps. Shrewd companies can also find ways to "localize" their products by offering different features or product configurations. One important point to remember is that transparency is two way. For many firms, not only will the cost of their end-product become more comparable, but also the cost of supplies sourced from within the euro-zone.[50] In fact, in a 1997 survey of 2,100 companies within the European Union, 65 percent of the respondents viewed "greater price transparency" as one of the key areas of cost saving (ranked second behind "reduction of exchange risks or costs").[51] Pricing implications of the euro will be discussed further in Chapter 13.

- **Intensified competitive pressure.** Many analysts predict that competitive pressure will intensify in scores of industries following the launch of the euro. Pressure to lower prices will increase. Some pessimists even foresee savage price wars that will squeeze company profits.[52] Most likely, the single currency will spur the pace

---

[47]"The Euro. Are You Ready?" *Business Week* (December 14, 1998), p. 35.

[48]Ibid., p. 35.

[49]"When the Walls Come Down," *Economist* (July 5, 1997), p. 69.

[50]"US Sop Giants' Million-$ Chances to Score," *Financial Times* (December 16, 1998), p. 4.

[51]www.euro.fee.be/Newsletter

[52]"The Euro. Are You Ready?" p. 41.

of cross-border competition. But then again, intensified competition should be seen as the outcome of an ongoing process, of which the euro is one single step. The euro plays a role but it is surely not the sole driver that accelerates rivalry within the European Union. To prepare their defenses, several companies have taken measures to lower their costs. This desire to cut costs has also spurred a wave of mergers and acquisitions to build up economies of scale. The Dutch supermarket chain Ahold, for example, is scouting opportunities in Britain, France, Germany, and Italy. By building up muscle, Ahold will be able to negotiate better prices with its suppliers.

- **Streamlined supply chains.** Another consequence of the euro is that companies will attempt to streamline their supply channels. When prices are quoted in euro, singling out the most efficient supplier becomes far easier. Cutting back the number of suppliers is one trend. Numerous firms also plan to build up partnerships with their suppliers. Xerox, for instance, is cutting its supplier base by a factor of ten.[53]

- **New opportunities for small and medium-sized companies.** The euro is most likely also a boon for small- and medium-sized enterprises (SMEs). So far, many SMEs have limited their operations to their home markets. One motivation for being provincial has often been the huge costs and hassle of dealing with currency fluctuations. According to one study, currency volatility has deterred almost a third of German SMEs from doing business abroad. An Arthur Andersen study of SMEs based in the Paris region found that nearly half of them expected to venture in new markets following the launch of the euro.[54]

- **Adaptation of internal organizational structures.** The euro also provides MNCs an incentive to rethink their organizational structure. In the past, firms maintained operations in each country to match supply and demand within each country, often at the expense of scale economies. Given that currency volatility, one of the factors behind such setups, significantly lessens with the introduction of the euro, many MNCs doing business on the continent are trimming their internal operations.[55] For instance, Michelin, the French tire maker, is closing down 90 percent of its 200 European distribution sites. The pharmaceutical concern Novartis is streamlining its European production and eliminating overlapping operations.[56] In the long run, firms like Michelin and Novartis will enjoy tremendous benefits of economies of scale. Once again, the euro should be viewed here as a catalyst stimulating a trend that has been ongoing for a number of years, rather than a trigger.

Roughly speaking, there will be two kinds of companies: proactive and reactive ones. Proactive firms go for a Big Bang approach. They started using the euro as the primary currency for their price lists and other marketing information almost from day one (January 1, 1999). Sales invoices are also quoted in the euro in most cases. Examples of firms adopting this approach include Philips Electronics and

---

[53]"Business Performance Will Need Sharper Edge," *Financial Times* (November 5, 1998), p. VIII.

[54]"When the Walls Come Down," *Economist* (July 5, 1997), p. 70.

[55]"Faster Forward," *Economist* (November 28, 1998), p. 84.

[56]"The euro," *Business Week* (April 27, 1998), p. 38.

Siemens. The second group of companies, the reactive ones, take a more passive approach. They will keep local currencies until the very end, when all firms are forced to switch to the euro. Their price lists will be prepared in local currencies. A recent survey sponsored by KPMG Consulting indicates that most large European firms are moving in the slow lane. For them, the euro will not become the major currency for purchasing and pricing until 2001. Interestingly enough, the same survey also showed strong geographic differences. Companies headquartered in Belgium and the Netherlands were moving much faster than firms based in France or Italy.[57]

SUMMARY

The international financial environment is constantly changing as a result of income growth, balance of payments position, inflation, exchange rate fluctuations, and unpredictable political events in various countries. The International Monetary Fund and World Bank also assist in the economic development of many countries, particularly those of developing countries, and promote stable economic growth in many parts of the world. In most cases, the change in a country's balance of payments position is an immediate precursor to its currency rate fluctuation and subsequent instability in the international financial market.

Thanks to the huge domestic economy and the international transaction currency role of the U.S. dollar, many U.S. companies have been shielded from the changes in the international financial market during much of the postwar era. However, as the U.S. economy depends increasingly on international trade and investment for its livelihood, few companies can ignore the changes.

Having been more dependent on foreign business, many European and Japanese companies have honed their international financial expertise as a matter of survival, particularly since the early 1970s. Accordingly, European countries and Japan have been better able to cope with foreign exchange rate fluctuations than the United States.

International marketers should be aware of the immediate consequences of exchange rate fluctuations on pricing. As increased cost pressure is imminent in an era of global competition, cost competitiveness has become an extremely important strategic issue to many companies. Astute companies have even employed an adverse target exchange rate for cost accounting and pricing purposes. Although accurate prediction is not possible, international marketers should be able to "guesstimate" the direction of exchange rate movements in major currencies. Some tools are available.

The Asian financial crisis and the introduction of the euro in the European Union are highlighted. We do not mean to imply that other issues, such as the Latin American financial crisis, the collapse of the Russian economy, and global warming are not equally important and have many business implications. We are sure that you are convinced of the importance of keeping constantly abreast of events around you to understand and cope with the ever-changing nature of international business.

We predict that companies from various Asian countries will emerge as leaner and more astute competitors in many different ways. U.S. and other foreign companies doing business in Asia should not pull out of the Asian markets simply because it is difficult to do business there. Doing so will likely damage corporate reputation and customer trust—the two features that are considered sacrosanct throughout Asia. U.S. and other foreign companies should have longer-term orientation in dealing with Asian consumers and competitors by developing strategies that emphasize value and reducing operational costs.

On the other hand, the European Union (EU) is going through a different kind of economic and political metamorphosis. The EU's new common currency, the euro, has begun to change the way companies do business in Europe. Price comparison across European countries has become easier than ever before. The ease of doing business across countries will permit small- and medium-sized companies to go "international" in the region. Competitive pressure is bound to increase. European companies can also enjoy broader economies of scale and scope, making themselves more competitive in and outside the EU. Again, U.S. and other foreign companies should not take for granted the changing face of the EU market and competition originating from it.

[57]"Companies 'Holding Back on Euro'," *Financial Times* (December 10, 1998).

KEY TERMS

Bretton Woods Conference
currency bloc
current account balance
euro
exchange rate pass-through

external market adjustment
fixed exchange rate
free float
hedging
internal market adjustment

International Monetary
Fund (IMF)
managed float
Price harmonization
purchasing power parity
(PPP)

special drawing rights
(SDRs)
target exchange rate
trade balance
World Bank

REVIEW QUESTIONS

1. How did the U.S. dollar become the international transaction currency in the post–World War II era?

2. Which international currency or currencies are likely to increasingly assume a role of the international transaction currency in international trade? Why?

3. Why is a fixed exchange rate regime that promotes the stability of the currency value inherently unstable?

4. Discuss the primary roles of the International Monetary Fund and World Bank.

5. What is the managed float?

6. How does a currency bloc help a multinational company's global operations?

7. Using the PPP argument, estimate whether the U.S. dollar is overvalued or undervalued relative to the

German deutsche mark, the French franc, and the Japanese yen.

8. Describe in your own words how the knowledge of spot and forward exchange rate markets helps international marketers.

9. Why is the exchange rate pass-through usually less than perfect (i.e., less than 100 percent)?

10. Define the four types of balance of payments measures.

11. Describe the sequence of events that took place to cause the Asian financial crisis in the late 1990s.

12. What are the advantages and disadvantages of having the euro as a common currency in the European Union?

DISCUSSION QUESTIONS

1. Fujitsu, a Japanese computer manufacturer, was recently quoted as taking various steps to prevent wild foreign exchange fluctuations from affecting the company's business. One step being taken is the balancing of export and import contracts. In 1999, the company entered into $3.4 billion of export contracts and $3.2 billion of import contracts. For the year 2000, these figures were expected to be balanced. Explain how this measure would help the firm. What are the advantages and disadvantages of this measure? Are there any alternate courses of action that would give the same end results?

2. One feature of the Japanese business with companies of the rest of the world has been an insistence of entering into import contracts only in U.S. dollar denomination. There has been a reluctance on the part of Japanese companies to enter into import contracts in yen. One reason could be what has been cited in the

Fujitsu case in the previous question. What could be the other reason/s?

3. The Big Mac Index of the *Economist* has been introduced as a guide in the popular press to whether currencies are at their "correct" exchange rate. Although the merits of this index have been mentioned, this index has various defects. Identify and explain the defects associated with this index.

4. Since the introduction of a new currency, real, in Brazil in July 1994, the country has experienced more than 50 percent domestic inflation over the period (i.e., at an annual rate of more than 15 percent). Yet, the value of real relative to the U.S. dollar remained relatively constant (1 real in 1994 to 1.15 real in mid-1998 per U.S. dollar). Brazil's trade deficit is expected to increase to more than 6 percent of the country's GDP by 1999 from a bal-

anced position in 1994. As a reference, the United States' largest trade deficit ever recorded in the country's history amounted to a mere 3 percent of its GDP in 1987. How would you advise companies such as Anheuser-Busch and Wal-Mart interested in further increasing their direct investment in local operations?

5. A recent reflection of the perils of foreign exchange fluctuations is steep depreciation in the value of many Asian currencies, including Thailand's baht, Indonesia's rupiah, Malaysia's ringgit, and Korea's won, referred to as the Asian financial crisis. For example, the value of the Indonesia rupiah plummeted from about 2,500 rupiah to the dollar in 1997 to its value of a little over 10,000 rupiah to the dollar by January 1999.

a. You are preparing a report for the marketing manager of the generator division of General Electric, based in the United States. In one section of the report, the marketing manager wants you to highlight the prospects of the Indonesian peso for the subsequent year and how it would affect likely sales of a large-size generator (currently being manufactured by only three companies, including GE, all of which are based outside Mexico).

b. You are preparing the same report for the marketing manager of 3M with manufacturing facilities in Indonesia. Would you change your forecast prospects for the firm's sales in the subsequent year?

FURTHER READING ◆

Clark, Terry, Masaaki Kotabe, and Dan Rajaratnam. "Exchange Rate Pass-Through and International Pricing Strategy: A Conceptual Framework and Research Propositions." *Journal of International Business Studies*, 30 (Second Quarter 1999): 249–268.

Cogue, Dennis E. "Globalization: First We Kill All the Currency Traders." *Journal of Business Strategy*, 17 (2) (March/April 1996): 12–13.

Donnely, Raymond, and Edward Shuhi. "The Share Price Reaction of U.S. Exporters to Exchange Rate Movements: An Empirical Study." *Journal of International Business Studies*, 27 (1) (First Quarter 1996): 157–65.

Genberg, Hans. *The International Monetary System: Its Institutions and Its Future.* New York: Springer, 1995.

Harvey, John T. "The International Monetary System and Exchange Rate Determination: 1945 to Present." *Journal of Economic Issues*, 29 (2) (June 1995): 493–502.

Miller, Kent D., and Jeffrey J. Reuer. "Firm Strategy and Economic Exposure to Foreign Exchange Rate Movements," *Journal of International Business Studies*, 29 (Third Quarter 1998): 493–513.

The Asian Financial Crisis

"A Survey of South-East Asia: The Tigers that Changed their Stripes," *Economist* (February 12, 2000): 1–16.

"Asia: How Real is the Recovery?" *Business Week* (May 3, 1999): 56–58.

Butler, Steven. "Still Pacific grim?" *U.S. News & World Report* (November 16, 1998): 55–58.

Radelet, Steven, and Jeffrey D. Sachs. "The East Asian Financial Crisis: Diagnosis, Remedies, Prospects." *Brookings Papers on Economic Activity*, 1 (1998): 1–90.

www.ilo.org/public/english/60empfor/cdart/bangkok/index.htm "The Social Impact of the Asian Financial Crisis" by International Labor Organization.

www.fas.org/man/crs/crs-asia2.htm The 1997-98 Asian Financial Crisis, CRS Report for Congress.

Marketing in Euro-Land

Knox, Andrea. "Pricing in Euroland." *World Trade* (January 1999): 52–56.

"The Euro—Special Report." *Business Week* (April 27, 1998): 24–45.

"The Euro. Are You Ready?—Special Report," *Business Week* (December 14, 1998): 34–43.

Scheerlinck, Willy, "The First Days of the Euro," *The Banker* (May 1999): 16–17.

www.sap.com/euro/index.htm Case studies and white papers.

www.euro.fee.be Case studies, legal background, newsletters.

www.abnamro.com/euro Frequently asked questions on the euro.

GLOBAL CULTURAL ENVIRONMENT

HAPTER OVERVIEW

1. DEFINING CULTURE

2. ELEMENTS OF CULTURE

3. CROSS-CULTURAL COMPARISONS

4. ADAPTING TO CULTURES

5. CULTURE AND THE MARKETING MIX

6. ORGANIZATIONAL CULTURES

7. CROSS-CULTURAL NEGOTIATIONS

Buyer behavior and consumer needs are largely driven by cultural norms. Managers running a company in a foreign country need to interact with people from different cultural environments. Global business means dealing with consumers, strategic partners, distributors, and competitors with different cultural mindsets. Cultures often provide the cement among members of the same society. A given country could be an economic basket case compared to the rest of the world, but its cultural heritage often provides pride and self-esteem to its citizens. Foreign cultures also intrigue. A stroll along Hong Kong's Nathan Road, Singapore's Orchard Road, or Shanghai's Nanjing Road reveals the appeal among Asian citizens of Western cuisine and dress codes. At the same time, cultures may also foster resentment, anxiety, or even division. When plans for Euro-Disney were revealed, French intellectuals referred to the planned theme park as a "cultural Chernobyl."[1] The Uruguay Round of GATT negotiations

---

[1]In contrast, the Hong Kong government actively pursued Disney in the hope of setting up a Disney theme-park in the territory. After intense negotiations, Disney and the SAR government finally came to an agreement to build a Disney theme park on Lantau Island by the year 2005.

almost got derailed because of the French government's efforts to protect the French movie industry against the Hollywood juggernaut.

In order to grasp the intricacies of foreign markets, it is imperative to get a deeper understanding of cultural differences. From a global marketing perspective, the cultural environment matters for two main reasons. First and foremost, cultural forces are a major factor in shaping a company's global marketing mix program. Global marketing managers constantly face the issue of to what degree cultural differences should force adaptations of the firm's marketing strategy. Cultural blunders can easily become costly for MNCs. Some of the possible liabilities of cultural faux pas include embarrassment, lost customers, legal consequences, missed opportunities, damage control, and tarnished reputation.[2] Second, cultural analysis often pinpoints market opportunities. Companies that meet cultural needs that competitors have ignored often gain a competitive edge. For instance, several Japanese diaper makers were able to steal market share away from Procter & Gamble by selling diapers that were much thinner than the ones marketed by P&G, thereby better meeting the desires of Japanese mothers.[3]

Evolving trends, as mapped out by changes in cultural indicators, also lead to market opportunities that can be leveraged by savvy marketers. Consider for a moment the opportunities created by the "little emperors and empresses" in China, altogether a market of around 300 million children. Children in China affect consumption patterns in three ways: (1) they have spending power, (2) they have

❖ ❖

$\mathcal{G}$LOBAL PERSPECTIVE 4–1

SELLING U.S.-STYLE FAST FOOD IN ASIA

At one time the skeptics said that Asians would never give up their diet for the blander tastes of American fast food. But the traditional corner coffee shop selling chicken, rice, and noodles is being replaced by McDonald's, Pizza Hut, or Kentucky Fried Chicken. The taste of food is only one element in the success story. "Our marketing people tell us that people here (Malaysia) love the American way. People come to the stores not only for the food but to enjoy American style and American service," says Syed Ghazali, general manager in Malaysia of Kenny Rogers Roasters, a Florida-based fast-food chain. The region's economic success has brought a rise of an increasingly affluent middle class. A plate of chicken and rice might only cost 95 cents in Kuala

Lumpur, the capital of Malaysia. But more and more city dwellers have the money to pay twice or three times as much for a Roasters meal.

A vital ingredient in the attractiveness of U.S.-style fast food is that it caters to the family. Fast-food chains make some adjustments to local conditions. Kenny Rogers Roasters cost about half as much in Malaysia as in the United States. Some chains use local sauces and ingredients. Others insist that all supplies come from the United States. Tony Roma's, a Texas-based chain specializing in ribs, ships a container of U.S. pork ribs each month into Indonesia, the world's largest Muslim country.

Not everyone is happy about the U.S. invasion of Asia's high streets. There are suspicions that along with the food, U.S. values are being imported. Asia's leaders worry about a directionless, undisciplined younger generation lounging at eating joints.

Source: "Feast your eyes on an Asian opportunity," *The Financial Times* (July 7, 1994), p. 6. Reprinted with permission.

---

[2]Tevfik Dalgic and Ruud Heijblom, "International Marketing Blunders Revisited—Some Lessons for Managers," *Journal of International Marketing*, 4(1) (1996), pp. 81–91.

[3]Alecia Swasy, *Soap Opera. The Inside Story of Procter & Gamble* (New York: Random House, 1993).

"pester power," and (3) they act as change agents. Giving pocket money to children is increasingly common in China. Chinese children—often being a single child due to China's one-child policy—also have a tremendous amount of "pester power." Finally, children are important change agents for scores of new products because they are often the first ones to be exposed (via friends, television) to the innovation. Capitalizing on these trends, Pepsi-Cola launched a fruit drink ("Fruit Magix") in China that targeted children.[4] Global Perspective 4–1 discusses how American-style fast-food restaurants grasped market opportunities in the Asian region.

To highlight the central role of culture, consider for a moment consumer behavior in the global marketplace. Within a given culture, consumption processes can be described via a sequence of four stages: access, buying behavior, consumption characteristics, and disposal (see Exhibit 4–1):[5]

- *Access.* Does the consumer have physical and/or economic access to the product/service?

- *Buying behavior.* How is the decision to buy made by the consumers in the foreign market?

- *Consumption characteristics.* What factors drive the consumption patterns?

- *Disposal.* How do consumers dispose of the product (in terms of resale, recycling, etc.)?

Each of these stages is heavily influenced by the culture in which the consumer thrives.

This chapter deals with the cultural environment of the global marketplace. We will first describe the concept of culture. Next, we explore various elements of culture. Cultures differ a great deal but they also have elements in common. We will discuss several schemes that can be used to compare cultures. Cultural mishaps are quite likely when conducting global business. As a global business manager, you should be aware of your own cultural norms and other people's values. To that end, we will discuss several ways to adapt to foreign cultures. Cultural forces shape the company's marketing mix. The chapter will also discuss the influence of culture on a firm's marketing mix policy. Most of the time this chapter will look at national cultures. However, organizations are also governed by their organizational culture. We will look at the different types of organizational cultures that exist. Finally, we will examine a special form of cross-cultural interactions: international negotiations.

DEFINING CULTURE
◆ ◆ ◆ ◆ ◆ ◆

Culture comes in many guises. A computer search of articles published in social science journals showed slightly more than 1,300 entries that contained the word *culture*. Recent books center on the *Culture of Contentment* (J. K. Galbraith) and *The Rise and Fall of Cattle Culture* (J. Rifkin). Given the manifold uses of the word

---

[4]Amit Bose and Khushi Khanna, "The Little Emperor. A Case Study of a New Brand Launch," *Marketing and Research Today* (November 1996), pp. 216–21.

[5]P. S. Raju, "Consumer Behavior in Global Markets: The A-B-C-D Paradigm and Its Application to Eastern Europe and the Third World," *Journal of Consumer Marketing*, 12, no. 5 (1995), pp. 37–56.

EXHIBIT 4–1
THE A-B-C-D PARADIGM

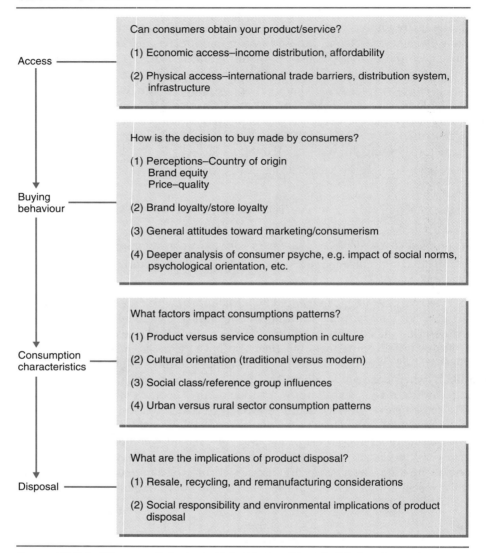

Access

Can consumers obtain your product/service?

(1) Economic access–income distribution, affordability

(2) Physical access–international trade barriers, distribution system, infrastructure

Buying behaviour

How is the decision to buy made by consumers?

(1) Perceptions–Country of origin
Brand equity
Price–quality

(2) Brand loyalty/store loyalty

(3) General attitudes toward marketing/consumerism

(4) Deeper analysis of consumer psyche, e.g. impact of social norms, psychological orientation, etc.

Consumption characteristics

What factors impact consumptions patterns?

(1) Product versus service consumption in culture

(2) Cultural orientation (traditional versus modern)

(3) Social class/reference group influences

(4) Urban versus rural sector consumption patterns

Disposal

What are the implications of product disposal?

(1) Resale, recycling, and remanufacturing considerations

(2) Social responsibility and environmental implications of product disposal

Source: P.S. Raju, "Consumer Behavior in Global Markets: The A-B-C-D Paradigm and Its Applications to Eastern Europe and the Third World," *Journal of Consumer Marketing,* 12, (5) (1995), p. 39. Reprinted with permission.

culture, the concept becomes quite murky. The literature offers a host of definitions. The Dutch cultural anthropologist Hofstede defines culture as: "the collective programming of the mind which distinguishes the members of one group or category from those of another."[6] Terpstra and David offer a more business-oriented definition:[7]

---

[6]Geert Hofstede, *Cultures and Organizations: Software of the Mind* (London: McGraw-Hill, 1991), p. 5.

[7]Vern Terpstra and Kenneth David, *The Cultural Environment of International Business* (Cincinnati, OH: South-Western Publishing Co., 1991), p. 6.

Culture is a learned, shared, compelling, interrelated set of symbols whose meanings provide a set of orientations for members of society. These orientations, taken together, provide solutions to problems that all societies must solve if they are to remain viable.

Despite the wide variety of definitions, common elements span the different formulations. First of all, culture is *learned* by people. In other words, it is not biologically transmitted via the genes (nurture, not nature). A society's culture is passed on (cultivated) by various peer groups (family, school, youth organizations, and so forth) from one generation to the next one. The second element is that culture consists of many different parts that are all *interrelated* with one another. One element (say, one's social status) of a person's culture does have an impact on another part (say, the language that this person uses). So, a person's cultural mind-set is not a random collection of behaviors. In a sense, culture is a very complex jigsaw puzzle where all the pieces hang together. Finally, culture is *shared* by individuals as members of society. These three facets—cultures being learned, shared, and composed of interrelated parts—spell out the essence of culture.

Cultures may be defined by national borders, especially when countries are isolated by natural barriers. Examples are island nations (e.g., Japan, Ireland, Taiwan) and peninsulas (e.g., Korea). However, most nations contain different subgroups (*subcultures*) within their borders. These subgroups could be defined along linguistic (Flemish versus Walloons in Belgium) or religious (Buddhist Sinhalese versus Hindu Tamils in Sri Lanka) lines. Few cultures are homogeneous. Typically, cultures contain subcultures that have little in common with one another. Needless to say, the wide variety of cultures and subcultures creates a tremendous challenge for global marketers.

ELEMENTS OF CULTURE   ◆ ◆ ◆ ◆ ◆ ◆

Culture consists of many interrelated components. Knowledge of a culture requires a deep understanding of its different parts. In this section, we describe those elements that are most likely to matter to international marketers: material life, language, social interactions, aesthetics, religion, education, and values.

A major component of culture is its material aspect. *Material life* primarily refers to the technologies that are used to produce, distribute, and consume goods and services within society. Differences in the material environment partly explain differences in the level and type of demand for many consumption goods. For instance, energy consumption is not only much higher in developed countries than in developing nations, but also relies on more advanced forms such as nuclear energy. To bridge material environment differences, marketers are often forced to adapt their product offerings. Consider, for instance, the soft-drink industry. In many countries outside the United States, store shelf space is heavily restricted and refrigerators have far less capacity (smaller kitchens) compared to the United States. As a result, soft-drink bottlers sell one- or one-and-a-half liter bottles rather than two-liter bottles. Also, in markets like China and India, the road infrastructure is extremely primitive, making distribution of products a total nightmare. In India, Coca-Cola uses large tricycles to distribute cases of Coke along narrow streets.[8]

Material Life

---

[8]"Coke pours into Asia," *Business Week* (October 21, 1996), pp. 22–25.

Technology gaps also affect investment decisions. The poor transportation and distribution infrastructure in many developing countries forces companies to improvise and look for alternative ways to deliver their products. Governments in host nations often demand technology transfers as part of the investment package. Companies that are not keen on sharing their technology are forced to abandon or modify their investment plans. When the Indian government asked Coca-Cola to share its recipe, Coke decided to jump ship and left the India marketplace in 1977 (Coke later re-entered via a joint venture).

Language

Language is often described as the most important element that sets human beings apart from animals. Language is used to communicate and to interpret the environment. Two facets of language have a bearing on marketers: (1) the use of language as a communication tool within cultures, and (2) the huge diversity of languages across, and often within, national boundaries.

Let us consider first the communication aspect. As a communication medium, language has two parts: the *spoken* and the so-called *silent* language. The spoken language is the vocal sounds or written symbols that people use to communicate with one another. Silent language refers to the complex of nonverbal communication mechanisms that people use to get a message across. Edward Hall identified five distinctive types of silent languages: space, material possessions, friendship patterns, time, and agreements. Space refers to the conversation distance between people: close or remote. The second type, material possessions, relates to the role of possessions in people's esteem of one another. Friendship patterns cover the notion and treatment of friends. Perceptions of time also vary across cultures. Differences exist about the importance of punctuality, the usefulness of "small talk," and so forth. The final type refers to the interpretation of agreements. People in some cultures focus on the explicit contract itself. In other cultures, negotiating parties put faith in the spirit of the contract and trust among one another.

Not surprisingly, a given gesture often has quite different meanings across cultures. In the United States, thumbs up is a sign of approval. In other countries, such a gesture is grossly insulting. Other examples abound of silent language forms that are harmless in one society and risky in others. It is imperative that managers familiarize themselves with the critical aspects of a foreign culture's hidden language. Failure to follow this rule will sooner or later lead to hilarious or embarrassing situations.

The huge diversity of languages poses another headache to multinational companies. Language is often described as the mirror of a culture. Differences exist

Contrast of the ancient and the modern. Businessman using mobile phone near the Forbidden City in Beijing, China.

across and within borders. Not surprisingly, populous countries such as India contain many languages. Even small countries show a fair amount of language variety. Luxembourg, a tiny country of fewer than 400,000 people nestled between Belgium, France, and Germany, possesses three official languages (French, German, and Letzeburgish).

Even within the same language, meanings and expressions vary a great deal. A good example is English. English words that sound completely harmless in one English-speaking country often have a silly or sinister meaning in another Anglo-Saxon country. Until a few years ago, Snickers bars were sold under the brand name Marathon in the United Kingdom. Mars felt that the Snickers name was too close to the English idiom for female lingerie (*knickers*). Cert, a London-based consultant, offers a few rules of thumb about talking in English to foreigners:[9]

1. *Vocabulary.* Go for the simplest words (e.g., use the word *rich* instead of loaded, affluent, or opulent). Treat colloquial words with care.

2. *Idioms.* Pick and choose idioms carefully (For instance, most non-U.S. speakers would not grasp the meaning of the expression *nickel-and-diming*).

3. *Grammar.* Express one idea in each sentence. Avoid subclauses.

4. *Cultural references.* Avoid culture-specific references (e.g., "Doesn't he look like David Letterman?").

5. *Understanding the foreigner.* This will be a matter of unpicking someone's accent. If you do not understand, make it seem that it is you, not the foreigner, who is slow.

Language blunders easily arise due to careless translation of advertising slogans or product labels. Golden Wonder, a British snack manufacturer, almost shipped potato chips to Greece in boxes marked "coffin" after a non–Greek translator picked the wrong word for *case*. The blunder was uncovered when the company checked the wording with its Greek distributors. The English version of a recent newspaper ad campaign run by Electricité de France, a French state-owned utility firm, said that the company offered "competitive energetic solutions" and was "willing to accompany your development by following you on all of your sites in Europe and beyond."[10] Exhibit 4–2 shows an example of *Chinglish*. The exhibit is part of a hotel manual that one of us found in a guest house in Shanghai.

Mistranslations may convey the image that the company does not care about its customers abroad. Several techniques exist to achieve good translations of company literature. With **back translation**, a bilingual speaker—whose native tongue is the target language—translates the company document first in the foreign language. Another bilingual translator—whose native tongue is the base language—then translates this version back into the original language. Differences between the versions are then resolved through discussion until consensus is reached on the proper translation.

Firms doing business in multilingual societies need to decide what languages to use for product labels or advertising copy. Multilingual labels are fairly common

---

[9]"When Fine Words Will Butter No Parsnips," *The Financial Times* (May 1), 1992.
[10]"The Case of the Misleading Coffin," *The Financial Times* (June 21, 1999), p. 12.

EXHIBIT 4–2
NOTICE TO GUESTS

---

1. show the valid ID. card as stated when registering with the Front Office.

2. Please don't make over or put up your guest or your relatives or your friends for the night without registing.

3. Please don't damage and take away, the furniture and equipment in the hotel or something borrowed from the Main Tower and change their usages. If happened, We will claim for damage and loss.

4. Please don't take the things which are subject to burning, explosion, rolling into the Main Tower. Please throw the cigrettend march into the ashtray when smoking in the room. Please don't smoking when lying in the bed.

5. Please don't commit illegal behaviours like gambling, smuggling, whoring, selling drugs. Please don't pick fruit and flower and vomit anywhere, Please don't take the animal and usuall smell things into the hotel.

6. Keep quiet in the hotel, please don't fight and get truck and create a disturbance in the hotel. The security department will handle the person who damage Severely, the order, endanger others' rest, even body safty, according to public security clauses.

7. Guest are advised to deposit their valuables in the Front Office safe. In case of burglary or theft, the hotel haven't responsibility for it.

8. Please don't use dangerous electrical equipment except hairdrier, shaver.

9. The service hour of the hotel is 8:00 am to 10:00 pm the visitor should leave the hotel before 11:00 pm.

10. Please pay attention to and observe all regulations of the hotel. The hotel have access to depriving the quanlity of staying of the people who transgress the rules above and neglect the dissuading.

Source: Hotel manual of a guesthouse in Shanghai.

now, especially in the Pan-European market. Advertising copy poses a bigger hurdle. To deal with language issues in advertising copy, advertisers can rely on local advertising agencies, minimize the spoken part of the commercial, or use subtitles. We will revisit these issues in much more detail in Chapter 14.

Social Interactions

The movie *Iron & Silk* is a neat illustration of the cultural misunderstandings that arise in cross-cultural interactions. The movie is based on the true-life story of Mark Salzman, a Yale graduate who, after his studies, went to China to teach English in a Chinese village. During his first day of class, his students, out of respect for their teacher, insist on calling him "Mister Salzman." Mark prefers to be addressed on a first-name basis. Ultimately, students and teacher compromise on "teacher Mark."

A critical aspect of culture is the social interactions among people. Social interplay refers to the manner in which members of society relate to one another. Probably the most crucial expression of social interactions is the concept of kinship. This concept varies dramatically across societies. In most Western countries, the family unit encompasses the **nuclear family**, being the parents and the children. The relevant family unit in many developing countries is the **extended family**, which comprises a much wider group of often only remotely related family members. The way families are structured has important ramifications. Family units fulfill many roles, including economic and psychological support. For instance, Sri Lankan banks promote savings programs that allow participants to build up savings to support their parents when they reach retirement. Such saving programs would be unthinkable in the United States. An income-tax filer in Hong Kong can claim deductions for contributions made to support one's parents or grandparents. Major purchase decisions are agreed upon by many individuals in countries where extended families are the norm. Within such communities, members of an extended family will pool their resources to fund the purchase of big-ticket items (e.g., sewing machines). A Los Angeles radio contest targeted toward Hispanic families offered two tickets to Disneyland. The contest failed, largely because it demanded that Hispanics pick two family members out of their extended family.[11]

Countries also vary in terms of the scope of the decision-making authority. A recent study by Asia Market Intelligence (AMI), a Hong Kong-based research firm, looked at the decision-making influence of husbands and wives on grocery shopping.[12] Across all twelve Asian markets surveyed, 31 percent of the decision makers were male. This contrasts with less than 10 percent in Western countries. The proportion of male decision makers was highest for Malaysia (47%), Singapore (41%), and Shanghai (40%). According to AMI, the reason for the more prominent role of male decision makers in Asia is that Asian men are more likely to view shopping as a family activity.

Another important aspect of social interactions is the individual's **reference groups**. Reference groups refer to the set of people to whom an individual looks for guidance in values and attitudes. As such, reference groups will have an enormous impact on people's consumption behavior patterns. The consumer research literature[13] identifies three kinds of reference groups. Membership groups are those to which people belong. Anticipatory groups are groupings of which one would like to be part. Dissociative groups are groups with which individuals do not want to be associated. Reference groups are especially influential for consumer products that are socially visible, such as most status goods and luxury items. Knowledge on reference group patterns could provide inputs in formulating product positioning strategies and devising advertising campaigns. A good example is a campaign that Allied Domecq developed to reposition Kahlua in Asia. During the Asian recession, Allied Domecq wanted to revamp Kahlua, a Mexican coffee liqueur brand, as the brand of choice among young Asians. To reach out to its target audience, Allied Domecq sponsored a dance program on MTV Networks Asia called "Party Zone Mixing With Kahlua." The prime motivation behind the sponsorship was that "young adults throughout Asia look to MTV as a trendsetter and representative of their lifestyle."[14] One study showed the

---

[11]"Slips of the Tongue Result in Classic Marketing Errors," *Advertising Age International* (June 20, 1994), pp. 1–15.

[12]"Men Have a Large Say on Choice of Groceries in Asia, Survey Finds," *Asian Wall Street Journal* (February 19/20, 1999), p. 11.

[13]James F. Engel, Roger D. Blackwell, and Paul W. Miniard, *Consumer Behavior* (Hinsdale, IL: Dryden, 1986), pp. 318–24.

[14]"Kahlua Gets New Sales Face in Asia," *Advertising Age International* (March 8, 1999), pp. 5–6.

critical role of group-conformity pressure in Confucian cultures (e.g., Korea, Japan). Although U.S. subjects in the study primarily relied on their own personal attitudes regarding their purchase intentions of a new brand of sneakers, their Korean counterparts put much more emphasis on social norms.[15]

Aesthetics

Aesthetics refers to the ideas and perceptions that a culture upholds in terms of beauty and good taste. Cultures differ sharply in terms of their aesthetic preferences, though variations are mostly regional, not national. In the Asia-Pacific region, aesthetic expressions are driven by three principles:[16] (1) complexity and decoration (multiple forms, shapes, and colors), (2) harmony, and (3) nature displays (e.g., mountains, flowers, trees).

Color also has different meanings and aesthetic appeals. Blue, America's prime corporate color, is seen in East Asia as a cold color, connoting evil and the sinister. In Chinese cultures, red is perceived as a lucky color. Yellow, on the other hand, is perceived as pleasant and associated with authority. In Japan, pastel tones, expressing softness and harmony, are preferred to bright colors.[17]

Religion

Religion plays a central role in many societies. To appreciate people's buying motives, customs and practices, awareness and understanding of their religion is often crucial. Religion refers to a community's set of beliefs that relate to a reality that cannot be verified empirically.[18] These beliefs usually involve reflections about after-life, but not always.

Exhibit 4–3 highlights the various influences of Islam on the marketing function.

Religious taboos often force companies to adapt their marketing mix program. To cater to Hindu believers, McDonald's restaurants in India do not sell hamburgers that contain beef. Out of respect for the local Muslims, there is no pork on the menu. Global Perspective 4–2 describes in detail the efforts that McDonald's undertook to respect local religious sensibilities in India. Elite Foods, a licensee of Pepsi-Cola Foods International, spent six months adapting Doritos corn chips for the launch in Israel. The Nacho Cheese flavor is made without cheese so that it would not be seen as a dairy product. Jewish dietary laws prescribe that meat and dairy products should not be eaten together. Therefore, nondairy snack foods have more appeal among observant Jews. Also, the name Nacho Mixx is used instead of Nacho Cheese.[19]

In numerous Asian countries, the ancient Chinese philosophy of *feng shui* (wind–water) plays an important role in the design and placement of corporate buildings and retail spaces. According to feng shui, the proper placement and arrangement of a man-made structure and its interior objects will bring good for-

---

[15]Chol Lee and Robert T. Green, "Cross-Cultural Examination of the Fishbein Behavioral Intentions Model," *Journal of International Business Studies* (Second Quarter 1991), pp. 289–305.

[16]Bernd H. Schmitt and Yigang Pan, "Managing Corporate and Brand Identities in the Asia-Pacific Region," *California Management Review*, 38 (Summer 1994), pp. 32–48.

[17]Bernd H. Schmitt, "Language and Visual Imagery: Issues in Corporate Identity in East Asia," *Journal of World Business* (Winter 1995), pp. 28-36.

[18]Terpstra and David, *The Cultural Environment: of International Business*, p. 73.

[19]"Doritos Tinkers with its Chips for Israel," *Advertising Age International* (October 1997), p. I-9.

EXHIBIT 4–3

MARKETING IN AN ISLAMIC FRAMEWORK

Elements	Implications for Marketing
I. Fundamental Islamic concepts	
A. Unity (Concept of centrality, oneness of God, harmony in life)	Product standardization, mass media techniques, central balance, unity in advertising copy and layout, strong brand loyalties, a smaller evoked size set, loyalty to company, opportunities for brand extension strategies.
B. Legitimacy (Fair dealings, reasonable level of profits)	Less formal product warranties, need for institutional advertising and/or advocacy advertising, especially by foreign firms, and a switch from profit maximizing to a profit satisfying strategy.
C. Zakaat (2.5 percent per annum compulsory tax binding on all classified as "not poor.")	Use of "excessive" profits, if any, for charitable acts, corporate donation for charity, institutional advertising.
D. Usury (Cannot charge interest on loans. A general interpretation of this law defines "excessive interest" charged on loans as not permissible.)	Avoid direct use of credit as a marketing tool; establish a consumer policy of paying cash for low value products; for high value products, offer discounts for cash payments and raise prices of products on an installment basis; sometimes possible to conduct interest transactions between local/foreign firm in other non-Islamic countries; banks in some Islamic countries take equity in financing ventures, sharing resultant profits (and losses).
E. Supremacy of human life (Compared to other forms of life or objects, human life is of supreme importance.)	Pet food and/or products less important; avoid use of statues, busts – interpreted as forms of idolatry; symbols in advertising and/or promotion should reflect high human values; use floral designs and artwork in advertising as representation of aesthetic values.
F. Community (All Muslims should strive to achieve universal brotherhood — with allegiance to the "One God." One way of expressing community is the required pilgrimage to Mecca for all Muslims at least once in their lifetime, if able to do so.)	Formation of an Islamic Economic Community — development of an "Islamic consumer" served with Islamic-oriented products and services, for example, "kosher" meat packages, gifts exchanged at Muslim festivals, and so forth; development of community services — need for marketing or nonprofit organizations and skills.
G. Equality of people	Participative communication systems; roles and authority structures may be rigidly defined but accessibility at any level relatively easy.
H. Abstinence (During the month of Ramadan, Muslims are required to fast without food or drink from the first streak of dawn to sunset — a reminder to those who are more fortunate	Products that are nutritious, cool, and digested easily can be formulated for Sehr and Iftar (beginning and end of the fast).

Continued

EXHIBIT 4–3 (continued)

Elements	*Implications for Marketing*
to be kind to the less fortunate and as an exercise in self-control.)	
Consumption of alcohol and pork is forbidden; so is gambling.	Opportunities for developing nonalcoholic items and beverages (for example, soft drinks, ice cream, milk shakes, fruit juices) and nonchance social games, such as Scrabble; food products should use vegetable or beef shortening.
I. Environmentalism (The universe created by God was pure. Consequently, the land, air, and water should be held as sacred elements.)	Anticipate environmental, antipollution acts; opportunities for companies involved in maintaining a clean environment; easier acceptance of pollution-control devices in the community (for example, recent efforts in Turkey have been well received by the local communities).
J. Worship (Five times a day; timing of prayers varies.)	Need to take into account the variability and shift in prayer timings in planning sales calls, work schedules, business hours, customer traffic, and so forth.
II. Islamic culture A. Obligation to family and tribal traditions	Importance of respected members in the family or tribe as opinion leaders; word-of-mouth communication, customers' referrals may be critical; social or clan allegiances, affiliations, and associations may be possible surrogates for reference groups; advertising home-oriented products stressing family roles may be highly effective, for example, electronic games.
B. Obligation toward parents is sacred	The image of functional products could be enhanced with advertisements that stress parental advice or approval; even with children's products, there should be less emphasis on children as decisionmakers.
C. Obligation to extend hospitality to both insiders and outsiders	Product designs that are symbols of hospitality, outwardly open in expression, rate of new product acceptance may be accelerated and eased by appeals based on community.
D. Obligation to conform to codes of sexual conduct and social interaction. These may include the following: 1. Modest dress for women in public	More colorful clothing and accessories are worn by women at home; so promotion of products for use in private homes could be more intimate—such audiences could be reached effectively through women's magazines; avoid use of immodest exposure and sexual implications in public settings.
2. Separation of male and female audiences (in some cases)	Access to female consumers can often be gained only through women as selling

Elements	Implications for Marketing
E. Obligations to religious occasions (For example, there are two major religious observances that are celebrated—Eid-ud-Fitr, Eid-ud-Adha.)	agents—salespersons, catalogs, home demonstrations, and women's speciality shops. Tied to purchase of new shoes, clothing, sweets, and preparation of food items for family reunions, Muslim gatherings. There has been a practice of giving money in place of gifts. Increasingly, however, a shift is taking place to more gift giving; because lunar calendar, dates are not fixed.

Source: Mushtaq Luqmani, Zahir A. Quareshi, and Linda Delene, "Marketing in Islamic Countries: A Viewpoint," *MSU Business Topics* (Summer 1980), pp. 20–21. Reprinted with permission.

tune to its residents and visitors. Good feng shui allows the cosmic energy to flow freely throughout the building and hinders evil spirits from entering the structure.[20] For instance, the doors of the Mandarin Hotel were placed at an angle to the street to discourage the entry of evil spirits.[21]

◆ ◆

GLOBAL PERSPECTIVE 4–2

THE GOLDEN ARCHES IN INDIA—NO PORK, NO BEEF

The morning the golden arches were unveiled on New Delhi's skyline, Ajay Seth and his two daughters braved the crowd at the first McDonald's in India to see how foreigners made one of the family's favorite snack: the vegetable burger. "It's very important that the food has an Indian taste," said Seth before sinking his teeth into the sesame-seed bun sandwiching his vegetable patty. He was only mildly impressed.

McDonald's may have to refine some recipes for the spice-loving Indian palate. But its entry into India on October 13 after three years of discreet planning crowned an unprecedented effort to go "local" from the outset—a lesson for other multinational companies investing in this proud and often prickly market. That's good business and smart politics at a time when India's center-left government is trying delicately to build a consensus for greater foreign investment and free-market reforms while preserving the coalition's "pro-poor" image.

Source: "Food for Politics," *Far Eastern Economic Review* (October 24, 1996), p. 72.

McDonald's strategy to woo customers centers on the menu. To avoid insulting Hindus, who revere cows, it dropped beef for the first time. To cater to Muslims, there's no pork. Burgers are made from mutton, including the Big Mac, which has been rechristened the Maharaja Mac. To win over the strictest vegetarians, designated staffers prepare veggie dishes in a separate area of the kitchen, another first for McDonald's. To blunt nationalist opposition, McDonald's India projects itself as a local enterprise. It sources virtually all of its ingredients from local suppliers and claims to be guided by its 50–50 Indian partners in two restaurant ventures in New Delhi and Mumbai. . . . Foreign food and consumer-product companies have touched the deepest nerve since India opened its economy five years ago. But the McDonald's entry indicates that the ground has shifted. The *Indian Express*, often critical of economic reforms, praised McDonald's in a lead editorial for respecting local culture and chastised the anti-multinational lobby for making food the "stuff of dubious politics."

[20]Bernd Schmitt and Alex Simonson, *Marketing Aesthetics. The Strategic Management of Brands, Identity, and Image* (New York: The Free Press, 1997), pp. 275–76.

[21]Jan Morris, *Hong Kong* (New York: Vintage Books, 1988), p. 132.

Religion also drives the holiday calendar in many countries. A country like Sri Lanka, with several officially recognized religions (e.g., Hinduism, Buddhism), forces a careful examination of one's calendar whenever meetings are to be scheduled. Israel's national airline El Al is not allowed to fly on the Sabbath or on Jewish holidays. This government restriction reportedly cut El Al's profits by nearly 50 percent in 1992.[22] On the other hand, religious holidays often steer advertising campaigns or may open up untapped market opportunities. In many Western European countries, Saint Nicholas Day (December 6) is the key event for toy companies and candy makers.

The role of women in society is sometimes largely driven by the local religion. In Islamic societies, conducting market research that involves women is extremely hard. For instance, mixing men and women in focus groups is prohibited in Saudi Arabia.[23]

Religious norms also influence advertising campaigns. In Iran, all ads need to be cleared by Islamic censors. This approval process can take up to three months. One print ad created for Chiquita was frowned upon by Iranian authorities because they considered showing only three bananas on a full-page ad a waste of space.[24] Also in Iran, Gillette's local advertising agency had a hard time placing an ad for the Gillette Blue II razor. Islam dictates that its followers refrain from shaving. Ultimately, Gillette's account executive was able to convince the advertising manager of one local newspaper by using the argument that shaving sometimes becomes necessary, such as in the case of head injuries resulting from a car accidents.[25]

Education

Education is one of the major vehicles to channel culture from one generation to the next. Two facets of education that matter to international marketers include: the level and the quality of education. The level of education varies a lot between countries. Most developed countries have mandatory education up to a certain age. In some countries, however, especially Muslim societies, education is largely the preserve of males. As a consequence, males are often far better educated than females in such societies. One powerful indicator of the education level is a country's illiteracy rate. Exhibit 4–4 gives you an overview of illiteracy levels around the world. In countries with low literacy levels, marketers need to exercise caution in matters such as product labeling, print ads, and survey research. One baby food company attributed its poor sales in Africa to the product label that was used. The label's picture of a baby was mistakenly thought by the local people to mean that the jars contained ground-up babies.[26]

---

[22]"And You Thought U. S. Airlines Had It Tough," *Business Week* (October 12, 1992), p. 107.

[23]"Programming Globally—With Care," *Advertising Age International* (September 18, 1995), p. I-14.

[24]"Multinationals Tread Softly While Advertising in Iran," *Advertising Age International* (November 8, 1993), p. I-21.

[25]"Smooth Talk Wins Gillette Ad Space in Iran," *Advertising Age International* (April 27, 1992), p. I-40.

[26]David A. Ricks, *Blunders in International Business* (Cambridge, MA: Blackwell Publishers, 1993).

EXHIBIT 4–4
EDUCATIONAL STATISTICS FOR A SAMPLE OF COUNTRIES

Country	Percentage of Illiterates (Age 15+)—1995 Estimates		Scientists and Engineers per Million Population (1995)
	Male	*Female*	
Africa:			
Egypt	36.4	61.2	458 (1991)
Nigeria	32.7	52.7	15 (1987)
South Africa	18.1	18.3	938 (1993)
Latin America:			
Brazil	16.7	16.8	168
Mexico	8.2	12.6	213
Peru	5.5	17.0	625 (1994)
Venezuela	5.7	7.5 (1993)	208 (1992)
Asia:			
China	10.1	25.5 (1996)	350
India	34.5	62.3	149 (1994)
Korea	0.7	3.3	2,636 (1994)
Thailand	4.0	8.4	119
United States	NA	NA	3,732 (1993)
Australia	NA	NA	3,166 (1994)
Europe:			
Italy	1.4	2.4	1,325 (1994)
Russia	0.5	3.2 (1989)	3,520
Spain	1.8	3.9	1,210 (1994)

Source: UNESCO, 1998 Statistical Yearbook, Tables 1.2 and 5.1. Reproduced with permission from UNESCO.

Companies are also concerned about the "quality" of education. Does education meet business needs? The last column in Exhibit 4–4 shows the number of scientists and engineers per million population. As you can see, there are some huge differences, even within countries with a similar level of economic development. Shortages in certain fields often force companies to bid against one another for the scarce talent that is available or to employ expatriates. Many companies try to build up a local presence by hiring local people. However, a shortage of qualified people in the local market usually forces them to rely on expatriates until local employees are properly trained.

All cultures have value systems that shape people's norms and standards. These norms influence people's attitudes toward objects and behavioral codes. Value systems tend to be deeply rooted. Core values are intrinsic to a person's identity and inner self. One study of the decision-making process made by executives from the People's Republic of China showed that even after almost four decades of Communist philosophy, traditional Chinese values (e.g., saving face, long-term exchange relationships, respect for leaders) heavily

Value Systems

influence market entry and product decisions.[27] The origins of many value systems are hidden in history. It is unlikely that people's value systems change in a short span of time. Exhibit 4–5 is an excerpt of a study commissioned by Dentsu, a Japanese advertising agency, on the beliefs and attitudes of Asian citizens. Note that the data were gathered between November 1996 and January 1997—prior to the start of the Asian crisis. The figures show that talk about "Asian values" may be a bit premature—there appears to be little common ground among Asian citizens. For instance, 85 percent of Mumbai citizens agree that children should look after aged parents, compared to a mere 15 percent agreement of Tokyo citizens.

For marketers, a crucial value distinction is a culture's attitude toward change. Societies that are resistant to change are usually less willing to adopt new products or production processes. Terspstra and David suggest several guidelines that are helpful to implement innovations in cultures hostile to changes:[28]

1. Identify roadblocks to change.
2. Determine which cultural hurdles can be met.
3. Test and demonstrate the innovation's effectiveness in the host culture.
4. Seek out those values that can be used to back up the proposed innovation.

From an international marketer's vantage point, a society's value system matters a great deal. Local attitudes toward foreign cultures will drive the product positioning and design decisions. In many countries, goods with American roots are strongly valued. U.S. companies are able to leverage on such sentiments by using Americana as a selling point. McIlhenny sells Tabasco with the same product label and formulation worldwide, emphasizing its American roots. In South Africa, Mars stresses the U.S. ties of Uncle Ben's rice with a "100% American" banner on its packaging.

Value systems often explain the dismal performance or phenomenal success of new product introductions. Despite Russia's low standard of living, canned pet food became very well accepted. Russians often pamper their pets, giving them choice cuts of meat. MasterFoods' marketing in Russia utilized a "more for your money" selling point by showing that canned pet food is more nutritious and cheaper than fresh food.[29]

Cultural norms might also dictate selling approaches. Dell's Japan operation uses a less aggressive tack to lure customers. Aggressiveness is not highly valued in Japan. In the United States Dell vigorously promotes low computer prices. In contrast, in Japan the firm shows how direct selling leads to a lower price.[30]

[27]David K. Tse, Kam-hon Lee, Ilan Vertinsky, and Donald A. Wehrung, "Does Culture Matter? A Cross-Cultural Study of Executives' Choice, Decisiveness, and Risk Adjustment in International Marketing," *Journal of Marketing*, 52 (4) (October 1988), pp. 81–95.

[28]Terpstra and David, *The Cultural Environment of International Business*, (Cincinnati, OH: Southwestern Publishing Company, 1991) pp. 124–25.

[29]"How to Sell Pet Food in Russia," *Advertising Age International* (May 17, 1993), p. I–21.

[30]"Direct Mail Defies Japan's Ad Recession," *Advertising Age International* (April 18, 1994), p. I–8.

EXHIBIT 4-5
DENTSU LIFESTYLE SURVEY

	Beijing	Mumbai	Tokyo	Singapore	Bangkok
BELIEFS (% who agree with statement)					
Children should look after aged parents	67	85	15	77	78
Parents should not rely on their children	21	11	39	9	8
Cannot say	12	5	46	14	14
Men work, women stay at home	20	37	21	26	24
CONCERNS (% agree)					
Personal safety	73	38	*	*	*
Economic development	70	62	48	67	87
Cost of living	60	*	56	50	62
Education and culture	46	49	*	39	49
Moral civilization	38	*	*	*	*
Health and welfare	*	48	68	55	49
Pollution	*	*	46	*	39
Employment	*	*	37	*	*
Citizens' rights	*	*	*	35	*
National security	*	50	*	*	*
IMAGE AS A NATION (% agree)					
Hard-working	86	59	65	65	**
Takes good care of family	63	**	**	21	31
Funny	**	53	**	**	**
Polite	41	47	30	29	38
Bad at negotiating	**	**	45	**	**
Loyal to company	**	**	42	**	**
Closed society	**	**	36	**	**
Clean	**	**	**	37	**
Appreciates Nature	**	**	**	**	**
WHAT THE STATE MUST DO (% agree)					
Adopt policies according to public opinion	65	56	68	50	67
Grant full social benefits	68	68	65	56	63
Regulate individual rights for greater good	47	67	11	42	51
Promote competition based on ability	33	26	25	26	38
Adopt Western systems	21	38	8	24	36
Have a strong leader push social reform	11	35	5	18	14

Source: Dentsu Institute for Human Studies.
*Not among top five concerns.
**Not among top 10 national attributes.
N.A.-Not Available.

◆ ◆ ◆ ◆ ◆ ◆ CROSS-CULTURAL COMPARISONS

Cultures differ from one another, but usually they share certain aspects. Getting a sense of the similarities and dissimilarities between your culture and the host country's culture is useful for scores of reasons. Cultural classifications allow the marketing manager to see how much overlap there can be between the marketing programs to be implemented in different markets. Further, most cultural traits tend to be regional instead of national. Certain regions in the world can be looked upon as culturally similar and thus approached in a marketing context. In terms of culture, the Walloons in French-speaking Belgium have much more in common with the French than with the Flemish of Northern Belgium. This section gives you an overview of the most common classification schemes.

High- versus Low-Context Cultures

One of the characters in the movie *Chan Is Missing* is a lawyer who describes a confrontation between her client who was involved in a traffic accident and a policeman at the scene of the accident. The client is a recent immigrant from mainland China. The policeman asks her client whether he stopped at the stop sign, expecting a yes or no for an answer. The Chinese immigrant instead starts talking about his driving record, how long he has been in the United States, and other matters that he feels are relevant. The policeman, losing his patience, angrily repeats his question. The events described in the movie are a typical example of the culture clash that arises when somebody from a high-context culture (China) is faced with a person from a low-context culture (United States).

The notion of cultural complexity refers to the way messages are communicated within a society. The anthropologist Edward Hall makes a distinction between so-called **high-context** and **low-context cultures**.[31] The interpretation of messages in high-context cultures heavily rests on contextual cues. What is left unsaid is often as important (if not more) as what is said. Examples of contextual cues include the nature of the relationship between the sender and receiver of the message (for instance, in terms of gender, age, balance of power), the time and site of the communication, and so forth. Typical examples of high-context societies are Confucian cultures (China, Korea, Japan) and Latin America.

Low-context cultures, on the other hand, put the most emphasis on the written or spoken word. What is meant is what is said. The context, within which messages are communicated, is largely discounted. The United States, Scandinavia, and Germany are all examples of low-context cultures. The distinction between high- and low-context cultures matters in many areas of international marketing. For example, in the field of personal selling, many U.S. companies like to rotate salespeople across territories. In high-context societies, where nurturing trust and rapport with the client plays a big role, firms might need to adjust such rotation policies. Research also indicates a faster rate of adoption of new products in high-context cultures than in low-context societies.[32] In the field of international advertising, campaigns that were developed with a high-context culture in mind are likely to be less effective when used in low-context cultures, and vice versa.

---

[31]Edward T. Hall, *Beyond Culture* (Garden City, NY: Anchor Press, 1976).

[32]Hirokazu Takada and Dipak Jain, "Cross-National Analysis of Diffusion of Consumer Durable Goods in Pacific Rim Countries," *Journal of Marketing*, 55 (April 1991), pp. 48–54.

Cultures differ in their attitude toward time. Hall makes a distinction between cultures with a **monochronic** and **polychronic** notion of time.[33] Monochronic people do one thing at a time. Their agendas are very well organized; they tend to be punctual; they don't want to waste time. In short, they are "time is money" type of people. Polychronic people have an entirely different concept of time. They tend to do several things at once. They are less organized; less rigid regarding their schedule; less punctual. For them, business is a form of socializing, not the other way round. For instance, at business luncheon meetings in France it is considered rude not to while away a couple of hours and finish off at least one bottle of wine.[34] Monochronic time cultures often are low-context cultures, while polychronic time cultures are usually high-context cultures.

Polychronic versus Monochronic Cultures

Cultures differ enormously in their degree of homogeneity. At one extreme are **homophilous** cultures, where people share the same beliefs, speak the same language, and practice the same religion. Examples are Korea, Japan, and Scandinavian countries. Most countries are **heterophilous** cultures with a fair amount of differentiation. In general, less homogeneity demands a more individualized marketing approach. Failure to do so is usually a recipe for disaster. A case in point is China. Top Green International is a Hong Kong–based joint venture that holds the master franchise for TCBY ("The Country's Best Yogurt") in China. One of the joint venture partners notes: "Each city (in China) is very different; each province has its own culture. You can't just make one single television commercial and broadcast it across the country. You have to find out what the interest is in each city or province."[35] Differences in cultural homogeneity underlie differences in adoption rates for new products or services. There is strong evidence that new products diffuse more rapidly in homogeneous countries.[36]

Cultural Homogeneity

The Dutch scholar Geert Hofstede has proposed several other cultural classification schemes.[37] His grid is based on a large-scale research project he conducted among employees of more than sixty IBM subsidiaries worldwide. The first dimension is termed **power distance**, referring to the degree of inequality among people that is viewed as being equitable. Societies that are high in power distance tolerate relatively high social inequalities. Members of such societies accept wide differences in income and power distribution. Examples of high power distance countries are the Arab countries, Mexico, and West Africa. On the other hand, low power distance societies tend to be more egalitarian. Low power distance countries are countries such as Germany, the United Kingdom, and the United States.

Hofstede's Classification Scheme

[33]Hall, *Beyond Culture*.
[34]"The Fall of Fun," *The New Yorker* (November 18, 1996), pp. 62–71.
[35]"Frozen Assets: TCBY takes a scoop out of the China market," *Far Eastern Economic Review* (November 14, 1996), p. 68.
[36]Takada and Jain, "Cross-National Analysis of Diffusion of Consumer Durable Goods in Pacific Rim Countries."
[37]Geert Hofstede, "Management Scientists are Human," *Management Science*, 40, 1 (January 1994), pp. 4–13.

The second dimension is labeled **uncertainty avoidance**, defined as the extent to which people in a given culture prefer structured situations with clear rules over unstructured ones. People tend to be more easygoing in countries with low degrees of uncertainty avoidance. Societies with high uncertainty avoidance tend to be rigid and risk averse. Examples of countries that score high on uncertainty avoidance are France, Japan, and Mexico.

The third dimension is called **individualism**. As the label suggests, this criterion describes the degree to which people prefer to act as individuals rather than group members ("me" versus "we" societies). In societies that are high on individualism, the focus is on people's own interests. In such cultures, a child early on realizes that one day he or she will need to stand on his or her own feet. There is little need for loyalty to a group. In **collectivist** societies the interests of the group take center stage. Members in such societies differentiate between in-group members who are part of its group and all other people. They expect protection from the group and remain loyal to their group throughout their life.

The fourth distinction, **masculinity**, considers the importance of "male" values such as assertiveness, success, competitive drive within society, and achievement, as opposed to "female" values like solidarity and quality of life. *Masculine* societies are those in which values associated with the role of men prevail. Cultures where people favor values such as solidarity, preserving the environment, and quality of life are more *feminine*. Japan is viewed as a masculine society, while Indonesia is an example of a feminine culture.

Follow-up research of Hofstede's work in Asia led to a fifth dimension: **long-termism**.[38] This final criterion refers to the distinction between societies with a **long-term** orientation and those with a **short-term** focus. People in long-term oriented societies tend to have values that center around the future (e.g., perseverance, thrift). On the other hand, members of short-term oriented cultures are concerned about values that reflect the past and the present (e.g., respect for tradition). Countries like Hong Kong and Japan score high on the long-termism dimension, whereas West Africa, the United States, and Great Britain score very low on this criterion.

Exhibit 4–6 portrays how different countries score on the various dimensions. One must be cautious when applying these schemes to global buyer behavior. It is important to bear in mind that the five dimensions and the respective country scores that were derived in Hofstede's work were not determined in a consumption context. In fact, questions have been raised about the ability of these values to make meaningful predictions about consumption patterns.[39] Countries with the same scores may have entirely different buying behaviors. Likewise, countries that have completely different scores on a given cultural dimension could have very similar consumption patterns. To illustrate this point, consider the linkage between uncertainty avoidance and brand loyalty. Earlier we noted that perceived risk can be viewed as one of the indicators of uncertainty avoidance. Numerous consumer research studies in the United States have established a strong relationship between perceived risk and brand loyalty.

---

[38]Geert Hofstede and Michael H. Bond, "The Confucius Connection: From Cultural Roots to Economic Growth," *Organizational Dynamics*, 16 (4) (Spring 1988), pp. 4–21.
[39]Marieke de Mooij, *Advertising Worldwide* (New York: Prentice-Hall, 1994), p. 159.

EXHIBIT 4–6(A)
UNCERTAINTY AVOIDANCE VERSUS POWER DISTANCE

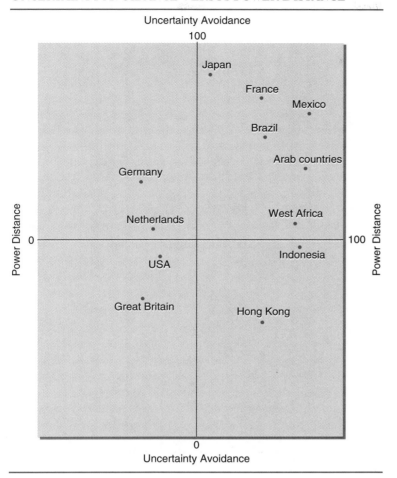

That is, brand loyalty is one of the major risk reduction relievers that consumers rely on when faced with a choice situation with a high level of perceived risk.[40] Given the overwhelming evidence for U.S. consumers, one would expect the same kind of relationship outside the United States: high levels of brand loyalty within societies where consumers tend to be high in perceived risk ("uncertainty avoidance"). However, a recent cross-cultural comparison found that outside the United States the relationship between the two measures is usually just flat (neither negative nor positive).[41]

---

[40]See for instance, T. Roselius, "Consumer Rankings of Risk Reduction Methods," *Journal of Marketing*, 35 (1971), pp. 56–61.

[41]Bronislaw J. Verhage, Ugur Yavas, and Robert T. Green, "Perceived Risk: A Cross-Cultural Phenomenon," *International Journal of Research in Marketing*, 7, (1990), pp. 297–303.

EXHIBIT 4–6(B)
MASCULINITY VERSUS INDIVIDUALISM

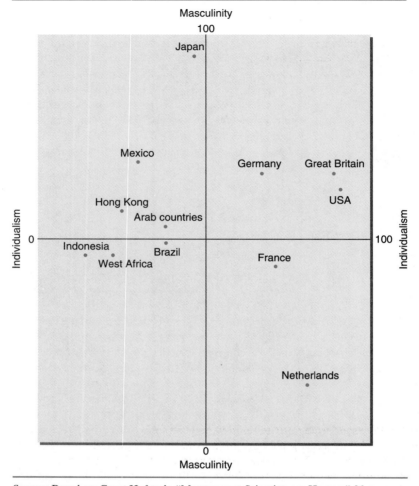

Source: Based on: Geert Hofstede, "Management Scientists are Human," *Management Science*, vol. 40 no. 1 (January 1994), pp. 4–13.

◆ ◆ ◆ ◆ ◆ ◆ ADAPTING TO FOREIGN CULTURES

To function in the global marketplace, you need to become sensitive to cultural biases that influence your thinking, behavior, and decision making. Given the diversity of cultures, cultural mishaps easily arise when global marketers interact with members of a "foreign" culture. Some of these cultural blunders are relatively harmless and easily forgiven. Unfortunately, many cultural mistakes put the company and its products in an unpleasant situation or even create permanent damage. There are numerous firms whose globalization efforts have been derailed by cultural mishaps.

Lack of cultural sensitivity takes many forms. Most of us hold cultural stereotypes that distort cultural assessments. Cultural blinders that occur at the subconscious level are hard to detect. When cultural misassessments do show up, it is usually after the fact. So cultural adaptation is absolutely necessary to make marketing decisions in line with the host culture. Such adaptation is hampered by the tendency to use a **self-reference criterion (SRC)**, a term coined by J. A. Lee, a cultural anthropologist. The SRC refers to people's unconscious tendency to resort to their own cultural experience and value systems to interpret a given business situation. Lee outlined a four-step procedure that allows global marketers to identify cross-cultural differences and take the necessary actions to cope with them. The four-step correction mechanism goes as follows:[42]

Step 1: Define the business problem or goal in terms of your own cultural traits, customs, or values.

Step 2: Define the business problem or goal in terms of the host culture's traits, customs, or values.

Step 3: Isolate the SRC influence in the problem and examine it scrupulously to see how it interferes with the business problem.

Step 4: Redefine the business problem, but this time without the SRC influence, and solve for the "optimal" business goal situation.

Even more dangerous than SRC interference is to fall into the trap of **ethnocentrism**, the belief that one's own culture is superior to another culture. Procter & Gamble's experience in Mexico exemplifies cultural adaptation. Ace detergent, launched in Mexico by P&G in the early 1950s, was clobbered by the local brands. Ace, developed for U.S. washing machines, had a low-suds formula. At that time, many Mexicans washed their clothes in the river. High-suds detergents were therefore preferable. Eventually, the formula was changed to have a higher-suds content. P&G also adapted the packaging: It made smaller sizes, using plastic bags (to keep the detergent dry) instead of cardboard.

Toy-maker Mattel's experience with the Barbie doll in Japan is another nice illustration of adaptation.[43] Mattel first introduced a Barbie doll designed specifically for the Japanese market, called Moba Barbie. Moba's looks were supposedly akin to what Japanese consumers desired, bearing a close resemblance to the major competing doll. Mattel never conquered more than a 5 to 6 percent share of the Japanese doll market. After eight years of lackluster sales, Mattel decided to re-introduce Barbie, taking on more Western looks. TV commercials also displayed Japanese girls playing with Barbies. Before the new campaign, most Japanese girls mistakenly believed that Moba Barbie was a display doll. As a result of these changes in Mattel's marketing strategy, the sales of Barbie dolls in Japan finally took off.

The lesson offered by the experience of marketing behemoths such as P&G and Mattel is that there is no magic bullet to avoid cultural mishaps. P&G mistakenly believed that what worked in the United States would also find a market across the Rio Grande. Mattel, on the other hand, mistakenly tried to cater to "Japanese" desires. While Lee's four-step SRC-correction procedure appears

---

[42]J.A. Lee, "Cultural Analysis in Overseas Operations," *Harvard Business Review* (March–April 1966), pp. 106–114.

[43]"Western Barbie: Mattel Makes Japan Push with Revamped Doll," *Advertising Age* (October 7, 1991).

"REMEMBER — WALK IN SIDEWAYS, DON'T LOOK AT THE CEILING, IF YOU AGREE WITH HIM, DON'T SMILE, IF YOU DON'T AGREE WITH HIM, SMILE..."

Cultural adaption may be necessary when doing business abroad.

flawless, it is often hard to put into practice. For ages, travelers and scholars of various backgrounds have gathered material on peoples and shared it with others. Exhibit 4–7 summarizes some of the "Twenty-Seven Articles" that T. E. Lawrence ("Lawrence of Arabia") put down to assist others in coping with desert Arabs. Probably the most valuable piece of advice is given in Lawrence's introduction to his recommendations: "Handling Hejaz Arabs is an art, not a science, with exceptions and no obvious rules." The same piece of advice applies to any culture or subculture.

Still, there are a couple of techniques that companies can rely on to prepare managers for cross-cultural differences.[44] Immersion through prolonged stays in the foreign market often helps. Intensive foreign language training is one of the more common tools to foster cultural sensitivity. Language skills, though, are not sufficient to become a successful international manager. Other qualities like humility—willing to accept that you will not be as competent as in your own environment—also play an important role.[45] Numerous resources exist to familiarize managers with other aspects of the host country's cultural environment. A good example is the "Culturgram" series (www.culturgram.com) published by

---

[44]Howard Tu and Sherry E. Sullivan, "Preparing Yourself for an International Assignment," *Business Horizons* (January–February 1994), pp. 67–70.

[45]"Culture Shock for Executives," *The Financial Times* (April 5, 1995), p. 12.

EXHIBIT 4–7
TWENTY-SEVEN ARTICLES BY T.E. LAWRENCE, AUGUST 1917

The following notes have been expressed in commandment form for greater clarity and to save words. They are, however, only my personal conclusions, arrived at gradually while I worked in the Hejaz and now put on paper as stalking horses for beginners in the Arab armies (. . .) They are of course not suitable to any person's need, or applicable unchanged in any particular situation. Handling Hejaz Arabs is an art, not a science, with exceptions and no obvious rules . . .

1. Go easy for the first weeks. A bad start is difficult to atone for, and the Arabs form their judgments on externals that we ignore.

2. Learn all you can about your Ashraf and Bedu. Get to know their families, clans, and tribes, friends and enemies, wells, hills and roads. Do all this by listening and by indirect enquiry. Do not ask questions. Get to speak their dialect of Arabic, not yours. . . . Be a little stiff at first.

3. In matters of business deal only with the commander of the army, column or party in which you serve. Never give orders to anyone at all, and reserve your directions or advice for the C.O. (commanding officer), however great the temptation of dealing direct with the underlings.

4. Win and keep the confidence of your leader. Strengthen his prestige at your expense before others when you can.

5. Remain in touch with your leader as constantly and unobtrusively as you can. . . . Formal visits to give advice are not so good as the constant dropping of ideas in casual talk. . . .

8. Your ideal position is when you are present and not noticed. Do not be too intimate, too prominent, or too earnest. . . .

11. The foreigner and Christian is not a popular person in Arabia. However friendly and informal the treatment of yourself may be, remember always that your foundations are very sandy ones.

12. Cling tight to your sense of humour. You will need it every day. . . . Reproof if wrapped up in some smiling form will carry further and last longer than the most violent speech. The power of mimicry or parody is valuable, but use it sparingly for wit is more dignified than humour. . . .

16. If you can, without being too lavish forestall presents to yourself. A well placed gift is often most effective in winning over a suspicious sheikh. Never receive a present without giving a liberal return. . . .

20. If you wear Arab things at all, go all the way. Leave your English friends and customs on the coast, and fall back on Arab habits entirely. . . .

25. In spite of ordinary Arab example avoid too free talk about women. It is as difficult a subject as religion, and their standards are so unlike your own, that a remark harmless in English may appear unrestrained to them . . .

27. The beginning and ending of the secret of handling Arabs is unremitting study of them. Keep always on your guard; never say an unconsidered thing, or do an unnecessary thing: watch yourself and your companions all the time: hear all that passes, search out what is going on beneath the surface, read their characters, discover their tastes and their weaknesses, and keep everything you find out to yourself.

Source: Abstracted from: Jeremy Wilson, *Lawrence of Arabia: The Authorized Biography of T. E. Lawrence* (New York: Atheneum, 1990), Appendix IV, pp. 960–965.

eMSTAR. Culturgrams provide environmental briefings on the customs, values, courtesies, and lifestyles of citizens in a given country. An online resource—though not as detailed as a Culturgram—is the Lonely Planet Web site (www.lonelyplanet.com). Many providers of cultural training programs (e.g., Berlitz International) offer a cultural orientation for executives. Such programs range from environmental briefings to cultural assimilator exercises where participants are exposed to various simulated settings that could arise during their assignment.[46]

◆ ◆ ◆ ◆ ◆ ◆ CULTURE AND THE MARKETING MIX

Culture is a key pillar of the marketplace. The success of international marketing activities is, to a large extent, driven by the local culture. These cultural variables may act as barriers or opportunities. In this section we show how culture and the firm's marketing mix interact.

Product Policy   Certain products are obviously more culture-bound than other products. In particular, food, beverages, and clothing products tend to be very culture-bound. Earlier we saw how American fast-food restaurants adjust their food items to local cultures (Global Perspectives 4–1 and 4–2). The changes that General Motors introduced for Buick in China are another good illustration of the role of culture in product design.[47] Whereas American drivers put their children in the back of the car, Chinese companies put their bosses there. As a result, the rear seats of Buicks made in China are raised and come with their own air-conditioning and radio controls. They also have more legroom than their American counterparts. To handle China's rough roads, the suspension for the Buick was adjusted. Interestingly enough, the engine size was cut from 3.5 liters to 2.8 to accommodate a rule that says that cars of over 3.0 liters are limited to government officials of minister level or above.

Cultural values also determine consumers' buying motivations. This is illustrated in Exhibit 4–8, which portrays the buying motives for car purchases in different cultures. As you can see, there are different clusters. In the upper-left quadrant are countries with weak uncertainty avoidance and high femininity. In this cluster, people look for safety and value when buying a car. In contrast, the bottom-right quadrant has clusters of countries that are masculine and have strong uncertainty avoidance. Car buyers in these countries aspire to buy cars that are big and fast.

Cultural norms sometimes open up new product opportunities. In most Asian countries, white skin is associated with positive values that relate to beauty, class, an upscale lifestyle. Dark skin is linked with hard labor and toil. In India, the skin whitener market has been growing at an annual rate of around 20 percent. Multinationals such as Unilever, Avon, and Beiersdorf have been able

---

[46]"Companies Use Cross-Cultural Training To Help Their Employees Adjust Abroad," *Wall Street Journal* (August 4, 1992), B1, B6.

[47]"Testing GM's Shock Absorbers," *The Economist* (May 1, 1999), p. 68.

to cash in on this phenomenon by marketing skin whiteners. Indeed, for Avon, its top-selling product in India is VIP Fairness Cream. The cream, that retails for 160 rupees (approximateley $3.60), promises a fairer skin in one month.[48]

As we will see in Chapter 13, pricing policies are driven by the interplay of the **Pricing** four Cs: customers, company (costs, objectives, strategies), competition, and collaborators (e.g., distributors). Customers' willingness-to-pay for your product will vary across cultures. Products that are perceived as good value in one culture may have little or no value in other cultures. In Western countries, a high price is often seen as a signal of premium quality for many product categories. However, in emerging markets, charging a high price may be looked upon as gouging the customer.

EXHIBIT 4–8
BUYING MOTIVES FOR AUTOMOBILES

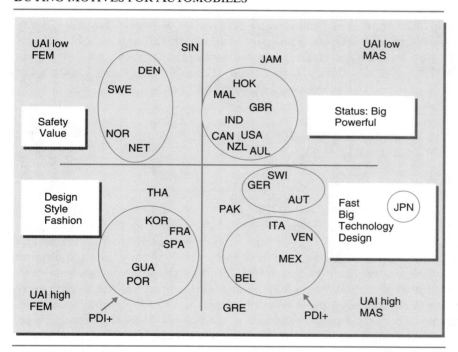

Note: AUL = Australia, AUT = Austria, BEL = Belgium, CAN = Canada, DEN = Denmark, FRA = France, GER = Germany, GBR = Great Britain, GRE = Greece, GUA = Guatemala, HOK = Hong Kong, IND = India, ITA = Italy, JAM = Jamaica, JPN = Japan, KOR = Korea, MAL = Malaysia, MEX = Mexico, NOR = Norway, NET = the Netherlands, NZL = New Zealand, PAK = Pakistan, POR = Portugal, SIN = Singapore, SPA = Spain, SWE = Sweden, SWI = Switzerland, THA = Thailand, USA = the United States, VEN = Venezuela.

Source: Marieke de Mooij, *Global Marketing and Advertising. Understanding Cultural Paradoxes*, (Thousand Oaks, CA: SAGE Publications, 1998), p. 147.

---

[48]"Creams for a Lighter Skin Capture the Asian Market," *International Herald Tribune* (April 24, 1998), p. 2.

One example of how pricing and culture interact is the practice of *odd pricing* where prices end with 9 (or 5) ($19.99 instead of $20). Specific price points like End-9 prices are known to increase unit sales substantially. This sales effect is due to the fact that these "magic prices" signal good value to the customers. In Chinese-speaking cultures like Hong Kong, however, the price points used often end with 8 instead of 9, since the Chinese word for eight ("ba") has the same sound as the word for wealth.

Distribution

Cultural variables may also dictate distribution strategies. Plagued with lifestyle changes, Avon, the U.S. cosmetics maker, has been forced to fine-tune its direct selling model. In places like Taiwan and China, Avon is experimenting with alternative distribution modes for selling its products. Some of the alternatives that Avon is looking into include the use of kiosks, small counters in department stores, the Internet, or selling products on home-shopping TV channels.

Cultural hurdles can sometimes be successfully mastered, as Dell Computer has shown in China. When Dell first launched its renowned direct-sales, built-to-order business model in China, many observers were very skeptical. Selling computers direct to corporate customers rather than through distributors was thought to be a recipe for disaster in China, where many deals are settled via wining and dining. Nevertheless, Dell's business model has been well accepted in China. Dell's sales have been growing at triple-digit rates.[49]

Promotion

Of the four marketing mix elements, promotion is the most visible one. People who do not buy your product for whatever reason may still be exposed to your advertising. Culture will typically have a major influence on a firm's communication strategy. Advertising styles that are effective in certain cultures can be counterproductive in other cultures. In high-context cultures (e.g., Spain, Italy, Japan), communication styles tend to be more indirect and subtle, using less copy and more symbols. In low-context cultures (e.g., Germany, Scandinavia), on the other hand, advertising uses more copy, factual data, and reasoning.[50] For instance, advertising in countries such as the United States and the United Kingdom often uses a lecture-format style where a celebrity "lectures" the audience about the good points of the product being advertised. Cultures in these countries are low in power distance and high in individualism. One recent study compared the reactions of Chinese and U.S. subjects to different advertising appeals. Not surprisingly, the study found that Chinese consumers favored a collectivistic appeal, whereas their U.S. counterparts preferred an individualistic appeal.[51]

Local cultural taboos and norms also influence advertising styles. In the United States, Gidget, a talking chihuahua, is a fixture in ads for Taco Bell, a Mexican-style fast food chain. However, Gidget does not feature in Taco Bell's Singapore ads.

---

[49]"Chasing the China Market," *Asiaweek* (June 11, 1999), p. 46.

[50]Marieke de Mooij, *Global Marketing and Advertising. Understanding Cultural Paradoxes* (Thousand Oaks, CA: SAGE Publications, Inc., 1998), p. 157–58.

[51]Yong Zhang and James P. Neelankavil, "The Influence of Culture on Advertising Effectiveness in China and the USA. A Cross-Cultural Study," *European Journal of Marketing*, 31 (1997), pp. 134–49.

Singapore's large Muslim population was the main motivation for dropping Gidget—Muslims view dogs as unclean animals.[52] In Malaysia, where Islam is the official religion, beer companies try to avoid direct contact with Muslims by not advertising on billboards or in Malay-language print media. Carlsberg, the Danish beer brewer, was forced to withdraw sponsorship of the 1998 Commonwealth Games after it started advertising the games on public buses in large cities. The Malay-language press took issue with the public nature of Carlberg's sponsorship campaign.[53]

ORGANIZATIONAL CULTURES ◆ ◆ ◆ ◆ ◆ ◆

So far, we have looked at the importance of national cultures for international marketing operations. At the same time, most companies are also characterized by their **organizational (corporate) culture**. Deshpandé and Webster[54] defined organizational culture as "the pattern of shared values and beliefs that help individuals understand organizational functioning and thus provide them with the norms for behavior in the organization" (p. 4). Shared beliefs relate to leadership styles, organizational attributes, bonding mechanisms within the organization, and overall strategic emphases.[55] As you can see in Exhibit 4–9, organizational culture types can be described along two dimensions. The vertical axis distinguishes between organizations with *organic* (emphasis on flexibility, spontaneity, individuality) and *mechanistic* processes (emphasis on control, stability, order). The horizontal axis describes whether the organizational emphasis is on *internal maintenance* (integration, efficient and smooth operations) or *external positioning* (competitive actions and achievement, differentiation). This scheme leads to four organizational culture types that are labeled *clan*, *adhocracy*, *hierarchical*, and *market*. Exhibit 4–9 lists for each of these organizational forms the dominant attributes, leadership styles, primary means of bonding, and strategic emphases.

Clan cultures (top-left quadrant) stress cohesiveness, participation, and teamwork. They are often headed by a father figure. The bonding glue is loyalty and tradition. Commitment to such firms runs high. In contrast, adhocracy cultures (top-right quadrant) are driven by values like entrepreneurship, creativity, adaptability, flexibility, and tolerance. Effectiveness in such cultures is viewed in terms of finding new markets and new opportunities for growth. The head of such organizations is usually an entrepreneur or an innovator. Such firms are committed to innovation and new product development. The third form is the hierarchy culture (bottom-left quadrant), which emphasizes order, rules, and regulations. Such organizations tend to be very formalized and structured. Maintaining a smooth-running operation is

---

[52]"As Taco Bell Enters Singapore, Gidget Avoids the Ad Limelight," *Advertising Age International* (January 11, 1999), pp. 13–4.

[53]"A Campaign Too Far for Carlsberg," *The Financial Times* (August 11, 1998), p. 8.

[54]Rohit Deshpandé and Frederick E. Webster, "Organizational Culture and Marketing: Defining the Research Agenda," *Journal of Marketing*, 53(1) (1989), pp. 3–15.

[55]Rohit Deshpandé, John U. Farley, and Frederick E. Webster, "Corporate Culture, Customer Orientation, and Innovativeness in Japanese Firms: A Quadrad Analysis," *Journal of Marketing*, 57 (1) (1993), pp. 23–37.

EXHIBIT 4–9
A MODEL OF ORGANIZATIONAL CULTURE TYPES*

ORGANIC PROCESSES (flexibility, spontaneity)

TYPE: **Clan**	TYPE: **Adhocracy**
DOMINANT ATTRIBUTES: Cohesiveness, participation, teamwork, sense of family	DOMINANT ATTRIBUTES: Entrepreneurship, creativity, adaptability
LEADER STYLE: Mentor, facilitator, parent-figure	LEADER STYLE: Entrepreneur, innovator, risk taker
BONDING: Loyalty, tradition, interpersonal cohesion	BONDING: Entrepreneurship, flexibility, risk
STRATEGIC EMPHASES: Toward developing human resources, commitment, morale	STRATEGIC EMPHASES: Toward innovation, growth, new resources

INTERNAL MAINTENANCE (smoothing activities, integration) — **EXTERNAL POSITIONING** (competition, differentiation)

TYPE: **Hierarchy**	TYPE: **Market**
DOMINANT ATTRIBUTES: Order, rules and regulations, uniformity	DOMINANT ATTRIBUTES: Competitiveness, goal achievement
LEADER STYLE: Coordinator, administrator	LEADER STYLE: Decisive, achievement-oriented
BONDING: Rules, policies, and procedures	BONDING: Goal orientation, production, competition
STRATEGIC EMPHASES: Toward stability, predictability, smooth operations	STRATEGIC EMPHASES: Toward competitive advantage and market superiority

MECHANISTIC PROCESSES (control, order, stability)

Note: *Adapted from Cameron and Freeman (1991) and Quinn (1988).

Source: Rohit Deshpandé, John U. Farley, and Frederick E. Webster, "Corporate Culture, Customer Orientation, and Innovativeness in Japanese Firms: A Quadrad Analysis," *Journal of Marketing*, 57 (1) (1993), pp. 23–37.

very important for such firms. Organizational effectiveness within hierarchical cultures is defined by consistency and achievement of clearly stated goals. Finally, market culture-like organizations (bottom-right quadrant) value competitiveness, tasks and goal achievement, and productivity. These organizations tend to be production-oriented. The major concern is getting the job done.

Most firms have elements of several types of cultures. However, one type of culture typically emerges as the dominant one.[56] Exhibit 4–10 presents the results

---

[56]Rohit Desphandé, John U. Farley, and Frederick E. Webster, "Factors Affecting Organizational Performance: A Five-Country Comparison," Working Paper, (Cambridge, MA: Marketing Science Institute, 1997).

EXHIBIT 4–10
ORGANIZATIONAL CULTURE TYPES

	Japan	U.S.	France	England	Germany
Organizational Culture Types					
Hierarchy	99.9	80.3	99.1	76.8	83.2
Market	103.3	112.5	93.7	116.3	89.4
Adhocracy	77.6	105.8	128.3	99.1	131.1
Clan	119.3	101.4	78.9	107.6	96.2

Source: Rohit Desphandé, John U. Farley, and Frederick E. Webster, "Factors Affecting Organizational Performance: A Five-Country Comparison," Working Paper, (Cambridge, MA: Marketing Science Institute, 1997).

of a recent study that contrasts organizations in five different countries. Japanese and French firms are clearly much more hierarchical than British and American firms. Anglo-Saxon companies tend to be much more market-type cultures than German or French firms. Not surprisingly, Japanese companies are also much more clan-driven than companies in other countries. The same study also found that organizations with a market culture tend to have a better business performance. On the other hand, firms governed by a clan or hierarchy culture are poor business performers.

CROSS-CULTURAL NEGOTIATIONS

◆ ◆ ◆ ◆ ◆ ◆

Conducting successful cross-cultural negotiations is a key ingredient for many international business transactions. International bargaining issues range from establishing the nuts and bolts of supplier agreements to setting up strategic alliances. Negotiation periods can run from a few hours to several months, if not years, of bargaining. Bargaining taps many resources, skills, and expertise. Scores of books have been devoted to negotiation "dos and don'ts."[57] Cross-cultural negotiations are further complicated by divergent cultural backgrounds of the participants in the negotiation process. In this section, our focus will be on the cultural aspects of international negotiations. Chapter 15 will revisit cross-cultural bargaining in the personal selling context.

Roughly speaking, there are four stages encountered in most negotiation processes: (1) nontask soundings, (2) task-related information exchange, (3) persuasion, and (4) concessions and agreement.[58] Nontask soundings include all activities that are used to establish a rapport among the parties involved. Developing a

Stages of Negotiation Process

---

[57]See, for example, R. Fisher and W. Ury, *Getting to Yes: Negotiation Agreement Without Giving In* (New York: Penguin, 1981), and, G. Kennedy, *Negotiate Anywhere!* (London: Arrow Books, 1987).

[58]John L. Graham and Yoshihiro Sano, "Across the Negotiating Table from the Japanese," *International Marketing Review*, 3 (Autumn 1986), pp. 58–71.

rapport is a process that depends on subtle cues.[59] The second stage relates to all task-related exchanges of information. Once the information exchange stage is completed, the negotiation parties typically move toward the persuasion phase of the bargaining process. Persuasion is a give-and-take deal. The final step involves concession-making, hopefully resulting into a consensus. Not surprisingly, negotiation practices vary enormously across cultures. Japanese negotiators devote much more time to nurture a rapport than U.S. negotiators. For Americans, the persuasion stage is the most critical part of the negotiation process. Japanese bargainers prefer to spend most of their time on the first two stages so that little effort is needed for the persuasion phase. Japanese and American negotiators also differ in the way concessions are made. Americans tend to make concessions during the course of the negotiation process, whereas Japanese prefer to defer this toward the end of the bargaining.[60]

Cross-Cultural Negotiation Strategies[61]

Exhibit 4–11 represents a framework of culturally responsive negotiation strategies, driven by the level of cultural familiarity that the negotiating parties possess about one another's cultures. Cultural familiarity is a measure of a party's current knowledge of his or her counterpart's culture and ability to use that knowledge competently. Depending on the particular situation, eight possible negotiation strategies could be selected. Let us briefly consider each of them:

1. *Employ an agent or advisor.* Outside agents, such as technical experts or financial advisors, could be used when cultural familiarity is extremely low. These agents can be used to provide information and to advise on action plans.

2. *Involve a mediator.* Whereas the previous strategy can be used unilaterally, both parties could also jointly decide to engage a mutually acceptable third party as a mediator. Successful mediation depends on maintaining the respect and trust of both parties.

3. *Induce the counterpart to follow one's own negotiation script.* Effective negotiators proceed along a **negotiation script**—the rules, conduct, ends they target, means toward those ends, and so forth. When the counterpart's familiarity with your culture is high, it might be feasible to induce the other party to follow your negotiation script. This strategy is especially useful when cultural knowledge is asymmetrical: The other party is knowledgeable about your culture, but you are not familiar with his or hers. Inducement could be via verbal persuasion or subtle cues.

4. *Adapt to the counterpart's negotiation script.* With moderate levels of familiarity about the counterpart's cultural mind-set, it becomes possible to adapt to the counterpart's negotiation script. Adaptation involves a deliberate decision to adjust some common negotiation rules.

[59]Kathleen K. Reardon and Robert E. Spekman, "Starting Out Right: Negotiation Lessons for Domestic and Cross-Cultural Business Alliances," *Business Horizons* (Jan.–Feb. 1994), pp. 71–79.

[60]John L. Graham, "Negotiating with the Japanese (Part 1)," *East Asian Executive Reports* (November 15, 1988), p. 8, 19–21.

[61]Stephen E. Weiss, "Negotiating with 'Romans'—Part 1," *Sloan Management Review* (Winter 1994), pp. 51–61; Stephen E. Weiss, "Negotiating with Romans—Part 2," *Sloan Management Review* (Spring 1994), pp. 85–99.

 How do you order tea in Cairo? When do you bow in Bangkok? In 275 locations worldwide there's someone to clue you in on the customs. And AT&T USADirect® Service to bring you closer to home. Call 800-228-9290 or your travel agent for reservations. We believe:

When you're comfortable you can do anything.™ **Marriott**
HOTELS·RESORTS·SUITES

Cultural differences do exist. In many cases, your willingness to accept differences is a key to your success in business.

5. *Coordinate adjustment of both parties.* When the circumstances lend themselves, both parties could jointly decide to arrive at a common negotiation approach that blends both cultures. Occasionally, they might propose to adopt the negotiation script of a third culture.

6. *Embrace the counterpart's script.* With this strategy, the negotiator volunteers to adopt the counterpart's negotiation approach. This demands a tremendous effort on part of the negotiator. It can only be effective when the negotiator possesses a great deal of familiarity about the other party's cultural background.

7. *Improvise an approach.* This strategy constructs a negotiation script over the course of negotiating. This approach is advisable when both parties feel very comfortable with their counterpart's culture. It might be effective when bargaining with members from a high-context culture where mutual bonding and other contextual cues are at least as important (nontask-related aspects) as the immediate negotiation concerns.

8. *Effect symphony.* The final strategy capitalizes on both parties' high cultural familiarity by creating an entirely new script or by following some other approach atypical to their respective cultures. For instance, the coordination might tap parts from both cultures.

EXHIBIT 4–11
CULTURALLY RESPONSIVE STRATEGIES AND THEIR
FEASIBILITY

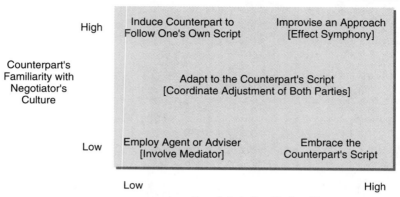

Brackets indicate a joint strategy, which requires deliberate consultation with counterpart. At each level of familiarity, a negotiator can consider feasible the strategies designated at that level and any lower level.

Reprinted from "Negotiating with 'Romans'—Part 1," by Stephen E. Weiss, *Sloan Management Review* (Winter 1994), pp. 51–61. Copyright 1994 by Sloan Management Review Association. All rights reserved.

The choice of a particular strategy partly depends on how familiar the negotiators are with the other party's culture. To pick a particular strategy, the following steps ought to be considered:

1. *Reflect on your culture's negotiation practices.* What negotiation model do you use? What is the role of the individual negotiator? What is the meaning of a satisfactory agreement?

2. *Learn the negotiation script common in the counterpart's culture.* This will help the negotiator to anticipate and interpret the other party's negotiating behaviors.

3. *Consider the relationship and contextual clues.* Different contexts necessitate different negotiating strategies. What circumstances define the interaction between the negotiation parties? Contextual clues include considerations such as the life of the relationship, gender of the parties involved, and balance of power.

4. *Predict or influence the counterpart's approach.* Prediction could be based on indicators like the counterpart's prenegotiation behavior or track record. In some cases, it is desirable to influence the other party's negotiation strategy via direct means (e.g., explicit request for a negotiation protocol) or through more subtle means (e.g., disclosing one's familiarity with the counterpart's culture).

5. *Choose a strategy.* The chosen strategy should be compatible with the cultures involved, conducive to a coherent pattern of interaction, in line with the relationship and bargaining context, and ideally acceptable to both parties.

$\mathcal{V}$IDEO BOX

CONSUMERS ACROSS BORDERS IN EUROPE

The European integration, which formed the European Union, is a political and economic success in the making. Now not only products but also people travel freely throughout the European Union. There is no denying that such a regional unification will enhance the gradual homogenization of product standards, industrial regulations, commercial codes, and fiscal and monetary policies in the long run. These factors will promote regional integration of corporate activities, such as standardizing products (or components) and services across national boundaries similar to the situation in the United States. However, the video clip clearly shows that culture, taste, and lifestyle differences tend to remain as diverse as they have been across national borders in the European Union. Furthermore, as a result of the political and economic unification movement *forced* onto them, people of different nationalities may even try to emphasize their national heritage and cultural differences more than ever before. Such nationalistic needs may even create a more complex cultural diversity in an end of homogenization.

What implications do you draw for marketing research and segmentation from these two forces at work in the European Union?

SUMMARY

Global marketing does not operate in a bubble. Culture is an intrinsic part of the global marketing environment. Cultural diversity brings along an immense richness. "Foreign" cultures may offer a breeding ground for new product ideas. Cultural changes may open up new market opportunities. At the same time, cultural diversity also poses enormous challenges to international marketers and managers in general. Usually, cultural blunders are easily forgiven. Occasionally, however, cultural mishaps create ill will and even lead to permanent damage of the firm's overseas business operations.

Preventive medicine is more effective than having to lick your wounds afterward. Dictums such as "When in Rome . . ." are nice catch-phrases but, unfortunately, it is seldom easy to learn what "do as the Romans" exactly means. Sensitivity to the host culture is a nice attribute, but for most people it will always stay an ideal rather than an accomplishment. There simply are no tricks of the trade or shortcuts. In fact, an often fatal mistake is to overestimate one's familiarity with the host culture.

In this chapter we analyzed what is meant by culture. We examined several elements of culture in detail. Cultures have differences, but they also share certain aspects. We examined several frameworks that you can use to analyze and classify different cultures. Once you are aware of the differences and commonalities, the next and most formidable task is to become sensitive to the host culture. We described several procedures to foster cultural adjustment. Cross-cultural training is one route toward cultural adaptation. The ideal, however, is to immerse oneself in the foreign culture through intensive language training, prolonged visits, or other means.

The interface between culture and the various marketing mix instruments was studied. Future chapters (Chapters 11 through 16) that look more closely at the global marketing mix will revisit these interactions. In this chapter, we also examined the notion of corporate or organizational culture. As we saw, to some extent corporate cultures are driven by the culture in which the company originated. Finally, we gave some background on a very complex form of cultural interface: cross-cultural negotiations. Several strategies were introduced to assist you in international bargaining situations.

KEY TERMS ✦

ethnocentrism

extended family

high- (low-) context culture

homophilous (heterophilous) culture

individualistic (collectivistic) culture

long-term (short-term) orientation

masculinity (femininity)

monochronic (polychronic) cultures

negotiation script

nuclear family

organizational culture

power distance

reference groups

self-reference criterion (SRC)

uncertainty avoidance

REVIEW QUESTIONS ✦ ✦ ✦ ✦ ✦ ✦ ✦ ✦ ✦ ✦ ✦ ✦ ✦ ✦ ✦ ✦ ✦ ✦ ✦

1. How does language complicate the tasks of global marketers?

2. Describe the importance of reference groups in international marketing.

3. What can marketers do to launch new products in countries that tend to resist change?

4. How do high-context cultures differ from low-context ones?

5. What are some possible issues in applying Hofstede's classification scheme in a global marketing context?

DISCUSSION QUESTIONS ✦ ✦ ✦ ✦ ✦ ✦ ✦ ✦ ✦ ✦ ✦ ✦ ✦ ✦ ✦ ✦ ✦

1. Focus group research conducted by advertising agencies like Leo Burnett shows that Asia's youngsters (the proverbial X-generation) mimic American trends but, at the same time, are pretty conservative. Gangsta rap, for instance, is extremely popular in Malaysia. But many of the values that Asian youths hold are quite traditional: family relations, respect for elders, marriage, and so on. Discuss this seeming contradiction.

2. A recent survey in China of 400 urban children aged 7–12 showed that 81.3 percent dreamed of international travel, 61.9 percent wanted space travel, 60.2 percent wanted to be more beautiful, and almost 90 percent wanted to be more intelligent. Given these aspirations,

what market opportunities do you see for Western companies that target China's child population?

3. What are some of the possible infrastructural roadblocks (e.g., in terms of transportation, storage) that ice cream manufacturers would face in South East Asia?

4. One of the cultural dimensions singled out by Hofstede is the individualism/collectivism distinction. What would this categorization imply in terms of setting up a sales force for international marketers? For instance, what incentive schemes might work in an individualistic culture? collectivistic?

5. The following table compares the economic affluence for different religious groups. Apparently, the world's

Religious Groups	GNP (US$) per capita (1994)	Religious Groups	GNP (US$) per capita (1994)
Top 10		**Bottom 10**	
Lutherans-Evangelical	28,700	Animist	804
Lutheran	28,600	Sikh	702
Shinto	26,900	Monotheism Official	680
Jehovah's Witnesses	23,300	Traditional Beliefs	644
Episcopalian	23,300	Voodoo	404
Mormon	22,900	Hindu	392
Mennonite	22,800	Jains	368
Baptist	22,700	Hoa-hao	245
Seventh-Day Adventists	22,600	Cadoaism	245
Church of God	22,000	Hinduism Official	179

Source: Philip M. Parker, *Religious Cultures of the World. A Statistical Reference,* Westport, CT: Greenwood Press, 1997, p. 5.

wealthiest religions are mostly Protestant groups (e.g., Lutherans, Episcopalians, Baptists). Do these figures suggest that Protestantism leads to more wealth?

6. Certain Muslim countries like Saudi Arabia do not allow advertisers to show a frontal picture of a woman with her hair. This creates a challenge for companies like Unilever or Procter & Gamble that want to advertise hair-care products (e.g., shampoo). How would you tackle this challenge?

7. Visit the Culturgrams Web site and download the free sample (www.culturgram.com/culturgram/ free-download.htm). Read the sample. What cultural differences exist between your culture and the one described in the sample? What are the similarities — if any?

8. A lot of advertising efforts in Japan tend to establish a mood related to the product instead of convincing the viewer why she/he should buy brand X. What cultural traits might lie behind this so-called "soft-sell" approach toward advertising in Japan?

FURTHER READING ✦ ✦ ✦ ✦ ✦ ✦ ✦ ✦ ✦ ✦ ✦ ✦ ✦ ✦ ✦ ✦ ✦ ✦ ✦

Baligh, H. Helmy. "Components of Culture: Nature, Interconnections, and Relevance to the Decisions on the Organization Structure." *Management Science*, 40(1), (1994): pp. 14–27.

Barber, Benjamin R. *Jihad vs. McWorld. How Globalism and Tribalism are Reshaping the World*. New York: Ballantine Books, 1995.

Graham, John L., Alma T. Mintu, and Waymond Rodgers. "Explorations of Negotiation Behaviors in Ten Foreign Cultures Using a Model Developed in the United States." *Management Science*, 40 (1), (1994): pp. 72–95.

Hall, Edward T. *Beyond Culture*. Garden City, NY: Anchor Press, 1976.

Hofstede, Geert. *Culture's Consequences: International Differences in Work-Related Values*. Beverly Hills, CA: Sage Publications, 1980.

Hofstede, Geert. *Cultures and Organizations: Software of the Mind*. London: McGraw-Hill, 1991.

Hofstede, Geert. "Management Scientists Are Human." *Management Science*, 40(1) (1994): 4–13.

Hofstede, Geert, and Michael Bond. "The Confucius Connection: From Cultural Roots to Economic Growth." *Organizational Dynamics* (1988): 4–21.

Neale, Margaret E. *Business Week's Guide to Cross-Cultural Negotiating. Maximizing Profitability in Intra- and Inter-Cultural Negotiations*. New York: McGraw-Hill, 1995.

Parker, Philip M. *Cross-Cultural Statistical Encyclopedia of the World. Volumes 1, 2, 3, and 4*. Westport, CT: Greenwood Press, 1997.

Ricks, David A. *Blunders in International Business*. Cambridge, MA: Blackwell Publishers, 1993.

Schwartz, Shalom H., and Lilach Sagiv. "Identifying Culture-Specifics in the Content and Structure of Values." *Journal of Cross-Cultural Psychology*, 26(1) (January 1995): 92–116.

Terpstra, Vern, and Kenneth David. *The Cultural Environment of International Business*. Cincinnati, OH: Southwestern Publishing Co., 1991.

Triandis, Harry C. "The Self and Social Behavior in Differing Cultural Contexts." *Psychological Review*, 96(3) (1989): 506–20.

POLITICAL AND LEGAL ENVIRONMENT

5

HAPTER OVERVIEW

1. POLITICAL ENVIRONMENT—INDIVIDUAL GOVERNMENTS

2. POLITICAL ENVIRONMENT—SOCIAL PRESSURES
   AND POLITICAL RISK

3. INTERNATIONAL AGREEMENTS

4. INTERNATIONAL LAW AND LOCAL LEGAL ENVIRONMENT

5. ISSUES TRANSCENDING NATIONAL BOUNDARIES

Business has been considered an integral part of economic forces. Indeed, economics was once called *political economy*, and as such, business could not be conducted devoid of political and legal forces. Although we tend to take political and legal forces for granted in doing business domestically, they could become central issues in international business and cannot be ignored. It is human nature that we tend to look at other countries' political and legal systems as peculiar because they differ from ours. We might even make some value judgment that our own country's political and legal system is always superior to other countries' and that they should change their system to our way. This ethnocentrism, however, hinders our proper understanding of, and sensitivity to, differences in the system that might have major business implications. By the very nature of their jobs, international marketers cannot afford to be ethnocentric as they interact with a multitude of political and legal systems, including their own at home.

International marketers should be aware that the economic interests of their companies can differ widely from those of the countries in which they do business, and sometimes even from those of their own home countries. Furthermore, they must abide by various international agreements, treaties, and laws. In this chapter, we will examine political and legal forces that affect the company's international marketing activities from the following three perspectives: the political and legal climates of the host country, those of the home country, and the international agreements, treaties, and laws affecting international marketing activities transcending national boundaries. Although political and legal climates are inherently related and inseparable because laws are generally a manifestation of a country's political processes, we will look at political climate first, followed by legal climate.

POLITICAL ENVIRONMENT—INDIVIDUAL GOVERNMENTS

Government affects almost every aspect of business life in a country. First, national politics affect business environments directly, through changes in policies, regulations, and laws. The government in each country determines which industries will receive protection in the country and which will face open competition. The government determines labor regulations and property laws. It determines fiscal and monetary policies, which then affect investment and returns. We will summarize those policies and regulations that directly influence the international business environment in a country.

Second, the political stability and mood in a country affect the actions a government will take—actions that may have an important impact on the viability of doing business in the country. A political movement may change prevailing attitudes toward foreign corporations and result in new regulations. An economic shift may influence the government's willingness to endure the hardships of an austerity program. We will discuss the strategic importance of understanding political risk in an international business context.

Home Country versus Host Country

Whenever marketing executives do business across national boundaries, they have to face the regulations and laws of both the home and host countries. A **home country** refers to a country in which the parent company is based. A **host country** is a country in which foreign companies are allowed to do business in accordance with its government policies and within its laws. Therefore, international marketing executives should be concerned about the host government's policies and their possible changes in the future, as well as their home government's political climate.

Because companies usually do not operate in countries that have been hostile to their home country, many executives tend to take for granted the political environment of the host country in which they currently do business. Sweeping political upheavals, such as the Cuban crisis in the 1960s, the Iranian Revolution in the 1980s, the breakup of the Soviet Union in the late 1980s, the Persian Gulf War in the 1990s, and more recently, the Kosovo crisis in Yugoslavia in 1999 have already made many business executives fully aware of dire political problems in some regions, and many companies have since stayed away from those areas. Despite the fact that those major political upheavals provide the largest single setting for an economic crisis faced by foreign companies, what most foreign companies are concerned about on a daily basis should be a much larger universe of low-key events that might not involve violence or a change in government regime but that do involve a fairly significant change in policy toward foreign companies.[1] In recent years, Vietnam has begun to attract foreign direct investment to spur its domestic economic growth and shift toward a more market-based economy.[2] Similarly, the end of apartheid in South Africa also signals foreign companies' cautious yet optimistic attitude toward resuming business relations with this African country.[3]

The intertwined nature of home and host government policies is illustrated by the U.S.–China diplomatic relationship having been re-established in the mid-1970s under the Nixon administration. As a result, the Chinese government finally opened its economy to foreign direct investment—mostly through joint ventures—in the 1980s. The first pioneer foreign companies stood to gain from the host government policies designed to protect the domestic producers they teamed up with in China. Thus, early beneficiaries were the United States' Chrysler (now DaimlerChrysler, based in Germany), Germany's Volkswagen, and France's Peugeot, with their respective Chinese partner companies. However, the U.S.–China relationship has since been anything but smooth. The United States, in particular, has been openly critical of China's human rights violations since the Tiannanmen Square massacre of 1989, and has tried to make its trade policy with China contingent upon measurable improvements in China's human rights policy.

Furthermore, a recent accidental NATO bombing of the Chinese embassy in Belgrade, Yugoslavia during its 1999 Kosovo campaign, the United States' continued criticism of China's threat to forcibly reunify Taiwan with the mainland, the widespread use of pirated U.S. software in China, and the European Union's failure to reach an accord to accept China's entry into the WTO might cause a setback in bringing China into the world economy. Although these issues may not damage the U.S. and European countries' relationships with China permanently, foreign companies operating in, or contemplating entry into, China are bound to experience undue uncertainties for the foreseeable future.[4]

The emergence of the Internet could also pose problems for Chinese trade relations. Though China seeks to free its markets in response to global pressure, particularly from the United States, the Internet undermines China's general censorship policies. This dilemma was recently shown when China imprisoned a Chinese Internet entrepreneur for exchanging lists of e-mail addresses with a U.S. organization in the hope of growing his Web-based business.[5] Nonetheless, encouraged by reformist leaders such as Premier Zhu Rongji, Internet use is growing explosively.

---

[1]Stephen J. Kobrin, "Selective Vulnerability and Corporate Management," in Theodore H. Moran, ed., *International Political Risk Assessment: The State of the Art, Landegger Papers in International Business and Public Policy*, Georgetown University, Washington, D.C. 1981, pp. 9–13.

[2]"Foreign Direct Investment Flows to Low-Income Countries: A Review of the Evidence," Overseas Development Institute Briefing Paper, September 1997, www.one.world.org/odi/briefing/3 97.html, accessed on August 20, 1999.

[3]"South Africa: Investment Climate Satement," Tradeport, www.tradeport.org/ts/countries/safrica/ climate.html, April 10, 1999, accessed on August 20, 1999.

[4]"China and EU Fail to Reach a WTO Accord–No Date Is Set to Resume, But an Opening Is Left; Clinton Presses His Case," *Wall Street Journal*, February 25, 2000, p. A12.

[5]Craig S. Smith, "China Imprisons Internet Entrepreneur," *Wall Street Journal* (January 21, 1999), p. A13.

In 1997, only 640,000 Chinese were connected. Now more than 4 million are. By 2001, the online population is estimated to hit 27 million—about as many as in Japan. And while only $42 million in e-commerce transactions were expected in 1999, they could approach $4 billion by 2003. However, there is some uncertainty as to how willing the Chinese government is to embrace the online commerce.[6]

International marketers must understand the fluid nature of the host country political climate in relation to the home country policies. Some countries are relatively stable over time; other countries experience different degrees of political volatility that make it difficult for international marketers to predict and plan ahead. Nonetheless, there are a few crucial political factors international executives should know that determines the nature of the host country's political climate.

Ideology.   One way to characterize the nature of government is by its political ideology, ranging from communism and socialism to capitalism. Under strict **communism**, the government owns and manages all businesses and no private ownership is allowed. As the recent breakup of the Soviet Union shows, the strict government control not only strips its people of private incentives to work but also is an inefficient mechanism to allocate scarce resources across the economy. On the other hand, **capitalism**, refers to an economic system in which free enterprise is permitted and encouraged along with private ownership. In a capitalistic society, free-market transactions are considered to produce the most efficient allocation of scarce resources. However, capitalism is not without critics. Even Wall Street financier George Soros has called attention to the threat that the values propagated by global laissez-faire capitalism pose to the very values on which open and democratic societies depend. Without social justice as the guiding principle of civilized life, life becomes a survival of the fittest.[7] For example, capitalism, if unfettered, may result in excessive production and excessive consumption, thereby causing severe air and water pollution in many parts of the world, as well as depleting the limited natural resources. Government roles would be limited to those functions that the private sector could not perform efficiently, such as defense, highway construction, pollution control, and other public services. An interesting example can be found in Japan. Although Japanese companies perfected an efficient just-in-time (JIT) delivery system, frequent shipments have caused increased traffic congestion and air pollution in Japan, and thus may not be as efficient in delivering social well being.[8] Now the Japanese government is trying to regulate the use of JIT production and delivery systems. **Socialism** generally is considered a political system that falls in between pure communism and pure capitalism. A socialist government advocates government ownership and control of some industries considered critical to the welfare of the nation.[9]

Structure of Government

---

[6]Bruce Einhorn and Dexter Roberts, "China's Web Masters," *Business Week Online*, International Edition, August 2, 1999.

[7]George Soros, *The Crisis of Global Capitalism* (New York: Public Affairs, 1998).

[8]Kamran Moinzadeh, Ted Klastorin, and Emre Berk, "The Impact of Small Lot Ordering on Traffic Congestion in a Physical Distribution System," *IIE Transactions*, 29 (August 1997), pp. 671–79.

[9]Refer to an excellent classic treatise on capitalism, socialism, and communism by Joseph A. Schumpeter, *Capitalism, Socialism, and Democracy* (New York: Harper & Brothers, 1947).

After the breakup of the Soviet Union, most East European countries converted to capitalist ideology.[10] China is in a transition stage, although uncertainties still remain. There remain few countries that adhere to the extreme communist doctrine other than North Korea and Cuba. Although many countries cherish capitalism and democracy, the extent of government intervention in the economy varies from country to country. (Both capitalistic and socialistic countries in which government planning and ownership play a major role are also referred to as *planned economies*).

Political Parties.   The number of political parties also influences the level of political stability. A one-party regime does not exist outside the communist country. Most countries have a number of large and small political parties representing different views and value systems of their population. In a *single-party-dominant* country, government policies tend to be stable and predictable over time. Although such a government provides consistent policies, they do not always guarantee a favorable political environment for foreign companies operating in the country. A dominant party regime may maintain policies (e.g., high tariff and nontariff barriers, foreign direct investment restrictions, and foreign exchange controls) that reduce the operational flexibility of foreign companies. For example, in Mexico a few political parties have always existed, but one party, called the Institutional Revolutionary Party, had been dominant in the past seventy years. However, since 1994, Mexico's ruling party has lost its firm grip on its politics. Although the opening of the Mexican political system may eventually lead to a stronger democracy over time, it is believed that its economy will experience an unknown degree of political instability for the foreseeable future.[11]

The trauma followed by the collapse of one-party-dominant systems can be relatively large, as experienced by the breakup of the Soviet Union. In a cabinet dialogue between then-President Nixon and then-Premier Nikita Kruschev in 1972, PepsiCo had cultivated ties with Soviet leaders that led to a deal providing the Soviet Union and its East European allies with Pepsi concentrate and state-of-the-art bottling technology in return for the inside track to the huge, unexploited soft-drink market within the Soviet Empire. However, when the Soviet Union collapsed in 1991, PepsiCo was devastated. Almost overnight, all the hard-earned skills and nepotism that PepsiCo had developed for operating in a centralized command economy counted for nothing. Making matters worse, PepsiCo was seen to be connected with the discredited former regime. Archrival Coca-Cola almost immediately launched a drive for market share. The results were striking. In Hungary, for example, PepsiCo's market share tumbled from 70 percent to 30 percent almost overnight.[12]

In a *dual-party system*, such as the United States and Britain, the parties are usually not divided by ideology but rather, have different constituencies. For example, in the United States, the Democrats tend to identify with working-class people

---

[10]Robert D. Russell, "The Emergence of Entrepreneurship in Eastern Europe: A Self-Organizing Perspective," *International Journal of Commerce and Management*, 6 (1–2) (1996), pp. 21–37.

[11]"PRI Loses a Mexico Governorship, but Clean Vote Could Help Image," *Economist* (February 14, 1995), p. 18; "The 5% Solution," *Economist* (November 23, 1996), p. 48.

[12]Hugh D. Menzies, "PepsiCo's Soviet Travails," *International Business* (November 1995), p. 42.

and assume a greater role for the federal government, while the Republicans tend to support business interests and prefer a limited role for the federal government. Yet both parties are strong proponents of democracy. In such a dual-party system, the two parties tend to alternate their majority position over a relatively long period. In 1995, the Democrats finally lost control of Congress to the Republican majority after many years. We have begun to see some sweeping changes in government policy, ranging from environmental protection to affirmative action, usually in support of business interests.

The other extreme situation is a *multiple-party system* without any clear majority, found in Italy and more recently in Japan. The consistency of government policies may be compromised as a result. Since there is no dominant party, different parties with differing policy goals form a coalition government. The major problem with a coalition government is a lack of political stability and continuity, and this portends a high level of uncertainty in the business climate. Since, in Japan, career bureaucrats, who are not political appointees, used to be in virtual control of government policy development and execution, the changes in government leadership did not seem to pose any measurable policy change. However, in recent years due to Japan's prolonged recession, those nonpolitical elite bureaucrats are under fire.[13]

Turkey offers another interesting example. Turkey's constitution mandates a secular national government. It has a multiple-party system, but the instability and bickering of coalition governments has led to three military coups since 1960. In 1998 the military generals were about to try another coup against modern Turkey's first Islamic fundamentalist–led government when Turkey's president, Suleyman Demirel, helped to persuade the fundamentalist party to step down quietly. If a coup had taken place, Turkey's fragile democracy might have collapsed in violence. Turkey's current prime minister, Bulent Ecevit, has a strong anti-Western orientation. Yet, Turkish President Demirel has managed to prevent Prime Minister Ecevit from renewing ambassadorial relationships with Iraq and has persuaded him to let NATO use Turkish bases from which to send bombers again the Serbs in the Kosovo conflict in 1999.[14]

Government Policies and Regulations

It is the role of government to promote a country's interests in the international arena for various reasons and objectives. Some governments actively invest in certain industries that are considered important to national interests. Other governments protect fledgling industries in order to allow them to gain the experience and size necessary to compete internationally. In general, reasons for wanting to block or restrict trade are as follows:

1. National security
   - Ability to produce goods necessary to remain independent (e.g., self-sufficiency)
   - Not exporting goods that will help enemies or unfriendly nations
2. Developing new industries
   - Idea of nurturing nascent industries to strength in a protected market
3. Protecting declining industries
   - To maintain domestic employment for political stability

---

[13]Peter Hartcher, *The Ministry* (Boston, MA: Harvard Business School Press, 1998).
[14]"Suleyman Demirel, Top Turk," *Economist* (July 24, 1999).

For example, Japan's active industrial policy by the MITI (Ministry of International Trade and Industry) in the 1960s and 1970s is well known for its past success, and has also been adopted by newly industrialized countries (NICs), such as Singapore, South Korea, and Malaysia.[15] Governments use a variety of laws, policies, and programs to pursue their economic interests.

This section focuses on describing those government programs, trade and investment laws, and macroeconomic policies that have an immediate and direct impact on the international business in a country. We will discuss laws regulating business behavior—such as antitrust laws and antibribery laws—in a subsequent section on international legal environments. Later sections of this chapter will discuss the legal systems that produce and enforce a countries' laws.

Incentives and Government Programs. Most countries use government loans, subsidies, or training programs to support export activities and specific domestic industries. These programs are important for host-country firms, as well as for firms considering production in one country for export to others. In the United States, the International Trade Administration (ITA) has a national network of district offices in every state, offering export promotion assistance to local businesses. Furthermore, in light of federal budget cuts and as a supplement to the ITA's trade promotion efforts, state governments have significantly increased their staff and budgets, not only for export assistance, particularly in nurturing small local businesses,[16] but also for attracting foreign direct investment to increase employment in their respective states.[17] Thus, the major objectives of any state government support are (1) job creation and (2) improving the state balance of trade (as in any country).

The state government's export promotion activities are more systematic, while its investment-attraction activities are characterized by their case-by-case nature. Foreign investment-attraction activities generally consist of seminars, various audiovisual and printed promotional materials, and investment missions, among others. Investment missions and various tax and other financial incentives appear to play the most important role in investment promotional efforts. Investment missions are generally made by government officials, particularly by the governor of the state, visiting with potential investors. One study has shown that whether or not they are active in foreign investment attraction activities, state governments that are active in export promotion tend to attract more foreign companies' direct investment in their states than those state governments that are not.[18]

---

[15]Masaaki Kotabe, "The Roles of Japanese Industrial Policy for Export Success: A Theoretical Perspective," *Columbia Journal of World Business*, 20 (Fall 1985), pp. 59–64; Mark L. Clifford, "Can Malaysia Take That Next Big Step?" *Business Week* (February 26, 1996), pp. 96–106.

[16]Masaaki Kotabe and Michael R. Czinkota, "State Government Promotion of Manufacturing Exports: A Gap Analysis," *Journal of International Business Studies*, 23 (Fourth Quarter 1992), pp. 637–58; and for the most recent comprehensive study, see Timothy J. Wilkinson, "American State Export Promotion Strategies for Entrepreneurs and Small- to Mid-Sized Businesses," Ph.D. dissertation, Department of Political Science, University of Utah, 1996.

[17]J. Myles Shaver, "Do Foreign-Owned and U.S.-Owned Establishments Exhibit the Same Location Pattern in U.S. Manufacturing Industries?" *Journal of International Business Studies*, 29 (Third Quarter 1998), pp. 469–92.

[18]Masaaki Kotabe, "The Promotional Roles of the State Government and Japanese Manufacturing Direct Investment in the United States," *Journal of Business Research*, 27 (June 1993), pp. 131–46.

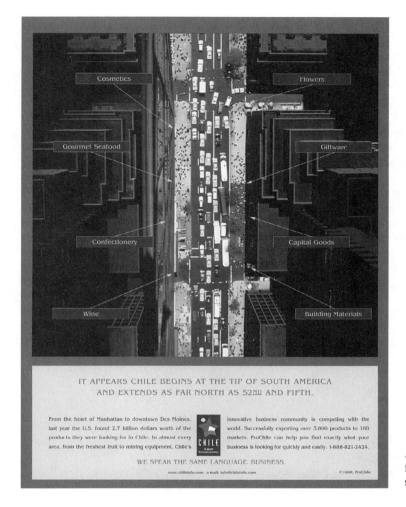

IT APPEARS CHILE BEGINS AT THE TIP OF SOUTH AMERICA
AND EXTENDS AS FAR NORTH AS 52ND AND FIFTH.

From the heart of Manhattan to downtown Des Moines, last year the U.S. found 2.7 billion dollars worth of the products they were looking for in Chile. In almost every area, from the freshest fruit to mining equipment, Chile's innovative business community is competing with the world. Successfully exporting over 3,800 products to 160 markets. ProChile can help you find exactly what your business is looking for quickly and easily. 1-888-821-2424.

WE SPEAK THE SAME LANGUAGE. BUSINESS.

www.chileinfo.com e-mail: info@chileinfo.com   © 1998, ProChile

A government agency actively solicits foreign buyers by helping them find sales leads with local firms.

For example, export-active states may be more politically favorable and receptive to foreign companies operating there. A well-known example is that to attract a Nissan plant, in 1985 Tennessee spent $12 million for new roads to the facility, and provided a $7 million grant for training plant employees and a $10 million tax break to the Japanese company.[19] Similarly, in the early 1990s, Alabama provided a $253 million package of capital investments and tax breaks to lure a Mercedes-Benz's sports utility vehicle production facility to the state.[20]

Most governments subsidize certain industries directly. Direct government subsidies are an important international consideration. In Europe, Airbus Industries was established in 1970 with joint government subsidies from the governments of Britain, France, Germany, and Spain to build a European competitor in the jet aircraft industry once dominated by U.S. companies, including Boeing and McDonnell-Douglas-Lockheed. The United States is no exception. When

---

[19]"Tennessee's Pitch to Japan," *New York Times* (February 27, 1985), pp. D1 and D6.
[20]"Tax Freedom Day Index Would Be Keen Indicator," *Orlando Sentinel* (May 8, 1994), p. D1.

threatened by Japanese competition in the semiconductor industry in the 1980s, the Reagan administration launched a Japanese-style government–industry joint industrial consortium known as SEMATECH (Semiconductor Manufacturing Technology) in 1987, with the federal government subsidizing half of its $200 million operating budget.[21] Thanks to SEMATECH, the U.S. semiconductor industry had recaptured the leading market share position by 1995.

The point is to recognize how government support for particular industries or for exporting in general will affect which industries are competitive and which are not. International businesses can benefit by planning for and utilizing home-country and host-country government programs.

Government Procurement. The ultimate government involvement in trade is when the government itself is the customer. It engages in commercial operations through the departments and agencies under its control. The U.S. government accounts for a quarter of the total U.S. consumption, so the government has become the largest single consuming entity in the United States. Thus, the government procurement policy has an enormous impact on international trade. In the United States, the Buy American Act gives a bidding edge to domestic suppliers. For foreign suppliers to win a contract from a U.S. government agency, their products must contain at least 50 percent of U.S.-made parts, or they must undercut the closest comparable U.S. product by at least 6 percent.[22] This "buy domestic" policy orientation is not limited to the United States, but applies to all other nations. In other words, when a U.S. company tries to sell to any foreign government agency, it should always expect some sort of bidding disadvantage relative to local competitors.

Trade Laws. National trade laws directly influence the environment for international business. Trade controls can be broken into two categories—economic trade controls and political trade controls. Economic trade controls are those trade restraints that are instituted for primarily economic reasons, such as to protect local jobs. Both **tariffs** and **nontariff barriers** (NTBs) work to impede imports that might compete with locally produced goods (see Exhibit 5–1). Tariffs tax imports directly, and also function as a form of income for the country that levies them. Average tariff rates on manufactured and mining products are 2.2 percent for Japan, 5.4 percent for the United States, and 5.7 percent for the European Union.[23] Nontariff barriers include a wide variety of quotas, procedural rules for imports, and standards set upon import quality that have the effect of limiting imports or making importing more difficult. For example, the biggest problem that equipment manufacturers will encounter if they try to sell into Mexico is that for any equipment that has an electrical connection (a TV, a router, or a server) they need a NOM, which is a Mexican certification (similar to UL, FCC in the United States) done by

---

[21]Due to the U.S. government's gradual budget cuts, SEMATECH became a technology consortium funded solely by member companies in 1998.

[22]David A. Vaughan, "The Buy American Act of 1988: Legislation in Conflict with U.S. International Obligations," *Law and Policy in International Business*, 20 (3), 1989, pp. 603–18; and "Part 1425: Foreign Acquisition," Department of the Interior Acquisition Regulation, U.S. Department of the Interior, www.ios.doi.gov/pam/1425-3.html, May 25, 1999, accessed on June 26, 2000.

[23]"MITI Angered by U.S. View of Trade Practices," *Financial Times* (May 3, 1994), p. 6.

EXHIBIT 5–1
TARIFF AND NONTARIFF BARRIERS

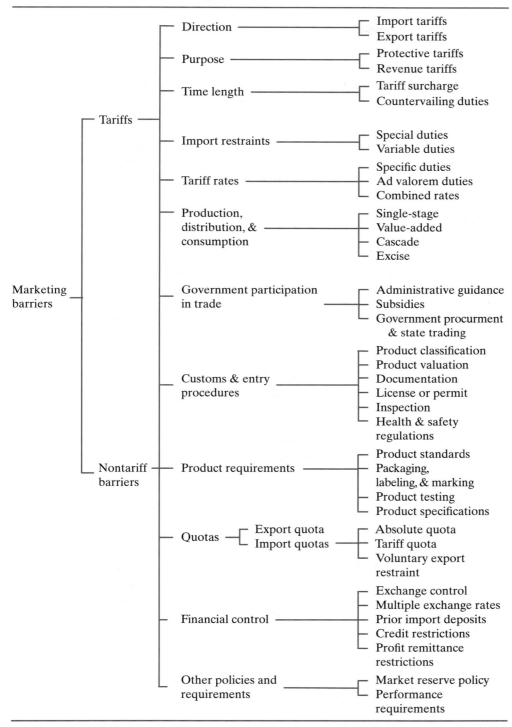

Source: Sak Onkvist and John J. Shaw, "Marketing Barriers in International Trade," *Business Horizons*, 31 (May–June 1988), p. 66.

authorized laboratories. This process takes money and time. Every different importer needs to get the NOM, even if two companies try to import a model number for which Compaq itself already has a NOM.[24]

Political trade controls are those trade restraints that are instituted for national interests or for international political reasons. **Embargoes** and **sanctions** are country-based political trade controls. Political trade restraints have become an accepted form of political influence in the international community. They are coercive or retaliatory trade measures often enacted unilaterally with the hopes of changing a foreign government or its policies without resorting to military force. Embargoes restrict all trade with a nation for political purposes. The United States maintains an economic embargo on Cuba today in an effort to change the country's political disposition. Sanctions are more narrowly defined trade restrictions, such as the U.S. government's threat in 1999 to impose retaliatory tariffs of 100 percent on hundreds of millions of dollars in European imports to compensate U.S. banana companies for their lost sales to Europe. A trade war waged by the U.S. government could make such seemingly unrelated items as Scottish cashmere sweaters, Pecorino cheese (but only the soft kind), German coffee makers, and French handbags scarce on American store shelves (See Chapter 2).[25]

Export license requirements are product-based trade controls. All exports officially require a specific export license from the Export Administration of the Department of Commerce. However, most products that are not sensitive to national security or are in short supply in the country may be sent to another country using only a general license. The application process for more sensitive products, including much high-technology exports, is quite extensive and can include review by numerous government agencies.

International businesses have a number of reasons to be concerned with trade restrictions. First, trade restrictions may completely block a company's ability to export to a country. Even if the company can export its goods, restrictions such as quotas or local modification requirements may make the product so expensive that an otherwise lucrative market is eliminated. Some companies attempt to benefit from import restrictions by establishing production facilities inside the foreign market country. For example, Brazil suddenly raised a tariff on imported cars from 20 percent to 70 percent in late 1994. As a result, foreign auto makers Fiat and Ford, with operating plants in Brazil, enjoyed a definite cost advantage over companies that exported cars to the country. Naturally, those latecomers decided to begin production in Brazil to avoid its hefty import tariffs. This is one illustration of strategic reasons why firms sometimes have plants in various countries rather than rely solely on exporting from home. The average price of a Volvo in Brazil is a whopping $85,000! Those companies, domestic or foreign, already manufacturing in the market can access the desired market with little competition from external producers.

However, trade restrictions are not necessarily good, even for companies inside a protected country. Trade restrictions often block companies from purchasing needed inputs at competitive prices. For example, in 1992 the U.S. International

---

[24]"Latin IT News" <latinitnews@mailer.latpro.com> posted by Gerard Dada of IT Marketing, September 8, 1999

[25]"Trade Fight Spills Over into Handbags, Coffee Makers," CNN Interactive, www.cnn.com, March 3, 1999.

Trade Commission levied an import tariff on the flat panel display screens used in laptop computers in response to a complaint that foreign companies were dumping the screens below cost on the U.S. market. Although local producers of computer screens benefited from the protection from competition, U.S. producers of laptop computers, which relied mostly on imported screens, could no longer compete. Many laptop producers were forced to ship their assembly plants overseas in order to stay in the market.

At a more macro level, if trade laws harm other countries, they are likely to invoke retaliation. For example, wrangling over China's inability to enforce intellectual property protection laws against pirating, the U.S. government announced the largest trade sanctions in U.S. history in 1995, slapping 100 percent tariffs on $1.1 billion of Chinese exports such as cellular phones, sporting goods, and plastic articles. China responded angrily, and promptly retaliated against U.S. exports of compact disks, video games, films, cigarettes, and alcohol.[26] Such a trade war also occurs frequently between seemingly friendly nations. For example, a recent skirmish over the inflow of American magazines into the Canadian market has escalated into warnings of a wide-ranging trade war. At the time of this writing, Canada is trying to introduce a law that would make it a criminal offense for Canadians to buy advertising in U.S.-based magazines, such as *Sports Illustrated*, transmitted via satellite to Canada for printing. The U.S. government is ready to retaliate with sanctions on specific Canadian exports to the tune of $2.5 billion a year.[27]

However, trade wars, if left unchecked, harm all countries by limiting the ability of competitive firms to export and generate the benefits created by specialization. One thing is clear—government trade laws have a complex and dynamic impact on the environment for international business.

Investment Regulations. International investments have been growing at a much faster pace than international trade. Many of these investments are being made by multinational corporations. Foreign direct investments are explained in terms of various market imperfections, including government-imposed distortions, but governments also have a significant role in constructing barriers to foreign direct investment and portfolio flows. These barriers can broadly be characterized as ownership and financial controls.

Ownership Controls. Most countries feel that some assets belong to the public—there is a sense of "national ownership." In a highly nationalistic country, this sentiment could apply to the ownership of any company. In many countries, the natural resources (e.g., the land and mineral wealth) are viewed as part of the national wealth, not to be sold to foreigners. For example, Kuwait has a constitutional ban on foreign ownership of its oil reserves. Recently, there has been a heated debate as to whether state-owned Kuwait Petroleum Corp. (KPC) has the right to sign agreements with foreign oil companies to produce local oil. The government argues that KPC is allowed under existing laws to forge foreign participation accords in return for cash incentives. But its efforts to advance the plan have

---

[26]Helene Cooper and Kathy Chen, "Sanctions Put U.S., China on Course to Trade War," *Wall Street Journal* (February 6, 1995), pp. A3, A11. Despite such bickerings, some improvement has also been observed. See, for example, "What's News—Worldwide," *Wall Street Journal* (April 30, 1997), p. 1.

[27]"Canada: What Your Read is What You Are?" *Economist* (February 6, 1999).

repeatedly come under attack by opposition members of parliament, who argue that foreign companies' provision of cash incentives amounts to foreign direct investment, thus foreign ownership.[28]

The United States has very few restrictions on foreign ownership; however, for reasons of national security, limitations do exist. For example, the Federal Communications Commission limits the control of U.S. media companies to U.S. citizens only. This was one of the motivating factors for Rupert Murdoch to relinquish his Australian citizenship for U.S. citizenship in order to retain control of his media network, Fox Television. Similarly, the U.S. Shipping Act of 1916 limits noncitizen ownership of U.S. shipping lines. The Federal Aviation Act requires airlines to be owned by U.S. citizens (defined as one where 75 percent of the voting rights of the firm are owned and controlled by U.S. citizens) in order to hold U.S. operating rights. The International Banking Act of 1978 limits interstate banking operations by foreign banks. Consequently, foreign banks cannot purchase or take over U.S. banks with interstate operations.

Financial Controls. Government-imposed restrictions can serve as strong barriers to foreign direct investments. Some common barriers include restrictions on profit remittances, and differential taxation and interest rates. Government-imposed restrictions can deter foreign investments. Restrictions of profit remittances can serve as a disincentive to invest, since returns cannot be realized in the home currency of the parent company. Although government controls on profit remittance are drawbacks in attracting investment, some governments also use such restrictions as a way to encourage foreign companies to increase exports from the host country. For example, Zimbabwe offers higher remittance rates—up to 100 percent—to foreign companies operating in that country that export significantly.[29]

Various MNCs have been able to exploit legal loopholes to circumvent this problem to some extent. Tactics include currency swaps, parallel loans,[30] countertrade activities, and charging for management services, among others. Also, various countries treat operations of foreign companies differently from those of local companies. Two means through which local companies are supported are lower tax rates and lower interest rates for loans secured from local financial institutions. These differences can put foreign companies at a significant disadvantage relative to domestic companies in that particular market, and can also act as a deterrent to foreign direct investments.

Macroeconomic Policies. Companies search internationally for stable growing markets where their profits will not be deteriorated by exchange loss or inflation. Government policies drive many economic factors such as the cost of capital, levels of economic growth, rates of inflation, and international exchange rates. Governments may directly determine the prime lending rate, or they may print or borrow the funds necessary to increase money supply. Governments may fix their currencies' exchange rates, or they may decide to allow the inter-

---

[28]Jeanne M. Perdue, "Kuwait Gets Green Light to Invite Majors," *Petroleum Engineer International*, 72 (September 1999), p. 7.

[29]Cris Chinaka, "Zimbabwe Announces Measures to Boost Investment," *Reuter Library Report* (April 27, 1993).

[30]For details, see Donald J. Smith and Robert A. Taggart, Jr., "Bond Market Innovations and Financial Intermediation," *Business Horizons*, 32 (November 1989), pp. 24–33.

national currency market to determine their exchange rates. The monetary and exchange policies a government pursues will affect the stability of its currency—which is of critical concern to any company doing business abroad. In the early 1990s, Mexico kept the peso's exchange rate artificially high despite its increasing trade deficit. One primary objective for such an exchange rate policy was to make it relatively easy for Mexico to import capital goods, such as machinery, from the United States for economic development. When Mexico's trade deficit rose to well over 8 percent of the country's GNP by 1994, Mexico could no longer hold on to an artificially high value of the peso and let it loose in December 1994. How serious was Mexico's trade deficit? Think, for a moment, that the United States had registered the large trade deficit of $172 billion in 1987, which once ushered in a doomsday prophecy of the decline of U.S. competitiveness. Yet, the U.S. trade deficit was no more than 3 percent of the country's GNP then!

Government fiscal policies also strongly influence macroeconomic conditions. The types of taxes a government employs will influence whether a particular type of business is competitive within a country. For example, if a government lowers long-term capital gains taxes or allows accelerated depreciation of corporate capital assets, it will encourage investment in manufacturing facilities. The Japanese government has been known for its pro-business tax abatement and depreciation policies that helped develop the world's leading manufacturing industries in Japan, ranging from steel and shipbuilding in the 1960s and 1970s, to machine tools, automobiles, and consumer electronics in the 1970s and 1980s, and to semiconductor and semiconductor manufacturing equipment in the 1980s and 1990s.

Although a government can play a role in a thriving economy and accessible capital, a number of other factors also determine a country's political environment. Historical considerations, social and political pressures, and the interests of particular constituencies will affect the political environment in important ways. For example, during the early 1990s China was enjoying an unprecedented economic boom. However, companies that tried to take advantage of China's open market policy have met with mixed results.[31] The next section will discuss such nonpolicy political considerations for international business.

POLITICAL ENVIRONMENT—SOCIAL PRESSURES AND POLITICAL RISK

The political environment in every country is regularly changing. New social pressures can force governments to make new laws or to enforce old policies differently. Policies that supported international investment may change toward isolationism or nationalism. In order to adequately prepare for international business or investment, the environment in each target country should be analyzed to determine its level of economic and political risk and opportunity. Global Perspective 5–1 shows how social pressures affect government and corporate policies.

[31]Erik Guyot and Craig S. Smith, "Chinese Crackdown Imperils Guaranteed Foreign Investment," *Wall Street Journal* (March 26, 1999), p. A23.

GLOBAL PERSPECTIVE 5–1

SOCIAL PRESSURES AFFECTING GOVERNMENT AND CORPORATE POLICIES: ANY FALLACY?

Steel workers mounted demonstrations in 1999, assailing that foreign steel is priced unfairly low. Under pressure, the U.S. government adopted a bill that would limit U.S. imports of steel to pre-1998 levels. Now the steel industry has filed complaints with the U.S. International Trade Commission and the Department of Commerce alleging that rolled steel from Argentina, Brazil, Japan, Russia, South Africa and Thailand is being dumped in the United States. So who are the American companies that are buying all that steel from those accused countries?

Interestingly, U.S. steelmakers themselves buy steel in slab form from various countries, which they process into finished steel. Those U.S. steelmakers have both complained vociferously about steel imports and bought foreign steel themselves. In all, American steelmakers, by some estimates, buy about 25 percent of the steel coming into the United States. Doesn't this seem hypocritical? Not at all, say the steelmakers. "Some will say, 'Gosh, it's wrong of you to be complaining about imports when you import so much yourself,'" says Bethlehem's chairperson, Curtis Barnette. "That view really misunderstands the marketplace and the issues." The problem arises only with particular types of steel, from particular countries, that under international trade rules are being unfairly dumped in the United States. Thus, "there is a big difference between imports and illegal imports," according to another executive.

Under the International Trade Commission (ITC) and the Department of Commerce requirements, the first test of dumping is that the steel is priced unfairly low—either below the selling price in the home country or below the cost of production. But what if the buyer is a U.S. steel company? Is it thus the beneficiary of the same unfair pricing about which it complains? Generally, U.S. steelmakers reply that they will not import steel if they think it has been priced in the United States at less than fair value. But this reply is tough to swallow. To qualify as dumped the ITC has to find that an import also has injured the domestic industry. But this is no easy test in real life. On March 3, 2000, the ITC commissioners finally arrived at a conclusion that steel product imports from the countries were not causing financial injury to domestic producers by undercutting local prices. As a result, the United States will not be imposing any duties or other penalties on this class of cold-rolled steel products imported from these six nations.

Similar political maneuvering is also shaping the trade policies across the Atlantic in the European Union (EU). EU prohibits importation of growth-hormone-treated beef from the United States. Now veterinary scientists argue that a hormone used by American cattle farmers is carcinogenic, dealing a severe blow to the U.S. campaign against an EU ban on hormones in beef. According to the EU scientists, one of the six growth-promoting hormones, known as 17 beta-oestradiol, fed to cattle in the United Sates has to be considered "a complete carcinogen." The findings mean that consumers will pressure the EU to maintain its ban on growth-hormone-treated beef imports from the United States.

The United States argues that the EU prohibition is not scientifically justified and even won backing for this stance from the World Trade Organization. The U.S. government has threatened to slap sanctions on about $300 million in EU exports if it continues to block U.S. exports of hormone-treated beef. Similar to the banana trade issue described in Chapter 2, political pressures from interest groups in and outside the United States continued to affect the nature of international trade.

Although generally unfounded by science, the European consumers' fear of "engineered" food is spreading into other categories of food products—genetically modified food products, and well beyond Europe into the United States and Japan. Some companies, such as Neslé and Unilever, have already announced to end the use of genetically modified ingredients in their foods. Now in the United States, Gerber and Heinz announced in July 1999 that they will not include genetically engineered ingredients in any baby foods. In Japan, even Japanese tofu makers are switching to nongenetically engineered soybeans, jeopardizing some 500,000 tons of soybean imports from the United States.

Sources: "Steelmakers Complain About Foreign Steel; They Also Import It," *Wall Street Journal* (March 22, 1999), p. A1 and p. A8; "U.S. Beef Hormone Is Carcinogenic, EU Scientists Say," *Wall Street Journal* (May 4, 1999), p. A14; and "Furor over 'Frankenfood'," *Business Week* (October 18, 1999), pp. 50–51; and "U.S. Trade Panel Rejects Claim That Cold-Rolled Steel Was Dumped," *Wall Street Journal Interactive*, http://interactive.wsj.com/, March 3, 2000.

Governments respond to pressures from various forces in a country, including the public at large, lobbyists for businesses, the church, and sometimes the personal interests of the members of the government. In order to assess the political stability of a country, it is critical to evaluate the importance of major forces on the government of the country. Many developing countries have undertaken significant liberalization programs during the 1980s and 1990s.[32] Although these programs have been regularly promoted by the International Monetary Fund (IMF), their success during recent years must be attributed to a larger social acceptance of the potential benefits of necessary austerity measures. For example, one study has shown that the IMF's Structural Adjustment Program helped improve the economic efficiency of both domestic and foreign companies operating in Nigeria in the 1980s.[33] The benefits of liberalization extend beyond the borders of the countries involved. Consider the liberalization in Mexico, where the privatization of the state telephone company (TelMex) led to large investments by Southwestern Bell. Similarly, private companies are moving rapidly to finance other large public projects. An international consortium composed of Mexico's Grupo Hermés, the United States' AES Corp., and the Japanese firm Nichimen have begun to construct Mexico's first independent power-producing plant in Yucatán State.[34] Although liberalization may provide unprecedented opportunities, the forces of special interests or the backlash of public sentiment may also cause governments to limit or curtail entirely certain international business operations.

Social Pressures and Special Interests

Feelings of national interest can act as a deterrent both to international trade and to foreign direct investments. As a manifestation of nationalistic sentiment, a boycott may be organized by an interest group or even by a government agency to refuse to buy a certain foreign product or products. A boycott represents an outburst of anger expressed by the interest group to protest a foreign company's activities that do not agree with the value system of the interest group. For example, abortion is a politically sensitive issue in the United States. An abortion pill, RU 486, developed by Hoechst AG (Germany's chemical and pharmaceutical giant) and its French subsidiary, Roussel Uclaf SA, was about to be introduced into the U.S. market. Stepping up its protest against the imminent arrival of the pill, a coalition of anti-abortion groups tried to boycott eleven prescription and over-the-counter drug products made by Hoechst and its affiliates in the United States, including the drug Allegra, which replaced the company's second-largest selling product, Seldane, a popular allergy medicine. Obviously, foreign companies have to be aware of the national sentiment of people in a foreign market.[35] Global Perspective 5–2 presents another set of contrasting examples about the way two similar companies coped with such a crisis.

How should a manager evaluate the opportunities and risks a country presents? Obviously this depends on too many factors to discuss them all. A manager

---

[32]Kate Gillespie and Hildy J. Teegen, "Market Liberalization and International Alliance Formation," *Columbia Journal of World Business*, 31 (Winter 1996), pp. 40–54.

[33]Sam C. Okoroafo and Masaaki Kotabe, "The IMF's Structural Adjustment Program and Its Impact on Firm Performance: A Case of Foreign and Domestic Firms in Nigeria," *Management International Review*, 33 (2) (1993), pp. 139–56.

[34]"Mexico's Energy Infrastructure Expanding to Match Growth," *NAFTA Works* (February 1997), pp. 1–2.

[35]Douglas Lavin, "Hoechst Will Stop Making Abortion Pill," *Wall Street Journal* (April 9, 1997), p. A3.

◆ ◆

𝒢LOBAL PERSPECTIVE 5–2

HOW TWO COMPANIES HANDLED A POLITICALLY SENSITIVE CRISIS SITUATION

Burger King and McDonald's recently experienced a flare-up in politically sensitive areas of the world. The following is how those two global hamburger chains handled the similar volatile political situations.

BURGER KING

In the face of a boycott threat by Arab and Muslim groups in late 1999, Burger King Corp. decided to revoke a franchise agreement for a restaurant in the Israeli-occupied West Bank. Burger King maintained that the decision to cancel the agreement with its Israeli franchisee, Rikamor Ltd., was the result of Rikamor's breach of contract. Rikamor told Burger King that the restaurant would be located in Israel proper, not the disputed West Bank. Rikamor has been asked to remove the Burger King name from the restaurant, although the chain has no power to force the restaurant to close. A statement released by Burger King said it had made it clear that it "would not approve Rikamor opening restaurants in the West Bank at this sensitive time in the peace process." Now backed by Jewish settlers who long for brand-name legitimacy, Burger King's Israeli franchisee swore to fight the fast-food giant's break with a branch in a West Bank Jewish settlement. Angry Israeli settlers called for a worldwide boycott of Burger King restaurants and a halt to Israeli–Palestinian peace talks, after the chain canceled its franchise in Maale Adumim,

a Jewish settlement near Jerusalem. Burger King said its decision was purely commercial and that it does not take sides in the Arab–Israeli peace process. Israel captured the West Bank in 1967, and Jewish settlements, located throughout the territory, are at the center of the Middle East conflict. Palestinians say the West Bank settlements are illegal.

MCDONALD'S

At the outset of the NATO's air war against Yugoslavia during the Kosovo Crisis in 1999, McDonald's, as a quintessential American trademark, was forced to temporarily close its fifteen restaurants in Yugoslavia due to vandalism by angry Serbian mobs. But when local managers re-opened the doors shortly after, they accomplished an extraordinary comeback using an unusual marketing strategy. They put McDonald's U.S. citizenship on the back burner. To help overcome animosity toward an American icon, the local restaurants promoted the Mc-Country, a domestic pork burger with paprika garnish. As a national flourish to evoke Serbian identity and pride, they produced posters and lapel buttons showing the golden arches topped with a traditional Serbian cap called the sajkaca. They also handed out free cheeseburgers at anti-NATO rallies. The basement of one restaurant in the Serbian capital even served as a bomb shelter. Anti-NATO sentiment runs high in Yugoslavia among Serbs, but many Serbians now associate McDonald's with Serbia rather than the United States.

Different companies have different corporate philosophies. If you had been in charge of international operations for either Burger King or McDonald's, how would you have addressed these political crises?

Source: "Burger King Revokes a Franchise in the West Bank," CNN.com, http://www.cnn.com; and Robert Block, "How Big Mac Was Able to Refrain From Becoming a Serb Archenemy," *Wall Street Journal Interactive*, http://interactive.wsj.com, September 3, 1999.

---

should certainly consider the political history of the country, as well as the history of similar industries within the country. In the following section we will discuss a number of factors that international managers should consider when determining the economic and political risks associated with a country.

Managing the Political Environment

International managers must manage the political environment in which the international firm operates. This means, first and foremost, learning to follow the customs of the country in which the firm is operating. But managing the political environment also means knowing which facets of the foreign country must be carefully monitored, and which can be manipulated. If managed correctly, the political environment could become a marketing support system, rather than an inhibitor, for the foreign company.[36]

In order to make informed decisions, the marketing manager must understand the political factors of the country, and also must understand the national strategies and goals of the country. The political factors in a country include the political stability, the predominant ideology toward business (and foreign business in particular), the roles that institutions have in the country (including the church, government agencies, and the legal systems), and the international links to other countries' legal and ideological structures.[37]

In order to be welcomed in a host country, the foreign firm has to offer some tangible benefits that the host government desires. Thus, it is critical that a manger recognize what the host country government's motivations and goals are. Most international business activities offer something to all parties involved. If the host country is actively pursuing job-creation goals, then a foreign firm that can offer jobs has leverage for obtaining concessions against other problems. The manager will want to understand what national policies are being pursued, and what policy instruments the government typically uses to pursue its interests (see Exhibit 5–2).

It is important to carefully assess the political power structure and mood in a country before making decisions regarding business operations. By evaluating various environmental factors (see Exhibit 5–3), marketing managers can arrive at a more thorough understanding of the likelihood of various problems or opportunities in a country. As shown in Exhibit 5–4, managers can also purchase or subscribe to country risk ratings provided by various risk-analysis agencies such as the Economist Intelligence Unit (EIU), International Country Risk Guide, and Business Environment Risk Intelligence (BERI).[38]

Irrespective of categories employed in their risk ratings, there are three general types of risks involved in operating in a foreign country: risks associated with changes in company ownership, risks associated with changes in company operations, and risks associated with changes in transfers of goods and money. Changes in ownership structure are usually due to dramatic political changes, such as wars or coups d'etat. A company may face the expropriation or confiscation of its property, or it may face the nationalization of its industry. **Expropriation** refers to a foreign government's takeover of company goods, land, or other assets, with compensation that tends to fall short of their market value. **Confiscation** is an outright takeover of assets without compensation. **Nationalization** refers to a foreign government's takeover for the purpose of making the industry a government-run industry. In nationalization, companies usually receive some level of compensation for their losses.

To reduce risk of expropriation or confiscation of corporate assets overseas, many companies use joint ventures with local companies or adopt a domestication policy. Joint ventures with local companies imply shared activities and tend to

---

[36]Michael G. Harvey, Robert F. Lusch, and Branko Cavarkapa, "A Marketing Mix for the 21st Century," *Journal of Marketing Theory and Practice*, 4 (Fall 1996), pp. 1–15.

[37]James E. Austin, *Managing in Developing Countries: Strategic Analysis and Operating Techniques* (New York: Free Press, 1990).

[38]Arno Backer, "A Politico-Economic View of the Debt-Servicing Capacity of Emerging Economies," *Intereconomics*, 33 (September/October 1998), pp. 230–37.

EXHIBIT 5–2
GOVERNMENT POLICY AREAS AND INSTRUMENTS

		POLICY INSTRUMENTS		
		Legal	*Administrative*	*Direct-market operations*
POLICY AREAS	Monetary	• Banking reserve levels	• Loan guarantee • Credit regulation	• Money creation
	Fiscal	• Tax rates • Subsidies	• Tax collection	• Government purchases
	Trade	• Government import controls	• Import quotas • Tariffs • Exchange rates and controls	• Government imports
	Foreign Investment	• Ownership laws	• Profit repatriation controls • Investment approvals	• Government joint ventures
	Incomes	• Labor laws	• Price controls • Wage controls	• Government wages
	Sectoral	• Land tenure laws	• Industry licensing • Domestic content	• State-owned enterprises

Source: Adapted from James E. Austin, *Managing in Developing Countries: Strategic Analysis and Operating Techniques* (New York: Free Press, 1990), p. 89. Reprinted with permission.

EXHIBIT 5–3
COUNTRY RISK ASSESSMENT CRITERIA

Index Area	*Criteria*
Political and economic environment	Stability of the political system Degree of control of economic system Constitutional guarantees Effectiveness of public administration Labor relations and social peace
Domestic economic conditions	Population size Per capita income Economic growth during previous five years Inflation during previous two years Accessibility of domestic capital market to foreigners Availability of high-quality local labor Possibility of giving employment to foreign nationals Legal requirements for environment Traffic system and communication channels
External economic relations	Restrictions imposed on imports Restrictions imposed on exports Restrictions imposed on foreign investments in the country Legal protection for brands and products Restrictions imposed on monetary transfers Revaluations of currency during previous five years Drain on foreign funds through oil or other energy imports Restrictions on the exchange of local money into foreign currencies

Source: Adapted from E. Dichtl and H. G. Koglmayr, *"Country Risk Ratings," Management International Review*, 26 (4) (1986), p. 6.

EXHIBIT 5–4

EXAMPLES OF COUNTRY RISK RATINGS

Country*	Political Risk	Financial Risk	Economic Risk	Composite Risk
1. Switzerland	92	50	43	94
2. Germany	83	49	41	87
3. Japan	85	49	42	88
4. United States	83	49	38	85
5. Canada	83	46	39	84
6. United Kingdom	81	48	36	82
7. France	80	44	38	81
8. Italy	74	44	37	77
9. Mexico	68	32	28	64
10. Hong Kong	67	41	39	74
11. China	67	39	33	69
12. India	49	30	31	55
13. Argentina	62	23	21	53
14. Romania**	55	29	15	49.5
15. Liberia**	10	8	12	15

Note: * Lower scores represent higher risk (highest risk = 1, lowest risk = 100).
  **Data from 1991.

Source: Extracted from *International Country Risk Guide*, 1996, reprinted in Claude B. Erb, Campbell R. Harvey, and Tadas E. Viskanta, "Expected Returns and Volatility in 135 Countries," *Journal of Portfolio Management*, 22 (Spring 1996), p. 46.

reduce nationalistic sentiment against the company operating in a foreign country. **Domestication policy** (also known as **phase-out policy**) refers to a company gradually turning over management and operational responsibilities, as well as ownership, to local companies over time.

However, these risks have been reduced in recent years, as many countries have realized the need for international support in order to receive the loans and investment they need to prosper. Consequently, the number of privatizations of once government-owned industries has increased in the last decade.[39]

Other changes in operating regulations can make production unprofitable. For example, local-content requirements may force a company to use inputs of higher cost or inferior quality, making its products uncompetitive. Price controls may set limits on the sales price for a company's goods that are too low to recover investments made. Restrictions on the number of foreign employees may force a company to train local citizens in techniques that require years of specialization.

Shifts in regulations on the transfer of goods and money can also dramatically affect the profitability of operating in a country. These changes include exchange rate restrictions or devaluations, input restrictions, and output price fixing. If a country is experiencing a shortage of foreign capital, it may limit the sale of foreign currencies to companies that need to buy some inputs from abroad or repatriate

---

[39]Michael S. Minor, "The Demise of Expropriation as an Instrument of LDC Policy, 1980–1992," *Journal of International Business Studies*, 25 (First Quarter 1994), pp. 177–88; Douglas L. Bartley and Michael S. Minor, "Privatization in Eastern Europe: A Field Report," *Competitiveness Review*, 6 (2) (1996), pp. 31–43; and John Nellis, "Time to Rethink Privatization in Transition Economies," *Finance & Development*, 36 (June 1999), pp. 16–19.

profits back home. Faced with such foreign exchange restrictions, companies have developed creative, if not optimal, means to deal with the foreign exchange restrictions. **Countertrade** is a frequently used method that involves trading of products without involving direct monetary payments. For example, in order to expand its operations in Russia, the Russian subsidiary of PepsiCo needed to import bottling equipment from the United States. However, the Russian government did not allow the company to exchange rubles for dollars, so it exported Russian vodka to the United States to earn enough dollars to import the needed equipment.

◆ ◆ ◆ ◆ ◆ ◆ INTERNATIONAL AGREEMENTS

International politics has always been characterized by the predominance of strong ideological links, centered around, and dominated by, a relatively small number of large powers. After World War II, those links centered on the two contending superpowers, the United States and the former Soviet Union. However, recently the hierarchical structure of world politics has been challenged by two processes.

First, the true independence of previously colonial countries has led to a much larger set of nations playing relatively independently on the international stage, entering into contracts and relations with new political and economic partners. Second, the loosening of the tight bipolarity in world politics, combined with the relative decline of the United States as the economic superpower in the free world and the breakup of the Soviet Union that had once led the communist world, has created an increased level of ambiguity in geopolitical stability.[40]

While most nations guard their independence by maintaining the ability to produce critical products domestically, citizens around the world have learned to expect and demand the lifestyle that international trade provides. Thus, domestic politics cannot be isolated from international politics. Political actions in one country will eventually influence the actions of other countries. For example, Mexico's recent decision to devalue its currency caused U.S. exports to Mexico to decrease. If the industries that are harmed by the decrease in sales have enough political force, they might ask the U.S. government to pressure Mexico to invest in strengthening its currency or face trade repercussions.

Not only do nations react to each other's actions, they develop relationships that determine their future actions. They form networks for achieving mutual goals, and they develop political and trade histories and dependencies that influence their perceptions of the world. Thus, the international political environment is determined by a dynamic process of the interactions of players each pursuing their own interests and working together for mutual interests. Coordination is required, for example, in order to establish and maintain a trade embargo as a viable alternative to military force. Similarly, coordination is required to avoid harmful currency devaluations or the financial insolvency of governments. The level at which governments rely on each other and are affected by each other's actions also leads to regular conflicts and tensions. Indeed, history has shown that a war—the ultimate

---

[40]Tom Nierop, *Systems and Regions in Global Politics—An Empirical Study of Diplomacy, International Organization and Trade, 1950–1991* (New York: Wiley, 1994).

form of international conflicts and tensions—is less likely to occur between two countries, the more trade they engage in with each other.[41]

The roles of the General Agreement on Tariffs and Trade (GATT) and the World Trade Organization that succeeded GATT in 1995 were explained earlier as part of the economic environment in Chapter 2. We limit our discussion to two major international agreements that have shaped and will reshape the political economies of the world.

The **G7** is an economic policy coordination group made up of political leaders from Canada, England, France, Germany, Italy, Japan, and the United States. The G7 began during the economic crises of the mid-1970s.[42] Russia joined the G7 in 1997; the group consisting of the original G7 and Russia is known as the **G8**. Heads of state, senior economic ministers, and heads of central banks typically meet once a year to further economic coordination. G7 meetings have primarily dealt with financial and macroeconomic issues (such as the Asian and Latin American financial crises), but since Russia's participation, the G8 has included some politically sensitive issues, such as an effort to make arrangements for the reconstruction of Kosovo—and indeed of the Balkan states as a whole—after the Kosovo conflict.[43]

G7 (Group of Seven) and G8 (Group of Eight)

The G8 provides a good example of the role and limitations of multinational agreements and economic groupings in the years to come. The 1990s reflected some of the limitations of coordinated actions, especially at a micro level. Recent coordinated actions of the federal banks of the G7 countries, in a bid to affect exchange rates, have had limited impact on the foreign exchange markets. At best, they have moderated the speed of the movements of exchange rates, rather than the extent of the movements. The primary reason is that the volume of foreign exchange traded on the exchanges worldwide far outstrips the combined resources of the federal banks. A recent report of the G7 finance ministers acknowledged that federal banks can only play a limited role through direct intervention in the markets.

However, a role in which coordinated action is believed to be feasible and effective is in ensuring adherence to world accepted political agendas. One example is on the issue of protection of human rights. The United States has had limited success in ensuring protection of human rights in China. Unilateral measures and bilateral negotiations have resulted in little change of China's human rights record. However, the United States is now determined to use the G8 forum to coordinate the action of the developed countries in linking China's trade status in all eight countries to its human rights record.

COCOM was founded in 1949 to stop the flow of Western technology to the former Soviet Union. Australia, Japan, and the NATO countries (except Iceland) are members. For example, even when U.S. franchises were already operating in the former Soviet Union, it was illegal to export personal computers for them to use!

COCOM (The Coordinating Committee for Multilateral Controls)

[41]Edward D. Mansfield, *Power, Trade, and War* (Princeton, NJ: Princeton University Press, 1994).

[42]Philip G. Cerny, ed., *Finance and World Politics: Markets, Regimes and States in the Post-hegemonic Era* (Cambridge, England: University Press, 1993).

[43]Michael Elliott, "What We Owe Them," *Newsweek* (June 21, 1999), p. 22.

The initial emphasis of COCOM was on all technology products. Subsequently, the focus shifted to various types of dual-purpose hardware and software technology products—that is, products that could be used for civilian as well as military purposes. Two trends, however, started exerting pressure on the policies adopted by COCOM. First, technologies that had primarily military applications were increasingly finding more civilian applications. Satellites, computers, and telecommunication technologies were prime examples of this trend. Second, the trend of economic liberalization in the newly industrializing and developing countries put further competitive pressures on Western companies to share technologies that were until then privy to the Western world. U.S. firms were particularly adversely affected. Many U.S. companies, including the large telecommunications companies, complained to the government that the restrictions were outdated and that they were losing valuable contracts to competitors from countries without such restrictions.

In 1992, COCOM reevaluated its mission and loosened restrictions on exports of computers, telecommunications equipment, machine tools, and other materials that might assist the newly independent nations of Eastern Europe and the former Soviet republics in their effort to develop market-driven economies. Due to the changed political and economic environment, COCOM ceased to exist in 1994. However, the spirit of the committee still lives on. There is a move to establish a new multilateral system, tentatively addressed by the name *New World Forum*, to replace COCOM. Two issues of primary importance for being considered within this multilateral system are nuclear technologies and missile (especially ballistic missile) technologies. Besides COCOM, the United States has used domestic legislatures to control exports of dual-use technologies through the U.S. Export Administrative Act. The act officially expired as of November 1995, but restrictions have still been maintained in the spirit of the act. Even today, the United States forbids the export of such generally available technology as software for encoding electronic messages and semiconductor-manufacturing equipment.[44]

◆ ◆ ◆ ◆ ◆ ◆ INTERNATIONAL LAW AND LOCAL LEGAL ENVIRONMENT

International marketing managers should understand two legal environments—the legal environment in each country in which they do business, and the more general international legal environment. At a macro level, international law and the bodies that evaluate it affect high-level international disputes and influence the form of lower-level arbitration and decisions. Local laws and legal systems directly determine the legal procedures for doing business in a foreign country. Local laws also determine the settlement of most international business conflicts—the country whose laws are used is determined by the jurisdiction for the contract.

---

[44]Anthony Cataldo and George Leopold, "China Feels Chill as Trade Tensions Rise," *Electronic Engineering Times* (March 22, 1999).

International law, or *the law of nations*, may be defined as a body of rules that is binding on states and other international persons in their mutual relations. Most nations and international bodies have voluntarily agreed to subjugate themselves to some level of constraint for the purpose of living in a world in which order, and not chaos, is the governing principle. In short, international law represents "gentlemen's agreements" among countries.

International Law

Although, technically speaking, there is no enforceable body of international law,[45] international customs, treaties, and court decisions establish a defined international legal environment. International bodies and policies exist for arbitrating cases that cannot be settled fairly in any given country.

International law comes from three main sources—*customs*, international *treaties*, and national and international *court decisions*. Customs are usages or practices that have become so firmly accepted that they become rules of law. For example, nations have historically claimed sovereignty over the resources in their offshore continental shelves. This historical practice has developed into a consensus that amounts to an international law. Custom-based laws develop slowly.

Treaties and international contracts represent formal agreements among nations or firms that set down rules and obligations to govern their mutual relationships. Treaties and contracts are only binding on those who are members to them, but if a great number of treaties or contracts share similar stipulations, these may take on the character of a custom-based law or a general rule.

National courts often make rulings in cases that apply to international issues. When these rulings offer an unusually useful insight into the settlement of international cases, or when they develop into a series of interpretations consistent with other nations' courts, then national rulings may be accepted as international laws. If the issue of conflict is one where a national court is not acceptable to one or both parties, international courts and tribunals may rule. International tribunals may be turned to for **arbitration** if the parties agree to let the case be tried. The International Court of Justice was established by the United Nations to settle international conflicts between nations, not between individual parties (such as firms) across national boundaries. However, it must be again noted that international court rulings do not establish precedent, as they might in the United States, but rather, apply only to the case at hand.

Legal systems and the laws they create differ dramatically in countries around the world. Many legal systems do not follow the common law system followed in the United States. We discuss a number of different legal systems and the types of laws that govern contracts and business in each system. We also discuss the issue of jurisdiction, which determines the critical issue of what courts, and what laws, are used in deciding a legal question. For most business issues, international law is primarily a question of which national laws apply and how to apply them to cases involving international contracts, shipping, or parties.

Local Legal Systems and Laws

---

[45]The government of a sovereign nation stipulates its laws with policing authority. Since there is no supranational government, no supranational (i.e., international) laws are binding. Although the United Nations is the most comprehensive political body, made up of more than 100 member nations, it is not a sovereign state, and therefore does not have enforceable laws that the member nations have to abide by other than voluntarily.

The laws that govern behavior within a country, as well as the laws that govern the resolution of international contractual disputes, are primarily local, or municipal, laws. Foreign subsidiaries and expatriate employees live within the legal bounds of their host countries' legal systems. Although U.S. embassy property is considered U.S. territory no matter where it is located, in general, companies and their employees must live within the local country laws. The inability of the U.S. government in 1994 to change the Singapore government's punishment by caning of Michael Fay, an American teenager charged of vandalism there, illustrates a clear example of the sovereignty of each country's laws.[46] The international marketing manager must be aware of the laws that will govern all business decisions and contracts.

Business Practices and the Legal System. Businesses face a myriad of legal issues every day. Questions relating to such issues as pricing policies and production practices must be clearly answered in order to avoid legal reproachment and punishment. Choices relating to legal industry constraints and various regulations on product specifications, promotional activities, and distribution must be understood in order to function efficiently and profitably. Legal systems in each country deal with these questions differently. For a brief summary of legal issues facing companies, see Exhibit 5–5.

For example, in many parts of the world, automobiles with engines larger than 2,000 cc displacement face a much stiffer commodity tax than those with smaller engines. Under the strict water purity law in Germany, foreign beers that contain any other additive or ingredient than the German law permits may not be exported to Germany. In China, the government allows passenger cars to be priced only in the range of $15,600 to $26,000. By law, foreign auto manufacturers can neither underprice their cars below $15,600 nor overprice them above $26,000. Due to recent cost inflation in China and due also to their low production volume, few foreign auto manufacturers can realize profits.[47] In Japan, the Large-Scale Retail Store Law, which regulated the retail store size, made it difficult for large U.S. retailers, such as Toys 'R' Us, to expand its retail distribution channel in the 1990s, although a new and revised Large-Scale Retail Store Law is expected to make determinations about the suitability of large retail stores based on an assessment of local environmental problems as opposed to the impact of new large retail stores on local businesses.[48]

In some countries it is illegal to mention a competitor's name in an advertisement. In some countries that follow Islamic law, it is even illegal to borrow money or charge interest! However, businesses need financial resources to grow; thus, they must learn how to acquire the resources they need within the legal limits established by the country in which they are operating. For example, in Pakistan, importers and exporters of raw materials rely on a technique that is known as *murabaha* to avoid the ban on interest. In this arrangement, a bank buys goods and sells them to customers, who then pay the bank at a future date and at a markup

---

[46]"Singapore's Prime Minister Denounces Western Society," *Wall Street Journal* (August 22, 1994), p. A8.

[47]"WTO Intimidates Chinese Auto Makers," *Wall Street Journal* (May 7, 1999), p. A16.

[48]Jack G. Kaikati, "The Large-Scale Retail Store Law," in Michael R. Czinkota and Masaaki Kotabe, *Japanese Distribution Strategy* (London, U.K.: Business Press, 2000), pp. 54–63.

EXHIBIT 5–5

LEGAL ISSUES FACING THE COMPANY

Type of Decision	Issue
Pricing decisions	Price fixing
	Deceptive pricing
Packaging decisions	Pollution regulations
	Fair packaging and labeling
Product decisions	Patent protection
	Warranty requirements
	Product safety
Competitive decisions	Barriers to entry
	Anticompetitive collusion
Selling decisions	Bribery
	Stealing trade secrets
Production decisions	Wages and benefits
	Safety requirements
Channel decisions	Dealers' rights
	Exclusive territorial distributor-ships

Source: Adapted from Kottler, Philip and Gary Armstrong, *Principles of Marketing*, 8th ed. (Englewood Cliffs, N.J.: Prentice Hall), 1998.

agreed upon by the bank and its customer. In Indonesia, credit card companies such as Visa and MasterCard receive collateral assets, such jewelry and cattle, which they can sell, from card users instead of charging interest.[49]

In recent years, some countries have started raising legal requirements for environmental protection. In Japan, the famed just-in-time delivery system, such as the one practiced by Toyota and 7-Eleven Japan, has been criticized as causing traffic congestion and air pollution. Laws are being considered to reduce the just-in-time practices.[50] **Green marketing** has become fashionable in an increasing number of countries. It is marketers' reaction to governments' and concerned citizens' increased call for reduction of unnecessary packaging materials and increased recycling and recyclability of materials used in the products. Recent developments in the European Union threaten to utilize environmental standards to control internal and external trade in consumer products. Marketers who do not conform may be restricted from participation. Meanwhile, those marketers who do meet the requirements enjoy the benefits of reduced competition and growing market share.[51]

---

[49]Kirk Albrecht, "Turning the Prophet's Words into Profits," *Business Week*, International Edition (March 16, 1998), p. 46; and also see Clement M. Henry, ed., "Special Issue: Islamic Banking," in *Thunderbird International Business Review*, 41 (July/August and September/October 1999).

[50]Eiji Shiomi, Hiroshi Nomura, Garland Chow, and Katsuhiro Niiro, "Physical Distribution and Freight Transportation in the Tokyo Metropolitan Area," *Logistics and Transportation Review*, 29 (December 1993), pp. 335–43.

[51]Barry N. Rosen and George B. Sloane, III, "Environmental Product Standards, Trade and European Consumer Goods Marketing: Processes, Threats and Opportunities," *Columbia Journal of World Business*, 30 (Spring 1995), pp. 74–86.

Regulations on E-Commerce. Local business laws also affect the use of the Internet. Although there are no measurable restrictions for e-commerce in the United States, it is not the case in foreign countries. For example, in Germany, there are strict regulations about providing "digital signatures" to ensure security when making purchases over the Internet.[52] Likewise, France has regulated that the use of *cookies* (software or hardware that identifies the user) should only be allowed when consent is granted.[53]

On the other hand, Singapore is introducing landmark legislation to boost the island republic's reputation as a safe harbor for e-commerce by creating a kind of uniform commercial code governing major aspects of trade via the Internet. The legislation sets out a process whereby electronic contracts can be digitally signed; sets an encryption standard to ensure security; and creates independent clearing-houses to authenticate the identities of sellers and buyers in a transaction. This local law is designed to attract Internet content companies to locate in Singapore.[54]

Types of Legal Systems. Four principal legal systems are used in the majority of counties: common law systems, code law systems, Islamic law systems, and social-ist law systems. **Common law** systems base the interpretation of law on prior court rulings—that is, legal precedents and customs of the time. The majority of the states in the United States follow common law systems (Louisiana is an exception). **Code (written) law** systems rely on statutes and codes for the interpretation of the law. In essence, there is very little "interpretation" in a code law system—the law must be detailed enough to prescribe appropriate and inappropriate actions. The majority of the world's governments rely on some form of code law system. **Islamic law** systems rely on the legal interpretation of the Koran and the words of Mo-hammed. Unlike common and code law systems, which hold that law should be manmade and can be improved through time, Islamic legal systems hold that God established a "natural law" that embodies all justice. Finally, **socialist laws**, devel-oped in the ex-Soviet Union after the Russian Revolution of 1917 and later assimi-lated by other communist states, are distinguished from other legal systems by the influence of state ownership of the means of production, the pervasive influence of the Communist Party, and the ties between the legal system and national central planning. Since the breakup of the Soviet Union, socialist laws have mostly faded from world political systems, except in countries such as Cuba and North Korea.

Legal systems address both criminal and civil law. Criminal law addresses stealing and other illegal activities. **Civil law** addresses the enforcement of con-tracts and other procedural guidelines. Civil laws regulating business contracts and transactions are usually called **commercial law**. International businesses are gener-ally more concerned with differences in commercial laws across different countries. For example, who is responsible if a shipper delivers goods that are not up to stan-dards and the contract fails to address the issue? What if the ship on which goods are being transported is lost at sea? What if goods arrive so late as to be worthless? What if a government limits foreign participation in a construction project after a foreign company has spent millions of dollars designing the project?

---

[52]Marcia Macleod, "Analysis: European E-Commerce Stands Divided," *Network News* (April 28, 1999), p. 14.

[53]John Leyden, "Online Data Protection Incites Worry," *Network News* (May 5, 1999), p. 4.

[54]Jim Erickson, "Taming the Wild Internet: Singapore Wants to Make E-Commerce Safer," *Asia Week* (July 17, 1998), p. 72.

EXHIBIT 5–6
THE NUMBER OF
LAWYERS PER 10,000
RESIDENTS

United States	307.4
Britain	102.7
Germany	82.0
Japan	12.1

Source: Michele Galen, Alice Cuneo, and David Greising, "Guilty," *Business Week* (April 13, 1992), pp. 60–65.

Sometimes the boundary between criminal and civil law will also be different across countries. For example, are the officers of a company liable for actions that take place while they are "on duty"? When a chemical tank leak in Bhopal, India, killed thousands of Indian citizens in 1984, it was not clear whether the officers of Union Carbide were criminally liable.[55]

Cultural Values and Legal Systems. In Japan, legal confrontations are very rare. As shown in Exhibit 5–6, Japan's population of lawyers is low, which makes it difficult to obtain evidence from legal opponents. Also, rules against class-action suits and contingency-fee arrangements make it difficult to bring suit against a person or company. There are disadvantages to Japan's system, but it supports the cultural value of building long-term business ties based on trust.

In the United States, there is a strong belief in the use of explicit contracts and a reliance on the legal system to resolve problems in business. In other countries, such as China, a businessperson who tries to cover all possible problems or contingencies in a contract may be viewed as untrustworthy. Chinese culture values relationships (known as *guanxi*) and therefore relies more heavily on trust and verbal contracts than does U.S. culture.[56] In Brazil, however, there is a value system different from both the United States' explicit contractual agreement and China's mutual trust and verbal contract. The Brazilian value system is known as *Jeitinho*, in which people believe that they can always find a solution outside the legal contract on a case-by-case basis.[57] If a culture does not respect the value of following through on an obligation, no legal system, whether written or verbal, will afford enough protection to make doing business easy.

Because there is no body of international law in the strictly legalistic sense, the key to evaluating an international contract is by determining which country's laws will apply, and where any conflicts must be resolved.

Jurisdiction

---

[55]Robert D. McFadden, "Labor and Class-Action Lawyer is Dead," *New York Times* (January 1, 1996), Section 1, p. 32.

[56]Steve Lovett, Lee C. Simmons, and Raja Kali, "Guanxi Versus the Market: Ethics and Efficiency," *Journal of International Business Studies*, 30 (Second Quarter 1999), pp. 231–48.

[57]Margaret Grieco and Richard Whipp, "Dismantling Logics of Action," *International Studies of Management and Organization*, 21 (Winter 1991), pp. 78–85.

Planning Ahead. By far the easiest way to ensure what laws will apply in a contract is to clearly state the applicable law in the contract. If both a home country producer and a foreign distributor agree that the producer's national laws of contracts will apply to a contract for the sale of goods, then both can operate with a similar understanding of the legal requirements they face. Similarly, to ensure a venue that will interpret these laws in an expected manner, international contracts should stipulate the location of the court or arbitration system that will be relied upon for resolving conflicts that arise.

If contracts fail to specify the jurisdiction of the contract, it is not so clear which laws apply. Courts may use the laws where the contract is made. Alternatively, courts may apply the laws where the contract is fulfilled.

Arbitration and Enforcement. Due to the differences in international legal systems, and the difficulty and length of litigating over a conflict, many international contracts rely on a prearranged system of arbitration for settling any conflict. Arbitration may be by a neutral party, and both parties agree to accept any rulings.

However, if one of the parties does not fulfill its contracted requirements and does not respond to or accept arbitration, there is little the injured party can do. There is no "international police" to force a foreign company to pay damages.

◆ ◆ ◆ ◆ ◆ ◆ ISSUES TRANSCENDING NATIONAL BOUNDARIES

ISO 9000 and 14000 In a bid to establish common product standards for quality management, so as to obviate their misuse to hinder the exchange of goods and services worldwide, the International Standards Organization (based in Geneva, Switzerland) has instituted a set of process standards. Firms who conform to these standards are certified and registered with International Standards Organizations. This common standard is designated **ISO 9000**. The ISO 9000 series was developed by its Technical Committee on Quality Assurance and Quality Management between 1979 and 1986 and was published in 1987. The series has been adopted widely by U.S. companies. The adoption of the ISO 9000 standards by member countries of the European Union has spurred widespread interest in companies worldwide to obtain this certification if they intend to trade with the European Union.

One of the reasons for the spurt of interest in ISO 9000 is the decision by the European Union to adopt ISO standards; the other main reason is the acknowledgment of the importance of quality by companies worldwide. It must be highlighted that ISO 9000 is not only concerned with standardized systems and procedures for manufacturing, but for all the activities of firms. These activities include management responsibility, quality systems, contract reviews, design control, document control, purchasing, product identification and tracing, (manufacturing) process control, inspection and testing, control of nonconforming products and necessary corrective actions, handling, storage, packaging and delivering, recordkeeping, internal quality audits, training, and servicing.

With the growing adoption of the ISO 9000 standards by firms worldwide, an ISO 9000 certification has become an essential marketing tool for firms. Firms that have it will be able to convince prospective buyers of their ability to maintain strict quality requirements. Firms that do not have ISO 9000 certification will increasingly be at a disadvantage relative to other competitors, not only in Europe but in most parts of the world.

Over the past decade, the need to pursue sustainable development has been at the center of discussion of environmental issues and economic development. Attainment of sustainable development was articulated as a goal in 1987 by the World Commission on the Environment and Development (World Commission), a body established by the United Nations. The World Commission defined *sustainable development* as development that "meets the needs of the present without compromising the ability of future generations to meet their own needs." Sustainable development was the focus of discussion at the United Nations Conference on the Environment and Development held in Rio de Janeiro in 1992, and its attainment was articulated as a goal in the Environmental Side Agreement to the North American Free Trade Agreement (NAFTA). In 1996, the International Organization for Standardization (ISO) named the attainment of sustainable development as a major goal in its new ISO 14000 Series Environmental Management Standards. The ISO 9000 standards served as a model for the ISO 14000 series.

The **ISO 14000** standards are receiving significant amounts of attention from business managers and their legal and economic advisors. Business managers view ISO 14000 as a market-driven approach to environmental protection that provides an alternative to "command and control" regulation by government. Businesses view implementation of ISO 14000 as a means to *self-regulate*, thereby minimizing their exposure to surveillance and sanctions by the U.S. Environmental Protection Agency and its state-level counterparts. For example, ISO 14000 is already strengthening chemical companies' relations with plant communities by providing third-party audits of a plant's environmental systems. It is an efficient way to show the community that companies are making environmental improvements. Therefore, any person or organization interested in environmental protection or business management should become familiar with the provisions and potential ramifications of ISO 14000.[58]

Intellectual Property Protection

Few topics in international business have attracted as much attention and discussion in recent years as intellectual property rights.[59] A recent news story, such as the discovery of a pirate video operation in the residence of Thailand's minister, presents a blatant violation of intellectual property rights. Unbeknown to Thailand's prime minister, a group of soldiers were using his official residence as a warehouse to store thousands of fake video compact disks, or VCDs, manufactured at a separate site. The size and reach of Southeast Asia's pirate VCD industry has exploded over the past year due to new digital technology and has skimmed billions of dollars from Hollywood. Analysts say 92 percent of the CDs sold in

[58]Paulette L. Stenzel, "Can the ISO 14000 Series Environmental Management Standards Provide a Viable Alternative to Government Regulation?" Working paper, Michigan State University, 1999.

[59]Clifford J. Shultz III and Bill Saporito, "Protecting Intellectual Property: Strategies and Recommendations to Deter Counterfeiting and Brand Piracy in Global Markets," *Columbia Journal of World Business*, 31 (Spring 1996), pp. 19–27.

Thailand are illegal copies—one of the highest percentages in the world, next to China, Russia, and Indonesia. Sales of pirated CDs in Thailand now top $90 million a year, with the bulk coming from fake copies of Hollywood blockbusters.[60]

Intellectual property refers to "ideas that are translated into tangible products, writings, and so on, and that are protected by the state for a limited period of time from unauthorized commercial exploitation."[61] Intellectual property rights broadly include patents, trademarks, trade secrets, and copyrights. These ideas typically involve large investments in creative and investigative work to create the product, but fairly low costs of manufacturing. As such, they are amenable to being duplicated readily by imitators. Imitation reduces the potential returns that would have accrued to the innovator, thereby limiting its ability to appropriate the large investments made. With increasing movements of goods and services across borders, the potential loss of revenues to innovator firms, most of which reside in industrialized countries, is significant. U.S. companies reportedly lose more than $50 billion a year as a result of inadequate protection from foreign infringement of intellectual property rights.[62] Governments of the developed countries, whose firms are losing the most, have been taking various steps at bilateral and multilateral levels. The United States has linked granting China most favored nation status for imports of Chinese-made products to the effective enactment and implementation of intellectual property rights, especially for entertainment products. This is bilateral action. On a multilateral level, an example is the agreement on **Trade-related aspects of intellectual property rights**, commonly known as the **TRIPs** agreement under the newly constituted World Trade Organization. An increasing number of developing countries have begun to endorse the TRIPs agreement in order to attract international investment through comprehensive and clear patent laws for ideas and innovation. For example, in 1996, Brazil signed into law the most far-reaching and forward-looking intellectual property protection of any nation in South America.[63]

Patent. Patent laws in the United States and Japan provide an example of the differences in laws across countries and their implications for corporations.[64] The most significant difference between the two countries is on the **first-to-file** and **first-to-invent principles**. Although most countries follow the first-to-file principle, only the United States (along with the Philippines) follows the first-to-invent principle. In the majority of countries, the patent is granted to the first person filing an application for the patent. In the United States, however, the patent is granted to the person who first invented the product or technology. Any patents granted prior to the filing of the patent application by the "real" inventor would be reversed in order to protect the rights of the inventor. The difference between the two principles is no small matter. See Global Perspective 5–3 for far-reaching implications.

---

[60]Robert Frank, "Thai Piracy Scandal Shows Scope of Industry in Asia," *Wall Street Journal Interactive*, http://interactive.wsj.com, October 26, 1999.

[61]Belay Sayoum, "The Impact of Intellectual Property Rights on Foreign Direct Investment," *Columbia Journal of World Business*, 31 (Spring 1996), pp. 51–59.

[62]Maxine Lans Retsky, "Curbing Foreign Infringement," *Marketing News* (March 31, 1997), p. 10.

[63]"Pfizer Forum: Brazil's Landmark Intellectual Property Law," *Economist* (March 22, 1997), p. 63.

[64]Masaaki Kotabe, "A Comparative Study of U.S. and Japanese Patent Systems," *Journal of International Business Studies*, 23 (First Quarter 1992), pp. 147–68.

*G*LOBAL PERSPECTIVE 5–3

TWO WORLDS APART: THE FIRST-TO-INVENT PRINCIPLE VERSUS THE FIRST-TO-FILE PRINCIPLE

FIRST TO FILE VERSUS FIRST TO INVENT

A fifteen-member advisory commission, consisting of corporate executives, lawyers, and academics, was appointed by then-Secretary of Commerce Mosbacher in 1990 to examine the virtues of the U.S. first-to-invent principle vis-à-vis the first-to-file principle espoused in the rest of the world. The commission's most controversial recommendation involved changing the law to award patents to the first to file. The first-to-invent principle had has guided the awarding of U.S. patents since Thomas Jefferson looked at the first ones filed in 1790.

Under current U.S. law, applicants for a patent must prove that they had the idea first, not simply that they won the race to the courthouse. An applicant can assert first priority to the invention at any time, and is entitled to a patent if thereafter he or she has not "suppressed, abandoned, or concealed" the invention. The U.S. system was established to protect inventors who lack the resources to keep up a stream of patent applications merely to invoke their priority. Not surprisingly, the system is championed today by resource-poor universities and independent inventors.

Supporters of the 'first-to-file' system, largely lawyers and corporations, argue that it would better serve the public because it is simpler and conforms with the systems in the rest of the world. Moreover, it would spur inventors to file for patents earlier and to disclose their inventions sooner, thus speeding the progression from idea to finished product. Many supporters also note that most U.S. companies are equipped to act on a first-to-file basis, since they typically apply for patents as soon as inventions are produced. With the adoption of the first-to-file system, this date would also affect patent rights abroad, and thus provide greater reliability for U.S. patents worldwide.

Source: Lee Edson, "Patent Wars," *Across the Board*, 30 (April 1993), pp. 24–29.

Many are apprehensive about such a change. The principal objection to the first-to-file system is that it fosters premature, sketchy disclosure in hastily filed applications, letting the courts work things out later. Although unlikely, it leaves the possibility of someone stealing the profits of an invention from the true inventor by beating him to the courthouse steps. In the end, the Patent Office could be deluged with applications filed for defensive purposes, as is the case in Japan, where this phenomenon is called *patent flooding*.

Sensitive to these criticisms, the commission recommended several other reforms to ensure fairness in implementing the first-to-file proposal. These reforms include issuing a provisional patent application at reduced cost while the patent itself is undergoing examination, and establishing a grace period for public disclosure without affecting patentability. Most importantly, the commission suggested adopting the rule of "prior-use right," allowing users of inventions to continue their use under certain conditions, even after a patent on the invention is obtained by another party.

The effect of first-to-file versus first-to-invent may be best illustrated by the case of the laser, a discovery generally credited to physicist Charles Townes, who won a Nobel Prize for elucidating the principle of the maser, the theoretical father of the laser. Townes owned the patent on the device. Years later, Gordon Gould, a former graduate student at Columbia University, where Townes taught physics, proved by contemporary notebooks and other means that he had developed the idea long before Townes patented it in 1958.

Gould could not have brought his case to the courts in foreign countries that give priority to the first to file. In the United States, however, the court accepted Gould's evidence of priority and awarded him the basic patents to the laser in 1977 and 1979, ruling that Townes and his employer, at the time AT&T had infringed on Gould's idea. Patlex Corp., of which Gould is a director, now collects fees from laser users throughout the world.

The marketing implications of this difference for U.S. companies as well as foreign companies are significant. To protect any new proprietary technologies, U.S. companies must ensure that their inventions are protected abroad through formal patent applications being filed in various countries, especially the major foreign markets and the markets of competitors and potential competitors. For foreign companies operating in the United States, the implications are that they must be extremely careful in introducing any technologies that have been invented in the United States. A "first-to-file" mentality could result in hasty patent applications and significant financial burden in the form of lawsuits that could be filed by competitors that claim to have invented the technology earlier.

Copyright. Copyrights protect original literary, dramatic, musical, artistic, and certain other intellectual works. (A computer program, for example, is considered a literary work.) A **copyright** provides its owner the exclusive right to reproduce and distribute the material or perform or display it publicly, although limited reproduction of copyrighted works by others may be permitted for fair use purposes. In the United States, the use of the copyright notice does not require advance permission, or registration with, the Copyright Office. In fact, many countries offer copyright protection without registration, while others offer little or no protection for the works of foreign nationals.[65]

Trademark. A **trademark** is a word, symbol, or device that identifies the source of goods and may serve as an index of quality. It is used primarily to differentiate or distinguish a product or service from another. Trademark laws are used to prevent others from offering a product or service with a confusingly similar mark. In the United States, registration is not mandatory, since *prior use* technically determines the rightful owner of a trademark. However, because determining who used the trademark prior to anyone else is difficult and subject to lawsuits, trademark registration is highly recommended. In most foreign countries, registration is mandatory for a trademark to be protected. In this sense, the legal principle that applies to trademarks is similar to the one that applies to patents: the *first-to-use* principle in the United States and the *first-to-file* principle in most other countries. Therefore, if companies are expected to do business overseas, their trademarks should be registered in every country in which protection is desired (see Global Perspective 5–4 for the extent to which U.S. firms could legally protect their own copyright and trademark used by other firms abroad).

Trade Secret. A **trade secret** is another means of protecting intellectual property and fundamentally differs from patent, copyright, and trademark in that protection is sought without registration. Therefore, it is not legally protected. However, it can be protected in the courts if the company can prove that it took all precautions to protect the idea from its competitors and that infringement occurred illegally by way of espionage or hiring employees with crucial working knowledge.

Although patent and copyright laws have been in place in the United States and other Western countries for well over a hundred years, laws on trademarks and trade secrets are of relatively recent vintage, having being instituted in the late nineteenth century and beginning of the twentieth century.[66] There are many international treaties to help provide intellectual property protection across national

---

[65]Subhash C. Jain, "Problems in International Protection of Intellectual Property Rights," *Journal of International Marketing*, 4(1) (1996), pp. 9–32.

[66]Bruce A. Lehman, "Intellectual Property: America's Competitive Advantage in the 21st Century," *Columbia Journal of World Business*, 31 (Spring 1996), pp. 8–9.

❖ ❖

𝒢LOBAL PERSPECTIVE 5–4

COULD U.S. FIRMS ALWAYS PROTECT THEIR OWN COPYRIGHT AND TRADEMARK USED BY OTHER FIRMS ABROAD? THE ANSWER IS CLEARLY NO!

Infringement of intellectual property rights is not confined to the United States. Inadequate protection of intellectual property rights in foreign countries could also result in copyrights and trademarks illegally used abroad making their way back to the United States. In many industrialized countries, it is possible to stem illegally used copyrights and trademarks from entering the home country. For example, in the United States, the U.S. Customs Service provides protection to copyrights and trademarks.

Prior to receiving U.S. Customs protection, copyrights and trademarks have to be registered first with the U.S. Copyright Office and the U.S. Patent and Trademark Office, respectively. Then for U.S. Customs protection, each copyright and trademark must be recorded at the U.S. Customs Service Office. The fee is $190. Although there are no standard application forms, the application requirements for recording a copyright and a trademark are listed in Section 133.1–133.7 of the U.S. Customs regulations. An application should include the following information: (1) a certified status copy and five photocopies of the copyright or trademark registration, (2) the name of its legal owner, (3) the business address of the legal owner, (4) the states or countries in which the business of the legal owner is incorporated or otherwise conducted, (5) a list of the names and addresses of all foreign persons or companies authorized or licensed to use the copyright or trademark to be protected, (6) a list of the names and addresses of authorized manufacturers of goods, and (7) a list of all places in which goods using the copyright or bearing the trademark are legally manufac-

tured. Although it is not necessary to submit a separate application for protection of each copyright or trademark, the filing fee of $190 still applies to each and every copyright or trademark being recorded with the Customs Service. Additional information can be obtained by contacting the U.S. Customs Service at the Intellectual Property Rights Branch, Franklin Court, 1301 Constitution Avenue, N.W., Washington, D.C. (Ph. 202-482-6960).

Unfortunately, the U.S. Patent and Trademark Office has little or no legal recourse when it comes to U.S. copyrights or trademarks used by foreign companies outside the United States. For example, in Brazil, America Online's famous aol.com domain is legally owned by StarMedia Network, a small Internet services Brazilian company in the fast-growing Latin American market. America Online (AOL) had sued Starmedia Network alleging trademark infringement and contested the Brazilian provider's use of domain name "aol.com.br." However, the Brazilian court ruled in May 1999 that since Brazil's America On Line registered the name first, it does not have to surrender the domain name to its U.S. rival.

The decision may touch off concerns about international cybersquatting as many Internet giants begin to launch overseas operations, only to find that a country-level version of the domain name is already registered. The AOL domain is registered in sixty countries, and not all of these registrations were made by the American company. AOL, which is currently marketing its Brazilian services under "br.aol.com," may appeal the São Paulo ruling. As a result of the Brazilian court's ruling in favor of StarMedia Network, its shares rose 74 percent in its first day of trading. The company provides e-mail, chat rooms, shopping, and personal Web pages for Spanish and Portuguese-speaking computer users, a market that analysts say is potentially huge.

Source: Maxine Lans Retsky, "Curbing Foreign Infringement," *Marketing News* (March 31, 1997), p. 10; "Brazilian ISP Prevails in AOL Lawsuit," a news report provided by "LatPro.com ejs@LatPro.com, May 31, 1999.

---

boundaries when, in fact, laws are essentially national. Three of the most important treaties are the Paris Convention, Berne Convention, and European Patent Convention.

Paris Convention.   The **Paris Convention** was established in 1883, and the number of signatory countries currently stands at 140. It is designed to provide "domestic" treatment to protect patent and trademark applications filed in other countries.

Operationally, the convention establishes rights of priority that stipulate that once an application for protection is filed in one member country, the applicant has twelve months to file in any other signatory countries, which should consider such an application as if it were filed on the same date as the original application.[67] It also means that if an applicant does not file for protection in other signatory countries within the grace period of twelve months of original filing in one country, legal protection cannot be provided. In most countries other than the United States, the first-to-file principle is used for intellectual property protection. Lack of filing within a grace period in all other countries in which protection is desired could mean a loss of market opportunities to a competitor who filed for protection of either an identical or a similar type of intellectual property.

Berne Convention. The **Berne Convention** is the oldest and most comprehensive international copyright treaty. This treaty provides reciprocal copyright protection in each of the fifteen signatory countries. Similar to the Paris Convention, it establishes the principle of national treatment and provides protection without formal registration. The United States did not join the Berne Convention until 1989.[68]

Although there are separate laws to protect the various kinds of intellectual property, there appears to be a strong correlation between the levels of intellectual property in various countries. Exhibit 5–7 provides some of the results of a recently published academic study based on survey questionnaires administered to experts/practitioners in the various countries.

Corporations as well as individual managers must deal with the growing importance of intellectual property as a significant form of competitive advantage. The laws to deal with this issue are not uniform across countries, nor are they extended across national boundaries (outside of the government pressure). Even if they are similar, the implementation levels vary significantly. Essentially, protection of intellectual property requires registration in all the countries in which a firm plans to do business. Managers need to be cognizant of this and take proactive measures to counteract any infringements.

European Patent Convention. The **European Patent Convention** is a treaty among seventeen European countries setting up a common patent office, the European Patent Office, headquartered in Munich, Germany. The European Patent Office examines patent applications designated for any of the seventeen countries under a common patent procedure and issues a European patent valid in all of the countries designated. The European Patent Office represents the most efficient way of obtaining protection in these countries if a patent applicant desires protection in two or more of the countries. The European Patent Convention is a party to the Paris Convention, and thus recognizes the filing date of an application by anyone in any signatory country as its own priority date if an application is filed within one year of the original filing date. The European Patent Office receives the application in English. The application will be published eighteen months after the filing, consistent with the

---

[67]World Intellectual Property Organization, *Paris Convention for the Protection of Industrial Property* www.wipo.org/eng/general/ipip/paris.htm, accessed March 4, 2000.

[68]Nancy R. Wesberg, "Canadian Signal Piracy Revisited in Light of United States Ratification of the Free Trade Agreement and the Berne Convention: Is This a Blueprint for Global Intellectual Property Protection?" *Syracuse Journal of International Law & Commerce*, 16 (Fall 1989), pp. 169–205.

EXHIBIT 5–7
RATINGS FOR THE LEVEL OF INTELLECTUAL PROPERTY
PROTECTION IN VARIOUS COUNTRIES SCALE OF 0 TO 10; 0 IS
MINIMUM

Country	Patents	Copyrights	Trademarks	Trade Secrets
Argentina	3.8	5.7	7.1	4.4
Brazil	3.3	5.2	3.3	3.3
Canada	8.1	7.7	9.0	7.8
Chile	5.7	5.7	7.6	7.8
China	2.4	2.9	6.2	3.3
Germany	8.6	8.6	9.0	10.0
India	3.3	5.7	3.8	3.3
Israel	7.1	7.1	8.6	8.9
Mexico	3.3	7.6	3.8	3.3
New Zealand	7.1	8.1	9.5	7.8
Philippines	7.1	6.2	7.6	7.8
South Korea	3.3	4.8	3.8	3.3
Singapore	7.1	6.7	8.6	5.6
Thailand	2.4	4.8	6.7	5.6
United States	9.0	8.1	9.0	7.8

Source: Adapted from Belay Seyoum, "The Impact of Intellectual Property Rights on Foreign Direct Investment," *Columbia Journal of World Business*, 31 (Spring 1996), p. 56.

first-to-file principle. Once a patent is approved, then registrations in and translations into the language of each designated country will be required. The European Patent Convention does not supersede any signatories' preexisting national patent system. Patent applicants can still file and obtain separate national patents, if they so desire.[69]

Antitrust Laws of the United States[70]

The antitrust laws of the United States have their foundation in the Sherman Antitrust Act of 1890, the Clayton Act of 1914, the Federal Trade Commission Act of 1914, and the Robinson Patman Act of 1936. U.S. antitrust laws have been, from the beginning, concerned with maximizing consumer welfare through the prevention of arrangements that increase market power without concurrently increasing social welfare through reduced costs or increased efficiency.

The Sherman Act specifically forbade every contract, combination, or conspiracy to restrain free and open trade, but it was soon argued that the law was intended to punish only unreasonable restraints. In the *Standard Oil* case of 1911, the courts ruled that an act must be an unreasonable restraint of trade for the Sherman Act to apply. Toward this end, a distinction developed between (1) cases in which a rule of reason should apply, and (2) cases considered to be per se violations of the law.

---

[69]William H. Needle, *An Intellectual Property Law Primer: An Overview of Patent, Trade Secrets, Copyrights and Trademarks*, Needle & Rosenberg, P.C., Atlanta, Georgia, 1996, www.needlepatent.com/artwhn1.htm, accessed April 20, 1999.

[70]This section draws from Masaaki Kotabe and Kent W. Wheiler, *Anticompetitive Practices in Japan: Their Impact on the Performance of Foreign Firms* (Westport, CT: Praeger Publishers, 1996).

The Clayton Act strengthened the U.S. antitrust arsenal by prohibiting trade practices that were not covered by the Sherman Act. It outlawed exclusive dealing and price discrimination. Both are subject to the rule of reason—that is, they are unlawful only if the effect may be to substantially lessen competition. This concept even applies to "any imaginary threat to competition, no matter how shadowy and insubstantial" as being reasonably probable of restraining trade.[71]

Concurrent with the enactment of the Clayton Act, Congress created the Federal Trade Commission (FTC) and empowered it to enjoin unfair methods of competition in commerce. Prior to the FTC, violations of antitrust laws were the jurisdiction of the Antitrust Division of the Justice Department. Since 1914, the organizations have pursued dual enforcement of the antitrust laws, with considerable, some argue inefficient, overlap. The Justice Department focuses largely on criminal price-fixing and merger review. The FTC, which does not handle criminal cases, concentrates about 60 percent of its total resources on merger review.

The U.S. antitrust laws were originally and primarily aimed at domestic monopolies and cartels, although the act expressly extends coverage to commerce with foreign nations. In the 1940s, the prosecution of Alcoa (*United States vs. Aluminum Company of America*, 148 F. 2d 416 1945) resulted in a clear extension of U.S. antitrust laws to activities of foreign companies, even if those actions occur entirely outside the United States, as long as they have a substantial and adverse effect on the foreign or domestic commerce and trade of the United States.

Successful extraterritorial enforcement, however, depends on effective jurisdictional reach. Detecting, proving, and punishing collusion and conspiracy to restrain trade among foreign companies is extremely difficult. From gathering evidence to carrying out retribution, the complexity of nearly every aspect of antitrust litigation is compounded when prosecuting a foreign entity. Issues of foreign sovereignty and diplomacy also complicate extraterritorial antitrust enforcement. If a foreign entity's actions are required by their own government, they are exempt from prosecution under U.S. law. Prior to the 1990s and the demise of the Soviet Union, U.S. trade and economic matters were typically a lower priority than defense and foreign policy concerns. This was particularly true with Japan. In nearly every major trade dispute over steel, textiles, televisions, semiconductors, automobiles, and so on, the Departments of State and Defense opposed and impeded retaliation against Japanese companies for violations of U.S. antitrust laws. A strong alliance with Japan and the strategic geographic military locations the alliance provided were deemed to be of more importance than unrestricted trade. This arrangement helped Japanese companies improve their competitive position.

The extraterritorial application of U.S. antitrust laws has recently been subject to considerably more debate. In 1977 the Antitrust Division of the Justice Department issued its *Antitrust Guidelines for International Operations*, which, consistent with the precedent established in the Alcoa case, reaffirmed that U.S. antitrust laws could be applied to an overseas transaction if there were a direct, substantial, and foreseeable effect on the commerce of the United States. The Foreign Trade Antitrust Improvements Act of 1982 again reiterated this jurisdiction. There has been controversy, however, over the degree of U.S. commerce to which jurisdiction extends.

The 1977 Justice *Guidelines* suggested that foreign anticompetitive conduct injuring U.S. commerce raises antitrust concerns when either U.S. consumers or U.S. exporters are harmed. In a 1988 revision of the *Guidelines*, the reference to

---

[71]Robert H. Bork, *The Antitrust Paradox* (New York: Basic Books, 1978), p. 48.

exporters was omitted. Later, in 1992, U.S. Attorney General William Barr announced that Justice would take enforcement action against conduct occurring overseas if it unfairly restricts U.S. exports, arguing that anticompetitive behavior of foreign companies that inhibits U.S. exports thereby reduces the economies of scale for U.S. producers and indirectly affects U.S. consumers through higher prices than might otherwise be possible.

Critics argue that comity concerns and the difficulties in gathering evidence and building a case around conduct occurring wholly within a foreign country make it unrealistic for the Justice Department to attempt such an extraterritorial application of U.S. laws. Perhaps the gravest concern, however, is that the policy may lead to prosecution of foreign business methods that actually promote U.S. consumer welfare, for it is predominantly believed in the U.S. economic and legal community that antitrust laws should be concerned solely with protecting consumer welfare. U.S. public opinion has also traditionally and strongly supported the government's role as the champion of consumer rights against commercial interests. U.S. antitrust laws have always reflected this grassroots backing. Such a tradition has not existed in Japan, and the development of antitrust laws there has been quite different.

Fully cognizant that there were many small- and medium-size firms with exportable products that were not currently exporting, the U.S. Congress passed the Export Trading Company legislation (ETC Act) in 1982 to encourage those firms to join forces to improve their export performance by exempting them from antitrust laws. Patterned after practices in Germany and Japan, the ETC Act also permits banks to own and operate export trading companies (ETCs) so that the export trading companies will have better access to capital resources, as well as market information through their banks.[72] As a result, the ETC Act assists in the formation of shippers' associations to reduce costs and increase efficiency, covers technology—licensing agreements with foreign firms, and facilitates contact between producers interested in exporting and organizations offering export trade services. However, those trading companies are not allowed to join forces in their importing businesses, hence they are called export trading companies. In reality, many manufacturing companies import raw materials and in-process components from abroad and export finished products using those imported materials. Japanese trading companies handle both exports and imports, and have many manufacturing companies as captive customers for both exports and imports. However, in the United States, those trading companies certified as ETCs under the ETC Act may not fully exploit economies of scale in their operation, as they cannot collectively handle manufacturing firms' imports.

U.S. Foreign Corrupt Practices Act of 1977

Among the many corrupt practices that international marketers face, bribery is considered the most endemic and murky aspect of conducting business abroad. However, special care must be taken to identify and accommodate the differences between international markets and those in the United States. Laws may vary widely from country to country, and these laws may on occasion conflict with one another, although international organizations such as the International Monetary

---

[72]Charles E. Cobb, Jr., John E. Stiner, "Export Trading Companies: Five Years of Bringing U.S. Exporters Together: The Future of the Export Trading Company Act," *Business America*, 10 (October 12, 1987), pp. 2–9.

Fund and the Organization of Economic Cooperation and Development (OECD) have increased global efforts to combat corrupt business practices.[73] Several countries in the Asia-Pacific Economic Cooperation (APEC) also joined the OECD Convention in criminalizing foreign commercial bribery in 1997.[74] Bribery is a means for one party to get from another party (at the cost of a third party) some special treatment that would otherwise not normally be obtainable. However, what constitutes bribery may also differ, depending on local customs and practices.

In order to create a level playing field for U.S. companies doing business abroad and to establish a high ethical standard to be followed by foreign countries, the United States passed the **Foreign Corrupt Practices Act** (FCPA) in 1977. The FCPA was designed to prohibit the payment of any money or anything of value to a foreign official, foreign political party, or any candidate for foreign political office for purposes of obtaining, retaining, or directing business. FCPA sets a high ethical standard for U.S. firms doing business abroad, but it cannot keep foreign firms from engaging in bribery and other anticompetitive acts in foreign countries, potentially giving undue competitive advantage to foreign firms over U.S. firms. However, there is no hard evidence that U.S. firms have suffered competitive loss because of the FCPA.[75]

The FCPA, although silent on the subject, does not prohibit so called *facilitating* or *grease payments*, such as small payments to lower-level officials for expediting shipments through customs or placing a transoceanic telephone call, securing required permits, or obtaining adequate police protection—transactions that simply facilitate the proper performance of duties. These small payments are considered comparable to tips left for waiters. Although some companies find such payments morally objectionable and operate without paying them, other companies do not prohibit such payments but require that employees seek advice in advance from their corporate legal counsel in cases where facilitating payments may be involved.[76]

The FCPA does not prohibit bribery payments to nongovernmental personnel, however. Nor does the United States have laws regulating other forms of payment that approach extortion. What constitutes bribery or extortion also becomes less transparent, and international marketers' ethical dilemma increases (see Global Perspective 5–5). From an ethical point of view, three major questions must be answered:

1. Does such an act involve unfairness to anyone or violate anyone's right?

2. Must such an act be kept secret, such that it cannot be reported as a business expense?

3. Is such an act truly necessary in order to carry on business?

---

[73]Carolyn Hotchkiss, "The Sleeping Dog Stirs: New Signs of Life in Efforts to End Corruption in International Business," *Journal of Public Policy & Marketing*, 17 (Spring 1998), pp. 108–15.

[74]Madeleine K. Albright, "APEC: Facing the Challenge," *U.S. Department of State Dispatch*, 8 (December 1997), pp. 3–5.

[75]Kari Lynn Diersen, "Foreign Corrupt Practices Act," *American Criminal Law Review*, 36 (Summer 1999), pp. 753–71.

[76]Mary Jane Sheffet, "The Foreign Corrupt Practices Act and the Omnibus Trade and Competition Act of 1988: Did They Change Corporate Behavior?" *Journal of Public Policy and Marketing*, 14 (Fall 1995), pp. 290–300.

CULTURAL RELATIVISM/ACCOMMODATION—SELLING OUT?

The following is an excerpt from an anonymous source circulating via e-mail on the GINLIST:

Cultural accommodation is an essential element in successful international and cross-cultural relationships. The question faced by the U.S. multinationals is whether to follow the advice, "When in Rome, do as the Romans do." Foreign firms operating in the U.S. are faced with a similar question, "When in America, should you do as the Americans do?" How far does an individual or a company go to accommodate cultural differences before they sell themselves out? . . . I will attempt to answer this question by looking at issues involving my personal core values, bribery and gift giving, and how these relate to the definitions presented. I will also discuss trust and credibility and how these qualities relate to the subject and present a case for marketplace morality. I will conclude by presenting what I feel is the answer to the question posed above.

The primary issue . . . is one of cultural relativism and its place in cross-cultural encounters. Cultural relativism is a philosophical position which states that ethics is a function of culture. . . . Ethical relativism is the belief that nothing is objectively right or wrong, and that the definition of right or wrong depends on the prevailing view of a particular individual, culture, or historical period.

Cultural or ethical relativists will find themselves in a constant state of conflict within their own society. By definition, it would be impossible to reach an agreement on ethical rights and wrongs for the society. An ethical relativist believes that whatever an individual (any individual) believes to be right or wrong is, in fact, correct. The only cultural norm would be one of chaos since it would be impossible to hold anyone accountable to a prevailing or arbitrary ethos due to the accepted fact that all is relative and all is correct by definition.

As an example, imagine trying to hold Hitler's Nazi government accountable for their crimes during World War II from this perspective. If ethics is relative and right and wrong are defined by the prevailing view of a particular individual, culture, or historical period, then Hitler's policies of racial purification were ethically correct. However, according to my ethical beliefs (and those of the world's representatives who presided over the Neurenburg Trials); that conclusion is completely unacceptable. There are some things that are moral and ethical absolutes. . . .

As we adapt to the differences in cultures, each individual and culture must still determine where the line is (which defines) the clear violations of moral absolutes. In pursuing this objective, understanding who we are and what we stand for are essential in identifying the sell-out point. We must come to terms with our core values and how they match up with both the company ethos and that of the host and home countries. . . .

It is interesting to note the Catch 22 that an international company can find itself in on this subject. In reference to China, if the company tries to avoid the appearance of a bribe by not participating in a culture's gift giving custom and just say "thanks," they may be seen as using the "verbal thanks as getting out of their obligation." The international manager must not only understand and respect the cultural subtleties, but know how to find the limits of the ethical behavior. One specific limit put in place by the U.S. Government is the Foreign Corrupt Practices Act (FCPA). This Act was passed in reaction to a "rash of controversial payments to foreign officials by American business in the 1970s." The Act specifically calls for "substantial fines for both corporations and individual corporate officers who engage in the bribery of foreign government officials."

U.S. firms are restricted from bribing; however, many companies in other countries engage in this practice routinely. American firms allege that restricting them from this practice puts them at a serious disadvantage to other nations' firms. In the short term, this may be true. Consider what would happen if every firm bribed. The cost of a project would be driven up so high that the country itself could no longer afford it. The bribe is not free and is always paid either by a higher contract price or through shortcuts in quality and material which may result in serious social costs. Consider a freeway overpass or a bridge not built to adequate safety standards or with poor quality materials. The result could be a collapsed bridge, resulting in loss of both life and property. The bribe also undermines the competitive process so that the purchaser pays more than the competitive price and erodes the trust in the public officials and the firm.

Is there a morality separate from the individual and from the culture? . . . A multinational corporation doing business in societies with differing moral norms must subscribe to a morality of the marketplace which is based on trust and credibility. Violating such norms would be self defeating. Companies engaging in business practices that result in a loss of trust or credibility will eventually lose their share of the market. . . .

A person who approaches the world from a cultural relativist perspective will change his or her position and standards depending on the prevailing view of the culture or sub-culture that person is in. Trust and credibility can neither be built nor retained from such a position. International or domestic businessmen want to know who they are dealing with. They want to know if they can trust the person and/or company they are about to join together with. . . .

Where is the line drawn that separates accommodation from selling out? In a large part it depends on the individual's value system, since what they're selling out on is really their own core values, trust, and credibility. There are moral absolutes, which, if violated, are always examples of stepping across the line.

Source: An anonymous source, distributed via e-mail on GIN-LIST, October 11, 1994.

Unless the answer to the first two questions is negative and to the third positive, such an act is generally deemed unethical.[77] It is advised that multinational firms maintain good "corporate citizenship" wherever they do business, since long-term benefits tend to outweigh the short-term benefit gained from bribes for the same reasons just mentioned—for example, corporate contributions to humanitarian and environmental causes, such as the Save the Rain Forest project in Brazil, and moral stands on oppressive governments, such as two European brewers, Carlsberg and Heineken, pulling out from Burma to protest this Asian country's dictatorship regime.[78]

◆ ◆

↻IDEO CASE

COULD THERE BE A UNIVERSAL DEFINITION OF BRIBERY, LET ALONE UNIVERSAL POLICING OF BRIBERY IN INTERNATIONAL BUSINESS?

The term "bribery" sounds bad. How about kickbacks, tips, contingency fees, consultation fees, etc.? Terms vary, objectives to be accomplished by not-so-easy-to-define payments vary, and to whom such payments are made varies. Personal income levels vary from country to country, and thus the levels of financial incentive provided by such payments vary. Also, as you learned from Chapter 4, cultural value systems vary; thus the degree of legality, or social acceptability, varies for such payments. In general, "facilitating" payments–legality or illegality aside–tend to be used more often in countries characterized by high levels of power distance, uncertainty avoidance, and collectivism than in other countries. As debated also in Global Perspective 5–5, could there be some things that are moral and ethical absolutes when it comes to payment of money to some third party to influence and/or facilitate business transactions in your favor?

How about the U.S. standard, as stipulated in the Foreign Corrupt Practices Act of 1977? The United States is a country characterized as having low levels of power distance and uncertainty avoidance and a high level of individualism–the opposite of those countries indicated above. Discuss how you would like to address this issue.

---

[77]Richard T. De George, *Business Ethics*, 4th ed. (Englewood Cliffs, N.J.: Prentice Hall, 1995), pp. 511–12.

[78]"Brewing Companies Pull Out," Asia OnLine, February 17, 1997, www.theage. com.au/special/asiaonline/burma/brewing.htm, accessed August 20, 1999.

SUMMARY ◆

When doing business across national boundaries, international marketers almost always face what is perceived to be political and legal barriers. It is due to the fact that government policies and laws can be very different from country to country. In most cases, a foreign company has to accept a host country's government policies and laws, as they are usually outside its control. Some large multinational firms, if backed by their home country government, may sometimes influence the host country's policies and laws. However, such an extraterritorial interference may have negative consequences in the long run for a short-term gain.

Despite various international agreements brought about by such international organizations as WTO, G8, and COCOM, which collectively strive toward freer and more equitable world trade, every nation is sovereign and maintains its special interests, which may occasionally clash with those of the international agreements. Although the world has been moving toward a freer trade and investment environment, the road has not necessarily been smooth. When considering entry or market expansion in foreign countries, their country risks need to be assessed. Multinational firms need to be aware of political risks arising from unstable political parties and government structure, changes in government programs, and social pressures and special interest groups in a host country. Political risks are further compounded by economic and financial risks. When disputes arise across national boundaries, they will most likely have to be settled in one country. Therefore before entering into a contract, companies must make careful plans for establishing the jurisdictional clause in the contract as needed.

Although government policies and laws of a country usually affect business transactions involving that country, increased business activities transcending national boundaries have tested the territoriality of some policies and laws of a country. The United States frequently applies its laws, such as antitrust laws and the Foreign Corrupt Practices Act, outside its political boundary to the extent U.S. businesses are affected or to the extent that its legal value system can be extended. On the other hand, despite the importance of intellectual property in international business, protection of intellectual property in foreign countries is granted essentially by registration in those countries. International marketing managers should be aware that domestic protection usually cannot be extended beyond their national boundaries.

KEY TERMS ◆

arbitration
first-to-file patent principle
first-to-invent patent
  principle
Berne Convention
capitalism
civil law
COCOM (The Coordinating Committee for Multilateral Controls)
code (written) law
commercial law

common law
communism
confiscation
copyright
countertrade
domestication (phase-out) policy
embargoes
European Patent Convention
Export license requirements

expropriation
Foreign Corrupt Practices Act of 1977
G7
G8
green marketing
home country
host country
international law
Islamic law
ISO 9000
ISO 14000

nationalization
nontariff barriers
Paris Convention
sanctions
socialism
socialist law
tariffs
trade secret
trademark
Trade-related Aspects of Intellectual Property Rights (TRIPS) agreement

REVIEW QUESTIONS ◆

1. Describe with examples the role of governments in promoting national interests pertaining to business activities.

2. What different types of trade controls influence international business? What are their intended objectives?

3. How do host country macroeconomic and fiscal policies affect foreign company operations?

4. What factors should international managers consider in determining the economic and political risks associated with a country?

5. International law is derived from three sources. What are they? Compare and contrast them.

6. Briefly describe the various types of local legal systems. How do differences in these legal systems affect international business?

7. Enumerate some of the legal issues that international business managers need to take cognizance of in host countries.

8. Describe the various types of barriers to international trade and investment.

DISCUSSION QUESTIONS ✦ ✦ ✦ ✦ ✦ ✦ ✦ ✦ ✦ ✦ ✦ ✦ ✦ ✦ ✦ ✦ ✦ ✦

1. Various foreign companies operating in Russia, especially in the oil and gas exploration business, have had to face the vagaries of Russian legislation, which changes frequently, making it difficult to plan activities. Besides being heavily taxed, foreign firms have had to face a change in export duties of crude oil over a dozen times in the past few years. Yet most companies continue to negotiate for making investments worth billions of dollars. Discuss some of the possible reasons for the actions of these companies. Companies take various steps to manage political risk. If you were representing a company negotiating investments in Russia, what steps would you take to manage (and/or reduce) the political risk associated with these investments?

2. The following examples highlight the impact of differences in laws and social norms on various aspects of the marketing program. What are the implications of such differences for using standardized product or advertising strategies (or using standardized advertising themes)?

(a) Pepsi International's humorous global ad campaign fronted by model Cindy Crawford, which includes the use of a Coke can, will not be seen in Germany because German regulations forbid the use of comparative advertising.

(b) Advertising laws in China have restricted the use of Budweiser posters, featuring young attractive women in Budweiser swimsuits, by Anheuser-Busch to bars and stores with adult clientele only. Furthermore, when Anheuser-Busch wanted models to wear swimsuits for a beer festival, the mothers of the models used insisted on the girls wearing T-shirts beneath the swimsuits.

(c) An Austin, Texas-based designer of computer games wants to market a game that involves humans fighting against aliens from different planets. One aspect of the game is that if the humans are shot, blood is shown to come out of their bodies. German laws, however, do not permit any depiction of red blood in computer games. The company wants to market this game in Germany, which is a huge market. One suggestion the company is working on is the use of an alternate color to depict human blood. However, it risks the prospect of making the game less realistic—"What would children make out of green liquid coming out of the human figure on being shot?"

3. KFC, a fast-food operator, faced immense resistance from some politically active consumer groups when it opened its operations in India. One group proclaimed that opening KFC outlets in the country would propagate a "junk-food" culture. Others proclaimed that this was "the return of imperialistic powers" and was an attempt to "Westernize the eating habits" of Indians. Overzealous local authorities in the city of Bangalore used a city law restricting the use of MSG (a food additive used in the chicken served by KFC) over a certain amount as a pretext for temporarily closing down the outlet, despite the fact that the authorities did not even have the equipment to measure the MSG content in the proportions stated in the law. In the capital city of New Delhi, a KFC outlet was temporarily closed down because the food inspector found a "house-fly" in the restaurant. While both of these issues got resolved through hectic consultations with these consumer groups and through legal orders issued protecting the interests of the outlets, they do reflect how political and social concerns of even a small segment of the population can adversely affect the operations of companies in foreign markets. If you were the country manager of KFC in India, what steps would you have taken to avoid these problems?

4. Enactment of intellectual property laws and their effective enforcement by developing countries, especially the newly industrializing countries and the high-growth economies of Asia, have been a prime concern of various Western countries. The academic literature has seen a dramatic increase in the discussion about the loss of revenue through infringement of intellectual property rights and the proactive steps that can be taken by companies to reduce their adverse effects. However, when the vice-

president of international operations for a division of a highly innovative and respected U.S.-based MNC was asked what steps the firm had taken in China to prevent intellectual property rights infringements, the executive's response was that the company did not take any specific measures—the company could not do anything about it. At best, it could approach the pirate company and think about collaborating with it to make the product legally for the multinational company. According to this executive, companies can do little to control intellectual property rights infringements, besides influencing, to some extent, their home governments to put political pressure on the governments of the host countries. Do you agree with the arguments of this executive, or do you consider them to be more a matter of exception rather than the rule? Give reasons for why you do or don't agree.

5. An extension of the antitrust laws into the arena of international trade has taken the form of anti-dumping laws, which have been enacted by most Western countries, and which are increasingly being enacted by developing countries. On the surface, most of the anti-dumping laws across the various countries seem to be similar to each other. However, since much of the content of these laws is open to interpretation, the results of these laws could vary significantly. The bottom line for the initiation of any anti-dumping investigation is that if a foreign manufacturer gets an "undue" advantage while selling its products (either through pricing its products higher in other protected markets or through government subsidies) in another country relative to the domestic manufacturer, and this hurts the domestic industry, the company is resorting to unfair competition and should be penalized for it. Although large firms are relatively more aware of the nuances of antidumping laws and have the resources, especially legal ones, to deal with this issue, it is the smaller firms, which often depend on governmental export assistance in various forms, that are the most susceptible to it.

One of your friends is planning to start exporting an industrial product to various countries in Europe. To help finance his export endeavor, he plans to utilize concessional export credit provided by the U.S. government to small exporters. This product is highly specialized, and caters to an extremely small niche market. Europe is a large market for this product. There are only two other manufacturers of this product, both based in Europe. One of these manufacturers is a $100-million company, which manufactures various other products besides the product in question. What would be your advice to your friend in terms of the significance of antidumping laws? What specific steps, if any, would you encourage your friend to take, especially in context of his limited financial resources?

FURTHER READING ◆

Boddewyn, Jean J., and Thomas L Brewer. "International-Business Political Behavior: New Theoretical Directions." *Academy of Management Review*, 19 (1) (1994): 119–43.

Butler, Kirt C., and Domingo Castelo Joaquin. "A Note on Political Risk and the Required Return of Foreign Direct Investment." *Journal of International Business Studies*, 29 (Third Quarter 1998): 599–607.

Duina, Francesco G. *Harmonizing Europe: Nation-States within the Common Market*. Albany, NY: State University of New York Press, 1999.

Gillespie, Kate, and J. Brad McBride. "Smuggling in Emerging Markets: Global Implications." *Columbia Journal of World Business*, 31 (Winter 1996): 40–54.

Giguere, Michael, and Paul E. Smith. "ISO 9000: Service Companies Can Benefit," *Business Quarterly*, 63 (May/ June 1999): 13–15.

Maskus, Keith E. "Implications of Regional and Multilateral Agreements for Intellectual Property Rights," *World Economy*, 20 (August 1997): 681–94.

Mittlestaedt, John D., and Robert A. Mittlestaedt. "The Protection of Intellectual Property: Issues of Origination and Ownership." *Journal of Public Policy and Marketing*, 16 (Spring 1997): 14–25.

Osland, Gregory E., and S. Tamer Cavusgil. "Performance Issues in US-China Joint Ventures," *California Management Review*, 38 (2) (1996): 106–30.

Naidu, G. M., V. Kanti Prasad, and Arno Kleimenhagen. "Purchasing's Preparedness for ISO 9000 International Quality Standards." *International Journal of Purchasing & Materials Management*, 32 (Fall 1996): 46–53.

Rugman, Alan, John Kirton, and Julie Soloway. *Environmental Regulations and Corporate Strategy: A NAFTA Perspective*. Oxford, England: Oxford University Press, 1999.

Sheffet, Mary Jane. "The Foreign Corrupt Practices Act and the Omnibus Trade and Competition Act of 1988: Did They Change Corporate Behavior?" *Journal of Public Policy and Marketing*, 14 (Fall 1995): 290–300.

Weiss, Linda. *The Myth of the Powerless State*. Ithaca, NY: Cornell University Press, 1998.

GLOBAL MARKETING RESEARCH

CHAPTER OVERVIEW

1. RESEARCH PROBLEM FORMULATION

2. SECONDARY GLOBAL MARKETING RESEARCH

3. PRIMARY GLOBAL MARKETING RESEARCH

4. MARKET SIZE ASSESSMENT

5. NEW MARKET INFORMATION TECHNOLOGIES

6. MANAGING GLOBAL MARKETING RESEARCH

Given the complexity of the global marketplace, solid marketing research is critical for a host of global marketing decisions. Skipping the research phase in the international marketing decision process can often prove a costly mistake. The following anecdotes illustrate that even marketing behemoths such as Wal-Mart and Procter & Gamble sometimes fail to live up to the "Test, Test, Test" maxim:

- When Wal-Mart first entered the Argentine market, its meat counters featured T-bone steaks—not the rib strips and tail rumps that Argentines prefer. Jewelry counters were filled with emeralds, sapphires, and diamonds. Argentine women, however, prefer wearing gold and silver. The hardware departments had tools and appliances for 110-volt electric power while the standard throughout Argentina is 220-volt.[1]

- In Japan, Procter & Gamble stumbled into a cultural minefield by showing a Camay commercial that featured a man walking into the bathroom while his spouse was taking a bath. This spot raised eyebrows in Japan, where a husband is not

---

[1]"Wal-Mart Learns a Hard Lesson," *International Herald Tribune* (December 6, 1999), p. 15.

supposed to impose on his wife's privacy in the bathroom. A Japanese ad campaign for its all-temperature Cheer laundry detergent brand mistakenly assumed that Japanese housewives wash clothes in different temperatures. Japanese women do their laundry in tap water or leftover bath water.[2]

Most of such cultural blunders stem from inadequate marketing research. Market research assists the global marketing manager in two ways:[3] (1) by making better decisions that recognize cross-country similarities and differences, and (2) by gaining support from the local subsidiaries for proposed marketing decisions.

To some degree, the procedures and methods that are followed to conduct global marketing research are close to those used in standard domestic research. Most of the marketing research tricks of the trade available for the domestic market scene (e.g., questionnaire design, focus group research, multivariate techniques such as cluster analysis, conjoint measurement) are fruitfully employed in the global marketplace. Also, the typical sequence of a multicountry market research process follows the familiar pattern used in domestic marketing research. In particular, there are six steps to follow in conducting global market research:

1. Define the research problem(s)
2. Develop a research design
3. Determine information needs
4. Collect the data (secondary and primary)
5. Analyze the data and interpret the results
6. Report and present the findings of the study

A typical example of a multicountry market research project is summarized in Exhibit 6–1. At each of these six steps, special problems may arise when the research activity takes place in foreign markets. The major challenges that global marketing researchers need to confront are:[4]

1. Complexity of research design due to environmental differences
2. Lack and inaccuracy of secondary data
3. Time and cost requirements to collect primary data
4. Coordination of multicountry research efforts
5. Difficulty in establishing comparability across multicountry studies

In this chapter, you will learn about the major issues that complicate cross-country research. We will also show ways to cope with these roadblocks. We then describe several techniques that are useful for market demand assessment. During the last two decades new market information technologies have emerged. We will discuss the impact of these technological advances on marketing research. Finally, we will consider several issues that concern the management of global market research.

---

[2]Alecia Swasy, *Soap Opera: The Inside Story of Procter & Gamble* (New York: Random House, 1993), p. 268.

[3]Kamran Kashani, "Beware the Pitfalls of Global Marketing," *Harvard Business Review* (Sept.–Oct. 1989), p. 97.

[4]Susan P. Douglas and C. Samuel Craig, *International Marketing Research* (Englewood Cliffs, NJ: Prentice-Hall, 1983).

EXHIBIT 6–1
A MULTI-COUNTRY MARKETING RESEARCH PROJECT AT ELI LILLY:
ESTIMATING THE MARKET POTENTIAL FOR A PRESCRIPTION WEIGHT LOSS
PRODUCT

Research Problem

Estimate the dollar potential for a prescription weight-loss product in the U.K., Spain, Italy, and Germany.

Research Hypothesis

Patients would be willing to pay a premium price for the product even without reimbursement by the government.

Secondary Data Research

- Market share of a similar product (Isomeride)
- Incidence of overweight and obesity in Europe*

Primary Data Research

- Sample size: 350 physicians from the U.K., Italy, Spain, and Germany
- Sampling procedure: random selection from a high prescribers doctor list based on company data
- Data collected:

  (1) Diary kept by physicians for two weeks
  (2) Questionnaires completed by patients who were judged to be prospect for the product by physician
  (3) Pricing study based on thirty additional phone interviews with physicians in the U.K., Italy, and Spain to measure price sensitivity

Source: Based on William V. Lawson, "The 'Heavyweights'—Forecasting the Obesity Market in Europe for a new compound," *Marketing and Research Today* (November 1995), pp. 270–74.

*Overweight people are people whose body weight is 25–29 percent more than recommended weight; obese people are people whose weight is more than 30 percent over their ideal weight.

◆ ◆ ◆ ◆ ◆ ◆ RESEARCH PROBLEM FORMULATION

Any research starts off with a precise definition of the research problem(s) to be addressed. The cliché of a well-defined problem being a half-solved problem definitely applies in a global setting. Fancy data-analytical tools will not compensate for wrong problem definitions. Once the nature of the research problem becomes clear, the research problem needs to be translated in specific research questions. The scope of market research questions extends to both strategic and tactical marketing decisions. For example, a product-positioning study carried out for BMW in the European market centered around the following three issues:[5]

1. What do motorists in the country concerned demand of their cars?

2. What do motorists believe they are getting from various brands?

3. What does that imply with regard to positioning the BMW brand across borders?

---

[5]Kern Horst, Hans-Christian Wagner, and Roswitha Hassis, "European Aspects of a Global Brand: The BMW Case," *Marketing and Research Today* (February 1990), pp. 47–57.

In an international context, the marketing research problem formulation is hindered by the self-reference criterion—that is, people's habit to fall back on their own cultural norms and values (see Chapter 4). This tendency could lead to wrong or narrow problem definitions. In a multicountry research process, the self-reference criterion also makes a meeting of the minds between headquarters and local people an immensely formidable task. To avoid such mishaps, market researchers must try to view the research problem from the cultural perspective of the foreign players and isolate the influence of the self-reference criterion. At any rate, local subsidiaries should be consulted at every step of the research process if the study will affect their operations, including the first step of the problem definition.

A major difficulty in formulating the research problem is the unfamiliarity with the foreign environment. Lack of familiarity may lead to false assumptions; misdefined research problems, and, ultimately, misleading conclusions about the foreign markets. To reduce part of the uncertainty, some exploratory research at the early stage of the research process is often very fruitful. A useful vehicle for such preliminary research is an **omnibus survey**.[6] Omnibus surveys are regularly scheduled surveys that are conducted by research agencies (e.g., ACNielsen) with questions from different clients. The surveys are administered to a very large sample of consumers, usually a panel created by the agency. The questionnaire contains a plethora of questions on a variety of topics. In most cases, clients are able to incorporate their own proprietary questions. The prime benefit of an omnibus survey is cost, as the expenses are shared by the subscribers to the survey. Another selling point is speed—results are quickly available. A major disadvantage is that only a limited amount of company-relevant information is obtainable through an omnibus. Also, the panel is usually not representative of the firm's target market profile.

Still, an omnibus survey is probably the most economical way to gather preliminary information on target markets. An omnibus is particularly suitable when you need to ask a few simple questions across a large sample of respondents. Findings from an omnibus may assist managers and researchers in fine-tuning the research problem(s) to be tackled. An omnibus is also an option to gauge the market potential for your product in the foreign market when you only have a limited budget. Omnibuses conducted on a regular basis can also be useful as a tracking tool to spot changes in consumer attitudes or behaviors. Exhibit 6–2 presents the key features of ACNielsen's China omnibus.

Once the research issues have been stated, management needs to determine the information needs. Some of the information will be readily available within the company or in publicly available sources. Other information will need to be collected from scratch.

SECONDARY GLOBAL MARKETING RESEARCH   ◆ ◆ ◆ ◆ ◆ ◆

Assessing the information needs is the next step after the research problem definition. Some pieces of information will already be available. That sort of information is referred to as **secondary data**. When the information is not useful, or

[6]David A. Aaker, V. Kumar, and George S. Day, *Marketing Research* (New York: John Wiley & Sons, 1998), p. 237.

EXHIBIT 6-2
ACNIELSEN CHINA OMNIBUS

Geographical Coverage
  (a) Key cities: Guangzhou, Shanghai, Beijing
  (b) Seven other cities: Chengdu, Fuzhou, Hangzhou, Nanjing, Shenyang, Tianjin, Wuhan

Timing
Four rounds

Sample Size
500 interviews in each city

Sampling Procedure
Random probability sampling with face-to-face interviews

Target Respondents
Individuals aged 9+

Deliverables
  - Self-explanatory charts and computer tables
  - Demographics (including gender, age, education, marital data, household size, household purchase decision maker, household head, occupation, nature of work unit, monthly household income) tabulated against proprietary questions

Examples of Omnibus Questions
  - Do you use X?
  - How often do you use X?
  - What do you like/dislike about X?
  - How much did you pay for X?
  - Have you seen any ad for Y?

Cost
Total cost depends on:

  (1) Number of questions
  (2) Nature of question: open-ended versus close-ended
  (3) Sample size
  (4) Number of cities

Fee per person is U.S. $1.00 or less (sample size) with setup cost of U.S. $2,000 for any project under U.S. $10,000. For instance, a project covering two cities and a sample size of 1,000 subjects will cost U.S .$3,000.

Source: Based on information provided by ACNielsen (China).

simply does not exist, the firm will need to collect the data. **Primary data** are data collected specifically for the purpose of the research study. Researchers will first explore secondary data resources, since that kind of information is usually much cheaper and less time consuming to gather than primary data. Both forms of data collection entail numerous issues in an international marketing setting. We will first touch on the major problems concerning secondary data research.

Market researchers in developed countries have access to a wealth of data that are gathered by government and private agencies. Unfortunately, the equivalents of such databases oftentimes are missing outside the developed world. Even when the information is available, it may be hard to track down. A starting point for data collection is the Web or a computerized service such as Lexis/Nexis that provides real-time online access to information resources based on user-provided keywords. Another example of an electronic databank is FINDEX, which offers a worldwide directory of market research intelligence reports. Exhibit 6–3 shows the wide variety of secondary data resources that are available to global market researchers. Also, a wealth of international business resources can be accessed via the Internet. One of the most comprehensive resources is the National Trade Data Bank (NTDB), maintained by the U.S. Department of Commerce (http://www.stat-usa.gov).[7] The NTDB includes market research reports, information on export opportunities, how-to-market guides, and so forth.[8] One of the nice features is a search engine that allows users to retrieve any information that is available on the NTDB for a given topic. Another valuable online resource is the International Business Resources Directory maintained by the CIBER center at Michigan State University (http://ciber.bus.msu.edu/busres.htm). This resource is an extremely well-organized directory that provides linkages to hundreds of online international business resources on the Internet.

Obviously, researchers can also tap information resources available within the company. Many companies have their own libraries that provide valuable data sources. Large companies typically compile enormous databanks on their operations. Government publications sometimes offer information on overseas markets. In the United States, the U.S. Department of Commerce offers detailed country reports and industry surveys. Many countries have a network of government-sponsored commercial delegations (e.g., Chambers of Commerce, the Japanese External Trade Organization—JETRO). These agencies will often provide valuable information to firms that desire to do business in their country, despite the fact that the raison d'être of most of these agencies is to assist home-grown companies in the foreign market.

Besides government offices, international agencies such as the World Bank, the Organization for Economic Cooperation and Development (OECD), the International Monetary Fund (IMF), and the United Nations gather a humongous amount of data. Reports published by these organizations are especially useful for demographic and economic information. Given that most of these documents report information across multiple years, their data can be used to examine trends in socioeconomic indicators. Unfortunately, reports published by such international agencies cover only their member states.

Several companies specialize in producing business-related information. Such information is usually far more expensive than government-based data. However, this sort of information often has more direct relevance for companies. Two prominent examples are The Economist Intelligence Unit (E.I.U.) and Euromonitor. One of the most useful resources put together by the E.I.U. are the country reports that appear on a quarterly basis. These country reports give a detailed update on the major political and economic trends in the countries covered. Euromonitor has several

---

[7]The National Trade Data Bank information is also available on CD-ROM.

[8]Though not free, at an annual subscription rate of U.S. $150 (individual rate), the information provided by the NTDB is a definite bargain.

EXHIBIT 6–3
RESOURCES FOR SECONDARY DATA

International Trade

- *Yearbook of International Trade Statistics* (United Nations)
- *US Imports* (U.S. Bureau of the Census)
- *US Exports* (U.S. Bureau of the Census)
- *Exporters' Encyclopaedia* (Dun and Bradstreet)

Country Information (Socioeconomic & Political Conditions)

- *Yearbook of Industrial Statistics* (United Nations)
- *Statistical Yearbook* (United Nations; Updated by *Monthly Bulletin of Statistics*)
- *Europa Yearbook*
- *OECD Economic Survey*
- *Country Reports* (The Economist Intelligence Unit)
- *Demographic Yearbook* (United Nations)
- *Statistical Yearbook* (United Nations)
- *UNESCO Statistical Yearbook*
- *World Factbook* (Central Intelligence Agency)

International Marketing

- *European Marketing Data and Statistics* (Euromonitor)
- *International Marketing Data and Statistics* (Euromonitor)
- *Consumer Europe* (Euromonitor)
- *European Advertising Marketing and Media Data* (Euromonitor)
- *Advertising Age International*
- *FINDEX: The Worldwide Directory of Market Research Reports, Studies & Surveys* (Cambridge Information Group Directories)
- *A Guide to Selling Your Service Overseas* (Northern California District Export Council)

Chambers of Commerce

See http://www.worldchambers.com/chambers.html on the World Wide Web for a global index

Directories of Foreign Firms

- *D & B Europa* (Dun & Bradstreet)
- *Directory of American Firms Operating in Foreign Countries* (World Trade Academy Press)
- *Directory of Foreign Firms Operating in the United States* (World Trade Academy Press)
- *Europe's 15,000 Largest Companies* (E L C Publishing)
- *International Directory of Importers: Europe* (Interdata)
- *Mailing Lists of Worldwide Importing Firms* (Interdata)
- *Moody's International Manual* (Moody's Investors Service)
- *Principal International Businesses; The World Marketing Directory* (Dun & Bradstreet)

publications that are extremely useful to global marketers. Two well-known reports are the *European Marketing Data and Statistics* and *International Marketing Data and Statistics*, annual volumes covering Europe and the global marketplace outside Europe, respectively.

A more recent form of secondary data sources are syndicated data sets sold by market research companies like ACNielsen Company and Taylor Nelson Sofres. These firms acquire data sets that cover purchase transactions from retail outlets whose cash registers are equipped with optical scanning equipment. Until about a

Some marketing research companies focus
on international marketing research with
branch offices strategically located around
the world.

decade ago, such data sources were only available in the United States. Optical
scanners are now well entrenched in most Western countries. Both giants in the
syndicated data business, ACNielsen and Taylor Nelson Sofres, have a major international presence now.

As firms move from government publications to syndicated data, the richness
of the information increases enormously. At the same time, the cost of collecting
and processing data goes up. Just as in a domestic marketing context, firms planning research in the global market place have to decide on the value added of additional information and make the appropriate trade-offs.

In the global market scene, some of the information sought by market researchers
does not exist. When data are missing, the researcher needs to infer the data by
using proxy variables or values from previous periods. Even if the data sets are
complete, the researcher will usually encounter many problems:

Problems with Secondary Data Research

Accuracy of Data. The accuracy of secondary data is often questionable, for
various reasons. The definition used for certain indicators often differs across countries. The quality of information may also be compromised by the mechanisms that
were used to collect it. Most developed countries use sophisticated procedures to
assemble data. Due to the lack of resources and skills, many developing countries
have to rely on rather primitive mechanisms to collect data. The purpose for which
the data were collected could affect their accuracy. International trade statistics do
not cover cross-border smuggling activities. Such transactions are, in some cases, far
more significant than legitimate trade.

Age of Data. The desired information may be available but outdated. Many countries collect economic activity information on a far less frequent basis than the United States. The frequency of census taking also varies from country to country. In the United States, a census is taken once every decade. In many emerging markets, census-taking seldom takes place.

Reliability over Time. Often companies are interested in historical patterns of certain variables to spot underlying trends. Such trends might indicate whether a market opportunity opens up or whether a market is becoming saturated. To study trends, the researcher has to know to what degree the data are measured consistently over time. Sudden changes in the definition of economic indicators are not uncommon. Juggling with economic variable measures is especially likely for variables that have political ramifications, such as unemployment and inflation statistics. For instance, government authorities may adjust the basket of goods used to measure inflation to produce more favorable numbers. Market researchers should be aware of such practices and, if necessary, make the appropriate corrections.

Comparability of Data. Cross-country research often demands a comparison of indicators across countries. Different sources on a given item often produce contradictory information. The issue then is how to reconcile these differences. One way to handle contradictory information is to **triangulate**—obtain information on the same item from at least three different sources and speculate on possible reasons behind these differences.[9] For instance, suppose you want to collect information on the import penetration of wine as a percentage of total consumption in various European countries. Triangulation might show that some of the figures you collected are based on value, while others are based on volume. It might also reveal that some sources include champagne and others do not.

Comparability may also be hindered by the lack of **functional** or **conceptual equivalence**.[10] Functional equivalence refers to the degree to which similar activities or products in different countries fulfill similar functions. Many products perform very different functions in different markets. In the United States bicycles are primarily used for leisure. In some countries (e.g., the Netherlands and China), bicycles are a major means of transportation. Absence of conceptual equivalence is another factor that undermines comparability. Conceptual equivalence reflects the degree to which a given concept has the same meaning in different environments. Many concepts have totally different meanings or may simply not exist in certain countries. The concept of *equal rights* for women is unfamiliar in many Muslim societies. Likewise, the notion of *intellectual property* is often hard to grasp in some cultures. Often, what one culture sees as obvious the other does not.

The comparison of money-based indicators (e.g., income figures, consumer expenditures, trade statistics) is hampered by the need to convert such figures into a common currency. The key issues are what currency to use and at what exchange rate (beginning of the year, year-end, or year-average). A further complication is that exchange rates do not always reflect the relative buying power between

---

[9]S. C. Williams, "Researching Markets in Japan—A Methodological Case Study," *Journal of International Marketing*, 4, 2, (1996), pp. 87–93.

[10]Yusuf A. Choudhry, "Pitfalls in International Marketing Research: Are You Speaking French Like a Spanish Cow?" *Akron Business and Economic Review*, vol. 17, no. 4 (Winter 1986), pp. 19–20.

countries. As a result, comparing economic indicators using market exchange rates can be very misleading.

Lumping of Data. Official data sources often group statistics on certain variables in very broad categories. This compromises the usefulness and the interpretation of such data for international market researchers. Managers should check what is included in certain categories.[11]

Given the hurdles posed by secondary data, it is important to verify the quality of collected information. To assess the quality of data, the researcher should seek answers to the following checklist:

1. When were the data collected? Over what time frame?
2. How were the data collected?
3. Have the variables been redefined over time?
4. Who collected the data?
5. For what purpose were the data gathered?

Of course, satisfactory answers to each of these questions does not assure total peace of mind. Researchers and managers should always be on guard regarding the quality of secondary data.

PRIMARY GLOBAL MARKETING RESEARCH ◆ ◆ ◆ ◆ ◆ ◆

Seldom will secondary data prove satisfactory for market research studies. The next step in the research process is to collect primary data specifically for the purpose of the research project. Primary data can be collected in several ways: (1) focus groups, (2) survey research, or (3) test markets. In this section we will concentrate on focus groups and survey research. Test marketing is discussed in Chapter 11 on global new product development.

Focus Groups

Before embarking on large-scale quantitative market research projects, most firms will conduct exploratory research. One of the most popular tools at this stage is the focus group. A focus group is a loosely structured, free-flowing discussion among a small group (eight to twelve people) of target customers guided by a professional moderator. They can be used for many different purposes: to generate information to guide the quantitative research projects, to reveal new product opportunities, to test out new product concepts, and so forth.

The rules for designing and running focus groups in a domestic marketing setting also apply for global market research projects.[12] Hiring well-trained moderators is critical in conducting focus groups for international market research. Moderators should be familiar with the local language and social interaction patterns. Cultural sensitivity is an absolute must with focus groups. For instance, Japanese consumers tend to be much more hesitant to criticize new product ideas than their

---

[11]Williams, p. 90.

[12]See, for example, Thomas C. Kinnear and James R. Taylor, *Marketing Research* (New York: McGraw-Hill, Inc., 1996), Chapter 10.

Western counterparts.[13] Also, many Asian societies like Japan are highly collective ("Confucian"). Strangers outside the group are excluded. As a result, getting the desired group dynamics for focus groups within such cultures is often very hard. To stimulate group dynamics, the following steps should be taken:[14]

- Be precise in recruitment to ensure group homogeneity and ease of bonding.
- Hire moderators who are able to develop group dynamics quickly through warm-ups, humor, and group-playing.
- Hire moderators who can spot and challenge "consensus"-claimed behaviors and attitudes.

When analyzing and interpreting focus group findings, market researchers should also concentrate on the nonverbal cues (e.g., gestures, voice intonations).[15] Information provided by these nonverbal cues is often as important as the verbal content of the focus groups.

Survey Methods for Cross-Cultural Marketing Research

Questionnaires are the most common vehicle to gather primary data in marketing research. Survey research begins with the design of a questionnaire. The next step is to develop a sampling plan to collect the data. Once these two tasks have been accomplished, the researcher moves to the next phase, the physical collection of information to the questionnaires. Each stage may lead to major headaches.

◆ ◆

𝒢LOBAL PERSPECTIVE 6–1
CONDUCTING FOCUS GROUPS WITH WOMEN IN THE ARAB GULF COUNTRIES

Dr. Nimir Eid, a Professor of Marketing at the American University of Beirut, offers the following guidelines for conducting focus group studies with women in the Arab Gulf countries:

1. *Moderator.* The focus group moderator should be female herself. Preferably, she has a similar age and nationality as the participants.

2. *Recruiting.* Often participants express a desire to bring along another "eligible" participant like a close friend or a relative. It is crucial that the researcher discreetly screens respondents before starting the focus group project. Otherwise, if participants have a very similar demographic profile, the validity of the research findings is likely to be compromised.

3. *Settings.* Focus groups should be run in the casual and nonthreatening setting of a private home. Avoid using one-way viewing facilities, and do not videotape the discussion.

4. *Transcripts.* The person responsible for analyzing the transcripts should be a female with a thorough understanding of the local culture and social norms.

Source: Nimir Eid, "Market Research with Women in the Arab Gulf Countries," *Marketing and Research Today* (May 1999), p. 54.

---

[13]David B. Montgomery, "Understanding the Japanese as Customers, Competitors, and Collaborators," *Japan and the World Economy*, vol. 3, no. 1 (1991), pp. 61–91.

[14]Chris Robinson, "Asian Culture: The Marketing Consequences," *Journal of the Market Research Society*, 38, no. 1 (1996), pp. 55–62.

[15]Naresh K. Malhotra, James Agarwal, and Mark Peterson, "Methodological Issues in Cross-cultural Marketing Research. A State-of-the-Art Review," *International Marketing Review*, 13, no. 5 (1996), pp. 7–43.

Questionnaire Design. By far the most popular instrument used to gather primary data is the questionnaire. Preparing questionnaires for global market research poses tremendous challenges. Just like in domestic marketing, care should be exercised with the wording and the sequencing of the questions. With multi-country projects, further care is needed to assure comparability of survey-based results across frontiers. Measurement issues in cross-country research center around the question: "Are the phenomena in countries A and B measured in the same way?" Absence of measurement equivalence will render cross-country comparisons meaningless. Earlier we discussed the need for **conceptual** and **functional equivalence** of secondary data. The same requirements apply to primary data in order to avoid cultural biases. Cross-country survey research needs to fulfill two further criteria: **translation** and **scalar equivalence**.

The first aspect deals with the translation of the instrument from one language into another one. Cross-cultural research, even within the same country or parent language (e.g., English, Spanish), demands adequate translations from the master questionnaire into other languages. Careless translations of questionnaires can lead to embarrassing mistakes. Good translations are hard to accomplish. Several methods exist to minimize translation errors. Two procedures often used in practice to avoid sloppy translations are **back-translation** and **parallel translation**. The back-translation method is a two-phase process. Suppose a company wants to translate a questionnaire from English into Arab. In the first step, the master questionnaire is translated into Arab by a (bilingual) translator whose native language is Arab, the target language. In the second stage, the Arab version is translated back into English by another bilingual interpreter whose native language is English, the base language. This version is then compared with the original survey to uncover any bugs or translation errors. The process is repeated until an acceptable degree of convergence is achieved. Parallel translation consists of using multiple interpreters who translate the same questionnaire independently. Alternative versions are compared by a committee of translators and differences are reconciled.

Most surveys typically have a battery of questions or "Agree/Disagree" statements with a (e.g., 7-point) scale to record responses. To make the findings of cross-country market research projects meaningful, it is paramount to pursue **scalar equivalence**: scores from subjects of different countries should have the same meaning and interpretation.[16] The standard format of scales used in survey research differs across countries. In the United States, a five- or seven-point scale is most common. In France, twenty-point scales prevail in survey research. Keep in mind that high scores in one country are not necessarily high scores elsewhere. Latin Americans, for example, tend to use the high end of the scale. An unenthusiastic respondent may still give your company a "7" or an "8" score on a ten-point scale. Asians, on the other hand, tend to use the middle of the scale.[17]

In some cases, you may also need to adjust the anchors of the scale. One recent study that measured attitudes of Japanese managers adopted scales that included "definitely true," "somewhat true," and "not all true." A pretest of the survey showed that the Japanese respondents had trouble with the concept of "agree/-disagree."[18] To make cross-country comparisons meaningful, it is advisable to

[16]Malhotra, Agarwal, and Peterson, p. 15.

[17]Jennifer Mitchell, "Reaching Across Borders," *Marketing News* (May 10, 1999), p. 19.

[18]Jean L. Johnson, Tomoaki Sakano, Joseph A. Cote, and Naoto Onzo, "The Exercise of Interfirm Power and Its Repercussions in U.S.–Japanese Channel Relationships," *Journal of Marketing*, vol. 57, no. 2 (April 1993), pp. 1–10.

adjust responses in each country by, for instance, taking deviations from country-averages on any given question. By the same token, in some societies people are cued to view "1" as best and the other endpoint of the scale as worst, while in others "1" is considered the worst, regardless of how the scale is designated.

Survey research in developing nations is further compounded by low levels of education. Specially designed visual scales like the Funny Faces scale (see Exhibit 6–4) are sometimes used to cope with illiteracy. In developing countries, market researchers should also try to reduce the verbal content and use visual aids. In countries that are unfamiliar with survey research (e.g., former East Bloc countries), it is advisable to avoid lengthy questionnaires or open-ended questions.[19]

Regardless of whether the survey is to be administered in Paris, Texas, or Paris, France, it is absolutely imperative to pretest the questionnaire. Pretesting is the only foolproof way to debug the questionnaire and spot embarrassing, and often expensive, mistakes. Speed is often critical when collecting data. However, rushing into the field without a thorough pretest of the questionnaire is a highly risky endeavor.

Sampling.   To collect data, the researcher has to draw a sample from the target population. A **sampling plan** basically centers around three issues:[20]

1. Who should be surveyed? What is our target population (*sampling unit*)?
2. How many people should be surveyed (*sample size*)?
3. How should prospective respondents be chosen from the target population (*sampling procedure*)?

Decisions on each of these issues will be driven by balancing costs, desired reliability, and time requirements. In multicountry research, firms also need to decide what countries should be researched. There are two broad approaches. The first approach starts with a large-scale exploratory research project covering many countries. This step might take the form of an omnibus survey. The alternative approach focuses on a few key countries. To choose these countries, a firm might group countries (e.g., along sociocultural indicators) and pick one or two representative members from each cluster. Depending on the findings coming from this first pool of countries, the research process is extended to cover other countries of interest.

The preparation of a sampling plan for multicountry research is often a daunting task. When drawing a sample, the researcher needs a sampling frame, that is, a listing of the target population (e.g., a telephone directory). In many countries, such listings simply do not exist or may be very inadequate. The proportion of individuals meeting the criteria of the target population could vary considerably. This forces the researcher to be flexible with the sampling methods employed in different countries.[21]

Computing the desired sample size in cross-country market research often becomes at best guesswork because the necessary pieces of information are missing. Desired sample sizes may also vary across cultures. Typically, heterogeneous cultures (e.g., India) demand bigger samples than homogeneous cultures (e.g.,

---

[19]Erdener Kaynak, *Marketing in the Third World*. (New York: Praeger, 1982), Chapter 4.

[20]See, for example, Naresh K. Malhotra, *Marketing Research. An Applied Orientation* (Englewood Cliffs, NJ: Prentice-Hall, 1993), Chapter 13.

[21]D.N. Aldridge, "Multi-Country Research," in *Applied Marketing and Social Research*, U. Bradley, Ed., 2nd Edition (New York: John Wiley, 1987), pp. 364–65.

EXHIBIT 6–4
THE FUNNY FACES SCALE

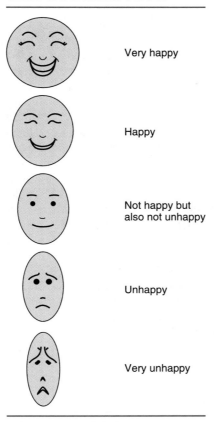

Very happy

Happy

Not happy but
also not unhappy

Unhappy

Very unhappy

Source: C. K. Corder, "Problems and Pitfalls in Conducting Marketing Research in
Africa." in *Marketing Expansion in a
Shrinking World*, ed. Betsy Gelb. Proceedings of American Marketing Association
Business Conference. (Chicago: AMA,
1978), pp. 86–90.

South Korea, Thailand).[22] This is due to the fact that diverse cultures typically have
much more variance in the traits to be measured than homogeneous ones.

Most researchers prefer some form of probabilistic sampling that enables them
to make statistical inferences about the collected data. The absence of sampling
frames and various cultural hurdles (e.g., inapproachability of women in Muslim societies) make a nonprobabilistic sampling procedure, such as convenience sampling,
the only alternative, especially in developing countries. Such handicaps do not apply
to all emerging markets. For instance, Chinese cities are divided into Administrative
Districts, Administrative Streets, and Resident Committees. Every household has to
register with its Resident Committee. One omnibus survey randomly picked ten

[22]Malhotra, Agarwal, and Peterson, p. 27.

Resident Committees in each target city. From each of the chosen Committees, one thousand households were drawn at random to be interviewed.[23]

Contact Method. When preparing a sampling plan, you also need to decide how to contact prospective subjects for the survey. The most common choices are mail, telephone, or person-to-person interviews (e.g., shopping mall intercepts). Exhibit 6–5 contrasts the usage of data collection methods in five European countries. Several factors explain why some methods prevail in some countries and are barely used elsewhere. Cultural norms often rule out certain data collection methods. Germans tend to show greater resistance to telephone interviewing than other Europeans.[24] By the same token, daytime phone calls will not work in Saudi Arabia, since social norms dictate that housewives do not respond to calls from strangers.[25] Cost differentials will also favor some methods over others. In many developing countries, the state of the infrastructure will make certain contact methods unattractive. In Brazil, for example, a significant portion of the mail faces large delays or never gets delivered. Lack of decent phone service in many developing countries creates a challenge for phone surveys. In China, researchers have to rely on very basic interviewing techniques because of poor phone coverage (about 7 percent versus 93 percent in the United States) and low response rates with mail surveys.[26]

These and other challenges imply that market researchers will often need to improvise and settle for the second best alternative. In recent years, marketers increasingly use the Internet as a research tool. For survey research, three types of online survey methods exist: (1) e-mail surveys, (2) random Web site surveys, and (3) panel Web site surveys.[27] E-mail surveys are self-administered questionnaires that are sent as an attachment to e-mails, to be completed by the addressee. With

EXHIBIT 6–5
COMPARISON OF EUROPEAN DATA COLLECTION METHODS

	France	The Netherlands	Sweden	Switzerland	U. K.
Mail	4%	33%	23%	8%	9%
Telephone	15	18	44	21	16
Central location/streets	52	37	—	—	—
Home/work	—	—	8	44	54
Groups	13	—	5	6	11
Depth interviews	12	12	2	8	—
Secondary	4	—	4	8	—

Source: Emanuel H. Demby, "ESOMAR Urges Changes in Reporting Demographics, Issues Worldwide Report," *Marketing News* (January 8, 1990), p. 24. Reprinted by permission of the American Marketing Association.

---

[23]Henry C. Steele, "Marketing Research in China: The Hong Kong Connection," *Marketing and Research Today* (August 1990), pp. 155–64.

[24]Aldridge, p. 365.

[25]Secil Tuncalp, "The Marketing Research Scene in Saudi Arabia," *European Journal of Marketing*, 22 (5) 1988, p. 19.

[26]Cyndee Miller, "China Emerges as Latest Battleground for Marketing Researchers," *Marketing News* (February 14, 1994), pp. 1–2.

[27]Jonathan Dodd, "Market Research on the Internet—Threat or Opportunity?" *Marketing and Research Today* (February 1998), pp. 60–66.

random Web site surveys, visitors to a site are asked to fill out a questionnaire. Panel Web site surveys rely on a panel of respondents where each panel member has an e-mail address. When eligible for a survey, panel members are contacted via e-mail and asked to complete a survey that is only accessible via a password. Exhibit 6–6 lists the pros and cons of online surveys.

Collecting the Information. Once the design of your questionnaire and sampling plan is completed, you need to collect the data in the field. This field will be covered with landmines, some of them fairly visible, others invisible. Primary data collection may be hindered by respondent- and/or interviewer-related biases.

Probably the most severe problem is nonresponse due to a reluctance to talk with strangers, fears about confidentiality, or other cultural biases. In many cultures, the only way to cope with nonresponse is to account for it when determining sample sizes. In China, surveys that are sanctioned by the local authorities will lead to a higher response rate.[28]

The **courtesy bias** refers to a desire to be polite towards the other person. This bias is fairly common in Asia and the Middle East.[29] The subject feels obliged to give responses that hopefully will please the interviewer. Another snag in survey research are biases toward **yea-** or **nay-saying**. In some countries, responses may reflect a **social desirability bias** where the subjects attempt to reflect a certain social status in their responses. Topics such as income or sex are simply taboo in some regions. There are no panaceas to handle these and other biases. Measures such as careful wording, thorough pretesting of the survey, and adequate training of the field workers will

EXHIBIT 6–6
PROS & CONS OF THE INTERNET AS A TOOL FOR GLOBAL MARKETING RESEARCH

Pros:

- Large samples are possible in small amount of time.
- There is global access to the Internet.
- Cost—in most cases, online surveys can be done much more cheaply than using other methods.
- Anonymity—this can be helpful for sensitive topics.
- Data analysis—data can port directly into statistical tools and databases.

Cons:

- Infrastructure—in many countries, access to the Internet is still fairly limited.
- Sample representativeness—for random Web-site surveys and e-mail surveys, representativeness can be a major issue. Likewise, there is also the risk of a self-selection bias.
- Technological problems such as incorrect e-mail addresses, poor connections.
- Low response rates—response rates can be fairly low; respondents may quit half-way.
- Multiple responses from same respondent.

Sources: Jonathan Dodd, "Market Research on the Internet—Threat or Opportunity?" *Marketing and Research Today* (February 1998), pp. 60–67, and Cheryl Harris, "Developing Online Market Research Methods and Tools—Considering Theorizing Interactivity: Models and Cases," *Marketing and Research Today* (November 1997), pp. 267–73.

[28]Steele, p. 160.
[29]Erdener Kaynak, *Marketing in the Third World*, p. 171.

minimize the incidence of such biases. In some cases, it will be worthwhile to incorporate questions that measure tendencies such as social desirability. Another option to handle cultural biases is to transform the data first before analyzing them. For instance, one common practice is to convert response ratings or scores to questions into rankings.

House-to-house or shopping-mall survey responses could also be scrambled by interviewer-related biases. Availability of skilled interviewers can be a major bottleneck in cross-country research, especially in developing countries and the former East Bloc countries. Lack of supervision or low salaries will tempt interviewers in some countries to cut corners by filling out surveys themselves or ignoring the sampling procedure. In many cultures, it is advisable to match interviewers to respondents. Disparities in cultural backgrounds may lead to misunderstandings.[30] Survey takers in some societies (e.g., Latin America) are regarded with suspicion by the local population.[31] Obviously, adequate recruiting, training, and supervision of interviewers will lessen interviewer-related biases in survey research. In countries where survey research is still in an early stage and researchers have little expertise, questionnaires should not be overcomplex.[32] When developing a survey instrument like a questionnaire for a global market research project, it is also helpful to have **redundancy**: ask the same question in different ways and in different parts of the questionnaire. That way, the researcher can cross-check the validity of the responses.[33]

♦ ♦ ♦ ♦ ♦ ♦ MARKET SIZE ASSESSMENT

When deciding whether to enter a particular country, one of the key drivers is the market potential. In most developed countries, a fairly accurate estimate of the market size for any particular product is easily obtainable. For many frequently purchased consumer goods, information suppliers like ACNielsen are able to give an up-to-date estimate of category volume and market shares based on scanning technology. Such information, however, does not come cheap. Before investing a substantial amount of money, you might consider less costly ways to estimate market demand. For many industries and developing countries, information on market demand is simply not readily available. Under such circumstances, there is a need to come up with a market size estimate, using "simple" ingredients.

In this chapter we introduce four methods that can be fruitfully employed to assess the size of the market for any given product:

1. Analogy method
2. Trade audit
3. Chain ratio method
4. Cross-sectional regression analysis

---

[30]Aldridge, p. 371.

[31]Douglas and Craig, p. 227.

[32]Stafford and Upmeyer, p. 40.

[33]Naghi Namakforoosh, "Data Collection Methods Hold Key to Research in Mexico," *Marketing News* (Aug. 29, 1994), p. 28.

All of these procedures can be used when very little data are available or the quality of the data is dismal, such as typically will be the case for many emerging markets. All four methods allow you to make a reasonable guesstimate of the market potential without necessitating intensive data-collection efforts. Market size estimates thus derived prove useful for country selection at the early stage. Countries that do not appear to be viable opportunities are weeded out. After this preliminary screening stage, richer data regarding market size and other indicators are collected for the countries that remain in the pool.

The first technique, the **analogy method**, starts by picking a country that is at the same stage of economic development as the country of interest and for which the market size is known. The method is based on the premise that the relationship between the demand for a product and a particular indicator (e.g., the demand for a related product) is similar in both countries.

Analogy Method

Let us illustrate the method with a brief example. Suppose that a consumer electronics company wants to estimate the market size for VCRs in Poland. For the base country, we take another Central European country, say Hungary, for which we know the sales of VCRs. We also need to choose a proxy variable that correlates highly with the demand for VCRs. In this case, we decide to choose color TV sales as an indicator. So, in this example, we assume that the ratio of VCR ownership to color-TV ownership in Hungary and Poland is roughly equivalent:

$$\frac{\text{VCR Demand}_{\text{Poland}}}{\text{Color TV Demand}_{\text{Poland}}} = \frac{\text{VCR Demand}_{\text{Hungary}}}{\text{Color TV Demand}_{\text{Hungary}}}$$

Since we are interested in the demand for VCRs in Poland, we can derive an estimate based on the following relationship:

$$\text{VCR Demand}_{\text{Poland}} = \text{Color TV Demand}_{\text{Poland}}\left(\frac{\text{VCR Demand}_{\text{Hungary}}}{\text{Color TV Demand}_{\text{Hungary}}}\right)$$

For this specific example we collected the following pieces of information:

	Annual Retail	Sales
	Color TV (000s)	VCR (000s)
Hungary	455	177
Poland	634	???

Source: European Marketing Data and Statistics 1992 (London: Euromonitor, 1992), Table 1416.

Plugging in those numbers, we get

Estimate VCR Demand$_{\text{Poland}}$ (Annual Retail Sales) = 634 (177/455) = 246.6

The critical part is finding a comparable country and a good surrogate measure (in this case the demand for color television sets). In some cases, the analogy exists between different time periods. So, the stage of economic development in country A ten years back is similar to the current state of the economy in country B. In the same fashion, we can derive an estimate for the product demand in country B, but this time you would apply the ratio between product demand and the surrogate measure in country A that existed ten years ago:

$$M_B^{2000} = X_B^{2000} * (M_A^{1990}/X_A^{1990})$$

where M refers to the market size for the product of interest and X is the surrogate measure. This variant is sometimes referred to as the **longitudinal method of analogy**.

Use of either approach will produce misleading estimates under these circumstances:[34]

1. Consumption patterns are not comparable across countries due to strong cultural disparities.

2. Other factors (competition, trade barriers) cause actual sales to differ from potential sales.

3. Technological advances allow use of product innovations in a country at an earlier stage of economic development ("leapfrogging").

McDonald's uses a variation of the analogy method to derive market size estimates:[35]

$$\left(\frac{\text{Population of Country X}}{\text{No. of People per McDonald's in U.S. (21,763)}}\right) \times \left(\frac{\text{Per Capita Income of Country X}}{\text{Per Capita Income of U.S. (\$30,200)}}\right)$$

$$= \text{Potential Penetration in Country X}$$

This method is illustrated in Exhibit 6–7, which contrasts the number of restaurants McDonald's could build with its current number of outlets for several countries. According to this formula, the worldwide market potential of McDonald's would be 42,000 restaurants. Currently, McDonald's has about 25,000 restaurants in 115 countries and territories, out of which about half are located outside the United States.[36]

Trade Audit   An alternative way to derive market size estimates is based on local production and import and export figures for the product of interest. A **trade audit** uses straightforward logic: Take the local production figures, add imports, and subtract exports. Thus:

Market Size in Country A = Local Production + Imports − Exports

Strictly speaking, one should also make adjustments for inventory levels. Although the procedure is commonsensical, the hard part is finding the input data. For many emerging markets (and even developed countries), such data are missing, inaccurate, outdated, or collected at a very aggregate level in categories that are often far too broad for the company's purposes.

---

[34]Lyn S. Amine and S. Tamer Cavusgil, "Demand Estimation in Developing Country Environment: Difficulties, Techniques and Examples," *Journal of the Market Research Society*, 28, no. 1 (1986), pp. 43–65.

[35]"How Many McDonald's Can He Build?" *Fortune* (October 17, 1994), p. 104. Figures are based on 1995 estimates as reported in the *CIA World Factbook 1996/7*.

[36]See http://www.mcdonalds.com.

EXHIBIT 6–7
MARKET POTENTIAL ESTIMATES FOR MCDONALD'S

Country	Current Number of Restaurants (1998)	Market Potential (in terms of number of restaurants)
Japan	2,852	4,714
Canada	1,085	1,017
Germany	931	2,608
United Kingdom	926	1,910
France	708	2,039
Brazil	672	1,634
Australia	666	609
Taiwan	292	475
China	220	6,539
Italy	201	1,865
Philippines	194	380
Spain	188	980
Netherlands	187	529
Sweden	177	267
Argentina	166	537
Hong Kong	152	275
New Zealand	145	98
Mexico	144	1,159
South Korea	131	972
Poland	130	428

Sources: "How Many McDonald's Can He Build?" *Fortune* (October 17, 1994), p. 104; *CIA World Factbook 1998*; and McDonald's Corp., *1998 Annual Report*.

The **chain ratio method** starts with a very rough base-number as an estimate for the market size (e.g., the entire population of the country). This base estimate is systematically fine-tuned by applying a string ("chain") of percentages to come up with the most meaningful estimate for total market potential.

Chain Ratio Method

To illustrate the procedure, let us use a simple example. Consider a firm that makes baby monitors and is planning to expand into China and/or India. Baby monitors are devices that track the baby's breathing while the baby is asleep. If for some reason the baby's breathing stops, an alarm will go off. The company wants to focus on urban areas, which are easier to access than the countryside. For the base number, we start with the overall population. Using the chain ratio method, you can compute a rough estimate of the market potential:[37]

	China	India	
Base Number— Total Population:	1,207.4	921.5	A
Urbanization Rate:	30.3%	26.8%	B
Urban Population:	365.8	247.0	$C = A \times B$
Birth Rates per 000s Population:	17.8	28.4	D
Market Potential Estimate:	6.5 million	7.0 million	$E = C \times D$

---

[37]The numbers for this illustration are taken from various tables in *International Marketing Data and Statistics 1997*. All numbers are in millions.

Evidently, these estimates could be refined even further, accounting for buying power, size of dwellings, and so forth, assuming the information is available.

Cross-Sectional Regression Analysis

Statistical techniques such as cross-sectional regression can be used to produce market-size estimates. With regression analysis, the variable of interest (in our case 'market size') is related to a set of predictor variables. To apply regression, you would first choose a set of indicators that are closely related to demand for the product of interest. You would then collect data on these variables and product demand figures for a set of countries (the cross-section) where the product has already been introduced. Given these data, you can then fit a regression model that will allow you to predict the market size in countries in your consideration pool.[38]

Again, let us illustrate the procedure with a simple example. Suppose a pharmaceutical company XYZ would like to introduce an antidepressant in Central and Eastern Europe. As predictor variables, we picked two indicators: per capita income (economic wealth) and suicide rate (number of suicides per thousand). The latter variable is chosen as a proxy for a country's mental well-being. We collected data on these two measures and per capita consumption (in U.S. dollars) of analgesics in thirteen Western European countries.[39] Using these data as inputs, we come up with the following regression model:

$$\text{Per Capita Consumption of Analgesics (in US\$)} = 0.72 + 0.000022 \times \text{Per Capita Income}$$

$$+ (0.17 \times \text{Suicide Rate})$$

$$\text{Goodness of Fit: } R_{adj}^2 = 0.49.[40]$$

The fit of the regression is fairly decent, especially since we only consider two predictor variables (see Exhibit 6–8). Based on this regression, we are able to predict the market size (in terms of per capita consumption in U.S. dollars) for analgesics in the Central and Eastern European markets. We plug in the income and suicide figures for the respective countries in this equation, with the following results:

Bulgaria	$ 3.40
Czech Rep. & Slovakia	$ 3.85
Hungary	$12.54
Romania	$ 4.36
Former Soviet Union	$ 3.76

From a per capita consumption perspective, it appears that Hungary is the most appealing market. Obviously, in overall market size, the former Soviet Union countries would offer the most attractive market opportunities.

When applying regression to come up with a market size estimate, you should be careful in interpreting the results. For instance, caution is warranted whenever the

---

[38]For further details, see, for example, David A. Aaker, V. Kumar, and George S. Day, *Marketing Research* (New York: John Wiley & Sons, 1995), Chapter 18.

[39]Our source for the data is *European Marketing Data and Statistics 1992*.

[40]The R_{adj}^2 is a measure for the goodness of fit of the regression: the closer to 1.0, the better the fit.

EXHIBIT 6–8
CROSS-SECTIONAL REGRESSION MODEL FOR ANALGESICS

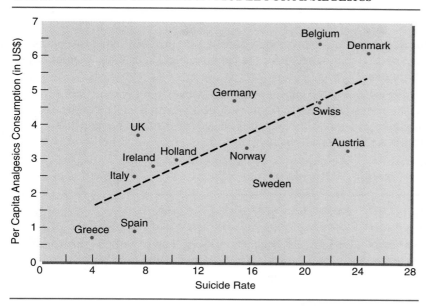

range of one of the predictors for the countries of interest is outside the range of the countries used to calibrate the regression. In fact, in the previous application, the suicide rates for the Central and Eastern European countries were far above the rates reported for the Western European countries. So, strictly speaking, we should be careful when using our results for decision making. Having said this, regression is probably one of the most handy tools to estimate market sizes, keeping in mind its constraints.

The methods we just described are not the only procedures you can use. Other, more sophisticated, procedures exist. Finally, some words of advice. Look at the three estimates for the size of the wallpaper market (in terms of number of rolls) in Morocco, based on different market size estimation techniques:[41]

Chain Ratio Method	484,000
Analogy Method	1,245,000
Trade Audit	90,500

You immediately notice a wide gap among the different methods. Such discrepancies are not uncommon. When using market size estimates, keep the following rules in mind:

1. Whenever feasible, use several different methods that possibly rely on different data inputs.

2. Don't be misled by the numbers. Make sure you know the reasoning behind them.

---

[41]Amine and Cavusgil, Table 4.

3. Don't be misled by fancy methods. At some point, increased sophistication will lead to diminishing returns (in terms of accuracy of your estimates), not to mention negative returns. Simple back-of-the-envelope calculations are often a good start.

4. When many assumptions are to be made, do a sensitivity analysis by asking what-if questions. See how sensitive the estimates are to changes in your underlying assumptions.

5. Look for interval estimates with a lower and upper limit rather than for point estimates. The range indicates the precision of the estimates. The limits can later be used for market simulation exercises to see what might happen to the company's bottom line under various scenarios.

◆ ◆ ◆ ◆ ◆ ◆ NEW MARKET INFORMATION TECHNOLOGIES

These days, almost all packaged consumer goods come with a bar code. For each purchase transaction, scanner data are gathered at the cash registers of stores that are equipped with laser scanning technology. The emergence of scanner data, coupled with rapid developments in computer hardware (e.g., workstations data storage disks) and software has led to a revolution in market research. Although most of the early advances in this information revolution took place in the United States, Europe and Japan rapidly followed suit. Exhibit 6–9 illustrates the penetration of scanning technology worldwide. Scanning technology has spurred several sorts of databases. The major ones include:[42]

- *Point-of-sale (POS) store scanner data.* Market research companies like ACNielsen, Taylor Nelson Sofres, and Information Resources obtain sales movement data from the checkout scanner tapes of retail outlets. These data are processed to provide instant information on weekly sales movements and market shares of individual brands, sizes, and product variants. Shifts in sales volume and market shares can be related to changes in the store environment (retail prices, display, and/or feature activity) and competitive moves. In the past, tracking of sales was based on store audits or warehouse withdrawal. The advantage of POS scanner data over these traditional ways of data-gathering is obvious: far better data quality.[43] The data are collected on a weekly basis instead of bimonthly. Further, they are gathered at a very detailed UPC-level, not just the brand level.

- *Consumer panel data.* Market research companies have consumer panels who record their purchases. There are two approaches to collect household level data. Under the first approach, panel members present an ID card when checking out at the cash register. That information is entered each time the household shops. The alternative approach relies on at-home scanning. Each time panel members

---

[42]See, for example, Del I. Hawkins and Donald S. Tull, *Essentials of Marketing Research* (New York: MacMillan Publishing Company, 1994), pp. 115–21.

[43]Gerry Eskin, "POS Scanner Data: The State of the Art, in Europe and the World," *Marketing and Research Today* (May 1994), pp. 107–17.

EXHIBIT 6–9
1993 WORLDWIDE SCANNING PENETRATION (PERCENT ACV[1] SCANNED)

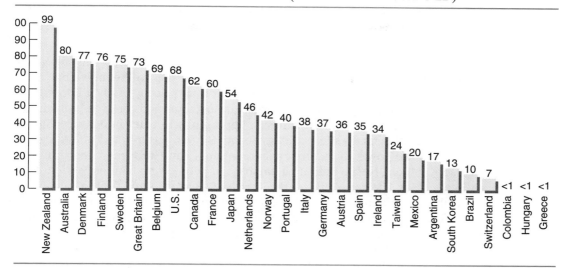

[1]ACV = All Commodity Volume.
Source: AC Nielsen.

return from a shopping trip, they scan the items that they bought. The home-scanning method is favored in Japan for two reasons:[44]

- Japanese supermarket chains are not very cooperative to install external scanner terminals.
- Japanese shoppers are highly mobile and shop a lot outside their "designated" panel area.

- *Single-source data.* Such data are continuous data that combine TV-viewing behavior with purchase transaction information for any given household member. Purchase transaction information includes product description, price, promotion, and other factors. TV-viewing behavior is tracked at the panel member's home via so-called Peoplemeters. The TV-audience measurement system usually requires cooperation of the panel member. Each time the family member watches a program, he or she has to push a button to identify him/herself. More advanced systems involve a camera that records which members of the household are watching TV. Single-source data allow companies to measure, among other things, the effectiveness of their advertising policy.

Outside the United States, most of the scanning data are store scanning data. Household-level data are available in some countries, such as the United Kingdom, Taiwan, and Japan, but are still in an infancy stage. In Europe, ACNielsen set up a partnership with the U.K.-based Safeway supermarket chain that allows companies

---

[44]Hotaka Katahira and Shigeru Yagi, "Marketing Information Technologies in Japan," in *The Marketing Information Revolution*, R. C. Blattberg, R. Glazer, and J. D. C. Little, Eds. (Boston, MA: Harvard Business School, 1994).

access to scanning data on all categories from all of the chain's 322 outlets.[45] In China, with 300 million TV homes and 900 TV stations, ACNielsen plans to cover the ten largest cities with Peoplemeters. Companies such as Nestlé are also putting together their own databases. These innovations in marketing decision support systems have spurred several major developments in the marketing area:

- *Shift from mass to micro marketing.*[46] Better knowledge on shopping and viewing behavior has moved the focus from mass marketing to the individual. New information technologies enable firms to tailor their pricing, product line, advertising, and promotion strategies to particular neighborhoods or even individuals. Database marketing gives companies an opportunity to enter into direct contact with their customers. Nestlé's strategy for its Buitoni pasta brand offers a good example of the power of database marketing in a Pan-European context. In the United Kingdom, Nestlé built up a database of people who had requested a free recipe booklet. The next step was the launch of a Casa Buitoni Club. Members of the club receive a magazine and opportunities to win a trip for cooking instruction. The goal of the strategy is to build up a long-term commitment to the Buitoni brand.[47] Likewise, in Malaysia Nestlé built up a database with information on consumption patterns, lifestyle, religion, race, and feelings about specific brands. By building up its database knowledge, Nestlé hopes to do a better job in target marketing and adapting its products to the local market.[48]

- *Continuous monitoring of brand sales/market share movements.* Sales measurement based on scanner data are more accurate and timely than, for instance, data from store audits. In Japan, thousands of new products are launched continuously. Accurate tracking information on new brand shares and incumbent brand shares is crucial information for manufacturers and retailers alike.[49]

- *Scanning data are used by manufacturers to support marketing decisions.* Initially, most scanning data were simply used as tracking devices. This has changed now. Scanning data are increasingly used for tactical decision support. The databases are used to assist all sorts of decisions in inventory management, consumer/trade promotions, pricing, shelf-space allocation, and media advertising. Scanning data are also increasingly used for category management.

- *Scanning data are used to provide merchandising support to retailers.* Many manufacturers also employ information distilled from scanning data to help out retailers with merchandising programs. Such support helps to build up a long-term relationship with retailers. Scanning data help manufacturers to show the "hard facts" to their distributors.

Richer market information should help global marketers to improve marketing decisions that have cross-border ramifications. Scanning data from the Pan-European region allows marketers to gauge the effectiveness of Pan-European adver-

[45]"IRI vs. Nielsen," *Advertising Age* (October 12, 1992), p. 50.
[46]David J. Curry, *The New Marketing Research Systems. How to Use Strategic Database Information for Better Marketing Decisions* (New York: John Wiley & Sons, 1994).
[47]Stan Rapp and Thomas L. Collins, *Beyond Maxi-Marketing: The New Power of Caring and Sharing* (New York: McGraw-Hill, Inc., 1994).
[48]"Nestlé Builds Database in Asia with Direct Mail," *Ad Age International* (January 1998), p. 34.
[49]H. Katahira and S. Yagi, "Marketing Information Technologies in Japan," p. 310.

tising campaigns, branding decisions, distribution strategies, and so forth. The information can also be used to monitor competitors' activities. With the emergence of consumer panel data, marketers are able to spot similarities and disparities in cross-border consumer behavior. In sum, the consequences of new market research systems are dramatic. Several environmental forces (e.g., single European market, cultural trends) promote the so-called *global village* with a convergence in tastes and preferences leading to "universal" segments. On the other hand, the new information technologies will ultimately allow marketers to enter into one-to-one relationships with their individual customers.

Despite the promises of scanner databases, their full potential is not yet exploited in many countries. Many users still simply view scanner data as an instrument to track market shares. Two factors are behind this state of affairs. One reason is the conservatism of the users of the data. Another factor is the attitude of local retailers toward data access. In countries like the United Kingdom, retailers are reluctant to release their data because they fear that by doing so they might inform their competition. Rivals are not just other retailers but in many cases the manufacturers who compete with the retailer's store brands.

State-of-the-art marketing research tools are also being developed to track the effectiveness of newer marketing mix media vehicles such as the Internet. For instance, the WebAudit is a package designed by ACNielsen Australia that allows subscribers to evaluate the performance of their Web site. Subscribers to the service receive information on user profiles by region, most requested pages, most downloaded files, and so on. The ultimate goal is to establish a "Nielsen rating" for World Wide Web sites similar to the ratings ACNielsen currently provides for television programming.[50]

MANAGING GLOBAL MARKETING RESEARCH ◆ ◆ ◆ ◆ ◆ ◆

Global marketing research projects have to cater to the needs of various interest groups: global and regional headquarters, and local subsidiaries. Different requirements will lead to tension among the stakeholders. In this section we center on two highly important issues in managing global marketing research: (1) who should conduct the research project and (2) coordination of global marketing research projects.

Selecting a Research Agency

Even companies with in-house expertise will often employ local research agencies to assist with a multicountry research project. The choice of a research agency to run a multicountry research project is made centrally by headquarters or locally by regional headquarters or country affiliates. Reliance on local research firms is an absolute must in countries such as China, both to be close to the market and to get around government red tape.[51] Local agencies may also have a network of contacts that give access to secondary data sources. Whatever the motive for using a local research agency, selection of an agency should be based on careful scrutiny and

[50]"Benchmark Standards for Worldwide Web Sites," *AC Nielsen SRG News* (October 1996), p. 3.
[51]Steele, p. 158.

screening of possible candidates. The first step is to see what sort of research support services are available to conduct the research project. Each year *Marketing News* (an American Marketing Association publication) puts together a directory of international marketing research firms (www.ama.org/pubs/mn/honglobal).

Several considerations enter the agency selection decision. Agencies that are partners or subsidiaries of global research firms are especially useful when there is a strong need for coordination of multicountry research efforts. The agency's level of expertise is the main ingredient in the screening process: What are the qualifications of the staff? the fieldworkers? The track record of the agencies is also a key factor: How long has the agency been in business? What sort of research problems has it dealt with? What experience does the agency have in tackling our type of research problem(s)? What clients has it worked for? In some cases, it is worthwhile to contact previous or current clients and explore their feelings about the prospective research supplier.

When cross-border coordination is an issue, companies should also examine the willingness of the agency to be flexible and be a good team player. Communication skills is another important issue. When secrecy is required, it is necessary to examine whether the candidate has any possible conflicts of interest. Does the agency have any ties with one of our (potential) competitors? Does it have a good reputation in keeping matters confidential? Again, a background check with previous clients may provide the answer.

Cost is clearly a crucial input in the selection decision. Exhibit 6–10 shows cost comparisons for different types of marketing research studies in various places. The comparisons are done on an index basis. For example, running a focus group in Western Europe would cost around 15,000 Swiss Francs (index = 100). In Japan (index = 194), however, the cost for a focus group would be almost twice as much. In Eastern Europe (index = 50), the cost for a focus group study would be only half the price of a focus group in Western Europe. Exhibit 6–10 illustrates that costs vary substantially, depending on the nature (e.g., telephone tracking versus usage survey) and the place of the study. For instance, attitude surveys are, on average, cheaper in the Pacific Rim countries (87) than in Western Europe (100 = Swiss Francs 40,800). On the other hand, in-home product tests tend to be more expensive in the Pacific Rim countries (144) than in Western Europe (100 = Swiss Francs 12,750). Budget constraints may force firms to go for a second-tier agency. Quality standards can vary a lot. One golden rule needs to be observed, though: Beware of agencies that promise the world at a bargain price. Inaccurate and misleading information will almost certainly lead to disastrous decisions.

William Lawson, a marketing manager with the pharmaceutical company Eli Lilly, offers the following tips on how to use market research agencies more productively for global market research projects:[52]

- *Use your agency creatively.* For example, to "sell" the research findings to the local subsidiaries, market research managers might consider asking the agency to present the results. A third "neutral" party might have more credibility among the local affiliates.

- *Take your agency into 100 percent confidence and share everything.* Create a partnership.

---

[52]William V. Lawson, "The 'Heavyweights'—Forecasting the Obesity Market in Europe for a New Compound," *Marketing and Research Today* (November 1995), pp. 270–74.

EXHIBIT 6–10
CROSS-COUNTRY COST COMPARISON FOR MARKET RESEARCH STUDIES

Usage & Attitude Survey

Western Europe (SwFrs 40,800)	100	
North America	220	
U.S.A.		234
Canada		202
Japan	181	
Australia	136	
Central/South America	100	
Brazil		114
Argentina		105
Mexico		92
Colombia/Chile/Venezuela		67
South Africa	102	
Middle East	96	
Saudi Arabia		106
U.A.E.		84
Pacific Rim	87	
Hong Kong		140
Indonesia		63
Taiwan/S. Korea		92
Eastern Europe	61	
Hungary		48
Czechoslovakia		65
Poland		62
Russia		81
North Africa	50	
Egypt		49
Turkey	45	
India	13	
Brazil	228	
Mexico	150	
South Africa	188	
Australia	157	
Middle East	151	
Saudi Arabia		165
U.A.E.		129
Pacific Rim	144	
Hong Kong		152
Indonesia		73
Taiwan/S. Korea		187
Eastern Europe	119	
Hungary		94
Czechoslovakia		111
Poland		127
Russia		155
North Africa	100	
Egypt		102
Turkey	77	
India	25	

Telephone Tracking Study

U.S.A. (SwFrs 36,120)	100
Canada	106
Japan	103
U.S.A.	100
Australia	80
Taiwan	78
Brazil	59
Hong Kong	48
South Africa	47
Argentina	34
Hungary	27
Turkey	26

In-Home Product Test

Western Europe (SwFrs 12,750)	100	
North America	318	
U.S.A.		283
Canada		362
Japan	297	
Central/South America	190	

Four Group Discussions

Western Europe (SwFrs 15,061)	100	
Japan	194	
North America	129	
U.S.A.		135
Canada		115
Pacific Rim	90	
Hong Kong		92
Indonesia		53
Taiwan/S. Korea		133
Central/South America	82	
Brazil		107
Argentina		53
Colombia/Chile/Venezuela		51
Mexico		83
Australia	74	
Middle East	70	
Saudi Arabia		72
U.A.E.		69
South Africa	51	
Eastern Europe	50	
Hungary		51
Czechoslovakia		53
Poland		48
Russia	45	
North Africa	33	
Egypt		32
Turkey	51	
India	17	

Source: ESOMAR. Permission for using this material has been granted by (E.S.O.M.A.R.) The European Society for Opinion and Marketing Research J. J. Viottastraat 29, 1071 JP, Amsterdam, The Netherlands.

- *Use your agency strategically.* Ask for their input, opinions, and their views on the implications of the study's findings.

Coordination of Multicountry Research

Multicountry research projects demand careful coordination of the research efforts undertaken in the different markets. The benefits of coordination are manifold.[53] Coordination facilitates cross-country comparison of results whenever such comparisons are crucial. It also can have benefits of timeliness, cost, centralization of communication, and quality control. Coordination brings up two central issues: (1) Who should do the coordinating? and (2) What should be the degree of coordination? In some cases, coordination is implemented by the research agency that is hired to run the project. When markets differ a lot, or when researchers vary from country to country, the company itself will prefer to coordinate the project.[54]

The degree of coordination centers around the conflicting demands of various users of marketing research: global (or regional) headquarters and local subsidiaries. Headquarters favor standardized data collection, sampling procedures, and survey instruments. Local user groups prefer country-customized research designs that recognize the peculiarities of their local environment. This conflict is referred to as the **emic** versus **etic** dilemma.[55] The **emic** school focuses on the peculiarities of each country. Attitudinal phenomena and values are so unique in each country that they can only be tapped via culture-specific measures. The other school of thought, the **etic** approach, emphasizes universal behavioral and attitudinal traits. To gauge such phenomena requires culturally unbiased measures. For instance, for many goods and services, there appears to be convergence in preferences across cultures. Therefore, consumer preferences could be studied from an etic angle. Buying motivations behind those preferences, however, often differ substantially across cultures. Hence, a cross-country project that looks into buying motivations may demand an emic approach.[56]

In cross-cultural market research, the need for comparability favors the **etic** paradigm with an emphasis on the cross-border similarities and parallels. Nevertheless, in order to make the research study useful and acceptable to local users, companies need to recognize the peculiarities of local cultures. So, ideally, survey instruments that are developed for cross-country market research projects should encompass both approaches—emic *and* etic.[57] There are several approaches to balance these conflicting demands. In a Pan-European positioning study conducted for BMW, coordination was accomplished via the following measures:[58]

1. All relevant parties (users at headquarters and local subsidiaries) were included from the outset in planning the research project.
2. All parties contributed in funding the study.

[53]Aldridge, p. 361.

[54]"Multi-country Research: Should You Do Your Own Coordinating?" *Industrial Marketing Digest* (1985), pp. 79–82.

[55]Douglas and Craig, pp. 132–37.

[56]Malhotra, Agarwal, and Peterson, p. 12.

[57]Malhotra, Agarwal, and Peterson, p. 12.

[58]H. Kern, H.-C. Wagner, and R. Hassis, "European Aspects of a Global Brand . . . ," pp. 49–50.

3. Hypotheses and objectives were deemed to be binding at later stages of the project.

4. Data collection went through two stages. First, responses to a country-specific pool of psychographic statements were collected. The final data collection in the second stage used a mostly standardized survey instrument containing a few statements that were country-customized (based on findings from the first run).

The key lessons of the BMW example are twofold. First, coordination means that all parties (i.e., user groups) should get involved. Neglected parties will have little incentive to accept the results of the research project. Second, multicountry research should allow some leeway for country peculiarities. For instance, questionnaires should not be overstandardized, but may include some country-specific items. This is especially important for collecting "soft" data (e.g., lifestyle/attitude statements).

◆ ◆

$\mathcal{G}$LOBAL PERSPECTIVE 6–2

HOW DOES JAPANESE MARKET RESEARCH DIFFER?

There is a philosophical difference in the role of marketing research between U.S./European and Japanese executives. Marketing researchers in the United States (and also, to some extent, within Europe) believe that various dimensions of consumer attitudes and behaviors can be measured with statistical tools. Japanese marketing researchers, however, believe that those tools are not sufficient to gauge the vagrant nature of consumer attitudes. As a result, Japanese marketing researchers rely far less on statistical techniques than their U.S. counterparts.

Toru Nishikawa, marketing manager at Hitachi, lists five reasons against "scientific" market research in the area of new product development:

1. *Indifference of respondents.* Careless random sampling leads to mistaken judgments, because some people are indifferent toward the product in question.

2. *Absence of responsibility.* The consumer is most sincere when spending, not when talking.

3. *Conservative attitudes.* Ordinary consumers are conservative and tend to react negatively to new product ideas.

4. *Vanity.* It is part of human nature to exaggerate and put on a good appearance.

5. *Insufficient information.* The research results depend on information about product characteristics given to survey participants.

Japanese firms prefer more down-to-earth methods of information gathering. Instead of administering surveys, Japanese market researchers will go into the field and observe how consumers use the product. For example, Toyota sent a group of engineers and designers to Southern California to observe how women get into and operate their cars. They found that women with long fingernails have trouble opening the door and handling various knobs on the dashboard. Consequently, Toyota altered some of its automobiles' exterior and interior designs.

Hands-on market research does not negate the importance of conventional marketing research. In fact, scores of Japanese firms assign more people to information gathering and analysis than U.S. firms. What is unique about Japanese market research is that Japanese research teams include both product engineers and sales and marketing representatives. Engineers gain insights from talking with prospective customers as much as their marketing peers. They can directly incorporate user comments into product specifications.

Sources: Michael R. Czinkota and Masaaki Kotabe, "Product Development the Japanese Way," *Journal of Business Strategy*, 11 (Nov./Dec. 1990), pp. 31–36, and Johny K. Johansson and Ikujiro Nonaka, *Relentless: The Japanese Way of Marketing* (New York: Harper Business, 1996).

SUMMARY ✦

Whenever you drive to an unknown destination, you will probably use a road map, ask for instructions to get there, and carefully examine the road signals. If not, you risk getting lost. By the same token, whenever you need to make marketing decisions in the global market place, market intelligence will guide you in these endeavors. Shoddy information invariably leads to shoddy decision making. Good information will spur solid decision making. In this day and age, having timely and adequate market intelligence also provides a competitive advantage. This does not mean that global marketers should do research at any cost. As always, it is important to examine at each step the costs and the value added of having more information. Usually it is not hard to figure out the costs of gathering market intelligence. The hard part is the benefit component. Views on the benefits and role of market research sometimes differ between cultures. Global Perspective 6–2 highlights the peculiarities of Japanese firms' approach to marketing research.

The complexities of the global marketplace are stunning. They pose a continuous challenge to market researchers. Hurdles are faced in gathering secondary and primary data. Not all challenges will be met successfully.

Mistakes are easily made. One American toiletries manufacturer conducted its market research in (English-speaking) Toronto for a bar soap to be launched in (French-speaking) Québec. The whole venture became a sad soap opera with a tragic ending.[59]

In this chapter we discussed the intricacies in developing and implementing a market research project in a cross-national setting. We also reviewed several techniques that prove useful to estimate the market size whenever few or only poor quality data are at your disposal.

To make cross-country comparisons meaningful, companies need to adequately manage and coordinate their market research projects with a global scope. Inputs from local users of the research are desirable for several reasons. When the locals feel that they were treated stepmotherly, it will be hard to "sell" the findings of the research project. As a result, getting their support for policies based on the study's conclusions becomes a formidable task. Local feedback also becomes necessary to uncover country-specific peculiarities that cannot be tapped with overstandardized measurement instruments.

KEY TERMS ✦

analogy method	courtesy bias	parallel translation	trade audit
back-translation	emic (etic)	scalar equivalence	translation equivalence
chain ratio method	functional equivalence	social desirability bias	triangulate
conceptual equivalence	omnibus survey		

REVIEW QUESTIONS ✦ ✦ ✦ ✦ ✦ ✦ ✦ ✦ ✦ ✦ ✦ ✦ ✦ ✦ ✦ ✦ ✦ ✦

1. What are the major benefits and limitations of omnibus surveys?
2. What is the notion of *triangulation* in global market research?
3. Discuss the major issues in running focus-group discussions in an international context.
4. Discuss why market size estimates may differ, depending on the method being used. How can such differences be reconciled?
5. Contrast the emic versus the etic approach in international marketing research.

---

[59]Sandra Vandermerwe, "Colgate-Palmolive: Cleopatra," Case Study, Lausanne: IMD, 1990.

DISCUSSION QUESTIONS ◆

1. Chapter 6 suggests two ways to select countries for multi-country market research projects: (1) start with a preliminary research in each one of them or (2) cluster the countries and pick one representative member from each cluster. Under what circumstances would you prefer one option over the other one?

2. Refer to Exhibit 6–7, which presents McDonald's market potential based on the formula given on page 205.

a. Using the same formula, estimate what McDonald's market potential would be for the following Pacific-Rim countries: India, Indonesia, Malaysia, Myanmar, the Philippines, Singapore, and Thailand.

b. Which ones of these markets looks most appealing in terms of market size? Compare your estimates with the actual number of restaurants in each of these countries (Information can be found in McDonald's 1998 Annual Report, which can be downloaded from McDonald's Web site — www.mcdonalds.com).

c. What factors are missing in the formula that McDonald's uses?

3. In most cases, standard data collection methods are still mail, phone, or personal interviewing. Tokyu Agency, Tokyo, a Japanese ad agency, has started using the Internet to find out how Japanese youngsters spend their money and what their views are on various issues (e.g., environment). What opportunities does the Internet offer as a data-gathering tool in international market research? What are its merits and disadvantages in this regard?

4. Clarion Marketing and Communications, a Connecticut-based marketing research firm, recently launched Global Focus, a technique that allows companies to run focus groups in different countries who interact with each other. The focus groups are held in videoconference centers in the different cities (e.g., one in New York; one in London) with a moderator in each location. Do you see a need for global focus groups? Why or why not? What are potential benefits? concerns?

5. Imagine that Nokia plans to expand its market in South America. Use the chain ratio method to come up with market size estimates for cellular phones in the following four countries: Argentina, Brazil, Chile, and Peru.

6. When developing a survey instrument for a cross-country study, market researchers often need to construct a scale (e.g., a 7-point disagree/agree scale). What are the major items that one should be concerned about when building such scales?

FURTHER READING ◆ ◆ ◆ ◆ ◆ ◆ ◆ ◆ ◆ ◆ ◆ ◆ ◆ ◆ ◆ ◆ ◆ ◆ ◆

Aldridge, D. N. "Multi-Country Research." In *Applied Marketing and Social Research*. U. Bradley, Ed., 2nd ed. New York, NY: John Wiley & Sons, 1987.

Amine, S. Lyn, and S. Tamer Cavusgil. "Demand Estimation in a Developing Country Environment: Difficulties, Techniques and Examples." *Journal of the Market Research Society*, 28(1) (1986): 43–65.

Choudhry, Yusuf A. "Pitfalls in International Marketing Research: Are You Speaking French Like A Spanish Cow?" *Akron Business and Economic Review*, 17(4) (Winter 1986): 18–28.

Douglas, Susan P., and C. Samuel Craig. *International Marketing Research*. Englewood Cliffs, NJ: Prentice Hall, 1983.

Eskin, Gerry. "POS Scanner Data: The State of the Art, in Europe and the World." *Marketing and Research Today* (May 1994): 107–17.

Hibbert, Edgar. "Researching International Markets — How Can We Ensure Validity of Results?" *Marketing and Research Today*. November 1993, pp. 222–28.

Johansson, K. Johny, and Ikujiro Nonaka. "Market Research the Japanese Way." *Harvard Business Review* (May–June 1987): 16–22.

Malhotra, Naresh K., James Agarwal, and Mark Peterson. "Methodological Issues in Cross-cultural Marketing Research. A State-of-the-Art Review." *International Marketing Review*, 13(5) (1996): 7–43.

Schroiff, Hans-Willi. "Creating Competitive Intellectual Capital." *Marketing and Research Today* (November 1998): 148–56.

Steele, Henry C. "Marketing Research in China: The Hong Kong Connection." *Marketing and Research Today* (August, 1990): 155–64.

Tuncalp, Secil. "The Marketing Research Scene in Saudi Arabia." *European Journal of Marketing*, 22(5) (1988): 15–22.

Williams, S. C. "Researching Markets in Japan — A Methodological Case Study." *Journal of International Marketing*, 4(2) (1996): 87–93.

GLOBAL SEGMENTATION AND POSITIONING

7

CHAPTER OVERVIEW

1. REASONS FOR INTERNATIONAL MARKET SEGMENTATION
2. INTERNATIONAL MARKET SEGMENTATION APPROACHES
3. SEGMENTATION SCENARIOS
4. BASES FOR COUNTRY SEGMENTATION
5. INTERNATIONAL POSITIONING STRATEGIES
6. GLOBAL, FOREIGN, AND LOCAL CONSUMER CULTURE POSITIONING

Few companies can be all things to all people. Instead of competing across the board, most companies will identify and target the most attractive market segments that they can serve effectively. Variation in customer needs is the primary motive for market segmentation. When consumer preferences vary, marketers can design a marketing mix program that is tailored toward the needs of the specific segments that the firm targets. Marketers select one or more segmentation bases (e.g., age) and slice up their prospective customer base according to the chosen criteria. Marketing programs are then developed that are in tune with the particular needs of each of the segments that the company wants to serve.

In global marketing, market segmentation becomes especially critical, given the sometimes incredibly wide divergence in cross-border consumer needs and preferences. In this chapter we will first focus on the motivations for international market segmentation. Given information on the segmentation criteria you plan to use, there are several country segmentation approaches you might take. We describe in detail several possible segmentation scenarios. We then consider several bases that marketers might consider for country segmentation. Once the company has chosen its target segments, management needs to determine a competitive positioning strategy for its products. The final sections focus on alternative international positioning strategies.

REASONS FOR INTERNATIONAL MARKET SEGMENTATION

The goal of market segmentation is to break down the market for a product or a service into different groups of consumers who differ in their response to the firm's marketing-mix program. That way, the firm can tailor its marketing mix to each individual segment, and, hence, do a better job in satisfying the needs of the target segments. This overall objective also applies in an international marketing context. In that sense, market segmentation is the logical outgrowth of the marketing concept.[1]

The requirements for effective market segmentation in a domestic marketing context also apply in international market segmentation. In particular, segments ideally should possess the following set of properties:[2]

1. *Measurable*. The segments should be easy to define and to measure. This criterion is easily met for "objective" country traits such as socioeconomic variables (e.g., per capita income). However, the size of segments based on cultural or lifestyle indicators is typically much harder to gauge.

2. *Sizable*. The segments should be large enough to be worth going after. Note that flexible manufacturing technologies enable companies to relax this criterion. In fact, many segments that might be considered too small in a single-country context become attractive once they are lumped across borders.

3. *Accessible*. The segments should also be easy to reach via the media. Differences in the quality of the media infrastructure (e.g., absence or presence of commercial television) imply that a given segment might be hard to reach in some countries and easy to target in other marketplaces.

4. *Actionable*. For market segmentation to be meaningful, it is important that effective marketing programs (the four Ps) can be developed to evoke the desired response from the target segment. When segments do not respond differently to the firm's marketing mix, there is basically no need to segment the market.

5. *Competitive intensity*. Preferably, the segments are not preempted by the firm's competition. In fact, in global marketing, small companies often use competitive pressure as one of their segmentation criteria when assessing international markets.

6. *Growth potential*. Finally, segments should hopefully have a significant growth potential. In practice, identifying market segments with promising growth prospects and low competitive pressure is quite challenging. Typically, marketers face a trade-off between competitive intensity and growth prospects.

---

[1]Yoram Wind and Susans P. Douglas, "International Market Segmentation," *European Journal of Marketing*, 6(1) (1972), pp. 17–25.

[2]Philip Kotler, *Marketing Management* (Upper Saddle River, N.J.: Prentice Hall, 2000), p. 274.

Let us consider now the major reasons why international marketers implement international market segmentation.

Country Screening

Companies usually do a preliminary screening of countries before identifying attractive market opportunities for their product or service. For preliminary screening, market analysts rely on a few indicators, for which information can easily be gathered from secondary data sources. At this stage, the international market analyst might classify countries in two or three piles. Countries that meet all criteria will be grouped in the "Go" pile for further consideration at the next stage. Countries that fail to meet most of the criteria will enter the "No Go" pile. The third set of countries are those that meet some of the criteria, but not all of them. They may become of interest in the future, but probably not in the short term.

Companies will use different sets of criteria to screen countries, depending on the nature of the product. For example, Kellogg uses the population size to classify candidate markets. Jordan, a small Norwegian toothbrush maker, groups countries based on competitive intensity and growth potential (measured via per capita consumption of toothbrushes). Given its small size, the firm's strategy is to be a niche player shooting for markets with low competitive pressure and favorable growth opportunities.[3]

Global Market Research

Country segmentation also plays a role in global marketing research. Companies increasingly make an effort to design products or services that meet the needs of customers in different countries. Certain features might need to be added or altered, but the core product is largely common across countries. Other aspects of the marketing mix program such as the communication strategy might also be similar. The benefits of a standardization approach often outweigh the possible drawbacks. Yet in order to successfully adopt this approach, companies need to do sufficient market research. Given the sheer number of countries in which many companies operate, doing market research in each one of them is often inefficient. Especially at the early stage, companies are likely to focus on a select few countries. The key question, then, is which countries to choose. One approach is to start grouping prospective markets into clusters of homogeneous countries. Out of each group, one prototypical member is chosen. Research efforts will be concentrated on each of the key members, at least initially. Presumably, research findings for the selected key member countries can then be projected to other countries belonging to its cluster. For example, Heineken chose four countries to do market research for Buckler, a nonalcoholic beer: the Netherlands, Spain, the United States, and France. The Dutch brewer wanted to assess the market appeal of Buckler and the feasibility of a Pan-European marketing strategy consisting of a roughly common targeting, positioning, and marketing mix strategy across the continent.[4]

---

[3]Per V. Jenster and Kamran Kashani, "Jordan A/S," Case Study, International Institute for Management Development, Lausanne, Switzerland, 1991.

[4]Sandra Vandermerwe, "Heineken NV: Buckler Nonalcoholic Beer," Case Study, International Institute for Management Development, Switzerland, 1991.

When a product or service does well in one country, firms often hope to replicate their success story in other countries. The strategic logic is to launch the product in countries that in some regards are highly similar to the country where the product has already been introduced.[5] For example, Cadbury-Schweppes was very confident about launching Schweppes tonic water in Brazil, given that the beverage was well accepted in culturally similar countries such as Mexico.

It is important, though, to realize that a host of factors make or break the success of a new product launch. Tabasco sauce is very popular in Asian countries that have a strong liking for spicy dishes (e.g., Japan). Hence, McIlhenny, the Louisiana-based maker of Tabasco sauce, might view entering Vietnam and India, two of the emerging markets in Asia with a palate for hot food, as the logical next step for its expansion strategy in Asia. Other factors, however, such as buying power, import restrictions, or the shoddy state of the distribution and media infrastructure, might lessen the appeal of these markets.

Entry Decisions

Segmentation decisions are also instrumental in setting the company's product positioning strategy. Once the firm has selected the target segments, management needs to develop a positioning strategy to embrace the chosen segments. Basically, the company must decide on how it wants to position its products or services in the mind of the prospective target customers. Environmental changes or shifting consumer preferences often force a firm to rethink its positioning strategy. Cathay Pacific's recent repositioning strategy is a good example. The Hong Kong–based airline carrier realized that its product offerings failed to adequately meet the needs of its Asian clients, who represent 80 percent of its customer base. To better satisfy this target segment the airline repositioned itself in the fall of 1994 to become the preferred airline among Asian travelers. To that end, Cathay wanted to project an Asian personality with a personal touch. Cathay now offers a wide variety of Asian meals and entertainment. Other measures include a new logo (by some people referred to as a shark-fin), new colors, repainted exteriors, and redesigned cabins and ticket counters. To communicate these changes to the public, Cathay launched a heavy advertising campaign with the slogan "The Heart of Asia."[6]

Positioning Strategy

In domestic marketing, segmentation and positioning decisions will dictate a firm's marketing-mix policy. By the same token, country segmentation will guide the global marketer's mix decisions. A persistent problem faced by international marketers is how to strike the balance between standardization and customization. International market segmentation could shed some light on this issue. Members falling in the same segment might lend themselves to a standardized marketing-mix strategy. The same *product* design, an identical *pricing* policy, similar advertising messages and media mixes, and the same distribution channels could be used in these markets. Of course, marketers need to be very careful when contemplating such moves. There should be a clear linkage between the segmentation bases and the target customers' responsiveness to any of these four Ps.

Marketing-Mix Policy

[5]Johny K. Johansson and Reza Moinpour, "Objective and Perceived Similarity for Pacific-Rim Countries," *Columbia Journal of World Business* (Winter 1977), pp. 65–76.
[6]John Pies, Cathay Pacific, private communication.

Usually, it is very hard to establish a linkage between market segments and all four elements of the marketing mix. For instance, countries with an underdeveloped phone infrastructure (e.g., Eastern Europe, China, Thailand) are typically prime candidates for mobile phone technologies. However, many of these countries differ dramatically in terms of their price sensitivities, given the wide gaps in buying power. So treating them as one group as far as the pricing policy goes might lead to disastrous consequences.

Exhibit 7–1 illustrates how country segmentation can be applied in developing international advertising strategies.[7] The mapping comes from a recent study that predicted the preference of a country in terms of rational ("think") and emotional ("feel") appeals based on the country's cultural and advertising industry environment (e.g., level of government regulation, per capita ad spending, media characteristics). The *think* strategy uses argumentation and the lecture format to address the target audience. *Feel* appeals are centered around emotions (psychological

EXHIBIT 7–1
"THINK" AND "FEEL" COUNTRY CLUSTERS

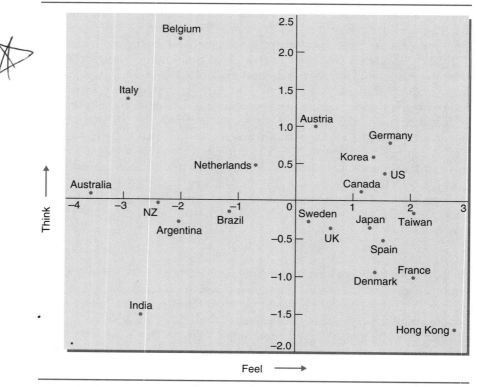

Source: Fred Zandpour and Katrin R. Harich, "Think and Feel Country Clusters: A New Approach to International Advertising Standardization," *International Journal of Advertising,* 15 (1996) p. 341. Copyright Advertising Association.

---

[7]Fred Zandpour and Katrin R. Harich, "Think and Feel Country Clusters: A New Approach to International Advertising Standardization," *International Journal of Advertising,* 15, (1996), pp. 325–44.

appeals), often phrased in a dramatic format. The map shows four distinctive clusters. For instance, five countries (Austria, Canada, Germany, South Korea, and the United States) fall into the high feel/high think region.

INTERNATIONAL MARKET SEGMENTATION APPROACHES

Global marketers approach the segmentation process from different angles. The standard country segmentation procedure classifies prospect countries on a single dimension (e.g., per capita Gross National Product) or on a set of multiple socioeconomic, political, and cultural criteria available from secondary data sources (e.g., the World Bank, UNESCO, OECD). Exhibit 7–2 presents a list of various country characteristics that analysts might consider for classifying countries in distinct segments. When there are numerous country traits, the segmentation variables are usually first collapsed into a smaller set of dimensions using data reduction techniques such as factor analysis. For instance, the set of variables listed in Exhibit 7–2 can be

EXHIBIT 7–2
MACRO-LEVEL COUNTRY CHARACTERISTICS

Construct	Items
1. Aggregate Production and Transportation (Mobility)	Number of air passengers/km
	Air cargo (ton/km)
	Number of newspapers
	Population
	Cars per capita
	Motor gasoline consumption per capita
	Electricity production
2. Health	Life expectancy
	Physicians per capita
	Political stability
3. Trade	Imports/GNP
	Exports/GNP
4. Lifestyle	GDP per capita
	Phones per capita
	Electricity consumption per capita
5. Cosmopolitanism	Foreign visitors per capita
	Tourist expenditures per capita
	Tourist receipts per capita
6. Miscellaneous	Consumer price index
	Newspaper circulation
	Hospital beds
	Education expenditures/Government budget
	Graduate education in population per capita

Source: Kristiaan Helsen, Kamel Jedidi, and Wayne S. DeSarbo, "A New Approach to Country Segmentation Utilizing Multinational Diffusion Patterns," *Journal of Marketing* 57(4) (October 1993), p. 64. Reprinted with permission from the *Journal of Marketing*, published by the American Marketing Association.

summarized via four constructs: mobility ("aggregate production and transportation"); health, trade, lifestyle, and cosmopolitanism.[8] The countries under consideration are then classified into homogeneous groups using statistical algorithms such as cluster analysis (see the Appendix for a brief overview of some of these techniques).

Exhibit 7–3 presents the results for a two- and three-segment country segmentation along the five constructs listed in Exhibit 7–2. Note that the United States forms a cluster of its own. We also observe that Japan is grouped with some of the European countries. In general, macro-level segments seldom match geographic groupings. The problem with macro-level segmentation is that the resulting country groupings do not necessarily correspond to market response measures (e.g., penetration rate, purchase intention, willingness to pay).

From a marketer's perspective, the practical usefulness of macro-level segments is questionable. To address this shortcoming of the standard country segmentation approach, an alternative procedure could be considered. This method proceeds as follows:[9]

EXHIBIT 7–3
TWO- AND THREE-SEGMENT SOLUTIONS

A. Two-Segment Solution

Segment 1	Segment 2
Austria	Japan
Belgium	Sweden
Denmark	U.S.
France	
Finland	
Holland	
Norway	
Switzerland	
U.K.	

B. Three-Segment Solution

Segment 1	Segment 2	Segment 3
Holland	Austria	U.S.
Japan	Belgium	
Sweden	Denmark	

Source: Kristiaan Helsen, Kamel Jedidi, and Wayne S. DeSarbo, "A New Approach to Country Segmentation Utilizing Multinational Diffusion Patterns," *Journal of Marketing*, 57(4) (October 1993), p. 66.
Reprinted with permission from the *Journal of Marketing*, published by the American Marketing Association.

---

[8]Arguably, the labeling of these constructs is somewhat subjective. Factor analysis solutions are seldom clear-cut.
[9]Sudhir H. Kale and D. Sudharshan, "A Strategic Approach to International Segmentation," *International Marketing Review* (Summer 1987), pp. 60–70.

Step 1   *Criteria Development.* Determine your cut-off criteria. For example, for Waste Management International, one of the requirements is the convertibility of the local currency. The criteria will be driven by product and company characteristics.

Step 2   *Preliminary Screening.* Examine which countries meet the thresholds for the criteria set forward in Step 1. Countries that do meet the cut-off will be retained. Those that fail to make the cut are thrown out.

Step 3   *Microsegmentation.* The next stage is to develop microsegments in each of the countries that are still in your consideration set. There are two ways to come up with these segments:

1. Derive microsegments in each country individually. Survey data collected from prospective customers in each of the countries are used as inputs. The variables are similar to those used in domestic segmentation applications (e.g., demographics, lifestyle). In the next step, the analyst consolidates the microsegments across countries based on similarities among the microsegments in the prospect countries.

2. Alternatively, you could jointly group individuals in all the prospect countries to come up directly with cross-border segments.

Marketing practitioners are more likely to benefit from the second approach, since it is more in tune with the marketing concept.

SEGMENTATION SCENARIOS   ◆ ◆ ◆ ◆ ◆ ◆

When segmenting your foreign markets, different scenarios may arise. A common phenomenon is illustrated in Exhibit 7–4, where we have one universal segment (A) while the other segments are either unique to the country or exist in only two of the three countries. Note also that the size of the different segments varies, depending on the country.

One possibility is that you uncover **universal** or **global segments**. These are segments that transcend national boundaries. They are universal in the sense that customers belonging to such segments have common needs. Note that this segment could also be a universal niche. The standard definition of a niche is a more narrowly defined group of consumers who seek a very special bundle of benefits. Examples of possible universal segments include the MTV generation, businesspeople, the affluent, and *cyberphiles*. The similarity of customer needs clearly depends on the product category.[10]

Commonality of consumer needs is high for high-tech consumer durables and travel-related products (e.g., credit cards, airlines). The Nokia 9000 Communicator is an example of a product that is targeted toward a universal segment—in this case, the international business traveler. The product combines phone, fax, e-mail, and Internet functions and weighs less than a pound. To roll out the innovation, Nokia used a global campaign with the slogan "Everything. Every-

[10]George S. Yip, *Total Global Strategy* (Englewood Cliffs, N.J.: Prentice Hall, 1995), pp. 30–32.

EXHIBIT 7–4
DIFFERENT SEGMENT SCENARIOS

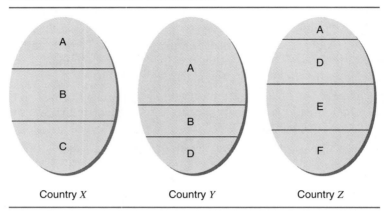

where."[11] At the other end of the spectrum are food products, where customer needs are usually very localized. Apart from global segments, you may also encounter **regional segments**. Here the similarity in customer needs and preferences exists at the regional level rather than the global level. While differences in consumer needs exist among regions, there are similarities within the region.

With universal or regional segments, you still need to decide to what extent you want to differentiate your marketing-mix strategy. At one end of the spectrum, management can adopt an undifferentiated marketing strategy that offers a more or less uniform package world- or region-wide. An undifferentiated marketing strategy allows the firm to capitalize on scale economies. To a large extent, this strategy suits high-tech companies. For instance, the corporate advertising director of Microsoft remarked in a recent forum that "The character of the (Microsoft) product is universal. Technology is an English-based thing, so there's a lot of willingness to embrace Western companies."[12] One company that pushes for a global approach is Polaroid. Polaroid's vice-president of global marketing observes that: "The world is global, and you can't win in a marketplace unless you have a global approach. If you have many products, you need to find some commonality, you need to seek universal themes."[13] At the other end of the spectrum are firms that tailor their marketing strategy to local markets. Although consumer needs and preferences may be similar, differentiation of positioning and other marketing-mix elements might be necessary to cope with variations in local market conditions. A differentiated strategy allows the company to stay better in tune with the local market and to be more flexible.

Unique (diverse) segments are the norm when gaps in cross-country customer needs and preferences are so substantial that it becomes very hard to derive meaningful cross-border segments. Under such a scenario, marketing-mix programs must

---

[11]"Nokia Trying to Lighten Business Travelers' Load," *Advertising Age International* (October 1996), pp. I-3, I-4.

[12]"U.S. Multinationals," *Advertising Age International* (June 1999), p. 41.

[13]Ibid., p. 40.

be localized in order to meet local needs. Rather than going after one common cross-border segment, management picks the most attractive target markets in each individual market. A case in point is the Canon AE-1 camera. When Canon launched this camera, it developed three different marketing programs: one for Japan, one for the United States, and one for Europe. In Japan, Canon targeted young replacement buyers. In the United States, it concentrated on upscale, first-time buyers of 35 mm single-lens reflex cameras. In Germany, Canon focused on older and technologically more sophisticated replacement buyers.[14] Jack Daniel's, the Tennessee-based whiskey brand, also pursues diverse target markets. In Australia and New Zealand, the beverage brand pursues young, hip, social drinkers. In China, where a bottle of Jack Daniel's costs $30 or more—double the U.S. price—the target is the 30- to 40-year-old urban professional who earns $1,000 a month working for a joint-venture company.[15]

In most instances, there is a mixture of universal, regional, and country-specific market segments. One final comment to be made here is that markets differ a great deal in terms of their degree of segmentation. Gaps in the degree of segmentation are most visible when contrasting the market structure in a developed country with the one in an emerging market. For most consumer goods, the market structure for a category in the emerging market is often pretty unsophisticated: premium versus economy. Industrialized countries, on the other hand, typically have many more segments and niches. This is, to a large extent, due to differences in the degree of market development. Early on in the product life cycle, the market is still relatively undersegmented. As consumers grow more sophisticated and demanding and as the category develops, new segments and niches emerge.

BASES FOR COUNTRY SEGMENTATION ◆ ◆ ◆ ◆ ◆ ◆

The first step in doing international market segmentation is deciding which criteria to use in the task. Just as in a domestic marketing context, the marketing analyst faces an embarrassment of riches. Literally hundreds of country characteristics could be used as inputs. In a sense, you can pick and choose the variables that you want. However, for the segmentation to be meaningful, there should be a linkage between the market segments and the response variable(s) that the company is interested in. Usually it is not a trivial exercise to figure out a priori which variables will contribute to the segmentation. Instead, the marketing analyst will need to rely on trial-and-error to find the "right" ingredients. Further, information on several segmentation criteria is typically missing, inaccurate, or outdated for some of the countries to be grouped.

We now briefly discuss different types of country variables that are most commonly used for country segmentation purposes. Most of these criteria can be used for the two segmentation approaches that we discussed earlier. For instance, one

---

[14]Hirotaka Takeuchi and Michael E. Porter, "Three Roles of International Marketing in Global Strategy," in *Competition in Global Industries*, ed. M. E. Porter (Boston, Mass.: Harvard Business School Press, 1986), pp. 139–40.

[15]"Jack Daniel's Goes Down Smooth in Australia, New Zealand, China," *Advertising Age International* (September 1997), pp. I-38, 39.

could use a socioeconomic variable like per capita income as a segmentation base to group countries. However, one could also use income to segment consumers within country first, and then derive pan-regional or global segments (e.g., pan-Asian middle class).

Demographics

Demographic variables are among the most popular segmentation criteria. They are easy to assess (recall the "measurability" requirement for effective market segmentation). Moreover, information on population variables is mostly reasonably accurate and readily available. An example of segmentation by age of the Chinese consumer market is shown in Exhibit 7–5. For many marketers in China, the most attractive age segment is Generation III, sometimes also known as the *s-generation* (single-child generation). Overall, Generation III consumers share five characteristics:[16]

1. *Luxury principle.* They spend a disproportionate amount of money on one thing at the expense of others. They have a strong drive toward a high personal consumption level.
2. *Consumption of Western feeling.* Material goods are a medium for them to experience Western culture.

EXHIBIT 7–5
CHINA'S THREE GENERATIONS

Generation I	• Age 45 to 59. • Generation of the socialistic society. • The talented got university education and have become high-ranking government officials but many work for state-owned enterprises. Some are already retired.
Generation II	• Age 30 to 44. • Lost opportunity to get proper education. • Mainly working for state-owned enterprises where income does not reflect job performance. • Those married are willing to spend as much as possible for "Little Emperor," their only child, at the expense of their pleasures. In many cases, what Generation II purchases is based on what the child wants or needs.
Generation III	• Age 18 to 29. • Good educational background, with opportunity to work for foreign-affiliated firms. They are blessed with a good aspect of the market economy system that promises a brighter future for people who earn enough money.

Source: Masaru Ariga, Mariko Yasue, and Gu Xiang Wen, "China's Generation III," *Marketing and Research Today* (February 1997), pp. 17–24.

---

[16]Masaru Ariga, Mariko Yasue, and Gu Xiang Wen, "China's Generation III," *Marketing and Research Today* (February 1997), pp. 17–24.

3. *Aspiration of big names.* They tend to be very fond of famous brand-name products.

4. *Newer-the-better syndrome.* They like to go after the newest products.

5. *One-cut-above-the rest mentality.* They like to impress others.

Other possible demographic segmentation bases include population size, urbanization degree, ethnic composition, and birth/death rates. For many consumer goods, especially low-ticket items, population size is a good proxy for market potential.

Countries with an aging population clearly offer market opportunities for consumer goods and services that cater to the elderly. Examples are geriatric care, travel-related services, leisure items, and medicines. Societies that are highly urbanized share many problems, such as traffic congestion, environmental pollution, and criminality, to mention a few. By the same token, countries with high birth rates have similar buying patterns. Examples of goods and services with high potential in such countries include baby food and clothing, toys, prenatal care services, and birth-control devices. Global Perspective 7–1 focuses on the buying habits of the Asian teenagers segment.

♦ ♦

*G*LOBAL PERSPECTIVE 7–1

THE ASIAN TEENAGERS SEGMENT: A BOON FOR THE NIKES OF THE WORLD

Two-thirds of Asia's population is under thirty, with about 250 million people between the ages of twelve and twenty-four. Marketers want to learn what makes Asian youngsters tick. Given the vastness of the region, it is hard to make generalizations. But there are certain similarities among Asia's teenagers.

Scores of marketing research studies show the importance of family, jobs, saving for the future, parental consent, taking care of the elderly, and other traditional values. Asian teenagers may mimic American trends in music and fashion, but they definitely are not carbon copies of their American counterparts. They are not as cynical or rebellious as Western teenagers according to an eight-country survey that was done by Bates Worldwide. However, differences exist. For instance, while Indian and Chinese youngsters prefer

Sources: "Building brand loyalty among hip Asian teens," *Advertising Age International* (June 1996), p. I-28, and "Rock Solid," *Far Eastern Economic Review* (December 5, 1996), pp. 50–52.

to conform, their Hong Kong and Korean counterparts like to stand out.

What is remarkable is the ease with which they straddle between two worlds: Asian traditional values and the onslaught of Western consumerism. Asia's X-generation has more pocket money, more free time, and fewer worries about the future, and it lives in much more open societies than their parents used to. So, why do they cling to many of the traditional values that their parents believe in? Part of the explanation is nationalism. The other binding force is the family. Surveys show again and again that families in Asia continue to play a key role in sharing and sustaining traditional values. One Thailand-based market researcher notes that "Superficially they [Asian teenagers] may look Western, they may prefer their McDonald's or Kentucky Fried Chicken to Thai food, or watch the same programmes as their counterparts in the West. But inside they hold lots of values they get from their parents that are hard to change: respect for age, respect for the family, collective not individual action and so on."

Socioeconomic Variables

If you draw a circle with a 250-mile (400-kilometer) radius around the German city Cologne, you cover 50 million of the wealthiest consumers in the Pan-European market.[17] This *Golden Circle* offers tremendous market opportunities to marketers of luxury goods (e.g., LVMH, BMW), high-end services (e.g., resorts, Internet access, mutual funds) and leisure-activity-related goods.

Consumption patterns for many goods and services are largely driven by the consumer wealth or the country's level of economic development in general. Consumers from countries at the same stage of economic development often show similar needs in terms of the per capita amount and types of goods they desire. One well known income-based schema considers five stages of economic development:[18]

1. *Traditional societies.* Countries at this stage are viewed as economic basket cases. Most of them remain in a relentless quagmire of enormous poverty, low productivity, high illiteracy, and low levels of technology. Many sub-Saharan African countries belong to this group.

2. *Preconditions for take-off.* The second stage includes countries that are making the transition to the take-off phase. Advances in science and technology enter the agricultural sector. Examples of countries belonging to this group are the Philippines, Myanmar, Vietnam, Albania, and Romania. The first steps are taken to develop the infrastructure needed for industrialization, leading to the next stage:

3. *The take-off.* At this step, the infrastructure is mainly in place, spurring city-centered industries. Most of the ASEAN-countries like Thailand and Malaysia can be considered as take-off economies. Modernization leads to rapid development in all sectors of the country's economy.

4. *The drive to maturity.* Countries entering this stage are able to produce a wide variety of products. The service sector gains prominence. Most Central European countries (e.g., Hungary, Poland, Czech Republic) and countries such as Singapore and South Korea have reached this stage.

5. *High mass-consumption.* The final stage includes countries that have a sizable middle class with significant discretionary incomes. The economies of these countries have a highly developed service sector. Most of these countries are major players in international trade. In fact, they have formed their own "club" so to speak: the OECD.

Not surprisingly, many consumer-goods marketers view per capita income, or a comparable measure, as one of the key criteria in grouping international markets. The usual caveats in using per capita income as an economic development indicator apply also when this measure is used for country segmentation:[19]

- *Monetization of transactions within a country.* To compare measures such as per capita GNP across countries, figures based on a local currency need to be trans-

---

[17]Graham Hinton and Jane Hourigan, "The Golden Circles: Marketing in the New Europe," *The Journal of European Business*, 1(6) (July/August 1990), pp. 5–30.

[18]W.W. Rostow, *The Stages of Economic Growth* (London: Cambridge University Press, 1960).

[19]Vern Terpstra and Kenneth David, *The Cultural Environment of International Business* (Cincinnati, OH: South-Western Publishing Co., 1991).

lated into a common currency (e.g., the U.S. dollar or the euro). However, official exchange rates seldom reflect the true buying power of a currency. So, income figures based on GNP or GDP do not really tell you how much a household in a given country is able to buy.

- *Gray and black sectors of the economy.* National income figures only record transactions that arise in the legitimate sector of a country's economy. Many countries have a sizable *gray* sector, consisting of largely untaxed (or under-taxed) exchanges that often involve barter transactions. In some cities (e.g., Moscow), many professors make ends meet by driving a taxi. In exchange for a dental checkup, a television repairman might fix the dentist's television set. Many societies also thrive on a substantial *black* sector, involving transactions that are outright illegal. Examples of such activities include the drug trade, smuggling, racketeering, gambling, and prostitution.

- *Income disparities.* Quantities such as the per capita GNP only tell part of the story. Such measures are misleading in countries with wide income inequalities. India, for example, has a sizable group of upscale consumers, despite its low per capita income.

To protect against these shortcomings of standard per capita income segmentation exercises, marketers might consider other methods to group consumers in terms of their buying power.[20] One alternative is to use the PPP (purchasing power parity) as a criterion. PPP reflects how much a household in each country has to spend (in U.S. dollars equivalent) to buy a standard basket of goods. The World Bank publishes PPP statistics every year now in its *World Bank Atlas*.

Another alternative to analyze buying power in a set of countries is via a **socioeconomic strata (SES) analysis**. For instance, Strategy Research Corporation applied an SES-analysis for Latin American households using measures like the number of consumer durables in the household, education level, and so on. Each country was stratified into five socioeconomic segments, each one designated with a letter: upper-class (A), middle- to upper-class (B), middle-class (C), lower-class (D), and poverty level (E). Exhibit 7–6 shows the relative sizes of the various SES segments (D and E are combined) in several Latin American countries.

Behavior-Based Segmentation

Just as in domestic marketing, segments can also be formed based on behavioral response variables. Behavioral segmentation criteria include degree of brand/supplier loyalty, usage rate (based on per capita consumption), product penetration (that is, the percentage of the target market that uses the product), and benefits sought. Exhibit 7–7 shows a behavior-based classification of European markets for a personal care company. Note that this particular company divides its markets into three groups: established markets, developmental markets, and underdeveloped markets. Two segmentation variables are used: sales per capita and amount of advertising done by the local distributor.

For new products, firms might consider segmenting countries on the basis of the new product diffusion pattern observed in the countries of interest. Diffusion-based criteria could relate to country traits such as the speed of adoption, the time-of-sales

[20]Chip Walker, "The Global Middle Class," *American Demographics* (September 1995), pp. 40–46.

EXHIBIT 7–6

LATIN-AMERICAN MARKETS: MANY LATIN HOUSEHOLDS HAVE LOTS OF SPENDING MONEY. (PERCENT DISTRIBUTION OF SELECTED LATIN-AMERICAN COUNTRIES BY SES SEGMENTS, 1994)

	upper class	middle-to-upper class	middle class	lower class and subsistence level
Argentina	2%	9%	35%	55%
Brazil	3	16	29	53
Chile	2	6	42	50
Colombia	2	8	37	53
Ecuador	2	15	22	61
Mexico	2	12	30	56
Paraguay	3	12	34	51
Peru	3	8	33	56
Uruguay	8	20	36	36
Venezuela	1	4	36	59

Note: Class designations correspond to Socioeconomic Strata (SES) segments.

Source: Chip Walker, "The Global Middle Class," *American Demographics* (September 1995), pp. 40–46. Reprinted with permission. ©1995 American Demographics.

peak, and the propensity to innovate. Exhibit 7–8 shows the groupings of a broad range of countries based on the diffusion patterns observed in each of these markets for three consumer durables: color televisions, VCRs, and CD players.

Note that the respective country groupings have little in common in terms of the number of segments and their composition. In fact, the only countries that consistently fall into the same grouping for all three consumer durables are Belgium and Denmark.

EXHIBIT 7–7

EUROPEAN MARKET CLASSIFICATIONS AS OF DECEMBER 31, 1994

Established Markets	*Developmental Markets*	*Underdeveloped Markets*
England	Austria	Czech Republic
Finland	Belgium	Denmark
Germany	Ireland	France
Holland	Italy	Hungary
Israel		Portugal
Norway		Spain
Switzerland		

Established = Above average sales/capita plus advertising.

Developmental = Average sales/capita; may or may not be advertising.

Underdeveloped = Below average sales/capita; no significant advertising.

EXHIBIT 7–8
SEGMENT ASSIGNMENTS BASED ON NEW PRODUCT PENETRATION PATTERNS

Consumer Durable	Segment I	Segment II	Segment III
Color TV	Austria	Finland, France, the Netherlands, Sweden, Switzerland, United Kingdom, United States	Belgium, Denmark, Japan, Norway
VCR	Austria, France Japan, the Netherlands, Switzerland	Norway, United Kingdom, United States	Belgium Denmark, Finland Sweden
CD-players	Austria, Belgium, Denmark, Finland, France, Japan, the Netherlands, United Kingdom	Norway, Sweden, Switzerland, United States	

Source: Kristiaan Helsen, Kamel Jedidi, and Wayne S. DeSarbo, "A New Approach to Country Segmentation Utilizing Multinational Diffusion Patterns," *Journal of Marketing*, 57 (October 1993), p. 67. Reprinted with permission from the *Journal of Marketing*, published by the American Marketing Association.

Lifestyle

Marketers can group consumers according to their lifestyle—that is, their attitudes, opinions, and core values. Lifestyle segmentation is especially popular in advertising circles. Many lifestyle segmentation schemes are very general and not related to a specific product category. Others are derived for a specific product field. Distinctions can also be made between whether a given typology was prepared for a specific country or a given region.

An example of the general-type lifestyle segmentation approach is a 1997 study conducted by Roper Starch Worldwide. The survey covered 1,000 people in 35 countries. Subjects were asked to rank 56 values. Based on the responses, the researchers came up with six global values segments:[21]

1. *Strivers (23 percent).* Strivers are slightly more likely to be men than women. They emphasize material things and professional goals. They value wealth, status, power, and ambition. They like products such as personal computers and cellular phones. Strivers are common in Asia (Japan, Philippines) and Russia. Their media habits are limited to newspapers.

2. *Devouts (22 percent).* Devouts include more women than men. They uphold more traditional values like faith, discipline, respect for elders, and obedience. They are concentrated in developing nations of Asia, the Middle East, and Africa. Their media habits are very limited. Western products hold very little appeal to them.

[21]Tom Miller, "Global Segments from 'Strivers' to 'Creatives'," *Marketing News* (July 20, 1998), p. 11 and "Research Finds That Consumers Worldwide Belong to Six Basic Groups that Cross National Lines," *The New York Times* (June 25, 1998).

3. *Altruists (18 percent)*. Altruists are very concerned about social issues and the welfare of society ("feminine" values, in Hofstede's terminology). They tend to be very well educated. Median age is 44 years, higher proportion of females. Altruists are primarily found in Russia and Latin America.

4. *Intimates (15 percent)*. Intimates are "people" people. They value above all else family, significant others, friends, and colleagues. They can be found in Europe (one out of four) and the United States. They are heavy users of media that allow bonding like television, movies, and radio.

5. *Fun seekers (12 percent)*. Fun seekers, as the label suggests, uphold values such as adventure, pleasure, excitement, and looking good. Not surprisingly, this group—the MTV generation—is the youngest segment. They frequent bars, restaurants, and clubs. They are heavily involved with electronic media. Though strongly represented in developed Asia, this group can be found anywhere else in the world.

6. *Creatives (10 percent)*. This segment has a strong interest in education, knowledge, and technology. Members of this groups are global trendsetters in terms of owning a PC, surfing the Web. Creatives are primarily located in Western Europe and Latin America. They are the heavy media consumers with a tilt toward newspapers, books, and magazines.

Exhibit 7–9 exemplifies the product-specific approach. It shows a typology that was derived for the pan-European car market. The distribution of the different types varies from country to country. Some of the types (e.g., the "prestige-oriented sporty driver") are more or less uniformly distributed. Other types, though (e.g., the "understatement" buyer) are prominent in some countries but far less visible in other countries.[22]

Lifestyle segmentation has been applied to position new brands, reposition existing ones, identify new product opportunities, and develop brand personalities.[23] Several concerns have been raised by practitioners and academics alike about the use of lifestyle segmentation:[24]

- Values are too general to relate to consumption patterns or brand choice behavior within a specific product category. As a result, lifestyle segmentation is not very useful as a tool to make predictions about consumers' buying responsiveness. Obviously, this criticism only applies to the general value schemes.

- Value-based segmentation schemes are not always "actionable." Remember that one of the requirements for effective segmentation is actionability. Lifestyle groupings do not offer much guidance in terms of what marketing actions should be taken. Also, many of the typologies have too many different types to be useful for practical purposes.

- Value segments are not stable, since values typically change over time.

---

[22]Horst Kern, Hans-Christian Wagner, and Roswitha Hassis, "European Aspects of a Global Brand: The BMW Case," *Marketing and Research Today* (February 1990), pp. 47–57.

[23]Marieke de Mooij, *Advertising Worldwide*, 2nd Ed., (Englewood Cliffs, N.J.: Prentice-Hall, 1994).

[24]Peter Sampson, "People are People the World Over: The Case for Psychological Market Segmentation," *Marketing and Research Today* (November 1992), pp. 236–44.

EXHIBIT 7–9

TYPOLOGY OF EUROPEAN CAR MARKET

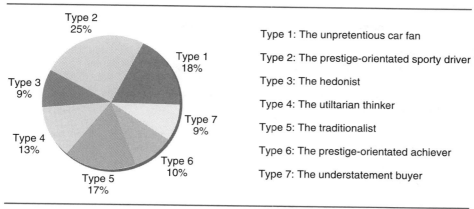

Type 1: The unpretentious car fan

Type 2: The prestige-orientated sporty driver

Type 3: The hedonist

Type 4: The utiltarian thinker

Type 5: The traditionalist

Type 6: The prestige-orientated achiever

Type 7: The understatement buyer

Source: Horst Kern, Hans-Christian Wagner, and Roswitha Hassis, "European Aspects of a Global Brand: The BMW Case," *Marketing and Research Today* (February 1990), p. 54.

Permission for using this material which was originally published in *Marketing and Research Today* has been granted by (E.S.O.M.A.R.) The European Society for Opinion and Marketing Research, J.J. Viottastraat 29, 1071 JP, Amsterdam, The Netherlands.

- Their international applicability is quite limited since lifestyles, even within the same region, often vary from country to country.

    Aside from the criteria already discussed, many other country characteristics may form a basis for segmentation. The proper criteria largely depend on the nature of the product and the objectives of the segmentation exercise.

INTERNATIONAL POSITIONING STRATEGIES ◆ ◆ ◆ ◆ ◆ ◆

Segmenting international markets is only part of the game. Once the multinational company has segmented its foreign markets, the firm needs to decide which target markets to pursue and what positioning strategy to use to appeal to the chosen segments. Some marketing scholars refer to positioning as the fifth P, next to product, price, promotion, and place. Developing a positioning theme involves the quest for a unique selling proposition (USP). In the global marketing scene, the positioning question boils down to a battle for the mind of your target customers, located not just within a certain country, but, in some cases, across the globe. The global positioning statement for Budweiser is shown in Exhibit 7–10. The formulation of a positioning strategy—be it local or global—moves along a sequence of steps:

1. Identify the relevant set of competing products or brands. What is the competitive frame?

2. Determine current perceptions held by consumers about your product/brand and the competition.

3. Develop possible positioning themes.

EXHIBIT 7–10
BUDWEISER GLOBAL POSITIONING

Budweiser maintains its leadership positioning in the global beer industry by consistently being a brand that is:

• Refreshingly different from local brands, with its clean, crisp taste and high drinkability
• A premium-quality beer, made using an all-natural process and ingredients
• Global in stature, representing heritage, quality, and American roots
• Well-known as a world-class sponsor of sports and entertainment events
• The world's best-selling beer

Source: www.anheuser-busch.com

4. Screen the positioning alternatives and select the most appealing one.

5. Develop a marketing mix strategy that will implement the chosen positioning strategy.

6. Over time, monitor the effectiveness of your positioning strategy. If it is not working, check whether its failure is due to bad execution or an ill-conceived strategy.

Uniform versus Localized Positioning Strategies

Obviously, for global marketers, a key question is to what degree a **uniform positioning strategy** can be used. Clearly, one key driver here is the target market decision. Roughly speaking, MNCs have two choices: target a universal segment across countries or pursue different segments in the different markets. When focusing on a uniform segment, management needs to decide whether to use the same positioning worldwide or positioning themes that are tailored to individual markets. If the firm decides to opt for different segments on a country-by-country basis, the norm is to also customize the positioning appeals. Exhibit 7–11 gives an overview of the different strategic options.

When the target customers are very similar worldwide, sharing common core values and showing similar buying patterns, a uniform positioning strategy may

EXHIBIT 7–11
GLOBAL POSITIONING AND
SEGMENTATION STRATEGIES

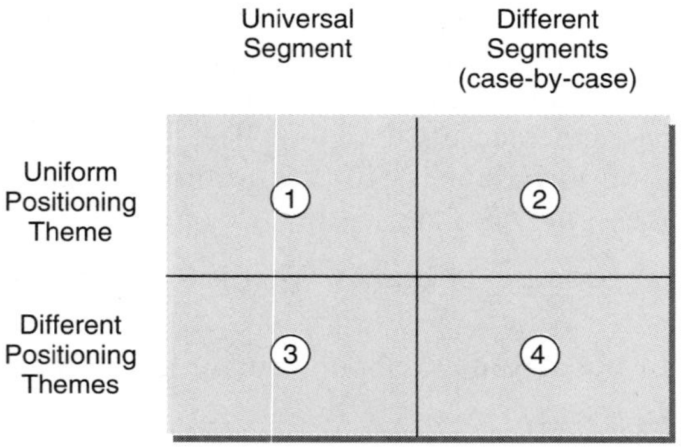

	Universal Segment	Different Segments (case-by-case)
Uniform Positioning Theme	①	②
Different Positioning Themes	③	④

work. By adopting a common positioning theme, the company can project a shared, consistent brand or corporate image worldwide. The need to have a consistent image is especially urgent for brands that have worldwide exposure and visibility. For instance, regarding Cadillac, General Motors Europe marketing director said, "One thing that is really important as we position the [Cadillac] brand around the world is that as customers travel around the world they need to see the same elements of styling, technology, and performance—the three pillars of our brand."[25] Having the same positioning theme also enables the firm to make use of global media. While a uniform positioning theme may be desirable, it is often very hard to come up with a good positioning theme that appeals in various markets. Universal themes often run the risk of being bland and not very inspired.

Very rarely do positioning themes "travel." Instead, management will usually modify or localize positioning themes. Appeals that work in one culture do not necessarily work in others. Differences in cultural characteristics, buying power, competitive climate, and the product life cycle stage force firms to tailor their positioning platform. Land Rover is an example of a brand where a global positioning strategy is hard to implement.[26] One of the core brand values that Land Rover has

◆ ◆

$\mathcal{G}$LOBAL PERSPECTIVE 7–2

HÄAGEN-DAZS'S POSITIONING STRATEGY IN CHINA

Legend has it that Marco Polo brought back the recipe for ice cream from China to Italy in the thirteenth century. Yet, today ice cream consumption in China is extremely low: around 0.2 liters per capita per year—less than a tenth of the consumption in North America. Over the last five years, several of the world's leading ice cream manufacturers have flocked to China.

In the premium segment, one of the most visible players is Häagen-Dazs. It has opened five ice cream cafés in Beijing, Shanghai, and Hangzhou. Oversupply has forced several local and foreign manufacturers to close down or cut their prices. Häagen-Dazs, however, charges prices that are comparable with those charged elsewhere in the world. For instance, a single scoop of ice cream at one of its cafes will cost you about $3.

A key success factor has been Häagen-Dazs's positioning strategy. The product is pitched toward young, educated professionals. It is touted as a luxury brand that can be experienced as "adult entertainment"—the positioning used worldwide. This positioning is backed up by a clever, well-executed marketing strategy. An extensive public relations campaign precedes each store launch. A buzz is created via sponsorship activities at places frequented by its target customers (e.g., discos, bowling alleys). Ice cream cafés are designed as leisure places where patrons can feel comfortable and at ease. Häagen Dazs's advertisements, though not as provocative as in the West, have a distinctive tone. One poster in Shanghai, for instance, showed a vampish Chinese woman in black leather holding two pints of Häagen-Dazs up to her chest.

Sources: "Luxury Ice-Cream Rivals Battle to Scoop the Chinese Market," *Financial Times* (August 18, 1998), p. 3; "Positioning Pleasure," *Business China* (September 27, 1999), pp. 2–3.

---

[25]"Cadillac Hits the Road to Rev Up Sagging Sales Around the World," *Advertising Age International* (January 1998), pp. 24–26.

[26]Nick Bull and Martin Oxley, "The Search for Focus—Brand Values across Europe," *Marketing and Research Today* (November 1996), pp. 239–47.

cultivated over the years in Europe is *authenticity*. This core value is based on Land Rover's heritage of fifty years as a 4×4-brand, in Europe. The North American market, which Land Rover only entered in the 1980s, presents a different picture. There, Jeep, the DaimlerChrysler 4×4-brand, is perceived as the authentic, original four-wheel drive. Hence, Land Rover would have a formidable task in creating the same image of authenticity in North America as it successfully did in Europe.

Many firms position a brand that is *mainstream* in its home market as a premium brand in their overseas markets, thereby targeting a narrower segment that is willing to pay a premium for imports. A case in point is the Ford Escort: Although the car is sold as a mainstream passenger car in the United States and Europe, the Escort is a premium car in India. It is not uncommon to see a chauffeur-driven Escort there.[27] Other examples of brands that are "mainstream" in their home market but perceived as premium in the international marketplace are Heineken, Levi's, and Budweiser. This strategy is especially effective in product categories where the local brands already are well entrenched (like beer in most countries) and imported brands have a potential to leverage the cachet of being "imported." Local brands usually enjoy a pioneering advantage by the fact of being the first one in the market. Therefore, instead of competing head-on with the local competition, foreign brands (despite the fact that they are a mainstream brand in their home market) are mostly better off by targeting the upscale segment. Though smaller in numbers, this segment is willing to pay a substantial premium price.

Universal Positioning Appeals

Universal positioning appeals are positioning themes that appeal to consumers anywhere in the world, regardless of their cultural background. Remember that positioning themes can be developed at different levels:

- Specific product features/attributes
- Product benefits (rational or emotional), solutions for problems
- User category
- User application
- Lifestyle

Products that offer benefits or features that are universally important would meet the criterion of a universal benefit/feature positioning appeal. In business-to-business markets, where buying behavior is often somewhat less culture-bound than for consumer goods, this is often true. Thus, a promise of superior quality, performance, or productivity for industrial products is one example of a positioning pitch with a universal ring. Benefit- or feature-based positioning can be universal for consumer goods when the core benefit is common worldwide. This would apply to superior quality or performance appeals for durables such as television sets (superior picture quality), washing machines (cleaning performance), and so forth. However, for products where buying motivations are very culture-bound (for instance, most food and beverage products), coming up with a universal benefit- or feature-related appeal is a much harder task.

---

[27]"GM, Ford Think Globally for Branding Strategies," *Advertising Age* (January 6, 1997), p. 35.

A special case where universal positioning clearly makes sense is the *global citizen theme* often used with corporate image strategies. Here the positioning strategy stresses a global leadership and/or global presence benefit. This strategy is often successfully used in industries where having a global presence is a major plus (e.g., credit cards, banking, insurance, telecommunications). Global Perspective 7–3 describes the recent global rebranding efforts of HSBC.

When positioning the product to a specific user category, a uniform approach might work when the user group shares common characteristics. An example where this approach works is the Pepsi-generation positioning going after the MTV generation. An example where a uniform positioning is likely to be futile are appeals that center on the "liberated women" group (e.g., Virginia Slims cigarettes: "You've come a long way, baby"), which is still a very culture-bound phenomenon.

Emotional appeals (e.g., lifestyle positioning) are usually difficult to translate into a universal theme. Values tend to be very culture bound. The trick is to come up with an emotional appeal that has universal characteristics and—at the same time—does not sound dull. A recent lifestyle survey found that "protecting the family" was seen as a top value in twenty-two countries, including the United States.[28] So, appeals based on family values might be prospective candidates.

◆ ◆

$\mathcal{G}$LOBAL PERSPECTIVE 7–3

HSBC'S DRIVE TOWARD GLOBAL RECOGNITION

The Hong Kong and Shanghai Banking Corp. (HSBC), with assets valued at more then $480 billion, is one of the biggest retail banking conglomerates in the world. With 5,000 offices serving 20 million clients in almost 80 countries, the bank is one of the few truly global banks. Still, the HSBC name does not have the resonance of banking brands like Citigroup or Deutsche Bank. To get more high-end accounts, HSBC decided that it must improve its name recognition around the world. In 1998 HSBC started to harmonize the bank's operations under one moniker—HSBC. Names of banks that HSBC acquired over the years are being phased out and replaced with the HSBC brand name. For instance, the name of the

U.K.'s Midland Bank, which HSBC acquired in 1992, was phased out by September 1999 ("HSBC, it's the new name for Midland Bank"). Customers worldwide are now greeted by a distinctive red-and-white hexagon-shaped logo. The end goal is to turn HSBC into a household name with worldwide recognition.

The first phase of the $100 million rebranding effort was a print ad campaign in international print media such as the *Financial Times* and *The Wall Street Journal*. The print ads featured three universally recognized highway symbols for eating, drinking, and sleeping facilities. The fourth symbol is HSBC's logo, communicating the message that HSBC is a premier banking brand. The print campaign was followed up with a TV campaign rolled out in 40 countries. Michael Broadbent, HSBC's director of corporate affairs, said at the time of the campaign's launch: "We want people from Bangkok to Buenos Aires to recognize HSBC and know that it stands for integrity, trust and excellent customer service."

Sources: "HSBC Uses Symbols to Stake Global Bank Claim," *Advertising Age International* (June 1999), p. 3; "HSBC Campaign Drives for Global Banking Recognition," *The Economist* (July 29, 1999); "John Bond's HSBC," *Business Week* (September 20, 1999), pp. 78–81.

---

[28]Tom Miller, "Global Segments from 'Strivers' to 'Creatives'," *Marketing News* (July 20, 1998), p. 11.

◆ ◆ ◆ ◆ ◆ ◆ GLOBAL, FOREIGN, AND LOCAL CONSUMER CULTURE POSITIONING[29]

Brand managers can position their brand as symbolic of a global consumer culture, a "foreign" culture, or a local culture. The first strategy can be described as **global consumer culture positioning (GCCP)**. This strategy tries to project the brand as a symbol of a given global consumer culture—buying the brand reinforces the consumer's feeling of being part of a global segment. It also fosters the buyer's self-image as being cosmopolitan, modern, and knowledgeable. Examples of brands that successfully use this strategy are Sony ("My First Sony") and Nike ("Just Do It").

At the other extreme is the **local consumer culture positioning (LCCP)** strategy. Despite the fact that the brand may be global, it is portrayed as an intrinsic part of the local culture. It is depicted as being consumed by local people, and, if applicable, manufactured by locals, using local supplies or ingredients. When Mercedes launched its mid-price E-class model in Japan, its ad campaign used Japanese scenery and images. The local imagery was underscored with the tagline: "Mercedes and a beautiful country."[30]

A third strategy is **foreign consumer culture positioning (FCCP)**. Here, the goal is to build up a brand mystique around a specific foreign culture, usually one that has highly positive connotations for the product (e.g., Switzerland for watches, Germany for household appliances). American brands like Nike, Timberland, Cadillac, and Budweiser have been able to position themselves very strongly in their foreign markets as an authentic piece of Americana.

Which positioning strategy is most suitable depends on several factors. One important determinant is obviously your target market. When target consumers share core values, attitudes, and aspirations, using a GCCP strategy could be effective. Another driver is the product category. Products that satisfy universal needs and are used in a similar manner worldwide lend themselves more to a GCCP-type approach. High-tech consumer brands (e.g., Siemens, Nokia, Sony) that symbolize modernism and internationalism would qualify. A third factor is the positioning approach used by the local competition. If every player in the local market is using a GCCP strategy, you might be able to break more easily through the clutter by going for an LCCP strategy (or vice versa). A final factor is the level of economic development. In emerging markets that are still in an early stage of economic development, a GCCP approach might be more beneficial than LCCP. In these markets, a brand with a global image enhances the owner's self-image and status.

Sometimes local brands fight it out with global brands by using a GCCP or FCCP strategy. For instance, Brand, a local Dutch beer, uses a U.S. setting and English in its advertising. Some brands also use a hybrid approach, by combining ingredients of each of the three strategies. McDonald's is portrayed as a global, cosmopolitan fast-food brand (GCCP) but also as an authentic piece of Americana (FCCP). At the same time, in many countries, McDonald's often highlights its local roots, stressing the

---

[29]Based on Dana L. Alden, Jan-Benedict E.M. Steenkamp, and Rajeev Batra, "Brand Positioning Through Advertising in Asia, North America, and Europe: The Role of Global Consumer Culture," *Journal of Marketing*, 63 (January 1999), pp. 75–87.

[30]"Mercedes-Benz Japan Drifts Down to Earth Alongside Economy," *Advertising Age International* (October 1997), p. 36.

fact that it provides local jobs, uses local ingredients, and so forth (LCCP). During the recent Kosovo conflict, McDonald's in Yugoslavia tried to evoke a Serbian identity. Local restaurants promoted the McCountry (a pork burger with paprika garnish) and produced posters showing the golden arches topped with a traditional Serbian cap.[31]

SUMMARY

A common theme in many writings on global marketing is the growing convergence of consumer needs.[32] Colorful phrases have been used to describe this phenomenon such as *"global village," "global mall,"* and *"crystallization of the world as a single place,"* just to mention a few. This phenomenon of increasing globalization is especially visible for many upscale consumer goods and a variety of business-to-business goods and services that are bought by multinational customers. One director of a global marketing research firm even went so far as to state that "marketers make too much of cultural differences."[33] She supports her claim with two reasons. First, technology has given consumers worldwide the same reference points. People see the same TV ads, share similar life experiences, they are exposed to the same products and services. Second, technology has also given us common aspirations. According to this school of thought, cultures do differ, but these differences do not have any meaningful impact on people's buying behavior.

In the other camp are people like Nicholas Trivisonno, the CEO of ACNielsen, who notes that: "There is no global consumer. Each country and the consumer in each country has different attitudes and different behaviors, tastes, spending patterns."[34] The truth of the matter is somewhere in between these two extreme opinions.

Without proper segmentation of your international markets, it is hard to establish whether the *global consumer* segment is myth or reality.

Global marketers have a continuum of choices to segment their customer base. At one end of the spectrum, the firm might pursue a "universal" segment. Essentially the same product is offered, using a common positioning theme. Most likely there are a few, mostly minor, adaptations of the marketing mix program to recognize cross-border differences. At the other end, the firm might consider treating individual countries on a case-by-case basis. In some circumstances, marketers might be able to offer the same product in each country, provided that the positioning is customized. However, typically, the product will need to be modified or designed for each country separately. In between these two extremes, there are bound to be many other possibilities.

By the same token, your positioning strategy can take different directions. Going after a uniform segment, you can adopt a universal positioning theme or themes that are custom-made. Universal appeals do have benefits. They allow the firm to develop a common communication strategy using global or pan-regional media channels. Unfortunately, coming up with a universal appeal that is appealing and not bland is often asking too much.

KEY TERMS

foreign culture consumer positioning (FCCP)
global culture consumer positioning (GCCP)

local culture consumer positioning (LCCP)
socioeconomic strata (SES) analysis

uniform (localized) positioning strategy
universal positioning appeals

universal (global) segments

[31]"McDonald's Dons a New Hat to Survive," *The Asian Wall Street Journal* (September 10–11, 1999), p. 9.

[32]Theodore Levitt, "The Globalization of Markets," *Harvard Business Review*, 61 (May–June 1983), pp. 92–102.

[33]Luanne Flikkema, "Global Marketing's Myth: Differences Don't Matter," *Marketing News* (July 20, 1998), p. 4.

[34]"The Global Consumer Myth," *The Financial Times* (April 23, 1991), p. 21.

REVIEW QUESTIONS ✦

1. Under what conditions should companies pursue universal market segments?

2. What are the major issues in using per capita GDP or GNP as a country segmentation criterion?

3. Discuss the weaknesses of lifestyle-based segmentation schemes. For what kind of applications would lifestyle segmentation be appropriate?

4. Sometimes local brands use a global consumer culture positioning approach. Explain. (*Key:* Some locally based marketers, fighting global brands, use GCCP to imply to their target customers that their products are "world-class" quality. For instance, in India, ads for local brands such as Videocon (consumer durables) and Amrutanjan (pain relievers) show visuals of foreign consumers using their products.)

DISCUSSION QUESTIONS ✦

1. Peter Sampson, a managing director of Burke Marketing Research, points out that "lifestyle and value-based segmentations are too general to be of great use in category specific studies . . . their international application is too limited as lifestyles vary internationally." Do you agree or disagree with his comment?

2. In a host of emerging markets (e.g., India, Brazil, Thailand), 50 percent-plus of the population is under 25. One marketer observes that: "teenagers are teenagers everywhere and they tend to emulate U.S. teenagers." (*Advertising Age International*, October 17, 1994, p. I-15) Is there a global teenager segment? Do teenagers in, say, Beijing really tend to emulate L.A. teenagers? Discuss.

3. Select a particular consumption product (e.g., ice cream). Try to come up with at least two variables that you believe might be related to the per capita demand for the chosen product. Collect data on the per capita consumption levels for your chosen product and the

selected variables for several countries. Segment the countries using, for example, cluster analysis (SAS users might consider PROC FASTCLUS). Derive two- and three-cluster solutions. Discuss your findings.

4. Browse through a recent issue of *The Economist*. As some of you may know, *The Economist* has regional editions. Most of the ads target an international audience (regional or global). Pick four ads and carefully examine each one of them. Who is being targeted in each print ad? What sort of positioning is being used?

5. A recent phenomenon in scores of emerging markets is a rising middle class. In a recent *Ad Age International* article (October 17, 1994) on the global middle class, one analyst referred to this phenomenon as the *Twinkie-ization* of the world (*Twinkie* being the brand name of a popular snack in the United States): "It's the little things that are treats and don't cost much and feel like a luxury." What are these "little things"? Do you agree with this statement?

FURTHER READING ✦

Alden, Dana L., Jan-Benedict E.M. Steenkamp, and Rajeev Batra. "Brand Positioning Through Advertising in Asia, North America, and Europe: The Role of Global Consumer Culture." *Journal of Marketing*, 63(1) (January 1999): 75–87.

Hassan, Salah S., and Lea P. Katsanis. "Identification of Global Consumer Segments." *Journal of International Consumer Marketing*, 3(2) (1991): 11–28.

Helsen, Kristiaan, Kamel Jedidi, and Wayne S. DeSarbo. "A New Approach to Country Segmentation Utilizing Multinational Diffusion Patterns." *Journal of Marketing*, 57 (October 1993): 60–71.

Hinton, Graham, and Jane Hourigan. "The Golden Circles: Marketing in the New Europe." *Journal of European Business*, 1(6) (July/August 1990): 5–30.

Johansson, Johny K., and Reza Moinpour. "Objective and Perceived Similarity for Pacific-Rim Countries." *Columbia Journal of World Business* (Winter 1977): 65–76.

Kale, Sudhir. "Grouping Euroconsumers: A Culture-Based Clustering Approach." *Journal of International Marketing*, 3(3) (1995): 35–48.

Kale, Sudhir, and D. Sudharshan. "A Strategic Approach to International Segmentation." *International Marketing Review* (Summer 1987): 60–70.

Sampson, Peter. "People are People the World Over: The Case for Psychological Segmentation." *Marketing and Research Today* (November 1992): 236–44.

Ter, Hofstede, Frenkel, Jan-Benedict E. Steenkamp, and Michel Wedel. "International Market Segmentation Based on Consumer-Product Relations." *Jour-nal of Marketing Research*, 36(1) (February 1999): 1–17.

Yavas, Ugur, Bronislaw J. Verhage, and Robert T. Green. "Global Consumer Segmentation versus Local Market Orientation: Empirical Findings." *Management International Review*, 32(3) (1992): 265–72.

APPENDIX ◆

In this appendix we give an overview of segmentation tools that can be used to do a country segmentation. A huge variety of segmentation methodologies has been developed in the marketing literature. Many of these techniques are quite sophisticated. We will just give you the flavor of two of the most popular tools, without going through all the technical nitty-gritty.

When only one segmentation variable is used, classifying countries in distinct groups is quite straightforward. You could simply compute the mean (or median) and split countries into two groups based on the value (above or below) on the criterion variable compared to the mean (or median). When more than two groups need to be formed, one can use other quantiles. Things become a bit more complicated when you plan to use multiple-country segmentation variables. Typically, the goal of market segmentation is to relate, in some manner, a battery of descriptive variables about the countries to one or more behavioral response variables:

$$\text{Response} = F(\text{Descriptor}_1, \text{Descriptor}_2, \text{Descriptor}_3, ...)$$

EXHIBIT 7–12
PRINCIPLES OF CLUSTER ANALYSIS

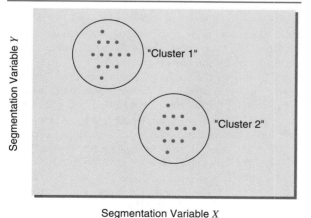

Segmentation Variable X

• Indicates location of country given its value for X and Y

For instance, the response variable might be the per capita consumption of a given product. The descriptor variables could be the stage in the product life cycle, per capita GNP, literacy level, and so on. We now describe two methods that can help you in achieving this goal: cluster analysis and regression.

Cluster Analysis. Cluster analysis is an umbrella term that embraces a collection of statistical procedures for dividing objects into groups (*clusters*). The grouping is done in such a manner that members belonging to the same group are very similar to one another but quite distinct from members of other groups.

Suppose information was collected for a set of countries on two variables, X and Y. The countries are plotted in Exhibit 7–12. Each dot corresponds to a country. In this case, the clusters are quite obvious. Just by eyeballing the graph, you can distinguish two clear-cut clusters, namely "Cluster 1" and "Cluster 2." Unfortunately, in real-world applications, clustering is seldom so easy. Consider Exhibit 7–13. This exhibit plots the values of chocolate volume growth rate and market concentration in eight countries.[35] For this example, it is far less obvious how many clusters there are, let alone how they are composed. In addition, most country segmentations involve many more than two criteria.

Luckily, there are many statistical algorithms available that will do the job for you. The basic notion is to group countries together that are similar in value for the segmentation bases of interest. Similarity measures come under many guises. The most popular way is to use some type of distance measure:

$$\text{Distance}^2_{\text{country A vs. B}} = (X_{\text{country A}} - X_{\text{country B}})^2 + (Y_{\text{country A}} - Y_{\text{country B}})^2$$

where X and Y are the segmentation variables. These distances would be computed for each pair of countries

---

[35]Measured via the combined market shares of the three largest competitors—Cadbury, Mars, and Nestlé.

EXHIBIT 7–13
PLOT OF CONCENTRATION VERSUS CATEGORY
GROWTH CHOCOLATE MARKET

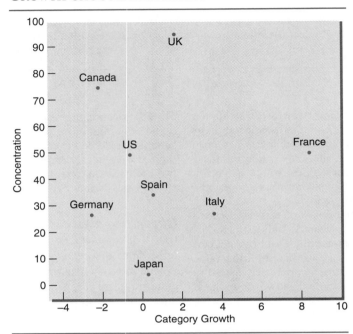

in the set.[36] The clustering algorithm takes these distances and uses them as inputs to generate the desired number of country groupings. Most "canned" statistical software packages (e.g., SAS, SPPS-X) have at least one procedure that allows you to run a cluster analysis. Exhibit 7–14 provides the two- and three-cluster solutions for the chocolate market example.

Regression. Alternatively, you might consider using regression analysis to classify countries. In regression, one assumes that there exists a relationship between a response variable, Y, and one or more so-called predictor variables, X_1, X_2 and so on:

$$Y = a + b_1X_1 + b_2X_2 + b_3X_3 + \ldots$$

The first term, a, is the intercept. It corresponds to the predicted value of Y when all the Xs are equal to 0. The other parameters, the bs, are the slope coefficients. For example, b_1 tells you what the predicted change in Y will be for a unit change in X_1.

In our context, the dependent variable, Y, would be a behavioral response variable (e.g., per capita consump-tion) and the predictor variables would be a collection of country characteristics that are presumed to be related to the response measure. For given values of the parame-ters, you can compute the predicted Y values, $\hat{Y}$. Very seldom, these predicted values will match the observed Ys. The goal of regression is to find estimates for the in-tercept, a, and the slope coefficients, the bs, that provide the "best" fit by minimizing the prediction errors, $Y - \hat{Y}$, between the predicted and observed values of Y. The most common regression procedure, ordinary least squares (OLS), minimizes the sum of the squared differ-ences of these prediction errors.

For each of the parameter estimates, the regression analysis will also produce a standard deviation. Dividing the parameter estimate by the standard deviation yields the *t*-ratio. This ratio tells you whether the predictor vari-able has a "significant" (statistically speaking) relation-ship with the dependent variable. As a rule of thumb, a *t*-ratio (in absolute value) larger than 2.0 would indicate a significant effect of the predictor variable on the re-sponse variable. The overall goodness of fit is captured via the R^2 statistic. The higher the R^2 value, the better the ability of your regression model to predict your data.

---

[36]Strictly speaking, these are "squared" distances.

EXHIBIT 7–14
CLUSTER ANALYSIS TWO-CLUSTER SOLUTION

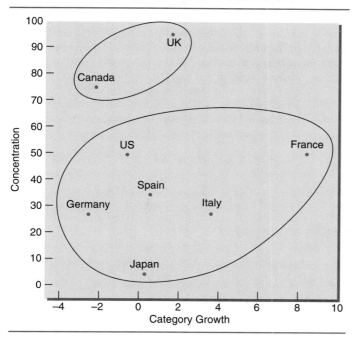

THREE-CLUSTER SOLUTION

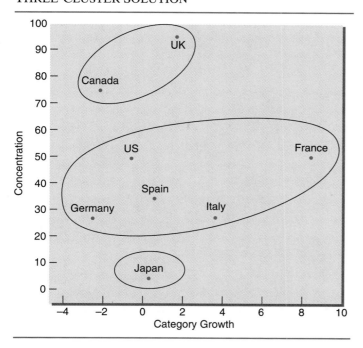

To illustrate the use of regression analysis as a segmentation tool, let us look at a numerical example. Consider a microwave oven maker who wants to explore market opportunities in the European market. Data were collected for several European countries on the penetration of microwave ovens (as a percentage of households owning a microwave). Data were also gathered on three potential segmentation variables: income (per capita GDP), participation of women in the labor force, and per capita consumption of frozen foods.[37] Using these data as inputs, the following results were obtained (*t*-ratios in parentheses):

$$\text{Microwave Ownership} = -76.7 - 0.5 \text{ Frozen Food } (-2.2) \ (-1.3) + 2.7 \text{ Women } - 0.03 \text{ Per cap GDP } (2.9) \ (-0.04)$$
$$R^2 = 0.52$$

Note that, apparently, the only meaningful segmentation base is the participation of women in the labor force: Microwave ownership increases with the proportion of women in the labor force. Since microwaves are a time-saving appliance, this result intuitively makes sense. The other variables appear to have (statistically speaking) not much of an impact on the adoption of microwave ovens. Somewhat surprisingly, high consumption of frozen foods does not lead to an increased ownership of microwave ovens. There is also no relationship with income. Thus, in this case, the European marketing manager could group countries simply on the basis of the degree of participation of women in the labor force.

Aside from these two commonplace tools, there are many other multivariate statistical procedures that can be used to do country segmentation analysis (e.g., latent class analysis, discriminant analysis, Automatic Interaction Detection).

---

[37]The data for this example were collected from the *European Marketing Data and Statistics 1992*, London: Euromonitor.

GLOBAL MARKETING STRATEGIES

8

HAPTER OVERVIEW

1. INFORMATION TECHNOLOGY AND GLOBAL COMPETITION

2. GLOBAL STRATEGY

3. GLOBAL MARKETING STRATEGY

4. REGIONALIZATION OF GLOBAL MARKETING STRATEGY

5. COMPETITIVE ANALYSIS

On a political map, country borders are as clear as ever. But on a competitive map, financial, trading, and industrial activities across national boundaries have rendered those political borders increasingly irrelevant. Of all the forces chipping away at those boundaries, perhaps the most important is the flow of information—information that governments previously monopolized, cooking it up as they saw fit and redistributing it in forms of their own devising. Their information monopoly on events happening around the world enabled them to fool, mislead, or even control the people, because only the government possessed the facts in detail.[1]

Today people can see for themselves what tastes and preferences are like in other countries. For instance, people in India watching CNN and Star TV now know instantaneously what is happening in the rest of the world. A farmer in a remote village in Rajasthan, India, asks the local vendor for Surf (the detergent manufactured by Unilever) because he has seen a commercial on TV. More than 10 million Japanese traveling abroad every year are exposed to larger-size homes and much lower consumer prices abroad. Such information access creates demand that would not have existed before, and it restricts the power of governments to influence consumer choice.

---

[1]Kenichi Ohmae, *The Borderless World* (London: Harper Collins, 1990).

The availability and explosion of information technology such as telecommunications has forever changed the nature of global competition. Geographical boundaries and distance have become less of a constraint in designing strategies for the global market. The other side of the coin is that not only firms that compete internationally but also those whose primary market is considered domestic will be affected by competition from around the world. In this chapter, we explain the nature of global competition and examine various ways to gain competitive advantage for the firm facing global competition.

◆ ◆ ◆ ◆ ◆ ◆ INFORMATION TECHNOLOGY AND GLOBAL COMPETITION

The development of transportation technology, including jet air transportation, cold storage containers, and large ocean carriers, changed the nature of world trade in the fifty years after the Second World War. Since the 1980s, the explosion of information technology, particularly telecommunications, and more recently, electronic commerce (e-commerce), has forever changed the nature of competition around the world. Geographical distance has become increasingly less relevant in designing global strategy.

In the 1980s telecommunications grew by more than 600 percent, and a similar level of growth took place in the 1990s. We are observing the emergence of a **Gross Information Product**, and it dwarfs the Gross Domestic Product. In 1998, the total combined value of physical exports of the United States, Germany, and Japan amounted to $1.61 trillion a year; in one week London's international electronic transactions in the form of foreign exchange, securities, funds transfer, and credit card transactions amounted to that much. The power of telecommunications was apparent during the Kosovo Conflict, when news about the war was in real time.

Also in the 1990s, we saw the explosive growth of e-commerce on the Internet. In 1995, only 4 percent of Americans used the Internet every day. Today, the figure is well over 25 percent, and still growing fast. There is no other marketing channel than e-commerce where revenues are growing at this pace. There is no other way a business can grow unimpeded by the need to build commercial space and hire sales staff. While traditional mass retailers, such as Wal-Mart in the United States and Carrefour in France, will not disappear any time soon, the Web will fundamentally change customers' expectations about convenience, speed, comparability, price, and service. Those new expectations will reverberate throughout the world, affecting every business, domestic or global, in many ways.

Electronic Commerce (E-Commerce)

Marketing beyond the home country has always been hampered by geographical distance and the lack of sufficient information about foreign markets, although transportation and communications technology has reduced, if not eliminated, many difficulties of doing business across the national boundary. Now as a result of an explosive growth of e-commerce on the Internet, those difficulties are increasingly becoming a thing of the past. In other words, product life cycle is becoming shorter and shorter. E-commerce breaks every business free of the concept of geographic distance. No longer will geography bind a company's aspirations or the scope of its market. Traditional bookstores used to be constrained to certain geographical areas—probably within a few miles of their physical locations. Now, Amazon.com and BarnesandNoble.com can reach any place on earth, as long as you have access to the Internet. For every early e-commerce mover to eliminate the geographic boundaries of its business, there will be dozens of companies that lose their local monopolies to footloose online businesses.[2] This is no longer limited to e-commerce businesses based in the United States.

Although Japan has been somewhat slower in adopting personal computers than the United States, the Internet has finally taken off in the world's second largest economy. For example, Rakuten Ichiba, the first successful Internet shopping mall, has achieved stellar growth since its launch in May 1997. Starting with just 13 stores, the mall had over 850 stores as of July 1999—a growth rate of 80 to 100 per month—and the mall was now receiving 15 million page hits per month. Founded with half a million dollars in capital, the Japanese Internet mall posted $300,000 in net profits on sales of $1.5 million in the fiscal year ended December 1998.[3] Even the same explosive Internet growth is being experienced in countries that are technologically behind the United States and Japan. Asia is expected to become the world's largest Internet market by 2006, with about 12 percent of the region—about 374 million people—going online, outnumbering U.S. Internet users.[4] For example, a Beijing-based entrepreneur, William Ding, launched Netease Systems Ltd., which has emerged as one of China's leading Internet portals, with 2.9 million page-views per day. It already offers e-mail, discussion groups, personal Web pages, and links to sixty mainland publications. In July 1999, Netease leaped into actual e-commerce, selling 110 PCs for $150,000 in one week in the country's first online auction.[5]

Managers receive information about the state of the firm's operations in almost real time. Routinely, the chief executive officer of a firm can know the previous day's sales down to a penny, and can be alerted to events and trends now instead of in several months, when it might be too late to do anything about them.

Real-Time Management

Top retailers such as Wal-Mart and Toys "R" Us get information from their stores around the world every two hours via telecommunications.[6] Industry analysts say that former leader Kmart fell behind due to the delay in installing point-of-sale information technology, which would have enabled it to get faster and more accurate information on inventories and shelf movement of products. Such access is now possible because advances in electronic storage and transmission technology have made it possible to store twenty-six volumes of *Encyclopaedia Britannica* on a single chip and transmit that material in a second; these figures are expected to improve by a factor of ten in every few years.

---

[2]"The E-Corporation: More than Just Web-Based, It's Building a New Industrial Order," *Fortune* (December 7, 1998), pp. 80–118.

[3]Teikoku Databank, 1999.

[4]"U.S. Companies Eye on an Asian Gold Rush," *Upside* (March 2000), p. 43.

[5]"China's Web Masters," *Business Week*, International Edition (August 2, 1999).

[6]Julia King, "OLAP Gains Fans among Data-Hungry Firms," *Computerworld*, 30 (January 8, 1996), pp. 43, 48.

The combination of information technology, access tools, and telecommunication has squeezed out a huge chunk of organizational slack from corporate operations that was previously inherent due to the slow and circuitous nature of information flow within the firm. Human "switches" created holdups throughout the process. Ordering and purchasing of components, which was once a cumbersome, time-consuming process, is now done by Electronic Data Interchange (EDI), reducing the time involved in such transactions from weeks to days and eliminating a considerable amount of paperwork. Levi-Strauss uses LeviLink, an EDI service for handling all aspects of order and delivery. Customers can even place small orders as needed (say, every week), and goods are delivered within two days. One of Levi-Strauss's customers, Design p.l.c., with a chain of sixty stores, was able to entirely eliminate its warehouses, which were used as a buffer to deal with the long lead times between order and delivery. Caterpillar's "plant with a future" is built around an integrated global production process, which itself is built around a global information network utilizing the latest advances in telecommunications and information technology.[7]

Online Communication

Sales representatives on field calls who were previously, in effect, tied to the regional or central headquarters due to lack of product information and limited authority, are now able to act independently in the field, because laptop computers, faxes, and satellite uplinks enable instant access to data from the company's central database. Changes in prices due to discounts can now be cleared online from the necessary authority. This reduces reaction time for the sales representative and increases productivity. Monitoring problems for the firm are also reduced, as is paperwork.

Multiple design sites around the world in different time zones can now work sequentially on the same problem. A laboratory in California can close its day at 5:00 P.M. local time when the design center in Japan is just opening the next day. That center continues work on the design problem and hands it over to London at the end of its day, which continues the work and hands over the cumulated work of Japan and London back to California. Finally, the use of telecommunications improves internal efficiency of the firm in other ways. For instance, when Microsoft came up with an upgrade on one of its applications that required some customer education, a customer, using videoconferencing on its global information network, arranged a single presentation for the relevant personnel, dispersed across the world, obviating travel and multiple presentations.

Internet Organization

The ultimate effect of information networks within the multinational company is expected to be on the nature of its organizational structure. As information flows faster across the organization and the number of "filtering" points between the source of information (e.g., POS information or market and industry analysis) and the user of the information (e.g., the brand manager or the chief executive officer) decreases, the nature of the organization chart in the MNC changes drastically. An increasing number of MNCs have begun to use internal Web servers on the

---

[7]Sidney Hill, Jr., "The Race for Profits," *Manufacturing Systems*, 16 (May 1998), pp. II–IV+.

Internet to facilitate communications and transactions among employees, suppliers, independent contractors, and distributors.[8]

An assembly-line worker in a Procter & Gamble plant, for instance, knows from his computer that stores have been selling a particular brand of facial cream more briskly than anticipated, and, having this information, can change production scheduling on his own, by giving the computer necessary instructions to cut down on some other brands and to increase the production of the brand in question. The foreman and the section manager of a conventional plant are no longer required. Similarly, a Xerox salesperson uploads and downloads sales-related data directly from the central database of the company using a laptop computer that communicates directly with the central computer. The information so obtained can be analyzed directly—the conventional functions of regional offices and the associated overheads decrease considerably.

Faster Product Diffusion

The obvious impact of information technology is the faster dispersion of technology and the shorter product life cycles in global markets than ever before. It suggests that the former country-by-country sequential approach to entering markets throughout the world, described in the international product cycle model in Chapter 1, is increasingly untenable.

This trend is reflected in many product markets already. The time lag for color televisions between the United States on one hand and Japan and Europe on the other was six years. With compact discs the household penetration rates had come down to one year. For Pentium-based computers, Taiwan, India, Japan, and U.S.-based companies released computers at about the same time in their respective national markets. Thus, a firm selling personal computers would have to launch a new product on a worldwide basis in order not to fall behind in the global sweepstakes.[9] This issue will be further discussed when we discuss new product development in Chapter 11.

Global Citizenship

Another important contributing factor in the globalization of markets is the spread of English as the language of international business. The transformation of the European Union into a monetary union has already taken place with the introduction of the euro as its common currency. **Global citizenship** is no longer just a phrase in the lexicon of futurologists. It has already become every bit as concrete and measurable as changes in GNP and trade flows. In fact, conventional measures of trade flows may have outlived their usefulness, as we will discuss later.

The global environment thus demands a strategy that encompasses numerous national boundaries and tastes, and that integrates a firm's operations across national borders. This strategy goes beyond the home-country-focused ethnocentric orientation or the multicountry-focused polycentric orientation of many

---

[8]John A. Quelch and Lisa R. Klein, "The Internet and International Marketing," *Sloan Management Review*, 37 (Spring 1996), pp. 60–75.

[9]Shlomo Kalish, Vijay Mahajan, and Eitan Muller, "Waterfall and Sprinkler New-Product Strategies in Competitive Global Markets," *International Journal of Research in Marketing*, 12 (July 1995), pp. 105–19.

multinational firms in the middle of the twentieth century. Global strategy requires that the firm adopt a geocentric orientation, where the entire world is viewed as a potential market and firm activities are integrated on a global basis.[10]

✦ ✦ ✦ ✦ ✦ ✦ GLOBAL STRATEGY

The acid test of a well-managed company is being able to conceive, develop, and implement an effective global strategy. A **global strategy** is to array the competitive advantages arising from location, world-scale economies, or global brand distribution. This is done by building a global presence, defending domestic dominance, and overcoming country-by-country fragmentation. Because of its inherent difficulties, global strategy development presents one of the stiffest challenges for managers today. Companies that operate on a global scale need to integrate their worldwide strategy, in contrast to the earlier multinational or multidomestic approach. The earlier strategies would more truly be categorized as multidomestic strategies rather than as global strategies.

Global Industry

We approach the issue of global strategy through various conceptualizations—the first conceptualization is that of a **global industry**.[11] Global industries are defined as *those where a firm's competitive position in one country is affected by its position in other countries, and vice versa*. Therefore, we are talking about not just a collection of domestic industries, but a series of interlinked domestic industries in which rivals compete against one another on a truly worldwide basis. For instance, part of the reason that General Motors managed to keep afloat during the late 1980s and early 1990s was the strength of its European operations. Its North American operations bled red ink for most of this period. On the other hand, the economic recessions in Brazil and Japan, two of its largest markets for Coca-Cola, sorely affected Coke's sales in the late 1990s. With more than three-quarters of its profits and 71 percent of its growth coming from overseas, this "American" firm is heavily dependent on the global market.[12]

Therefore, the first question that faces managers is the extent of globalization of their industry. Assuming that the firm's activities are indeed global or, alternatively, that the firm wishes to grow toward global operations and markets, managers must design and implement a global strategy. This is because virtually every industry has global or potentially global aspects—some industries have more aspects that are global and more intensely so. Indeed, a case has been made that the globalization of markets has already been achieved, that consumer tastes around the world have converged, and that the global firm attempts, unceasingly, to drive

---

[10]Yoram Wind, Susan P. Douglas, and Howard V. Perlmutter, "Guidelines for Developing International Marketing Strategies," *Journal of Marketing*, 37 (April 1973), pp. 14–23, Jaishankar Ganesh, V. Kumar, and Masaaki Kotabe, "International Marketing Standardization vs. Adaptation: A Synthesis and Empirical Investigation," A working paper, 1999.

[11]Michael E. Porter, ed., *Competition in Global Industries* (Boston, Mass.: Harvard University Press, 1986).

[12]Dean Foust, "Man on the Spot," *Business Week* (May 3, 1999), pp. 142–51.

consumer tastes toward convergence.[13] Four major forces determining the globalization potential of industry are presented in Exhibit 8–1.

The implications of a distinction between multidomestic and global strategy are quite profound. In a multidomestic strategy, a firm manages its international activities like a portfolio. Its subsidiaries or other operations around the world each control all the important activities necessary to maximize their returns in their area of operation independent of the activities of other subsidiaries in the firm. The subsidiaries enjoy a large degree of autonomy, and the firm's activities in each of its national markets is determined by the competitive conditions in that national market. In contrast, a global strategy integrates the activities of a firm on a worldwide basis to capture the linkages among countries and to treat the entire world as a single, borderless market. This requires more than the transferring of intangible assets between countries.

In effect, the firm that truly operationalizes a global strategy is a geocentrically oriented firm. It considers the whole world as its arena of operation, and its managers maintain equidistance from all markets and do not permit any intrinsic national preferences to influence decisions concerning the global firm. This is in contrast to an ethnocentric orientation, where managers operate under the dominant influence of home country practices, or a polycentric orientation, where managers of individual subsidiaries operate independently of each other—the polycentric manager in practice leads to a multidomestic orientation, which prevents integration and optimization on a global basis. Until the early 1980s the global operations of Unilever were a good example of a multidomestic approach. Unilever's various country operations were largely independent of each other, with headquarters restricting itself to data collection and helping out subsidiaries when required. As presented in Global Perspective 8–1, Unilever has begun to add some geocentric dimensions to its global strategy.

Competitive Structure

A second aspect of global strategy is the nature of competitive industry structure. Customized flexible manufacturing as a result of CAD/CAM (computer-aided design and computer-aided manufacturing) technology has shown some progress. However, it proved to be more difficult operationally than was thought, so economies of scale still remain the main feature of market competition. The theory is that the greater the economies of scale, the greater the benefits to those firms with a larger market share. As a result, many firms try to jockey for larger market shares than their competitors. Economies of scale come about because larger plants are more efficient to run, and their per-unit cost of production is less as overhead costs are allocated across large volumes of production. Further economies of scale also result from learning effects: the firm learns more efficient methods of production with increasing cumulative experience in production over time. All of these effects tend to intensify competition. Once a high level of economies of scale is achieved, it provides the firm strong barriers against new entrants to the market. The firm that builds its competitive advantage on economies of scale is known as using a **cost leadership** strategy. In the 1970s and early 1980s, many Japanese companies became cost leaders in such industries as automobiles and consumer electronics.

---

[13]Theodore Levitt, "The Globalization of Markets," *Harvard Business Review*, 61 (May–June 1983), pp. 92–102.

EXHIBIT 8–1
INDUSTRY GLOBALIZATION DRIVERS

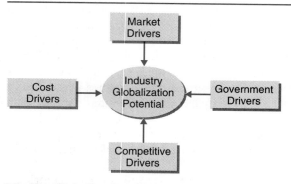

Market Globalization Drivers

Market drivers depend on the nature of customer behavior and the structure of channels of distribution. Some common market drivers are:

1. *Common Customer Needs.* Factors that affect whether customer needs are similar in different countries include economic development, climate, physical environment, and culture.
2. *Global Customers and Channels.* Global customers buy on a centralized or coordinated basis for decentralized use. Their existence affects the opportunity or need for global market participation, global products and services, global activity location, and global marketing.
3. *Transferable Marketing.* Certain elements of the marketing mix (e.g., brand name, pricing strategy) may be transferable across markets. The implications are that these elements can be effectively used both for increasing as well as reducing barriers.
4. *Lead Countries.* Lead countries represent countries where innovations in particular industries are prone to take place (e.g., Japan for consumer electronics, Germany for industrial control equipment, and the United States for computer software).

Cost Globalization Drivers

Cost drivers depend on the economics of the business. These drivers particularly affect production location decisions, as well as global market participation and global product development decisions. Some of these cost drivers are:

1. *Global Economies of Scale and Scope.* Global economies of scale apply when single-country markets are not large enough to allow competitors to achieve optimum scale. One of the most visible examples of this has been in the electronics industry. In many cases, economies of scope may be available by using facilities and processes in a single operating unit to produce a larger variety of goods or services with or without the presence of scale economies. Areas where economies of scope may be visible include consumer research, product development, and the creation of marketing programs.
2. *Steep Experience Curve.* Besides economies of scope and scale, steep learning activity associated with concentration of activities can result in significant cost advantages.
3. *Global Sourcing Efficiencies.* Efficiencies arise out of coordination of procurement activities of raw materials and components.
4. *Favorable Logistics.* A favorable ratio of sales value to transportation cost increases the ability to concentrate production and take advantage of economies of scale. Other logistic factors that have a bearing on global strategy development are nonperishability of products, absence of time urgency, and little need for location close to customer facilities.
5. *Differences in Country Costs.* This is based on the classical theories of differences in factor costs that do exist and can be exploited by firms to achieve comparative advantage.

Besides factor cost differences, exchange rate differences also have a significant bearing on the absolute costs and the stability of costs.

6. *High Product Development Costs.* High product development costs relative to the size of national markets act as a driver to globalization. These costs can be reduced by developing few global or regional products.

7. *Fast-Changing Technology.* Fast-changing technologies in products or processes lead to high product development costs, which increase their globalization potential.

Government Globalization Drivers

Rules set by national governments can affect the use of global strategic decision making. Some of these rules/policies include:

1. *Favorable Trade Policies.* Import tariffs and quotas, nontariff barriers, export subsidies, local content requirements, currency and capital flow restrictions, ownership restrictions, and requirements on technology transfer are some means governments can use to influence firm behavior. These policies can have a significant negative impact on standardization of products and programs.

2. *Compatible Technical Standards.* Differences in technical standards among countries also affect the extent of product standardization.

3. *Common Marketing Regulations.* Restrictions on various marketing activities can also act as a barrier to the use of uniform marketing approaches. For example, restrictions on the use of certain kinds of media for advertisements, differences in ad content like the use of sex and comparative advertising, and so on.

4. *Government-Owned Competitors.* The presence of government-owned competitors spurs the development of global plans as a means of counteracting the advantages of protected home markets.

5. *Government-Owned Customers.* Presence of government-owned customers could provide a barrier to globalization since such customers usually favor national suppliers.

Competitive Globalization Drivers

Competitive drivers raise the globalization potential of their industry and spur the need for a response on the global strategy levels. The common competitive drivers include:

1. *High Exports and Imports.* The level of exports and imports of final and intermediate products and services (i.e., the extent of interaction between countries) has a significant bearing on the use of a global strategy.

2. *Competitors from Different Continents and Countries.* Global competition among rivals from different continents tends to be more severe.

3. *Interdependent Countries.* Competitive interdependence among countries through shared business activities can help such firms to subsidize attacks on competitors in different countries. This can spur greater coordination of efforts by competitors to counterattack these subsidies.

4. *Globalized Competitors.* When a business's competitors use global strategy to exploit industry globalization potential, the business needs to match or preempt these competitors.

Source: Adapted from George S. Yip, *Total Global Strategy: Managing for Worldwide Competitive Advantage* (Englewood Cliffs, N.J.: Prentice Hall, 1992), pp. 223–31.

However, there is no guarantee that cost leadership will last. Until flexible manufacturing and customized production becomes fully operational, cost leaders may be vulnerable to firms that use **product differentiation** strategy to better serve the exact needs of customers. Although one could argue that lower cost will attract customers away from other market segments, some customers are willing to pay a premium price for unique product features that they desire. Uniqueness may come

❖ ❖

𝒢LOBAL PERSPECTIVE 8–1

GLOBALIZING THE MULTIDOMESTIC CORPORATE CULTURE

In Unilever, three main groups are involved in strategic management: operating companies, management groups that oversee them, and the corporation as a whole. To be a successful global company, the strategies at different levels need to interrelate, considering bottom-up and top-down approaches. The dilemma is to find the right equilibrium between instructions from the top and inputs from the bottom in order not to stifle management creativity at the bottom as well as to provide sufficient direction to achieve the interests of all the corporation's stakeholders.

The company's culture and philosophy influence this equilibrium. Unilever, for example, used to be highly decentralized, with individual operating companies, each with their own identity, linked by a common corporate culture and some common services such as research, finance, and management development. After having experimented with various organizational structures to encourage global strategic management, Unilever has adopted a full-time Corporate Development board member, who is on staff with an advisory role, free from major line responsibilities.

Unilever's culture still emphasizes the relative independence of operating companies, where headquarters imposes changes only when there are clear advantages. As the problems faced by Unilever did not require an immediate strong reaction, the senior managers could proceed comparatively gradually, having the opportunity to feel a part of the strategy process. The gradual change in strategy orientation fit the company's corporate culture, demanding a gradual dosage rather than a sudden shock, with senior managers being able to feel a greater sense of commitment to the company's strategy.

Unilever is now undertaking its biggest organizational shake-up since 1996, with a review of the way it plans and buys advertising campaigns. The review is designed to increase the efficiency of Unilever's $3.3 billion media expenditure. The review is likely to mean the world's second-largest advertiser adopts an integrated approach to promoting its products, ranging across detergents, deodorants, and food. The search for cost savings is likely to mean media will be bought globally rather than locally.

Sources: F.A. Maljers, "Strategic Planning and Intuition in Unilever," *Long Range Planning*, 23 (2) (1990), pp. 63–68; and David Benady, "Unilever in Global Ad Shake-Up," *Marketing Week*, 22 (February 11, 1999), p. 7.

---

in the form of comfort, product performance, and aesthetics, as well as status symbol and exclusivity. Despite the Japanese juggernaut in the automobile industry in the 1970s and 1980s, BMW of Germany and Volvo of Sweden, for example, managed to maintain their competitive strengths in the high-end segments of the automobile market. Smaller companies may pursue a limited differentiation strategy by keeping a niche in the market. Firms using a **niche** strategy focus exclusively on a highly specialized segment of the market and try to achieve a dominant position in that segment. Again in the automobile industry, Porsche and Saab maintain their competitive strengths with high-powered sports-car enthusiasts. However, particularly in an era of global competition, niche players may be vulnerable to large-scale operators due to sheer economies of scale needed to compete on a global scale.

Competition is not limited to the firms in the same industry. As just discussed, companies may adopt different strategies for different competitive advantages. If firms in an industry collectively have insufficient capacity to fulfill demand, the incentive is high for new market entrants. However, such entrants need to consider the time and investment it takes to develop new or additional capacity, the likelihood of such capacity being developed by existing competitors, and the possibility of changes in customer demand over time. Indirect competition also comes from suppliers and customers, as well as substitute products or services. A conceptual framework that portrays the multidimensional nature of competitive industry structure is presented in Exhibit 8–2.

1. **Industry competitors** determine the rivalry among existing firms.

2. **Potential entrants** may change the rule of competition but can be deterred through entry barriers. For example, Hyundai and Daewoo, two large Korean automobile manufacturers entering into the already crowded automobile industry, may change the nature of competition in the U.S. automobile industry. However, they have also been kept at bay by existing domestic and foreign automakers operating in the United States.

3. The **bargaining power of suppliers** can change the structure of industries. Intel has become a dominant producer of microprocessors for personal computers. Its enormous bargaining power has caused many PC manufacturers to operate on wafer-thin profit margins, making the PC industry extremely competitive.

4. The **bargaining power of buyers** may affect the firm's profitability. It is particularly the case when governments try to get price and delivery concessions from foreign firms. Similarly, Nestlé, whose subsidiaries used to make independent decisions on cocoa purchases, has centralized its procurement decision at its headquarters to take advantage of its consolidated bargaining power over cocoa producers around the world. In the case of Holzmann AG, the German construction giant had 440 separate subsidiaries, each doing its own procurement,

EXHIBIT 8–2
NATURE OF COMPETITIVE INDUSTRY STRUCTURE

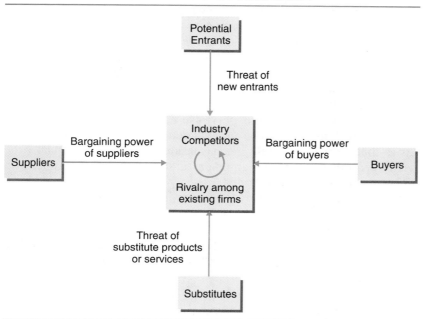

Source: Reprinted with the permission of the Free Press, a division of Simon & Schuster, from *Competitive Strategy: Techniques for Analyzing Industries and Competitors* by Michael E. Porter, p. 4. Copyright © 1980 by The Free Press.

leading to one division paying twice as much for cement as another division from the same supplier. Consolidating its buying power has led to greater efficiency and lower costs for the firm.[14]

5. The **threat of substitute products or services** can restructure the entire industry above and beyond the existing competitive structure. For example, a recent *Economist* article alerts that Playstation II, the successor to Sony's best-selling Playstation, a computer-game console due out in 2000, is a 128-bit computer more powerful than a Pentium III. It can play DVD movies, decode digital TV, and surf the Internet for less than $400; and it may even challenge the Microsoft-Intel PC standard.[15]

Hyper-competition[16] In any given industry, firms jockey among themselves for better competitive position, given a set of customers and buyers, the threat of substitutes, and the barriers to entry in that industry. However, Exhibit 8–2 represents a description of a situation without any temporal dimension; there is no indication as to how a firm should act so as to change the situation to its advantage. For instance, it is not clear how tomorrow's competitor may differ from today's. A new competitor may emerge from a completely different industry, given the convergence of industries. Ricoh, a facsimile and copier maker, has now come up with a product that records moving images digitally, which is what a camcorder and a movie camera do using different technologies. This development potentially pits Ricoh as a direct competitor to camcorder and movie camera makers—something not possible ten or twenty years ago.

Such a shift in competition is referred to as *creative destruction*. This view of competition assumes continuous change, which is a basic assumption behind the concept of **hypercompetition**, where the firm's focus is on disrupting the market. In a hypercompetitive environment, a firm competes on the basis of price–quality, timing, and know-how. It creates strongholds in the markets in which it operates (this is akin to entry barriers) and pools financial resources to outlast competitors.

The basic premise of hypercompetition is that all firms are faced with a form of aggressive competition that is tougher than oligopoly or monopolistic competition, but is not perfect competition, where the firm is atomistic and cannot influence the market at all. This form of competition is pervasive not just in fast-moving, high-technology industries like computers and deregulated industries like airlines, but also in industries that have traditionally been considered more sedate, like processed foods. The central thesis of this argument is that no type of competitive advantage can last—it is bound to get eroded.

For many firms, technology is the key to success in markets where significant advances in product performance are expected. A firm uses its technological leadership for rapid innovation and introduction of new products. The timing of such introductions in the global marketplace is an integral part of the firm's strategy. However, the dispersion of technological expertise means that any technological

---

[14]Richard C. Morais, "Cross-Border Shakeup," *Fortune* (February 22, 1999), p. 111.

[15]"Playing the Big Boys," *Economist* (May 15, 1999), pp. 65–66.

[16]Richard D'Aveni, *Hypercompetition: Managing the Dynamics of Strategic Maneuvering* (New York: The Free Press, 1994).

advantage is temporary, so the firm should not rest on its laurels. The firm needs to move on to its next source of temporary advantage to remain ahead. In the process, firms that are able to continue creating a series of temporary advantages are the ones that survive and thrive.

Hypercompetition postulates that firms compete in the following four arenas of competition.

Cost and Quality. The first arena is that of **cost and quality**. Japanese firms, in particular, have made U.S. and other Western competitors keenly aware that low cost and high quality can be achieved simultaneously. In the first arena, firms compete on price and quality—analogous to cost leadership, differentiation, and niche strategy, discussed earlier. As time goes by, the firms that are successful and that are still players in the market tend to become closer to one another in terms of price and quality. In other words, more firms become similar and the categorization of cost leadership and differentiation breaks down as firms attempt to deliver higher quality for lower cost. In effect, as shown in Exhibit 8–3, all firms attempt to move toward the ultimate value point—higher quality at lower costs. Improvements in manufacturing technology have enabled more firms to access this strategy than before.

Timing and Know-How. The second arena of competition is that of **timing and know-how**. They refer to factors such as technological leadership and being first to the market. Once competition shifts to the arena of timing and know-how, the technology, marketing skills, and other assets that a firm possesses become its weapons to gain advantages in time over its competitors. The firm now attempts to

EXHIBIT 8–3
THE PRICE/QUALITY TRADE-OFF AND THE
ULTIMATE VALUE POINT

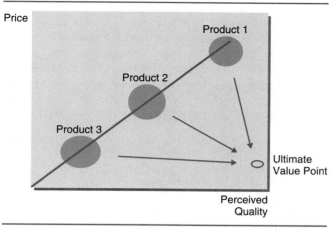

be among the pioneers, or first-movers, in the market for the product categories that it operates in.[17] Sony offers an excellent example of a company in constant pursuit of first-mover advantage with Trinitron color television, Betamax video-recorder, Walkman, 8mm videorecorder, and DVD (digital video disc), although not all of its products succeeded in the market. Indeed, there can even be some first-mover disadvantages.[18]

Strongholds. The third arena of competition is that of **strongholds**, referring to geographic and other market segments where the firm is strong (through, for example, the creation of barriers). A strong competitive position in some market segments provides the firm with the capability for attacking a competitor in another segment. Here again, many Japanese companies built their initial competitive strengths by becoming strong domestic competitors in the large Japanese market, which constitutes a little over half the size of the U.S. market (in terms of GDP) and which is known for quality-conscious, demanding customers.[19]

Financial Resources. The final arena of competition is the firm's **financial resources** that are used to make or purchase the latest technological advances or to monitor its competitors anywhere they compete, eliminating surprises. For example, the merger of Asea of Sweden and Brown-Boveri of Switzerland has created a global company that can compete with General Electric in any part of the world on the basis of its resources and global reach. Competition among firms now takes place, simultaneously or sequentially, through attempts to develop strongholds and to utilize the financial resources of the firm.

Black & Decker, a U.S.-based manufacturer of hand tools, switched to a global strategy using its strengths in the arenas of cost and quality and timing and know-how. In the 1980s Black & Decker's position was threatened by a powerful Japanese competitor, Makita. Makita's strategy of producing and marketing globally standardized products worldwide made it into a low-cost producer and enabled it to steadily increase its world market share. Within the company, Black & Decker's international fiefdoms combined with nationalist chauvinism to stifle coordination in product development and new product introductions, resulting in lost opportunities.

Then, responding to the increased competitive pressure, Black & Decker moved decisively toward globalization. It embarked on a program to coordinate new product development worldwide in order to develop core standardized products that could be marketed globally with minimum modification. The streamlining of R & D also offered scale economies and less duplication of effort—and new

[17]Gerard J. Tellis and Peter N. Golder, "First to Market, First to Fail?: Real Causes of Enduring Market Leadership," *Sloan Management Review*, 37 (Winter 1996), pp. 65–75; and Richard Makadok, "Can First-Mover and Early-Mover Advantages be Sustained in an Industry with Low Barriers to Entry/Imitation?" *Strategic Management Journal*, 19 (July 1998), pp. 683–96.

[18]Marvin B. Lieberman and David B. Montgomery, "First-Mover (Dis)advantages: Retrospective and Link with the Resource-Based View," *Strategic Management Journal*, 19 (December 1998), pp. 1111–1125.

[19]Michael E. Porter, "The Competitive Advantage of Nations," *Harvard Business Review*, 68 (March–April, 1990), pp. 73–93.

products could be introduced faster. Its increased emphasis on design made it into a global leader in design management. It consolidated its advertising into two agencies worldwide in an attempt to give a more consistent image worldwide. Black & Decker also strengthened the functional organization by giving the functional manager a larger role in coordinating with the country management. Finally, Black & Decker purchased General Electric's small appliance division to achieve world-scale economies in manufacturing, distribution, and marketing.

The global strategy initially faced skepticism and resistance from country managers at Black & Decker. The chief executive officer took a visible leadership role and made some management changes to start moving the company toward globalization. These changes in strategy helped Black & Decker increase revenues and profits by as much as 50 percent from 1986 to 1996.[20]

However, a word of caution is in order. A sudden strategy shift from a multidomestic to a global orientation could be more harmful than beneficial. A classic example of a failure is Parker Pen, as illustrated in Global Perspective 8–2. Indeed, it was not a global strategy that was at fault, but rather, implementation of the global strategy—it was too quick and too sudden, without due consideration of the company's organizational inertia.

Another ongoing example is Intel, which, having established a premier position in microprocessors, is now attempting to create a stronghold in that area by adding more and more components to the basic microprocessor design, such as video and graphic controllers. Intel is also utilizing its financial muscle to create powerful brand-name recognition for a product that is not really an end product but only a component in the end product—albeit a critical one. Competition based on financial resources is akin to the utilization of a large war chest by a country to win a war. As more firms attempt to compete on this basis, status quo again reigns with no basic differentiation among firms. Firms may then shift back to cost- and quality-based competition.

In essence, competitive advantage goes to firms that disrupt the existing status quo in the market and take advantage of the disruption. Managers, therefore, seek actively to create a market disequilibrium and then profit from it. In this scenario, the traditional economists' market equilibrium cannot exist because the market is continuously lurching from one "equilibrium" to another. The manager's job is to manage these continuous transitions so that the firm makes profits and gains on market share.

To disrupt the market, the firm must have its ear close to the ground so that it picks up customer requirements early enough to take advantage of market feedback ahead of its competitors. In other words, the firm needs to be market- and customer-oriented. Market orientation has been defined to be the organizationwide generation, dissemination, and responsiveness to the intelligence from customers and the market. If a firm is to maintain a market orientation consistently, it requires leadership from top executives, who have to send the correct signals to personnel in the organization.

There appear to be primarily two approaches to gaining competitive advantage. The competitor-centered approaches involve comparison with the competitor

---

[20]Black & Decker, various annual reports.

◆ ◆

𝒢LOBAL PERSPECTIVE 8–2

ROME COULD NOT BE BUILT IN A DAY AT PARKER PEN COMPANY

Parker Pen was a successful company until the early 1980s. It used to be a completely decentralized company, whose country managers had a great degree of operational flexibility. Parker Pen's subsidiaries used to develop their own marketing strategies, independently deciding what products to produce and selecting their own advertising agencies. Parker Pen was proud of its decentralized operational structure.

The Parker name was strongly associated with pens, having a strong reputation for quality and style. The company was able to charge premium prices in the past, when pens were considered as a gift item.

In the 1960s, however, a fundamental change occurred in the market: the development of the disposable, ball-point market. Despite this trend, Parker Pen had remained in the upper end of the market with high-priced pens. When Parker Pen decided to enter the lower end of the market, however, it failed, because its management team did not know how to market the product in this new market segment.

When the U.S. dollar rose in the early 1980s, Parker Pen began to see its operational inefficiencies and consequently lower profits due to its fragmented production and marketing around the world. To address this issue, a new management team was brought in, with James

Peterson as president and chief executive officer. Peterson decided to go "global," standardizing product and promotion strategies.

As a result, the product line was slashed from 500 to the 100 most profitable items. The company began to use Ogilvy & Mather as its sole global advertising agency; its manufacturing facilities were updated—especially the one used to produce the lower-end product: the Vector, a roller-ball pen.

Peterson believed that his global marketing effort could save Parker Pen, and decided to enter in every viable segment. Peterson intensified the identical global advertising, forgetting that pens could mean different things to different people. His strategy backfired.

Parker Pen's global marketing strategy also failed because Peterson tried to transform his managers abroad from independently operating executives into simple implementers of the global marketing strategy. With the abrupt change imposed on the country managers, Peterson failed to consider the corporate culture and its organizational inertia.

Eventually, Gillette, the world's largest razor maker, purchased Parker Pen Holdings in 1993. Gillette now organizes its businesses by product, rather than geography. In other words, Gillette's Parker Pen division now has a truly global responsibility. Furthermore, Gillette intends to accomplish local integration across its divisions, including Parker Pen, in order to create within-country synergies. Tapping the power of global brands often requires acknowledging country differences and respecting local norms—thus strengthening, rather than weakening, the local country unit and enhancing relationships across functions and divisions with it.

Source: Laurie Freeman, "Parker Pen Dropping Its Global Plans," *Advertising Age* (May 13, 1985), p. 66; "Gillette: Blade-Runner," *Economist* (April 10, 1993), p. 68; and Rosabeth Moss Kanter and Thomas D. Dretler, "'Global Strategy' and Its Impact on Local Operations: Lessons from Gillette Singapore," *Academy of Management Executive*, 12 (November 1998), pp. 60–68.

on costs, prices, technology, market share, profitability, and other related activities. Such an approach may lead to a preoccupation with some activities, and the firm may lose sight of its customers and various constituents. Customer-focused approaches to gaining competitive advantage emanate from an analysis of customer benefits to be delivered. In practice, finding the proper links between required customer benefits and the activities and variables controlled by management is needed. Besides, there is evidence to suggest that listening too closely to customer requirements may cause a firm to miss the bus on innovations, because current customers might not want innovations that require them to change how they operate.

A fourth aspect of global strategy is **interdependency** of modern companies. Recent research has shown that the number of technologies used in a variety of products in diverse industries is rising.[21] Access to resources limits how many distinctive competencies a firm can gain, so firms must draw on outside technologies to be able to build a state-of-the-art product. Since most firms operating globally are limited by a lack of all required technologies, it follows that for firms to make optimal use of outside technologies, a degree of components standardization is required. Such standardization would enable different firms to develop different end products, using, in a large measure, the same components.[22] Research findings do indicate that technology intensity—that is, the degree of R & D expenditure a firm incurs as a proportion of sales—is a primary determinant of cross-border firm integration.[23]

The computer industry is a good instance of a case where firms use components from various sources. Compaq, Dell, and Acer all use semiconductor chips from Intel, AMD, or Cyrix, hard drives from Seagate or Conner, and software from Microsoft. The final product—in this case, the personal computer—carries some individual idiosyncrasies of Compaq, Dell, or Acer, but at least some of the components are common and, indeed, are portable across the products of the three companies.

In the international context, governments also tend to play a larger role and may, directly or indirectly, affect parts of the firm's strategy. Tariffs and nontariff barriers such as voluntary export restraints and restrictive customs procedures might change cost structures so that a firm may need to change its production and sourcing decisions. It is possible, however, that with the end of the Cold War and the spread of capitalism to previously socialist economies, such factors may decrease in importance. The successful completion of the Uruguay Round of GATT talks in December 1993 and the signing of the agreement in April 1994 is an encouraging sign because it leads to greater harmonization of tariff rules and less freedom for national governments to make arbitrary changes in tariff and nontariff barriers and in intellectual property laws.

GLOBAL MARKETING STRATEGY

◆ ◆ ◆ ◆ ◆ ◆

As a whole, multinational companies using global marketing have been highly successful. Examples include Nestlé with its common brand name applied to many products in all countries, Coca Cola with its global advertising themes, Xerox with its global leasing policies, and Dell Computer's "sell-direct" strategy.[24] But **global**

---

[21]Aldor R. Lanctot, "Technology Reliance Strategy in a Globally Competitive Environment: Empirical Investigation and Managerial Implications," a Ph.D. dissertation, The University of Texas at Austin, 1995.

[22]Masaaki Kotabe, Arvind Sahay, and Preet S. Aulakh, "Emerging Roles of Technology Licensing in Development of Global Product Strategy: A Conceptual Framework and Research Propositions," *Journal of Marketing*, 60 (January 1996), pp. 73–88.

[23]Stephen Kobrin, "An Empirical Analysis of the Determinants of Global Integration," *Strategic Management Journal*, 12 (1991), pp. 17–31.

[24]Silvia Ascarelli, "Dell Finds U.S. Strategy Works in Europe," *Wall Street Journal* (February 3, 1997), p. A8; and Jaikumar Vijayan and Stacy Collett, "Compaq: Is Dell or IBM the Model?" *Computerworld*, 33 (April 26, 1999), pp. 1, 14.

EXHIBIT 8–4
VARIATION IN CONTENT AND COVERAGE
OF GLOBAL MARKETING

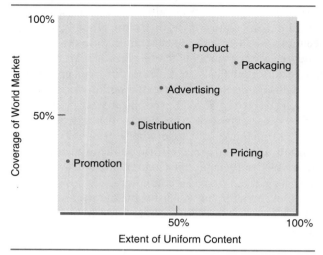

Source: George S. Yip, *Total Global Strategy: Managing for Worldwide Competitive Advantage* (Englewood Cliffs, NJ: Prentice Hall, 1992), p. 136.N

marketing strategy is not about standardizing the marketing process on a global basis. Although every element of the marketing process—product design, product and brand positioning, brand name, packaging, pricing, advertising strategy and execution, promotion, and distribution—may be a candidate for standardization, standardization is just one part of a global marketing strategy. It may or may not be used by a company, depending on the mix of the product-market conditions, stage of market development, and the inclinations of the management of the multinational firm. For instance, a marketing element can be global without being 100 percent uniform in content or coverage. Exhibit 8–4 illustrates a possible pattern.

Let us take an instance from Exhibit 8–4 and look at distribution with a magnitude of less than 50 percent on both coverage of world market and on extent of uniform content. If we assume that the firm in question (represented in the diagram) does not have a manufacturing facility in each of the markets it serves, then to the extent that various markets have a uniform content, and presumably similar operations, there is a requirement for coordination with manufacturing facilities elsewhere in the firm's global network. Also, where content is not uniform, any change requirements for the nonuniform content of distribution require corresponding changes in the product and/or packaging. Thus, a global marketing strategy requires more intimate linkages with a firm's other functions, such as research and development, manufacturing, and finance.[25]

In other words, a global marketing strategy is but one component of a global strategy. For an analogy, you may think of a just-in-time inventory and

---

[25]Masaaki Kotabe, *Global Sourcing Strategy: R & D, Manufacturing, and Marketing Interfaces* (New York: Quorum Books, 1992).

manufacturing system that works for a single manufacturing facility to optimize production. Extend this concept now to finance and marketing, and include all subsidiaries of the firm across the world as well. One can imagine the magnitude and complexity of the task when a manager is attempting to develop and implement a global strategy. One implication is that without a global strategy for R & D, manufacturing, and finance that meshes with the various requirements of its global marketing strategy, a firm cannot best implement that global marketing strategy.

Global marketing strategy can achieve one or more of four major categories of potential globalization benefits: cost reduction, improved quality of products and programs, enhanced customer preference, and increased competitive advantage.[26] General Motors and Ford approach global marketing somewhat differently; such a strategic difference suggests that the two U.S. automakers are in search of different benefits of global marketing (see Global Perspective 8–3).

Benefits of Global Marketing

Cost Reduction. This arises from savings in both work force and materials. When multiple national marketing functions are consolidated, personnel outlays are reduced through the avoidance of duplicated activities. Costs are also saved in producing global advertisements, commercials, promotional materials, and packaging. Savings from standardized packaging include reduction in inventory costs. With typical inventory carrying costs at 20 percent of sales, any reduction in inventory can significantly affect sales. With the availability of a global span of coverage by various forms of modern communication media, multicountry campaigns capitalizing on countries' common features would also reduce advertising costs considerably. Exxon's "Put a Tiger in Your Tank" campaign is a good example of a campaign that used the same theme across much of the world, taking advantage of the fact that the tiger is almost universally associated with power and grace.

Cost savings can also translate into increased program effectiveness by allowing more money and resources into a smaller number of more focused programs. British Airways was able to afford spectacular and expensive special effects for its highly memorable "Manhattan Landing" global television commercial, in which Manhattan was shown landing on a small English village.

Improved Products and Program Effectiveness. This may often be the greatest advantage of a global marketing strategy. Good ideas are relatively scarce in the business arena. So a globalization program that overcomes local objections to allow the spread of a good marketing idea can often raise the effectiveness of the program when measured on a worldwide basis. Traditionally, R & D has been concentrated in the headquarters country of a global company. This has sometimes circumscribed a possible synergy from amalgamation of good ideas from around the world.

Procter & Gamble has solved this problem by setting up major R & D facilities in each of its major markets in the Triad—North America, Japan, and Western Europe—and by putting together the pertinent findings from each of the laboratories. As in the saying, "Necessity is the mother of invention," different needs in

---

[26]George S. Yip, Total *Global Strategy: Managing for Worldwide Competitive Advantage* (Englewood Cliffs, N.J.: Prentice Hall, 1992), pp. 21–23.

GLOBAL PERSPECTIVE 8–3

GM AND FORD PURSUE DIFFERENT BENEFITS FROM GLOBAL MARKETING

Ford and General Motors approach globalization differently. In its quest for a "world car," Ford has developed the so-called Ford 2000 program by creating five new vehicle centers—four in the United States and one in Europe—each responsible for designing and developing a different type of car worldwide. Ford's plan was put to test when it built a mid-size world car in 1993 known as the Mondeo in Europe and the Ford Contour in North America. Its plan was to manufacture 700,000 cars a year in Europe and North America for nearly a decade, with only a "refreshing" after four or five years. Ford executives say they can no longer afford to duplicate efforts and they want to emulate the Japanese, who develop cars that with minor variations can be sold around the world. While the Mondeo/Contour sold 642,000 units in the first two years in Europe, it had disappointing sales in the United States, attributed to its comparably higher price relative to the car's predecessors. Successful product development efforts require that the company avoid two problems that can arise from pursuing global design. First, the high cost of designing products or components that are acceptable in many settings could negatively affect efficiency. Second, the product, in this case a world car, may be low cost but only meet the lowest common denominator of taste in all countries.

Alternatively, General Motors has taken a more regional tack by retaining strong regional operations that develop distinctly different cars for their own. If a car has a strong crossover potential, engineers and marketers cross the Atlantic to suggest customization. Thus, Cadillac got an Americanized version of the Opel Omega small luxury sedan developed by GM's Opel

subsidiary in Germany. GM managers contend that ad hoc efforts are cheaper and more flexible. John Oldfield, vice-president of new product programs at Ford of Europe, counters that "doing two conventional car programs would have cost substantially more than doing one global program. If we did it again, we could do it in three and a half years."

The two automakers' contrasting product development and marketing programs illustrate the traditionally viewed trade-offs of efficiency and adaptiveness, global standardization versus customization, market segmentation versus product differentiation, and product orientation versus customer orientation. These debates are framed by the tension between bending demand to the will of supply (i.e., driving the market) versus adjusting to market demand (i.e., driven by the market).

It is difficult to conclude that one strategy is genuinely better than the other. One has to be reminded that while the Ford Mondeo/Contour project cost $6 billion and took six years to develop, potential cost savings could also be enormous for years to come from the global strategy. On the other hand, GM's regional strategy could also make sense if regional taste differences remain so large that a Ford-style global strategy could, indeed, end up producing a "blandmobile" that hits the lowest common denominator of taste in different markets.

Which seems to be a winning strategy? Ford's new president, Jacques Nasser, wants to keep the efficiencies generated from central thinking about design and production. But he wants to reintroduce the market focus in regions across the globe that will give Ford stronger brands and more appealing products. It appears that the Ford 2000 was a good idea carried a bit too far. Nasser is trying to redefine the Ford 2000 program with a heightened emphasis on the company's brands and give the various regional and brand units more autonomy.

Source: "Ford: Alex Trotman's Daring Global Strategy," *Business Week* (April 3, 1995), pp. 94–104; and "Ford Be Nimble," *Business Week Online*, http://www.businessweek.com/, September 27, 1999.

different parts of the world may lead to different inventions. For example, Procter & Gamble's Liquid Tide laundry detergent was an innovative product developed in an innovative way by taking advantage of both the company's technical abilities and various market requirements in key markets around the world. Germans had been extremely concerned about polluting rivers with phosphate, a key whitening ingredient in the traditional detergent. To meet the German customer demand, Procter & Gamble in Germany had developed fatty acid to replace phosphate in the detergent. Similarly, Procter & Gamble Japan had developed surfactant to get out grease effectively in the tepid water that Japanese use in washing their clothes. In the United States, Procter & Gamble in Cincinnati, Ohio, had independently developed "builder" to keep dirt from settling on clothes. Putting all these three innovations together, the company introduced Liquid Tide and its sister products around the world.

Three benefits followed from this multiple R & D location strategy. By being able to integrate required product attributes from three separate markets, P & G was able to introduce a much better product than would otherwise be possible and increase its chances of success. Second, its development costs were spread over a much larger market—a market that was more inclined to receive the product favorably because of the incorporation of the product features described. Third, it increased the sources from which product ideas are available to it. Thus, not only does P & G have immediate returns, but also it has secured for itself a reliable resource base of future products.

Enhanced Customer Preference. Awareness and recall of a product on a worldwide basis increase its value. A global marketing strategy helps build recognition that can enhance customer preferences through reinforcement. With the rise in the availability of information from a variety of sources across the world and the rise in travel across national borders, more and more people are being exposed to messages in different countries. So a uniform marketing message—whether communicated through a brand name, packaging, or advertisement—reinforces the awareness, knowledge, and attitudes of people toward the product or service. Pepsi has a consistent theme in its marketing communication across the world—that of youthfulness and fun as a part of the Pepsi-drinking experience.

Increased Competitive Advantage. By focusing resources into a smaller number of programs, global strategies magnify the competitive power of the programs. Although larger competitors might have the resources to develop different high-quality programs for each country, smaller firms might not. Using a focused global marketing strategy could allow the smaller firm to compete with a larger competitor in a more effective manner. However, the most important benefit of a global strategy may be that the entire organization gets behind a single idea, thus increasing the chances of the idea's success. Avis created a global campaign communicating the idea "We are number two, therefore we try harder," not only to customers, but also to its employees. As a result, the entire organization pulled together to deliver on a global promise, not just in marketing but in all activities that directly or indirectly affected the company's interface with the customer.

Equally, if not more, important are the benefits of market and competitive intelligence provided by the increased flow of information due to the worldwide coordination of activities. As the global firm meshes the different parts of the organization into the framework of a focused strategy, information flow through the organization improves and enables the functioning of the strategy. A byproduct is that the organization as a whole becomes much better informed about itself and about the activities of its competitors in markets across the world. Access to more timely information results in the organization being more prepared and able to respond to signals from the marketplace.

Limits to Global Marketing

Although national boundaries have begun losing their significance both as a psychological and as a physical barrier to international business, the diversity of local environments (particularly cultural, political, and legal environments) still inhibits optimal global marketing strategy development. Indeed, we still debate the very issue raised more than twenty years ago: counteracting forces of "unification versus fragmentation" in developing operational strategies along the value chain. As early as 1969, John Fayerweather wrote emphatically:

> What fundamental effects does (the existence of many national borders) have on the strategy of the multinational firm? Although many effects can be itemized, one central theme recurs; that is, their tendency to push the firm toward adaptation to the diversity of local environments which leads toward fragmentation of operations. But there is a natural tendency in a single firm toward integration and uniformity that is basically at odds with fragmentation. Thus the central issue . . . is the conflict between unification and fragmentation—a close-knit operational strategy with similar foreign units versus a loosely related, highly variegated family of activities.[27]

The same counteracting forces have since been revisited by many authors in such terms as *standardization versus adaptation* (1960s), *globalization versus localization* (1970s), *global integration versus local responsiveness* (1980s), and most recently, *scale versus sensitivity* (1990s).[28] Terms have changed, but the quintessence of the strategic dilemma that multinational firms face today has not changed and will probably remain unchanged for years to come.

Now the question is to what extent successful MNCs can circumvent the effect of local environmental diversity. In some industries, product standardization may result in a product that satisfies customers nowhere. For processed foods, for example, national tastes and consumption patterns differ sufficiently to make standardization counterproductive. In Latin America, a variety of canned spicy peppers, such as jalapeño peppers, is a national staple in Mexico, but is virtually unheard of in Brazil and Chile. Obviously, firms cannot lump together the whole of Latin America as one regional market for condiments.

On the other hand, Merck, the world's second largest pharmaceutical company, faces a different kind of problem with global marketing. The company can market the same products around the world for various ailments, but cultural and political differences make it very difficult to approach different markets in a similar way. Merck, which operates internationally as MSD, has to increase public awareness of health care issues in Mexico, Central America, and much of South America by bringing top journalists from these countries together on a regular basis to meet with health care experts ranging from physicians to government officials. In the Pacific Rim, the company is trying to change the way it does business there. It used to operate through local distributors and licensees, never learning the local quirks of pharmaceutical business. Now, the company is creating subsidiaries in nearly all of the main Asian countries, including Korea, China, the Philippines, Taiwan, Singapore, and Malaysia, in order to learn what goes on inside those markets. In Eastern

[27]John Fayerweather, *International Business Management: Conceptual Framework* (New York: McGraw-Hill, 1969), pp. 133–34.

[28]Martin Sorrell, Group Chief Executive, WPP Group, "Globalization: Scale versus Sensitivity," A speech, Joint Conference of the Korean Marketing Association and the American Marketing Association, May 14–17, 1995.

Europe, Merck is starting from scratch, as its entry had been previously barred under the region's strict communist control. For example, in Hungary, the company has devoted its initial investment to establishing resource centers that are affiliated with local hospitals and universities in order to create a special image for Merck.[29]

Even in supposedly similar cultures, there can be huge differences in what are effective marketing campaigns. The Body Shop found this out when it took a successful ad campaign in Britain and brought it to the United States, assuming it would have the same appeal. The ad showed the naked buttocks of three men and completely misfired in the U.S. market. In the words of Body Shop founder Anita Roddick, "We thought it was funny and witty here, but women in New Hampshire fainted."[30]

However, despite such cultural and political constraints in the markets, Nestlé, for example, has managed to integrate procurement functions in order to gain bargaining power in purchasing common ingredients such as cocoa and sugar. In other industries, such as computers and telecommunications, consumption patterns are in the process of being established and the associated cultural constraint is getting less prominent. Also, the simultaneous launch of most products in these categories across the world precludes large differences. For these products, governments frequently attempt to exert national control over technological development, the products or the production process.[31] However, while it is the multinational firms that are the vehicle through which technology, production, and economic activity in general are integrated across borders, *it is the underlying technology and economic activity that are global*. National markets, regardless of how they are organized economically, are no longer enough to support the development of technology in many industries. See Exhibit 8–5 for some generalizations about the degree of product standardization around the world.

Thus, if critical technologies are transnational, then, to an extent, meanings of borders, sovereignty, and nation-states themselves are compromised. More specifically, terms such as *national control of technology* and *national industrial competitiveness* lose some of their meaning—the more so because national governments, which represent nations, do not "produce" anything or sell any of "their" product. Indeed, governments may then make themselves more useful by finding ways to provide the means to enhance the strengths and to access appropriate partners for the areas of weakness of the firms which call that government the home country government.

REGIONALIZATION OF GLOBAL MARKETING STRATEGY

◆ ◆ ◆ ◆ ◆ ◆

Some firms may have difficulty in organizing, or may not be willing to organize, operations to maximize flexibility and encourage integration across national borders. Beyond various cultural, political, and economic differences across national

---

[29]Fannie Weinstein, "Drug Interaction: Merck Establishes Itself, Country by Country, in Emerging Markets," *Profiles* (September 1996), pp. 35–39.

[30]Ernest Beck, "Body Shop Gets a Makeover to Cut Costs," *Wall Street Journal* (January 27, 1999), p. A18.

[31]C. K. Prahalad and Yves L. Doz, *The Multinational Mission* (New York: The Free Press, 1987).

EXHIBIT 8–5
DEGREE OF STANDARDIZABILITY OF PRODUCTS IN WORLD MARKETS

Local ←→ Universal

Factors limiting universality	Culture/ habits	Design taste	Language	Size/package	Technical system	User/ application	None
Example	• Fish sausage • Root beer • Boxer shorts • Rice cooker	• Furniture • Refrigerator • Processed food	• Word processor • Computer	• Textile • Automotive (seat size) • Soft drinks	• Color TV (PAL system in European voltage	• Portable radio/cassette player (youths in U.S.) • While liqueur (young females in Japan)	• Watch • Motorcycle • Petrochemical products • Piano • Money (capital market)

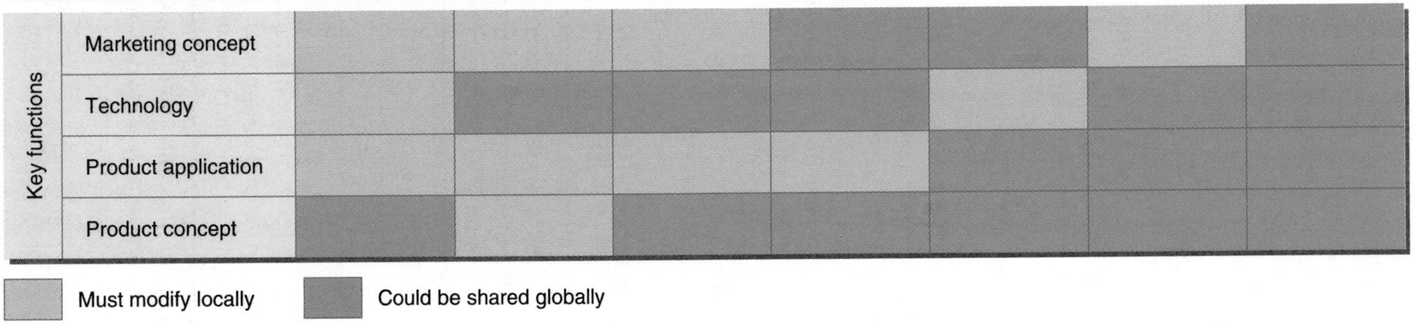

Key functions:

	Culture/habits	Design taste	Language	Size/package	Technical system	User/application	None
Marketing concept							
Technology							
Product application							
Product concept							

Must modify locally ▢   Could be shared globally ▢

Source: Competition by Kenichi Ohmae, p. 193. Copyright © 1985 by Kenichi Ohmae and McKinsey & Company, Inc.

borders, organizational realities also impair the ability of multinational firms to pursue global marketing strategies. Not surprisingly, integration has often been opposed by foreign subsidiaries eager to protect their historical relative independence from their parent companies. As described earlier, the successful and gradual adoption of global orientation in Global Perspective 8–1 and the debacle of Parker Pen's attempt to shift to globally uniform marketing in Global Perspective 8–2 offer good contrasting examples.

In finding a balance between the need for greater integration and the need to exploit existing resources more effectively, many companies have begun to explore the use of regional strategies in Europe, North America, and the Pacific Rim. **Regionalization** can be defined as the cross-subsidization of market share battles in pursuit of regional production, branding, and distribution advantages.[32] Regional strategies in Europe and North America have been encouraged by the economic, political, and social pressures resulting from the development of regional trading blocs, such as the European Union, North American Free Trade Agreement (NAFTA), and Southern Common Market (MERCOSUR).[33]

There are two favorable effects of the formation of regional trading blocs. First, the volatility of foreign exchange rates within a bloc seems to be reduced.[34] Second, with the growing level of macroeconomic integration with regions, there is also a trend toward greater harmonization of product and industry standards, pollution and safety standards, and environmental standards, among other things.[35] These regional commonalities further encourage firms to develop marketing strategies on a regional basis.[36] Global marketing strategy cannot be developed without considering competitive and other market forces from different regions around the world. To face those regional forces proactively, three additional strategies need to be considered at the firm level. These are cross subsidization of markets, identification of weak market segments, and the lead market concept.[37] See also Global Perspective 8–4 for an example of global competition between Nike and Reebok, employing these three strategies on an ongoing basis.

---

[32]Allen J. Morrison and Kendall Roth, "The Regional Solution: An Alternative to Globalization," *Transnational Corporations*, 1 (August 1, 1992), pp. 37–55; and Gerald Millet, "Global Marketing and Regionalization—Worlds Apart?" *Pharmaceutical Executive*, 17 (August 1997), pp. 78–81.

[33]Masaaki Kotabe and Maria Cecilia Coutinho de Arruda, "South America's Free Trade Gambit," *Marketing Management*, 7 (Spring 1998), pp. 38–46.

[34]Marc Hendriks, "Prospects for the European Financial System," *Business Economics*, 30 (July 1995), pp. 11–16; Alan David MacCormack, Lawrence James Newmann, and Donald B. Rosenfield, "The New Dynamics of Global Manufacturing Site Location," *Sloan Management Review*, 35 (Summer 1994), pp. 69–80.

[35]Edmund W. Beaty, "Standard Regionalization: A Threat to Internetworking?" *Telecommunications*, Americas Edition, 27 (May 1993), pp. 48–51.

[36]Maneesh Chandra, "The Regionalization of Global Strategy," A paper presented at 1997 Academy of International Business Annual Meeting, Monterrey, Mexico, October 8–12, 1997.

[37]Gary Hamel and C.K. Prahalad, "Do You Really Have a Global Strategy?" *Harvard Business Review* (July–August 1985), pp. 139–48.

GLOBAL PERSPECTIVE 8–4

NIKE AND REEBOK BATTLING FOR GLOBAL DOMINANCE

Sneakers have become an obsession—from sports enthusiasts to people concerned about health to junior executives, and to people who follow fashion, and housewives. Two giants dominate this market: Nike and Reebok. Nike was founded thirty years ago by Philip Knight, a University of Oregon track star, who began importing high-quality running shoes to the United States. Reebok, originally a British-made sneaker with a line of white-leather women's aerobic shoes, had its North American rights acquired in 1979 by Paul Fireman for his family's sporting-goods business.

Nike's first years were spent shuttling across the Pacific in search of capital and cheap labor from Japan to Korea to Taiwan. But the force that made this company fly was Knight's ability to attract popular sports heroes, the most dominant and charismatic, to his cause and then build new product lines and marketing campaigns around them. This formula had a great success—for a decade the company revenues grew at nearly triple-digit rates: they created a need.

By 1976, the jogging craze took off across the United States, and people desired a pricey pair of sneakers. In 1980s Nike went public as the market leader in the United States. The global dominance of German manufacturers Puma and Adidas was threatened.

In the mid-1980s the jogging fever suddenly broke. Reebok's sales exploded through the 1980s, as more women got into exercise and more people began to use good sneakers for several activities besides sports. In 1984 Fireman bought out the parent company, and in 1985 the company went public. When it passed Nike in annual sales in 1987, Knight decided to return to his core strategy—building new products around a popular athlete, this time with Michael Jordan. Nike's ad campaigns are legendary and have changed sports marketing forever, redefining what is celebrity and positioning Nike as the brand of athletic performance.

The Air Jordan line of footwear and apparel put Nike back on track. By 1990 it was the leader again. Reebok remains a great competitor, and the two companies together have more than half the share of the U.S. market and also control more than 40 percent of the global market. In the global arena, Adidas is the only significant competitor, with a 10 percent share of the global sales.

Until the 1990s Reebok had Nike's attention but was perceived to be a different company, whose main market was women's fitness, with a product line including a range of lower-priced casual shoes. Nike's strategic focus was to deliver high-quality, high-priced products to male athletes and wannabes. Their similarities were to act in the athletic footwear and apparel business, and both maintained the bulk of their manufacturing base in low-cost countries.

Around 1990 Fireman had launched sallies into men's team sports, boosted product development budget, and tried to broaden his products' appeal. He started using Nike's core strategy, then the two companies began to compete by sport heroes. Both companies know that their success heavily depends on celebrity marketing and consumer fad. That is also the reason they are trying to diversify. Nike is in retail with outlets called Nike Towns—conceived as sports museums—and Reebok has a fitness-club business and videos. They target every sport activity that can interest the under-18-year-old crowd.

In the future, the main arena will be outside the United States. Reebok makes half its sales overseas, and Nike sells about 40 percent of its goods abroad. The most important global battleground is soccer, an arena dominated by Adidas, with some 300 million people playing the game worldwide. Reebok has been chipping away at Adidas for several years, using sponsorship, signing global superstars, and marking its presence in important championships such as the World Cup. Nike entered this market more recently, but is already shaking up the sport—sponsoring men's and women's U.S. national teams, besides the Italian national team, and putting together a lineup of superstar endorsers, from Italy to Brazil.

Reebok's global strategy is to find a place in minor sports, by identifying the one that has an emotional appeal in a particular country—for example, handball in Denmark, cricket in Great Britain, and baseball in Japan. For Nike, its marketing power—sports celebrities—is no longer a secret. And both companies may have problems in the future with the overuse of heroes and emotions by so many advertisers.

Source: Kenneth Labaich, "Nike vs. Reebok—A Battle for Hearts, Minds & Feet," *Fortune* (September 18, 1995), pp. 58–69; and Bill Richards, "Nike Says It Plans to Slash $100 Million On Spending for Star Endorsements," *Wall Street Journal* (October 2, 1998), p. B6.

Cross-subsidization of markets refers to multinational firms using profits gained in a market where they have a strong competitive position to beef up their competitive position in a market where they are struggling to gain foothold. For example, Michelin used its strong profit base in Europe to attack the home market of Goodyear in the United States. Reducing prices in its home market (by Goodyear) would have meant that Goodyear would have reduced its own profits from its largest and most profitable market without substantially affecting Michelin's bottom line, because Michelin would have exposed only a small portion of its worldwide business by competing with Goodyear in the United States. Goodyear chose to strike back by expanding operations and reducing prices in Europe.

Kodak's ongoing rivalry with Fuji in the photographic film market provides another example of the importance of not permitting a global competitor unhindered operation in its home market. Kodak did not have a presence in Japan until the early 1980s. In this omission, Kodak was making the same mistake that many other Western companies have done—avoiding Japan as unattractive on a stand-alone basis, while not seeing its strategic importance as the home base of a global competitor and a source of ideas.[38]

Cross-Subsidization of Markets

The second strategy that firms should always keep an open eye for is the identification of **weak market segments** not covered by a firm in its home market. Small-screen portable TVs were used by Japanese TV makers to get a foot in the door of the large U.S. market for TVs. RCA and Zenith did not think this segment attractive enough to go after. Another classic example is Honda's entry into the U.S. motorcycle market in the 1960s. Honda offered small, lightweight machines that looked safe and cute, attracting families and an emerging leisure class with an advertising campaign, "You can meet the nicest people on a Honda." Prior to Honda's entry, the U.S. motorcycle market was characterized by the police, military personnel, aficionados, and scofflaws like Hell's Angels and Devil's Disciples. Honda broke away from the existing paradigms about motorcycles and the motorcycle market, and successfully differentiated itself by covering niches that did not exist before.[39] Once the Japanese companies were established in the small niche, they had a base to expand on to larger and more profitable product lines. More recently in 1997, Labatt International of Canada took advantage of freer trading relationships in NAFTA and Canadian consumers awakening to things Mexican by importing a Mexican beer, Sol, brewed by Cerveceria Cuauhtemoc Moctezuma, to fill a newly found market segment in Canada. These examples show that firms should avoid pegging their competitive advantage entirely on one market segment in their home market.

Identification of Weak Market Segments

What directions can this lead to in terms of a global product strategy—or a worldwide distribution, pricing, or promotion strategy? Let us discuss some aspects of a global product strategy for an automobile company. Suppose market data tell the managers that four dozen different models are required if the company desires to design separate cars for each distinct segment of the Triad market. But the

---

[38]Chanoine Webb, "The Picture Just Keeps Getting Darker at Kodak," *Fortune* (June 21, 1999), p. 206.

[39]Richard P. Rumelt, "The Many Faces of Honda," *California Management Review*, 38 (Summer 1996), pp. 103–11; and Richard D. Pascale, "Reflections on Honda," *California Management Review*, 38 (Summer 1996), pp. 112–17.

company has neither the financial nor the technological resources to go in for so many product designs. Also, there is no single global car that will solve the problems for the entire world. The United States, Japan, and Europe are different markets, with different mixes of needs and preferences. Japan requires right-hand drive cars with frequent inspections; many parts of Europe need small, right-hand drive cars. As a top manager of an automobile company the option of leaving out a Triad market would not be a good one. The company needs to be present in all of these three markets with good products.

Use of Lead Market Concept

The solution may be to look at the main requirements of each lead market in turn. A **lead market** is where unique local competition is nurturing product and service standards to be adopted by the rest of the world over time. In the U.S. automobile market, a utility truck model as well as a four-door family car is required. And now utility trucks are catching on in other parts of the world. Japanese consumers fond of high-tech gadgets may set the world standard for gas pumps that come equipped with on-line services that offer motorists access to weather forecasts and traffic information, as BP Amoco has decided to offer such gas pumps in Japan before any other place.[40]

Another example is wireless financial services. Although many U.S. banks are globally competitive, banks in Europe and Asia have already surpassed those in the United States when it comes to offering such services. In late 1999, around 1.6 million people were using wireless financial services in Europe and 1.3 million in Asia, mainly Japan, compared to only 30,000 in the United States. There are several reasons, some technological and some cultural. Although the push toward smart digital phones that can use the Web and e-mail has started, only one person in five has digital devices of any kind in the United States. Analog phones still account for 75 percent of cell phones in the United States. Digital has caught on earlier in Europe, where 36 percent of people have some sort of wireless digital device. Asia is not far behind. In Scandinavia and Japan, more than half the population has digital devices. In addition, Europe has one generally accepted standard for mobile phones—the Global System for Mobile Communications—that allows for short, two-way messages. The United States has a hodgepodge of competing technologies, making it expensive for financial institutions to reach a broad range of customers. Europe and Japan may serve as lead markets or better learning grounds for U.S. financial institutions to compete in the U.S. market down the road.[41]

As indicated earlier, this is a strategic response to the emergence of lead countries as a market globalization driver. Each can be a lead country model—a product carefully tailored to meet distinct individual needs. With a short list of lead country models in hand, minor modifications may enable a fair amount of sales in other Triad markets and elsewhere. This will halve the number of basic models required to cover the global markets and, at the same time, cover a major proportion of sales with cars designed for major markets. Additional model types could be developed through adaptation of the lead country models for specific segments. This approach in each of the largest core markets permits development of a pool of supplemental designs that can be adapted to local preferences.

---

[40]"BP Amoco to Pump Out Online Data with the Gas," *Philadelphia Inquirer* (August 18, 1999), p. C1.

[41]"Banking without a Wire: Europe, Asia Surpass U.S. in Offering Wireless Digital Financial Services," CNN.com, www.cnn.com, October 22, 1999.

In line with our earlier example of Procter & Gamble, it is not necessary that the design and manufacturing of a lead country model be restricted to one R & D and manufacturing facility. Ford has now integrated the design and manufacturing process on a global basis. It has design centers at Dearborn (Michigan), England, Italy, and Japan, which are connected by a satellite uplink. Designers using fast workstations and massively parallel computers simulate a complete model and the working of the model for various conditions. Separate parts of the car are simulated at different facilities. Thereafter, the complete design for a lead country is integrated in the facility assigned for the purpose. For instance, the complete design for the new Ford Mustang was put together in Dearborn, but it incorporated some significant changes in body design that were made in England based on designs of Jaguar, which Ford had acquired. Similarly, different components of an automobile may be sourced from different parts of the global network of the firm or even from outside the firm. As firms move toward concentrating on developing expertise in a few core competencies,[42] they are increasingly outsourcing many of the components required for the total product system that constitutes the automobile.

This increase in outsourcing raises another question for firms that practice it. How can firms ensure uninterrupted flow of components when the component makers are independent companies? The answer to this question and the set of issues that it raises takes us into the area of cooperation between firms and strategic alliances, which will be discussed in Chapter 9.

As stated earlier in Chapters 1 and 2, one salient aspect of the globalization of markets is the importance of the emerging markets, known as *big emerging markets* (BEMs)—China, India, Indonesia, and Brazil. As multinational companies from North America, Western Europe, and Japan search for growth, they have no choice but to compete in those BEMs despite the uncertainty and the difficulty of doing business there. A vast consumer base of hundreds of millions of people—the middle class market, in particular—is developing rapidly. When marketing managers working in the developed countries hear about the emerging middle-class markets in China or Brazil, they tend to think in terms of the middle class in the United States or Western Europe. In the United States, people who earn an annual income of between $35,000 and $75,000 are generally considered middle class.[43] In China and Brazil, people who have the purchasing power equivalent of $20,000 or more constitute only 2 and 9 percent of their respective populations and are considered upper class. In these emerging countries, people with the purchasing-power equivalent of $5,000 to $20,000 (and most of them in the $5,000 to $10,000 equivalent bracket) are considered middle class and constitute a little more than 25 percent of the population. Indeed, the vast majority (67 percent of the population) in China and Brazil are in the low-income class with the purchasing-power equivalent of less than $5,000. Obviously, the concept of the middle-class market segment differs greatly between developed and emerging countries. So does what they can afford to purchase.[44]

Marketing Strategies for Emerging Markets

---

[42]C. K. Prahalad and Gary Hamel, "The Core Competence of the Corporation," *Harvard Business Review*, 68 (May–June 1990), pp. 79–91.

[43]"The Billionaire Next Door," *Forbes* (October 11, 1999), pp. 50–62.

[44]C.K. Prahalad and Kenneth Lieberthal, "The End of Corporate Imperialism," *Harvard Business Review*, 76 (July–August 1998), pp. 69–79.

Consumers in BEMs are increasingly aware of global products and global standards, but they often are unwilling—and sometimes unable—to pay global prices. Even when those consumers appear to want the same products as sold elsewhere, some modification in marketing strategy is necessary to reflect differences in product, pricing, promotion, and distribution. Some unnecessary frills may need to be removed from the product to reduce price, while maintaining its functional performance. Packaging may need to be strengthened because the distribution problems, such as poor road conditions and dusty air, in emerging markets can hamper smooth handling. Promotion may need to be adapted to address local tastes and preferences. As these emerging markets improve their economic standing in the world economy, they tend to assert their local tastes and preferences over existing global products. Further, access to local distribution channels is often critical to success in emerging markets because it is difficult and expensive for multinational companies from developed countries to understand local customs and the labyrinthine network of distributors in the existing channel. Some companies (e.g., Unilever) have broadened the scope of their market by addressing these issues and also competing for the low-income classes. In Indonesia, Unilever does brisk business by selling inexpensive, smaller-size products, that are affordable to everyone and available anywhere. For instance, it sells Lifebuoy soap with the motto: "With a price you can afford." Unilever's subsidiary in India, Hindustan Lever, approaches the market as one giant rural market. It uses small, cheap packaging, bright signage, and all sorts of local distributors. In fact, Unilever has been so successful and profitable in Indonesia that its biggest rival, P & G, is now following suit.[45]

Local companies from those emerging markets are also honing their competitive advantage by offering better customer service than foreign multinationals can provide. They can compete with established multinationals from developed countries either by entrenching themselves in their domestic or regional markets or by extending their unique home-grown capabilities abroad. For example, Honda, which sells its scooters, motorcycles, and cars worldwide on the strength of its superior technology, quality, and brand appeal, entered the Indian market. Competing head-on with Honda's strength would be a futile effort for Indian competitors. Instead, Bajaj, an Indian scooter manufacturer, decided to emphasize its line of cheap, rugged scooters through an extensive distribution system and a ubiquitous service network of roadside-mechanic stalls. Although Bajaj could not compete with Honda on technology, it has been able to stall Honda's inroads by catering to consumers who looked for low-cost, durable machines. Similarly, Jollibee Foods, a family-owned fast-food company in the Philippines, overcame an onslaught from McDonald's in its home market not only by upgrading service and delivery standards but also by developing rival menus customized to local Filipino tastes. Along with noodle and rice meals made with fish, Jollibee developed a hamburger seasoned with garlic and soy sauce, capturing more than half of the fast-food business in the Philippines. Using similar recipes, this Filipino company has now established dozens of restaurants in neighboring markets and beyond, including Hong Kong, the Middle East, and as far as California.[46]

---

[45]Prahalad and Lieberthal, 1998.

[46]Niraj Dawar and Tony Frost, "Competing with Giants. Survival Strategies for Local Companies in Emerging Markets," *Harvard Business Review*, 77 (March–April 1999), pp. 119–29.

COMPETITIVE ANALYSIS

As we have discussed so far, a firm needs to broaden the sources of competitive advantage relentlessly over time. However, careful assessment of a firm's current competitive position is also required. One particularly useful technique in analyzing a firm's competitive position relative to its competitors is referred to as **SWOT (strengths, weaknesses, opportunities, and threats) analysis**. A SWOT analysis divides the information into two main categories (*internal factors* and *external factors*) and then further into positive aspects (*strengths* and *opportunities*) and negative aspects (*weaknesses* and *threats*). The framework for a SWOT analysis is illustrated in Exhibit 8–6. The internal factors that may be viewed as strengths or weaknesses depend on their impact on the firm's positions; that is, they may represent a strength for one firm but a weakness, in relative terms, for another. They include all of the marketing mix (product, price, promotion, and distribution strategy); as well as personnel and finance. The external factors, which again may be threats to one firm and opportunities to another, include technological changes, legislation, sociocultural changes, and changes in the marketplace or competitive position.

Based on this SWOT framework, marketing executives can construct alternative strategies. For example, an S*O strategy may be conceived to maximize both the company's strengths and market opportunities. Similarly, an S*T strategy may be considered in such a way as to maximize the company's strengths and minimize external threats. Thus, a SWOT analysis helps marketing executives identify a wide range of alternative strategies to think about.

EXHIBIT 8–6
SWOT ANALYSIS

SWOT Analysis

	Strengths	Weakness
Internal Factors / External Factors	Brand Name, Human Resources, Management Know-How, Technology, Advertising, etc.	Price, Lack of Financial Resources, Long Product Development Cycle, Dependence on Independent Distributors, etc.
Opportunities: Growth Market Favorable Investment Environment, Deregulation, Stable Exchange Rate, Patent Protection, etc.	S*O Strategy — Develop a strategy to maximize strengths and maximize opportunities	W*O Strategy — Develop a strategy to minimize weaknesses and maximize opportunities
Threats: New Entrants, Change in Consumer Preference, New Environmental Protection Laws, Local Content Requirement, etc.	S*T Strategy — Develop a strategy to maximize strengths and minimize threats	W*T Strategy — Develop a strategy to minimize weaknesses and minimize threats

You should note, however, that SWOT is just one aid to categorization. It is not the only technique. One drawback of SWOT is that it tends to persuade companies to compile lists rather than think about what is really important to their business. It also presents the resulting lists uncritically, without clear prioritization; so that, for example, weak opportunities may appear to balance strong threats. Furthermore, using the company's strengths against its competitors' weaknesses may work once or twice, but not over several dynamic strategic interactions, as its approach becomes predictable and the competitors begin to learn and outsmart it.

The aim of any SWOT analysis should be to isolate the key issues that will be important to the future of the firm and that will be addressed by subsequent marketing strategy.

◆ ◆

ⅴIDEO CASE

GLOBAL COMPETITION IN JAPAN'S AUTOMOBILE MARKET AND BEYOND

Japan remains one of the toughest markets for foreign automakers since there are many domestic car makers vying for the market share, led by Toyota, Honda, Nissan, Mazda, and Mitsubishi. Among foreign imports, Mercedes-Benz, BMW, Volvo, and Ford, among others, have also established their niches in the already congested auto market in Japan.

Now attracted to the resurgence of the Asian markets since the Asian financial crisis, U.S. and European automakers are increasingly aligning with Japanese automakers, such as Ford-Mazda and Renault-Nissan relationships. This is also timely for Japanese automakers, as many of them have been struggling with Japan's long recession since the early 1990s. The end result will be that more and more automakers are collaborating among themselves by sharing R&D, platforms, and access to new markets.

Discuss how the nature of competition may change over time in the automobile industry in Asia.

SUMMARY ◆

Market-oriented firms, facing greater competitiveness in world markets, find it essential to assume a global perspective in designing and implementing their marketing strategies. Cost containment, rising technology costs and the dispersal of technology, a greater number of global competitors in many industries, and the advent of hypercompetition in many markets mean that international business practices need to undergo continuous refinement in order to keep them aligned with company goals. The explosive growth of e-commerce has added urgency to competitive analysis involving not only established multinational firms but also an increasing number of entrepreneurial start-ups leapfrogging geographical constraints via the Internet.

Strategic planning and the integration of the global activities into one coherent whole needs to be implemented for a firm to maximize its activities and for the firm to remain a viable player in international markets. In doing so, the multinational firm needs to mesh information technology and telecommunications with its global operations in order to make relevant data available to managers in real time. In the end, a global strategy of any kind has to resolve a number of apparent contradictions. Firms have to respond to national needs, yet seek to exploit know-how on a worldwide basis. At the same time it must strive to produce and distribute goods and services globally as efficiently as possible.

In recent years, however, as a result of the formation of regional trading blocs, an increasing number of companies have begun to organize their marketing strategies on a regional basis by exploiting emerging regional similarities. Globally minded, proactive firms increasingly exploit their competitive position in some regions by funneling abundant resources and regionally successful marketing programs to other regions where they do not necessarily occupy a strong market position. SWOT analysis helps isolate the key issues that will be important to the competitiveness of the firm and that will be addressed by its subsequent marketing strategy.

KEY TERMS ◆

bargaining power of
    buyers
bargaining power of
    suppliers
cost and quality
cost leadership
cross-subsidization of
    markets

financial resources
global citizenship
global industry
global marketing strategy
global strategy
Gross Information
    Product

hypercompetition
interdependency
lead market
niche
potential entrant
product differentiation
regionalization

strongholds
SWOT (strengths, weak-
    nesses, opportunities,
    and threats) analysis
threat of substitute
    product (or service)
timing and know-how
weak market segments

REVIEW QUESTIONS ◆ ◆ ◆ ◆ ◆ ◆ ◆ ◆ ◆ ◆ ◆ ◆ ◆ ◆ ◆ ◆ ◆ ◆ ◆

1. How are the developments in information technology *affecting* the global strategies of firms?

2. What are the various factors/forces/drivers that determine the globlization potential of industries? How are global industries different from multidomestic industries?

3. What do you understand by the term *hypercompetition*? What, according to hypercompetition, are the various arenas of competition?

4. How are the concepts of *interdependency* and *standardization* related? What are the implications for global strategy?

5. How is a global marketing strategy distinct from standardization?

6. What are the benefits and limitations of global marketing strategies?

7. How are regional and global strategies different? What are some advantages and disadvantages of a regional strategy?

DISCUSSION QUESTIONS ◆ ◆ ◆ ◆ ◆ ◆ ◆ ◆ ◆ ◆ ◆ ◆ ◆ ◆ ◆ ◆ ◆

1. Food habits have been known to vary considerably across countries and regions. Would you describe the food industry as primarily multidomestic or global in nature? Use the fast-food chain McDonald's as a case example to explain your answer. Note that while there are certain similarities in all of the McDonald's outlets around the world, there are differences, especially in the menu, in various countries. Can the McDonald's example be generalized across the food industry?

2. In the summer of 1995, Procter & Gamble, the U.S. multinational giant, announced that it would be modifying its global operational structure. Its new structure would include a top-tier management team consisting of four vice-presidents, each representing a particular region, namely North America, Europe (and also to include the Middle East and Africa), Asia and Pacific Rim, and Latin America. One of the main reasons cited for this organizational change was the elimination of duties and regulations that now allows P & G to distribute its products to foreign consumers cheaper and quicker. While acknowledging that more than 50 percent of the company's sales come from North America, and so, too, a bulk of its prof-

its, the top management mentioned that it took care not to emphasize a particular region over the other. Yet, there is no doubt that most of the company's new products originated in the United States. Few dominant products and brands have been originated from its foreign subsidiaries. There are, however, examples of brands, such as Tide, which involved the cross-fertilization of ideas and technologies from its operations around the world.

Based on the facts provided, and any popular press information about P & G you have been exposed to, what would you consider to be P & G's predominant international strategy—global (integrated on a worldwide basis), regional (integrated on a regional level), ethnocentric (predominantly influenced by its operations in North America), or polycentric (primarily independent and autonomous functioning of its international subsidiaries)?

3. Since the early 1980s, the benefits of globalization have been acknowledged by researchers in academia and by business practitioners. However, practitioners have continually indicated the constraints on human management resources in actually implementing global strategies—to implement a global strategy, you need

globally thinking managers. In your opinion, are business schools making progress in developing more global managers? Are corporations doing a good job of training their managers to think globally? What are the deficiencies? What steps would recommend to business schools, as well as corporations, in order to promote the development of executives who think globally?

4. One of the many advantages of globalization suggested is economies of scale and scope. There is, however, a counterargument to this advantage. Mass customization production techniques could lead to erosion of scale and scope economies with the added advantage of being able to customize products, if not for individual customers, definitely for individual markets. Discuss the strengths and weaknesses of this counterargument.

5. Present-day business competition is increasingly being characterized by two opposite perspectives. On the one hand, the reduced trade barriers and duty reductions are making competition more global in nature. One example is the multinational consumer non-durable manufacturing corporations such as Unilever, Procter & Gamble, and Colgate-Palmolive, which are integrating their activities at a regional and global level. At the same time, these companies are being faced with the problem of losing market share to in-store brands. Are these perspectives really opposite to each other? What are the implications of these market drivers for the retail chains such as Wal-Mart? What are the implications for the consumer nondurable goods manufacturers?

FURTHER READING ✦

Angelides, Marios C. "Implementing the Internet for Business: A Global Marketing Opportunity," *International Journal of Information Management*, 17 (December 1997): 405–19.

Bartlett, Christopher, and Sumantra Ghoshal. "What Is A Global Manager?" *Harvard Business Review*, 70 (September/October, 1992): 124–32.

Dawar, Niraj, and Tony Frost. "Competing with Giants. Survival Strategies for Local Companies in Emerging Markets," *Harvard Business Review*, 77 (March–April 1999): 119–29.

Emmerji, Louis. "Globalization, Regionalization, and World Trade." *Columbia Journal of World Business*, 27 (Summer 1992): 6–13.

Ger, Güliz. "Localizing in the Global Village," *California Management Review*, 41 (Summer 1999): 64–83.

Kaynak, Erdener. *The Global Business: Four Key Marketing Strategies*. New York: International Business Press, 1993.

Kanter, Rosabeth Moss, and Thomas D. Dretler. "'Global Strategy' and its Impact on Local Operations: Lessons from Gillette Singapore," *Academy of Management Executive*, 12 (November 1998): 60–68.

Lovelock, Christopher H., and George S. Yip. "Developing Global Strategies for Service Businesses." *California Management Review*, 38 (Winter 1996): 64–86.

Mascarenhas, Briance, Alok Baveja, and Mamnoon Jamil. "Dynamics of Core Competencies in Leading Multinational Companies," *California Management Review*, 40 (Summer 1998): 117–32.

Mitchell, Jennifer. "Reaching Across Borders," *Marketing News* (May 10, 1999): 19.

O'Brian, Richard. *Global Financial Integration: The End of Geography*. New York: Council on Foreign Relations Press, 1992.

Piturro, Marlene, "What Are You Doing about the Global Realities?" *Management Review*, 88 (March 1999): 16–22.

GLOBAL MARKET ENTRY STRATEGIES

CHAPTER OVERVIEW

1. TARGET MARKET SELECTION

2. CHOOSING THE MODE OF ENTRY

3. EXPORTING

4. LICENSING

5. FRANCHISING

6. CONTRACT MANUFACTURING

7. JOINT VENTURES

8. WHOLLY OWNED SUBSIDIARIES

9. STRATEGIC ALLIANCES

After the U.S. government lifted its trade embargo against Vietnam, Procter & Gamble entered Vietnam through a joint venture with Phuong Dong in 1995.[1] Phuong Dong, the local partner, is an entity under the state-owned Vietnam Chemical Corp. (Vinachem), a subsidiary of the Ministry of Industry. Phuong Dong has its own stable of competing laundry brands. Moreover, the parent company, Vinachem, also had a joint venture with Unilever, P&G's archrival. At the inception of P&G Vietnam, Procter & Gamble held a 70 percent share in the joint

---

[1]The P&G Vietnam discussion is based on the following sources: "P&G's Venture in Vietnam Has a Bit of Soap in Its Eyes," *The Asian Wall Street Journal* (October 21, 1997), p. 6; "Ebb Tide? Procter & Gamble's Spat in Vietnams Nears a Crest," *The Asian Wall Street Journal* (February 26, 1998); www.pg.com (corporate news releases).

venture. In its first two fiscal years, P&G Vietnam racked up $28 million in losses due to unforeseen start-up costs and weak demand for the company's brands. The honeymoon between the two partners did not last long. In the fall of 1997, P&G wanted to inject more cash into the business. However, Phuong Dong, being cash-poor, did not want to pour more money in the venture. P&G offered to buy out the Vietnamese stake, but its partner flatly refused to sell. Phuong Dong blamed the venture's losses on P&G's extravagant spending for advertising and expatriate salaries. P&G wanted to build brand-name recognition and boost market share by heavy advertising. Phuong Dong, like other state-run companies, preferred to emphasize distribution channels. The local press described P&G as "arrogant." Government officials accused P&G of deliberately making losses to undermine its Vietnamese partner. After intense haggling with Vinachem, P&G was finally able to increase its stake in the partnership from 70 to 93 percent.

Procter & Gamble's high-profile spat with its Vietnamese partner may be a bit unusual, but it highlights the importance of making sound strategic entry decisions. Making the "right" entry decisions will heavily impact the company's performance in global markets. Granted, other strategic marketing-mix decisions also play a big role. A major difference here is that many of these other decisions can easily be corrected, sometimes even overnight (e.g., pricing decisions), while entry decisions are far more difficult to redress.

We can hardly overemphasize the need for a solid market entry strategy. Entry decisions will heavily influence the firm's other marketing-mix decisions. Several decisions need to be made. The firm has to decide on: (1) the target product/market, (2) the goals of the target markets, (3) the mode of entry, (4) the time of entry, (5) a marketing-mix plan, and (6) a control system to monitor the performance in the entered market.[2] This chapter will cover the major decisions that constitute market entry strategies. It starts with the target market selection decision. We then consider the different criteria that will impact the entry mode choice. Following that, we will concentrate on the various entry strategy options that MNCs might look at. Each of these will be described in some detail and evaluated. The final section focuses on cross-border strategic alliances.

◆ ◆ ◆ ◆ ◆ ◆ ◆ TARGET MARKET SELECTION

A crucial step in developing a global expansion strategy is the selection of potential target markets. Companies adopt many different approaches to pick target markets. A flowchart for one of the more elaborate approaches is given in Exhibit 9–1.

To identify market opportunities for a given product (or service) the international marketer usually starts off with a large pool of candidate countries (say, all Central European countries). To narrow down this pool of countries, the company will typically do a preliminary screening. The goal of this exercise is twofold: you want to minimize the mistakes of (1) ignoring countries that offer viable opportunities for your product, and (2) wasting time on countries that offer no or little

---

[2]Franklin R. Root, *Entry Strategies for International Markets* (New York: Lexington Books, 1994), p. 23.

EXHIBIT 9–1
A LOGICAL FLOW MODEL OF THE ENTRY DECISION PROCESS

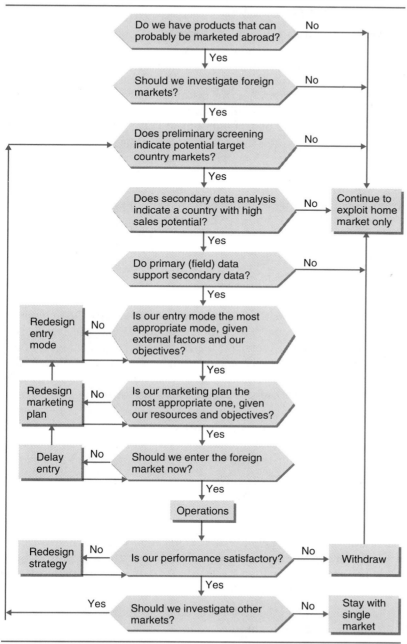

potential.[3] Those countries that make the grade are scrutinized further to determine the final set of target countries. A four-step procedure that you can employ for the initial screening process goes as follows:

Step 1:   *Select indicators and collect data.*
First, you need to pick a set of socioeconomic and political indicators you believe are critical. The indicators that a company selects are, to a large degree, driven by the strategic objectives spelled out in the company's global mission. Colgate-Palmolive, for instance, views per capita purchasing power as a major driver behind market opportunities.[4] Coca-Cola looks at per capita income and the number of minutes that it would take somebody to work to be able to afford a Coca-Cola product.[5] McDonald's starts with countries that are similar to the United States in lifestyle, with a large proportion of women working, and shorter hours for lunch.[6] Information on these country indicators can easily be gathered from publicly available data sources. Typically, countries that do well on one indicator (say, market size) rate poorly on other indicators (say, market growth). Somehow, we need to combine our information to come up with an overall measure of market attractiveness for these candidate markets.

Step 2:   *Determine importance of country indicators.*
The second step is to determine the importance weights of each of the different country indicators identified in the previous step. One common method is the "constant-sum" allocation technique. Here, you simply allocate one hundred points across the set of indicators according to their importance in achieving the company's goals (e.g., market share). So, the more critical the indicator, the higher the number of points it gets allocated. The total number of points should add up to 100.

Step 3:   *Rate the countries in the pool on each indicator.*
Next, you give each country a score on each of the indicators. For instance, you could use a 7-point scale (1 meaning very unfavorable; 7 meaning very favorable). The better the country does on a particular indicator, the higher the score.

Step 4:   *Compute overall score for each country.*
The final step is to derive an overall score for each prospect country. To that end, you simply sum up the weighted scores that the country obtained on each indicator. The weights are the importance weights that were assigned to the indicators in the second step. Countries with the highest overall scores are the ones that are most attractive. An example of this four-step procedure is given in Exhibit 9–2.

Sometimes, the company might desire to weed out countries that do not meet a cut-off for criteria that are of paramount importance to the company. For instance,

---

[3]Ibid., p. 55.

[4]"Tangney is bullish on L. America," *Advertising Age International* (May 17, 1993), p. I-23.

[5]www.thecoca-colacompany.com/investors/Divester.html.

[6]"Lifestyle flux lures McD's to Mideast," *Advertising Age International* (November 21, 1994), p. I-20.

EXHIBIT 9–2
METHOD FOR PRE-SCREENING MARKET OPPORTUNITIES: EXAMPLE

Country	Per Capita Income	Population	Competition	Political Risk	Score
A	50	25	30	40	3400*
B	20	50	40	10	3600
C	60	30	10	70	3650
D	20	20	70	80	3850
Weights	25	40	25	10	

*(25 × 50) + (40 × 25) + (30 × 35) + (40 × 10) = 3400.

Wrigley, the U.S. chewing gum maker, was not interested in Latin America until recently because many of the local governments imposed ownership restrictions.[7] In that case, the four-step procedure would be done only for the countries that stay in the pool.

Other far more sophisticated methods exist to screen target markets. Kumar and colleagues, for example, developed a screening methodology that incorporates multiple objectives of the firm, resource constraints, and its market expansion strategy.[8] One procedure, which is a bit more sophisticated than the method described here, is described in the appendix.

Over time, companies sometimes must fine-tune their market selection strategy. Grolsch, the Dutch premium beer brewer, used to export to emerging markets like China and Brazil. In the wake of flagging profits, Grolsch decided to focus on mature beer markets where buying power is high and the premium segment is growing. Markets that meet those criteria include the United States, the United Kingdom, Canada, Australia, and continental Europe.[9] Exhibit 9–3 shows the market opportunity matrix for the Asia–Pacific division of Henkel, a German conglomerate. The shaded area highlights the countries that look most promising from Henkel's perspective.

CHOOSING THE MODE OF ENTRY ◆ ◆ ◆ ◆ ◆ ◆

Several decision criteria will influence the choice of entry mode. Roughly speaking, two classes of decision criteria can be distinguished: internal (firm-specific) criteria and external (environment-specific) criteria. Let us first consider the major external criteria.

Decision Criteria for Mode of Entry

[7]"Guanxi Spoken Here," *Forbes* (November 8, 1993), pp. 208–10.
[8]V. Kumar, A. Stam and E.A. Joachimsthaler, "An Interactive Multicriteria Approach to Identifying Potential Foreign Markets," *Journal of International Marketing*, 2 (1) (1994), pp. 29–52; see also Lloyd C. Russow and Sam C. Okoroafo, "On the Way Towards Developing a Global Screening Model," *International Marketing Review*, 13 (1) (1996), pp. 46–64.
[9]"Grolsch Targets Mature Markets," *Financial Times* (February 10, 1999), p. 20.

EXHIBIT 9–3
OPPORTUNITY MATRIX FOR HENKEL IN ASIA PACIFIC

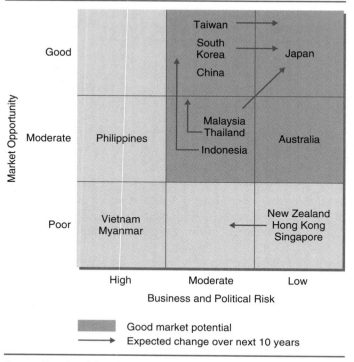

Source: Reprinted from Hellmut Schütte, "Henkel's Strategy for Asia Pacific," *Long Range Planning*, 28 (1), p. 98. Copyright 1995, with kind permission from Elsevier Science Ltd., The Boulevard, Langford Lane, Kidlington OX5 1GB, UK.

Market Size and Growth. In many instances, the key determinant of entry choice decisions is the size of the market. Large markets justify major resource commitments in the form of joint ventures or wholly owned subsidiaries. Market potential can relate to the current size of the market. However, future market potential as measured via the growth rate is often even more critical, especially when the target markets include emerging markets.

Risk. Another major concern when choosing entry modes is the risk factor. The role of risk in global marketing is discussed in Chapter 5 (pp. 124–30). Risk relates to the instability in the political and economic environment that may impact the company's business prospects. Generally speaking, the greater the risk factor, the less eager companies are to make major resource commitments to the country (or region) concerned. Evidently, the level of country risk changes over time. For instance, the peace process in the Middle East and the abolishment of the apartheid regime in South Africa have lured many MNCs to these regions. Many companies opt to start their presence with a liaison office in markets that are high-risk but, at the same time, look very appealing because of their size or growth potential. For instance, MetLife, the insurance company, opened a liaison office in Shanghai and Beijing while it is waiting for permission from the Chinese government to start operations. A liaison office functions then as a low-cost listening post to gather market intelligence and establish contacts with potential distributors.

Government Regulations. Government requirements are also a major consideration in entry mode choices. In scores of countries, government regulations heavily constrain the set of available options. Trade barriers of all different kinds restrict the entry choice decision. In the car industry, local content requirements in countries such as France and Italy played a major role behind the decision of Japanese car makers like Toyota and Nissan to build up a local manufacturing presence in Europe.

Competitive Environment. The nature of the competitive situation in the local market is another driver. The dominance of Kellogg Co. as a global player in the ready-to-eat cereal market was a key motivation for the creation in the early 1990s of Cereal Partners Worldwide, a joint venture between Nestlé and General Mills. The partnership gained some market share (compared to the combined share of Nestlé and General Mills prior to the linkup) in some of the markets, though mostly at the expense of lesser players like Quaker Oats and Ralston Purina.

Local Infrastructure. The physical infrastructure of a market refers to the country's distribution system, transportation network, and communication system. In general, the poorer the local infrastructure, the more reluctant the company is to commit major resources (monetary or human).

All these factors combined determine the overall market attractiveness of the countries being considered. Markets can be classified in five types of countries based on their respective market attractiveness:[10]

- *Platform countries* can be used to gather intelligence and establish a network. Examples include Singapore and Hong Kong.
- *Emerging countries* include Vietnam and the Philippines. Here the major goal is to build up an initial presence for instance via a liaison office.
- *Growth countries* such as China and India can offer early mover advantages. These often encourage companies to build up a significant presence in order to capitalize on future market opportunities.
- *Maturing and established countries* include South Korea, Taiwan, and Japan. These countries have far fewer growth prospects than the other types of markets. Often times, local competitors are well entrenched. On the other hand, these markets have a sizable middle class and solid infrastructure. The prime task here is to look for ways to further develop the market via strategic alliances, major investments or acquisitions of local or smaller foreign players. A case in point is General Electric, an American megacorporation. In the hope of achieving big profits in Europe, GE invested more than $10 billion from 1989 to 1996, half of it for building new plants and half for almost fifty acquisitions, despite the fact that Europe is a fairly mature market.[11]

---

[10]Philippe Lasserre, "Corporate Strategies for the Asia Pacific Region," *Long Range Planning*, 28 (1) (1995), pp. 13–30.
[11]"If Europe's Dead, Why is GE Investing Billions There?" *Fortune* (September 9, 1996).

As you can see in Exhibit 9–4, different types of countries require different expansion paths, although deviations cannot be ruled out.

We now give an overview of the key internal criteria:

Company Objectives. Corporate objectives are a key influence in choosing entry modes. Firms that have limited aspirations will typically prefer entry options that entail a minimum amount of commitment (e.g., licensing). Proactive companies with ambitious strategic objectives, on the other hand, will usually pick entry modes that give them the flexibility and control they need to achieve their goals. Bridgestone, the Japanese tire maker, needed a strong foothold in the U.S. market to become a leading firm in the tire industry. To that end, Bridgestone entered into a bidding war with Pirelli to acquire Firestone. More recently, the company is setting up factories in Central Europe and China and a joint venture in India with Tata, a major truck company, to achieve its goal of a 20 percent market share of the global tire market.[12]

EXHIBIT 9–4
ENTRY MODES AND MARKET DEVELOPMENT

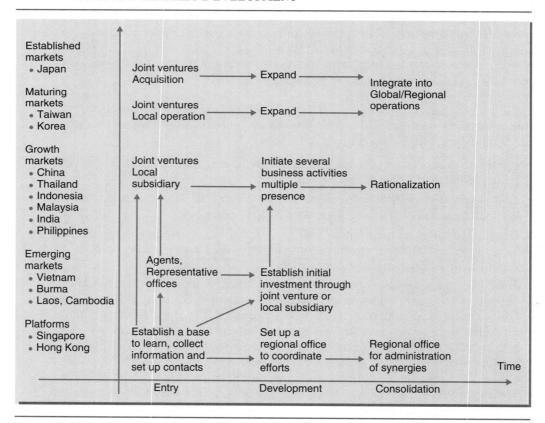

Source: Reprinted from Philippe Lasserre, "Corporate Strategies for the Asia Pacific Region," *Long Range Planning*, 28 (1), p. 21. Copyright 1995, with kind permission from Elsevier Science Ltd., The Boulevard, Langford Lane, Kidlington OX5 1GB UK.

---

[12]"The Buck Stops Here," *Forbes* (March 10, 1997), p. 44.

Need for Control. Most MNCs would like to possess a certain amount of control over their foreign operations. Control may be desirable for any element of the marketing-mix plan: positioning, pricing, advertising, product design, branding, and so forth. Caterpillar, for instance, prefers to stay in complete control of its overseas operations to protect its proprietary know-how. For that reason, Caterpillar avoids joint ventures.[13] To a large degree, the level of control is strongly correlated with the amount of resource commitment: the smaller the commitment, the lower the control. So, most firms face a trade-off between the degree of control over their foreign operations and the level of resource commitment they are willing to take.

Internal Resources, Assets, and Capabilities. Companies with tight resources (human and/or financial) or limited assets are constrained to low commitment entry modes such as exporting and licensing that are not too demanding on their resources. Even large companies should carefully consider how to allocate their resources between their different markets, including the home market. In some cases, major resource commitments to a given target market might be premature given the amount of risk. On the other hand, if a firm is overly reluctant with committing resources, the firm might miss the boat by sacrificing major market opportunities. Internal competencies also influence the choice-of-entry strategy. When the firm lacks certain skills that are critical for the success of its global expansion strategy, the company can try to fill the gap by forming a strategic alliance.

Flexibility. An entry mode that looks very appealing today is not necessarily attractive five or ten years down the road. The local environment changes constantly. New market segments emerge. Local customers become more demanding or more price conscious. Local competitors become more sophisticated. To cope with these environmental changes, global players need a certain amount of flexibility. The flexibility offered by the different entry-mode alternatives varies a great deal. Given their very nature, contractual arrangements like joint ventures or licensing tend to provide very little flexibility. When major exit barriers exist, wholly owned subsidiaries are hard to divest, and, therefore offer very little flexibility compared to other entry alternatives.

Mode-of-Entry Choice: A Transaction Cost Explanation[14]

Although some of the factors just listed favor high-control entry modes, other criteria suggest a low-control mode. The different modes of entry can be classified according to the degree of control they offer to the entrant from low-control (e.g., indirect exporting) to high control modes (e.g., wholly owned subsidiary, majority stake partnerships). To some extent, the appropriate entry-mode decision boils down to the issue of how much control is desirable. Ideally, the entrant would like to have as much control as possible. However, entry modes that offer a large degree of control also entail substantial resource commitments and huge amounts of risk. Therefore, the entrant faces a trade-off between the benefits of increased control and the costs of resource commitment and risk.

---

[13]"Engine Makers Take Different Routes," *Financial Times* (July 14, 1998), p. 11.

[14]Erin Anderson and Hubert Gatignon, "Modes of Foreign Entry: A Transaction Cost Analysis and Propositions," *Journal of International Business Studies*, 11 (Fall 1986), pp. 1–26.

One useful framework to resolve this dilemma is the so-called **transaction-cost analysis (TCA)** perspective. A given task can be looked at as a "make-or-buy" decision: either the firm contracts the task out to outside agents or partners (low-control modes) or the job can be done internally (high control modes). TCA argues that the desirable governance structure (high- versus low-control mode) will depend on the comparative transaction costs—that is, the cost of running the operation.

The TCA approach begins with the premise that markets are competitive. Therefore, market pressure minimizes the need for control. Under this utopian scenario, low-control modes are preferable since the competitive pressures force the outside partner to comply with his contractual duties. When the market mechanism fails, high-control entry modes become more desirable. From the TCA angle, market failure typically happens when **transaction-specific assets** become valuable. These are assets that are only valuable for a very narrow range of applications. Examples include brand equity, proprietary technology, and know-how. When these types of assets become very important, the firm might be better off to adopt a high-control entry mode in order to protect the value of these assets against opportunitistic behaviors and uncertainty.

An empirical study of entry decisions made by the 180 largest MNCs over a fifteen-year period found that MNCs are most likely to enter with wholly owned subsidiaries when one of the following conditions holds:[15]

- The entry involves an R & D-intensive line of business
- The entry involves an advertising-intensive line of business (high brand-equity)
- The MNC has accumulated a substantial amount of experience with foreign entries.

On the other hand, MNCs are most likely to prefer a partnership when one of these holds:

- The entry is in a highly risky country
- The entry is in a socioculturally distant country
- There are legal restrictions on foreign ownership of assets.

◆ ◆ ◆ ◆ ◆ ◆   EXPORTING

Most companies start their international expansion with exporting. For many small businesses, exporting is very often the sole alternative for selling their goods in foreign markets. A fair number of Fortune 500 companies, such as Boeing and Caterpillar, also generate a major part of their global revenues via export sales. In 1998 Caterpillar's exports from the United States were about $6 billion—this translates into $400,000 per Caterpillar job in the United States.[16]

---

[15]Hubert Gatignon and Erin Anderson, "The Multinational Corporation's Degree of Control over Foreign Subsidiaries: An Empirical Test of a Transaction Cost Explanation," *Journal of Law, Economics, and Organization*, 4 (2) (Fall 1988), pp. 305–36.

[16]www.cat.com

Chapter 17 discusses in detail export and import management matters. In this chapter we will give you a snapshot overview of exporting as an entry mode. Companies that plan to engage in exporting have a choice between three broad options: **indirect**, **cooperative**, and **direct exporting**. Indirect exporting means that the firm uses a middleman based in its home market to do the exporting. With cooperative exporting, the firm enters into an agreement with another company (local or foreign) where the partner will use its distribution network to sell the exporter's goods. Direct exporting means that the company sets up its own export organization within the company and relies on a middleman based in a foreign market (e.g., a foreign distributor).

Indirect Exporting

Indirect exporting happens when the firm sells its products in the foreign market via an intermediary located in the firm's home country. The middleman could be an export management company (EMC), a trading house, or simply a broker. Indirect exporting offers several advantages to the exporting company compared to other entry modes. The firm gets instant foreign market expertise. Very little risk is involved. Generally speaking, no major resource commitments are required.

There are some downsides with indirect exporting. The company has little or no control over the way its product is marketed in the foreign country. Lack of adequate sales support, wrong pricing decisions, or poor distribution channels will inevitably lead to poor sales. Ill-fated marketing-mix decisions made by the intermediary could also damage the company's corporate or brand image. The middleman may have very limited experience with handling the company's product line.

Given the low commitment, indirect exporting is often seen as a good beachhead strategy for "testing" the international waters: once the demand for the product takes off, the manufacturer can switch to another, more pro-active, entry mode.

Cooperative Exporting

Companies that are not willing to commit the resources to set up their own distribution organization but still want to have some control over their foreign operations should consider cooperative exporting. One of the most popular forms of cooperative exporting is **piggyback exporting**. With piggybacking, the company uses the overseas distribution network of another company (local or foreign) for selling its goods in the foreign market. Wrigley, the U.S. chewing gum company, recently entered India by piggybacking on Parrys, a local confectionery firm. Through this tie-up, Wrigley is able to plug into Parrys' distribution network, thereby providing Wrigley immediate access to 250,000 retail outlets. The two major attractions that Parrys' network offered to Wrigley were the overlap in product category and the size of the distribution network.

The quality of the distribution network can also play a role. Gillette tied up with Bangalore-based TTK, an Indian manufacturer of pressure cookers and kitchenware for the distribution of Braun products, despite the fact that Gillette has its own distribution network in India. Gillette needed department-store-type outlets for its Braun product range, precisely the type of distribution channels that TTK uses for the distribution of its merchandise.[17]

[17]"India—Distribution Overview," IMI960321, U.S. Department of Commerce, International Trade Administration.

Direct Exporting

Under direct exporting, the firm sets up its own exporting department and sells its products via a middleman located in the foreign market. Once the international sales potential becomes substantial, direct exporting often looks far more appealing than indirect exporting. To some degree, the choice between indirect and direct exporting is a "make-or-buy" decision: Should we as a company perform the export task, or are we better off delegating the task to outsiders? Compared to the indirect approach, direct exporting has a number of pluses. The exporter has far more control over its international operations. Hence, the sales potential (and profit) is often much more significant than under indirect exporting. It also allows the company to build up its own network in the foreign market and get better market feedback.

There is a price to be paid, though. Given that the responsibility for the exporting tasks is now in the hands of the company, the demands on resources—human and financial—are much more intense than with indirect exporting. Besides the marketing-mix tasks, these tasks involve choosing target markets, identifying and selecting representatives in the foreign market, and scores of logistical functions (e.g., documentation, insurance, shipping, packaging).

◆ ◆ ◆ ◆ ◆ ◆ LICENSING

Companies can also penetrate foreign markets via a licensing strategy. **Licensing** is a contractual transaction where the firm—the *licensor*—offers some proprietary assets to a foreign company—the *licensee*—in exchange for royalty fees. Examples of assets that can be part of a licensing agreement include trademarks, technology know-how, production processes, and patents. Royalty rates range between one-eighth of 1 percent and 15 percent of sales revenue.[18] For instance, Tokyo Disneyland is owned and operated by Oriental Land Company under license from Disney. In return for being able to use the Disney name, Oriental Land Company pays royalties to Disney. In some industries, companies' cross-licensing agreements are fairly common. In 1999, Qualcomm and Ericsson settled their patent disputes regarding CDMA-based wireless communications-technology by entering into cross licenses for their patent portfolios. Qualcomm receives royalties from each mobile phone unit sold that incorporates CDMA-technology.

Benefits

For many companies, licensing has proven to be a very profitable means for penetrating foreign markets. In most cases, licensing is not very demanding on the company's resources. Therefore, it is especially appealing to small companies that lack the resources and the wherewithal to invest in foreign facilities. One licensing expert notes that overseas licensing accounts for up to one third of the profits of some small companies.[19] Compared to exporting, another low-commitment entry

---

[18]"Licensing May Be Quickest Route to Foreign Markets," *Wall Street Journal* (September 14, 1990), p. B2.
[19]Ibid.

mode, licensing allows the licensor to navigate around import barriers or get access to markets that are completely closed to imports. For instance, several foreign tobacco companies in China use licensing agreements to avoid the 240 percent import tax levied on imported cigarettes.[20] Local governments may also favor licensing over other entry modes.

Companies that use licensing as part of their global expansion strategy lower their exposure to political or economic instabilities in their foreign markets. The only volatility that the licensor faces are the ups and downs in the royalty income stream. Other risks are absorbed by the licensee.

In high-tech industries, technology licensing has two further appeals. In highly competitive environments, rapid penetration of global markets allows the licensor to define the leading technology standard and to rapidly amortize R & D expenditures.[21] A case in point is Motorola's licensing of proprietary microprocessor technology to Toshiba.

Caveats

Licensing comes with some caveats, though. Revenues coming from a licensing agreement may be dwarfed by the potential income that other entry modes such as exporting could have generated. Another possible disadvantage is that the licensee may not be fully committed to the licensor's product or technology. Lack of enthusiasm on the part of the licensee will greatly limit the sales potential of the licensed product. When the licensing agreement involves a trademark, there is the further risk that misguided moves made by the licensee tarnish the trademark covered by the agreement.

The biggest danger is that a licensing arrangement could nurture a future competitor: Today's comrade-in-arms often becomes tomorrow's villain. The licensee can leverage the skills it acquires during the licensing period once the agreement expires. Global Perspective 9–1 chronicles the mishaps that Borden went through when its relationship with Meiji Milk, its licensee in Japan, turned sour.

There are several moves that companies can make to protect themselves against the risks of licensing arrangements.[22] If doable, the company should seek patent or trademark protection abroad. A thorough profitability analysis of a licensing proposal is an absolute must. Such an analysis must single out all the costs that are entailed by the venture, including the opportunity costs that stem from revenues that need to be sacrificed. Careful selection of prospective licensees is extremely important. Once a partner has been singled out, the negotiation process starts, which, if successful, will produce a licensing contract. The contract will cover parameters like the technology package, use conditions (including territorial rights and performance requirements), compensation, and provisions for the settlement of disputes.

---

[20]"Smoke Signals Point to China Market Opening," *South China Sunday Post* (October 6, 1996), p. 5.

[21]M. Kotabe, A. Sahay and P.S. Aulakh, "Emerging Role of Technology Licensing in the Development of a Global Product Strategy: Conceptual Framework and Research Propositions," *Journal of Marketing*, 60 (1) (January 1996), pp. 73–88.

[22]Franklin R. Root, *Entry Strategies for International Markets*, Chapter 5.

◆ ◆

$\mathcal{G}$LOBAL PERSPECTIVE 9–1

THE BORDEN–MEIJI MILK SAGA: THE MELTDOWN OF LADY BORDEN

When Borden, a U.S. multinational food company, entered Japan in 1971, it decided to tie up through a licensing arrangement with Meiji Milk. Borden's licensing agreement with Meiji Milk, Japan's leading dairy company, was the envy of many companies. Borden could benefit from Meiji Milk's vast distribution network. Meiji Milk, in turn, was able to acquire the expertise to manufacture various kinds of dairy products. The partnership also developed the premium ice cream market in Japan with its Lady Borden brand.

But the venture was not a fairytale—other brands entered the market, and Lady Borden's market share started to flounder. As a result Borden wanted to dissolve its partnership with Meiji Milk, marketing Lady Borden on its own. Borden wanted to have more control over the marketing of its products in Japan so that it could respond more rapidly to the competitive challenges. Meiji Milk retaliated by rolling out two ice cream brands of its own, one of which, Lady Breuges, was in direct competition with Lady Borden. When Borden cut its ties with Meiji Milk, it also lost access to Meiji Milk's distribution channels. The company hoped that brand clout would pull Japanese customers to the Lady Borden brand. However, the pull of the Borden brand name did not make up for the loss of Meiji Milk's distribution muscle.

In June 1994, Borden, in a desperate move, licensed its trademarks and formulations for the Lady Borden brand to the confectionery maker Lotte Co. When Borden split with Meiji Milk in 1991, its share of Japan's premium ice cream market was around 50 percent. Three years later, when a Japanese newspaper compiled a scorechart of the ice cream market, Meiji had 12 percent, while Borden's share was so negligible that it didn't make the list.

Sources: "Borden's Breakup with Meiji Milk Shows How a Japanese Partnership Can Curdle," *The Wall Street Journal* (February 21, 1991), p. B1, B4, and, "Borden's Hopes Melt in Japanese Market," *Advertising Age* (July 18, 1994), p. 38.

◆ ◆ ◆ ◆ ◆ ◆ ◆ FRANCHISING

Scores of service industry companies use **franchising** as a means for capturing opportunities in the global marketplace. For instance, of the 8,000 Tricon[23] restaurants around the world, about 4,400 are franchised.[24] The internationalization efforts of ten well-known franchise companies are summarized in Exhibit 9–5. Franchising is to some degree a "cousin" of licensing: it is an arrangement whereby the **_franchisor_** gives the **_franchisee_** the right to use the franchisor's trade names, trademarks, business models, and/or know-how in a given territory for a specific time period, normally ten years.[25] In exchange, the franchisor gets royalty payments and other fees. The package might include the marketing plan, operating manuals, standards, training, and quality monitoring.

To snap up opportunities in foreign markets, the method of choice is often **master franchising**. With this system, the franchisor gives a master franchise to a local entrepreneur, who will, in turn, sell local franchises within his territory. The territory could be a certain region within a country or a group of countries

---

[23]Formerly PepsiCo.

[24]PepsiCo, Inc., *1995 Annual Report*, p. 10.

[25]Albert Kong, "How to Evaluate a Franchise," *Economic Bulletin* (October 1998), pp. 18–20.

EXHIBIT 9–5

INTERNATIONALIZATION EFFORTS OF TEN WELL-KNOWN FRANCHISE COMPANIES

Company	Industry	Year Established	Year of First Franchise	Year First Intnl. Franchise	Nr. of Operating Units	Planned New Intnl. Units (within 12 months)
A&W	Fast food	1919	1925	1956	USA: 683 CAN: 470 RoW: 144*	40
Mrs. Fields	Cookies	1977	1990	1992	USA: 849 CAN: 11 RoW: 60	25
Global Travel Network	Travel agencies	1982	1983	1992	USA: 429 CAN: 2 RoW: 55	30
Subway	Sandwiches	1965	1974	1984	USA: 11452 CAN: 1259 RoW: 693	300
Gloria Jean's	Gourmet coffee	1979	1986	1993	USA: 240 CAN: 0 RoW: 12	6
Midas	Automotive services	1956	1956	1968	USA: 1898 CAN: 246 RoW: 561	50
Mailboxes Etc.	Business support	1980	1981	1988	USA: 2971 CAN: 209 RoW: 377	170
Kwik Copy	Print & copying services	1967	1968	1978	USA: 517 CAN: 84 RoW: 420	46
Berlitz Intnl.	Language training	1878	1996	1996	USA: 65 CAN: 8 RoW: 280	30
World Gym Fitness	Fitness	1977	1985	1985	USA: 276 CAN: 3 RoW: 9	13

*RoW = Rest of the World.

Source: www.franchiseintl.com

(e.g., Greater China). Usually, the master franchise holder agrees to establish a certain number of outlets over a given time horizon. Exhibit 9–6 is a listing of some of the international franchise resources that are available on the Internet.

The benefits of franchising are clear. First and foremost, companies can capitalize on a winning business formula by expanding overseas with a minimum of investment. Just as with licensing, political risks for the rights-owner are very limited. Further, since the franchisees' profits are directly tied to their efforts, franchisees are usually highly motivated. Finally, the franchisor can also capitalize on the local franchisees' knowledge of the local market place. They usually have a much better understanding of local customs and laws than the foreign firm.

Benefits

EXHIBIT 9–6
FRANCHISE RESOURCES ON THE INTERNET

- **Central Information Sites**

    The International Franchise Association (IFA):
    www.franchise.org
    Franchise Doctor:
    www.franchise.doc.com
    Frannet:
    www.frannet.com
    International Herald Tribune (Guide to International Franchising):
    www.franchiseintl.com

- **U.S. Corporations and Trade Associations**

    American Bar Association Forum on Franchising:
    www.abanet.org
    Franchise Development Services Ltd.:
    www.ds.dial.pipex.com/fds1

    National (non-U.S.) Agencies & Associations

    Argentina:
    www.copyshow.com.ar/aaf
    Australia & New Zealand:
    www.franchise.net.au
    www.halledit.com.au/bizops
    www.franchise.co.nz
    Austria:
    www.telecom.at/wklms/franchise
    Brazil:
    www.abf.com.br
    Canada:
    www.cfaexpo.com
    France:
    www.club-internet.fr/perso/fff/
    Hong Kong:
    www.franchise.org.hk
    Italy:
    www.infodata-italy.com
    South Africa:
    africa.cis.co.za:81/buy/ad/fasa/fasa1.html
    United Kingdom:
    www.franchise-group.com

Sources: "International Franchising," *International Herald Tribune*
(November 19, 1997), p. 14; and Colin McCosker, "Trends and Opportunities
in Franchising," *Economic Bulletin* (October 1998), p. 16.

Caveats   Franchising carries some risks, though. Just as in the case of licensing, the franchisor's income stream is only a fraction of what it would be if the company held an equity stake in the foreign ventures. Finding suitable franchisees or a master franchisee can be a stumbling block in many markets. In many countries, the concept of franchising as a business model is barely understood.[26] A major con-

---

[26]Colin McCosker, "Trends and Opportunities in Franchising," *Economic Bulletin* (October 1998), pp. 14–17.

cern is the lack of control over the franchisees' operations. Dissatisfied with the performance of its franchisees in Mexico and Brazil, Blockbuster Video changed tracks in 1995. The entertainment company decided to set up joint ventures and equity relations in Mexico and Brazil to replace the franchising arrangements held there, thereby getting more control and oversight.[27] Given the largely intangible nature of many franchising systems, cultural hurdles can also create problems. In fact, a recent study showed that cultural and physical proximity are the two most popular criteria used by companies for picking international markets in franchising.[28]

CONTRACT MANUFACTURING   ◆ ◆ ◆ ◆ ◆ ◆ ◆

With **contract manufacturing**, the company arranges with a local manufacturer to manufacture parts of the product or even the entire product. Marketing the products is still the responsibility of the international firm.

Numerous companies have become very successful by specializing in contract manufacturing. NatSteel Electronics (NEL) is one of the leading global electronics contract manufacturers. The company, based in Singapore, has facilities in countries such as Indonesia, Malaysia, China, and Mexico. Its customers include Fortune 500 companies such as Compaq, IBM, Apple, and Hewlett-Packard.

Cost savings are the prime motivation behind contract manufacturing. Significant cost savings can be achieved for labor-intensive production processes by sourcing the product in a low-wage country. Typically, the countries of choice are places that have a substantial comparative labor cost advantage. Labor cost savings are not the only factor. Savings can also be achieved via taxation benefits, lower energy costs, raw materials costs, or overhead.

Benefits

Some of the benefits listed for the previous entry modes also apply here. Subcontracting leads to a small amount of exposure to political and economic risks for the international firm. It is also not very demanding on the company's resources. Contract manufacturing also allows access to markets that, because of import barriers, would otherwise be closed.

Contract manufacturing is not without drawbacks though. The "nurture-a-future-competitor" concern raised for licensing and franchising also applies here. Because of this risk, many companies prefer to make high-value items or products that involve proprietary design features in-house. A fixation with low labor costs can often have painful consequences. Low-labor-cost countries typically have very low labor productivity. Some of these countries, such as India and South Korea, also have a long tradition of bad labor relations. Too much reliance on low-cost labor could also create a backlash in the company's home-market among its employees

Caveats

[27]"Blockbuster's Fast-forward," *Advertising Age International* (September 18, 1995), p. I-32.
[28]John F. Preble and Richard C. Hoffman, "Franchising Systems Around the Globe: A Status Report," *Journal of Small Business Management* (April 1995), pp. 80–88.

and customers. Monitoring of quality and production levels is a must, especially during the start-up phase when "teething problems" are not uncommon.

When screening foreign subcontractors, the ideal candidate should meet the following criteria:[29]

- Flexible and geared toward just-in-time delivery
- Able to meet quality standards and implement Total Quality Management
- Solid financial footing
- Able to integrate with company's business
- Have contingency plans to handle sudden changes in demand

◆ ◆ ◆ ◆ ◆ ◆ JOINT VENTURES

For many MNCs who want to expand their global operations, joint ventures prove to be the most viable way to enter foreign markets, especially in emerging markets. With a joint venture, the foreign company agrees to share equity and other resources with other partners to establish a new entity in the target country. The partners typically are local companies, but they can also be local government authorities, other foreign companies, or a mixture of local and foreign players. Depending on the equity stake, three forms of partnerships can be distinguished: majority (more than 50 percent ownership), fifty-fifty, and minority (50 percent or less ownership) ventures. Huge infrastructure or high-tech projects that demand a large amount of expertise and money often involve multiple foreign and local partners. Another distinction is between cooperative and equity joint ventures. A **cooperative joint venture** is an agreement to collaborate between the partners that does not involve any equity investments. For instance, one partner might contribute manufacturing technology whereas the other partner provides access to distribution channels. Cooperative joint ventures are quite common for partnerships between well-heeled MNCs and local players in emerging markets. A good example of the collaborative approach is Cisco's sales strategy in Asia. Instead of investing in its own sales force, Cisco builds up partnerships with hardware vendors (e.g., IBM), consulting agencies (e.g., KPMG), or systems integrators (e.g., Singapore-based Datacraft). These partners in essence act as front people for Cisco. They are the ones that sell and install Cisco's routers and switches.[30] An **equity joint venture** goes one step further. It is an arrangement where the partners agree to raise capital in proportion to the equity stakes agreed upon. A typical example is the entry strategy of Cable & Wireless (C&W), a British telecommunications firm, in Japan. To gain credibility with the Japanese government, C&W set up a partnership with big Japanese corporations. The three major stakeholders—C&W, Toyota, and C. Itoh—each hold roughly 17 percent. The other partners share the balance. The alliance has gained a 16 percent market share of Japan's international telecommunications market.

---

[29]E. P. Hibbert, "Global Make-or-buy Decisions," *Industrial Marketing Management*, 22 (1993), pp. 67–77.

[30]"Cisco's Asian Gambit," *Fortune* (January 10, 2000), pp. 52–54.

A major advantage of joint ventures, compared to lesser forms of resource commitment such as licensing, is the return potential. With licensing, for instance, the company solely gets royalty payments instead of a share of the profits. Joint ventures also entail much more control over the operations than most of the previous entry modes we have discussed so far. MNCs that like to maximize their degree of control prefer full ownership. However, in many instances, local governments (e.g., China) discourage or even forbid wholly owned ventures in certain industries. Under such circumstances, partnerships are a second-best or temporary solution.

Apart from the benefits listed above, the **synergy** argument is another compelling reason for setting up a joint venture. Partnerships not only mean a sharing of capital and risk. Possible contributions brought in by the local partner include: land, raw materials, expertise on the local environment (culture, legal, political), access to a distribution network, personal contacts with suppliers, government officials, and so on. Combined with the skills and resources owned by the foreign partner, these inputs offer the key to a successful market entry. A recent fifty-fifty joint venture between Canada's Sun Life Assurance and China Everbright Group, a large financial conglomerate, is one example. Sun Life, which got approval to sell life insurance in China in April 1999, chose China Everbright because it can provide the venture access to a large distribution network and local contacts.[31]

Benefits

For many MNCs, lack of full control is the biggest shortcoming of joint ventures. There are a number of ways for the MNC to gain more leverage. The most obvious way is via a majority equity stake. However, government restrictions often rule out this option. Even when for some reason majority ownership is not a viable alternative, MNCs have other means at their disposal to exercise control over the joint venture. MNCs could deploy expatriates in key line positions, thereby controlling financial, marketing, and other critical operations of the venture. MNCs could also offer various types of outside support services to back up their weaker joint ventures in areas such as marketing, quality control, and customer service.[32]

Caveats

Lack of trust and mutual conflicts turn numerous international joint ventures into a marriage from hell. Conflicts could arise over matters such as strategies, resource allocation, transfer pricing, ownerships of critical assets like technologies and brand names. In many cases, the seeds for trouble exist from the very beginning of the joint venture. Exhibit 9–7 contrasts the mutually conflicting objectives that the foreign partner and the local Chinese partner may hold when setting up a joint venture in China. Cultural strains between partners often spur mistrust and mutual conflict, making a bad situation even worse. Autolatina, a joint venture set up by Ford Motor Co. and Volkswagen AG in Latin America, was dissolved after seven years in spite of the fact that it remained profitable to the very end. Cultural differences between the German and American managers were a major factor. One participating executive noted that "there were good intentions behind Autolatina's formation but they never really overcame the VW–Ford culture shock."[33]

[31]"Sun Life, Everbright Tie Up," *China Daily* (December 16, 1999), p. 6.

[32]Johannes Meier, Javier Perez, and Jonathan R. Woetzel (1995), "Solving the Puzzle— MNCs in China," *The McKinsey Quarterly*, No. 2, pp. 20–33.

[33]"Why Ford, VW's Latin Marriage Succumbed to 7-Year Itch," *Advertising Age International* (March 20, 1995), p. I–22.

EXHIBIT 9–7
CONFLICTING OBJECTIVES IN CHINESE JOINT VENTURES

	Foreign Partner	*Chinese Partner*
Planning	Retain business flexibility	Maintain congruency between the venture and the state economic plan
Contracts	Unambiguous, detailed, and enforceable	Ambiguous, brief, and adaptable
Negotiations	Sequential, issue by issue	Holistic and heuristic
Staffing	Maximize productivity; fewest people per given output level	Employ maximum number of local people
Technology	Match technical sophistication to the organization and its environment	Gain access to the most advanced technology as quickly as possible
Profits	Maximize in long term; repatriate over time	Reinvest for future modernization; maintain foreign exchange reserves
Inputs	Minimize unpredictability and poor quality of supplies	Promote domestic sourcing
Process	Stress high quality	Stress high quantity
Outputs	Access and develop domestic market	Export to generate foreign currency
Control	Reduce political and economic controls on decision making	Accept technology and capital but preclude foreign authority infringement on sovereignty and ideology

Reprinted from M. G. Martinsons and C.-S. Tsong, "Successful Joint Ventures in the Heart of the Dragon," *Long Range Planning*, 28 (5), p. 5. Copyright 1995, with kind permission from Elsevier Science Ltd., The Boulevard, Langford Lane, Kidlington OX5 1GB UK.

When trouble undermines the joint venture, the partners can try to resolve the conflict via mechanisms built in the agreement. If a mutually acceptable resolution is not achievable, the joint venture is scaled back or dissolved. For instance, a joint venture between Unilever and AKI in South Korea broke up after seven years, following disagreements over brand strategies for new products, resource allocation, advertising support, and brand ownership.[34]

Drivers Behind Successful International Joint Ventures

There are no magic ingredients to foster the stability of joint ventures. Yet, there are some important lessons that can be drawn from past JV fairytales and horror stories:

Pick the Right Partner. Most joint venture marriages prosper by choosing a suitable partner. That means that the MNC should invest the time in identifying proper candidates. A careful screening of the joint venture partner is an absolute necessity. Michael Bonsignore, CEO of Honeywell, observes, "Nothing reinforces our success more than choosing the right partner. We pick well."[35] One issue is that it is not easy to sketch a profile of the "ideal" partner. The presence of complementary skills and resources that lead to synergies is one characteristic of successful joint ventures. Prospective partners should also have compatible goals.

[34]"How Unilever's South Korean Partnership Fell Apart," *Advertising Age* (August 31, 1992), p. 3 and p. 39.
[35]"Investing in Emerging Asia," *Asiaweek* (December 20, 1996), p. 54.

Some evidence suggests that partners should be similar in terms of size and resources. Partners with whom the MNC has built up an existing relationship (e.g., distributors, customers, suppliers) also facilitate a strong relationship.[36] One issue that latecomers in a market often face is that the "best" partners have already been snapped up. Note though that the same issue arises with acquisition strategies. A recent study on joint venture performance in China offers five guidelines for partner selection.[37] First, integrate partner selection with your strategic goals. Second, obtain as much information as possible about the candidate (e.g., company brochures, business license). Third, visit the site. Fourth, check whether the potential partner shares your investment objective. And, finally, do not put too much emphasis on the rule of guanxi (relationships).

Establish Clear Objectives from the Beginning.[38]   It is important to clearly spell out the objectives of the joint venture from day one. Partners should know what their respective contributions and responsibilities are before signing the contract.[39] They should also know what to expect from the partnership.

Bridge Cultural Gaps.   Many joint venture disputes stem from cultural differences between the local and foreign partners. A lot of agony and frustration can be avoided when the foreign investor makes an attempt to bridge cultural differences. For instance, when setting up joint ventures in China, having an ethnic Chinese or an "old China hand" as a middleman often helps a great deal. The problem is that knowledgeable people who share the perspectives of both cultures are often very hard to find.[40]

Gain Top Managerial Commitment and Respect.   Short of a strong commitment from the parent companies' top management, most international joint ventures are doomed to become a failure. The companies should be willing to assign their best managerial talent to the joint venture. Venture managers should also have complete access to and support from their respective parent companies.[41]

Use Incremental Approach.   Rather than being overambitious, an incremental approach toward setting up the international joint venture appears to be much more effective. The partnership starts on a small scale. Gradually, the scope of the joint venture is broadened by adding other responsibilities and activities to the joint venture's charter. An example of the incremental approach is Bausch & Lomb's expansion strategy in China, described in Global Perspective 9–2.

---

[36]Karen J. Hladik, "R&D and International Joint Ventures," in *Cooperative Forms of Transnational Corporation Activity*, edited by P.J. Buckley (London: Routledge, 1994).

[37]Yadong Luo, "Joint Venture Success in China: How Should We Select a Good Partner," *Journal of World Business*, 32 (2) (1998), pp. 145–66.

[38]Dominique Turpin, "Strategic Alliances with Japanese Firms: Myths and Realities," *Long Range Planning*, 26 (4) (1993), pp. 11–16.

[39]Maris G. Martinsons and Choo-sin Tseng, "Successful Joint Ventures in the Heart of the Dragon," *Long Range Planning*, 28 (5) (1995), pp. 45–58.

[40]Ibid., p. 56.

[41]Turpin, p. 15.

◆ ◆

$\mathcal{G}$LOBAL PERSPECTIVE 9–2

BAUSCH & LOMB'S EXPANSION STRATEGY IN CHINA

Bausch & Lomb, the U.S.-based health care and optical products manufacturer, first entered China in 1987 via a cooperative joint venture. The joint venture, lasting for three years, was set up with Beijing No. 608 Eyeglass Factory. B&L agreed to provide manufacturing technology, semi-finished goods, and a small amount of capital. The domestic partner contributed part of its existing site, staff, and market knowledge. The key factor for choosing Factory 608 was the partner's distribution system which B&L regarded as one of the most important assets in the relationship. The connections of the partner also played a role. In 1989, the JV started to make a profit.

In 1991, B&L made the next move by converting its cooperative JV into an equity joint venture. B&L was able to negotiate a 60 percent majority stake, which at that time was very unusual for foreign investors in China. The new JV structure also obtained permission to sell its entire production in China. Under the previous cooperative contract, the JV was subject to a 20 percent export quota. Since 1992, B&L has also had a wholly owned subsidiary based in Guangdong province to manufacture and distribute sunglasses. More recently, B&L set up a holding company in Shanghai. The charter of the holding company is to explore new business opportunities in China and to enhance the synergies between the different operations.

Source: Tobias Newland, "Bausch & Lomb: Focusing on Expansion," *China Joint Venturer* (April 1996), pp. 14–19.

◆ ◆ ◆ ◆ ◆ ◆ WHOLLY OWNED SUBSIDIARIES

Multinational companies often prefer to enter new markets with 100 percent ownership. Ownership strategies in foreign markets can essentially take two routes: **acquisitions**, where the MNC buys up existing companies, or **greenfield operations** that are started from scratch. As with the other entry modes, full ownership entry entails certain benefits to the MNC but also carries risks.

Benefits   Wholly owned subsidiaries give MNCs full control of their operations. It is often the ideal solution for companies that do not want to be saddled with all the risks and anxieties associated with partnerships like joint venturing. Full ownership means that all the profits go to the company. Fully owned enterprises allow the investor to manage and control its own processes and tasks in terms of marketing, production, and sourcing decisions. Setting up fully owned subsidiaries also sends a strong commitment signal to the local market. In some markets—China, for example—wholly owned subsidiaries can be erected much faster than joint ventures with local companies, which may consume years of negotiations before their final take-off.[42] The latter point is especially important when there are substantial advantages to being an early entrant in the target market.

---

[42]Wilfried Vanhonacker, "Entering China: An Unconventional Approach," *Harvard Business Review* (March–April 1997).

Despite the advantages of 100 percent ownership, many MNCs are quite reluctant to choose this particular mode of entry. The risks of full ownership cannot be easily discounted. Complete ownership means that the parent company will have to carry the full burden of possible losses. Developing a foreign presence without the support of a third party is also very demanding on the firm's resources. Obviously, apart from the market-related risks, substantial political risks (e.g., nationalization) must be factored in. **Caveats**

Companies that enter via a wholly owned enterprise are sometimes also perceived as a threat to the cultural and/or economic sovereignty of the host country. Shortly after Daewoo's initially successful bid for the multimedia arm of the French group Thomson–CSF in the fall of 1996, the deal sparked controversy among French trade unions and the media. In the end, the French government vetoed the sale of the Thomson group following the negative opinion of the French privatization commission.[43]

One way to address hostility to foreign acquisitions in the host country is by *localizing* the firm's presence in the foreign market by hiring local managers, sourcing locally, developing local brands, sponsoring local sports or cultural events, and so forth.[44] Global Perspective 9–3 describes how Eastman Kodak expanded its presence in China.

✦ ✦

$\mathcal{G}$LOBAL PERSPECTIVE 9–3

KODAK EXPANDS ITS MANUFACTURING AND MARKETING CAPABILITIES IN CHINA

In the spring of 1998, Eastman Kodak astonished the business world when it announced a pact to invest $1 billion in China to expand its manufacturing and marketing skills there. From Kodak's perspective, the China market represents a tremendous opportunity. George Fisher, the then-CEO of Eastman Kodak, noted that "If only half the people in China shot a single 36-exposure roll of film a year—a fraction of the usage rates in other countries—that would swell the number of worldwide 'clicks' by 25 percent. Each second, 500 more photos would be taken. That's the equivalent of adding another U.S. or Japan to the world photographic market. China offers more potential for Kodak than any other market in the world."

The agreement required Kodak to invest $380 million in two newly formed companies, Kodak (China) Co. and Kodak (Wuxi) Co. (see Exhibit 9–8 for the ownership structure). Kodak owns 80 percent of the shares of Kodak (China) and 70 percent of the shares of Kodak (Wuxi); the balance is owned by local investors. These two companies took over the primary business assets of three ailing state-owned enterprises. Kodak also promised to invest $700 million over a five-year period. Further, Kodak agreed to set up compensation funds for three other domestic money-losing photographic filmmakers. In exchange, those three firms pledged that they would not tie up with a non-Kodak partner until 2001.

David Swift, president of Kodak's Greater China Region, commented, that "The investment guarantees that Chinese consumers will continue to receive superior products and first-class service that Kodak is famous for." With the deal, Kodak hopes to accomplish three things: (1) lower costs by producing domestically, (2) better distribution, and (3) exclusivity, in light of the Chinese government's promise not to approve other similar ventures for four years in the photographic industry.

Sources: www.kodak.com (press-releases); "Kodak's China Moment," *Asiaweek*, (May 1, 1998), p. 56; "Out of the Strait-Jacket," *Business China* (April 27, 1998), pp. 1–3; Wilfried R. Vanhonacker, "Structuring Foreign Direct Investments in China: A Strategic Opportunity," Working Paper, (December 1998), HKUST.

---

[43]http://www.asiatimes.com/96/12/05/05129601
[44]Vanhonacker.

EXHIBIT 9–8
OWNERSHIP STRUCTURE OF KODAK'S INVESTMENT DEAL IN CHINA

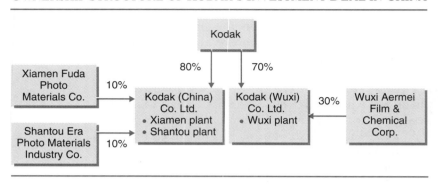

Acquisitions and Mergers

Companies such as Sara Lee have built up strong global competitive positions via cleverly planned and finely executed acquisition strategies. MNCs choose acquisition entry to expand globally for a number of reasons. First and foremost, when contrasted with greenfield operations, acquisitions provide a rapid means to get access to the local market. For relative latecomers in an industry, acquisitions are also a viable option to obtain well-established brand names, instant access to distribution outlets, or technology. In recent years, some of the South Korean *chaebols* have used acquisition entries in foreign markets to gain a foothold in high-tech industries. Highly visible examples include Samsung's acquisition of the American computer maker AST and LG Electronics' takeover of Zenith. LG would have needed to invest more than $1 billion to build up a strong global TV brand from scratch.[45]

Sara Lee, a U.S. conglomerate, has been extremely successful in building up growth via well-chosen acquisitions. Instead of milking the acquired local brands and replacing them with a global brand, Sara Lee heavily invests in its local brand assets in the hope that one day they can be converted into prestigious regional or even global brand names. Success stories of local brands that became leading European brands include Douwe Egberts in coffee, Pickwick in tea, and Dim in hosiery. Sara Lee is also following the acquisition path in emerging markets, with an equal amount of success.

Expansion via acquisitions or mergers carries substantial risks, though. Differences in the corporate culture of the two companies between managers are often extremely hard to bridge. A well-publicized example of a company that has been plagued with corporate culture disease is Pharmacia & Upjohn, a pharmaceutical company that was formed in 1995 via the merger of Sweden-based Pharmacia AB and the American drug firm Upjohn. Swedish managers were stunned by the hard-driving, mission-oriented approach of Upjohn executives. Their U.S. counterparts were shocked about European vacation habits.[46]

The assets of the acquisition do not always live up to the expectations of the acquiring company. Outdated plants, tarnished brand names, or an unmotivated work force are only a few of the many possible disappointments that the acquiring

---

[45]"Guess Who's Betting on America's High-Tech Losers," *Fortune* (October 28, 1996).
[46]"A Case of Corporate Culture Shock in the Global Arena," *International Herald Tribune* (April 23, 1997), pp. 1, 11.

company could face. The local government might also attach certain conditions to the acquisition. Daewoo, for instance, promised the French government to hire 5,000 more people when it was bidding for the consumer electronics division of Thomson. A careful screening and assessment of takeover candidates can avoid a lot of heartburn on the part of the acquiring company. Another drawback is that acquisition entry can be a very costly global expansion strategy. Good prospects are usually unwilling to sell themselves. If they are, they do not come cheap. Other foreign or local companies are typically interested too, and the result is often a painful bidding war. The costs and strains of integrating the acquisition with the company can also be a substantial burden.

Acquisition strategies are not always feasible. Good prospects may already have been nabbed by the company's competitors. In many emerging markets, acceptable acquisition candidates often are simply not available. Overhauling the facilities of possible candidates is sometimes much more costly than building an operation from scratch. In the wake of these downsides, companies often prefer to enter foreign markets through greenfield operations that are established from scratch. Greenfield operations offer the company more flexibility than acquisitions in areas such as human resources, suppliers, logistics, plant layout, or manufacturing technology. Greenfield investments also avoid the costs of integrating the acquisition into the parent company.[47] Another motivation is the package of goodies (e.g., tax holidays) that host governments sometimes offer to whet the appetite of foreign investors. The down side of greenfield operations is that they require enormous investments of time and capital.

Greenfield Operations

STRATEGIC ALLIANCES ◆ ◆ ◆ ◆ ◆ ◆

A distinctive feature of the activities of global corporations today is that they are using cooperative relationships like licensing, joint ventures, R & D partnerships, and informal arrangements—all under the rubric of alliances of various forms—on an increasing scale. More formally, **strategic alliances** can be described as *a coalition of two or more organizations to achieve strategically significant goals that are mutually beneficial.*[48] The business press reports like clockwork the birth of strategic alliances in various kinds of industries. Eye-catching are especially those partnerships between firms that have been archenemies for ages. A principal reason for the increase in cooperative relationships is that firms today no longer have the capacity of a General Motors of the 1940s which developed all its technologies in-house. As a result, firms, especially those operating in technology intensive industries, may not be at the forefront of all the required critical technologies.[49] This implies that there should be a rise in cooperative relationships, and this is indeed the case.

[47]Jiatao Li, "Foreign Entry and Survival: Effects of Strategic Choices on Performance in International Markets," *Strategic Management Journal*, 16 (1995), pp. 333–51.

[48]Edwin A. Murray, Jr. and John F. Mahon, "Strategic Alliances: Gateway to the New Europe?" *Long Range Planning* (August 1993), pp. 102–11.

[49]Noel, Capon and Rashi Glazer, "Marketing and Technology: A Strategic Co-alignment," *Journal of Marketing*, 51 (July 1987), 1–14.

Types of Strategic Alliances

Strategic alliances come in all kinds of shapes. At one extreme, alliances can be based on a simple licensing agreement between two partners. At the other extreme, they may consist of a thick web of ties. The nature of alliances also varies depending on the skills brought in by the partners. A first category, very common in high-tech industries, is based on technology swaps. Given the skyrocketing costs of new product development, strategic alliances offer a means to companies to pool their resources and learn from one another. Such alliances must be struck from a position of strength. Bargaining chips might be patents that the company holds. A second type of cross-border alliances involves marketing-based assets and resources such as access to distribution channels or trademarks. A case in point is the partnership established by Coca-Cola and Nestlé to market ready-to-drink coffees and teas under the Nescafé and Nestea brand names. This deal allowed the two partners to combine a well-established brand name with access to a vast proven distribution network. In India, Huggies, Kimberly-Clark's diapers, are manufactured and distributed through an alliance with Hindustan Lever, the local unit of Unilever, whose powerful distribution network covers 400,000 retail outlets. A third category of alliances is situated in the operations and logistics area. In their relentless search for scale economies for operations/logistics activities, companies may decide to join forces by setting up a partnership. Finally, operations-based alliances are driven by a desire to transfer manufacturing know-how. A classic example is the NUMMI joint venture set up by Toyota and General Motors to swap car-manufacturing expertise.

The Logic Behind Strategic Alliances

The strategic pay-offs of cross-border alliances are alluring, especially in high-tech industries. Lorange and colleagues[50] suggest that there are four generic reasons for forming strategic alliances: defense, catch-up, remain, or restructure (see Exhibit 9–9). Their scheme centers around two dimensions: the strategic importance of the business unit to the parent company and the competitive position of the business.

- *Defend*. Companies create alliances for their core businesses to defend their leadership position. Basically, the underlying goal is to sustain the firm's leadership position by learning new skills, getting access to new markets, developing new technologies, or finessing other capabilities that help the company to reinforce its competitive advantage.[51]

- *Catch-Up*. Firms may also shape strategic alliances to catch up. This happens when companies create an alliance to shore a core business in which they do not have a leadership position. Nestlé and General Mills launched Cereal Partners Worldwide to attack the Kelloggs-dominated global cereal market. PepsiCo and General Mills, two of the weaker players in the European snack food business, set up a joint venture for their snack-food business to compete more effectively in the European market.

- *Remain*. Firms might also enter a strategic alliance to simply remain in a business. This might occur for business divisions where the firm has established a leadership position but which only play a peripheral role in the company's

---

[50]Peter Lorange, Johan Roos, and Peggy S. Brønn, "Building Successful Strategic Alliances," *Long Range Planning*, 25 (6) (1992), pp. 10–17.

[51]See also David Lei and John W. Slocum, Jr., "Global Strategy, Competence-Building and Strategic Alliances," *California Management Review* (Fall 1992), pp. 81–97.

EXHIBIT 9–9
GENERIC MOTIVES FOR STRATEGIC
ALLIANCES

		Business' Market Position	
		Leader	Follower
Strategic Importance in Parent's Portfolio	Core	Defend	Catch Up
	Peripheral	Remain	Restructure

Source: Reprinted from P. Lorange, J. Roos and P.S. Brønn, "Building Successful Strategic Alliances," *Long Range Planning*, 25 (6), p. 10. Copyright 1992, with kind permission from Elsevier Science Ltd., The Boulevard, Langford Lane, Kidlington OX5 1GB, UK.

business portfolio. That way, the alliance enables the company to get the maximum efficiency out of its position.

- *Restructure.* Last, a firm might also view alliances as a vehicle to restructure a business that is not core and in which it has no leadership position. The ultimate intent here is that one partner uses the alliance to rejuvenate the business, thereby turning the business unit in a "presentable bride," so to speak. Usually, one of the other partners in the alliance will end up acquiring of the business unit.

The formula for a successful strategic alliance will probably never be written. Still, a number of studies done by consulting agencies and academic scholars have uncovered several findings on what distinguishes enduring cross-border alliances from the floundering ones. An analysis of cross-border alliances done by McKinsey came up with the following recommendations:[52]

Cross-Border Alliances that Succeed

- *Alliances between strong and weak partners seldom work.* Building up ties with partners that are weak is a recipe for disaster. The weak partner becomes a drag on the competitiveness of the partnership. As David Logan, Hewlett-Packard's corporate development director puts it: "One should go for the best possible partners—leaders in their field, not followers."[53]

- *Autonomy and flexibility.* These are two key ingredients for successful partnerships. Autonomy might mean that the alliance has its own management team and its own board of directors. This speeds up the decision-making process. Autonomy also makes it easier to resolve conflicts that arise. To cope with environmental changes over time, flexibility is essential. Market needs change, new technologies emerge, competitive forces regroup. Being flexible, alliances can more easily adapt to these changes by revising their objectives, the charter of the venture, or other aspects of the alliance.

[52]Joel Bleeke and David Ernst (1991), "The Way to Win in Cross-border Alliances," *Harvard Business Review* (Nov.–Dec. 1991), pp. 127–35.
[53]"When Even a Rival Can Be a Best Friend," *Financial Times* (October 22, 1997), p. 12.

Equal ownership. Fifty-fifty ownership means that the partners are equally concerned about the other's success. Both partners should contribute equally to the alliance.[54] Thereby, all partners will be in a win–win situation where the gains are equally distributed. However, fifty-fifty joint ventures between partners from developed countries and developing countries are more likely to get bogged down in decision-making deadlocks. One recent study of equity joint ventures in China found that partnerships with minority foreign equity holding run much more smoothly than other equity sharing arrangements. Fifty-fifty partnerships ran into all sorts of internal managerial problems like joint decision-making and coordination with local managers. Majority foreign equity ventures had fewer internal problems but encountered many external issues such as lack of local sourcing, high dependence on imported materials.[55] So, in spite of the findings of the McKinsey study, the ownership question—fifty-fifty versus majority stake—remains murky.

To these we would like to add a few more success factors. Stable alliances have the commitment and support of the top of the parents' organization. Strong alliance managers are key.[56] Alliances between partners that are related (in terms of products, markets, and/or technologies) or have similar cultures, assets sizes and venturing experiencing levels tend to be much more viable.[57] Further, successful alliances tend to start on a narrow basis and broaden over time. A partnership between Corning, a U.S. glassmaker, and Samsung, a Korean electronics firm, started with one plant making television tubes in South Korea. Over time, the partnership broadened its scope, covering much of east Asia. Finally, a shared vision on the goals and the mutual benefits is the hallmark of viable alliances.

SUMMARY

Companies have a smorgasbord of entry strategy choices to implement their global expansion efforts. Each alternative has its pros and cons (see Exhibit 9–10). There is no shoe that fits all sizes. Many firms use a hodgepodge of entry modes. Motorola established a $300 million-plus manufacturing venture in Tianjin (China), which is a fully owned enterprise. However, the marketing and sales of the products is to be done via a range of equity joint ventures with local partners.[58]

Within the same industry, rivals often adopt different approaches to enter new markets. Cummins Engines, a leading U.S.-based diesel engines maker, uses a strategy based on joint ventures with outside groups—mostly customers but also competitors like Komatsu. Caterpillar, on the other hand, prefers having total control over its new ventures using acquisitions as a route to expand overseas.[59] Companies often adopt a phased entry strategy: They start off with a

[54]Godfrey Devlin and Mark Bleackley, "Strategic Alliances—Guidelines for Success," *Long Range Planning*, 21(5) (1988), pp. 18–23.

[55]Yigang Pan and Wilfried R. Vanhonacker, "Equity Sharing Arrangements and Joint Venture Operation in the People's Republic of China," Working Paper, February 1994, Hong Kong University of Science & Technology.

[56]Devlin and Bleackley, pp. 18–23.

[57]Kathryn R. Harrigan, "Strategic Alliances and Partner Assymetries," in *Cooperative Strategies in International Business*, F.J. Contractor and P. Lorange, eds. (Lexington, MA: Lexington Books, 1988).

[58]Vanhonacker.

[59]"Engine Makers Take Different Routes," *Financial Times* (July 14, 1998), p. 11.

EXHIBIT 9-10
ADVANTAGES AND DISADVANTAGES OF DIFFERENT MODES OF ENTRY

Entry Mode	Advantages	Disadvantages
Indirect exporting	• Low commitment (in terms of resources) • Low risk	• Lack of control • Lack of contact with foreign market • No learning experience • Potential opportunity cost
Direct exporting	• More control (compared to indirect exporting) • More sales push	• Need to build up export organization • More demanding on resources
Licensing	• Little or no investment • Rapid way to gain entry • Means to bridge import barriers • Low risk	• Lack of control • Potential opportunity cost • Need for quality control • Risk of creating competitor • Limits market development
Franchising	• Little or no investment • Rapid way to gain entry • Managerial motivation	• Need for quality control • Lack of control • Risk of creating competitor
Contract manufacturing	• Little or no investment • Overcome import barriers • Cost savings	• Need for quality control • Risk of bad press (e.g., child labor) • Diversion to gray and/or black markets
Joint venture	• Risk sharing • Less demanding on resources (compared to wholly-owned) • Potential of synergies (e.g., access to local distribution network)	• Risk of conflicts with partner(s) • Lack of control • Risk of creating competitor
Acquisition	• Full control • Access to local assets (e.g., plants, distribution network, brand assets) • Less competition	• Costly • High risk • Need to integrate differing national/corporate cultures • Cultural clashes
Greenfield	• Full control • Latest technologies • No risk of cultural conflicts	• Costly • Time consuming • High political & financial risks

minimal-risk strategy. Once the perceived risk declines, they switch to a higher commitment mode, such as a wholly owned venture. Caterpillar, Inc., the U.S.-based manufacturer of earth-moving and construction equipment, entered the former Soviet bloc in 1992 via direct exporting to minimize its financial risk exposure. Once sales took off, Caterpillar upped the ante by establishing joint ventures with Russian and American firms.[60]

As this chapter made clear, a broad range of variables impact the entry mode choice. The three major dimensions include the resource commitment the firm is willing to make, the amount of risk (political and market) the firm is willing to take, and the degree of control that is desirable.

To compete more effectively in the global arena, more and more companies use cross-border strategic alliances to build up their muscle. Depending on the strategic role and the competitive position of the business unit involved, the goal of the alliance could be to defend, strengthen, sustain, or restructure the SBU. The benefits that the partners can derive from the synergies of the alliance often downplay the concerns the parent companies might have about the partnership. Still, the formation of the alliance should always be preceded by a meticulous analysis of questions such as these:[61]

* What are the mutual benefits for each partner?
* What learning can take place between firms?
* How can the parties complement each other to create joint capabilities?
* Are the partners equal in strength, or is this the case of the "one-eyed guiding the blind"?

Satisfactory answers to these questions improve the chances of the cross-border alliance becoming a win–win situation for all partners involved.

KEY TERMS

acquisitions
contract manufacturing
cooperative exporting
cooperative joint venture
direct (indirect) exporting
equity joint venture
franchising
greenfield operations
licensing
master franchising
strategic alliances

REVIEW QUESTIONS

1. Why do some MNCs prefer to enter certain markets with a liaison office first?
2. What are the possible drawbacks of fifty–fifty joint ventures?
3. Draw up a list of the respective pros and cons of licensing.
4. What are the respective advantages and disadvantages of greenfield operations over acquisitions?
5. What mechanisms can firms use to protect themselves against ill-fated partnerships?

DISCUSSION QUESTIONS

1. The table at the top of p.311 lists in chronological order the countries that Starbucks, the Seattle-based coffee retailer, entered up to 1999. As you can see, Starbucks concentrated on the Pacific Rim to date. Why do you think did Starbucks decide to concentrate on this region?
2. Waste Management International heavily relies on acquisitions in Europe. In Asia, though, the company follows an entirely different entry strategy. What could be the reasons why companies use different entry choices in different regions?

[60]Avraham Shama, "Entry Strategies of U.S. Firms to the Newly Independent States, Baltic States, and Eastern European Countries," *California Management Review*, 37 (3) (Spring 1995), pp. 90–109.
[61]Lorange, Roos, and S. Brønn, pp. 12–13.

COUNTRIES
ENTERED BY
STARBUCKS

Year	Countries
1996	Japan
	Singapore
1997	Philippines
1998	Taiwan
	Thailand
	Malaysia
	New Zealand
1999	China
	Kuwait

3. Companies tend to begin their internationalization process in countries that are culturally very close. For instance, U.S-based companies would enter Canada and/or the United Kingdom first, before moving on to other countries. The so-called psychic distance between the United States and Canada (or Britain) is small, given that these countries are supposedly very similar. A recent survey, however, found that only 22 percent of Canadian retailers thought that they were operating suc-cessfully in the United States. Explain why culturally close countries are not necessarily easy to manage.

4. Check some recent issues of the *Wall Street Journal* and/or the *Financial Times*. Look for articles on cross-border strategic alliances. Pick one or two examples and find out more about the alliances you chose via a search on the Internet. Why were the alliances formed? What do the partners contribute to the alliance? What benefits do they anticipate? What concerns/issues were raised?

5. Helmut Maucher, former chairman of Nestlé was quoted saying: "I don't share the euphoria for alliances and joint ventures. First, very often they're an excuse, and an easy way out when people should do their own homework. Second, all joint ventures create additional difficulties—you share power and cultures, and decisions take longer." Comment.

6. Visit the online guide to international franchising set up by the *International Herald Tribune* (www.franchiseintl.com). Note that this guide lists franchises based on industry type. Pick any industry type and two or more competing franchise companies within that industry (e.g., Subway and Blimpie). Contrast their international franchising strategy (in terms of geographic coverage, training, provided services, etc.).

FURTHER READING ◆ ◆ ◆ ◆ ◆ ◆ ◆ ◆ ◆ ◆ ◆ ◆ ◆ ◆ ◆ ◆ ◆

Anderson, Erin, and Hubert Gatignon. "Modes of Foreign Entry: A Transaction Cost Analysis and Propositions," *Journal of International Business Studies*, 11 (Fall 1986): 1–26.

Bleeke, Joel, and David Ernst. "The Way to Win in Cross-Border Alliances," *Harvard Business Review* (Nov–Dec. 1991): 127–35.

Cavusgil, S. Tamer. "Measuring the Potential of Emerging Markets: An Indexing Approach." *Business Horizons*, 40 (January–February 1997): 87–91.

Devlin, Godfrey, and Mark Bleackley. "Strategic Alliances—Guidelines for Success," *Long Range Planning*, 21 (5) (1988): 18–23.

Kumar, V., A. Stam, and E.A. Joachimsthaler. "An interactive Multicriteria Approach to Identifying Potential Foreign Markets," *Journal of International Marketing*, 2 (1) (1994): 29–52.

Lorange, Peter, Johan Roos, and Peggy S. Brønn. "Building Successful Strategic Alliances," *Long Range Planning*, 25 (6) (1992): 10–17.

Martinsons, M. G., and C.-S. Tseng. "Successful Joint Ventures in the Heart of the Dragon," *Long Range Planning*, 28 (5) (1995): 45–58.

Ostland, Gregory E, and S. Tamer Cavusgil. "Performance Issues in U.S.-China Joint Ventures," *California Management Review*, 38 (2) (Winter 1996): 106–30.

Preble, John F., and Richard C. Hoffman. "Franchising Systems Around the Globe: A Status Report," *Journal of Small Business Management* (April 1995): 80–88.

Root, Franklin R. *Entry Strategies for International Markets*. New York, NY: Lexington Books, 1994.

Shama, Avraham. "Entry Strategies of U.S. Firms to the Newly Independent States, Baltic States, and Eastern European Countries." *California Management Review*, 37 (3) (Spring 1995), pp. 90–109.

Turpin, Dominique. "Strategic Alliances with Japanese Firms: Myths and Realities," *Long Range Planning*, 28 (5) (1993): 45–58.

APPENDIX ◆

Alternative Country Screening Procedure.

When the product has already been launched in some regions, the firm might consider using a variant of the country screening procedure described in this chapter. The alternative method leverages the experience the firm gathered in its existing markets. It works as follows: Suppose the MNC currently does business in Europe and is now considering an expansion into Asia.

Step 1: *Collect historical data on European market.*
Go back to your files and collect the historical data for the European markets on the indicators that you plan to use to assess the market opportunities for the Asian region. Let us refer to these pieces of information as X_{iec}, that is, the score of European country ec on indicator i;

Step 2: *Evaluate the MNC's post-entry performance in each of its existing European markets.*
Assess the MNC's post-entry performance in each European country by assigning a success score (e.g., on a ten-point scale). If performance is measured on just one indicator, say, market-share achieved five years after entry, you could also simply use that indicator as a performance measure. Let us refer to the performance score for country ec as S_{ec}.

Step 3: *Derive weights for each of the country indicators.*
The next step is to come up with importance weights for each of the country indicators. For this, you could run a cross-sectional regression using the European data gathered in the previ-

ous two steps. Our dependent variable is the post-entry success score (S_{ec}) while the predictor variables are the country indicators (X_{iec}):

$$S_{ec} = a + w_1 X_{1ec} + w_2 X_{2ec} + \ldots + w_I X_{Iec}$$
$$ec = 1, 2, \ldots, EC$$

By running a regression of the success scores, S_{ec}, on the predictor variables, X_{iec} ($i = 1, \ldots, I$), you can derive estimates for the importance weights of the different indicators.

Step 4: *Rate the Asian countries in the pool on each indicator.*
Each of the Asian candidate markets (ac) in the pool is given a score on each of the indicators that are considered: X_{iac}.

Step 5: *Predict performance in prospect Asian countries.*
Finally, predict the post-entry performance in the prospective Asian markets by using the weights estimated in the previous step and data collected on each of the indicators (the X_{iac}'s) for the Asian countries. For instance, the regression estimates might look like:

$$\begin{aligned} \text{Performance} = {} & -0.7 + 6.0 \, (\text{Market Size}) \\ & + 2.9 \, (\text{Growth}) \\ & - 1 \, (\text{Competition}) \end{aligned}$$

By plugging in the ratings (or actual values) for the Asian markets in this equation, you can then predict the MNC's performance in each of these countries.

GLOBAL SOURCING STRATEGY: R&D, MANUFACTURING, AND MARKETING INTERFACES 10

CHAPTER OVERVIEW

1. EXTENT AND COMPLEXITY OF GLOBAL SOURCING STRATEGY

2. TRENDS IN GLOBAL SOURCING STRATEGY

3. VALUE CHAIN AND FUNCTIONAL INTERFACES

4. PROCUREMENT: TYPES OF SOURCING STRATEGY

5. COSTS AND CONSEQUENCES OF GLOBAL SOURCING

6. OUTSOURCING OF SERVICE ACTIVITIES

During the last decade or so, international business has experienced a major metamorphosis of an irreversible kind. Gone are the days when international business meant the one-way expansion of U.S. companies to the rest of the world. Also gone are the days when European and Japanese companies simply exported to, or manufactured in, the United States. Today, executives of the same companies have come to accept a new reality of global competition and global competitors. The United States, Western Europe, and Japan, still dominate global competition, but an increasing number of countries are competing head-on for global leadership. Global competition suggests a drastically shortened life cycle for most products. Companies do not have the luxury of developing a polycentric, country-by-country approach to international business. If they follow such an approach, a globally oriented competitor will likely overcome their initial competitive advantages by blanketing the world markets with similar products in a shorter period of time.

One successful example of a globally oriented strategist is Sony. Sony developed transistorized solid-state color TVs in Japan in the 1960s and marketed them initially in the United States, then followed up quickly by introducing them in the rest of the world, including the Japanese market. Mass marketing initially in the United States and then throughout the world in a short time period gave this Japanese company a first-mover advantage, as well as economies of scale advantages.

In contrast, EMI provides a historic case example of the failure to take advantage of global opportunities. This British company developed and began marketing CAT (computer-aided tomography) scanners in 1972, for which its inventors, Godfrey Houndsfield and Allan Cormack, won a Nobel Prize. Despite an enormous demand for CAT scanners in the United States, the largest market for state-of-the-art medical equipment, EMI failed to export them to the United States immediately and in sufficient numbers. Instead, the British company slowly, and probably belatedly, began exporting them to the United States in the mid-1970s, as if to follow the evolutionary pattern suggested by the international product cycle model. Some years later, the British company established a production facility in the United States, only to be slowed down by technical problems. By then, EMI was already facing stiff competition from global electronics giants including Philips, Siemens, General Electric, and Toshiba. Indeed, it was General Electric that, in a short period of time, blanketed the U.S. market and subsequently the rest of the world with its own version of CAT scanners, which were technologically inferior to the British model.[1]

In both cases, technology diffused quickly. Today, quick technological diffusion is virtually assured. Without established sourcing plans, distribution, and service networks, it is extremely difficult to exploit both emerging technology and potential markets around the world simultaneously. General Electric's swift global reach could not have been possible without its ability to procure crucial components internally and on a global basis. As a result, the increased pace of new product introduction and reduction in innovational lead time calls for more proactive management of locational and corporate resources on a global basis. In this chapter, we emphasize global management of the *interfaces* of R&D, manufacturing, and marketing activities on one hand and procurement on the other—which we call **global sourcing strategy**—such that companies can proactively standardize either components or products. Global sourcing strategy requires a close coordination among R&D, manufacturing, and marketing activities across national boundaries.[2]

Differing objectives tend to create a tug-of-war-like situation among R&D, manufacturing, and marketing. For example, the demands of marketing for repeated product modification and proliferation for the sake of satisfying the ever-changing customer needs may be contrary to the objectives of manufacturing at lowering costs, since repeated modifications lead to increased costs and loss of production efficiencies. Similarly, designing products and features as desired by customers may indeed be innovative, but might not be conducive to efficient manufacturing. An exception to this situation would be a perfectly flexible computer-aided design (CAD) and computer-aided manufacturing (CAM) facility, which would allow various modifications to be made in the products without significantly increasing the associated manufacturing costs. (One must note, however, that while CAD/CAM technology has improved tremendously in recent years, the full benefit

---

[1]Fillipo Dell'Osso, "Defending a Dominant Position in a Technology Led Environment," *Business Strategy Review* (Summer 1990), pp. 77–86.

[2]Masaaki Kotabe, *Global Sourcing Strategy: R & D, Manufacturing, and Marketing Interfaces* (New York: Quorum Books, 1992).

of flexible manufacturing is still many years away).[3] Contrarily, excessive product standardization for the sake of lowering manufacturing costs will also be likely to result in unsatisfied or undersatisfied customers. Therefore, topics such as product design for manufacturability and components/product standardization have become increasingly important strategic issues today. It has become imperative for many companies to develop a sound sourcing strategy in order to exploit most efficiently R&D, manufacturing, and marketing on a global basis.

EXTENT AND COMPLEXITY OF GLOBAL SOURCING STRATEGY

In this chapter, we introduce you to subject matters not ordinarily covered in a marketing textbook. It is our strong belief that marketing managers should understand and appreciate the important roles that product designers, engineers, production managers, and purchasing managers, among others, play in marketing decision making. Marketing decisions cannot be made in the absence of these people.[4] The overriding theme throughout the chapter is that successful management of the interfaces of R&D, manufacturing, and marketing activities determines a company's competitive strengths and consequently its market performance. Now we will look at logistical implications of this interface management.

One successful interface management is illustrated by Toyota's global operations. The Japanese car maker is equipping its operations in the United States, Europe, and Southeast Asia with integrated capabilities for creating and marketing automobiles. The company gives the managers at those operations ample authority to accommodate local circumstances and values without diluting the benefit of integrated global operations. Thus, Calty Design Research, a Toyota subsidiary in California, designs the bodies and interiors of new Toyota models, including Lexus and Solara, for production in the United States. Toyota has technical centers in the United States and in Brussels to adapt engine and vehicle specifications to local needs.[5] Toyota operations that make automobiles in Southeast Asia supply each other with key components to foster increased economies of scale and standardization in those components—gasoline engines in Indonesia, steering components in Malaysia, transmissions in the Philippines, and diesel engines in Thailand.

Undoubtedly, these multinational companies, including Toyota, not only facilitate the flow of capital among various countries through direct investment abroad, but also significantly contribute to the world trade flow of goods and services. Multinational companies combine this production and distribution to supply those

---

[3]James H. Gilmore and Joseph B. Pine, II, "The Four Faces of Mass Customization," *Harvard Business Review*, 75 (January/February 1997), pp. 91–101.

[4]David B. Montgomery and Frederick E. Webster, Jr., "Marketing's Interfunctional Interfaces: The MSI Workshop on Management of Corporate Fault Zones," *Journal of Market Focused Management*, 2 (1997), pp. 7–26.

[5]Fumiko Kurosawa and John F. Odgers, "Global Strategy of Design and Development by Japanese Car Makers—From the Perspective of the Resource-Based View," *Association of Japanese Business Studies 1997 Annual Meeting Proceedings* (June 13–15, 1997), pp. 144–46.

EXHIBIT 10–1
HONDA'S WORLDWIDE PRODUCTION AND SOURCING NETWORK

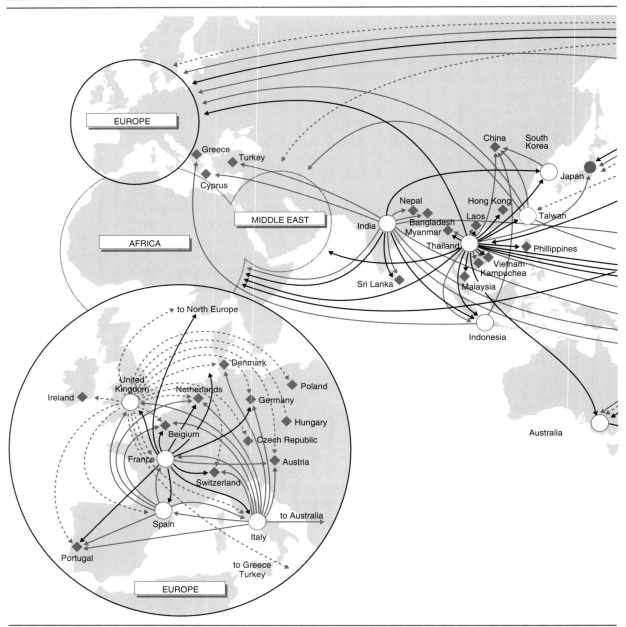

Source: Honda Motor Company Annual Report 1996.

local markets hosting their foreign subsidiaries, and then export what remains to other foreign markets or back to their parent's home market.

Let us revisit the significance of multinational companies' foreign production relative to their exports from their home base. U.S. MNCs are the most experienced in the industrialized world, and sell more than three times as much overseas through their subsidiaries as they export to the world. For U.S. multinationals, the

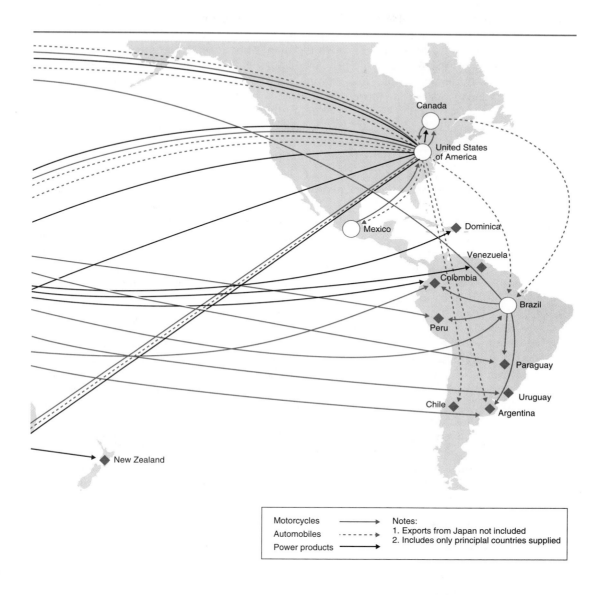

Motorcycles	———→	Notes:
Automobiles	- - - - -→	1. Exports from Japan not included
Power products	———→	2. Includes only principlal countries supplied

3:1 ratio of foreign sales to exports has remained largely unchanged since the mid-1960s. This ratio for European multinationals has grown from 3:1 in the 1970s to 5:1 by 1990. Similarly, the ratio for Japanese multinationals has increased from 1:1 in the mid-1970s to 2.5:1 by 1990. Also, both American and Japanese subsidiaries sell more than 20 percent of their foreign sales in third-country markets (third-country markets are defined as markets other than the country where the parent company is based and the country where the particular manufacturing facility is based), including their home markets, while European subsidiaries in the United States and Japan sell approximately 10 percent in third-country markets.[6]

This intra-firm trade, through the management of foreign production by multinational firms, is one of the primary factors leading to the total volume of international trade among the Triad regions (i.e., the United States, European Community, and Japan) increasing more than tenfold in twenty years—to $514.7 billion in 1995 from $44.4 billion in 1970—or by more than four times in real terms.

Two notable changes have occurred in international trade. First, in the last thirty years there has been a secular decline in the proportion of trade between the European Community and the United States in the Triad regions, and conversely, there has been an increase in trade between the United States and Japan, and in particular, between the European Community and Japan. It strongly indicates that European countries and Japan have found each other as increasingly important markets above and beyond their traditional market of the United States. Second, newly industrialized countries (NICs) in Asia, including South Korea, Taiwan, Hong Kong, and Singapore, have dramatically increased their trading position relative to the rest of the world. Not only have these NICs become prosperous marketplaces, but more significantly, they have become important manufacturing and sourcing locations for many MNCs.

From the sourcing perspective, U.S. and other MNCs were procuring a less expensive supply of components and finished products in NICs for sale in the United States and elsewhere. As a result, U.S. bilateral trade with NICs has increased more than eightyfold, to $150 billion in 1996 from $1.8 billion in 1970. Trade statistics, however, do not reveal anything other than the amount of bilateral trade flows between countries. It is false to assume that trade is always a business transaction between independent buyers and sellers across national boundaries. It is equally false to assume that a country's trade deficit in a certain industry equates with the decline in the competitiveness of companies in that industry. For example, Honda's production and sourcing network is presented in Exhibit 10–1. Clearly, an increasing segment of international trade of components and finished products is strongly influenced by multinational companies' foreign production and sourcing investment activities.

◆ ◆ ◆ ◆ ◆ ◆ TRENDS IN GLOBAL SOURCING STRATEGY

Over the last twenty years or so, gradual yet significant changes have taken place in global sourcing strategy. Most of the changes are in the way that business executives think of the scope of global sourcing for their companies and exploit various resultant opportunities as a source of competitive advantage. Peter Drucker, a famed management guru and business historian, once said that sourcing and logistics would remain "the darkest continent of business"—the least exploited area of business for competitive advantage. Naturally, many companies that have a limited scope of global sourcing are at a disadvantage over those that exploit it to their fullest extent in a globally competitive marketplace. Five trends in global sourcing

---

[6]Dennis J. Encarnation, "Transforming Trade and Investment, American, European, and Japanese Multinationals Across the Triad," a paper presented at the Academy of International Business Annual Meetings, November 22, 1992.

EXHIBIT 10–2
FACTORS THAT AFFECT GLOBAL SOURCING STRATEGY

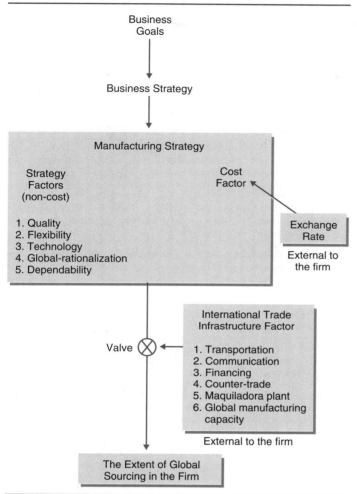

Source: Paul M. Swamidass, "Import Sourcing Dynamics: An Integrative Perspective," *Journal of International Business Studies* (Fourth Quarter 1993), p. 682.

are identified.[7] Exhibit 10–2 shows various factors that affect the scope of global sourcing strategy.

Since the 1970s, exchange rates have fluctuated rather erratically. If the dollar appreciates, U.S. companies find it easy to procure components and products from abroad. Such was the case in the first half of the 1980s when the dollar appreciated precipitously. The appreciation of the dollar was reflected in the surge of U.S. imports. Contrarily, if the dollar depreciates, U.S. companies would find it increasingly

Trend 1: The Decline of Exchange Rate Determinism of Sourcing

---

[7]This section draws from Paul M. Swamidass, "Import Sourcing Dynamics: An Integrative Perspective," *Journal of International Business Studies*, 24 (Fourth Quarter 1993), pp. 671–91.

difficult to depend on foreign supplies, as they have to pay higher dollar prices for every item sourced from abroad. In these scenarios, companies consider the exchange rate determining the extent to which they can engage in foreign sourcing.

However, this exchange rate determinism of sourcing is strictly based on the price factor. Indeed, a recent study shows that exchange rate fluctuations have little impact on the nature of sourcing strategy for crucial components.[8] Foreign sourcing also occurs for noncost reasons such as quality, technology, and so on. First of all, since it takes time to develop overseas suppliers for noncost purposes, purchasing managers cannot easily drop a foreign supplier when exchange rate changes have an adverse effect on the cost of imported components and products. Second, domestic suppliers are known to increase prices to match rising import prices following exchange rate changes. As a result, switching to a domestic supplier may not ensure cost advantages. Third, many companies are developing long-term relationships with international suppliers—whether those suppliers are their subsidiaries or independent contractors. In a long-term supply relationship, exchange rate fluctuations may be viewed as a temporary problem by the parties involved. Finally, some companies with global operations are able to shift supply locations from one country to another to overcome the adverse effects of exchange rate fluctuations, or even developing localized procurement plans to shield their operations completely from exchange rate fluctuations.[9]

Trend 2: New Competitive Environment Caused by Excess Worldwide Capacity

The worldwide growth in the number of manufacturers has added excess production capacity in most industries. The proliferation of manufacturers around the world in less sophisticated, less capital-intensive manufactured products, such as cement, is much greater than in more complex, knowledge-intensive products such as computers. Thus, there has been tremendous downward pressure on prices of many components and products around the world. Although the ability to deliver a high volume of products of satisfactory quality at a reasonable price was once the hallmark of many successful U.S. companies, the increasing number of global suppliers has effectively rendered the prompt delivery of volume no longer a competitive weapon. There has since occurred a strategic shift from price and quantity to quality and reliability of products as a determinant of competitive strength.[10] According to a recent survey (see Exhibit 10–3), better product and component quality, lower price, unavailability of item in the United States, and more advanced technology abroad are among the most important reasons for increased sourcing from abroad.

Trend 3: Innovations in and Restructuring of International Trade Infrastructure

Advances in structural elements of international trade have made it easier for companies to employ sourcing for strategic purposes. The innovations and structural changes that have important influences on sourcing strategy are (1) the increased number of purchasing managers experienced in sourcing, (2) improvements made in transportation and communication (e.g., fax and intranet), (3) new

---

[8]Janet Y. Murray, "A Currency Exchange Rate-Driven vs. Strategy-Driven Analysis of Global Sourcing," *Multinational Business Review*, 4 (Spring 1996), pp. 40–51.

[9]"Manufacturers Reshape Asian Strategies," *Nikkei Weekly* (January 12, 1998), p. 1 and p. 5; and "The World's Most Admired Companies," *Fortune* (October 26, 1998), pp. 206–26.

[10]Martin K. Starr and John E. Ullman, "The Myth of Industrial Supremacy," in Martin K. Starr, ed., *Global Competitiveness* (New York: W. W. Norton and Co., 1988).

EXHIBIT 10-3
KEY FACTORS FOR SOURCING FROM
ABROAD

Factor
Very Important
1. Better quality
2. Lower price
3. Unavailability of items in the United States
Important
4. More advanced technology abroad
5. Willingness to solve problems
6. More on-time delivery
7. Negotiability
8. Association with foreign subsidiary
Neutral
9. Geographical location
10. Countertrade requirements
11. Government assistance

Source: Adapted from Hokey Min and William P. Galle, "International Purchasing Strategies of Multinational U.S. Firms," *International Journal of Purchasing and Materials Management* (Summer 1991), p. 14.

financing options, including countertrade (barter that includes all variations of exchange of goods for goods), new incentives and opportunities for exports from countries without hard currency, (4) manufacturing facilities diffused throughout the world by globally minded companies, and (5) maquiladora plants (Mexico's version of free-trade-zone manufacturing facilities, mostly located close to the U.S.–Mexico border) providing a unique form of sourcing options to manufacturers operating in the United States.

Trend 4: Enhanced Role of Purchasing Managers

During the last ten to fifteen years, U.S. manufacturers were under pressure to compete on the basis of improved cost and quality. Many U.S. companies adopted just-in-time (JIT) production. JIT production requires close working relationships with component suppliers, and places an enormous amount of responsibility on purchasing managers. Furthermore, sourcing directly from foreign suppliers requires greater purchasing know-how and is riskier than other alternatives that use middlemen, who are generally U.S.-based wholesalers and representatives. Middlemen based in the United States are subject to U.S. laws and assume some of the currency risk associated with importing. However, now that purchasing managers are increasingly making long-term commitments to foreign suppliers and the level of market-information processing in the purchasing system has improved, dealing directly with suppliers is justified.[11] The finding suggests that U.S. purchasing managers are confident

---

[11]G. Tomas M. Hult, "A Global Learning Organization Structure and Market Information Processing," *Journal of Business Research*, 40 (October 1997), pp. 155–66.

about their international know-how and that they may be seeking long-term sourcing arrangements. The key to achieving effective global sourcing is securing management involvement at both the strategic (top) and the tactical (middle) levels.[12]

Trend 5: Trend Toward Global Manufacturing

During the 1980s, while U.S. companies continued to locate their operations in various parts of the world, companies from other countries such as Japan, Germany, and Britain expanded the magnitude of their foreign manufacturing operations at a much faster pace. The share of foreign-owned companies in U.S.-based manufacturing activities has increased from 5.2 percent in 1977 to close to 15 percent recently. As a global company adds another international plant to its network of existing plants, it creates the need for sourcing of components and other semiprocessed goods to and from the new plant to existing plants (see Global Perspective 10–1). Global manufacturing adds enormously to global sourcing activities, either within the same company across national boundaries or between independent suppliers and new plants.

Since the late 1980s, statistical trends have clearly shown that U.S. companies have increased sourcing from abroad, despite the overall depreciation of the U.S. dollar. Their continued sourcing from abroad represents a strategic expansion and rationalization over time. In response to slow productivity growth in the United States relative to other major trading nations in the 1980s, U.S. parent companies' technology had transferred directly to their foreign affiliates for production instead of in the form of equipment and components for local modification in the foreign markets. By the early 1990s those companies had built an increasingly integrated global manufacturing and delivery structures. Despite the rapid economic and productivity growth at home since the mid-1990's to this day, many U.S. companies are increasingly assigning design and other R&D responsibilities to satellite foreign units so as to design a regional or world product. As a result, foreign affiliates have also developed more independent R&D activities to manufacture products for the U.S. markets in addition to expanding local sales.[13]

◆ ◆ ◆ ◆ ◆ ◆ VALUE CHAIN AND FUNCTIONAL INTERFACES

The design of global sourcing strategy is based on the interplay between a company's competitive advantages and the comparative advantages of various countries. **Competitive advantage** influences the decision regarding what activities and technologies a company should concentrate its investment and managerial resources in, relative to its competitors in the industry. **Comparative advantage** affects the company's decision on where to source and market, based on the lower

---

[12]S. Tamer Cavusgil, Attila Yaprak, and Poe-lin Yeoh, "A Decision-making Framework for Global Sourcing," *International Business Review*, 2 (2) (1993), pp. 143–56; and A. Coskin Samli, John M. Browning, and Carolyn Busbia, "The Status of Global Sourcing as a Critical Tool of Strategic Planning: Opportunistic versus Strategic Dichotomy," *Journal of Business Research*, 43 (November 1998), pp. 177–87.

[13]Masaaki Kotabe and K. Scott Swan, "Offshore Sourcing: Reaction, Maturation, and Consolidation of U.S. Multinationals," *Journal of International Business Studies*, 25 (First Quarter 1994), pp. 1–27.

$\mathcal{G}$LOBAL PERSPECTIVE 10–1

TRADE FOLLOWS INVESTMENT

"Trade follows investment in the 1990s. . . . If you can't invest, you can't trade." As you recall from the Appendix to Chapter 1, the international product cycle argument was used to explain many companies' foreign expansion in the 1960s–1980s. It posits that companies tend to engage in exports to similar countries with similar per capita income levels and invest in foreign production in those "export" markets, as they are threatened by local competition there. In other words, "trade was generally followed by direct investment." Foreign direct investment was generally considered a *reactive* move for exporters to defend their hard-earned market position in foreign countries by setting up their local operations to better compete with local companies. Then why has the relationship between trade and investment reversed in the 1990s? The fundamental reason for such a reversed relationship is that many companies have to act more *proactively* to the ever-increasing tides of global competition. Today, companies do not have the luxury of time to follow the defensive strategic paths described by the international product cycle argument. As mentioned in Chapter 1, we all have to keep in mind what Mark Twain once wrote: "If you stand still, you could get run over." In an era of global competition, companies cannot stay put or stay satisfied with their current market position domestically as well as internationally. They need to invest and put their production and delivery systems in place in foreign markets much earlier than in the past. If they stood still, they could get "run over" by the onslaught of competitors from many parts of the world.

First, the U.S. Department of Commerce data support that argument. More than 80 percent of all Japanese imports are bought by U.S. affiliates of Japanese multinationals for local production and assembly in the United States. Meanwhile, parts now account for almost half the value of all Japanese imports, up from 10 percent in the mid-1980s. Similarly, U.S. companies such as Motorola and 3M that want to expand distribution networks in Japan would likely bring in more U.S.-made components. If there are no American companies abroad, there is not much to pull other U.S. goods into Japan.

Second, it is not only Japanese companies operating in the United States sourcing components from Japan, but U.S. companies also procuring components from Japan. Japanese high-tech firms shipped more than $20 billion worth of integrated circuits and other electronic components into the United States. Shipments from Japan-based purchasing offices of U.S. companies made up a hefty chunk of that. Companies such as Texas Instruments, Apple Computer, and Digital Equipment now have big purchasing operations in Japan. U.S. companies could no longer rely solely on necessary components either from domestic suppliers or from their in-house production.

Third, a shorter product cycle means that competitive pressure to reduce cost comes immediately after product introduction. Again, there is no luxury of time to see the international product cycle argument fulfill its prophesy. For example, Russia's economy is a mess, its currency shaky, its government gripped by crisis-a country, it would seem, to avoid at all costs. But the battle for Russia's consumer market has never been fiercer. With the ruble down 75 percent, Russians can no longer afford imported goods, so multinational consumer companies are defending their hard-won market shares by switching from importing to local manufacturing. McDonald's has set up local companies, and its Russian operations have remained profitable despite the currency turmoil. Similarly, Danone, the French food company, has switched from 80 percent of its Russian sales coming from imports to quadrupling its production at one Russian factory, while building a new $100 million plant. This local production and delivery has enabled the food giant to lower its costs in order to keep its prices low for consumers after the ruble crash, while solidifying its position in the Russian market for the long haul.

Sources: "The Secret of Weapon that Won't Start a Trade War," *Business Week* (March 7, 1994), p. 45; and Carol Matlack, "Betting on a New Label: Made in Russia," *Business Week* (April 12, 1999), p. 122.

EXHIBIT 10–4
VALUE CHAIN CONCEPT

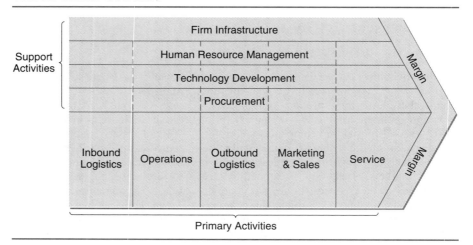

Source: Reprinted with the permission of The Free Press, a division of Simon & Schuster from *Competitive Advantage: Creating and Sustaining Superior Performance* by Michael E. Porter, p. 37. Copyright © 1985 by Michael E. Porter.

cost of labor and other resources in one country relative to another.[14] As shown in Exhibit 10–4, the **value chain concept** offers a general framework for understanding what it takes to manage the interrelated value-adding activities of a company on a global basis.[15] A company is essentially a collection of activities that are performed to design, manufacture, market, deliver, and support its product. This set of interrelated corporate activities is called the *value chain*. Therefore, to gain competitive advantage over its rivals in the marketplace, a company must perform these activities either at a lower cost or in such a way as to offer differentiated products and services, or must accomplish both. For example, Daewoo, Korea's new entrant into the automobile industry, introduced the Nubira, the Lanos, and the Leganza models whose prototypes were developed at its Worthing Technical Center in Britain and styled at Italdesign, a creative Italian design firm, with help from Daewoo's new Design Forum in Korea. They were manufactured in Korea for export to the European market.[16]

The value chain can be divided into two major activities performed by a company: (1) *primary activities* consisting of inbound logistics (procurement of raw materials and components), manufacturing operations, outbound logistics (distribution), sales, and after-sale service, and (2) *support activities* consisting of human

---

[14]Bruce Kogut, "Designing Global Strategies: Comparative and Competitive Value-Added Chains," *Sloan Management Review*, 26 (Summer 1985), pp. 15–28.

[15]Michael E. Porter, *Competition in Global Industries* (Cambridge, Mass.: Harvard Business School Press, 1986).

[16]Michael Schuman, "Daewoo Lifts Its Sights to U.S. and Europe," *Wall Street Journal* (March 4, 1997), p. A15; Nick Maling, "Korea Opportunities: Following Korean Economic Meltdown, Car Makers Were Expected to Flood the UK with Cheap Imports. Instead, They Have Defied Conventional Wisdom and Continue Building Brand Identity," *Marketing Week* (August 20, 1998), pp. 26–28.

resource management, technology development, and other activities that help promote primary activities. Competing companies constantly strive to create value across various activities in the value chain. Of course, the value that a company creates is measured ultimately by the price buyers are willing to pay for its products. Therefore, the value chain is a useful concept that provides an assessment of the activities that a company performs to design, manufacture, market, deliver, and support its products in the marketplace.

Five continuous and interactive steps are involved in developing a global sourcing strategy along the value chain.[17]

1. Identify the separable links (R&D, manufacturing, and marketing) in the company's value chain.

2. In the context of those links, determine the location of the company's competitive advantages, considering both economies of scale and scope.

3. Ascertain the level of transaction costs (e.g., cost of negotiation, cost of monitoring activities, and uncertainty resulting from contracts) between links in the value chain, both internal and external, and select the lowest cost mode.

4. Determine the comparative advantages of countries (including the company's home country) relative to each link in the value chain and to the relevant transaction costs.

5. Develop adequate flexibility in corporate decision making and organizational design so as to permit the company to respond to changes in both its competitive advantages and the comparative advantages of countries.

In this chapter, we focus on the three most important interrelated activities in the value chain: namely, R&D (i.e., technology development, product design, and engineering), manufacturing, and marketing activities. Management of the *functional interfaces*, or linkages, among these value-adding activities is a crucial determinant of a company's competitive advantage. A basic framework of management of R&D, manufacturing, and marketing interfaces is outlined in Exhibit 10–5. Undoubtedly, these value-adding activities should be examined as holistically as possible, by linking the boundaries of these primary activities. Thus, global sourcing strategy encompasses management of (1) the interfaces among R&D, manufacturing, and marketing on a global basis and (2) logistics identifying which production units will serve which particular markets and how components will be supplied for production. As presented in Global Perspective 10–2, linking R&D and manufacturing with marketing provides enormous direct and indirect benefits to companies operating in a highly competitive environment.

R & D/Manufacturing Interface

Technology is broadly defined as know-how. Technology can be classified based on the nature of know-how—know-how composed of product technology (the set of ideas embodied in the product) and process technology (the set of ideas involved in the manufacture of the product or the steps necessary to combine new materials to produce a finished product). However, executives tend to focus solely on product-related technology as the driving force of the company's

---

[17]Richard D. Robinson, ed., *Direct Foreign Investment: Costs and Benefits* (New York: Praeger Publishers, 1987).

EXHIBIT 10–5
INTERFACES AMONG R & D, MANUFACTURING, AND MARKETING

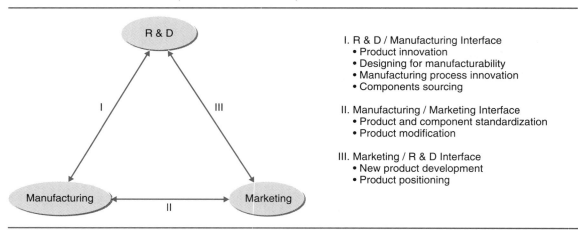

I. R & D / Manufacturing Interface
 • Product innovation
 • Designing for manufacturability
 • Manufacturing process innovation
 • Components sourcing

II. Manufacturing / Marketing Interface
 • Product and component standardization
 • Product modification

III. Marketing / R & D Interface
 • New product development
 • Product positioning

competitiveness. Product technology alone may not provide the company a long-term competitive edge over competition unless it is matched with sufficient manufacturing capabilities.[18]

The earlier example of EMI's CAT (computer-aided tomography) scan technology represents a classic case of such a product technology orientation. Similar cases exist throughout history. The British discovered and developed penicillin, but it was a small U.S. company, Pfizer, that improved on the fermentation (i.e., manufacturing) process and, as a result, became the world's foremost manufacturer of penicillin. The first jet engine was developed in Britain and Germany, but it was again U.S. companies, Boeing and Douglas, that improved on the technology and eventually dominated the jet plane market.

Ignoring manufacturing as a strategic weapon, many U.S. companies have historically emphasized product innovations (i.e., product proliferation and modifications). However, the U.S. technological lead over foreign competition has virtually evaporated, so there will be fewer products that U.S. companies can export simply because no one else has the technology to manufacture the products. Stressing the historical linkage of imitation and product innovations, it is contended that imitation (manufacturing process learning), followed by more innovative adaptation, leading to pioneering product design and innovation, forms the natural sequence of industrial development.[19] In other words, product innovation and manufacturing activities are intertwined, such that continual improvement in manufacturing processes can enable the company not only to maintain product innovation-based competitiveness, but also to improve its product innovative abilities in the future.[20]

These examples amply suggest that manufacturing processes should also be innovative. To facilitate the transferability of new product innovations to manufacturing, a team of product designers and engineers should strive to design

---

[18]Bruce R. Guile and Harvey Brooks, ed., *Technology and Global Industry: Companies and Nations in the World Economy* (Washington, D.C.: National Academy Press, 1987).

[19]Starr and Ullman, 1988.

[20]Guile and Brooks.

❖ ❖

𝒢LOBAL PERSPECTIVE 10–2

POWER OF GOOD LINKAGE MANAGEMENT

In today's world of global competition and high-speed product development, linkage among R & D, manufacturing, and marketing is more vital to successful business than ever before. Delivering a competitive product to the market at the right time, with the right specifications and feature benefits, all at a manufacturing cost that allows for profit, is one tough assignment. Add to this the global complexity of marketing, R & D, and manufacturing not being co-located in the same place, competing in an environment where world-class product development time is under fifty weeks, and you have a challenge that few companies are dealing with appropriately today.

International marketing executives no longer have the luxury of time to consider R & D and manufacturing as activities remotely related and remotely relevant to them. They have to deal with all of this complexity and be fully aware that without adequate understanding of the linkages necessary among R & D, manufacturing, and marketing, their businesses run a very high risk of failure.

John A. Bermingham, who has worked as executive vice president at Sony Corporation of America, president and CEO of AT&T Smart Cards Systems, and most recently as president and CEO of Rolodex Corporation, has a keen appreciation of how important and beneficial it is to manage linkages among R & D, manufacturing, and marketing activities on a global basis. The following is his advice:

When marketing determines a product need, the very first thing that marketing managers must do is to bring R & D and manufacturing together to establish a powerful linkage for the duration of the project. Marketing should also include finance, sales, and operations in this project, but the key linkage for the purpose of the product development is among marketing, R & D, and manufacturing.

According to John Bermingham, good linkage management has many benefits for these teams.

- A powerful linkage develops the requisite personal/business relationship needed among the three groups

that allows for the understanding and empathy for each other's responsibilities. These relationships cannot be fostered via faxes and teleconferences. They need to be developed on a face-to-face basis as well as throughout the project, especially if the marketing, R & D, and manufacturing teams are in different countries.

- A powerful linkage is necessary to ensure that issues are on top of the table at the beginning of the project and also as they develop throughout the project. Marketing must ensure that R & D and manufacturing are aware of the marketing strategy, competitive environment, and global implications. Any situations arising during the project must be discussed openly and positively with mutual understanding and with decisions being made to minimize impairment to the project with full understanding among the teams.

- A powerful linkage allows for speed. When you consider that world-class product development time is less than fifty weeks, and some say it will be less than forty weeks in the not too distant future, a powerful linkage is imperative. Teams must be working a series parallel effort. While certain things have to happen before others, certain things can be accomplished simultaneously, but this can only be accomplished with linkage.

- A powerful linkage develops a high sense of urgency. Teams really begin to understand how important speed is in this type of environment when they go past understanding their own needs and problems and begin to understand the other linked teams' needs and problems. Hence, urgency surrounds everything that these linked teams set out to accomplish. They see their linkage to the others and want to meet the needs of the entire team.

- A powerful linkage fosters mutual ownership individually and collectively. It is very important that there be individual ownership in the project, but it is just as important that the teams understand and accept collective ownership in the project. A tight linkage across the teams develops this collective ownership.

- A powerful linkage develops a true team environment that is essential and obligatory for success. Therefore, one of the most important roles for today and for the future for R & D and manufacturing in global marketing management is to ensure that these powerful linkages are established and strengthened.

Source: John A. Bermingham, "Executive Insights: Roles of R & D and Manufacturing in Global Marketing Management," *Journal of International Marketing*, 4 (4) (1996), pp. 75–84.

components such that they are conducive to manufacturing without undue retooling required and that components may be used interchangeably for different models of the product. Low levels of retooling requirements and interchangeability of components are necessary conditions for efficient sourcing strategy on a global scale. If different equipment and components are used in various manufacturing plants, it is extremely difficult to establish a highly coordinated sourcing plan on a global basis.

Manufacturing/ Marketing Interface

There exists a continual conflict between manufacturing and marketing divisions. It is to the manufacturing division's advantage if all the products and components are standardized to facilitate for standardized, low-cost production. The marketing division, however, is more interested in satisfying the diverse needs of customers, requiring broad product lines and frequent product modifications adding cost to manufacturing. How have successful companies coped with this dilemma?

Recently, there has been an increasing amount of interest in the strategic linkages between product policy and manufacturing long ignored in traditional considerations of global strategy development. With aggressive competition from European and Japanese MNCs emphasizing corporate product policy and concomitant manufacturing, many companies have realized that product innovations alone cannot sustain their long-term competitive position without an effective product policy linking product and manufacturing process innovations. So the strategic issue is how to design a robust product or components with sufficient versatility built in across uses, technology, and situations.[21]

Four different ways of developing a global product policy are generally considered an effective means to streamline manufacturing, thus lowering manufacturing cost, without sacrificing marketing flexibility: (1) core components standardization, (2) product design families, (3) universal product with all features, and (4) universal product with different positioning.[22]

Core Components Standardization. Successful global product policy mandates the development of universal products, or products that require no more than a cosmetic change for adaptation to differing local needs and use conditions. A few examples illustrate the point. Seiko, a Japanese watchmaker, offers a wide range of designs and models, but they are based on only a handful of different operating mechanisms. Similarly, the best-performing German machine tool-making companies have a narrower range of products, use up to 50 percent fewer parts than their less successful rivals, and make continual, incremental product and design improvements, with new developments passed rapidly on to customers.

Product Design Families. This is a variant of core component standardization. For companies marketing an extremely wide range of products due to cultural differences in product-use patterns around the world, it is also possible to reap

---

[21]K. Scott Swan, "Robust Design for Global Product Development: An Data Envelope Analysis," a Ph.D. dissertation, Management Science and Information Systems, The University of Texas at Austin, 1997.

[22]Hirotaka Takeuchi and Michael E. Porter, "Three Roles of International Marketing in Global Strategy," in Michael E. Porter, ed., *Competition in Global Industries* (Boston, Mass.: Harvard Business School Press, 1986), pp. 111–46.

economies of scale benefits. For example, Toyota offers several car models based on a similar family design concept, ranging from Lexus models to Toyota Avalons, Camrys, and Corollas. Many of the Lexus features well received by customers have been adopted into the Toyota lines with just a few minor modifications (mostly downsizing). In the process, Toyota has been able to cut product development costs and meet the needs of different market segments. Similarly, Electrolux, a Swedish appliance manufacturer, has adopted the concept of "design families," offering different products under four different brand names, but using the same basic designs. A key to such product design standardization lies in standardization of components, including motors, pumps, and compressors. Thus, White Consolidated in the United States and Zanussi in Italy, Electrolux's subsidiaries, have the main responsibility for components production within the group for worldwide application.

Universal Product with All Features. As just noted, competitive advantage can result from standardization of core components and/or product design families. One variant of components and product standardization is to develop a universal product with all the features demanded anywhere in the world. Japan's Canon has done so successfully with its AE-1 cameras and newer models. After extensive market analyses around the world, Canon identified a set of common features customers wanted in a camera, including good picture quality, ease of operation with automatic features, technical sophistication, professional looks, and reasonable price. To develop such cameras, the company introduced a few breakthroughs in camera design and manufacturing, such as use of an electronic integrated circuitry brain to control camera operations, modularized production, and standardization and reduction of parts.

Universal Product with Different Positioning. Alternatively, a universal product can be developed with different market segments in mind. Thus, a universal product may be positioned differently in different markets. This is where marketing promotion plays a major role to accomplish such a feat. Product and/or components standardization, however, does not necessarily imply either production standardization or a narrow product line. For example, Japanese automobile manufacturers have gradually stretched out their product line offerings, while marketing them with little adaptation in many parts of the world. This strategy requires manufacturing flexibility. The crux of global product or component standardization, rather, calls for proactive identification of homogeneous segments around the world, and is different from the concept of marketing abroad a product originally developed for the home market. A proactive approach to product policy has gained momentum in recent years as it is made possible by intermarket segmentation.[23] In addition to clustering countries and identifying homogeneous segments in different countries, targeting different segments in different countries with the same products is another way to maintain a product policy of standardization.

For example, Honda has marketed almost identical Accord cars around the world by positioning them differently in the minds of consumers from country to country. Accord has been promoted as a family sedan in Japan, a relatively inexpensive sports car in Germany, and a reliable commuter car in the United States.

---

[23]Theodore Levitt, "The Globalization of Markets," *Harvard Business Review*, 61 (May–June 1983), pp. 92–102.

In recent years, however, Honda has begun developing some regional variations of the Accord for the United States, European, and Japanese markets. Nonetheless, Honda adheres to a policy of core component standardization such that at least 50 percent of the components, including the chassis and transmission, are shared across the variations of the Accord.[24]

Marketing/ R & D Interface

Both R&D and manufacturing activities are technically outside marketing managers' responsibility. However, marketing managers' knowledge of the consumers' needs is indispensable in product development. Without a good understanding of the consumers' needs, product designers and engineers are prone to impose their technical specifications on the product, rather than fitting them to what consumers want. After all, consumers, not product designers or engineers, have the final say in deciding whether to buy the product.

Japanese companies, in particular, excel in management of the marketing/ R&D interface.[25] Indeed, their source of competitive advantage often lies in marketing and R&D divisions' willingness to coordinate their respective activities. In a traditional product development, either a new product was developed and pushed down from the R&D division to the manufacturing and to the marketing division for sales or a new product idea was pushed up from the marketing division to the R&D division for development. This top-down or bottom-up new product development takes too much time in an era of global competition, when a short product development cycle is crucial to meet constant competitive pressure from new products introduced by rival companies.

R&D and marketing divisions of Japanese companies are always on the lookout for use of emerging technologies initially in existing products to satisfy customer needs better than their existing products and their competitors'. This affords them an opportunity to gain experience, debug technological glitches, reduce costs, boost performance, and adapt designs for worldwide customer use. As a result, they have been able to increase the speed of new product introductions, meet the competitive demands of a rapidly changing marketplace, and capture market share.

In other words, *the marketplace becomes a virtual R&D laboratory for Japanese companies to gain production and marketing experience, as well as to perfect technology*. This requires close contact with customers, whose inputs help Japanese companies improve their products on an ongoing basis.

In the process, they introduce new products one after another. Year after year, Japanese companies unveil not-entirely-new products that keep getting better in design, reliability, and price. For example, Philips marketed the first practical VCR in 1972, three years before Japanese competitors entered the market. However, Philips took seven years to replace the first-generation VCR with the all-new V2000, while the late-coming Japanese manufacturers launched an onslaught of no fewer than three generations of improved VCRs in this five-year period.

---

[24]"Can Honda Build a World Car?" *Business Week* (September 8, 1997), pp. 100–108.

[25]X. Michael Song and Mark E. Parry, "A Cross-National Comparative Study of New Product Development Processes: Japan and the United States," *Journal of Marketing*, 61 (April 1997), pp. 1–18.

Another example worth noting is the exploitation of *fuzzy logic* by Hitachi and others.[26] When fuzzy logic was conceived in the mid-1960s by Lotfi A. Zadeh, a computer science professor at the University of California at Berkeley, nobody other than several Japanese companies paid serious heed to its potential application in ordinary products. The fuzzy logic allows computers to deal with shades of gray or something vague between 0 and 1—no small feat in the binary world of computers. Today, Hitachi, Matsushita, Mitsubishi, Sony, and Nissan Motors, among others, use fuzzy logic in their products. For example, Hitachi introduced a "fuzzy" train that automatically accelerates and brakes so smoothly that no one reaches for the hanging straps. Matsushita, maker of Panasonics, began marketing a "fuzzy" washing machine with only one start button that automatically judges the size and dirtiness of the load and decides the optimum cycle times, amount of detergent needed, and water level. Sony introduced a palm-size computer capable of recognizing written Japanese, with a fuzzy circuit to iron out the inconsistencies in different writing styles. Now fuzzy circuits are put into the autofocus mechanisms of video cameras to get constantly clear pictures. Although fuzzy chips have already been incorporated into a wide range of products in Japan, they have yet to be widely introduced in the rest of the world.[27]

The continual introduction of newer and better-designed products also brings a greater likelihood of market success.[28] Ideal products often require a giant leap in technology and product development, and naturally are subject to a much higher risk of consumer rejection. Not only does the Japanese approach of incrementalism allow for continual improvement and a stream of new products, but it also permits for quicker consumer adoption. Consumers are likely to accept improved products more quickly than very different products, since the former are more compatible with the existing patterns of product use and lifestyles.

PROCUREMENT: TYPES OF SOURCING STRATEGY

Sourcing strategy includes a number of basic choices that companies make in deciding how to serve foreign markets. One choice relates to the use of imports, assembly, or production within the country to serve a foreign market. Another decision involves the use of internal or external supplies of components or finished goods.

Sourcing decision making is multifaceted and entails both contractual and locational implications. From a contractual point of view, the sourcing of major components and products by multinational companies takes place in two ways: (1) from the parents or their foreign subsidiaries on an "intra-firm" basis and (2) from independent suppliers on a "contractual" basis. The first type of sourcing is known

---

[26]Larry Armstrong, "Why 'Fuzzy Logic' Beats Black-or-White Thinking," *Business Week* (May 21, 1990), pp. 92–93.

[27]Robert J. Crawford, "Reinterpreting the Japanese Economic Miracle," *Harvard Business Review* 76 (January/February 1998), pp. 179–84.

[28]Michael R. Czinkota and Masaaki Kotabe, "Product Development the Japanese Way," *Journal of Business Strategy*, 11 (November/December 1990), pp. 31–36.

EXHIBIT 10–6
TYPES OF SOURCING STRATEGY

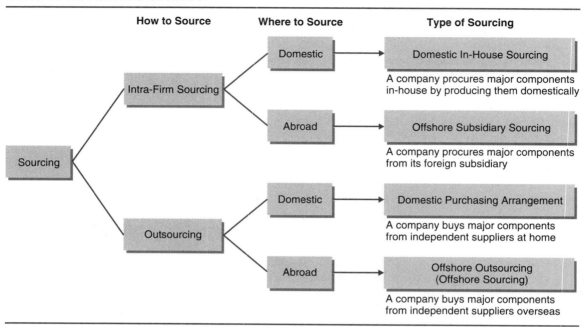

as **intra-firm sourcing**. The second type of sourcing is commonly referred to as **out-sourcing**. Similarly, from a locational point of view, MNCs can procure components and products either (1) domestically (i.e., *domestic sourcing*) or (2) from abroad (i.e., *offshore sourcing*). Therefore, as shown in Exhibit 10–6, four possible types of sourcing strategy can be identified.

In developing viable sourcing strategies on a global scale, companies must consider not only manufacturing costs, the costs of various resources, and exchange rate fluctuations, but also availability of infrastructure (including transportation, communications, and energy), industrial and cultural environments, the ease of working with foreign host governments, and so on. Furthermore, the complex nature of sourcing strategy on a global scale spawns many barriers to its successful execution. In particular, logistics, inventory management, distance, nationalism, and lack of working knowledge about foreign business practices, among others, are major operational problems identified by both U.S. and foreign multinational companies engaging in international sourcing.

Many studies have shown, however, that despite, or maybe as a result of, those operational problems, *where* to source major components seems much less important than *how* to source them. Thus, when examining the relationship between sourcing and competitiveness of MNCs, it is crucial to distinguish between sourcing on a "contractual" basis and sourcing on an "intra-firm" basis, for these two types of sourcing will have a different impact on their long-run competitiveness.

Intra-Firm Sourcing   MNCs can procure their components in-house within their corporate system around the world. They produce major components at their respective home base and/or at their affiliates overseas to be incorporated in their products marketed in various

various parts of the world. Thus, trade takes place between a parent company and its subsidiaries abroad, and also between foreign subsidiaries across national boundaries. This is often referred to as *intra-firm sourcing*. If such in-house component procurement takes place at home, it is essentially **domestic in-house sourcing**. If it takes place at a company's foreign subsidiary, it is called **offshore subsidiary sourcing**. Intra-firm sourcing makes trade statistics more complex to interpret, since part of the international flow of products and components is taking place between affiliated companies within the same MNC system, which transcends national boundaries. As you recall from a discussion on intra-firm trade in Chapter 1, about 30 percent of U.S. exports is attributed to U.S. parent companies transferring products and components to their affiliates overseas, and about 40 percent of U.S. imports is accounted for by foreign affiliates exporting to their U.S. parent companies. For both Japan and Britain, intra-firm transactions account for approximately 30 percent of their total trade flows (exports and imports combined), respectively.[29] Although statistics on intra-firm trade between foreign affiliates are limited to U.S. firms, the share of exports to other foreign affiliates in intra-firm exports of foreign affiliates rose from 37 percent in 1977 to 60 percent in 1993, and has been stable since then on, also suggesting the increased role of foreign affiliates of U.S. multinational firms outside the United States.[30]

In the 1970s, foreign competitors gradually caught up in a productivity race with U.S. companies, which had once commanded a dominant position in international trade. It coincided with U.S. corporate strategic emphasis drifting from manufacturing to finance and marketing. As a result, manufacturing management gradually lost its organizational influence. Production managers' decision-making authority was reduced, such that R&D personnel prepared the specifications with which production complied and marketing personnel imposed delivery, inventory, and quality conditions. Productivity considerations were ignored. In a sense, production managers gradually took on the role of outside suppliers within their own companies.[31]

Outsourcing

Production managers' reduced influence in the organization further led to a belief that manufacturing functions could, and should, be transferred easily to independent operators and subcontractors, depending on the cost differential between in-house and contracted-out production. A company's reliance on domestic suppliers for major components and/or products[32] is basically a **domestic purchase**

---

[29]United Nations Center on Transnational Corporations, *Transnational Corporations in World Development: Trends and Perspectives* (New York: United Nations, 1988); Organization for Economic Cooperation and Development, *Intra-Firm Trade*, Paris, OECD, 1993; Stefan H. Robock, "U.S. Multinationals: Intra-Firm Trade, Overseas Sourcing and the U.S. Trade Balance," a paper presented at the 1999 Academy of International Business-Southeast Conference, June 4–5, 1999.

[30]*World Investment Report 1996*, pp. 13–14; and *World Investment Report* 1998 (New York: United Nations, 1996 and 1998).

[31]Stephen S. Cohen and John Zysman, "Why Manufacturing Matters: The Myth of the Post-Industrial Economy," *California Management Review*, 29 (Spring 1987), pp. 9–26.

[32]Rodney Ho, "Small Product-Development Firms Show Solid Growth," *Wall Street Journal* (April 22, 1997), p. 32: This article shows that entrepreneurial companies have begun to fill a void of new product development role as large companies trim their internal R & D staff and expenditures in the United States. Although it makes financial sense, at least in the short term, those outsourcing companies will face the same long-term concern as explained in this chapter.

arrangement. Furthermore, in order to lower production costs under competitive pressure, U.S. companies turned increasingly to *outsourcing* of components and finished products from abroad, particularly from newly industrialized countries including Singapore, South Korea, Taiwan, Singapore, Hong Kong, Brazil, and Mexico. Initially, subsidiaries were set up for production purposes (i.e., offshore subsidiary sourcing), but gradually, independent foreign suppliers took over component production for U.S. companies. This latter phenomenon is usually called *offshore outsourcing* (or offshore sourcing, for short).

Component procurement from overseas (i.e., offshore subsidiary sourcing and offshore outsourcing) is receiving an increasing amount of attention, as it not only affects domestic employment and economic structure but also sometimes raises ethical issues (see Global Perspective 10–3). Companies using such strategy have been described pejoratively as **hollow corporations**.[33] It is occasionally argued that those companies are increasingly adopting a "designer role" in global competition—offering innovations in product design without investing in manufacturing process technology.

This widespread international sourcing practice could have a deleterious impact on the ability of companies to maintain their initial competitive advantage based on product innovations.[34] Indeed, keeping abreast of emerging technology through continual improvement in R&D and manufacturing is essential for the company's continued competitiveness.

◆ ◆ ◆ ◆ ◆ ◆ **COSTS AND CONSEQUENCES OF GLOBAL SOURCING**

Need for Coordination

Global sourcing strategy requires close coordination of R&D, manufacturing, and marketing activities, among others, on a global basis. In Chapter 8, we discussed the two fundamental forces that have shaped the nature of competition for firms across national boundaries over the years: the firm's desire to integrate and streamline its operations and the diversity of markets. One thing that has changed, however, is the *ability* and *willingness* of these companies to integrate various activities on a global basis in an attempt either to circumvent or to nullify the impact of differences in local markets to the extent possible. It might be *more* correct to say that these companies have been increasingly compelled to take a global view of their businesses, due primarily to increased competition, particularly among the Triad regions of the world: namely, the United States, Western Europe, and Japan. Remember, "If you stand still, you could get run over"—a contemporary view of competitive urgency that is shared by an increasing number of executives of multinational firms, irrespective of nationality.

[33]"Special Report: The Hollow Corporation," *Business Week* (March 3, 1986), pp. 56–59; and Robert Heller, "The Dangers of Deconstruction," *Management Today* (February 1993), p. 14 and p. 17.

[34]Constantinos Markides and Norman Berg, "Manufacturing Offshore Is Bad Business," *Harvard Business Review*, 66 (September–October 1988), pp. 113–20.

❖ ❖

𝒢LOBAL PERSPECTIVE 10–3

OFFSHORE SOURCING AND SWEATSHOPS OVERSEAS

The rapid globalization linking manufacturing companies, investors, and consumers around the world has touched off some ethical questions in recent years. Offshore sourcing is the practice of companies manufacturing or contracting out all or parts of their products abroad. Outsourcing makes it possible for those companies to procure products and components much more cheaply than manufacturing them in their home country. In many cases, labor cost savings are a strong motive for companies to engage in offshore sourcing. For example, Nike, the leading U.S. footwear company, has subcontractors in Taiwan, South Korea, and Indonesia, which collectively run twelve factories in Indonesia, producing 70 million pairs of Nike sneakers a year. Like any other footwear factories everywhere in Asia, work conditions are tough, with mandatory overtime work and constant exhaustion. Although these factories may be modern, they are drab and utilitarian, with vast sheds housing row upon row of mostly young women working many hours. The basic daily wage in Indonesia for these workers is a mere $2.23 a day. Here a pair of Pegasus running shoes costs about $18 to put together, and retails for $75 once shipped to the United States. The condition is similar in Vietnam, where 35,000 workers producing Nike shoes at five plants put in twelve hours a day to earn $1.60—less than the $2 or so it costs to buy three meals a day.

Although the working conditions at these subcontractors' factories have improved over time at Nike's initiatives, the company has a long way to go before it lives up to its stated goal of providing a fair working environment for all its workers. In Indonesia, police and factory managers have a not-so-subtle cozy relationship where police help keep workers under control. Despite its strong political clout, Nike has not challenged the Indonesian government's control over labor. Nike's code of conduct seems to remain vague, despite its intentions.

The linking of the firm's private interests with the larger public good has been referred to as corporate citizenship. Multinational companies cannot claim ignorance about the workers who produce the products they buy or the conditions in which they work. Large companies have the resources to investigate those with whom they do business. Ethically speaking, they should set standards that their contractors have to meet in order to continue their contracts. Indeed, in recent years, socially responsible investing (SRI) has increasingly become the practice of making investment decisions on the basis of both financial and social performance. The SRI movement has grown into a $1.185 trillion business, accounting for about one in ten U.S. invested dollars.

Sources: "Pangs of Conscience: Sweatshops Haunt U.S. Consumers," *Business Week* (July 29, 1996), pp. 46–47; "Report Alleges Abuses by Nike Contractors," *Austin-American Statesman* (March 28, 1997), p. D8; R. Bruce Hutton, Louis D'Antonio, and Tommi Johnsen, "Socially Responsible Investing: Growing Issues and New Opportunities," *Business and Society*, 37 (September 1998), pp. 281–305; and Richard T. De George, *Business Ethics*, 5th ed., (Englewood Cliffs, N.J.: Prentice Hall, 1999).

The last thirty years have seen a tremendous growth and expansion of European and Japanese MNCs encroaching on the competitive strengths of U.S. MNCs in almost all the markets around the world. Although U.S. MNCs have subsidiaries all over the world, they have been somewhat reluctant to develop an integrated and well-coordinated global strategy that successful European and Japanese MNCs have managed to establish. At the core of an integrated global strategy lies the company's ability to coordinate manufacturing activities with R&D, engineering, and marketing on a global basis. Indeed, European and Japanese MNCs have heavily invested in, and improved on, their strengths in manufacturing that many U.S. MNCs have ignored. As a result, many U.S. companies tend to have an ill-coordinated manufacturing strategy that results in a poor match between their manufacturing system capability and markets.

As explained earlier, Honda has been successful in developing its Accord model as a truly world car based on the same platform, yet promoted differently in different key markets around the world. On the contrary, Ford's global car project with the Coutour/Mystique model in the United States and the Mondeo model in Europe has not been successful, despite a total investment in excess of $6 billion. Its failure is attributed primarily to the lack of design, engineering, and marketing coordination between European and American development teams.[35]

Functional Mismatch

This functional mismatch has been traced to a drift in U.S. management's strategic emphasis from manufacturing to marketing and to finance over the years.[36] U.S. management's attention was focused on marketing in the 1960s, followed by a preoccupation with finance in the 1970s, culminating in the merger and acquisition craze of the 1980s and the 1990s—aptly called *paper entrepreneurship*.[37]

In order to lower production costs under competitive pressure, U.S. MNCs outsourced more components and finished products from newly industrializing countries such as South Korea, Taiwan, Singapore, Hong Kong, Brazil, and Mexico, among others. Akio Morita, a co-founder of Sony, a highly innovative Japanese electronics company, chided such U.S. MNCs as *hollow corporations* that simply put their well-known brand names on foreign-made products and sold them as if the products were their own.[38] The main characteristics of hollow corporations are illustrated in Global Perspective 10–4.

However, we should not rush to a hasty conclusion that outsourcing certain components and/or finished products from foreign countries will diminish a company's competitiveness. Thanks to the explosive growth of the Internet, outsourcing activities have actually increased and become more efficient.[39] Many multinational companies with plants in various parts of the world are exploiting not only their own competitive advantages (e.g., R&D, manufacturing, and marketing skills) but also the locational advantages (e.g., inexpensive labor cost, certain skills, mineral resources, government subsidy, and tax advantages). Thus, it is also plausible to argue that these multinational companies are in a more advantageous competitive position than are domestic-bound companies.

Then, isn't the "hollowing-out" phenomenon indicative of a superior management of both corporate and locational resources on a global basis? What is wrong, if at all, with Caterpillar procuring more than 15 percent of components for its tractors from foreign suppliers? How about Honeywell marketing in the United States the products manufactured in its European plants? Answers to these questions hinge on a company's ability and willingness to integrate and coordinate various ac-

---

[35] Alex Taylor III, "Ford's $6 Billion Baby, *Fortune* (June 28, 1993), pp. 76–81; and Jerry Flint, "Ford: Global or Bust," *Ward's Auto World* (March 1998), p. 23.

[36] Elwood S. Buffa, "Making American Manufacturing Competitive," *California Management Review*, 26 (Spring 1984), pp. 29–46.

[37] Robert Reich, *The Next American Frontier* (New York: Times Books, 1983).

[38] "Special Report: The Hollow Corporation," *Business Week* (March 3, 1986), pp. 56–59.

[39] Ira Sager, "Go Ahead, Farm Out Those Jobs," *Business Week* (March 22, 1999), p. EB35.

GLOBAL PERSPECTIVE 10-4

HOLLOW CORPORATIONS

The following discussion appeared in a now-classic article in the *Business Week* in 1986.

By shifting production overseas or shopping abroad for parts and components, U.S. companies are whittling away at the critical mass essential to a strong industrial base. For example,

- General Electric Co. spent $1.4 billion in 1995 to import products sold in the United States under the GE label. Virtually all of its consumer electronics goods are already made in Asia. By the end of summer, the company plans to shut down its last domestic color-TV plant. In appliances, GE now buys its microwave ovens from Japan and began going offshore for room air conditioners as early as 1987.
- Eastman Kodak Co. is counting on foreign-made products to fuel much of its growth. To diversify from the stagnant film business, Kodak is buying video camera recorders and videotape from Japan, along with its midsize copying machines. It also imports floppy disks from a Kodak factory in Britain.
- Honeywell Inc. gets the central processing "brain" for its biggest mainframe computer from a Japanese manufacturer, and two other mainframes that Honeywell sells in the United States are imported as finished products from Europe. The Minneapolis company also goes abroad for a host of components used in its factory-automation equipment and commercial air-conditioning systems.

If this trend continues, warns Jack D. Kuehler, senior vice-president of International Business Machines Corp., companies will gradually become less adept at understanding how new technology can be exploited and eventually "lose the ability to design." Adds Robert A. Lutz, chairman of Ford of Europe Inc.: "You're seeing a substantial deindustrialization of the U.S., and I can't imagine any country maintaining its position in the world without an industrial base." Only now U.S. companies are also shifting far more valuable things overseas: fundamental technology, management functions, and even the design and engineering skills that are crucial to innovation.

BACKING AWAY

When Sony Corp. unveiled the first VCRs in 1975, they carried price tags of more than $1,000, so most U.S. companies dismissed them as too expensive and complex ever to command a major market. Besides, they were already backing away from tape recorders, the source of the technology that went into the VCR. Now, with product simplification and automated production, VCRs are selling—like hotcakes—at less than $300.

Here, too, not one is made in the United States, although Sony plans to start building a U.S. VCR factory this year. And now it has spun off its VCR technology into the so-called camcorder, a combination video camera recorder that promises to be the last straw for movie cameras and film. Alarmed, Kodak has jumped into the video market—with a camcorder made by Matsushita Electric Industrial Co.

However, as RCA has learned, selling goods made by a foreign competitor can be a rocky partnership. RCA has leveraged its name and distribution resources to grab the biggest share of domestic VCR sales, an estimated 20 percent. Its machines now get stamped with the RCA logo in a Hitachi Ltd. factory. Matsushita used to do that for RCA. But in 1984, with Matsushita gaining market share by undercutting RCA's prices with Panasonic VCRs that were clones of RCA's units, RCA turned to Hitachi. RCA suspects the deal with Hitachi will also prove temporary. "You can only source for a limited time," admits Jack K. Sauter, an RCA group vice-president. But RCA, GE, and Zenith are compelled to endure the situation. Not only do the profits from VCRs help subsidize their manufacturing losses on color TV sets, but also they lack the expertise to produce competitively.

WAITING IN THE WINGS

Of course, not all companies are oblivious to the implications of deindustrialization. A small but growing band is feverishly working to develop the technologies that will be used in the totally automated factory. Caterpillar has launched a major effort to automate production, both in the United States and abroad. And Cat is encouraging managers to think long term, planning ten years ahead. "That's a dramatic difference" in philosophy, says Caterpillar's Ranney.

A decade and a half since the source of this article was published, we still debate the same issue, although we have better understanding of the logic about the "boundaries" of the firm. The argument is based on internalization/transaction cost theory (as described in the

Source: "Even American Knowhow is Headed Abroad," *Business Week* (March 3, 1986), pp. 60–63; and Jay B Barney, "How a Firm's Capabilities Affect Boundary Decisions," *Sloan Management Review*, 40 (Spring 1999), pp. 137–145.

Appendix to Chapter 1). However, the real issue is not how far a firm can "hollow out" or outsource its business functions, but how far it should do so for its long-term sustainable competitive advantage.

tivities. The real issue is not how far a firm can "hollow out" or outsource its business functions, but how far it should do so for its long-term sustainable competitive advantage.

Sustainable Core Competence versus Transitory Core Competence	There are two opposing views of the long-term implications of offshore sourcing. One school of thought argues that many successful companies have developed a dynamic organizational network through increased use of joint ventures, subcontracting, and licensing activities across international borders.[40] This flexible network system is broadly called **strategic alliances**. Strategic alliances allow each participant to pursue its particular competence. Therefore, each network participant can be seen as complementing rather than competing with the other participants for the common goals. Strategic alliances may even be formed by competing companies in the same industry in pursuit of complementary abilities (new technologies or skills) from each other. The other school of thought argues, however, that while this may be true in gaining transitory advantages in the short run, there could also be negative long-term consequences resulting from a company's dependence on independent suppliers. Such reliance on outsourcing may make it inherently difficult for the company to sustain its long-term competitive advantages, as it could not keep abreast of constantly evolving design and engineering technologies without engaging in those developmental activities.[41] These two opposing arguments will be elaborated here.

Strategic Alliances.   The advantage of forming a strategic alliance is claimed to be its structural flexibility. Strategic alliances can accommodate a vast amount of complexity while maximizing the specialized competence of each member, and provide much more effective use of human resources that would otherwise have to be accumulated, allocated, and maintained by a single organization. In other words, a company can concentrate on performing the task at which it is most efficient. This approach is increasingly applied on a global basis with countries participating in a dynamic network as multinational companies configure and coordinate product development, manufacturing, and sourcing activities around the world.

First, due to the need for fast internationalization and related diversification, strategic alliances provide a relatively easy option to access the world markets and to combine complementary technologies. Thus, AT&T needed Olivetti's established European network to enter the European market for telephone

---

[40]Raymond E. Miles and Charles C. Snow, "Organizations: New Concepts for New Forms," *California Management Review*, 28 (Spring 1986), pp. 62–73.

[41]Masaaki Kotabe, "Efficiency vs. Effectiveness Orientation of Global Sourcing Strategy: A Comparison of U.S. and Japanese Multinational Companies," *Academy of Management Executive*, 12 (November 1998), pp. 107–119.

switchboard equipment. Similarly, Toyota established a joint venture with General Motors so that the Japanese car maker could learn to work with UAW union members while General Motors could learn just-in-time inventory management from Toyota.

Second and more relevant to sourcing issues, an increasing number of companies have funneled out manufacturing functions to independent partners. In 1989, for example, Apple Computer enlisted Sony to design and manufacture a new notebook-size Macintosh computer called the PowerBook 100. In this arrangement, Apple gave Sony the basic blueprint, and Sony engineers, who had little experience building personal computers, developed Apple's smallest and lightest machine from drawing board to factory floor in less than thirteen months.[42] This is a strategic alliance in which Apple's basic design ability was complemented by Sony's miniaturization technology. The result has been a spectacular success for Apple that could not have materialized without Sony's participation.

However, it has also become apparent that Apple could lose manufacturing capabilities for the next generations of notebook-size computers without Sony's participation. On the other hand, Sony, having mastered engineering and manufacturing of Apple's notebook computers, gradually increased its role upstream to assisting Apple in product designing. Such a relationship could prove to be detrimental to Apple's competitiveness if Sony were able to take over most of what it takes to develop a notebook computer. Later, being concerned about this, Apple decided to sever its relationship with Sony.

Dependence. Companies that rely on independent external sources of supply of major components tend to forsake part of the most important value-creating activities to, and also become dependent on, independent operators for assurance of component quality. Furthermore, those MNCs tend to promote competition among independent suppliers, ensure continuing availability of materials in the future, and exploit full benefits of changing market conditions. However, individual suppliers are forced to operate in an uncertain business environment that inherently necessitates a shorter planning horizon. The uncertainty about the potential loss of orders to competitors often forces individual suppliers to make operating decisions that will likely increase their own long-term production and materials costs. In the process, this uncertain business environment tends to adversely affect the MNCs sourcing components and/or finished products from independent suppliers.

The decline of IBM in the personal computer market in recent years offers the most vivid example of the problems caused by its dependence on independent suppliers for crucial components in the personal computer market.[43] As a relatively late entrant into the burgeoning personal computer market in the early 1980s, IBM decided, contrary to its long-held policy of developing proprietary technology in-house, to rely on microprocessors from Intel and operating software from Microsoft. Given its massive size and marketing abilities, IBM was able to become a market leader in the personal computer business in a short period of time. However, Intel and Microsoft were also free to market their wares to any other companies. As a result, many small and nimble personal computer companies rushed into

---

[42]Brenton R. Schlender, "Apple's Japanese Ally," *Fortune* (November 4, 1991), pp. 151–52.
[43]Bruce Lloyd, "IBM: Decline or Resurrection?" *Management Decision*, 32 (8) (1994), pp. 5–10.

the personal computer market and began marketing IBM-compatible personal computers at the cost of IBM's market share position. IBM was slow to respond to this competition, so it lost both its dominant position and control of the personal computer market that it had helped create.

Gradual Loss of Design and Manufacturing Abilities. Multinational companies that depend heavily on independent suppliers could also lose sight of emerging technologies and expertise in the long run that could be incorporated into the development of new manufacturing processes, as well as new products. Apple–Sony and IBM–Intel–Microsoft alliances may be illustrative of such possibilities. Thus, continual sourcing from independent suppliers is likely to forebode those companies' long-term loss of the ability to manufacture at competitive cost and, as a result, loss of their global competitiveness. However, if technology and expertise developed by a multinational company are exploited within its MNC system (i.e., by its foreign affiliates and by the parent company itself), the company can retain its technological base without unduly disseminating expertise to competitors. The benefit of such internalization is likely to be great, particularly when technology is highly idiosyncratic or specific with limited alternative uses, or when it is novel in the marketplace. For such a technology, the market price mechanism is known to break down, as a seller and potential buyers of the technology tend to see its value very differently. Potential buyers, who do not have perfect knowledge of how useful the technology will be, tend to undervalue its true market value. As a result, the seller of the technology is not likely to get a full economic benefit of the technology by selling it in the open market.

In a relationship with a foreign supplier, it is particularly essential that a lead company devise methods to ensure the continued product and service quality. For example, in entering the Chinese industrial tire market recently, Industrial Tires Co. (ITL), Canada's top industrial tire maker, continues to provide technology, patterns, compounds, and trade names, takes care of equipment selection and process and product engineering, and maintains a high-level quality assurance program for Yantai, a manufacturing and marketing partner in China.[44]

In addition, by getting involved in design and production on its own, the multinational company can keep abreast of emerging technologies and innovations originating anywhere in the world for potential use in the future. Furthermore, management of the quality of major components is required to retain the goodwill and confidence of consumers in the products. As a result, "intra-firm" sourcing of major components and finished products between the parent company and its affiliates abroad and between its foreign affiliates themselves would more likely enable the company to retain a long-term competitive edge in the world market.

◆ ◆ ◆ ◆ ◆ ◆ OUTSOURCING OF SERVICE ACTIVITIES

In 1998, the United States was ranked the largest exporter and importer of services, providing $233.6 billion of services to the rest of the world and receiving $161.5 billion worth of services. Furthermore, according to a recent government

---

[44]Bruce Meyer, "ITL Building on Global Strategy," *Rubber and Plastics* (July 4, 1994).

estimate, approximately 16 percent of the total value of U.S. exports and imports of services were conducted across national boundaries on an intra-firm basis (i.e., between parent companies and their subsidiaries). Increasingly, U.S. companies have expanded their service procurement activities on a global basis in the same way they procure components and finished products.

As we have discussed, firms have the ability and opportunity to procure components/finished goods that have proprietary technology on a global basis. This logic also applies equally to service activities. The technological revolution in data processing and telecommunications (trans-border data flow, telematics, etc.) either makes the global tradability of some services possible or facilitates the transactions economically. Furthermore, because the production and consumption of some services do not need to take place at the same location or at the same time, global sourcing may be a viable strategy.

Thanks to the development of the Internet and e-commerce, certain service activities are increasingly outsourced from independent service suppliers. The Internet will also accelerate growth in the number of e-workers. This net-savvy and highly flexible corps will be able to perform much or all of their work at home, or in small groups close to home, irrespective of their locations. International e-workers can also operate in locations far from corporate headquarters. They will be part of the growth in *intellectual outsourcing*. Already such e-workers can write software in India for a phone company in Finland, provide architectural services in Ireland for a building in Spain, and do accounting work in Hong Kong for an insurance company in Vancouver. Globalization of services through the Internet is likely to expand considerably in the future.[45]

Particularly, Bangalore, India, should be noted. The region is described as the Silicon Valley of that country. Bangalore has rapidly become the center of offshore programming activities. Many U.S. companies are outsourcing an increasing portion of software development from companies in Bangalore. For example, Aztec Software & Technology Services Ltd., and Indian company, has worked with Microsoft Corp.'s SQL Server group for more than eighteen months on the SQL Server 7.0 release and even developed a few tools for the technology. The company also collaborated with programmers at IBM's Almaden Research Center, San Jose, to develop the Datalinks linking technology for databases. BFL Software Ltd., employing more than four hundred technical people in two factories, is another Indian software company with close U.S. ties. Its client roster includes Compaq Computer Corp. and Federal Express Corp. Alternatively, those U.S. companies could set up their own support operations in Bangalore, if they wanted tighter control of their local operations.[46]

Outsourcing of service activities has been widely quoted in the popular press as a means to reduce costs and improve the corporate focus; that is, concentrating on the core activities of the firm. However, outsourcing may also serve other purposes, including (a) reducing time to implement internal processes, (b) sharing risk in an increasingly uncertain business environment, (c) improving customer service, (d) improving access to expertise not available in-house, (e) reducing head count,

---

[45]Robert D. Hormats, "High Velocity," *Harvard International Review*, 21 (Summer 1999), pp. 36–41.

[46]Tim Scannell, "U.S. Skills Shortage Prompts Integrators to Search Offshore," *Computer Reseller News* (March 15, 1999), pp. 1–2.

and (f) instilling a sense of competition, especially when departments within firms develop a perceptible level of inertia.[47]

In the case of service companies, the distinction between core and supplementary services is necessary in strategy development. **Core services** are the necessary outputs of an organization that consumers are looking for, while **supplementary services** are either indispensable for the execution of the core service or are available only to improve the overall quality of the core service bundle. Using an example of the health care industry, the core service is providing patients with good-quality medical care. The supplementary services may include filing insurance claims, arranging accommodations for family members (especially for overseas patients), handling off-hour emergency calls, and so on. The same phenomenon arises in the computer software industry. When the industry giant, Microsoft, needed help in supporting new users of Windows operating software, it utilized outsourcing with Boston-based Keane, Inc. to set up a help desk with 350 support personnel.

Core services may gradually partake of a "commodity" and lose their differential advantage vis-à-vis competitors as competition intensifies over time. Subsequently, a service provider may increase its reliance on supplementary services to maintain and/or enhance competitive advantage. "After all, if a firm cannot do a decent job on the core elements, it is eventually going to go out of business."[48] In other words, the reason a service firm exists is to provide good-quality core services to its customers. However, in some instances, it simply cannot rely solely on core services to stay competitive. We can expect that core services are usually performed by the service firm itself, regardless of the characteristics of the core service. On the other hand, contrary, although supplementary, services are provided to augment the core service for competitive advantage, the unique characteristics of supplementary services may influence "how" and "where" they are sourced.[49]

SUMMARY ✦

The scope of global sourcing has expanded over time. Whether or not to procure components or products from abroad was once determined strictly on price and thus was strongly influenced by the fluctuating exchange rate. Thus, the appreciation of the dollar prompted companies to increase offshore sourcing, while the depreciation of the dollar encouraged domestic sourcing. Today many companies consider not simply price but also quality, reliability, and technology of components and products to be procured. Those companies design their sourcing decisions based on the interplay between their competitive advantages and the compara-

---

[47]Maneesh Chandra, "Global Sourcing of Services: A Theory Development and Empirical Investigation," a Ph.D. dissertation, The University of Texas at Austin, 1999.

[48]C. H. Lovelock, "Adding Value to Core Products with Supplementary Services," in C. H. Lovelock, ed., *Services Marketing*, 3rd ed. (Englewood Cliffs, NJ: Prentice-Hall, 1996).

[49]Terry Clark, Daniel Rajaratnam, and Timothy Smith, "Toward a Theory of International Services: Marketing Intangibles in a World of Nations," *Journal of International Marketing*, 4(2) (1996) pp. 9–28; and Janet Y. Murray and Masaaki Kotabe, "Sourcing Strategies of U.S. Service Companies: A Modified Transaction-Cost Analysis," *Strategic Management Journal*, 20 (September 1999), pp. 791–809.

tive advantages of various sourcing locations for long-term gains.

Trade and foreign production managed by multinational companies are very complex. In growing global competition, sourcing of components and finished products around the world within the multinational company has increased. The development of global sourcing and marketing strategies across different foreign markets has become a central issue for many multinational companies. Traditionally, a polycentric approach to organizing operations on a country-by-country basis allowed each country manager to tailor marketing strategy to the peculiarities of local markets. As such, product adaptations were considered a necessary strategy to better cater to the different needs and wants of customers in various countries. Product adaptation tends to be a reactive, rather than a proactive, strategic response to the market. A high level of product adaptation may make it difficult for multinational companies to reap economies of scale in production and marketing and to coordinate their networks of activities on a global scale.

Global sourcing strategy requires close coordination of R & D, manufacturing, and marketing activities on a global basis. Managing geographically separated R & D, manufacturing, and marketing activities, those companies face difficult coordination problems of integrating their operations and adapting them to different legal, political, and cultural environments in different countries. Furthermore, separation of manufacturing activities involves an inherent risk that manufacturing in the value chain will gradually become neglected. Such a neglect can be costly, as continued involvement in manufacturing leads to pioneering product design and innovation over time. An effective global sourcing strategy calls for continual efforts to streamline manufacturing without sacrificing marketing flexibility. To accomplish this, a conscious effort to develop either core components in house or develop product design families or universal products is called for.

A caveat should be also noted. Although a company's ability to develop core components and products and to market them in the world markets on its own is preferred, the enormousness of such a task should be examined in light of rapid changes in both technology and customer needs around the world. Those changes make the product life cycle extremely short, sometimes too short for many multinational companies to pursue product development, manufacturing, and marketing on a global basis without strategic alliance partners. Benefits of maintaining an independent proprietary position should always be weighed against the time cost of delayed market entry.

Although most of our knowledge about sourcing strategy comes from manufacturing industries, a similar logic applies to sourcing of service activities. As a result of the explosive growth of the Internet and e-commerce, supplementary service activities—a type of services that help improve the delivery of the company's core businesses—are increasingly outsourced from independent suppliers around the world.

KEY TERMS ✦

comparative advantage	domestic purchase	intra-firm sourcing	supplementary services
competitive advantage	arrangement	offshore subsidiary	value chain concept
core services	functional interfaces	sourcing	
domestic in-house	global sourcing strategy	outsourcing	
sourcing	hollow corporation	strategic alliance	

REVIEW QUESTIONS ✦ ✦ ✦ ✦ ✦ ✦ ✦ ✦ ✦ ✦ ✦ ✦ ✦ ✦ ✦ ✦ ✦ ✦ ✦

1. Discuss the reasons why trade statistics do not capture the intricacies of global sourcing.

2. Discuss the trends in global sourcing strategy. Why is it necessary for companies to keep up with those trends?

3. Why was manufacturing ignored by U.S. multinational companies in the 1980s?

4. Discuss the relationships between paper entrepreneurship and hollow corporations.

5. How do multinational companies exploit the value chain on a global basis?

6. What are inherent difficulties in coordinating (a) R & D/manufacturing, (b) manufacturing/marketing, and (c) marketing/R & D interfaces?

7. What are strategic motivations for standardizing either components or products or both?

8. Under what conditions can a company develop its global sourcing strategy without an alliance partner?

DISCUSSION QUESTIONS

1. Sirena Apparel Group Inc. is a manufacturer and distributor of men's and women's clothing. Recently, it decided to establish its own manufacturing facility in San Luis Rio Colorado, Mexico. The reason was the intense cost pressures that it faced from foreign imports. The establishing of this manufacturing facility in Mexico would, according to the company, give it a competitive edge with other foreign manufacturers. Sirena is not an isolated example. It is just one of the many companies that have been establishing manufacturing facilities across the border. Would you consider the move by the company as one step toward the hollowing out of the company? Why or why not? Hewlett-Packard is one of the many personal manufacturers that has established its own manufacturing facilities abroad, especially in Southeast Asia. Are these companies being hollowed out?

2. According to Nobuhiko Kawamoto, the president of Honda Motor Company, its global sourcing strategy can help the company considerably in its new emphasis on the Japanese market. Until recently, Honda has been one of the star performers among foreign automobile manufacturers in the United States. However, its position in the domestic Japanese market has been less formidable. It continues to hold a less impressive fifth position in sales of automobiles in Japan. As part of its strategy, Honda Motor Company plans to introduce more than fifteen new models of cars in a short span of time. The high costs involved would in part be met by "skimming" more models off fewer platforms and with fewer parts. Lower costs due to more efficient sourcing of components and subassemblies are expected to reduce manufacturing costs to counter some of the high costs involved with the strategy. Skeptics point out that overemphasis on common platforms may lead to coming out with products that might not be well received by the domestic customers, who are known to be extremely discerning and are becoming more style conscious. Would you agree with the view of the skeptics?

3. There has been considerable emphasis on the declining productivity of U.S. manufacturing firms since the early 1980s when Japanese and Korean manufacturers made their presence felt in the United States. An argument could be made that this emphasis on manufacturing activity may be slightly misplaced, especially given the fact that today only 25 percent of the GNP of the United States comes from manufacturing activities, while nearly 70 percent of the GNP is attributable to service activities. Do you agree with this argument? Why or why not?

4. The integration–adaptiveness dichotomy has long plagued international marketers as two opposing forces in the formulation of international strategies. The pressures for integrated strategies include the importance of multinational customers and competitors, high investment intensity, high technology intensity, pressure for reducing costs, universal customer needs, and access to raw materials and energy. The pressures of adaptiveness include differences in customer needs, differences in markets structure, differences in distribution channels, availability of substitutes and need to adapt, and host government demands. What are the implications of these opposing pressures on the sourcing strategy chosen by the firm? Describe two industries in which a global and integrated sourcing strategy would seem more appropriate. Describe two industries in which a local decentralized sourcing strategy may be more appropriate. Which sourcing strategy would be more appropriate for the microprocessor (semiconductor) industry?

5. An important impediment to the implementation of global sourcing strategies is the fluctuations in the foreign exchange rates. You are the executive assistant to the vice-president of the international operations of a multibillion-dollar and multinational manufacturer of earth-moving equipment. The company has manufacturing facilities in all three countries in North America, in seven countries in Europe, in three countries in South America, and in six countries in East and Southeast Asia. Approximately 50 percent of the components of each manufacturing facility come from one of the other manufacturing facilities (25 percent from within the same continent and 25 percent from a different continent). The vice-president would like you to suggest ways in which the risks of foreign exchange rate fluctuations can be reduced and yet the benefits of an integrated sourcing strategy can be derived. What are some of the suggestions that you would make?

FURTHER READING ◆

Fawcett, Stanley E., and Joseph I. Scully. "Worldwide Sourcing: Facilitating Continued Success," *Production and Inventory Management Journal*, 39 (First Quarter 1998): pp. 1–9.

Kotabe, Masaaki. *Global Sourcing Strategy: R & D, Manufacturing, and Marketing Interfaces*. New York: Quorum Books, 1992.

Laseter, Timothy M. *Balanced Sourcing: Cooperation and Competition in Supplier Relationships*. San Francisco: Jossey-Bass Publishers, 1998.

Lovelock, Christopher H., and George S. Yip. "Developing Global Strategies for Service Business," *California Management Review*, 38 (2) (1996): 64–86.

Murray, Janet Y., Masaaki Kotabe, and Albert R. Wildt. "Strategic and Financial Performance Implications of Global Sourcing Strategy: A Contingency Analysis." *Journal of International Business Studies*, 26 (First Quarter 1995): 181–202.

Quinn, James Brian. "Strategic Outsourcing: Leveraging Knowledge Capabilities." *Sloan Management Review*, 40 (Summer 1999): 9–21.

Samli, A. Coskin, John M. Browning, and Carolyn Busbia. "The Status of Global Sourcing as a Critical Tool of Strategic Planning: Opportunistic versus Strategic Dichotomy." *Journal of Business Research*, 43 (November 1998): 177–87.

Zou, Shaoming, and Matthew B. Myers. "The R & D, Manufacturing and Marketing Competencies and the Firm's Global Marketing Position: An Empirical Study." *Journal of Global Marketing*, 12 (3) (1999): 5–21.

GLOBAL PRODUCT POLICY DECISIONS I: DEVELOPING NEW PRODUCTS FOR GLOBAL MARKETS

11

A cornerstone of a global marketing mix program is the set of product policy decisions that multinational companies (MNCs) constantly need to formulate. The range of product policy questions that need to be tackled is mindboggling: What new products should be developed for what markets? What products should be added, removed, or modified for the product line in each of the countries in which the company operates? What brand names should be used? How should the product be packaged and serviced? Clearly, product managers in charge of the product line of a multinational company have their work cut out for them.

Improper product policy decisions are easily made, as the following anecdotes illustrate:

- *Ikea in the United States*. Ikea, the Swedish furniture chain, insists that all its stores carry the basic product line with little room for adaptation to local tastes. In the United States, Ikea was initially puzzled by the reluctance of customers to buy its beds and bed linen. Eventually, the firm uncovered that Americans liked bigger beds than Swedes. Ikea remedied the situation by ordering larger beds and sheets from its suppliers.[1]

---

[1] "Struggle to save the soul of Ikea," *Financial Times* (March 27, 1995), p. 12.

- *Procter & Gamble in Australia.* Rather than manufacturing disposable diapers locally in Australia, as does Kimberly-Clark, P & G decided to import them. The size of the Australian and New Zealand markets did not warrant local manufacturing according to P & G. Unfortunately, by using packaging designed for the Asian region with non-English labeling, P & G alienated its customers in Australia.[2]

- *U.S. car makers in Japan.* Historically, U.S. car sales in Japan have been pretty dismal. Analysts have blamed import barriers and the fact that most U.S.-made cars were originally sold with the steering wheel on the lefthand side. There are other factors at play, though. Sales of Chrysler's Neon car during the first year of introduction in Japan were far below target. Japanese car buyers disliked the Neon's rounded curves; they preferred boxier designs. The sales of Ford's Taurus in Japan were also lackluster. Part of the problem was that, initially, the Taurus did not fit in Japanese parking spaces. In order for a car to be registered in Japan, the police need to certify that it will fit in the customer's parking lot (see also Global Perspective 11–1 on Saturn's marketing strategy in Japan).[3]

- *Ford in Brazil.* When Ford introduced the Pinto model in Brazil, it was unaware that *Pinto* stands for small male genitals in Brazilian slang. Sales of the Pinto, not surprisingly, were pretty dismal. Once Ford figured out why sales for the Pinto model were so low, it renamed the model Corcel, meaning horse.[4]

These anecdotes amply show that even seasoned blue-chip companies commit the occasional blunder when making product decisions in the global marketplace. Product blunder stories, aside of being entertaining (at least for outsiders), sometimes teach valuable lessons. (See Global Perspective 11–1.) This chapter focuses on new product development strategies for global markets. The first part of this chapter looks at the product strategic issues that MNCs face. The second part gives an overview of the new product development (NPD) process in a global setting. Finally, we examine some of the cross-cultural challenges in running global NPD projects.

GLOBAL PRODUCT STRATEGIES   ◆ ◆ ◆ ◆ ◆ ◆

Companies can pursue three global strategies to penetrate foreign markets.[5] Some firms will simply adopt the same product or communication policy used in their home market. They **extend** their homegrown product/communication strategies to their foreign markets. Other companies prefer to adapt their strategy to the local marketplace. This strategy of **adaptation** enables the firm to cater to the needs and

---

[2]"P&G Puts Nappies to Rest in Australia," *Advertising Age International* (September 19, 1994), p. I-31.

[3]"Success Continues to Elude U.S. Car Makers in Japan," *The Asian Wall Street Journal* (January 10–11, 1997), pp. 1, 7.

[4]Jack Mingo, *How the Cadillac Got Its Fins* (New York: Harper Business, 1994).

[5]Warren J. Keegan, "Multinational Product Planning: Strategic Alternatives," *Journal of Marketing*, 33 (January 1969), 58–62.

GLOBAL PERSPECTIVE 11–1

SELLING SATURNS IN JAPAN

Saturn, a unit of General Motors Corp., has been phenomenally popular in the United States with its refreshing approach to selling cars. The car's popularity in the U.S. market is due to its unique formula of customer-friendly retailing and no-haggle pricing. In light of its success story in the United States, G.M. figured that Saturn might also do well in fiercely competitive Japan. The car premiered in Japan in April 1997. Saturn's launch strategy in Japan was to take on the local competition by competing as an everyday car. It installed right-hand drive steering and added features such as folding side mirrors. Saturn also established its own dealer network—a rather unusual move for car imports. Saturn's goal was to sign up twenty exclusive dealers who would only sell Saturns. It took the firm longer than expected to achieve its target. The car was priced at $14,000—competitive with local brands and cheaper than most other imports. Saturn also invested heavily in advertising to build brand recognition. Ads showed scenes of Saturn's headquarters in Tennessee and Japanese salespeople sporting Saturn's casual look.

Despite all the enthusiasm and G.M.'s gung ho attitude, sales have been disappointing so far. In 1998, Saturn sold just 1,400 vehicles. Several factors seemed to be behind this setback. One was bad timing. When Saturn was introduced in Japan, the country was going through a deep economic slump. The launch date happened a few days after the government hiked the sales tax to 5 percent (from 3 percent), a move that weakened the car market overall. Sales of sedans—the only subcategory in which Saturn initially competed—were plunging around the launch time. Some analysts also felt that the Saturn strategy would not appeal to import-car buyers in Japan. The typical foreign-car buyer wants a car that makes him stand out of the crowd. Successful imports from the United States are quintessentially "American" cars like DaimlerChrysler's Jeep Cherokee and G.M.'s Cadillac Seville. Setting up an own dealership network posed some challenges, too. The economic recession meant that few potential dealers were willing to take the risk of selling a relatively unknown car model. Those who were interested had a hard time raising the money. With only twenty dealerships, potential customers may also have had a hard time locating a dealer outlet.

Sales picked up a bit in 1999 with the launch of a three-door coupé model. In October 1998, Saturn announced plans to open eighty new stores over the coming five years. Saturn also set up an Internet showroom (www.saturn.co.jp) to better serve the needs of Internet savvy car shoppers. Whether Saturn's uphill struggle in Japan will ultimately pay off remains to be seen. Still, Saturn seems to have had some impact on the Japanese car market: Toyota adopted Saturn's no-haggle approach toward pricing at some of its dealerships in Japan.

Sources: "Saturn Signs 6 Firms to Sell Cars in Japan," *The Asian Wall Street Journal* (July 9, 1996), p. 6; "In Japan, Saturn Finds the Going Has Been Slow," *The Asian Wall Street Journal* (August 26, 1998), p. 1, 7; "Saturn in Japan Slows to Crawl," *Advertising Age International* (January 1998), p. 26; "Despite Problems in Japan, GM's Saturn Not Giving Up," *Dow Jones Business News* (April 14, 1999).

---

wants of its foreign customers. A third alternative is to adopt an **invention** strategy, where products are designed from scratch for the global marketplace. These three basic strategies can be further finessed into five strategic options, as shown in Exhibit 11–1. Let us look at each one of these options in greater detail.

Strategic Option 1: Product and Communication Extension— Dual Extension

At one extreme, a company might choose to market a standardized product using a uniform communications strategy. Early entrants in the global arena will often opt for this approach. Also, small companies with few resources typically prefer this option. For them, the potential payoffs of customized products and/or advertising campaigns usually do not justify the incremental costs of adaptation. Dual extension might also work when the company targets a "global" segment with

EXHIBIT 11–1
GLOBAL EXPANSION STRATEGIES

Strategy	Product function or need satisfied	Conditions of product use	Ability to buy product	Recommended product strategy	Recommended communications strategy	Rank order from least to most expensive	Product examples
1	Same	Same	Yes	Extension	Extension	1	Soft drinks
2	Different	Same	Yes	Extension	Adaptation	2	Bicycles, motor-scooters
3	Same	Different	Yes	Adaptation	Extension	3	Gasoline, deter-gents,
4	Different	Different	Yes	Adaptation	Adaptation	4	Clothing, greeting cards
5	Same	—	No	Invention communica-tions	Develop new	5	Hand-powered washing machines

Source: From Warren J. Keegan, "Multinational Product Planning: Strategic Alternatives." Reprinted from *Journal of Marketing,* 33 (January 1969) pp. 58–62, published by the American Marketing Association.

similar needs. Blistex's marketing efforts for its namesake product in Europe is a typical example. The product, a lip balm, offers identical needs in each of the various European markets. Except for some minor modifications (e.g., labeling), the same product is sold in each country. Starting in 1995, Blistex ran a uniform European advertising campaign, using identical positioning ("Care-to-Cure") and advertising themes across countries.[6] In Asia, Kao, the Japanese P & G, launched a shampoo brand called Lavenus with the same formulation, packaging, and basic advertising message—change your hairstyle to the trendiest of the moment, whatever that may be.[7]

Generally speaking, a standardized product policy coupled with a uniform communication strategy offers substantial savings coming from economies of scale. This strategy is basically product-driven rather than market-driven. The downside is that it is likely to alienate foreign customers, who might switch to a local or another foreign competing brand that is more in tune with their needs. In many industries, modern production processes such as CAD/CAM[8] manufacturing technologies obviate the need for large production batch sizes.

---

[6]Mark Boersma, Supervisor International Operations, Blistex, Inc., Personal Communication.
[7]"Kao Makes Adjustments To Meet Local Tastes, Based on Product Type," *The Asian Wall Street Journal* (April 8, 1999), p. 14.
[8]Computer-Aided-Design/Computer-Aided-Manufacturing.

Strategic Option 2: Product Extension — Communications Adaptation

Due to differences in the cultural or competitive environment, the same product often is used to offer benefits or functions that dramatically differ from those in the home market. Such gaps between the foreign and home market drive companies to market the same product using customized advertising campaigns. Although it retains the scale economies on the manufacturing side, the firm sacrifices potential savings on the advertising front. Wrigley, the Chicago-based chewing gum company, is a typical practitioner of this approach. Most of the brands marketed in the United States are also sold in Wrigley's overseas markets. Wrigley strives for a uniformly superior quality product. To build up the chewing gum category, Wrigley sells its products at a stable and low price. Given that chewing gum is an impulse item,[9] Wrigley aims for mass distribution. The company sees an opportunity to sell its product at any place where money changes hands. Despite these similarities in Wrigley's product and distribution strategies, there are wide differences in its communication strategy. The benefits that are promoted in Wrigley's advertising campaigns vary from country to country. In the United States, Wrigley has capitalized on smoking regulations by promoting chewing gum as a substitute for smoking. In several European countries, Wrigley's advertising pitches the dental benefits of chewing gum. In the Far East, Wrigley promotes the benefit of facial fitness in its advertising campaigns.[10]

Strategic Option 3: Product Adaptation — Communications Extension

Alternatively, firms might adapt their product but market it using a standardized communications strategy. Local market circumstances often favor the case of product adaptation. Another source behind product adaptation is the company's expansion strategy. Many companies add brands to their product portfolio via acquisitions of local companies. To leverage the existing brand equity enjoyed by the acquired brand, the local brand is usually retained. Although these factors lead to product adaptation, similar core values and buying behaviors among consumers using the product might present an opening for a harmonized communications strategy. Within such a context, clever marketing ideas can be transferred from one country to another country, despite the product-related differences. For instance, a Taiwan-produced commercial for P & G's Pantene shampoo was successfully transferred with a few minor changes to Latin America. Likewise, an ad campaign developed in Mexico for Vicks Vaporub was used throughout Latin America.[11]

Strategic Option 4: Product and Communications Adaptation — Dual Adaptation

Differences in *both* the cultural and physical environments across countries call for a dual adaptation strategy. Under such circumstances, adaptation of the company's product and communication strategy is the most viable option for international expansion.

Slim-Fast adapts both product and advertising to comply with varying government regulations for weight-loss products. When Slim-Fast was first launched in Germany, its ads used a local celebrity. In Great Britain, testimonials for diet aids

---

[9]Impulse goods are products that are bought without any planning.

[10]Doug Barrie, Group Vice-President International, Wrigley Cy., Personal Communication.

[11]"P&G Sees Success in Policy of Transplanting Ad Ideas," *Advertising Age International* (July 19, 1993), p. I-2.

are not allowed to feature celebrities. Instead, the British introduction campaign centered around teachers, an opera singer, a disk jockey, and others. Also, the product gets adapted to the local markets. In the United Kingdom, banana is the most popular flavor, but this flavor is not sold in continental Europe.[12]

Genuinely global marketers try to figure out how to create products with a global scope rather than just for a single country. Instead of simply adapting existing products or services to the local market conditions, their mind-set is to zero in on global market opportunities. Black & Decker is a good example of a company that adopts the **product invention** approach to global market expansion. Black & Decker aims to bring out new products that cater to common needs and opportunities around the world. To manage its global product development process, Black & Decker set up a Worldwide Household Board. This steering committee approves global plans, allocates resources, and gives direction and support, among other tasks. One of the product innovations flowing from this global product planning approach is the SnakeLight Flexible Flashlight. The SnakeLight was first launched in North America, and then, six months later, in Europe, Latin America, and Australia. The product addresses a global need for portable lighting. The SnakeLight proved to be major hit around the world.[13]

> **Strategic Option 5: Product Invention**

Other companies increasingly adhere to the invention strategy. In the past, Procter & Gamble Europe was a patchwork of country-based operations, each with its own business. These days, P & G aims to develop products that appeal to the entire European region. Many other companies also recently jumped on the "produce globally, market locally" bandwagon. Not all of these efforts have been successful, though. The Ford Mondeo was part of the Ford 2000 project to put Ford's product development projects on a global basis. The car was among Ford's first efforts toward a world-car strategy. Developed in Europe, the car was sold in the United States as the Contour and Mercury Mystique sedan. Although the European version sold pretty well, the American versions were major fiascos.[14] American car buyers considered the models too small and too expensive, given their size.[15]

STANDARDIZATION VERSUS CUSTOMIZATION ◆ ◆ ◆ ◆ ◆ ◆

A recurrent theme in global marketing is whether companies should aim for a standardized or country-tailored product strategy. **Standardization** means offering a uniform product on a regional or worldwide basis. Minor alternations are usually made to meet local regulations or market conditions (for instance, voltage adjustments for electrical appliances). However, by and large, these changes only lead to minor cost increases. A uniform product policy capitalizes on the commonalities in customers' needs across countries. The goal is to minimize costs. These cost savings

---

[12]"Slim-Fast Beefs Up in Europe," *Advertising Age International* (May 17, 1993), p. I-4.

[13]Don R. Garber, "How to Manage a Global Product Development Process," *Industrial Marketing Management*, 25 (1996), pp. 483–89.

[14]"The Revolution at Ford," *The Economist* (August 7, 1999), pp. 55–56.

[15]"The World Car Wears New Faces," *The New York Times* (April 10, 1998), p. 1.

Due to competitive pressure, Coca-Cola's product assortment in Japan is unusually large.

can then be passed through to the company's customers via low prices. With **customization**, on the other hand, management focuses on cross-border differences in the needs and wants of the firm's target customers. Under this regime, appropriate changes are made to match local market conditions. While standardization has a product-driven orientation—lower your costs via mass production—customization is inspired by a market-driven mind-set—increase customer satisfaction by adapting your products to local needs.

Five forces favor a globalized product strategy:

1. Common customer needs
2. Global customers
3. Scale economies
4. Time to market
5. Regional market agreements

Common Customer Needs

For many product categories, consumer needs are very similar in different countries. The functions for which the product is used might be identical. Likewise, the usage conditions or the benefits sought might be similar. An example of a product that targets a global segment is Pepsi Max, a sugar-free cola that Pepsi rolled out in 1993. Pepsi Max is a one-calorie soda with the "mouth-feel" of a regular cola. The product caters toward consumers who shunned traditional diet drinks because of taste.[16] Many product categories also show a gradual but steady convergence in consumer preferences. Exhibit 11–2 portrays changes over time in worldwide alcohol consumption patterns. There is apparently a shift in the consumption mix toward one focal point: 20 percent spirits/40 percent wine/40 percent beer. Growing similarities in consumer preferences have also been observed in the car industry.[17] In the Triad markets (Japan,

---

[16]"Double Entendre: The Life and the Life of Pepsi Max," *Brandweek* (April 18, 1994), p. 40.

[17]Takashi Hisatomi, "Global Marketing by the Nissan Motor Company Limited—A Simultaneous Market Study of Users' Opinions and Attitudes in Europe, USA and Japan," *Marketing and Research Today* (February 1991), pp. 56–61.

EXHIBIT 11-2
CONVERGENCE IN DRINKING PATTERNS

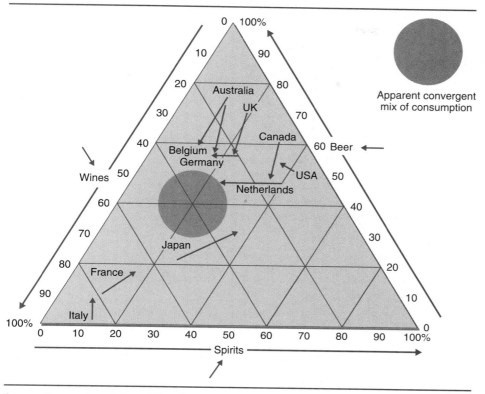

Source: Brewers Association of Canada.

Europe, and the United States) the preferred car size in terms of length-by-width has shifted toward a space of 7 to 9 square meters. The size of cars in Europe has not changed much during the last two decades. In the United States fuel conversation efforts following the 1973 oil crisis spurred a move to more compact cars during the 1970s and 1980s. On the other hand, Japan witnessed an increase in the demand of large cars driven by changes in the tax regime and consumer preferences. People's expectations from a car in the Triad markets are also becoming increasingly alike. Marketing research done by Nissan showed that car buyers in all three Triad markets rank self-expression, pleasantness of operation, and comfort among their top values. Obviously, the importance of such similarities should not be exaggerated. Despite a convergence of consumer needs in some regards, cultural differences persist and should not be overlooked. A multi-country market research project carried out for BMW underscores the importance of market peculiarities.[18] European motorists have a common desire for reliability, safety, quality, and advanced technology. These are the basic criteria that any decent car should meet. However, once you go beyond these basic requirements, there is a set of other requirements that differ from country to

---

[18]Horst Kern, Hans-Christian Wagner and Roswitha Hassis, "European Aspects of a Global Brand: The BMW Case," *Marketing and Research Today* (February 1990), pp. 47–57.

EXHIBIT 11–3
DIFFERENCES IN CAR REQUIREMENTS FOR VARIOUS
EUROPEAN COUNTRIES

Country	Requirements
Netherlands	• Understatement • High reputation of brand
France	• Self-confident posture • Good road-holding ability
Switzerland	• Demanding but discreet
Austria	• Prestige thinking • Car for presenting oneself to the outside world
Italy	• In accordance with personal style • Dynamic driving • Road holding

Source: Horst Kern, Hans-Christian Wagner and Roswitha Hassis, "European Aspects of a Global Brand: The BMW Case," *Marketing and Research Today*, February 1990, p. 53.

Permission for using this material which was originally published in *Marketing and Research Today* has been granted by (E.S.O.M.A.R.) The European Society for Opinion and Marketing Research J.J. Viottastraat 29, 1071 JP, Amsterdam, The Netherlands.

country (see Exhibit 11–3). In Austria prestige is key: a car is expected to reflect "who" the owner is. Italian car drivers, on the other hand, attach importance to dynamic driving performance, design, and aesthetic qualities.

Global Customers

In business-to-business marketing, the shift toward globalization means that for many companies a significant part of their business comes from MNCs that are essentially global customers. Buying and sourcing decisions are commonly centralized, or at the least regionalized. As a result, such customers typically require services or products that are harmonized worldwide.

Scale Economies

Scale economies in the manufacturing and distribution of globalized products is in most cases the key driver behind standardization moves. Savings are also often realized because of sourcing efficiencies or lowered R & D expenditures. These savings can be passed through to the company's end-customers via lower prices. Scale economies offer global competitors a tremendous competitive advantage over local or regional competitors. In many industries though, the "economies of scale" rationale has lost some of its allure. Production procedures such as flexible manufacturing and just-in-time production have shifted the focus from size to timeliness. CAD/CAM techniques allow companies to manufacture customized products in small batch sizes at reduced cost. Although size often leads to lower unit costs, the diseconomies of scale should not be overlooked. Hidden costs associated with size can often be ascribed to bureaucratic bloat and shop-floor alienation.[19]

---

[19]"Big is Back: A Survey of Multinationals," *The Economist* (June 24, 1995), p. 4.

In scores of industries being innovative is not enough to be competitive. Companies must also seek ways to shorten the time to bring new product projects to the market. By centralizing research and consolidating new product development efforts on fewer projects, companies are often able to reduce the time-to-market cycle. Procter & Gamble notes that a recent Pan-European launch of liquid laundry detergents could be done in 10 percent of the time it took in the early 1980s, when marketing efforts were still very decentralized.[20]

Time to Market

The formation of regional market agreements such as the Single European Market encourages companies to launch regional (e.g., Pan-European) products or redesign existing products as pan-regional brands. The legislation leading to the creation of the Single European Market in January 1993 aimed to remove most barriers to trade within the European Union. It also provided for the harmonization of technical standards in many industries. These moves favor Pan-European product strategies. Mars, for instance, now regards Europe as one giant market. It modified the brand names for several of its products, turning them into Pan-European brands. Marathon in the United Kingdom became Snickers, the name used in Continental Europe. The Raider bar in Continental Europe was renamed Twix, the name used in the United Kingdom.[21]

Regional Market Agreements

Whether firms should strive for standardized or localized products is a bogus question. The issue should not be phrased as an either-or dilemma. Instead, product managers should look at it in terms of degree of globalization: What elements of my product policy should be tailored to the local market conditions? Which ones can I leave unchanged? At the same time, there are strategic options that allow firms to modify their product while keeping most of the benefits flowing from a uniform product policy. Two of these product design policies are the **modular** and the **core-product** approach.[22]

Degree of Standardization

Modular Approach. The first approach consists of developing a range of product parts that can be used worldwide. The parts can be assembled into numerous product configurations. Scale economies flow from the mass-production of more-or-less standard product components at a few sites. This approach has become very popular in the automotive industry. Ford, for instance, aspires to develop cars from the same kits of parts, thereby spreading its product development costs over a broad range of car brands, each with its distinct consumer appeal.[23]

Core-Product (Platform) Approach. As discussed in Chapter 10, the core-product (platform) approach starts with the design of a mostly uniform core-product or platform. Attachments are added to the core product to match local market needs. Savings are achieved by reduced production and purchasing costs.

---

[20]Procter & Gamble, *Annual Report* (1993).

[21]Dale Littler and Katrin Schlieper, "The Development of the Eurobrand," *International Marketing Review*, 12 (2) (1995), pp. 22–37.

[22]Peter G. P. Walters and Brian Toyne, "Product Modification and Standardization in International Markets: Strategic Options and Facilitating Policies," *Columbia Journal of World Business*, 24 (Winter 1989), pp. 37–44.

[23]"The Revolution at Ford," *The Economist* (August 7, 1999), pp. 55–56.

❖ ❖

𝒢LOBAL PERSPECTIVE 11–2

TWO ILLUSTRATIONS OF THE PLATFORM APPROACH WITH GLOBAL PRODUCT DESIGN

DEERE

Deere is one of the world's biggest manufacturers of farm machinery. Deere's tractors worldwide are based on six "families": platforms, on which different elements (e.g., engines, gear boxes) can be fitted to suit needs in local markets. With that system, Deere can easily swap design ideas. For instance, some tractors made in Mannheim, Deere's European tractor plant, use a new gear box designed in the United States. Likewise, some of the tractors made in the U.S. plant contain a new axle suspension concept developed in the European site. The platform system allows Deere to meet customers' expectations worldwide while at the same time minimizing costs.

Sources: "Difficult Furrow to Plough," *Financial Times* (March 9, 1999), p. 12; "Electrolux Sees Future in Fewer, Stronger Brands," *Financial Times* (February 20, 1999), p. 23.

ELECTROLUX

Electrolux has become the world's largest household appliance maker—owning more than forty different brands such as Electrolux, Frigidaire, Kelvinator, AEG, Zanussi. In Europe alone, the firm sells 6,500 different types of ovens. In February 1999, the Stockholm-based company announced plans to streamline its brand portfolio and to rationalize its product design process. The company aspires to move its broad product portfolio of 15,000 different product variants toward common product platforms and fewer brands. This move would result in lower purchasing and manufacturing costs. Electrolux plans to have common platforms in refrigerators and ovens, with customers able to choose particular features in different markets. Whether Electrolux will succeed is to be seen. When Whirlpool, its global rival, introduced a world washing machine, consumer response was lukewarm.

At the same time, companies adopting this approach have the flexibility that allows them to modify the product easily. The model design procedures of the French car maker Renault exemplify this approach. More than 90 percent of Renault's sales revenues comes from the European market. The body, engines, transmissions, and chassis of a given model are the same in the different markets. Minor changes, such as stronger heaters in Nordic countries or better air conditioning for cars sold in Southern Europe, are easily implemented.[24] Global Perspective 11–2 describes how Deere and Electrolux use the core-product approach in designing their products.

The balancing act between standardization and adaptation is very tricky. One scholar[25] describes **overstandardization** as one of the five pitfalls that global marketers could run into. Too much standardization stifles initiative and experimentation at the local subsidiary level. However, one should not forget that there is also a risk of **overcustomization**. Part of the appeal of imported brands is often their *foreignness*. By adapting too much to the local market conditions, an import runs the risk of losing that cachet and simply becoming a me-too brand, barely differentiated from the local brands. Such a mistake was made by Carlsberg when it entered Thailand. Carlsberg tried to imitate Singha, the leading local brand. It raised the

---

[24]"Auto Marketers Gas Up for World Car Drive," *Advertising Age International* (January 16, 1995), p. I-16.

[25]Kamran Kashani, "Beware the Pitfalls of Global Marketing," *Harvard Business Review* (September–October 1989).

alcohol level to 6 percent for its flagship brand, thereby matching Singha's level. It launched a second brand, Chang, as a "local" beer. Prices were set at par with Singha. As a result, Thai beer drinkers had little reason to switch to Carlsberg's offerings. Dealers tried to get rid of their inventory by lowering the price, thereby cheapening Carlsberg's brand image.[26]

MULTINATIONAL DIFFUSION   ◆ ◆ ◆ ◆ ◆ ◆ ◆

The speed and pattern of market penetration for a given product innovation usually differs substantially between markets. It is not uncommon for new products that were phenomenally successful in one country or region to turn out to be flops in other markets. Dry beers rejuvenated the beer market in Japan during the late 1980s but never gained a foothold in the United States and Europe. Another example is dishwashers. Although dishwashers are quite common in U.S. homes, such appliances are not very popular in Asia (or Europe, for that matter). Most Chinese households, for example, see little benefit in buying a dishwasher. Attachment to traditional dishwashing techniques and Chinese cooking styles[27] are the major hurdles that hinder the development of the dishwasher market.[28] In this section we will introduce several concepts and insights from multinational new product diffusion research. These explain some of the differences in new product performance between different countries.

In general, the adoption of new products is driven by three types of factors: individual differences, personal influences, and product characteristics. Individuals differ in terms of their willingness to try out new products. Early adopters are eager to experiment with new ideas or products. Late adopters take a wait-and-see attitude. Early adopters differ from laggards in terms of socioeconomic traits (income, education, social status), personality, and communication behavior. A prominent role is also played by the influence of prior adopters. Word-of-mouth spread by previous adopters often has a much more significant impact on the adoption decision than nonpersonal factors such as media advertising. For many product categories, peer pressure will often determine whether (and when) a person will adopt the innovation. The third set of factors relates to the nature of the product itself. Five product characteristics are key:[29]

1. *Relative advantage.* To what extent does the new product offer more perceived value to potential adopters than existing alternatives?

2. *Compatibility.* Is the product consistent with existing values and attitudes of the individuals in the social system? Are there any switching costs that people might incur if they decide to adopt the innovation?

3. *Complexity.* Is the product easy to understand? Easy to use?

---

[26]"Foreigners Go Home," *Forbes* (October 9, 1995), p. 68.

[27]Chinese cooking uses a lot of oil, which is difficult to wash away with a dishwasher.

[28]"Dishwasher Companies Given Cold Shoulder," *China Daily* (July 25, 1999), p. 9.

[29]Thomas S. Robertson, *Innovative Behavior and Communication* (New York: Holt, Rinehart and Winston, 1971).

4. *Triability*. Are prospects able to try out the product on a limited basis?

5. *Observability*. How easy is it for possible adopters to observe the results or benefits of the innovation? Can these benefits easily be communicated?

Aside from these variables there are several country characteristics that can be used to predict new product penetration patterns. Communication leading to the transfer of ideas tends to be easier when it happens between individuals who have a similar cultural mind-set. Therefore, the adoption rate for new products in countries with a **homogeneous** population (e.g., Japan, South Korea, Thailand) is usually faster than in countries with a highly diverse culture. When a new product is launched at different time intervals, there will be **lead countries**, where it is introduced first, and **lag countries**, which are entered afterward. Generally, adoption rates seem to be higher in lag countries than in the lead country. Potential adopters in lag countries have had more time to understand and evaluate the innovation's perceived attributes than their counterparts in the lead country. Also, over time, the product's quality tends to improve and its price usually lowers due to scale economies.[30]

One research study that looked at the penetration patterns for consumer durables in Europe identified three more country characteristics that are relevant.[31] The first variable is **cosmopolitanism**. *Cosmopolitans* are people who look beyond their immediate social surroundings, while *locals* are oriented more toward their immediate social system. The more cosmopolitan the country's population, the higher the propensity to innovate. The second country trait is labeled **mobility**. Mobility is the ease with which members of a social system can move around and interact with other members. It is largely determined by the country's infrastructure. Mobility facilitates interpersonal communication, and, hence does have a positive impact on the product's penetration in a given market. Finally, the *percentage of women in the labor force* affects the spread of certain types of innovations. Higher participation of women means higher incomes and hence more spending power. Time-saving products (such as washing machines and dishwashers) appeal to working women. By the same token, time-consuming durables will be less valued in societies where working women form a substantial portion of the labor force.

Recent research has also identified a strong relationship between two of Hofstede's (see Chapter 4) cultural dimensions, individualism and uncertainty avoidance, and national innovativeness (see Exhibit 11–4).[32] Individualistic cultures value autonomy. They also tend to be more hedonistic and materialistic than group-oriented cultures. Empirical findings show a positive relationship between individualism and an index of national innovativeness, meaning: the more individualistic the nation's culture, the higher national innovativeness. Members from societies that score high on uncertainty avoidance are less inclined to take risks or experiment. Since new product adoption involves some degree of risk taking, one would expect lower rates of new product adoption in countries with high levels of

---

[30]Hirokazu Takada and Dipak Jain, "Cross-National Analysis of Diffusion of Consumer Durable Goods in Pacific Rim Countries," *Journal of Marketing*, 55 (2) (April 1991), pp. 48–54.

[31]Hubert Gatignon, Jehoshua Eliashberg and Thomas S. Robertson, "Modeling Multinational Diffusion Patterns: An Efficient Methodology," *Marketing Science*, 8 (3) (Summer 1989), pp. 231–47.

[32]Michael Lynn and Betsy D. Gelb, "Identifying Innovative National Markets for Technical Consumer Goods," *International Marketing Review*, 13 (6) (1996), pp. 43–57.

EXHIBIT 11–4

NATIONAL INNOVATIVENESS VS. INDIVIDUALISM

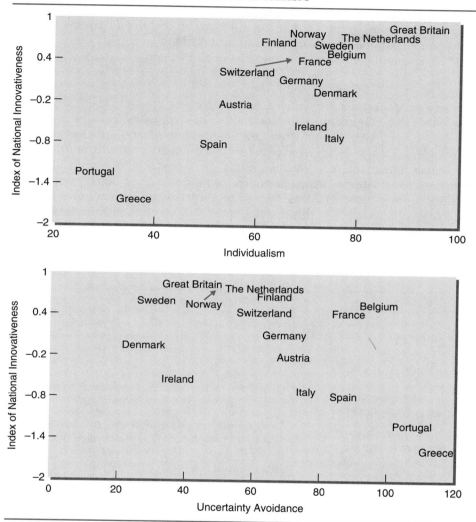

Source: Michael Lynn and Betsy D. Gelb, "Identifying Innovative National Markets for Technical Consumer Goods," *International Marketing Review*, 13 (6) 1996, pp. 43–57.

uncertainty avoidance. The data show indeed that there is a negative association between a country's innovativeness and uncertainty avoidance.

DEVELOPING NEW PRODUCTS FOR GLOBAL MARKETS   ◆ ◆ ◆ ◆ ◆ ◆

For most companies, new products are the bread and butter of their growth strategy. Unfortunately, developing new products is time consuming and costly, with immense challenges. The new product development process becomes a major headache for multinational organizations that try to coordinate the process on a regional or sometimes even worldwide basis. The steps to be followed in the global new product development (NPD) process are, by and large, similar to domestic marketing situations. In this section, we will focus on the unique aspects that take place when innovation efforts are implemented on a global scope. Global Perspective 11–3 describes the launch of a new fruit drink by Pepsi.

Identifying New Product Ideas

Every new product starts with an idea. Sources for new product ideas are manifold. Companies can tap into any of the so-called 4 Cs—*company*, *customers*, *competition*, and *collaborators* (e.g., distribution channels, suppliers)—for creative new product ideas. Obviously, many successful new products originally started at the R & D labs. Other internal sources include salespeople, employees, and market researchers. Multinational companies often capitalize on their global know-how by transplanting new product ideas that were successful in one country to other markets. A good example of this practice is the Dockers line of casual slacks. This product was introduced in Japan by Levi Strauss Japan in 1985. The line became

◆ ◆ ◆ ◆ ◆ ◆ ◆ ◆ ◆ ◆ ◆ ◆ ◆ ◆ ◆ ◆ ◆ ◆ ◆ ◆

$\mathcal{G}$LOBAL PERSPECTIVE 11–3

THE LAUNCH OF "FRUIT MAGIX"

WINDOW OF OPPORTUNITY:

- China has more than 300 million kids aged 4–12.
- Parents spend much more on kids than they used to (one-child policy; growth of buying power).
- Power of kids (spending power; pester power; change agents).
- No fruit drink brands targeted towards kids.

MARKETING GOAL:

- To develop a juice drink brand for the "Little Emperors" and "Empresses."

MARKET RESEARCH:

- A pack-price trade-off analysis amongst mothers to determine "optimal" price and packaging form.

Sources: Olivia Kan, Senior Executive, Pepsi-Cola International, and A. Bose and K. Khanna, "The Little Emperor. A Case Study of a New Brand Launch," *Marketing and Research Today* (November 1996), pp. 216–21.

- Quantitative taste tests amongst 300 children each in Guangzhou, Shanghai, and Beijing.
- Two rounds of focus groups in Shanghai and Guangzhou amongs boys and girls aged 7 to 10 years to identify relevant icon, key brand property, and most effective style/tone of communication.

NEW PRODUCT INTRODUCTION LAUNCH PLAN:

• Brand Name:	Fruit Magix
• Brand Device:	Fruitman
• Product Variants:	Orange, Strawberry/Grape, and Mango (10% juice)
• Package:	250 ml. Tetra Pak
• Price:	RMB 2.00 per pack (approx. US $0.25)
• Target Audience:	Primary—kids aged 6-12; Secondary—mothers
• Positioning:	"Fruit Magix is delicious and fun fruit drink for cool kids of today"

THE WORLD AT A GLANCE

CONTENTS

Maps from Goode's World Atlas used with permission,
© by Rand McNally, 2000

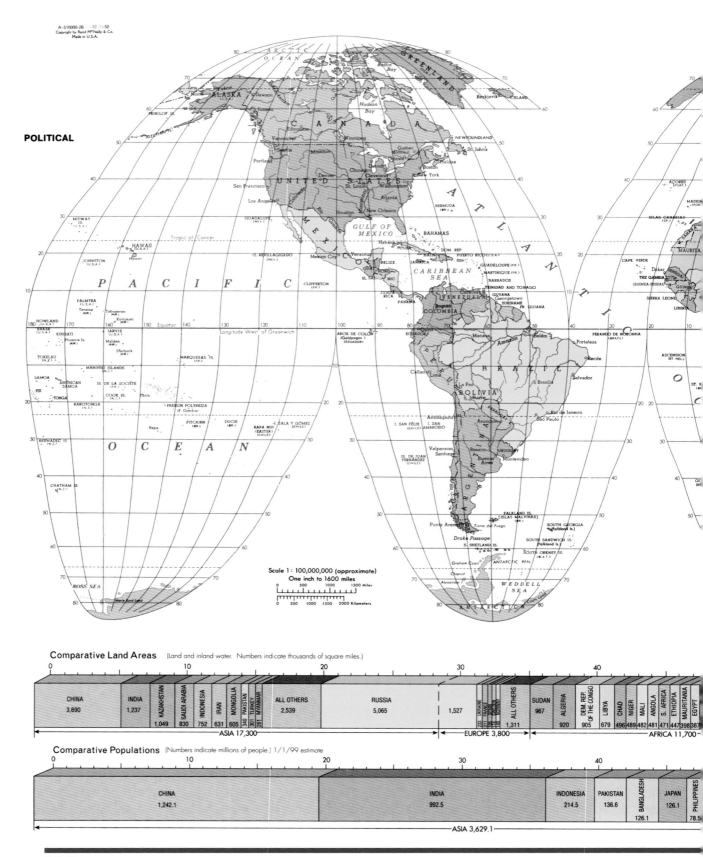

POLITICAL

ARCTIC OCEAN

Scale 1 : 100,000,000 (approximate)
One inch to 1600 miles

0   500   1000   1500 Miles

0   500   1000   1500   2000 Kilometers

Comparative Land Areas (Land and inland water. Numbers indicate thousands of square miles.)

0	10	20	30	40

| CHINA 3,690 | INDIA 1,237 | KAZAKHSTAN 1,049 | SAUDI ARABIA 830 | INDONESIA 752 | IRAN 631 | MONGOLIA 605 | PAKISTAN 340 | TURKEY 301 | MYANMAR 261 | ALL OTHERS 2,539 | RUSSIA 5,065 | 1,527 | ALL OTHERS 1,311 | SUDAN 967 | ALGERIA 920 | DEM. REP. OF THE CONGO 905 | LIBYA 679 | CHAD 496 | NIGER 489 | MALI 482 | ANGOLA 481 | S. AFRICA 471 | ETHIOPIA 447 | MAURITANIA 398 | EGYPT 387 |

ASIA 17,300 ◀——————————▶ EUROPE 3,800 ◀——▶ AFRICA 11,700

Comparative Populations (Numbers indicate millions of people.) 1/1/99 estimate

0	10	20	30	40

| CHINA 1,242.1 | INDIA 992.5 | INDONESIA 214.5 | PAKISTAN 136.6 | BANGLADESH 126.1 | JAPAN 126.1 | PHILIPPINES 78.5 |

ASIA 3,629.1

M-2

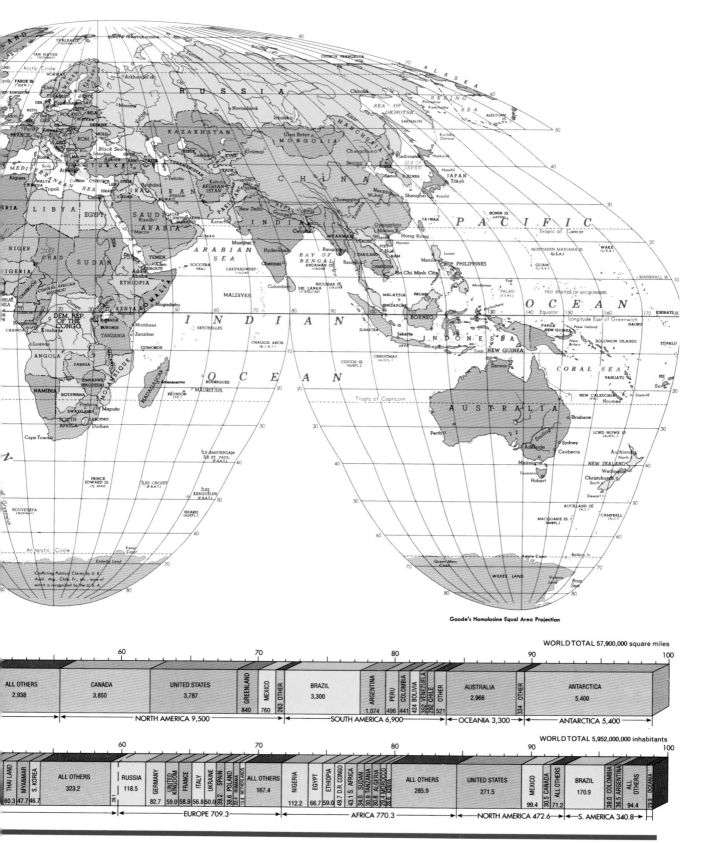

Goode's Homolosine Equal Area Projection

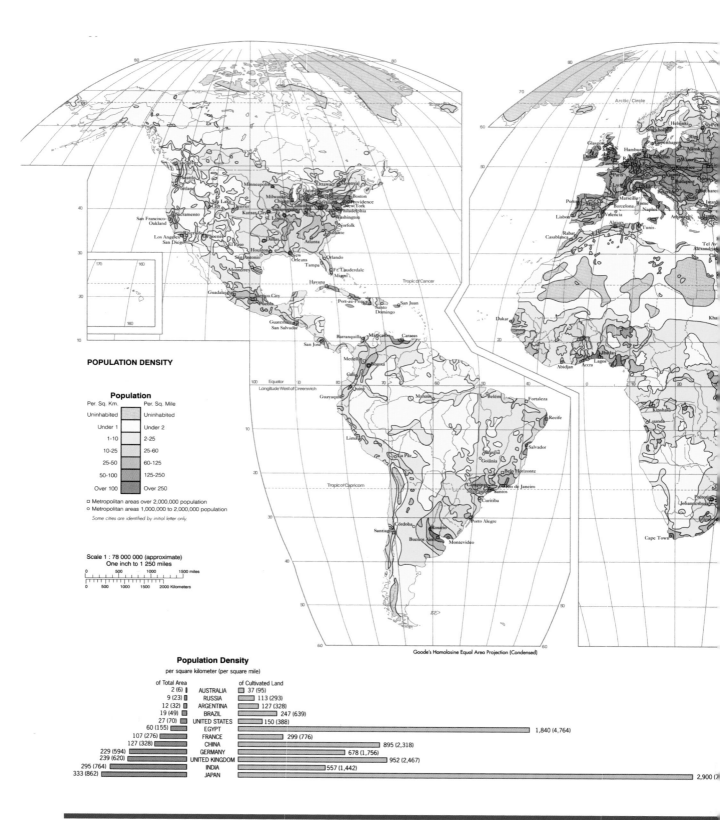

POPULATION DENSITY

Population

Per. Sq. Km.	Per. Sq. Mile
Uninhabited	Uninhabited
Under 1	Under 2
1-10	2-25
10-25	25-60
25-50	60-125
50-100	125-250
Over 100	Over 250

□ Metropolitan areas over 2,000,000 population
○ Metropolitan areas 1,000,000 to 2,000,000 population

Some cities are identified by initial letter only.

Scale 1 : 78 000 000 (approximate)
One inch to 1 250 miles

0   500   1000   1500 miles
0   500   1000   1500   2000 Kilometers

Goode's Homolosine Equal Area Projection (Condensed)

Population Density

per square kilometer (per square mile)

of Total Area		of Cultivated Land
2 (6)	AUSTRALIA	37 (95)
9 (23)	RUSSIA	113 (293)
12 (32)	ARGENTINA	127 (328)
19 (49)	BRAZIL	247 (639)
27 (70)	UNITED STATES	150 (388)
60 (155)	EGYPT	1,840 (4,764)
107 (276)	FRANCE	299 (776)
127 (328)	CHINA	895 (2,318)
229 (594)	GERMANY	678 (1,756)
239 (620)	UNITED KINGDOM	952 (2,467)
295 (764)	INDIA	557 (1,442)
333 (862)	JAPAN	2,900 (7...

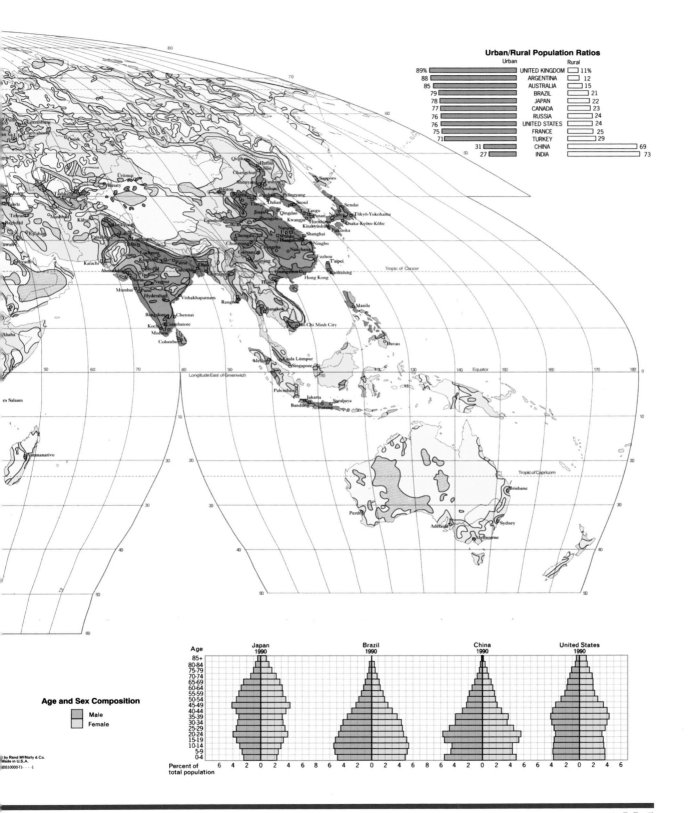

Urban/Rural Population Ratios

	Urban		Rural	
UNITED KINGDOM	89%		11%	
ARGENTINA	88		12	
AUSTRALIA	85		15	
BRAZIL	79		21	
JAPAN	78		22	
CANADA	77		23	
RUSSIA	76		24	
UNITED STATES	76		24	
FRANCE	75		25	
TURKEY	71		29	
CHINA	31		69	
INDIA	27		73	

Age and Sex Composition

Male
Female

Age and Sex Composition pyramids: Japan 1990, Brazil 1990, China 1990, United States 1990

Age: 85+, 80-84, 75-79, 70-74, 65-69, 60-64, 55-59, 50-54, 45-49, 40-44, 35-39, 30-34, 25-29, 20-24, 15-19, 10-14, 5-9, 0-4

Percent of total population

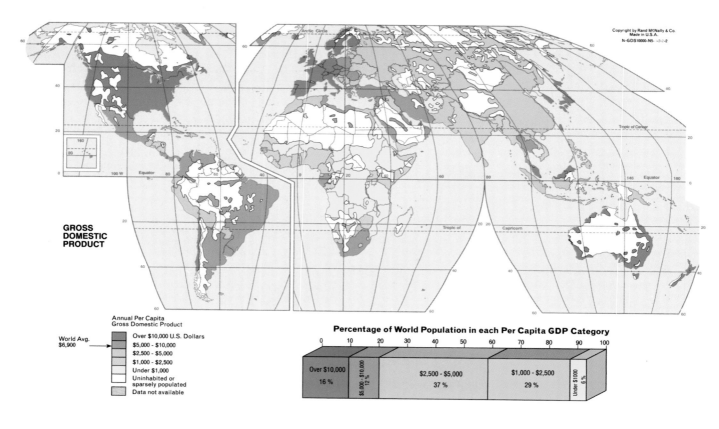

GROSS DOMESTIC PRODUCT

Annual Per Capita
Gross Domestic Product

World Avg.
$6,900

- Over $10,000 U.S. Dollars
- $5,000 - $10,000
- $2,500 - $5,000
- $1,000 - $2,500
- Under $1,000
- Uninhabited or sparsely populated
- Data not available

Percentage of World Population in each Per Capita GDP Category

Over $10,000	$5,000 - $10,000	$2,500 - $5,000	$1,000 - $2,500	Under $1000
16 %	12 %	37 %	29 %	6 %

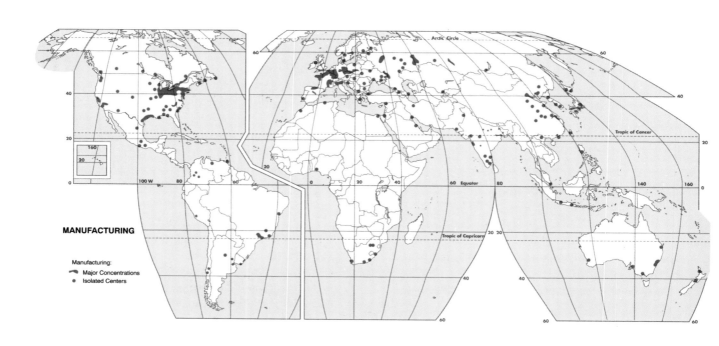

MANUFACTURING

Manufacturing:
- Major Concentrations
- Isolated Centers

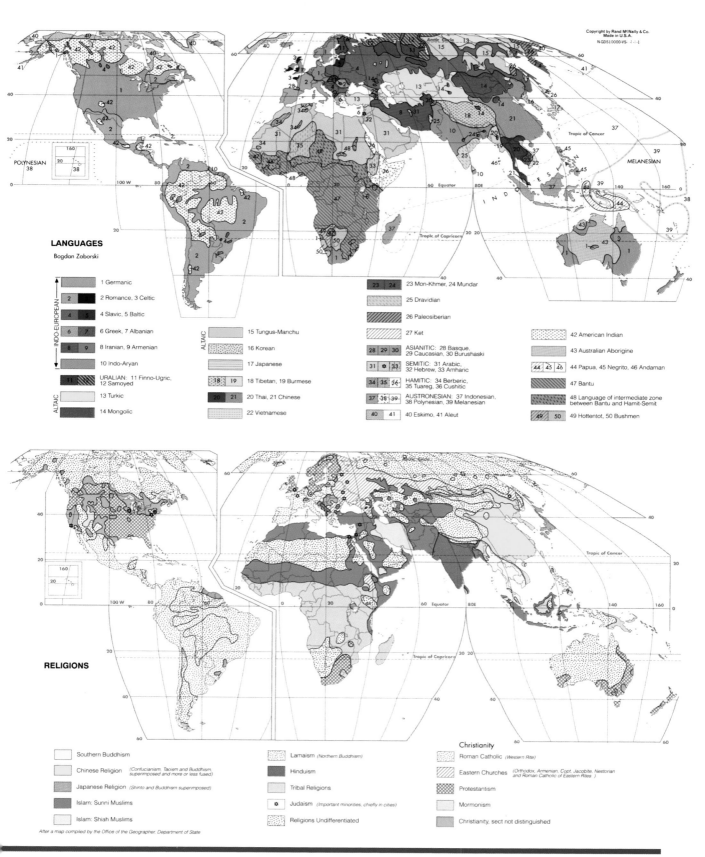

LANGUAGES

Bogdan Zaborski

INDO-EUROPEAN
- 1 Germanic
- 2 Romance, 3 Celtic
- 4 Slavic, 5 Baltic
- 6 Greek, 7 Albanian
- 8 Iranian, 9 Armenian
- 10 Indo-Aryan

URALIAN: 11 Finno-Ugric, 12 Samoyed

ALTAIC
- 13 Turkic
- 14 Mongolic
- 15 Tungus-Manchu
- 16 Korean
- 17 Japanese
- 18 Tibetan, 19 Burmese
- 20 Thai, 21 Chinese
- 22 Vietnamese

- 23 Mon-Khmer, 24 Mundar
- 25 Dravidian
- 26 Paleosiberian
- 27 Ket
- ASIANITIC: 28 Basque, 29 Caucasian, 30 Burushaski
- SEMITIC: 31 Arabic, 32 Hebrew, 33 Amharic
- HAMITIC: 34 Berberic, 35 Tuareg, 36 Cushitic
- AUSTRONESIAN: 37 Indonesian, 38 Polynesian, 39 Melanesian
- 40 Eskimo, 41 Aleut

- 42 American Indian
- 43 Australian Aborigine
- 44 Papua, 45 Negrito, 46 Andaman
- 47 Bantu
- 48 Language of intermediate zone between Bantu and Hamit-Semit
- 49 Hottentot, 50 Bushmen

POLYNESIAN 38
MELANESIAN

RELIGIONS

- Southern Buddhism
- Chinese Religion (Confucianism, Taoism and Buddhism, superimposed and more or less fused)
- Japanese Religion (Shinto and Buddhism superimposed)
- Islam: Sunni Muslims
- Islam: Shiah Muslims

- Lamaism (Northern Buddhism)
- Hinduism
- Tribal Religions
- ✿ Judaism (Important minorities, chiefly in cities)
- Religions Undifferentiated

Christianity
- Roman Catholic (Western Rite)
- Eastern Churches (Orthodox, Armenian, Copt, Jacobite, Nestorian and Roman Catholic of Eastern Rites.)
- Protestantism
- Mormonism
- Christianity, sect not distinguished

After a map compiled by the Office of the Geographer, Department of State

M-7

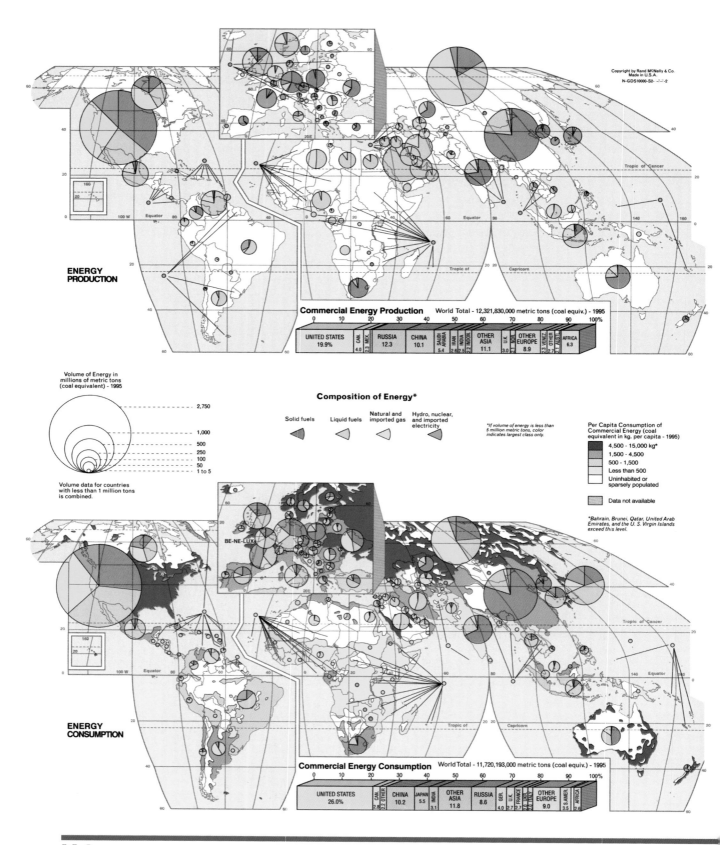

ENERGY PRODUCTION

Commercial Energy Production World Total - 12,321,830,000 metric tons (coal equiv.) - 1995

0	10	20	30	40	50	60	70	80	90	100%

| UNITED STATES 19.9% | CAN 4.0 | MEX 2.3 | RUSSIA 12.3 | CHINA 10.1 | SAUDI ARABIA 5.4 | IRAN 2.6 | INDIA 2.6 | INDON 2.2 | OTHER ASIA 11.1 | U.K. 3.0 | NOR 2.1 | OTHER EUROPE 8.9 | VENEZ 2.3 | OTHER 2.7 | AUST 2.1 | AFRICA 6.3 |

Volume of Energy in millions of metric tons (coal equivalent) - 1995

2,750
1,000
500
250
100
50
1 to 5

Volume data for countries with less than 1 million tons is combined.

Composition of Energy*

Solid fuels   Liquid fuels   Natural and imported gas   Hydro, nuclear, and imported electricity

*If volume of energy is less than 5 million metric tons, color indicates largest class only.

Per Capita Consumption of Commercial Energy (coal equivalent in kg. per capita - 1995)

4,500 - 15,000 kg*
1,500 - 4,500
500 - 1,500
Less than 500
Uninhabited or sparsely populated

Data not available

*Bahrain, Brunei, Qatar, United Arab Emirates, and the U. S. Virgin Islands exceed this level.

ENERGY CONSUMPTION

Commercial Energy Consumption World Total - 11,720,193,000 metric tons (coal equiv.) - 1995

0	10	20	30	40	50	60	70	80	90	100%

| UNITED STATES 26.0% | CAN 2.8 | OTHER 2.2 | CHINA 10.2 | JAPAN 5.5 | INDIA 3.1 | OTHER ASIA 11.8 | RUSSIA 8.6 | GER. 4.0 | U.K. 2.7 | FRANCE 2.1 | ITALY 2.7 | OTHER EUROPE 9.0 | S. AMER. 3.5 | AFRICA 2.6 |

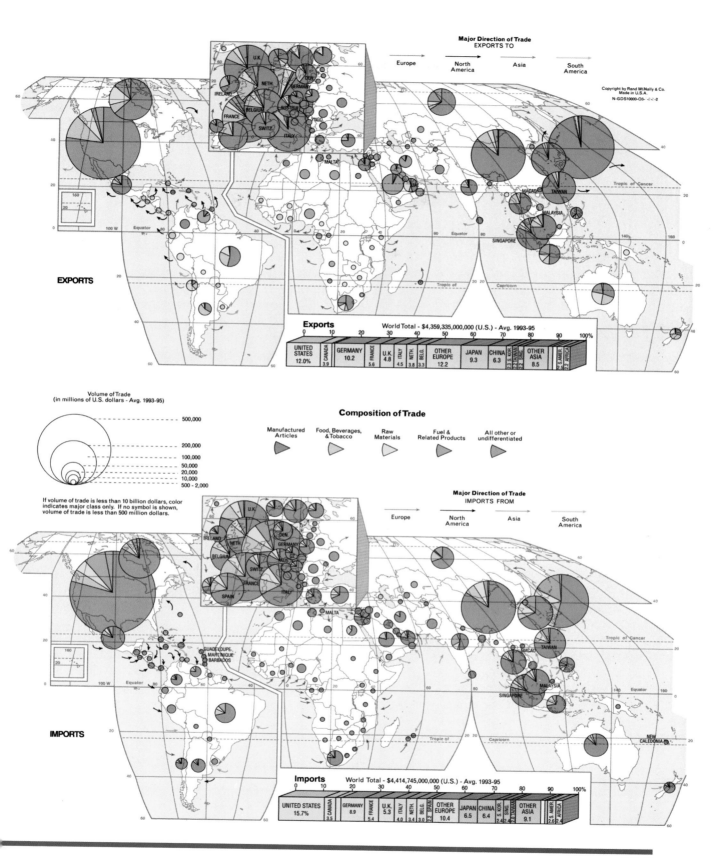

Major Direction of Trade
EXPORTS TO

Europe → North America → Asia → South America

Copyright by Rand McNally & Co.
Made in U.S.A.
N-GDS10000-O3- -2-2 -2

EXPORTS

Exports		World Total - $4,359,335,000,000 (U.S.) - Avg. 1993-95											
UNITED STATES 12.0%	CANADA 3.9	GERMANY 10.2	FRANCE 5.6	U.K. 4.8	ITALY 4.5	NETH. 3.8	BELG. 3.3	OTHER EUROPE 12.2	JAPAN 9.3	CHINA 6.3	S. KOR. 2.3 TAIWAN 2.2 SING.	OTHER ASIA 8.5	S. AMER. 2.3 AFRICA

Volume of Trade
(in millions of U.S. dollars - Avg. 1993-95)

500,000
200,000
100,000
50,000
20,000
10,000
500 - 2,000

If volume of trade is less than 10 billion dollars, color indicates major class only. If no symbol is shown, volume of trade is less than 500 million dollars.

Composition of Trade

Manufactured Articles   Food, Beverages, & Tobacco   Raw Materials   Fuel & Related Products   All other or undifferentiated

Major Direction of Trade
IMPORTS FROM

Europe → North America → Asia → South America

IMPORTS

Imports		World Total - $4,414,745,000,000 (U.S.) - Avg. 1993-95											
UNITED STATES 15.7%	CANADA 3.5	GERMANY 8.9	FRANCE 5.4	U.K. 5.3	ITALY 4.0	NETH. 3.4	BELG. 3.0 SPAIN 2.2	OTHER EUROPE 10.4	JAPAN 6.5	CHINA 6.4	S. KOR. 2.4 TAIWAN 2.0 SING.	OTHER ASIA 9.1	S. AMER. 2.6 AFRICA 2.4

M-9

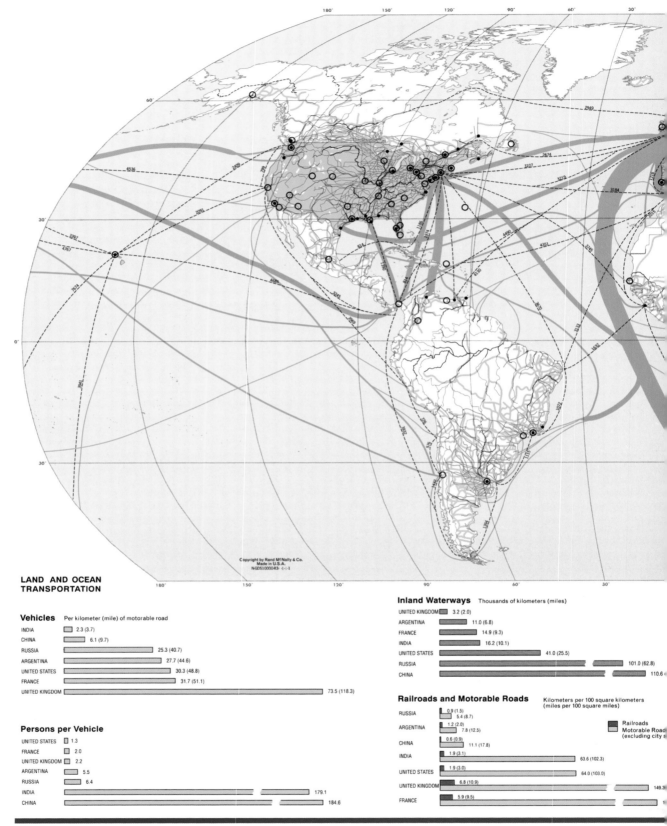

LAND AND OCEAN TRANSPORTATION

Vehicles Per kilometer (mile) of motorable road

INDIA	2.3 (3.7)
CHINA	6.1 (9.7)
RUSSIA	25.3 (40.7)
ARGENTINA	27.7 (44.6)
UNITED STATES	30.3 (48.8)
FRANCE	31.7 (51.1)
UNITED KINGDOM	73.5 (118.3)

Persons per Vehicle

UNITED STATES	1.3
FRANCE	2.0
UNITED KINGDOM	2.2
ARGENTINA	5.5
RUSSIA	6.4
INDIA	179.1
CHINA	184.6

Inland Waterways Thousands of kilometers (miles)

UNITED KINGDOM	3.2 (2.0)
ARGENTINA	11.0 (6.8)
FRANCE	14.9 (9.3)
INDIA	16.2 (10.1)
UNITED STATES	41.0 (25.5)
RUSSIA	101.0 (62.8)
CHINA	110.6

Railroads and Motorable Roads Kilometers per 100 square kilometers (miles per 100 square miles)

Railroads
Motorable Road
(excluding city s

	Railroads	Motorable Roads
RUSSIA	0.9 (1.5)	5.4 (8.7)
ARGENTINA	1.2 (2.0)	7.8 (12.5)
CHINA	0.6 (0.9)	11.1 (17.8)
INDIA	1.9 (3.1)	63.6 (102.3)
UNITED STATES	1.9 (3.0)	64.0 (103.0)
UNITED KINGDOM	6.8 (10.9)	149.3
FRANCE	5.9 (9.5)	1

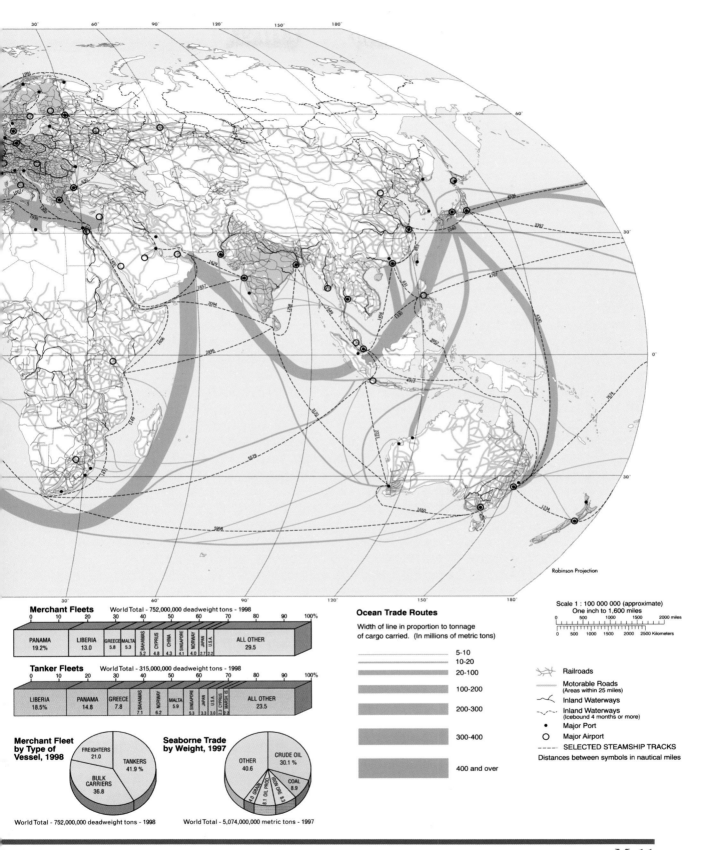

Merchant Fleets World Total - 752,000,000 deadweight tons - 1998

0	10	20	30	40	50	60	70	80	90	100%

| PANAMA 19.2% | LIBERIA 13.0 | GREECE 5.8 | MALTA 5.3 | BAHAMAS 5.2 | CYPRUS 4.8 | CHINA 4.3 | SINGAPORE 4.1 | NORWAY 4.0 | JAPAN 2.7 | U.S.A. 2.2 | ALL OTHER 29.5 |

Tanker Fleets World Total - 315,000,000 deadweight tons - 1998

0	10	20	30	40	50	60	70	80	90	100%

| LIBERIA 18.5% | PANAMA 14.8 | GREECE 7.8 | BAHAMAS 7.1 | NORWAY 6.2 | MALTA 5.9 | SINGAPORE 5.3 | JAPAN 3.3 | U.S.A. 3.0 | CYPRUS 2.3 | MARSH.IS. 2.2 | ALL OTHER 23.5 |

Merchant Fleet by Type of Vessel, 1998

FREIGHTERS 21.0
TANKERS 41.9 %
BULK CARRIERS 36.8

World Total - 752,000,000 deadweight tons - 1998

Seaborne Trade by Weight, 1997

OTHER 40.6
CRUDE OIL 30.1 %
COAL 8.9
IRON ORE 8.3
OIL PROD. 8.1
GRAIN 4.0

World Total - 5,074,000,000 metric tons - 1997

Ocean Trade Routes

Width of line in proportion to tonnage of cargo carried. (In millions of metric tons)

	5-10
	10-20
	20-100
	100-200
	200-300
	300-400
	400 and over

Scale 1 : 100 000 000 (approximate)
One inch to 1,600 miles

0   500   1000   1500   2000 miles
0   500   1000   1500   2000   2500 Kilometers

Railroads
Motorable Roads (Areas within 25 miles)
Inland Waterways
Inland Waterways (Icebound 4 months or more)
• Major Port
O Major Airport
----- SELECTED STEAMSHIP TRACKS
Distances between symbols in nautical miles

Robinson Projection

M-11

POPULATION

Note: Size of each country is proportional to population.

Tints indicate rate of natural increase.

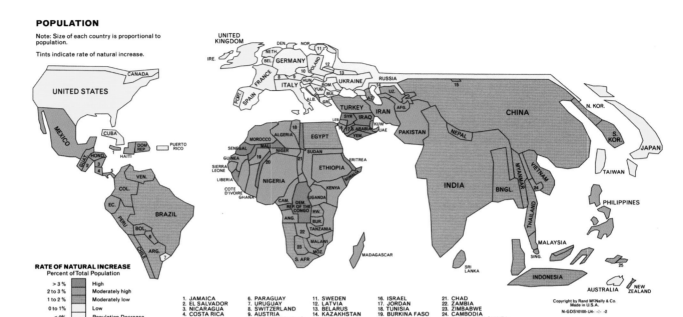

RATE OF NATURAL INCREASE
Percent of Total Population

> 3 %	High
2 to 3 %	Moderately high
1 to 2 %	Moderately low
0 to 1%	Low
< 0%	Population Decrease

1. JAMAICA
2. EL SALVADOR
3. NICARAGUA
4. COSTA RICA
5. PANAMA

6. PARAGUAY
7. URUGUAY
8. SWITZERLAND
9. AUSTRIA
10. CZECH REPUBLIC

11. SWEDEN
12. LATVIA
13. BELARUS
14. KAZAKHSTAN
15. MONGOLIA

16. ISRAEL
17. JORDAN
18. TUNISIA
19. BURKINA FASO
20. BENIN

21. CHAD
22. ZAMBIA
23. ZIMBABWE
24. CAMBODIA
25. PAPUA NEW GUINEA

incredibly successful in Japan. As a result, Levi Strauss subsequently decided to launch the line in the United States and Europe as well.[33]

These days many MNCs create organizational structures to foster global (or regional) product development. Unilever set up a network of worldwide innovation centers (ICs) for personal care and food products. Each IC unit consists of marketing, advertising agency, and technical people, and is headed by the company chairman of the country subsidiary where the IC is based. The centers are responsible for developing product ideas and research, technology, and marketing expertise. One example of an innovation spurred by a Unilever IC based in Thailand is Asian Delight, a new Asian ice cream brand. The ice cream is mixed with a variety of fruits and vegetables used in desserts throughout the region.[34] Black & Decker sets up business teams to develop global products. Each team is headed by a Product General Manager and has representatives from the various geographic regions. The charter of the teams is to develop new products with "the right degree of commonality and the right amount of local market uniqueness." Project leadership is assigned to the country or region that has a dominant category share position.[35]

Screening

Evidently, not all new product ideas are winners. Once new product ideas have been identified, they need to be screened. The goal here is to weed out ideas with little potential. This filtering process can take the form of a formal scoring model. One example of a scoring model is NewProd, which was based on almost two hundred projects from a hundred companies.[36] Each of the projects was rated by managers on about fifty screening criteria and judged in terms of its commercial success. Exhibit 11–5 lists the most important screening dimensions. The model has been validated in North America, Scandinavia, and the Netherlands.[37] Looking at Exhibit 11–5, you can see that the most important success factor is product advantage (superiority, quality, and uniqueness). Recent studies that interviewed Chinese[38] and Japanese[39] product managers reinforced the major role of product advantage in screening new product winners from losers. However, the study done in China also showed the following:

1. Competitive activity was negatively correlated with new product success.
2. Being first in the market (pioneer entry) was an important success factor.
3. Product ideas derived from the marketplace were much more likely to be successful than ideas that came from technical work or in-house labs.

---

[33]"The Jeaning of Japan," *Business Tokyo* (February 1991), pp. 62–63.

[34]"Unilever's Tinkering with Asian Delight Yields Regional Hit," *Advertising Age International* (October 1997), p. 10.

[35]Don R. Graber, "How to Manage a Global Product Development Process," *Industrial Marketing Management*, 25 (1996), pp. 483–89.

[36]Robert G. Cooper, "Selecting New Product Projects: Using the NewProd System," *Journal of Product Innovation Management*, 2 (1) (March 1985), pp. 34–44.

[37]Robert G. Cooper, "The NewProd System: The Industry Experience," *Journal of Product Innovation Management*, 9 (2) (June 1992), pp. 113–27.

[38]Mark E. Parry and X. Michael Song, "Identifying New Product Successes in China," *Journal of Product Innovation Management*, 11 (1994), pp. 15–30.

[39]X. Michael Song and Mark E. Parry, "What Separates Japanese New Product Winners from Losers," *Journal of Product Innovation Management*, 13 (1996), pp. 422–39.

EXHIBIT 11–5
NEWPROD SCREENING MODEL

Key Dimensions (factor name)	Regression Coefficient (weight of factor)	F-Value	Variables or Items Loading on Factor
Product superiority, quality, and uniqueness	1.744	68.7	Product: • Is superior to competing products • Has unique features for user • Is higher quality than competitors' • Does unique task for user • Reduces customers' costs • Is innovative—first of its kind
Overall project/resource compatibility	1.138	30.0	A good "fit" between needs of project and company resource base in terms of: • Managerial skills • Marketing research skills • Sales force/distribution resources • Financial resources • Engineering skills • Production resources
Market need, growth, and size	0.801	12.5	High need level customers for product class Large market (S volume) Fast growing market
Economic advantage of product to end user	0.722	10.2	Product reduces customers' costs Product is priced lower than competing products
Newness to the firm (negative)	−0.354	2.9	Project takes the firm into new areas for the firm such as: • New product class to company • New salesforce/distribution • New types of users' needs served • New customers to company • New competitors to company • New product technology to firm • New production process to firm
Technology resource compatibility	0.342	2.5	A good "fit" between needs of project and company resource base in terms of: • R & D resources and skills • Engineering skills and resources
Market competitiveness (negative)	−0.301	2.0	Intense price competition in market Highly competitive market Many competitors Many new product intros into market Changing user needs
Product scope	0.225	0.9	Market-driven new product idea Not a custom product, i.e., more mass appeal A mass market for product (as opposed to one or a few customers)
Constant	0.328		

Source: Robert G. Cooper, "Selecting New Product Projects: Using the NewProd System," *Journal of Product Innovation Management*, 2 (1) (March 1985), p. 39.

Once the merits of a new product idea have been established in the previous stage, they must be translated into a product concept. A product concept is a fairly detailed description, verbally or sometimes visually, of the new product or service. To assess the appeal of the product concept, companies often rely on focus group discussions. The focus group members discuss the likes and dislikes of the proposed product and the current competing offerings. They also state their willingness to buy the new product if it were to be launched in the market. The discussion is guided by a moderator.

A more sophisticated procedure to measure consumer preferences for product concepts is **conjoint analysis** (sometimes also referred to as trade-off analysis). Most products and services can be considered as a bundle of product attributes. The starting premise of conjoint analysis is that people make trade-offs between the different product attributes when they evaluate alternatives (e.g., brands) from which they have to pick a choice. The purpose, then, of conjoint analysis is to gain an understanding of the trade-offs that consumers make. The outcome of the exercise will be a set of *utilities* for each level of each attribute, derived at the individual household or consumer segment level. By summing these utilities for any specific product concept, we can see how attractive that concept is to a particular consumer. The higher this utility score, the more attractive the concept. This information allows the company to answer questions such as how much more their customers are willing to pay for additional product features or superior performance. The tool can also be used to examine to what degree a firm should customize the products it plans to launch in the various target markets.

To illustrate the use of the conjoint for the design of products in an international setting, let us look at a hypothetical example. In what follows, we focus on the use of conjoint analysis in the context of global NPD.[40] Imagine that company XYZ considers selling satellite TV dishes in two Southeast Asian countries: Thailand and Malaysia.

The first step is to determine the salient attributes for the product (or service). Exploratory market research (e.g., a focus group discussion) or managerial judgment can be used to figure out the most critical attributes. At the same time, we also need to consider the possible levels ("values") that each of the attributes can take. In our example (see Exhibit 11–6) four attributes are considered to be important: (1) the number of channels, (2) the purchase price,[41] (3) the installation fee, and (4) the size of the dish (in terms of inches). Each of the attributes has three possible levels.

For instance, the diameter of the dish could be 18, 25, or 30 inches, and it could cost $100, $200, or nothing to have the dish installed. The next step is to construct product profiles by combining the various attribute levels. Each profile would represent a description of a hypothetical product. In most applications it is unrealistic to consider every possible combination because the number of possibilities rapidly explodes. Instead, one uses an experimental design to come up with a small but manageable number of product profiles. This number varies from study to study. Obviously, the number of profiles will depend on the number of attributes

Concept Testing

---

[40]Those of you who are interested in the technical background should consult Paul E. Green and Yoram Wind, "New Ways to Measure Consumers' Judgments," *Harvard Business Review*, 53 (1975), pp. 107–17.

[41]In the example we assume that no middlemen will be used, so the retail price is the same as the ex-factory price.

EXHIBIT 11–6
SALIENT ATTRIBUTES AND
ATTRIBUTE LEVELS FOR SATELLITE
DISHES

Product Attributes	Attribute Levels
Number of channels	1) 30
	2) 50
	3) 100
Purchase price	1) $500
	2) $600
	3) $700
Installation fee	1) Free
	2) $100
	3) $200
Size of dish	1) 18"
	2) 25"
	3) 30"

and attribute levels, but also on other factors like the amount of information you want to collect. In most studies, the number of profiles ranges between 18 and 32. For example, Product Profile 18 might look like this:

Number of channels :	30	Installation fee:	$100
Purchase price :	$500	Size of dish :	25 inches

Once the profiles have been finalized, you can go into the field and ask subjects to evaluate each concept. In each country several prospective target customers will be contacted. For instance, you might ask the respondent to rank the product profiles from most to least preferred. In addition, other data (e.g., demographics, lifestyle) are collected that often prove useful for benefit segmentation purposes.

Once you have collected the preference data, you need to analyze them using a statistical software package (e.g., SAS). The computer program will assign utilities to each attribute level based on the product evaluation judgment data that were gathered. Hypothetical results for our example are shown in Exhibit 11–7. Each country has two segments: a price-sensitive and quality-sensitive segment. The entries in the columns represent the utilities for the respective attribute levels. For instance, the utility of 100 channels in Thailand would be 5.6 for segment II compared to 2.5 for Malaysia's performance segment II. The results can be used to see which attributes matter most to each of the segments in the different target markets. The relative range of the utilities indicates the attribute importances. In this example, price is most critical for the first Thai segment (utility range: 0 to −4.6), whereas the number of channels (utility range: 0 to 5.6) matters most for the second Thai segment. The technical nitty-gritty is less important here, but we would like you to get a flavor of how conjoint can be used to settle product design issues in a global setting. Let us consider the standardization versus customization issue.

To Standardize or Not to Standardize. For the sake of simplicity, suppose that currently there is one incumbent competitor, ABC, in the satellite dish industry in Thailand and Malaysia. The ABC brand has the following features:

EXHIBIT 11–7
RESULTS OF CONJOINT ANALYSIS FOR SATELLITE DISHES

Attributes	Thailand Segment I	Thailand Segment II	Malaysia Segment I	Malaysia Segment II
Number of channels:				
30	0.0	0.0	0.0	0.0
50	1.5	3.4	1.4	1.8
100	3.2	5.6	3.0	2.5
Purchase price:				
$500	0.0	0.0	0.0	0.0
$600	−3.2	−1.5	−2.8	−2.5
$700	−4.6	−2.0	−4.8	−3.0
Installation fee:				
Free	0.0	0.0	0.0	0.0
$100	−1.5	−0.2	−1.4	−1.0
$200	−1.8	−0.4	−2.1	−1.7
Size of dish (diameter):				
18"	0.0	0.0	0.0	0.0
25"	−0.5	−1.0	−0.4	−2.0
30"	−0.8	−1.5	−1.0	−5.0
Size of segment	12,000	28,000	15,000	16,000

Number of channels:	30	Installation fee:	Free
Purchase price:	$500	Size of dish:	30 inches

XYZ is looking at two possibilities: (1) sell a uniform product (model XYZST) or (2) launch a customized product for each of the two markets (models XYZTH and XYZMA). The profiles for each product are presented in Exhibit 11–8 for comparison.

In this example, the selling price for the uniform product is less than the price for the standardized product because of scale economies. By computing the overall utility for each of the alternatives, we are able to estimate the market share that each product would grab in the two countries. This overall score is simply the sum of the utilities for the attribute levels. The respective utilities for the various product configurations are shown in Exhibit 11–9.

EXHIBIT 11–8
PRODUCT PROFILES FOR XYZ SATELLITE DISH COMPANY

Attribute	Product XYZST (Standardized)	Product XYZTH (Thailand)	Product XYZMA (Malaysia)
Number of channels	30	100	30
Selling price	$500	$700	$700
Installation fee	Free	$200	Free
Size of dish	30"	25"	18"

EXHIBIT 11–9
UTILITIES FOR RESPECTIVE ALTERNATIVES DERIVED VIA CONJOINT STUDY

Alternative	Thailand Segment I	Thailand Segment II	Malaysia Segment I	Malaysia Segment II
ABC (Competitor)	− 0.8	− 1.5	− 1.0	− 5.0
XYZST (Standardized)	− 3.7[1]	0.7	− 3.2	− 3.7
XYZTH (Customized for Thailand)	− 4.0	2.2	Not offered	Not offered
XYZMA (Customized for Malaysia)	Not offered	Not offered	− 4.8	− 3.0

[1] $1.5 + (-3.2) + (-1.5) + (-0.5) = -3.7$

Assuming that each customer will pick the alternative that gives the highest overall utility, we can derive market share estimates in the two countries for the two product alternatives. For instance, looking at the uniform dish in Thailand, we find that customers in the quality segment II would prefer it over the competing model (since $0.7 > -1.5$). On the other hand, the first segment in Thailand would pick ABC (since $-3.7 < -0.8$). Hence, the market share for the standardized model (XYZST) in the Thai market would equal 70 percent: the number of households in the quality segment, 28,000 (see bottom row of Exhibit 11–7) divided by the entire market size for satellite dishes in Thailand, 40,000. In the same manner, we can compute XYZ's market share for the standardized model in Malaysia and for the customized models in the two countries:

Market share standardized product XYZST in Malaysia = 51.6% (16,000/31,000)

Market share customized product XYZTH in Thailand = 70% (28,000/40,000)

Market share customized product XYZMA in Malaysia = 51.6% (16,000/31,000)

In our example, the market share estimates for the two alternatives (standardized versus customized) end up being equal. Once we have cost estimates for the manufacturing and marketing of the different alternatives, we can come up with an estimate of their expected profits. For instance, let us assume that the variable costs are equal (say, $400 per unit) but the fixed costs (combined across the two markets) differ: $5 million for the standardized product option as opposed to $10 million for the customized product option. The unit contribution equals the purchase price plus the installation fee, minus the variable cost. Plugging in our market share estimates and the cost estimates, we can assess the profit potential of the various options.

Profits for standardized product approach (combined across the two countries) =

(Unit Sales Thailand + Unit Sales Malaysia) (Unit Contribution) − (Fixed Costs)

or

$$(28,000 + 16,000) \times (\$600 + \$100 - \$400) - \$5,000,000 = \$8.2 \text{ million}$$

Profits for the customized product strategy =

$$(28,000) \times (\$700 + \$200 - \$400) + (16,000) \times (\$700 + \$0 - \$400) - \$10,000,000 =$$
$$\$8.8 \text{ million}$$

Given the higher profit potential for the second alternative, launching two customized models (model XYZTH targeted toward Thailand and model XYZMA toward Malaysia) is clearly the winning option here. Obviously, aside of the economics, other factors need to be taken into consideration before settling such issues.

In many Western countries, test marketing new products before the full-fledged rollout is the norm for most consumer goods industries. Test marketing is essentially a field experiment where the new product is marketed in a select set of cities to assess its sales potential and scores of other performance measures. In a sense, a test market is the dress rehearsal prior to the product launch (assuming the test market results support a "GO" decision). There are several reasons why companies would like to run a test market before the rollout. It allows them to make fairly accurate projections of the market share, sales volume, and penetration of the new product. In countries where household scanning panels are available, firms can also get insights into likely trial, repeat purchase, and usage rates for the product. Another boon of test marketing is that companies can contrast competing marketing-mix strategies to decide which one is most promising in achieving the firm's objectives.

Test Marketing

Despite these merits, test markets also have several shortcomings. They are typically time consuming and costly. Apart from the direct costs of running the test markets, there is also the opportunity cost of lost sales that the company would have achieved during the test market period in case of a successful global rollout. Moreover, test market results can be misleading. It may be difficult to replicate test market conditions with the final rollout. For instance, certain communication options that were available in the test market cities are not always accessible in all of the final target markets. Finally, there is also a strategic concern: test markets might alert your competitors, allowing them to preempt you.

In light of these drawbacks, MNCs often prefer to skip the test market stage. Instead they use a market simulation or immediately launch the new product. In fact, one survey indicated that Pan-European financial institutions conducted test markets less than 20 percent of the time.[42] One alternative to test marketing is the laboratory test market. Prospective customers are contacted and shown commercials for the new item and existing competing brands. After the viewing, they are given a small amount of money and are invited to make a purchase in the product category in a simulated store setting ("lab"). Hopefully, some of the prospects will pick your new product. Those who purchase the new product take it home and consume it. Those who choose a competing brand are given a sample of the new product. After a couple of weeks the subjects are contacted again via the phone. They are asked to state their attitude toward the new item in terms of

---

[42]Aliah Mohammed-Salleh and Chris Easingwood, "Why European Financial Institutions Do Not Test-Market New Consumer Products," *International Journal of Bank Marketing*, 11 (3) (1993), pp. 23–27.

likes and dislikes, satisfaction, and whether they would be willing to buy the product again.

Such procedures, though relatively cheap, still give valuable insights about the likely trial and repeat buying rates, usage, and customer satisfaction for the new product, price sensitivities, and the effectiveness of sampling. The collected data are often used as inputs for a marketing computer simulation model to answer "what if" questions.

Another route that is often taken is to rely on the sales performance of the product in one country, the lead market, to project sales figures in other countries that are considered for a launching decision. In a sense, an entire country is used as one big test market. A practitioner of this approach is Colgate-Palmolive. For example, Colgate used Thailand as a bellwether for the worldwide introduction of Nouriché, a treatment shampoo.[43] Thailand was chosen as a springboard because of the size and growth potential of its hair-care market. BMW used Australia as a global test market for a chain of BMW Lifestyle concept stores selling accessories (e.g., wallets, garments) under the BMW brand name. The concept is a way of keeping in touch with BMW customers to build a long-term relationship.[44] Miller, the U.S. beer brewer, also employed Canada as a test market for Red Dog for the United States.[45] The new brand is red in color, low in carbonation, and easy to drink. Miller planned to position Red Dog as interactive, liberating, nonconformist, and confident. The new product strategy for Red Dog was first implemented and tested in Canada. After the successful launch in Canada, Red Dog was introduced in the United States in 1994. By and large, the segmentation and positioning strategies used in Canada were replicated for the U.S. rollout. Some changes were made, though, to allow for the peculiarities of the American beer market. Other recent cases of the use of an entire country as a test market are summarized in Exhibit 11-10.

Using a country as a test market for other markets raises several issues. How many countries should be selected? What countries should be used? To what degree can sales experience garnered in one country be projected to other countries? Generally speaking, cross-cultural and other environmental differences (e.g., the competitive climate) turn cross-country projections into a risky venture. The practice is only recommendable when the new product targets cross-border segments.

Timing of Entry: Waterfall versus Sprinkler Strategies

A key element of a global product launch strategy is the entry timing decision: When should we launch the new product in the target markets? Roughly speaking, there are two broad strategic options: the **waterfall** and the **sprinkler model** (see Exhibit 11-11).[46] The first option is the global phased rollout or **waterfall strategy**, where new products trickle down in a cascade-like manner.[47] The typical pattern is

---

[43]"Colgate Tries Thai for Global Entry," *Advertising Age International* (May 16, 1994), p. I-22.

[44]"In Australia, BMW to Test New Concept in Dealerships: Branded Fashion Sales," *Advertising Age International* (March 8, 1999), p. 2.

[45]Donna J. Neal, "Crossing Borders with New Brand Introductions," in Sanjay Sood, ed., *Brand Equity and the Marketing Mix: Creating Customer Value*, Marketing Science Institute, Report No. 95-111, September 1995.

[46]Hajo Riesenbeck and Anthony Freeling, "How Global are Global Brands?" *The McKinsey Quarterly*, (4) (1991), pp. 3–18.

[47]Kenichi Ohmae, "The Triad World View," *Journal of Business Strategy*, 7 (Spring 1985), pp. 8–19.

EXHIBIT 11–10
EXAMPLES OF TEST MARKET COUNTRIES

Company	Product	Test Market Used	Geographic Coverage
Colgate-Palmolive	Nouriché (shampoo)	Thailand	World
Unilever	Organics (shampoo)	Thailand	World
Toyota	Toyota Soluna	Thailand	Asia
Honda	Honda City	Thailand	Asia
Miller	Red Dog (beer)	Canada	North America
BMW	Concept Stores	Australia	World
Tricon	Taco Bell (fast food)	Australia and Singapore	Asia
Colgate-Palmolive	Palmolive Naturals (antiperspirant spray)	Romania	Central and Eastern Europe
KFC	Breakfast menu	Singapore	World
Fiat	Palio (car)	Brazil	World

EXHIBIT 11–11
"WATERFALL" VERSUS "SPRINKLER" MODEL

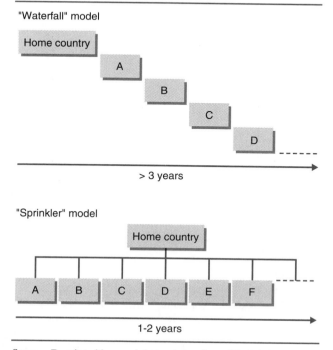

"Waterfall" model

> 3 years

"Sprinkler" model

1-2 years

to introduce the new product first in the company's home market. Next, the innovation is launched in other advanced markets. In the final phase, the multinational firm markets the product in less advanced countries. This whole process of geographic expansion may last several decades. The time span between the U.S. launch and the foreign launch was twenty-two years for McDonald's, twenty years for Coca-Cola, and thirty-five years for Marlboro.[48] The prime motive for the waterfall model is that customization of the product for the foreign market launch can be very time consuming. A phased rollout is also less demanding on the company resources. Other constraints may block a global rollout. Starbucks's desire to find good local partners explains why Starbucks has been launched early on in countries like Singapore but much later in Hong Kong.[49] On the other hand, staggered rollouts are not always acceptable. In many industries—especially business-to-business markets—consumers worldwide do not want to be left behind. They all want to have access to the latest generation. Further, a phased rollout gives competitors time to catch up.

The second timing decision option is the **sprinkler strategy** of simultaneous worldwide entry. Under this scenario, the global rollout takes place within a period of one to two years. The growing prominence of universal segments and concerns about competitive preemption in the foreign markets are the two major factors behind this expansion approach. In June 1999, Colgate-Palmolive launched a new deodorant line under the Palmolive Naturals brand name across Central and Eastern Europe and the Far East.

The waterfall strategy of sequential entry is preferable over the sprinkler model under these conditions:[50]

1. The lifecycle of the product is relatively long.

2. Nonfavorable conditions govern the foreign market. These might include
   · Small foreign markets (compared to the home market)
   · Slow growth
   · High fixed costs of entry

3. The competitive climate in the foreign market is weak because competitors are weak or willing to cooperate, or there are no competitors.

◆ ◆ ◆ ◆ ◆ ◆ GLOBAL NPD AND CULTURE

In this final section we touch on the linkages between the new product development process and national cultures. Cultural differences heavily influence the NPD process. A recent study that contrasted European and North American new product programs led to the following conclusions:[51]

---

[48]Numbers quoted in Riesenbeck and Freeling.
[49]"Starbucks Ships its Coffee Craze to Pacific Rim," *Advertising Age* (April 27, 1998), p. 28.
[50]Shlomo Kalish, Vijay Mahajan and Eitan Muller, "Waterfall and Sprinkler New-Product Strategies in Competitive Global Markets," *International Journal of Research in Marketing*, 12 (July 1995), pp. 105–119.
[51]E. J. Kleinschmidt, "A Comparative Analysis of New Product Programmes," *European Journal of Marketing*, 28 (7) (1994), pp. 5–29.

- The NPD process among European firms is much more formalized.
- European Go/No Go standards tend to be far stricter than American norms.
- In terms of organization, NPD projects within European firms more likely have a well-defined project leader and an assigned team of players than projects run by North American companies. Also, when teams do exist, they are much more multifunctional than American teams.
- Incentive schemes also differ. Compared to American firms, European companies punish project leaders less in case of failure, reward intrapreneurs more generously, and offer more seed money for pet projects.

Another study contrasted the trade-offs that German and U.S. new-product managers make.[52] The study showed that U.S. managers put the greatest emphasis on meeting the product development budget. Least important is beating the development schedule. For German companies, the priorities are reversed: their top priority is meeting the product development schedule.

Peculiarities have also been observed for the Japanese NPD process. The Japanese approach takes an incremental perspective with the emphasis being on continuous technological improvements.[53] One of the consequences of this "incrementalist" approach is parallel new product development.[54] While developing the first generation of a new product, Japanese firms will work on the second- and third-generation products. Thereby, as soon as competitors launch a me-too product, the Japanese firm can counter by introducing the next generation product.[55] Japanese companies also strongly believe in **product churning**: they rush new products to the market with little or no market research and then gauge the market's reaction.[56] Another characteristic of Japanese NPD are the close and ongoing linkages with the customer. Japanese NPD managers constantly listen to the "voice of the customer."[57]

The precise role of culture depends on the stage of the NPD process. We can make a distinction between the "initiation" (idea generation, screening, concept development) and "implementation" (test marketing, product launch) stages of global NPD.[58] Decentralization, often found in egalitarian (low power distance — see Chapter 4) cultures, encourages idea generation and feedback. On the other hand, a centralized structure (high power distance) is probably a strength for the

---

[52]Ashok K. Gupta, Klaus Brockhoff, and Ursula Weisenfeld, "Making Trade-Offs in the New Product Development Process: A German/US Comparison," *Journal of Product Innovation Management*, 9 (March 1992), pp. 11–18.

[53]Michael Czinkota and Masaaki Kotabe, "Product Development the Japanese Way," *Journal of Business Strategy* (Nov./Dec. 1990), pp. 31–36.

[54]R. B. Kennard, "From Experience: Japanese Product Development Process," *Journal of Product Innovation Management*, 8 (September 1991), pp. 184–88.

[55]Paul A. Herbig and Fred Palumbo, "A Brief Examination of the Japanese Innovative Process: Part 2," *Marketing Intelligence & Planning*, 12 (2) (1994), pp. 38–42.

[56]David McHardy Reid, "Perspectives for International Marketers on the Japanese Market," *Journal of International Marketing*, 3 (1) (1995), pp. 63–84.

[57]Kennard.

[58]Cheryl Nakata and K. Sivakumar, "National Culture and New Product Development: An Integrative Review," *Journal of Marketing*, 60 (1) (January 1996), pp. 61–72.

implementation steps of the NPD when rigor and control become more critical. Cultures with low uncertainty avoidance—characterized with risk taking and little need for planning and structure—are probably beneficial for the initial steps of the NPD process. At later stages, risk avoidance and planning become more desirable. These traits are typically found in cultures with high uncertainty avoidance. Similar contrasts can be made for other cultural dimensions. To tap into the benefits of differing cultural mind-sets, MNCs like Baxter International, Black & Decker, Procter & Gamble, and Colgate-Palmolive increasingly opt for cross-cultural new product project teams. Global Perspective 11–4 describes Colgate-Palmolive's approach toward global new product development.

$\mathcal{G}$LOBAL PERSPECTIVE 11–4

COLGATE-PALMOLIVE'S GLOBAL NPD APPROACH

1. GLOBAL PRODUCT DEVELOPMENT

Colgate researchers create products for the world—not for a single country. The process begins with consumer research in multiple countries with a broad range of economic and cultural characteristics. Once products with potential global appeal are identified, development work begins. Here, Colgate's global marketing experts and global scientists work in teams—organized around the specific core consumer business and its strategic growth plan.

2. MULTIYEAR ACTIVITY GRIDS

In the late stages of development, regional and country managers prioritize and plan all aspects of the launch using a three-year horizon. That way, everything—from raw materials to manufacturing to distribution to media advertising—is most efficiently coordinated.

3. COUNTRY—NOT CITY—TEST MARKETS

Concurrent test marketing begins with anywhere from one to six countries to identify the best plan to use for the subsequent rapid global rollout. For example, early results from introduction in Australia, the Philippines,

New Zealand, Greece, Portugal, and Colombia indicated that Colgate Total, a new toothpaste containing a long-lasting antibacterial formula that fights plaque, tartar and cavities, would be a popular addition to the Colgate product line throughout the world. Colgate Total turned out to be a major success story for Colgate. During 1998, Total captured market leadership in the U.S. toothpaste market and was rated as one of *Business Week's* "Best New Products of 1998."

4. "BUNDLE BOOKS" LEAVE NOTHING TO CHANCE

Modifications suggested by lead country testing are then incorporated into a *Bundle Book*, a detailed manual explaining everything a country manager needs to know about a product—its formula, packaging, marketing strategy, advertising—to launch it quickly and successfully.

5. WORLDWIDE PRODUCT EXPANSION

The final stage of taking Colgate's products from development to market involves the managers of a specific country orchestrating the product launch. Local Colgate experts, from manufacturing to marketing, working with the original global product development team, execute the launch strategy consistent with the unique characteristics of the particular market.

Source: Colgate-Palmolive, *1998 Annual Report*, pp. 12–13.

SUMMARY ✦

Global product policy decisions are tremendously important for the success of an MNC's global marketing strategies. In this chapter, the focus was on managing the NPD process in a global context. We first gave an overview of the different product strategy options that companies might pursue. Roughly speaking, a multinational company has three options: *extension* of the domestic strategy, *adaptation* of home-grown strategies, or *invention* by designing products that cater to the common needs of global customers. One of the major issues that firms wrestle with is the standardization-versus-customization issue. By now, you should realize that this issue should not be stated in "either-or" terms. Instead, it is a matter of degree: To what extent should we adapt (or if you want: standardize) our product strategy? We described the major forces that favor a globalized (or regionalized) product strategy. At the same time, there will always be forces that push your product strategy in the direction of customization.

Ideally, companies strike a neat balance between product standardization and adaptation. We described two product design approaches that enable a firm to capture the benefits of either option: the *modular* and the *core-product* approach. By adopting these approaches or their variants, firms minimize the risk of overstandardizing their product offerings while still grabbing the scale economies benefits that flow from a uniform product policy. We also demonstrated how you can use one market research tool—conjoint analysis—to make global product design decisions in practice.

The last part of this chapter highlighted the different stages in the new product development process. By and large, the pattern is similar to the steps followed in developing new products for the home market. However, there are a number of complicating factors that need to be handled: How do we coordinate global NPD efforts across different cultures? What mechanisms and communication channels can we use to stimulate idea exchanges? What alternatives do we have when certain steps of the NPD sequence are not doable (e.g., test marketing)?

Finally, we showed how cultural differences translate into different NPD approaches. It is fitting to conclude this chapter with the insights of a seasoned practitioner. In a recent speech Don Graber, president of Worldwide Household Products at Black & Decker, offered the following set of guidelines on global product development:[59]

- Start with the consumer. Understand the commonalities and differences in regional needs.
- Do not try to make a product more global than it really is. A good, well-executed regional product is better than a poorly executed global product.
- Global business teams that are multifunctional and multigeographic are very helpful in supporting a global product program.
- Top managerial commitment and support is absolutely essential.

KEY TERMS ✦

adaptation	extension	modular approach	overcustomization
core-product approach	invention	product churning	(overstandardization)
customization	lead (lag) country	sprinkler strategy	standardization
			waterfall strategy

REVIEW QUESTIONS ✦ ✦ ✦ ✦ ✦ ✦ ✦ ✦ ✦ ✦ ✦ ✦ ✦ ✦ ✦ ✦

1. Under what conditions is a dual extension strategy advisable? When is product invention more appropriate?

2. Explain the difference between the modular and core-product approaches.

3. Discuss the forces that favor a globalized product design strategy.

4. In what sense is the "standardize versus customize" question in global product design a bogus issue?

---

[59]Don R. Graber, "How to Manage a Global Product Development Process," *Industrial Marketing Management*, 25 (1996), pp. 483–89.

5. MNCs tend to move more and more toward a sprinkler strategy in terms of their global launch timing decisions. What forces lie behind this trend?

6. What are the major dangers in using an entire country as a test market for new products that are to be launched globally (or regionally)?

DISCUSSION QUESTIONS ◆ ◆ ◆ ◆ ◆ ◆ ◆ ◆ ◆ ◆ ◆ ◆ ◆ ◆ ◆ ◆ ◆

1. Do you agree/disagree with the following statement recently made by John Dooner, chairman-CEO of Mc-Cann-Erickson Worldwide, a global advertising agency (*Advertising Age International*, September 1996, p. I-21): "The old global view was that a centrally developed brand idea could be made relevant in just about any market, depending on how it was adapted. The reality of the new globalism is that a brand viewpoint that starts out being relevant in one market can become relevant in others, because of the nature of converging consumers. Creative ideas literally can come from anywhere, as long as there is a coordinated system for recognizing and disseminating these ideas. Countries that were once thought of as only being on the receiving end of global ideas can now also be the creators and exporters of these ideas."

2. The median income of consumers in emerging markets like India, Vietnam, and the Philippines is a small fraction of the median income level in developed markets. Given the low buying power, the price charged in Western countries for many impulse items would represent a major expense in developing countries. The retail price for a pack of Wrigley chewing gum in the United States is a quarter for a five-stick package. What product policy options might Wrigley consider to make its product more affordable to local consumers in, say, the Philippines?

3. A few years ago, Discovery Communications, the parent company of the Discovery Channel, made a decision to create a global TV brand. It now reaches almost 90 million subscribers in ninety countries. The Discovery Channel's programming includes history, nature, science, travel, and technology. In light of McLuhan's "global village," do you think that there is potential for simply offering the U.S. program schedule or should the Discovery Channel adapt its product to local markets?

4. Recently, Whirlpool's Swedish division developed the VIP microwave oven. This microwave oven uses state-of-the-art technology and has several very advanced features. Imagine that Whirlpool would like to introduce this new model in Asia. In its 1995 Annual Report, Whirlpool notes that microwave ovens have become "global products." Would Whirlpool be able to launch the VIP as a truly global product, or do you think they probably would need to adapt the product?

5. Many Japanese companies do not follow the typical new product development process (idea generation → screening → · · · → commercialization). Instead, they practice "product churning": make a batch of the new product and then see whether Japanese consumers buy the product. After the product is launched, other entrants often introduce me-too versions. What are the possible benefits of this approach compared to the Western NPD model?

6. What particular challenges do you see for companies introducing product categories that are truly new—recent examples include frozen yogurt (TCBY) and breakfast cereals (Kellogg's) in China; iced tea (Snapple) in Europe—into the foreign market? How might the marketing-mix strategies used by the companies involved differ from the strategies used in the more developed markets?

7. *Assignment.* Most annual reports have some discussion on the product strategies that is used. Get a recent annual report of at least two multinational companies in the same industry (many companies now put their annual report on the World Wide Web). How do their global product strategies differ? What do they have in common? How do the companies organize their global product development efforts?

FURTHER READING ◆ ◆ ◆ ◆ ◆ ◆ ◆ ◆ ◆ ◆ ◆ ◆ ◆ ◆ ◆ ◆ ◆

Bose, Amit, and Khushi Khanna. "The Little Emperor: A Case Study of a New Brand Launch." *Marketing and Research Today* (November 1996): 216–21.

Czinkota, Michael, and Masaaki Kotabe. "Product Development the Japanese Way." *Journal of Business Strategy* (Nov./Dec. 1990): 31–36.

Duarte, Deborah, and Nancy Snyder. "Facilitating Global Organizational Learning in New Product Development at Whirlpool Corporation." *Journal of Product Innovation Management*, 14 (1997): 48–55.

Garber, Don. "How to Manage a Global Product Development Process." *Industrial Marketing Management*, 25 (1996): 483–89.

Gatignon, Hubert, Jehoshua Eliashberg, and Thomas S. Robertson. "Modeling Multinational Diffusion Patterns: An Efficient Methodology." *Marketing Science*, 8 (Summer 1989): 231–47.

Herbig, Paul A., and Fred Palumbo. "A Brief Examination of the Japanese Innovative Process: Part 2." *Marketing Intelligence & Planning*, 12 (2) (1994): 38–42.

Kalish, Shlomo, Vijay Mahajan, and Eitan Muller. "Waterfall and Sprinkler New-Product Strategies in Competitive Global Markets." *International Journal of Research in Marketing*, 12 (July 1995): 105–19.

Keegan, Warren J., and C. S. Mayer (eds.). *Multinational Product Management*. Chicago: American Marketing Association, 1977.

Kleinschmidt, E. J. "A Comparative Analysis of New Product Programmes." *European Journal of Marketing*, 28 (7) (1994): 5–29.

Lynn, Michael, and Betsy D. Gelb. "Identifying Innovative National Markets for Technical Consumer Goods." *International Marketing Review*, 13 (6) (1996): 43–57.

Nakata, Cheryl, and K. Sivakumar. "National Culture and New Product Development: An Integrative Review." *Journal of Marketing*, 60 (January 1996): 61–72.

Song, X. Michael, and Mark E. Parry. "The Dimensions of Industrial New Product Success and Failure in State Enterprises in the People's Republic of China." *Journal of Product Innovation Management*, 11 (2) (1994): 105–18.

Song, X. Michael, and Mark E. Parry. "The Determinants of Japanese New Product Successes." *Journal of Marketing Research*, 34 (February 1997): 64–76.

Song, X. Michael, and Mark E. Parry. "A Cross-National Comparative Study of New Product Development Processes: Japan and the United States." *Journal of Marketing*, 61 (April 1997): 1–18.

Song, X. Michael, C. Anthony Di Benedetto, and Yuzhen Lisa Zhao. "Pioneering Advantages in Manufacturing and Service Industries: Empirical Evidence From Nine Countries." *Strategic Management Journal*, 20: 811–36.

Takada, Hirokazu, and Dipak Jain. "Cross-National Analysis of Diffusion of Consumer Durable Goods in Pacific Rim Countries." *Journal of Marketing*, 55 (April 1991): 48–54.

Walters, Peter G. P., and Brian Toyne. "Product Modification and Standardization in International Markets: Strategic Options and Facilitating Policies." *Columbia Journal of World Business*, 24 (Winter 1989): 37–44.

GLOBAL PRODUCT POLICY DECISIONS II: MARKETING PRODUCTS AND SERVICES

CHAPTER OVERVIEW

1. GLOBAL BRANDING STRATEGIES

2. MANAGING MULTINATIONAL PRODUCT LINES

3. PRODUCT PIRACY

4. COUNTRY-OF-ORIGIN EFFECTS

5. GLOBAL MARKETING OF SERVICES

Lee Kum Kee is a brand that is relatively obscure in the West.[1] However, in Asia, Lee Kum Kee is to oyster sauce what Heinz is to ketchup. In 1999, the brand was ranked as the fourth most valuable Asian brand (excluding Japan) by Inter-brand—ahead of brands like LG Electronics, Foster's, and Cathay Pacific. The brand is owned by a privately held company, headquartered in Hong Kong. The company aspires now to develop its brand in the rest of the world. To that end, Lee Kum Kee redesigned the product label, emphasizing the English "Lee Kum Kee" part of its brand name, not the Chinese ideograms, which might alienate Western shoppers. The firm also widened its product line to appeal to the palates of Western consumers. Flavors added include sweet-and-sour fish, black-bean chicken, and spicy tofu. In Australia, the company increased the size of its single-serving sauce packets after research indicated that Australians prefer more sauce with their food. The challenges that Lee Kum Kee is struggling with—global brand and product line management—are the focal issues in this chapter.

---

[1]This discussion is based on "Spreading the Sauce," *Far Eastern Economic Review* (May 20, 1999), pp. 60–61.

Companies that brand their products have various options when they sell their goods in multiple countries. More and more companies see global (or at least regional) branding as a must. Nevertheless, quite a few firms still stick to local branding strategies. In between these two extreme alternatives, there are numerous variations. This chapter will consider and assess different branding approaches. Next, we shift our attention to the managing of an international product line. Multinational product line management entails issues such as these: What product assortment should the company launch when it first enters a new market? How should the firm expand its multinational product line over time? What product lines should be added or dropped?

Another concern that global marketers face is the issue of product piracy. In this chapter we will suggest several approaches that can be employed to tackle counterfeiting. A lot of research has investigated the impact of country-of-origin effects on consumer attitudes toward a product. We will explore the major findings of this research stream and examine different strategies that firms can use to handle negative country-of-origin stereotypes. The balance of this chapter covers the unique problems of marketing services internationally. Services differ from tangible products in many respects. What these differences imply in terms of market opportunities, challenges, and marketing strategies will be discussed in the last section.

GLOBAL BRANDING STRATEGIES ◆ ◆ ◆ ◆ ◆ ◆ ◆

Sara Lee, a U.S. Fortune 500 company, has 25,000 trademarks registered worldwide, 80 percent of which are in current use.[2] One of the major tasks that international marketers like Sara Lee face is the management of their company's brand portfolio. For many firms the brands they own are their most valuable assets. A brand can be defined as "a name, term, sign, symbol, or combination of them which is intended to identify the goods and services of one seller or group of sellers and to differentiate them from those of competitors."[3] Linked to a brand name is a collection of assets and liabilities—the **brand equity** tied to the brand name. These include brand-name awareness, perceived quality, and any other associations invoked by the brand name in the customer's mind. The concerns that are to be addressed when building up and managing brand equity in a multinational setting include the following:[4]

- How do we strike the balance between a global brand that shuns cultural barriers and one that allows for local requirements?

- What aspects of the brand policy can be adapted to global use? Which ones should remain flexible?

- Which brands are destined to become "global" megabrands? Which ones should be kept as "local" brands?

---

[2]Keith Alm, formerly senior vice-president Pacific Rim, Sara Lee, private communication.

[3]Philip H. Kotler, *Marketing Management* (Upper Saddle River, NJ: Prentice-Hall, 2000).

[4]Jean-Noel Kapferer, *Strategic Brand Management. New Approaches to Creating and Evaluating Brand Equity* (London: Kogan Page, 1992).

- How do you condense a multitude of local brands (like in the case of Sara Lee) into a smaller, more manageable number of global (or regional) brands?
- How do you execute the changeover from a local to a global brand?
- How do you build up a portfolio of global megabrands?

Suffice it to say, there are no simple answers to these questions. In what follows, we will touch on the major issues regarding international branding.

Global Brands Reflect on your most recent trip overseas and some of the shopping expeditions that you undertook. Several of the brand names that you saw there probably sounded quite familiar: McDonald's, Coca-Cola, Levi Strauss, Canon, Rolex. On the other hand, there were most likely some products that carried brand names that you had never heard of before or that were slight (or even drastic) variations of brand names with a more familiar ring. A key strategic issue that appears on international marketers' agenda is whether there should be a **global brand**. What conditions favor launching a product with a single brand name worldwide? the same logo? maybe even the same slogan? When is it more appropriate to keep brand names local? In between these two extremes, there are several other options that you might consider. For instance, some companies use local brand names but at the same time put a corporate banner brand name on their products (e.g., "Findus by Nestlé"). See Global Perspective 12–1 for another approach.

Exhibit 12–1 is a list of the most valuable brands in the world put together by Interbrand, a consulting agency. For each brand, Interbrand assessed the

◆ ◆

GLOBAL PERSPECTIVE 12–1

MAYBELLINE — CREATION OF A GLOBAL MAKE-UP BRAND

In 1996, Maybelline, a U.S. brand that specializes in mass-market make-up, generated 90 percent of its revenue in the United States. In that year, L'Oréal, the French cosmetics giant, acquired Maybelline. Since then, L'Oréal has pushed Maybelline into more than 70 countries. Three years after the acquisition, more than half of the brand's sales originate from outside the United States. In China, the brand is sold through more than 2,000 stores. Maybelline is now the leading mass-market make-up brand there.

Sources: "L'Oréal Exports America," *Advertising Age International* (January 11, 1999), p. 9; "L'Oréal. The Beauty of Global Branding," *Business Week* (June 28, 1998), pp. 30–34; www.loreal.com; Alain Evrard, "L'Oréal: Achieving Success in Emerging Asian Markets," in *Brand Warriors*, Fiona Gilmore, ed. (London: HarperCollinsBusiness, 1997).

The Maybelline brand is one of the ten brands on which L'Oréal has founded its global expansion. L'Oréal's mission is to convey the charm of different cultures through its multicultural brand portfolio: Italian values with Giorgio Armani, the French slice of life with L'Oréal Paris or Lancôme, American values with Ralph Lauren or Maybelline, and so on. Where most other MNCs try to homogenize their brands, L'Oréal wants its brands to embody their country heritage.

The launch of Maybelline in India is a fine example of L'Oréal's branding philosophy. When Maybelline was rolled out in India, L'Oréal stressed the brand's American roots and urban chic. The ads featured supermodel Christy Turlington, Maybelline's embodiment since 1992. Print ads appeared in magazines such as *Elle, Cosmopolitan*, and *Femina*. TV spots were aired on satellite channel Star Plus.

profit stream likely to be generated by products carrying the brand name.[5] Note that the league is heavily dominated by American brands. This is not too surprising, because companies based in the United States have had much more experience with brand management than firms from other countries. It also reflects on the strength of the U.S. domestic market as a springboard for companies with global aspirations.[6]

A truly global brand is one that has a consistent identity with consumers across the world. This means the same product formulation, the same core benefits and

EXHIBIT 12–1
TOP 60 BRANDS WORLDWIDE

	Brand Name	Country of Origin	Industry	Brand Value ($US m)	Brand Value % of Market Capitalization
1	Coca-Cola	U.S.	beverages	83,845	59
2	Microsoft	U.S.	software	56,654	21
3	IBM	U.S.	computers	43,781	28
4	General Electric	U.S.	diversified	33,502	10
5	Ford	U.S.	automobiles	33,197	58
6	Disney	U.S.	entertainment	32,275	61
7	Intel	U.S	computers	30,021	21
8	McDonald's	U.S.	food	26,231	64
9	AT&T	U.S.	telecoms	24,181	24
10	Marlboro	U.S.	tobacco	21,048	19
11	Nokia	Finland	telecoms	20,694	44
12	Mercedes	Germany	automobiles	17,781	37
13	Nescafé	Switzerland	beverages	17,595	23
14	Hewlett-Packard	U.S.	computers	17,132	31
15	Gillette	U.S.	personal care	15,894	37
16	Kodak	U.S.	imaging	14,830	60
17	Ericsson	Sweden	telecoms	14,766	32
18	Sony	Japan	electronics	14,231	49
19	Amex	U.S.	financial services	12,550	35
20	Toyota	Japan	automobiles	12,310	14
21	Heinz	U.S.	food	11,806	64
22	BMW	Germany	automobiles	11,281	77
23	Xerox	U.S.	office equipment	11,225	40
24	Honda	Japan	automobiles	11,101	37
25	Citibank	U.S.	financial services	9,147	22
26	Dell	U.S.	computers	9,043	9
27	Budweiser	U.S.	alcohol	8,510	33
28	Nike	U.S.	sports goods	8,155	77
29	Gap	U.S.	apparel	7,909	39
30	Kelloggs	U.S.	food	7,052	52
31	Volkswagen	Germany	automobiles	6,603	30
32	Pepsi-Cola	U.S.	beverages	5,932	14

[5]Some of you may notice that some major brands like Levi's and Lego appear to be missing. The reason is that Interbrand's calculation method relies on publicly available financial data. Privately owned companies like Levi Strauss or Lego do not offer sufficient financial information.

[6]"Assessing a Name's Worth," *Financial Times* (June 22, 1999), p. 12.

EXHIBIT 12-1 (continued)

	Brand Name	Country of Origin	Industry	Brand Value ($US m)	Brand Value % of Market Capitalization
33	Kleenex	U.S.	personal care	4,602	21
34	Wrigley's	U.S.	food	4,404	50
35	AOL	U.S.	software	4,329	18
36	Apple	U.S.	computers	4,283	77
37	Louis Vuitton	France	fashion	4,076	34
38	Barbie	U.S.	toys	3,792	46
39	Motorola	U.S.	telecoms	3,643	15
40	Adidas	Germany	sports goods	3,596	N.A.
41	Colgate	U.S.	personal care	3,568	18
42	Hertz	U.S.	car hire	3,527	75
43	IKEA	Sweden	housewares	3,464	N.A.
44	Chanel	France	fashion	3,143	N.A.
45	BP	U.K.	oil	2,985	3
46	Bacardi	Cuba	alcohol	2,895	N.A.
47	Burger King	U.S.	food	2,806	8
48	Moet & Chandon	France	alcohol	2,804	23
49	Shell	U.K.	oil	2,681	2
50	Rolex	Switzerland	luxury	2,423	N.A.
51	Smirnoff	U.K.	alcohol	2,313	7
52	Heineken	Holland	alcohol	2,184	15
53	Yahoo!	U.S.	software	1,761	14
54	Ralph Lauren	U.S.	fashion	1,648	66
55	Johnnie Walker	U.K.	alcohol	1,634	5
56	Pampers	U.S.	personal care	1,422	1
57	amazon.com	U.S.	books	1,361	7
58	Hilton	U.S.	leisure	1,319	35
59	Guinness	Ireland	leisure	1,262	4
60	Marriott	U.S.	leisure	1,193	52

Source: www.interbrand.com/league_chart.html

values, the same positioning. Very few brands meet these strict criteria. Even a company like Procter & Gamble has only a few brands in its portfolio that can be described as truly global, namely: Always/Whisper (feminine protection), Pringles (potato chips), and Pantene (hair care). Four other brands—Ariel/Tide, Safeguard, Oil of Olay, Pampers—are beginning to establish a common positioning.[7]

What is the case for global branding? One advantage of having a global brand name is obvious: economies of scale. First and foremost, the development costs for products launched under the global brand name can be spread over large volumes. This is especially a bonus in high-tech industries (e.g., pharmaceuticals, computing, chemicals, automobiles) where multibillion dollar R & D projects are the norm. Scale economies also arise in manufacturing, distribution (warehousing and shipping), and, possibly, promotion of a single-brand product. As we noted in the last chapter, computerized design and manufacturing processes allow companies to

---

[7]"Even at P & G, Only 3 Brands Make Truly Global Grade So Far," *Advertising Age International* (January 1998), p. 8.

harvest the scale benefits of mass production while customizing the product to the needs of the local market. Even then, substantial scale advantages on the distribution and marketing front often strongly favor global branding.

The scale advantage is only one of the reasons for using a global brand name.[8] Part of the task of brand managers is building up brand awareness. By its very nature, a global brand has much more visibility than a local brand. Prospective customers who travel around may be exposed to the brand both in their home country and in many of the countries they visit. Therefore, it is typically far easier to build up brand awareness for a global brand than for a local brand. A global brand can also capitalize on the extensive media overlap that exists in many regions. Cable-TV subscribers in Europe and many Asian countries have access to scores of channels from neighboring countries. Having a global brand that is being advertised on one (or more) of these channels can mean more bang for the bucks.

A further benefit is the prestige-factor. Simply stated, the fact of being *global* adds to the image of your brand. It signals that you have the resources to compete globally, and it signals that you have the willpower and commitment to support your brand worldwide.[9] Positioning yourself as a global brand can be very effective if you are able to claim leadership in your home country, especially when there is a favorable match between the product and the country image. After years of an uphill struggle, Marlboro quickly became the leading cigarette brand in Hong Kong when it positioned itself as being the leading brand in the United States. Those global brands that can claim worldwide leadership in their product category have even more clout: Colgate, Intel, Marlboro, Coca-Cola, and Nike, to mention just a few.

In some cases global brands are also able to leverage the country association for the product: McDonald's is U.S. fast food, L'Oréal is French cosmetics, Swatch is a Swiss watch, Nissin Cup is Japanese noodles, and so on. A desire to reflect its American roots also motivated Disney to change the name for its Paris themepark from Euro Disney to Disneyland Paris.[10] Of course, such positioning loses some of its appeal when your competition has the same heritage. For instance, Marlboro is an American cigarette brand, but so are Camel and Salem.

The arguments for global branding sound very powerful. Note, though, that like many other aspects of global marketing, the value of a brand, its *brand equity*, usually varies a great deal from country to country. A large-scale brand assessment study done by the advertising agency DDB Needham in Europe illustrates this point:[11] brand equity scores for Kodak ranged from 104 in Spain to 130 in the United Kingdom and Italy.[12] Inter-country gaps in brand equity may be due to any of the following factors:

1. *History.* By necessity, brands that have been around for a long time tend to have much more familiarity among consumers than latecomers. Usually, early

---

[8]David A. Aaker, *Managing Brand Equity, Capitalizing on the Value of a Brand Name* (New York: The Free Press, 1991).

[9]David A. Aaker, *Building Strong Brands* (New York: The Free Press, 1996).

[10]"The Kingdom Inside a Republic," *The Economist* (April 13, 1996), pp. 68–69.

[11]Jeri Moore, "Building Brands Across Markets: Cultural Differences in Brand Relationships Within the European Community," in D. A. Aaker and A. L. Biel, eds. *Brand Equity & Advertising: Advertising's Role in Building Strong Brands* (Hillsdale, NJ: Erlbaum Associates, 1993).

[12]The scores were derived via a multiplication formula: Brand Awareness × Brand Liking × Brand Perception.

entrants also will have a much more solid brand image if they have used a consistent positioning strategy over the years.

2. *Competitive climate.* The battlefield varies from country to country. In some countries the brand faces only a few competitors. In others, the brand constantly has to break through the clutter and combat scores of competing brands that nibble away at its market share.

3. *Marketing support.* Especially in decentralized organizations, the communication strategy used to back up the brand can vary a great deal. Some country affiliates favor *push strategies*, using trade promotions and other incentives targeted toward distributors. Others might prefer a *pull strategy* and thus focus on the end consumers. It is not uncommon for the positioning theme used in the advertising messages to vary from country to country.

4. *Cultural receptivity to brands.* Another factor is the cultural receptivity towards brands. Brand receptivity is largely driven by risk aversion. Within Europe, countries such as Spain and Italy are much more receptive toward brand names than Germany or France.[13] Asian societies tend to be very group-oriented. Being part of a group means sharing values and product experiences. As a result, this sense for collectivism leads to high levels of brand loyalty in Asian countries.

5. *Product category penetration.* A final factor is the salience of the product category in which the brand competes. Because of lifestyle differences, a given category will be established much more solidly in some countries than in others. In general, brand equity and product salience go together: the higher the product usage, the more solid will be the brand equity.

Local Branding

Coca-Cola has four core brands in its brand portfolio (Coke, Sprite, Diet Coke, and Fanta). At the same time, it also owns numerous regional and local brands worldwide. Although the advantages of a global brand name are numerous, there are also substantial benefits of using a local brand. In some cases legal constraints force the company to adopt a local brand name or "localize" an existing brand. In 1996 the Vietnamese government imposed new regulations that required that all brand names be localized. Billboards that did not comply with the new legislation were painted over. Government pressure could be another factor. In China, Coca-Cola promised to help develop China's soft-drink industry. To that end, Coca-Cola assisted in developing the Tian Yu Di brand—an umbrella brand for mineral water, tea, and juices.[14]

In some cases, a local brand becomes necessary because the name or a very similar name is already used within the country in another (or even the same) product category. Use of a global brand name may also be limited because someone already owns the right for the trademark in the foreign market. Heublein, a division of Britain's Diageo, was forbidden to use the Smirnoff name on any of its exports to Russia after a bitter court battle with Russian descendants of the Smirnoff name. By the same token, a decades-old trademark dispute prevents Anheuser Busch from using the Budweiser name in many European countries. Budweiser

---

[13]Moore.

[14]"Providing the Best Products at Best Price," *China Daily Business Weekly* (September 19/25, 1999), p. 7.

Budvar, a Czech brewery, claims ownership rights to the name stretching back to medieval times. Because of that, in countries like France and the Netherlands, Anheuser's beer is branded *Bud*.[15]

Cultural barriers also often justify local branding. Without localizing the brand name, the name might be hard to pronounce or may have undesirable associations in the local language. Soft drinks like the Japanese brew Pocari Sweat and the Dutch beverage Sisi would have a hard sell in Anglo-Saxon countries. Associations linked to the brand name often lose their relevance in the foreign market.[16] Brand names like 'Snuggle', 'Healthy Choice', 'Weight Watchers', or 'I Can't Believe It's Not Butter' don't mean much in non–English-speaking foreign markets.

A local linkage can also prove helpful in countries where patriotism and buy-local attitudes matter. Under such circumstances, the local brand name offers a cue that the company cares about local sensitivities. A case in point is the beer industry. Karel Vuursteen, Heineken chairman, states, "There is strong local heritage in the [beer] industry. People identify with their local brewery, which makes beer different from detergents or electronic products."[17] For that reason, beer brewers like Heineken expand by promoting global brands and, at the same time, buying local brands, distribution assets, and breweries. In many emerging markets, once the novelty and curiosity value of Western brands is gone, consumers often switch back to less expensive, local brands. To cope with such trends, many global marketers sell local brands side by side with their global brands. In Russia, Mars has created two products specifically for Russian consumers, the nutty Topic and the sugary mint Rondel. Although Snickers is still the leading brand, these two local brands are close behind.[18]

When the local brand name stems from an acquisition, keeping the local brand can be preferable to changing it into a global brand name. The brand equity built up over the years for the local brand can often be a tremendous asset. Thus, one motive for sticking with the local brand name is that the potential pay-offs from transforming it into a global brand name do not outweigh the equity that would have to be sacrificed. See Global Perspective 12–2 for further discussion.

Global or Local Brands?

By now you probably realize that there are no simple answers to the global-versus-local brand dilemma. Companies such as Nestlé, Philip Morris, or Unilever have a portfolio of local, regional, and global brands. Take Nestlé for example. The Swiss food multinational owns nearly 8,000 different brands worldwide. Exhibit 12–2 shows Nestlé's brand architecture. As you can see, Nestlé's brands are organized in a branding tree. At the root are ten worldwide corporate brands—brands like Carnation, Nestlé, and Perrier. The next level consists of forty-five strategic brands that are managed at the strategic business unit level. Examples include Kitkat, After

[15]"This Bud's for Them: Anheuser-Busch Takes Closer Aim at Foreign Markets," *The New York Times* (June 23, 1999).

[16]Rajeev Batra, "The Why, When, and How of Global Branding," in Sanjay Sood, ed., *Brand Equity and the Marketing Mix: Creating Customer Value*, Marketing Science Institute, Report No. 95-111, September 1995.

[17]"Time for Another Round," *Financial Times* (June 21, 1999).

[18]"The Cold War Over Chocolate," *Business Week* (July 21, 1997), p. 48.

◆ ◆

*G*LOBAL PERSPECTIVE 12–2

CHINESE BRANDS—UP AND COMING

Brand names like Haier, Legend, and Meidi are probably not yet household names for most non-Chinese people. While the "Made in China" label is fairly common, what is still unusual are products sold under Chinese brand names. Only a handful of mainland Chinese companies have the resources and the stamina to establish global brands. The Interbrand list of top fifty non-Japanese Asian brands that was published in 1999 included only one Chinese brand, namely Tsingtao. However, this situation is likely to change in the near future. According to Viveca Chan, Hong Kong-based managing director of Grey China, an advertising agency: "If there's one country in the world that has ample opportunity for taking brands global, it's China."

In the near term, the biggest potential is with goods strongly associated with China (e.g., Chinese medicine, tea, cuisine) or products that can leverage the mystique associated with China (fashion, music, cosmetics). Several state-owned enterprises (SOEs) and joint ventures are setting their eyes on overseas markets. They strongly believe that their products can compete with the best in the world. Many of them have given global giants a run for their money in China, their home turf. Apart from the extra revenues, there are other reasons why Chinese companies would like to create a global brand presence. Having a global brand bolsters a company's image in China, thereby boosting sales at home.

Sources: "The Long March," *Far Eastern Economic Review* (January 14, 1999), pp. 66–68; "Out of the Shadows," *The Economist* (August 28, 1999), pp. 52, 55; "Haier: Innovation Yields Growth," *China Daily Business Weekly* (Sept. 26–Oct. 2, 1999), p. 6.

One of the most successful companies so far in this regard is a household white goods maker with a German ring: Haier, an SOE managed by Zhang Ruimin. Zhang Ruimin, the charismatic president of the Haier group, has turned his company from a small collectively owned factory into a large transnational company, able to compete with the likes of Whirlpool and Electrolux. Zhang regards the only strong brands as those that are recognized in the international market. The group has grown more than 80 percent annually during the past fifteen years. Haier is governed by a strong market orientation, which is fairly unusual for a Chinese SOE. In October 1997, when Zhang visited Sichuan province, he heard complaints about the quality of Haier-made washers. Further probing indicated that the local people used their washers to wash sweet potatoes, in addition to clothes. This inspired Haier to develop a new kind of washing machine that could be used to wash potatoes.

Zhang's goal is to transform Haier into a world brand. Haier started making forays in international markets in 1997. Zhang's maxim—"First hard, then easy"—meant that he entered first Japan, Korea, the United States, and Europe rather than emerging markets in Asia or Latin America. Haier's international expansion did not always go smoothly. It took the firm almost a year to pass authentication procedures in Germany. The firm set up a plant in South Carolina and a design center in Los Angeles to localize its products in the United States. The company also opened a shop on New York's Fifth Avenue. Haier now holds around 20 percent share of the American market in small refrigerators (capacity less than 180 liters).

Eight, and Smarties. Climbing further, you can spot the regional strategic brands, managed at the regional level. For instance, in the frozen food category, Nestlé markets the Stouffer's brand in America and Asia and the Findus brand in Europe. At the very top of the tree is a multitude of local brands that are the responsibility of the local subsidiaries.

Although there is often a drive to build up global brands, there are solid reasons to make an in-depth analysis before converting local brands into regional or global ones. In fact, local brands sometimes can have much more appeal among consumers than their global competing brands. This is especially true when there is not much benefit from being global. In the Polish detergent market, P & G

EXHIBIT 12–2
NESTLÉ BRANDING TREE

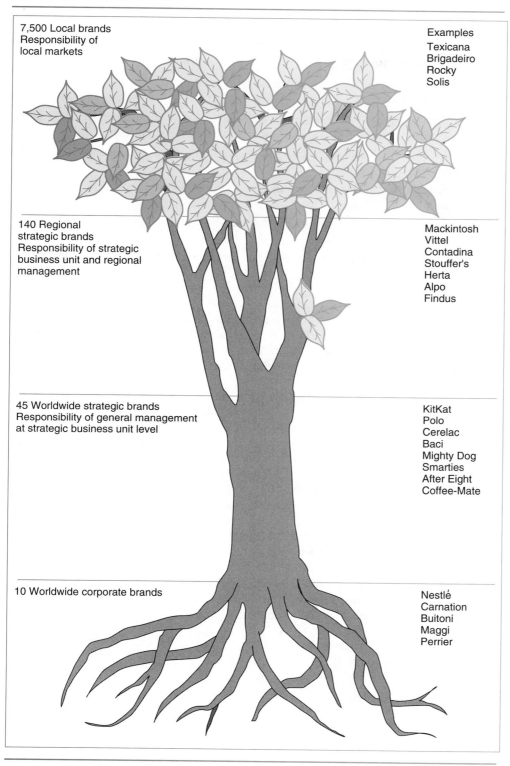

7,500 Local brands
Responsibility of
local markets

Examples
Texicana
Brigadeiro
Rocky
Solis

140 Regional
strategic brands
Responsibility of strategic
business unit and regional
management

Mackintosh
Vittel
Contadina
Stouffer's
Herta
Alpo
Findus

45 Worldwide strategic brands
Responsibility of general management
at strategic business unit level

KitKat
Polo
Cerelac
Baci
Mighty Dog
Smarties
After Eight
Coffee-Mate

10 Worldwide corporate brands

Nestlé
Carnation
Buitoni
Maggi
Perrier

launched Ariel and Unilever introduced Omo. The leading detergent brand, however, is Pollena 2000, a local brand owned by Unilever.[19]

David Aaker, an expert on branding, offers the following checklist for analyzing globalization propositions:[20]

1. What is the cost of creating and maintaining awareness and associations for a local brand versus a global one?

2. Are there significant economies of scale in the creation and running of a communication program globally (including advertising, PR, sponsorships)?

3. Is there value to associations of a global brand or of a brand associated with the source country?

4. What local associations will be generated by the global name? symbol? slogan? imagery?

5. Is it culturally and legally doable to use the brand name, symbol, or slogan across the different countries?

6. What is the value of the awareness and associations that a regional brand might create?

Brand Name Changeover Strategies

When the case for a transition from a local to a global (or regional) brand name is made, the firm needs to decide how to implement the changeover in practice. Four broad strategic options exist:[21] (1) fade-in/fade-out, (2) combine brands via co-branding or under one umbrella brand, (3) transparent forewarning, and (4) summary axing.

With **fade-in/fade-out**, the new global brand name is somehow tied with the existing local brand name. After a transition period, the old name is dropped. A typical example is the brand name change that Disney implemented for its Paris theme park. It first shrunk the *Euro* part in Euro Disney and added the word *land*. In October 1994 the word *Euro* was dropped altogether and the theme park is now branded as *Disneyland Paris*.[22]

The second route combines the "old" local brand and the global or regional brand in some manner. One tactic that is sometimes employed is to have the global brand as an umbrella or endorser brand. For example, Pedigree was launched in the late 1980s in France as "Pedigree by Pal." Another possibility is **dual branding**. When Whirlpool acquired the white goods division of Philips, the company initially employed a dual branding strategy—Philips and Whirlpool. After a transition period, the Philips brand name was dropped. Likewise, AXA, the French insurance group, uses **co-branding** to consolidate its multiple brands into a single global brand in those markets where the local brand has high awareness. For instance, in

[19]"Unilever Chief: Refresh Brands," *Advertising Age International* (July 18, 1994), p. I-20.

[20]David A. Aaker, *Managing Brand Equity* (New York: The Free Press, 1991).

[21]Trond Riiber Knudsen, Lars Finskud, Richard Törnblom, and Egil Hogna, "Brand Consolidation Makes a Lot of Economic Sense," *The McKinsey Quarterly*, 4 (1997), pp. 189–93.

[22]"The Kingdom Inside a Republic," *The Economist* (April 13, 1996), p. 69.

the United States, Equitable was turned into AXA Equitable. After several years, the Equitable part of the brand will be dropped.[23]

The third approach, **transparent forewarning**, alerts the customers about the brand name change. The forewarning can be done via the communication program, in-store displays, and product packaging. A good example is the transition made by Mars in the Pan-European market for Raider, one of its candy products. Mars launched a TV-advertising campaign to launch the change, saying: "Now Raider becomes Twix, for it is Twix everywhere in the world." The print ad in Exhibit 12–3 is part of a campaign that HSBC, the London-based banking group, undertook when it replaced its local banking brands with the HSBC name.

Far less compelling is the fourth practice, **summary axing**, where the company simply drops the old brand name almost overnight and immediately replaces it with the global name. This is only appropriate when competitors are rapidly gaining global clout by building up global brands.

To manage the transition effectively, there are some rules that should be respected.[24] When the name is changed gradually, one of the key concerns is the proper length for the transition period. Coming back to the Philips–Whirlpool example, the two companies had agreed that Whirlpool could use the Philips brand name until 1999. In principle, the firm should allow sufficient time for the customers to absorb the name change. How long this process will take depends on the product and the strength of the image associated with the old brand name. For some product categories, the purchase cycle matters, too. Sometimes the phase-out can be done sooner than scheduled. Whirlpool discovered through its research that the Philips brand name could be dropped far ahead of the originally planned drop date.

It is also important that consumers that are exposed to the changeover messages, via advertising or product packaging or both, associate the new brand name with the old one. One of the primary goals of Whirlpool's advertising campaign was to maintain awareness of the Philips brand name while building up association with Whirlpool.[25]

To avoid negative spillovers on the global brand name, companies should also ensure that the local products have acceptable quality before attaching the global brand name to them. Otherwise, the goodwill of the global brand name could be irreparably damaged. As a result, other products launched under the global brand name might be viewed with skepticism by consumers in the foreign market. Part of Whirlpool's geographic expansion in China involved a joint venture that makes air conditioners based on Japanese designs. The air conditioners, sold under a local brand name, Raybo, initially had about half the life expectancy of U.S.-made Whirlpool models. Whirlpool's president declared that his company would not put the Whirlpool name on the product until its quality problems were fixed.[26]

---

[23]"AXA Spends $70 Million to Create Global Brand," *Advertising Age International* (April 13, 1998), p. 2.

[24]Marieke de Mooij, *Advertising Worldwide: Concepts, Theories and Practice of International, Multinational and Global Advertising* (Prentice-Hall, 1994).

[25]Jan Willem Karel, "Brand Strategy Positions Products Worldwide," *The Journal of Business Strategy* (May/June 1991), pp. 16–19.

[26]"For Whirlpool, Asia Is the New Frontier," *The Wall Street Journal* (April 25, 1996), p. B-1.

EXHIBIT 12–3

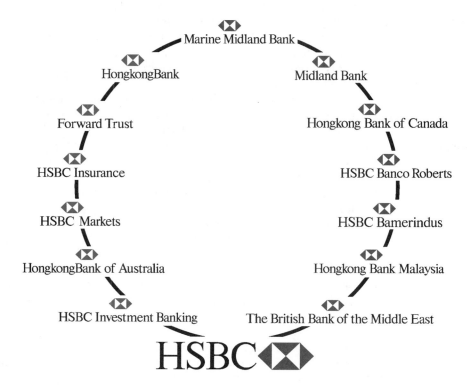

ONE FAMILY, NOW ONE NAME.

We are uniting our family around the world under one name. HSBC.

Why? Because as one of the world's most successful financial services organizations we would like you to understand us better.

You may have met our people already. You talk to them every time you are in touch with one of our family members. But you may not yet know just how much we can do for you around the corner and around the world.

With more than $41 billion in capital resources, and 5,500 offices in 79 countries and territories, we are big enough to help and close enough to care.

Talk to us and see. You can be sure of a warm welcome.

Finally, companies should monitor the marketplace's response to the brand name change with marketing research. Such tracking studies enable the firm to ensure that the changeover runs smoothly. They also assist firms in determining how long promotional programs that announce the name change should last. Whirlpool tracked brand recognition and buying preference of consumers on a weekly basis during the brand-change period.

We now consider two other branding practices that companies use, namely private branding and corporate branding:

Heinz is one of the leading canned soup brands in the United Kingdom. The company also sells soup in the United States. In fact, Heinz has captured a 7 percent share of the overall soup category. But the soup that Heinz makes in the United States is not sold under the Heinz brand name.[27] Instead, it is sold under store brand names. Heinz has an 87 percent share of the private label soup market in the United States.[28]

One of the most visible retailing phenomena during the last decade is the spread of **private labels** ("store brands"). Private labels come under various guises. At one extreme are the generic products that are packaged very simply and sold at bottom prices. At the other extreme are premium store brands that deliver quality sometimes superior to national brands. Private labels have made big inroads in several European countries. They account for almost one-third of supermarket sales in the United Kingdom and one-fourth in France.[29] In Japan and most other Asian countries, on the other hand, store brands are still marginal players. Consumers in this region tend to be extremely brand loyal.[30] Private labels, however, are definitely on the rise in the Asia, as can be seen in Exhibit 12-4.

Private Label Branding ("Store Brands")

EXHIBIT 12-4
PRIVATE LABELS AS PERCENTAGE OF RETAIL SALES IN ASIA

	1990	1995
Taiwan	5.0	12.0
Singapore	3.8	6.6
Hong Kong	4.2	6.5
South Korea	4.0	6.0
Malaysia	2.9	5.3
Thailand	2.2	5.0
Philippines	2.2	3.3
Japan	1.0	2.5
Indonesia	0.0	0.3

Source: "Asian Private Label," *Retail Monitor International* (April 1997), p. 115. Reprinted with kind permission of Euromonitor.

[27]Heinz once did market canned soup under its own name in the United States.
[28]"Your Global Portfolio," Heinz, Corporate Affairs Department, 1995.
[29]Erich Joachimsthaler, "Marketing Metamorphosis: From Products to Brand to Consumers," *mimeo*, IESE, Barcelona, 1994.
[30]"No Global Private Label Quake—Yet," *Advertising Age International* (January 16, 1995), p. I-26.

Several factors explain the success of private labels:[31]

1. *Improved quality of private label products.* Many years ago private labels used to have a quality stigma: only cheapskates would buy a store brand. Today the quality gap between store brands and their brand-name competitors is gone in most countries. The improved quality image is probably the key success factor behind the spread of store brands. In many product categories, consumers now have the option to buy a good-quality store brand at a lower price than the brand-name alternative.

2. *Development of premium private-label brands.* Not only has the quality gap disappeared, but retailers in North America and Europe in collaboration with private-label manufacturers have developed private-label products that offer premium quality. In some cases, store brand products have even become far more innovative than the competing name brand products.

3. *Shift in balance of power between retailers and manufacturers.* A third factor is the shift in the balance of power from manufacturers to retailers. This reversal has been strong, especially in Europe, where large-scale national chains dominate the retailing landscape. Italy is one of the few countries in Europe where private labels have made little progress. It is also a market where government regulations have dampened the development of big chain stores.

4. *Expansion into new product categories.* Private labels used to be limited to a small range of product categories. These days private labels are marketed in an ever-widening range of categories. This spread has helped to make private labels more acceptable among consumers.

5. *Internationalization of retail chains.* Another factor is the growing internationalization of large supermarket chains. In recent years, French hypermarchés like Carrefour invaded Spain, the German food-store chain Aldi entered the Benelux countries, France, and the United Kingdom, and the Dutch retailer Ahold started to penetrate the U.S. market. Many of these international retailers plan to replicate their private-label program in the host country.

6. *Economic downturns.* When disposable income drops, consumers usually become more value conscious and tend to switch from national brands to private labels.[32] Without doubt, the persistent economic malaise in many European countries has been a major driver behind the success of store brands in Europe.

As a branding strategy, private labeling is especially attractive to MNCs that face well-entrenched incumbent brands in the markets they plan to enter. Under such circumstances, launching the product as a store brand enables the firm to get the shelf space access which it would otherwise be denied.

The private labels boom offers for many manufacturers an opportunity to penetrate markets that would otherwise be hard to crack. In Japan, manufacturers that do not have the resources to set up a distribution channel network have tied up with local retailers to penetrate the market. Agfa-Gevaert, the German/Belgian photographic film maker agreed to supply a store brand film to Daiei, a major Japanese supermarket chain.[33] Eastman Kodak also decided to offer private-label film in Japan. Most of the distribution system is locked up by the local competitors,

---

[31]John A. Quelch and David Harding, "Brands versus Private Labels: Fighting to Win," *Harvard Business Review* (January-February 1996), pp. 99–109.

[32]Stephen J. Hoch and Shumeet Banerji, "When Do Private Labels Succeed?" *Sloan Management Review* (Summer 1993), pp. 57–67.

[33]"Japan' Brands Feel the Pinch, Too," *Financial Times* (April 28, 1994), p. 9.

Fuji and Konica. Kodak hoped to grab a larger share of the Japanese film market by making a private-label film for the Japanese Cooperative Union, a group of 2,500 retail stores.[34]

Umbrella branding is a system where a single banner brand is used worldwide, often with a sub-brand name, for almost the entire product mix of the company. Often times, the banner is the company's name: Sony, Kodak, Siemens, Virgin, to name a few. Some companies also use noncompany names. For example, Matsushita, the Japanese consumer electronics maker, employs banner brands like JVC and Panasonic. Umbrella branding is particularly popular among Japanese firms, though there are also quite a few non-Japanese companies that opt for this branding system.

> **Umbrella (Corporate) Branding**

What is the appeal of corporate branding in a global marketing context? Researchers have identified several reasons. First and foremost, in many cultures a good corporate image will have a strong positive impact on the evaluation of the attributes of the product endorsed by the banner brand. For the customers, the presence of the banner brand's logo on the product means trust, a seal of approval, and a guarantee for quality and excellence.[35] The umbrella brand basically serves as a risk-reducing device for the customer.[36] London International Group (LIG), the world's leading condom marketer, mentions this benefit as the reason behind its drive to make the Durex brand the umbrella for its condom business world wide.[37] Local brand names are now tied with the Durex name. In Germany, the packaging was altered to say "From the house of Durex." One observer described the motives behind this move as follows:

> The idea behind it is that anywhere you go in the world, you will see the Durex name, rather than lots of sub-brands. People want security and safety when they are buying these products.

A second benefit is that umbrella branding facilitates brand-building efforts over a range of products. Having a banner brand makes it easier to build up global share of mind and brand integrity.[38] Instead of splitting marketing dollars over scores of different brands, the advertising support focuses on a single umbrella brand. A case in point is Nokia, one of the leading makers of cellular phones. Nokia used to have scores of brand names. These days the company pushes the corporate brand name in the global marketplace where the Nokia brand is far less familiar than in Scandinavia. As one company official commented: "We had many brand names but now we believe it is better to stick to one brand."[39]

---

[34]"Kodak Pursues a Greater Market Share in Japan with new Private-Label Film, *"Wall Street Journal* (March 7, 1995), p. B-4

[35]Camillo Pagano, "The Management of Global Brands," in Paul Stobart, ed., *Brand Power* (London: The MacMillan Press, Ltd., 1994).

[36]Cynthia A. Montgomery and Birger Wernerfelt, "Risk Reduction and Umbrella Branding," *Journal of Business*, 65 (1) (1992), pp. 31–50.

[37]"LIG Stretches Durex Identity Around World," *Advertising Age International* (March 11, 1996), p. I-4.

[38]Gary Hamel and C.K. Prahalad, *Competing for the Future* (Boston, MA: Harvard Business School Press, 1994).

[39]"Scandinavia's Nokia Phones Japan," *Advertising Age International* (December 13, 1993), p. I-6.

A final rationale is that a corporate branding system makes it easier to add or drop new products.[40] High-tech companies like Siemens and Motorola tend to rely very heavily on product innovation to defend their market share. Nurturing a single strong banner brand is far more efficient than creating a distinct brand from scratch for every new product launch.

Protecting Brand Names

Visitors in Kathmandu who are getting tired of Nepalese cuisine can always try out the local Pizza Hut. Just like Pizza Hut restaurants elsewhere in the world, it serves pizza. But except for the name and the main menu items, the Kathmandu Pizza Hut has nothing in common with a U.S. Pizza Hut. Exhibit 12–5 presents another example of trademark infringement: Pizza Domino, a pizza chain based in Israel, with a logo (and name) that bears a striking resemblance to a well-known pizza chain.

Brands are vital assets to brand owners. The Coca-Cola trademark is estimated to be worth almost $84 billion, nearly 60 percent of the company's market value.[41] Given the strategic importance of brands, protection of the brand name is one of the major tasks faced by the brand owner. The protection challenge entails several questions: How should the brand be protected? Which aspects of the brand? When? Where? For what product classes? Answers to these questions are largely driven by an analysis of the costs and benefits of protecting the brand.

Consider the first issue: How? The most common way to seek protection is by legal registration. The first step is to hire legal counsel in each country where the brand should be protected. There are several international agreements in force that help this process. The oldest treaty is the Paris Convention for the Protection of

EXHIBIT 12–5
PIZZA DOMINO IN ISRAEL: TWIN BROTHER OF DOMINO'S PIZZA?

Source: Courtesy Edmund Wong.

---

[40]Hiroshi Tanaka, "Branding in Japan," in D. A. Aaker & A. L. Biel, eds., *Brand Equity & Advertising: Advertising's Role in Building Strong Brands* (Hillsdale, NJ: L. Erlbaum Associates, 1993).

[41]"Assessing a Name's Worth," *Financial Times* (June 22, 1999), p. 12.

Intellectual Property supported by almost a hundred countries. The Paris Convention is based on the principle of reciprocity: (1) people of member states have the same rights that the state grants to its own nationals, and (2) foreigners have equal access to local courts to combat trademark infringement. In the European Union, the Single Market Act also had ramifications for brand protection: trademark registration in any of the EU member states is now effective for the entire European Union.

One major stumbling block is the difference in opinion held by industrialized and developing countries on intellectual property protection. Developed countries view intellectual property right protection as the reward for innovativeness. Taking the protection away would mean that companies lose their incentive to invest in new product development. Many developing countries, on the other hand, regard intellectual property (IP) as a public good. Easy access to IP spurs economic development and, thereby, enables the developing country to narrow the gap with the developed world.[42] The two opposing views are summarized in Exhibit 12–6.

What should be protected? Many elements of the brand franchise may require protection. Obviously, one should register the brand name. But in some countries, you might also consider protecting the translation of the brand name, or even the transliteration equivalent—that is, representations in the local language that have

EXHIBIT 12–6
DIFFERING VIEWS ON INTELLECTUAL PROPERTY PROTECTION

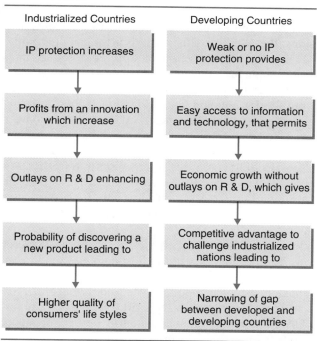

Source: Subhash C. Jain, "Problems in International Protection of Intellectual Property Rights," *Journal of International Marketing*, 4 (1) (1996), pp. 9–32.

---

[42]Subhash C. Jain, "Problems in International Protection of Intellectual Property Rights," *Journal of International Marketing*, 4 (1) (1996), pp. 9–32.

the same sound.[43] Other forms of intellectual property that might need protection include slogans, jingles, visual aspects (e.g., McDonald's golden arches)—in short, any distinctive elements that are part of the brand's imagery.

The "when" and "where" issues at first sight appear trivial: ideally, you would like to register the brand's trademarks in as many places and as soon as possible. But some constraints enter the picture here. The costs of registration itself are usually quite modest. But legal counsel fees are far more significant. However, the major cost item is often the use cost. In many countries, the company is obliged to "use" the trademarks in order to enjoy the protection benefits. *Use* means that the company has to sell commercially significant volumes of the product under the protected brand name. Most countries, however, give a grace period of several years (usually five) before the brand owner has to use the registered trademarks.

The last concern deals with the scope of the protection: What product classes should be covered? Many companies register their brands in virtually all product categories. A more sensible rule is to register the trademarks in all classes covering goods for which the brand is currently used and related classes.[44] The related classes are product categories that the company might enter in the future via brand extensions, using the protected brand name.

◆ ◆ ◆ ◆ ◆ ◆ MANAGING MULTINATIONAL PRODUCT LINES

Most companies sell a wide assortment of products. The product assortment is usually described on two dimensions: the width and the length of the product mix.[45] The first dimension—*width*—refers to the collection of different product lines marketed by the firm. For most companies these product lines are very related. Heinz has a broad mix of product lines. Besides ketchup, Heinz's flagship product, the company sells baby food, pet food, ice cream, and so forth. All these product lines are food items. Other companies, especially Japanese and Korean ones, have a much more diverse product mix. Kao, one of Japan's biggest consumer goods manufacturers, has a product mix that covers personal care products, cosmetics, laundry products, and food items. But Kao also sells chemicals, floppy disks and CD-ROMs. The second dimension—*length*—refers to the number of different items that the company sells within a given product line. Thus, the product mix for a particular multinational could vary along the width and/or length dimension across the different countries where the firm operates.

When comparing the product mix in the company's host and home markets, there are four possible scenarios. The product mix in the host country could be an extension of the domestic line, a subset of the home market's product line, a mixture of local and nonlocal product lines, or, lastly, a completely localized product line.

Small firms with a narrow product assortment will simply extend their domestic product line. Blistex, a tiny U.S. company that makes primarily lip-care products, has a very limited range of product lines that are marketed in all of its foreign

---

[43]Garo Partoyan, "Protecting Power Brands," in P. Stobart, ed., *Brand Power* (London: MacMillan, 1994).

[44]Ibid.

[45]See, for instance, Douglas J. Dalrymple and Leonard J. Parsons, *Marketing Management* (New York: John Wiley & Sons, Inc., 1995).

markets. Companies that enter new markets carefully select a subset of their product mix. When Coca-Cola goes into a new market, the focus is obviously first on Coca-Cola. Once the flagship brand is well established, the next introduction is typically Fanta, the flavor line. Fanta is followed by Sprite and Diet Coke. Once the infrastructure is in place, other product lines—including local ones—are added over time.[46] Most MNCs have a product mix that is partly global (or regional) and partly home-grown. A typical example is presented in Exhibit 12–7,

EXHIBIT 12–7
INTERNATIONAL PRODUCT MIX OF BEST FOODS

Market Positions Worldwide

1 Leader in Market Share
2 Second in Market Share
• Present in the Market
◆ Technical or Licensing Agreement

	Soups*	Sauces*	Bouillons	Mealmakers*	Potato Products	Pasta	Mayonnaise	Pourable Dressings	Corn Oil	Foodservice**	Peanut Butter	Starches	Desserts (Ambient)	Premium Baking
	Worldwide Businesses										Key Business			
North America, Caribbean														
Canada	2	2	1				1		1	•	2	1		
United States	•	•	2	•	•	•	1	•	1	•	2	1	•	1
Dominican Republic	2		2				•		•	•		1		
Europe, Africa/Middle East														
Austria	1	1	1	1	1				1	•		1		
Belgium	1	1	1	1						•		1		
Bulgaria	•	•	•		•					•				
Czech Republic	2	2	2	2	•		1	1		•				
Denmark	1	1	1	1	2			2	1	•		1	•	
Finland	1	1	1	2					1	•		2		
France	1	2	2				2	2		•		1	1	
Germany	2	2	2	2	1		•		1	•		1	•	
Greece	1	1	1		2	1	1	1		•		2	2	
Hungary	1	1	2	2	1		2			•				•
Ireland	1	1	1	1	1	•	1	2	•	•		2	1	
Italy	1	•	2		1		•		•	•		1		
Netherlands	2	1	2	2	•				•	•		2		
Norway	•	2	•						•	•		1		
Poland	1	1	1	1	1		2			•				•
Portugal	1	•	1		2		1	2		•		1	2	
Romania	1		1		•					•				•
Russia	2	•	2		1		•		•	•	•			
Slovak Republic	•	•	•	•	•		1			•				
Spain	2	•	2	•		•	•	•		•		1	2	
Sweden	1	2	1	1				•	1	•	1	1		
Switzerland	1	1	1	1	1		•	•	•			1	•	
United Kingdom	2	•	2	•		•	1	2	1	•		1	1	
Israel	1	2	2	1	•	•	1		1	•	1		2	

---

[46]www.thecoca-colacompany.com/investors/Divester.html

EXHIBIT 12–7 (continued)

Market Positions Worldwide

1 Leader in Market Share
2 Second in Market Share
• Present in the Market
◆ Technical or Licensing Agreement

	Soups*	Sauces*	Bouillons	Mealmakers*	Potato Products	Pasta	Mayonnaise	Pourable Dressings	Corn Oil	Foodservice**	Peanut Butter	Starches	Desserts (Ambient)	Premium Baking
					Worldwide Businesses							Key Business		
Europe, Africa/Middle East														
Jordan	2		2							•				
Kenya	1		1							•	•	2	1	
Morocco	1	•	1							•			1	1
Saudi Arabia							2		2	•	•	•		
South Africa	1	2	1	1			•	1		•	•		1	•
Tunisia	1	•	1				•			•		2		•
Turkey	1		2	•						•			1	•
Latin America														
Argentina	1		1	•	1		1	1	2	•			1	•
Bolivia	•		•				2						1	
Brazil	2	•	1			2	1	1	1	•			1	•
Chile	2	•			2		1	1	1	•			1	•
Colombia	•	2	2	2	•		1	•	•	•			1	1
Costa Rica	2	1	2				1	1	1	•	•		1	•
Ecuador	2	•	•	2			•		1	•			•	
El Salvador		•					•	•	1		•		1	
Guatemala	•		•				•	1	1	•	•		1	
Honduras		•					•		1				2	
Mexico	1	•	1	1		1	2	•	2	•			1	•
Panama	•		•				•	•	•	•			1	
Paraguay	2		2		2	•	1		2	•			1	•
Peru	2	•	2		2		1	•	1	•			1	•
Uruguay	1		1		1	•	1	1	2				1	•
Venezuela	2	•	2	1			•	•		•			1	•
Asia														
China	•	•	2				•			•	•	•	•	•
Hong Kong	•		1			•	2		•	•		1	1	1
India	1			•						•			1	1
Indonesia	1		•				2	2	1	•	2			
Japan◆	1	•	1	•			2	2	1	•	•			
Malaysia	1		2				1	1	1	•		1		2
Pakistan	1	•	1	•			2		1	•			1	1
Philippines	1	•	1			1	1			•		1		1
Singapore	1		1				1	•	•	•		1	1	1
Sri Lanka	2	1	2						•	•				
Taiwan	1		1				2	1	•	•		1		
Thailand	1	1	1	2		1	1		1	•		1	•	•
Vietnam	2		1				•			•				

*Dehydrated products only.

**Best Foods foodservice (catering) products hold leading share positions in many of the categories in which they compete.

Source: BestFoods, *1998 Annual Report.*

which gives an overview of the wordwide product mix of Bestfoods, an American food company.

Several drivers affect the composition of a firm's international product line. These include customer preferences, the price spectrum, the competitive climate, the firm's organizational structures, and the product's history.

Customer Preferences.   In many product categories, consumer preferences vary from country to country. Especially for consumer packaged goods, preferences are still very localized. To cater to their distinctive customer needs, marketers may add certain items to the country's product lines that are not offered elsewhere. This point is illustrated in Exhibit 12–8, which shows the leading Campbell's soup flavors for a sample of countries around the globe. Although there is some overlap ("Cream of Mushroom" is highly popular in the United Kingdom, the United States, and Mexico) some of the other popular flavors (e.g., "Cream of Pumpkin" in Australia) are not even offered in the U.S. market.

Price Spectrum.   In emerging markets, companies often compete across the price spectrum by offering premium and budget products. The upscale products are targeted toward prosperous consumers. Budget products are offered as entry-level or value products for other consumers. Colgate exemplifies this approach. For small mom-and-pop stores, Colgate adapts its package designs to provide single-size sachets, small refillable bottles, and paperboard cartons. The giant supermarkets, on the other hand, stack the same brands in larger sizes.

Competitive Climate.   Differences in the competitive environment often explain why a company offers certain product lines in some countries but not in others. A telling example is the canned soup industry. In the United States, the soup category is basically owned by the Campbell Soup Company: eight out of

EXHIBIT 12–8
TOP-SELLING CAMPBELL'S SOUPS AROUND THE WORLD

Country	Top-Selling Soup Flavour
United States	Chicken Noodle (No. 2: Cream of Mushroom; (No. 3: Tomato)
Australia	Cream of Pumpkin
Canada	Tomato
Hong Kong	Cream Style Corn with Chicken
Mexico	Cream of Mushroom
U.K.	Cream of Mushroom

Source: Campbell Soup Company, *1995 Annual Report*, pp. 18–19. (Photo courtesy of Campbell Soup Company.)

every ten cans of soup are sold under the Campbell's brand name.[47] Given the clout of the Campbell's brand name, it is virtually impossible to penetrate the U.S. canned soup market. The picture is quite different in the United Kingdom, where Campbell's was a relative latecomer. In the United Kingdom, the leading canned soup brand is Heinz with a 36 percent share of the market.[48] Coca-Cola's product line strategy in Japan is also driven to a large degree by the local rivalry in the Japanese beverage market. One of the pillars of Coke's Japan-marketing strategy is to improve on its rivals' products. As a result, Coke sells an incredible variety of beverages in Japan that are not available anywhere else (see Exhibit 12–9).

Organizational Structure. Especially in MNCs that are organized on a country basis, product lines may evolve to a large degree independently in the different countries. The scope of the country manager's responsibility is increasingly being limited in many MNCs (see Chapter 18). Nevertheless, country managers still have a great deal of decision-making autonomy in many functional areas, including product policy.

History. Product lines often become part of an MNC's local product mix following geographic expansion efforts. Companies like Procter & Gamble, Heinz, and Sara Lee penetrate new and existing markets via acquisitions. Some of these acquisitions include product lines that are outside the MNC's core business. Rather

EXHIBIT 12–9
LIST OF COCA-COLA'S LOCAL BRANDS IN JAPAN

Brand	Launch Year	Product Description
Ambasa	1981	Noncarbonated, lactic soft drink with familiar smooth taste for everyday use.
Calo	1997	"Functional" soft drink with cocoa taste; helps build healthy bones.
Georgia	1975	Authentic, real coffee drink with variety of flavors sourced from around the world.
Ko Cha Ka Den	1992	Line of blended teas.
Lactia	1996	Lactic, noncarbonated soft drink; offers healthy digestion and quick refreshment.
Perfect Water	1997	Mineral-balanced water; helps restore balance to daily life.
Real Gold	1981	Carbonated, herb-mix flavored drink; provides quick energy.
Saryusaisai	1993	Non-sugar Oolong tea drink.
Seiryusabo	1994	Green and Barley tea drinks.
Shpla	1996	Citrus flavored soft drink; helps overcome mental stress and dullness.
Vegitabeta	1991	Peach-flavored soft drink; helps maintain healthy balance.

[47]Campbell Soup Company, *1995 Annual Report.*
[48]H.J. Heinz Company, *1995 Annual Report.*

than divesting these noncore businesses, a company often decides to keep them. As part of its growth strategy in Central Europe, Heinz acquired Kecskemeti Konzerv-gyar, a Hungarian canning company. The company makes a broad range of food products, including baby food, ketchup, pickles—staple items for Heinz—but also products like jams and canned vegetables—items that are not really part of Heinz's core business lines.

Global marketers need to decide for each market of interest which product lines should be offered and which ones are to be dropped. When markets are entered for the first time, market research can be very helpful for designing the initial product assortment. Market research is less useful for radically new products (e.g., frozen yogurt, electric vehicles) or newly emerging markets. In such situations, the company should consider using a "probing-and-learning" approach. Such a procedure has the following steps:

1. Start with a product line that has a minimum level of product variety.
2. Gradually adjust the amount of product variety over time by adding new items and dropping existing ones.
3. Analyze the incoming actual sales data and other market feedback.
4. Make the appropriate inferences.
5. If necessary, adjust the product line further.[49]

The gist of this procedure is to use the product line as a **listening post** for the new market to see what product items work best.

By and large, add/drop decisions should be driven by profit considerations. In the global marketing arena, it is crucial not just to look at profit ramifications within an individual country. Ideally, the profitability analysis should be done on a regional or even global basis. A good start is to analyze each individual country's product portfolio on a sales turnover basis. Product lines can be categorized as (1) core products, (2) niche items, (3) seasonal products, or (4) filler products.[50] Core products are the items that represent the bulk of the subsidiary's sales volume. Niche products appeal to small segments of the population, which might grow. Seasonal products have most of their sales during limited times of the year. Finally, filler products are items that account for only a small portion of the subsidiary's overall sales. These might include "dead-weight" items whose sales were always lackluster or prospective up-and-coming products. From a global perspective, a comparison of the product mix make-up across the various countries provides valuable insights. Such an analysis might provide answers to questions like:

- Could some of our "seasonal" products in country A be turned into "core" items in country B?
- Given our track record in country A, which ones of our filler products should be considered as up-and-coming in country B and which ones should be written off as dead-weight products?

---

[49]Anirudh Dhebar, "Using Extensive, Dynamic Product Lines for Listening in on Evolving Demand," *European Management Journal*, 13 (2) (June 1995), pp. 187–92.

[50]John A. Quelch and David Kenny, "Extend Profits, Not Product Lines, *Harvard Business Review* (Sept.–Oct. 1994), pp. 153–60.

- Is there a way to streamline our product assortment in country A by dropping some of the items and consolidating others, given our experience in country B?

◆ ◆ ◆ ◆ ◆ ◆ ◆ PRODUCT PIRACY

Product piracy is one of the downsides that marketers with popular global brand names face. Any aspect of the product is vulnerable to piracy, including the brand name, the logo, the design, and the packaging.

The impact on the victimized company's profits is twofold. Obviously, there are the losses stemming from lost sales revenues. The monetary losses due to piracy are potentially staggering (see Exhibit 12–10). Losses in sales revenues incurred by U.S. software manufacturers in China are estimated to be around $500 million. Worldwide, the retail value of pirated music was assessed to be around $2.25 billion in 1994, or 6 percent of legitimate sales.[51] Counterfeiters also depress the MNC's profits indirectly. In many markets, MNCs often are forced to lower their prices in order to defend their market share against their counterfeit competitors.

Even more worrisome than the monetary losses is the damage that pirated products could inflict to the brand name. Pirated products tend to be of poor quality. As one Levi-Strauss official remarked: "If someone is buying a pair of what they assume are Levi's that fall apart after a day and a half, obviously that hurts our image."[52]

EXHIBIT 12–10
PIRACY AROUND THE WORLD
(MM = MILLION)

Leaders for motion picture losses	
Italy	$ 321 MM
Japan	$ 156 MM
Russia	$ 145 MM
Saudi Arabia	$ 100 MM
Mexico	$ 74 MM
Leaders for music recordings losses	
China	$ 345 MM
Russia	$ 300 MM
Bulgaria	$ 126 MM
United Arab Emirates	$ 72 MM
Germany	$ 70 MM
Leaders for software losses	
Japan	$1,106 MM
Germany	$1,076 MM
China	$ 351 MM
Korea	$ 313 MM
Russia	$ 310 MM

Source: Reprinted with permission from the March 20, 1995 issue of *Advertising Age.* Copyright, Crain Communications Inc. 1995.

---

[51]"Skull and CD," *The Economist* (Dec. 23–Jan. 5, 1995), p. 78.

[52]"Modern Day Pirates a Threat Worldwide," *Advertising Age International* (March 20, 1995), pp. I-3, I-4.

MNCs have several strategic options at their disposal to combat counterfeiters. The major weapons are as follows:

Strategic Options Against Product Piracy

Lobbying Activities. Lobbying governments is one of the most common courses of action that firms use to protect themselves against counterfeiting. Lobbyists pursue different types of objectives. One goal is to toughen legislation and enforcement of existing laws in the foreign market. However, improved intellectual property rights (IPR) protection is more likely to become reality if one can draw support from local stakeholders. For instance, Chinese technology developers increasingly favor a tighter IPR system.[53] Another route is to lobby the home government to impose sanctions against countries that tolerate product piracy. Intellectual property rights infringement has been one of the major stumbling blocks for China's application to the World Trade Organization (WTO) and renewal of "Most Favored Nation" (MFN) status by the U.S. government.[54] Lastly, MNCs might also lobby their government to negotiate for better trademark protection in international treaties such as the WTO agreement and NAFTA.

Legal Action. Prosecuting counterfeiters is another alternative that companies can employ to fight product piracy. China has set up special IP courts now to stamp out product piracy. In order to sue infringers, companies need to track them down first. In countries like China foreign firms can hire private agencies to help them with investigations of suspected infringers. Legal action has numerous downsides, though. A positive outcome in court is seldom guaranteed. The whole process is time consuming and costly. Court action can also generate negative publicity.[55] Microsoft's experience in China illustrates this point. When the company sued Yadu Group, a local humidifier maker, for pirating Microsoft products, the Chinese press had a field day bashing Microsoft for going after a local company. The case was dismissed because of a legal technicality. The only party that gained (apart from the lawyers involved) was the defendant whose brand awareness increased enormously because of all the publicity surrounding the case.[56]

Customs. Firms can also ask customs for assistance to conduct seizures of infringing goods. In countries with huge trade flows like China, customs can only monitor a small proportion of traded goods for IP compliance. Customs officers will most likely attach low priority to items such as Beanie Babies or Hello Kitty dolls. However, courtesy calls can be very effective. IP owners could also pinpoint broader concerns to the customs officials such as risks to consumers of fake goods or to the reputation of the host country.[57]

Product Policy Options. The third set of measures to cope with product piracy entails product policy actions. For instance, software manufacturers often protect their products by putting holograms on the product to discourage counterfeiters.

[53]Pitman B. Potter and Michel Oksenberg, "A Patchwork of IPR Protections," *The China Business Review* (Jan.–Feb. 1999), pp. 8–11.

[54]"US Seeks to Dog Chinese Copycats," *Financial Times* (February 16, 1994), p. 8.

[55]"Counter Feats," *The China Business Review* (Nov./Dec. 1994), pp. 12–15.

[56]"Microsoft-Bashing Is Paying Off For Software Giant's Foes in China," *The Asian Wall Street Journal* (January 3, 2000), pp. 1, 4.

[57]Joseph T. Simone, "Countering Counterfeiters," *The China Business Review* (Jan.–Feb. 1999), pp. 12–19.

Holograms are only effective when they are hard to copy. Microsoft learnt that lesson the hard way when it found out that counterfeiters simply sold MS-DOS 5.0 knockoffs using counterfeit holograms.[58] LVMH, the owner of a wide variety of upscale liquor brands, redesigned its bottles to make it harder for copycatters to re-use LVMH bottles for their own brews.[59]

Communication Options. Companies also use their communication strategy to counter rip-offs. Through advertising or public relations campaigns, companies warn their target audience about the consequences of accepting counterfeit merchandise. In Japan, LVMH distributed a million leaflets at three airports. The goal of this campaign was to warn Japanese tourists that the importation of counterfeit products is against the law.[60] Anti-counterfeiting advertising campaigns that target end consumers could also try to appeal to people's ethical judgments: a "good citizen" does not buy counterfeit goods.[61] The target of warning campaigns is not always the end customer. Converse, the U.S. athletic shoemaker, ran a campaign in trade journals throughout Europe alerting retailers to the legal consequences of selling counterfeits.[62]

◆ ◆ ◆ ◆ ◆ ◆ COUNTRY-OF-ORIGIN STEREOTYPES

Two of the biggest cosmetics companies in the world are Japanese: Kao and Shiseido. While successful in Japan and other Asian countries, Kao and Shiseido have had a hard time penetrating the European and American markets. Apparently, part of the problem is that they are Japanese. One image study conducted by a London-based advertising agency revealed that European consumers view Japanese-made products as "technically advanced and reliable, but short on soul."[63]

Country-of-Origin (COO) Influences on Consumer

There is ample evidence that shows that for many products, the "made in" label matters a great deal to consumers. Consumers often seem to rely very heavily on **country-of-origin** cues to evaluate products. Most of us prefer a bottle of French champagne over a Chinese-made bottle, despite the huge price gap. As the Kao/Shiseido story tells us, consumers hold cultural stereotypes about countries that will influence their product assessments. At the same time, research studies of COO effects clearly show that the phenomenon is pretty complex. Some of the key research findings are:

[58]"Catching Counterfeits," *Security Management* (December 1994), p. 18.
[59]Mr. Joël Tiphonnet, vice-president LVMH Asia Pacific, personal communication.
[60]"Modern Day Pirates a Threat Worldwide," *Advertising Age International* (March 20, 1995), pp. I-3, I-4.
[61]Alexander Nill and Clifford J. Shultz II, "The Scourge of Global Counterfeiting," *Business Horizons* (Nov.–Dec. 1996), pp. 37–42.
[62]"Converse Jumps on Counterfeit Culprits with Ad," *Marketing* (October 21, 1993), p. 11.
[63]"The Softer Samurai," *The Economist* (May 12, 1990), p. 73.

- COO effects are not stable; perceptions change over time.[64] Country images will change when consumers become more familiar with the country, the marketing practices behind the product improve over time, or when the product's actual quality improves. A classic example are Japanese-made cars where COO effects took a 180° turn during the last couple of decades, from a very negative to a very positive country image.[65]

- In general, consumers prefer domestic products over imports. The number 1 selling car is Renault in France, Toyota in Japan, Volkswagen in Germany, and Fiat in Italy. Not surprisingly, there is a COO bias against products coming from developing countries. For example, a recent study conducted in the Philippines found that products made in developing countries are only marketable when they are priced far less than products offered by regional or global competitors.[66]

- Research also shows that both the country of design and the country of manufacturing/assembly play a role. Foreign companies can target patriotic consumers by becoming a local player in the host market. For instance, they might set up an assembly base in the country. At the same time, they can capitalize on their country image to attract those customers who recognize the country's design image. For instance, Toyota pitches its Camry model as "the best car built in America."[67]

- Demographics make a difference. COO influences are particularly strong among the elderly,[68] less educated, and politically conservative.[69] Consumer expertise also makes a difference: novices tend to use COO as a cue in evaluating a product under any circumstances, experts only rely on COO stereotypes when product attribute information is ambiguous.[70]

- Consumers are likely to use the origin of a product as a cue when they are unfamiliar with the brand name carried by the product.[71]

---

[64]Wood, Van R., John R. Darling, and Mark Siders (1999), "Consumer Desire To Buy and Use Products In International Markets: How to Capture It, How to Sustain It," *International Marketing Review*, 16 (3), pp. 231–56.

[65]Akira Nagashima, "A Comparison of Japanese and US Attitudes Toward Foreign Products," *Journal of Marketing* (January 1970), pp. 68–74.

[66]John Hulland, Honorio S. Todiño, Jr., and Donald J. Lecraw, "Country-of-Origin Effects on Sellers' Price Premiums in Competitive Philippine Markets," *Journal of International Marketing*, 4 (1) (1996), pp. 57–80.

[67]Glen H. Brodowsky and J. Justin Tan, "Managing Country of Origin: Understanding How Country of Design and Country of Assembly Affect Product Evaluations and Attitudes Toward Purchase," in Steven Brown and D. Sudharshan, eds., *American Marketing Association Summer Educators' Conference Proceedings* (Chicago: American Marketing Association, 1999), pp. 307–20.

[68]Terence A. Shimp and Subhash Sharma, "Consumer Ethnocentrism: Construction and Validation of the CETSCALE," *Journal of Marketing Research*, 24 (August 1987), pp. 280–89.

[69]Thomas W. Anderson and William H. Cunningham, "Gauging Foreign Product Promotion," *Journal of Advertising Research* (February 1972), pp. 29–34.

[70]Durairaj Maheswaran, "Country of Origin as a Stereotype: Effects of Consumer Expertise and Attribute Strength on Product Evaluations," *Journal of Consumer Research*, 21 (September 1994), pp. 354–65.

[71]Victor V. Cordell, "Effects of Consumer Preferences for Foreign Sourced Products," *Journal of International Business Studies* (Second Quarter 1992), pp. 251–69.

- Finally, COO effects depend on the product category. Japan is strongly linked in consumers' minds with "high-tech" and performance-type attributes but is perceived poorly on attributes like "design," "hedonism," or "style." So, in Japan's case, a product-country match should occur for products like cars or consumer electronics, while COO effects would be less relevant for cosmetics or designer clothing. As shown in Exhibit 12–11, there are four possible outcomes, depending on (1) whether there is a match between the product and country, and, (2) whether the (mis-)match is favorable.[72]

Strategies to Cope with COO Stereotypes

Before exploring strategic options to deal with COO, firms should conduct market research to investigate the extent and the impact of COO stereotypes for their particular product. Such studies would reveal whether the country of origin really matters to consumers and to what degree COO hurts or helps the product's

EXHIBIT 12–11
PRODUCT-COUNTRY MATCHES AND MISMATCHES: EXAMPLES AND STRATEGIC IMPLICATIONS

| | *Country Image Dimensions* | |
	Positive	*Negative*
Dimensions as Product Features — *Important*	**I Favorable Match** Examples: • Japanese auto • German watch Strategic Implications: • Brand name reflects COO • Packaging includes COO Information • Promote brand's COO • Attractive potential manufacturing site	**II Unfavorable Match** Examples: • Hungarian auto • Mexican watch Strategic Implications: • Emphasize benefits other than COO • Non-country branding • Joint-venture with favorable match partner • Communication campaign to enhance country image
Dimensions as Product Features — *Not Important*	**III Favorable Mismatch** Example: • Japanese beer Strategic Implications: • Alter importance of product category image dimensions • Promote COO as secondary benefit if compensatory choice process	**IV Unfavorable Mismatch** Example: • Hungarian beer Strategic Implications: • Ignore COO—such information not

Source: Martin S. Roth and Jean B. Romeo, "Matching Product Category and Country Image Perceptions: A Framework for Managing Country-of-Origin Effects," *Journal of International Business Studies* (Third Quarter 1992), p. 495.

---

[72]Martin S. Roth and Jean B. Romeo, "Matching Product Category and Country Image Perceptions: A Framework for Managing Country-of-origin Effects," *Journal of International Business Studies* (Third Quarter 1992), pp. 477–97.

evaluation. One useful technique makes use of a *dollar preference* scale. Participants are asked to indicate how much they are willing to pay for particular brand/country combinations.[73]

Country-image stereotypes can either benefit or hurt a company's product. Evidently, when there is a favorable match between the country image and the desired product features, a firm could leverage this match by touting the origin of its product, provided its main competitors do not have the same (or better) origin. Our focus below is on strategies that can be used to counter negative COO stereotypes. The overview is organized along the four marketing mix elements:

Product Policy. A common practice to cope with COO is to select a brand name that disguises the country of origin or even invokes a favorable COO.[74] It is probably no coincidence that two of the more successful local apparel retailers in Hong Kong have Italian-sounding names (Giordano and Bossini). Another branding option to downplay negative COO feelings is to use private-label branding. A recent study that looked at COO influences on prices in the Philippines shows that marketers can overcome negative COO effects by developing brand equity.[75] Sheer innovation and a drive for superior quality will usually help firms to overcome COO biases in the long run.

Pricing. Selling the product at a relatively low price will attract value-conscious customers who are less concerned about the brand's country of origin. Obviously, this strategy is only doable when the firm enjoys a cost advantage. At the other end of the pricing spectrum, firms could set a premium price to combat COO biases. This is especially effective for product categories in which price plays a role as a signal of quality (e.g., wine, cosmetics, clothing).

Distribution. Alternatively, companies could influence consumer attitudes by using highly respected distribution channels. In the United Kingdom, Hungarian and Chilean wines are becoming increasingly popular. One reason for their success is the fact that they are sold via prestigious supermarket chains in Britain, like Tesco and J. Sainsbury.[76]

Communication. Finally, the firm's communication strategy can be used to alter consumer's attitudes toward the product. There are two broad objectives that such strategies could pursue: (1) improve the country image or (2) bolster the brand image. The first goal, changing the country image, is less appealing because it could lead to "free-rider" problems. Efforts carried out by your company to change the country image would also benefit your competitors from the same

---

[73]Usually the respondents are also given an anchor point (e.g., "Amount above or below $10,000?"). For further details see: Johny K. Johansson and Israel D. Nebenzahl, "Multinational Production: Effect on Brand Value," *Journal of International Business Studies* (Fall 1986), pp. 101–26.

[74]France Leclerc, Bernd H. Schmitt, and Laurette Dubé, "Foreign Branding and Its Effects on Product Perceptions and Attitudes," *Journal of Marketing Research*, 31 (May 1994), pp. 263–70.

[75]John Hulland et al., "Country-of-Origin Effects on Sellers' Price Premiums," ibid.

[76]"Non-traditional Nations Pour into Wine Market," *Advertising Age International* (May 15, 1995), p. I-4.

country of manufacture, even though they don't spend a penny on the country-image campaign. For that reason, country-image type of campaigns are mostly done by industry associations or government agencies. For instance, in the United States, Chilean wines were promoted with wine tastings and a print advertising campaign with the tag line: "It's not just a wine. It's a country." The $2 million to 3 million campaign was sponsored by ProChile, Chile's Ministry of Foreign Affairs' trade group.[77] Seagram UK, on the other hand, developed a strategy to build up the Paul Masson brand image when the California wine was first launched in the United Kingdom.[78]

◆ ◆ ◆ ◆ ◆ ◆ GLOBAL MARKETING OF SERVICES

Most of the discussion in this chapter so far has focused on the marketing of so-called "tangible" goods. However, as countries grow richer, services tend to become the dominant sector of their economy. Looking at Asia, the service sector now accounts for more than half of the GDP in countries like Hong Kong (more than 60 percent there), Singapore, Taiwan, and Thailand.[79] Worldwide, the service sector accounts for more than 60 percent of the world output.[80] These statistics show the increasing clout of services in global marketing.

In this section we will first focus on the challenges and opportunities that exist in the global service market. We will then offer a set of managerial guidelines that might prove fruitful to service marketers who plan to expand overseas.

Challenges in Marketing Services Internationally

Compared to marketers of *tangible* goods, service marketers face several unique hurdles on the road to international expansion. The major challenges include the following:

Protectionism. Trade barriers to service marketers tend to be much more cumbersome than for their physical goods counterparts. Many parts of the world are littered with service trade barriers coming under many different guises. Most cumbersome are the non-tariff trade barriers, where the creative juices of government regulators know no boundaries. In the past, the service sector has been treated very stepmotherly in trade agreements. The rules of the GATT system, for instance, only applied to visible trade. Its successor, the World Trade Organization (WTO), now expands at least some of the GATT rules to the service sector.[81]

[77]Ibid.
[78]Paul E. Breach, "Building the Paul Masson Brand," *European Journal of Marketing*, 23 (9) (1989), pp. 27–30.
[79]"Asia, at Your Service," *The Economist* (February 11, 1995), p. 53.
[80]Joseph A. McKinney, "Changes in the World Trading System," *Baylor Business Review* (Fall 1995), p. 13.
[81]Ibid.

Immediate Face-to-Face Contacts with Service Transactions.   The human aspect in service delivery is much more critical than for the marketing of tangible goods. Services are *performed*. This performance feature of services has several consequences in the international domain. Given the intrinsic need for people-to-people contact, cultural barriers in the global marketplace are much more prominent for service marketers than in other industries. Being in tune with the cultural values and norms of the local market is essential to survive in service industries. As a result, services are typically standardized far less than are tangible products.[82] At the same time, service companies usually aspire to provide a consistent quality image worldwide. Careful screening and training of personnel to assure consistent quality is extremely vital for international service firms. To foster the transfer of know-how between branches, many service companies set up communication channels such as regional councils.

The need for direct customer interface also means that service providers often need to have a local presence. This is especially the case with support services such as advertising, insurance, accounting, law firms, or overnight package delivery. In order not to lose MNC customer accounts, many support service companies are often obliged to follow in their clients' footsteps.

Difficulties in Measuring Customer Satisfaction Overseas.   Given the human element in services, monitoring consumer satisfaction is imperative for successful service marketing. Doing customer satisfaction studies in an international context is often a frustrating job. The hindrances to conducting market research surveys also apply here. In many countries, consumers are not used to sharing their opinions or suggestions. Instead of expressing their true opinions about the service, foreign respondents may simply state what they believe the company wants to hear (the "courtesy" bias).[83]

Despite the challenges just described, many international service industries offer enormous opportunities to savvy service marketers. The major ones are listed here:

Opportunities in the Global Service Industries

Deregulation of Service Industries.   Although protectionism is still rampant in many service industries, there is a steady improvement in the international trade service climate. Some of the GATT rules that only applied to tangible goods are now extended to the international service trade under the new WTO regime. Several individual countries are taking steps to lift restrictions targeting foreign service firms. Even sectors that are traditionally off-limits to foreigners are opening up now in numerous countries. India and the Philippines, for example, opened up their telephone industry to foreign companies.[84] Once China's access to the WTO has

---

[82]B. Nicolaud, "Problems and Strategies in the International Marketing of Services," *European Journal of Marketing*, 23 (6), pp. 55–66.
[83]Gaye Kaufman, "Customer Satisfaction Studies Overseas Can Be Frustrating," *Marketing News* (August 29, 1994), p. 34.
[84]"Asia, at Your Service," pp. 53–54.

EXHIBIT 12–12

HIGHLIGHTS OF SERVICE-RELATED PROVISIONS OF THE SINO-U.S. WTO AGREEMENT

Sector	Provisions
Audiovisual	Maximum 40 foreign movies upon entry; growing to 50 within 3 years upon entry (compared to max. 10 prior to agreement).
Banking	• Full market access within 5 years. • Foreign banks allowed to conduct local currency business with Chinese enterprises (within 2 years upon entry) and individuals (within 5 years). • Geographic and customer restrictions to be removed within 5 years upon entry.
Distribution	Restrictions phased out within 3 years upon entry.
Insurance	• Geographic limitations: Phased out within 3 years. • Scope: China will expand scope to include group, health, and pension lines of insurance. • Investment: 50 percent ownership allowed for life insurance; 51 percent for non-life upon entry and wholly owned foreign ownership within 2 years; reinsurance completely open.
Professional services	Foreign majority control allowed except for practicing Chinese law.
Securities	• Minority-owned foreign joint ventures allowed to engage in fund management on same terms as Chinese firms. • Minority owned foreign joint ventures allowed to underwrite domestic securities.
Logistical services (e.g., air courier, storage)	• Restrictions phased out within 3 to 4 years upon entry. • Service suppliers able to establish wholly owned subsidiaries.
Telecommunications	• Regulatory principles: Foreign suppliers can use any technology they choose. • Scope of services: China will phase out all geographic restrictions for paging (in 2 years upon entry), mobile (5 years), and fixed lines (6 years). Immediate access to Beijing, Shanghai, and Guangzhou (these 3 cities combined represent 75 percent of all domestic traffic) upon entry. • Investment: 49% foreign ownership in all services (including Internet); 50% in paging within 2 years; 49% in mobile within 5 years; 49% in international and domestic telephony within 6 years.
Tourism and travel	• Wholly owned foreign hotels allowed within 3 years; majority ownership allowed upon entry. • Foreign travel operators can provide full range of travel agency services.

Source: www.uschina.org/public/991115a.html

been approved, trade barriers in China should fall dramatically in most service areas (see Exhibit 12–12).

Increasing Demand for Premium Services.

Demand for premium-quality services expands with increases in consumers' buying power. International service providers that are able to deliver a premium product often have an edge over their local competitors. There are two major factors behind this competitive advantage.

One of the legacies of years of protectionism is that local service firms are typically unprepared for the hard laws of the marketplace. Notions such as customer orientation, consumer satisfaction, and service quality are marketing concepts that are especially hard to digest for local service firms that, until recently, did not face any serious competition. For example, local funeral companies in France invested very little in funeral homes. Prior to the de-monopolization of the industry, funeral business in France was basically a utility: firms bid for the right to offer funeral services to a municipality at fixed prices. Service Corp. International, a leading American funeral company, now plans to gain a foothold in France by selling premium products and upgraded facilities.[85]

Global service firms can also leverage their "global know-how" base. A major strength for the likes of Waste Management International, Federal Express, and AT&T is that they have a worldwide knowledge base into which they can tap instantly. Some of McDonald's American restaurants switched to a face-to-face ordering system for drive-in meals after their experience in Japan showed that customers preferred this system to placing orders via intercoms.[86]

Increased Value Consciousness. As customers worldwide have more alternatives to choose from and become more sophisticated, they also grow increasingly value conscious. Service companies that compete internationally also have clout on this front versus local service providers, since global service firms usually benefit from scale economies. Such savings can be passed through to their customers. McDonald's apparently saved around $2 million by centralizing the purchase of sesame seeds.[87] In Thailand, Makro, a large Dutch retailer, uses computerized inventory controls and bulk selling to undercut its local rivals.[88] Given the size of its business, Toys "R" Us, the U.S. discount toy retailer, was able to set up its own direct import company in Japan, allowing the firm to deliver merchandise straight from the docks to its warehouses, thereby bypassing distributors' margins.[89]

To compete in foreign markets, service firms resort to a plethora of different strategies.

Global Service Marketing Strategies

Capitalize on Cultural Forces in the Host Market. To bridge cultural gaps between the home and host market, service companies often customize the product to the local market. Successful service firms grab market share by spotting cultural opportunities and setting up a service product around these cultural forces.

Standardize and Customize. As noted in the last chapter, one of the major challenges in global product design is striking the right balance between standard-

---

[85]"Funereal Prospects," *Forbes* (September 11, 1995), pp. 45–46.

[86]"Big Mac's Counter Attack," *The Economist* (November 13, 1993), pp. 71–72.

[87]Ibid.

[88]"Asia, at Your Service," pp. 53–54.

[89]"Revolution in Toyland," *The Financial Times* (April 8, 1994), p. 9.

410 • **Part 4. Global Marketing Strategy Development**

ization and customization. By their very nature (service delivery at the point of consumption) most services do not need to wrestle with that issue. Both standardization and adaptation are doable. The core service product can easily be augmented with localized support service features that cater to local market conditions.[90]

Central Role of Information Technologies (IT).   Information technology forms a key pillar of global service strategies. Service firms add value for their customers by employing technology such as computers, intelligent terminals, and state-of-the-art telecommunications. Many service firms have established Internet access to communicate with their customers and suppliers. IT is especially valued in markets that have a fairly underdeveloped infrastructure. Companies should also recognize the potential of realizing scale economies by centralizing their IT functions via "information hubs."[91]

Add Value by Differentiation.   Services differ from tangible products by the fact that it is usually far easier to find differentiation possibilities. Service firms can appeal to their customers by offering benefits not provided by their competitors and/or lowering costs. Apart from monetary expenses, cost items include psychic costs (hassles), time costs (waiting time), and physical efforts.[92] Especially in markets where the service industry is still developing, multinational service firms can add value by providing premium products. AIG allows its customers in China to settle their bills by bank transfers. Most local insurance companies require their customers to wait in line to pay the premiums in cash.

Establish Global Service Networks.   Service firms with a global customer base face the challenge of setting up a seamless global service network. One of the key questions is whether the company should set up the network on its own or use outside partners. Given the huge investments required to develop a worldwide network, more and more companies are choosing the latter route. Trends of firms grouping together to establish global network can be observed in service industries such as the international telephone business (e.g., Concert by AT&T and BT), airline travel (e.g., the STAR alliance), and advertising.

SUMMARY ✦

Mission statements in annual reports reflect the aspiration of countless companies to sell their products to consumers worldwide. This push toward global expansion raises many tricky questions on the product policy front.

Mastering these global product issues will yield success and, possibly, even worldwide leadership.

Companies need to decide what branding strategies they plan to pursue to develop their overseas business.

---

[90]Christopher H. Lovelock and George S. Yip, "Developing Global Strategies for Service Businesses," *California Management Review*, 38 (2) (Winter 1996), pp. 64–86.

[91]Ibid.

[92]"Services Go International," *Marketing News* (March 14, 1994), pp. 14–15.

There is plenty of ammunition to build a case for global brands. At the same time, there are also many arguments that can be put forward in favor of other branding strategies. Developing a global branding strategy involves tackling questions such as these:

- Which of the brands in our brand portfolio have the potential to be globalized?

- What is the best route toward globalizing our brands? Should we start by acquiring local brands, develop them into regional brands, and, ultimately, if the potential is there, into a "truly" global brand?

- What is the best way to implement the change-over from a local to a global (or regional) brand?
- How do we foster and sustain the consistency of our global brand image?
- What organizational mechanisms should we as a company use to coordinate our branding strategies across markets? Should coordination happen at the regional or global level?

The ultimate reward of mastering these issues successfully is regional—or sometimes even wordwide—leadership in the marketplace.

KEY TERMS

country-of-origin stereotype
dual branding

fade-in/fade-out
global brand

product piracy
summary axing

transparent forewarning
umbrella branding

REVIEW QUESTIONS

1. For what types of product/service categories would you expect global brand names? For which ones would you anticipate localized names?

2. Why is the market share of private labels much higher in Europe than in Asia?

3. Explain why the strength of a global brand may vary enormously from country to country.

4. What factors should MNCs consider when implementing a brand-name facelift in their foreign markets?

5. Describe the key success factors behind private labels in Europe.

6. What strategies can MNCs adopt to cope with product piracy?

7. How does the marketing of global services differ from marketing tangible goods worldwide?

DISCUSSION QUESTIONS

1. The Advanced Photo System (APS) is a new digital photography system that was launched in 1996 by several companies in the camera industry. APS cameras have features like simple loading, adjustable print size, and the ability to download pictures onto computers. The major photo industry companies use quite different branding strategies. Companies like Kodak and Nikon use a global brand name: Advantix and Nuvis, respectively. Other competitors, such as Fuji and Canon, use several brand names for their APS camera and film products. Brand names used by Fuji, for example, are:

Endeavor in the United States, Fotonex in Europe, and Epion in Japan.

Why would some competitors (e.g., Kodak) use a global brand name for this product while others (e.g., Fuji, Canon) use several brand names?

2. Interbrand, a consulting firm, recently compiled a list of the most valuable brands in the world. This list is accessible on Interbrand's Web site—www.interbrand.com. Except for Sony, Toyota, and Honda, no Asian brands made the list of the top sixty brands. Explain why

Asian companies have been less successful in building global brands than American or European firms.

3. In September 1999, Unilever announced that it will trim more than 1,000 brands. The company wants to focus on 400 of its current 1,600 brands, with a core group of so-called power brands that are known globally or region-wide (e.g., Magnum ice cream, Lipton tea, Vaseline skin cream). These 400 brands accounted for 90 percent of Unilever's 1998 sales revenues. The brands outside the core group will gradually lose marketing support, and will be ultimately sold, withdrawn, or consolidated into bigger brands. Discuss Unilever's decision. What do you see as possible advantages? Disadvantages?

4. As already noted, developing and industrialized countries hold different views about intellectual copyright protection. Developing countries claim that stringent copyright protection does not enable them to close the gap with the industrialized world. Discuss what rewards developing countries might derive from intellectual property right protection.

5. Most luxury watches have a Swiss-made label. Consider strategies that a "Made in India" watch maker might consider to target the premium segment in the Western world.

6. Nestlé, the Swiss food conglomerate, has created a Nestlé Seal of Guarantee that it puts on the back of some of its products (e.g., Maggi sauces). The Seal of Guarantee is not used for many of its other products, such as pet food and mineral water. What might be Nestlé's motivations for adding or dropping its Nestlé Seal of Guarantee stamp to the brand name?

7. The Rover Mini is a squat, boxy car that was designed in the late 1950s when the Suez Canal crisis prompted gas rationing in Europe (if you are not familiar with the car, check out its Web site: www.mini.co.uk). Rover, now owned by BMW, started exporting the car to Japan in 1985. The Mini sells for between 1.8 million yen and 2.4 million yen. A Japanese model of the same size costs about half that. Yet, the Mini has many takers. Rover rarely does TV ads. Instead, it relies on word of mouth. Despite the price tag and little advertising, Rover sells more Minis in Japan than anywhere else in the world. The car has been far more successful in Japan than most other imported car makes like GM's Saturn or DaimlerChrysler's Neon. What factors do you think explain the Rover Mini's success in Japan?

8. The intangible nature of many service businesses leads to uncertainty on the part of the customer. Describe how global service providers can lessen this uncertainty by marketing their services globally.

FURTHER READING ✦ ✦ ✦ ✦ ✦ ✦ ✦ ✦ ✦ ✦ ✦ ✦ ✦ ✦ ✦ ✦ ✦ ✦

Aaker, David A., and Erich Joachimsthaler. "The Lure of Global Branding." *Harvard Business Review* (Nov.-Dec. 1999): 137–44.

Cordell, Victor V. "Effects of Consumer Preferences for Foreign Sourced Products." *Journal of International Business Studies* (Second Quarter 1992): 251–69.

Dahringer, Lee D. "Marketing Services Internationally: Barriers and Management Strategies." *The Journal of Services Marketing*, 5 (3) (Summer 1991).

Darling, John R., and Van R. Wood. "A Longitudinal Study Comparing Perceptions of U.S. and Japanese Consumer Products in a Third/Neutral Country: Finland 1975 to 1985." *Journal of International Business Studies* (Third Quarter 1990): 427–50.

Harvey, Michael G., and Ilkka A. Ronkainen. "International Counterfeiters: Marketing Success Without the Cost and the Risk." *Columbia Journal of World Business* (Fall 1985): 37–45.

Jain, Subhash C. "Problems in International Protection of Intellectual Property Rights," *Journal of International Marketing*, 4 (1) (1996): 9–32.

Kapferer, Jean-Noel. *Strategic Brand Management: New Approaches to Creating and Evaluating Brand Equity.* London: Kogan Page, 1992.

Leclerc, France, Bernd H. Schmitt, and Laurette Dubé. "Foreign Branding and Its Effects on Product Perceptions and Attitudes." *Journal of Marketing Research*, 31 (May 1994): 263–70.

Lovelock, Christopher H., and George S. Yip. "Developing Global Strategies for Service Businesses." *California Management Review*, 38 (2) (Winter 1996): 64–86.

Moore, Jeri. "Building Brands Across Markets: Cultural Differences in Brand Relationships Within the European Community." In D. A. Aaker and A. L. Biel, eds., *Brand Equity & Advertising: Advertising's Role in Building Strong Brands.* Hillsdale, NJ: Erlbaum Associates, 1993.

Pagano, Camillo. "The Management of Global Brands." In P. Stobart, ed., *Brand Power.* London: The MacMillan Press, Ltd., 1994.

Partoyan, Garo. "Protecting Power Brands." In P. Stobart, ed., *Brand Power.* London: The MacMillan Press, Ltd., 1994.

Roth, Martin S., and Jean B. Romeo. "Matching Product Category and Country Image Perceptions: A Framework for Managing Country-of-Origin Effects." *Journal of International Business Studies* (Third Quarter 1992): 477–97.

Shultz, C., and B. Saporito. "Protecting Intellectual Property: Strategies and Recommendations to Deter Counterfeiting and Brand Piracy in Global Markets." *Columbia Journal of World Business* (Spring 1996): 18–28.

Tanaka, Hiroshi. "Branding in Japan." In D.A. Aaker and A.L. Biel, eds., *Brand Equity & Advertising: Advertising's Role in Building Strong Brands*. Hillsdale, NJ: Erlbaum Associates, 1993.

GLOBAL PRICING

13

CHAPTER OVERVIEW

1. DRIVERS OF FOREIGN MARKET PRICING
2. PRICE ESCALATION
3. PRICING IN INFLATIONARY ENVIRONMENTS
4. GLOBAL PRICING AND CURRENCY FLUCTUATIONS
5. TRANSFER PRICING
6. GLOBAL PRICING AND ANTIDUMPING REGULATION
7. PRICE COORDINATION
8. PRICING POLICIES AND THE EURO
9. COUNTERTRADE

Global pricing is one of the most critical and complex issues that global firms face. Price is the only marketing mix instrument that creates revenues. All other elements entail costs. Thus, a company's global pricing policy may make or break its overseas expansion efforts. Furthermore, a firm's pricing policy is inherently a highly cross-functional process based on inputs from the firm's finance, accounting, manufacturing, tax, and legal divisions. Predictably, the interests of one group (say, marketing) may clash with the objectives of another group (say, finance).

Multinationals also face the challenge of how to coordinate their pricing policy across different countries. A lack of coordination will create gray market (*parallel imports*) situations (see Chapter 17). In gray markets, products marketed in low-priced countries are shipped and resold by unauthorized channels in high-priced markets. These imports will compete with the high-priced equivalent products offered by legitimate distributors. Efforts to trim big price gaps between countries may be hampered by stonewalling attempts of local country managers or distribution channels.

This chapter will focus on global pricing strategies. After giving an overview of the key drivers (customers, competition, company goals and costs, distribution channels, and government policies) of foreign market pricing, we will discuss several strategic international pricing issues. The chapter concludes with a discussion of countertrade, which is a form of noncash pricing.

DRIVERS OF FOREIGN MARKET PRICING   ◆ ◆ ◆ ◆ ◆ ◆

Even within the same geographic area such as the Pan-European market, wide cross-border price differences are quite common. Shortly after the arrival of the euro, KPMG Consulting conducted a survey of retail prices for 33 directly comparable products in the eleven euro countries and the United Kingdom. Of the 33 products, 29 showed price differentials of more than 50 percent between the highest- and lowest-price countries (see Exhibit 13–1). Almost half (15) had gaps of 100 percent or more. The biggest price difference was recorded for household salt (1,200 percent). Why these enormous price variations? A potpourri of factors governs global pricing decisions. Some of the drivers are related to the 4 Cs: *company* (costs, company goals), *customers* (price sensitivity, segments), *competition* (nature, intensity), and *channels*. Aside from these, in many countries, multinationals' pricing decisions are often influenced by government policies. We now consider the main drivers that may affect global pricing.

Company Goals.   When developing a pricing strategy for its global markets, the firm needs to decide what it wants to accomplish with its strategy. These goals might include maximizing current profits, penetrating the market, projecting a premium image, and so forth. According to one study,[1] the most important pricing objectives of companies doing business in the United States (including foreign-based firms) are (1) to achieve a satisfactory return on investment, (2) to maintain market share, and (3) to meet a specified profit goal (in that order). Company objectives will vary from market to market, especially in multinationals with a large degree of local autonomy. New Balance, the U.S.-based maker of high-tech running shoes, sells its shoes in France as haute couture items rather than simply athletic shoes (as it does in the United States, for instance). To beef up the premium image, the price is about 800 francs (around $130) a pair—almost twice the U.S. price![2] Company goals will also change over time. Initially, when a firm enters a country, it may set a relatively low price (compared to other countries) to penetrate the market. Once the firm is well entrenched, it may shift its objectives and bring them in line with the goals pursued in other countries.

[1]S. Samiee, "Pricing in Marketing Strategies of U.S.- and Foreign-Based Companies," *Journal of Business Research*, 15 (1987), pp. 17–30.
[2]"The Road to Richesse," *Sales & Marketing Management* (November 1999), pp. 89–96.

EXHIBIT 13–1

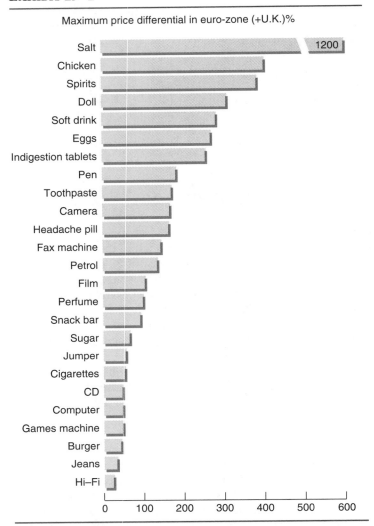

Maximum price differential in euro-zone (+U.K.)%

© The Economic Intelligence Unit Limited 1999.

Company Costs. Company costs figure prominently in the pricing decision. Costs set the floor: the company wants to set at least a price that will cover all costs needed to make and sell its products. Cost differentials between countries can lead to wide price gaps. It is important that management considers all relevant costs of manufacturing, marketing, and distributing the product. Company costs consist of two parts: variable costs, which change with sales volume, and fixed costs (e.g., overhead) that do not vary.

Export pricing policies differ depending on the way costs are treated.[3] The most popular practice is **cost-plus pricing**. This approach adds international costs

[3] S. Tamer Cavusgil, "Unraveling the Mystique of Export Pricing," *Business Horizons*, 31 (May–June 1988), pp. 54–63.

and a mark-up to the domestic manufacturing cost. At times, the company will offer discounts or rebates to reward its customer. An alternative approach is **dynamic incremental pricing**. This strategy arrives at a price after removing domestic fixed costs. The premise is that these costs have to be born anyhow, regardless of whether the goods are exported. Only variable costs generated by the exporting efforts and a portion of the overhead load (the *incremental costs*) should be recuperated. Examples of exporting-related incremental costs include manufacturing costs, shipping expenses, insurance, and overseas promotional costs. Although the second approach is more kosher from an economic perspective, there are certain risks. Situations where the export list price is far below the domestic price could trigger dumping accusations in the export market.

When demand is highly price sensitive, the company needs to consider how it can reduce costs from a global perspective. Manufacturing scale economies provide an incentive to standardize product offerings or to consolidate manufacturing facilities. In some markets, logistics costs can be trimmed by centralizing distribution centers or warehouse facilities. By the same token, significant marketing costs may prompt a multinational operating in Europe to develop Pan-European advertising campaigns. In developing countries, MNCs are often able to make their goods affordable by relying on local materials and labor. In Thailand and Malaysia, Coca-Cola operates with local sugar, local materials, local labor, and local transportation so that it can get a very affordable product in the local consumers' hands.[4]

Whereas costs set a floor, consumers' perceived value attached to your product will set a ceiling to the price. Consumer demand is function of buying power, tastes, habits, and substitutes. These demand conditions will vary from country to country. For instance, Nescafé is fairly expensive in Italy because the Italian demand for instant coffee is very minor.[5]

Customer Demand

Buying power is a key consideration in pricing decisions. Countries with low per capita incomes pose a dilemma. Consumers in such countries are far more price-sensitive than in developed markets. Therefore, price premiums are often a major hurdle for consumers in these markets. One option is to go for the mass-market by adjusting the product. Firms might consider downsizing the product (smaller volume, size, fewer units per package) or lowering the product quality. In the Philippines, Wrigley markets tiny individual pieces of chewing gum (rather than five-stick packages) while the quality is maintained (see Exhibit 13–2). Retailers charge customers one Philippine peso[6] for three pieces of chewing gum.[7] In Egypt, one of the moves that Procter & Gamble undertook to revitalize the sales of Ariel, its high-suds laundry detergent brand, was to downsize the package size from 200 grams to 150 grams, thereby lowering the cash outlay for ordinary consumers.[8] In Russia, Procter & Gamble chose the

---

[4]www.thecoca-colacompany.com/investors/Divester.html.

[5]"Counting Costs of Dual Pricing . . . ," *The Financial Times* (July 9, 1990), p. 4.

[6]40 Philippine pesos equals about $1.

[7]Douglas S. Barrie, group vice-president International, Wrigley Company, personal communication.

[8]Mahmoud Aboul-Fath and Loula Zaklama, "Ariel High Suds Detergent in Egypt—A Case Study," *Marketing and Research Today* (May 1992), pp. 130–35.

EXHIBIT 13–2
AN EXAMPLE OF DOWNSIZING WITH PRICE
ADJUSTMENT

second route—lower quality—by rolling out an economy laundry detergent product carrying the Tide brand name—a premium-brand U.S. brand.[9]

Another strategic option is to charge prices in the same range as Western prices and target the upper-end of the foreign market. Generally speaking, a market consists of a quality-sensitive and a price-sensitive market segment. In some markets the quality segment dominates. In other countries, the price segment prevails. A case in point is the personal computer market. PC prices in Germany are far lower than in Britain. German PC buyers focus on price. In Britain, on the other hand, consumers tend to buy more powerful machines. British consumers are also less sophisticated buyers than their German counterparts.[10]

Typically, the nature of demand will change over time. In countries that were entered recently, the firm may need to stimulate trial via discounting or a penetration pricing strategy. In more mature markets, the lion's share of customers will be repeat buyers. Once brand loyalty has been established, price will play less of a role as a purchase criterion, and the firm may be able to afford the luxury of a premium pricing strategy. The success of such a pricing strategy will evidently hinge on the company's ability to differentiate its product from the competition.

Competition   Competition is another key factor in global pricing. Differences in the competitive situation across countries will usually lead to cross-border price differentials. The competitive situation may vary for a number of reasons. First, the number of competitors typically differs from country to country. In some countries, the firm faces very few competitors (or even enjoys a monopoly position), whereas in others, the company has to combat numerous competing brands. Also, the nature of competition will differ: global versus local players, private firms versus state-owned companies. Even when local companies are not state-owned, they often are viewed as "national champions" and treated accordingly by their local governments. Such a status entails subsidies or other goodies (e.g., cheap loans) that enable them to undercut their competitors. In some markets, firms have to compete with a knock-off

[9]"P&G Accelerates International Pace," *Advertising Age International* (March 21, 1994), pp. I-3, I-23.
[10]"A Byte of the Market," *Financial Times* (November 22, 1998), p. 7.

version of their own product. The presence of counterfeit products could force the firm to lower its price in such markets. Also, in many emerging markets, legitimate distributors of global brands need to compete with smugglers. In China, for instance, industry analysts estimated that 100,000 cars were smuggled in 1996 from Japan and South Korea.[11] Smuggling operations put downward pressure on the price of the affected product. The strength of private labels (store brands) is another important driver. In countries where store brands are well entrenched, companies are forced to accept lower margins than elsewhere.

A company's competitive position typically varies across countries. Companies will be price leaders in some countries and price takers in other countries. Heinz's policy is to cut prices in markets where it is not the leading brand.[12] Finally, the rules of the game usually differ. Nonprice competition (e.g., advertising, channel coverage) may be favored in some countries. Elsewhere, price combats are a way of life. In France, a ban on cigarette advertising leaves price as the only competitive device to gain market share.[13]

Another driver behind global pricing is the distribution channel. The pressure exercised by channels can take many forms. Variations in trade margins and the length of the channels will influence the ex-factory price charged by the company. The balance of power between manufacturers and their distributors is another factor behind pricing practices. Countries such as France and the United Kingdom are characterized by large retailers who are able to order in bulk and to bargain for huge discounts with manufacturers. In the Pan-European market, several smaller retailers have formed cross-border coops to strengthen their negotiation position with their common suppliers. The power of large-scale retailers in Europe is visibly illustrated by the hurdles that several manufacturers faced in implementing Every Day Low Pricing (EDLP). With EDLP, the manufacturer offers consistently lower prices to the retailer (and the ultimate shopper) instead of promotional price discounts and trade promotions. Several German supermarket chains delisted P & G brands like Ariel, Vizir, and Lenor detergent products and Bess toilet tissue when P & G introduced EDLP in Germany in early 1996.[14] Another example is the personal computer industry. The cheaper markets (e.g., the United States and Germany) offer consumers a broad assortment of channel choices: direct marketers, supermarkets (e.g., Aldi in Germany), big speciality retail chains, and so on. However, in Britain, where PC prices are on average 50 percent or more higher than in Germany, the market is dominated by Dixons, a retail chain that—according to Intel's chief executive—charges "ridiculous margins."[15]

Large cross-country price gaps open up arbitrage opportunities that lead to **parallel imports (gray markets)** from low-price countries to high-price ones. These parallel imports are commonly handled by unauthorized distributors at the expense of legitimate trade channels. To lessen parallel imports, firms might consider narrowing cross-border price disparities. Thus, preemption of cross-border bargain hunting is often a strong motivation behind a company's pricing practices.

Distribution Channels

---

[11]"Where's the Pot of Gold?" *Business Week (Asian Edition)* (February 3, 1997), pp. 14–15.

[12]"Counting Costs of Dual Pricing . . . ," p. 4.

[13]"Marlboro Price Cut Stays on Home Soil," *Advertising Age International* (June 21, 1993), p. I-18.

[14]"Heat's on Value Pricing," *Advertising Age International* (January 1997), pp. I-21, I-22.

[15]"A Byte of the Market," *Financial Times* (November 22, 1998), p. 7.

Government Policies

Even after the launch of the euro, car prices in the European Union can still vary by up to 50 percent. One of the main reasons for these car price disparities is the sales tax rate for new cars. These vary from as low as 15 percent in Luxembourg to 213 percent in Denmark. This taxation gap also affects pretax car prices. In fact, most car makers in Europe subsidize the pretax prices in high-tax countries by charging more in low-tax countries.[16]

Government policies can have a direct or indirect impact on pricing policies. Factors that have a direct impact include sales tax rates (e.g., value added taxes), tariffs, and price controls. Sometimes government interference is blatant. The Chinese government sets minimum prices in twenty-one industries, ranging from electronic appliances to sugar processing. The goal is to stamp out price wars and protect the Chinese economy against deflation pressures. Firms that ignore the pricing rules are slapped with hefty fines.[17]

An increase in the sales tax rate will usually lower overall demand. However, in some cases taxes may selectively affect imports. For instance, in 1990, the U.S. government introduced a 10-percent luxury tax on the part of a car's price that exceeds $30,000. This luxury tax primarily affected the price of luxury import cars since few U.S.-made luxury cars sold for more than the $30,000 threshold. In August 1996 President Clinton signed a bill to phase out the tax over seven years. Tariffs obviously will inflate the retail price of imports. Another concern is price controls. These either affect the whole economy (for instance, in high-inflation countries) or selective industries. In many countries, a substantial part of the health care costs are borne by the government. As a result, drug prices in many of these countries are negotiated with the host government. Many pharmaceutical companies face the dilemma of accepting lower prices for their drugs or having their drugs registered on a negative list, which contains drugs that the government will not reimburse.[18] Further, several governments heavily encourage the prescription of generics or stimulate parallel imports from low-price countries to put price pressure on drug companies.

Aside from direct intervention, government policies can have an indirect impact on pricing decisions. For instance, huge government deficits spur interest rates (cost of capital), currency volatility, and inflation. The interplay of these factors will affect the product cost. Inflation might also affect labor costs in those countries (e.g., Belgium, Brazil) that have a wage indexation system. Such a system adjusts wages for increases in the cost of living.

Earlier we pinpointed the main factors that will drive global pricing decisions. We now highlight the key managerial issues in global pricing.

◆ ◆ ◆ ◆ ◆ ◆ MANAGING PRICE ESCALATION

Exporting involves more steps and substantially higher risks than domestic marketing. To cover the incremental costs (e.g., shipping, insurance, tariffs, margins of various intermediaries), the final foreign retail price will often be much higher than

---

[16]"Car Price Disparities Highlighted," *The Financial Times* (January 7, 1999), p. 2.

[17]"So Much for Competition," *Business Week (Asian edition)*, (November 30, 1998), pp. 22–23.

[18]Some countries have a positive list of drugs from which physicians can prescribe.

the domestic retail price. This phenomenon is known as **price escalation**. Price escalation raises two issues that management needs to confront: (1) Will our foreign customers be willing to pay the inflated price for our product ("sticker shock")? and (2) Will this price make our product less competitive? If the answer is no, the exporter needs to decide how to cope with price escalation.

There are two broad approaches to deal with price escalation: (1) find ways to cut the export price, or (2) position the product as a (super) premium brand. Several options exist to lower the export price:[19]

1. *Rearrange the distribution channel.* Channels are often largely responsible for price escalation, either due to the length of the channel (number of layers between manufacturer and end-user) or due to exorbitant margins. In some circumstances, it is possible to shorten the channel. Alternatively, firms could look into channel arrangements that provide cost efficiencies. In recent years, several U.S. companies have decided to penetrate the Japanese consumer market through direct marketing (e.g., catalog sales, telemarketing). This allows them to bypass the notorious Japanese distribution infrastructure and become more price-competitive.

2. *Eliminate costly features (or make them optional).* Several exporters have addressed the price escalation issue by offering no-frills versions of their product. Rather than having to purchase the entire bundle, customers can buy the core product and then decide whether they want to pay extra for optional features.

3. *Downsize the product.* Another route to dampen sticker shock is downsizing the product by offering a smaller version of the product or a lesser count. This option is only desirable when consumers are not aware of cross-border volume differences. To that end, manufacturers may decide to go for a local branding strategy.

4. *Assemble or manufacture the product in foreign markets.* A more extreme option is to assemble or even manufacture the entire product in foreign markets (not necessarily the export market). Closer proximity to the export market will lower transportation costs. To lessen import duties for goods sold within European Union markets, numerous firms have decided to set up assembly operations in EU member states.

5. *Adapt the product to escape tariffs or tax levies.* Finally, a company could also modify its export product to bring it into a different tariff or tax bracket. When the United States levied the 10 percent tax on plus-$30,000 luxury cars, Land Rover increased the maximum weight of Range Rover models sold in America to 6,019 lbs. As a result, the Range Rover was classified as a truck (not subject to the 10% luxury tax) rather than a luxury car.

These measures are different ways to counter price escalation. Alternatively, an exporter could exploit the price escalation situation and go for a premium positioning strategy. LEGO, the Danish toymaker, sells building block sets in India that are priced between $6 and $223, far more than most other toys that Indian parents can purchase. To justify the premium price, LEGO uses a marketing strategy that targets middle-class parents and stresses the educational value of LEGO toys.[20] Of course, for this strategy to work, other elements of the export marketing-mix

---

[19]S. Tamer Cavusgil, "Unraveling the Mystique of Export Pricing," *Business Horizons* (May–June 1988), p. 56.
[20]"LEGO Building Its Way to China," *Advertising Age International* (March 20, 1995), p. I-29.

should be in tandem with the premium positioning. In Europe and Japan, Levi Strauss sells its jeans mainly in upscale boutiques rather than in department stores.[21]

❖ ❖ ❖ ❖ ❖ ❖ PRICING IN INFLATIONARY ENVIRONMENTS

When McDonald's opened its doors in January 1990, a Big Mac meal (including fries and a soft drink) in Moscow cost 6 rubles. Three years later, the same meal cost 1,100 rubles.[22] Rampant inflation is a major obstacle to doing business in many countries. Moreover, high inflation rates are usually coupled with highly volatile exchange rate movements. In such environments, price setting and stringent cost control become extremely crucial. Not surprisingly, in such markets, companies' financial divisions are often far more important than other departments.[23]

There are several alternative ways to safeguard against inflation.

1. *Modify components, ingredients, parts, and/or packaging materials.* Some ingredients are subject to lower inflation rates than others. This might justify a change in the ingredient mix. Of course, before implementing such a move, the firm should consider all its consequences (e.g., consumer response, impact on shelf life of the product).

2. *Source materials from low-cost suppliers.* Supply management plays a central role in high inflation environments. A first step is to screen suppliers and determine which ones are most cost efficient without cutting corners. If feasible, materials could be imported from low-inflation countries. Note, though, that high inflation rates are coupled with a weakening currency. This will push up the price of imports.

3. *Shorten credit terms.* In some cases, profits can be realized by juggling around with terms of payment. For instance, a firm that is able to collect cash from its customers within fifteen days, but has one month to pay its suppliers, can invest its money during the fifteen-day grace period. Thus, firms strive to push up the lead time in paying their suppliers. At the same time, they also try to shorten the time to collect from their clients.[24]

4. *Include escalator clauses in long-term contracts.* Many business-to-business marketing situations involve long term contracts (e.g., leasing arrangements). To hedge his position against inflation, the vendor could negotiate to include escalator clauses that will provide the necessary protection.

5. *Quote prices in a stable currency.* To handle high inflation, companies often quote prices in a stable currency such as the U.S. dollar or the euro.

6. *Pursue rapid inventory turnovers.* High inflation also mandates rapid inventory turnarounds. As a result, information technologies (e.g., scanning techniques, computerized inventory tracking) that facilitate rapid inventory turnovers or even just-in-time delivery will yield a competitive advantage.

---

[21]"The Levi Straddle," *Forbes* (January 17, 1994), p. 44.

[22]"Inflation Bites Russians, Who Still Bite into Big Mac," *Advertising Age International* (March 15, 1993), pp. I-3, I-23.

[23]"A Rollercoaster Out of Control," *The Financial Times* (February 22, 1993).

[24]Ibid.

7. *Draw lessons from other countries.* Operations in countries with a long history of inflation offer valuable lessons for ventures in other high-inflation countries. Cross-fertilization by drawing from experience in other high inflation markets often helps. Some companies—McDonald's[25] and Otis Elevator International,[26] for example—have relied on expatriate managers from Latin America to cope with inflation in the former Soviet Union. One of the lessons drawn from Brazil was that McDonald's negotiates a separate inflation rate with each supplier. These rates are then used for monthly realignments, instead of the government's published inflation figures.

To combat hyperinflation, governments occasionally impose price controls (usually coupled with a wage freeze). For instance, Brazil went through five price freezes over a six-year interval. Such temporary price caps could be selective, targeting certain products, but, in extreme circumstances, they will apply across-the-board to all consumer goods. Price freezes have proven to be very ineffective in dampening inflation (witness the experience of Brazil). Often, expectations of an imminent price freeze start off a rumor mill that will spur companies to implement substantial price increases, thereby setting off a vicious cycle. One consequence of price controls is that goods are diverted to the black market, leading to shortages in the regular market.

Companies faced with price controls can consider several action courses:

1. *Adapt the product line.* To reduce exposure to a government-imposed price freeze, companies diversify into product lines that are relatively free of price controls.[27] Of course, before embarking on such a changeover, the firm has to examine the long-term ramifications. Modifying the product line could imply loss of economies of scale, an increase in overheads, and adverse reactions from the company's customer base.

2. *Shift target segments or markets.* A more drastic move is to shift the firm's target segment. For instance, price controls often apply to consumer food products but not to animal-related products. So, a maker of corn-based consumer products might consider a shift from breakfast cereals to chicken-feed products. Again, such action should be preceded by a thorough analysis of its strategic implications. Alternatively, a firm might consider using its operations in the high-inflation country as an export base for countries that are not subject to price controls.

3. *Launch new products or variants of existing products.* If price controls are selective, a company can navigate around them by systematically launching new products or modifying existing ones. Also here, the firm should consider the overall picture by answering questions such as these: Will there be a demand for these products? What are the implications in terms of manufacturing economies? inventory management? How will the trade react? Further, if these products are not yet available elsewhere, this option is merely a long-term solution.

---

[25]"Inflation Lessons Over a Big Mac," *The Financial Times* (February 22, 1993).
[26]"Russians Up and Down," *The Financial Times* (October 18, 1993), p. 12.
[27]Venkatakrishna V. Bellur, Radharao Chaganti, Rajeswararao Chaganti, and Saraswati P. Singh, "Strategic Adaptations to Price Controls: The Case of the Indian Drug Industry," *Journal of the Academy of Marketing Science*, 13 (1) (Winter 1985), pp. 143–59.

4. *Negotiate with the government.* In some cases, firms are able to negotiate for permission to adjust their prices. Lobbying can be done individually, but is more likely to be successful on an industrywide basis.

5. *Predict incidence of price controls.* Some countries have a history of price-freeze programs. Given historical information on the occurrence of price controls and other economic variables, econometric models can be constructed to forecast the likelihood of price controls. That information can be used by managers to see whether price adjustments are warranted, given the likelihood of an imminent price freeze.[28]

A drastic action course is simply to leave the country. Many consumer goods companies chose this option when they exited their South-American markets during the 1980s. However, companies that hang on and learn to manage a high-inflation environment will be able carry over their expertise to other countries. Further, they will enjoy a competitive advantage (due to entry barriers such as brand loyalty and supplier ties) versus companies that reenter these markets once inflation has been suppressed.

◆ ◆ ◆ ◆ ◆ ◆ GLOBAL PRICING AND CURRENCY MOVEMENTS

In May 1992, two of the most expensive car markets in the European Union were Spain and Italy. One year later, Italy and Spain were the two lowest priced markets.[29] Currency volatility within the European Union was mostly responsible for these car price reversals. With a few exceptions (e.g., the Eastern Caribbean, some former French colonies in West Africa), most countries have their own currency. Exchange rates reflect how much one currency is worth in terms of another currency. Due to the interplay of a variety of economic and political factors, exchange rates continuously float up- or downward. Even membership to a monetary union does not guarantee exchange rate stability. In September 1992, the Italian lira and the pound sterling were forced to withdraw from the European Monetary System. At the same time, the bands within which the remaining currencies could move without intervention were broadened. In early 1994, the CFA, the currency unit shared by several former French African colonies, was devalued by 50 percent. Given the sometimes-dramatic exchange rate movements, setting prices in a floating exchange rate world poses a tremendous challenge.[30] Exhibit 13–3 lists several exporter strategies under varying currency regimes.

Currency Gain/Loss Pass Through

Two major managerial pricing issues result from currency movements: (1) How much of a exchange rate gain (loss) should be passed through to our customers? and (2) In what currency should we quote our prices? Let us first address the **pass-**

---

[28]James K. Weekly, "Pricing in Foreign Markets: Pitfalls and Opportunities," *Industrial Marketing Management*, 21 (1992), pp. 173–79.

[29]"Fluctuating Exchange Rates Main Factor in European Car Price Comparisons," *The Financial Times* (July 5, 1993).

[30]Llewlyn Clague and Rena Grossfield, "Export Pricing in a Floating Rate World," *Columbia Journal of World Business* (Winter 1974), pp. 17–22.

EXHIBIT 13-3
EXPORTER STRATEGIES UNDER VARYING CURRENCY CONDITIONS

When domestic currency is WEAK...	*When domestic currency is STRONG...*
• Stress price benefits	• Engage in nonprice competition by improving quality, delivery, and aftersale service
• Costly features expand product line and add more	• Improve productivity and engage in vigorous cost reduction
• Shift sourcing and manufacturing to domestic market	• Shift sourcing and manufacturing overseas
• Exploit export opportunities in all markets	• Give priority to exports to relatively strong-currency countries
• Conduct conventional cash-for-goods trade	• Deal in countertrade with weak-currency countries
• Use full-costing approach, but use marginal-cost pricing to penetrate new/competitive markets	• Trim profit margins and use marginal-cost pricing
• Speed repatriation of foreign-earned income and collections	• Keep the foreign-earned income in host country, slow collections
• Minimize expenditures in local, host country currency	• Maximize expenditures in local, host country currency
• Buy needed services (advertising, insurance, transportation, etc.) in domestic market	• Buy needed services abroad and pay for them in local currencies
• Minimize local borrowing	• Borrow money needed for expansion in local market
• Bill foreign customers in domestic currency	• Bill foreign customers in their own currency

Source: S. Tamer Cavusgil, "Unraveling the Mystique of Export Pricing," reprinted from *Business Horizons* (May–June 1988). Copyright 1988 by the Foundation for the School of Business at Indiana University. Used with permission.

through issue. Consider the predicament of American companies exporting to Japan. In principle, a weakening of the U.S. dollar versus the Japanese yen will strengthen the competitive position of U.S.-based exporters in Japan. A weak dollar allows U.S.-based firms to lower the yen-price of American goods exported to Japan. This enables American exporters to steal market share away from the local Japanese competitors without sacrificing profits. By the same token, a stronger U.S. dollar will undermine the competitive position of American exporters. When the dollar appreciates versus the yen, we have the mirror picture of the previous situation: the retail price in yen of American exports goes up. As a result, American exporters might lose market share if they leave their ex-factory prices unchanged. To maintain their competitive edge, they may be forced to lower their ex-factory dollar prices. Of course, the ultimate impact on the exporter's competitive position will also depend on the impact of currency movement on the exporter's costs and the nature of the competition in the Japanese market. The benefits of a weaker dollar could be washed out when many parts are imported from Japan, since the weaker dollar will make these parts more expensive. When most of the competitors are U.S.-based manufacturers, changes in the dollar's exchange rate might not matter.

Let us illustrate these points with a numerical example. Consider the situation in Exhibit 13–4, which looks at the dilemmas that a hypothetical U.S.-based exporter to Japan faces when the exchange rate between the U.S. dollar and the Japanese yen changes. In the example we assume a simple linear demand schedule:

Demand (in units) in Japanese export market = 2,000 − 50 × yen price

We also make an admittedly dubious assumption: Our exporter does not face any costs (in other words, total revenues equal total profits). Initially, one U.S. dollar equals 100 yen and the firm's total export revenue is $55.5 million. Suppose now that the U.S. dollar has strengthened by 30 percent versus the Japanese yen, moving from an exchange rate of 100 yen to one U.S.$ to a 130-to-1 exchange rate (row 2 in Exhibit 13–4). If the U.S.$ ex-factory price remains the same (i.e., $30,000), Japanese consumers will face a 30 percent price increase. Total demand decreases (from 1,850 units to 1,805 units) and also U.S.$ revenue goes down by $1.35 million. Our American exporter faces the problem of whether to pass through exchange rate losses, and if so, how much of the loss he should absorb. If our exporter does not lower the U.S. dollar ex-factory price, he is likely to lose market share to his Japanese (or European) competitors in Japan. So, to sustain its competitive position, the U.S.-based manufacturer would be forced to lower its ex-factory price. In this situation, American exporters face the trade-off between sacrificing short-term profits (maintaining price) and sustaining long-term market share in export markets (cutting ex-factory price). For example, in the extreme case, the U.S. firm might consider sustaining the yen-based retail price (i.e., 3 million yen). In that case, US$ revenues would go down by $11.45 million.

Generally speaking, the appropriate action will depend on four factors, namely: (1) customers' price sensitivity, (2) the impact of the dollar appreciation on the firm's cost structure, (3) the amount of competition in the export market, and (4) the firm's strategic orientation. The higher consumers' price sensitivity in the

EXHIBIT 13–4
A NUMERICAL ILLUSTRATION OF PASS-THROUGH AND LOCAL CURRENCY STABILITY

Demand in Japan (Units) = 2,000 − 50 × Price (in Yen)
Costs = $0.0

Panel A: 100% Pass-Through

Exchange Rate	Unit Price in US$	Unit Price in Yen	Units Sold	US$ Revenue
100 Yen = $1	$30,000	3.0m	1,850	$55.50m
130 Yen = $1	$30,000	3.9m	1,805	$54.15m
70 Yen = $1	$30,000	2.1m	1,895	$56.85m

Panel B: Local-Currency Price Stability

Exchange Rate	Unit Price in US$	Unit Price in Yen	Units Sold	US$ Revenue	Revenue Gain/(Loss) vs. 100% PT
100 Yen = $1	$30,000	3.0m	1,850	$55.50m	$0.00m
130 Yen = $1	$23,077	3.0m	1,850	$42.69m	($11.45m)
70 Yen = $1	$42,857	3.0m	1,850	$79.28m	$22.45m

export market, the stronger the case for lowering the ex-factory price. One route to lower price sensitivity is by investing in brand equity. High brand equity provides a buffer to global price competition. A decline in costs resulting from the strengthening of the U.S. dollar (e.g., when many parts are imported from Japan) broadens the price adjustment latitude. The more intense the competition in the export market, the stronger the pressure to cut prices. The fourth factor is the firm's strategic orientation. Firms could be market-share oriented or focus on short-term profits. Naturally, market-share oriented firms would tend to pass through less of the cost increase than their financial performance-oriented counterparts.[31] The bottom row of Exhibit 13–4 shows what happens when the U.S. dollar weakens by 30 percent. In that case we have the mirror picture of the previous scenario.

American exporters might lower their mark-ups much higher in price-conscious export markets than in price-insensitive markets. Such destination-specific adjustments of mark-ups in response to exchange rate movements is referred to as **pricing-to-market (PTM)**. PTM behaviors differ across source countries. One study of export pricing adjustments in the U.S. automobile market contrasted pricing decisions of Japanese and German exporters over periods where both the Japanese yen and the German mark depreciated against the U.S. dollar.[32] The results of the study showed that there was much more pass-through (and less PTM) by German exporters than by their Japanese rivals (see Exhibit 13–5).

EXHIBIT 13–5
RETAIL PRICE CHANGES DURING DOLLAR APPRECIATIONS: JAPANESE AND GERMAN EXPORTS TO THE U.S. MARKET

Model	Real dollar appreciation	Real retail price change in US market
Honda Civic 2-Dr. Sedan	39%	−7%
Datsun 200 SX 2-Dr.	39	−10
Toyota Cressida 4-Dr.	39	6
BMW 320i 2-Dr. Sedan	42	−8
BMW 733i 4-Dr. Sedan	42	−17
Mercedes 300 TD Sta. Wgn.	42	−39

Note: The real dollar appreciation measures the movement of the U.S. producer price index relative to the Japanese and German producer price indices converted into dollars by the nominal exchange rate. The real retail price change measures the movement of the dollar retail price of specific auto models relative to the retail unit value of all domestically produced cars.

Source: Reprinted from Joseph A. Gagnon and Michael M. Knetter, "Markup Adjustment and Exchange Rate Fluctuations: Evidence from Panel Data on Automobile Exports," *Journal of International Money and Finance*, vol. 14, no. 2, p. 304. Copyright 1995, with kind permission from Elsevier Science Ltd., Langford Lane, Kidlington OX5 1GB, UK.

---

[31]Terry Clark, Masaaki Kotabe, and Dan Rajaratnam, "Exchange Rate Pass-Through and International Pricing Strategy: A Conceptual Framework and Research Propositions," *Journal of International Business Studies*, 30 (Second Quarter 1999), pp. 249–68.

[32]Joseph A. Gagnon and Michael M. Knetter, "Markup Adjustment and Exchange Rate Fluctuations: Evidence from Panel Data on Automobile Exports," *Journal of International Money and Finance*, 14 (2) (1995), pp. 289–310.

Playing the pricing-to-market game carries certain risks. Frequent adjustments of prices in response to currency movements will distress local channels and customers. When local currency prices move up, foreign customers may express their disapproval by switching to other brands. On the other hand, when prices go down, it will often be hard to raise prices in the future. Therefore, often times, the preferred strategy is to adjust mark-ups in such a way that local currency prices remain fairly stable. This special form of pricing-to-market has been referred to as **local-currency price stability (LCPS)** where mark-ups are adjusted to stabilize prices in the buyer's currency.[33] The bottom panel of Exhibit 13–4 reports the revenue losses or gains of an exporter who maintains LCPS. To pass through exchange rate gains from U.S. dollar devaluations, U.S.-based exporters could resort to temporary price promotions or other incentives (e.g., trade deals) rather than a permanent cut of the local currency regular price.

Currency Quotation

Another pricing concern rising from floating exchange rates centers on the currency unit to be used in international business transactions. Sellers and buyers usually prefer a quote in their domestic currency. That way, the other party will have to bear currency risks. The decision largely depends on the balance of power between the supplier and the customer. Whoever yields will need to cover currency exposure risk through hedging transactions on the forward exchange market. A survey of currency choice practices of Swedish, Finnish, and American firms found that firms using foreign currencies have higher export volumes and transaction values than exporters using their home currency. However, profit margins suffer.[34] Some firms decide to use a common currency for all their business transactions, world- or regionwide. Dow Chemical embraces the deutsche mark for all its business dealings in Europe. In the wake of the euro, companies such as DaimlerChrysler and Siemens are switching to a euro-regime both for their internal (e.g., transfer pricing) and external (suppliers and distributors) transactions.

◆ ◆ ◆ ◆ ◆ ◆ TRANSFER PRICING

Determinants of Transfer Prices

Most large multinational corporations have a network of subsidiaries spread across the globe. Sales transactions between related entities of the same company can be quite substantial, involving trade of raw materials, components, finished goods, or services. **Transfer prices** are prices charged for such transactions. Transfer pricing decisions in an international context need to balance off the interests of a broad range of stakeholders: (1) parent company, (2) local country managers, (3) host government(s), (4) domestic government, and (5) joint venture partner(s) when the transaction involves a partnership. Not surprisingly, reconciling the conflicting interests of these various parties can be a mind-boggling juggling act.

---

[33]Michael M. Knetter, "International Comparisons of Pricing-to-Market Behavior," *American Economic Review*, 83 (3) (1993), pp. 473–86.

[34]Saeed Samiee and Patrik Anckar, "Currency Choice in Industrial Pricing: A Cross-National Evaluation," *Journal of Marketing*, 62 (July 1998), pp. 112–27.

A number of studies have examined the key drivers behind transfer pricing decisions. One survey of U.S.-based multinationals found that transfer pricing policies were primarily influenced by the following factors (in order of importance):

1. Market conditions in the foreign country
2. Competition in the foreign country
3. Reasonable profit for foreign affiliate
4. U.S. federal income taxes
5. Economic conditions in the foreign country
6. Import restrictions
7. Customs duties
8. Price controls
9. Taxation in the foreign country
10. Exchange controls[35]

Other surveys have come up with different rankings.[36] However, a recurring theme appears to be the importance of market conditions (especially, the competitive situation), taxation regimes, and various market imperfections (e.g., currency control, custom duties, price freeze). Generally speaking, MNCs should consider the following criteria when making transfer pricing decisions:[37]

- *Tax regimes.* Ideally, firms would like to boost their profits in low-tax countries and dampen them in high-tax countries. To shift profits from high-tax to low-tax markets, companies would set transfer prices as high as possible for goods entering high-tax countries and vice versa for low-tax countries. However, manipulating transfer prices to exploit corporate tax rate differentials will undoubtedly alert the tax authorities in the high-tax rate country and, in the worst case, lead to a tax audit. We will revisit the taxation issue shortly.

- *Local market conditions.* Another key influence is local market conditions. Examples of market-related factors include the market share of the affiliate, the growth rate of the market, and the nature of local competition (e.g., nonprice-versus price-based). To expand market share in a new market, multinationals may initially underprice intra-company shipments to a start-up subsidiary.[38]

- *Market imperfections.* Market imperfections in the host country, such as price freezes and profit repatriation restrictions, hinder the multinational's ability to move earnings out of the country. Under such circumstances, transfer prices can be used as a mechanism to get around these obstacles. Also, high import duties might prompt a firm to lower transfer prices charged to subsidiaries located in that particular country.

---

[35]Jane Burns, "Transfer Pricing Decisions in U.S. Multinational Corporations," *Journal of International Business Studies*, 11 (2) (Fall 1980), pp. 23–39.

[36]See, e.g., Seung H. Kim and Stephen W. Miller, "Constituents of the International Transfer Pricing Decision," *Columbia Journal of World Business* (Spring 1979), p. 71.

[37]S. Tamer Cavusgil, "Pricing for Global Markets," *Columbia Journal of World Business* (Winter 1996), pp. 66–78.

[38]Mohammad F. Al-Eryani, Pervaiz Alam, and Syed H. Akhter, "Transfer Pricing Determinants of U.S. Multinationals," *Journal of International Business Studies*, 21 (Third Quarter 1990), pp. 409–25.

- *Joint venture partner.* When the entity concerned is part of a joint venture, parent companies should also factor in the interests of the local joint venture partner. Numerous joint venture partnerships have hit the rocks because of disagreements over transfer pricing decisions.
- *Morale of local country managers.* Finally, firms should also be concerned about the morale of their local country managers. Especially when performance evaluation is primarily based on local profits, transfer price manipulations might distress country managers whose subsidiary's profits are artificially deflated.

Setting Transfer Prices

There are two broad transfer pricing strategies: market-based transfer pricing, and nonmarket-based pricing. The first perspective uses the market mechanism as a cue for setting transfer prices. Such prices are usually referred to as **arm's-length prices**. Basically, the company charges the price that any buyer outside the MNC would pay, as if the transaction had occurred between two unrelated companies (at '*arm's length*'). Tax authorities typically prefer this method over other transfer pricing approaches. Since an objective yardstick is used—the *market price*—transfer prices based on this approach are easy to justify to third parties (e.g., tax authorities). The major problem with arm's length transfer pricing is that an appropriate benchmark is often lacking, due to the absence of competition. This is especially the case for intangible services. Many services are only available within the multinational. Payments of royalties and license fees within U.S.-based multinationals were $13 billion in 1990, far beyond the $4 billion paid between unrelated companies.[39]

Nonmarket-based pricing covers various policies that deviate from market-based pricing, the most prominent ones being **cost-based pricing** and **negotiated pricing**. Cost-based pricing simply adds a mark-up to the cost of the goods. Issues here revolve around getting a consensus on a "fair" profit split and allocation of corporate overhead. Further, tax authorities often do not accept cost-based pricing procedures. Another form of nonmarket-based pricing is negotiated transfer prices. Here conflicts between country affiliates are resolved through negotiation of transfer prices. This process may lead to better cooperation among corporate divisions.[40]

A recent study shows that compliance with financial reporting norms, fiscal and custom rules, anti-dumping regulations prompt companies to use market-based transfer pricing.[41] Government-imposed market constraints (e.g., import restrictions, price controls, exchange controls) favor nonmarket-based transfer pricing methods. To the question, which procedure works best, the answer is pretty murky: there is no "universally optimal" system.[42] In fact, most firms use a mixture of market-based and non-market pricing procedures.

[39]"Taxing Questions," *The Economist* (May 22, 1993), p. 73.

[40]R. Ackelsberg and G. Yukl, "Negotiated Transfer Pricing and Conflict Resolution in Organization," *Decision Sciences* (July 1979), pp. 387–98.

[41]M. F. Al-Eryani et al., "Transfer Pricing Determinants," p. 422.

[42]Jeffrey S. Arpan, "International Intracorporate Pricing: Non-American Systems and Views," *Journal of International Business Studies* (Spring 1972), p. 18.

Cross-country tax rate differentials encourage many MNCs to set transfer prices that shift profits from high-tax to low-tax countries to minimize their overall tax burden. At the same time, MNCs need to comply with the tax codes of their home country and the host countries involved. Noncompliance may risk accusations of tax evasion and lead to tax audits. So the issue that MNCs face can be stated as follows: How do we as a company draw the line between setting transfer prices that maximize corporate profits and compliance with tax regulations?

Minimizing the Risk of Transfer Pricing Tax Audits[43]

To avoid walking on thin ice, experts suggest to set transfer prices that are as close as possible to the Basic Arm's Length Standard (BALS). This criterion is now accepted by tax authorities worldwide as the international standard for assessing transfer prices. In practice, there are three methods to calculate a BALS price: comparable/uncontrollable price, resale price, and cost-plus. The first rule—comparable/uncontrollable—states that the parent company should compare the transfer price of its "controlled" subsidiary to the selling price charged by an independent seller to an independent buyer of similar goods or services. The resale price method determines the BALS by subtracting the gross margin percentage used by comparable independent buyers from the final third-party sales price. Finally, the cost-plus method fixes the BALS by adding the gross profit mark-up percentage earned by comparable companies performing similar functions to the production costs of the controlled manufacturer or seller. Note that this rule is somewhat different from the cost method that we discussed earlier since, strictly speaking, the latter method does not rely on mark-ups set by third parties.

Exhibit 13–6 gives a flowchart that can be used to devise transfer pricing strategies that minimize the risk of tax audits. Decisions center around the following five questions:

1. Do comparable/uncontrolled transactions exist?
2. Where is the most value added? Parent? Subsidiary?
3. Are combined profits of parent and subsidiary shared in proportion to contributions?
4. Does the transfer price meet the benchmark set by the tax authorities?
5. Does the MNC have the information to justify the transfer prices used?

GLOBAL PRICING AND ANTIDUMPING REGULATION ◆ ◆ ◆ ◆ ◆ ◆

The antidumping laws that most governments use to counter dumping practices are a potential minefield for global pricing policies. Dumping occurs when imports are being sold at an "unfair" price. To protect local producers against the encroachment of low-priced imports, governments may levy countervailing duties or fines. Thus, it is important for exporters to realize that pricing policies, such as penetration pricing, may trigger antidumping actions. The number of antidumping initiatives has staggered in recent years. Most of the action takes place in the United States and the European Union. However, antidumping cases are increasingly

---

[43]This section is based on John P. Fraedrich and Connie Rae Bateman, "Transfer Pricing by Multinational Marketers: Risky Business," *Business Horizons* (Jan.–Feb. 1996), pp. 17–22.

EXHIBIT 13–6
DECISION MAKING MODEL FOR ASSESSING RISK OF TP STRATEGY

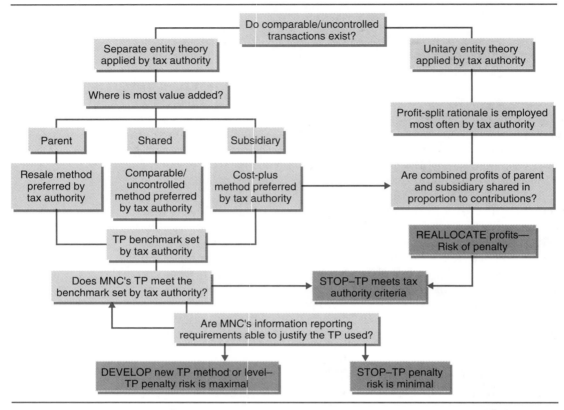

Source: John P. Fraedrich and Connie Rae Bateman, "Transfer Pricing by Multinational Marketers: Risky Business." Reprinted from *Business Horizons*, January-February 1996. Copyright 1996 by the Foundation for the School of Business at Indiana University. Used with permission.

initiated in Japan, India and other developing countries. Economists often refer to this trend as a rise in protectionism.[44]

There are several possible reasons to explain the growing popularity of antidumping litigation. The removal of traditional trade barriers (tariffs, quotas) has encouraged several countries to switch to nontariff barriers such as antidumping to protect their local industries. A World Bank study showed that the impact of dumping duties in the U.S. manufactured goods sector has boosted average tariffs in that sector from a nominal 6 percent rate to 23 percent.[45] There is also a huge imbalance between plaintiffs (local producer(s)) and defendants (importer(s)) in antidumping cases. Plaintiffs typically face no penalties for frivolous complaints. Moreover, plaintiffs clearly have a home advantage (local legislation, local judge).[46] Allegedly, antidumping action is often utilized as a tactical tool to foster voluntary export restraints (VER). Foreign competitors, faced with the prospect of antidump-

---

[44]Jagdish Bhagwati, *Protectionism* (Cambridge, MA: The MIT Press, 1988), Chapter 3.

[45]"Negotiators Down in the Dumps over US Draft," *The Financial Times* (November 25, 1993), p. 6.

[46]J. Bhagwati, *Protectionism*, pp. 48–49.

ing action, may decide to fall back on VERs as the lesser of two evils.[47] Finally, the concept of a "fair" price is usually pretty murky. The U.S. trade law defines dumping to occur when imports are sold below the home-country price (price discrimination) or when the import price is less than the "constructed value" or average cost of production ("pricing below cost"). Either concept can be very vague. In some situations, the imported good is not sold in the home country so that no basis of comparison exists (absence of domestic price).

Antidumping actions will persist in the future. Multinationals need to take antidumping laws into account when determining their global pricing policy. Aggressive pricing may trigger antidumping measures and, thus, jeopardize the company's competitive position. Global companies should also monitor changes in antidumping legislation and closely track antidumping cases in their particular industry.

To minimize risk exposure to antidumping actions, exporters might pursue any of the following marketing strategies:[48]

- *Trading up.* Move away from low-value to high-value products via product differentiation. Most Japanese car makers have stretched their product line upward to tap into the upper-tier segments of their export markets.

- *Service enhancement.* Exporters can also differentiate their product by adding support services to the core product. Both moves—trading up and service enhancement—are basically attempts to move away from price competition, thereby making the exporter less vulnerable to dumping accusations.

- *Distribution and communication.* Other initiatives on the distribution and communication front of the marketing mix include: (1) the establishment of communication channels with local competitors, (2) entering into cooperative agreements with them (e.g., strategic alliances), or (3) reallocation of the firm's marketing efforts from vulnerable products (that is, those most likely to be subjected to dumping scrutiny) to less sensitive products.

PRICE COORDINATION   ◆ ◆ ◆ ◆ ◆ ◆

When developing a global pricing strategy, one of the thorniest issues is how much coordination should exist between prices charged in different countries. This issue is especially critical for global (or regional) brands that are marketed with no or very few cross-border variations. Economics dictate that firms should price discriminate between markets such that overall profits are maximized. So, if (marginal) costs are roughly equivalent, multinationals would charge relatively low prices in highly price sensitive countries and high prices in insensitive markets. Unfortunately, reality is not that simple. In most cases, markets cannot be perfectly separated. Huge cross-country price differentials will encourage gray markets where goods are shipped from low-price to high-price countries by unauthorized distributors. Thus, some coordination will usually be necessary. In deciding how much coordination, several considerations matter:

[47]James E. Anderson, "Domino Dumping, I: Competitive Exporters," *American Economic Review*, 82 (1) (March 1992), pp. 65–83.
[48]Michel M. Kostecki, "Marketing Strategies between Dumping and Antidumping Action," *European Journal of Marketing*, 25 (12) (1991), pp. 7–19.

1. *Nature of customers.* When information on prices travels fast across borders, it is fairly hard to sustain wide price gaps. Under such conditions, firms will need to make a convincing case to their customers to justify price disparities. With global customers (e.g., multinational clients in business-to-business transactions), price coordination definitely becomes a must. General Motors applies "global enterprise pricing" for many of the components it purchases. Under this system, suppliers are asked to charge the same universal price worldwide.[49] In Europe, Microsoft sets prices that differ by no more than 5 percent between countries due to pressure from bargain-hunting multinational customers.[50]

2. *Nature of channels.* In a sense, distribution channels can be viewed as intermediate customers. So, the same logic applies here: Price coordination becomes critical when price information is transparent and/or the firm deals with cross-border distribution channels. Pricing discipline becomes mandatory when manufacturers have little control over their distributors.

3. *Nature of competition.* In many industries, firms compete with the same rivals in a given region, if not worldwide. Global competition demands a cohesive strategic approach for the entire marketing mix strategy, including pricing. From that angle, competition pushes companies toward centralized pricing policies. On the other hand, price changes made by competitors in the local market often require a rapid response. Should the subsidiary match a given price cut? If so, to what extent? Local subsidiaries often have much better information about the local market conditions to answer such questions than corporate or regional headquarters. Thus, the need for alertness and speedy response to competitive pricing moves encourages a decentralized approach toward pricing decisions.

4. *Market integration.* When markets integrate (e.g., Single European Market), barriers to cross-border movement of goods come down. Given the freedom to move goods from one member state to another, the Pan-European market offers little latitude for perfect price discrimination.[51] Many of the transaction costs plaguing parallel imports that once existed, have now disappeared. In fact, the European Commission imposes heavy penalties against companies that try to limit gray market transactions. The Commission fined Volkswagen almost $110 million when it accused VW of competition abuses. VW had ordered its Italian dealers not to sell cars to citizens from outside Italy. Austrian and German shoppers tried to buy VW cars in Italy where they were 30 percent cheaper.[52]

   Several multinationals doing business in the European Union harmonize their prices to narrow down price gaps between different member states. Mars and Levi Strauss reduced their Pan-European price gaps to no more than 10 percent.[53] In the same manner, Compaq limits price variations to 5 percent around a central price.

[49]"GM Powertrain Suppliers Will See Global Pricing," *Purchasing* (February 12, 1998).

[50]"European Software-Pricing Formulas, Long Abstruse, Develop a Rationale," *The Wall Street Journal* (June 11, 1993).

[51]Wolfgang Gaul and Ulrich Lutz, "Pricing in International Marketing and Western European Economic Integration," *Management International Review*, 34 (2) (1994), pp. 101–24.

[52]"On the Road to Price Convergence," *Financial Times* (November 12, 1998), p. 29.

[53]"Counting Costs of Dual Pricing in the Run-Up to 1992," *The Financial Times* (July 9, 1990), p. 4.

5. *Internal organization.* The organization setup is another important influence. Highly decentralized companies pose a hurdle to price coordination efforts. In many companies, the pricing decision is left to the local subsidiaries. Moves to take away some of the pricing authority from country affiliates will undoubtedly spark opposition and lead to bruised egos. Just as with other centralization decisions, it is important that performance evaluation systems are fine-tuned if necessary.

6. *Government regulation.* Government regulation of prices puts pressure on firms to harmonize their prices. A good example is the pharmaceutical industry. In many countries, multinationals need to negotiate the price for new drugs with the local authorities. Governments in the European Union increasingly use prices set in other EU member states as a cue for their negotiating position. This trend has prompted several pharmaceutical companies to negotiate a common EU-price for new drugs.

Given the pressure toward increased globalization, some degree of price coordination becomes absolutely necessary. In some cases, firms set a uniform pricing formula that is applied by all affiliates. Elsewhere, coordination is limited to general rules that only indicate the desired pricing positioning (e.g., premium positioning, middle-of-the-road positioning).

Aligning Pan-Regional Prices

Simon and Kucher[54] propose a three-step procedure to align prices in the Pan-European market. Pressure to narrow down price gaps could lead to two scenarios (see Exhibit 13–7). The disaster scenario (panel (A) in Exhibit 13–7) is a situation

EXHIBIT 13–7
PAN-EUROPEAN PRICE COORDINATION

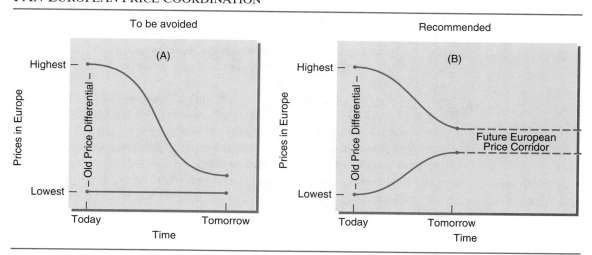

Source: Hermann Simon and Eckhard Kucher, "The European Pricing Time Bomb—and How to Cope with It," *Marketing and Research Today* (March 1992), pp. 3–14.

Permission for using this material which was originally published in *Marketing and Research Today*, has been granted by (E.S.O.M.A.R.) The European Society for Opinion Research J.J. Viottastraat 29, 1071 JP, Amsterdam, The Netherlands.

[54]Hermann Simon and Eckhard Kucher, "The European Pricing Time Bomb—And How to Cope With It," *Marketing and Research Today* (February 1993), pp. 25–36.

where all prices sink to the lowest price. Calculations by Lehman Brothers, an investment bank, have shown that, if all car prices in the euro area fell to the lowest levels, the revenues of the French car makers Peugeot and Renault would drop by 12 percent and 9 percent, respectively.[55] At the other extreme, companies may try to sustain cross-border price gaps. The desired scenario (panel B in Exhibit 13–7) tries to find the middle ground by upping prices in low-price countries and cutting them in high-price countries. To pursue this scenario, firms should set a **pricing corridor** within the region.

The procedure works as follows:

Step 1: **Determine Optimal Price for Each Country.** Find out what price schedules will maximize overall profits. Given information on the demand schedule and the costs incurred in each market, managers are able to figure out the desirable prices in the respective markets.

Step 2: **Find out whether parallel imports ("gray markets") are likely to occur at these prices.** Parallel imports arise when unauthorized distributors purchase the product (sometimes repackaged) in the low-price market and then ship it to high-price markets. The goal of step 2 is not to preempt parallel imports altogether but to boost profits to the best possible degree. Given the "optimal" prices derived in the first step, the manager needs to determine to what extent the proposed price schedule will foster parallel imports. Parallel imports become harmful insofar as they inflict damage on authorized distributors. They could also hurt the morale of the local sales force or country managers. Information is needed on the arbitrage costs of parallel importers. For instance, in the European drug industry, parallel importers target drugs with more than 20 percent price differentials. Conceivably, firms might decide to abandon (or not enter) small, low-price markets, thereby avoiding pricing pressure on high-price markets. MNCs should also consider the pros and cons of nonpricing solutions to cope with parallel imports. Possible strategies include product differentiation, intelligence systems to measure exposure to gray markets, and creating negative perceptions in the mind of the end-user about parallel imports.[56]

Step 3: **Set a pricing corridor.** If the "optimal" prices that were derived in Step 1 are not sustainable, firms need to narrow the gap between prices for high-price and low-price markets. Charging the same price across the board is not desirable. Such a solution would sacrifice company profits. Instead, the firm should set a pricing corridor. The corridor is formed by systematically exploring the profit impact from lowering prices in high-price countries and upping prices in low-price countries, as shown in panel B of Exhibit 13–7. The narrower the price gap, the more profits the firm has to sacrifice. At some point, there will be a desirable trade-off between the size of the gray market and the amount of profits sacrificed.

---

[55]"Faster Forward," *The Economist* (November 28, 1998), pp. 83–84.

[56]"Peggy A. Chaudhry and Michael G. Walsh, "Managing the Gray Market in the European Union: The Case of the Pharmaceutical Industry," *Journal of International Marketing*, 3 (3) (1995), pp. 11–33.

Of course, this method is not foolproof. Competitive reactions (e.g., price wars) need to be factored in. Also, government regulations may restrict pricing flexibility. Still, the procedure is a good start when pricing alignment becomes desirable.

Global marketers can choose from four alternatives to promote price coordination within their organization.[57]

Implementing Price Coordination

1. *Economic measures.* Corporate headquarters are able to influence pricing decisions at the local level via the transfer prices that are set for the goods that are sold to or purchased from the local affiliates. Another option is rationing. That is, headquarters sets upper limits on the number of units that can be shipped to each country.

2. *Centralization.* In the extreme case, pricing decisions are made at corporate or regional headquarters level. Centralized price decision-making is fairly uncommon, given its numerous shortcomings. It sacrifices the flexibility that firms often need to respond rapidly to local competitive conditions.

3. *Formalization.* Far more common than the previous approach is formalization where headquarters spells out a set of pricing rules that the country managers should comply with. Within these norms, country managers have a certain level of flexibility in determining their ultimate prices.

4. *Informal coordination.* Finally, firms can use various forms of informal price coordination. The emphasis here is on informing and persuasion rather than prescription and dictates. Examples of informal price coordination tactics include discussion groups and "best-practice" gatherings.

Which one of these four approaches is most effective is contingent on the complexity of the environment in which the firm is doing business. When the environment is fairly stable and the various markets are highly similar, centralization is usually preferable over the other options. However, highly complex environments require a more decentralized approach.

PRICING POLICIES AND THE EURO

◆ ◆ ◆ ◆ ◆ ◆

Since January 1, 1999, eleven European Union members states have adopted the euro as their common currency.[58] The euro will not be a physical reality until July 1, 2002, when the old currencies (e.g., deutsche mark, Italian lira) in the euro-zone will disappear. With the arrival of the euro, currency exposure will decline, thereby eliminating the need to hedge against exchange rate movements. However, new challenges arise that managers doing business in the euro-zone will need to tackle. The major consequence of the euro is that prices will become more transparent for distributors and consumers alike. Increased price transparency does not mandate price consistency, but

---

[57]Gert Assmus and Carsten Wiese, "How to Address the Gray Market Threat Using Price Coordination," *Sloan Management Review* (Spring 1995), pp. 31–41.

[58]See Chapter 3 (pages 96–102) for a more detailed discussion of the euro and its implications. As per January 1, 2000, Greece will join the euro-zone.

it sure makes strategic pricing decisions within Europe more complicated. Cross-border price differences can no longer hide behind exchange rate fluctuations.

How should companies operating in the euro-zone adjust their pricing policies in wake of the euro? With respect to pricing, marketing executives will primarily need to make strategic decision in four areas.

Harmonization of Prices

The biggest impact of the euro is likely to be price harmonization. Volkswagen expects its prices to arrive within a 5–10 percent band.[59] As price comparisons across borders become easier, it is harder for firms to justify the substantial price gaps witnessed in many product categories. The pressure to harmonize will be biggest for commodity-like products for which consumers tend to be price sensitive. Products and brands that are well differentiated across borders may be able to shield themselves against the price-leveling pressures of the euro. For instance, an Opel Astra bought in Germany comes with a standard CD player and air conditioner, far more luxurious than the same model sold in Portugal.[60]

Harmonization does not have to mean that prices sink to the lowest level. As described earlier, the ideal approach is to up the prices in the low-price countries and cut them in the high-price countries. For some companies, existing pricing policies are so complex that it would be very costly to revise them. Instead of adjusting prices across-the-board, one approach is to draw the line between new and existing products. Sun Microsystems, for instance, decided that the only workable solution was to introduce a common price for new products only.[61]

Differences in cross-border prices will only be workable when they are rational and defensible. For instance, differences in the cost of doing business might justify different price levels. Likewise, performance differences among distributors might be a reason for setting different prices.

Dual Pricing

A recent KPMG survey on the preparedness of companies for the euro found that dual labeling—that is, posting prices in euro and the local currency—was the trickiest issue associated with the launch of the euro. For instance, in Germany, almost 60 percent of companies interviewed rated dual labeling as the most significant issue. Companies and retailers will need to decide how quickly to introduce dual labeling. Some firms start with a trial run. Marks & Spencer, the British retailing group, started with a trial in the Netherlands and then used its experience there to roll out dual labeling to other countries in the region.[62] Several large firms like DaimlerChrysler now require their suppliers to begin the changeover to the euro.[63]

Transfer Pricing

One other consequence of the euro is that prices not only become more transparent for consumers and distributors but also for tax authorities. In the past, transfer price documentation could rely heavily on exchange rate differences to

---

[59]"Car Price Disparities Highlighted," *Financial Times* (January 7, 1999), p. 2.

[60]Ibid.

[61]"Pricing for the Euro," *Business Europe* (May 5, 1999), p. 4.

[62]"Getting Ready on the Shop Floor," *Financial Times* (October 29, 1998), p. 25.

[63]Manfred Gentz, "The Coming Competitive Shakeout," *Harvard Business Review* (Jan.–Feb. 1999), pp. 52–54.

justify the allocation of profits and losses. However, with the euro, tax audits on transfer pricing become much more efficient. In light of the increased price transparency, multinational companies will need to review their transfer pricing policies.[64]

Another nettlesome issue is how to handle the price thresholds (e.g., price points ending with "9") that many firms use when quoting their prices. In the Netherlands, a VCR with a price tag of Dfl. 599 would have a euro-price of €275 (€1 = Dfl. 2.18). For that price, the two closest price thresholds would be €269 and €279. What price threshold should be taken? If the higher price threshold is chosen, the firm runs the risk of being accused of profiteering. The lower price threshold cuts into the firm's profit margin. Essentially, firms will have three options:[65]

Price Points

1. Lower price in euro to the next price threshold (€269 in our example) when the euro is formally introduced.

2. Increase the price well before the launch of the euro in 2002 so you get a "nice" price when the official exchange rate is applied.

3. Apply the official exchange rate when the euro is introduced and adjust prices later if necessary.

The latter strategy makes sense for goods where the importance of price thresholds is minimal. Global Perspective 13–1 describes how one Japanese company, Matsushita, adopted the euro for its European operations.

◆ ◆

𝒢LOBAL PERSPECTIVE 13–1

MATSUSHITA — AN EARLY ADOPTER OF THE EURO

Matsushita, maker of consumer electronics with brand names like Panasonic, JVC, and National, believes that the euro represents costs but also opportunities. In the past, the company's operations had to cope with more than twenty different currencies. Since April 1999, it has held only four: the euro, the pound sterling, the yen, and the dollar.

The group's costs to prepare for the euro changeover were enormous. It needed to put in place the information technology infrastructure for billing in euro

Sources: "Plenty of Gain but Pain, Too," *Financial Times* (December 17, 1998), p. 4; "Financial harmony," *Financial Times* (May 18, 1999), p. 16.

or local currency—depending on the desire of its suppliers and customers. One of the biggest cost items is the lost revenues from price harmonization. In the past, prices differed by as much as 15 percent. The range today is no more than 5 percent. Since the beginning of 1999, Matsushita's sales catalog for the 11 euro-zone countries has displayed prices in euro and local currencies. Big European retail chains, such as Kingfisher, still prefer to settle their invoices in local currency.

Matsushita also adopted the euro for internal use. All cash flow from its euro-zone operations is now pooled and centrally managed. All payments for goods supplied by the Japanese parent to the European operations are settled in euro.

---

[64]"Time to Tackle the Most Taxing Issue," *Financial Times* (September 24, 1998), p. 25.

[65]Raimund Wildner, "The Introduction of the Euro. The Importance of Understanding Consumer Reactions," *Marketing and Research Today* (November 1998), pp. 141–47.

◆ ◆ ◆ ◆ ◆ ◆ COUNTERTRADE

Countertrade is an umbrella term used to describe unconventional trade-financing transactions that involve some form of noncash compensation. During the last decade, companies have increasingly been forced to rely on countertrade. The number of countries mandating countertrade has jumped from about fifteen (mostly former East Bloc and developing countries) in 1975 to more than a hundred in 1991.[66] Estimates on the overall magnitude of countertrade vary but the consensus estimate is that it covers 10 percent to 15 percent of world trade.[67] A search on the Internet lists 1,172 Web sites on countertrade. One of the most publicized deals was PepsiCo's $3 billion arrangement with the former Soviet Union to swap Pepsi for profits in Stolichnaya vodka and ocean freighters and tankers.[68] Given the growth of countertrade, global marketers should be aware of its nuts and bolts.

Forms of Countertrade

Countertrade comes in six guises: Barter, clearing arrangements, switch trading, buyback, counterpurchase, and offset. Exhibit 13–8 classifies these different forms of countertrade.

The main distinction is whether or not the transaction involves monetary compensation. Let us look at each form in more detail:[69]

- *Simple barter.* Simple barter is a swap of one product for another product without the use of any money. Usually, no third party is involved to carry out the transaction. Though one of the oldest forms of countertrade, it is very seldom used these days. China's Farm Chemical Sales Promotion Group and the Moroccan government arranged a barter agreement in which $260 million worth of plant-protection chemicals were swapped for the equivalent value of Moroccan phosphate products.[70]

- *Clearing agreement.* Under this form, two governments agree to import a set specified value of goods from one another over a given period. Each party sets up an account that is debited whenever goods are traded. Imbalances at the end of the contract period are cleared through payment in hard currency or goods. A clearing agreement between Indonesia and Iran specified that Indonesia would supply paper, rubber, and galvanized sheets in exchange for 30,000 barrels per day of Iranian crude oil.[71]

[66]Kwabena Anyane-Ntow and Santhi C. Harvey, "A Countertrade Primer," *Management Accounting*, April 1995, pp. 47–49.

[67]Jean-François Hennart and Erin Anderson, "Countertrade and The Minimization of Transaction Costs," Working Paper no. 92-012R, The Wharton School, University of Pennsylvania, Philadelphia, PA.

[68]"Worldwide Money Crunch Fuels More International Barter," *Marketing News*, March 2, 1992, p. 5.

[69]Costas G. Alexandrides and Barbara L. Bowers, *Countertrade: Practices, Strategies, and Tactics*, New York: John Wiley & Sons, 1987, Chapter 1.

[70]Aspy P. Palia and Oded Shenkar, "Countertrade Practices in China," *Industrial Marketing Management*, 20 (1991), pp. 57–65.

[71]Aspy P. Palia, "Countertrade Practices in Indonesia," *Industrial Marketing Management*, 21 (1992), pp. 273–79.

EXHIBIT 13–8
CLASSIFICATION OF FORMS OF COUNTERTRADE

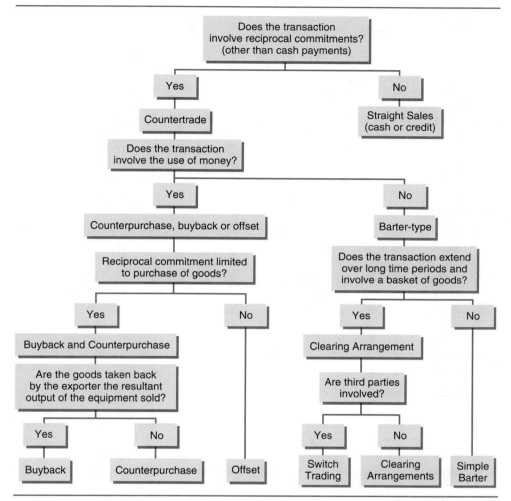

Source: Jean-François Hennart, "Some Empirical Dimensions of Countertrade," *Journal of International Business Studies* (Second Quarter 1990), p. 245.

- *Switch trading.* This is a variant of clearing arrangements where a third party is involved. In such deals, rights to the surplus credits are sold to specialized traders (**switch traders**) at a discount. The third party uses then the credits to buy goods from the deficit country.

  All these types do not entail cash payment flows. The remaining forms involve some use of money. They lead to two parallel agreements: the original sales agreement between the foreign customer and supplier, and a second contract where the supplier commits to purchasing goods in the customer's country.

- *Buyback (compensation).* Buyback arrangements typically occur with the sale of technology, turn-key plants, or machinery equipment. In such transactions, the seller provides the equipment and agrees to be paid (partially or fully) by the products resulting from using the equipment. Such agreements are much more mutually beneficial than the other forms of countertrade. A typical example of a buyback contract is an agreement that was settled between PALMCO Holdings, Malaysia's biggest palm oil refiner, and Japan's Kao Corporation. The contract set up a $70 million joint venture to produce palm oil byproducts in Malaysia. Kao was to be compensated by 60 percent of the output which it could use as inputs for producing detergents, cosmetics, and toiletries.[72]

- *Counterpurchase.* Counterpurchase is the most popular form of countertrade. Similar to buyback arrangements, two parallel contracts are set up. Each party agrees to buy a specified amount of goods from the other for hard currency over a set period. Contrary to buybacks, the products are unrelated. Typically, the importer will provide a shopping list from which the Western exporter can choose. In October 1992, PepsiCo set up a joint-venture in Ukraine with three local partners. Under the agreement, the partnership was to market Ukranian-built ships. Proceeds from the ship sales were to be used to buy soft-drink equipment, to build bottling plants, and to open Pizza Hut restaurants in Ukraine.[73]

- *Offset.* Offset is a variation of counterpurchase: the seller agrees to "offset" the purchase price by sourcing from the importer's country or transferring technology to the other party's country. Offset is very common with defense contracts. An offset contract concluded between Indonesia and General Dynamics to buy F-16 aircraft stipulated that some of the parts would be supplied by PT Nusantara, an Indonesian manufacturer.

Motives Behind Countertrade

Companies engage in countertrade for a variety of reasons. The most commonly cited benefits are as follows:

- *Gain access to new or difficult markets.* Countertrade in many ways is a "necessary evil." It can be very costly and risky. Nevertheless, being prepared to accept countertrade deals offers for many companies a competitive edge that allows them to penetrate markets with a lack of hard currency cash. Many exporters accept countertrade arrangements because their rivals offer it. A U.K. survey found that 80 percent of the exporters' competitors were also involved in countertrade.[74]

- *Overcome exchange rate controls or lack of hard currency.* Shortages of hard currency often lead to exchange controls. To navigate around government-imposed currency restrictions, firms use countertrade.

- *Overcome low country credit worthiness.* This benefit applies to trade with parties located in countries with low credit ratings. Under such conditions, the other party faces high interest rates or difficult access to credit financing. Countertrade allows both parties to overcome such hurdles.

- *Increase sales volume.* Firms with a substantial amount of overheads face a lot of pressure to increase sales. Despite the risks and costs of countertrade, such deals

---

[72]Aspy P. Palia, "Countertrade Practices in Japan," *Industrial Marketing Management*, 22, (1993), pp. 125–32.

[73]"PepsiCo to Finance Ukraine Expansion with Ship Exports," *The Financial Times* (October 23, 1992).

[74]David Shipley and Bill Neale, "Industrial Barter and Countertrade," *Industrial Marketing Management*, 16 (1987), pp. 1–8.

provide a viable opportunity to achieve full capacity utilization. Also, companies often engage in countertrade to dispose of surplus or obsolete products.

- *Generate long-term customer goodwill.* A final payoff is that willingness to accept countertrade deals fosters long-term customer goodwill. Once the credit and/or currency situation in the client's country eases, sellers will be able to capitalize on customer goodwill cemented over the years.

Among these marketing objectives, a recent survey of industrial firms located in twenty-three countries showed that the most important ones are: (1) sales increase (mean response of 3.91 on a 5-point scale), (2) increased competitiveness (3.90), and (3) entry to new markets (3.54).[75] Note that several of these motives are long-term oriented (e.g., gaining entry to new markets, generate goodwill), while some of the other motives are short-term oriented (e.g., use excess production capacity). Firms that are driven by long-term benefits tend to be much more proactive in soliciting countertrade business and pursuing countertrade transactions than short-term oriented firms.[76] Whatever the motive for entering a countertrade agreement, it is important to realize the drawbacks of such arrangements.

Not every exporter is willing to jump on the countertrade bandwagon. In many cases, the risks and costs of a countertrade deal far outweigh its potential advantages. Some of the shortcomings that have been identified by exporters include:[77]

Shortcomings of Countertrade

- *No "in-house" use for goods offered by customers.* Exporters often face the problem of what to do with the goods they are offered. Goods that cannot be used in-house need to be resold. Getting rid of the goods can be a major headache, especially when the quality of the merchandise is poor or when there is an oversupply. Some firms will rely on specialist brokers to sell their goods.

- *Timely and costly negotiations.* Arranging a countertrade deal requires a time-consuming and complex bargaining process. A prospective customer with a long track record usually has a tremendous edge over an exporter with little negotiation skills. Parties will need to haggle over the goods to be traded, their respective valuation, the mixture cash/merchandise, the time horizon, and so on.

- *Uncertainty and lack of information on future prices.* When part of the traded goods involve commodities, firms run the risk that the price sinks before the goods can be sold. Apart from price uncertainty, there is uncertainty about the quality of the goods.

- *Transaction costs.* Costs flowing from countertrade quickly add up: cost of finding buyers for the goods (if there is no in-house use), commissions to middlemen (if any), insurance costs to cover risk of faulty or nondelivery, hedging costs to protect against sinking commodity prices. Given the potential risks and costs an

---

[75]Dorothy A. Paun, "An International Profile of Countertrading Firms," *Industrial Marketing Management*, 26 (1) (1997), pp. 41–50.
[76]Dorothy A. Paun and Aviv Shoham, "Marketing Motives in International Countertrade: An Empirical Examination," *Journal of International Marketing*, 4 (3) (1996), pp. 29–47.
[77]Shipley and Neale, pp. 5–6.

exporter might run, one of the key questions is whether to handle deals in-house or to use specialist middlemen. This decision will basically be driven by a trade-off of the benefits of using outsiders (reduction of risks and transaction costs) with the costs to be incurred (mainly commission).

Countertrade has probably reached its peak now. In fact, some former East Bloc countries are trying to avoid such trade in order to signal their commitment to free markets.[78] Still, countertrade will survive, as many countries remain strapped for hard-currency cash.[79] Finally, here are a few words of advice:[80]

1. Always evaluate the pros and cons of countertrade against other options.
2. Minimize the ratio of compensation goods to cash.
3. Strive for goods that can be used in-house.
4. Assess the relative merits of relying on middlemen versus an in-house staff.
5. Check whether the goods are subject to any import restrictions.
6. Assess the quality of the goods.

SUMMARY ◆

When setting the price in foreign markets, two kinds of mistakes could be made: pricing the product too high or pricing it too low. When the price is set too high, customers will stay away from the firm's products. As a result, profits will be far less than they might have been. In India, Procter & Gamble's Ariel detergent brand initially led to a flow of red ink, partly because P&G charged a retail price far higher than Unilever's Surf Ultra.[81] Setting prices too low might also generate numerous pains. Local governments may cry foul and accuse the firm of dumping. Local customers might interpret the low price as a signal of low quality and avoid your product. Local competitors might perceive the low price as an aggressive move to grab market share and start a price war. And when the price is far lower than in other markets, distributors (local and nonlocal) might spot an arbitrage opportunity and ship the product to your high-price markets, thereby creating a gray market situation. Making pricing decisions is one of the most formidable tasks that international marketers face. Many different elements influence global pricing decisions. Aside of the roles played by the 4 Cs (customers, competition, channels, and company), marketers also need to factor in the impact (direct or indirect) of local government decisions.

In this chapter, we covered the major global pricing issues that matter to marketers: export price escalation, inflation, currency movements, antidumping regulations, and price coordination. In spite of the fact that pricing is typically a highly decentralized marketing decision, cross-border price coordination becomes increasingly a prime concern. We introduced several approaches through which international marketers can implement price coordination. Especially in industrial markets, firms increasingly become aware of the long-term rewards of countertrade as a way of doing business in the global arena. In many cases, countertrade is the sole means for gaining access to new markets. Companies that decide to engage in countertrade should bear in mind the numerous road bumps that these transactions involve.

---

[78]"A Necessary Evil," *The Economist* (November 25, 1989), p. 79.

[79]"Worldwide Money Crunch Fuels More International Barter," *Marketing News* (March 2, 1992), p. 5.

[80]Based on Shipley and Neale, and J. R. Carter and J. Gagne, "The Dos and Don'ts of International Countertrade," *Sloan Management Review* (Spring 1988).

[81]"Ariel Share Gain Puts P&G India Through the Wringer," *Advertising Age International* (November 8, 1993), pp. I-3, I-22.

KEY TERMS

arm's-length price
cost-plus pricing
countertrade
dumping

dynamic incremental pricing
local-currency price stability (LCPS)

pass-through
pricing corridor
price escalation

pricing-to-market
transfer price

REVIEW QUESTIONS

1. What mechanisms can exporters use to curtail the risks of price escalation in foreign markets?

2. How does competition in the foreign market affect your global pricing decisions?

3. One recent study quoted in Chapter 13 reports that there was much more pass-through by German car makers than their Japanese counterparts in the U.S. car market when both currencies depreciated against the U.S. dollar. What might explain these different responses?

4. Should MNCs always try to minimize their transfer in high corporate tax countries? Why (or why not)?

5. What measures might exporters consider to hedge themselves against antidumping accusations?

6. Explain why countertrade is often viewed as a necessary evil.

DISCUSSION QUESTIONS

1. Many MNCs that consider entering emerging markets face the issue that the regular price they charge for their goods (that is, the retail price in developed markets) is far beyond the buying power of most local consumers. What strategic options do these companies have to penetrate these markets?

2. Company XYZ sells a body-weight control drug in countries A and B. The demand schedules in the two countries are:

Country A: Sales in A = 100 − 10 × Price in A

Country B: Sales in B = 100 − 6.67 × Price in B

The marginal costs are 4 in both countries. There are no fixed costs.

(a) What prices should XYZ set in A and B if it optimizes the price in A and B individually? What would be total profits?

(b) Suppose that due to parallel imports, prices in the high-price countries drop to the level of the low-price country? What would be total profits under that scenario?

(c) Suppose now that the two countries are treated as one big market? What would be the optimal price then? What would be total profits?

Price Corridor (in %)	Price in A	Price in B	Sales Revenue in A	Sales Revenue in B	Profits in A	Profits in B	Total Profit	Profit Sacrifice (in %)
0								
5								
10								
20								
25								

(d) Set a pricing corridor between A and B by completing the following table:

3. Countertrade accounts for a substantial proportion of international trade. Do you foresee that the share of countertrade will increase or decline? Why?

4. How will a weakening of the German mark versus the Japanese yen affect German car makers such as BMW and Volkswagen in Japan? What measures do you suggest German car makers might consider taking to cope with a weaker German mark?

5. How can local competitors use antidumping procedures as a competitive tool against foreign competitors?

6. In Russia, Procter & Gamble markets Tide, its U.S. premium laundry detergent brand, as an economy brand with the slogan "Tide is a guarantee of clean clothes." Except for the brand name and the product category, all aspects of the products (formula, price, positioning) are different between the U.S. and the Russian product. What might be the rationale behind this strategy? Was this strategy a good idea?

FURTHER READING ◆

Adler, Ralph A. "Transfer Pricing for World-Class Manufacturing." *Long Range Planning*, 29 (1): 69–75.

Assmus, Gert, and Carsten Wiese. "How to Address the Gray Market Threat Using Price Coordination." *Sloan Management Review* (Spring 1995): 31–41.

Carter, Joseph R, and James Gagne. "The Dos and Don'ts of International Countertrade." *Sloan Management Review*, 29 (3) (Spring 1988): 31–37.

Cavusgil, S. Tamer. "Unraveling the Mystique of Export Pricing." *Business Horizons*, 31 (May–June 1988), pp. 54–63.

Cavusgil, S. Tamer. "Pricing for Global Markets," *The Columbia Journal of World Business*. (Winter 1996): 66–78.

Fraedrich, John P., and Connie Rae Bateman. "Transfer Pricing by Multinational Marketers: Risky Business." *Business Horizons* (Jan.–Feb. 1996), pp. 17–22.

Gaul, Wolfgang, and Ulrich Lutz. "Pricing in International Marketing and Western European Economic Integration." *Management International Review*, 34 (2) (1994): 101–24.

Kostecki, Michel M. "Marketing Strategies between Dumping and Anti-Dumping Action." *European Journal of Marketing*, 25 (12) (1991): 7–9.

Paun, Dorothy. "An International Profile of Countertrading Firms." *Industrial Marketing Management*, 26 (1997): 41–50.

Paun, Dorothy, and Aviv Shoham. "Marketing Motives in International Countertrade: An Empirical Examination." *Journal of International Marketing*, 4 (3) (1996): 29–47.

Rabino, Samuel, and Kirit Shah. "Countertrade and Penetration of LDC's Markets." *The Columbia Journal of World Business* (Winter 1987): 31–38.

Samiee, Saeed. "Pricing in Marketing Strategies of U.S.- and Foreign-Based Companies." *Journal of Business Research*, 15 (1987): 17–30.

Shipley, David, and Bill Neale. "Industrial Barter and Countertrade." *Industrial Marketing Management*, 16 (1987): 1–8.

Simon, Hermann, and Eckhard Kucher. "The European Pricing Time Bomb—and How to Cope with It." *Marketing and Research Today* (February 1993): 25–36.

Sims, Clive, Adam Phillips, and Trevor Richards. "Developing a Global Pricing Strategy." *Marketing and Research Today* (March 1992): 3–14.

Weekly, James K. "Pricing in Foreign Markets: Pitfalls and Opportunities." *Industrial Marketing Management*, 21 (1992): 173–79.

COMMUNICATING WITH THE WORLD CONSUMER

CHAPTER OVERVIEW

1. GLOBAL ADVERTISING AND CULTURE

2. SETTING THE GLOBAL ADVERTISING BUDGET

3. CREATIVE STRATEGY

4. GLOBAL MEDIA DECISIONS

5. ADVERTISING REGULATIONS

6. CHOOSING AN ADVERTISING AGENCY

7. COORDINATING INTERNATIONAL ADVERTISING

8. OTHER COMMUNICATION TOOLS

9. GLOBALLY INTEGRATED MARKETING COMMUNICATIONS

One of Procter & Gamble's biggest advertising blunders happened in Japan when the firm introduced its disposable diapers Pampers brand. Around that time, P & G aired a TV commercial in the United States showing an animated stork delivering Pampers diapers at home. P & G's American managers in Japan figured that this could be an excellent piece of advertising they could transplant into the Japanese market to back up the launch of Pampers. The copy was dubbed in Japanese and the Japanese package replaced the American one. Unfortunately, this cute commercial failed to create business. After some consumer research, P & G discovered that Japanese consumers were confused about why a bird was delivering disposable diapers. Contrary to Western folklore, storks in Japan are not supposed to deliver babies. Instead, babies allegedly arrive in giant peaches that float on the river to deserving parents.[1] These days, P & G uses a more relevant advertising model to promote Pampers to Japanese consumers: the testimonial of a nurse who also happens to be a mother—the *expert mom*.[2]

The first part of this chapter will focus on global advertising. We will first cover the cultural challenges that advertisers face. We will then examine the major international advertising planning decisions that marketers need to address. In particular, we will look at budgeting and resource allocation issues, message strategy, and media decisions. One hurdle that advertisers face is the maze of advertising regulations across the world. We will highlight the different types of regulations and discuss several mechanisms to cope with them. Next we will turn to another important global advertising concern: advertising agency selection for foreign markets. When running regional or global campaigns, coordination of multicountry communication efforts becomes paramount. We will discuss several approaches that you can use to coordinate multicountry advertising campaigns. The second part of this chapter explores other forms of communication tools that global marketers utilize.

◆ ◆ ◆ ◆ ◆ ◆ GLOBAL ADVERTISING AND CULTURE

Advertising is to some extent a cultural phenomenon. As the P & G example in the introduction demonstrated, when advertising appeals are not in sync with the local culture, the ad campaign will falter. In the worst-case scenario, the ad might even stymie the advertised product's sales. Since most advertising has a major verbal component, we will first look at the language barriers.

Language Barriers

Language is one of the most formidable barriers that international advertisers need to surmount. Numerous promotional efforts have misfired because of language related mishaps. Apart from translation, another challenge is the proper interpretation of ideas. The IBM global slogan "Solutions for a Small Planet" became *small world* in Argentina, as *planet* failed to convey the desired conceptual thrust there.[3] Given the bewildering variety of languages, advertising copy translation mistakes are easily made. One can identify three different types of translation errors: simple carelessness, multiple-meaning words, and idioms.[4] The following examples are typical instances of translation blunders that can be ascribed to pure carelessness:

---

[1]The story goes as follows. A long time ago—in the Japan of the fourteenth century—an old man and his wife had been childless. They were very sad. When the old lady went to a nearby river to do the laundry, she saw a huge *momo* (peach) floating on the river. She brought it back home. And lo and behold, the peach suddenly broke into two halves and a baby came out from inside. They named this baby *Momotaro*—a boy from a peach.

[2]"Even at P&G, Only 3 Brands Make Truly Global Grade So Far," *Advertising Age International* (January 1998), p. 8.

[3]David A. Aaker and Erich Joachimsthaler, "The Lure of Global Branding," *Harvard Business Review* (Nov.–Dec. 1999), p. 144.

[4]David A. Ricks, *Blunders in International Business* (Cambridge, MA: Blackwell Publishers, 1993).

Original slogan: "It takes a tough man to make a tender chicken."
Translation: "It takes a sexually excited man to make a chick affectionate."

Original slogan: "Body by Fisher."
Translation: "Corpse by Fisher."

Original slogan: "When I used this shirt, I felt good."
Translation: "Until I used this shirt, I felt good."

The second group of translation mishaps relates to words that have multiple meanings. Consider a campaign run by the Parker Pen Company in Latin America. When entering Latin America, Parker used a literal translation of a slogan the company was using in the United States: "Avoid embarrassment—use Parker Pens." However, the Spanish word for *embarrassment* also means *"pregnancy."* As a result, Parker was unconsciously advertising its products as a contraceptive.[5]

The third class of language-related advertising blunders stems from idioms or local slang. Idioms or expressions that use slang from one country may inadvertently lead to embarrassing meanings in another country. One U.S. advertiser ran a campaign in Britain that used the same slogan as the one that was used back home: "You can use no finer napkin at your dinner table." Unfortunately, in Britain, the word *napkin* is slang for *diapers*.[6] Exhibit 14–1 lists the different words that Goodyear has singled out for saying *tires* in Spanish.

So, what are the solutions for overcoming language barriers? One obvious cure is to involve local advertising agencies or translators in the development of your promotional campaigns. Their feedback and suggestions are often highly useful.

Another tactic is simply not to translate the slogan into the local language. Instead, the English slogan is used worldwide. The Swiss luxury watch maker TAG Heuer used the tag line "Don't crack under pressure" without translating it in each of its markets, even Japan, where more than 60 percent of the audience had no clue

EXHIBIT 14–1
FIVE DIFFERENT WAYS FOR SAYING
TIRES IN SPANISH

Spanish Word for Tires	Countries Using Each Word
Cauchos	Venezuela
Cubiertas	Argentina
Gomas	Puerto Rico
Llantas	Mexico, Peru, Guatemala, Colombia, and elsewhere in Central America
Neumaticos	Chile

Source: D.A. Hanni, J.K. Ryans, Jr. and I.R. Vernon, "Coordinating International Advertising—The Goodyear Case Revisited for Latin America." This article originally appeared in *Journal of International Marketing*, 3 (2) (1995), published by Michigan State University Press, p. 84.

---

[5]Ibid.

[6]Ibid.

of the slogan's meaning.[7] Other examples of universally used slogans that were left untranslated are "Coke is it" and "United Colors of Benetton." For TV commercials, one can add local subtitles to translate the "foreign" language. IBM did this for its global "Subtitles" campaign.[8]

For radio or TV commercials, voice-overs that use the local slang often become necessary. However, this rule cannot be generalized. For instance, whereas Egyptian consumers prefer colloquial Egyptian Arabic in their advertising, usage of local slang is less advisable for Gulf Arabs.[9] Finally, meticulous copy research and testing should enable advertisers to pick up translation glitches.

Other Cultural Barriers

Many of the trickiest promotional issues occur in the domain of religion. In Saudi Arabia, for example, only veiled women can be shown in TV commercials, except from the back. As you can imagine, such restrictions lead to horrendous problems for hair-care advertisers. Procter & Gamble navigated around that constraint by creating a spot for Pert Plus shampoo that showed the face of a veiled woman and the hair of another woman from the back. In Brazil, Pirelli, the Italian tire maker, used an ad with a Christ-like depiction of Ronaldo, the Brazilian soccer star. The ad shows Ronaldo with his arms spread and a tire tread on the sole of his foot, standing in place of the "Christ the Redeemer" statue. The ad drew heavy criticism from the Brazilian church authorities and the Vatican. After protests from local bishops, Volkswagen withdrew a billboard campaign in France of an ad for the Golf relaunch with a modern version of the Last Supper.[10]

Just as with language barriers, advertisers can escape falling into cultural traps by getting input from local staff, distributors, or ad agency people. One framework that helps with studying the influence of culture on global advertising is the Hofstede cultural grid that we discussed in Chapter 4. As you may recall, the model classifies national cultures based on their value systems. Five dimensions were derived: power distance, uncertainty avoidance, individualism, masculinity, and long-termism.[11] This model can then be used to assess the effectiveness of advertising campaigns.[12] Ideally, advertising campaigns should match the cultural value systems of the target audience.

Let us consider each of these five cultural dimensions. Power distance refers to the degree of inequality that is seen as acceptable within the country. Ads that position products or services as status symbols are most likely to be effective in countries with large power distance (e.g., Arab countries, Indonesia, Mexico).

Uncertainty avoidance relates to the extent that people within the culture prefer structured situations with clear-cut rules and little ambiguity. Campaigns that center around the hard-sell approach (e.g., testimonials) are advisable for cultures with high uncertainty avoidance (e.g., France, Japan, Mexico). Countries that score high on individualism (e.g., Great Britain, United States) are societies where the

[7]"TAG Heuer: All Time Greats?" *Director* (April 1994), pp. 45–48.

[8]Wayne R. McCullough, "Global Advertising Which Acts Locally: The IBM Subtitles Campaign," *Journal of Advertising Research* (May/June 1996), pp. 11–15.

[9]"Peace Process Forges New Middle East Future," *Advertising Age International* (April 1996), p. I-13.

[10]"Brazilian Ad Irks Church," *Advertising Age International* (April 13, 1998), p. 11.

[11]Geert Hofstede, "Managements Scientists Are Human," *Management Science*, vol. 40 (1), (January 1994), pp. 4–13.

[12]"Individualism is Major Element in Effective Global Advertising," *Advertising Age International* (February 12, 1996), p. I-8.

members see themselves as individuals rather than part of a group. This cultural trait might determine whether ads should feature people alone or in a group setting.

Masculinity is an umbrella term that reflects typically "male" values such as performance, success, and competition. Ad campaigns ought to recognize these values in highly masculine societies (e.g., Japan). The final dimension is the long-term versus short-term orientation of a society. Cultures with a long-term orientation are driven by future-directed values such as thrift, perseverance, longevity. Ads developed for audiences in countries that score relatively high on long-termism (e.g., Japan, Hong Kong) might consider projecting long-term oriented values in their message appeals.

Exhibit 14–2 shows how the Hofstede grid can be used to assess the appropriateness of comparative advertising campaigns where one brand is contrasted with a competing brand (identified or unidentified). The upper left-hand quadrant is the combination of collectivism/femininity. In group-oriented cultures, comparison with the competition is not acceptable because the other party will lose face. For feminine cultures, comparative advertising is too aggressive. Moving to the right, we have a mixture of collectivism and masculinity. Overt comparative advertising that focuses on competing brands is again not acceptable because of the "losing

EXHIBIT 14–2
Comparative Advertising*

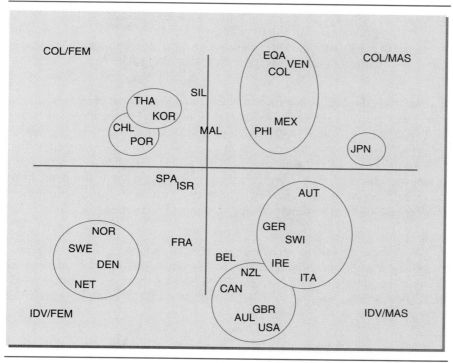

Note: AUL = Australia, AUT = Austria, BEL = Belgium, CAN = Canada, CHL = Chile, COL = Colombia, DEN = Denmark, EQA = Equador, FRA = France, GER = Germany, GBR = Great Britain, IRE = Ireland, ISR = Israel, ITA = Italy, JPN = Japan, KOR = Korea, MAL = Malaysia, MEX = Mexico, NET = the Netherlands, NOR = Norway, NZL = New Zealand, PHI = Philippines, POR = Portugal, SIN = Singapore, SPA = Spain, SWE = Sweden, SWI = Switzerland, THA = Thailand, USA = the United States, VEN = Venezuela.

COL = Collectivism, IDV = Individualism, MAS = Masculine, FEM = feminine.

*Source: See footnote 13.

face" issue. However, advertisers can make comparisons with another product from the same company to show how much better the new product is than the old one. The third quadrant has cultures that combine individualism with femininity. Here, comparative advertising works as long as it is done in a modest, nonaggressive manner. An excellent example is the slogan used by Carlsberg, a Danish beer brewer: "Probably the best beer in the world." The final quadrant—masculinity mixed with individualism—comprises cultures where comparative advertising is most likely to work best.[13]

While such categorizations are useful, it is important to bear in mind that value systems change over time. Otherwise you risk falling into the trap of cultural stereotypes. For instance, Japan has become much more family-oriented during the 1990s. This shift from materialism and status toward family values in Japan has spurred commercials that center around family life.[14]

◆ ◆ ◆ ◆ ◆ ◆ ◆ SETTING THE GLOBAL ADVERTISING BUDGET

One of the delicate decisions that marketers face when planning their communication strategy centers around the "money" issue. As an illustration, Exhibit 14–3 contrasts the spending levels of two global rivals, P & G and Unilever, in several countries where the two compete. The key questions here are: How much should we spend? What budgeting rule shall we use? How should we allocate our resources across our different markets? Let us first look at the budgeting question. Companies rely on different kinds of advertising budgeting rules.[15]

Percentage of Sales

This rule simply sets the overall advertising budget as a **percentage of sales**. The base is either past or expected sales revenues. The obvious appeal of this decision rule is its simplicity. One question here is what percentage to choose. The biggest downside of this rule is that sales revenue (past or projected) drives advertising spending, whereas the purpose of advertising is to impact sales. The method is clearly not a sound strategy for markets that were recently entered, especially if the percentage base is historical sales revenues. A survey of advertising practices worldwide showed that the percentage-of-sales method was used by almost half of the respondents.[16]

Competitive Parity

The principle of the **competitive parity** rule is extremely simple: Use your competitors' advertising spending as a benchmark. For instance, one could simply match their spending amounts. The rationale for this approach is that the competitors' collective wisdom signals the "optimal" spending amount. The rule also allows the

---

[*,13]Marieke de Mooij, *Global Marketing and Advertising* (Thousand Oaks, CA: SAGE Publications, 1998), pp. 252–54.

[14]"It's All in the Family for Japan Ads," *Advertising Age International* (July 19, 1993), pp. I-3, I-22.

[15]See, for instance, Rajeev Batra, John G. Myers and David A. Aaker, *Advertising Management* (5th ed. Englewood Cliffs, NJ: Prentice-Hall, 1996).

[16]N.E. Synodinos, C.F. Keown and L.W. Jacobs, "Transnational Advertising Practices: A Survey of Leading Brand Advertisers in Fifteen Countries," *Journal of Advertising Research* (April/May 1989), pp. 43–50.

EXHIBIT 14–3
AD SPENDING COMPARISON PROCTER & GAMBLE VERSUS
UNILEVER (1998)

Country	Procter & Gamble	Unilever	Spending Ratio: Column (2): Column (3)
Asia:			
China	$124,188	$21,312	5.83
India	$38,602	$240,904	0.16
Philippines	$70,266	$70,716	0.99
Taiwan	$90,018	$31,344	2.87
Thailand	$24,004	$53,121	0.45
Vietnam	$3,837	$7,289	0.53
Europe:			
Czech Republic	$29,367	$16,304	1.80
Italy	$128,578	$194,402	0.66
Netherlands	$99,338	$107,057	0.93
Poland	$104,727	$70,532	1.48
Russia	$105,720	$36,853	2.87
Sweden	$40,628	$49,356	0.82
United Kingdom	$327,953	$412,587	0.79
Americas:			
Argentina	$42,315	$133,489	0.32
Colombia	$61,500	$36,120	1.70
United States	$1,729,300	$691,200	2.50
Middle East:			
Egypt	$7,592	$4,776	1.59
Saudi Arabia	$3,213	$4,689	0.69
Turkey	$64,119	$124,331	0.52

Figures in 000s of US$.

Source: Based on database available on www.adage.com/dataplace/
GLOBAL_MARKETERS.html

company to sustain a minimum "share of voice" (brand advertising as a share of total industry advertising) without rocking the boat. Advertising scholars have pointed out several shortcomings of competitive parity as a budgeting norm. Obviously, the industry's spending habits may well be questionable. Also, marketers that recently entered a new market probably should spend far more relative to the incumbent brands to break through the clutter.

The most popular budgeting rule is the so-called **objective-and-task method**. Conceptually, this is also the most appealing budgeting rule: promotional efforts are treated here as a means to achieve the advertiser's stated objectives. This method was found to be used by almost two-thirds of the respondents in the same survey mentioned earlier.[17] The concept is straightforward. The first step of the procedure

Objective-and-Task Method

[17]Ibid.

is to spell out the goals of the communication strategy. The next step is to determine the tasks that are needed to achieve the desired objectives. The planned budget is then the overall costs that the completion of these tasks will amount to. The objective-and-task method necessitates a solid understanding of the relationship between advertising spending and the stated objectives (e.g., market share, brand awareness). One way to assess these linkages is to use field experiments. With experimentation, the advertiser systematically manipulates the spending amount in different areas within the country to measure the impact of advertising on the brand's awareness, sales volume, or market share.

Resource Allocation

Part of the budgeting process is also the allocation of the resources across the different countries. At one extreme are companies like FedEx, where each country subsidiary independently determines how much should be spent within its market and then requests the desired resources from headquarters. This is known as bottom-up budgeting. Top-down budgeting is the opposite approach. Here headquarters sets the overall budget and then splits up the pie among its different affiliates. EDS, a U.S.-based information technology consulting company, allocated advertising budgets proportional to the revenue contribution of the different regions for a recent global ad campaign.[18] Motorola Corp. also centralizes budget decisions. The company puts its budget together centrally and then allocates it depending on regional and local needs. Other companies that centralize budgeting decisions include Sun Microsystems, AT&T Corp., Bausch & Lomb, and Delta Airlines.[19] A third approach, which becomes increasingly more common, takes a regional angle. Each region decides the amount of resources that are needed to achieve its planned objectives and then proposes its budget to headquarters. A survey conducted by *Advertising Age International* in 1995 found that the most favored approaches are bottom-up (28 percent of respondents) or region-up budgeting (28 percent)—see Exhibit 14–4.[20] Only 20 percent of the responses indicated that the headquarters office has direct control over funding decisions. The survey also indicated substantial cross-industry differences in resource allocation practices.

◆ ◆ ◆ ◆ ◆ ◆ CREATIVE STRATEGY

The Standardization versus Adaptation Debate

One of the thorniest issues that marketers face when developing a communication strategy is the choice of a proper advertising theme. Companies that sell the same product in multiple markets need to establish to what degree their advertising campaign should be standardized. *Standardization* simply means that one or more elements of the communication campaign are kept the same. The major elements of a campaign are the message (strategy, selling proposition, platform) and the execution.

[18]"EDS in Global Push to Boost Understanding of Who It Really Is," *Media* (October 1, 1999), p. 30.
[19]"U.S. Multinationals," *Advertising Age International* (June 1999), pp. 39–40.
[20]"Ad Decision-makers Favor Regional Angle," *Advertising Age International* (May 15, 1995), pp. I-3, I-16.

EXHIBIT 14–4

SURVEY ON INTERNATIONAL AD BUDGET ALLOCATION PRACTICES

Current Budget Allocation	*Response by Industry*						
	Total	Airlines	Automotive	Consumer products	High-tech/ telecom	Hotels	Luxury goods
Each pan-geographic region determines its own needs, petitioning headquarters for a budget	28%	46%	29%	30%	25%	23%	17%
Each individual market has a different strategy with a different means of funding advertising budgets	28%	8%	29%	45%	39%	14%	22%
Worldwide headquarters determines the total allocation, controlling the budget directly	20%	29%	11%	9%	25%	23%	26%
Several budget sources (e.g., corporate/worldwide and local budgets)	15%	13%	14%	6%	11%	32%	17%
Other allocation method	9%	4%	18%	9%	—	4%	17%
No answer	1%	—	—	—	—	4%	—

Source: "Ad Decision-Makers Favor Regional Angle." Reprinted with permission from the May 15, 1995, issue of *Advertising Age*. Copyright, Crain Communications Inc. 1995.

The issue of standardize-versus-adapt has sparked a fierce debate in advertising circles. A truly global campaign is uniform in message and often also in execution (at least, in terms of visuals). Where necessary, minor changes might need to be made in the execution to comply with local regulations or to make the ad more appealing to local audiences (voice-overs, local actors). They typically also heavily rely on global or pan-regional media channels. "Truly" global campaigns are still quite uncommon. Exhibit 14–5 summarizes several examples of recent global advertising campaigns.

What makes the case of standardization so compelling in the eyes of many marketers? A variety of reasons have been offered to defend global, if not, pan-regional advertising campaigns. The major ones are listed here.

Merits of Standardization

Scale Economies. Of the factors encouraging companies to standardize their advertising campaigns, the most appealing one is the positive impact on the advertiser's bottom line. The savings coming from the economies of scale of a single campaign (as opposed to multiple country-level ones) can be quite eye-catching. Levi Strauss reportedly saved around £1.5 million (±$2.2 million) by shooting a single TV ad covering six European markets.[21] By the same token, advertising for Martini & Rossi, the Italian vermouth brand, would probably cost three times as much if the ads were to be developed on a country-by-country basis.[22] There are several factors behind such

---

[21]"A Universal Message," *The Financial Times* (May 27, 1993).
[22]Rein Rijkens, *European Advertising Strategies* (London: Cassell, 1992).

EXHIBIT 14–5
FOUR RECENT EXAMPLES OF GLOBAL AD CAMPAIGNS

	AXA	HSBC	Enron	EDS
Industry	Insurance	Banking	Energy	IT Consulting
Budget	$70 million	$100 million	$50 million	$100 million–200 million
Target	• Financial community • Business leaders • AXA employees	• Existing and potential customers	• Consumers • Foreign governments	• Government officials • Business leaders • Very large companie (plus $1 billion sales revenue)
Tagline	"Go Ahead. Go Ahead with AXA."	"Your world of financial services."	• "Natural gas. Electricity. Endless possibilities."	"from idea to implementation."

Objectives	• Establish brand awareness.
	• Build brand identity around the world.
		• Turn HSBC into a household name worldwide.	• Unveil new company name, logo, and image.
			• Create goodwill.
				• Ensure customers understand array of services provided.
				• Change consumer perceptions.
				  • Clarify EDS's strength, resources, and expertise in IT.
				  • Show how EDS can help companies to become e-businesses.

Creative Strategy	A boy reduces his risk when jumping across a gorge by using the AXA logo as a bridge.	Print ads feature three universally recognized highway symbols for eating, drinking, and sleeping accommodations. The fourth symbol is HSBC's logo as a sign for banking.	Ads depict charming children and adults whose communities now benefit from Enron power.	Simple, lively visuals.
Media Strategy	TV Int'l and domestic financial print media	TV International business titles (e.g., *Financial Times, The Wall Street Journal, The Economist*)	TV (e.g., CNNI) Business publications	TV (e.g., CNNI, CNBC) International and domestic financial print media (e.g., *Wall Street Journal, Business Week, Asiaweek*)

savings. Producing a single commercial is often far cheaper than making several different ones for each individual market. Savings are also realized because firms can assign fewer executives to develop the campaign at the global or pan-regional level.

Consistent Image. For many companies that sell the same product in multiple markets, having a consistent brand image is extremely important. Consistency was one of the prime motives behind the Pan-European campaign that Blistex, a U.S.-based lip-care manufacturer, began in 1995. Prior to the campaign, advertising

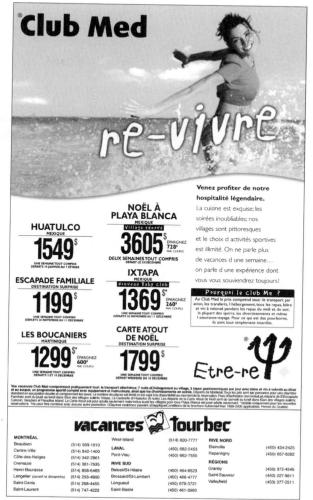

Club Med's magazine ad is one example of global marketing at work. The same promotional message as well as the global image transcends across different cultures.

themes varied from country to country, often highlighting only one item of Blistex's product line. The entire product range consists of three items, each one standing for a different need. In many of its markets, brand awareness was dismally low. The objectives for the new Pan-European campaign were (1) to increase brand awareness, and (2) to have the same positioning theme by communicating the so-called "care-to-cure" concept behind Blistex' product line.[23] Campbell's pan-European advertising strategy for the Delacre cookie brand is also driven by a desire to establish a single brand identity across Europe. The brand's platform is that Delacre is a premium cookie brand with the finest ingredients based on French know-how. The same campaign is aired in English reaching 30 million people in more than twenty countries.[24] Message consistency matters a great deal in markets

---

[23]Mark Boersma, Blistex, personal communication.

[24]"Rebuilding in a Crumbling Sector," *Marketing* (February 18, 1993), pp. 28–29.

with extensive media overlap or for goods that are sold to "cosmopolitan" customers who travel the globe. Banking is a typical example: "Those customers span the globe and travel the globe. They can only know one Chase in their minds, so why should we try to confuse them?"[25]

Global Consumer Segments. Cross-cultural similarities are a major impetus behind efforts toward a standardized advertising approach. The "global village" argument often pops up in discussions on the merits of global or pan-regional advertising campaigns. The argument of cultural binding especially has clout with respect to product categories that appeal to the elites or youngsters as pointed out by David Newkirk, a consultant with Booz Allen & Hamilton: "The young and the rich have very similar tastes the world over, and that's what's driving the convergences in advertising and media."[26] Bausch & Lomb's first Pan-Asian campaign for Ray-Ban sunglasses is a good example. The campaign targets Asia's Generation X—young (age 16 to 25) and trendy Asians with buying power. Loughlin, president for North Asia of Bausch & Lomb, observed, "We are trying to talk to Asian youth in a language that they understand and relate to across the region. It's a language of music and fast-paced images." The campaign was built around a series of questions that youngsters ask. Each one of the spots ended with the tag line: "Whatever you're looking for. Ray-Ban the new look."[27]

Creative Talent. Creative talent among ad agencies is a scarce supply. It is not uncommon that the most talented people within the agency are assigned to big accounts, leaving small accounts with junior executives. The talent issue matters especially in countries that are plagued with a shortage of highly skilled advertising staff.

Cross-Fertilization. More and more companies try to take advantage of their global scope by fostering cross-fertilization. In the domain of advertising, cross-fertilization means that marketers encourage their affiliates to adopt, or at least consider, advertising ideas that have proven successful in other markets. This process of exploiting "good" ideas does not even need to be restricted to "global" brands. Nestlé used the idea of a serialized "soap-mercial" that it was running for the Nescafé brand in the United Kingdom for its Tasters Choice coffee brand in the United States. The campaigns, chronicling a relationship between two neighbors that centers around coffee, were phenomenally successful in both markets. Likewise, when Procter & Gamble introduced Pantene shampoo in Latin America, it used a spot that was originally produced in Taiwan. Only a few minor changes were made to allow for local cultural differences.[28] Coming up with a good idea typically takes a long time. Once the marketer has hit on a creative idea, it makes common sense to try to leverage it by considering how it can be transplanted to other countries.[29]

---

[25]"Ads Going Global," *Advertising Age* (July 22, 1991), p. 42.

[26]"A Universal Message," *The Financial Times* (May 27, 1993).

[27]"Ray-Ban Ogles 16–25 Group in Southeast Asia Blitz," *Advertising Age International* (June 1996), p. I-30.

[28]"P&G Sees Success in Policy of Transplanting Ad Ideas," *Advertising Age International* (July 19, 1993), p. I-2.

[29]T. Duncan and J. Ramaprasad, "Standardizing Multinational Advertising: The Influencing Factors," *Journal of Advertising*, 24 (3) (Fall 1995), pp. 55–68

Apart from these reasons, there are other considerations that might justify standardized multinational advertising. A survey conducted among ad agency executives identified the single brand image factor as the most important driver for standardizing multinational advertising. Two other critical factors are time pressure and corporate organizational setup.[30] Obviously, developing a single campaign is less time consuming than creating several ones.

Another crucial variable is the corporation's organizational setup. In general, if the advertiser is highly centralized, it is highly likely that theme development is standardized. Advertising is usually very localized in decentralized organizations. On the other hand, for many small companies, local advertising is the responsibility of local distributors. The shift toward regional organizational structures is definitely one of the major drivers behind the growing popularity of regional campaigns.

Barriers to Standardization

Faced with these arguments for standardization, advocates of adaptation can easily bring forward an equally compelling list to build up the case for adaptation. The four major barriers to standardization relate to (1) cultural differences, (2) advertising regulations, (3) differences in the degree of market development, and (4) the "Not Invented Here" (NIH) syndrome.

Cultural Differences. Notwithstanding the "global village" headlines, cultural differences still persist for many product categories. Cultural gaps between countries may exist in terms of lifestyles, benefits sought, usage contexts, and so forth. As a result, many companies think twice before standardizing their multinational advertising campaigns, especially for culturally sensitive products such as food. Global Perspective 14–1 describes how Blue Diamond, a California-based cooperative of almond growers, tailors its advertising messages to individual markets.

◆ ◆

*G*LOBAL PERSPECTIVE 14–1

BLUE DIAMOND—A WINNING MESSAGE IN THE U.S. DOES NOT TRAVEL

In the United States, Blue Diamond aired an award-winning campaign showing farmer waist deep in almonds, begging viewers to buy "A can a week, that's all we ask." Despite the success of the spots in Blue Diamond's home market, the ads were never shown in the export markets. A pretest of the spot in Canada found that the ad was just too silly for Canadians' tastes. Also, Canadians would prefer buying their "can a week" from Canadian farmers. Instead, a series of local commercials were created in French and English with the tagline "Blue Diamond Almonds. The Classic Snack." In Japan, where

almonds were still a relatively novel item when Blue Diamond first entered the market, the main challenge was to educate the market. One commercial was aired that used animation, describing the nutritional value of almonds. Another ad illustrated the different possible uses of almonds.

The Korean commercial featured a guitar-player singing "Blue, Blue Diamond" to the tune of Blue Hawaii. In Hong Kong, "Ode to Almond" ads touted almonds' Californian roots, flavor, and nutritional value. The spots used in Germany also emphasized Blue Diamond's California origin. Ads aired in the Middle East used a taste positioning theme: "The luxurious taste of Blue Diamond almonds in seven unique flavors."

Adapted from: "Every Market Needs a Different Message," *IABC Communication World* (April 1990), pp. 16–18.

[30]Ibid.

Cultural gaps may even prevail for goods that cater toward global segments. A case in point are luxury goods that target global elites. The user benefits of cognac are by and large the same worldwide. The usage context, however, varies a lot: in the United States, cognac is consumed as a stand-alone drink, in Europe, often as an after-dinner drink, and in China it is consumed with a glass of water during dinner. As a result, Hennessy cognac, while promoting the same brand image, adapts its appeals according to local customs.[31] Even in industrial marketing, advertisers occasionally need to make allowances for cultural differences. A print ad originally created for Siemens in Germany to convey "energy" was deemed unsuitable for the Hong Kong market (see Exhibit 14–6). The German ad showed a crowd of en-

EXHIBIT 14–6
ADAPTATION OF SIEMENS PRINT AD

Print ad used in Hong Kong   Print ad used in Germany

---

[31]"Cachet and Carry," *Advertising Age International* (February 12, 1996), p. I-18.

thusiastic youngsters at a pop concert. Audiences at Canto-pop concerts tend to be much more subdued than their Western counterparts. Instead of using the German print ad, Siemens Hong Kong came up with an ad that showed a fireworks display with a view of the Hong Kong skyline.[32]

Advertising Regulations. Local advertising regulations pose another barrier for standardization. Regulations usually affect the execution of the commercial. Coming back to the Ray-Ban example, whereas the theme that was used in the Pan-Asian campaign was the same across Asia, the execution sometimes differed due to local rules. In Malaysia, for instance, foreign-made commercials or ads featuring Caucasians are not allowed. Hence, Ray-Ban was forced to shoot local commercials for Malaysian TV.[33]

Market Maturity. Differences in the degree of market maturity also rule out a standardized strategy. Following the breakup of the former East Bloc, the prime challenge faced by Procter & Gamble, for example, in these new markets was to educate consumers by giving them product information. Gaps in cross-market maturity levels mandate different advertising approaches. When Snapple, the U.S.-based "New Age" beverage, first entered the European market, the biggest challenge was to overcome initial skepticism among consumers about the concept of "iced tea." Typically, in markets that were entered very recently, one of the main objectives is to create brand awareness. As brand awareness builds up, other advertising goals gain prominence. Products that are relatively new to the entered market also demand education of the customers.

"Not-Invented-Here" (NIH) Syndrome. Finally, efforts to implement a standardized campaign often also need to cope with the NIH-syndrome. Stonewalling attempts at standardization may come from local subsidiaries and/or local advertising agencies. Local offices generally have a hard time accepting creative materials from other countries. Later on in this chapter we will suggest some guidelines that can be used to overcome NIH attitudes.

Approaches to Creating Advertising Copy

Marketers adopt several approaches to create multinational ads. At one extreme, the entire process may be left to the local subsidiary or distributor, with only a minimum of guidance from headquarters. At the other extreme, global or regional headquarters makes all the decisions, including all the nitty-gritty surrounding the development of ad campaigns. Most companies adopt an approach that falls somewhere in between these two extremes.

Export Advertising. With **export advertising**, the creative strategy is highly centralized. A universal copy is developed for all markets. The same positioning theme is used worldwide. Visuals and most other aspects of the execution are also the same. Minor allowances are made for local sensitivities, but by and large the same copy is used in each of the company's markets. Obviously, export advertising delivers all the

---

[32]Monika Sturm, senior communications manager, Siemens Hong Kong Ltd., personal communication.

[33]"Ray-Ban Ogles 16–25 Group in Southeast Asia Blitz," p. I-30.

EXHIBIT 14–7
EXAMPLES OF UNIVERSAL APPEALS

Superior quality. Clearly, the promise of superior quality is a theme that makes any customer tick. A classic example here is the "Ultimate Driving Machine" slogan that BMW uses in many of its markets.

New product/service. A global rollout of a new product or service is often coupled with a global campaign announcing the launch. A recent example is the marketing hype surrounding the launch of Windows 2000 by Microsoft.

Country of origin. Brands in a product category with a strong country stereotype often leverage their roots by touting the "made in" cachet. This positioning strategy is especially popular among fashion and luxury goods marketers.

Heroes and celebrities. Tying the product with heroes or celebrities is another form of universal positioning. A recurring issue on this front is whether advertisers should use "local" or "global" heroes. When sports heroes are used, most advertisers will select local, or at least regional, celebrities. Reebok International's advertising strategy in the Asian region heavily relies on Asian athletes such as tennis player Michael Chang, Indian cricketer Mohammed Azharuddin, or New Zealand rugby player Jonah Lomu.* With movie personalities the approach usually differs. Swiss watchmaker SMH International promoted its Omega brand with a TV commercial featuring the actor Pierce Brosnan after the release of the James Bond movie *Golden Eye*.

Lifestyle. The mystique of many global upscale brands is often promoted by lifestyle ads that reflect a lifestyle shared by target customers, regardless of where they live. As one media buyer commented: "It's not just a question of money. It's being able to afford it and having the lifestyle that lets you say, 'I need a pen worth $300.'"**

Global presence. Many marketers try to enhance the image of their brands via a "global presence" approach—telling the target audience that their product is sold across the globe. Obviously, such a positioning approach can be adopted anywhere. The "global scope" pitch is often used by companies that sell their product or services to customers for whom this attribute is crucial. The concept is also used by other types of advertisers, though. Warner-Lambert created commercials for its Chiclets chewing gum brand that tried to project the cross-cultural appeal of the brand. One spot showed a young man in a desert shack rattling a Chiclets box. The sound of Chiclets triggers the arrival of a cosmopolitan group of eager customers.***

Market leadership. Regardless of the country, being the leading brand worldwide or within the region is a powerful message to most consumers. For products that possess a strong country image, a brand can send a strong signal by making the claim that it is the most preferred brand in its home country.

Corporate image. Finally, corporate communication ads that aspire to foster a certain corporate image also often lend themselves to a uniform approach.

* "Reebok-Sets Strategy to Get Sales on Track in Fast-growing Asia," p.12
** "Cachet and Carry," p. I-15.
*** "Chiclets Tries New Language," *Advertising Age International* (April 19, 1993), pp. I-1, I-21.

benefits of standardized campaigns: (1) the same brand image and identity worldwide, (2) no confusion among customers, (3) substantial savings, and (4) strict control over the planning and execution of your global communication strategy.[34] On the creative strategy front, a centralized message demands a universal positioning theme that travels worldwide. Exhibit 14–7 offers several examples of universal appeals. Export advertising is very common for corporate ad campaigns that aim to create awareness, to reposition the company, or reinforce an existing company image.

Global Prototype Advertising.

With **prototype advertising** guidelines are given to the local affiliates concerning the execution of the advertising. These

[34] M.G. Harvey, "Point of View: A Model to Determine Standardization of the Advertising Process in International Markets," *Journal of Advertising Research* (July/August 1993), pp. 57–64.

guidelines are conveyed via manuals or VCR tapes. Mercedes uses a handbook to communicate its advertising guidelines to the local subsidiaries and sales agents. Instructions are given on the format, visual treatment, print to be employed for headlines, and so on.[35] Likewise, the Swiss watchmaker TAG Heuer has a series of guidebooks covering all the nuts and bolts of its communication approach, including rules on business card design.[36] Wrigley, the Chicago-based chewing gum maker, produced a videotape for its international advertising program. The tape offers guidelines on ad execution, including minutiae such as how the talent should put the gum in his or her mouth, the background of the closing shot, tips on the handling of the gum before the shooting of the commercial, and so forth. It shows examples of clips that follow and do not follow the guidelines. The tape also tells under what circumstances deviations from the norms are acceptable.

Pattern Standardization Advertising. With **pattern standardization**, headquarters spells out guidelines on the positioning theme (platform) and the brand identity to be used in the ads. Worldwide brand values are mapped out centrally. Responsibility for the execution, however, is left to the local markets. That way, brand consistency is sustained without sacrificing the relevance of the ad campaign to local consumers. Smirnoff's "pure thrill" campaign exemplifies this approach. All of its global advertising shows distorted images becoming clear when viewed through the Smirnoff bottle. However, the specific scenes that are used vary across countries, as consumers hold different perceptions about what is "thrilling."[37] Seagram, the liquor marketer, took a **modular approach** for a campaign it ran for Chivas Regal. After doing a copy test in seven countries, Seagram picked a campaign that consisted of a series of twenty-four ads, each using the slogan "There will always be a Chivas Regal." Marketing executives in each country, however, were able to cherry-pick the specific ads from the series for their market. Just as with the previous approach, instructions on proper positioning themes and concepts are shared with the local agencies and affiliates through manuals, videotapes, or other means.

GLOBAL MEDIA DECISIONS   ◆ ◆ ◆ ◆ ◆ ◆

Another task that international marketers need to confront is the choice of the media in each country where the company is doing business. In some countries, media decisions are much more critical than the creative aspects of the campaign. In Japan, for instance, media buying is crucial, given the scarce supply of advertising space. Given the choice between an ad agency that possesses good creative skills and one that has enormous media-buying clout, most advertisers in Japan would pick the latter.[38]

International media planners have to surmount a wide range of issues. The media landscape varies dramatically across countries or even between regions within

---

[35]Rijkens.

[36]"TAG Heuer: All Time Greats?" pp. 45–48.

[37]Aaker and Joachimsthaler, p. 144.

[38]"The Enigma of Japanese Advertising," *The Economist* (August 14, 1993), pp. 59–60.

a country. Differences in the media infrastructure exist in terms of media availability, accessibility, media costs, and media habits.

Media Infrastructure

Most Western countries offer an incredible abundance of media choices. New media channels emerge continuously. Given this embarrassment of riches, the marketer's task is to decide how to allocate its promotional dollars to get the biggest bang for the bucks. In other countries, though, the range of media channels is extremely limited. Many of the media vehicles that exist in the marketer's home country are simply not available in the foreign market. Government controls heavily restrict the access to mass-media options such as television in a host of countries. For instance, advertising is not allowed on Saudi Arabian radio. In Germany, TV commercials are only allowed during limited time frames.

The media infrastructure differs dramatically from country to country, even within the same region. Whereas TV viewers in the West can surf dozens of TV channels, their Asian counterparts have access, on the average, to a measly choice of 2.4 channels. The standard media vehicles such as radio, cinema, and TV are well established in most countries. New media such as cable, satellite TV, and pay-TV are steadily growing. Given the media diversity, advertisers are forced to adapt their media schedule to the parameters set by the local environment. Exhibit 14–8 contrasts typical media allocation patterns in various countries.

Media Limitations

One of the major limitations in many markets is media availability. The lack of standard media options challenges marketers to come up with creative options. Intel, the U.S. computer chip maker, builds brand awareness in China by distributing bike reflectors in Shanghai and Beijing with the words "Intel Inside Pentium Processor." Advertisers in Bangkok have taken advantage of the city's notorious traffic jams by using

EXHIBIT 14–8
AD SPENDING BY MEDIUM (1999 ESTIMATES)

	Television	Newspaper	Magazines	Radio	Outdoor	Cinema
Australia	34.2%	42.2%	11.2%	7.9%	3.7%	0.8%
Brazil	65.0%	21.0%	8.0%	3.3%	2.7%	n/a
Canada	37.6%	39.1%	7.1%	12.9%	3.1%	0.1%
China (98 Est.)	45.0%	37.1%	2.5%	4.1%	n/a	n/a
France	34.9%	23.0%	23.2%	6.5%	11.8%	0.6%
Germany	23.1%	45.4%	24.2%	3.3%	3.1%	0.9%
Italy	54.7%	22.2%	14.5%	4.7%	3.5%	0.4%
Japan	44.3%	27.2%	9.8%	5.0%	13.7%	n/a
Mexico (98 Est.)	64.8%	7.0%	8.5%	19.6%	n/a	n/a
South Kor	24.5%	47.3%	3.7%	2.8%	n/a	n/a
Spain (98 Est.)	38.5%	33.8%	12.3%	9.9%	4.6%	1.0%
Thailand	65.0%	17.0%	5.0%	10.0%	3.0%	1.0%
U.K.	33.2%	34.5%	23.0%	4.0%	4.5%	0.8%
U.S.A.	44.3%	27.2%	9.8%	5.0%	13.7%	n/a

Various Sources

media strategies that reach commuters. Some of the selected media vehicles include outdoor advertising, traffic-report radio stations, and three-wheeled taxis (*tuk-tuk*).[39]

Marketers must also consider media costs. For all kinds of reasons, media costs differ enormously between countries. Exhibit 14–9 gives some cost-per-thousand (CPM) estimates for the major media. In general, high CPMs are found in areas that have a high per capita GNP. The amount of competition within the media market is another important factor. In the United Kingdom, TV ad rates are relatively low because it is a mature market and there are many competing channels.[40] In China, for example, advertising rates differ greatly across regions. Also, different TV advertising rates are charged to local firms, foreign companies, and joint ventures, although the gap is narrowing.[41]

A major obstacle in many emerging markets is the overall quality of the local media. Take China, for instance. For many print media, no reliable statistics are available on circulation figures or readership profiles. Print quality of many newspapers and magazines is appalling. Newspapers may demand full payment in advance when the order is booked and ask for additional money later on. There are no guarantees that newspapers will run your ad or TV broadcasters will show your spot on the agreed date.

To illustrate the rapid changes in the media landscape, we would like to pinpoint six major trends:

Recent Developments in the Global Media Landscape

- *Growing commercialization and deregulation of mass media.* One undeniable shift in scores of countries is the growing commercialization of the mass media, especially the broadcast media. Take a country like Belgium. Ten years ago, commercial TV was basically nonexistent in Belgium. Advertisers who wanted to use TV as a medium had to rely on either cinema as a substitute or TV channels in neighboring countries. Following the introduction of several commercial TV stations, the situation is totally different now. Similar moves toward commercialization and the lifting of government restrictions on the local media can be observed in many other countries.

- *Shift from radio and print to TV advertising.* The rise of commercial TV has turned TV into the medium of choice for advertisers worldwide.[42] Some advertisers who traditionally focused mostly on print media are shifting some of their advertising dollars to television. Luxury-goods marketers such as the Swiss watch maker SMH have started to run ad campaigns on channels like CNN International and Star TV.[43] Television also offers novel ways of reaching target customers. TVSN ("Television Shopping Network") is a 24-hour shopping network seen by satellite and cable TV viewers in Japan, Korea, Taiwan, Hong Kong, and the Philippines. Mer-

[39]"Bangkok is Bumper to Bumper with Ads," *Advertising Age International* (February 20, 1996), p. I-4.

[40]"TV is Advertisers' Big Pick in Europe," *Advertising Age International* (June 21, 1993), p. I-19.

[41]"China TV Stations Narrow Pricing Gap," *Media* (March 15, 1996), p. 4.

[42]John M. Eger, "Global Television: An Executive Overview," *Columbia Journal of World Business* (Fall 1987), pp. 5–10.

[43]"Marketers at High End Try New Media Mixes," *Advertising Age International* (February 12, 1996), p. I-16.

EXHIBIT 14–9
MEDIA ADVERTISING COSTS

(a) Print Media

Title	Region	Circulation	Ad Rate - Full Page, 1x, Color	CPM
Business Week	Latin America	25,000	$6,900	$276.0
	Europe	82,597	$15,900	$192.5
	Asia	67,000	$12,000	$179.1
Cosmopolitan	Latin America	526,984	$29,925	$56.8
	Europe	2.5 million	$156,87	$62.7
	Asia	1.1 million	$50,975	$46.3
The Economist	Latin America	17,432	$6,480	$371.7
	Europe	285,678	$33,000	$115.5
	Asia	79,500	$9,500	$119.5
National Geographic	Latin America	138,075	$12,730	$92.1
		1.1 million	$57,000	$51.8
		479,679	$26,400	$55.0
Newsweek	Latin America	60,000	$19,280	$271.3
	Europe	340,000	$44,565	$131.1
	Asia	240,000	$40,845	$170.0
Reader's Digest	Latin America	1.7 million	$61,986	$36.5
	Europe	7.3 million	$176,718	$24.2
	United States	15.7 million	$208,000	$13.2
	Asia	1.9 million	$64,359	$33.8
Wall Street Journal	Latin America	60,000	$19,280 (b & w)	$321.3
	Europe	340,000	$44,565 (b & w)	$131.0
	Asia	240,000	$40,845 (b & w)	$170.0
	United States	1.78 million	$137,303 (b & w)	$77.1

(b) TV

Network	Region	No. of households	Average rate (:30 spot)	(CPM)
BBC World	Latin America	3 million	$100	$.03
	Europe	42 million	$800	$.02
	Asia	15 million	Varies	N.A.
CNN International	Latin America	6.7 million	$1,000	$.15
	Europe	103.2 million	$3,000	$.03
	Asia	25.1 million	$2,000	$.08
CNBC	Europe	52.2 million	$1,500	$.03
	Asia	13 million	$900	$.07
TNT	Latin America	9.8 million	$1,000	$.10
	Europe	38.9 million	$2,000	$.05
	Asia	17 million	$1,000	$.06

Source: Extracted from "Global Media," *Advertising Age International* (February 8, 1999), pp. 23–30.

chandise can be ordered via a toll-free number, paid for with a credit card, and delivered by courier.[44] Global marketers also increasingly recognize the power of infomercials as a selling tool. In Japan, for instance, infomercial marketers now have access to more than half of Japan's population. The head of one infomercial marketing firm underscores the opportunities available in international markets as follows: "Down the road we'll be able to put a product simultaneously into the homes of 300 to 500 million people around the globe. Now that's powerful."[45]

• *Rise of global media.* One of the most dramatic developments in the media world has been the mushrooming spread of regional and global media. Several factors explain the appeal of global or regional media to international advertisers. In some countries it is very hard to get access to the local media. By using international media, advertisers get a chance to target customers who would otherwise be hard to reach. International media also facilitate the launch of global or pan-regional ad campaigns. Another major asset is that most international media have well-defined background information on their audience reach and profile. In contrast to most local media, they tend to have a very well-defined audience. The major barrier to advertising on global media has been the cultural issue. Satellite TV broadcasters, for instance, initially planned to broadcast the same ads and programs globally. Because of that, viewership for many of the satellite channels was extremely low. As a result, very few advertisers were interested in airing spots on satellite TV. Lately, however, more and more satellite networks have started to customize the content of their programs. NBC Super Channel even broadcasts many of its programs in Europe with subtitles now or local voice-overs to overcome the language barrier. ESPN Asia, a sports channel, plans to have seven subregional networks in Asia, each with its own fare to cater toward local sports preferences. Once the new setup is completed, ESPN will be able to bring Asian viewers their local sports and global sports. Advertisers will be offered packages that leverage on the new program portfolio.[46] A push toward localization also exists among many publishing houses of international magazine titles. In Japanese bookstores, magazine racks offer Japanese editions of titles such as *GQ, National Geographic*, and *Cosmopolitan.*

• *Growing importance of multimedia advertising tools.* More and more advertisers worldwide are experimenting with multimedia.[47] The most visible form is the Internet, though clearly interest in the Internet as an advertising vehicle is still very minimal.[48] While some markets (e.g., Hong Kong) have scores of consultants that can assist marketers with the setup and upkeep of a Web site, in most other countries such expertise is lacking. Access to and use of the Internet medium dif-

[44]"As Advertised on TV," *Asiaweek* (July 12, 1996), p. 48.

[45]"Infomercial Audience Crosses Over Cultures," *Advertising Age International* (January 15, 1996), p. I-8.

[46]"ESPN Splits Asia into Subregions, Targeted Markets," *Advertising Age International* (March 20, 1996), p. I-14.

[47]"Scoping Out Europe's Interactive Activity," *Advertising Age International* (January 16, 1995), p. I-12.

[48]John A. Quelch and Lisa R. Klein, "The Internet and International Marketing," *Sloan Management Review* (Spring 1996), pp. 60–75.

fers substantially across countries. In many countries, there is also a lot of skepticism about the cost efficiencies of the Internet as an advertising tool.[49]

- *Improved monitoring.* A few years ago, Speedo, a Kenyan pen maker, tried to boost its sales in Kenya during the Christmas season with a massive advertising campaign. The results were pretty discouraging. Follow-up on the campaign quickly pointed out the reason: none of the scheduled TV spots was ever broadcast.[50] Obviously, having an infrastructure in place that allows advertisers to monitor broadcast and print media is highly desirable to avoid these kinds of problems. Moreover, advertisers can track how much, when, and in what media their competitors advertise. Fortunately, in more and more countries, watchdog agencies exist that provide the wherewithal for monitoring the media landscape.

- *Improved TV-viewership measurement.* To plan a TV ad campaign, high-quality viewership data are an absolute must for marketers. In many markets, measurement of TV viewership relied on diary data collected by a local market research agency from household panel members. Not surprisingly, the value of such data was highly questionable. The advent of new technologies has led to monitoring devices that allow far more precise data collection than past tools. The most advanced tool is the *people meter*, a device hooked up to the TV set of a household panel member, that automatically registers viewing behavior. Exhibit 14–10 illustrates how the introduction of people meters in various countries affected TV ratings. Note that the previous ratings methods grossly overestimated TV ratings in most of the countries.

◆ ◆ ◆ ◆ ◆ ◆ ADVERTISING REGULATIONS

Global advertisers often face a bewildering set of locally imposed advertising regulations. In many countries the advertising industry is governed by some form of self-regulation. Self-regulation can take various forms.[51] One possibility is that local advertisers, advertising agencies, and broadcast media jointly agree on a set of rules. Alternatively, the local advertising industry and government representatives may decide on a code of advertising ethics. There are several reasons behind self-regulation of the advertising industry, including protection of consumers against misleading or offensive advertising, and protection of legitimate advertisers against false claims or accusations made by competitors. Another forceful reason to set up self-regulatory bodies is to prevent more stringent government-imposed regulation or control of the advertising industry.

Advertising regulations come under many different guises. This section summarizes the major types of advertising regulations and offers some recent examples for each one of them:

---

[49]"Internet Foreign Turf to Some Marketers," *Advertising Age International* (March 11, 1996), p. I-12.

[50]"Watchdog Agency Monitors Ad Space in Kenya's Media," *Advertising Age International* (June 19, 1995), p. I-11.

[51]Marieke de Mooij, *Advertising Worldwide*, 2nd ed. (New York: Prentice-Hall, 1994).

EXHIBIT 14–10
HOW SWITCHING TO PEOPLE METERS AFFECTED TV RATINGS WORLDWIDE

Country	Ratings Change	Prior Ratings Method
Argentina*	Down 50% for popular programs. Down 20% to 25%	Meter/diary
Australia	Up 10% to 25%	Diary sweeps
Brazil	Down 25%	Diary
Canada	News, sports, networks, young viewers down	Diary
Chile	Smaller stations up, bigger stations down	Daily diaries
Finland	Slight increase	Diary panel
France	Prime down 10%, day down 5%	Meter/telephone
Greece	Down 20% to 40%	Diary sweeps
Ireland	No change	People meter
Mexico	Down 30%	Meter/diary
Netherlands	High-rated shows down, low-rated shows up	Diary panel
New Zealand	Slight increase overall (news down, but off-peak viewing up)	Diary sweeps
Philippines	Down 25%	Telephone coincidental
Puerto Rico	Down 4%	Meter/diary
Spain	Down 15%	Aided recall
Switzerland	Up before and after peak time	Readership survey
Thailand	Prime down	Diary sweeps
U.K.	Up 15% to 20%	Meter/diary
U.S.	Down 5% to 10%	Meter/diary

*Before people meters, Argentina had two ratings services with different methods.

Source: "People Meters Shake Up Global TV Ratings." Reprinted with permission from the July 18, 1994 issue of *Advertising Age.* Copyright, Crain Communications Inc. 1994.

Tough restrictions, if not outright bans, apply to the advertising of pharmaceuticals and so-called *vice* products in many countries. Japan, for example, prohibits the use of the word *safe* or *safety* or any derivatives when promoting over-the-counter drugs (e.g., pain relievers, cold medicines).[52] Despite opposition of advertising agencies, advertisers, and media channels, rules on the advertising of tobacco and liquor products are becoming increasingly more severe.

Vice Products and Pharmaceuticals

Another area of contention is comparative advertising, where advertisers disparage the competing brand. Such advertising practices are commonplace in the United States, but other countries heavily constrain or even prohibit comparative advertising. For example, until recently, advertisers in South Africa were forbidden to name competitors, show rival brands, or make comparisons that allude to the competing brand.[53] In other markets, such as Colombia, marketers that use comparative ad-

Comparative Advertising

[52]John Mackay, McCann-Erickson Japan, private communication.
[53]"Comparative Ads Mulled," *Advertising Age International* (March 15, 1993), p. I-6.

vertising must substantiate their claims. In Japan, comparative advertising—though not illegal—is a cultural taboo. It is seen as immodest and underhanded. Often, the Japanese side with the competitor![54]

Content of Advertising Messages

The content of advertising messages could be subject to certain rules or guidelines. Dorf Industries, an Australian plumbing fixtures marketer, ran a campaign that featured a spurned lover getting even with her boyfriend by turning on all taps. The slighted girlfriend leaves the house, which, in the mean time, is filling up with water. The spots were aired during an Australian drought. The campaign was banned by the Advertising Standards Council for its "wanton and irresponsible waste of water."[55] Also in Australia, Toyota was forced to withdraw a series of spots advertising the Celica model because of their content. One of the spots was a "Jaws" spoof in which shark-like Celicas speed down a jetty. The ad violated the Advertising Standards Council's guidelines on "dangerous behavior or illegal or unsafe road usage practices."[56]

In Vietnam, the Ministry of Trade, The Ministry of Culture and Information, the Customs department, and any single TV station or newspaper can censor ads. A pan-Asian campaign that San Miguel, the Philippine beer brewer, planned to run in Vietnam got nixed by the Ho Chi Minh City authorities. The campaign, showing a Western businessman who offered a San Miguel to an Asian colleague, used the slogan "San Miguel: A Sign of Friendship." The ad was banned because the local authorities claimed that beer couldn't be a sign of friendship.[57]

Ads may also be banned or taken off the air because they are offensive or indecent. For example, ads that show skin or revealing lingerie are banned from TV advertising in Singapore.[58] Many countries also have regulations against sexist advertising or ads with exaggerated ("puffery") claims.

Advertising toward Children

Another area that tends to be heavily regulated is advertising targeted toward children. Some markets (e.g., Québec) simply prohibit TV stations from airing children's ads.[59] In Europe, rules on advertising to children are widespread. In Finland, for example, children cannot speak or sing the name of a product in commercials. In Turkey, children are only allowed to watch TV ads with "parental guidance." Italy bans commercials in cartoon programs that target children. China poses a series of rules that advertisers to children need to respect. Contrary to regulations in Western countries, most of the standards center around cultural values: respect for

---

[54]John Mackay, McCann Erickson Japan, private communication.

[55]"Aussie Ad Probe Comes to a Boil over Dorf Ads," *Advertising Age International* (February 20, 1995), p. I-6.

[56]"ASC Slams Brakes on Australian Toyota Ads," *Advertising Age International* (May 16, 1994), p. I-6.

[57]"Get My Censor Sensor," *Far Eastern Economic Review* (June 6, 1996), p. 61.

[58]"Sensitive Sensors," *Advertising Age International* (November 23, 1992), p. I-13.

[59]"Group Wants Children's Ads in Quebec," *Advertising Age International* (April 1996), p. I-10.

elders and discipline. For instance, one of the rules bans ads that "shows acts that children should not be doing alone." This standard would conflict with Michelin's celebrated baby commercials.[60]

Scores of other sorts of advertising regulations usually litter the marketing landscape. Some countries only allow advertising in the local language or commercials that were produced with local talent. A number of countries view advertising as an easy source to raise money: ad spending is taxed in Italy and Colombia, for example. China, Vietnam, and other developing markets have a multitiered advertising rate structure—charging a local rate, a foreign rate, and a joint venture rate.

Although many ad regulations often sound frivolous, having a clear set of advertising rules and restrictions is a boon. If not, the law of the jungle applies. Marketers in Taiwan did not face any restrictions on ad claims until recently. Lack of regulation fostered a climate where advertisers misled consumers or even lied to them about their products' performance.[61]

How should marketers cope with advertising regulations? There are a couple of possible actions:

1. *Keep track of regulations and pending legislation.* Monitoring legislation and gathering intelligence on possible changes in advertising regulations is crucial. Bear in mind that advertising regulations change continuously. In many countries the prevailing mood is in favor of liberalization with the important exception of tobacco and alcohol advertising. European Union member states are also trying to bring their rules in line with EU regulations. Many companies have in-house legal counsels to assist them in handling pending advertising legislation.

2. *Lobbying activities.* A more drastic action is to lobby local governments or international legislative bodies such as the European Parliament. Lobbying activities are usually sponsored jointly by advertisers, advertising agencies, and the media. As usual, too much lobbying carries the risk of generating bad publicity, especially when the issues at hand are highly controversial.

3. *Challenge regulations in court.* Advertisers may also consider fighting advertising legislation in court. In Chile, outdoor board companies, advertisers, and sign painters filed suit in civil court when the Chilean government issued new regulations that required outdoor boards to be placed several blocks from the road.[62] In European Union member states, advertisers have also been able to overturn local laws by appealing to the European Commission or the European Court of Justice. A French law that heavily restricted tobacco and liquor advertising was found to be in violation of European Union rules.[63]

---

[60]Louisa Ha, "Concerns About Advertising Practices in a Developing Country: An Examination of China's New Advertising Regulations," *International Journal of Advertising*, 15 (1996), pp. 91–102.

[61]"Taiwanese Consumer Law May Rein in Wild Ad Claims," *Advertising Age International* (June 20, 1994), p. I-6.

[62]"Chilean Fight for Outdoor Ads," *Advertising Age International* (April 27, 1992), p. I-8.

[63]"Ad Restrictions Back Under Fire," *Advertising Age International* (March 11, 1996), p. I-6.

4. *Adapt marketing-mix strategy*. Tobacco marketers have been extremely creative in handling advertising regulations. A widely popular mechanism is to use the brand extension path to cope with tobacco ad bans. For instance, the Swedish Tobacco Co., whose brands have captured more than 80 percent of the Swedish cigarette market, started promoting sunglasses and cigarette lighters under the Blend name, its best-selling cigarette brand, to cope with a complete tobacco ad ban in Sweden.[64] In the United Kingdom, Hamlet, the leading cigar brand, shifted to other media vehicles following the ban on all TV tobacco advertising in the United Kingdom in October 1992. Hamlet started using outdoor boards for the first time, installing them at 2,250 sites. It ran a sales promotion campaign at a horse race where losing bettors got a free Hamlet cigar. It also developed a videocassette with about twenty of its celebrated commercials. The videotape was made available for purchase or rent.[65] South Korea is the only country where Virginia Slims is pitched as the successful man's cigarette. Why? Because Korean law forbids advertising cigarettes to women and young adults.[66]

Global Perspective 14–2 summarizes some of the advertising regulations that were recently imposed in Vietnam.

$\mathcal{G}$LOBAL PERSPECTIVE 14–2

DOS AND DON'TS FOR ADVERTISERS IN VIETNAM

* *Content.* The content of advertising must be accurate, truthful, and correctly reflect the function, effect, and quality of goods and services.
* *Language.* The voice and words must be in Vietnamese, except if licensed business names, phrases, and words cannot be replaced by Vietnamese words. When Vietnamese is used with another language, the Vietnamese words should be shown larger and above the foreign words.
* *National symbols.* Use of national symbols such as the Vietnamese flag, anthem, leaders' pictures, and the "International" anthem are forbidden.

Source: "Advertising Industry Regulations to Help Boost Vietnam's Profile," Media (February 3, 1995), p. 14.

* *Media restrictions.* No ads on the front page of newspapers or magazines. No ads may be inserted in news stories, television or radio programs. Outdoor advertising that may affect traffic safety, cause difficulties to firefighting operations, or affect the aesthetic value of streetscapes, landscapes, or structures is banned. Ad space should be no more than 10 percent of the total newspaper space and maximum 5 percent of a TV/radio program.
* *Duration of ads.* An ad cannot run more than five consecutive days for newspapers and radio, with no more than ten airings per day for radio spots. Limits for TV spots are eight days and five showings per day.

---

[64]"Swedish Marketers Skirt Tobacco Ad Ban," *Advertising Age International* (June 20, 1994), p. I-2.

[65]"Hamlet Shifts to Other Media Since TV Spots are Banned," *Advertising Age International* (April 27, 1992), p. I-8.

[66]"Real Men May Not Eat Quiche . . . But in Korea They Puff Virginia Slims," *Asian Wall Street Journal* (December 27/28, 1996), pp. 1, 7.

CHOOSING AN ADVERTISING AGENCY ◆ ◆ ◆ ◆ ◆ ◆ ◆

Although some companies (e.g., Benetton, Hugo Boss, and Chanel) develop their advertising campaigns in-house, most firms heavily rely on the expertise of an advertising agency. In selecting an agency, the international marketer has several options:

1. Work with the agency that handles the advertising in the firm's home market.
2. Pick a purely local agency in the foreign market.
3. Choose the local office of a large international agency.
4. Select an international network of ad agencies that spans the globe.

When screening ad agencies, the following set of criteria can be used:

- *Market coverage.* Does the agency cover all relevant markets? What is the geographic scope of the agency?

- *Quality of coverage.* What are the core skills of the agency? Does the level of these skills meet the standards set by the company? Also, is there a match between the agency's core skills and the market requirements? For instance, in a market like Japan where media space is scarce, media buying skills are far more critical than creative development.

- *Expertise with developing a central international campaign.* When the intent of the marketer is to develop a global or pan-regional advertising campaign, expertise in handling a central campaign becomes essential.

- *Scope and quality of support services.* Most agencies are not just hired for their creative skills and media buying. They are also expected to deliver a range of support services, like marketing research, developing other forms of communication (e.g., sales promotions, public relations, event-sponsorships).

- *Desirable image ("global" versus "local").* The image—global or local—that the company wants to project with its communication efforts also matters a great deal. Companies that aspire to develop a "local" image often assign their account to local ad agencies. The Citrus Marketing Board of Israel uses local advertising agencies for precisely this reason: "We can't translate campaigns from Israel into another culture, so we get into these cultures by using local promoters."[67]

- *Size of the agency.* Generally speaking, large agencies have more power than small agencies. This is especially critical for media buying where a healthy relationship between the media outlet and the ad agency is critical.

- *Conflicting accounts.* Does the agency already work on an account of one of our competitors? The risk of conflicting accounts is a major concern to many advertisers. There are two kinds of risks here. First of all, there is the confidentiality issue: marketers share a lot of proprietary data with their advertising agency. Second, there is also the fear that superior creative talent might be assigned by the ad agency to the competing brand's account.

---

[67]"Using Culture to Promote Fruit," *Advertising Age International* (May 1996), p. I-4.

Note that sometimes these criteria may conflict with one another. A characteristic of the Japanese agency industry is that the large agencies service competing brands. Hence, companies that approach a big Japanese ad agency like Dentsu or Hakuhodo may need to accept the fact that the agency also handles the accounts of competing brands.

◆ ◆ ◆ ◆ ◆ ◆ COORDINATING INTERNATIONAL ADVERTISING

Global or pan-regional advertising approaches require a great deal of coordination across and communication among the various subsidiaries. In this section we discuss a number of mechanisms that can be used to facilitate this process.

Monetary Incentives (Cooperative Advertising)

Small companies often assign the advertising responsibility to their local distributors. In such a setup, the marketer might face two possible issues. First, relative advertising efforts may vary a great deal across the different distributors. Second, there is usually little consistency in the message that is conveyed in each of the different markets where the product is sold. To tackle these concerns, marketers often provide monetary incentives to their respective distributors to get some level of coordination. Most often, the incentive takes the form of cooperative advertising where the firm contributes to the local distributor's advertising spending activities.

Blistex, an American maker of lip-care products, set up a cooperative advertising system to implement a Pan-European advertising campaign. One objective of the campaign was to get all distributors to advertise Blistex. The second major priority was to use a common advertising theme across all European markets. To achieve these goals, Blistex set up an advertising fund from which each distributor could withdraw money up to a certain amount to fund its advertising activities.[68]

Advertising Manuals

The use of an **advertising manual (brand book)** or videotape to guide international advertising efforts is fairly common. Mercedes-Benz puts together a handbook that spells out its advertising guidelines for its European subsidiaries and sales agents. Likewise, Seiko, the Japanese watchmaker, guides its local affiliates and advertising agencies via an advertising manual.[69]

Lead-Country Concept

Colgate-Palmolive has implemented a lead-country system for its international advertising campaigns. For instance, for Colgate Tartar Control Formula, the lead country was the United Kingdom. Aside of the lead country, inputs are provided by

---

[68] Mark Boersma, Blistex Inc., private communication.
[69] Rijkens.

the advertising agency and the global business development manager. The details of the campaign are summarized in a *bundle*, which is sent to the various subsidiaries.[70] Dupont's handling of its Lycra brand advertising is another interesting example.[71] The synthetic brand is used in a wide variety of applications (e.g., swimsuits, running shorts). Its brand identity is communicated via the global tagline "Nothing moves like Lycra." However, each application also needs its own positioning. Responsibility for coming up with application-specific positioning themes is delegated to country managers in the country where the application is most prominent. For instance, the Brazilian country manager is in charge of swimsuit positioning, as Brazil is the lead market for this particular use of Lycra.

Numerous multinationals rely on global or pan-regional meetings to coordinate their international advertising. These meetings can be very informal. To create a new communication campaign for the Latin American region, Goodyear, the US tire maker, set up an informal two-day working conference in Miami. Participants included the marketing executives from each country, regional senior executives, and several key creative staff people from Leo Burnett's Latin American offices, the ad agency in charge of the account.[72] The different steps behind the development of Goodyear's 1992 Latin American ad campaign are presented in Exhibit 14–11. Note that the entire process took about six months.

Global or Pan-Regional Meetings

Robert Jordan, a senior advertising executive, offers six guidelines to implement a global or pan-regional advertising approach:[73]

1. Top management must be dedicated to going global.
2. Use a third party (e.g., the ad agency) to help sell key managers the benefits of a global advertising approach.
3. A global brief based on cross-border consumer research can help persuade managers to think in terms of global consumers.
4. Find product champions and give them a charter for the success of the global marketing program.
5. Convince local staff that they have an opportunity in developing a global campaign.
6. Get local managers on the global marketing team—have them do the job themselves.

---

[70]Ibid.

[71]Aaker and Joachimsthaler, p. 143.

[72]D.A. Hanni, J.K. Ryans, Jr., and I.R. Vernon, "Coordinating International Advertising—The Goodyear Case Revisited for Latin America," *Journal of International Marketing*, 3 (2) (1995), pp. 83–98.

[73]R. O. Jordan, "Going Global: How to Join the Second Major Revolution in Marketing. Commentary," *The Journal of Consumer Marketing*, 5 (1) (Winter 1988), pp. 39–44.

EXHIBIT 14–11
FRAMEWORK FOR PAN-REGIONAL AD CAMPAIGN DEVELOPMENT AT GOODYEAR

1. Preliminary Orientation
September 1992
Subsidiary strategic information input on business and communications strategy on country-by-country basis.
Home Office Review

2. Regional Communications Strategy Definition
Strategy Definition Meeting
October 1992
Outputs: Regional positioning objective, communication objectives, and creative assignment for advertising agency.

3. Advertising Creative Review
Creative Review Meeting
November 12, 1992
Outputs: Six creative concepts (story boards). Research questions regarding real consumer concerns to guide research.

4. Qualitative Research Store
Qualitative Research
November–December 1992
Consistent research results across five countries on purchase intentions and consumer perceptions of safety.

5. Research Review
Research Review Meeting
January 15, 1993
Sharply defined "consumer proposition" identified and agreed upon with new creative assignment for agency.

6. Final Creative Review
Final Creative Review Meeting
March 12, 1993
Campaign Adoption

7. Budget Approval—Home Office

8. Campaign Execution—Media Buys Local Countries

Source: D.A. Hanni, J.K. Ryans, Jr. and I.R. Vernon, "Coordinating International Advertising—The Goodyear Case Revisited for Latin America."

This article originally appeared in *Journal of International Marketing*, 3 (2) (1995), published by Michigan State University Press.

◆ ◆ ◆ ◆ ◆ ◆ OTHER FORMS OF COMMUNICATION

For most companies, media advertising is only one part of the communication package. Although advertising is the most visible form, the other communication tools play a vital role in a company's global marketing-mix strategy. In this section, we will review four key tools: sales promotions, sponsorships, direct marketing, and trade shows. Managing a sales force—which can be regarded as both a promotion and distribution tool—will be discussed in Chapter 15.

Sales promotions refer to a collection of short-term incentive tools that lead to quicker and/or larger sales of a particular product by consumers or the trade.[74] There are basically two kinds of promotions: consumer promotions that target end users (e.g., coupons, sweepstakes, rebates) and trade promotions that are aimed at distributors (e.g., volume discounts, advertising allowances). For the majority of MNCs, the sales promotion policy is a local affair. Several rationales explain the local character of promotions:[75]

Sales Promotions

- *Economic development.* Low incomes and poor literacy in developing countries make some promotional techniques unattractive but, at the same time, render other tools more appealing. One study of promotional practices in developing countries found above-average use of samples and price-off packs.[76]

- *Market maturity.* For most product categories, there is a great deal of variation in terms of market maturity. In countries where the product is still in an early stage of the product life cycle, trial-inducing tools such as samples, coupons and cross-promotions are appropriate. In more established markets, one of the prime goals of promotions will be to encourage repeat purchase. Incentives such as bonus packs, in-pack coupons, and, trade promotions that stimulate brand loyalty tend to be favored.

- *Cultural perceptions.* Cultural perceptions of promotions differ widely across countries. Some types of promotions (e.g., sweepstakes) may have a very negative image in certain countries. According to one study, Taiwanese consumers have less-favorable attitudes toward sweepstakes than consumers in Thailand or Malaysia. Nor are Taiwanese concerned about losing face when using coupons. Malaysians, on the other hand, favor sweepstakes over coupons.[77] Shoppers in Europe redeem far fewer coupons than their counterparts in the United States.[78]

- *Trade structure.* One of the major issues companies face is how to allocate their promotional dollars between consumer promotions—that are directly aimed at the end user (*pull*)—and trade promotions (*push*)—that target the middlemen. Because of differences in the local trade structure, the balance of power between manufacturers and trade is tilted in favor of the trade in certain countries. When Procter & Gamble attempted to cut back on trade promotions by introducing EveryDay Low Pricing in Germany, several major German retailers retaliated by delisting P & G brands.[79] Differences in distributors' inventory space and/or costs also play a role in determining which types of promotions are effective.

[74]Kotler, Philip, *Marketing Management* (Upper Saddle River, NJ: Prentice-Hall, 2000).

[75]K. Kashani and J.A. Quelch, "Can Sales Promotions Go Global?" *Business Horizons*, 33 (3) (May-June 1990), pp. 37–43.

[76]J.S. Hill and U.O. Boya, "Consumer Goods Promotions in Developing Countries," *International Journal of Advertising*, 6 (1987), pp. 249–64.

[77]Lenard C. Huff and Dana L. Alden, "An Investigation of Consumer Response to Sales Promotions in Developing Markets: A Three-Country Analysis," *Journal of Advertising Research* (May-June 1998), pp. 47–56.

[78]"Coupon FSIs Dropped," *Advertising Age International* (October 11, 1993), p. I-8.

[79]"Heat's on Value Pricing," *Advertising Age International* (January 1997), pp. I-21, I-22.

- *Government regulations.* Probably the most critical factor in designing a promotional package is local law. Certain practices may be heavily restricted or simply forbidden. In Germany, for instance, coupon values cannot be more than 1 percent of the product's value. Vouchers, stamps, and coupons are banned in Norway.[80] Exhibit 14–12 shows which promotion techniques are allowed in nine European countries. As you can see, Germany appears to be one of the most restrictive environments for promotion campaigns. The United Kingdom, on the other hand, seems to be very liberal.

Kashani and Quelch suggest that multinational companies appoint an international sales promotion coordinator. The manager's agenda would involve tasks such as these:[81]

- Promote transfer of successful promotional ideas across units.
- Transplant ideas on how to constrain harmful trade promotional practices.
- Gather performance data and develop monitoring systems to evaluate the efficiency and effectiveness of promotions.
- Coordinate relations with the company's sales promotion agencies worldwide.

EXHIBIT 14–12
WHAT TECHNIQUES ARE ALLOWED IN EUROPE

What Techniques Are Allowed In Europe

PROMOTION TECHNIQUE	UK	NL	BEL	SP	IR	IT	FR	GER	DK
On-pack promotions	✓	✓	?	✓	✓	✓	?	✓	✓
Banded offers	✓	?	?	✓	✓	✓	?	✓	✓
In-pack premiums	✓	?	?	✓	✓	✓	?	?	?
Multi-purchase offers	✓	?	?	✓	✓	✓	?	✓	✓
Extra product	✓	✓	✓	✓	✓	✓	?	X	✓
Free product	✓	?	✓	✓	✓	✓	✓	X	?
Reusable/other use packs	✓	✓	✓	✓	✓	✓	✓	?	✓
Free mail-ins	✓	✓	?	✓	✓	✓	✓	✓	✓
With purchase premiums	✓	?	✓	✓	✓	✓	?	X	?
Cross-product offers	✓	✓	X	✓	✓	✓	?	✓	✓
Collector devices	✓	✓	✓	✓	✓	✓	✓	✓	✓
Competitions	✓	?	?	✓	✓	?	✓	✓	?
Self-liquidating premiums	✓	✓	✓	✓	✓	✓	✓	✓	✓
Free draws	✓	X	?	✓	✓	✓	✓	✓	✓
Share outs	✓	✓	?	✓	✓	?	?	✓	?
Sweepstake/lottery	?	X	?	✓	X	?	?	✓	X
Money off vouchers	✓	✓	✓	✓	✓	✓	✓	?	✓
Money off next purchase	✓	✓	✓	✓	✓	✓	✓	X	✓
Cash backs	✓	✓	✓	✓	✓	X	✓	X	✓
In-store demos	✓	✓	✓	✓	✓	✓	✓	✓	✓

Key ✓ = permitted   X = not permitted   ? = may be permitted

Source: Global Marketing and Advertising—Understanding Cultural Paradoxes. www.isp.org.uk/europa.html

---

[80]"Coupon FSIs dropped." See footnote 78.

[81]Kashani and Quelch, pp. 37–43.

Direct marketing refers to various forms of interactive marketing where the company uses media that enables it to get direct access to the end consumer and establish a one-to-one relationship. The most prominent forms of direct marketing are direct mail, telemarketing, door-to-door selling, the Internet,[82] and catalog selling. In a sense, direct marketing is a promotional tool and a distribution tool. For companies like Avon, Amazon.com, Dell, E-Trade, and Amway, direct marketing goes even beyond just being a marketing mix instrument: it is basically a business model for them.

Direct marketing is growing very fast internationally. Many of the celebrated firms in the area have been able to successfully transplant their direct marketing model to other markets. About one year after Dell entered China, it has been able to become one of the leading PC brands there, despite skepticism that its practice of selling direct would not work in a country where salesmanship centers around connections.[83] In Russia and the Czech Republic, where direct marketing is still a novelty, junk mail is opened and read scrupulously.[84]

Though still rare, some firms have been able to successfully implement global direct marketing campaigns. A good illustration is a campaign run by Unisys, a U.S.-based information technology company. Its "Customer Connection" program is a million-dollar-plus, multilingual program that combines direct mail and telemarketing worldwide. Every quarter, Unisys sent out direct mail to key decision-makers in 23 countries. The mailing described product and technology offerings in seven languages and came with a personalized letter signed by a Unisys region or country manager. Native-speaking telemarketers would then follow up by asking if the client manager recalls the mailing, if they had any queries, and if they would like to remain on the mailing list. Follow-up surveys showed that 70 percent of the contacted executives responded positively to the program.[85]

As with other promotion tools, direct marketing might also encounter hurdles in foreign markets. A notorious case was the complete ban on direct selling that the Chinese government imposed in the Spring of 1998. Well-established selling companies such as Avon, Amway, and Mary Kay basically had to shut down their operations. As a result, these companies had to rethink their way of doing business in China. Avon struck a deal with Watson's, a Hong Kong–based drugstore chain, to set up small counters in its stores.[86] Land's End, the American catalog company, was forced to drop its no-questions-asked, money-back guarantee in Germany, after protests from local retailers.[87]

Direct Marketing

Sponsorship is one of the fastest growing promotion tools. In 1999, companies spent almost $20 billion on sponsoring.[88] Given the global appeal of sports, more and more MNCs are using sports sponsorships as their weapon of choice in their

Event Sponsorships

[82]More discussion on the use of the Internet as a promotion tool in Chapter 19.

[83]"Chasing the China Market," *Asiaweek* (June 11, 1999), p. 46.

[84]"Direct Hit," *The Economist* (January 9, 1999), pp. 57–59.

[85]"Unisys Cuts Clear Path to Int'l Recovery," *Marketing News* (September 27, 1999), pp. 4–6.

[86]"Avon Scrambles to Reinvent Itself in China after Beijing's Ban on Direct Selling," *Far Eastern Economic Review* (October 22, 1998), pp. 64–66.

[87]"Lands' End Guarantee is Beached in Germany," *International Herald Tribune* (Sept. 25/26, 1999), p. 11.

[88]www.sponsorship.com

global battle for market share. Sponsorship also stretches to other types of events, such as concert tours and art exhibitions. A case in point is Heineken, the Dutch beer brewer. In 1995 Heineken pumped money in various sports activities world-wide, including, the Rugby World Cup in South Africa, the Davis Cup and the U.S. Open Tennis tournament. However, the brewer also organized a Heineken Night of the Proms in the Netherlands, Spain and Switzerland.[89]

Ideally, the sponsored event should reinforce the brand image that the company is trying to promote. TAG Heuer, the Swiss watchmaker, is a prime example of a company that relies on sponsorship to build up its brand reputation by being the official timer of various Olympic games. The company spends about $10 million annually on sponsorship activities.[90] Likewise, United Distillers sponsors interna-tional golf events to reinforce the brand image of Johnnie Walker Black Label.[91]

There are three major risks with event sponsorship. The organizers of the event may let nonsponsors in, thereby discounting the value of the sponsorship to the of-ficial sponsors. They might also sell too many sponsorships, leading toward clutter. The third risk is known as ambush marketing. With ambush marketing, a company seeks to associate with an event (e.g., the Olympics) without payment to the event owner. The culprit hereby steals the limelight from its competitor who sponsors the event. By associating with the event, the ambushing company misleads the public by creating the impression that it is a legitimate sponsor. For example, some U.S. mail trucks still carried the Olympic rings years after the U.S. Post Office gave up its sponsorship of the Olympics.[92] Aside of these risks, there is also the issue of response measurement. In general, measuring the effectiveness of a particular sponsorship activity is extremely hard. Some firms have come up with very creative procedures to do just that. In Asia, Reebok tested out a campaign on Star TV's Channel V music channel in which the veejays wear Reebok shoes. To gauge the impact of the campaign, TV viewers were directed to Reebok's Web site on the Internet. Once the viewers got access to Reebok's site, they were able download a coupon that could be used for the next shoe purchase.[93]

Trade Shows

Trade shows (trade fairs) are a vital part of the communication package for many international business-to-business marketers. The number of trade shows outside North America was more than 16,000 in 1999. Spending on trade shows accounts for almost one-fifth of the total communications budget of U.S. indus-trial firms and one-fourth for European companies.[94] Trade shows have a direct sales effect—the sales coming from visitors of the trade show booth—and indi-rect impacts on the exhibitor's sales.[95] Indirect sales effects stem from the fact

---

[89]Heineken N.V., *Annual Report 1995*.

[90]"TAG Heuer: All Time Greats?" pp. 45–48.

[91]"Tiger Woods Played Here," *Forbes* (March 10, 1997), pp. 96–97.

[92]"Javelins are Already Flying—at Billy Payne," *Business Week* (July 22, 1996), p. 43.

[93]"Reebok Sets Strategy to Get Sales on Track in Fast-growing Asia," *The Asian Wall Street Journal* (May 31–June 1, 1996), p. 12.

[94]Jacobson, D. (1990), "Marketers Say They'll Boost Spending," *Business Marketing*, 75 (March), pp. 31–32.

[95]S. Gopalakrishna, G. L. Lilien, J. D. Williams and I. K. Sequeira, "Do Trade Shows Pay Off?" *Journal of Marketing*, 59 (July 1995), pp. 75–83.

that visitors become more aware of and interested in the participating company's products. The indirect effects matter especially for new products. Trade fairs are often promoted in trade journals. Government agencies like the U.S. Department of Commerce, also provide detailed information on international trade fairs.

There are some notable differences between overseas trade shows and North American ones.[96] Overseas fairs are usually much larger than the more regional, niche-oriented shows in the United States. Because of their size, international shows attract a much wider variety of buyers. Hospitality is another notable difference between trade show affairs in the United States and in foreign markets. For instance, even at the smallest booths at German shows, visitors are offered a chair and a glass of orange juice. Larger booths will have kitchens and serve full meals. Empty booths are filled with a coffee table and water cooler. In the United States, trade show events tend to be pure business. While trade shows are on the rise, events in Latin America still lack the sophistication and infrastructure one encounters in Europe and North America.

When attending an international trade show, the following guidelines might prove useful:[97]

- Decide on what trade shows to attend at least a year in advance. Prepare translations of product materials, price lists, selling aids.
- Bring plenty of literature. Bring someone who knows the language or have a translator.
- Send out, ahead of time, direct-mail pieces to potential attendees.
- Find out the best possible space—for instance, in terms of traffic.
- Plan the best way to display your products and to tell your story.
- Do your homework on potential buyers from other countries.[98]
- Assess the impact of trade show participation on the company's bottom line.[99] Performance benchmarks may need to be adjusted when evaluating trade show effectiveness in different countries since attendees might behave differently.[100]

Online information resources on trade show events are plentiful (e.g., www.tscentral.com). A recent phenomenon is the emergence of "virtual trade shows," which allow buyers to walk a "show floor," view products, and request information without physically being there.[101] One example is E-Expo USA, a pilot virtual trade show promoted by the U.S. Department of Commerce. For one flat fee, booths remain online for an entire year.

---

[96]"Trading Plätze," *Marketing News* (July 19, 1999), p. 11.

[97]B. O'Hara, F. Palumbo and P. Herbig, "Industrial Trade Shows Abroad," *Industrial Marketing Management*, 22 (1993), pp. 233–37.

[98]"Trading Plätze."

[99]See S. Gopalakrishna and G.L. Lilien, "A Three-Stage Model of Industrial Trade Show Performance," *Marketing Science*, 14 (1) (Winter 1995), pp. 22–42 for a formal mathematical model to assess trade show effectiveness.

[100]Marnik G. Dekimpe, Pierre François, Srinath Gopalakrishna, Gary L. Lilien, and Christophe Van den Bulte, "Generalizing About Trade Show Effectiveness: A Cross-National Comparison," *Journal of Marketing*, 61 (October 1997), pp. 55–64.

[101]"All Trade Shows, All the Time," *Marketing News* (July 19, 1999), p. 11.

◆ ◆ ◆ ◆ ◆ ◆ GLOBALLY INTEGRATED MARKETING COMMUNICATIONS (GIMC)

For most companies, media advertising is only one element of their global communications efforts. As we saw in the previous section, marketers use many other tools. In recent years, advertising agencies and their clients have recognized the value of an **integrated marketing communications (IMC)** program—not just for domestic markets but globally. The goal of IMC is to coordinate the different communication vehicles—mass advertising, sponsorships, sales promotions, packaging, point-of-purchase displays, and so forth—to convey one and the same idea to the prospective customers with a unified voice.[102] Instead of having the different promotional mix, elements send out a mish-mash of messages with a variety of visual imagery, each and every one of them centers around that single key idea. By having consistency, integration, and cohesiveness, marketers will be able to maximize the impact of your communication tools.

A five-nation survey of ad agencies found that the use of IMC varies a lot. The percentage of client budgets devoted to IMC activities was low in India (15 percent) and Australia (22 percent). The percentage was far higher in New Zealand (40 percent) and the United Kingdom (42 percent).[103] A **globally integrated marketing communications (GIMC)** program goes one step further. GIMC is a system of active promotional management that strategically coordinates global communications in all of its component parts both horizontally (country-level) and vertically (promotion tools).[104]

To run a GIMC program effectively places demands on both the advertiser's organization and the advertising agencies involved. Companies that want to pursue a GIMC for some or all of their brands should have the mechanisms in place to coordinate their promotional activities vertically (across tools) and horizontally (across countries). By the same token, ad agencies should be willing to integrate and coordinate the various communication disciplines across countries. GIMC also requires frequent communications both internally and between ad agency branches worldwide.[105]

SUMMARY ◆

Global advertising is for many marketers one of the most daunting challenges they face. There are a multitude of decisions that need to be carried out on the front of international advertising. This chapter gave you an overview of the major ones: creating advertising campaigns, setting and allocating the budget, selecting media vehicles to carry the campaign, choosing advertising agencies, and coordinating cross-country advertising programs. The development of a global advertising plan involves many players—headquarters, regional and/or local offices, advertising agencies—which typically makes the entire process pretty frustrating. However, the poten-

---

[102]"Integrated Marketing Communications: Maybe Definition Is in the Point of View," *Marketing News* (January 18, 1993).

[103]Philip J. Kitchen and Don E. Schultz, "A Multi-Country Comparison of the Drive for IMC," *Journal of Advertising Research* (Jan.–Feb. 1999), pp. 21–38.

[104]Andreas F. Grein and Stephen J. Gould, "Globally Integrated Marketing Communications," *Journal of Marketing Communications*, 2 (3) (1996), pp. 141–58.

[105]Stephen J. Gould, Dawn B. Lerman, and Andreas F. Grein, "Agency Perceptions and Practices on Global IMC," *Journal of Advertising Research* (Jan.–Feb. 1999), pp. 7–20.

tial rewards—in the form of increased market share and an improved profit picture—of a brilliant and well-executed international advertising strategy are tantalizing.

One of the front-burner issues that scores of international advertisers face is to what degree they should push for pan-regional or even global advertising campaigns. The arguments for standardizing campaigns are pretty compelling: (1) cost savings, (2) a coherent brand image, (3) similarity of target groups, (4) transplanting of creative ideas. By now, you should also be quite familiar with the counterarguments: (1) cultural differences, (2) different markets having different degree in market maturity, (3) role of advertising regulations, and (4) variations in the media-environment. Despite years of debate, it is almost impossible to establish waterproof general guidelines.

Overall, there seems to be a definite move toward more pan-regional (or even globalized) campaigns. Numerous explanations have been put forward to explain this shift: the "global" village rationale, the mushrooming of global and pan-regional media vehicles, restructuring of marketing divisions and brand systems along global or pan-regional lines. Another important development is the emergence of new media outlets, including the Internet. While it is hard to gaze in a crystal ball and come up with concrete predictions, it is clear that international advertisers will face a drastically different environment ten years from now.

KEY TERMS ✦

advertising manual (brand book)
competitive parity
export advertising

globally integrated marketing communications (GIMC)

modular approach
objective-and-task method
pattern standardization

percentage of sales
prototype advertising

REVIEW QUESTIONS ✦

1. Most luxury products appeal to global segments. Does that mean that global advertising campaigns are most appropriate for such kind of products?

2. Discuss the major challenges faced by international advertisers.

3. Spell out the steps that international advertisers should consider to cope with advertising regulations in their foreign markets.

4. What factors entice international advertisers to localize their advertising campaigns in foreign markets?

5. What are the major reasons for standardizing an international advertising program?

6. What will be the impact of satellite TV on international advertising?

7. What do you see as the major drawbacks of the Internet as a communication tool from the perspective of an international advertiser?

8. What mechanisms should MNCs contemplate to coordinate their advertising efforts across different countries?

DISCUSSION QUESTIONS ✦

1. Poland recently imposed a ban on advertising for alcoholic beverages. How do you think brewers like United Distillers and Seagram should adjust their marketing-mix strategy to cope with this ban?

2. The allocation of promotional dollars between "pull" (consumer promotions + media advertising) and "push" varies drastically for many advertisers across countries. What are the factors behind these variations?

3. Consider Exhibit 14–4. What does the information in this exhibit suggest in terms of possible advertising strategies in the different countries listed there?

4. For a particular brand, select at least three different print ads from different countries that came out during the same period. What do the ads have in common? How do they differ? Speculate about the reasons behind the commonalities and differences.

FURTHER READING ◆

Al-Makaty, Safran S., G. Norman van Tubergen, S. Scott Whitlow, and Douglas A. Boyd. "Attitudes toward Advertising in Islam." *Journal of Advertising Research* (May/June 1996): 16–26.

Davison, Andrew, and Erik Grab. "The Contributions of Advertising Testing to the Development of Effective International Advertising: The KitKat Case Study." *Marketing and Research Today* (February 1993): 15–24.

De Mooij, Marieke. *Advertising Worldwide*, 2nd ed., Englewood Cliffs, NJ: Prentice-Hall, 1994.

Domzal, Teresa J., and Jerome B. Kernan. "Mirror, Mirror: Some Postmodern Reflections on Global Advertising." *Journal of Advertising*, 22 (4) (December 1993): 1–20.

Duncan, Tom, and Jyotika Ramaprasad. "Standardizing Multinational Advertising: The Influencing Factors." *Journal of Advertising*, 24 (3) (Fall 1995): 55–68.

Hanni, D. A., J. K. Ryans, Jr., and I. R. Vernon. "Coordinating International Advertising—The Goodyear Case Revisited for Latin America." *Journal of International Marketing*, 3 (2) (1995): 83–98.

Harvey, M. G., "Point of View: A Model to Determine Standardization of the Advertising Process in International Markets." *Journal of Advertising Research* (July/August 1993): 57–64.

Hill, John S., and Unal O. Boya. "Consumer Goods Promotions in Developing Countries." *International Journal of Advertising*, 6 (1987): 249–64.

James, W. L., and J. S. Hill. "International Advertising Messages: To Adapt or Not to Adapt (That is the Question)." *Journal of Advertising Research* (June/July 1991): 65–71.

Johansson, Johny K. "The Sense of "Nonsense": Japanese TV Advertising." *Journal of Advertising,* 23 (1) (March 1994): 17–26.

Kashani, Kamran, and John A. Quelch. "Can Sales Promotions Go Global?" *Business Horizons*, 33 (3) (May–June 1990): 37–43.

Kaynak, Erderer. *The Management of International Advertising*. New York, NY: Quorum Books, 1989.

McCullough, Wayne R. "Global Advertising which Acts Locally: The IBM Subtitles Campaign." *Journal of Advertising Research* (May/June 1996): 11–15.

Maynard, Michael L., and Charles R. Taylor. "A Comparative Analysis of Japanese and U.S. Attitudes toward Direct Marketing." *Journal of Direct Marketing*, 10 (Winter 1996): 34–44.

Meenaghan, Tony. "Current Developments & Future Directions in Sponsorship." *International Journal of Advertising*, 17 (1): 3–28.

Mehta, Raj, Rajdeep Grewal, and Eugene Sivadas. "International Direct Marketing on the Internet: Do Internet Users Form a Global Segment?" *Journal of Direct Marketing*, 10 (Winter 1996): 45–58.

Mueller, Barbara. "An Analysis of Information Content in Standardized vs. Specialized Multinational Advertisements." *Journal of International Business Studies* (First Quarter 1991): 23–39.

O'Hara, B., F. Palumbo, and P. Herbig. "Industrial Trade Shows Abroad." *Industrial Marketing Management*, 22 (1993): 233–37.

Plummer, Joseph T. "The Role of Copy Research in Multinational Advertising." *Journal of Advertising Research* (Oct./Nov. 1986): 11–15.

Quelch, John A. and Lisa R. Klein. "The Internet and International Marketing." *Sloan Management Review* (Spring 1996): 60–75.

Rijkens, Rein. *European Advertising Strategies*. London: Cassell, 1992.

SALES MANAGEMENT

CHAPTER OVERVIEW

1. MARKET ENTRY OPTIONS AND SALES FORCE STRATEGY

2. CULTURAL CONSIDERATIONS

3. IMPACT OF CULTURE ON SALES MANAGEMENT
   AND PERSONAL SELLING

4. EXPATRIATES

U.S. automakers still have great difficulty making inroads into the Japanese market, although Japan does not impose any tariffs on foreign cars and has eliminated nearly all nontariff barriers to automobile trade. One major, yet little known, reason is in the way cars are sold in Japan. Unlike the United States, where customers visit car dealers, a majority of cars are peddled by door-to-door salespeople in Japan, much the same way Avon representatives sell personal care and beauty products (see Global Perspective 15–1). This example vividly illustrates the importance of international sales management.

What does the salesperson do in a company? We can think of many different types of salespeople, from entry-level laborers who stand behind the counter at an ice cream store to industrial experts who work entirely within the offices of a corporate client. Some salespeople are selling products, others are selling services. Some are focused on the immediate sale, some are primarily concerned with building the confidence and goodwill of a client. Salespeople take orders, deliver products, educate buyers, build relationships with clients, and provide technical knowledge.

In all cases the salesperson is the front line for the company. The customer sees only the salesperson and the product. Through the salesperson, the customer develops an opinion of the company. And the success or failure of the company

GLOBAL PERSPECTIVE 15–1

DIRECT MARKETING: CAR SALES DOOR-TO-DOOR — WHY THE U.S. BIG THREE STILL HAVE DIFFICULTY CRACKING INTO THE JAPANESE MARKET

Autos are always a contentious issue in the U.S.–Japan trade relationship. Roughly two-thirds of the U.S. trade deficit with Japan is auto-related. Why can't U.S. automakers crack into the Japanese market?

The answer is hidden in the way cars are sold. For example, Eiko Shiraishi, a Tokyo housewife, has never visited an auto dealership, kicked a tire, or taken a test drive. So how does she end up with a $30,000 gleaming silver Toyota in her driveway?

In Japan, a door-to-door salesperson peddles cars the way the Avon Lady sells cosmetics. Japanese cars may be high-tech, but Japanese salesmanship is very old-fashioned. The Japan Automobile Dealers Association estimates that half the cars sold in Japan are peddled by door-to-door salespeople. No wonder U.S. automakers still have difficulty competing against Toyota, Nissan, Honda, and so on in Japan.

J. Michael Durrie, the head of General Motors Japan, sighs, "There isn't any silver bullet that would make it easier to sell products in this very competitive, very expensive marketplace." U.S. trade negotiators want the Japanese to assure that substantially more auto dealerships in Japan will stock U.S. vehicles. Even if Japanese auto dealerships did carry more U.S. cars on their lots, sales of U.S. cars would not materially increase — until, and unless, door-to-door salespeople were assigned to making the door-to-door rounds peddling U.S. cars in Japan.

Toyota alone boasts more than 100,000 door-to-door salespeople in Japan, the size of California. This figure amounts to half as many as the entire sales force in the United States for all domestic and foreign cars. "Indeed, Toyota's sales force is so strong that they just blow everybody else off the face of the earth," says Keith Donaldson, an auto analyst at Salomon Brothers Asia Ltd.

Ford Motor Co., the most aggressive of the U.S. Big Three in Japan, is trying to attract customers the American Way: mounting a media and advertising blitz aimed at bringing prospective buyers into the showroom. Ford dealers do not knock on doors, as such a sales tactic is too costly and inefficient. However, a Ford executive admits, "We need to come up with some ideas to sell more cars without door-to-door sales, but the reality is that we haven't come up with any."

One word of small consolation to the U.S. Big Three in Japan is that with the recent Japanese recession, Japanese automakers have been forced to reassess their successful but relatively inefficient, unique way of selling cars. For example, Nissan and Isuzu have both announced reductions in marketing subsidies as part of a companywide cost-cutting program. In addition, as Japan shifts to two-income households, less and less people are home during the day, so door-to-door salespeople have increased difficulty in reaching customers at home. Instead, door-to-door salespeople have begun invading corporate offices to meet prospective customers. However, expecting Japanese customers, who also expect door-to-door delivery service should their cars ever need repairs, to start visiting auto dealerships any time soon remains a tall order.

Source: Summarized from Valerie Reitman, "In Japan's Car Market, Big Three Face Rivals Who Go Door-to-Door," *Wall Street Journal* (September 28, 1994), p. A1, A11; and Alexandra Harney, "Death of the Salesman Spells Boost For Japan," *Financial Times* (January 5, 1999), p. 6.

rests largely on the ability of the sales force. We cannot overstate the importance of making good decisions when those decisions affect the quality and ability of the company's sales force. This chapter investigates how the processes of sales management and personal selling are changed when taken overseas into another culture.

So what is international about sales management and personal selling? First, we can break international sales management issues into two categories that provide a clarification of the use of the term *international*:

EXHIBIT 15–1

INTERNATIONAL SALES STRATEGY AND INTERCULTURAL CONSIDERATIONS

International Sales Strategy Issues	Intercultural Issues within the Foreign Country
Sales force skill availability	Motivation
Country image	Cultural sensitivity
Expatriate recruiting	Ethical standards
Centralized training	Fairness
Home to host communications	Relationship building
	Selling style differences

1. *International strategy considerations*: These issues analyze more than one country's assets, strengths, and situations, or that deal directly with cross-border coordination.

2. *Intercultural considerations*: These issues focus on the culture of the foreign country and its effect on operations within that country.

Although these two categories are not mutually exclusive, they help to clarify what makes international sales management considerations different from domestic sales management. A list of examples appears in Exhibit 15–1.

In this chapter, we highlight issues related to the choice of market entry method and the sales management step to setting sales force objectives. In relating foreign entry choices to sales management, we provide a framework for thinking about the effects of various sales force management issues. Subsequently, we ask you to carefully consider the cultural generalizations that influence international decisions and interactions. Poor generalizations will produce flawed sales management. Good tools for generalizing about cultures can help the international manager make decisions that accurately take into account cultural differences.

We also discuss how cultural differences, in general, will affect issues central to sales management. We consider cultural impacts on recruiting, training, supervising, and evaluating salespeople, as well as on the personal sales process. We evaluate the issues of recruiting, training, supervising, and evaluating the sales force with a focus on the host country, local salesperson.

Finally, we discuss the complex issues involved when a company sends its employees overseas. The successful use of expatriates gives a company significant advantages, but requires careful selection, training, supervision, and evaluation.

MARKET ENTRY OPTIONS AND SALES FORCE STRATEGY

♦ ♦ ♦ ♦ ♦ ♦

In the sales force management "process," we start with setting objectives and strategy. These steps include determining the goals and purposes of the sales force and the structure that will best meet those goals. To a large extent, these initial steps determine the requirements for the subsequent steps in the process—recruiting, training, supervising, and evaluating.

The question of *how to enter the market* is central to marketing. As a company decides what form its market entry will take, it is making a decision that limits and defines key underlying aspects of its future sales force management. For example, if a company decides to sell its products in the United States through a large, integrated distributor, it may only need a small, highly mobile sales force.

In international sales, the form of entry has even greater implications in international sales. The form of entry will determine how large the sales force needs to be, and will influence how much training it will require. It will also influence whether the sales force is predominantly local foreign citizens or whether it is primarily expatriates. This composition will then influence the compensation scale required. As we can see, the form of entry directly influences many of the *downstream* sales-force management options. This section reviews various options for entering a foreign market and summarizes the principle implications and questions each option raises.

The entry method we have been referring to is also termed the *level of integration* in the market. Forward integration refers to greater ownership and control of the distribution channel. For example, a company might begin its foreign sales by exporting through a merchant distributor who takes title to the product and performs all of the necessary foreign sales functions. Later, the company might integrate forward into the distribution channel by hiring its own commissioned sales agents in the foreign country. Still greater forward integration might consist of the company purchasing a sales subsidiary and establishing product warehouses abroad.[1]

Determining the best level of integration is an issue more appropriate for a chapter on international strategy than sales management. However, in determining the entry form, the company must consider the subsequent influences it will have on its sales management options. In general, a greater forward integration is preferred when (1) the operation is large enough to spread out the overhead costs of owning and maintaining infrastructure and training and supervising employees, (2) an inability to enforce contractual obligations on outside intermediaries or some other need for greater control of the sales process requires a strong presence in the host country, or (3) sales of a service usually require a presence in the country earlier than would otherwise be considered.

A number of typical entry approaches and the sales management concerns each raises are presented in Exhibit 15–2.

Low-Involvement Options

Selling through an Export Management Company (EMC) or an Export Trading Company (ETC) is considered a low-involvement approach to international sales. **Export management companies (EMCs)**, in general, serve the needs of their clients in entering a market or sourcing goods from a market. They are characterized by their "service" nature and efforts to interact with and meet the needs of the exporter client. Many EMCs have specific expertise in selecting markets abroad and finding customers due to their language capabilities, previous business experience in the country, or a network of their business contacts. The EMC works with an exporter in one of two ways. First, the EMC may act as an agent distributor performing marketing services for the exporter client, primarily responsible for developing foreign business and sales strategies and estab-

[1]Saul Kline, Gary L. Frazier, and Victor J. Roth, "A Transaction Cost Analysis Model of Channel Integration in International Markets," *Journal of Marketing Research*, 27 (May 1990), pp. 196–208.

EXHIBIT 15–2
DEGREE OF INVOLVEMENT AND SALES MANAGEMENT ISSUES

Degree of Involvement	Examples	Description	Sales Management Concerns
Limited foreign involvement and visibility	Export Management Companies (EMC), Export Trading Companies (ETC), direct exporting, licensing	• Concerned with contract for sales from the U.S. • No sales force or representatives abroad • Little or no control over foreign marketing process	• Goals of the company may not take precedence • Low foreign image and stability • Impossibility of training sales force
Local management and sales force	Piggybacking, selling through chains	• Little attempt to make foreign sales imitate U.S. sales culture. May "borrow" a sales force or sell via direct contracts from abroad with multidistributor outlets	• Ineffective customs (lack of influence) • Low product knowledge • Control (trust, commitment) • Poor communications
Expatriate management and local sales force (mixed)	Selling through chains with locals, direct selling with locals	• Expatriates oversee sales regions, lead training	• Perceptions of equality and fairness • Cultural interactions
Heavy to complete expatriate sales force	Traveling global sales force, high technology experts	• Client-by-client sales by expatriate sales force	• Lack of local understanding of insiders and market workings • High cost • Difficulty in recruiting expatriates • Country limits on expatriates or rules, such as taxes, which vary depending on foreign presence

lishing contact abroad. For this prospecting role, the EMC earns its income from a commission on the products it sells on the exporter's behalf. Second, the EMC may alternatively act as a merchant distributor who purchases products from the domestic exporter, takes title, sells the product in its own name, and consequently assumes all trading risks. The domestic exporter selling directly to the merchant EMC receives its money without having to deal with the complexities and trading risks in the international market. On the other hand, the exporter is less likely to build its own international experience. Many inexperienced exporters use EMCs services mainly to test the international arena, with some desire to become direct participants once a foreign customer base has been established. This can cause conflict between the interests of the EMC and those of the client exporter.

Export trading companies (ETCs) are usually large conglomerates that import, export, countertrade, invest, and manufacture in the global arena. The ETC can purchase products, act as a distributor abroad, or offer services. Mitsubishi, Mitsui, Sumitomo, and Marubeni, among others, are major examples of an ETC, which are known in Japan as *sogoshosha* (general trading companies).[2] ETCs utilize their vast size to benefit from economies of scale in shipping and distribution. In the United States, the Export Trading Company Act of 1982 authorized an exemption from antitrust laws for ETCs.[3] The intent was to improve the export performance of small and medium-sized companies by allowing them joint participation with banks in an ETC. ETCs offer the exporting company a stable, known distributor, but they do not offer the exporting company much control over or knowledge about the international sales process.

Licensing also represents a low-involvement approach to foreign sales. The company licenses its product or technology abroad and allows the contracting foreign company to coordinate the production and foreign distribution of the product.

Limited involvement approaches to international market entry simplify sales management greatly by reducing it to a predominantly domestic activity. There is little need to recruit, train, supervise, or evaluate a foreign or expatriate sales force. However, companies that follow a limited involvement approach sacrifice the benefits that hiring and training their own sales force can provide. These benefits include the ability to motivate and monitor the sales force and to train them to better serve the customer, the customer loyalty that a dedicated sales force can generate, and the perception of permanence and commitment that a dedicated sales force conveys. Many foreign companies look for such an indication of stability and commitment when selecting suppliers.

Mid-level involvement approaches to foreign sales are those approaches in which the company controls some portion of the distribution process. Thus, the company must employ some management or sales force abroad. This work force may be either predominantly host country employees or it may include a large share of expatriates. In either case, the company will deal face to face with the foreign culture, and intercultural communication becomes a significant issue. Training can help reduce misunderstandings and miscommunications, and can provide both sides with tools to understand the perspectives of the others. For example, training helps the local salespeople better understand the company's policies by reviewing its history and goals. And training also helps the expatriates understand the local market by reviewing the norms of business within their industry and country.

The choice of whether to rely on expatriate involvement is not an easy one. Without expatriate involvement, the company might decide it is difficult to control the sales process, even though it owns part of the process. With expatriate involvement, local nationals may envy the expatriates' higher levels of pay or resent the limitations on their career opportunities with the company.

High involvement approaches are those in which the company substantially controls the foreign distribution channels. The company may own warehouses to store products. The company may own outlets where the products are sold, and it may manage a large, dedicated sales force abroad. Typically, if a U.S. company is highly involved in a foreign country, at least some of that presence will be expa-

[2]Alan T. Shao, "The Future of Sogo Shosha in a Global Economy," *International Marketing Review*, 10 (December 1993), pp. 37–55.
[3]Daniel C. Bello and Nicholas C. Williamson, "The American Export Trading Company: Designing A New International Marketing Institution," *Journal of Marketing*, 49 (Fall 1985), pp. 60–69.

triates. For some companies only the top officer abroad is an expatriate. For others the expatriate presence is much stronger.

The benefits of controlling distribution include the ability to recruit, train, and supervise a foreign sales force that can best represent the company abroad. However, controlling distribution requires that the sales volume be large enough to justify the costs, and it also requires enough experience to avoid costly errors.

Role of Foreign Governments

At the time the company is considering its entry strategy, it should take into consideration foreign government rules and practices. Many host country governments design regulations to protect local firms from international competition and ensure that local citizens benefit from experience in management positions at international companies. Thus, governments limit the number of international companies they allow to sell in the market, and they require that foreign companies fill a large number of positions with local citizens. Even the United States follows such practices. The U.S. Immigration and Naturalization Service does not let foreign managers enter the United States to work when it believes that there are U.S. citizens capable of performing the same jobs. Foreign countries often dictate who can enter, for how long, and for what jobs. These requirements may determine which entry strategy makes sense for a company.

A second issue in deciding the entry approach is the role expected of companies as "corporate citizens" in the country. If a company sets up a complete sales and distribution subsidiary, it may be expected to build local infrastructure or support local politicians or take part in local training initiatives. Such considerations will weigh in on the choice of the sales approach.

CULTURAL CONSIDERATIONS

◆ ◆ ◆ ◆ ◆ ◆

Personal Selling

At the level of **personal selling** there is little true *international* selling. The sales task tends to take place on a national basis. Generally, salespeople carry out the majority of their sales within one country—probably even within one region or area of a country. A salesperson selling big-ticket items, such as airplanes or dam construction, may sell to many countries. But even then, each sale is a sale within one country, and the entire sales process takes place in one country. Further, despite growing "international sales," salespeople typically work only in one region. Even in the European Union (EU), for example, where close borders and similar economies might encourage salespeople to work over larger areas, personal selling activities still remain bound mostly to a country or a region. Thus, an analysis of *international* personal selling is a study of how differences in culture impact the forms, rules, and norms for personal selling within each country.

Personal selling is predominantly a personal activity. It requires that the salesperson understand the needs and wants of the customer. The salesperson must understand local customs well enough to be accepted. And the salesperson must be able to form relationships with the customers. Do customers require a close, supportive relationship where the salesperson regularly checks up on them and knows the names of relatives? Does the customer expect favors to "lubricate

An Avon sales representative selling to a customer in a rural area in São Paulo, Brazil. This local sales rep has good personal knowledge of this rural community and customers.

the process"? Each culture has different norms for the process of selling and buying.[4]

Throughout this chapter, we refer to the need to adapt sales and management techniques to the local culture to be successful.[5] It would be wonderful if a diagram were available that could help managers plot the appropriate solutions for each country. Although such a diagram is too much to hope for, we can take a look at some common generalizations and categorizations of cultural traits and think how they might affect our sales approach. We must take care, though, not to imply that any culture can be described accurately in a few words or categories.

Cultural Generalization

As an example of a cultural generalization with both helpful insights and misleading oversights, consider the foreign view of Germans. Germans are typically viewed as scientifically exacting and industrious people. We might therefore approach sales in Germany by building a small core of technically trained, independent sales agents. But if we think Germans look at work the same way Americans do, we will be misguided! The typical German manufacturing work week is only thirty hours. Also, Germans jealously guard their free time and show little interest in working more to earn more.[6]

We must also be careful not to group people from what may appear to us as very similar cultures, but who consider themselves, and react to situations, in a very distinct manner. Consider, for example, South Korea and Japan. We may think that Koreans would be accustomed to the same bottom-up, consensual decision-making approach the Japanese are known for. Korean workers, however, tend to work

---

[4]Bruce Money, "The Influence of World-of-Mouth Referrel Activity on Industrial Service Customer Loyalty in an International Context," *Enhancing Knowledge Development in Marketing*, 1999 American Marketing Association Educators' Proceedings, Summer 1999, p. 216.

[5]Chanthika Pornpitakpan, "The Effects of Cultural Adaptation on Business Relationships: Americans Selling to Japanese and Thais," *Journal of International Business Studies* 30 (Second Quarter 1999), pp. 317–38.

[6]Daniel Benjamin and Tony Horwitz, "German View: You Americans Work Too Hard—And For What?" *Wall Street Journal* (July 14, 1994), p. B1.

within a top-down, authoritarian leadership structure,[7] and require a higher level of definition in their job structure to avoid suffering from role conflict. A Korean salesperson might accept as normal a short-term position with few prospects for long-term progress, whereas a Japanese salesperson would not dream of it.[8]

Another example is the differences in the orientation of salespeople in Australia and New Zealand. Most of us tend to think that their cultures are very similar. However, salespeople in New Zealand tend to be more committed to, and generally more satisfied with, their work than their Australian counterparts. Additionally, there are differences in preferences toward compensation (Australians preferring greater security in the form of larger salary) and special incentives (New Zealanders having a much higher preference toward travel with other winners and supervisory staff).[9] In a way, salespeople in New Zealand share more similarities in their value system with their Japanese counterparts than their Australian neighbors.

These and other observations suggest that cultural generalizations may be risky even among seemingly similar countries, particularly at the operational level. As discussed in Chapters 4 and 14, one of the most widely used tools for categorizing cultures for managerial purposes is Hofstede's scale of five cultural dimensions (reproduced in Exhibit 15–3). Hofstede's scale uses many questions to determine where countries stand on each dimension.

Corporate Culture

Companies also have their own distinct **corporate cultures**. The culture at a company helps determine the norms of behavior and the mood at the workplace. This corporate culture acts in conjunction with national or country culture to set the values and beliefs that employees carry in the workplace.

The differences between the cultures of any two companies have been found to be determined significantly by the *practices* of those already in the company, especially the founders. By contrast, the differences between the cultures of companies in two countries are based more on the ingrained cultural *values* of the employees.[10] Values are learned earlier in life and are much more difficult to change than practices. Consider an example of the difference in trying to modify each. We might expect to initiate novel work practices without strong negative reactions from the employees. For example, we might ask salespeople to report to a group instead of to a boss in an effort to instill a sense of group responsibility. However, if we attempt to change procedures that are strongly rooted in the values of a country's culture, we may be asking for a negative response. Consider the troubles we might encounter if we attempted to integrate men and women in the sales force in Saudi Arabia. At the very least, we would not bring out the best the sales force has to offer.

Thus, while corporate cultures determine much about the working environment and even the success of an organization, the practices that characterize them

[7]Hak Chong Lee, "Managerial Characteristics of Korean Firms," in K. H. Chung and H. C. Lee, eds. *Korean Managerial Dynamics* (New York: Praeger, 1989), pp. 147–62.

[8]Alan J. Dubinsky, Ronald E. Michaels, Masaaki Kotabe, Chae Un Lim, and Hee-Cheol Moon, "Influence of Role Stress on Industrial Salespeople's Work Outcomes in the United States, Japan, and Korea," *Journal of International Business Studies*, 23 (First Quarter 1992), pp. 77–99.

[9]William H. Murphy, "Hofstede's National Culture as a Guide for Sales Practices across Countries: The Case of a MNC's Sales Practices in Australia and New Zealand," *Australian Journal of Management*, 24 (June 1999), pp. 37–58.

[10]Geert Hofstede, Bram Neuijen, Denise Daval Ohayv, and Geert Sanders, "Measuring Organizational Cultures: A Qualitative and Quantitative Study Across Twenty Cases," *Administrative Science Quarterly*, 35 (1990), pp. 286–316.

EXHIBIT 15–3
FIVE CULTURAL DIMENSIONS

Dimension	Definition	Examples
Power Distance	The concentration of power (physical and intellectual capabilities, power, and wealth) in certain groups and the acceptance of it	High power distance: Korea, India, Japan, Mexico Low power distance: Australia, United States, Germany
Individualism vs. Collectivism	The importance of the individual vs. the group; or the pursuit of self-interests vs. subordination to group interests (i.e., "I" vs. "we" orientation)	High individualism: United States, Australia, Great Britain, Canada Low individualism: Japan, Venezuela, China, Pakistan, Thailand, Mexico
Masculinity vs. Femininity	The need for achievement, assertiveness, and material success vs. the need for relationships and modesty (Masculine cultures have segregated roles, think big is beautiful, and need to show off. Feminine cultures care more for quality of life and environment than money.)	Feminine: Sweden, France, Netherlands Masculine: Japan, Mexico, Britain, Germany
Uncertainty Avoidance	Extent of ability to cope with uncertainty about the future without stress	High uncertainty avoidance: Japan, France, Mexico Low uncertainty avoidance: United States, Hong Kong, Great Britain
Long-Term Orientation	Values oriented toward the future, thrift, and perseverance	Long-term orientation: Hong Kong, Japan Short-term orientation: United States, Great Britain, Germany

Source: Geert H. Hofstede, *Cultures and Organizations: Software of the Mind* (New York: McGraw-Hill 1991).

are fairly malleable. Country cultures, and more specifically, the values people build at an early age in life, also greatly influence which management practices will succeed. However, cultural values are fairly fixed—do not underestimate the importance of cultural values and people's unwillingness to change them.[11]

Myers–Briggs Type Indicator

One popular tool for characterizing people that addresses their cognitive styles is the **Myers–Briggs Type Indicator (MBTI)**. As shown in Exhibit 15–4, the MBTI is based on the following four personal dimensions: (1) extrovert versus introvert, (2) sensing versus intuitive, (3) thinking versus feeling, and (4) judging versus perceiving.

[11]Ibid.

EXHIBIT 15–4
MYERS–BRIGGS TYPE INDICATOR OF PERSONAL CHARACTERISTICS

Personal Dimension	Description
Extrovert vs. Introvert	An extrovert tends to rely on the environment for guidance, be action-oriented, sociable, and communicate with ease and frankness. An introvert tends to show a greater concern with concepts and ideas than with external events, relative detachment, and enjoyment of solitude and privacy over companionship.
Sensing vs. Intuitive	A sensing person tends to focus on immediate experience, become more realistic and practical, and develop skills such as acute powers of observation and memory for details. An intuitive person tends to value possibility and meaning more than immediate experience, and become more imaginative, theoretical, abstract, and future oriented.
Thinking vs. Feeling	A thinking person tends to be concerned with logical and impersonal decision making and principles of justice and fairness, and is strong in analytical ability and objectivity. A feeling person tends to make decisions by weighing relative values and merits of issues, be attuned to personal and group values, and be concerned with human, rather than technical, aspects of a problem.
Judging vs. Perceiving	A judging person tends to make relatively quick decisions, be well planned and organized, and seek closure. A perceiving person tends to be open to new information, not move for closure to make quick decisions, and stay adaptable and open to new events or change.

Source: Neil R. Abramson, Henry W. Lane, Hirohisa Nagai, and Haruo Takagi, "A Comparison of Canadian and Japanese Cognitive Styles: Implications for Management Interactions," *Journal of International Business Studies*, 24 (Third Quarter 1993), pp. 575–87.

Using this scale, Abramsom, Lane, Nagai, and Takagi[12] found significant cognitive distinctions between Canadian and Japanese MBA students. The English-speaking Canadian students preferred intuition, judgment, and thinking, whereas the Japanese students preferred sensing, perceiving, and thinking, but were more feeling-oriented than the Canadian students. In summary, the English-speaking Canadians displayed a logical and impersonal, or objective, style that subordinates the human element. The Japanese displayed a more feeling style, which emphasized the human element in problem solving—such as being sympathetic and building trust in human relations. English-speaking Canadians have a tendency to seek fast decisions and rush to closure on data collection. The Japanese were found to resist fast decision making because of a preference to obtain large amounts of information. Another recent study by Cannon, Doney, and Mullen also

[12]Neil R. Abramson, Henry W. Lane, Hirohisa Nagai, and Haruo Takagi, "A Comparison of Canadian and Japanese Cognitive Styles: Implications for Management Interactions," *Journal of International Business Studies*, 24 (Third Quarter 1993), pp. 575–87.

shows that French-speaking Canadians in Quebec, unlike the English-speaking Canadians, are a bit more similar to Japanese in terms of their emphasis on trust building.[13] Indeed, Japanese salespeople, who emphasize trust building, use more word-of-mouth referrals in consummating sales than American counterparts.[14]

Such differences in style must be taken into consideration whenever two cultures interact. In international sales, cross-cultural interaction takes place between the home office and the subsidiary, between expatriate managers and the sales force, or between an expatriate salesperson and the customer. If the cultural norms and cognitive styles of both sides are more clearly understood, it will help reduce misconceptions and miscommunications.

◆ ◆ ◆ ◆ ◆ ◆ IMPACT OF CULTURE ON SALES MANAGEMENT AND PERSONAL SELLING PROCESS

In general, human resource practices of multinational corporations (MNCs) closely follow the local practices of the country in which they operate.[15] These human resource practices include time off, benefits, gender composition, training, executive bonuses, and participation of employees in management. However, human resource practices also depend on the strategy desired, the culture of the company, and even the country from which the company originated.

Thus, while we can say that the sales management process should adapt to the local environment,[16] we acknowledge the difficult give and take involved in adapting a U.S. company's culture and procedures with the sales and management practices of a foreign country:

> When host-country standards seem substandard from the perspective of the home country (manager), the manager faces a dilemma. Should the MNC implement home country standards and so seem to lack respect for the cultural diversity and national integrity of the host (country)? Or, should the MNC implement seemingly less optimal host country standards?[17]

One good exemplary hiring policy is presented in Global Perspective 15–2.

---

[13]Joseph P. Cannon, Patricia M. Doney, and Michael R. Mullen, "A Cross-Cultural Examination of the Effects of Trust and Supplier Performance on Long-Term Buyer-Supplier Relationships," *Enhancing Knowledge Development in Marketing*, 1999 American Marketing Association Educators' Proceedings, Summer 1999, p. 101.

[14]R. Bruce Money, Mary C. Gilly, and John L. Graham, "Explorations of National Culture and Word-of-Mouth Referral Behavior in the Purchase of Industrial Services in the United States and Japan," *Journal of Marketing*, 62 (October 1998), pp. 76–87.

[15]Philip M. Rosenzweig, and Ritin Nohria. "Influences on Human Resource Management Practices in Multinational Corporations," *Journal of International Business Studies*, 25 (Second Quarter 1994), pp. 229–51.

[16]A recent study proves that when management practices are adapted to the national culture of a country in which the company operates, its financial performance tends to improve. See Karen L. Newman and Stanley D. Nollen, "Culture and Congruence: The Fit between Management Practices and National Culture," *Journal of International Business Studies*, 27 (Fourth Quarter 1996), pp. 753–79.

[17]Thomas Donaldson, "Multinational Decision-Making: Reconciling International Norms," *Journal of Business Ethics*, 4 (1985), pp. 357–66.

❖ ❖

$\mathcal{G}$LOBAL PERSPECTIVE 15-2

TGI FRIDAY'S, INC.

In setting up overseas, the restaurant chain TGI Friday's follows a key series of guidelines:

- Choose a local development partner to guide through government obstacles, local hiring practices, and on-site business hurdles.

- Concentrate on hiring fun employees who "fit" the company's image—"fun" people willing to sing "Happy Birthday" to a customer.

- Entrust the entire operation to the overseas management after business practices and philosophy have been completely transferred.

- In seeking new overseas managers, look for foreign nationals on assignment or pursuing studies in the United States and offer them an opportunity to return home, bringing back with them the knowledge they have acquired about U.S. culture and business and service standards. But just as important, they are experts in the traditions, ethics, and ways of life of the customers (we) want to serve in foreign markets.

An example of these guidelines put into practice is TGI Friday's expansion into England. Its success can be attributed to the chain's strong local partner, Whitbread PLC, and a successful initial launch in the city of Birmingham.

Source: Mark Hamstra, "Operators Bullish About Opportunities in Overseas Markets, Despite Turmoil," *Nation's Restaurant News* (October 5, 1998), p. 86.

The process of sales force management provides a framework for a closer look at the challenges involved in adapting management practices to a new culture. Sales force management consists of the following six steps:[18]

1. Setting sales force objectives
2. Designing sales force strategy
3. Recruiting and selecting salespeople
4. Training salespeople
5. Supervising salespeople
6. Evaluating salespeople

Setting sales force objectives is dependent on having already determined the larger, strategic objectives of the company. A company may have the strategic objective of adding value by providing the customer with more understanding of a product's use. Or the company may want to enter the market as the low-cost provider. Once such strategic objectives are decided upon, the company can evaluate what roles the sales force will play in reaching these goals. These roles are the sales force objectives. They explicitly state *what* the sales force will be asked to do, whether it is solving customer complaints or pushing for publicity of the product.

Sales force objectives will then influence much of the rest of the sales management process. If a sales force objective is to expand market share, then the sales

Sales Force Objectives

---

[18]See Philip Kotler, *Marketing Management*, 9th ed. (Englewood Cliffs, NJ: Prentice-Hall, 1997), pp. 685–704.

force will be designed, recruited, trained, supervised, and evaluated using that objective as a guideline. Sales force objectives will guide how much sales force time and effort will be required for digging up leads versus working with existing customers, or how much effort will be placed on new products versus older products, or how much effort will be spent on customer satisfaction compared to sales volume.

Setting international sales force objectives will require a similar approach used to determine domestic agendas. In fact, many "international" sales force issues are really local issues in a foreign country. However, setting the best international sales force objectives will depend not only on the company goals, but also on an analysis of the culture and values of the country it is entering. The company might use a standardized approach for all countries, or it might customize its sales force management approach from the ground up for each country. Most companies will probably customize some aspects of each country's sales force objectives, but will follow previously held beliefs about the purpose of the sales force to decide most objectives. Once the objectives are known, the company can begin designing the structure of the proposed sales force.

Sales Force Strategy

With the sales force's objectives set, the company can concentrate on the strategies needed to achieve those objectives. Sales force strategy addresses the structure, size, and compensation of the sales force.

The structure determines the physical positioning and responsibilities of each salesperson. A company selling one product to a dispersed client base might consider a *territorial sales force*, with each salesperson responsible for a particular area, and reporting up the line to regional sales managers. Another company, with numerous, unrelated, complex products, might consider a *product sales force* structure, where each salesperson sells only one product or product line, even when selling to a single customer. A third company, which requires close contact with its customers to keep up on customer needs and build tight relationships, might employ a *customer sales force* structure, where account managers are responsible for particular clients. Each of these approaches has advantages and disadvantages. Internationally, choosing the most appropriate sales force strategy will require analyzing many of the same considerations as it does domestically. However, additional considerations might arise concerning the lack of capable local salespeople, the cultural expectations of clients, and the dramatically increased costs of maintaining expatriate personnel abroad.

The size of the sales force depends on the sales structure. The company often calculates how many salespeople are needed by determining how many visits or calls each type of customer should receive and how many salespeople will be needed to make the necessary number of visits. In a foreign culture, customers' distinct expectations may modify the calculations. Although a client in the United States might be satisfied with buying large quantities of a product and hearing from the salesperson every six months, the foreign client might expect a salesperson to be in regular contact and might want to buy smaller quantities more regularly. Such considerations will impact the sales force size.

Sales force compensation is the chief form of motivation for salespeople. However, companies do not pay sales forces equally in all countries. The purchasing power of the "same" quantity of money may not be the same. And more importantly, pay expectations, or the "going rate," varies dramatically from country to country. The company must carefully consider the social perceptions of its compensation scale. A commission-based compensation may not motivate salespeople in some other countries. A salary scale with large rewards for success may be viewed as unfair. The company must evaluate the impact the compensation system will have on the employees, and then consider what impact the system will also have on the final customer. The pay system must motivate salespeople to leave customers with the appropriate, desired perceptions of the company.

In order to successfully recruit and select salespeople, the company must understand what it wants in its salespeople and know how to find and attract people with the necessary skills. The first decision is whether the company will recruit from the local, foreign labor force for the jobs it is creating or whether it will fill them by sending U.S. employees overseas. The company may find a strong cultural bias against salespeople in the local market and find it difficult to recruit the necessary talent. Even if it can recruit "talented" people, the company may not clearly know what skills and character traits will work the best in the unfamiliar culture. If the company tries to recruit employees at home, it may have a tough time convincing salespeople or managers with the necessary skills to take the time off from the "fast track" at home.

Recruiting and Selecting

Complicating the search for talent is that the desired skills and characteristics are not as clear as it first appears. Employers may base their expectations for salespeople on U.S. standards. For example, the employer may look for candidates with an outgoing attitude. However, in some cultures it requires a quieter, more patient approach to truly maximize sales. The skills required for success as a salesperson depend on the culture in which the sales take place.

Finally, the employer must consider the strong influences of tribal, religious, or other group relations within a country. A Hindu might not want to make purchases from a Muslim. English companies might do better to hire Irish salespeople to make sales in Ireland. History may give one group a distinct advantage, especially where they have become accepted as a strong business force. For example, the Parsees in India manage an unusually large portion of the nation's business, and Chinese salespeople, the descendants of the Chinese merchant clan, are prominent throughout Asia.[19] A wise sales manager will look for and recruit a sales force that takes advantage of each country's natural distinctions.

One way for the company to accelerate the difficult process of building a sales force from scratch is to establish a joint venture with or acquire a local company that already has a functional sales force. For example, when Merck wanted to expand its pharmaceutical business in Japan, it acquired Banyu Pharmaceutical instead of building its subsidiary and distribution channel from scratch. Merck had immediate access to Banyu's field sales force of more than 1,000. In Japan, where personal relationships probably weigh in importance more than the quality of products per se, personal selling is all the more critical in relationship-building and -maintaining purposes. Similarly, when Wal-Mart wanted to expand into Europe, its first move was to buy out Wertkauf, a German national chain store, in order to have instant distribution channel members working for it and supply channels already established, as well as a beachhead for the rest of Europe.[20]

[19]See an excellent treatise, Min Chen, *Asian Management Systems: Chinese, Japanese and Korean Styles of Business* (London: Routledge, 1995), pp. 69–83.
[20]Garth Alexander, "Wal-Mart Weighs Up Plan to Invade UK," *Sunday London Times* (March 7, 1999).

Training   Most sales training takes place in the country where the salespeople reside. The company determines how much technical, product knowledge, company history and culture, or other training its sales force requires. IBM puts its sales force through an initial training of thirteen months and expects all salespeople to spend 15 percent of their time each year in additional training.[21] International training can require trainers who speak the appropriate foreign languages. It may require building training facilities in the host country.

An additional consideration of international sales training is adapting the training to the needs of the local market. For example, a computer salesperson in Japan may need an exceptionally detailed technical understanding of the product to make the sale, whereas in Paraguay a salesperson may benefit more from training about company values and warranty procedures. The training the sales force receives must reflect cultural differences in purchasing patterns, values, and perspective of the selling process.

For some high-technology or highly standardized global products, sales training may be held at the international or regional level. Training for such products may require expensive training tools or materials, and is probably more similar across countries than training in sales techniques, so it makes more sense to centralize training. IBM, for example, has a European training center with average attendance of 5,000 people a day. Another good example is McDonald's Hamburger University in the outskirts of Chicago, where all franchisees from around the world have to receive centralized training.

Although international companies often benefit in the local market by offering their employees better training than local competitors, they face the problem of protecting their investment in their employees. Companies with well-trained sales forces are often "raided" for employees by national companies. In order to protect their investments, the MNCs must offer higher compensation and better promotion opportunities than their competitors.

Supervising   Supervising the sales force means directing and motivating the sales force to fulfill the company's objectives, and it means providing the resources that allow them to do so. The company may set norms concerning how often a salesperson should call each category of customer, and how much of his or her time the salesperson should spend on various activities. The company may motivate the salesperson by establishing a supportive, opportunity-filled organizational climate, or by establishing sales quotas or positive incentives for sales. The company often provides the salesperson with tools, such as portable computers or research facilities, so as to provide better chances to achieve his or her goals. International sales management addresses how each of these supervising approaches will be received by the sales force, and what the cultural implications are. For example, cultures that cherish group identity over individuality will probably not respond well to a sales contest as a motivator.

Motivation and Compensation.   Financial compensation is one of the key motivators for employees in all cultures. However, successful sales programs make use of a wide variety of motivators. The sales manager will want to adapt the incentive structure to best meet local desires and regulations. The use of commissions in motivating salespeople is not publicly acceptable in many countries. Commissions reinforce the negative image of the salesperson benefiting from the sale, with no

---

[21]"How IBM Teaches Techies to Sell," *Fortune* (June 6, 1988), pp. 141–46.

regard for the purchaser's well-being. Salary increases may substitute for commissions to motivate salespeople to consistently perform highly. However, under certain circumstances, large salary discrepancies between employees are also not acceptable. Strong unions may tie a company's hands in setting salaries. Or the "collectivist" culture of a country like Japan may not accept that one person should earn substantially more than another in the same position. Koreans, for example, are used to working under conditions where compensation is not directly contingent on performance, but rather, on seniority. When financial rewards are not acceptable, the company must rely more heavily on nonfinancial rewards, such as recognition, titles, and perquisites for motivation.

Foreign travel is another reward employed by international companies. For example, Electrolux rewards winning sales teams in Asia with international trips. When necessary, companies can combine an international trip with training and justify it as an investment in top salespeople.

Management Style. Management style refers to the approach the manager takes in supervising employees. The manager may define the employee's roles explicitly and require a standardized sales pitch. Or the manager may set broad, general goals that allow salespeople to develop their own skills. A number of studies have found that the best management approach varies by culture and country. For example, Dubinsky et al.[22] found that role ambiguity, role conflict, job satisfaction, and organizational commitment were just as relevant to salespeople in Japan and Korea as in the United States, and that role conflict and ambiguity have deleterious effects on salespeople in any of the countries. However, specific remedies for role ambiguity, such as greater job formalization (or more hierarchical power, defined rules, and supervision), have a distinct effect on the salespeople in different countries.

One fair generalization is that greater formalization invokes negative responses from the sales force in countries in which the power distance is low and the individualism is high (such as in the United States). And greater formalization invokes positive responses from the sales force in countries in which the power distance is high and the individualism is low (such as in India).[23]

Ethical Perceptions. Culture, or nationality, also influences salespeople's beliefs about the ethics of common selling practices and the need for company policies to guide those practices. Why is this important? Salespeople need to stay within the law, of course. But more importantly, in order to maintain the respect of customers, salespeople must know what is ethically acceptable in a culture. For example, in the United States, giving a bribe is tantamount to admitting that your product cannot compete without help. However, in many cultures, receiving a bribe is seen as a privilege of having attained a position of influence. An understanding of the ethical norms in a culture will help the company maintain a clean image and will also help the company create policies that keep salespeople out of the tense and frustrating situations where they feel they are compromising their ethical standards.

As an example of differences in ethical perceptions, consider the results of a study in which, salespeople in Korea, Japan, and the United States were presented

---

[22]Dubinsky et al., "Influence of Role Stress . . . ," pp. 77–99.

[23]Sanjeev Agarwal, "Influence of Formalization on Role Stress, Organizational Commitment, and Work Alienation of Salespersons: A Cross-National Comparative Study," *Journal of International Business Studies*, 24 (Fourth Quarter 1993), pp. 715–40.

with written examples of "questionable" sales situations:[24] Examples of the situations used include the following:

- Having different prices for buyers for which you are the sole supplier
- Attempting to circumvent the purchasing department and reach other departments directly when it will help sales
- Giving preferential treatment to customers who management prefers or who are also good suppliers

The salespeople were asked to rate to what extent it was unethical to take part in the suggested activity. The results indicated that in general, U.S. salespeople felt the situations posed less ethical problems than did salespeople from Japan and Korea. Another interesting finding of the study—the assumption that Japanese "gift-giving" would extend into the sales realm—was found to be untrue. In fact, Japanese felt it was more of an ethical problem to give free gifts to a purchaser than did U.S. salespeople. For Koreans, however, gift-giving was less of an issue.

Paradoxically, U.S. salespeople indicated that they wanted their companies to have more policies explicitly addressing these ethical questions. Why? Apparently, salespeople in the United States feel more comfortable when the ethical guidelines are explicitly stated, whereas in other countries (Korea and Japan here), the cultural exchange of living in a more community-oriented society provides the necessary guidelines.

Evaluating   Evaluating salespeople includes requiring that salespeople justify their efforts and provide the company with information about their successes, failures, expenses, and time. Evaluations are important to motivate the sales force, to correct problems, and to reward and promote those who best help the company achieve its goals. Two types of evaluations are common: *quantitative* evaluations and *qualitative* evaluations. Examples of quantitative evaluations are comparisons of sales, of sales percents, or increases in sales. Examples of qualitative evaluations include tests of the knowledge and manner of the salesperson. Since net profit is often the company's primary objective, evaluations should serve to promote long-term net profits. In some foreign cultures, however, evaluations may be seen as an unnecessary waste of time, or they may invade the sense of privacy of salespeople.

Evaluations help management keep up on sales progress, and they help employees receive feedback and set goals. International sales force evaluations must take into consideration the culture's built-in ability to provide feedback to employees. For example, in Japan the "collectivist" nature of the culture may provide the salesperson with much more sense of performance feedback than the "individualistic" culture in the United States would. Thus, it makes sense that U.S. sales managers use more regular, short-term performance evaluations than Japanese sales managers in order to provide their sales force with more feedback.[25]

---

[24]Alan J. Dubinsky, Marvin A. Jolson, Masaaki Kotabe, and Chae Un Lim, "A Cross-National Investigation of Industrial Salespeople's Ethical Perceptions," *Journal of International Business Studies*, 22 (Fourth Quarter 1991), pp. 651–70.

[25]Ueno Susumu, and Uma Sekaran, "The Influence of Culture on Budget Control Practices in the U.S. and Japan: An Empirical Study," *Journal of International Business Studies*, 23 (Fourth Quarter 1992), pp. 659–74.

Evaluations in international sales management can provide useful information for making international comparisons. Such comparisons can help management identify countries where sales are below average and refine the training, compensation, or sales force strategy as necessary to improve performance.

EXPATRIATES

Most companies with a sales force abroad will, at the very least, send a few expatriates abroad as operations begin in a new country. **Expatriates** are home-country personnel sent overseas to manage local operations in the foreign market. The general trend of the last decade has been a decreasing use of expatriate managers overseas and an increasing reliance on local foreign talent.[26] This trend reflects the increasingly international perspective of MNCs, increasing competence of foreign managers, and the relatively increasing competitive disadvantage of the cost of maintaining Americans abroad. Despite the relative decline, there are more employees than ever involved in international assignments due to the increase in international sales and production.[27] Expatriates have a number of advantages over foreign nationals for companies that sell their products internationally.

Better Communication. Expatriates understand the home office, its politics, and its priorities. They are intimately familiar with the products being sold and with previously successful sales techniques. Expatriates may be able to rely on personal relationships with home office management, which increases trust on both sides of the border and may give the expatriate an ability to achieve things that a third-country national or a host-country national could not achieve. With an expatriate abroad, communications with the home country will be easier and more precise due to the groundwork of cultural and corporate understanding. And the expatriate will give the home office the sense that they have someone in place who they can be sure understands the company intent and expectations.

Development of Talent. Sending employees to a foreign country provides the company with another advantage that hiring foreign locals may not provide: The company develops future managers and executives who can later use their international perspective in management. The expatriate executive will need to understand the workings of the home office, as well as the cultural distinctions of doing business in that country. He or she will weave personal contacts abroad with an understanding of production techniques.[28] As a Whirlpool Corporation executive was quoted saying, "The CEO in the twenty-first century must have multienvironment, multicountry, multifunctional, and maybe even multicompany, multiindustry experience."

Advantages of Using Expatriates

[26]Stephen J. Kobrin, "Expatriate Reduction and Strategic Control in American Multinational Corporations," *Human Resource Management*, 27 (Spring 1988), pp. 63–75.
[27]Michael Harvey, "Empirical Evidence of Recurring International Compensation Problems," *Journal of International Business Studies*, 24 (Fourth Quarter 1993), pp. 785–99.
[28]Amanda Bennett, "The Chief Executives in Year 2000 Will Be Experienced Abroad," *Wall Street Journal* (February 27, 1990), p. A1.

Indeed, of the eight members of Whirlpool's executive committee, five had international experience, and four of those have had international postings within the last three years.[29] Thus, by sending their most promising rising stars overseas, companies are sowing the seeds to harvest the next generation of executives.

Difficulties of Sending Expatriates Abroad

Cross-Cultural Training. As with so many other complex situations in life, a little shared understanding goes a long way. In the case of the expatriate, training can significantly help in understanding the cultural differences of the foreign country. Such "cultural sensitivity training" used to be overlooked by U.S. companies; expatriates were expected to "pick it up as they go."

However, the impact of cultural misunderstandings can be large. As a result, **cross-cultural training** is on the rise in recent years because more globally oriented companies moving fast-track executives overseas want to curb the cost of failed expatriate stints. A premature expatriate return has been estimated to cost as much as $1.2 million.[30] The total cost of expatriate failures has been estimated to cost nearly $2.5 billion a year for U.S. corporations.[31] These figures do not include hidden or indirect costs such as lost business opportunities, damage to the organization's reputation, potential damage to customers, suppliers, and even host government officials.

Now nearly half of major U.S. companies provide formal cross-cultural training programs before foreign transfers, compared with a mere 10 percent a decade ago. On average, a cross-cultural training program costs $3,000 to $6,000 per expatriate-to-be. Although cultural orientation and foreign language training are two of the most important parts of the cross-cultural training program, companies need cultural orientation (including culture, history, and background of country) more than foreign-language training.[32]

Once the expatriate is overseas, training becomes more difficult to provide, but it is even more important. The expatriates are not in constant contact with colleagues, and may not be picking up the newest technology in their company's field. They may be missing out on important policy or procedural changes that the company is undertaking. Ongoing training, whether in country or back in the United States, can make a huge difference in the success of an overseas assignment.

It is advised that the more different the culture into which people are venturing, the more specific and rigorous the training needs to be, and the more the training needs to incorporate such experiential tactics such as simulations and role plays aimed at specific differences.[33]

However, the expatriates must recognize that within a two- to four-year average time frame abroad they will never internalize enough of the local culture to overcome all social and communication concerns. Even with appropriate training,

---

[29]"GE Redesigns Rungs of Career Ladder," *Wall Street Journal* (Match 15, 1993),p. B1, B7

[30]Donald J. McNerney, "Global Staffing: Some Common Problems and Solutions," *HR Focus* 73 (June 1996), pp. 1–5.

[31]Maali H. Ashamalla, "International Human Resource Management Practices: The Challenge of Expatriation," *Competitiveness Review*, 8 (2) (1998), pp. 54–65.

[32]Ibid.

[33]J. Stewart Black, Mark Mendenhall, and Gary Oddou, "Toward a Comprehensive Model of International Adjustment. An Integration of Multiple Theoretical Perspectives," *Academy of Management Review*, 16 (April 1991), pp. 291–317.

the expatriates are the product of their home culture. They will eat with a fork when a hand is more polite, shake on a deal and thereby show their lack of faith, or require that a contract with all possible legal contingencies spelled out be signed in triplicate when honor and trust dictate that the deal go through on a shared local drink. These may appear small social problems, but such social problems may keep the expatriate out of important deals. As Black and Porter[34] noted in their article title, "a successful manager in Los Angeles may not succeed in Hong Kong." The expatriate may find, after some time, that the best place to make sales is not his or her client's offices but sitting at the bar watching soccer (or better known as football outside the United States) with other executives.

Motivation. Motivating expatriates to accept and succeed at positions abroad requires a combination of carefully planned policies and incentives. Appropriate policies help make the prospects of going overseas attractive before, during, and after it takes place. Expatriates often express concern that their stints abroad not hinder their career progress. Companies should set up and publicize career paths that reward and make use of skills expatriates acquire overseas. Additionally, while the expatriate is overseas, regular communication with the home office will help allay fears that career progress will not be hindered by "out of sight, out of mind."[35]

Compensation. According to General Motors, the average cost of sending an American executive and his or her family overseas for a three-year assignment is between $750,000 an $1 million above and beyond his or her salary.[36] As presented in Exhibit 15–5, estimates are that the cost of sending a home country employee abroad is, on average, 2.5 to 3 times his or her base salary.[37] Compensation packages may include overseas premiums, housing allowances, cost-of-living allowances, tax equalizations, repatriation allowances, all-expense-paid vacations, and performance-based bonuses. Yet despite this, one study found that 77 percent of expatriates were dissatisfied with their expatriation salaries and benefits and their international compensation packages in general. In fact, more than 25 percent were contemplating leaving their company.[38] How much should overseas assignments pay?

One approach has been to pay expatriates a premium for their willingness to live in adverse conditions. Such special "hardship packages" can cause problems, however. Overseas employees may notice the discrepancy in remuneration between expatriates, local nationals, and third-country nationals. An expatriate sales manager in Japan may be motivated by an incentive system through which he or she would earn a higher salary for stellar performance. However, such an individual approach would not sit well with Japanese colleagues, who subscribe to a collective approach that does not favor standing out from others of similar seniority.

---

[34]J. Stewart Black and Lyman W. Porter, "Managerial Behaviors and Job Performance: A Successful Manager in Los Angeles May Not Succeed in Hong Kong," *Journal of International Business Studies*, 22 (First Quarter 1991), pp. 99–113.

[35]Thomas F. O'Boyle, "Little Benefit to Careers Seen in Foreign Stints," *Wall Street Journal* (December 11, 1989), p. B1, B4.

[36]Patrick Oster, "The Fast Track Leads Overseas," *Business Week*, November 1, 1993, pp. 64–86.

[37]Hoann Lubin, "Companies Try to Cut Subsidies for Employees," *Wall Street Journal* (December 11, 1989), p. B1.

[38]J. Stewart Black, "Returning Expatriates Feel Foreign in Their Native Land," *Personnel*, 68 (August 1991), p. 17.

EXHIBIT 15–5
THE PRICE OF AN EXPATRIATE

An employer's average first-year direct cost of sending a U.S. executive to Britain, with a $100,000 salary and a family of four:

Direct Compensation Costs	
Base salary	$100,000
Foreign assignment premium	15,000
Cost of living adjustment	21,000
Housing costs	39,000
Transfer Costs	
Relocation allowance	$5,000
Airfare to London	2,000
Moving expenses	25,000
Other Costs	
Company car	15,000
Schooling for two children	20,000
Annual home leave (four people)	4,000
U.K. personal income tax	56,000
TOTAL	$302,000

Source: Organization Resource Counselors, Inc., 1997.

Furthermore, expatriates who receive a generous compensation package while abroad may lose motivation upon returning home to a previous salary scale.[39] A more recent approach has been to consider the overseas assignment a necessary step for progress within the company, viewed more as a learning experience than as a hardship.

The company must also consider the impact of family life cycle on compensation.[40] Expatriates with spouses and children encounter higher needs abroad, including the need to make up for the loss of a spouse's income and the cost of enrolling children in private schools. A program must be flexible enough to adjust to the varying needs of different employees.

Family Discord. The typical candidate for an international assignment is married, has two school-aged children, and is expected to stay overseas for three years. In the age of two-career families, an international assignment means that a spouse may have to suspend a stateside career. Thus, many employees are reluctant to move abroad. Others who accept transfers grow frustrated as they find that their spouses cannot get jobs or even work permits abroad. Schools where English is spoken must be found, or children must learn the local language. Concerns about the safety and happiness of family members may keep the candidate from accepting an overseas position. Given such complexities, it is clear why it might be difficult to motivate typical candidates to accept an overseas stint.[41]

Unsuccessful family adjustment is the single most important reason for expatriate dissatisfaction compelling an early return home. Expatriates as well as their

[39]Harvey 1993.
[40]Harvey, pp. 785–99.
[41]Ashamalla, pp. 54–65.

family members are in crisis because of culture shock and stress. As a result, marriages break up and some people become alcoholic.

Thus, international companies try to cut costs by reducing the problems that can hurt expatriates' job satisfaction and performance. For example, AT & T has begun putting prospective expatriates through management interviews, a written test, and a self-assessment checklist of "cultural adaptability," as well as interviews with a psychologist (see Global Perspective 15–3). To help spouses find jobs abroad, Philip Morris Company hired an outplacement firm to provide career counseling and job leads.[42]

Repatriation is the return of the expatriate employee from overseas. Although efforts are being made by companies, many returning expatriates have difficulty finding good job assignments when their foreign positions end. The post-return concern that an overseas assignment can damage a career back home will discourage employees to take up a foreign position. According to one 1989 study, 65 percent of personnel managers surveyed indicated that expatriates' foreign assignments are not integrated into their overall career planning; and worse yet, 56 percent of them felt that a foreign assignment could be either detrimental to or immaterial in one's career.[43] The most recent extensive study conducted by the Conference Board in 1997 reported an equally deplorable picture. Repatriated managers in U.S. firms leave their companies at twice the rate of domestic managers without international experience. It also shows that 20 percent of repatriate

The Return of the Expatriate— Repatriation

GLOBAL PERSPECTIVE 15–3

SCREENING CANDIDATES FOR EXPATRIATION

An increasing number of companies are screening prospective expatriates and their spouses for cross-cultural adaptability. The following are some of the questions asked at AT & T.

1. Would your spouse's career be put on hold to accompany you on an international assignment? If so, how would this affect your spouse and your relationship with each other?

2. Would you enjoy the challenge of making your own way in new environments?

3. How would you feel about the need for networking and being your own advocate to secure a job upon return from your foreign assignment?

4. How willing and able are you to initiate and build new social contacts abroad?

5. Could you live without television?

6. How important is it for you to spend a significant amount of time with people of your own ethnic, racial, religious, and national background?

7. Have you ever been genuinely interested in learning about other peoples and cultures?

8. Do you like vacationing in foreign countries?

9. Do you enjoy ethnic and foreign cuisine?

10. How tolerant are you of having to wait for repairs?

Source: Adapted from Gilbert Fuchsberg, "As Costs of Overseas Assignments Climb, Firms Select Expatriates More Carefully," *Wall Street Journal* (January 9, 1992), p. B1.

---

[42]Carla Joinson, "Relocation Couseling Meets Employees' Changing Needs," *HRMagazine*, 43 (February 1998), pg. 63–70.
[43]O'Boyle, p. B1, B4.

managers leave their companies within one year after returning from overseas assignments and as high as 50 percent leave within the first three years.[44] In the past two decades, U.S. companies have failed to make any measurable improvement in their repatriation policies.

Repatriation is distinct from other forms of relocation. After an average absence of 3.5 years, expatriates themselves have changed, adopting certain values, attitudes, and habits of their host countries. And the United States has changed, politically, economically, and technologically. The results of poor handling of repatriation are poor employee performance and high employee turnover—both very costly to the organization.

Expatriates face a long list of difficulties upon returning home. Their standard of living often declines. And they often face a lack of appreciation for the knowledge they gained overseas. Without a clear use for their skills, returned expatriates often suffer from a lack of direction and purpose. New stateside assignments often do not give the repatriated employee the same responsibility, freedom, or respect that was enjoyed overseas. It is difficult to adjust to being just another middle manager at home. And poor communications with the home office while abroad leave the returnee cut off from the internal happenings and politics of the company, limiting opportunities for career growth.

Black, Gregersen, and Mendenhall[45] proposed a number of suggestions for enhancing repatriation adjustment. These include (1) post-arrival training, (2) a repatriation center to help employees reform their objectives with the company, (3) spouse adjustment assistance, (4) pre-return training, (5) increased contact with the home office while abroad, and (6) setting up a "sponsor" or partner back in the home office to keep the expatriate up to date and in touch. Pre-trip training should lay out the details for the candidate, including future training expected, help the company will provide, and, importantly, the career path that the move will help. The effort and cost of such comprehensive planning sends a strong signal of the importance of foreign assignments to expatriate candidates.

Generalizations about When Using Expatriates Is Good or Bad

Expatriates are important whenever communication with the home country office is at a premium. Communication is facilitated among managers of the same nationality.[46] Thus, the company is better off with a stronger expatriate base abroad when the overseas situation puts pressure on communications with the home office. Thus, expatriates are especially important in complex operating environments, or when elevated political risk requires constant monitoring, or when a high cultural distance separates the home and host countries. On the other hand, in very competitive environments, local nationals may provide important links to the local business community and perhaps play a key strategic role in gaining business.[47]

[44]Valerie Frazee, "Welcome Your Repatriates Home," *Workforce* (April 1997), pp. 24–28.

[45]J. Stewart Black, Hal B. Gregersen, and Mark E. Mendenhall, "Toward a Theoretical Framework of Operational Adjustment," *Journal of International Business Studies*, 23 (Fourth Quarter 1992), pp. 737–60.

[46]Nakiye Boyacigiller, "The Role of Expatriates in the Management of Interdependence, Complexity and Risk in Multinational Corporations," *Journal of International Business Studies*, 21 (Third Quarter 1990), pp. 357–81.

[47]Ibid., p. 371.

SUMMARY ✦

No matter how global a company becomes, its sales force remains the front line for the company. On the other hand, actual sales activities are truly local activities, far detached from decision making at headquarters. Particularly, in Latin European, Latin American, and Asian countries, salespeople's ability to build trust with prospective customers prior to sales is extremely important. An effective sales force management is most elusive, yet crucial in developing a coherent international marketing and distribution strategy.

Because sales activities are local activities, they tend to be strongly affected by cultural differences (e.g., shopping habit, negotiation style) around the world, making it difficult, if not impossible, for the international marketing manager to integrate overseas sales operations. Many companies rely on merchant distributors at home or sales agents in the foreign market who have more intimate knowledge of the marketplace. As sales increase, these companies begin to increase their commitment to developing their own distribution and sales force in the foreign market.

The development of an effective sales organization requires sales force objectives and sales force strategy adapted to local differences and calls for careful recruiting, training, supervising, motivating, and compensating of local salespeople. Furthermore, an increasing number of expatriate managers are sent to overseas posts to directly manage the company's local sales force. Expatriate managers function as a bridge between headquarters and local operations, and have to be culturally adaptive and versatile.

Although international assignments have increasingly become a necessary requirement for fast-track managers, cultural adaptability is not always an inborn qualification of many expatriate managers. Cross-cultural training is crucial, as failed expatriate assignments cost the company dearly in terms of lower business performance and dejected employee morale. Recently, companies have begun to develop a repatriation program to ease returned expatriates back into their stateside positions. Such a well-organized repatriation program is important to encourage managers to take up expatriate assignments.

KEY TERMS ✦

corporate culture	export management	Myers–Briggs Type	repatriation
cross-cultural training	company (EMC)	Indicator (MBTI)	*sogoshosha* (general
expatriate	export trading company	personal selling	trading company)
	(ETC)		

REVIEW QUESTIONS ✦ ✦ ✦ ✦ ✦ ✦ ✦ ✦ ✦ ✦ ✦ ✦ ✦ ✦ ✦ ✦ ✦ ✦

1. In what ways does international sales management differ from domestic sales management?

2. Discuss why mode of entry and sales management are closely related.

3. For what type of business does a company employ a traveling global sales force?

4. How might foreign government affect a company's sales force management?

5. Why is it generally considered difficult to adopt a U.S.-style commission-based sales force management in such countries as Japan and Mexico?

6. Discuss why expatriate managers are important to a parent company, despite the enormous cost of sending them overseas.

7. Suppose you are developing a cultural training program for employees to be sent to overseas posts. What courses would you include in your two-week program? Why?

DISCUSSION QUESTIONS ✦ ✦ ✦ ✦ ✦ ✦ ✦ ✦ ✦ ✦ ✦ ✦ ✦ ✦ ✦

1. One feature in international selling that is becoming more common is the idea of piggybacking (i.e., tying up with existing sales channels to distribute and sell your

products). Examples include Dunkin Donuts (as the name suggests, the confectionery chain) combining with Baskin-Robbins (the ice-cream chain) units to sell in

Canada, Mexico, and Indonesia. According to business proponents of piggybacking, it allows a significant reduction in costs and risks by the ability to share resources such as dining space and staff, leading to better profitability. However, the concern is that a foreign partner, who is often chosen as the piggybacking partner (unlike the example just stated) may devote less attention to the foreign product. If the piggybacking is with a unit in the same business, considerable cannibalization can also take place. Discuss the conditions under which a piggyback strategy would be appropriate and under which conditions it would not be appropriate.

2. A trend that has been worrying most manufacturers, especially of consumer nondurable products, is the increasing transfer of power from the manufacturers to large and multinational retailing chains. Manufacturers now have relatively less control on how to sell a product to the consumers—less, say, in in-store displays and pass-through of discounts, for example. A case example of this problem is the recent standoff between a multi-billion-dollar retail chain and a multinational, multibillion-dollar food specialty giant. The retailer insisted that it be given certain discounts (which it deemed reasonable) for a certain product sold in China, given the strong relationship between these firms in the U.S. market. The Chinese subsidiary of the manufacturer refused to give these discounts. The retailing giant retaliated by saying that for each subsequent week that it did not receive a discount in China, it would remove one selling unit (brand) from all of the retailer's stores in the United States. Given the size of the U.S. market, the manufacturer finally gave in and accepted giving the discounts. Ten years back, no retailer would have dared using the same tactic with such a large manufacturer. Another troubling fact is that many of these retailing chains are promoting their own brands (e.g., Wal-Mart promoting the Sam's brand), and various grocery chains are promoting their own brands. What are the implications of these changes for the manufacturers of these consumer nondurable products? What proactive steps can manufacturing firms take to counter this trend?

3. Domino's Pizza International, the Ann Arbor, Michigan, based pizza chain, is known worldwide for its delivery service. Its initial policy of giving away its pizza free if not delivered within half an hour was a legendary service theme, and it earned them a unique position in the consumer's mind. However, recently, the company's foray into Poland in 1994 proved how modifications to positioning strategies might become essential in certain international markets. In 1994, the company wanted to open franchises in Poland. It was keen on opening delivery units as it has in most other countries. However, the lack of reliable and appropriate infrastructure in terms of telephone service in Poland posed a problem. "Its delivery concept wouldn't ride very far if potential customers couldn't phone in their orders." So, in stark contrast to its policy in other countries, Domino opened a sit-in restaurant in Poland in March 1994, followed by another one a couple of months later. Only after some time did it open its standard delivery unit. While this was one way of tiding over the selling constraints peculiar to this market, there was the risk that they were deviating from their most salient positioning theme. Do you think the strategy adopted by Domino's was a wise one? If so, give reasons. If not, provide an alternate strategy, giving your justification for the same.

4. Many firms have followed an incremental approach in the past to the sales channels used in international markets. Typically, these companies started by selling in foreign markets through sales agents or distributors. This was followed by opening of liaison offices to assist and monitor the activities of the appointed distributors. With subsequent growth in business, the company would set up its own sales subsidiary to manage sales and customer service. This incremental strategy has worked quite effectively for many companies in the past. In your opinion, would the current emphasis being placed on globalization have any bearing on the effectiveness of this incremental strategy? If so, what would this effect be, and why?

FURTHER READING ✦ ✦ ✦ ✦ ✦ ✦ ✦ ✦ ✦ ✦ ✦ ✦ ✦

Cook, Roy A., and Joel Herche. "Assessment Centers: An Untapped Resource for Global Salesforce Management." *Journal of Personal Selling and Sales Management*, 12 (Summer 1992): 31–37.

Cort, Kathryn T., and William L. Shanklin. "The Wall." *Marketing Management*, 7 (Fall 1998): 42–46.

Gorchels, Linda, Thani Jambulingam, and Timothy W. Aurand. "International Marketing Managers: A Comparison of Japanese, German, and U.S. Perceptions." *Journal of International Marketing*, 7 (1) (1999): 97–105.

Money, R. Bruce, Mary C. Gilly, and John L. Graham. "Explorations of National Culture and Word-of-

Mouth Referral Behavior in the Purchase of Industrial Services in the United Sates and Japan." *Journal of Marketing,* 62 (October 1998): 76–87.

Scheneider, Fred. "Shopping on the Information Superhighway." *International Journal of Retail and Distribution Management* (Spring 1995): 9–10.

Segal-Horn, Susan, and Heather Davison. "Global Markets, The Global Consumer, and International Retailing." *Journal of Global Marketing,* 5(3) (1992): 31–61.

Solomon, Charlene Marmer. "HR's Helping Hand Plus Global Inpatriates Onbound." *Personnel Journal,* 74 (November 1995): 40.

Talbott, Shannon Peters. "Building a Global Workforce Starts with Recruitment." *Personnel Journal,* 75 (March 1996): 59.

"Towards an International Salesforce." *Journal of Management Development,* 14(9) (1995): 6–8.

GLOBAL LOGISTICS AND DISTRIBUTION

16

HAPTER OVERVIEW

1. DEFINITION OF GLOBAL LOGISTICS

2. MANAGING GLOBAL LOGISTICS

3. FREE TRADE ZONES

4. MAQUILADORA OPERATION

5. U.S. SPECIAL IMPORT TARIFF PROVISIONS

6. GLOBAL RETAILING

Global logistics and distribution have played a critical role in the growth and development of world trade and in the integration of manufacturing on a world-wide scale. In fact, the level of world trade in goods and, to some extent, services, depends to a significant degree on the availability of economical and reliable international transportation services. Decreases in transportation costs and increases in performance reliability expand the scope of manufacturing operations and increase the associated level of international trade and competition.[1] The use of appropriate distribution channels in international markets increases the chances of success dramatically. Coca-Cola succeeded in Japan, in part, because it spent the time and money to set up its own bottlers and distribution.

---

[1]John H. Dunning, "Reappraising the Eclectic Paradigm in an Age of Alliance Capitalism," *Journal of International Business Studies*, 26 (Third Quarter 1995), pp. 461–91.

The concept of business logistics is relatively new. John F. Magee is generally credited with publishing the first article on logistics theory in 1960.[2] As far back as 1954, Peter Drucker said that logistics would remain "the dark continent of business"[3]—the least well understood area of business—and his prediction proved true until well into the 1980s. It is not too difficult to demonstrate the importance of the physical handling, moving, storing, and retrieving of material. In almost every product, more than 50 percent of product cost is material related, while less than 10 percent is labor. Yet, over the years this fact has not received much attention. In the United States, the total logistics cost has amounted to 10 percent to 11 percent of the country's GDP every year in the last decade. It was about $900 billion in 1998, roughly four times as large as the current U.S. trade deficit.[4]

In the 1990s, a variety of issues drove the increased emphasis on logistics and distribution management. It was epitomized by General Motors' recent lawsuit against Volkswagen over the defection of José Ignacio Lopez, the former vice-president of purchasing at General Motors and one of the most renowned logistics managers in the automobile industry.[5] His expertise is said to have saved General Motors several billion dollars from its purchasing and logistic operations, which would directly affect the company's bottom line. The importance of distribution channels is further evidenced by the recent mergers in the auto industry, in which giant multinationals are gobbling up smaller manufacturers with strong brand names but inadequate global distribution, such as Ford's takeover of Volvo.[6]

As firms start operating on a global basis, logistics managers need to manage shipping of raw materials, components, and supplies among various manufacturing sites at the most economical and reliable rates. Simultaneously, they need to ship finished goods to customers in markets around the world at the desired place and time. The development of intermodal transportation and electronic tracking technology has caused a quantum jump in the efficiency of the logistic methods employed by firms. Intermodal transportation refers to the seamless transfer of goods from one mode of transport (e.g., aircraft or ship) to another (e.g., truck) and vice versa without the hassle of unpacking and repackaging of goods to suit the dimensions of the mode of transport being used. Tracking technology refers to the means for keeping continuous tabs on the exact location of the goods being shipped in the logistic chain. This enables quick reaction to any disruption in the shipments because (a) the shipper knows exactly where the goods are in real time and (b) the alternative means can be quickly mobilized.

---

[2]John F. Magee, "The Logistics of Distribution," *Harvard Business Review*, 38 (July 1960), pp. 89–101.

[3]Peter F. Drucker, *The Practice of Management* (New York: Harper & Brothers, 1954).

[4]Thomas A. Foster, "1999 Annual Report: Logistics Productivity Goes Flat," *Logistics Management and Distribution Report*, 38 (July 1999), pp. 51–56.

[5]"Business: The Decline and Fall of General Motors," *Economist* (October 10, 1998), pp. 63–65.

[6]Keith Bradsher, "Ford Seen in Deal to Pay $6 Billion for Volvo Car Unit," *The New York Times* (January 28, 1999), p. A1.

◆ ◆ ◆ ◆ ◆ ◆ Definition of Global Logistics

Global logistics is defined as the design and management of a system that directs and controls the flows of materials into, through and out of the firm across national boundaries to achieve its corporate objectives at a minimum total cost. As shown in Exhibit 16–1, it encompasses the entire range of operations concerned with products or components movement, including both exports and imports simultaneously. Global logistics, like domestic logistics, encompasses materials management and physical distribution.[7]

Materials management refers to the inflow of raw materials, parts, and supplies through the firm. This topic has been explored earlier in Chapter 10 in the context of global sourcing strategy, or management of R & D, manufacturing, and marketing interfaces. **Physical distribution** refers to the movement of the firm's finished products to its customers, consisting of transportation, warehousing, inventory, customer service/order entry, and administration. In this chapter, we focus on physical distribution management.

Although the functions of physical distribution are universal, they are affected differently by the tradition, culture, economic infrastructure, laws, and topography, among others, in each country and each region. In general, in geographically large countries, such as the United States, where products are transported for a long distance, firms tend to incur relatively more transportation and inventory costs than in smaller countries. On the other hand, in geographically concentrated countries, such as Japan and Britain, firms tend to incur relatively more warehousing, customer service/order entry, and general administrative costs than in geographically larger countries. This is primarily because a wide variety of products with different features have to be stored to meet the variegated needs of customers in concentrated areas. The results of a recent survey of physical distribution costs in various European countries relative to the United States are presented in Global Perspective 16–1. Although it is possible to attribute all cost differences to topography, customs, laws of the land, and other factors, the cost differences could also reflect how efficiently or inefficiently physical distribution is managed in various countries and regions.

EXHIBIT 16–1
GLOBAL LOGISTICS

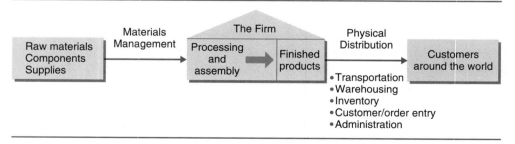

---

[7]Donald F. Wood, *International Logistics* (New York: Chapman & Hall, 1995).

$\mathcal{G}$LOBAL PERSPECTIVE 16–1

REGIONAL VARIATIONS IN PHYSICAL DISTRIBUTION COSTS IN EUROPE AND ROOM FOR IMPROVEMENT

Despite the allegedly more integrated and more efficient European economy under the aegis of the European Union, physical distribution costs in Europe have not declined yet, and worse yet, seem to have increased. According to Herbert W. Davis and Company's estimate, the Europeans paid 9.17 percent of revenue for physical distribution in 1993, up from 8.1 percent in 1992. The comparable rate for the United States was 8.07 percent in 1993.

Regional variations exist, however. Germany experienced a slight drop in distribution cost from 10.4 percent to 10.1 percent, while its average was still above the continental average. Costs in the Netherlands declined from 9.7 percent to 9.0 percent in the same period. The United Kingdom registered the highest increase, from 6.8 percent to 8.0 percent, but still enjoyed the lowest in the continent. Similarly, French distribution costs went up to 8.3 percent from 7.3 percent. Sweden remained the highest distribution-cost country in the European Union, registering at 11.3 percent.

The physical distribution costs consist of transportation, warehousing, inventory, customer service/order entry, and administration. Let us make a comparison in terms of these components of the distribution costs between the two continents across the Atlantic. The following table shows cost comparisons (as a percentage of revenue).

The largest disparity was in warehousing, where European costs measured 3.03 percent, almost a third of total distribution costs, compared to 1.98 percent in the United States. These expenses are the cost of both plant and field warehouses, including labor, space, and direct materials. Similarly, a large difference was observed in customer service/order entry—the cost of people, space, and materials needed to take orders and handle inquiries—with 0.83 percent in Europe, compared to 0.49 percent in the United States.

	European Union	The United States
Transportation	2.79%	3.23%
Warehousing	3.03%	1.98%
Inventory	1.73%	1.93%
Customer Service/ Order Entry	0.83%	0.49%
Administration	0.79%	0.44%
Total	9.17%	8.07%

These disparities mean opportunities to logisticians involved with Europe. They are hopeful of the promises of the single market for the continent's distribution industry by erasing national borders, deregulating industries, establishing a common currency, and so on, over time.

Information technology is a key to improvement. For example, an effective tool in managing truck transportation and its attendant costs is software that determines the shortest mileage between two points. The fewer miles traveled, the less cost. In 1997, PC*MILER/Europe software was introduced that permits coordination with Global Positioning System (GPS) satellite tracking. The software was originally developed by ALK Associates in the United States and has become a popular and effective measurement tool for shippers in North America. Refinements to the North American version of PC*MILER are designed to keep it current with the expanding needs of the market. There has been a bit more involved in amassing the European data for thirty-eight countries, as opposed to dealing with up to three central data sources for the North American system. There are 563,000 miles (or 900,000 kilometers) of highway in the PC*MILER/Europe version, and 62,000 accessible locations. The program's functionality is virtually identical to the North American version with the addition of the European latitude-longitude coordinates, enabling ties to the GPS satellite tracking system in Europe.

Source: James Thomas, "Mountain High, River Wide; Physical Distribution Costs in Europe," *Distribution*, 93 (May 1994), pp. 62–65; and Roger Morton, "Software Can Ease Your Transportation Troubles," *Transportation & Distribution,* 38 (March 1997), pp. 60–66.

◆ ◆ ◆ ◆ ◆ ◆   MANAGING GLOBAL LOGISTICS

Logistics management is inextricably tied with international trade and multinational manufacturing and sourcing of raw materials, components, and supplies. The rate of growth in the volume of world merchandise exports slowed to 3.5 percent in 1998, from some 10 percent per year in the past several years, due largely to continuing economic contraction in much of Asia. World output growth slipped to 2 percent in 1998, compared to 3 percent in 1997. However, world trade is expected to increase at a much faster rate than world output, as in the past. Global logistics, however, has become considerably more complex, more costly, and as a result, more important for the success of a firm. A variety of factors contribute to the increased complexity and cost of global logistics, as compared to domestic logistics.

- *Distance*. The first fundamental difference is distance. Global logistics frequently require transportation of parts, supplies, and finished goods over much longer distances than is the norm domestically. A longer distance generally suggests higher direct costs of transportation and insurance for damages, deterioration, and pilferage in transit and higher indirect costs of warehousing and inventory.

- *Exchange rate fluctuation*. The second difference pertains to currency variations in international logistics. The corporation must adjust its planning to incorporate the existence of currencies and changes in exchange rates. For example, as the U.S. dollar appreciated and the Japanese yen soared in value in the mid-1990s, Honda found it much cheaper to ship its Accord models to Europe from its U.S. plant in Marysville, Ohio, rather than from its plants in Japan.

Depending upon a local market's stage of economic development and infrastructural conditions, a foreign company may need to adjust its mode of transportation drastically.

- *Foreign intermediaries*. Additional intermediaries participate in the global logistics process because of the need to negotiate border regulations of countries and deal with local government officials and distributors. Although home country export agents, brokers, and export merchants work as middlemen providing an exporting service for manufacturing firms, those home-based middlemen may not have sufficient knowledge about the foreign countries' market conditions or sufficient connections with local government officials and distributors. In Oriental countries (e.g., Japan, Korea, and China), personal "connections" of who knows whom frequently seem to outweigh the Western economic principle of profit maximization or cost minimization in conducting business.[8] Therefore, working with the local distributors has proved very important in building initial connections with the local business community as well as local government regulators.

The global logistics manager must understand the specific properties of the different modes of transport in order to use them optimally. The three most important factors in determining an optimal mode of transportation are the value-to-volume ratio, perishability of the product, and the cost of transportation. The **value-to-volume ratio** is determined by how much value is added to the materials used in the product. **Perishability** of the product refers to the quality degradation over time and/or product obsolescence along the product life cycle. The **cost of transportation** should be considered in light of the value to volume and perishability of the product.

Modes of Transportation

Ocean Shipping. Ocean shipping offers three options. **Liner service** offers regularly scheduled passage on established routes. **Bulk shipping** normally provides contractual service for prespecified periods of time, while the third category is for *irregular runs*. Container ships carry standardized containers that greatly facilitate

A major container port in Singapore used as a hub of global distribution.

[8]See, for example, Jean L. Johnson, Tomoaki Sakano, and Naoto Onzo, "Behavioral Relations in Across-Culture Distribution Systems: Influence, Control, and Conflict in U.S.-Japanese Marketing Channels," *Journal of International Business Studies*, 21 (Fourth Quarter 1990), 639–55; and Min Chen, *Asian Management Systems: Chinese, Japanese, and Korean Styles of Business* (New York: Routledge, 1995).

the loading and unloading of cargo and intermodal transfer of cargo. Ocean shipping is used extensively for the transport of heavy, bulky, or nonperishable products, including crude oil, steel, and automobiles. Although most manufacturers rely on existing international ocean carriers, some large exporting companies, such as Toyota and Hyundai, have their own fleets of cargo ships. Over the years, shipping rates have been falling as a result of a price war among shipping lines. For example, an average rate for shipping a forty-foot container from Asia to the United States fell from $4,000 in 1992 to $3,500 in 1997. However, in a move to reclaim its power to set prices on the biggest American ocean trade line, a shipping cartel is trying to raise rates on goods imported from Asia to the United States.[9] Such a move by the shipping cartel, known as the *Trans-Pacific Stabilization Agreement*, may encourage large companies with a major stake in trans-Pacific trade to purchase their own fleets of cargo ships.

Air Freight. Shipping of goods by air has seen rapid growth over the last thirty years. Although the total volume of international trade using air shipping remains quite small—it still constitutes less than 2 percent of international trade in goods—it represents more than 20 percent of the value of goods shipped in international commerce. High-value goods are more likely to be shipped by air, especially if they have a high value-to-volume ratio. Typical examples are semiconductor chips, LCD screens, and diamonds. Perishable products like produce and flowers also tend to be airfreighted. Changes in aircraft design have now enabled air transshipment of relatively bulky products. Three decades ago, a large propeller aircraft could hold only 10 tons of cargo. Today's cargo jumbo jets carry more than 30 tons, and medium- to long-haul transport planes like the C-130 and the AN-32 can carry more than 80 tons of cargo. These supersize transport planes have facilitated the growth of global courier services, such as FedEx and DHL. In terms of sheer bulk, however, this is dwarfed by the million-ton-plus tankers that ferry crude oil from the Gulf to the United States and Japan.

Intermodal Transportation. More than one mode of transportation is usually employed. Naturally, when shipments travel across the ocean, surface or air shipping is the initial mode of transportation crossing national borders. Once landed, they may be further shipped by truck, barge, railroad, or air. Even if countries are contiguous, such as Canada, the United States, and Mexico, for example, various domestic regulations prohibit use of the same trucks between and across the national boundaries. When different modes of transportation are involved, or even when shipments are transferred from one truck to another at the national border, it is important to make sure that cargo space is utilized at full load so that the per-unit transportation cost is minimized.

Managing shipments so that they arrive in time at the desired destination is critical in modern-day logistics management. Due to low transit times, greater ease of unloading and distribution, and higher predictability, many firms use airfreight, either on a regular basis or as a backup to fill in when the regular shipment by an ocean vessel gets delayed. For footwear firms Reebok and Nike, and for fashion firms such as Pierre Cardin, use of air freight is becoming almost a required way of doing business, as firms jostle to get their products first into the U.S. market from their production centers in Asia and Europe. The customer in a retail store often

[9]Anna Wilde Mathews, "Ocean-Shipping Cartel to Raise U.S.-Asia Rates," *Wall Street Journal* (June 8, 1998), p. A2.

buys a product that may have been airfreighted in from the opposite end of the world the previous day or even the same day. Thus, the face of retailing is also changing as a result of advances in global logistics.

Distance between the transacting parties increases transportation costs and requires longer-term commitment to forecasts and longer lead times. Differing legal environments, liability regimes, and pricing regulations affect transportation costs and distribution costs in a way not seen in the domestic market. Trade barriers, customs problems, and paperwork tend to slow the cycle times in logistics across national boundaries. Although this is true, the recent formation of regional trading blocs, such as the European Union, the North American Free Trade Agreement, and the MERCOSUR (The Southern Cone Free Trade Area) is also encouraging integration and consolidation of logistics in the region for improved economic efficiency and competition (see Global Perspective 16–2).

Warehousing and Inventory Management

A firm's international strategy for logistics management depends, in part, on the government policy and, in part, on the infrastructure and logistic services environment available. The traditional logistics strategy involves anticipatory demand management based on forecasting and inventory speculation.[10] In this scenario, a multinational firm estimates the requirements for supplies as well as the demand from its customers and then attempts to manage the flow of raw materials and components in its worldwide manufacturing system and the flow of finished products to its customers in such a manner as to minimize the holding of inventory without jeopardizing manufacturing runs and without losing sales due to stockouts.

In the past, the mechanics and reliability of transportation and tracking of the flow of goods was a major problem. With the increasing use of information technology, electronic data interchange, and intermodal transportation, the production, scheduling, and delivery of goods across national borders is also becoming a matter of just-in-time delivery, while some structural problems still remain. For instance, the current restrictions on U.S.–Canada air freight services, and U.S.–Mexico cross-border trucking slow the flow of goods and add to the lead times. Such government restrictions need to be changed to facilitate faster movement of goods across borders.

Despite those restrictions, forward-looking multinational firms can still employ near just-in-time inventory management. For example, Sony has an assembly plant in Nuevo Laredo, Mexico, just across the Texas border, importing components from its U.S. sister plants in the United States. Although transportation across the U.S.–Mexico international bridges is occasionally delayed by traffic congestion, Sony has been able to manage just-in-time inventory management with a minimum of safety stock in its warehouse.

Hedging Against Inflation and Exchange Rate Fluctuations. Multinational corporations can also use inventory as a strategic tool in dealing with currency fluctuations and as a hedge against inflation. By increasing inventories before imminent depreciation of a currency instead of holding cash, the firm may reduce its exposure to currency depreciation losses. High inventories also provide a hedge against inflation, because the value of the goods/parts held in inventory remains the same compared to the buying power of a local currency, which falls with a devaluation. In such cases the international logistics manager has to coordinate operations with that of

[10]Louis P. Bucklin, "Postponement, Speculation and the Structure of Distribution Channels," *Journal of Marketing Research*, 2 (February 1965), pp. 26–31.

◆ ◆

$\mathcal{G}$LOBAL PERSPECTIVE 16–2

REDESIGNING LOGISTICS IN THE EMERGENCE OF THE EUROPEAN UNION

European governments have begun to privatize transportation services. Since January 1, 1993, the European Union (EU) movement presents opportunities for reducing logistics costs and boosting efficiency. And it is not just Europeans but also foreign manufacturers, including those in North America, who are finding that political changes in Europe have created opportunities for greater efficiency and lower costs in their logistics.

However, there still are many political, legal, and technical issues to be settled before Europe truly is unified. Across the region, borders have all but disappeared with the advent of high-speed passenger trains, highways without customs posts, and now a single currency. Europe's state-owned phone monopolies, electric utilities, airlines, and other national franchises have all been pried open to competition. However, rail freight remains a bastion of Europe's old ways, a patchwork of protected, antiquated national networks. No two European countries use the same signaling systems or electric current for their trains. For example, trains in Britain and France run on the left side of dual-track lines, while those in the rest of Europe run on the right. Since Britain and France, however, use two different gauges of track, trains crossing their shared border must stop to let each car be lifted so that its wheels can be changed.

As a result, European industry has taken to the highways for transportation. Railways' share of goods transport with the European Union has fallen to about 14 percent now from 32 percent in 1970. In the United States, railways account for 41 percent of freight traffic. The downside to the increase in truck traffic is increased traffic congestion, which hampers efficient transportation despite the unified European economy. The most conservative estimate of the cost of traffic jam is a little over 2 percent of Europe's GDP at minimum. It could be as high as 6 percent.

Thus, logistics managers must plan how to respond to changes as they occur. Here are some of the many changes reshaping European logistics strategies:

CUSTOMS PROCEDURES

For the most part, customs check points as a shipment crosses each nation's border have been eliminated. Duties and trade statistics now are a matter strictly between the originating and destination countries, and intermediate countries no longer are involved. Consequently, transit times and paperwork between EU countries, particularly for truck traffic, are steadily being reduced.

HARMONIZED PRODUCT STANDARDS

Prior to unification, each European country had its own manufacturing, packaging, labeling, and safety standards for almost every item sold within its borders. Under the European Union, Pan-European harmonized standards are being developed and replacing most of those country-by-country regulations. As a result, companies can manufacture a single version of a product for sale in all parts of the EU, rather than design and manufacture different versions of the same item for each member country. Product harmonization will allow shippers to redesign not only their distribution patterns and facilities, but also their customer-service strategies.

TRANSPORTATION DEREGULATION

The European Commission is deregulating transportation in Europe in order to open markets in member states to competition and to eliminate conflicting regulations that impede the flow of traffic between EU countries. The deregulation promises to promote the development of efficient, cost-effective services in all modes.

TRANSPORTATION INFRASTRUCTURE

As in Japan and the United States, growing demand for just-in-time deliveries increases traffic and exacerbates transportation bottlenecks (particularly, inter-regional trucking). The European Commission and individual governments are actively encouraging private development of rail and water alternatives.

Source: "Logistics Strategies for a New Europe," *Traffic Management*, 33 (August, 1994), p. 49A; and "In the Unified Europe, Shipping Freight by Rail is a Journey into the Past," *Wall Street Journal* (March 29, 1999), pp. A1 and A8.

the rest of the firm, so that the cost of maintaining an increased level of inventories is more than offset by the gains from hedging against inflation and currency fluctuations. Many countries, for instance, charge a property tax on stored goods. If the increase in the cost of carrying the increased inventory along with the taxes exceeds the saving from hedging, then the increased inventory may not be a good idea.

Benefiting from Tax Differences.   There are creative ways in which costs can be written off before taxes so that internal transit arrangements can actually make a profit. This implies that what and how much a firm transfers within its global manufacturing system is a function of the tax systems in various countries to and from which the transfers are being made. When the transfer of a component A from country B to country C is tax-deductible in country B (as an export) and gets credit in country C for being part of a locally assembled good D, then the transfer makes a profit for the multinational firm. Access to and use of such knowledge is the forte of logistics firms that sell these services to the multinational firm interested in optimizing its global logistics.

Logistic Integration and Rationalization.   More dramatic changes are taking place in the wake of the European Union. According to a recent study conducted by Andersen Consulting and the U.K.'s Cranfield School of Management, an increasing number of European firms have begun to integrate European operations, rationalize those operations, or do both.[11] **Logistic integration** refers to coordinating production and distribution across geographic boundaries—a radical departure from the traditional country-by-country-based structure consisting of separate sales, production, warehousing, and distribution organizations in each country. **Rationalization**, on the other hand, means reducing resources to achieve more efficient and cost-effective operations. Although conceptually separate, most companies' strategies include both aspects of the logistics strategy.

For example, Baxter Healthcare, a U.S. medical-supplies manufacturer, has recently reorganized its production and logistics management by product lines for all of Europe. Previously, the company had separate organizations in each country, offering a full range of products. Now, each of its manufacturing, distribution, and administrative facilities specializes in one type of product and markets that product throughout Europe (integration). Furthermore, the company may consolidate warehouses so that it serves the entire region from one or a few strategically located distribution centers (rationalization). The cost savings as a result of redesigning European logistics systems has been reported to amount, on average, to as much as 40 percent to 50 percent from the current country-by-country–based approach.[12] Similarly, in expectation of the upcoming maritime deregulation, Proctor & Gamble centralized its global shipping functions at a single U.S. site in Cincinnati, Ohio. By centralizing its logistics operations before May 1, 1999, when the Ocean Shipping Reform Act took effect, Procter & Gamble was poised to begin shipping U.S. and foreign-to-foreign cargo together and capitalize on the forthcoming economies of scale.[13]

---

[11]This section draws from "Logistics Strategies for a New Europe," *Traffic Management*, 33 (August, 1994), p. 49A.

[12]Ibid., p. 49A.

[13]Terry Brennan, "Riding the Crest of Deregulation," *Journal of Commerce* (February 11, 1999), p. 1A.

It must be remembered, however, that while the laws of the European Union point toward economic integration, there still are and will continue to be political, cultural, and legal differences among countries. Similarly, as shown in Global Perspective 16–3, the North American Free Trade Agreement is not free of arcane regulations, either. Consequently, despite the promised benefit of logistics integration and rationalization, international marketers as well as corporate planners have to have specialized local knowledge to ensure smooth operations. Particularly, customer service strategies need to be differentiated, depending on the expectations of local consumers. For example, German buyers of personal computers may be willing to accept Dell Computer's mail-order service or its Web site ordering service,[14] but French and Spanish customers may assume that a delivery person will deliver and install the products for them.

E-Commerce and Logistics.   Another profound change in the last decade is the proliferation of the Internet and electronic commerce (e-commerce). The Internet opened the gates for companies to sell direct to consumers easily across national boundaries. We stated in Chapter 1 that manufacturers that traditionally sell

❖ ❖

$\mathcal{G}$LOBAL PERSPECTIVE 16–3

CABOTAGE RULES IN THE NORTH AMERICAN FREE TRADE AGREEMENT

Cabotage refers to the right of a trucker to be able to carry goods in an assigned territory. Traditionally, countries have restricted cabotage rights of foreign truckers. If the American trucking company has a scheduled load to the United States from Toronto, then the truck may carry the load but the driver must be Canadian. Similarly, an American trucker, after delivering goods in Toronto, cannot pick up another load and deliver it in Ottawa—that is a violation of current cabotage rules. Even under the North American Free Trade Agreement (NAFTA), Canada, the United States, and Mexico have varying degrees of—even sometimes confusing—regulations on cabotage rights. In theory, the NAFTA should have worked out truly free mobility of goods by allowing the cabotage rights of truckers from Canada, the United States, and Mexico. But the reality is still far from it.

In the United States, President Bill Clinton still refuses to allow Mexican truckers to have full access to four border states. The president cited safety concerns in

keeping Mexican trucks from operating throughout the states of Arizona, New Mexico, Texas, and California, although those fears may not be supported by facts. Similarly, the Mexican trucking association, Camara Nacional del Autotransporte de Carga, continues to oppose opening up cabotage to allow point-to-point coverage in Mexico by U.S. trucking companies.

The United States does not have a coherent cabotage regulation with Canada. The U.S. Immigration and Naturalization Service is going after Canadian drivers who have "violated" cabotage rules by moving trailers within the United States even though U.S. Customs permits such movements. A number of Canadian drivers have had their trucks seized, been fined, and kicked out of the United States. Under an agreement engineered by the Canadian and American trucking associations, Canadian officials have been allowing American drivers to perform such cabotage movements in Canada. Now the Canadian government is thinking about retaliating against the United States by mounting a crackdown on American truck drivers entering Canada to parallel the aggressive treatment Canadian drivers are facing from the U.S. Immigration and Naturalization Service.

Source: John D. Schulz, "Open Up, President Clinton!" *Traffic World* (January 18, 1999), p. 28; and Alex Binkley, "Tit for Tat," *Traffic World* (July 12, 1999), p. 24.

---

[14]Silvia Ascarelli, "Dell Finds U.S. Strategy Works in Europe," *Wall Street Journal* (February 3, 1997), p. A8; Eryn Brown, "Could the Very Best PC Maker Be Dell Computer?" *Fortune* (April 14, 1997), p. 26.

through the retail channel *may* benefit the most from e-commerce. Furthermore, customer information no longer is held hostage by the retail channel.

We emphasize *may* because *logistics cannot go global as easily as e-commerce in reality*. This revolutionary way of marketing products around the world is epitomized by Dell Computer, which put pressure on the industry's traditional players with a simple concept: sell personal computers directly on the Internet to customers with no complicated channels. Michael Dell has successfully introduced a new way for PC companies to compete—not by technology alone, but by emphasizing the needs of the customers with an ability to satisfy and serve them quickly and efficiently and above and beyond the traditional national boundary. By 1999, major PC companies were compressing the supply chain via such concepts as "build to order" rather than "build to forecast." However, order taking may take place globally, but shipping of PCs needs to be rather local or regional for various reasons.

You may ask: "If the Web makes any company instantly global, then why don't most e-businesses ship overseas? And why don't more companies make their Internet-powered supply chains globally accessible?" The answer is that it remains very difficult to manage the complex logistics, financial, and regulatory requirements of global trade. For instance, leading e-commerce sites, such as Amazon.com, Dell.com, and eToys.com, still have the disclaimers indicating they either do not ship overseas or cannot calculate the added charges for overseas shipping. Syntra, a software company, started offering modular and hosted versions of its core global commerce engines to help users overcome the obstacles of international e-commerce. Xerox's Offsite Document Services, which reproduces, ships, and fulfills documents for international customers, is using Syntra's services to ensure it is complying with U.S. export rules.[15]

Such services alleviate various problems associated with physical distribution for e-commerce. However, they could not address logistical problems associated with local competition and exchange rate fluctuations. For example, in Australia, Ozbooks.com sells 800,000 books and Dymocks, Australia's largest bookseller, offers just 80,000 books online. These Australian companies are no comparison in size to Amazon.com, with some 4.5 million books. Yet, these smaller Australian online booksellers' competitive advantage over Amazon.com is that they have a comprehensive offering of books published in Australia, while Amazon.com does not. Furthermore, competing on price for international sales without local distribution is tricky because exchange rates fluctuate. When the Australian dollar depreciated during the Asian financial crisis, buying from Amazon.com and other U.S. Web retailers became more expensive in Australia. Australian consumers log on to local alternatives like Ozbook.com instead.[16]

Another example is Compaq Computer in Latin America. The Houston, Texas-based company announced it would sell computers over the Internet throughout Latin America starting in October 1999. The company guaranteed delivery within 72 hours of Compaq computers bought online. Latin Americans shopping online can buy the computers in local currency and do not have to bring the computers through customs. This requires local assembly of Compaq computers. Compaq has offices in Mexico, Ecuador, Argentina, Brazil, Venezuela, Chile, Puerto Rico, Colombia, and Peru.[17]

---

[15]Richard Karpinski, "Software Simplifies Overseas Commerce," *Internetweek* (July 19, 1999), p. PG9.

[16]"Here Comes the Fight-Back," *The Industry Standard* (March 29, 1999), pp. 32–38.

[17]"Compaq Expands Latin America Net Sales," *Latin IT News*, http://latinitnews@mailer.latpro.com, posted on August 17, 1999.

The Web may have dispensed with physical stores, but local adaptation of product offerings and setting-up of local distribution centers remain as crucial as ever. The local competition is forcing Amazon.com and other American e-commerce companies to reassess what it means to operate globally on the Internet.

Third-party Logistic (3PL) Management

International shipping between a company's own facilities can be as tricky as dealing with an outside company. The trend seems to be decentralization, in varying degrees, accompanied, paradoxically, by a degree of centralization, as suggested by sourcing and logistics executives at some larger U.S. multinationals like General Motors, AT&T, DuPont, Dow Chemical, and Westinghouse.

According to Armstrong & Associates, a consulting firm that tracks the logistics outsourcing industry, in 1998, U.S. companies spent almost $40 billion on **third-party logistics (3PL) services**. The largest 3PL sector is the value-added warehousing and distribution industry. Survey statistics show two important trends: (1) the 3PL industry has a tremendous untapped opportunity for growth with the Fortune 500 companies, and (2) the mid-sized companies are making the best use of savings and service advantages that outsourcing can offer.[18] To stay with the trend, information technology companies such as IBM have established a consulting group selling supply-chain management services to other manufacturing firms. IBM is one of the top importing and exporting companies in the United States. Like a number of large shippers, Big Blue has turned its expertise in global logistics into a profit-making, third-party service consulting group, known as International Trade Management Services (ITMS). ITMS's forte is global supply-chain management, and the Boulder, Colorado, center processes about $15 billion worth of trade volume annually. Several years ago, Kmart was making plans to move into Mexico. While Kmart had a state-of-the-art softlines distribution center in Sunnyvale, Texas, and another for hardlines in Corsicana, Texas, both distribution centers were designed to ship products to U.S. stores only. Kmart turned to ITMS's expertise to help it bring its Mexico stores online within schedule. ITMS developed compliant processes for cross-border goods, information, and financial flows for five different supply options, covering all U.S. and Mexican trade requirements. ITMS designed a state-of-the-art trade system that preclassifies goods, provides Spanish descriptions, and interfaces with the government systems to generate Special Economic Zone Documents and invoices. This involved coordination.[19]

Although it lags behind the U.S. trend, Britain leads Europe with 38 percent of its overall logistics market contracted out to third parties. The European third-party logistics market is expected to grow at 8 percent a year, reaching a value of $34.5 billion in 2003. Italy and Spain have the greatest potential, as their relatively large markets have a low rate of outsourcing. A survey of leading contract logistics companies highlights two main factors in the next five years. The euro has meant greater transparency for supply chain managers, allowing them to compare cost structures. This has resulted in tougher competition.[20] And constant re-engineering

---

[18]"1999 Annual Report—Third-Party Logistics: No End to the Good News," *Logistics Management and Distribution Report*, 38 (July 1999), pp. 73–74.

[19]William McKee, "Innovation to a Third-party," *Distribution*, 93 (December 1994), pp. 50–53.

[20]"UK Top on Outsourcing," *Supply Management*, 4 (July 8, 1999), p. 13.

of supply chains has forced contract logistics suppliers to create pan-European networks in order to win large contracts, resulting in fewer suppliers in Europe.

Logistical Revolution with the Internet. The trend toward third-party logistics is a result of the Internet and the intranet (a specialized, secure Internet channel established between the companies) as well as concentrating on core competencies (See Global Perspective 16–4). The Internet and the intranet facilitate on-time inventory and distribution coordination without constraint of geographical boundaries. Core competencies refer to the mix of skills and resources that a firm possesses that enable it to produce one set of goods and/or services in a much more effective manner than another. Also, competent logistic firms can save money for a multinational firm shipping components between its facilities in different countries, because shipping costs paid internally can vary according to the fluctuation of foreign currencies. There is much diversity in how payments are made, in whether shipments are paid for straight through to a recipient or left at a port of entry, and in the rate charged, which is often different for a company and for its customers.

General Motors has one corporate office at headquarters at Detroit that oversees the logistics of all component operations reflecting a degree of centralization. Actual shipping operations, including implementation and documentation, are handled by two independent support companies—Burlington Air Express, which handles GM business in North America and Europe, and Air Express International,

◆ ◆

$\mathcal{G}$LOBAL PERSPECTIVE 16–4

LOGISTICAL REVOLUTION WITH THE INTERNET

Beverage companies, such as Coca Cola and Heineken, usually have to rely on local bottlers and distributors, which could not be outsourced to specialized third-party logistics providers. Nonetheless, they could improve their ability to process sales forecasts and orders by relying on third-party data management companies. For example, Heineken turned to Logility, an Atlanta-based provider of integrated value-chain planning software. In the past, Heineken's U.S. district managers had to sit down with distributors to plan orders three months in advance. The distribution manager would then fax the order to Heineken's U.S. headquarters in White Plains, and then the order would be transmitted to the company's brewery and world headquarters in Amsterdam. Then it took ten to twelve weeks for U.S. distributors to receive shipments. The solution devised by Heineken and Logility uses the Internet to eliminate order-taking via telephone and hand calculations for faxing, all of which used to

lead to human error as well. Heineken also implemented an intranet, a private network connecting the company to customers and suppliers using the Internet based on Logility's Value Chain Solutions program. This system is known as HOPS (Heineken Operational Planning System), which allows for real-time sales forecasting and ordering interaction with distributors.

Distributors log on to the customized Web pages using a standard browser and Internet connection. They only need Netscape Navigator to access the program, eliminating the high cost of a direct line from the distributor to Heineken's offices. Once they enter identification and password, they can view sales forecasts, and they can modify and submit orders by pressing a button. Order submissions are available in real time at the Heineken brewery in Europe, which can then adjust its brewing and shipment schedules.

Heineken USA's new collaborative planning has reduced order cycle times from three months to four weeks, and simplified planning for its distributor customers. A shorter lead time means fresher beer delivered to customers.

Source: "Heineken Redefines Collaborative Planning through the Internet," *Beverage Industry,* 89 (September 1998), p. 47.

which covers South America and Asia. Until some time back, GM used to handle its own shipping, but turned to external contractors to maximize efficiency. The support companies do their own billing, itemized for review by the logistics office at GM headquarters.

At Dell Computer, the international logistics manager makes certain that the third-party logistics provider is state of the art and keeps them involved in Dell's strategic planning. Dell buys monitors finished and packaged, ready to deliver directly to the customer the world over. Since it does not add any value to the monitor itself, Dell tries to avoid handling the monitor, preferring instead to have the logistic provider warehouse it and move it to Dell when the information system link with Dell drops an order into the warehouse computer. This saves Dell inventorying costs and gives it more operational flexibility.[21]

Pharmaceutical giant Eli Lilly has gradually outsourced more of its global logistics to Swiss-based Danzas AG. Danzas was recently put in charge of customs handling and the delivery of Eli Lilly's airborne and ocean imports. Based in the pharmaceutical hub of Basel, Switzerland, Danzas has increasingly specialized in pharmaceutical products, also working with SmithKline Beecham and Hoffman-La Roche.[22]

As the market for third-party logistics has increased substantially in the 1990s, many traditional shippers, such as DHL, UPS, Federal Express, and TNT, have developed large business units solely devoted to integrated logistics. Many logistic companies are now moving to provide tailored logistic solutions in international markets for their clients. One major player is Ryder, the truck-rental and shipping company. Its Integrated Logistics Unit is looking to become number one in the industry, and is increasingly looking toward high technology to do it. By developing state-of-the-art networks that combine cutting-edge software with the Internet, Ryder hopes to gain an advantage over the competition. Ryder is also consolidating into 'multiclient service'—that is, consolidating shipments from different companies, even if they are competitors, such as Ford and Chrysler. "Car companies are realizing they have to compete in the showroom, and who delivers the part to the back door doesn't matter," observed Ryder President Raymond Greer.[23]

Circle International of Canada provides another excellent example. With 350 offices located worldwide, this Canadian company provides all logistical services including logistics information systems, global communications, air freight, ocean freight, inland transportation, customs brokerage, warehousing and distribution, and transportation insurance. For instance, a typical automobile manufacturer uses about twenty-five freight forwarders and vendors who share responsibility for exporting vehicles and parts to worldwide markets. Excess inventory and poor-response time contribute to low return on assets and poor customer service. First, Circle develops a plan tailored to meet their needs to reduce inventory, shorten transit time, streamline administration, and offer higher customer service. To accomplish these goals, this Canadian company establishes a central service center for all exports with its onsite staff that can reduce administrative costs by some 30

---

[21]Silvia Ascarelli, "Dell Finds U.S. Strategy Works in Europe," *Wall Street Journal* (February 3, 1997), p. A8.

[22]Robert Koenig, "Danzas Expands Pharmaceutical Logistics Business with Eli Lilly," *Journal of Commerce* (December 7, 1998), p. 14A.

[23]Helen Atkinson, "Greer Maps Path for Ryder Unit," *Journal of Commerce* (January 5, 1999), p. 12A.

percent. Second, the company develops a logistics database to coordinate, track, and schedule material flows from the United States and other locations. This system enables employees to transmit data electronically to the client each day. Third, parts and vehicles are received at strategically located consolidation points where they are inspected, packed, assembled, and processed through the company's automated inventory system. This centralized approach to managing inventory allows for reduction of material handling and greater control over material. Fourth, the logistics company provides clients with customs brokerage services. Using its global information network, commercial invoice data are summarized and transmitted to the destination's customs operations. Finally, from the central service center, Circle coordinates material flow of goods, working directly with vendors and carriers around the world to ensure competitive shipping rates, accurate delivery time, and expedited distribution from origin to destination.[24] Since moving to one such logistic provider, Sun Microsystems reduced its year-end inventory level in Europe from $62 million to $12 million.

Some distribution companies even find the best way to be successful is to create a distribution alliance, and pool their logistics resources together. An example is the global distribution alliance between three international electronics distribution companies: the U.S. company Pioneer-Standard, the British company Eurodis, and Taiwan's World Peace Industrial. By the alliance's ability to cover almost the entire globe, it has been able to obtain worldwide exclusive distribution contracts from electronics manufacturers.[25]

FREE TRADE ZONES ◆ ◆ ◆ ◆ ◆ ◆

A **free trade zone (FTZ)** is an area that is located within a nation (say, the United States), but is considered outside of the customs territory of the nation. Many countries have similar programs. In the United States, a free trade zone is officially called a Foreign Trade Zone. FTZs are licensed by the Foreign Trade Zone Board and operated under the supervision of the Customs Service. The level of demand for FTZ procedures has followed the overall growth trend for global trade and investment. Currently, about 150 FTZs are in operation and, as part of their activity, more than 180 manufacturing plants are operating with subzone status. Warehousing and manufacturing activity combined account for incoming zone shipments of some $170 billion annually, and more than 2,800 firms employing over 315,000 persons are now using FTZ procedures.[26] Subzones are adjuncts to the main zones when the main site cannot serve the purpose and are usually found at manufacturing plants. Legally, goods in the zone remain in international commerce as long as they are held within the zone or are exported. In other words, those goods (including materials, components, and finished products) shipped into an FTZ in the United States from abroad are legally considered not

---

[24]Circle International Home Page, http://www.circleintl.com/index.htm, accessed June 20, 1997.

[25]Matthew Sheerin, "Distribution Alliance Shopping for Global Partners," *Electronic Buyers' News* (November 23, 1998).

[26]John J. Da Ponte. Jr. "The Foreign-Trade Zones Act: Keeping Up with the Changing Times," *Business America* (December 1997), pp. 22–25.

having landed in the customs territory of the United States and thus are not subject to U.S. import tariffs, as long as they are not sold outside the FTZ in the United States.

As summarized in Exhibit 16–2, an FTZ provides many cash flow and operating advantages to zone users. No duties, tariffs, or taxes are levied on any goods imported into an FTZ, until or unless they are brought into U.S. territory. Even when these goods enter the United States, customs duties can be levied on the lesser of the value of the finished product or its imported components.

Operationally, an FTZ provides an opportunity for every business engaged in international commerce to take advantage of a variety of efficiencies and economies in the manufacture and marketing of their products. Merchandise within the zone may be unpacked and repacked; sorted and relabeled; inspected and tested; repaired or discarded; reprocessed, fabricated, assembled, or otherwise manipulated. It may be combined with other imported or domestic materials; stored or exhibited; transported in bond to another FTZ; sold or exported. Foreign goods may be modified within the zone to meet U.S. import standards and processed using U.S. labor.

Aging of imported wine is an interesting way of taking advantage of an FTZ. A U.S. wine importer purchases what is essentially newly fermented grape juice from French vineyards and ships it to an FTZ in the United States for aging. After several years, the now-aged French wine can be shipped throughout the United States, when an appropriate U.S. import tariff will be assessed on the original value of the grape juice instead of on the market value of the aged wine. If tariff rates are sufficiently high, then cost savings from using an FTZ can be enormous.

Another effective use of an FTZ is illustrated by companies such as Ford and Dell Computer. These companies rely heavily on imported components such as auto parts and computer chips, respectively. In such a case, the companies can get part of their manufacturing facilities designated as subzones of an FTZ. This way,

---

EXHIBIT 16–2
BENEFITS OF USING A FREE TRADE ZONE (FTZ)

---

1. **Duty deferral and elimination:** Duty will be deferred until products are sold in the United States. If products are exported elsewhere, no import tariff will be imposed.
2. **Lower tariff rates:** Tariff rates are almost always lower for materials and components than for finished products. If materials and components are shipped to an FTZ for furtherprocessing and finished products are sold in the United States, a U.S. import tariff will be assessed on the value of the materials and components, rather than on the value of the finished products.
3. **Lower tariff incidence:** Imported materials and components that through storage or processing undergo a loss or shrinkage may benefit from FTZ status, as the tariff is assessed only on the value of materials and components that actually found their way into the product.
4. **Exchange rate hedging:** Currency fluctuations can be hedged against by requesting customs assessment at any time.
5. **Import quota not applicable:** Import quotas are not generally applicable to goods stored in an FTZ.
6. **"Made in U.S.A." designation:** If foreign components are substantially transformed within an FTZ located in the United States, the finished product may be designated as "Made in U.S.A."

---

they can use their facilities as ordinarily as they can, yet enjoy all the benefits accruing from an FTZ.

At the macro-level, all parties to the arrangement benefit from the operation of trade zones. The government maintaining the trade zone achieves increased investment and employment. The firm using the trade zone obtains a beachhead in the foreign market without incurring all the costs normally associated with such an activity. As a result, goods can be reassembled, and large shipments can be broken down into smaller units. Duties may be payable only on the imported materials and the component parts rather than on the labor that is used to finish the product.

In addition to free trade zones, various governments have also established export processing zones and special economic areas. As shown in Global Perspective 16–5, Japan, which has had a large trade surplus over the years, has developed a unique trade zone program specifically designed to increase imports rather than exports. The common dimensions for all these zones are that special rules apply to them, when compared with other regions of the country, and that the purpose of these rules is the desire of governments to stimulate the economy—especially the export side of international trade. Export processing zones usually provide tax- and

◆ ◆

𝒢LOBAL PERSPECTIVE 16–5

JAPAN'S FOREIGN ACCESS ZONE TO INCREASE IMPORTS AND INWARD DIRECT INVESTMENT

Japan has made some of its major trading partner countries turn protectionist as it has run a huge trade surplus over the years. To increase imports into Japan rather than to encourage exports from Japan, the Japanese government announced "A Basic Plan for the Expansion of Imports" in 1993. It is a $20 billion program to create a national network of thirty-one import promotion areas scattered across the country, or as the Japanese call them, *foreign access zones.* Importers and foreign investors would get special tax breaks and other advantages. The foreign access zones could provide a major opportunity for American and other foreign businesses setting up beachhead in Japan.

Operations based in the access zones would also get around most, if not all, of the existing impediments to foreign investment in Japan. The zones will provide inexpensive warehousing and storage, free or low-cost translation and marketing assistance, access to less expensive regional labor, and most important of all, local marketing opportunities that bypass the large trading companies and their traditional keiretsu distribution channels.

Source: Ronald A. Morse, "Foreign Access Zones: A Billion Dollar Opportunity with Japan," *Forum* (September 15, 1993), p. 5; and Alan Kitchin, "Japan: A Place in the Sun," *Director,* 51 (September 1997), pp. 77–80.

Kyushu, Japan's southernmost island, has been selected as the testing ground for this open approach. It is being promoted as the "crossroads of Asia" (it is closer to Shanghai and Seoul than it is to Tokyo). Also known as "Silicon Island," Kyushu hosts a clutch of US high-tech manufacturers (including Texas Instruments, which employs 1,000 people at its Hiji plant). The island's two main cities, Fukuoka and Kitakyushu, have fully espoused the Japanese government's foreign access zone concept. Across Kyushu, cities and prefectures are competing with one another to offer the best incentives to incoming-business.

In 1997, Kitakyushu raised its cash incentives for building new factories and software houses from $1.8 million to $4.5 million. Other incentives include discounted office space in a newly constructed Asian trade center, a land leasing program at 8 percent of evaluated cost, and joint venture opportunities with local companies boasting private electricity supplies.

Kitakyushu's port, Hibikinada, is being deepened and a new $1.5 billion international airport is being constructed on reclaimed land nearby. Kyushu is committed to a future role as an Asian production base - but for the moment it is more likely to be used as an entry point for the Japanese market.

duty-free treatment of production facilities whose output is destined abroad. The maquiladoras of Mexico are one example.[27]

For the logistician, the decision of whether to use such zones is framed by the overall benefit for the logistics system. Clearly, transport and retransport are often required, warehousing facilities need to be constructed, and material handling frequency will increase. However, the costs may well be balanced by the preferential government treatment or by lower labor costs.

◆ ◆ ◆ ◆ ◆ ◆ MAQUILADORA OPERATION

The **maquiladora** industry, also known as the *in-bond* or *twin-plant program*, is essentially a special Mexican version of a free trade zone. Mexico allows duty-free imports of machinery and equipment for manufacturing as well as components for further processing and assembly, as long as at least 80 percent of the plant's output is exported. Mexico permits 100 percent foreign ownership of the maquiladora plants in the designated maquiladora zone.

Mexico's Border Industrialization Program developed in 1965 set the basis for maquiladora operations in Mexico. It was originally intended to attract foreign manufacturing investment and increase job opportunities in areas of Mexico suffering from chronic high unemployment. Most of them are located along the U.S.–Mexico border, such as Tijuana across from San Diego, Ciudad Juarez across from El Paso, and Nuevo Laredo across from Laredo. Over the years, however, Mexico has expanded the maquiladora programs to industrialized major cities such as Monterrey, Mexico City, and Guadalajara, where more skilled workers can be found.

Mexico has been an attractive location for labor-intensive assembly because, while hour wage rates in most developing countries have increased since 1980, in Mexico they have declined in dollar terms from $2.96 per hour in 1980 to $1.20 per hour in 1990, and to about $0.50 per hour in 1999. This decline has resulted from a series of peso depreciations beginning in 1976, including the devastating depreciation that shook the Mexican economy in late 1994 and 1995. Employment in the maquiladora industry grew from 120,000 in 1980 to 300,000 in 1987, and has since more than doubled to 750,000 in 1999.[28] Automobile and electronics product assembly makes up the bulk of maquiladora industries.

In Tijuana, electronics manufacturers alone, including Samsung, Sony, Hitachi, and JVC, assemble more than 9 million television sets a year. In the United States, where more than ninety companies once built TV sets, television-manufacturing jobs—mostly production of picture tubes, receivers, and cabinets—have fallen to 30,000 nationwide, according to the Electronics Industry Association. Mexican workers now have the ability to handle complex and sophisticated manufacturing processes. Now with trade barriers falling as a result of the North American Free Trade Agreement (NAFTA), it has become easier for MNCs, particularly those

---

[27]Lance Eliot Brouthers, John P. McCray, and Timothy J. Wilkinson, "Maquiladoras: Entrepreneurial Experimentation to Global Competitiveness," *Business Horizon*, 42 (March/April 1999), pp. 37–44.

[28]National Statistics Institute database, 1999.

from the United States, to make high-tech products in border towns like Tijuana and ship them worldwide.[29]

The competitive pressures of the world economy have forced many large manufacturing companies to abandon their assembly plants in the United States and move to Mexican maquiladoras. Furthermore, in order to meet local content requirements imposed by NAFTA, foreign firms, too, have been expanding their manufacturing operations in the maquiladoras. Particularly, Asian companies, such as Panasonic, Sanyo, Sony, Samsung, and Daewoo, have invited some of their traditional components suppliers to join them in the maquiladoras to increase local procurement.

U.S. SPECIAL IMPORT TARIFF PROVISIONS ◆ ◆ ◆ ◆ ◆ ◆

The dramatic growth of maquiladoras in Mexico is not entirely attributed to Mexico's Border Industrialization Program and inexpensive labor cost. Special U.S. tariff provisions have also encouraged U.S.-based companies[30] to export U.S.-made components and other in-process materials to foreign countries for further processing and/or assembly and subsequently to reimport finished products back into the United States. U.S. imports under these tariff provisions are officially called **U.S. imports under Items 9802.00.60 and 9802.00.80 of the U.S. Harmonized Tariff Schedule** (the 9802 tariff provisions, for short).

The 9802 tariff provisions permit the duty-free importation by U.S.-based companies of their components previously sent abroad for further processing or assembly (i.e., tariffs are assessed only on the foreign value-added portion of the imported products). More specifically, item 9802.00.60 applies to reimportation for further processing in the United States of any metal initially processed or manufactured in the United States that was shipped abroad for processing. Item 9802.00.80 permits reimportation for sale in the United States of finished products assembled abroad in whole or in part made up of U.S.-made components.[31] Therefore, the higher the U.S. import tariff rates, the more beneficial it is for U.S.-based companies to be able to declare U.S. imports under the 9802 tariff provisions. Consequently, many U.S.-based companies have taken full advantage of both the 9802 tariff provisions of the United States and the maquiladora laws of Mexico in pursuit of cost competitiveness.

Under the provisions of NAFTA, however, U.S. import tariffs on products originating from Canada and Mexico continue to be reduced over the next decade or so. As a result, the tariff advantage for products reimported from Mexico into the United States under the 9802 tariff provisions will eventually diminish over time. However, as many items still have five, ten, and some fifteen-year phase-in periods before elimination of tariffs, the 9802 tariff provisions will remain useful even within NAFTA for the foreseeable future.[32] These tariff provisions still benefit

---

[29]"Economics Lesson in a Border Town: Why That Asian TV Has a 'Made in Mexico' Label," *New York Times* (May 23, 1996), p. D1.

[30]U.S.-based companies refer to both U.S. and foreign companies that are manufacturing in the United States.

[31]Martha L. Celestino, "Manufacturing in Mexico," *World Trade*, 12 (July 1999), pp. 36–42.

[32]Ibid.

U.S.-based companies manufacturing outside of the NAFTA region as long as U.S.-made materials and components are used in production.

U.S. imports under the 9802 tariff provisions have increased at a much faster rate than the overall U.S. imports. In recent years, some 20 percent of total U.S. imports come under the 9802 tariff provisions. At a glance, this percentage figure does not appear significant. It is to be noted that about 40 percent of total U.S. manufactured imports are attributed to U.S. firms' foreign affiliates exporting back to the United States. For example, 45 percent of Canada's exports, 53 percent of Mexico's exports, and 36 percent of Taiwan's exports came to the United States under the 9802 tariff provisions.[33] This phenomenon is also called intra-firm sourcing or intra-firm trade. A good portion of the provision 9802 imports is of intra-firm nature, thus representing a significant portion of intra-firm trade managed by U.S. multinational firms.[34]

◆ ◆ ◆ ◆ ◆ ◆ GLOBAL RETAILING

The face of distribution that consumers interact with is the retail store at which they shop. In developed parts of the world, retailing employs between 7 percent and 12 percent of the work force and wields enormous power over manufacturers and consumers. Retailers have grown into some of the world's largest companies, rivaling or exceeding manufacturers in terms of global reach. Wal-Mart, a U.S. discount chain, has grown to be the world's largest retailer with annual revenues of $138 billion in 1999, which exceed many times over the annual revenues of some of its top suppliers. It is Procter & Gamble's single largest customer, buying as much as the household product giant sells to Japan. Each of Europe's top half-dozen food retailers, such as Carrefour, Kingfisher, Ahold, and Metro, has larger sales than any of the continent's food manufacturers except Nestlé and Unilever.

Retailing involves very locally entrenched activities, including stocking of an assortment of products that local consumers prefer, catering to local shopping pattern (e.g., shopping frequency, time of shopping, and traffic jam), seasonal promotion, and meeting local competition on a daily basis. International retailers that are willing to adapt their strategy to local ways of doing things while taking advantage of their managerial and information technology capabilities seem to be more successful than those that try to extend their ways of doing things abroad. In general, European retailers tend to be more willing to customize their marketing and procurement strategies to various local market peculiarities than U.S. or Japanese retailers.[35] Wal-Mart, which tended to extend its U.S.-based procurement and product assortment strategies in its earlier foreign expansion, resulting in a huge market adjustment problem, is now moving very slowly to convert the stores it has acquired in Europe into anything Americans would recognize as Wal-Marts.[36]

[33]U.S. International Trade Commission, *1999 Tariff Database*, http://dataweb.usitc.gov/scripts/tariff.asp, accessed September 10, 1999.

[34]Masaaki Kotabe, "Efficiency vs. Effectiveness Orientation of Global Sourcing Strategy: A Comparison of U.S. and Japanese Multinational Companies," *Academy of Management Executive*, 12 (November 1998), pp. 107–119.

[35]Brenda Sternquist, *International Retailing* (New York: Fairchild Publications, 1998).

[36]Earnest Beck and Emily Nelson, "As Wal-Mart Invades Europe, Rivals Rush to Match Its Formula," *Wall Street Journal Interactive Edition*, http://interactive.wsj.com/, October 6, 1999.

At the heart of this retailing revolution is the fundamental change in the way goods and services reach the consumer. Earlier, the distribution chain across the world was controlled by the manufacturer or the wholesaler. The retailer's main competitive advantage lay in merchandising—his or her skills in choosing the assortment of goods for sale in the store. The main use of a second advantage of the retailer—closeness to the customer—was to beat the rival retailer across the street. It was the manufacturer who decided what goods were available, and in most countries at what price they could be sold to the public.

That distribution system of earlier times has now been turned upside down. The traditional supply chain powered by the manufacturing *push* is becoming a demand chain driven by consumer *pull*—especially in the developed countries where the supply and variety of goods is far above base-level requirements of goods and services. In most industrialized countries, resale price maintenance—which allows the supplier to fix the price at which goods can be sold to the final customer—has either been abolished or bypassed. The shift in power in the distribution channel is fundamentally a product of the application of information technology to store management.

Now many MNCs from industrialized countries are entering markets and developing their distribution channels in developing countries. A recent study by New York University's Tish Robinson shows that companies from Western countries seem to have difficulty competing with Japanese companies in fast-growing Southeast Asian markets and that it is attributed to different styles in managing distribution channels. In just three decades, the consumer electronics distribution systems in Malaysia and Thailand have come to be characterized by a striking presence of exclusive dealerships with Japanese multinational manufacturers such as Matsushita, Sanyo, and Hitachi.

For example, Matsushita (a maker of Panasonics, National, and Technics brand names) practices a push strategy with 220 exclusive dealerships in Malaysia and 120 in Thailand. In Malaysia, these exclusive dealerships represent 65 percent of total Matsushita sales although their numbers represent only 30 percent of the retailers selling Matsushita products. On the other hand, General Electric and Philips use a pull strategy, relying on the multivendor distribution system without firm control of the distribution channel as practiced in Western countries. Competitors from the United States and Europe are feeling locked out of Japanese companies' tightly controlled distribution channels in Southeast Asia.[37] A push strategy appears to be more effective than a pull strategy in emerging markets.

"Push" versus "Pull"

Computer systems can now tell a retailer instantly what they are selling in hundreds of stores across the world, how much money they are making on each sale, and increasingly, who their customers are. This information technology has had two consequences.

On-Time Retail Information Management

Reduced Inventory. First, a well-managed retailer no longer has to keep large amounts of inventory—the stock burden has been passed upstream to the manufacturer. The retailer has a lower chance of running out of items, as well. At Wal-Mart,

---

[37]Patricia Robinson, "The Role of Historical and Institutional Context in Transferring Distribution Practices Abroad: Matsushita's Monopolization of Market Share in Malaysia," *The American Marketing Association and the Japan Marketing Association Conference on the Japanese Distribution Strategy* (November 22–24, 1998).

more than half of its 5,000 vendors get point-of-sale data. The moment a 7–Eleven customer in Japan buys a soft drink or a can of beer, the information goes directly to the bottler or the brewery. It immediately becomes the production schedule and the delivery schedule, actually specifying the hour at which the new supply has to be delivered and to which of the 4,300 stores. In effect, therefore, Ito-Yokado Co. controls the product mix, the manufacturing schedule and the delivery schedule of major suppliers such as Coca-Cola or Kirin Breweries. The British retailer Sainsbury's supply chain is geared to provide inputs on demand from the stores with a scheduled truck service to its 350 stores. The stores' ordering cycle is also set to match the loading and arrival of the trucks, which almost run according to a bus schedule.

Market Information at the Retail Level. Second, it is the retailer who has real time knowledge of what items are selling and how fast they are selling. This knowledge is used to extract better terms from the manufacturers. This trend in the transfer of power to the retailer in the developed countries has coincided with the lowering of trade barriers around the world and the spread of free-market economies in Asia and Latin America. As a result, retailers such as America's Toys "R" Us, Tower Records, and Wal-Mart; Britain's Mark & Spencer and J. Sainsbury; Holland's Mark; Sweden's IKEA; and France's Carrefour are being transformed into global businesses.

Strong logistics capabilities can be used as an offensive weapon to help a firm gain competitive advantage in the marketplace by improving customer service and consumer choice, and by lowering the cost of global sourcing and finished goods distribution.[38] These capabilities become increasingly important as the level of global integration increases, and as competitors move to supplement low-cost manufacturing strategies in distant markets with effective logistic management strategies. This point is well illustrated by Ito-Yokado's takeover in 1991 of the Southland Corporation that had introduced 7–Eleven's convenience store concept in the United States and subsequently around the world. Ito-Yokado of Japan licensed the 7–Eleven store concept from Southland in the 1970s and has invented just-in-time inventory management and revolutionized its physical distribution system in Japan. The key to Ito-Yokado's success with 7–Eleven Japan has been the use of its inventory and physical distribution management systems which result in lower on-hand inventory, faster inventory turnover, and most importantly, accurate information on customer buying habits. Ito-Yokado's 7–Eleven Japan now implements its just-in-time physical distribution system in 7–Eleven stores in the United States.[39]

Distribution is, thus, increasingly becoming concentrated; manufacturing, by contrast, is splintering. Thirty-five years ago, the Big Three automakers shared the U.S. auto market. Today the market is split among ten—Detroit's Big Three, five Japanese car makers, and two German car makers. Thirty-five years ago, 85 percent of all retail car sales were done in single-site dealerships; even three dealership chains were uncommon. Today, a fairly small number of large-chain dealers account for 40 percent of the retail sales of cars.

---

[38]Roy D. Shapiro, "Get Leverage from Logistics," *Harvard Business Review*, 62 (May–June 1984), pp. 119–26.

[39]Masaaki Kotabe, "The Return of 7–Eleven . . . from Japan: The Vanguard Program," *Columbia Journal of World Business*, 30 (Winter 1995), pp. 70–81.

Given the increased bargaining power of distributors, monitoring their performance has become an important management issue for many multinational companies. Although information technology has improved immensely, monitoring channel members' performance still remains humanistic. In general, if companies are less experienced in international operations, they tend to invest more resources in monitoring their channel members' activities.[40] As they gain in experience, they may increasingly build trust relationships with their channel members and depend more on formal performance-based control.[41]

The density of retail and wholesale establishments in different countries varies greatly. As a general rule, industrialized countries tend to have a lower distribution outlet density than the emerging markets. Part of the reason for this stems from the need in emerging markets for very small purchase lots and more frequent purchases due to low incomes and the lack of facilities in homes to refrigerate and preserve foods. At the same time, the advanced facilities available in the developed world allow a much higher square footage of retail space per resident, due to the large size of the retail outlets. The United States, for instance, has about 18.5 square feet of retail space per resident, compared to figures below 10 square feet for Western Europe.

Retailing Differences Across the World

Japan's retail industry has a number of features that distinguish it from retailing in Western countries. The major ones are a history of tight regulation—albeit being increasingly deregulated—less use of cars for shopping, and the importance of department stores in the lives of most people. For more than forty years until recently, the Large-Scale Retail Store Law[42] in Japan helped to protect and maintain small retail stores (12 retail stores per 1,000 residents in Japan vs. 6 retail stores per 1,000 residents in the United States in 1994) and, partly in consequence, a multilayered distribution system. Consequently, there has been the relatively poor proliferation of megastores and large-scale shopping centers. Since Japan's urban areas are crowded, roads are congested and parking is expensive or nonexistent, many people use public transport to shop. Consequently, shopping is usually within a rather small radius of the home or workplace and products, especially food, generally are bought in smaller quantities. Shopping, therefore, is more frequent. This situation is further encouraged by the requirement of Japanese cooking for fresh ingredients. Retail stores that not only stay open 24 hours a day throughout the week but also practice just-in-time delivery of fresh perishable foods, such as 7–Eleven and Lawson, are extremely popular in Japan. Discount stores have also gained in popularity among recession-weary, now price-conscious Japanese consumers. Similarly, department stores are crucial in everyday Japanese life. The variety of goods and services offered by the average department store ranges way beyond that in most retail outlets abroad. Larger department stores stock everything from fresh food and prepared dishes to discount and boutique clothing, and household and garden goods. Many have children's play-

---

[40]Esra F. Gencturk and Preet S. Aulakh, "The Use of Process and Output Controls in Foreign Markets," *Journal of International Business Studies*, 26 (Fourth Quarter, 1995), pp. 755–86.

[41]Preet S. Aulakh, Masaaki Kotabe, and Arvind Sahay, "Trust and Performance in Cross Border Marketing Partnerships: A Behavioral Approach," *Journal of International Business Studies*, 27 (Special Issue 1996).

[42]Jack G. Kaikati, "The Large-Scale Retail Store Law: One of the Thorny Issues in the Kodak-Fuji Case," *The American Marketing Association and the Japan Marketing Association Conference on the Japanese Distribution Strategy*, November 22–24, 1998.

grounds and pet centers—some with displays resembling a miniature zoo. Museum-level art and craft exhibitions often are housed on upper floors, and both family and exquisite restaurants are usually on the top floor.[43] It is a very different—and often difficult—market for foreign retailers to enter. See Global Perspective 16–6 for international retailers cracking into the Japanese market.

In Germany, store hours are limited. Stores may not open on Sundays and should close on weekdays by 6 P.M. They may open one Saturday a month until 2:30 P.M. The IFO Economic Research Institute in a German government–commissioned report has recommended that stores be allowed to remain open from 6 A.M. to 10 P.M. on weekdays and until 6 P.M. on Saturdays; however, stores are still expected to be closed on Sundays.[44] Hence, while these laws are now being reviewed, even the situation after the proposed changes is still in contrast to the United States, where retail stores may remain open seven days a week, twenty-four hours a day. Keeping stores open in this manner requires very strong logistics management on the part of retailers and the manufacturing firms supplying the retailers. The sending organization, the receiving organization, and the logistics provider (if applicable) have to work very closely together.

E-Commerce and Retailing. Despite those cultural differences and regulations in retailing still in place, countries such as Japan and Germany are warming up to the same electronic commerce revolution as the United States has already experienced. In Japan, for example, Rakuten Ichiba Internet Mall has achieved stellar growth since its launch in May 1997. Starting with just 13 stores, the mall had more than 850 stores as of January 2000—a growth rate of 80–100 per month—and the mall is now receiving 15 million page hits per month.[45] Founded with $500,000 in capital, Rakuten posted $300,000 in profits on sales of $15 million in the fiscal year ended December 1998, up from a loss of $150,000 on sales of $400,000 the previous year. Rakuten is well on its way to reaching its goal of 1,000 stores and $8 million in retail sales by the end of 1999 (at the time of this writing). In Germany, SAP already dominates the $12 billion market for so-called enterprise software. Its primary goal is to develop a software system with which entire industries could run as efficiently as a single plant, with razor-thin inventories and the leanest of work forces. It has another plan to push into consumer markets, from department stores to Internet malls.[46]

E-commerce is not limited to the developed countries. China, the world's most populous country, is expected to become the one of the world's largest Internet markets as early as 2003. China is already the fastest-growing Internet market in Asia, with the number of online users expected to reach 6.7 million by the end of 1999, up 319 percent from 1998, according to a report entitled "The Internet in China," jointly published by BDA China and the Strategis Group. The number of Chinese PC users going online is proliferating at nearly the same rate. At this rate of growth, China's Internet user base will hit 33 million in 2003, about double the size

[43]"Country Profiles–Japan," *Stores* (Jan 1998), pp. S45–S47.

[44]Marco Grühnhagen, Robert A. Mittelstaedt, and Ronald D. Hampton, "The Effect of the Relaxation of 'Blue Laws' on the Structure of the Retailing Industry in the Federal Republic of Germany," presented at 1997 AMA Summer Educators' Conference, August 2–5, 1997.

[45]Rakuten Ichiba Home Page, http://www.rakuten.co.jp, accessed February 10, 2000.

[46]Stephen Baker, "Sap's Expanding Universe—The Software Giant's Ambitious New Goal: To Be Everywhere Business is Taking Place," *Business Week* (September 14, 1998), p. 168.

GLOBAL PERSPECTIVE 16–6

FOREIGN RETAILERS AND DIRECT MARKETERS ENTERING INTO JAPAN EN MASSE

When U.S. President George Bush visited Japan in January 1992, Japan's retail distribution was a major issue between the United States and Japan. Toys "R" Us had been trying to open its stores in Japan since 1989, but Japan's Large-Scale Retail Store Law and tight relationships among local toy manufacturers, retailers, and wholesalers thwarted the American toy retailer's entry to the Japanese market.

The Large-Scale Retail Store Law gave small retailers and wholesalers disproportionate influence over the Japanese market by requiring firms planning to open a large store to submit their business plan to the local business regulation council, the local chamber of commerce (made up of those small retailers and wholesalers to be affected), and the Ministry of International Trade and Industry. As a result of this Catch-22 requirement, the process would take between one year and eighteen months, and was seen by foreign retailers as an almost insurmountable entry barrier.

Under U.S. government pressure, the Large-Scale Retail Store Law was relaxed in 1992 and also in 1994. Under the amendments, the task of examining applications for new stores was transferred from the local business regulation council to the Large-Scale Retail Store Council, a government advisory board under the Ministry of International Trade and Industry (MITI). Consequently, the maximum time required for various applications and approvals is now set at 12 months. These two revisions of the Large-Scale Retail Store Law have contributed to the increase in the number of applications requesting approval to establish a large retail store. According to the Japan Council of Shopping Centers, it is estimated that shopping centers have opened at the rate of more than 100 per year since 1992.

Toys "R" Us exploited this opportunity and was ultimately successful in cracking the Japanese market. It boasted a total of thirty-seven stores in 1996, and plans to open an average of ten more per year across the country. Following the success of Toys "R" Us, other foreign-based retailers have begun to crack the Japanese market. Nearly a dozen other such foreign retailers have recently opened their stores in Japan. Foreign firms face more difficulties when opening a store for general merchandise than one for a niche product, because the large Japanese general merchandise stores, such as Daiei, Ito-Yokado, and Seiyu, are well entrenched and already dominate the market. On the other hand, foreign niche retailers who face few competitors have been fairly successful.

For example, U.S.-based Tower Records, U.K.-based HMV, and Virgin Megastores have opened comparably large stores, selling both imported and domestic music tapes and CDs at competitive prices. Specialty retailers of outdoor goods and clothes are another brand of retailers to pour into the Japanese market recently. Among them, U.S.-based L.L. Bean and Eddie Bauer are the market leaders.

While Toys "R" Us and Tower Records have a wholly owned subsidiary in Japan, L.L. Bean and Eddie Bauer team up with a well-known Japanese company. L.L. Bean Japan is a Japanese franchise 70 percent owned by Japan's largest retailing group, Seibu, and 30 percent by Matsushita Electric, a maker of Panasonics, Technics, JVC, and Quasar brands. Eddie Bauer Japan is a joint venture of Otto-Sumitomo, a Sumitomo Group mail-order retailer, and Eddie Bauer USA. The contrasting experiences of Toys "R" Us, Tower Records, L.L. Bean, and Eddie Bauer raise an important question for future entrants to the Japanese market: whether to team up with a Japanese partner or open a wholly owned Japanese subsidiary. In general, forming a joint venture or a franchise allows new entrants to start faster, although they might lose control of the company's operation in Japan. Future would-be entrants should bear in mind that Japan is not an easy place to do business because, in addition to regulations, land and labor costs are extremely high.

On the other hand, direct marketing—another form of retailing—has blossomed into a $20 billion industry despite Japan's continued recession. Ten percent of this market belongs to foreign companies like Lands' End, an outdoor clothing maker, and Intimate Brands, which distributes Victoria's Secret catalogs. "For those companies and individuals who say that Japan is a closed market, I really can't think of an example of an easier market entry than catalog sales," says Cynthia Miyashita, president of mail-order consultant Hemisphere Marketing Inc. in Japan. Foreign mail-order companies sidestep Japan's notoriously complex regulations, multilevel distribution networks, and even import duties. Here are a few cases in point:

· Japan's post offices are unequipped to impose taxes on the hundreds of thousands of mail-order goods that flood the postal system, making direct marketing products virtually duty-free. Local competitors who import products in bulk have to pay duties, forcing up their prices.

- Many products, such as vitamins and cosmetics, are subject to strict testing regulations in Japan, but those

Source: Hayden Stewart, "Foreign Retailers Follow Toys "R" Us Path to Success," Journal of Japanese Trade and Industry, 15 (3) (1996), pp. 52–54; Joji Sakurai, "Firms Challenge Image of Japan's Closed Markets," *Marketing News* (July 20, 1998), p. 2; and Jack G. Kaikati, "The Large-Scale Retail Store Law: One of the Thorny Issues in the Kodak-Fuji Case," in Michael R. Czinkota and Masaaki Kotabe, *Japanese Distribution Strategy* (London: Business Press, 2000).

rules do not apply if the products are sold through mail order for personal consumption. That gives direct-mail customers in Japan access to a wide array of otherwise-unavailable products.

- American mailing costs are so cheap that it is more economical to send a package from New York to Tokyo than from Tokyo to Osaka, which reduces overhead costs for direct-mail products.

- Although Japanese companies are not allowed to mail goods from foreign post offices for sale at home, foreign companies face no such restrictions.

of Japan's user base today.[47] Similarly, the number of people using the Internet in Brazil grew 130 percent in 1999, making it Latin America's most wired nation, accounting for half of the region's six million people on the Web, according to the International Data Corporation. And despite a weak economy and huge gaps between rich and poor, industry experts expect the number of Internet users in Brazil to grow 60 to 100 percent over the next three years.[48] Along with the growth of Internet access is expected a similar growth in entrepreneurial e-commerce operators.

Despite the rapid growth of Internet-wired people and e-commerce operators around the world, it is to be noted, as explained earlier in this chapter, that the need for local or regional distribution of products is likely to remain as important as it was the case before the Internet revolution.

VIDEO CASE

HYPERMARKETS IN JAPAN

Japan experienced eight years of recession, characterized as the "Burst of the Bubble Economy," caused primarily by a decline in overinflated land prices, from 1992 to 2000. This long recession triggered price deflation across Japan. Furthermore, during the same time period, the Japanese yen appreciated drastically relative to the U.S. and other major currencies, making foreign imports cheaper in Japan.

Until recently, the Japanese distribution system was characterized as having stable relationships between manufacturers and their distributors. In a way, the channel was in large part controlled by large Japanese manufacturing companies such as Toyota,

Panasonic, and Kao. The reduction in consumer demand and the rapid increase in less expensive imports from abroad made Japanese consumers very price-sensitive. Price discounters, such as large discount stores and hypermarkets, have suddenly become popular among the budget-weary Japanese consumers in recent years.

Procter & Gamble in Japan (P&G Japan), albeit an American company, manufactures almost all the products locally for the Japanese market, and has been affected by price deflation the same way Japanese companies have. What advice would you give P&G Japan in terms of its distribution and logistics strategy?

[47]"China's Net Market Booming," CNN.com, July 2, 1999.

[48]"Brazilians Take to the Web with Uncommon Speed," Latin IT News, http://latinitnews@mailer.latpro.com, June 28, 1999.

SUMMARY

Logistics and distribution have traditionally been a local issue and have had to do with getting goods to the final customer in a local market. However, while the intent of serving the customer remains, retailers have been transformed into global organizations that buy and sell products from and to many parts of the world. At the same time, with the increase in the globalization of manufacturing, many firms are optimizing their worldwide production by sourcing components and raw materials from around the world. Both these trends have increased the importance of global logistic management for firms.

The relevance of global logistics is likely to wax in the coming years because international distribution often accounts for between 10 percent and 25 percent of the total landed cost of an international order. The international logistics manager has to deal with multiple issues, including transport, warehousing, inventorying, and the connection of these activities to the corporate strategy of the firm. Not only are these logistics issues compounded by inflation, currency exchange, and tax rates that differ across national boundaries, but the international logistics manager can exploit those differences to their advantage—advantages not available to domestic firms.

Logistics management is closely linked to manufacturing activities, even though a new trend shows that logistics management can be outsourced from third-party logistics specialists. Many companies, particularly those in the European Union, are trying to develop a consolidated production location so that they can reduce the number of distribution centers and market their products from one or a few locations throughout Europe. Federal Express, Airborne Express, and TNT, for example, have evolved from document shippers to providing complete logistics functions—indeed, all these firms now sport a business logistics division whose function is to handle the outsourced logistics functions of corporate clients.

Various governments, including the United States, have developed free trade zones, export processing zones, and other special economic zones designed chiefly to increase domestic employment and exports from the zone. Various tax and other cost benefits available in the zones attract both domestic and foreign firms to set up warehousing and manufacturing operations. Many U.S.-based multinational firms, both domestic and foreign, take advantage of U.S. tariff provisions 9802.00.60 and 9802.00.80 and many of Mexico's maquiladoras (a special Mexican version of free trade zones). Historically, cost advantage accruing from use of a combination of the U.S. tariff provisions and Mexico's maquiladoras has benefited many large MNCs that could easily relocate labor-intensive assembly or processing operations there. As a result of NAFTA, however, maquiladoras have begun to attract increasingly high-tech industries as well.

Retailing has long been considered a fairly localized activity subject to different customer needs and different national laws regulating domestic commerce. Nevertheless, some significant change is taking place in the retail sector. Information technology makes it increasingly possible for large retailers to know what they are selling in hundreds of stores around the world. Given this intimate knowledge of customers around the world, those retailers have begun to overtake the channel leadership role from manufacturers. The United States' Wal-Mart and Toys "R" Us, Japan's Ito-Yokado, and Britain's Mark & Spencer are some of the major global retailers changing the logistics of inventory and retail management on a global basis.

Finally, e-commerce is increasingly dispensing with physical stores. However, local adaptation of product offerings and setting-up of local distribution centers remain as important as it was before the Internet revolution. Furthermore, complex international shipping requirements and exchange rate fluctuations hamper smooth distribution of products around the world.

KEY TERMS

bulk shipping
cost of transportation
free trade zone (FTZ)
global logistics
liner service

logistic integration
maquiladora operation
materials management
perishability
physical distribution

rationalization
third-party logistics (3PL) services
value-to-volume ratio

U.S. imports under Items 9802.00.60 and 9802.00.80 of the U.S. Harmonized Tariff Schedule

REVIEW QUESTIONS ✦

1. Define the term *global logistics*. Enumerate and describe the various operations encompassed by it.

2. What factors contribute to the increased complexity and cost of global logistics as compared to domestic logistics?

3. What role do third-party logistics companies play in international trade? What are the advantages of using these companies over internalizing the logistics activities?

4. Describe the role of free trade zones (FTZs) in global logistics.

5. What are the reasons for the dramatic increase in cross-border trade between the United States and Mexico?

6. How is information technology affecting global retailing?

7. The United States and Japan have similar income and purchasing power levels. Yet, there are significant differences in the retail structures between the two countries. Describe some reasons for these differences.

DISCUSSION QUESTIONS ✦ ✦ ✦ ✦ ✦ ✦ ✦ ✦ ✦ ✦ ✦ ✦ ✦ ✦ ✦ ✦ ✦ ✦ ✦

1. Some economists have brought attention to the importance of the role of geography in international trade. One example of this is the dramatic rise in trade between the United States and Mexico. This increase is attributed primarily to wage differences between the two countries and the proximity, with both countries sharing a joint border more than 2,000 miles in length. Geographic proximity allows for the relative cheap movement of goods by train from the heart of Mexico to any corner of the United States within three to four days. On the other hand, advocates of globalization claim that the role of geography in international trade is limited and is reducing constantly. They contend that direct transportation costs as a percentage of the total value of the goods for most goods is low and is declining. Furthermore, it is not actual transportation costs, but the coordination of managerial resources and information that is the key to savings through global logistics. This reduces the role of geography in international trade to a minimal level. Comment on the two views.

2. Taking advantage of advancements in information technology and increased lowering of trade barriers, various catalog merchandisers have been increasing their global presence at a rapid rate. L.L. Bean is an example of one such success case. Its international sales in 1994 grew by more than 62 percent and now account for 13 percent of its total sales. However, problems of infrastructure (e.g., telephone and postal service in general, and the lack of international services such as 1-800 numbers in particular) are significant barriers to the centralization of this business. These problems have led to 70 percent of L.L. Bean's international sales coming from one country (Japan).

Assume that you are part of the top management team of a large retail chain that has a moderate presence in the domestic catalog business, but no presence in the international market. However, this company would like to enter the international catalog merchandising business and was willing to make long-term financial commitments for this endeavor. Given the constraints just mentioned, the relative nascent state of the business at a global level, and the significant advantages to be gained through coordination of global logistics, what would you recommend the company do in terms of choice of market, the centralization vs. decentralization of logistics activities, and the decision to outsource vs. internalize the logistic activities?

3. The world is moving closer to an era of free trade and global economic interdependence. The worldwide reduction in tariff and nontariff barriers and the increasing levels of world trade are testimony to this fact. These reductions in trade barriers will in the very near future make free trade zones an anachronistic concept. Hence, if you were making an investment decision, on behalf of your company, to establish a manufacturing facility in a developing country, placing too much emphasis on investing in free trade zones may be a short-term workable proposition, but a long-term mistake. Do you agree or disagree with this statement? Give reasons for your answer.

4. Reduced trade barriers and saturation of domestic markets are two forces in the 1990s that are encouraging large retail chains to move overseas. Large retail chains in the United States, Japan, and Europe are aggressively making forays into international markets, although there is a significant regional bias in these efforts. U.S. retail chains such as Wal-Mart have primarily focused on

Canada and have now turned their focus to Mexico. Japanese retail chains such as JUSCO and Daimaru have made significant inroads into Southeast Asia, while Western European chains such as Julius Meinl (Austria), Promodes (France), Ahold (The Netherlands), and TESCO (U.K) are diversifying into Eastern Europe and other countries within Europe. Industry analysts point out that this internationalization of retail business will significantly alter the nature of competition. Significant rationalization through acquisitions of retail businesses is bound to take place. The verdict on the expected effects of this rationalization and increased competition on specialty chains is still unclear. What would you predict the retail business to look like ten years from now? What would be the role of specialty stores and specialty chains?

5. The concept of one-stop-shopping for global logistics is fast catching on. There are now more than thirty large logistic companies, called *mega-carriers*, who can provide truly global and integrated logistic services. What are the opportunities and threats that these trends offer to small and large transporters, freight-forwarders, and shippers (exporters)?

FURTHER READING ◆

Celestino, Martha L. "Electronic Commerce." *World Trade*, 12 (February 1999): 76–79.

Dowlatshahi, Shad. "The Role of Purchasing and TQM in the Maquiladora Industry." *Production and Inventory Management Journal*, 39 (Fourth Quarter 1998): 42–49.

Fawcett, Stanley E., Laura Birou, and Barbara Cofield Taylor. "Supporting Global Operations Through Logistics and Purchasing." International Journal of Physical Distribution and Logistics Management, 23(4) (1993): 3–11.

Hanks, George F., and Lucinda Van Alst. "Foreign Trade Zones." *Management Accounting*; 80 (January 1999): 20–23.

Johnson, Jean L., John B. Cullen, and Tomoaki Sakano. "Opportunistic Tendencies in IJVs with the Japanese: The Effects of Culture, Shared Decision Making, and Relationship Age." *International Executive*, 38(1) (1996).

Mathur, Lynette Knowles, and Ike Mathur. "The Effectiveness of the Foreign-Trade Zone as an Export Promotion Program: Policy Issues and Alternatives." *Journal of Macromarketing* 17 (Fall 1997): 20–31.

Rao, Kant, and Richard R. Young. "Global Supply Chains: Factors Influencing Outsourcing of Logistics Functions." *International Journal of Physical Distribution and Logistics Management*, 24 (6) (1994): 11–19.

Rapoport, Carla. "Retailers Go Global." *Fortune*, 131(3) (1995): 102–108.

Sternquist, Brenda. *International Retailing* (New York: Fairchild Publications, 1998).

Wood, Donald F. *International Logistics*. New York: Chapman & Hall, 1995.

EXPORT AND IMPORT MANAGEMENT

17

CHAPTER OVERVIEW

1. ORGANIZING FOR EXPORTS

2. INDIRECT EXPORTING

3. DIRECT EXPORTING

4. LINKAGE BETWEEN FOREIGN DIRECT INVESTMENT AND EXPORTS

5. MECHANICS OF EXPORTING

6. ROLE OF THE GOVERNMENT IN PROMOTING EXPORTS

7. MANAGING IMPORTS—THE OTHER SIDE OF THE COIN

8. MECHANICS OF IMPORTING

9. GRAY MARKETS

Exporting is the most popular way for many companies to become international. There are two main reasons for this: (1) exporting requires minimum resources while allowing high flexibility, and (2) it offers substantial financial, marketing, technological, and other benefits to the firm. As exporting is usually the first mode of foreign entry used by many companies, exporting early on tends to give them first-mover advantage.[1] However, selling to a foreign market involves numerous high risks, arising from a lack of knowledge about and unfamiliarity with

---

[1]Yigang Pan, Shaomin Li, and David K. Tse, "The Impact of Orfer and Mode of Market Entry on Profitability and Market Share," *Journal of International Business Studies*, 30 (First Quarter 1999), pp. 81–104.

foreign environments, which can be heterogeneous, sophisticated, and turbulent. Furthermore, conducting market research across national boundaries is more difficult, complex, and subjective than its domestic counterpart. For successful development of export activities, systematic collection of information is critical. Market information helps managers to assess the attractiveness of foreign markets and decide whether to engage in exporting. Once a firm has decided to start exporting, information is required on how to handle the mechanics of it, including how to enter overseas markets, or what adaptations to make to the marketing mix elements. As a firm proceeds through the export involvement over time, information is necessary to tackle strategic issues, such as what market expansion strategy to adopt; where to introduce new products; and how to appraise corporate export performance.[2]

The nature of world exports and imports has also changed radically. The notion of developing countries as exporters of raw materials from which they earn revenue to pay for imports of manufactured goods is already hopelessly inappropriate. Raw materials' prices fell sharply in 1998 and 1999, pushing the share of primary products in world exports below 20 percent in current-price terms for the first time in the postwar period. Prices of internationally traded manufactured goods and services also declined in 1998, but by considerably less than those of primary products. Manufactured goods accounted for almost 60 percent of the exports of developing countries. Also, the effect of exports from the industrial countries to the developing nations on the economies of industrial nations is now considerable.[3]

Due largely to continuing economic contraction in much of Asia, the rate of growth in the volume of world merchandise exports slowed to 3.5 percent in 1998, from over 10 percent in 1997. World output growth slipped to 2 percent in 1998, compared to 3 percent in 1997. Although trade growth still exceeded output growth in 1998, it was by a smaller margin than the average for the 1990s. International trade is expected to pick up steam into the next century once Asian economies recover from the financial crisis.[4] *This said, as Exhibit 17–1 shows, the world's top six exporting countries still account for about 45 percent of total world exports.*

Although the United States is still relatively more insulated from the global economy than other nations (see Chapter 2), exporting has become increasingly important as a driver of new job creation and better paying jobs. Exports represent about 11 percent of the U.S. gross domestic product, yet account for fully one-third of total U.S. economic growth since 1990. An estimated 12 million American jobs depend on international trade and export expansion. In the 1990s, export-related jobs grew several times faster than the overall U.S. employment rate, and those jobs directly related to exports pay about 20 percent more than the average hourly U.S. wage.[5]

This chapter will look primarily at the export function; it will simultaneously attempt to understand the import function as the counterpart of the export

---

[2]Leonidas C. Leonidou and Athena S. Adams-Florou, "Types and Sources of Export Information: Insights from Small Business," *International Small Business Journal*, 17 (April–June 1999), pp. 30–48.

[3]World Trade Organization, *World Trade Growth Slower In 1998 After Unusually Strong Growth In 1997*, Press Release, April 16, 1999, http://www.wto.org/wto/intltrad/internat.htm, Accessed June 24, 1999.

[4]World Trade Organization, 1999.

[5]Paul J. Kullman, "The Commerce Department's Trade Compliance Center Gears up," *Business America*, 118 (May 1997), pp. 28–31.

EXHIBIT 17–1
SHARE OF WORLD EXPORTS (PERCENT) OF TOP SIX EXPORTERS

	1980–84	*1985–89*	*1990*	*1992*	*1994*	*1996*	*1998*	*1999*
United States	11.6	11.2	11.5	11.9	12.1	11.9	12.7	12.4
Germany	9.3	11.1	11.9	11.4	10.1	9.9	10.0	9.6
Japan	7.7	9.3	8.3	9.0	9.4	7.8	7.2	7.5
France	5.4	5.8	6.3	6.3	5.6	5.5	5.7	5.3
United Kingdom	5.2	5.1	5.4	5.1	4.8	5.2	5.1	4.8
Canada	4.0	4.2	3.7	3.6	3.9	3.8	4.0	4.2

Source: "1995: The Year We Turned the Corner on Trade," *Business America* (Washington, D.C.: U.S. Department of Commerce, March 1996), pp. 9–13; "Current International Trade Position of the United States," *Business America* (Washington, D.C.: U.S. Department of Commerce, December 1997), pp. 34–36; *World Trade Growth Slower In 1998 After Unusually Strong Growth In 1997*, World Trade Organization, Press Release, April 16, 1999, http://www.wto.org/wto/intltrad/internat.htm; and *World Trade Organization Annual Report 2000* (World Trade Organization, 2000).

function, because for every export transaction there is, by definition, an import transaction as well. Aside from some differences between the procedure and rationale for exports and imports, both are largely the same the world over.

◆ ◆ ◆ ◆ ◆ ◆ # ORGANIZING FOR EXPORTS

Research for Exports

For a firm beginning exports for the first time, the first step is to use available secondary data to research potential markets. Increasingly, international marketing information is available in the form of electronic databases, ranging from the latest news on product developments to new material in the academic and trade press. Well over 6,000 databases are available worldwide, with almost 5,000 available online. The United States is the largest participant in this database growth, producing and consuming more than 50 percent of these database services. When entering a culturally and linguistically different part of the world, managers need to understand a completely new way of commercial thinking that is based on a different culture and works on a different set of premises. It is to be noted, however, that export research for markets such as China and Russia and most of the former command economies must still be done largely in the field, because very little prior data exist and, even when available, they are often not reliable (See Global Perspective 17–1).

The identification of an appropriate overseas market and an appropriate segment involves grouping by the following criteria:

1. Socioeconomic characteristics (e.g., demographic, economic, geographic, and climatic characteristics)

2. Political and legal characteristics

3. Consumer variables (e.g., lifestyle, preferences, culture, taste, purchase behavior, and purchase frequency)

4. Financial conditions

Global Perspective 17-1

Research for Exports: Where Official Statistics are either Non-Existent or Unreliable

Any company seeking to create or expand a distribution network in transition economies is faced with difficulties in locating and evaluating distributors (usually on the basis of capital, expertise, location, and talent), and in controlling and motivating them (given the uncertain legal enforceability of distribution contracts). Given the difficulty of obtaining market information and of locating suitable distributors (in terms of capital, expertise, entrepreneurial flair, and good location), many companies have made poor selection decisions.

In Russia, where a vast underground economy still exists side by side with the official one, the first rule of doing business is that nothing is what it seems. When U.S. companies want financial or market information on Russian companies, they turn to Tom Tirone. Tirone created Tirone Corp., a research firm in Champagne, III., that helps sift through the Russian rubble. Using a database built from scratch, Tirone tries to locate the very few profitable companies operating in the former Soviet Union.

Clients seem pleased with the results. "I've got Tom, or I've got Moscow firms that give out government data, which I'm not sure I trust," says Chris Elbring of International Business Management, a consulting firm that serves Westerners doing business in the Ural Mountains.

Tirone Corp. began when Tirone was completing his MBA and sought to do a study on the behaviors of successful and failed new businesses in Russia. There was just one hitch: there was no data on Russian businesses. So in mid-1995, Tirone assembled a team of experts to knock on the doors of more than 200 Russian businesses. "If someone asked me the detailed questions about my business that I asked these Russians, I'd throw them out a window," Tirone says now. Luckily, they hadn't yet sorted out issues like what is and what isn't competitive information, so they were very open."

Source: Rajeev Batra, "Marketing Issues and Challenges in Transitional Economies," *Journal of International Marketing* 5 (4) (1997), pp. 95–114; and Eileen P. Gunn, "Sifting for Profits Amid the Russian Rubble," *Fortune* (December 7, 1998), pp. 60, 64.

On the basis of these criteria an exporter can form an idea of the market segments in a foreign market.[6] First, regions within countries across the world are grouped by macroeconomic variables indicating the levels of industrial development, availability of skilled labor, and the purchasing power. For example, from an exporter's point of view the Bombay–Thane–Pune area in Western India has more in common with the Monterrey area and the Mexico City area in Mexico and the Shanghai–Wuxi area in China than with other areas in India. All these three areas already have a well-developed industrial base and purchasing power that is equal to that of the middle class in the developed nations. Such economically homogenous groups across the world are a result of the globalization of markets. These apparently similar markets may, however, differ on political and legal dimensions. An exporter or importer has legal recourse in India if the importer or exporter violates terms and the court of adjudication is in India. Legal recourse is still largely wishful thinking in China. By tackling the consumer variables in addition to the macroeconomic ones, the exporter can successfully segment the international market into homogenous segments where similar elements of the marketing mix can be applied.

[6]For a comprehensive review of the export development process, see Leonidas C. Leonidou and Constantine S. Katsikeas, "The Export Development Process: An Integrative Review of Empirical Models," *Journal of International Business Studies*, 27 (Third Quarter 1996), pp. 517–51.

Data for grouping along macroeconomic criteria are available from international agencies such as the World Bank, which publishes the *World Development Report*. In addition, the United Nations produces a series of statistical abstracts on a yearly basis covering economic, demographic, political, and social characteristics that are very useful for grouping analysis. Data on international trade and finance are published quarterly and annually by the International Monetary Fund. Both the Organization for Economic Cooperation and Development (OECD—a group of advanced nations) and the European Union (EU) publish a variety of statistical reports and studies on their member countries.

Export Market Segments

As discussed in Chapter 7, the grouping of countries and regions among countries enables the firm to link various geographical areas into one homogeneous market segment that the firm can cater to in meeting its export objectives. The next task is to develop a product strategy for the selected export markets. The export market clusters obtained by clustering regions within different nations would fall into various levels. At the country level would be countries with the same characteristics as the U.S. market. At a regional level within nations there would be geographical and psychographic segments in many different types of countries where the firm can export the same core product it sells in domestic markets without any significant changes. It is a form of market diversification in which the firm is selling a standardized, uniform product across countries and regions.[7] Mercedes automobiles and Rolex watches sell to the same consumer segment worldwide. Another example of a standardized product that sells worldwide is soft drinks. The Coca-Cola Company markets essentially one Coke worldwide.

Products that can be standardized may satisfy basic needs that do not vary with climate, economic conditions, or culture. A standardized product is the easiest to sell abroad logistically, since the firm incurs no additional manufacturing costs and is able to use the same promotional messages across different regions in different countries across the world. If those different regions have comparable logistics and infrastructural facilities, then the distribution requirements and expenses would also be similar.

Where it is not possible to sell standardized products, the firm may need to adapt its products for the overseas marketplace. In such instances, either the firm's product does not meet customer requirements or it does not satisfy the administrative requirements of foreign countries. Such markets may require modification of the product to succeed in the foreign market.[8] Brand names, for example, need to be changed before a product can be sold, because the brand name may mean something detrimental to the prospect of the product. Ford has recently released the new European Ka model in Japan. Ka means *mosquito* in Japanese, a less than popular disease-carrying pest. Analysts are calling the Ka dead on arrival.[9] A per-

---

[7]Lloyd C. Russow, "Market Diversification: Going International," *Review of Business*, 17 (Spring 1996), pp. 32–34.

[8]S. Tamer Cavusgil and Shaoming Zou, "Marketing Strategy-Performance Relationship: An Investigation of the Empirical Link in Export Market Ventures," *Journal of Marketing*, 58 (January 1994), pp. 1–21.

[9]Keith Naughton, "Tora, Tora, Taurus," *Business Week* (April 12, 1999), p. 6.

fume named Mist probably will not sell in Germany, because *mist* means manure in German slang. Sometimes, a new product has to be developed from a manufacturing viewpoint because the product is not salable as it is in the export market. Room air-conditioner units being exported to Egypt have to have special filters and coolers, and have to be sturdy enough to handle the dust and heat of Egyptian summer.

INDIRECT EXPORTING ◆ ◆ ◆ ◆ ◆ ◆

Indirect exporting involves the use of independent middlemen to market the firm's products overseas. These middlemen, known as export representatives, assume responsibility for marketing the firm's products through their network of foreign distributors and their own sales force. It is not uncommon for a U.S. producer who is new to exporting to begin export operation by selling through an export representative. Many Japanese firms have also relied on the giant general trading companies known as Sogoshosha. Use of middlemen is not uncommon when it is not cost-effective for an exporter to set up its own export department. Such a firm may initiate export operations through export representatives who know the market and have experience in selling to them. There are several types of export representatives in the United States. The most common are the combination export manager (CEM), the export merchant, the export broker, the export commission house, the trading company, and the piggyback exporter.

The **combination export manager (CEM)** acts as the export department to a small exporter or a large producer with small overseas sales. CEMs often use the letterhead of the company they represent and have extensive experience in selling abroad and in the mechanics of export shipments. CEMs operate on a commission basis and are usually most effective when they deal with clients who have businesses in related lines. Since credit plays an increasingly important role in export sales, CEMs have found it increasingly difficult to consummate export sales on behalf of clients without their credit support. As more and more firms begin exporting on a regular basis, CEMs have become a vanishing breed, though a list of CEMs can be found in the *American Register of Exporters and Importers* and in the telephone yellow pages.

Export merchants, in contrast to the CEM, buy and sell on their own accounts and assume all the responsibilities of exporting a product. In this situation, the manufacturers do not control the sales activities of their products in export markets and are entirely dependent on the export merchant for the export of their products. This loss of control over the export marketing effort is a major drawback to using export merchants. The **export broker**, as the name implies, is someone who brings together an overseas buyer and a domestic manufacturer for the purpose of an export sale and earns a commission for establishing a contact that results in a sale.

Foreign buyers of U.S. goods sometimes contract for the services of a U.S. representative to act on their behalf. This resident representative is usually an **export commission house**, which places orders on behalf of its foreign client with U.S. manufacturers and acts as a finder for its client to get the best buy. The export com-

Similar to a manufacturing firm that relies on an indirect export channel member for an exporting, a service company may also work with a local agent for exporting services to (i.e., getting its business solicited in) a foreign country.

mission house acts on behalf of its clients and does not buy on its own behalf. **Trading companies** are large, foreign organizations engaged in exporting and importing. They buy on their own account in the United States and export the goods to their country of origin. Most of the well-known trading companies are Japanese or Western European in origin. Japanese trading companies, known as *sogoshosha* (e.g., Mitsui, Mitsubishi, and Sumitomo) operate worldwide and handle a significant proportion of Japanese foreign trade. United Africa Company, a subsidiary of Unilever, operates extensively in Africa. Another European trading company is Jardine Matheson in Hong Kong, a major trading force in Southeast Asia. Exhibit 17–2 gives an idea of the major types of trading companies.

Piggyback exporting refers to the practice where firms that have an established export departments assume, under a cooperative agreement, the responsibility of exporting the products of other companies. The carrier buys the rider's products and markets them independently. The rider plays a peripheral role in the export marketing overseas. Piggybacking may be an option to enter an export market, but is normally avoided by firms who wish to be in exports over the long haul because of the loss of control over the foreign marketing operations.

EXHIBIT 17–2

MAJOR TYPES OF TRADING COMPANIES AND THEIR COUNTRIES OF ORIGIN

Type	Rationale for Grouping	Some Examples by Country of Origin
General trading companies	Historical involvement in generalized imports/exports	Mitsui (Japan), East Asiatic (Denmark), SCOA (France), Jardine Matheson (Hong Kong)
Export trading companies	Specific mission to promote growth of exporters	Daewoo (Korea), Interbras (Brazil), Sears World Trade (US)
Federated export marketing groups	Loose collaboration among exporting companies supervised by a third party, usually market-specific	Fedec (UK), SBI Group (Norway), IEB Project Group (Morocco)
Trading arms of MNCs	Specific international trading operations in parent company operations	General Motors (US), Volvo (Sweden)
Bank based or affiliated trading groups	A bank at the center of a group extends commercial activities	Mitsubishi (Japan), Cobec (Brazil)
Commodity trading companies	Long-standing export trading in a specific market	Metallgesellschaft (Germany), Louis Dreyfus (France)

Source: Lyn Amine, "Toward a Conceptualization of Export Trading Companies in World Markets," in S. Tamer Cavusgil, ed., *Advances in International Marketing*, 2 (Greenwich, Conn.: JAI Press, 1987), pp. 199–208.

DIRECT EXPORTING ◆ ◆ ◆ ◆ ◆ ◆

Direct exporting occurs when a manufacturer or exporter sells directly to an importer or buyer located in a foreign market. It requires export managers' full commitment both in their attitudes and in their behavior for export success.[10] Direct exporting can manifest itself in various organizational forms, depending on the scale of operations and the number of years that a firm has been engaged in exporting. In its most simple form, a firm will have an export sales manager with some clerical help. The export manager is responsible for the actual selling and directing of activities associated with the export sales. Most of the other export marketing activities (advertising, logistics, and credit, for example) are performed by a regular department of the firm that also handles international trade transactions.

As export activities grow in scale and complexity, most firms create a separate **export department** that is largely self-contained and operates independent of domestic operations. An export department may be structured internally on the basis of function, geography, product, customer, or some other combination. Some firms prefer to have an **export sales subsidiary** instead of an export department in order to keep export operations separate from the rest of the firm. In terms of internal operations and specific operations performed, an export sales subsidiary differs very little from an export department. The major difference is that the subsidiary,

---

[10]Stump, Rodney L., Gerard A. Athaide, Catherine N. Axinn, "The Contingent Effect of the Dimensions of Export Commitment on Exporting Financial Performance: An Empirical Examination," *Journal of Global Marketing*, 12 (1) (1998), pp. 7–25.

EXHIBIT 17–3
COMPARISON OF DIRECT AND INDIRECT EXPORTING

Indirect Exporting	Direct Exporting
• Low set-up costs • Exporter tend not to gain good knowledge of export markets	• High set-up costs • Leads to better knowledge of export markets and international expertise due to direct contact
• Credit risk lies mostly with the middlemen • Since it is not in the interest of the middlemen doing the exporting, customer loyally rarely develops	• Credit risks are higher, especially in the early years • Customer loyalty can be developed for the exporter's brands more easily

being a separate legal entity, must purchase the products it sells in the overseas markets from its parent manufacturer. This means that the parent has to develop and administer a system of transfer pricing. A subsidiary has the advantage of being an independent profit center and is therefore easier to evaluate; it can also offer tax advantages, ease of financing, and greater closeness to the customer.

Instead of a foreign sales subsidiary, a firm also has the option of establishing a **foreign sales branch**. Unlike a subsidiary, a branch is not a separate legal entity. A foreign sales branch handles all of sales, distribution, and promotional work throughout a designated market area and sells primarily to wholesalers and dealers. Where used, a sales branch is the initial link in the marketing channel in the foreign market. Often there will be a storage and warehousing facility available so the branch can maintain an inventory of products, replacement parts, and maintenance supplies.

Indirect exporting and direct exporting are compared in Exhibit 17–3. Both have advantages and disadvantages, though over the long-term—for a firm desiring a permanent presence in international markets—direct exports tend to be more useful.

◆ ◆ ◆ ◆ ◆ ◆   **MECHANICS OF EXPORTING**

To the uninitiated, the mechanics of exporting can seem to be cumbersome and full of meaningless, irrelevant paperwork. Form 7525-V, which is one of the many forms required to be filed by a prospective exporter (See Exhibit 17–4), gives a glimpse of the details that the government requires if you are in the exporting business. However, it is precisely a summarized, collated, and edited version of such data that was the basis of at least some of the secondary data that prospective exporters use in their research when exploring foreign markets. These data are also used to compile trade statistics, which are barometers of the health of an economy, the stock market, and foreign exchange rates.

The Automated Export System (AES) on the Internet

The paperwork involved in export declaration forms is complex and time consuming, no matter how useful information provided on the forms can be. At the time of this writing, however, the Commerce Department's Census Bureau launched a new system, called the **Automated Export System (AES)**, on October 1, 1999. AES enables exporters to file export information at no cost over the Internet—part of an effort to make government more efficient and boost U.S. exports.

EXHIBIT 17–4

FORM 7525-V: INFORMATION TO BE REPORTED ON THE SHIPPER'S EXPORT DECLARATION

1(a) **Exporter**—The name and address of the U.S. exporter—the principal party responsible for effecting export from the United States. The exporter as named on the validated export license. Report only the first five digits of the ZIP code.

1(b) **Exporter Identification Number**—The exporter's Internal Revenue Service Employer Identification Number (EIN) or Social Security Number (SSN) if no EIN has been assigned. Report the nine-digit numerical code as reported on your latest Employer's Quarterly Federal Tax Return, Treasury Form 941. The EIN is usually available from your accounting or payroll department.

1(c) **Related Party Transaction**—One between a U.S. exporter and foreign consignee (e.g., parent company or sister company), where there is at least 10 percent ownership of each by the same U.S. or foreign person or business enterprise.

2 **Date of Exportation**—The date of departure or date of clearance, if date of departure is not known (not required for vessel and postal shipments).

3 **Bill of Lading or Air Waybill Number**—The exporting carrier's bill of lading or air waybill number.

4(a) **Ultimate Consignee**—The name and address of the party actually receiving the merchandise for the designated end-use or the party so designated on the validated export license. For overland shipments to Mexico, also include the Mexican state in the address.

4(b) **Intermediate Consignee**—The name and address of the party in a foreign country who makes delivery of the merchandise to the ultimate consignee or the party so named on the export license.

5 **Agent of Exporter**—The name and address of the duly authorized forwarding agent.

6 **Point (State) of Origin or Foreign Trade Zone (FTZ) Number**

(a) The two-digit U.S. Postal Service abbreviation of the state in which the merchandise actually starts its journey to the port of export, *or*

(b) The state of the commodity of the greatest value, *or*

(c) The state of consolidation, *or*

(d) The Foreign Trade Zone Number for exports leaving an FTZ.

7 **Country of Ultimate Destination**—The country in which the merchandise is to be consumed, further processed, or manufactured; the final country of destination as known to the exporter at the time of shipment; or the country of ultimate destination as shown on the validated export license. Two-digit (alpha character) International Standards Organization (ISO) codes may also be used.

8 **Loading Pier**—The number or name of the pier at which the merchandise is laden aboard the exporting vessel (for vessel shipments only).

9 **Method of Transportation**—The mode of transport by which the merchandise is exported. Specify by name, (i.e., vessel, air, rail, truck, etc.). Specify "own power" if applicable.

10 **Exporting Carrier**—The name of the carrier transporting the merchandise out of the United States. For vessel shipments, give the vessel's flag also.

11 **U.S. Port of Export**

(a) Overland—The U.S. Customs port at which the surface carrier crosses the border.

(b) Vessel and Air—The U.S. Customs port where the merchandise is loaded on the carrier that is taking the merchandise out of the United States.

(c) Postal—The U.S. Post Office where the merchandise is mailed.

12 **Foreign Port of Unloading**—The foreign port and country at which the merchandise will be unloaded from the exporting carrier (for vessel and air shipments only).

13 **Containerized**—Cargo originally booked as containerized cargo and that placed in containers at the vessel operator's option (for vessel shipments only).

14 **Commodity Description**—A sufficient description of the commodity to permit verification of the Schedule B Commodity Number or the description shown on the validated export license.

EXHIBIT 17–4 (CONTINUED)

15 **Marks, Numbers, and Kinds of Packages**—Marks, numbers, or other identification shown on the packages and the numbers and kinds of packages (boxes, barrels, baskets, etc.).

16 **"D" (Domestic) or "F" (Foreign)**

(a) Domestic exports—Merchandise grown, produced, or manufactured in the United States (including imported merchandise which has been enhanced in value or changed from the form in which imported by further manufacture or processing in the United States).

(b) Foreign exports—Merchandise that has entered the United States and is being re-exported in the same condition as when imported.

17 **Schedule B Commodity Number**—The ten-digit commodity number as provided in Schedule B, Statistical Classification of Domestic and Foreign Commodities Exported from the United States. Check Digit (CD) is no longer required. See item 5 for a discussion of not repeating the same Schedule B numbers on the SED. See the Appendix showing a list of telephone numbers for assistance with Schedule B numbers.

18 **Net Quantity**—Report whole unit(s) as specified in Schedule B with the unit indicated. Report also the unit specified on the validated export license if the units differ. See the Appendix showing a list of telephone numbers for assistance with units of quantity.

19 **Gross Shipping Weight**—(For vessel and air shipments only) The gross shipping weight in kilograms for each Schedule B number, including the weight of containers but excluding carrier equipment (pounds multiplied by 0.4536 = kilos. Report whole units.)

20 **Value**—Selling price or cost if not sold, including freight, insurance, and other charges to U.S. port of export, but excluding unconditional discounts and commissions (nearest whole dollar, omit cents). Report one value for each Schedule B number.

21 **Export License Number or General License Symbol**—Validated export license number and expiration date or general license symbol. See the Appendix showing a list of telephone numbers for assistance with licensing information.

22 **Export Control Classification Number**—(When required)—ECCN number of commodities listed on the Commerce Control List in the Export Administration Regulations. See the Appendix showing telephone numbers for assistance with the ECCN.

23 **Designation of Agent**—Signature of exporter authorizing the named agent to effect the export when such agent does not have formal power of attorney.

24 **Signature/Title/Date**—Signature of exporter or authorized agent certifying the truth and accuracy of the information on the SED, title of exporter or authorized agent, and date of signature.

25 **Authentication**—For Customs use only.

Source: http://www.census.gov/foreign-trade/correct/corway1.txt, accessed August 4, 2000.

AES is a joint venture between the U.S. Customs Service, the Foreign Trade Division of the Bureau of the Census (Commerce), the Bureau of Export Administration (Commerce), the Office of Defense Trade Controls (State), other federal agencies, and the export trade community. It is the central point through which export shipment data required by multiple agencies is filed electronically on the Internet to Customs, using the Electronic Data Interchange (EDI). AES is a completely voluntary system that provides an alternative to filing paper Shipper's Export Declarations. Export information is collected electronically and edited immediately, and errors are detected and corrected at the time of filing. AES is a nationwide system operational at all ports and for all methods of transportation. It was designed to improve trade statistics, reduce duplicate reporting to multiple agencies, improve customer service, and ensure compliance with and enforcement of laws relating to exporting.[11]

---

[11]More information on AES is available at the U.S. Customs' Internet site <http://www.customs.ustreas.gov/impoexpo/auto_exp.htm>, the Census Bureau's Foreign Trade Division site <http://www.census.gov/foreign-trade/aes/aes.html> or by calling 1-800-549-0595.

This Internet-based system will allow exporters, freight forwarders, and consolidators to file shippers' export-declaration information in an automated, cost-free way. AES has the goal of paperless reporting of export information by the year 2002. The new system will reduce the paperwork burden on the trade community, make document storage and handling less costly, improve the quality of export statistics, and facilitate exporting in general. Before AES, the export system was paper-bound, expensive, labor intensive, and error prone.

Exporting starts with the search for a buyer abroad. It includes research to locate a potential market and a buyer and the process of closing a sale. We covered the process of getting an order earlier in this chapter. Once an export contract has been signed, the wheels are set in motion for the process that results in the export contract. The *first* stage has to do with the legality of the transaction. The exporter has to check to see that the goods can be imported by the importing party—importing country licensing law can trip up a transaction unless looked at in advance.

Legality of Exports

Standard specifications for products and services are especially important for Europe and Japan, as far as American exporters are concerned. As far as export transactions to third-world countries are concerned, the convertibility of the importing country's currency is something that needs to be checked even in this day of liberalization. If that country's currency is not convertible, then the importing party must have permission to remit hard currency. Finally, the exporter needs to make sure that there are no export restrictions on the goods proposed to be exported from the United States. Security concerns on encryption technology, for example, permit the exports of encryption technology that incorporate no more than 40 bits. All exports from the United States (except those to Canada and U.S. territories) require an **export license**, which may be a general export license or a validated export license. A *general license* permits exportation within certain limits without requiring that an application be filed or that a license document be issued. A *validated license* permits exportation within specific limitations; it is issued only on formal application. Most goods can move from the United States to the free world countries under a general license. A validated license is required to export certain kinds of strategic goods regardless of destination. For most goods, the license is granted by the U.S. Department of Commerce's Office of Export Administration. For certain specific products, however, the license is granted by other U.S. government agencies, as shown in Exhibit 17–5.

The logistics of the export transaction is the second pillar of an export transaction, which includes (1) the terms of the sale, including f.o.b./c.i.f. payment mode and schedule, dispute settlement mechanism, and service requirements (if applicable); (2) monitoring the transportation and delivery of the goods to the assigned party—the assignee in the bill of lading and obtaining proof of delivery—the **customs receipt**; and (3) shipping and obtaining the bill of lading.

Export Transactions

Once a company has a firm order for exports, it has to execute the order so as to deliver the product or service promised to the overseas customer. A **bill of lading** is a contract between the exporter and the shipper indicating that the shipper has accepted responsibility for the goods and will provide transportation in return for payment. The bill of ownership can also be used as a receipt and to prove ownership of the merchandise, depending on the type of the bill of lading. A *straight bill of lading* is nonnegotiable and is usually used in prepaid transactions. The goods are delivered to a specific individual or company. A *shipper's order bill of lading* is negotiable; it

EXHIBIT 17–5

U.S. EXPORT LICENSING AUTHORITIES FOR SPECIFIC COMMODITIES

Commodity	Licensing Authority
Arms, ammunition, and other war-related products	Department of State
Atomic energy material (including fissionable material and facilities for their manufacture)	Atomic Energy Commission
Gold and silver	Department of Treasury
Natural gas and electric energy	Federal Power Commission
Narcotic drugs	Department of Justice
Tobacco plants and seeds	Department of Agriculture
Endangered wildlife	Maritime Commission
Vessels	Maritime Commission

Source: U.S. Department of Commerce. The Export Administration Regulations, http://bxa.fedworld.gov/, Washington, D.C., 1999.

can be bought, sold, or traded while the goods are still in transit (i.e., title of the goods can change hands). A shipper's order bill of lading is used for letter-of-credit transactions. The customer usually (depending on the terms of the export contract) needs the original or a copy of the bill of lading to take possession of the goods.[12]

A **commercial invoice** is a bill for the goods stating basic information about the transaction, including a description of the merchandise, total cost of the goods sold, addresses of the buyer and the seller, and delivery and payment. The buyer needs the invoice to prove ownership and to arrange payment terms. Commercial invoices are also used by some governments to assess customs duties. Other export documentation that may be required includes export licenses, certificates of origin, inspection certification, dock and/or warehouse receipts, destination control certificates (to inform shippers and other foreign parties that the goods may only be shipped to a particular country), shippers' export declaration (Form 7525-V provided in Exhibit 17–4 used to compile export trade statistics) and export packaging lists. To ensure that all required documentation is accurately completed and to minimize potential problems, firms entering the international market for the first time with an export order should consider using **freight forwarders**—who are specialists in handling export documentation.

Terms of Shipment and Sale

The responsibilities of the exporter, the importer, and the logistic provider should be spelled out in the export contract in terms of what is and what is not included in the price quotation and who owns title to the goods while in transit. **INCOTERMS**, which went into effect from July 1, 1990, and is an acronym for International Commercial Terms, are the internationally accepted standard definitions for the terms of sale by the International Chamber of Commerce.[13] The commonly used terms of shipment are summarized in Exhibit 17–6.

---

[12]A Basic Guide to Exporting, U.S. Department of Commerce, Washington, D.C., 1986.

[13]http://www.ltdmgmt.com/incoterms.htm, accessed June 28, 2000.

EXHIBIT 17–6
TERMS OF SHIPMENT

Ex-works (EXW) at the point of origin	The exporter agrees to deliver the goods at the disposal of the buyer to the specified place on the specified date or within a fixed period. All other charges are borne by the buyer.
Free Alongside Ship (FAS) at a named port of export	The exporter quotes a price for the goods, including charges for delivery of the goods alongside a vessel at a port. The seller covers the costs of unloading and wharfage; loading on to the ship, ocean transportation, insurance, unloading and wharfage at a port of destination and transport to the site required by the buyer are on the importer's account.
Free on Board (FOB) at a named port of export	In addition to FAS, the exporter undertakes to load the goods on the vessel to be used for ocean transportation and the price quoted by the exporter reflects this cost.
Cost and Freight (CFR) to a named overseas port of disembarkation	The exporter quotes a price for the goods including the cost of transportation to a named overseas port of disembarkation. The cost of insurance and the choice of the insurer are left to the importer.
Cost, Insurance and Freight (CIF) to a named overseas port of disembarkation	The exporter quotes a price including insurance and all transportation and miscellaneous charges to the port of disembarkation from the ship or aircraft. CIF costs are influenced by port charges (unloading, wharfage, storage, heavy lift, demurrage), documentation charges (certification of invoice, certification of origin, weight certificate) and other miscellaneous charges (fees of freight forwarder, insurance premiums).

The terms of shipment used in the export transaction and their acceptance by the parties involved are important so that subsequent disputes will not occur. These terms of shipment also have significant implications on costing and pricing. The exporter should therefore learn what terms of shipment importers prefer in a particular market and what the specific transaction may require. A CIF quote by an exporter clearly shows the importer the cost to get the product to a port in a desired country. An inexperienced importer may be discouraged by an EXW quote because the importer may not have the knowledge of how much the EXW quote translates in terms of landed cost at home.

Payment Terms

The financing and payments of an export transaction constitute the third set of things to do with regard to an export transaction. For example, is export credit available from an Ex-Im Bank or a local agency supporting exports? What payment terms have been agreed on? Customary payment terms for noncapital goods transactions include cash with order, confirmed irrevocable letter of credit, irrevocable letter of credit, revocable letter of credit, sight draft—documents against payment (D/P), time draft—documents against acceptance (D/A), open account, and consignment basis payments. These terms are explained in Exhibit 17–7. The terms of payment between the exporter and the importer are a matter of negotiation and depend on a variety of factors. These factors include the buyer's credit

EXHIBIT 17–7
TERMS OF PAYMENT IN AN EXPORT TRANSACTION

Cash with order	Cash payment when order is placed
Confirmed irrevocable letter of credit	A letter of credit issued by the importer's bank and confirmed by a bank, usually in the exporter's country. The obligation of the second bank is added to the obligation of the issuing bank to honor drafts presented in accordance with the terms of credit.
Unconfirmed irrevocable letter of credit	A letter of credit issued by the importer's bank. The issuing bank still has an obligation to pay.
Revocable letter of credit	A letter of credit that may be withdrawn from the beneficiary at any time without prior notice to the exporter. It does not carry a bank's obligation to pay.
Sight draft	A draft so drawn as to be payable on presentation to the drawee (usually the buyer).
Time draft	A draft maturing at a certain fixed time after presentation or acceptance.
Open account	No draft drawn. Transaction payable when specified on invoice
Consignment	A shipment that is held by the importer until the merchandise has been sold, at which time payment is made to the exporter.

Source: John S. Gordon, *Profitable Exporting: A Complete Guide to Marketing Your Products Abroad*, 2nd ed. (New York: John Wiley & Sons, 1993), p. 141.

standing, the amount of the sale transaction, the availability of foreign exchange in the buyer's country, the exchange control laws in the buyer's country, the risks associated with the type of merchandise to be shipped, the usual practice in the trade, and market conditions—i.e., a buyer's market or a seller's market and payment terms offered by competitors.

When negotiating payment terms with an importer, an exporter must be guided by the risks associated with the importer and the importer's country. **Credit risk** is the risk that the importer will not pay or will fail to pay on the agreed terms. The exporter has to consider this, along with foreign exchange risks, transfer risks, and the political risks of the importer's country. **Foreign exchange risk** exists when the sale is in the importer's currency and that currency depreciates in terms of the home currency, leaving the exporter with less in the home currency.[14] **Transfer risk** refers to the chances that payment will not be made due to the importer's inability to obtain foreign currency (usually, U.S. dollars) and transfer it on the exporter, while **political risks** refer to the risks associated with war, confiscation of the importer's business, and other unexpected political events.

If an exporter sells for cash, there is virtually no risk. The possible nominal risk is associated with the timing of the order, as compared to the receipt of payment. A sale on a **confirmed irrevocable letter of credit** has slightly more risk. The confirmation places a U.S. bank or other known bank acceptable to you in front of the

_____

[14]A recent study shows that exporters who accept foreign currency as a medium of payment tend to sell a higher volume and have more satisfied customers (i.e., importers) but tend to have lower profit margins than those exporters who accept domestic currency. This is due probably to foreign exchange rate risk. For detail, see Saeed Samiee and Patrik Anckar, "Currency Choice in Industrial Pricing: A Cross-National Evaluation," *Journal of Marketing*, 62 (July 1998), pp. 112–27.

importer's bank—the payment risk assumed by the exporter devolves almost completely on this bank. If the sale is in a foreign currency, the exporter is still exposed to the risk of depreciation of the foreign currency relative to the dollar. An **unconfirmed letter of credit** exposes the exporter to the creditworthiness of the buyer's bank in the foreign country because a U.S. bank is no longer guaranteeing payment. The exporter thus faces the additional risk of a change in the value of the foreign currency (if the sale is not in U.S. dollars), the risk that the payment cannot be transferred to the United States, and the risk that the political conditions in the buyer's country will change to the exporter's detriment.

A **draft** is an IOU, or a promise for payment, from an importer. The two most frequently used drafts are sight and time drafts. A *sight draft* is an importer's promise to send payment upon seeing the merchandise at the port of entry. A *time draft* is an importer's promise to make payment on a prespecified date. Exports on sight draft basis further increase the payment risk in an export transaction because there is no financial institution like a bank that has assumed the risk of payment. A time draft further escalates the risk because the buyer by "accepting the draft" will receive the title documents and can pick up the goods without payment. Finally, an **open account** sale has no evidence of debt (promissory note, draft, etc.) and the payment may be unenforceable. Usually, done on the basis of an invoice, an open account transaction is recommended only after the exporter and the importer have established trust in their relationship.

Associated with the payment and shipment terms is the marine insurance (applicable to all forms of shipping) of the goods being shipped. The exporter and the importer have to decide and mutually agree on the insurance terms as part of the contract. The exporter will be unable to enforce the provisions of an insurance coverage unless he or she holds an insurable interest in the transaction at the time of the loss. The exporter has such an interest if the cargo is lost, damaged, or destroyed and the exporter suffers a loss or fails to make an expected profit. Lack of clarity usually has a greater adverse impact on the exporter, as shown by the following example.

An exporter delivered goods to the docks to be loaded for export to a foreign buyer. The terms of sale were FOB (exporter's dock) and the seller received an on-board bill of lading (which means that the goods were supposed to be on board the ship). A fire engulfed the dock and the ship left the dock to save itself before the goods could actually be loaded. The buyer had insured the goods from the FOB point (on board the ship). The goods left on the dock perished in the fire. The seller's insurance company claims that it is not liable, as the shipper received the on-board bill of lading, and the buyer's insurance company claims that it is not liable, as the goods were never actually loaded. The transaction continues to be in dispute by the concerned parties. In this case the dispute arose because of the unforeseen contingency of the goods not actually being on board the ship when they were legally supposed to be.

Currency Hedging

The fourth task of an exporter is to arrange a foreign exchange cover transaction with the banker or through the firm's treasury in case there is a foreign exchange risk in the export transaction. Such arrangements include reversing the forward currency transaction if required and hedging the foreign exchange risk using derivative instruments in the foreign exchange markets—for example, currency options and futures. Where the U.S. exporter is receiving some currency other than the dollar, covering a trade transaction through forward sales, currency options, and currency futures enables the exporter to lock in the dollar value of the export transaction up to a year in the future, thus enabling more certain cash flows and forecasting. Due care needs to be exercised in the uses of financial derivative instruments, because an unwary or uninformed firm can lose large amounts of money (see Chapter 3 for detail).

◆ ◆ ◆ ◆ ◆ ◆ ROLE OF THE GOVERNMENT IN PROMOTING EXPORTS[15]

Export promotion activities generally comprise (1) export service programs (e.g., seminars for potential exporters, export counseling, how-to-export handbooks, and export financing) and (2) market development programs (e.g., dissemination of sales leads to local firms, participation in foreign trade shows, preparation of market analysis, and export news letters).[16] In addition, program efforts can be differentiated as to whether the intent is to provide informational or experiential knowledge. Informational knowledge typically would be provided through "how-to" export assistance, workshops, and seminars, while experiential knowledge would be imparted through the arrangement of foreign buyers' or trade missions, trade and catalog shows, or participation in international market research.

Government expenditures on export promotion seem to make sense. One billion dollars' worth of exports creates, on average, 22,800 jobs. It has been estimated that $2 billion of GNP are generated per billion dollars of exports, together with $400 million in state and federal tax revenues.[17]

Although exports may be considered a major engine of economic growth in the U.S. economy, many U.S. firms do not export. Many firms, particularly small- to medium-sized ones, appear to have developed a fear of international market activities. Their management tends to see only the risks—informational gaps, unfamiliar conditions in markets, complicated domestic and foreign trade regulations, the absence of trained middle managers for exporting, and lack of financial resources— rather than the opportunities that the international market can present. Yet, these very same firms may well have unique competitive advantages to offer that may be highly useful in performing successfully in the international market.

For example, small- and medium-sized firms can offer their customers shorter response times. If some special situation should arise, there is no need to wait for the "home office" to respond. Responses can be immediate, direct, and predictable

---

[15]This section draws from Esra F. Gencturk and Masaaki Kotabe, "Performance Implications of Export Marketing Involvement and Export Promotion Assistance Usage," A Working Paper, 2000.

[16]William C. Lesch, Abdolreza Eshghi, and Golpira S. Eshghi, "A Review of Export Promotion Programs in the Ten Largest Industrial States," in S. Tamer Cavusgil and Michael R. Czinkota, eds. *International Perspectives on Trade Promotion and Assistance* (New York: Quorum Books, 1990), pp. 25–37.

[17]Masaaki Kotabe and Michael R. Czinkota, "State Government Promotion of Manufacturing Exports: A Gap Analysis," *Journal of International Business Studies*, 23 (Fourth Quarter 1992), pp. 637–58.

to the customer, therefore providing precisely those competitive ingredients that increase stability in a business relationship and reduce risk and costs. These firms often can also customize their operations more easily. Procedures can be adapted more easily to the special needs of the customer or to local requirements. One could argue that in a world turning away from mass marketing and toward niche marketing, these capabilities may well make smaller-sized firms the export champions of the future.

Through the **Export Enhancement Act of 1992**, the U.S. government announced the National Export Strategy—a strategic, coordinated effort to stimulate exports.[18] As part of this strategy, the U.S. Trade Promotion Coordinating Committee had set a goal of increasing the level of exports of goods and services from the $700 billion achieved in 1994 to $1 trillion by the year 2000.[19] In pursuit of this objective, the International Trade Administration of the U.S. Department of Commerce has devoted a substantial amount of the tax dollars allocated to it to help U.S. firms export their goods and services. For instance, the Japan Export Information Center (JEIC), established in April 1991, is the primary contact point within the Department of Commerce for U.S. exporters seeking business counseling and commercial information necessary to succeed in the Japanese market. The JEIC's principal functions are to provide guidance on doing business in Japan, as well as information on market entry alternatives, market data and research, product standards and testing requirements, intellectual property protection, tariffs, and nontariff barriers. On the flip side, the Japanese External Trade Organization (JETRO), affiliated with Japan's Ministry of International Trade and Industry has also in recent years switched from promoting Japanese exports to helping U.S. and other foreign companies export and invest in Japan. The new emphasis on import promotion is part of the Japanese government's broader strategy to pull more foreign business into Japan, particularly from small to mid-size companies. These efforts are also an attempt to chip away at Japan's roughly $64 million trade surplus with the United States, and hopefully encourage a greater balance of trade for the future.[20]

The U.S. Department of Commerce also has industry specialists and country specialists in Washington, D.C. The industry specialists are available to give exporters information on the current state of the exporter's products overseas, comment on marketing and sales strategies, inform on trade shows and events and give other counsel. The country specialists are available to give information on the target country, current trade issues with the United States, customs and tariff information, insight on the business climate and culture, and any other information on a country required by the exporter.

The **Ex–Im Bank**—short for **Export–Import Bank**—plays a crucial role in promoting exports. The Ex–Im Bank is a federally supported bank whose mission is to support exporters with the necessary credit. Ex–Im Bank is not an aid or development agency, but a government held corporation, managed by a board of directors

Export–Import Bank

---

[18]Richard T. Hise, "Globe Trotting," *Marketing Management*, 6 (Fall 1997), pp. 50–58.

[19]"Stocktaking: Implementing the National Export Strategy," *Business America* (October 1995), pp. 28–65.

[20]Rosalind McLymont, "In an About Face, Japanese Group Provides Help to Foreign Exporters," *Journal of Commerce* (April 19, 1999), p. 5A.

consisting of a chairman, vice-chairman, and three additional board members. Members serve for staggered terms and are chosen and serve at the discretion of the president of the United States. The Ex–Im Bank's accomplishments in 1998 are presented in Exhibit 17–8.

EXHIBIT 17–8
EXPORT ASSISTANCE FROM THE U.S. EXPORT–IMPORT BANK

Total Financing
- Ex–Im Bank financing helped 2,060 U.S. exporters make foreign sales in FY 1998.
- Ex–Im Bank authorized $10.5 billion in loans, guarantees, and export credit insurance, supporting nearly $13 billion of U.S. exports to markets worldwide.

Small Business
- Ex–Im Bank authorized $2.2 billion in financing to support exports by small businesses— 21 percent of total authorizations, well beyond the 10 percent set-aside of financing for small business mandated by Congress.
- Ex–Im Bank approved 1,864 small business transactions—85 percent of the total number of Ex–Im Bank transactions.
- In FY 1998, 369 businesses used Ex–Im Bank programs for the first time.
- Ex–Im Bank authorized a total of $388 million in working capital guarantees, $369 million of which benefited small businesses. Of the 275 working capital guarantee transactions authorized, 265 were for small businesses, representing 96 percent of the transaction volume.
- Small businesses were issued 1,534 export credit insurance policies—nearly 90 percent of the total number of Ex–Im Bank's policies. Small business insurance authorizations totaled $1.7 billion, 39 percent of the total amount of insurance authorizations.

Export Credit Insurance
- Ex–Im Bank authorized $4.3 billion to support 1,731 insurance policies under the Export Credit Insurance Program.
- Filling the gap in export credit caused by the Asian financial crisis, Ex–Im Bank authorized approximately $1 billion to support short-term letters of credit for U.S. goods and services sold to Korea.

Aircraft
- Ex–Im Bank authorized $2.6 billion to finance the export of U.S. large commercial aircraft to emerging markets throughout the world.

Environment
- Ex–Im Bank authorized more than $284 million in loans, guarantees, and export credit insurance to support environmentally beneficial U.S. exports.

Energy
- Ex–Im Bank supported transactions involving U.S. exports to foreign power projects, with a total export value of $1.3 billion.

Services
- Ex–Im Bank's loan guarantee, and insurance authorizations assisted in the export of a wide range of U.S. services (such as engineering, design, consulting, and training), of which the total export value was $332.5 million.

Agriculture
- Ex–Im Bank helped to finance the export of $74 million of U.S. agricultural commodities, livestock, foodstuffs, and related products, and $189 million of agricultural equipment, chemicals, supplies, and services.

Source: Export–Import Bank of the United States, *1998 Annual Report: Rising to Meet Today's Export Challenges,* Washington, D.C., 1999.

Ex–Im Bank is designed to supplement, not compete with, private capital. Ex–Im Bank has historically filled gaps created when the private sector is reluctant to engage in export financing. Ex–Im Bank (1) provides guarantees of *working capital loans* for U.S. exporters, (2) guarantees the *repayment of loans* or makes loans to foreign purchasers of U.S. goods and services and (3) provides *credit insurance* against nonpayment by foreign buyers for political or commercial risk. To carry out the U.S. government's strategy for continuing export growth, the Ex–Im Bank is focusing on critical areas such as emphasizing exports to developing countries, aggressively countering trade subsidies of other governments, stimulating small business transactions, promoting the export of environmentally beneficial goods and services, and expanding project finance capabilities. The Ex–Im Bank made $10.5 billion in loans, guarantees, and export letters of credit financing in 1998, helping 2,060 exporters make foreign sales.[21]

The Ex–Im Bank has two major programs in place, among other things. Its *Project Finance Division* was formed in 1994 to meet the growing global demand for project financing. It provides financing for ventures to go forward based on their earnings rather than relying on government funding or direct guarantees, enabling more U.S. companies to successfully compete for massive infrastructure development projects in big emerging markets. Annual spending on infrastructure projects like roads, railways, telecommunications, power generation, and mining outside the United States is estimated to exceed $200 billion a year. The Project Finance Division completed its twenty-second transaction in 1997, bringing Ex–Im Bank support for this type of financing to $6 billion by the end of that year. The *Working Capital Guarantee Program*, an important source of export financing for small and medium-sized businesses, authorized working capital loans of $388 million in 1998, of which $369 million benefited small businesses.[22]

For example, for construction equipment manufacturers, such as Caterpillar, Komatsu and Case, government agencies and the Ex–Im Bank play a crucial role in making the sale. For Mack Truck Sales of South Florida, a dealer and exporter, exports account for about 55 percent of its $96 million in business. The company recently took advantage of the Ex–Im Bank insurance program to sell trucks in Ecuador. In addition, this Miami-based Mack Truck dealer often sells to mining and road-building companies that are funded by the World Bank and the Inter-American Development Bank.[23]

The Ex–Im Bank is also combating the "trade distorting" loans of foreign governments through the aggressive use of its Tied Aid Capital Projects Fund. The idea is that the Ex–Im Bank is willing to match foreign tied-aid offers that are commercially viable and pending, on a case-by-case basis, in order to be able to preemptively counter foreign tied-aid offer. For instance, if a highway project in China gets a bid from a European or Japanese consortium of firms that offer to give concessional aid for the project but stipulate that in return the Chinese should buy machinery and materials from suppliers to be specified by the Europeans (or the Japanese), then a U.S. firm bidding for the same project can depend

---

[21]Neil Earle, "Financing the Deal," *World Trade* 12 (July 1999), pp. 44–48.

[22]Export–Import Bank of the United States, *1998 Annual Report: Rising to Meet Today's Export Challenges* (Washington, D.C., U.S. Government Printing Office 1999).

[23]Richard Barovick, "Exporters Scrambling for Financing," *Journal of Commerce* (March 22, 1999), p. 10 A.

on being able to provide concessional financing through the resources of the Ex–Im Bank. In addition, the U.S. government is no longer shy of representing American firms openly and of being powerful advocates on behalf of American businesses. Cabinet secretaries in the Clinton administration have led groups of top business executives to many emerging markets. Accompanying administration officials on foreign missions gives business executives a chance to get acquainted with decision makers in foreign governments—and many infrastructure projects are awarded by governments.[24] The U.S. government lobbied hard to obtain airplane orders for Boeing from Singapore Airlines, Cathay Pacific and Saudia, all of which were being lobbied hard by the French government to buy from Airbus-European consortium.

Critics may cavil at this active role of the U.S. government in promoting exports; however, if U.S. firms are to retain their position in existing markets and if they are to gain access to new markets, then they have to have the same facilities that are available to firms from other nations. It is for this reason that the policy of advocacy on behalf of U.S. firms fighting to enter new markets or to retain existing markets is a cornerstone of the national export policy.[25]

U.S. Tariff Concessions

Other areas in which the government plays a role in promoting exports include the establishment and maintenance of foreign trade zones (FTZs), foreign sales corporations (FSCs), and the Export Trading Company Act of 1982.

Foreign Trade Zones. As discussed in detail in Chapter 16, foreign trade zones (free trade zones) let businesses store, process, assemble, and display goods from abroad without paying a tariff. Once these goods leave the zone and enter the United States they have to pay a tariff—but not on the cost of assembly or profits. If the product is re-exported, no duties or tariffs have to be paid. Thus, a U.S. firm can assemble foreign parts for a camera in a Florida FTZ and ship the finished cameras to Latin America without paying duty.

Foreign Sales Corporations. A foreign sales corporation (FSC) is a foreign corporation not located in a free trade zone that is allowed to earn some exempt and nontaxable income on its exports from the United States. Most FSCs operate as commission agents and are located in the U.S. Virgin Islands or Barbados. Although the FSC requirements appear complex, the proliferation of FSC management companies suggests that most U.S. exporters can establish and maintain such entities at a modest annual cost (around $10,000). A less costly and simpler alternative, the *small FSC*, provides tax benefits to businesses with up to $5 million in annual foreign trading gross sales. For most products exported, the FSC tax benefit is 15 percent. For example, if a U.S. company normally pays U.S. tax at a 35 percent rate, the use of an FSC results in an effective tax rate of only 29.75 percent (0.35×0.85) on export profits. For high-volume, low-profit items such as grain, the FSC benefit can range between 15 percent and 30 percent.[26]

---

[24]"Why Executives Tour World With Politicians," *Wall Street Journal* (April 4, 1996), p. B1.

[25]"Advocacy: Supporting U.S. Jobs in Global Competition," *Business America* (October 1995), pp. 66–89.

[26]For detail, see Ernest R. Larkins, Ellwood F. Oakley III., and Gary M. Winkle, "Tax and Accounting Aspects of Global Expansion," *The Tax Adviser*, 30 (June 1999), pp. 416–22.

American Export Trading Company. The Export Trading Company Act of 1982 encourages businesses to join together and form export trading companies. It provides antitrust protection for joint exporting, and permits banking institutions to own interests in these exporting ventures. This act makes it practical for small- and medium-size exporting firms to pool resources without the fear of antitrust persecution and inadequate capitalization. A bank may hold up to 100 percent stock in an export trading company and is exempted from the collateral requirements contained in the Federal Reserve Act for loans to its export trading company.

Export Regulations

Although the U.S. government has become earnest in promoting exports, it also has a hand in regulating exports. The Trade Act of 1974 bars the Ex–Im Bank credit to most communist countries. The Foreign Corrupt Practices Act of 1977 (as amended in 1986) imposes jail terms and fines for overseas payoffs that seek to influence overseas government decisions—though payments to expedite events that are supposed to take place under local laws are no longer illegal. Many U.S. exporters, especially exporters of big-ticket items, are of the opinion that the Foreign Corrupt Practices Act provides an unfair advantage to exporters from Europe and Japan who have been able to make such payments and get tax write-offs for the payments under export expenses. In 1996, under newly agreed provisions of the World Trade Organization (WTO), firms from other countries will no longer be able to make such payments without incurring penalties—thus leveling the playing field somewhat for U.S. exporters. Regulatory mechanisms such as COCOM (Coordinating Committee on Exports) restrict what can be exported to former communist countries, though with the breakdown of the Soviet Union, COCOM has lost much of its relevance. Laws remain in place, however, that restrict exports of security-sensitive technology like sophisticated machine tools and encryption technology for computer software and hardware (See Global Perspective 17–2).

Antitrust laws prevent U.S. firms from bidding jointly on major foreign projects. Human rights legislation and nuclear nonproliferation policies require that the federal government has to recertify every year the Most Favored Nation status of major foreign trade partners like China. These are examples of the U.S. exporting its own rules to other nations under the aegis of WTO. To the extent that such actions result in the same rules for all nations engaging in international trade, such behavior benefits trade; however, such behavior can also be perceived as an infringement of national sovereignty by many nations.

Sometimes the actions of a foreign government can affect exports. These actions relate to tariffs and local laws relating to product standards and classification. For example, computer networking equipment exported from the United States to the European Union is charged a 3.9 percent tariff. A recent EU ruling decided that computer networking equipment like adopters, routers, and switches do not crunch data but transport data and so should be classified as telecommunication equipment. Telecommunication equipment, however, carries a higher tariff rate of 7.5 percent, increasing the landed price of these products in Europe.[27] Such actions by foreign governments are usually attempts to provide protection to local industry.

Finally, a government may tax exports with the purpose of satisfying domestic demand first or to take advantage of higher world prices. For example, in 1998, two typhoons damaged trees in the northern Philippines, stripping away mature coconuts.

[27]"Europe's Computer Networking Tariffs May Lead to U.S. Complaint to WTO," *Wall Street Journal* (May 1, 1996), p. B7.

✦ ✦

𝒢LOBAL PERSPECTIVE 17–2

RISK OF EXPORT VIOLATIONS IN THE UNITED STATES

The more high-tech the exports become, the more likely they could be classified as national security-sensitive technology. In October 1999, the U.S. Justice Department indicted the U.S. aerospace company, McDonnell Douglas Corp. (now owned by Boeing) and a Chinese government-owned technology firm on charges that they tried to circumvent U.S. export controls and ship sophisticated machine tools to China for military production.

The issue at hand is whether McDonnell Douglas knew beforehand that the machine tools would be diverted for military use. The case involves McDonnell Douglas's sale in 1994 of nineteen surplus machine tools to the Chinese company for $5 million. The U.S. government licensed the export of the tools only for use in a joint Chinese–McDonnell Douglas program to build forty civilian airliners in China. Six of the sophisticated machine tools, which use sophisticated, precision engineering technology to shape parts for the U.S. B-1 Bomber and the Peacekeeper missile, were diverted to the Nanchang Aircraft Corp., where China makes Silkworm cruise missiles and A-5 fighter jet. Because of the capabilities of the tools, the sale was closely scrutinized

Source: Michael J. Sniffen, "McDonnell Douglas, Chinese Firm Charged with Export Violations," *Philadelphia Inquirer* October 20, 1999, p. A13.

by U.S. officials. U.S. Attorney William Lewis said, "Although none of the equipment was used by the Chinese military aerospace industry, this criminal conspiracy was a serious attempt to circumvent the export control laws which are designed to protect the national security of the United States and to further our non-proliferation goals."

This incident raises two important issues. First, even *after* sales have been consummated, exporters of high-tech, security-sensitive products (both hardware and software) have to monitor whether their products are being used in accordance with the specified usage as stipulated on the export license. Technically, it is the exporter's obligation to do so. Second, the post-sale monitoring activity can be very expensive. In the McDonnell Douglas case, it was a major transaction, and the U.S. government had decided to keep a close eye on the products. As this American company is large and has ample internal resources to conduct self-monitoring, such an activity itself would not be prohibitively costly. However, for many small high-tech companies, such a monitoring activity might be too costly. What if those small companies did not—and could not—"invest" in monitoring activities, and their foreign customers did divert the product into illicit use? Would the U.S. export control and validation system discourage small high-tech companies from exporting?

Coconut oil shipments during the fourth quarter of 1998 were 60 percent below their normal level. The coconut oil market continues to face production declines and the threat of higher prices. Indonesia, the second largest producer, continues to impose high export duties on coconut oil.[28] The goal of such measures is to curb exports and try to keep a lid on internal food industry costs as coconut oil prices soar.

✦ ✦ ✦ ✦ ✦ ✦ ## MANAGING IMPORTS—THE OTHER SIDE OF THE COIN

So far the chapter has been devoted exclusively to exports. We now turn to imports. For organizations in the United States, importing is considerably easier than for most firms in the rest of the world. One of the primary reasons for this is that, unlike importers in most of the rest of the world, U.S. importers can pay the seller abroad in their own currency—the U.S. dollar—because the U.S. dollar is an inter-

[28]Jim Papanikolaw, "Coconut Oil Market Tightens because of Bad Weather in 1998," *Chemical Market Reporter* (January 25, 1999), p. 8.

nationally accepted denomination of exchange. Thus, unlike importers in Brazil or Indonesia who have to find U.S. dollars (or other hard currencies) to pay for imports, an importer in the United States can manage by shelling out U.S. dollars. About 60 percent of the world's trade is still denominated in U.S. dollars—the exporter wants dollars in return for the goods or services sold.

However, denomination of trade in dollars is changing, especially in Europe, where the euro is emerging as the currency in which trade is denominated. Most of the time, therefore, a U.S. importer does not have to bother with hedging foreign exchange transactions or with trying to accumulate foreign currency to pay for imports. On occasion, a U.S. importer may not even need a confirmed letter of credit. This same advantage has become available to the European Union (EU) member countries. EU member countries are now able to pay in euro for their imports from other member countries. Similarly, in Asia, where the Japanese yen is emerging as the currency in which trade is denominated. Japan benefits from this on a more limited geographical basis. Japan is now able to pay in Japanese yen for much of its imports from Southeast Asia.

This is not to suggest that a firm can import anything for sale in the United States. There are restrictions on trade with Iran, Libya, Iraq, and Cuba, for example. Iran and Libya are thought to be supporters of state sponsored terrorism. Since the Gulf War, Iraq had been, until May 1996, under United Nations sanctions, which prevented it from exporting oil, while Cuba has been a pariah as far as the United States is concerned since 1959. The same restrictions have existed with respect to North Korea since the Korean War that ended in 1953. Production and marketing considerations also limit what can be imported and sold profitably in the United States. For goods like soaps and cosmetics, the demand for imports is minimal. However, the United States is a surplus producer of many categories of goods including aircraft, defense equipment, medical electronics, computer software, and agricultural goods.

Importing any good is, thus, predicated upon the existence of a situation where the domestic production of the good in question is not sufficient to satisfy demand. For example, annual sales of cut flowers in the U.S. is close to $10 billion, but domestic production meets only about 30 percent of the demand, with Americans purchasing flowers not just for special occasions but also for sending messages, as a token of friendship, as a get-well wish, or just to convey "have a nice day" to someone. Imports of cut flowers are primarily from Columbia, Mexico, Costa Rica, Ecuador, Peru, and Kenya.[29] The imported flowers must satisfy the selective U.S. consumer—in addition, the product must comply with the U.S. Plant Protection Quarantine Inspection Program and antidumping regulations. Since the product is highly perishable, air transportation and rapid transit through customs have to be ensured. Thus, the importer of flowers has to go through many hoops in terms of locating a reliable seller and arranging the logistics. Importer behavior will, of course, depend on the category of goods being purchased abroad.

However, importer buyer behavior is a relatively under-researched area in the field of international trade—partly on account of most nations being more interested in maximizing exports rather than imports—and restricting imports is relatively simple, as compared to being a successful exporter. The most important of the organizational buying models is the BuyGrid model.[30] Besides elaborating on

---

[29]Edward Lewine, "The $4 Bouquet," *New York Times* (May 9, 1999), p. 6 and 26.

[30]Patrick J. Robinson, Charles W. Faris and Yoram Wind, *Industrial Buying and Creative Marketing* (Boston: Allyn and Bacon, 1967).

EXHIBIT 17–9

MODEL OF IMPORTER BUYER BEHAVIOR

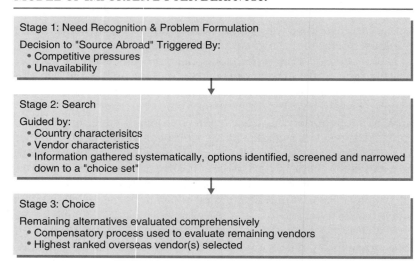

Stage 1: Need Recognition & Problem Formulation

Decision to "Source Abroad" Triggered By:
- Competitive pressures
- Unavailability

Stage 2: Search

Guided by:
- Country characterisitcs
- Vendor characteristics
- Information gathered systematically, options identified, screened and narrowed down to a "choice set"

Stage 3: Choice

Remaining alternatives evaluated comprehensively
- Compensatory process used to evaluate remaining vendors
- Highest ranked overseas vendor(s) selected

Source: Neng Liang and Rodney L. Stump, "Judgmental Heuristics in Overseas Vendor Search and Evaluation: A Proposed Model of Importer Buyer Behavior," *International Executive,* Copyright (November, 1996). Reprinted by permission of John Wiley & Sons, Inc.

how the purchasing process evolves and highlighting the role of buyers' search in choice decisions, this framework was the first to categorize buy decisions as (1) straight buys, (2) modified rebuy, and (3) new tasks.

Although this framework was developed primarily for domestic purchases, it is applicable to import decisions as well. Applying the framework for an import decision and taking into account the increased uncertainty in international markets would translate into a procedure presented in Exhibit 17–9. This sequence of actions in an import situation appears logical, as in exports, but many international supplier relationships start with an *unsolicited export order,* where importers place an order with a selected foreign vendor without any systematic vendor search and evaluation. The lack of a systematic approach to vendor identification and evaluation may stem from a difficulty in accessing all relevant information and from the idea of bounded rationality—the notion that due to limited cognitive abilities, humans tend to satisfice and not optimize. Thus, given the information available, which cannot be complete, managers will not be able to make the best decision.[31]

◆ ◆ ◆ ◆ ◆ ◆ MECHANICS OF IMPORTING

An import transaction is like looking at an export transaction from the other end of the transaction. Instead of an exporter looking for a prospective buyer, an importer looks for an overseas firm that can supply it with the raw materials, compo-

---

[31]Neng Liang and Rodney L. Stump, "Judgmental Heuristics in Overseas Vendor Search and Evaluation: A Proposed Model of Importer Buyer Behavior," *International Executive,* 38 (November/December 1996), pp. 779–806.

nents, or finished products that it needs for its business. Once an importer in the United States locates a suitable overseas exporter, it has to negotiate the terms of the sale with the exporter, including, but not restricted to the following:

- Finding a bank that either has branches in the exporter's country or has a correspondent bank located in the exporter's country, and establishing a line of credit with the bank if the importer not already done so.

- Establishing a letter of credit with a bank with the terms of payment and how payment is to be made. This includes terms of clearing the goods from the docks/customs warehouse (sometimes with title for goods going temporarily to the bank), insurance coverage, terms of transfer of title, and so on.

- Deciding on the mode of transfer of goods from exporter to importer and transfer of funds. Transportation party provides proof of delivery to the exporter's bank or the exporter. The exporter (or its bank) presents the proof of delivery to the importer's bank (branch in importer's own country/correspondent bank). The importer's bank transfers funds to the exporter's bank and simultaneously debits the importer's account or presents a demand draft to the importer.

- Checking compliance with national laws of the importing country and the exporting country. Import restrictions into the U.S. include quotas on automobiles, textiles and steel and quarantine checks on food products. They also include a ban on imports from Cuba, North Korea, Libya, Iraq, and Iran.

- Making allowances for foreign exchange fluctuations through making covering transactions through the bank so that the dollar liability for the importer either remains fixed or gets lower.

- Fixing liability for payment of import duties and demurrage and warehousing in case the goods get delayed due to congestion at ports. These payments are normally the responsibility of the importer.

An examination of these mechanics of an import transaction reveals that the transaction is materially the same as an export transaction. The differences that are of interest to managers involved in the import of goods into the United States include the following:

- An exporter faces the risk of receiving no payment due to a variety of factors, whereas nonpayment is not an issue in imports. However, the quality of goods and services imported can be an issue for imports—this is not usually an issue in exports.

- The importer can pay in its own currency (most of the time)—a facility not available to importers in almost any other country.

- Everything else equal, it is easier for a U.S. firm to import than to export because of the primacy of the U.S. dollar despite the gradual depreciation of the U.S. dollar over time.

Import Documents and Delivery in the United States

When a shipment reaches the United States, the consignee (normally the importer) will file entry documents with the port director at the port of entry. The bill of lading or the airway bill properly endorsed by the consignor in favor of the consignee serves as the evidence of the right to make entry. The entry documents also include an entry manifest, Customs Form 7533, Customs Form 3461, packing lists if appropriate, and the commercial invoice. The entry should be accompanied by evidence that a bond is posted with customs to cover any potential duties, taxes, and penalties that may accrue. A **bond** is a guarantee by someone that the duties and any potential penalties will be paid to the customs of the importing country. In the event that a custom broker is employed for the purpose of making entry, the broker may permit the use of the bond to provide the required coverage.

Entry may be for immediate delivery, for ordinary delivery, for a warehouse or may be unentered for a period of time. Merchandise arriving from Canada and Mexico, trade fair goods, perishable goods and shipments assigned to the U.S. government almost always utilize the **Special Permit for Immediate Delivery** on Customs Form 3461 prior to the arrival of the goods to enable fast release after arrival. An entry summary is then filed within ten days of the release of the goods. Imported goods coming in under ordinary delivery use normal channels, including Form 7533. Under warehousing, goods are placed in a custom bonded warehouse if the entry of the imported goods is desired to be delayed. The goods may remain in a bonded warehouse for a period of five years. At any time during the period warehoused goods may be re-exported without payment of duty, or they may be withdrawn for consumption upon the payment of duty. If there is a failure to enter the goods at the port of entry or the port of destination within five working days after arrival, the imported goods may be placed in the general warehouse at the risk and expense of the importer.

Import Duties in the United States

Import duties that have to be paid may be ad valorem, specific, or compound. An **ad valorem duty**, which is the one most frequently applied, is a percentage of the value of the merchandise, such as 5 percent ad valorem. Thus, an auto shipment worth $100 million that has an ad valorem rate of 3.9 percent will pay $3.9 million as customs duty. A **specific duty** rate is a specified amount per unit of weight or other quantity, such as 5.1 cents per dozen, 20 cents per barrel, or 90 cents per ton. A **compound duty** rate is a combination of an ad valorem rate and a specific rate, such as 0.7 cents per kilogram plus 10 percent as valorem. Average import duty rates in Japan (3.4 percent), the United States (5.2 percent), and the European Union (7.7 percent) are relatively low compared to many other countries (e.g., Mexico with 18.0 percent).[32] The entry of imported merchandise into the United States is complete after the goods are cleared by the customs from the port of entry or the port of destination.

Antidumping import duties are assessed on imported merchandise sold to importers in the United States at a price that is less than the fair market value. The fair market value of merchandise is defined under articles of the WTO as the price at which the good is normally sold in the manufacturer's home market. For some goods, countervailing duties are assessed to counter the effects of subsidies provided by foreign governments to goods that are exported to the United States, because without the **countervailing duty** the price of these imported goods in the U.S. market would be artificially low, causing economic injury to U.S. manufacturers. Duty drawbacks are a refund of 99 percent of all ordinary customs duties. **Duty drawback** may be a direct identification drawback or a substitution drawback. *Direct identification drawback* provides a refund of duties paid on imported merchandise that is partially or totally used within five years of the date of import in the manufacture of an article that is exported. *Substitution drawback* provides a refund of duties paid on designated imported merchandise upon exportation of articles manufactured or produced with the use of substituted domestic or imported merchandise that is of the same quality as the designated import merchandise.

---

[32]"Trends in Market Openness," *OECD Economic Outlook*, 65 (June 1999), pp. 207–21.

As explained in Chapter 16, importing firms can also utilize foreign trade zones profitably. They can set up facilities in a FTZ to import finished goods, component parts, or raw materials for eventual domestic consumption or import merchandise that is frequently delayed by customs quota delays or import merchandise that must be processed, generating significant amounts of scrap. An important feature of foreign trade zones for foreign merchants entering the American market is that the goods may brought to the threshold of the market, making immediate delivery certain and avoiding the possible cancellation of orders due to shipping delays. Foreign sales corporations can be set up in the U.S. by the overseas subsidiaries of U.S. corporations to take advantage of the provisions governing foreign sales corporations.

GRAY MARKETS

Gray market channels refer to the legal export/import transaction involving genuine products into a country by intermediaries other than the authorized distributors. From the importer's side, it is also known as **parallel imports**. Distributors, wholesalers, and retailers in a foreign market obtain the exporter's product from some other business entity. Thus, the exporter's legitimate distributor(s) and dealers face competition from others who sell the exporter's products at reduced prices in that foreign market. High-priced branded consumer goods like cameras, jewelry, perfumes, watches, and so on, where production lies principally in one country are particularly prone to gray market imports. Brand reputation is a critical element in gray market goods exports and the distribution is typically through exclusive wholesalers and distributors.

For example, if purchased on the gray market, a $101,500 brand-new Mercedes-Benz SL600 Convertible, which meets all the U.S. safety and pollution control requirements, can be purchased for 20 percent less than the price ($126,900) charged by the local authorized dealer. Similarly, in the luxury boat market, many foreign dealers of U.S. manufacturers are seriously affected by gray market activity. To avoid higher prices abroad, foreign retailers often come to the U.S. and purchase their boats from U.S. dealers, and then arrange their own transportation, circumventing the licensed dealer in their own home country.[33] Although gray market products look similar to their domestic counterparts, they may not be identical and may not carry full warranties. Nevertheless, the volume of gray market activities is significant.

Three conditions are necessary for gray markets to develop. First, the products must be available in other markets. In today's global markets, this condition is readily met. Second, trade barriers such as tariffs, transportation costs, and legal restrictions must be low enough for parallel importers to move the products from one market to another. Again, under the principle of GATT, now WTO, the trade barriers have been reduced so low that parallel importation has become feasible. Third, price differentials among various markets must be great enough to provide the basic motivation for gray marketers. Such price differences arise for various

[33]Frank Reynolds, "Senior Management Apathy Could Sink U.S. Pleasure Boat Exports," *Journal of Commerce* (March 24, 1999), p. 9A.

reasons, including currency exchange rate fluctuations, differences in demand, and segmentation strategies employed by international marketing managers.[34]

- *Currency fluctuations.* The fluctuating currency exchange rates among countries often produce large differences in prices for products across national boundaries. Gray marketers can take advantage of changes in exchange rates by purchasing products in markets with weak currencies and selling them in markets with strong currencies.

- *Differences in market demand.* Similarly, price differences may be caused by differences in market demand for a product in various markets. If the authorized channels of distribution cannot adjust the market supply to meet the market demand, a large enough price difference may develop for unauthorized dealers to engage in arbitrage process—that is, buying the product inexpensively in countries with weak demand and selling it profitably in countries with strong demand.

- *Segmentation strategy.* Although currency exchange rates and differences in market demand may be beyond the control of international marketing managers, segmentation strategy may result in (1) planned price discrimination and (2) planned product differentiation among various markets. Even for an identical product, different pricing strategy may be adopted for various reasons, including differences in product life cycle stage, customer purchase behavior, and price elasticity across different markets. Different prices across different markets motivate gray marketers to exploit the price differences among the markets.

Alternatively, the product may be modified to address the specific needs of different markets. Contradictory to common sense, adaptation of individual products for specific market also leads to substantially more gray marketing. This occurs for two reasons. First, when, for example, a stripped version of the product is marketed in Europe and an enhanced version is marketed in the United States, some American consumers, who may not be willing to pay for the enhanced model with too many refinements, import the simpler, less expensive version from an unauthorized distributor through a gray marketing channel. Second, some consumers simply want to purchase the product models that are not marketed in their domestic markets in order to differentiate themselves from the rest of the consumers. This is increasingly likely, as markets around the world become more homogeneous.[35]

A key question for the exporter of branded products is whether a gray market will cause a global strategy to become less desirable. Closer control and monitoring of international marketing efforts can certainly reduce the threat of gray market goods to negligible levels.[36] As presented in Exhibit 17–10, international marketers not only try to confront existing gray markets reactively, but also are increasingly developing more proactive approaches to gray market problems before they arise.

---

[34]This section draws from Dale F. Duhan and Mary Jane Sheffet, "Gray Markets and the Legal Status of Parallel Importation," *Journal of Marketing*, 52 (July 1988), pp. 75–83; and Tunga Kiyak, "International Gray Markets: A Systematic Analysis and Research Propositions," A paper presented at 1997 AMA Summer Educators' Conference, August 2–5, 1997.
[35]Matthew B. Myers, "Incidents of Gray Market Activity among U.S. Exporters: Occurrences, Characteristics, and Consequences," *Journal of International Business Studies*, 30 (First Quarter 1999), pp. 10–126.
[36]Ibid.

EXHIBIT 17–10

HOW TO COMBAT GRAY MARKET ACTIVITY

A. *Reactive Strategies to Combat Gray Market Activity*

Type of Strategy	Implemented by	Cost of Implementation	Difficulty of Implementation	Does It Curtail Gray Market Activity at Source?	Does It Provide Immediate Relief to Authorized Dealers?	Long-term Effectiveness	Legal Risks to Manufacturers or Dealers	Company Examples
Strategic confrontation	Dealer with manufacturer support	Moderate	Requires planning	No	Relief in the medium term	Effective	Low risk	Creative merchandising by Caterpillar and auto dealers
Participation	Dealer	Low	Not difficult	No	Immediate relief	Potentially damaging reputation of manufacturer	Low risk	Dealers wishing to remain anonymous
Price cutting	Jointly by manufacturer and dealer	Costly	Not difficult	No, if price cutting is temporary	Immediate relief	Effective	Moderate to high risk	Dealers and manufacturers remain anonymous
Supply interference	Either party can engage	Moderate at the wholesale level; high at the retail level	Moderately difficult	No	Immediate relief or slightly delayed	Somewhat effective if at wholesale level; not effective at retail level	Moderate risk at wholesale level; low risk at retail	IBM, Hewlett-Packard, Lotus Corp., Swatch Watch USA, Charles of the Ritz Group, Ltd., Leitz, Inc., NEC Electronics

EXHIBIT 17–10 (CONTINUED)

Type of Strategy	Implemented by	Cost of Implementation	Difficulty of Implementation	Does It Curtail Gray Market Activity at Source?	Does It Provide Immediate Relief to Authorized Dealers?	Long-term Effectiveness	Legal Risks to Manufacturers or Dealers	Company Examples
Promotion of gray market product limitations	Jointly, with manufacturer leadership	Moderate	Not difficult	No	Slightly delayed	Somewhat effective	Low risk	Komatsu, Seiko, Rolex, Mercedes-Benz, IBM
Collaboration	Dealer	Low	Requires careful negotiations	No	Immediate relief	Somewhat effective	Very high risk	Dealers wishing to remain anonymous
Acquisition	Dealer	Very costly	Difficult	No	Immediate relief	Effective if other gray market brokers don't creep in	Moderate to high risk	No publicized cases
B. Proactive Strategies to Combat Gray Market Activity								
Product/service differentiation and availability	Jointly, with manufacturer leadership	Moderate to high	Not difficult	Yes	No; impact felt in medium to long term	Very effective	Very low risk	General Motors, Ford, Porsche, Kodak
Strategic pricing	Manufacturer	Moderate to high	Complex; impact on overall profitability needs monitoring	Yes	Slightly delayed	Very effective	Low risk	Porsche
Dealer development	Jointly, with manufacturer leadership	Moderate to high	Not difficult; requires close dealer participation	No	No; impact felt the long term	Very effective	No risk	Caterpillar, Canon

Strategy	Responsibility	Cost	Difficulty			Effectiveness	Risk	Companies
Marketing information systems	Jointly, with manufacturer leadership	Moderate to high	Not difficult; requires dealer participation	No	No; impact felt in after implementation	Effective	No risk	IBM, Catepillar, Yamaha, Hitachi, Komatsu, Lotus Development, Insurance companies
Long-term image reinforcement	Jointly	Moderate	Not difficult	No	No; impact felt in the long term	Effective	No risk	Most manufacturers with strong dealer networks
Establishing legal precedence	Manufacturer	High	Difficult	Yes, if fruitful	No	Uncertain	Low risk	COPIAT, Coleco, Charles of the Ritz Group, Ltd.
Lobbying	Jointly	Moderate	Difficult	Yes, if fruitful	No	Uncertain	Low risk	COPIAT, Duracell, Porsche

Note: Company strategies include, but are not limited to, those mentioned here.

Source: S. Tamer Cavusgil and Ed Sikora, "How Multinationals Can Counter Gray Market Imports," *Columbia Journal of World Business*, 23 (Winter 1988), pp. 75–85.

SUMMARY

The United States was the largest importer and exporter in the world in 1999. The U.S. government has a variety of programs to support exports, though many government policies—which are sometimes dictated by political compulsions—hinder exports from the U.S. export markets provide a unique opportunity for growth, but competition in these markets is fierce. With the rise of the big emerging markets like Brazil, China, and India, competition is likely to intensify even more.

Procedurally, exporting requires locating customers, obtaining an export license from the federal government (a general or validated license); collecting export documents (such as the bill of lading, commercial invoice, export packing list, insurance certificate); packing and marketing; shipping abroad; and receiving payment—most of the time through a bank using a letter of credit. Conversely, imports require locating a seller, obtaining an import license, usually establishing a letter of credit, turning over import documents (like the bill of lading, etc.) to indicate receipt of goods, and making payment through the banking system. Methods of payment include cash in advance, open account, consignment sale, dollar draft, and a letter of credit. Of these, the last two are the most popular. Depending on the nature of the payment terms and the currency of payment the exporter may need to make foreign exchange hedging transactions. The U.S. government is now taking a more active role in promoting exports of U.S. firms as they bid for big ticket items in the emerging markets.

Imports are the obverse of exports. A U.S. importer can make payments in U.S. dollars unlike an importer in many other countries. Any good coming in through a U.S. port has to pass through customs and pay the appropriate duty and be authorized by customs at the port of entry or the port of destination for entry. Unlike an exporter who faces a payment risk, the importer's risks are associated with delivery schedules and product quality. Foreign exchange risk is common to both imports and exports. Entry of some goods into the United States is restricted by bilateral and multilateral quotas as well as by political considerations.

Finally, globalization of markets has spawned gray marketing activities by unauthorized distributors taking advantage of price differences that exist among various countries due to currency exchange rate fluctuations, different market demand conditions, and price discrimination, among other factors. For companies marketing well-known branded products, gray markets have become a serious issue to be confronted proactively as well as reactively.

KEY TERMS

ad valorem duty
American Export Trading Company of 1982
antidumping import duties
Automated Export System
bill of lading
bond
combination export manager (CEM)
commercial invoice
compound duty

Countervailing duty
credit risk
customs receipt
direct exporting
draft
duty drawback
Ex–Im Bank (Export–Import Bank)
export broker
export commission house
export department

Export Enhancement Act of 1992
export license
export merchant
export sales subsidiary
foreign exchange risk
foreign sales branch
Foreign Sales Corporation
freight forwarder
gray market (parallel imports)

Incoterms
indirect exporting
letter of credit
open account
piggyback exporting
political risk
Special Permit for Immediate Delivery
specific duty
trading company
transfer risk

REVIEW QUESTIONS

1. How does a prospective exporter choose an export market?

2. What are the factors that influence the decision of the exporter to use a standardized product strategy across countries and regions?

3. What are the direct and indirect channels of distribution available to exporters? Under what conditions would the use of each be the most appropriate?

4. Terms of payment are an extremely important facet of export transactions. Describe the various terms of payments in increasing order of risk.

5. Describe the various terms of shipment and sale.

6. What is the role of government (home country) in export activities? Explain in the context of U.S. exporters.

7. Managing imports in the United States is by and large more easy and less risky than managing exports? Give reasons why this is true.

8. What are gray markets? What are the factors that lead to the development of gray markets?

DISCUSSION QUESTIONS ◆

1. A friend of yours, who owns a small firm manufacturing and selling CD-ROM–based computer games, would like to market the company's products abroad. Your friend seeks information from you on the following:

a. Which markets should the firm target (what sources of information to tap)?

b. How should it tap these markets (what are the steps you would advise)?

c. What are the direct and indirect costs involved in exports?

d. What kind of assistance can he get from governmental and nongovernmental agencies at any of the stages involved? What would your advice be?

2. General trading companies have played and continue to play a leading role in the exports and imports of products from and to Japan. The effectiveness of these companies is evident from the fact that in the recent Fortune 500 list of the world's largest corporations, five of the top ten corporations (including the top three) are Japanese trading firms. Although there is little question about the effectiveness of these firms, various business executives, especially outside Japan, interpret the directing of exports and imports through such firms as adding to significant inefficiencies in terms of higher costs and lost opportunities. Do you agree with this contention? Why or why not? The top three trading houses, Mitsubishi, Mitsui, and Itochu, had profitability ratios (profits after taxes / total revenues) of 0.18 percent, 0.17 percent, and 0.07 percent, respectively. Would this information have any bearing on your answer?

3. You are the manager for international operations of a manufacturer of steel in the United States. You have received an offer at a very attractive price to purchase 5,000 metric tons of wires rods (used to draw wires for the manufacture of nails) from a large nail manufacturer located in a developing country X. What would you deem to be the most appropriate choice of export terms of payment and terms of shipment, given the following information (include any precautions that you would take to ensure the successful execution of the order):

a. The prospective importer has its account at a local bank. Local government rules stipulate making payments only through this bank.

b. The local bank does not have any international operations/branches.

c. The currency of country X has been extremely unstable, with its value having depreciated by more than 20 percent recently.

d. The interest rates are extremely high in this country.

e. The legal system is weak in this country, but the firm that is willing to place the order has a good reputation based on past experience with other international manufacturers.

f. Rain and summer heat can cause the product to deteriorate if kept for a time longer than necessary.

g. This country exports a larger amount by the sea route than it imports. Hence, many ships have to go empty to get cargo from this country to the United States.

4. Nontariff barriers to international trade have significant implications, both for exporters as well as for importers. One of the most prevalent nontariff barriers used is antidumping duties or the threat of initiating antidumping investigations. The use of antidumping duties has recently received some criticisms as affecting certain high-growth industries adversely, while protecting some smaller inefficient (as claimed) industries. One typical example quoted is the manufacture of laptop computers. Antidumping duties were levied against Japanese manufacturers of flat-panel screens (used in the manufacture of laptop computers) at the behest of would-be flat-panel manufacturers in the United States. It was the contention of these U.S. producers that if the flat panels were not dumped by Japanese manufacturers, the U.S. producers would be able to raise capital to initiate production of this product. As a result of the duties levied, which would have added significant costs to the computers manufactured in the United States, most U.S. manufacturers (many of whom had plans to manufacture laptop computers within the United States) shifted to sites abroad. According to the computer manufacturers, the antidumping decision sacrificed the fastest-growing segment of the computer industry to a nonexistent domestic flat-panel industry. The proponents of antidumping legislation, however, contend that the threat of predatory practices is real and antidumping procedures take care of this threat. Whom would you side with, the proponents or the critics of antidumping actions?

5. You are part of the management team of a U.S. computer manufacturer. Recently, the Texas distributors of the company's products have been complaining of significant gray imports taking place from Mexico that is adversely affecting their margins. The main reason for gray imports is attributed to the recent volatility of the Mexican peso, especially the downward pressures on its value. What steps would you suggest to take care of the current problem? What would be your advice to curb gray marketing in the future?

FURTHER READING

Bello, Daniel C., and Ritu Lohtia. "Export Channel Design: The Use of Foreign Distributors and Agents." *Journal of Academy of Marketing Science*, 23 (2) (1995): 83–93.

Burgel, Oliver, and Gorden C. Murray. "The International Market Entry Choices of Start-Up Companies in High-Technology Industries." *Journal of International Marketing*, 8 (2) (2000): 33–62.

Katsikeas, Constantine S., Shengliang L. Deng, and Lawrence H. Wortzel. "Perceived Export Success Factors of Small and Medium-Sized Canadian Firms." *Journal of International Marketing*, 5 (4) (1997): 53–72.

Leonidou, Leonidas C., and Constantine S. Katsikeas. "The Export Development Process: An Integrative Review of Empirical Models." *Journal of International Business Studies*, 27 (3) (1996): 517–51.

Liang, Neng, and Arvind Parkhe. "Importer Behavior: The Neglected Counterpart of International Exchange." *Journal of International Business Studies*, 28 (Third Quarter 1997): 495–530.

Michael, James. "A Supplemental Distribution Channel?: The Case of U.S. Parallel Export Channels," *Multinational Business Review*, 6 (Spring 1998): 24–35.

Moini, A. H. "Small Firms Exporting: How Effective are Government Export Assistance Programs?" *Journal of Small Business Management*, 36 (January 1998): 1–15.

Russow, Lloyd C., and Andrew Solocha. "A Review of the Screening Process within the Context of the Global Assessment Process." *Journal of Global Marketing*, 7(1) (1993): 65–85.

Wilkinson, Timothy J. "The Effect of State Appropriations on Export-Related Employment in Manufacturing." *Economic Development Quarterly*, 13 (May 1999): 172–82.

PLANNING, ORGANIZATION, AND CONTROL OF GLOBAL MARKETING OPERATIONS

18

CHAPTER OVERVIEW

1. GLOBAL STRATEGIC MARKETING PLANNING

2. KEY CRITERIA IN GLOBAL ORGANIZATIONAL DESIGN

3. ORGANIZATIONAL DESIGN OPTIONS

4. ORGANIZING FOR GLOBAL BRAND MANAGEMENT

5. LIFECYCLE OF ORGANIZATION STRUCTURES

6. TO CENTRALIZE OR DECENTRALIZE?

7. CONTROLLING GLOBAL MARKETING EFFORTS

8. GUIDELINES FOR CHOOSING THE RIGHT ORGANIZATION STRUCTURE

The capstone of a company's global marketing activities will be its strategic marketing plan. To implement its global plans effectively, a company needs to reflect on the best organizational setup that enables it to successfully meet the threats and opportunities posed by the global marketing arena. The global marketer must confront organizational issues such as these: What is the proper communication and reporting structure? Who within our organization should bear responsibility for each of the functions that need to be carried out? How can we as an organization leverage the competencies and skills of our individual subsidiaries? Where should the decision-making authority belong for the various areas?

We will consider the major factors that will influence the design of a global organizational structure. Multinational companies (MNCs) can choose from a wide variety of organizational structures. In this chapter, we will expose you to the major alternative configurations. We will also highlight the central role played by country managers within the MNC's organization. More and more companies try to build up and nurture global brands. We will look at several organizational mechanisms that firms can adopt to facilitate such efforts. Change requires flexibility. This chapter will look into different ways that MNCs can handle environmental changes. MNCs must also decide where the decision-making locus belongs. The challenge is to come up with a structure that bridges the gap between two forces: being responsive to local conditions and integrating your global marketing efforts. The final section focuses on control mechanisms that companies can utilize to achieve their strategic goals.

◆ ◆ ◆ ◆ ◆ ◆ GLOBAL STRATEGIC MARKETING PLANNING

The vast majority of multinational companies prepare a **global strategic marketing plan** to guide and implement their strategic and tactical marketing decisions. Such plans are usually developed on an annual basis and look at policies over multiple years. The content of a global strategic marketing plan can be very broad in scope, but it usually covers four areas:[1]

1. *Market situation analysis.* Management makes a situation analysis on a global basis of the company's customers (market segments, demand trends, etc.), the competition (SWOT analysis), the company itself, and the collaborators (e.g., suppliers, distribution channels, alliance partners).
2. *Objectives.* For each country, management states goals that are both achievable and challenging.
3. *Strategies.* Once the objectives have been determined, management needs to formulate marketing strategies for each country to achieve the set goals, including resource allocation.
4. *Action plans.* Strategies need to be translated into concrete actions that will implement those strategies. Specific actions are to be spelled out for each marketing mix element.

These are the core areas of a global strategic marketing plan; such a plan will also discuss anticipated results and include contingency plans.

Bottom-Up versus Top-Down Strategic Planning

International planning can be top-down (centralized) or bottom-up (decentralized). Obviously, hybrid forms that combine both options are also possible. With **top-down planning**, corporate headquarters guides the planning process. **Bottom-up planning** is the opposite. Here, the planning process starts with the local subsidiaries and is then consolidated at headquarters level. The bottom-up approach has the advantage of embracing local responsiveness. Top-down planning, on the other hand, facilitates performance monitoring. A centralized approach also makes it easier to market products with a global perspective. A recent survey of large multinational corporations found that pure bottom-up planning was most popular

[1]See, for instance, Douglas J. Dalrymple and Leonard J. Parsons, *Marketing Management* (New York: John Wiley & Sons, 1995), Chapter 17.

(used by 66 percent of the companies surveyed). Only 10 percent of the interviewed companies, on the other hand, relied on a pure top-down planning process. The balance used a hybrid format (11 percent) or no planning at all (12 percent).[2]

Marketing plans can go awry. Exhibit 18–1 is a listing of the internal obstacles that can undermine the global strategic marketing plan preparation. As you can see, the top-three stumbling blocks are lack of proper information, too little emphasis on the development of alternative strategic options, and unrealistic strategic

Pitfalls

EXHIBIT 18–1
INTERNAL OBSTACLES TO GLOBAL STRATEGIC MARKETING PLAN
PREPARATION

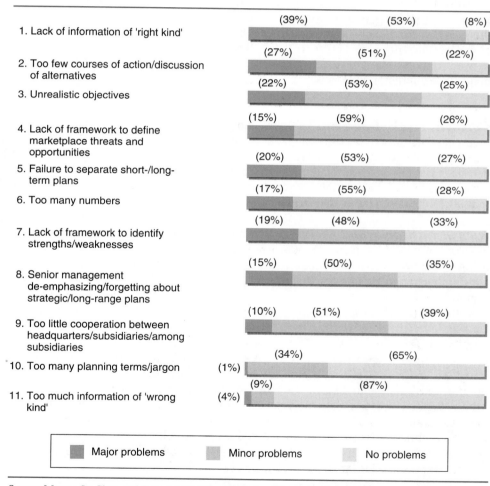

1. Lack of information of 'right kind'   (39%) (53%) (8%)
2. Too few courses of action/discussion of alternatives   (27%) (51%) (22%)
3. Unrealistic objectives   (22%) (53%) (25%)
4. Lack of framework to define marketplace threats and opportunities   (15%) (59%) (26%)
5. Failure to separate short-/long-term plans   (20%) (53%) (27%)
6. Too many numbers   (17%) (55%) (28%)
7. Lack of framework to identify strengths/weaknesses   (19%) (48%) (33%)
8. Senior management de-emphasizing/forgetting about strategic/long-range plans   (15%) (50%) (35%)
9. Too little cooperation between headquarters/subsidiaries/among subsidiaries   (10%) (51%) (39%)
10. Too many planning terms/jargon   (1%) (34%) (65%)
11. Too much information of 'wrong kind'   (4%) (9%) (87%)

■ Major problems   Minor problems   No problems

Source: Myung-Su Chae and John S. Hill, "The Hazards of Strategic Planning for Global Markets," *Long Range Planning,* 29 (6) (1996), p. 885.

[2]Myung-Su Chae and John S. Hill, "The Hazards of Strategic Planning for Global Markets," *Long Range Planning,* 29 (6) (1996), 880–91.

objectives. Obviously, external factors can also interfere. Changes in the political and the economic environment can upset the finest strategic plans. China's sudden clampdown on direct selling created upheaval for Avon, Amway, and Mary Kay, among other companies. The suddenness and severity of the recent Asian financial crisis wreaked havoc for the plans of most Western MNCs. Other external factors include changes in the competitive climate (e.g., deregulation), technological developments, and consumer-related factors.[3]

◆ ◆ ◆ ◆ ◆ ◆ **KEY CRITERIA IN GLOBAL ORGANIZATIONAL DESIGN**

As with most other global managerial issues there is no magic formula that prescribes the "ideal" organizational setup under a given set of circumstances. Yet, there are some factors that companies should consider when engineering their global organizational structure. In the following discussion, we make a distinction between environmental and firm-specific factors. Let us start with a look at the major environmental factors.

Environmental Factors

Competitive Environment. Global competitive pressures force MNCs to implement structures that facilitate quick decision making and alertness. In industries where competition is highly localized, a decentralized structure where most of the decision making is made at the country-level is often appropriate. Nevertheless, even in such situations, MNCs can often benefit substantially from mechanisms that allow the company to leverage its global knowledge base.

Rate of Environmental Change. Drastic environmental change is a way of life in scores of industries. New competitors or substitutes for your product emerge. Existing competitors form or disband strategic alliances. Consumer needs worldwide constantly change. Businesses that are subject to rapid change require an organizational design that facilitates continuous scanning of the firm's global environment and swift responsiveness to opportunities or threats posed by that environment.

Regional Trading Blocs. Companies that operate within a regional trading bloc (e.g., the European Union, NAFTA, Mercosur) usually integrate to some extent their marketing efforts across the affiliates within the block area. A case in point is the European Union. In light of the European integration, numerous MNCs decided to rationalize their organizational structure. Many of these companies still maintain their local subsidiaries, but the locus of most decision making now lies with the Pan–European headquarters. As other trading blocs such as Asia's APEC and South America's Mercosur evolve towards the European model, one can expect similar makeovers in other regions.

Nature of Customers. The company's customer base also affects its desired organizational setup. Companies that have a "global" clientele (e.g., DHL, IBM, and

---

[3]Ibid.

AT & T) need to develop structures that permit a global reach while allowing them to stay "close" to their customers.

These are the major external drivers. We now turn to the prime firm-specific determinants.

Strategic Importance of International Business. Typically, when overseas sales account for a very small fraction of the company's overall sales revenues, simple organizational structures (e.g., an export department) can easily handle the firm's global activities. As international sales grow, the organizational structure will evolve to mirror the growing importance of the firm's global activities. For instance, companies may start with an international division when they test the international waters. Once their overseas activities expand, they are likely to adopt an area-type (country- and/or region-based) structure.

Product Diversity. The diversity of the company's foreign product line is another key factor in shaping the company's organization. Companies with substantial product diversity tend to go for a global product division configuration.

Company Heritage. Differences in organizational structures within the same industry can also be explained via corporate culture. Nestlé and Unilever, for example, have always been highly decentralized MNCs. A lot of the decision-making authority has always been made at the local level. When Unilever realized that its marketing efforts required a more Pan–European approach to compete with the likes of Procter & Gamble, the company transformed its organization and revised its performance measures to provide incentives for a European focus. One of Unilever's senior executives, however, noted that the change-over "comes hard to people who for years have been in an environment where total business power was delegated to them."[4] As long as a given formula works, there is little incentive for companies to tinker with it. Revamping an organization to make the structure more responsive to new environmental realities can be a daunting challenge.

Quality of Local Managerial Skills. Decentralization could become a problem when local managerial talents are missing. Granted, companies can bring in expatriates, but this is typically an extremely expensive remedy, and it does not always work out. For instance, expatriate managers might find it hard to adapt to the local environment.

Firm-Specific Factors

ORGANIZATIONAL DESIGN OPTIONS ◆ ◆ ◆ ◆ ◆ ◆

Firms can adopt four principal designs to organize their global activities:

- **International division.** Under this design, the company basically has two entities: the domestic division, which is responsible for the firm's domestic activities, and the international division, which is in charge of the company's international operations.

---

[4]"Unilever Adopts Clean Sheet Approach," *The Financial Times* (October 21, 1991).

- **Product-based structure.** With a product structure the company's global activities are organized along its various product divisions.
- **Geographic structure.** This is a setup where the company configures its organization along geographic areas: countries, regions, or some combination of these two levels.
- **Matrix structure.** This is an option where the company integrates two approaches—for instance, the product and geographic dimensions—so there is a dual chain of command.

We will now consider each of these options in greater detail. At the end of this section, we will also discuss **global networking** as a possible organization model.

International Division Structure

Most companies that engage in global marketing will initially start off by establishing an export department. Once international sales reach a threshold, the company might set up a full-blown international division. The charter of the international division is to develop and coordinate the firm's global operations. The unit also scans market opportunities in the global marketplace. In most cases, the division has equal standing with the other divisions within the company.

This option is most suitable for companies that have a product line that is not too diverse and does not require a large amount of adaptation to local country needs. It is also a viable alternative for companies whose business is still primarily focused on the domestic market. Over time, as international marketing efforts become more important to the firm, most companies tend to switch to a more globally oriented organizational structure.

Global Product Division Structure

The second option centers around the different product lines or strategic business units (SBUs) of the company. Each product division, being a separate profit center, is responsible for managing worldwide the activities for its product line. This alternative is especially popular among high-tech companies with highly complex products and MNCs with a very diversified product portfolio. The approach is adopted by Ericsson, John Deere, and Sun Microsystems (see Exhibit 18–2). Global Perspective 18–1 describes how Whirlpool implemented the global SBU approach for its microwave ovens and air treatment products.

There are several benefits associated with a global product structure. The product focus offers the company a large degree of flexibility in terms of cross-country resource allocation and strategic planning. For instance, market penetration efforts in recently entered markets can be cross-subsidized by profits generated in developed markets. In many companies, a global product structure goes in tandem with consolidated manufacturing and distribution operations. This approach is exemplified by Honeywell, the U.S. maker of control tools, which has set up centers of excellence that span the globe.[5] That way, an MNC can achieve substantial scale economies in the area of production and logistics, thereby improving the firm's competitive cost position. Another appeal is that global product structures facilitate the development of a global strategic focus to cope with challenges posed by global players.[6]

[5]Honeywell, *1995 Annual Report.*
[6]W. H. Davidson and P. Haspeslagh, "Shaping a Global Product Organization," *Harvard Business Review* (July–August 1982), 125–32.

$\mathcal{G}$LOBAL PERSPECTIVE 18-1

WHIRLPOOL'S GLOBAL BUSINESS UNITS

Whirlpool has managed its worldwide operations principally through a regional business unit structure. Microwave ovens and air treatment products (e.g., room air conditioners, dehumidifiers) have become such global products that Whirlpool established two product-oriented business units. These units are responsible for product planning, development, manufacturing, and distribution on a global basis. The regional business units continue to be in charge of sales and marketing.

Source: Whirlpool Corporation, *1995 Annual Report.*

The Global Microwave Oven Business Unit was launched in mid-1994 based on a manufacturing facility in Norrkäping, Sweden, and a joint venture in Shunde, China. The Shunde facility offers low-cost, large-scale production capability, while the Norrkäping plant offers leading-edge technology. Swedish and Chinese engineers were rotated between the two facilities to integrate the two units and to address quality, logistics, and procurement issues.

The Global Air Treatment Business Unit was formed in 1995 after the creation of a Shenzen-based Chinese joint venture. Also for this SBU, Whirlpool exchanged staff between the Tennessee facility and the Chinese unit to foster global integration.

EXHIBIT 18-2
THREE EXAMPLES OF A GLOBAL PRODUCT STRUCTURE

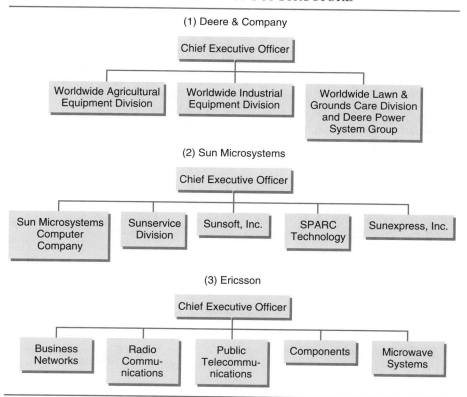

The shortcomings of a product division are not insignificant. Lack of communication and coordination among the various product divisions could lead to needless duplication of tasks. A relentless product-driven orientation can distract the company from local market needs. The global product division system has also been criticized for scattering the global resources of the company.[7] Instead of sharing resources and creating a global know-how pool, international resources and expertise get fragmented. A too narrow focus on the product area will lead to a climate where companies fail to grasp the synergies that might exist between global product divisions.

Geographic Structure

The third option is the geographic structure, where the MNC is organized along geographic units. The units might be individual countries or regions. In many cases, MNCs use a combination of country-based subsidiaries and regional headquarters. There are other variants. Coca-Cola, for instance, used to have five different regions, each one of them being further divided into subregions, as is shown in Exhibit 18–3. Area structures are especially appealing to companies that market closely related product lines with very similar end-users and applications around the world.

EXHIBIT 18–3
THE COCA-COLA COMPANY: EXAMPLES OF A GEOGRAPHIC STRUCTURE

Operating Officers

Africa Group
President
    North Africa Division
    Southern Africa Division

Middle and Far East Group
President
    Middle East Division
    Southeast and West Asia Division
    South Pacific Division
    China Division
    North Pacific Division
    Philippines Division

Latin America Group
President
    Brazil Division
    Coca-Cola Interamerican
    River Plate Division
    North Latin America Division
    Central America and Caribbean Division
    Andean Division

Greater Europe Group
President
    Nordic and Northern Eurasia Division
    Northwest European Division
    East Central European Division
    Iberian Division
    Central Mediterranean Division
    German Division
    Coca-Cola G.m.b.H.

Coca-Cola Foods
President

North America Group
President
    Coca-Cola Operations
    Coca-Cola Fountain
    Coca-Cola Ltd., Canada

Source: The Coca-Cola Company, *1995 Annual Report.*

---

[7]Ibid., p. 129.

Country-Based Subsidiaries.   Scores of MNCs set up subsidiaries on a country-by-country basis. To some degree, such an organization reflects the marketing concept. By setting up country affiliates, the MNC can stay in close touch with the local market conditions. The firm can thereby easily spot and swiftly respond to local market developments.

Country-focused organizations have several serious handicaps, though. They tend to be costly. Coordination with corporate headquarters and among subsidiaries can easily become extremely cumbersome. A country focus often leads to a not-invented-here mentality that hinders cross-fertilization. Some critics of the country model derisively refer to the country model as a mini-United Nations with a multitude of local fiefs run by scores of country managers.[8] Kenichi Ohmae sums up the weaknesses of the country structure as follows:

> One of the prime difficulties of organizing a company for global operations is the psychology of managers who are used to thinking by country-based line of authority rather than by line of opportunity. Lots of creative ideas for generating value are overlooked because such managers are captive to nation state–conditioned habits of mind. Once that constraint is relaxed . . . a nearly infinite range of new opportunities comes into focus: building cross-border alliances, establishing virtual companies, arbitraging differential costs of labor or even services . . . . I strongly believe that, as head-to-head battles within established geographies yield less and less incremental value, changing the battleground from nation to cross-border region will be at the core of 21st-century corporate strategy.[9]

New Role of Country Managers.   Some corporate strategy gurus foresee the demise of the country manager. According to their opinion, the role of the country manager of the twenty-first century will be minimal.[10] Several forces are held responsible for this change of affairs.[11]

* The threats posed by global competitors who turn the global marketplace into a global chess game
* The growing prominence of global customers who often develop their sourcing strategies and make their purchase decisions on a global (or pan-regional) basis
* The rise of regional trading blocs that facilitate the integration of manufacturing and logistics facilities but also open up arbitrage opportunities for gray marketers

At the same time, several developments create a need for strong country managers.[12] Nurturing good links with local governments and other entities (e.g., the European Union) becomes increasingly crucial. Local customers are still the lion's share of most companies' clientele. Local competitors sometimes pose a far bigger

---

[8]However, some of the major MNCs operate in more countries than the number of UN member states.

[9]Kenichi Ohmae, *The End of the Nation State. The Rise of Regional Economies* (New York: The Free Press, 1995), p. 112.

[10]Ibid., p. 115.

[11]John A. Quelch, "The New Country Managers," *The McKinsey Quarterly*, 4 (1992), 155–65.

[12]John A. Quelch and Helen Bloom, "The Return of the Country Manager," *The McKinsey Quarterly*, 2 (1996), 30–43.

threat than global rivals. In many emerging markets, strong local brands (e.g., Legend Computers in China) often have a much more loyal following than regional or global brands. Many winning new-product or communication ideas come from local markets rather than regional or corporate headquarters.

To strike the balance between these countervailing forces, country managers of the twenty-first century should strive to fit any of the following five profiles, depending on the nature of the local market:[13]

- The *trader* establishes a beachhead in a new market or heads a recently acquired local distributor. Traders should have an entrepreneurial spirit. Their roles include sales and marketing, scanning the environment for new ideas, and gathering intelligence on the competition.

- The *builder* develops local markets. Builders are entrepreneurs who are willing to be part of regional or global strategy teams.

- The *cabinet member* is a team player with profit and loss responsibility for a small- to medium-sized country. Team-manship is key here, since marketing efforts may require a great deal of cross-border coordination, especially for global and pan-regional brands. Major strategic decisions are often made at the regional level rather than by the country subsidiary.

- The *ambassador* is in charge of large and/or strategic markets. Responsibilities include handling government relations, integrating acquisitions and strategic alliances, and coordinating activities across SBUs. Ideally a seasoned manager, the ambassador should be somebody who is able to manage a large staff. For instance, Asea Brown Boveri, a Swiss/Swedish consortium, views the tasks of its Asia-based country managers as "to exploit fully the synergies between our businesses in the countries, to develop customer based strategies, to build and strengthen relationships with local customers, governments, and communities."[14]

- The *representative* in large, mature markets must handle government relations and legal compliance, among other things.

Regional Structures. Many MNCs that do not feel entirely comfortable with a pure country-based organization opt for a region-based structure with regional headquarters. To some extent, a regional structure offers a compromise between a completely centralized organization and the country-focused organization. The intent behind most region-based structures is to address two concerns: lack of responsiveness of headquarters to local market conditions and parochialism among local country managers. In more and more industries, markets tend to cluster around regions rather than national boundaries. In some cases, the regions are formal trading blocs like the European Union or NAFTA, which allow almost complete free movement of goods across borders. In other cases, the clusters tend to be more culture-driven.

A recent survey done in the Pacific region singles out five distinct roles for regional headquarters (RHQ):[15]

---

[13]Ibid., pp. 38–39.

[14]Gordon Redding, "ABB—The Battle for the Pacific," *Long Range Planning*, 28 (1) (1995), 92–94.

[15]Philippe Lasserre "Regional Headquarters: The Spearhead for Asia Pacific Markets," *Long Range Planning*, 29 (February 1996), 30–37.

- *Scouting.* The RHQ serves as a listening post to scan new opportunities and initiate new ventures.

- *Strategic stimulation.* The RHQ functions as a "switchboard" between the product divisions and the country managers. It helps the strategic business units understand the regional environment.

- *Signaling commitment.* By establishing an RHQ, the MNC signals a commitment to the region that the company is serious about doing business in that region.

- *Coordination.* Often the most important role of the RHQ is to coordinate strategic and tactical decisions across the region. Areas of cohesion include developing pan-regional campaigns in regions with a lot of media overlap, price coordination, especially in markets where parallel imports pose a threat, and consolidation of manufacturing and logistics operations.

- *Pooling resources.* Certain support and administrative tasks are often done more efficiently at the regional level instead of locally. RQH might fulfill support functions like after-sales services, product development, and market research.

Matrix Structure

Imposing a single-dimensional (product, country, or function-based) management structure on complex global issues is often a recipe for disaster. In the wake of the serious shortcomings of the geographic or product-based structures, several MNCs have opted for a matrix organization. The matrix structure explicitly recognizes the multidimensional nature of global strategic decision making. With a matrix organization, two dimensions are integrated in the organization. For instance, the matrix might consist of geographic areas and business divisions. The geographic units are in charge of all product lines within their area. The product divisions have worldwide responsibility for their product line. So, there is a dual chain of command, with managers reporting to two superiors.

A somewhat unorthodox example of a matrix organization was the initial marketing organization of DaimlerChrysler's automotive businesses created after the company was formed in 1998 (see Exhibit 18–4).[16] Along geographic lines, the organization was divided into three regions (North America, Latin America, and the rest of the world). Along product lines, the organization was split into three areas: Chrysler car brands (Chrysler, Dodge, Plymouth, and Jeep), Mercedes-Benz car brands, and the commercial vehicle brands. Sometimes, the MNC might even set up a three-dimensional structure (geography, function, and business area). The various dimensions do not always carry equal weight. For instance, at Siemens the locus of control is shifting more and more toward the business areas, away from the geographic areas.

There are two major advantages of the matrix structure.[17] Matrices reflect the growing complexities of the global market arena. In most industries MNCs face global *and* local competitors; global *and* local customers; global *and* local

---

[16]"DaimlerChrysler decides on new Global Sales and Marketing Organization for passenger cars and commercial vehicles," Press-wire (December 15, 1998).

[17]Thomas H. Naylor, "The International Strategy Matrix," *Columbia Journal of World Business* (Summer 1985), 11–19.

EXHIBIT 18-4
DAIMLERCHRYSLER'S MATRIX ORGANIZATION FOR PASSENGER
CARS AND COMMERCIAL VEHICLES

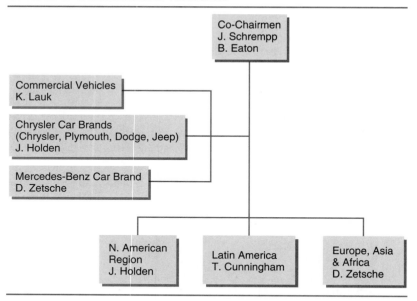

Source: www.daimlerchrysler.com.

distributors. In that sense, the matrix structure facilitates the MNC's need to "think globally and act locally"—to be *glocal*—or, in Unilever's terminology, to be a *multilocal multinational*. The other appeal of the matrix organization is that, in principle at least, it fosters a team spirit and cooperation among business area managers, country managers, and/or functional managers on a global basis.

In spite of these benefits, some companies, (e.g., British Petroleum and Imperial Chemical Industries) have disbanded their matrix structure. Others, such as IBM and Dow Chemical, have streamlined their matrix setup.[18] There are several reasons why matrix structures have lost their appeal among many MNCs. Dual (or triple) reporting and profit responsibilities frequently lead to conflicts or confusion. For instance, a product division might concentrate its resources and attention on a few major markets, thereby upsetting the country managers of the MNC's smaller markets. Another shortcoming of the matrix is bureaucratic bloat. Very often, the decision-making process gets bogged down, thereby discouraging swift responsiveness toward competitive attacks in the local markets. Overlap among divisions often triggers tensions, power clashes, and turf battles.[19]

The four organizational structures that we covered so far are the standard structures adopted by most MNCs. The simplicity of the one-dimensional structures and the shortcomings of the matrix model have led several companies to look for better solutions. Below, we discuss one of the more popular forms: the **networked organization**.

[18]"End of a Corporate Era," *The Financial Times* (March 30, 1995), p. 15.
[19]Christopher A. Bartlett and Sumantra Ghoshal, "Matrix Management, Not a Structure, a Frame of Mind," *Harvard Business Review* (July-August 1990), 138–45.

Global networking is one solution that has been suggested to cope with the short-comings associated with the classical hierarchical organization structures. The network model is an attempt to reconcile the tension between two opposing forces: the need for local responsiveness and the wish to be an integrated whole.[20] Strictly speaking, the network approach is not a formal structure but a mind-set. That is, a company might still formally adopt, say, a *matrix* structure, but at the same time develop a global network. The networked global organization is sometimes also referred to as a *transnational*.[21]

According to advocates of the network model, MNCs should develop processes and linkages that allow each unit to tap into a global knowledge pool. A good metaphor for the global network is the atom (see Exhibit 18–5). At the center is a common knowledge base. Each national unit can be viewed as a source of ideas, skills, capabilities, and knowledge that can be harnessed for the benefit of the total organization.[22]

Ideally, the entire global organization functions as a "sphere." When one unit within the organization anywhere around the world faces a problem or an opportunity, the sphere rotates, thereby giving the unit immediate access to the company's global resource and expertise pool.[23]

EXHIBIT 18–5

A New Organizational Metaphor

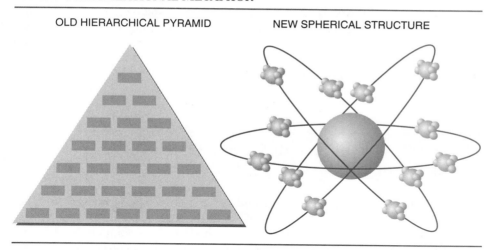

OLD HIERARCHICAL PYRAMID   NEW SPHERICAL STRUCTURE

Source: Raymond E. Miles and Charles C. Snow, "The New Network Firm: A Spherical Structure Built on a Human Investment Philosophy." Reprinted by permission of the publisher, from ORGA-NIZATIONAL DYNAMICS SPRING 1995 © 1995. American Management Organization, New York. All rights reserved.

---

[20]Christopher A. Bartlett and Sumantra Ghoshal, "Organizing for Worldwide Effectiveness: The Transnational Solution," *California Management Review* (Fall 1988), 54–74.

[21]Ibid.

[22]Christopher A. Bartlett, "Building and Managing the Transnational: The New Organizational Challenge," in *Competition in Global Industries*, Michael E. Porter, Ed., (Boston: Harvard Business School Press, 1986), 367–401.

[23]Raymond E. Miles and Charles C. Snow, "The New Network Firm: A Spherical Structure Built on a Human Investment Philosophy," *Organizational Dynamics*, v. 23, no. 4 (Spring 1995) 5–18.

Asea Brown Boveri (ABB), the Swiss-Swedish engineering consortium, is often touted as a prime example of a global networking.[24] Percy Barnevik, former CEO and one of the major forces behind ABB's reorganization, describes ABB's vision as follows:

> Our vision was to create a truly global company that knows no borders, has many home countries and offers opportunities for all nationalities. While we strived for size to benefit from economies of scale and scope, our vision was also to avoid the stigma of the big company with a large headquarters and stifling bureaucracy, countless volumes of instructions, turf defenders and people working far from their customers. With our thousands of profit centers close to customers we wanted to create a small company culture with its huge advantages of flexibility, speed and the power to free up the creative potential of each employee.[25]

There are several mechanisms to develop the required vision and cement the necessary linkages. One approach, to which we will return shortly, is the international teaming concept. The charter of the international management team might cover areas such as communicating the overall corporate vision ("missionary" work, so to speak), new product development, technology transfer, strategy development, and so forth. ABB uses a company *bible* to tie together the different companies within its organization. ABB's bible describes the firm's mission and values, the long-term objectives, and guidelines on how to behave internally.[26] Heineken NV, the Dutch beer brewery, uses a set of *Rules and Guidelines* to cement the ties between its local operations. Rules for the Heineken brand cover the product formula, the use of its brand identity, its positioning, and procedures to maintain consistency in the brand's communication strategies. Less strict guidelines cover pricing, packaging, promotions and so on.[27]

◆ ◆ ◆ ◆ ◆ ◆ ORGANIZING FOR GLOBAL BRAND MANAGEMENT

Global branding is the rage for more and more companies. However, to foster and nurture global brands, companies often find it useful to put organizational mechanisms in place. This is especially so for decentralized companies where local decisions compromise the global branding strategies. Several options exist: (1) a global branding committee, (2) a brand champion, (3) global brand manager, and (4) informal, ad hoc brand meetings. Let us look each one of these in detail.

---

[24]William Taylor, "The Logic of Global Business: An Interview with ABB's Percy Barnevik," *Harvard Business Review* (March–April 1991), 91–105.

[25]Asea Brown Boveri, *1995 Annual Report*, p. 5.

[26]Manfred F.R. Kets de Vries, "Making a Giant Dance," *Across the Board* (October 1994), 27–32.

[27]Karel Vuursteen, "Decision Making at Heineken," *Marketing and Research Today* (February 1996), 42–45.

Global branding committees are usually made up of top-line executives from head-quarters, regional, and/or local offices. Their charter is to integrate and steer global and local branding strategies. Visa International's "Global Branding Marketing Group" exemplifies this approach.[28] The group's goal is to establish better communications among regions and to leverage global media buying power. It is made up of the heads of marketing from each region. Hewlett-Packard created a "Global Brand Steering Committee" in 1998. Its primary tasks include brand positioning and vision. Polaroid's recent reorganization led to the establishment of a "Brand Franchise Council." The group meets every other month to discuss global brand issues and direction changes, review brand strategies and advertising copy strategy, and monitor local executions. The council consists of general managers from the United States, Europe, and Japan, and is headed by the senior VP-worldwide marketing.[29]

Global Brand-ing Committee

A brand champion is a top-line executive (sometimes a CEO) who serves as the brand's advocate.[30] The approach works well for companies whose senior executives have a passion and expertise for branding. One practitioner of brand championship is Nestlé. The company has a brand champion for each of its twelve corporate strategic brands. The brand champion approves all brand and line extension decisions[31]; monitors the presentation of the brand worldwide; and spreads insights on best practices within the organization.[32]

Brand Champion

This is a steward of the brand whose main responsibility is to integrate branding efforts across countries and combat local biases. In the corporate hierarchy, the position is usually just below top-line executives. The position is most suitable for organizations where top management lacks marketing expertise, such as many high-tech firms. For the global brand manager to be effective, the following conditions should hold:[33]

Global Brand Manager

- *The top of the organization is committed to branding.* Top-line executives—though most likely lacking a marketing background—should share the vision and a belief in strong branding.
- *There is a solid strategic planning process in place.* Country managers should adopt the same format, vocabulary, and planning cycle.
- *Managers see the need to travel to learn about local management and best practices.* Managers must meet local customers and/or distributors and learn local customs.
- *There is a system to identify, mentor, and train prospects who can fill the role.*

---

[28]"U.S. Multinationals," *Advertising Age International* (June 1999), 44.

[29]Ibid.

[30]"David A. Aaker and Erich Joachimsthaler, "The Lure of Global Branding," *Harvard Business Review* (Nov.–Dec. 1999), 142.

[31]A brand extension is using the same brand for a new product in another product category; a line extension is launching new varieties (e.g., a new flavor, a new package format) of the brand within the same product category.

[32]Aaker and Joachimsthaler, p. 142.

[33]Ibid., p. 142.

Informal, Ad-hoc Branding Meetings

Even if, for some reason, a company decides against a formal structure, it might still find it worthwhile to have informal mechanisms to guide global branding decisions. This usually takes the form of ad-hoc branding meetings. A good example is Abbott International, a U.S.-based pharmaceutical company. Whenever a new product is planned, international executives meet with local staff to discuss the global brand. The ad-hoc committee reviews patents and trademarks for each country to decide whether to use the U.S. name in the other countries.[34]

◆ ◆ ◆ ◆ ◆ ◆ LIFE CYCLE OF ORGANIZATION STRUCTURES

A drastic change in the MNC's environment or internal circumstances sometimes requires a rethinking of the ideal way to organize the firm's global operations. In some cases companies have moved from one extreme to another before finding a suitable configuration. A case in point is Kraft General Foods Europe (KGFE).[35] In the early 1980s, KGFE tried to impose uniform marketing strategies across Europe. This attempt led to so much ill-will among KGFE's local units that Kraft soon abandoned its centralized system. It was replaced by a loose system where country managers developed their own marketing strategies for all Kraft brands, including the regional (e.g., Miracoli pasta) and global brands (e.g., Philadelphia cream cheese). Not surprisingly, this system created a great deal of inconsistency in the marketing strategies used. More recently, in the early 1990s, KGFE introduced a system of core teams. With the new setup, KGFE hopes to be able to coordinate its marketing operations across Europe while still remaining alert to local market peculiarities. Global Perspective 18–2 reports the overhaul Procter & Gamble recently undertook to streamline its organization.

Several management theorists have made an attempt to come up with the "right" fit between the MNC's environment (internal and external) and the organizational setup. One of the more popular schemas is the stages model shown in Exhibit 18–6, which was developed by Stopford and Wells.[36] The schema shows the relationship between the organizational structure, foreign product diversity, and the importance of foreign sales to the company (as a share of total sales). According to their model, when companies first explore the global marketplace they start off with an international division. As foreign sales expand without an increase in the firm's foreign product assortment diversity, the company will most likely switch to a geographic area structure. If instead the diversity of the firm's foreign product line substantially increases, it might organize itself along global product lines. Finally, when both product diversity and international sales grow significantly, MNCs tend to adopt a two-dimensional matrix structure.

Several scholars have criticized the Stopford–Wells staged model. First, the model is a purely descriptive representation of how MNCs develop over time based on an analysis of U.S.-based MNCs. Thus, it would be misleading to apply the framework in a prescriptive manner, as several people have done.[37] Second, the structure of the organization is only one aspect of a global organization. Other,

---

[34]"U.S. Multinationals," p. 44.

[35]"Cross-border Kraftsmen," *The Financial Times* (June 17, 1993).

[36]John M. Stopford and Louis T. Wells Jr., *Managing the Multinational Enterprise: Organization of the Firm and Ownership of the Subsidiary* (New York: Basic Books, 1972).

[37]Bartlett, 1986, pp. 367–401.

◆ ◆

𝒢LOBAL PERSPECTIVE 18-2

REVAMPING PROCTER & GAMBLE: ORGANIZATION 2005

(Until recently, Procter & Gamble was split into four regional divisions: North America; Europe, Middle East, and Africa; Asia; and Latin America. Each division was responsible for its profits and losses. After a lackluster sales performance during the mid-90s, P&G decided to embark on a self-improvement plan. Top executives of the firm traveled around the country, visiting the CEOs of a dozen major companies such as Kellogg, Hewlett-Packard and 3M in search for advice. The result of the whole exercise was "Organization 2005," a new bold plan to revamp the P&G organization.

Under Organization 2005, P&G is reshaped into seven Global Business Units (GBUs) based on product categories, such as baby care, laundry detergents, shampoos, and beauty care. Each GBU will have all the resources it needs to understand consumer needs in its product area and to do product innovation. The GBUs will develop and sell products on a worldwide basis. They will replace a system where country managers ruled their local fiefs, setting prices and devising product policies as they saw fit.

There are two other elements of Organization 2005. One is the creation of Global Business Services (GBS). This new unit brings support services such as accounting, information technology, and data management under one roof. The other aspect is a streamlining of corporate functions. Most corporate staff has moved into the new business units.

P&G sees the revamped organization as a continuation of the strategy it started in the 1980s when it moved from brand management to category management. With the new setup, category management will be run on a global basis. Durk Jager, P&G's CEO, makes the case for Organization 2005 as follows: "Organization 2005 is focused on one thing: leveraging P&G's innovative capability. Because the single best way our growth(...) is to innovate bigger and move faster consistently and across the entire company. The cultural changes we are making will also create an environment that produces bolder, more stretching goals and plans, bigger innovations and greater speed."

Sources: "P&G's Hottest New Product: P&G," *Business Week* (October 5, 1998), pp. 58–59; "The What, Not the Where, to Drive P&G," *Financial Times* (September 3, 1998), p. 18.

equally important, components are the mind-sets of the managers and managerial processes. The MNC's environment is dynamic; it changes all the time. Thus, fit between the environment and the MNC's organizational structure is not enough. Global organizations also need flexibility.[38]

An in-depth study of a sample of ten successful U.S.-based MNCs shows that the key challenge for MNCs is building and sustaining the right management process instead of looking for the proper organizational structure.[39] According to the study, the installation of such a process moves through three stages. The first step is to recognize the complexity of the MNC's environment. Country and regional managers must look at strategic issues from multiple perspectives—a **glocal mind-set**, so to speak. During the second stage, the company introduces communication channels and decision-making platforms to facilitate more flexibility. In the final stage, the MNC develops a corporate culture that fosters collaborative thinking and decision making. Such an agenda might include activities such as formulating common goals and values, developing reward systems and evaluation criteria that encourage a cooperative spirit, and providing role models.

---

[38]Sumantra Ghoshal and Nitin Nohria, "Horses for Courses: Organizational Forms for Multinational Corporations," *Sloan Management Review* (Winter 1993), 23–35.

[39]Christopher A. Bartlett, "MNCs: Get Off the Reorganization Merry-go-round," *Harvard Business Review* (March–April 1983), 138–46.

EXHIBIT 18–6
STOPFORD-WELLS INTERNATIONAL STRUCTURAL STAGES MODEL

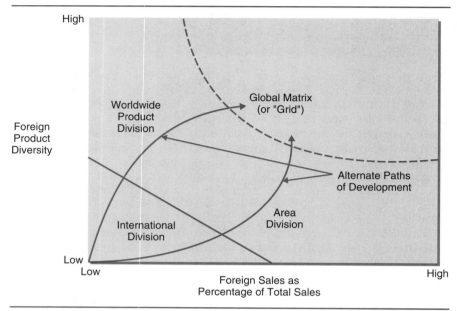

Source: Reprinted by permission of Harvard Business School Press. From: Christopher A. Barlett, "Building and Managing the Transnational: The New Organizational Challenge," in *Competition in Global Industries*, M. E. Porter (Ed.). (Boston, MA: Harvard University Press, 1987), p. 368. Copyright © 1986 by the President and Fellows of Harvard College.

◆ ◆ ◆ ◆ ◆ ◆ TO CENTRALIZE OR DECENTRALIZE?

Power sharing between headquarters and local business units is a delicate but extremely important matter. Roughly speaking, companies can move in two opposite directions. With decentralized organizations the national operating companies are highly autonomous. Each one of the local units represents a profit center. Corporate headquarters may provide guidance and advice, but when push comes to shove it is the local subsidiary that makes the decisions. Peter Brabeck-Letmathe, Nestlé's CEO, describes the decision-making process within his company as follows:

> *"We respond to what the local market says, and they may take another look and change their mind. But if they don't want something, we don't force them. We might send a couple of people to offer encouragement, but that's as far as it goes."*[40]

Centralized organizations, on the other hand, consolidate most decision-making power at corporate headquarters. In practice, most MNCs are somewhere between these two extremes: certain tasks like finance and R & D are typically centralized, other tasks like pricing and advertising are the realm of the local subsidiaries. Forces for global integration such as global brands, global customers, and

---

[40]Andrew J. Parsons, "Nestlé: The Visions of Local Managers," *The McKinsey Quarterly*, 2 (1996), 5–29.

scale economies push companies toward globalized decision making. Drivers towards local responsiveness favor a local autonomy approach. The two forces can jointly have a high impact. Under such conditions, a *transnational solution* is needed, where companies strike a delicate balance between centralization and decentralization.

Recently, several management theorists have offered *federalism* as a way to combine the autonomy of the local units with the benefits of coordination.[41] MNCs that follow this model share the following characteristics:[42]

- *Noncentralization.* Power is diffused. It belongs to the local units. Power cannot be taken away unilaterally by corporate headquarters. Charles Handy, a longtime preacher of federalism, notes that federal organizations are decentralized *and* centralized.[43]

- *Negotianalism.* Decisions are made via a bargaining process. Each local unit has a voice. Each local unit is listened to.

- *Constitutionalism.* Another feature is that many of these companies often have a "constitution," like the Asea Brown Boveri company bible that we mentioned earlier.

- *Territoriality.* There are clear boundary markers based on geography or business areas.

- *Balance of power.* Federations seek balance of power between headquarters and units and among units.

- *Autonomy.* The units are self-governing. They can experiment with new ideas as long as they respect the principles spelled out in the company's constitution. As a result, a proper-working federal organization enables the company to gather the benefits of "big" and "small" companies.

What do companies do in practice? Exhibit 18–7 is a ranking of the most popular initiatives, based on a survey of CEOs of leading U.S.-based consumer goods companies. In general, the more successful companies coordinate their international decision making worldwide. Coordination is especially crucial for brand positioning, package design, advertising strategy, and pricing policies (Exhibit 18–8).

CONTROLLING GLOBAL MARKETING EFFORTS   ◆ ◆ ◆ ◆ ◆ ◆

To make global marketing strategies work, companies need to establish a control system. The main purpose of controls is to ensure that the behaviors of the various parties within the organization are in line with the company's strategic goals. We will first concentrate on formal control methods. We will then turn to less formal means to implement control: establishing a corporate culture and management development.

---

[41]See, for instance, Charles Handy, "Balancing Corporate Power: A New Federalist Paper," *Harvard Business Review* (November–December 1992), pp. 59–72.

[42]James O'Toole and Warren Bennis, "Our Federalist Future: The Leadership Imperative," *California Management Review* (Summer 1992), 73–90.

[43]Barbara Ettorre, "A Conversation With Charles Handy. On the Future of Work and an End to the Century of the Organization," *Organizational Dynamics* (Summer 1996), 15–26.

EXHIBIT 18–7
INITIATIVES TAKEN BY MNCS TO COORDINATE GLOBAL ACTIVITIES

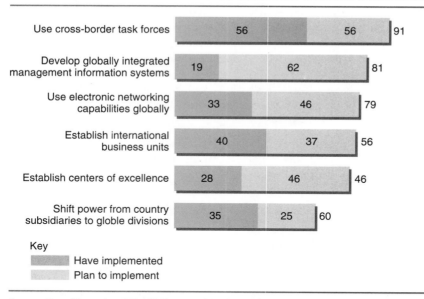

Use cross-border task forces — 56 | 56 | 91

Develop globally integrated management information systems — 19 | 62 | 81

Use electronic networking capabilities globally — 33 | 46 | 79

Establish international business units — 40 | 37 | 56

Establish centers of excellence — 28 | 46 | 46

Shift power from country subsidiaries to globle divisions — 35 | 25 | 60

Key

▓ Have implemented

░ Plan to implement

Source: Ingo Theuerkauf, David Ernst, and Amir Mahini, "Think Local, Organize . . . ?" *International Marketing Review,* 13 (3) (1996), p. 11.

EXHIBIT 18–8
INTERNATIONAL DECISION MAKING: MORE VERSUS LESS SUCCESSFUL COMPANIES

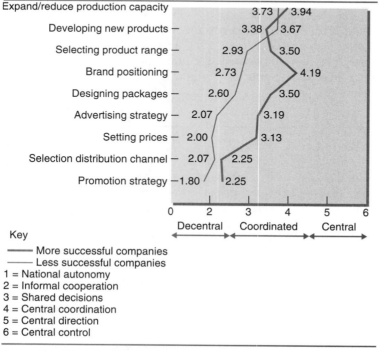

Expand/reduce production capacity — 3.73 / 3.94

Developing new products — 3.38 / 3.67

Selecting product range — 2.93 / 3.50

Brand positioning — 2.73 / 4.19

Designing packages — 2.60 / 3.50

Advertising strategy — 2.07 / 3.19

Setting prices — 2.00 / 3.13

Selection distribution channel — 2.07 / 2.25

Promotion strategy — 1.80 / 2.25

0   2   3   4   5   6

Decentral   Coordinated   Central

Key

—— More successful companies
—— Less successful companies
1 = National autonomy
2 = Informal cooperation
3 = Shared decisions
4 = Central coordination
5 = Central direction
6 = Central control

Source: Ingo Theuerkauf, David Ernst, and Amir Mahini, "Think Local, Organize . . . ?" *International Marketing Review,* 13 (3) (1996), p. 11.

Any formal control system consists of basically three building blocks: (1) the establishment of performance standards, (2) the measurement and evaluation of performance against standards, and (3) the analysis and correction of deviations from standards.

Formal ("Bureaucratic") Control Systems

Establishing Standards. The first step of the control process is to set standards. These standards should be driven by the company's corporate goals. There are essentially two types of standards: behavior- and outcome-based. Behavior-based control means specifying the actions that are necessary to achieve good performance. Managers are told through manuals/policies how to respond to various scenarios. Rewards are based on whether the observed behavior matches the prescribed behavior. Examples of behavior-based standards include distribution coverage, branding policies, pricing rules, and R & D spending. Output-based control depends on specific standards that are objective, reliable, and easy to measure. Outcome standards focus on very specific outcome-oriented measures such as profit–loss statements, return on investment, market share, sales, and customer satisfaction.

When applied too rigorously, behavior-based standards restrain local management's ability to respond effectively to local market conditions. An example is Johnson & Johnson's experience in the Philippines.[44] In the early 1990s, J & J's managers found out that young Philippine women used J & J's baby talcum to freshen their makeup. To cater toward their needs, local management developed a compact holder for talcum powder. However, a few days before the planned launch of the new product, corporate headquarters asked the local managers to drop the product, claiming that the cosmetics business is not a core business for J & J. Only after the local marketing head made a personal plea for the product at J & J's headquarters was the subsidiary given the green light. The product became a big hit, though it was never launched in other markets since J & J does not want to run the risk of being perceived as a cosmetics maker.

Output-based standards could also create problems, especially when internal and external factors undermine the validity of the output norm as a performance measure. For instance, profits of the local subsidiary might be distorted by the firm's transfer pricing rules.[45]

For most companies, the two types of standards matter. Let us show you why with a simple illustration. Imagine headquarters wants country A to increase its market share by 3 percentage points over a one-year period. Country A could take different approaches to achieve this target. One path is to do a lot of promotional activities—couponing, price promotions, trade deals, and so on. Another route is to spend more on advertising. In both cases, the outcome might be achieved. However, with the first option—heavy dealing—the company risks cheapening the product's image and possibly even diluting the brand's equity. With the second option, the subsidiary would invest in brand equity. Thus, the same outcome can be realized through two totally different behaviors, one of which can ruin the long-term viability of the company's brand assets.

Ideally, standards are developed via a "bottom-up" and "top-down" planning process of listening, reflecting, dialoguing, and debating between headquarters and

[44]Niraj Dawar and Tony Frost, "Competing with Giants. Survival Strategies for Local Companies in Emerging Markets," *Harvard Business Review* (March–April 1999), 119–29.
[45]Robert D. Hamilton III, Virginia A. Taylor, and Roger J. Kashlak, "Designing a Control System for a Multinational Subsidiary," *Long Range Planning*, 29 (6), 857–68, 1996.

the local units. Standards should also strike a delicate balance between long- and short-term priorities.[46]

Evaluating Performance. Formal control systems also need mechanisms to monitor and evaluate performance. The actual performance is compared against the established standards. In many instances, it is fairly straightforward to measure performance, especially when the standards are based on within-country results. To make global or pan-regional strategies work, MNCs also need to assess and reward individual managers' contributions to the "common good." For example, two-thirds of the bonuses payable to Unilever's senior executives in Europe are now driven by Unilever's performance in that region.[47] In practice, it is tremendously hard to gauge managers' contributions to the regional or global well-being of the firm.

Analyzing and Correcting Deviations. The third element is to analyze deviations from the standards and, if necessary, make the necessary corrections. If actual performance does not meet the set standard, one needs to analyze the cause behind the divergence. If necessary, corrective measures will be taken. This part of the control system also involves devising the right incentive mechanisms—checks and balances—that make subsidiary managers tick. Although proper reward systems are crucial to motivate subsidiary managers, a recent study has shown the key role played by the presence of **due process**.[48] Due process encompasses five features:

1. The head office should be familiar with the subsidiaries' local situation.
2. There should be two-way communication in global strategy-making decision processes.
3. The head office is relatively consistent in making decisions across local units.
4. Local units can legitimately challenge headquarter's strategic views and decisions.
5. Subsidiary units get explanations for final strategic decisions.

Informal Control Methods

Aside of formal control mechanisms, most MNCs also establish informal control methods. Here we cover the two most common informal control tools, namely, corporate culture and human resource development.

Corporate Culture. For many MNCs with operations scattered all over the globe, shared cultural values are often a far more effective "glue" to incite subsidiaries than formal bureaucratic control tools. Corporate cultures can be *clan-based* or *market-based*.[49] **Clan cultures** embody a long socialization process; strong,

---

[46]Guy R. Jillings, "Think Globally, Act Locally," *Executive Excellence* (October 1993), p. 15.

[47]"Unilever Adopts Clean Sheet Approach," *The Financial Times* (October 21, 1991).

[48]W. Chan Kim and Renée A. Mauborgne, "Making Global Strategies Work," *Sloan Management Review*, Spring 1993, pp. 11–24.

[49]David Lei, John W. Slocum Jr., and Robert W. Slater, "Global Strategy and Reward Systems: The Key Roles of Management Development and Corporate Culture," *Organizational Dynamics* (Winter 1989), pp. 27–41.

powerful norms; and a defined set of internalized controls. **Market cultures** are the opposite: norms are loose or absent; socialization processes are limited; control systems are purely based on performance measures. For most global organizations where integration is an overriding concern, a clan-like culture is instrumental in creating a shared vision.

Corporate values are more than slogans that embellish the company's annual report. To shape a shared vision, cultural values should have three properties:[50]

- *Clarity.* Meaning that the stated values should be simple, relevant, and concrete.
- *Continuity.* Values should be stable over time, long-term oriented—not flavor-of-the-month type values.
- *Consistency.* To avoid confusion, everyone within the organization should share the same vision. Everybody should speak the same language. Everyone should pursue the same agenda.

Exhibit 18–9 gives an overview of the vision and the cultural values defined by Whirlpool Corp., a leading household appliance maker. With a few key words, Whirlpool is able to communicate its vision to its global stakeholders.

Human Resource Development. The company's management development programs are another major informal control tool. Their role is critical in at least three regards.[51] First and foremost, training programs can help managers worldwide in understanding the MNC's mission and vision and their part in pursuing them. Second, such programs can speed up the transfer of new values when changes in the company's environment dictate a "new" corporate mentality. Finally, they can also prove fruitful in allowing managers from all over the world to share their best practices and success stories.

EXHIBIT 18–9
WHIRLPOOL CORPORATION VISION STATEMENT

Our Vision:
Every Home . . . Everywhere
with Pride, Passion, Performance
We create the world's best home appliances, which make life easier and more enjoyable for all people. Our goal is a Whirlpool product in every home, everywhere. We will achieve this by creating:
Pride . . . in our work and each other
Passion . . . for creating unmatched customer loyalty for our brands
Performance . . . results that excite and reward global investors with superior returns
We bring this dream to life through the power of our unique global enterprise and our outstanding people . . . working together . . . everywhere.

Source: Whirlpool Corp., *1999 Annual Report.*

---

[50]Bartlett and Ghoshal, "Matrix Management . . . ," pp. 138–45.
[51]David Lei et al., p. 39.

◆ ◆ ◆ ◆ ◆ ◆ GUIDELINES FOR CHOOSING THE RIGHT ORGANIZATION STRUCTURE

In their search for the proper structure and strategic coherence, countless MNCs have come up with schemes that led to confusion, frustration, and ill-will among subsidiary managers. We can offer some pieces of advice, though:

- *Recognize the need for business asymmetry.* Due to relentless environmental changes, power sharing between the center and the periphery will vary over time, over business units, and even across activities (product development, advertising, pricing) within business units. Different SBUs within the organization have different needs for responsiveness and global co-ordination.[52] Especially widely diversified companies should recognize that each business unit needs a different format, depending on its particular circumstances and needs. For instance, Asea Brown Boveri has businesses that are *superlocal* (e.g., electrical installation) and *superglobal* (e.g., power plant projects). The principle of **business asymmetry** is illustrated in Exhibit 18–10 for Goodyear, the world's leading tire-maker. Depending on the business area, units are structured on a regional or global basis.

EXHIBIT 18–10
GOODYEAR: EXAMPLE OF "BUSINESS ASYMMETRY"

Strategic Business Unit	Products and Markets	Geographic Markets Served
North American Tire	Original equipment, replacement tires for autos, trucks, farm, aircraft, construction	United States, Canada, Export
Kelly-Springfield	Replacement tires for autos, trucks, tractors	United States, Canada, Export
Goodyear Europe	Original equipment, replacement tires for autos, trucks, farm, construction	Europe, Africa, Middle East, Export
Goodyear Latin America	Original equipment, replacement tires for autos, trucks, tractors	Central, South America, Export
Goodyear Asia	Original equipment, replacement tires for autos, trucks, farm, aircraft, construction	Southeast, Western Asia, North Pacific Rim, Export
Engineered Products	Auto belts, hose, body components, industrial products	Worldwide
Chemicals	Synthetic and natural rubber, chemicals for internal, external customers	Worldwide
Celeron	Crude oil transportation, related services	Operates only pipeline from U.S. West Coast to Texas
Goodyear Racing	Tires for all major motor racing series	Worldwide

Source: The Goodyear Tire & Rubber Company, *1994 Annual Report.*

---

[52]"Fashionable Federalism," *The Financial Times* (December 18, 1992).

- *Democracy is a must.* Getting the balance right also requires democracy. When building up a global organization, make sure that every country subsidiary has a voice. Subsidiaries of small countries should not be concerned about getting pushed over by their bigger counterparts.

- *A shared vision is important.* Getting the organizational structure right—the "arrows" and "boxes," so to speak—is important. Far more critical, though, is the organizational psychology.[53] People are key in building an organization. Having a clear and consistent corporate vision is a major ingredient in getting people excited about the organization. To instill and communicate corporate values, companies should also have human resource development mechanisms in place that will facilitate the learning process.

- *There is a need for a good mix of specialists of three types—country; functional; business.* There is no such a thing as a *transnational manager.*[54] Companies should breed specialists of three different kinds: country, functional, and global business (SBU). Country managers, in particular—once feared to become part of the endangered species list—play a key role. As we discussed earlier in this chapter, the country manager's skills and role will differ from country to country. Some subsidiaries need a "trader"; others need an "ambassador."

- *Moving unit headquarters abroad seldom solves the organization's problems.* In recent years, companies like IBM, Hewlett-Packard, and Siemens have moved business unit headquarters abroad. Several of these moves were done for very sensible reasons: getting closer to the customer or supplier, being in the big guys' backyard, cutting costs. Unfortunately, in many cases the relocation typically turns out to be mere window-dressing in a drive to become more global-oriented. Sometimes transfers can even be counterproductive. They may weaken your corporate identity when it is strongly linked to your firm's home country.

SUMMARY ✦

In this chapter we discussed the structures and control mechanisms that MNCs can use to shape a global organization. Companies can pick from a variety of structures, ranging from a single international division to a global network operation. Formal and informal (culture, management development) control mechanisms are available to run global operations. However, the dynamics of the global marketing arena mean that building a global organization is much more than just choosing the "right" organizational configuration and control systems. Global players constantly need to reflect on how to strike the balance between centralization *and* decentralization, local responsiveness *and* global integration, center *and* periphery. As with many other challenges in global marketing, there are no easy 1-2-3 solutions. This chapter has offered some guidance in choosing the appropriate organization structure.

KEY TERMS ✦ ✦ ✦ ✦ ✦ ✦ ✦ ✦ ✦ ✦ ✦ ✦ ✦ ✦ ✦ ✦ ✦ ✦ ✦

bottom-up planning	geographic structure	global teamwork	matrix structure
business asymmetry	global networking	glocal mind-set	networked organization
clan culture	global strategic marketing	international division	product-based structure
due process	plan	market culture	top-down planning

---

[53]Bartlett and Ghoshal, "Matrix Management . . . ," pp. 138–45.

[54]"Global Executives Walk a Tightrope," *The Financial Times*, October 12, 1992.

REVIEW QUESTIONS ◆

1. How does a global networked organization differ from the matrix structure?

2. Describe how external environmental drivers influence the organizational design decision.

3. What are the pros and cons of a regional organization structure?

4. What mechanisms can companies use to foster a global corporate culture?

5. What does it take for an MNC to be a multilocal multinational?

FURTHER READING ◆

Bartlett, Christopher A. "Building and Managing the Transnational: The New Organizational Challenge." In *Competition in Global Industries*, M. E. Porter, Ed. Boston, MA: Harvard University Press, 1986, pp. 367–401.

Bartlett, Christopher A., and Sumantra Ghoshal. "Organizing for Worldwide Effectiveness: The Transnational Solution." *California Management Review* (Fall 1988): 54–74.

Davidson, W. H., and P. Haspeslagh. "Shaping a Global Product Organization." *Harvard Business Review* (July-August 1982): 125–32.

Hamilton, Robert D. III, Virginia A. Taylor, and Roger J. Kashlak. "Designing a Control System for a Multinational Subsidiary." *Long Range Planning*, 29(6): 857–68 (1996).

Lasserre, Philippe. "Regional Headquarters: The Spearhead for Asia Pacific Markets." *Long Range Planning*, 29 (February 1996): 30–37.

Naylor, Thomas H. "The International Strategy Matrix." *Columbia Journal of World Business* (Summer 1985): 11–19.

Quelch, John A. "The New Country Managers." *The McKinsey Quarterly*, 4 (1992): 155–65.

Quelch, John A., and Helen Bloom. "The Return of the Country Manager." *The McKinsey Quarterly*, 2 (1996): 30–43.

Snow, Charles C., Sue C. Davison, Scott A. Snell, and Donald C. Hambrick. "Use Transnational Teams to Globalize Your Company." *Organizational Dynamics* (Spring 1996): 50–67.

Theuerkauf, Ingo, David Ernst, and Amir Mahini. "Think Local, Organize . . . ?" *International Marketing Review*, 13(3) (1996): 7–12.

GLOBAL MARKETING AND THE INTERNET

19

HAPTER OVERVIEW

1. THE INTERNET AND THE GLOBAL MARKETPLACE

2. STRUCTURAL BARRIERS TO GLOBAL E-COMMERCE

3. USING THE INTERNET FOR UNDERSTANDING GLOBAL BUYERS

4. COMPETITIVE ADVANTAGE AND CYBERSPACE

5. RAMIFICATIONS OF THE INTERNET FOR GLOBAL MARKETING STRATEGIES

Patagon.com International Ltd. (www.patagon.com) has become one of Latin America's hottest online brokerage firms. The firm was created by a pair of twenty-something Argentines with funding from U.S.-based venture capitalists. The firm hopes to become a financial service empire soon that offers credit cards, mutual funds, and mortgages online.[1] Seven-Eleven Japan, Sony Corp. and five other Japanese companies recently set up a joint venture that aspires to become Japan's largest e-commerce venture.[2] The partnership plans to use two e-commerce channels. One channel will sell CDs and travel packages to Japanese consumers over their mobile phones. Customers will be able to pick up their tickets or CDs at a 7-Eleven store and pay in cash. The other channel is to install in all 8,000 convenience store outlets a terminal that will offer the same services as the other e-commerce channel. Boo.com (www.boo.com) claimed to be the world's first online

---

[1]"The Rise and Rise of Patagon.com," *Business Week* (October 25, 1999), 40.
[2]"Seven-Eleven Japan to Set Up Joint Venture for E-Commerce," *The Asian Wall Street Journal* (January 7–8, 2000), 3.

global sports and urban fashion store.[3] The site targeted "outward-looking young people who're passionate about international fashion styles." The company—founded by three Swedes (including a former catwalk model)—allowed customers to order the latest fashion items in six languages. Visitors to the site could zoom in for close-ups of clothes and were guided by an animated shopping assistant ("Miss Boo"). The film, however, went bust around mid-2000. For scores of small and large companies worldwide, the Internet proves to be a major boon.

The Internet has revolutionized the international business arena and global marketing in particular. Roughly speaking, the Internet is a network of computers interconnected throughout the world operating on a standard protocol that allows data to be transmitted. Participants in the network include universities, governments, companies, and research organizations, among others.[4] The Internet has been around for more than three decades. The launch of Sputnik in 1957 spurred the foundation of the Advanced Research Projects Agency (ARPA). One of ARPA's major achievements was the development of a standard protocol that allowed otherwise incompatible computers to communicate with one another. This protocol was basically the umbilical cord for the Internet. Until the early 1990s, the Internet was primarily the preserve of the military and academic researchers. However, the development of new software (e.g., Java, Netscape) during the early 1990s turned the Internet into a commercial medium that has transformed businesses worldwide. In the advent of the forces unleashed by this new technology, this final chapter will focus on the impact of the Internet on global marketing. We will first give an overview of Internet developments in Asia, Europe, and Latin America. We will then discuss the major challenges that the use of the Internet poses for global marketers. The final part of the chapter looks at the impact of the World Wide Web (WWW) on global marketing activities.

THE INTERNET AND THE GLOBAL MARKETPLACE

Internet usage worldwide is growing rapidly. Exhibit 19–1 shows the number of Internet users on a country-by-country basis. Although the Internet originated in the United States, it has rapidly turned into a global phenomenon. According to Nua, an Irish Internet consulting company, the global online population was about 171 million Web users in 1999. Of those, around 50 percent originate from outside the United States.[5] By 2002, Internet users from outside North America are expected to account for 65 percent of the total number of Net surfers.[6] The number of Internet addresses is expected to grow from less than 1 billion in 1999 to more than 7.5 billion in 2002.[7] The **global e-commerce** market is predicted to reach $1.2

[3]"Boo.com Delays Prove To Be Lesson In Int'l E-commerce," *Advertising Age International* (December 1999), 3, 20.

[4]Jim Hamill, "The Internet and International Marketing," *International Marketing Review*, 14 (5) (1997), 300–323.

[5]www.internetindicators.com/global.html.

[6]"Global Facts About the Internet," *Advertising Age International* (June 1999), 2.

[7]Ibid.

EXHIBIT 19–1

INTERNET USERS BY COUNTRY

Country	Number of people (in million)	% of Total Population	Year Surveyed*
USA/Canada	79.4–106.3	29.3–39.4	1999
Europe			
United Kingdom	7.5–10.6	16.0–18.0	1998
Germany	7.3–8.4	8.7–10.0	1998–99
France	2.5–6.2	5.2–12.9	1998–99
Sweden	2.9–3.6	33.0–40.9	1998–99
Italy	2.6–5.0	4.1–8.0	1998–99
Spain	2.2–2.7	6.6–7.7	1998–99
Finland	1.4–1.8	32.0–35.0	1998
Netherlands	1.3–2.3	7.8–13.7	1998–99
Denmark	1.1–1.7	22.0–23.0	1998–99
Norway	1.0–1.6	22.7–36.3	1998–99
Russia	1.0–1.2	.7–.8	1998
Switzerland	.9–1.2	12.0–16.2	1998
Belgium	.4–1.4	3.9–16.0	1998
Slovak Republic	.51	9.5	1998
Austria	.36–.40	4.5–5.5	1998
Ireland	.3–.4	11.0–13.5	1998–99
Czech Republic	.27	2.6	1998
Hungary	.2	2.0	1998
Portugal	.19	1.9	1998
Estonia	.15	10.0	1998
Iceland	.12	45.0	1998
Poland	.7	1.8	1997
Turkey	.6	1.0	1997
Asia/Pacific			
Japan	14.0–18.0	11.1–14.4	1998–99
Australia	4.2–5.5	23.4–30.5	1998–99
Taiwan	2.2–3.0	10.0–14.3	1998–99
South Korea	1.8–3.1	3.9–6.7	1998–99
China	1.2–4.0	.1–.3	1998–99
Hong Kong	.85	13.4	1998
Malaysia	.6	3.0	1998
New Zealand	.56	15.8	1998
Singapore	.5	14.7	1997
India	.5	.5	1998
Philippines	.32	.03	1998
Thailand	.13	< .01	1998
Indonesia	.08	< .01	1998
Latin America			
Brazil	2.35–3.5	1.4–2.1	1998
Mexico	.5–.7	.5–.7	1998–99
Argentina	.25–.33	.7–.9	1998–99
Chile	.15	1.0	1999
Columbia	.09–.3	.2–1.0	1999
Uruguay	.09	2.7	1999
Venezuela	.08	3.3	1999
Costa Rica	.03	3.4	1999
Peru	.02	.08	1999

EXHIBIT 19–1 (CONTINUED)

Country	Number of people (in million)	% of Total Population	Year Surveyed*
Middle East			
Israel	.5–.6	9.0–10.8	1998–99
U.A.E.	.09	3.0	1998
Bahrain & Saudi Arabia	.05	.23	1998
Kuwait	.04	2.2	1998
Jordan	.02	.5	1998
Africa			
South Africa	1.0–1.6	2.4–3.7	1998–99
Egypt	.04–.06	.06–.09	1998–99

Source: Compiled from information available from *Nua Internet Surveys*, Nua, Ltd., http://www.nua.ie/index.html, accessed September 30, 1999.

*Estimates vary by the agency that provided information. Estimates shown here are the high and low estimates provided by various survey agencies since mid-1998.

trillion by 2001.[8] These projections underscore the growing importance of the Internet for marketers around the world. In this section, we will explore the spread of the Web in three regions: Asia-Pacific, Latin America, and Europe.

Asia-Pacific   Although the Internet was pioneered in the United States, the Asia-Pacific region is quickly catching up. Most of the action in the region is in the business-to-business area, which is the fastest growing segment of e-commerce. Online e-commerce sales revenue in the area is expected to grow from $2 billion in 1999 to $32.6 billion in 2003.[9] There seem to be two key drivers behind this increase. First, scores of government initiatives entice Asian companies to move online. Thailand passed a law that requires all export and import documents to go online by the year 2000. Hong Kong has planned a *Cyberport* and Singapore a *wired island*. The Taiwanese government hopes to have 50,000 firms online by 2001.[10] Likewise, the Chinese government has boosted the spread of e-commerce by cutting access charges and encouraging government departments to put up their own Web sites. It also declared 1999 the year of "getting on the Internet."

A second factor is competitive pressure. In many industries, response time—the time to take orders and ship products—is often at least as critical as the cost factor. Asian manufacturers that are not able to slash their response times risk losing foreign customer accounts. Digital links between customers and suppliers offer a solution for Asian businesses that want to stay ahead of their competitors.[11] Some overseas customers such as Kmart and J.C. Penney now do only business with suppliers that know how to handle orders online.

[8]www.internetindicators.com/global.html.
[9]"A Biz-to-Biz E-boom," *Business Week* (October 25, 1999), 26–27.
[10]Ibid.
[11]"Racing to Get Globally Wired," *Business Week* (April 20, 1998), 24–25.

In most countries, personal computers are the most common Internet access tool. However, in Japan, cellular phones, are becoming increasingly popular for access to the Web. DoCoMo's "i-mode" service offers continuous Internet access via mobile phones, using the latest cellular phone technology.

Online shopping, on the other hand, is still a relatively new phenomenon. Currently, there are about 1,400 Asian Internet retailers. Of those, more than half are located in South Korea (409) and Greater China (405)—China, Taiwan, and Hong Kong—combined.[12] Although the number of Asians shopping online is growing, most of them spend their money on non-Asian Web sites. The most common products bought online by Asian users include books, magazines, and computer software.[13]

Though Web mania has taken hold of the region, several obstacles hinder the spread of e-commerce. In many Asian countries, business people prefer to do business on a face-to-face basis instead of via anonymous channels. Cultivating relationships and networking is what really matters. Over time, this mind-set will most

[12]"E-Commerce Takes Root in the Biggest Continent," *The Asian Wall Street Journal* (October 27, 1999), 1, 8.
[13]"More Asians Shop Online But on Non-Asian Sites," *The Asian Wall Street Journal* (November 1, 1999), p. 8.

likely change, but this may take a while. Another stumbling block for business-to-business e-commerce is the deeply rooted secrecy that many Asian businesses, especially family-owned ones, adhere to. Because of that mind-set, companies are reluctant to share information with their suppliers. Another formidable hurdle to e-commerce growth is the knowledge barrier.[14] Talent to create and maintain Web sites is rare.

Online shopping in Asia is hampered by numerous barriers. Especially in emerging markets, access to home computers and telephone lines is still fairly limited. The credit-card culture common in most Western countries has not taken off yet in Asia. Asian consumers are reluctant to share credit-card numbers and other personal data with online retailers. Instead, they prefer to put a check in the mail or fax credit-card information. Global Perspective 19–1 discusses e-commerce developments in China.

❖ ❖

$\mathcal{G}$LOBAL PERSPECTIVE 19–1

CHINA ONLINE

By 2001, China is expected to have more Internet users than any other Asian-Pacific country. By 2005, China is predicted to have the largest number of Internet users in the world. In many ways, China is well-placed for a rapid development of e-commerce. The key drivers include the following:

- The explosion of Internet use

- The government's interest in developing e-commerce

- Underdeveloped distribution and retail infrastructure

Consider the first force. In the middle of 1998, China had about 1.2 million Internet users. Its user base is expected to grow to 33 million in 2003. A key factor behind this rise is the drop in online costs. In 1997, 40 hours a month would cost a whopping $80. China Net has slashed this rate to a monthly charge of only $14. Currently, most users are young, well-educated, and concentrated in the richest areas of China (Beijing, Shanghai, and Guang-

Sources: "Net Gains," *Business China* (January 18, 1999), 5–6; "Surf's Up," *Far Eastern Economic Review* (March 4, 1999), 10–12; "The Promise of e-commerce," *Business China* (August 16, 1999), 5–7; "Internet Growth in China Drives Easy Access, Calls for Relaxation of Regulations," *Media* (October 29, 1999), 22.

dong). The government is heavily in favor of fostering a *knowledge economy*. The Beijing government has announced plans to get at least 80 percent of local governments linked to the Internet by the end of 2000 and 80 percent of Chinese companies wired by 2001. It hopes to be able to use the Internet as a tool to boost Chinese exports. The Internet also allows consumers to overcome some of the hurdles associated with China's dismal distribution infrastructure.

Obstacles to e-commerce are still tremendous, though. One roadblock is the low penetration of credit cards: less than 2 percent of Chinese consumers own a credit card. Likewise, ownership of personal computers among Chinese is extremely low: 1 out of every 150 Chinese households owns a PC. This compares with penetration rates of 28 percent in Hong Kong and 17 percent in Taiwan. Conservative consumer attitudes pose another challenge. It is hard to convince Chinese consumers to buy anything by computer. China's legal system has not adapted yet to the development of e-commerce. Regulations in areas such as privacy, consumer rights, and recognition of digital signatures have yet to be spelled out. Foreign exchange controls hamstring foreign vendors' ability to sell goods and services to Chinese Internet users. Still, many of these barriers to e-commerce will gradually disappear. The surf is definitely up in China.

---

[14]"Report for APEC Cites Barriers to E-Commerce Growth," *International Herald Tribune* (September 8, 1999), p. 15.

European businesses and consumers have embraced the Internet with gusto. Consumer spending on e-commerce in Europe is expected to surpass U.S. spending by the year 2002. Exhibit 19–2 shows that consumer spending at European Web sites is growing at an amazing rate. Forty-seven million European households are expected to have Internet access by 2003.[15] The most popular items are computer hardware (44 percent), air travel (23 percent), books (14 percent), and music and software (5 percent each).[16]

Europe

Small and medium-sized European companies are finding the Internet a cheap way to broaden their geographic scope. Just like in Asia, customers increasingly expect their vendors to become wired in order to sustain a business relationship. One major catalyst in Europe for e-commerce is the launch of the euro. The euro makes it much easier for online European retailers to sell across borders. Other drivers behind the rise in e-commerce include free Internet access (excluding phone charges) in countries like Germany and the United Kingdom (www.freeserve.net), a drop in security concerns, and word of mouth.

Several challenges to e-commerce in Europe persist, however. One major stumbling block is government red tape. An incredible maze of rules, laws, and regulations burden the development of e-commerce in the region, especially in Germany. For example, Germany's discount law (*Rabattgesetz*) forbids special price offers to individual customers. The price of the product or service has to be identical for everybody. Therefore, it would be illegal in Germany to operate a reverse auction like Priceline.com, where customers state the price they are willing to pay for a certain item. European firms, just like their Asian counterparts, also face a knowledge barrier. A survey conducted by Andersen Consulting found that 85 percent of European executives do not believe that their company has the skills necessary to exploit e-commerce successfully. One more hurdle is Europe's lack of a credit card

EXHIBIT 19–2

CONSUMER SPENDING AT EUROPEAN SITES 1997–2002

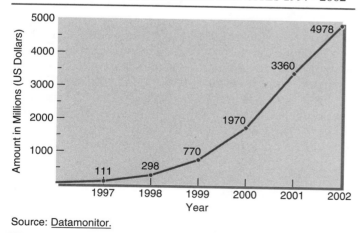

Source: Datamonitor.

---

[15]www.internetindicators.com/global.html.

[16]"E-Shop Till You Drop," *Business Week* (February 9, 1998), 18–19.

culture. Unlike Americans, Europeans are reluctant to reveal credit card numbers on the Internet. European Internet users also face higher costs of going online. Penetration of PCs in Southern Europe is still very low. According to Datamonitor, only 10 percent of households in Spain and Italy will be online by 2002, compared to 35 percent in Sweden.[17]

Latin America

Net fever is also spreading rapidly in Latin America. According to International Data Corp., the number of Internet users in Latin America will grow from 4.8 million in 1998 to 19 million in 2003. Over the same period, revenue from online sales is expected to soar from a mere $167 million to $8 billion. Business-to-business sales are expected to account for $6.1 billion of the total revenue. A recent survey by IDC found that 90 percent of businesses in Latin America had or were developing a Web site by the end of 1998. Brazil, with 88 percent of online sales in 1999, has been one of the strongest e-commerce markets in the region. The country boasts almost fifty Internet service providers (ISPs), including local players such as Universo Online and global players such as AOL and Telefónica, a Spanish telecommunications company. Brazil also has the largest number of online retailers in the region. Two factors set Brazil apart from other Latin American markets: the high penetration of PCs and a technically sophisticated banking system. For instance, Bradesco, Brazil's largest private commercial bank, has more than 750,000 online customers and is adding 1,000 per day.[18] Online shopping habits of Latin American Internet users are similar to the rest of the world except for grocery shopping, which is far more popular in the area than elsewhere.

E-commerce in Latin America is spurred by several factors. The Internet helps to level the playing field for companies bidding for contracts by offering fewer opportunities for corruption. Companies will also be able to slash their costs and increase productivity by linking up with their supply chain members. There are also cultural factors. People in Latin America do not enjoy shopping in person as much as their American counterparts. Most would rather stay at home and shop online.[19]

E-commerce faces a number of obstacles, though. One hurdle is the high cost of Internet access. Latin American users spend, on average, $53 per month on service fees and local phone charges, double the amount forked over by U.S. users. One other major barrier is the maze of customs regulations and import duties, which delay the arrival of goods and increase costs. Dell's online customers in Brazil and Argentina need to travel to the main international airport to clear their purchases through customs.[20] Not unlike Asian and European consumers, Internet users in Latin America are reluctant to release their credit card number.[21]

---

[17]Ibid.

[18]"Battle for the Net," *Business Week* (October 25, 1999), 36–44.

[19]Ibid.

[20]Ibid.

[21]Check out the Internet surveys on www.nua.ie for updates on Internet developments in these regions and in other areas.

STRUCTURAL BARRIERS TO GLOBAL E-COMMERCE

◆ ◆ ◆ ◆ ◆ ◆

Although most forecasts about the future of global e-commerce are rosy, several structural barriers might slow down its expansion. In particular, the following obstacles might interfere: (1) language barriers, (2) cultural barriers, (3) spread of personal computers (PCs), (4) knowledge barriers, (5) access charges, and (6) government regulations. Let us look at each one of these in turn.

Language Barriers

Given the Internet's origins in the United States, it is not surprising that much of the content is U.S.-focused and that the English language has dominated the Web so far. However, as the number of Internet users rises, English messages will not be understood by a growing number of non-English speakers. By 2005, 57 percent of the Internet audience will speak a language other than English, according to a recent report.[22] A study by Forrester research found that business users on the Web are three times more likely to purchase when the Web site "speaks" their native language.[23] Hence, a company that plans to become a global e-business player may need to localize its Web sites in order to communicate with target customers in their native tongue.

The demand for Web site localization services has boosted a new Web-oriented translation industry. For instance, WorldPoint (www.worldpoint.com) is a Honolulu-based firm with a network of ten thousand translators. The company offers a Web-based "localization" service that translates and edits documents such as annual reports, manuals, and marketing materials into eighteen languages—not just text, but also currencies, dates, and even color and image conventions. Translation fees range between 20 and 30 cents a word, depending on the languages involved. Daimler-Chrysler hired WorldPoint to expand its Web presence into sixty-five markets.

Generally speaking, companies that want to make their Web sites international by translating the content into other languages have three options. The first one is to hire a firm like WorldPoint or use local people to do the translation job. This will be very time-consuming and costly, however. Another alternative is to use software that offers instantaneous translations. Although this option is less costly and time-consuming than the first one, the results can be very imprecise. A third method is to pick a few key languages. Gillette, for example, set up a Web site for its Mach3 razor blade in Japanese and German after studying the number of Internet users in these countries.[24]

Cultural Barriers

Cultural norms and traditions can also hinder the spread of the Internet. In Confucian-based cultures like most East Asian nations, business is conducted on a personal basis. Networking and personal relationships play a major role in business transactions. Nonetheless, Dell was able to gain a foothold in markets like China and Hong Kong with its Dell Online business concept. One other impediment is

---

[22]"Majority of Users Will Be Non-English Speakers," www.nua.ie (June 10, 1999).

[23]www.internetindicators.com/global.html.

[24]"The Internet," *Advertising Age International* (June 1999), 42, 44.

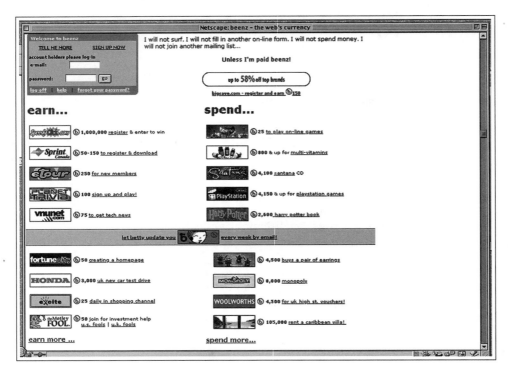

Beenz is a new digital currency launched by beenz.com, a New York-based company. It is used by more than 300 website merchants worldwide.

the lack of a credit card culture and security concerns. In many countries outside North America, credit card penetration is still very low. For example, less than one-fourth of German households are credit card holders. Even where credit card penetration is high, online shoppers may not be too keen to release their credit card number and other personal data. Instead, Internet users end up giving the information through fax or over the phone to the vendor. For instance, in 1998, more than 80 percent of Chinese-speaking Internet users who shopped online preferred to complete their transactions offline.[25] Probably, advances in encryption- and smart card-technology will provide a solution on this front. However, even with all the enhanced security features, many Internet users still prefer to pay for their transactions offline.

Another worry is that managers may overlook the need for cultural alertness when setting up a global e-commerce operation. Traditionally, managers would scout local markets and communicate with local partners to become familiar with the local culture. With a virtual business, face-to-face contacts are minimal, especially for small and medium-sized enterprises (SMEs). One suggestion here is to join Internet discussion groups and bulletin boards to gain knowledge about cultural norms and values in the foreign market.[26]

---

[25]"More Asian Shop Online But on Non-Asian Sites," *The Asian Wall Street Journal* (November 1, 1999), 8.

[26]John Q. Quelch and Lisa R. Klein, "The Internet and International Marketing," *Sloan Management Review* (Spring 1996), 60–75.

In many emerging markets, ownership of personal computers (PCs) is still very low. Even in some developed countries, ownership of PCs can be very limited. Less than 40 percent of small companies in Japan own PCs, and less than 20 percent have Internet access.[27] Some analysts view the low level of PC ownership as a major obstacle toward Internet adoption. Traditionally, expensive PCs have indeed constrained the growth of the Internet in many of these countries. However, just like in most Western countries, prices of PCs are dropping rapidly. In China, local computer firms such as Legend have introduced low-price PC's. In other countries (e.g., Mexico), Internet Service providers are giving PCs away for free or at a very low price to clients who sign up to their Internet access service. Moreover, ownership of a PC is no longer a prerequisite in order to get online access. Internet kiosks and cybercafés are some of the channels available to Internet users who do not own a home PC. In Peru, RCP (ekekos.rcp.net.pe) manages a network of thirty *Net cabins* across the country. Each cabin is a walk-in office equipped with PCs that are linked to the Web. Subscribers who pay a monthly fee of $15 can log on for up to 15 hours, including phone charges.[28]

In China, where PC penetration is extremely low (0.7 percent of homes in 1999), companies such as Microsoft are pursuing an innovative strategy to get Chinese consumers online by using television sets as a gateway. Ninety-one percent of Chinese households own a TV. TV set-top boxes like Microsoft's Venus product connect regular TV sets to the Internet. Prices start at $180, a fraction of the cost of a low-end PC (see also Global Perspective 19–2).[29] Other non-PC devices that can offer Internet access include Web-enabled cellular phones, personal digital assistants (PDAs), and videogame consoles. International Data Corp. has predicted that by 2002 the shipment of non-PC devices will account for up to half of all Web-enabled units.

Another hardware-related problem to Internet access is speed. According to John Roth, CEO of Nortel Networks, an estimated 2.5 billion hours were wasted in 1998 as people waited for pages to download. Slow Internet access still remains a major problem in many countries. As bandwidth increases, Internet access will presumably become more attractive.

A recent report prepared for an APEC meeting warned that none of the promises that the Internet holds can be exploited unless the **knowledge barrier** is dismantled.[30] Setting up an e-business requires certain knowledge skills that are not readily available. The hardware infrastructure problems and software-related challenges flowing from e-commerce will burden small and large companies alike. Although the Internet has been touted as a level playing field for smaller businesses, such companies may have a hard time finding and hiring the talent needed to assist them in running an electronic storefront. Especially in emerging markets, scarcity of proper talent and skills will restrain the development of a digital economy.

Personal Computer Ownership

Knowledge Barrier

---

[27]"Web Cuts Out an Entire Order of Middlemen," *Financial Times* (January 5, 2000), 14.

[28]"Putting the Net in the Corner Store," *Business Week* (October 25, 1999), 44.

[29]"TV May Be China's Preferred Web Portal," *The Asian Wall Street Journal* (November 1, 1999), 8.

[30]"Report for APEC Cites Barriers to E-Commerce Growth," *International Herald Tribune* (September 8, 1999), 15.

❖ ❖ ❖ ❖ ❖ ❖ ❖ ❖ ❖ ❖ ❖ ❖ ❖ ❖ ❖ ❖ ❖ ❖ ❖ ❖

$\mathcal{G}$LOBAL PERSPECTIVE 19–2

MICROSOFT'S SET-TOP BOX STRATEGY FOR THE CHINA INTERNET MARKET

According to International Data Corp. Asia Pacific, there were 2.4 million Chinese households with a PC by the end of 1999—this translates into 0.7 percent of Chinese homes. The percentage of the Chinese population online was about 0.3 percent. Instead of waiting for computer ownership to reach a critical mass, Microsoft has come up with a new strategic approach for getting Chinese people online: through their TV sets. TVs are much more widespread in China: 91 percent of Chinese households own a set.

In the fall of 1999, Microsoft launched the Venus set-top box. Based on a fully localized version of Microsoft Windows CE operating system, the device allows users to surf the Web. It also comes with other features such as

word-processing, spreadsheets, games, video CD. The Venus set-top box connects with a standard TV monitor and uses PC-like input devices such as a keyboard, joystick, and mouse. "By delivering this technology in low-cost and easy-to-use format, we hope to increase access to educational software, and ultimately, the Internet for China's consumers," said Bill Gates. Microsoft foresees that more than 80 percent of Venus customers will be people who cannot afford a full-scale PC or who do not want to deal with the complexity of a computer. If the product turns out to be a hit in China, Microsoft will consider offering it in other developing countries as well.

The Venus concept is supported by several manufacturers, including Acer Inc., Haier Group Co., Legend Group Co., and Philips Consumer Electronics. Microsoft receives licensing fees from Venus hardware manufacturers and derives revenue from sales of software applications written for Venus.

Sources: www.microsoft.com/PressPass/press/1999/Mar99/ChinaPR.html and "TV May Be China's Preferred Web Portal," *The Asian Wall Street Journal* (November 1, 1999), p. 8.

Computer illiteracy in some countries will also slow down the adoption of the Internet. This obstacle, however, will likely be removed as training and education improves. Also, new user-friendly devices and software products will sooner or later bridge the computer illiteracy gap for even the most computer-anxious consumers.

Access Charges   Early 1999, the Campaign for Unmetered Telecommunications (CUT) organized a Web boycott in several European countries. Internet users in Belgium, France, Italy, Poland, Portugal, Spain, and Switzerland were asked to go offline for 24 hours in protest of high access charges. In October 1998, Italian Netizens repeatedly downloaded information from the Web site of Telecom Italia, thereby blocking access to the site for other users. The move was organized to protest an increase in local telephone rates. Similar campaigns have occurred in other countries as a means to protest against high telecommunication charges.

In numerous countries, high Internet access charges are a sore point. Until March 1999, when the Chinese government cut the cost of Internet access by half, the cost to Chinese Internet users was thirty times greater than in the United States. The cost of surfing the Web typically consists of two parts: Internet subscription rates and telephone charges. While Internet subscription fees are often low or free of charge, telephone charges can be prohibitive. Exhibit 19–3 compares average monthly Internet access charges in Latin America. As you can see, rates vary a great deal across countries. In developing countries, high charges effectively make the Web the preserve of the wealthy. Elsewhere, like in many European markets, consumers end up spending less time surfing the Web because of high telecommunication charges.

EXHIBIT 19-3

AVERAGE RATES OF INTERNET ACCESS IN LATIN AMERICA

Country	Cost of Monthly Access	Number of ISPs
Argentina	$41.90	42
Belize	$20.00	3
Brazil	$26.96	48
Chile	$40.27	12
Colombia	$35.56	16
Costa Rica	$40.00	4
Ecuador	$45.00	1
French Guyana	$23.80	1
Honduras	$39.29	12
Mexico	$26.10	45
Puerto Rico	$29.00	1
Suriname	$17.50	1
Trinidad and Tobago	$81.71	4
Uruguay	$29.55	11
Venezuela	$54.35	7

Source: Inter-American Biodiversity Information Network (www.nua.ie/-surveys).

Government deregulation, increased competition, and new access alternatives (e.g., through cable TV) will probably reduce the cost of going online. Internet users in Germany used to pay between $6 and $28 per month to ISPs, and then pay Deutsche Telekom 4 cents for each minute on the phone to their ISP. Even for moderate users, these charges easily led to bills of over $50 per month. New competitors like Mannesmann Arcor and Interkom, a joint venture between Viag AG and British Telecom, now offer Internet access at much lower rates. Access to the Web in Japan used to be dominated by NTT, which charged sky-high fees. However, as new rivals such as Sony and SpeedNet (a joint venture between Softbank, Microsoft, Tokyo Electric Power) enter the Web access market in Japan, access rates are falling rapidly.[31]

Legal Constraints and Government Regulations

Most governments are enthusiastic about the Internet and the opportunities that e-commerce offers. And yet, red tape and government regulations stall e-commerce in dozens of countries. Regulations on issues such as data protection, intellectual property rights, taxation, customs, and import duties vary across countries.

E-commerce is global. The law, on the other hand, is mostly local. Hence, one of the fundamental issues is the question of jurisdiction: Whose contract and consumer laws apply? These issues remain unsolved. Problems related to national laws are compounded by a shortage of legal precedents and experts who can interpret existing legislation. The European Union recently drafted legislation that states that the consumer's home jurisdiction would apply for e-commerce purchases. In general, companies have two alternatives to handle legal concerns. They can either

[31]"Finally, Japan's Netizens May Be Able to Afford the Net," *Business Week* (November 22, 1999).

set up separate Web sites that comply with local laws or one mega-site that copes with every conceivable local legal requirement.[32]

To see how fragmented government regulations and laws affect e-commerce, consider the experience in Europe of Gateway, the U.S.-based PC maker. When Gateway wanted to sell computers in Europe online, it initially planned to set up a single electronic storefront with different views for each separate market, listing a different price. However, differences in value-added tax rates, currencies, and culture forced Gateway to create separate Web sites for each individual European market.[33]

Several governments have been trying to come to terms with global e-commerce issues by issuing legislation that covers the various areas of concern. A listing of Web sites of various governments' policy initiatives can be found on www. doc.gov/ecommerce/internat.htm.

Legal conflicts also arise about domain names. AOL, for example, has been engaged in a lengthy legal battle over the use of the "aol.com.br" domain name in Brazil with Curitiba America, a small local Internet concern.[34] A recent attempt to resolve these kinds of domain disputes was the establishment of ICANN (Internet Corporation for Assigned Names and Numbers). This nongovernmental body would handle such disputes through a process of mandatory arbitration.[35]

◆ ◆ ◆ ◆ ◆ ◆ USING THE INTERNET FOR UNDERSTANDING GLOBAL BUYERS

The Internet opens up new avenues for gathering market intelligence about consumers and competitors worldwide. It is—without any doubt—one of the richest pools of secondary data available. One shortcoming is that the sheer wealth of data has led to an embarrassment of riches: how to separate out the useful from the not-so-useful information. Advances in search engine technology will hopefully provide a solution.

In terms of primary research, the possibilities created by the Internet are stunning.[36] Marketers can get instant feedback on new product concepts or advertising copy. They can also set up worldwide consumer panels that can be used to track buying behavior and test out marketing-mix programs. Other new measurement tools are available as well:[37]

- *Online surveys.* **Online surveys** include e-mail surveys that are sent as attachments to e-mails, to be filled out and sent back by the respondent. An alternative is a Web site survey where visitors are invited to fill out a questionnaire on the Web site in question. A third possibility is the panel Web site survey. Here a panel

---

[32]"Global E-commerce Law Comes Under the Spotlight," *Financial Times* (December 23, 1999), 4.

[33]"Net Marketers Face Hurdles Abroad," *Advertising Age International* (June 1999), 42.

[34]"AOL Waltzes Into Brazil, Unprepared for the Samba," *The New York Times* (December 11, 1999), B2.

[35]"Global E-commerce," p. 4.

[36]Quelch and Klein, pp. 60–75.

[37]Ibid.

is set up, with each panel member having a password. When eligible for a survey, members are e-mailed a request to visit the Web site and fill out the survey.[38]

- *Bulletin boards and chat groups.* Online bulletin boards are virtual cork boards where visitors can post questions and responses. Chat groups are virtual discussion groups that hold online conversations on a topic of their choice. Companies can monitor and participate in bulletin board and chat group discussions in many countries simultaneously.

- *Web visitor tracking.* Servers automatically collect a tremendous amount of information on the surfing behavior of visitors—for instance, on the time spent on each page. Marketers can access and analyze this information to see how observed patterns relate to purchase transactions.

- *Virtual panels.* Web sites often request visitors for registration. Visitor profiles can be used to run global virtual panels. Obviously, such panels will not be as reliable as traditional panels as the information thus collected may be inaccurate or incomplete.

- *Focus groups.* An online focus groups is set up by selecting participants that meet certain criteria. Subjects are asked which chat-room to enter and when. They are run like ordinary focus groups. Not only can they be run worldwide but transcripts are immediately available.[39]

Although online research can produce high-quality intelligence, it is imperative to be aware of its shortcomings.[40] Sample representativeness could be a major issue when Internet users are not representative of the target population as a whole. This is especially a concern in countries where Internet access is still very low. When a sample is to be drawn, online research could be hampered through incorrect or outdated e-mail addresses. With some of the survey methods described above (e.g., Web site surveys), there is also a self-selection bias. Web site visitors might also fill out the same questionnaire multiple times. It is also difficult to find out whether respondents are honest. Identity validation can also be a problem, especially when the same e-mail address is used by multiple people.

COMPETITIVE ADVANTAGE AND CYBERSPACE ◆ ◆ ◆ ◆ ◆ ◆

The Internet offers two major benefits to companies that use the tool as a gateway to global marketing: cost/efficiency savings and accessibility (*connectivity*). Compared to traditional communication tools (e.g., media advertising, catalogs) and distribution channels, the costs of the Internet as a delivery channel are far lower. The Internet also offers access to customers around the world. As a result, the value of some of the pre-Internet sources of competitive advantage has been deflated. One of these sources is scale. Some observers have argued that one of the major consequences of the Internet is that small and large firms are on an equal footing now as far as global competition is concerned. Barriers to entry due to size have been

---

[38]Jonathan Dodd, "Market Research on the Internet—Threat or Opportunity," *Marketing and Research Today* (February 1998), 60–66.

[39]Ibid.

[40]Ibid.

dismantled. The advantages of size will disappear.[41] Barriers due to geographical space and time zones are no longer relevant.[42]

Although size-related advantages will probably lessen, claims that the Internet provides a level playing field to small and large global players alike are somewhat overblown. Large multinationals will still maintain an edge in most industries over their smaller competitors, especially in the global arena. Large firms still enjoy a substantial competitive advantage because of larger resources and more visibility among prospective customers worldwide. Deep pockets allow them to hire the best talent and buy the latest technologies in the area. It is also more likely that target customers will find the Web site of a well-known large multinational than of a small upstart.[43]

Instead of size, technology is now being touted as a key source for competitive advantage. Although technology matters, marketing skills will still play a major role in global marketing: A site with the latest technologies but one that doesn't meet customer expectations will not make the cut.[44]

◆ ◆ ◆ ◆ ◆ ◆ RAMIFICATIONS OF THE INTERNET FOR GLOBAL MARKETING STRATEGIES

The Internet has been hyped as one of the most important marketing tools for the global marketers. Even after downplaying all the euphoria surrounding this new medium, it is clear that the Internet means a lot for international marketers. Companies can use the Web to contact internal users (e.g., staff, salespeople) or external users (e.g., customers, suppliers, distributors) around the globe. Regardless of the target, the medium can be effectively used as a business model to generate revenues and/or cut costs. Let us now consider in more detail how the Internet affects the various areas of international marketing.

One-to-One Marketing

The interactive nature of the Internet turns the medium into the holy grail for global marketers. Mass customization—both in terms of product offerings and promotion—on a global scale is now much easier because of the Internet. One celebrated practitioner of this approach is Dell. Dell's online customers can select a computer from a wide range of options offered online. Through its built-to-order system, Dell offers customers variety while still sustaining margins via its flexible manufacturing system and on-time inventory management.[45]

The mantra—target, aim, personalize, sell—is now much more than just a catchphrase. With traditional marketing, one-way communication was the norm. The Web, however, allows buyers and sellers worldwide to develop close relation-

---

[41]Quelch and Klein, p. 71.

[42]Howie Lau How Sin, "The Integration of Internet Marketing," *Economic Bulletin* (May 1998), 13–15.

[43]Saeed Samiee, "The Internet and International Marketing: Is There a Fit?" *Journal of Interactive Marketing*, 12 (Autumn 1998), 5–21.

[44]"The Integration of Internet Marketing," p. 15.

[45]Ted Fan, "Discovering What Works in Cyberspace," *Economic Bulletin* (May 1998), pp. 17–19.

ships. Customers can get the information, products, and services that match their needs. Companies can communicate with their customers and prospects in a personalized and interactive manner through e-mail or other Internet tools.[46] By analyzing past buying patterns and conversing online with their consumers, firms are able to build up customer profiles. For example, Amazon.com sends book recommendations to its customers, based on previous purchases and books bought by readers with similar tastes. Buyers are also invited to submit book reviews.

Product Policy

From a product policy perspective, the Internet offers rich opportunities. Given the intrinsic nature of the Internet, the medium can be used to foster global brand building. The Internet also enables firms to develop new Internet-based products that can be rolled out globally if necessary.

Global Branding. One of the challenges that global Internet marketers face is the management of global brands on the Web.[47] Many MNCs have allowed their local subsidiaries to set up their own Web sites. Often, these Web sites lack coordination. As a result, these sites project different images, visuals, content, and messages for the brand and/or company. Consequently, consumers who visit sites associated with the brand or the company may get confused. With global cult brands (e.g., Land Rover, Harley Davidson), the issue of multiple sites becomes further compounded as individual dealers and brand enthusiasts set up their own Web sites figuring the brand. This problem becomes especially thorny when the company tries to broadcast a single brand or corporate image. Therefore, just as with more traditional communication media such as advertising, some amount of coordination of the content and tone of Web sites under the MNC's control is a must when a uniform brand or company image is desirable.

Internet-Based New Products. Savvy marketers can use the Web to develop new Internet-based products. These new products can immediately be rolled out on a global scale or tested out first via a pilot on a limited basis. A prime example is a new online shopping venture that Visa International developed in Australia.[48] The project, christened shopwithVisa (www.shopwithVisa.com.au), markets leading brands with special merchant offers to customers who pay with a Visa credit card. Offerings include global brands (e.g., Dell), local brands (e.g., Aussie Greengrocer) and Internet startups (e.g., www.wineplanet.com.au). If the pilot is successful, Visa will roll out the venture to other markets.

Marketing of Services

The Internet heralds changes in the marketing of international services. Services differ from goods in four respects:[49] (1) intangibility, (2) simultaneity, (3) heterogeneity, and (4) perishability. Intangibility means that services cannot be stored,

---

[46]Howie Lau How Sin, "The Integration of Internet Marketing," *Economic Bulletin* (May 1998), 13–15.

[47]Quelch and Klein, p. 70.

[48]"Visa Int'l Internet Project Targets Australia Shoppers," *Advertising Age International* (October 1999), pp. 3, 6.

[49]See, for instance, Valarie A. Zeithaml, A. Parasuraman, and Leonard L. Berry, "Problems and Strategies in Services Marketing," *Journal of Marketing*, 49 (Spring 1985), pp. 33–46.

protected through patents, or displayed. Simultaneity refers to the fact that services are typically produced and consumed at the same time. Service delivery is also heterogeneous. It depends on many uncontrollable factors. There is no guarantee that the service delivered will match the service that was promised. The final characteristic, perishability, refers to the fact that services cannot be saved, stored, resold, or returned. In the global marketplace, these issues become even more taxing because of environmental differences between the foreign markets and the domestic market.

The Internet allows global service marketers to break the logjam posed by these challenges.[50] Consider the tangibility issue first. International service providers can use the Web to substantiate the service promises they make. For instance, international travelers who rent a car or book a hotel online can print out the confirmation note. They thereby get instant tangible evidence of the transaction. Another way to manage intangibility is by offering samples of the service online. Visitors to Amazon.com's Web site can sample music or read book extracts before placing their orders.

The Web also offers solutions to overcome the simultaneity issue. The fact that services in general need to be "manufactured," so to speak, at the point of sale makes mass production difficult. However, simultaneity becomes less of an issue with the Internet. Indeed, mass customization is one of the major pluses of the Web, based on information technology, data storage, and data processing capabilities. Services can be tailored very easily via the Internet to the individual needs of the customer.

The Web also makes it easier for international service marketers to deal with the heterogeneity issue. The medium offers opportunities to standardize many aspects of the service provision, thereby making service transactions less unpredictable and more consistent. Elements such as greetings, reminders, and thank-you expressions can easily be standardized. Obviously, one risk here is that in some cultures customers might resent having the human element removed from service encounters. Therefore, one of the dilemmas that international service firms face is what elements of the service provision could be standardized. Because of cultural differences, these choices might differ across countries.

Finally, the Web also enables companies to manage perishability. Marketers can use their Web site to balance demand and supply.[51] A Web site gives service marketers the ability to offer 24-hour service to customers around the world. Geographic boundaries and time zones no longer matter. Marketers can also use their site to manage demand. Airlines occasionally use their Web site to sell seats via online auctions.

Global Pricing   For many MNCs who have set up a Web presence, a downside of the Internet is that it makes global pricing decisions less flexible. The Web provides a window to customers and distributors alike on price levels for competing brands. Prospective customers around the world have access to an incredible wealth of price and prod-

---

[50]Pierre Berthon, Leyland Pitt, Constantine S. Katsikeas, and Jean Paul Berthon, "Virtual Services Go International: International Services in the Marketspace," *Journal of International Marketing* 7 (3) (1999), pp. 84–105.

[51]Leyland Pitt, Pierre Berthon, and Richard T. Watson, "Cyberservice: Taming Service Marketing Problems with the World Wide Web," *Business Horizons* (Jan.–Feb. 1999), pp. 11–18.

uct-related information. Most European retailers who set up an electronic store-front have failed miserably to attract buyers. A key reason is that European Internet users quickly found out that they could order identical items from competing U.S.-based Web sites at a fraction of the European prices, even after shipping costs and other charges.

In Chapter 13, we saw how the euro will lead to more **cost transparency** within the eleven member states of the euro-zone. By the same token, the Internet facilitates cost transparency for customers and distributors around the world. It now takes only a few mouse clicks to gather and compare price and product attribute information for a given product from the different markets where the product is sold. Various Web sites like Germany's DealPilot.com or Britain's Shop-Guide.co.uk offer price comparisons of different shopping sites, thereby lowering the search effort for e-shoppers. Customers can also sample the *price floor* through various auction sites sponsored by firms such as eBay.com or qxl.com. The information advantage that sellers traditionally enjoyed over buyers has dissipated due to the very nature of the Internet technology.

For global marketers, cost transparency creates several issues.[52] First and foremost, it severely impairs the firm's ability to sustain high margins for its products. In Europe, for example, powerful mega-retailers increasingly press their suppliers to charge one single price throughout the region. Transparency may also transform differentiated products into commodity-like goods, where the only point of difference is price. A third consequence, coupled to the previous one, is that cost transparency might undermine consumers' brand loyalties and make them more price conscious. The number-one purchase criterion becomes price. Rather than being loyal to a particular brand, consumers become more and more deal-prone, buying the cheapest brand available within their consideration set of acceptable brands. Finally, cost transparency may also raise questions among consumers about price unfairness. Because of various restrictions, customers in one country may not be able to order via the Internet the same product at a lower price from another country. However, when they realize that the product is much cheaper outside their country, consumers in high-price markets may feel that they're being taken for a ride, unless the price gaps can be fully justified. Another consequence of increased cost transparency is that cross-border price wars are now much more likely. Amazon.com and bol.com, the book-selling Web site recently launched by the German publisher Bertelsmann, have been engaged in fierce price wars in markets like Britain.

To cope with cost transparency due to the Internet, companies can pursue various routes. First, firms can align their prices by, for instance, cutting prices in high-price countries and upping them in low-price markets (see Chapter 13). Second, they can also "localize" their products so that offerings differ across countries and comparison-shopping becomes less easy. In some industries (e.g., pharmaceuticals, consumer electronics), manufacturers can also alert buyers about the adverse consequences (e.g., limited or no warranty coverage, lack of service support) of buying from low-price overseas suppliers. Finally, outright refusal to handle orders from overseas buyers is another tactic. Despite the euro and customs-free trade, several online European retailers will not ship goods across national borders.[53] Examples

---

[52]Indrajit Sinha, "Cost Transparency and the Net," *Harvard Business Review* (forthcoming).
[53]"Europe's Not-So-Merry E-Christmas," *Business Week* (November 15, 1999), 98–99.

include the German shopping site Karstadt.com (department store) and the British Web site ELC.co.uk (toys).

Distribution

The Internet also brings momentous changes for international distribution strategies. Firms that plan to make the Internet an integral part of their international distribution channel need to reflect on issues such as these: Should Internet distribution complement or replace our existing channels? Will the role of our current distributors change as a result of having the Internet as an additional channel medium? Should we allow our distributors to set up their own Internet channels? Global retailers, facing the onslaught of online sellers, need to decide whether they should remain a bricks-and-mortar business or transform themselves into a click-and-mortar business by setting up a Web presence.

Role of Existing Channels. Connectivity means that in many industries buyers can now hook up directly through the Internet with manufacturers, thereby bypassing existing channels. Some observers have gone so far as to claim that the Internet heralds the end of the middleman. Especially in Japan, where there are sometimes up to seven layers of distribution between the manufacturer and the end user, the Internet is likely to cut out many middlemen. Because of this redundancy, some people foresee that the business-to-business e-commerce will grow more rapidly in Japan than in the United States.[54]

Although the Internet may diminish the role of intermediaries in certain businesses, in most industries distributors might still play a key role. Manufacturers who plan to add the Internet to their existing international channels need to ponder the effects of this new medium on the incumbent channels. In general, there are two possibilities: a **replacement effect** or a **complementary effect**. With the former, the Internet mostly cannibalizes existing distribution channels. With the latter, on the other hand, the Internet expands the overall business by offering a more attractive value proposition to prospective buyers. The extent to which the Internet has mostly a replacement or complementary impact will depend on the nature of the industry (see Exhibit 19–4).[55] Most likely, the effects will also depend on the country. Manufacturers may have different distribution channels in place in the various countries where they operate. Also, when the product life cycle stage varies across markets, the effect of the Internet on incumbent channels will probably differ.

The most successful distributors will be those who are able to build up new competences that leverage the Internet. The reason for having a distribution channel in the first place is the value added that the middleman offers. Traditionally, sources of value added might have been scale, inventory, assortment, and so forth. With the rise of the Internet, distributors will need to look into novel ways to build competences. For instance, one potential downside of the Internet is *information overload*. Intermediaries can add value for their customers by collecting, interpreting, and disseminating information.[56]

[54]"Web Cuts Out an Entire Order of Middlemen," *Financial Times* (January 5, 2000), 14.
[55]"Internet Distribution Strategies: Dilemmas for the Incumbent," *Mastering Information Management. Part Seven—Electronic Commerce.* Supplement to the *Financial Times* (March 15, 1999), 6–7.
[56]Quelch and Klein, p. 66.

EXHIBIT 19–4

COMPLEMENTARY VERSUS REPLACEMENT EFFECT OF
THE INTERNET

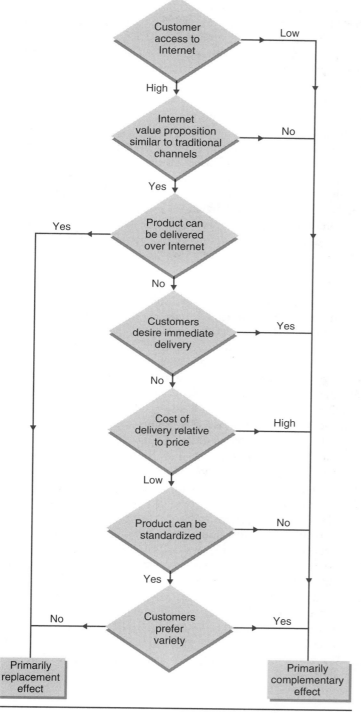

Source: Nirmayala Kumar, "Internet Distribution Strategies: Dilemmas for
the Incumbent," *Mastering Information Management. Part Seven.* Supplement to the *Financial Times* (March 15, 1999), p. 6.

Manufacturers who decide to incorporate the Web in their international distribution strategy also need to decide on what approach to adopt.[57] The first approach is to decide not to use the Internet for purchase transactions and forbid distributors also from using the Internet as a sales medium. In that case, Web sites accessible to outsiders would merely function as a product information tool. A second approach consists of allowing middlemen to sell goods over the Internet. However, the manufacturer herself would not sell directly via the Internet. One downside with this strategy is that sales from middlemen via the Internet may impinge on existing pricing policies and territorial restrictions. In the worst case scenario, Internet sales might spur gray market activity. The third strategy is the complete opposite of the previous one. Here, Internet sales are restricted to the manufacturer. A major risk here is that sales thus generated simply cannibalize incumbent resellers, thereby leading to channel conflicts. One way to counter such a risk is by selling different product lines through the various channels. However, resellers may dislike such differentiation strategy if it turns out that the product lines sold directly over the Internet are more popular than the ones allocated to them. Finally, companies can also pursue a free-for-all strategy where goods are sold direct through the Internet and manufacturers allow their resellers to sell online. It is then up to the market to settle on the ultimate winning combination.

Retailing Landscape. Some people have seen the battle between conventional bricks-and-mortar retailers and Internet retailers as a beauty contest with the cards stacked in favor of the latter. Consumers enjoy the convenience, the broad product assortment, and the product information provided by shopping Web sites. Pure Web retailers often also have a price advantage over traditional retailers. They have lower property and warehousing costs, and they are often exempt from sales tax. Dozens of large retail chains are trying to meet the challenge posed by pure Web retailers by setting up a Web site presence. These chains are sometimes referred to as **click-and-mortar retailers**. Some examples include Wal-Mart and Barnes & Noble (www.bn.com) in the United States, Bertelsmann (bol.com) in Germany, and FNAC in France. By going online, these chains are able to combine the advantages of having a Web site presence with those of a physical presence.[58] Click-and-mortar retailers can cross-market between their Web site and their store outlets. Customers have the advantage of getting a touchy-feel of the goods before buying them online. Products bought online can easily be returned to the local store. Click-and-mortar retailers also often enjoy substantial brand equity, whereas most pure Web retailers still need to invest a lot to build up a brand. As a result, their customer acquisition costs are generally much higher than for their click-and-mortar competitors. Most of them also have a financial advantage. Whereas retailers such as Wal-Mart, FNAC, or Bertelsmann have plenty of cash available, most pure cyber-retailers (e.g., CDNOW, Amazon) have only seen huge losses so far. One final benefit is that local chains often have a better feel of the local culture. Most of the well-known brands in pure Web retailing (e.g., e-trade, Amazon.com, CDNOW) still have rather limited international expertise.

---

[57]"Internet Distribution Strategies: Dilemmas for the Incumbent," p. 7.
[58]"The Real Internet Revolution," *The Economist* (August 21, 1999), 53–54.

A good example of the clash between click-and-mortar and pure Internet retailers is the rivalry in France between FNAC, a leading French music and bookstore chain, and CDNOW, a U.S.-based online music vendor.[59] CDNOW recently entered France and Germany. It added local language "gateways" to its U.S. Web site. For instance, French shoppers can place orders in French and pay in French francs. FNAC launched a pre-emptive strike by setting up a music Web site to compete with CDNOW. CDNOW enjoys several competitive advantages. Sony and Time Warner, two leading music content companies, have a major stake in CDNOW (37 percent each). This enables CDNOW to offer international Internet shoppers the lastest releases at bargain prices. As one of the pioneers in online retailing, CDNOW also enjoys a technology advantage over FNAC. FNAC, on the other hand, also has several competitive advantages. It can use its Web site as an extension of its store network and vice versa. In France and other European countries, the FNAC brand name is a trusted brand with much more familiarity among consumers in France and other European markets than the CDNOW brand name.

Global Promotion and the Web

According to Forrester Research, worldwide advertising spending on the Internet will rise from $3.3 billion in 1999 to $15 billion by 2003 (see Exhibit 19–5). Not surprisingly, most of that amount will be spent in the United States. Though these estimates look huge, online advertising's share of total ad spending is still rather low. In 1998, the amount spent on online advertising was a meager 0.6 percent of total worldwide ad spending. This proportion is projected to increase to 3.1 percent by 2001.[60]

As a global, interactive broadcast medium, the Internet offers several advantages to international advertisers. One potent quality is the Internet's global reach. In principle, customers anywhere around the world can be targeted via Web advertisements. Another highly useful feature is the interactive nature of the Internet. While most other advertising medium tools are one-way, the Internet is a two-way broadcast medium. Buyers and vendors can communicate with one another. The Internet also allows precision. Internet marketers can get precise information

EXHIBIT 19–5
ONLINE AD REVENUE FORECASTS

Region	1998	1999	2000	2001	2002
North America	1,300*	2,340	3,995	5,425	7,890
Europe	105	235	525	1,050	1,840
Asia–Pacific	80	130	250	475	815
Latin America	20	45	110	230	420
% of media advertising	0.1	0.2	0.4	0.7	1.1

in U.S. Millions.

Source: Forrester Research.

[59]"Storming a CD Bastille," *Business Week* (November 15, 1999), 46–47.
[60]"Global Facts About the Internet," *Advertising Age International* (June 1999), 2.

QXL is a pan-European auction Website. The service has three options: you can sell to/buy from another customer, a company or QXL directly.

about Web site visitors based on visitor feedback, browsing behavior, and historical buying patterns. Interactivity and precision offer a potent mix to international Internet advertisers. Advertising messages can be customized to individual prospects. Advertisers can save money by sending the right message to the right people.[61] Lord Lever's maxim that half of the advertising money is being wasted may no longer be true. One more useful characteristic that sets the Internet apart from conventional advertising media is the fact that advertisers can instantly assess whether a particular advertisement is working.

Internet advertising uses a wide spectrum of techniques. Exhibit 19–6 shows the findings of a survey of U.S. and European Internet advertisers. As you can see, the most popular form still is *banner advertising*. By clicking on the **banner ad**, users are taken to the advertiser's Web site, where they can have more product information. Banners combined with buttons comprise about 60 percent of all online advertising.[62] Unfortunately, it is also the least effective technique. Some of the other online advertising techniques are described in Global Perspective 19–3.

Despite the appeal of Internet advertising as a medium, many advertisers are still skeptical about its potential as a global promotion tool. Several of the advertising techniques (e.g., interstitials) take a long time to download. Such ads can be irritating to users in countries where access and/or phone charges are high, especially in places where Internet access is slow. In most countries, access to the Internet is still quite lim-

---

[61]"Advertising that Clicks," *The Economist* (October 9, 1999), 75–81.

[62]Ibid., p. 76.

GLOBAL PERSPECTIVE 19–3

ONLINE ADVERTISING TECHNIQUES

- *Banners.* Banners are the straps at the top of a Web page. They carry a company or brand name, a message, and an incentive to click. They can be static or animated. Banners are not interactive. Once you click on them, they carry you to another Web site.

- *Permanent buttons.* Buttons are smaller in size than banners. They are typically placed close to relevant content. Just like banners, they are not interactive and take you to the site of interest once you click on it.

- *Affiliate programs.* Affiliate deals split an advertiser's revenue with the site in exchange for free advertising.

- *Sponsorships.* With sponsorships, payment is up front, whether or not there is a sale.

- *E-mailing lists.* E-mail messages are sent directly to the consumer with an offer (e.g., coupon) or product information.

- *Rich-media expanding banners.* These are "sophisticated" banners. They use technology such as Java, Shockwave, or Flash to combine video, audio, and/or animation. Viewers can click on them without leaving the original Web page.

- *Interstitials.* These are Web ads that pop up on their own page in between content pages.

Source: Based on "Netymology," *The Economist* (October 9, 1999), p. 76.

EXHIBIT 19–6

WEBSITES' ONLINE TECHNIQUES FOR ATTRACTING VISITORS*

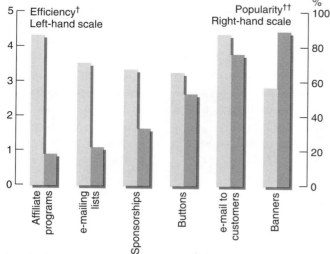

Websites' Online Techniques for Attracting Visitors*

*Survey of US and European online marketers, Apr 1999
†Five equals most effective ††% of respondents using technique
Source: Forrester Research

ited. Therefore, the scope of Internet advertising may be restricted to a very narrow segment of the target population. Also, the agency talent to create attractive Internet advertisements is lacking in many countries. Finally, international marketers that plan to use the Web as an advertising tool should familiarize themselves with advertising regulations and restrictions that apply in the foreign markets.[63]

SUMMARY ◆

To international marketers the Internet offers many promises. It can be leveraged to save costs and time and to generate revenues. Customers previously outside the marketer's reach now become easily accessible. The medium can be used to build up brand equity. For scores of business around the world, it has proven to be a cost-efficient distribution channel. It offers great potential as a global interactive advertising channel. One-to-one marketing to customers anywhere in the world is no longer a pipe dream.

In spite of all these goodies, marketers should not overlook the challenges that international Internet marketing poses. Some of those barriers are structural and may be difficult to overcome: government regulations, cultural barriers, lack of Internet access, the knowledge barrier, and so forth. Other challenges are strategic. Companies who want to embrace the Internet have to think about the implications of this medium for their global marketing strategy. Building a Web site does not automatically mean that consumers worldwide will beat a path to your door. Customers need to be lured to the site. Also, the site should be continuously updated and refreshed to entice first-time visitors to come back. Global marketers also need to balance off the advantages of customized content versus the rewards of having a consistent worldwide image.

The Internet has brought profound changes for businesses around the world. It has created a new business paradigm: e-commerce. In a recent cover article in *The Atlantic* magazine, Peter Drucker rightfully points out: "In the mental geography of e-commerce, distance has been eliminated. There is only one economy and only one market . . . every business must be globally competitive . . . the competition is not local anymore—in fact, it knows no boundaries."[64] For marketers, probably the biggest consequence of the Web is indeed that competition is no longer local. Any firm can set up a global business on the Internet from day one. Having an Internet presence has become for scores of companies a matter of survival. Suppliers who are reluctant to go online risk losing out to those who are not. Companies that do not develop a Web site presence soon risk having their customers browsing their competitors' sites for information.

KEY TERMS ◆

banner ad	cost transparency	knowledge barrier	replacement effect
click-and-mortar retailer	global e-commerce	online survey	virtual panel
complementary effect			

---

[63]Richard C. Balough, "Web Sites Shouldn't Advertise Trouble," *Marketing News* (August 16, 1999), p. 15.

[64]Peter Drucker, "Beyond the Information Revolution," *The Atlantic* (October 1999), pp. 47–57.

REVIEW QUESTIONS

1. What structural barriers affect the use of the Internet as an international marketing medium?

2. What advantages do click-and-mortar retailers have over pure Web retailers? What are the disadvantages?

3. Explain the notion of cost transparency in the context of the Internet. What are the possible solutions that marketers can have to cope with the problem?

4. In many countries, the Internet infrastructure is far less sophisticated than in the United States. Phone lines are of poor quality. Transmission rates are slow. What does poor infrastructure imply for "internationalizing" e-commerce?

5. For international Web marketers, one major dilemma is to what degree they should localize their Web sites. What forces favor centralization? Which factors might tilt the balance toward localization?

DISCUSSION QUESTIONS

1. Global Perspective 19–2 discusses Microsoft's set-top box strategy in China. Other companies are following Microsoft's alternative Internet access devices strategy. What are the possible downsides and risks of this strategy?

2. Would a typical mid-sized manufacturer in high-context societies like Taiwan, China, or Thailand enter into a strategic business relationship with companies and people that they only encounter over the Web instead of face-to-face?

3. Some observers claim that the Internet revolutionizes the way small and medium-sized companies (SMEs) can compete in the global marketplace. In essence, the Internet has created a level playing field for SMEs. Where before SMEs had a hard time to internationalize, now any mom-and-pop outfit can open an electronic storefront with a global reach. Do you agree? What downsides do small e-businesses face vis-à-vis large companies?

4. Dozens of Internet research firms such as Forrester Research and International Data Corp. issue projections and studies about the future of e-commerce and the Internet market in general. The figures usually vary wildly. For instance, when forecasts were made for the number of Internet users worldwide during 2000, predictions ranged from a low of 157 million (Morgan Stanley) to a high of 327 million users (Internet Industry Almanac). What explains this huge data disparity?

FURTHER READINGS

Berthon, Pierre, Leyland Pitt, Constantine S. Katsikeas, and Jean Paul Berthon. "Virtual Services Go International: International Services in the Marketspace." *Journal of International Marketing*, 7 (3) (1999): 84–105.

Cronin, Mary J. *Global Advantage on the Internet. From Corporate Connectivity to International Competitiveness.* New York: Van Nostrand Reinhold, 1996.

Dodd, Jonathan. "Market Research on the Internet—Threat or Opportunity?" *Marketing and Research Today* (February 1998): 60–67.

Garton, Steve. "An Assessment of Internet Users Across and Within Regions of the World." *Marketing and Research Today* (May 1999): 77–83.

Hamill, Jim. "The Internet and International Marketing." *International Marketing Review*, 14 (5) (1997): 300–23.

Pitt, Leyland, Pierre Berthon, and Richard T. Watson. "Cyberservice: Taming Service Marketing Problems with the World Wide Web." *Business Horizons* (January/February 1999): 11–18.

Quelch, John A., and Lisa R. Klein. "The Internet and International Marketing." *Sloan Management Review* (Spring 1996): 60–75.

Samiee, Saeed. "The Internet and International Marketing: Is There a Fit?" *Journal of Interactive Marketing*, 12 (4) (Autumn 1998): 5–21.

Samli, A. Coskun, James R. Wills Jr., and Paul Herbig. "The Information Superhighway Goes International: Implications for Industrial Sales Transactions." *Industrial Marketing Management*, 26 (1997): 51–58.

CASES

CASE OUTLINE

WEB CASES

ASE OUTLINE

ADDITIONAL CASES AVAILABLE ON THE WORLDWIDE WEB

go to www.wiley.com/college/kotabe

$\mathcal{C}$ASE 1

CLUB MED: THE PARTY IS OVER

Club Méditerranée (Club Med), a corporation in the all-inclusive resort market, manages 140 resort villages in Mediterranean, snow, inland, and tropical locales in more than 35 countries. Its resorts do business under the Club Med, Valtur, Club Med Affaires (for business travelers), and Club Aquarius brand names. Club Med also operates tours and two cruise liners: Club Med 1 cruises the Caribbean and the Mediterranean, and Club Med 2 sails the Pacific. The company also arranges specialized sports facilities. Club Mediterranee's clientele is about 1/3 French, with the rest being mainly from North America and Japan.

Club Med found that its all-inclusive price is not as widely accepted as it has been in the past. The firm has found that consumers' preferences have changed. Vacationers are not willing to spend large amounts of money for vacations that include many activities that the vacationers are not using as much as they had been in the past. This change in preference poses a problem for the company because Club Med's competition has been able to customize travel packages for each consumer at prices that vacationers feel more comfortable with.

Though it appears easy for Club Med to also customize travel packages, the company is at a disadvantage compared to its competition. Most of the competitors are found in a small number of locations, while Club Med has resorts scattered all over the world. Currency devaluation and political boycotts are some of the situations that Club Med faces worldwide on an ongoing basis. These external factors are reducing the company's ability to increase sales and gain new customers.

BACKGROUND AND HISTORY

Club Méditerranée, otherwise known as "Club Med," was originally founded by a group of travelers, headed by Gerald Blitz, in 1950. However, through the years, as

This case was prepared by Karen Bartoletti; Alexandra Doiranlis, Steven Kustin, and Sharon Salamon of New York University's Stern School of Business and updated by John Graham of Temple University under the supervision of Professor Masaaki Kotabe for class discussion rather than to illustrate either effective or ineffective management of a situation described (July 2000).

this group was increasing in size, it was becoming increasingly more difficult to manage. Blitz, therefore, took the opportunity to turn this "association" into a business, with the aid of Gilbert Trigano, in 1954. Trigano sought to establish this organization, and by 1985, Club Méditerranée S.A. was transformed into a publicly traded company on the Paris Stock Exchange. Club Med Inc. became the U.S.-based subsidiary of Club Mediterranee, headed by Trigano's son Serge. Today, Club Med encompasses over 114 villages, on six continents, and thirty-three countries (see Exhibit 1). In addition, Club Med has two cruise ships.

The Club Med style can be best described by the sense of closeness found among the managers. All managers are former village chiefs and are therefore knowledgeable of the company's everyday operations. This immediately reflects on the "friendly" relationships that the GO's (Club Med-speak for assistants) and GM's (Club Med-speak for guests) have with each other, making every vacationer's experience a memorable one. A distinguishing feature of a Club Med resort is the living area, which is much simpler than that of a typical hotel chain. Rooms are sparsely decorated (i.e., no phones, televisions, etc.). This simpler approach has made Club Med very successful. Another key to success was Club Med's image as a place to go when you want to escape. Finally, unlike typical hotel chains, Club Med measures its capacity in each resort by the number of beds, not the number of rooms, since singles have roommates.

INDUSTRY STRUCTURE

Until 1986, Club Med had a very strong position in the all-inclusive resort market. The corporation's level of bargaining power with buyers, suppliers, and labor was high (see Exhibit 2). During that time period a client interested in duplicating "the Club Med experience" would have had to pay an additional 50 percent to 100 percent to have an identical experience at other resorts (see Exhibit 3). With regard to suppliers, companies that provided vacation-related services, such as airlines, were willing to give Club Med significant discounts in exchange for mass-bookings. Finding labor was not a problem for this resort chain because thousands of people were interested in working at such a pleasurable location.

EXHIBIT 1
THE CLUB MEDITERRANÉE GROUP VILLAGES WORLDWIDE

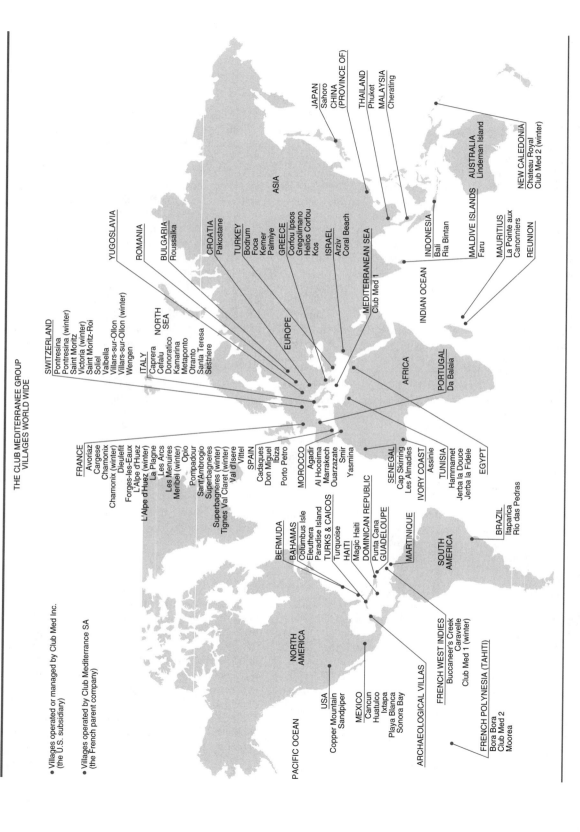

THE CLUB MEDITERRANEE GROUP
VILLAGES WORLD WIDE

• Villages operated or managed by Club Med Inc.
  (the U.S. subsidiary)

• Villages operated by Club Mediterrance SA
  (the French parent company)

EXHIBIT 2
FORCES DRIVING INDUSTRY COMPETITION

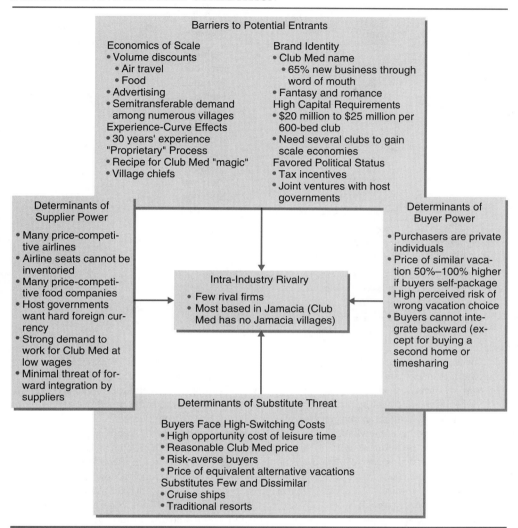

Barriers to Potential Entrants

Economics of Scale
• Volume discounts
  • Air travel
  • Food
• Advertising
• Semitransferable demand among numerous villages
Experience-Curve Effects
• 30 years' experience
"Proprietary" Process
• Recipe for Club Med "magic"
• Village chiefs

Brand Identity
• Club Med name
  • 65% new business through word of mouth
• Fantasy and romance
High Capital Requirements
• $20 million to $25 million per 600-bed club
• Need several clubs to gain scale economies
Favored Political Status
• Tax incentives
• Joint ventures with host governments

Determinants of Supplier Power
• Many price-competitive airlines
• Airline seats cannot be inventoried
• Many price-competitive food companies
• Host governments want hard foreign currency
• Strong demand to work for Club Med at low wages
• Minimal threat of forward integration by suppliers

Intra-Industry Rivalry
• Few rival firms
• Most based in Jamacia (Club Med has no Jamacia villages)

Determinants of Buyer Power
• Purchasers are private individuals
• Price of similar vacation 50%–100% higher if buyers self-package
• High perceived risk of wrong vacation choice
• Buyers cannot integrate backward (except for buying a second home or timesharing

Determinants of Substitute Threat

Buyers Face High-Switching Costs
• High opportunity cost of leisure time
• Reasonable Club Med price
• Risk-averse buyers
• Price of equivalent alternative vacations
Substitutes Few and Dissimilar
• Cruise ships
• Traditional resorts

COMPETITION

As of 1986, Club Med began facing competition. This company was no longer the only all-inclusive resort. Many of the firm's competitors were realizing similar success. In 1986, most of the all-inclusive competitors had adopted Club Med's style of recreational activities with staff members acting as directors of these organized games. By then, the only major difference that Club Med maintained was the fact that their price did not include drinks.

One competitor, Jack Tar Village, the Jamaica-based company, operates resorts located mostly in the Caribbean. Jack Tar positions the resorts as more glam-orous and modern than those of Club Med. This can be seen in advertisements where the company implicitly criticizes the spartan rooms and methods of Club Med. Jack Tar's claim to fame in relation to Club Med is its open bar policy.

Another competitor that the firm must consider is the SuperClubs Organization, which operates four resorts in Jamaica. These resorts have reputations for being the most uninhibited and sexually oriented resorts. SuperClubs also follow a system of having drinks included in their price, but the other distinction from Club Med is the vacation's packaging and distribution. Club Med bundles the ground transportation with the rest of their

EXHIBIT 3
COST COMPARISON

Average Costing of a 7-Day Holiday in Don Miguel	Normal Marbella Prices	Typical Club Med Holiday
Return airfare London/Malaga	£199	Included
Coach transfer to resort	£20	Included
UK government departure taxes	£5	Included
Hotel (3-star equivalent) & breakfast	£300	Included
Seven three-course lunches (@£15)	£105	Included
Wine with lunch & dinner (7 bottles @ £5)	£35	Included
Seven three-course dinners (@£17)	£119	Included
Cycling (6 days @ £5/hr)	£30	Included
Tennis lessons (6 days @ £8/hr)	£48	Included
Night club entrance (6 × £5)	£30	Included
Tips to staff (7 × £2)	£14	Included
Child care facilities (6 × 4 hrs @ £5/hr)	£120	Included
TOTAL	£1,025	From £569

Other activities/facilities included in the price at Club Med Don Miguel:

Swimming Pool, Circus School, Archery, Weights Room, Keepfit Classes, Specialty Restaurant, Bridge, Evening Entertainment/Shows, Ping Pong, Jacuzzi, Sauna, Hamman.

Other on-site conveniences at Club Med:
Bank, Boutique, Medical Center, Bar(s)-(bar drinks extra cost), Car Rental, Laundry Service.

packages while air transportation was to be distributed directly to consumers or travel agencies. SuperClubs, on the other hand, bundled ground transportation packages to be sold through large tour wholesalers, who, in turn, grouped these packages to be sold to the travel agencies.

Activities that Club Med and their competition offer are similar, but the way they are offered is somewhat different. Club Med's competitors offer the same activities but do not include them in the initial price of the vacation. A few of SuperClubs' activities that were included were tennis, basketball, and exercise rooms, but jet-skiing and parasailing were available for an additional fee. This allowed Club Med's competitors to offer lower prices and take away potential clients from Club Med. This concept has worked for the competition because consumers find that they are not using all the activities offered. Therefore, there is no reason to pay an all-inclusive price. Club Med, on the other hand, suffers from ecological, economical, and political constraints that prevent the firm from using this individual pricing method, which could lead to customized packages for vacationers.

THE SERVICE CONCEPT

Club Med's worldwide presence in the resort vacation business has allowed the firm to grow and dominate this industry. The original mission statement includes the idea that the company's goal is to take a group of strangers away from their everyday lives and bring them together in a relaxing and fun atmosphere in different parts of the world. This feeling can be expected in any of the 114 resorts. This mission is the key to Club Med's competitive advantage. Consumers anywhere in the world know they will get the same preferential treatment while they are in the Club Med villages.

The company's strategy of keeping members coming back is carried out by having their guests join a club as members with an initiation fee as well as annual dues. With the membership, they receive newsletters, catalogs featuring their resorts, and discounts on future Club Med vacations. This makes people feel more like a part of the Club Med and creates strong brand loyalty. In fact, an average Club Med vacationer revisits four times after their initial stay at one of its resorts.

All Club Med villages are similar in their setup regardless of what part of the world they are in. The resort sites are carefully chosen by taking into consideration the natural beauty (i.e., scenic views, beachfront, woodland, no swampland, etc.), good weather, and recreational potential. Each resort has approximately forty acres to accommodate all the planned activities: windsurfing, sailing, basketball, volleyball, tennis, etc. The resorts' secluded atmosphere is further exemplified by the lack of daily "conveniences" such as TV, clocks, radios, even writing paper. This is done to separate individuals from civilization so they can relax as much as possible.

Club Med organizes everything in a manner that encourages social interaction between guests. The rooms are built around core facilities such as the pool. Meals are done buffet style and the tables seat six to eight people so guests can sit and meet with many different people at every meal.

All activities and meals are included in the fee paid before the vacation begins. The only exceptions are bar drinks and items purchased in the small shops; those items are put on a tab and paid for at the end of the vacation as guests check out. The goal behind this all-inclusive price is to limit the amount of financial decisions made by the guests so, once again, they do not have to think of the pressures of the "real world."

Each day the guests have a choice of participating in a variety of activities. As evening sets in there are choices for after-dinner activities like dancing and shows. All activities are designed to encourage guests to join in. Even the shows allow for audience participation.

PROBLEMS

Until recently, Club Méditerranée was predicted to have strong sales growth due to successful market penetration in other countries. Now, however, that same expansion which helped the firm become famous may be the cause of the firm's disadvantage in relation to its competitors. Club Med does not have as great of a sales increase as it had anticipated. This is due to economic and ecological disasters in countries where Club Med resorts are located. This makes it difficult for Club Med to maintain its beautiful resorts in countries that suffer from such disasters.

With this knowledge taken into consideration, contracts are drawn up between Club Med and the government of the corresponding country. The key clause in these contracts states that if Club Med is allowed to enter the country, the firm will increase tourism in the area. In turn, the government will provide financial aid to help pay for the costs of maintaining the new resort facilities.

Joint ventures with host governments have proven to be not as profitable as expected. An example of such a disappointment is when the Mexican government agreed to maintain Club Med's facilities if the corporation would increase Mexico's tourism level. However, unexpected occurrences, such as depreciation in the country's currency, limited the amount of capital the Mexican government could allocate to maintain the resort's facilities. This put Club Med in a difficult situation when the firm had to suddenly maintain its facilities with less government funds than expected. Though Club Med's resorts are very profitable in Mexico, the devaluation of the peso has caused Club Med's maintenance costs to rise dramatically. This, in turn, prevents Club Med from reducing its prices and offering customized packages to its vacationers.

A second example of how international resorts reduce the firm's ability to compete effectively is Club Med's penetration into France. The resorts in the area had been doing well until March 1996. At that time, it became known that France had been conducting nuclear tests in the South Pacific. This caused Club Mediterranee to receive less bookings than expected in its Tahiti-based resorts. These resorts were avoided by tourists due to riots among residents concerned about the testing; this resulted in negative publicity in this part of the world. The riots, which occurred often in airports, deterred potential tourists from flying into this region.

The effects in one area where Club Med is based often indirectly affect other Club Med resorts as well. With a lower clientele in its Tahiti-based resorts, and in the surrounding territories, Club Med experiences lower revenues and, therefore, acquires less money to maintain these resorts. As a result, the firm compensates for such losses by using the profits from other resorts that have not suffered from similar disasters. Problems such as these prevent Club Med from reducing prices by implementing a customized travel package, which would enable the firm to compete more effectively in the vacation resort market.

WHAT LIES AHEAD?

Club Med fell on hard financial times through much of the 1990s, a result of rundown properties, a reputation for mediocre food and amenities, the aging of the baby boomers, a backlash against the sexual revolution, and an inconsistent message that was filtered through eight advertising agencies in different countries.

In 1998, Philippe Bourguignon, who is credited with turning around Euro Disney, was brought in as new chairman to stem the decline. He immediately instigated a $500-million, three-year rescue program. Unprofitable villages and some sales offices were closed, and older resorts are being refurbished. Thanks to the new chairman's leadership, Club Med is making a comeback. Attendance is rising, the company turned a modest profit last year, and 74 villages are undergoing a $350 million restructuring. Recently, the stock bounced back from a twelve-month low of $63.67 to close at $84.17 in April 1999. Occupancy rose to 72.3 percent last year, up from 69.1 percent in the 1997 fiscal year and 66.9 percent in the 1996 fiscal year. In fiscal 1998, attendance at Club Med rose 5 percent, to almost 1.6 million, although it is still well below the record 1.8 million set in 1989. Equally important, after huge losses in both 1997 ($215 million) and 1996 ($130 million), the company earned $30 million in revenue on $1.5 billion in sales. While there are still many problems confronting the resort club, such as a 10 percent loss of room space due to renovations, Club Med appears to be back on track to success.

Current management is well aware of the strong brand recognition that Club Med holds. It is synonymous with the pursuit of pleasure. However, management would like to alter this perception. It would like to eliminate the perception of Club Med as a "swingers" paradise. Even if Club Med wanted it to be such a resort, it would be virtually impossible to compete with resorts that have sprung up in Europe, Asia and the Caribbean in recent years catering exclusively to hedonistic life styles. But Club Med has not just been renovating properties. A big change is the decision to concentrate its sales and marketing efforts on France, the United States, Canada, Belgium, Japan, Italy, Germany, and Switzerland. These countries account for 74 percent of visitors.

With Japan in an economic slump and American attendance lagging for the last six years, Club Med's financial turnaround last year came largely from European vacationers. But with its millions of people with abundant disposable incomes, the United States is Club Med's No. 1 target. Combined United States and Canadian visitors totaled 189,000 in 1998, far behind the 598,200 visitors from France. This is the lowest total in the last six years.

To increase U.S. visitors, Club Med is considering building another village in Florida, to complement its family village at Port St. Lucie, and plans to build its second United States ski resort in Colorado or Utah.

It has invested millions into advertising to rejuvenate its strong brand name, which has been misunderstood because of poor advertising campaigns. Each village is now ranked with two, three, or four tridents, based on amenities and comfort level, with the result that the thirteen budget Club Aquarius villages are being folded into the two-trident category. A major expansion is underway around the Pacific Rim, including new resorts in Indonesia, China, the Philippines and Vietnam. By 2003, Club Med intends to open minicenters in fifteen cities, including Paris, Singapore, Brussels, Montreal, and Barcelona, Spain, to give local residents a daylong sample of the Club Med experience and to reacquaint former customers with that experience.

CASE 2

STARBUCKS COFFEE: EXPANSION IN ASIA

HISTORY

Starbucks Coffee Company was founded in 1971 by three coffee aficionados. Starbucks, named after the coffee-loving first mate in *Moby Dick*, opened its first store in Seattle's Pike Place Public Market. During this time, most coffee was purchased in a can directly from supermarket shelves. Starbucks' concept of selling fresh-roasted whole beans in a specialty store was a revolutionary idea.

In 1987, Howard Schultz, a former Starbucks employee, acquired the company. When Schultz first joined Starbucks in the early 1980s as director of retail operations, Starbucks was a local, highly respected roaster and retailer of whole bean and ground coffees. A business trip to Milan's famous coffee shops in 1983 opened Schultz's eyes to the rich tradition of the espresso beverage. Schultz recalls, "What I saw was the unique relationship that the Italian people had with the ubiquitous coffee bars around Italy. People used the local coffee bar as

the third place from home and work. What I wanted to try and do was re-create that in North America."[1] Inspired by the Italian espresso bars, Schultz convinced executives to have Starbucks' stores serve coffee by the cup. And the rest is history!

Starbucks went public in 1993 and has done extremely well in turning an everyday bever age into a premium product. The green and white mermaid logo is widely recognized; the brand is defined by not only its products, but also by attitude. It is all about the Starbucks experience, the atmosphere and the place that is a refuge for most people to get away from everyday stresses. The average customer visits a Starbucks eighteen times in a month, and about 10 percent of all customers visit twice a day. They have created an affinity with customers that is almost cult-like. Today, Starbucks is the leading roaster and retailer of specialty coffee in North America with more than 1,000 retail stores in thirty-two markets.

This case was prepared by Valerie Darguste, Ana Su, Ai-Lin Tu, and Peggy Wei of New York University and John Graham of Temple University under the supervision of Professor Masaaki Kotabe for class discussion rather than to illustrate either effective or ineffective management of a situation described (January 2000).

MISSION STATEMENT

Starbucks' corporate mission statement is as follows: "Establish Starbucks as the premier purveyor of the finest coffee in the world, while maintaining our uncompromising principles as we grow. The following guiding principles will help us measure the appropriateness of our decisions":

1. Provide a great work environment and treat each other with respect and dignity.

2. Apply the highest standards of excellence to the purchasing, roasting, and fresh delivery of our coffee.

3. Develop enthusiastically satisfied customers all of the time.

4. Contribute positively to our communities and our environment.

5. Recognize that profitability is essential to our future success.

6. Embrace diversity as an essential component in the way we do business.

Starbucks' corporate objective is to become the most recognized and respected brand of coffee in the world. To achieve this goal, Starbucks plans to continue to expand its retail operations rapidly in two ways. First, to increase its market share in existing markets and secondly, to open stores in new markets. Starbucks' retail objective is to become a leading retailer and coffee brand in each of its target markets by selling the first quality coffees and related products. In addition, Starbucks provides a superior level of customer service, thereby building a high degree of customer loyalty.

SALES & PROFITS

Starbucks' net earnings in 1998 were $68.4 million, which is a significant increase from the $26.1 million earnings three years earlier. Furthermore, its revenues grew more than twelve times from $103.2 million in 1992 to $1.3 billion in 1998 (see Exhibit 1). The increase in revenues and sales was a direct result of the numerous new stores that were opened. During this period Starbucks stores grew 508 percent from 165 stores to over 1,400.

EXHIBIT 1
NET REVENUES AND NET EARNINGS FOR STARBUCKS (IN $MILLIONS)

Year	Net Revenues (in $million)	Net Earnings (in $million)
1992	103.2	4.5
1993	176.5	8.3
1994	284.9	10.2
1995	465.2	26.1
1996	696.5	42.1
1997	966.9	57.4
1998	1,300.0	68.4

COMMITMENT TO COFFEE

Starbucks is committed to selling only the finest whole bean coffees and coffee beverages. Starbucks roasts more than thirty varieties of the world's finest Arabica coffee beans; therefore, the company goes to extreme lengths to buy the very finest Arabica coffee beans available on the world market, regardless of price. Arabica beans have a very refined flavor and contain about 1 percent caffeine by weight. These beans account for 75 percent of the world production, and are sought by specialty roasters.

To ensure compliance with its rigorous standards, Starbucks is vertically integrated, controlling its coffee sourcing, roasting, and distribution through its company-operated retail stores. It purchases green coffee beans for its many blends and varieties from coffee-producing regions throughout the world and custom roasts them to its exacting standards. Currently, there are three roasting plants in the United States. Roasts that do not meet the company's rigorous specifications, or beans that remain in bins more than a week, are all donated to charity. Starbucks sells the fresh beans, along with rich-brewed coffees and Italian-style espresso beverages, primarily through its company-operated and licensed stores.

COMMITMENT TO THE COMMUNITY

Despite becoming extremely profitable, Starbucks has not lost sight of being socially responsible. Starbucks has contributed to CARE, a nonprofit charity organization for the needy in coffee-growing countries, since 1991. As North America's leading corporate sponsor, Starbucks has helped establish health and literacy programs in Guatemala, Indonesia, Kenya, and Ethiopia. This long-term charity program has helped improve living conditions in the coffee-producing countries that Starbucks buys from. It is the company's way of providing assistance to those developing nations with which it does business. In addition, in 1996, Starbucks established a Code of Conduct policy, which is the first step in a long-term commitment to improving social conditions in the world's coffee-growing nations.

CURRENT SITUATION

Coffee consumption in the United States has climbed to its highest level in nearly a decade. In 1989, there were only 200 specialty coffee stores in the United States. Today, there are more than 5,000; the Specialty Coffee Association projects 10,000 stores by 1999. The entire coffee market is estimated to be a $30 billion industry.

In keeping with its corporate mission, Starbucks is expanding its retail outlets at an incredible rate. Most recently, Starbucks has entered several new markets including Toronto, Rhode Island, North Carolina, and Tokyo. In 1997, Starbucks is looking forward to enter Phoenix, Miami, Hawaii, and Singapore, and by the year 2000, Starbucks plans to have 2,000 locations throughout North America. Today, three million people a week visit Starbucks.

In addition to retail operations expansion, the company plans to selectively pursue other opportunities to leverage and grow the Starbucks brand through the introduction of new products and the development of new distribution channels (see Exhibit 2). Joint ventures with companies like Dreyer's Grand Ice Cream, Inc., Pepsi-Cola, and Capitol Records have enabled Starbucks to introduce new product lines into the market. In 1994, the company entered a joint venture agreement with Pepsi-Cola to develop ready-to-drink coffee products. In the spring of 1996, the company launched a new bottled coffee drink called Frappuccino™, a low-fat, creamy blend of Starbucks brewed coffee and milk. On October 31, 1995, a long-term joint venture with Dreyer's Grand Ice Cream was announced. The joint venture yielded a premium line of coffee ice creams distributed to leading grocery stores nationwide. This line has become the number-one-selling super-premium coffee-flavored ice cream in the nation. Finally, joint ventures with record companies such as Capitol Records have enabled Starbucks to sell customized music CDs in its stores.

Starbucks specialty sales and marketing team has continued to develop new channels of distribution as the company is growing. Its plan to become a nationally known brand is being pushed forward by last year's deal with United Airlines, which gives Starbucks exclusive access to 75 million domestic and international travelers.

EXHIBIT 2
STARBUCKS' BUSINESS VENTURES

March 1995	Released Blue Note blend coffee and CD jointly with Capitol Records.
September 1995	First Starbucks retail store opened within an existing and newly opened state-of-the-art Star Markets.
October 1995	Signed an agreement with SAZABY Inc., a Japanese retailer and restaurateur, to form a joint venture partnership to develop Starbucks retail stores in Japan. The joint venture was called Starbucks Coffee Japan, Ltd. The first store opened in Tokyo in the summer of 1996 and marked Starbucks' first retail expansion outside of North America.
October 1995	A long-term joint venture with Dreyer's Grand Ice Cream was formed to market a premium line of coffee ice creams. Nationwide distribution to leading grocery stores occurred in the spring of 1996.
November 1995	Formed a strategic alliance with United Airlines to become the exclusive coffee supplier on every United flight.
January 1996	The North American Coffee Partnership was formed between Pepsi-Cola and Starbucks New Venture Company, a wholly owned subsidiary of Starbucks. The partnership announced its plan to market a bottled version of Starbucks' Frappuccino™ beverage.
February 1996	Formed an agreement with Aramark Corp. to put licensed operations at various locations marked by Aramark. The first licensed location opened in the end of 1996.
September 1996	Introduced Double Black Stout™, a new dark roasted malt beer with the aromatic and flavorful addition of coffee with the Redhook Ale Brewery.
October 1996	Formed an agreement with U.S. Office Products Company, a nationwide office products supplier to corporate, commercial and industrial customers. The alliance will allow Starbucks to distribute its fresh-roasted coffee and related products to the workplace through U.S. Office Products' extensive North American channels.
1998	Formed a joint venture with Intel Corp. The venture will help push Starbucks into the market of cybercafes.
1998	Formed an alliance with eight companies to enable the gift of over 320,000 new books for children through the All Books for Children Holiday Book Buy.
1998	Acquired Seattle Coffee Company, UK's leading specialty coffee company.
1998	Formed a joint venture with Mack Johnson's Johnson Development Corp. to develop Starbucks locations in underserved, inner-city urban neighborhoods.
1998	Formed long-term licensing agreement with Kraft Foods to accelerate growth of the Starbucks brand into the grocery channel across the United States.

However, the company's goal of expansion does not stop at airports. For two years, Starbucks has been the only coffee brand served in ITT Sheraton Corporate Hotels. In 1996, it also became the coffee of choice in Westin Hotels & Resorts. More recently it formed an alliance with U.S. Office Products to sell Starbucks coffee to offices throughout the United States. This alliance is a tremendous opportunity for Starbucks to serve the workplace environment, and overall strengthen its customers' relationship with the Starbucks brand. Finally, Starbucks wants to grow its direct response and specialty sales operations. Starbucks' direct response group launched a new America Online Caffe Starbucks store to sell its products via Internet.

Though profits for Starbucks have increased significantly over the years, there is still cause for the company to be worried. Overall sales are still growing quickly, but the rate of growth is slowing at existing stores. Annual sales growth at stores has slid from 19 percent in 1993 to 7 percent in 1996. The biggest cause of sluggish sales growth is attributed to store cannibalization. Starbucks has been known to open stores within one block of each other in hopes of saturating the market. In addition, growth has also been hurt by poor merchandising efforts that has left many products—like mugs and coffee makers—on display for years.

INTERNATIONAL EXPANSION

With a stable business in North America, Starbucks plans on extensively expanding abroad. Its international strategy is to utilize two expansion strategies—licensing and joint-venture partnerships. The success of expanding into foreign markets is dependent on Starbucks' ability to find the right local partners to negotiate local regulations and other country-specific issues.

Currently, Starbucks exists in only two foreign countries—Japan and Singapore. The company felt that Asia offered more potential than Europe. According to one executive, "The region is full of emerging markets. Consumers' disposable income is increasing as their countries' economies grow, and most of all, people are open to Western lifestyles." Finally, coffee consumption growth rates in Southeast Asia are estimated to increase between 20 percent to 30 percent a year. With this in mind, Starbucks has plans to invest $10 million in developing its Asian operations and up to $20 million with its joint venture partners in Asia. The countries Starbucks is currently looking at include Taiwan, South Korea, Hong Kong, Malaysia, and Indonesia.

Starbucks does not have a roasting plant in Asia as of yet. Instead, one shipment of coffee beans arrives in Asia every other week to supply the company's shops in Singapore and Japan.

Japan

On October 25, 1995, Starbucks Coffee International signed a joint venture agreement with SAZABY Inc., a Japanese retailer and restauranteur, to develop Starbucks retail stores in Japan. The joint venture partnership is called Starbucks Coffee Japan, Ltd. This alliance proves to be a strong one because it combines two major lifestyle companies that will provide the Japanese consumer a new and unique specialty coffee experience. Under this partnership, Starbucks opened its flagship Tokyo store in the upscale Ginza shopping district, its first retail store expansion outside of North America.

Japan is an essential part of Starbucks' international expansion plan because the nation is the third largest coffee consuming country in the world, behind the United States and Germany. Japan is also an ideal country because it has the largest economy in the Pacific Rim.

Demand for coffee blends in Japan has doubled in the past five years, and specialty blends are the fastest growing segment of the industry. One industry analysts said, "The Japanese have taken to coffee like a baby to milk." Gourmet coffee accounts for 2.5 percent of the 1.2 billion pounds of coffee bought by Japan each year. The average per capita consumption among gourmet drinkers in 1997 was 1.5 cups a day from more than a half cup in 1990. The company picked Japan for its first big overseas venture because it is the third-largest coffee-consuming country in the world, but the quality of its coffee products provides a major opportunity for Starbucks' specialty drinks. Japanese vending machines, for instance, dispense $1 billion worth of cold, canned coffee drinks. A similar bottled beverage jointly produced by Starbucks and Pepsi is in the process.

Starbucks currently has nineteen stores in Tokyo and is expecting to open more. The stores offer the same menu as Starbucks does in its U.S. stores, although portions are smaller. The names of items, such as *tall* and *grande* are also the same as the ones used in the United States. All of the stores will also feature the company's trademark decor and logo. In addition, Japanese customers are able to purchase Starbucks coffee beans, packaged food, coffee-making equipment, as well as fresh pastries and sandwiches.

Currently Starbucks' Japanese sales are 25 percent above the originally expected sales figures. On opening day, the Japanese crowded into Starbucks and as many as 200 customers formed lines around the block to get a taste of Starbucks high-quality coffee. Starbucks hopes to cultivate the same kind of coffee craze in Japan as the one it had created in North America. However, profits from the Japanese venture will not happen for several years. Operating costs, like rent and labor, in Japan are extremely high, and Starbucks will also have to pay for coffee shipment from its roasting facility in Kent to Japan. Retail space in downtown Tokyo is also more than double that of Seattle's rent.

Starbucks plans to eventually open a roasting plant in Japan to help keep costs down. However, this is contingent if the stores in Japan prove to be a success.

Singapore

Economic Background. According to the 1990 U.S. Department of State, Singapore, otherwise known as the Lion State, has an annual growth rate (1998-in real terms) of 11 percent. The country's per capita income is $8,782, which is the third highest in Asia after Japan and Brunei. However, Singapore is a country that relies heavily on industry with the industrial sector (including food and beverages) making up about 17 percent of Singapore's real GDP. It imports about $44 billion in crude oil, machinery, manufactured goods and foodstuff from the United States, European Community, Malaysia and Japan. In addition, Singapore is constantly looking for new products and new markets to drive its export-led economy. It is attempting to become a complete business center, offering multinationals, a manufacturing base, a developed financial infrastructure, and excellent communications to service region and world markets.

However, the late 1990s was not a very good period for Singapore as the country was affected to some extent by the Asian financial crisis. The economy grew at an annual rate of 8.7 percent from 1990 to 1996, but has since slowed down significantly. The main sector that was hurt by this slow growth was the manufacturing industry, which grew by less than 3 percent, down from 10 percent in 1995. In addition, the commerce sector grew by less than 4 percent, down from 9 percent in 1995. Analysts claim that weak economic growth, global competition, and a very slow tourist season made Singapore's retail industry very sluggish. The restaurants and hotels also recorded weak growth.

Living in Singapore. Singapore has one of the best living conditions in Asia. In 1999, its per capita GNP was U.S. $27,480. Furthermore, Singapore is known for its diversity. There are 3.4 million Singaporeans: ethnic Chinese, Malays and Indians make 77 percent, 14 percent, and 7 percent of the population, respectively. The most practiced religions are Buddhism/Taoism (53.9%), Islam (14.9%), Christianity (12.9%) and Hinduism (3.3%). The main languages are Malay, Chinese (Mandarin), Tamil and English. English is the language of administration, while Malay is the national language.

With a moderately high cost of living, Singaporeans are able to indulge in luxury goods. Much of Singapore's entertainment is influenced by Western culture.

For instance, many theaters show Broadway musicals such as *Les Miserables* and pop concerts like Michael Jackson. Television programs are in English, Chinese, Malay, and Tamil. In 1992, pay TV channels such as CNN, Movievision, HBO, and Chinese Variety were introduced.

Singaporeans are known to indulge themselves with food. "So discriminating have the Singaporeans become on the subject of quality and price that eating has become a national obsession." Singapore has an array of restaurants, coffeehouses, fast-food outlets and food centers that are easily accessible and offer a variety of foods at affordable prices. Most of these food places are not air-conditioned except for those located in shopping complexes. However, eating in an air-conditioned restaurant, regardless of income level, is an affordable luxury. "The average lunch or high tea buffet spread offering a wide variety of dishes is available at many hotel coffee houses and restaurants, and it costs about $15 (Singaporean currency) or more per person. Most restaurants and coffeehouses impose a 10 percent service charge, but tipping is not encouraged."

Singapore's Love Affair with Coffee. According to Singaporean social commentator Francis Yim, "Coffeehouses are a sign that Singaporeans have achieved the status of a developed nation and we are breaking new ground in the area of becoming a cultured society." In the past during the construction of Singapore, Singaporeans did not have the time to enjoy their cup of Java. Regardless of their religion and beliefs, Singaporeans went to coffeehouses in the evenings for their meals and drank coffee in order to keep themselves awake. Now coffee is viewed as a beverage instead of a drink. People want to take the time to savor their coffee. It is not just a drink, but a personality altogether. The various flavors that coffeehouses offer reflect the different moods as well as taste.

The first Starbucks coffee outlet in Singapore opened on December 14, 1996, in Liat Towers, with the help of BonStar Pte. Ltd., a subsidiary of Bonvests Holding Ltd., a Singaporean company with food services and real estate interests. The store in Liat Towers is located in Singapore's main shopping district on Orchard Road, which is a very trendy shopping center where the French department store, Gallery Lafayette, and Planet Hollywood reside. There are plans to open ten to twelve more Starbucks in Singapore within the next year. The licensing agreement with Starbucks currently only covers Singapore, but Bonvests hopes to expand the franchises into other Asian markets. Starbucks' expansion into Singapore is its first expansion into Southeast Asia. Bonvests Holdings anticipates that the Starbucks retail stores will generate at least $40 million in sales over the next five to six years.

Bonvests is an ideal partner for several reasons. Bonvests has acquired expertise in running food businesses, like the local Burger King chain. They also know and understand the local consumer market, government regulations, and the local real estate market.

Starbucks chose Singapore for its entry in the Southeast Asian market because of the highly "western-ized" ideas and lifestyles it had adopted. Some have described Starbucks as being another American icon, like McDonald's. Some even say that Starbucks has created an American coffee cult. Slowly, but surely, gourmet coffee bars have been penetrating into the food scene in Singapore. It is estimated that Singaporeans drink more than 10,000 gourmet cups a day. In addition, the market

EXHIBIT 3
COMPETITOR PROFILES

SPINELLI

Spinelli Coffee Company, long-regarded by many as San Francisco's best coffee retailer, has been licensed by Equinox for expansion into Southeast Asia. Equinox is a joint venture between Golden Harvest, a Hong Kong film company, and Singapore Technologies Industrial Corp., a Singapore Conglomerate. Seven outlets were opened in Singapore's central business district by the fall of 1997, with up to forty locations targeted for the region by the year 2000. In addition, Spinelli is also in the process of setting up roasting factories to supply the Asian Market. Spinelli brings to Asia years of experience in sourcing, producing and selling premium coffee drinks and whole bean coffee.

SUNTEC DOME HOLDINGS

Dome Café is a cafe modeled on European lines and was discovered by a Singaporean lawyer. It is best known for its distinctive sidewalk and atrium cafes, where, the food menu is longer than the coffee list. They serve light snacks and full meals served all day, from sandwiches made with foccacia (a flat, Italian bread) to exotic entrees like duck and pumpkin risotto.

Suntec Dome Holdings was formed in 1996 when Suntec Investment, an investment vehicle for a group of Hong Kong tycoons, bought 51 percent stakes in the Dome Chain. Ronald Lee and Sebastian Ong, founders of Dome, imported the European-style Dome concept from Australia. They are expecting to increase the numbers of outlets from seven to seventeen within three years, an estimated $7 million is expected to be allocated for the expansion of outlets. Plans to build more roasting plants to distribute Dome's coffee in Asia are to follow, though roasting factories in Singapore and Australia exist already. Their growth strategy is to expand into several Asian countries, with six outlets within two years in Malaysia and plans for further expansion into Indonesia, Thailand, Hong Kong, and China are in the development stage.

COFFEE CLUB

Established coffee trading company Hiang Kie, now sixty years old, sniffed out the gourmet coffee trend and whipped up its first outlet in Holland Village in 1991. There are thirty-seven variations, from the humble Kopi Baba to the spicy, vintage tones of Aged Kalossi Coffee. The best attraction is the Iced Mocha Vanilla—Macciato coffee and milk topped with vanilla ice cream and a drizzle of chocolate syrup. In addition, they serve light meals of cakes, salads, sandwiches, and home-made ice cream.

COFFEE CONNECTION

Coffee Connection is the latest, trendier incarnation of Suzuki Coffee House, started in the 1980s by Sarika Coffee to showcase its Suzuki Coffee Powder. So far it is the mothership of coffee bars, with sixty-nine different drinks ranging from cool coffee jelly to Bleu Mountain Chaser. The best attraction is the Cappuccino Italiano—espresso infused with hot milk, topped with a frothy milk cap and dusted lightly with chocolate powder. They also serve ice cream, pasta, pizza, and foccacia sandwiches.

BURKE'S COFFEE

The origins of Burke's Coffee started from four Singaporean students who studied in Seattle, liked the espresso bars, and brought back the concept. Burke's Coffee is a Seattle-styled cafe, bringing the lifestyle of the Pacific Northwest to Singapore. Burke has made a name for itself as a friendly and inviting place in the midst of the hustle and bustle of downtown Singapore. The store has established a loyal customer base of young professionals who visit the store frequently. Burke's serve sandwiches, soups, and desserts. There are seven basic coffee drinks, plus twelve Italian syrups that you can add on request. The best attraction is the Mocha Freeze and Hazelnut Latte.

in Singapore has tremendous growth potential. According to Bruce Rolph, head of research at Saloman Brothers Singapore Pte. Ltd., "People should increasingly focus on Singapore not as a mature market with low earnings and growth potential, but as a uniquely positioned beachhead to get leverage over what's happening in Asia." Finally, the Singaporean market still has no clear leader in the specialty coffee industry. This means that Starbucks still has a good chance to become one of the top contenders in this market.

Despite the opportunities that exist for Starbucks in Singapore, there are still obstacles that it must overcome to be successful there. Competition is fierce, with fourteen players and thirty-eight stores between them (see Exhibit 3). With Starbucks' entry into the Asian market, bigger retail stores are already gearing up for a coffee battle. However, smaller companies like Burke's Cafe and Spinelli are welcoming Starbucks' entry. Their strategy is to open an outlet right next to Starbucks to attract the customers that overflow from Starbucks.

One of Starbucks' biggest competitors, Suntec Dome Holdings, has already established itself in Singapore. Suntec Dome Holdings already has good name recognition with Suntec Walk, Suntec City, Dome Cafe, and so on. Suntec is distinctive from the other retail coffee stores in that it is seen more as a restaurant than a coffee chain. It targets a broader market segment with a lower budget range. They are also backed by major supporters with the capital to counter Starbucks' expansion strategy. In addition to Singapore, Suntec Dome Holdings has plans to expand to other markets such as Malaysia, Indonesia, Thailand, Hong Kong, and China. Spinelli, a smaller competitor, also plans to expand into the region. With these plans of expansion to be completed by the year 2000, Spinelli will be potentially a major threat to Starbucks.

More well-known coffee spots to Singaporeans are Coffee Connection and Coffee Club, which are also direct competitors of Starbucks. The customers that go to Coffee Connection and Coffee Club like the atmosphere and the service they receive there. As reflected here, Singapore has seen a proliferation of gourmet coffee outlets in the past few years; therefore, the market is slowly becoming overcrowded.

Starbucks will need to turn some heads and create the brand equity they need to stay in competition with their competitors. However, they do have an advantage entering this market. Starbucks packages a coffee-drinking experience that the Singaporeans want, both trendy and American. As mentioned earlier, Singaporeans love American products and hopefully, that will translate into major dollars for Starbucks in Singapore.

Second, Starbucks faces a challenge in Singapore amid a prolonged and still-deepening crisis in the retail industry. Major retailers, like Kmart and France's Galeries Lafayette, have recently left Singapore after much failure.

◆ ◆

ASE 3

DOWBRANDS ZIPLOC™: THE CASE FOR GOING INTERNATIONAL

In October 1990, Stewart James, vice president of international for DowBrands, Inc., was reviewing the success of Ziploc™ brand zippered bags outside the United States:

> The jury is still out. In Canada, we're at about break even. In Latin America, we've built a plant—we've put a

stake in the ground for Ziploc™—but have yet to show operating profits. We're in the process of buying back a joint venture in Japan, after which we should make some money. We sell some product in Europe through our own organization, but none of our European subsidiaries is convinced that there is much of a future for Ziploc™; and some recent market research seems to support the conclusion that it will never be more than a niche product in those countries. Sometimes in these cases, the only way to find out for sure is to make a commitment and go for it.

In my view, DowBrands should grow Ziploc™ at all costs, and this means taking it to the rest of the world. It is our number one product in sales and profitability, and my experience has shown that estimating volume potential where behavioral changes are required is a very difficult question to research anyway. We are the low-cost producer in this category, and for a product which is as much a production art as it is a science, we are still far ahead on the learning curve. We are facing increased competition and margin erosion in the U.S. market, and now is the time to go forth in the international arena. The only problem is; how do we get the rest of the organization fired up about this opportunity?

DOWBRANDS, INC.

As a separate corporate entity, the DowBrands subsidiary of the Dow Chemical Company was only five years old, although its genesis was with the marketing of Saran Wrap™ in 1953. Saran Wrap™, a thin plastic film, was originally conceived to protect military arsenal stored at the end of World War II, but someone discovered it made an excellent wrap for the preservation of fresh and/or leftover foods. In time, Dow added other food-care products and such cleaning products as Dow Bathroom Cleaner™ to the line.

The parent company was a successful, $18 billion, multinational chemical company, but the consumer-prod-

EXHIBIT 1
DOWBRANDS[a]
SELECTED DOWBRANDS INTERNATIONAL DIVISION PRODUCTS

Canada:	Dow Bathroom Cleaner, Glass Plus, Fantastik spray cleaner, bathroom cleaner, and upholstery cleaner; K2r, Spray'N Wash, Spray'N Starch, Ziploc™, Saran Wrap™, Handi-Wrap™, Stretch'N Seal
Italy:	Domopak brand aluminum foils, aluminum containers, plastic wraps, food and garbage bags
Brazil:	Zipy (Ziploc™), Mr. Magic (Fantastik lemon), Thunder (Dow Bathroom Cleaner)
Argentina:	Radiante brand cleaners
Japan:	Reed/Ziploc™ food bags and microwave cooking bags
Hong Kong:	Ziploc™
Singapore:	Ziploc™
Europe:	Albal aluminum foils and containers, Albal food and garbage bags; Glad aluminum products, plastic film, food and garbage bags.

Source: Company records, dated 3/24/90.

[a]Ziploc™ trademark of DowBrands. Saran Wrap™ and Handi-Wrap™ trademarks of the Dow Chemical Company. "Glad" used under license to DowBrands.

ucts portion had never reached what many executives believed was its full potential. Dow spent $1 billion for research and development, and its inventors—dubbed "the molecule movers"—had an excellent track record for inventing new chemical compounds, but the company had been less successful in realizing the full market potential from those inventions. A notable example was a moisture-absorbing technology that Dow developed but sold to Procter & Gamble. It became one of P&G's most profitable products ever. Needless to say, Dow believed that the rewards of such inventions were reaped more by the successful marketer than by the successful inventor. Based on the idea that a dollar in sales, of a specialty product would deliver more profit than a dollar of basic commodity sales, an ongoing discussion at DowBrands was how to exploit markets for its inventions.

The mission for the consumer-products division was to become a *technology-driven* packaged-goods concern, with the basis for excellence coming from highly protected technical advantages. The importance of good marketing skills could not be ignored, however, so in 1985, Dow bought the Texize Division of Morton Thiokol, who not only made and manufactured a line of complementary cleaning products, but also employed personnel skilled in the design and marketing of consumer packaged goods. Texize was combined with the consumer-products division to form the new DowBrands business unit. In 1989, DowBrands acquired the European operations of the First Brands Company, which marketed the well-known Glad brand of plastic bags and wraps in the United States. Its Glad and Albal brands of household wrappers were well established in Europe. (See Exhibit 1 for a listing of major DowBrands products sold internationally.)

Division sales for 1990 were forecast at $1 billion, with food care representing about a third of this amount and international sales about 20 percent. Ziploc™ sales at retail were about $300 million and represented about 70 percent of the division's food-care business. The president and chief executive officer of DowBrands reported to the chairman of the board of DowBrands.

ZIPLOC™ STORAGE BAGS

With the rise of private automobiles, home refrigerators and freezers, and large supermarkets in the United States after World War II, shopping trips for groceries became less frequent than daily and the need arose for a way to protect fresh food (and leftovers) from becoming stale and hard. The need was met by aluminum foil, wax paper, and plastic wraps, augmented in 1962 by small plastic bags. The plastic bag (using a thin polyethylene film) was first introduced as a wrap for sandwiches and it grew in sales at more than 15 percent a year. Dow tried to protect its own plastic-wrap business with the Handi-

Wrap™ sandwich bag but was unsuccessful in coming up with a form and packaging that was competitive. At the same time, the use of plastic bags for large storage (garbage, leaves, etc.) was introduced; this market grew at 10 percent a year.

In 1966, Dow R&D personnel saw a custom bag with a plastic "zipper" at a trade show; the zipper used a unique technology that allowed the open end of a plastic bag to be closed by gently pressing a plastic ridge on one edge into a plastic track on the opposing edge. Not only did the zipper offer a convenient, reusable closure, but consumers believed it also served to seal out hostile air more thoroughly than traditional twist-tie closures then in use. Dow obtained exclusive rights to the manufacture of zippered bags for grocery-store distribution, but lack of consistent quality led to high consumer returns, and the project was dropped.

Dow continued to work on perfecting the manufacture of zippered bags while looking for untapped applications for nonzippered bags, especially at the premium end of the price spectrum. By 1970, Dow had determined that "unique, leak-proof seal" was a more important benefit to stress to consumers than "convenient/easy-to-use"; in fact, the zipper seal was perceived as *not* easy-to-use, because beginning the zippering process was not always easy, and ascertaining whether the zipper had "caught" or closed fully enough to make a perfect seal was not always clear. Dow changed the name of the product to Ziploc™ and introduced it nationally in 1972 with heavy advertising to educate consumers about the benefits and use of the zipper system.

A number of favorable elements in the climate helped Ziploc™ sales take off in 1973—increased U.S. disposable income, which reduced importance of the premium price, and a shortage of glass products for food storage and freezing. New positioning for the storage bag included nonfood uses, and in 1975, Ziploc™ storage bags led the market with a 33 percent share. A Ziploc™ sandwich bag was also introduced in 1975. A premium pricing strategy was effected by (1) offering fewer bags at the same price as competitors' packages while (2) continuing to advertise heavily and consistently to demonstrate zipper-seal benefits. While competitors tended to offer consumer and trade discounts, Dow did neither; it used its advertising to build strong consumer loyalty.

When consumer research revealed that a third of Ziploc™ bags were used in freezers, a bag especially 4 designed for this harsh environment was offered in 1980. A period of high inflation in 1981–1983 led to an advertising theme of cutting high food costs through the use of high-quality storage protection. Consumers still complained about the difficulty of using the zipper, however, and in 1983, a new, wide-track seal was developed. Nevertheless, market research showed that, given products of equal "ease of use," to claim "ultimate in food protection" would still capture more business.

In 1984, continued consumer-behavior research confirmed three distinct uses for Ziploc™: storage (refrigerator and cupboard), lunch bag/box sandwiches, and freezer. In addition, the Ziploc™ positioning was changed to focus on an end benefit of fresh, good-tasting food. The zipper feature was no longer the chief focus, but was used to support the "fresh" promise. Advertisements differentiated the three product types (storage, sandwich, and freezer), and Dom Deluise was selected as the Ziploc™ spokesperson.[2]

Dow continued to make product improvements and line extensions, including pint-sized freezer bags for single servings, jumbo bags for nonfood use, wide-track zippers on freezer bags, "grip strips" for easier opening on all products, "pleated" bags for easier use, "write-on labels" for freezer bags, and "Microfreez" bags for storing/reheating/cooking in the microwave oven (which was not successful).

Dow management believed that a consumer "information overload" was forming by the late 1980s (because of the proliferation of new products) that would lead to a "big brand" era. Because consumers had less time or desire to experiment than in the past, this trend would benefit major brands that had established good recall based on dependability and value. Hence, in 1989, Dow advertising began to emphasize Ziploc™'s quality heritage. A new advertisement campaign focused on "put your trust in a Ziploc™ bag," and new package graphics were aimed at improving the product's positioning of high quality.

By 1990, zippered bags had obtained a 70 percent share of the $600 million U.S. retail storage/freezer/sandwich bag market (60 percent of 365 million cases). Ziploc™ accounted for about half of the total dollar market (about 40 percent of the total unit market); it was the seventeenth largest-selling nonfood item in U.S. food stores.

Competitors were First Brands' Glad bags (about 25 percent of the total dollar market, split between zippered and regular products), private-label bags (about 20 percent of the dollar market, roughly split between zippered and regular), and Reynolds Metals' Sure-Seal Zippered Bags and Mobil Oil's twist-tie Baggies, which together accounted for the remainder. First Brands had bought the Glad business from Union Carbide in 1986 and, soon after, introduced a bag with a unique seal that changed colors when the bags had been properly sealed. Despite Reynolds' small share, Dow was watching its Sure-Seal brand carefully, because whereas Ziploc™'s strategy had consistently been to use consumer advertising and pro-

---

[2]Deluise was a well-known television comedian whose ample frame was augmented by his notorious love of good food. Advertisements showing Deluise peering into a refrigerator, cooling zover "my precious little [. . . sausage . . . coq-au-vin, . . . etc.]" protected by Ziploc were designed to create viewer involvement in a low-salience product.

motions with few trade incentives, Reynolds' strategy was apparently to round out its protective-packaging line, rather than make early profits, by offering a parity product with heavy trade and consumer promotion. This strategy yielded Reynolds a price advantage versus Ziploc™ of 30–40 cents for a package of twenty quart storage bags. Glad had responded with heavy trade promotions, while Ziploc™ maintained its strategy of heavy advertising reminding consumers of its premium protection.

By summer 1990, Glad seemed to be maintaining its share, while Sure-Seal had gained five share points, mostly from Ziploc™. The group brand manager for Ziploc™ bags, Dawn Miller, responded to this threat by a consumer deal offering "get three for the price of two." Response was great, but Miller was concerned by eventual price erosion of Ziploc™. The possibility of introducing a lower priced "fighter brand" was rejected, since the slotting allowances of almost $500,000 would reduce the return to an unacceptable level. As Miller said,

> Our main task will be to continue improving the product through performance features. However, this is tricky, since the production process is so complex: one small change might affect many other parts of the production process. It is far from a trivial act to tinker with any part of it! Gone is the time when we were the only product on the market, able to establish and hold our premium positioning through advertising alone. Consumers understand our concept well: Ziploc™ is a high-quality, low-volume storage product, almost like a disposable Tupperware, only better, because it seals better while taking up less room.

> The challenge is whether we can continue to add value to command a premium price. While we may be the low-cost producer because we can make the bags faster, I wonder whether the large investments required to support our automated factories offsets this advantage. If a price war starts, we will learn fast how far our cost advantage extends! I know that there is a segment for whom quality or price/value is no issue, but I am concerned that this segment is a shrinking one. This is an interesting time to be in this job!

FIRST BRANDS/EUROPE ACQUISITION, 1989

The acquisition of the First Brands/Europe wholly owned subsidiary (FBE) in early 1989 was consistent with DowBrands' strategic plan to increase international sales to $230 million by 1995. The strategic objective was to become a leader in the food-care/disposables (fcd)[3] category in Japan, Latin America, and Europe, with Europe targeted as a priority area.

In assessing world opportunities, the DowBrands strategic planners noted that, because no large plastics or

hydrocarbon firms were selling fcds outside the United States, given Ziploc™'s U.S. position, it could be considered the strongest premium fcd brand in the world. Unlike other DowBrands categories, the worldwide fcd market was serviced mostly by small regional manufacturers whose strengths seemed to be more in manufacturing than in marketing; only First Brands/Europe appeared to have built any meaningful multinational business. The planners also based Dow's strong future potential in this category on its a superior and protectable technology.

Europe seemed to be especially attractive. Although household expenditures for fcds were just half ($10.62 per household) those of the United States ($20.43), the number of 1987 households in the five countries of France, Italy, Germany, Spain, and the United Kingdom exceeded that of the United States (100 million in Europe vs. the United States' 91 million). Moreover, annual fcd growth rate in Europe was attractive (10 percent, compared to 3 percent in the United States). The leading 4 competitors held only 30 percent of the business (versus 70 percent in the United States).

The premium category was of special interest. It consisted of products that offered the extra benefits of convenience or product strength, such as Ziploc™, drawstring garbage bags, and pleated food bags. Industry experts estimated that these products had high gross margins (50 percent or better) but that selling expenses were also high (typically 35 percent), The premium fcd business was estimated to be 36 percent of all fcd sales dollars in the United States (annual growth was 10 percent), but it was only a "few millions dollars" in Europe (less than 1 percent of the fcd market). The gross margin potential differed substantially by country, as did trade margins, as the following table indicated:

	Average Price/ Nielsen Unit	Estimated Average Trade Margin
Germany	$1.06	36%
U.K.	.98	40
France	2.20	27
Italy	1.22	33

Source: Company records.

The DowBrands planners expected such factors as increasing numbers of European home-makers in the work force and the growing penetration of large refrigerators and freezers to push this segment's growth. Appendix A gives selected data on major European markets.

FBE had sales of $96 million in 1988 with pretax profits of $3 million. It marketed a full line of fcds with strong shares in France and Spain (the Albal brand) and in Scandinavia and Belgium (the Glad brand). The Glad brand was sold in all the European countries except

---

[3]The term "fcd" as used here covers all nondurable products used to transport, store, freeze, and dispose of food, including foils, wraps, papers, and bags.

Ireland. Over 40 percent of FBE's business was in France, 30 percent in Spain and Portugal, and the rest in Germany (private label only), Scandinavia, and the Benelux countries. Of its 312 employees, 200 were in manufacturing and the rest in sales and administration. FBE had a plastic bag and wrap factory in Germany and an aluminum rewinding plant in France. Some 54 percent of its dollar sales were in aluminum foil (the most important fcd in Europe), 14 percent in garbage bags, 13 percent in food bags, 8 percent in plastic wraps, and 11 percent in other products. Branded sales represented 75 percent of FBE's total sales.

DowBrands planners summed up their arguments for acquiring First Brands/Europe this way:

> The acquisition appeal is due to First Brands' strength in France and Spain, two of DowBrands target markets where we currently have no position. It also has a leading position in food bags and wraps in Scandinavia and Belgium. It is unique in Europe because it has pioneered the premium product segment by introducing both state-of-the-art zippered food bags and drawstring trash bags into France. Together with Domopak [DowBrands' existing operation in Italy] this acquisition would form a potent food care/disposables company, competing for the strongest position in the category in Europe.

(See Appendix B for the planners' detailed comments on FBE's strengths.)

Upon the acquisition of FBE in March 1989, DowBrands created a new position of managing director for Europe, which reported to the vice president of international. Under the managing director were regional managers for four country subsidiaries, each with a full-functioned organization (Italy, France, Spain, Germany); the German subsidiary was also responsible for sales organizations in Scandinavia, the Benelux countries, and the United Kingdom. In the managing director's headquarters were the European managers for manufacturing, marketing research and business development, human resources, and so on.

STEWART JAMES

As vice president and global product director, James had responsibility for all DowBrands' businesses abroad. Reporting to him were the general managers of the company's operations in Canada, South America (headquarters in Sao Paulo and a plant in Rio de Janeiro, Brazil), the Pacific Rim (headquarters in Tokyo), and Europe (the former First Brands/Europe companies; headquarters in Germany).

James, 40, came to his job in October 1989 from previous positions in marketing and sales at DowBrands and at a southeastern food manufacturer; his most recent assignment had been vice president of Sales for DowBrands. While he had no prior experience in international sales, he was perceived by his colleagues as accomplished, aggressive, and well suited to lead DowBrands into the international arena because of his energy and all-consuming desire to succeed.

He made these comments in the most recent DowBrands newsletter:

> We're going to do about $235 million this year—that's in excess of 20 percent of DowBrands overall sales. But I'm not so concerned about that increasing in terms of percentage as I am in terms of the quality of our business. My vision for the future is that we should, given our size, be considered a multinational company and not a global package good company at this time.
>
> My vision is to build critical mass in the top strategic countries. Strategic countries are those countries that have a large concentrated urban population and gross domestic product and have the type of homemakers that can afford to buy our products. . . . For example, Japan, with half the population of the states and more gross per capita income than the U.S., is a tremendous opportunity. We must stop thinking of Japan as a $20 million market and then go to Taiwan, Korea and Hong Kong, etc. Instead, we ought to think of Japan as a potential $100 million market five years from now and therefore use these other satellite countries to feed that investment. The top strategic countries are the ones that count and the ones that in the long-term will enable us to do other things.

FINDINGS FROM CONSUMER RESEARCH ON THE FCD MARKET IN EUROPE

In the fall of 1987, the U.K. office of DowBrands had conducted a set of comparison "awareness and usage" surveys for fcd products in Great Britain, France, and Germany in order to set priorities for the Ziploc™ opportunities in those three countries. (Spain had been eliminated as a possible candidate in an earlier study.) Data were collected regarding the types of uses for fcds, perceptions regarding strengths and weaknesses of the existing brands of wrappings, and those brands' respective images. About 425 in-depth home interviews conducted in each country asked what had been wrapped (fish, meat, etc.), for where (fridge, freezer, etc.), what material was used (aluminum foil, plastic, etc.), and how frequently respondents usually performed such an action (e.g., "wrapped fish for the freezer with aluminum foil less than three times a month"). A summary report was issued in May 1988; following are selected findings from that report:

Overall, the extrapolated monthly "fcd occasions" ranged from 1.3 billion in Germany to 1.1 billion in the United Kingdom to .8 billion in France. Exhibit 2 gives the extrapolation calculations for this study, Exhibit 3 presents a breakdown by materials and destinations, and

Exhibit 4 is a summary graph of destination and materials combined. (The second part of Exhibit 4 compares the usage of bags in these countries with earlier data from the United States.) As shown in Exhibit 5, the ten most frequently specific uses varied considerably by country.

The researchers clustered respondents psychographically based on their answers to a number of lifestyle questions. The relative size of the six clusters for each country and their use of major fcd materials are shown in Exhibit 6.

Respondents were asked to name what material they would have used as an alternative if the material actually used had not been available (the materials were

EXHIBIT 2
DOWBRANDS
EXTRAPOLATED NUMBER OF MONTHLY
OCCASIONS FOR TOTAL POPULATIONS IN
EACH COUNTRY

	D*	F	GB
Percentage of households represented by survey:	85%	92%	84%
Household universe (millions) represented:	21.9	19.4	17.8
Average number occasions per month, per HW:	80.9	48.3	65.6

EXTRAPOLATED NUMBERS (in millions)

Monthly food-care occasions for the total household population	1,771	937	1,167
• Monthly fcd usage occasions (aluminum, wraps, or bags):	1,332	834	1,063
• Monthly fcd usage occasions using rigid containers or "other" materials:	(439)	(103)	(104)

* "D" was the international symbol for West Germany, "F" is France, and "GB" is Great Britain.

Source: Company records, dated May 1988.

EXHIBIT 3
DOWBRANDS
FCD USAGE OCCASIONS, WEIGHTED
INCIDENCE: SHARES OF THE GRAND TOTAL
NUMBER OF USAGE OCCASIONS/MONTH

	Germany	France	G.B.
	%	%	%
Base 100% =	36,919	21,436	30,816
• MATERIALS:			
Aluminum:	23	56	30
Wraps:	33	14	35
Bags:	17	15	21
Containers:	25	11	13
Other:	2	4	1
	100	100	100
• DESTINATION:	%	%	%
Freezer:	19	21	15
Fridge:	64	62	33
Kitchen:	9	2	6
Oven:	1	4	10
MWO:	–	1	9
Out of home:	7	9	27
	100	100	100

Notes: Kitchen = out in the open in the kitchen

MWO = microwave oven

Source: Company records, dated May 1988.

aluminum, plastic wraps, plastic bags, and rigid containers). In France, the biggest "winner" was rigid containers; in Germany, aluminum; and in Great Britain, aluminum. Plastic bags did not show a material "win" in any country. Exhibit 7 details the substitution data within each country.

A test of "satisfaction with each wrap" compared with use revealed that in France, aluminum foil was highest in use and in satisfaction; in Germany, plastic wrap was highest in use but rigid containers were highest in satisfaction; and in Great Britain, plastic wrap had the highest use but plastic bags had the highest satisfaction, higher than in the other two countries.

In general, homemakers in all three countries displayed average-to-high levels of satisfaction with all materials across the majority of destinations and use occasions. German homemakers tended to be less satisfied with substitutes than those in France and Great Britain. A summary of the three most important material attributes is given in Exhibit 8. A perceptual map of users of each of the fcds in each country is reproduced in Exhibit 9.

Respondents were shown a number of "photoprompts" of the major fcd brands and asked, for a number of image items (e.g., "high quality," "good value for money," etc.), which brands were best or worst for that

EXHIBIT 4
DOWBRANDS
FCD USAGE OCCASIONS SUMMARY

• BY DESTINATIONS & MATERIALS COMBINED   •   USAGE SHARES   •   IN THREE EUROPEAN COUNTRIES

–F

	Aluminum foils	Plastic wraps	Plastic food bags	Rigid containers
Freezer	6	1	11	3
Fridge	29	10	3	4
Kitchen	1			
Cooking	4	1		
Out of the house	7	1		

H.B. : Total = 94%, Excl. "other materials" + occasions < 1%

–D

	Aluminum foils	Plastic wraps	Plastic food bags	Rigid containers
Freezer	4	2	9	4
Fridge	14	27	4	17
Kitchen	1	3	2	2
Cooking	1			
Out of the house	3	1	2	1

H.B. : Total = 87%, Excl. "other materials" + occasions < 1%

–GB

	Aluminum foils	Plastic wraps	Plastic food bags	Rigid containers
Freezer	2	3	8	2
Fridge	9	14	4	6
Kitchen	3	2		1
Cooking	10	7		1
Out of the house	6	9	9	3

H.B. : Total = 90%, Excl. "other materials"

Cooking-conventional or microwave oven

Source: Opportuniry Study, 1987

EXHIBIT 4 (continued)
COMPARISON OF DESTINATION OF BAGS IN FOUR COUNTRIES

	F	D	GB	USA*
Base: (Usage Occasions)	(3,119)	(5,914)	(6,294)	(45,647)
	%	%	%	%
• Fridge	24	27	18	22
• Freezer	76	61	37	14
• Microwave	–	–	1	–
• Oven	–	1	1	–
• Out of home	–	11	43	63
	100	100	100	100

*USA data from diary panel, 1984.

Note: Europe, 1987; United States, 1984.

Source: Company records, dated May 1988.

EXHIBIT 5
DOWBRANDS
RECAP FCD USAGE OCCASIONS:
THE 10 MOST FREQUENT INDIVIDUAL OCCASIONS BY
COUNTRY (WEIGHTED INCIDENCE)

	Germany	France	G.B.
Base 100% =	36,919	21,436	30,816
• Occasions within 10 most frequent in at least 2 countries:	%	%	%
Cheese/fridge	12.7	14.7	7.9
Veg-fruit/fridge	10.4	6.8	3.2
Raw meat/freezer	4.8	7.7	3.1
Bread-cakes/out of house	3.6	2.5	3.1
Veg-fruit/freezer	4.1	4.3	3.6
Raw meat/fridge	2.3	8.6	–
Sandwiches/out of house	–	4.3	21.6
Cooked meat/fridge	–	10.9	6.3
Leftovers/fridge	–	10.7	6.0
• Other frequent occasions specific to one country:			
Deli meat/fridge	18.4		
Bread-cakes/kitchen	6.1		
Bread-cakes/fridge	5.3		
Bread-cakes/freezer	4.5		
Fish/fridge		2.6	
Veg-fruit/microwave			3.1
Raw meat/oven			6.9
TOTAL 'TOP 10'	72.2	73.1	64.8

Source: Company records, dated May 1988.

EXHIBIT 6
DowBRANDS
USAGE OF MATERIAL TYPES BY CLUSTER GROUPS

Cluster sizes:		NF	EG	HO	OP	EXP	RE
	D	13	16	16	20	12	23
	F	18	15	23	14	16	14
	GB	12	18	38	14	9	9
ALU							
	D index:	99	47	118	91	128	118
	share:	13	8	19	18	15	27
	F index:	123	109	82	77	130	80
	share:	22	16	19	11	21	11
	GB index:	76	93	106	104	134	84
	share:	9	17	40	15	12	8
WRAPS							
	D index:	84	84	89	138	113	87
	share:	11	13	14	28	14	20
	F index:	83	103	113	48	142	100
	share:	15	15	26	7	23	14
	GB index:	73	98	84	125	113	159
	share:	9	18	32	18	10	14
BAGS							
	D index:	46	58	99	121	108	137
	share:	6	9	16	24	13	32
	F index:	61	69	97	101	131	156
	share:	11	10	22	14	21	22
	GB index:	96	82	96	113	60	178
	share:	12	15	36	16	5	16

An earlier Awareness and Usage study uncovered six cluster groups based on an analysis of the pattern of respondents' answers. The groups were described as follow:

RE = *Role Enhancer*
High positive association with all items relating to home cooking, make own foods, home care, etc., but negative with "spend most of the day away from home." High awareness and usage of fcd brands. (Not found in Spain.)

EXP = *Experimentalist*
High purchase of recently launched products. Tend to be "away from home most of day." High microwave ownership.

OP = *Own Produce Preserver*
High scores for freezing produce grown by self or bought directly from producer. Not experimental. High deep freezer ownership.

HO = *Home Oriented*
High scores for "home" and "cooking" items. Not necessarily high for "freezing." Tend to be non-working.

EG = *Easy Going*
Lowest scores for home-oriented items. Tendency to score low on freezing items. Often spend day away from home. Youngest group.

NF = *Non Freezing*
Lowest scores on freezing items. May have high home-oriented scores. Low freezer ownership. Older group, lower social class.

The box on the previous page shows the percentage of each cluster by country (e.g., the NF cluster represents 13% of the German sample but 18% of the French sample). An index is the ratio of a cluster's share of usage compared to its size (e.g., the NF cluster in France uses 22% of aluminum which, compared with its 18% of the sample, yields an index of 123.)

Source: Company records, dated May 1988.

(*Note:* See following page for explanatory notes)

EXHIBIT 7
DOWBRANDS
SUBSTITUTION BETWEEN MATERIALS

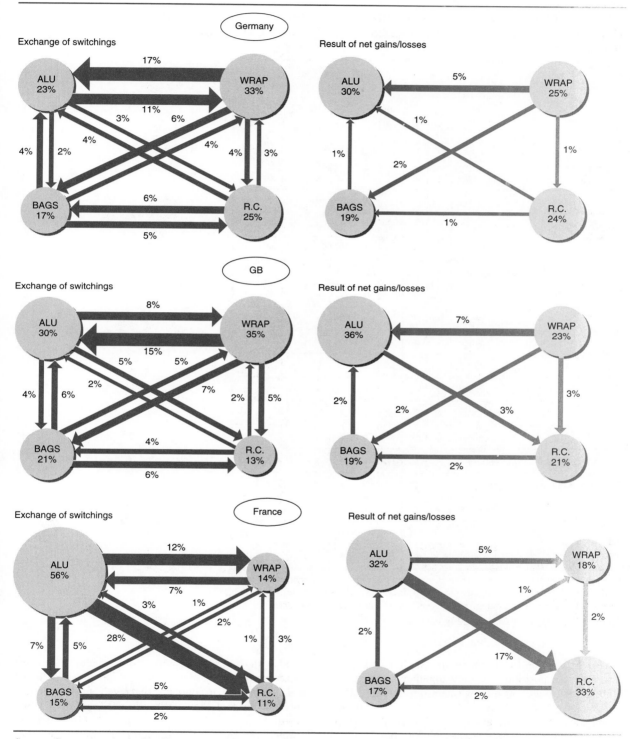

Source: Company records, dated May 1988.

EXHIBIT 8
DOWBRANDS
IMPORTANCE OF FCD MATERIAL ATTRIBUTES IN THREE
EUROPEAN COUNTRIES (% FOR LEAST, SECOND/THIRD, MOST
IMPORTANT)*

	Least			Second/third			Most		
Important attribute in	F	D	GB	F	D	GB	F	D	GB
Keeps food fresh and tasty				●	●	●	•	●	●
Isolates odors well	•	•	•	●	●	•	•	•	•
Easy to handle	•	•	•	●	•	•	•	●	•
Very higienic		•		●	•	•	•	●	•
Airtight closure	•	•	•	•	•	●	•	•	•
Space saving	•	•	•	●	●	•	•	•	•
Prevents food spoiling		•		•	●	•	•	•	•
Resistant	•		•	•	●	•	•	●	•
Moisture proof	•	•	•	•	•	•	•	•	•
Safe with all foods	•			•	•	●	•	•	•
Good value for money	•	•	•	•	•	•	•	•	•
Can recognize contents	•	●	•	●	•	•	•	•	•
Inexpensive	•	•	●	•	•	•	•	•	•
Adapts itself well around shapes	•	●	•	•	•	•	•	•	•
Stays in place once wrapped	•	●	•	•	•	●	•	•	•
Easy to dispense	•	•	•	•	•	•	•	•	•
Safe for the environment	•	•	•	•	•			•	
Re-useable	●	●	●	•	●	•		•	•

*The sizes of the circles are relative to "keeps food fresh & tasty" in Germany, which received the greatest percentage response across all questions and countries.
Source: Company records, dated May 1988.

image or feature. In Germany, the Melitta and Frapan brands were positioned closely together at the quality end of the high/low quality spectrum for all fcds; in France, again for all fcds, the Propsac, Handy Bag, Sopalin, and Albal (foil and bags only) brands were perceived as "national brands with high availability"; not surprisingly, the major brands in all countries were associated with "high availability," and retailers' (private) brands were associated with "not available everywhere." In all countries, respondents perceived most positively those brands that they "currently use" and/or the one they designated as the "leading brand." In Great Britain, however, retailers' brands often had a good image, especially with respect to "good value for the money."

EXHIBIT 9
DOWBRANDS
IMAGES OF FCD MATERIALS

ANALYSIS OF CORRESPONDENCE BASED ON USERS OF ALUMINIUM FOIL (A), PLASTIC WRAP (W), PLASTIC FOOD BAGS (B), PERMANENT (PC) AND DISPOSABLE (DC) RIGID CONTAINERS IN EACH COUNTRY. AXIS 1 (VERT.) AND 2 (HOR.) VARIANCE EXPLAINED = 86%

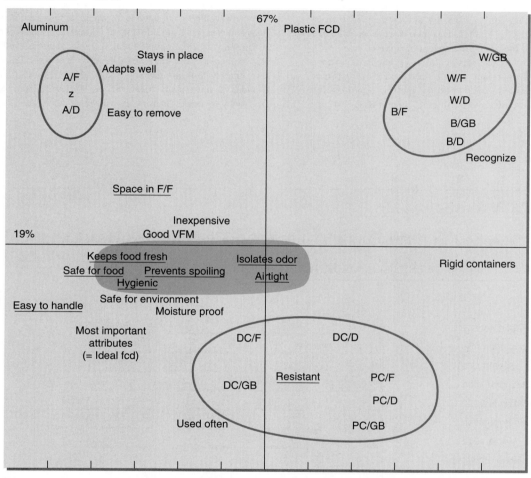

Source: Company records, dated May 1988.

In general, the researchers concluded that the greatest opportunity for Ziploc™ in Great Britain was for the sandwich-bag market, but in France and Germany, it was for Ziploc™ freezer bags. They were encouraged that one of the most important fcd attributes discovered for all countries was "airtight closure," a major Ziploc™ selling feature; they also noted the importance given to "keeping food fresh and tasty" and "isolating odors well."

THE DECISION

James was familiar with the marketing research results, but he felt that they might not provide enough support for launching an aggressive Ziploc™ program in Europe:

As detailed and well executed as it is, the research only shows that there is promise in Europe, especially in the large markets of France, Germany, and the U.K. It has the usual defect in that it shows more about what *is* with respect to current products and segments than what *might be* the prospects for an emerging premium segment. The detailed study was not carried out in Spain, since refrigerators tend to be small and freezers non-existent, and everyday shoppers apparently don't perceive the need for the superior protection of Ziploc™. And frankly, this is the attitude that some of our people still have about food-shopping habits even in France and Germany. So, you can picture the resistance I am getting from my management in Europe against making the kind of investment spends we will need to do to build the premium segment of zippered bags.

We have to use imagination: we might have done more research in Spain, and we should do it in the rest of Europe, all with an open mind for spotting opportunities. When you ask customers to relate current usage to new ideas, they have great difficulty in doing that. I wonder if the typical A&U [attitude and usage] studies are up to the task. What they do is to give my European management the wrong kind of ammunition. And these people remind me that we can't expect the same high profit margins abroad that we have here in the States and that start-up expenses will be high. But even with a lower margin in Europe, I still see Ziploc™ improving the overall margin mix after the expenses of the sell-in are absorbed. . . .

How would I go? I need to hammer, hammer, hammer my vision. Perhaps I should set up a "President of Ziploc™" in Europe. The Glad people there are not convinced; with $130 million in sales, they don't need it. They say, "Look how long it took to develop the Ziploc™ business in Canada." I must show them success stories in Europe. That's why we bought Europe, and now it's time to act.

APPENDIX A ◆

DOWBRANDS SELECTED DATA ON MAJOR EUROPEAN MARKETS*

DEMOGRAPHIC PROFILES OF THE 5 MAJOR EUROPEAN COUNTRIES

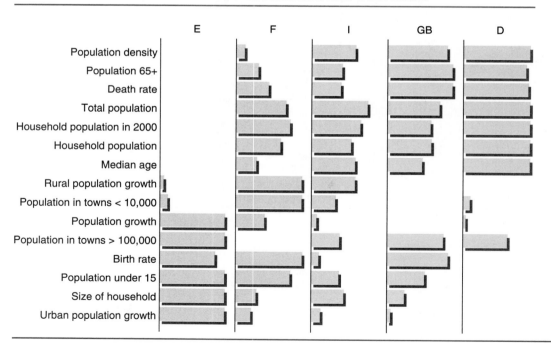

Notes: * See definition of each indicator in data table below.

* The graph above highlights differences along countries by using, for each indicator, the minimum and maximum values as the edge of constant scale.

	E	F	I	GB	D	USA
Population density Pers/Km2.1948	78	102	131	233	245	26
Population 65+%, 1984	12.8	13.6	14.0	15.5	15.3	12.3
Death rate Deaths per 1,000, 1944	8.3	10.1	8.8	11.8	11.7	8.8
Total population Millions	39.2	55.8	57.5	54.8	81.0	248.8
Household popul in 2000 Estimated Millions	15.2	23.8	23.1	22.1	25.8	184.4
Household population Millions, 1967	11.7	21.1	20.4	21.2	25.8	94.5
Median Age 1988	32.5	34.3	36.2	35.5	38.2	32.4
Rural population growth Av. annual 1940–86	−1.7	−2	−.5	−1.8	−1.8	.7
Population in towns < 10,000 %	26	50	33	23	26	NA
Population growth Total % Change 1964–80	33	19	10	8	9	33
Population in towns > 100,000 %	42	16	27	38	33	NA
Birth rate Births per 1,000, 1968	13.1	13.6	11.0	13.4	10.8	15.3
Population under 15% 1984	21.7	20.4	17.7	18.7	14.7	21.5
Size of household Av. number of persons	3.76	2.77	3.04	2.72	2.31	2.87
Urban population growth AV. Annual 1980–86	1.4	.4	−.3	−.2	−.1	.2

Source: Trends & Opportunities abroad, 1984 American Demographics Inc. IBM 87, European Basic Market Data, G.F.K.

*"E" is the international symbol for Spain and "I" for Italy.

SOCIOECONOMIC PROFILES OF THE 5 MAJOR EUROPEAN COUNTRIES AND THE USA

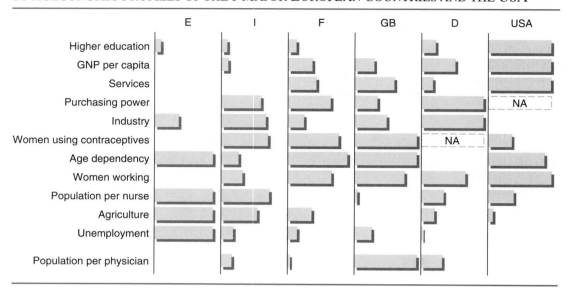

Notes: * See definition of each indicator in data table below.

    * The graph above highlights differences along countries by using, for each indicator, the minimum values as the edge of constant scale

    * The indicator population per physican is isolated because of the peculiarity shown.

	E	F	I	GB	D	USA
Higher education enrollement in	26	25	27	20	29	57
GNP per capita $	4.290	8.520	8.540	8.460	10.940	16.650
Services % labor force 84	46	48	56	59	50	84
Index Purchasing power 1994 (100-Av. 16 European countries)	57	109	112	48	133	NA
Industry % labor force in	37	41	35	38	44	31
Women using contraceptives married 16–40	59	78	79	83	NA	88
Aged dependency Ratio (6 of 0–14 & 86% aged 15–44)	52	46	52	52	43	51
Women working % women 14–44 working	27	41	53	56	52	62
Population per nurse	280	250	110	120	170	180
Agriculture % labor force in	17	12	9	3	8	4
Unemployment rate 1986	22.0	10.8	9.8	11.5	7.5	7.1
Population per physician	39.0	75.0	480	1,881	420	500

FOODCARE APPLIANCES OWNERSHIP—1987
IN THE FIVE MAJOR EUROPEN COUNTRIES BY MULTI-OWNERSHIP GROUPS

Country (household millions) →	D (25.8)	GB (21.2)	F (21.1)	I (20.4)	E (11.7)
None of the three appliances	3	2	3		3
Fridge only	20	21	25	20	
Combined fridge-freezer only	18	33	30	59	52
Separate freezer only	49	36	29	9	41
Both types of freezers	10	8	12	12	3

% Housewives owning

	D	I	GB	F	E
Separate deep freezer	(59)	(44)	(41)	21	4
Combined fridge-freezer	28	(41)	(42)	(71)	(42)
Any freezer	(77)	(77)	(72)	(80)	48

Source: Company records dated April, 1988

APPENDIX B ◆

DOWBRANDS SELECTED DETAILS OF FIRST BRANDS/EUROPE STRENGTHS, 1989

FRANCE

First Brands/Europe has a solid No. 2 position in the $300 million French market, the largest food care/disposables market in Europe. And at just under 12 percent growth over the last four years, France is Europe's second fastest growing market. FBE's sales force has done a good job in getting its products onto French supermarket shelves and the consumer awareness of the Albal brand is the best among all fcd brands in France. FBE's French business originated with the acquisition of the Albal trademark from the French national aluminum company in 1985. Following this, FBE added plastic wraps and bags into what was previously an aluminum-based business. FBE's plastics business and its overall share of the French market have grown steadily ever since.

SPAIN

Spain's fcd market is $60 million and is the fastest growing European market at over 12 percent a year. FBE has become increasingly enthusiastic about the growing Spanish market and purchased the operating business from its distributor in October 1988. They are the market leader with Albal in aluminum and with Glad in wraps and bags.

PREMIUM BAGS

FBE launched a zipper-closure food bag in France in late 1987, under the brand name AlbaZip. This product is identical to the colored-zipper Glad Lock product which competes with Ziploc™ in America. This market is still very small, but after only months on the market, AlbaZip has already captured more than half of the premium food bag market. The key competitors, by the way, are utilizing bags with the outdated Mini-Grip-style zipper. Both the Ziploc™ and the Glad Lock closures (used on AlbaZip) are overwhelmingly preferred by the consumer.

FBE has also recently launched a premium drawstring trash bag into France called Lock-Up. Premium trash bags represent a promising growth area for us throughout Europe.

COMPETITORS

There are no dominant leaders across the continent [see table attached]. Only FBE has a major position in more than one country. The significant role played by private labels is evident, especially in the UK and, to a lesser extent, in France. FBE is a major private label supplier in Germany (and also in France and in Spain). Melitta's dominant share in Germany gives it the overall lead in these five markets. When combined with our strong position in Italy, the marriage of FBE and Domopak not only puts us in a solid position in three of the five key Western European markets, but it also positions DowBrands well to compete effectively in Europe 1992.

Source: Company records, dated 11/23/88.

WESTERN EUROPE COMPETITIVE ENVIRONMENT, 1987

	France ($360M)		United Kingdom ($281M)		Germany ($245M)		Italy ($163M)		Spain ($60M)	
	Leaders	Share	Leaders	Share	Leaders	Share	Leaders	Share	Leaders	Share
ELF/Aquitaine (Handy Bag)		22%	Polylina	17%	Melitta	45%	Cuki	22%	FBE	37%
FBE		12	Br. Alcan	11	Pely	6	Domopak	21	Reynolds	21
Akzo (Propsac)		11	HD. Plastics	3	Kraft	5	Comiset	2		
Private Label		36%		65%		22%		N/A		N/A

Share of Total 5 Countries	
Melitta	10.8%
Elf/Aquitaine	6.3
FBE	8.6
Domopak	8.2
Private Label	32.7
Total	66.6%

Source: Company records, dated 11/23/88.

CASE 4

NOVA INCORPORATED: TWO SOURCING OPPORTUNITIES

After notifying his management team of their assignments for the following week's meeting, Fisher contemplates taking a short vacation, and, perhaps, reacquaint-

This case was developed by Profs. Jack Muckstadt, School of Operations Research and Industrial Engineering, Cornell University; David Murray, Operations and Information Technology, School of Business, College of William & Mary; Dennis G. Severance, Computers and Information Systems, The University of Michigan; and K. Scott Swan, Marketing and International Business, School of Business, College of William & Mary. © 2000 For discussion purposes only: None of this material is to be quoted or reproduced without the expressed permission of the authors.

ing himself with the game of golf. As he is preparing to leave, he receives two memos. The first is from Claudio Spiguel, requesting authority to purchase all products for South America from a local source. The second is from Wei Chang, the president of the Asia Pacific region, seeking permission to conduct negotiations that would lead to joint manufacturing and distribution ventures in India and China. After reading these memos, he sends copies of them to his management team asking them for advice, and informing them that they should be prepared to discuss both issues at next week's meeting.

Copies of Chang's and Spiguel's memos are attached.

Nova Manufacturing, Inc.
"Your Global Assembly Supplier"

MEMORANDUM

To: John Fisher, CEO

From: Wei Chang, President, Nova Asia Pacific

Date: June 17, 2000

Subject: Implications For Market Growth Opportunities In The Asia Pacific Region

For the past year you have encouraged me to grow my business substantially. After careful analysis of the opportunities in this region I have concluded that it is possible to dramatically increase sales over the next five years. In fact, I believe it is likely that we can increase business by a factor of ten. While this may sound optimistic, I am confident that we can achieve this level of growth.

I have spent several months making contacts in both India and China and have succeeded in establishing appropriate government and industry ties in both countries. As I toured these countries, I found that there is an enormous requirement for our products driven by the explosive growth in construction in both countries.

Two reasons make it possible for us to penetrate these markets First, the local production of widget equivalents is limited, since the technology for modern widget manufacturing is not known in these places. The outdated production methods, which are both capital and labor intensive, have made growth in domestic production capacity appear unprofitable. Thus, the governments are eager for us to provide our products to them. Second, the quality of the current local supply is very poor. Where the domestically prduced widgets are used, their reliability and durability are a source of great concern to their users. In fact, numerous accidents have resulted from the poor product design and manufacturing processes. Our reputation for high quality is therefore a major source of competitive advantage for us.

To date, our major competitors have not succeeded in penetrating these markets, in spite of several concerted attempts to do so. I suspect that their lack of success so far is due to their failure to appreciate the distinctive cultures of these countries, and how business must be transacted within them. Nonetheless, our competitors are active and their products are also well regarded.

For us to compete successfully in these markets, we must have technical support, low prices (much lower than our current ones), and high quality and reliable supply. Furthermore, it is important to understand the limitations of the logistics infrastructure in these countries. The major consumers of widgets are not located in places that can be reliably resupplied from port cities or by air.

I believe that for us to compete, we must undertake joint ventures for manufacturing and distribution in both countries. The reason for this is twofold: first, to be price competitive we must take advantage of the low labor costs that are available in both India and China, and we must avoid the tariffs and overheads associated with transporting and importing products from London or Cincinnati. The second reason that we must have a manufacturing presence is to gain access to distribution channels. Both governments are looking for technology transfer, and have made it clear that without licensing our product and process technologies to a locally owned partner, they will be of little help in providing market access. It would, of course, be folly for us to attempt to build a marketing, sales, and distribution infrastructure from scratch, and totally on our own. Accordingly, I have begun preliminary discussions with the appropriate government and industry officials and have identified potential joint venture partners.

I have also gathered preliminary cost data, and estimate that we can produce and sell products with a 40 percent margin at a cost basis equal to 60 percent of the current transfer price. I have taken the cost of capital, labor, transportation facilities and land into account when making these calculations. I estimate that our return on net assets (RONA) will be approximately 55 percent.

This is an opportunity that we cannot ignore. We must act soon or others will seize it. I would like permission to pursue detailed negotiations so that we can begin production within a year. Of course, I will submit a Capital Appropriations Request for formal approval once you agree in principle with the project. I will also need technical support from both Julie Anderson and Jerry Jackson to set up the manufacturing and technical information system, and assistance from our legal department in working out the licensing agreements.

I look forward to seeing you at our next meeting, and to discussing my idea with you in greater detail at that time.

Nova Manufacturing, Inc.
"Your Global Assembly Supplier"

MEMORANDUM

To: John Fisher, CEO
From: Claudio Spiguel, President, Nova South America
Date: June 18, 2000
Subject: Maintaining Customer Service and Improving Nova Profitability

Attached is a copy of your recent memo on **Customer Service and Cost** as well as a copy of Larry Judge's memo on **Lean Production**. Sometimes it takes a combination of reminders like this to shake us loose from old habits and to drive home the point that we can't make marginal changes if we seek major improvements. Let me explain.

First, I am sure that my South America operations were a significant contributor to your memo. Recently we have been maintaining generous amounts of inventory of finished goods in an attempt to provide superior service to our customers. In addition, we have found that deliveries from Cincinnati and London have been more reliable. As a result, we have succeeded in providing excellent service, which has led to a substantial growth in our business. While I knew at the time I decided to increase my cycle stock and safety stock levels that costs would rise, I believed that it was the right thing to do for our customers.

Then later, Larry Judge's memo on RONA arrived. It reminded me that customer service was not the only goal for Nova managers. Making a "fair profit" for our share holders on the assets they had provided us with was also important. Since inventories are the greatest of the assets under my local control and their holding costs contribute heavily to our operating expense, inventory reduction is my key lever for RONA improvement. I am torn between the goals of reducing inventory and maintaining a high level of customer service. When I improve one the other gets worse.

When I shared this dilemma with a cousin who runs a manufacturing firm here in São Paulo, he asked for a sample of each of the products that Nova sells in South America. After reverse engineering our ten products, he designed a manufacturing process to build each and lined up a set of local suppliers. He has now offered me the following contract. If I guarantee to purchase all Nova products sold in South America during the next five years from him, he will make the capital investment required to manufacture them. He will sell them to us at our current Nova transfer price, quoted in dollars to eliminate Nova's exposure to Brazilian currency fluctuation, and he will guarantee the price for three years (which Cincinnati will not do for me). Moreover, he will require no minimum order size and he will guarantee one day delivery of any order quantity up to 2 percent of annual demand. Finally, he will pay all transportation costs and will guarantee that product quality will meet or exceed Nova's existing standards.

This is the answer to a prayer. He will own the pipeline stock, and I will need only two days of safety stock and about a day of cycle stock. My fill rates will remain very high and my transportation costs will be negligible. From your perspective, the risk of profit erosion from the wild currency fluctuations that we have experienced in recent years will be eliminated. I estimate that my RONA bonus will exceed 40 percent and he feels that he will make an acceptable profit. This is a win-win-win situation.

Do I have your approval to sign the contract and proceed with this new alliance?

Nova Manufacturing, Inc.
"Your Global Assembly Supplier"

MEMORANDUM

To: All Nova Distribution Center Managers

From: John Fisher, CEO

Date: June 1, 2000

Subject: Customer Service and Cost

In the last two weeks I ran into a board member and then a college classmate, who each informed me that during the past 6 months their companies had increased their purchases of our products. They were amazed at the increase in our ability to serve them given that in the past we always were late and erratic in our shipping performance. Without having details on products, regions and dates, they assured me that what was a problem is now a real strategic advantage for us. They wondered how we moved from last to first as a supplier in their industry.

While you all should be commended for following my instructions to improve customer service, recognize that our costs have risen to the point where the increased demand and service reduces profitability. Let me be blunt. Unless we can maintain the improved service levels at substantially lower operating costs, we will be out of business. You must reduce your expenses—transportation, holding, and other overhead costs. Our "success" at increased customer service has caused the additional problem of consistent overtime at factories that degrades factory performance through increased scrap rates, increased setup times, and expedited transportation. At the management committee meeting this month, we will review your plans and progress.

Nova Manufacturing, Inc.
"Your Global Assembly Supplier"

MEMORANDUM

To: All Nova Distribution Center Managers
From: Larry Judge, CFO
Date: June 8, 2000
Subject: Lean Production

To survive in our increasingly competitive business environment, it is imperative that we all strive continuously to improve financial performance. Return on net assets, RONA, is a traditional and important measure of the effectiveness with which productive assets are deployed by a company's management. I have therefore decided to establish last year's RONA numbers as a benchmark for company performance. Hereafter, monthly RONA numbers at each location will be used as a barometer to measure performance improvement as we move forward during the year.

I have calculated your 1999 RONA and will tie your compensation to your ability to improve it in 2000. The company improvement goal of 10 percent *must be* met by all locations. Managers who exceed this goal will receive a salary bonus percentage equal to twice their percentage improvement beyond 4 percent. I know you will each do the right thing.

Based on the financial data from Nova, the results of *pro forma* numerical analysis for each of the four alternative sourcing strategies are provided in Table 1. The numbers represent expected return on net assets (RONA) at various points in the company's sourcing operations. Additional qualitative issues that need to be considered are summarized in Table 2.

TABLE 1
NUMERICAL ANALYSIS

	(a) Current In-house Production/ No change RONA	(b) Outsource/ No change to bonus structure RONA	(c) In-house Production/ Transfer price change RONA	(d) In-house Production/ N. American factory payment to S. America (Rebate) RONA
Distribution Centers				
N. America	14.67%	14.67%	42.52%	14.67%
Euro. Union	11.08	11.08	11.08	11.08
E. Bloc Euro	9.09	9.09	9.09	9.09
S. America	5.24	17.92	17.92	17.92
Asia Pacific	7.38	7.38	7.38	7.38
Factories				
Cincinnati, Ohio	12.86	− 6.62	− 1.49	8.25
London, UK	20.80	20.80	20.80	20.80
Nova Corp				
Cincinnati Margin	13.21	8.77	13.40	13.21
N.A. rebate	12.11	− 10.32	− 3.18	12.11
				$734,500

TABLE 2
QUALITATIVE ANALYSIS

	(a) No change	(b) Outsource	(c) Transfer price	(d) NA rebate
Benefits				
Customer Service	Doing well but very expensive	Similar service	Accounting change	Accounting change
Internal Operations	Maintain internal	Less expensive. Frees manufacturing capacity for other opportunities. Less overtime.	Treat as "short" relationship—why penalize because factory in Cincinnati artifact?	Treat as "short" relationship—why penalize because factory in Cincinnati artifact?
Innovation, etc.	Maintain ability to innovate and learn	Learning opportunity?		
Financial Performance	No manipulation of transfer pricing		Improve RONA through transfer pricing	
Risks				
Customer Service		Quality concerns		
Internal Operations	Demotivate DC managers with innovative solutions?	Loss of process and product secrets. How to deal with Cincinnati factory RONA?	How to deal with distortion in NA DC RONA? No real change How to deal with Cincinnati factory RONA?	No real change. How to deal with Cincinnati factory RONA?
Innovation, etc.		Loss of innovation & learning? Improved adaptability?		
Financial Performance	Transfer pricing gains lost	Large RONA hit to corporate		

Discussion Questions

1. Evaluate the risks and rewards of internationalization/globalization through cooperative strategies via the opportunities to (1) enter into joint ventures in China and India in exchange for licenses to NOVA's process and product technology and (2) outsource manufacturing in Brazil.

2. Discuss market orientation in the context of sourcing strategies: "How do we assure that we provide our customers the right product/service at the right place, at the right time, at the right price, at our best total cost?

3. Raise some fundamental questions about core competencies and company identity:

- "Why do we manufacture anything internally?"

- "Where is our value-added?"

- "How do we capture and share information that will enable the required communication, coordination, cooperation, and control among value-chain partners?"

CASE 5

SHISEIDO COMPANY, LTD.: FACING GLOBAL COMPETITION

INTRODUCTION

Shiseido was founded by Yushin Fukuhara as Japan's first Western-style pharmacy in 1872, and has shifted its focus back and forth between cosmetics and pharmaceuticals since 1915. Its strength in both areas has enabled it to weather the Great Earthquake of 1923 and World War II. It leads the cosmetic industry technologically, and has offered Japan many "firsts" in products.

It introduced Japan to its first toothpaste in 1888. In 1902, Shiseido introduced Japan's first soda fountain/drugstore. Three years later, it established the chain store system, which became the backbone of the firm and the standard distribution system for the industry.

Shiseido began international expansion in 1957 and is currently represented by 17 subsidiaries and more than 8,700 outlets in 69 countries. Offshore production accounts for about 50 percent of its global sales, which amounted to 64.9 billion yen in fiscal 1997.

In 1987, Yoshiharu Fukuhara, grandson of the founder, took over as president. The same year, Shiseido announced a 6 percent decrease in sales and a write-off in inventory worth $239 million; net income fell 34 percent to $72 million. The company also abolished separate sales volume budgeting for sales companies and retail outlets, which had been faulted for the tendency of salesmen to push sales to retailers in order to meet in-house quotas. The 1998 product mix consisted of cosmetics (74% of sales), fine toiletries (16%), and other businesses (10%).

With the implementation of the "Global No.1" long-term vision, Shiseido identified three goals: technological excellence, diversified operations, and customer satisfaction. It continued to streamline domestic cosmetics lines to reduce inventory, eliminating products with a consistent turnover, while developing new technology and items.

This case was prepared by Narin Sihavong and Erik Surono of the University of Hawaii at Manoa under the supervision of Masaaki Kotabe of the Fox School of Business and Management at Temple University for class discussion rather than to illustrate either effective or ineffective management of a situation described (August 1999).

THE ORGANIZATION

Corporate Philosophy

Shiseido's basic management policies for the twenty-first century are embodied in its "Global No.1" long-term vision. While most CEOs might define No.1 as being top in terms of revenues or market share, Fukuhara equates the number-one ranking with quality-dedicated people making sophisticated products and providing high level of customer service. If you do this, he reasons, sales, market share and profits will follow naturally.

Shiseido interprets the "benefit desired by customers" as the "desire, of customers, for enhanced beauty." Shiseido's mission as a company is to accelerate and reinforce its efforts to provide such customer benefits. *The Shiseido Way* is a charter of principles guiding the company activities. This charter incorporates its ideas and determination to work together with its customers, business partners, shareholders, employees, and society. Its determination to work with shareholders is clearly defined in its stated desire to "strive to earn the understanding and responsiveness of all shareholders and other investors, by achieving appropriate and sound business performances, based on high-quality growth, and by pursuing transparent corporate policies."

Research and Development

Shiseido has placed central importance on research and development since opening the Shiseido Chemistry Research Laboratories in 1939. Shiseido's president, Fukuhara, stressed the strong commitment towards R&D, "We are all trying to achieve a greater understanding of body and soul synergy. It all start with research." Shiseido employs around 1,000 people globally in R&D-related positions. In the fiscal year 1998, its R&D investments reached nearly 4 percent of nonconsolidated net sales, illustrating the company's commitment to creating new value for its product. Shiseido's research and development are a major strength of the firm, yet only about 5 percent of its products are patented.

Shiseido maintains R&D facilities in each major region around the world. These are networked to form a global R&D system. In Japan, it operates the Research

Center (1) and Research Center (2), as well as the Institute of Beauty Sciences and the Beauty Creation Center. The two research centers, in particular, adopt a diversified and global approach and work jointly with R&D entities in Japan and overseas, conducting comprehensive research in human science.

In 1989, the company established the Harvard Cutaneous Biology Research Center—the first of its kind in the world—in partnership with Massachusetts General Hospital at the Harvard Medical School, which has documented the biological relationship between the nervous system and the immune system. Also located in the United States are the R&D Center of Zotos International and the Shiseido America Techno-Center. In Paris, it operates the Shiseido Europe Techno-Center. With these facilities, it is steadily building a global R&D network.

Environmental Protection

In 1990, Shiseido was the pioneer in the Japanese cosmetics industry in eliminating chlorofluorocarbons from its aerosol lines. In 1992, it formulated the *Shiseido Ecopolicy*, a set of action plans covering the environmental protection efforts of all its divisions.

By 2001, it plans to eliminate the use of polyvinyl chloride in its product containers and packaging and raise the level of industrial waste recycling to 60 percent. This would result in a 50 percent reduction in unusable waste.

By 2011, it plans to cut carbon dioxide emissions by 15 percent on a basic unit scale from 1991 levels. Moreover, it is on schedule for obtaining the ISO 14001 certification, an international standard for environmental management, for its domestic production facilities by 1999 and for its overseas facilities by 2001.

MARKETING ISSUES

When Shiseido marketing managers discuss their marketing system, they do not use the conventional four Ps approach. Their framework consists of the distribution (store), product, and communications concept. In line with this approach, the company's "innovative marketing concepts" include brand marketing, store marketing, and area marketing.

Product Line

Shiseido introduces at least one new product to the domestic market each month and tries to span the entire market. Shiseido offers about 3,000 products, which is 30 percent greater than Kanebo, its close competitor. Its main products are in cosmetics and toiletries. It pro-

motes basic products (the cleanser, lotion, and milky lotion) and personal products (such as those addressing wrinkles and other specific problems or needs) for each customer.

In 1996, Shiseido concentrated its efforts on revamping or expanding the Revital, UV White, Whitesse, Premier, and Cle-de-Peau lines. Also anticipating growth in the domestic fragrance market, Shiseido introduced its "import" fragrance Chant de Coeur, which is manufactured in France. The company also emphasized *Brand Marketing*, which is an establishment of individual identities for each of the principal product lines described above.

Major brands currently promoted are Elserie, PJ Rapis (Perky Jean), Premier, Recientem and Revital, which are aimed at certain age groups. UV White, Whitesse, Cle de Peau, Inoue, Whitia, and Lordes Neues are aimed at specific personal needs. The three top selling lines for women are New Elixir, UV White, and Revital, while the top lines for men are Auzleze, Bravas, and Flowline.

Since 1986, Shiseido has launched the inexpensive Cosmenity lines and four brands, collectively referred to as out-of-Shiseido products, which do not carry the Shiseido name. Cosmenity items pass through the nonselective route to address the needs of customers seeking more affordable, easy-to-use products. For example, Ipsa (the out-of-Shiseido line product) is independently displayed in Tokyo department stores such as Isetan and has become very successful.

Distribution

Forty years ago, Shiseido's relationship with wholesalers was discontinued. Currently, the majority of Shiseido's cosmetics are distributed through the selective system. With the establishment of its chain store system, Shiseido's efforts extended to consulting, merchandising, sales corner development, and other marketing areas. Through the mutually dependent relationship with the chain store, Shiseido was able to achieve a consistent image and establish itself in the premium market. Shiseido currently has contracts with about 25,000 exclusive stores nationwide. Contracts, including conditions for consultation sales, sales strategies, and inventory, management, are renegotiated each year. Shiseido divides its customer base into five different life stages or age groups, with which it targets different brands. Therefore, these stores are ranked according to sales of Shiseido products in five different classes. The higher the class, the more benefits the store receives from Shiseido such as greater rebates, more beauty consultant support and more samples for customers.

As consumer needs have shifted to self-selection products (as opposed to those requiring counseling), Shiseido has had to reconsider its strategies and seems to have focused most of its attention on the retail store and retail marketing strategies. *Store marketing* refers to the creation of clear operating concepts and the development of individual identities of chain stores. The chain store division within Shiseido, including one section for "Shop Designing and Store Promotion Planning," has worked to develop "software," shop concepts. Working with the advertising section, it has developed "hardware," POP (point of purchase) displays and other merchandising tools for the stores.

Communication with Customers

Advertising. Shiseido is unique in that it has established and maintained in-house advertising. Often a model or artist is consistently used in the advertisement to create an image for a product. The use of well-known artists such as Ezumi Mariko, Koizumi Kyoko, and Yamaguchi Tomoko, suggests that Shiseido cosmetics are for women who resemble or would like to resemble the artists in age, style, and so on. As a result of increasing competition, Shiseido is moving toward a blend of its traditional romantic style to a more practical, informational style for certain products, while turning to outside ad agencies such as Dentsu for some toiletries advertisements.

Shiseido invests heavily in local advertising, especially through television (60% of advertising expenses) and magazines (25%). Selling and general expenses rose rapidly by 7.2% in 1999 to ¥372.9 billion ($3.24 billion) due to expansion of advertising and promotional expenses.

Membership Club. The Hanatsubaki or Camellia Club provides another means of communication to its customers. Membership lists provide the store with names and addresses for direct mail follow-up. Members also receive notice of special promotions and a copy of the club magazine. Camellia Club members account for an estimated 70 percent of domestic sales.

Shiseido also supplies tools to help retailers maintain information on customers and to communicate with customers. Shop owners use the Hanatsubaki Club notebook to keep track of its members. The Kizuna Karute (Customer/Patient Chart) includes forms for names and addresses as well as lifestyle information, suggestions, and advice sheets. The advice according to the lifestyle card, includes forms for housewives, working women, and sportswomen. Publications like the Beauty Circle offer customers season-specific beauty advice, and general beauty tips.

Shiseido has also started the Elserie Club for high school students. Members can attend one-day beauty school classes and receive free samples and mailings. They, in turn, provide information to the company by filling out questionnaires.

Shiseido Representatives. A major means of communication is through MAs (merchandising advisors, or salesmen), MALs (merchandising advisor ladies), BCs (beauty consultants), and other representatives from the sales companies. MAs and MALs visit shops, for which they are responsible, one to five times a week. BCs are assigned to shops to help perform facials, set up displays, and assist customers and shop owners.

In addition, storeowners attend Tento Katsudo Seminars on new products once a month and selected storeowners chosen as CLs (Counseling Leaders) attend special seminars on sales strategies. Retailers learn how to give advice to consumers regarding Shiseido products. As the concept of beauty inside and out spreads, counseling content has extended to health and fitness as well. Through these channels, information flows from the research center of Shiseido to the customer.

Regional Center and Consumer Communication Center. Information gathered through various routes mentioned above could aid greatly in *area marketing*, which refers to the matching of the store and its regional products to the region and its characteristics. Shiseido's 15 regional sales companies gather market information regarding consumers in their areas, which are used for product development, marketing, production, and distribution plans. In this, each sales company branch identifies core spots to target within their territory. In response to the increasingly individualized and diversified needs of customers and the rapid social changes fueled by the growing importance of information, Shiseido will soon establish a *Consumer Communication Center* and build a framework to facilitate creation and transmission of new values via real-time, two-way communication.

Target Consumer and Competition

Target Consumer. Shiseido divides its target into five stages, according to age. Stage I includes women ages 15–17, which accounts for about 2 percent of sales. Stage II includes women ages 18–24, accounting for about 14 percent of sales. Stage III runs from ages 25–34 (17 percent) and almost 50 percent of sales are made to women in Stage IV, ages 35–54. Stage V includes women ages upwards of 55 years.

Women account for about 85 percent of sales versus men who account for about 15%. According to a recent Shiseido Consumer Center Survey, about 40% of Shiseido's customers are repeat buyers. Reasons cited for purchasing Shiseido products included: referral by friends (18.5%), magazine/poster (15.5%), took the products in hand (presumably the tester) (14.5%) and others (11.5%).

Competition and Challenges

Foreign companies such as Max Factor, Revlon and Clinique entered the Japanese market in the early 1980s and have pursued the selective distribution through a limited number of prestigious department stores. In 1991, there was a strong pressure applied on Japan by the U.S. to open its ¥1.3 trillion ($13 billion) cosmetics industry to foreign competition, longstanding retail price controls were lifted on cosmetics, drugs, and other small products priced under ¥1,030 ($10). (The major cosmetics companies in Japan are listed in Exhibit 1). Other issues affecting the industry in 1992 included the new Ministry of Health regulations governing imports and the manufacturing of cosmetics involved lengthy approval processes. Moreover, common ingredients approved for use in cosmetics outside Japan were prohibited by the Ministry of Health, which required the reformulation of most products.

In 1987, Shiseido's marketing section was overstaffed and its sales force was more interested in meeting quotas than in pursuing the firm's long-term interests. Rising inventory at its outlets was masked by still-impressive sales and profit figures. However bloated and unresponsive to market conditions, Shiseido's position was protected by an exclusionary retail system that enabled it to dictate prices and tightly control retailers. At that time, Yoshiharu Fukahara, grandson of the founder, took over as president. Fukuhara held back sales to retailers to squeeze their inventories and streamlined the firm marketing operations. The gains worked to the long-term health of the company. Inventories with retailers showed a drop to four months in the fiscal year ending March 31, 1992, from a record of 62 months in 1987. The number of marketing subsidiaries has been reduced to 15 from 72 in 1988, and supporting staff to 1,000 from 4,000 over the same period.

Currently, Shiseido's cosmetic sales, which account for 74 percent of its businesses, are under attack from all sides. Inexpensive imports from rivals such as Max Factor is on the increase. Supermarket chains are forcing suppliers to lower their prices: From 1994 to 1995, in a span of 18 months, the price of cosmetics fell by over 10 percent in real terms. Shiseido was able to keep prices from plummeting by imitating the marketing tactics of its Western rivals: that means differentiating its product line and providing its customers with more personal service.

Despite the fierce competition, Shiseido has been able to keep its position as the undisputed leader in the cosmetic industry in Japan with 27 percent of the market and its president serving as a chair of the cosmetics industry association. The other top five domestic manufacturers in 1992 were Kao with 16 percent; Kanebo with 11 percent; Pola with 8 percent, and Kose

EXHIBIT 1
MAJOR COSMETICS COMPANIES IN JAPAN

Company	Total Sales $ million	Skin Care	Makeup	Hair Care	Fragrances	Men's Cosmetics
Top 5 Cosmetics Companies						
Shiseido	$1,963.2	49%	31%	3%	3%	10%
Kanebo	$1,331.2	39	36	5	3	12
Pola	704.1	54	28	2	3	2
Kose	553.8	51	36	5	1	3
Kao	470.8	46	42	2	0	10
Top 5 Foreign Cosmetics Companies						
Max Factor	$440.8	37%	54%	1%	2%	1%
Avon	$303.8	35	30	4	0	0
Revlon	92.3	25	52	10%	7	0
Clinique	80.7	72	25	1	0	0
Chanel	76.1	21	21	0	58%	0

Source: Adapted from Cosmetics and Toiletries Marketing Strategies, Fuji Keizai.

with 7 percent. Many of its rivals, have used Shiseido as a company to be benchmarked in the cosmetic industry. Another problem is that many advertisements have taken on the Shiseido flare, with notebooks resembling Hanatsubaki Club registers, but bearing other makers names displayed at many counters. Beauty consultants of other makers appear in many of the same stores, and most makers promote the use of a beauty analysis machine. Stores even encourage competition among manufacturers by making sales figures for all makers available.

While customer loyalty to Shiseido is strong in the rural areas, it is weaker in the urban areas. Shiseido also plans to increase its *terminal marketing*, which refers to distribution of samples at major commuter stations such as Shinjuku. The terminal marketing strategy will probably be used to combat stiffening competition in the urban areas, specifically Tokyo and Osaka.

FINANCIAL HIGHLIGHTS

In the fiscal year 1998 ending in March 31, 1998, Shiseido Company, Limited, and its 61 consolidated subsidiaries reported net sales of ¥620.9 billion ($5.4 billion), up 5.5 percent from fiscal 1997 (see Exhibit 2).

Sales by Area

In Japan, Shiseido worked to increase trust and mutual relationships with customers amid an operating environment characterized by overcautious consumer attitudes and a deepening market recession. As a result, domestic sales grew by 0.9 percent.

Overseas, Beauté Prestige International S.A., a French subsidiary handling fragrances, continued to steadily expand its business, and Shiseido-brand products performed solidly in Europe, the Americas and Asia. During the year, Taiwan Shiseido Co., Ltd., became a consolidated subsidiary, and the North American Professional (Hair Salon) Division of Helene Curtis Inc. in the United States, which the Company acquired in December 1996, contributed to sales throughout fiscal 1998. As a result, overseas sales jumped 42.9 percent, to ¥92.2 billion ($802 million) and constituted 14.9 percent of net sales, up from 11.0 percent in fiscal 1997.

Sales by Product (See Exhibit 3)

Cosmetics.   In fiscal 1998, sales of cosmetics, Shiseido's mainstay business, grew 4.7percent, to ¥457.3 billion (3.98 billion), and accounted for 73.7 percent of net sales.

EXHIBIT 2
3-YEAR FINANCIAL HIGHLIGHTS

	Millions of Yen			Thousand US$
For the Year:	1998	1997	1996	1998
Net sales	¥620,910	¥588,572	¥560,821	$4,776,231
Inc. from operations	39,278	42,898	37,012	302,139
Net income	16,868	19,152	17,507	129,754
Divsional Sales:				
Cosmetics	¥457,333	¥436,705	¥404,181	$3,517,946
Toiletries	99,310	94,610	101,675	763,923
Others	64,267	57,257	54,965	494,362
At Year-End:				
Total assets	¥626,435	¥610,132	¥580,513	$4,818,731
Shareholders' equity	413,801	388,145	357,861	3,183,085
Per Share Data (in yen and US$)				
Net income	¥40.1	¥47.5	¥43.7	$0.31
Cash dividends	13.25	12.5	12.5	0.102
Shareholders equity	977.4	941	894.2	7.52
Return on Equity	4.20%	5.10%	5.00%	
Number of Employees	22,718	22,045	22,305	

1. Net income per share is calculated on the average number of shares outstanding in each year.
2. For Exhibits 3 & 4, U.S. dollar amounts are converted from yen, at the rate of ¥130 = US$1, the approximate rate of exchange effective March 31, 1998.

EXHIBIT 3
SALES BY PRODUCT

		(and percentage of net sales) Millions of Yen					Thousands US$
		1998	1997	1996	1995	1994	1998
Cosmetics		¥457,333	¥436,705	¥404,181	¥387,314	¥390,188	$3,517,946
		(73.70%)	(74.20%)	(72.10%)	(71.70%)	(71.00%)	(73.70%)
	Domestic	379,604	377,141	359,997	353,056	359,402	2,920,031
	Overseas	77,729	59,564	44,184	34,258	30,786	597,915
Toiletries	(Domestic)	99,310	94,610	101,675	97,606	102,132	763,923
		(16.00%)	(16.10%)	(18.10%)	(18.10%)	(18.60%)	(16.00%)
Others		64,267	57,257	54,965	55,441	56,858	494,362
		(10.30%)	(9.70%)	(9.80%)	(10.20%)	(10.40%)	(10.30%)
	Domestic	49,778	52,272	48,717	49,416	50,433	382,908
	Overseas	14,489	4,985	6,248	6,025	6,425	111,454
Net sales		¥620,910	¥588,572	¥560,821	¥540,361	¥549,178	$4,776,231
		(100.00%)	(100.00%)	(100.00%)	(100.00%)	(100.00%)	(100.00%)
Overseas sales		¥92,218	¥64,549	¥50,432	¥40,283	¥37,211	$709,369

Toiletries. Toiletries, its second mainstay business, principally consist of hair-care products, facial cleansers, soaps and bath additives. In fiscal 1998, sales in this category rose 5.0 percent, to ¥99.3 billion ($863.5 million), representing 16.0 percent of net sales.

Others. This category covers the manufacture and sale of salon products, foodstuffs, pharmaceuticals, fashion goods, fine chemicals and other items, as well as event planning and health-related activities. In the fiscal year 1998, sales grew 12.2 percent, to ¥64.3 billion ($559.1 million), or 10.3 percent of net sales.

Cost of Goods Sold

Shiseido endeavored to raise productivity and reduce costs from the product design stage, and thus was able to limit cost of sales to 33.6 percent of net sales, approximately the same level as in the previous year. Selling, general and administrative (SG&A) expenses increased 7.2 percent (fiscal 1999, ended March 31), due to such factors as reinforced advertising in the self-selection market, as well as added advertising, promotional, personnel and other expenses from twelve newly consolidated subsidiaries.

Net Income

Income from operations decreased 8.4 percent, and ¥15.6 billion ($135.7 million) in net other expenses were incurred for a number of reasons. First, the company allocated ¥20.0 billion ($173.9 million) for restructuring expenses, with specific actions including the liquidation of SFC Co., Ltd., a finance subsidiary, and the withdrawal from the fitness club business by the planned closing of Shiseido Wellness Co., Ltd. Second, the company posted losses on the devaluation of securities, stemming from the depressed Japanese stock market. Due to restructuring, income taxes were down substantially compared with the fiscal year 1997 level. As a result, the decrease in net income was limited to 11.9 (see Exhibit 4).

DIVERSIFICATION AND INTERNATIONAL EXPANSION

Diversification

To maintain its competitive advantage, Shiseido has launched an inexpensive line of cosmetics to meet market demands in the lower end products, which are becoming popular during the Japanese recession. These products are marketed under different names and do not bare the Shiseido name. Other lines of businesses that Shiseido has pursued are beauty foods, pharmaceuticals, accessory shops and a fitness club.

International Expansion

Shiseido began full-scale marketing internationally in 1957 when it entered the Taiwanese market, and the company has since been active in various regions around the world. The early days of overseas expansion were not successful for Shiseido because of inconsistent

EXHIBIT 4

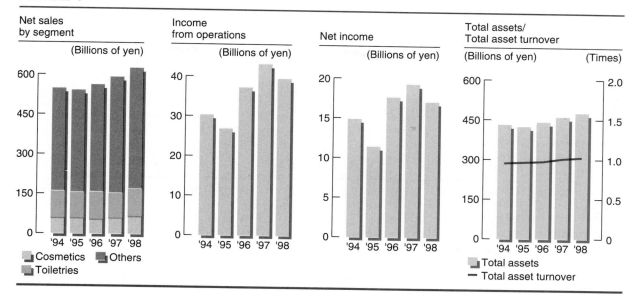

marketing. In the 1970s, for instance, it had to reduce the number of retail outlets in the United States because of sluggish sales.

During the bubble economic period, cash-rich Shiseido has opted to acquire existing production facilities abroad rather than build its own. It also acquired the French salon Carita in 1986 for ¥9 billion and U.S. hair product company Ezotos International Inc, 1988 for US$345 million. In 1998, it established three regional headquarters—one each in Europe, the Americas, and Asia. These regional headquarters provide a support framework for the global development of the Shiseido Group. At the same time, each headquarters will reinforce its marketing activities to meet the specific characteristics of its region. Shiseido felt that it has a strong position in the cosmetic business but weak in the toiletries and salon businesses. In 1997, the company rank fourth globally with well-established brands and products in all major markets.

To globalize its toiletries business, Shiseido made a strategic alliance with Johnson and Johnson of the United States in 1999. The alliance already calls for two projects to be launched. First, Shiseido's successful Super Mild Japanese shampoo brand will be developed and marketed by Johnson and Johnson as Johnson's Super Mild throughout Asia Pacific region outside Japan, starting in Australia and China. Second, Johnson and Johnson's Neutrogena skin care product will be developed and marketed in Japan by a new Shiseido company named Prier Co., Ltd. In the cosmetic business lines. Shiseido is trying

to decrease its emphasis on Japanese-oriented products and has moved toward skin care and color products that are more suitable for the American woman.

To prepare itself for a more crowded domestic market, Shiseido is aiming for further overseas expansion, an area in which the company should pay more attention, given the fact that its current foreign sales is only 15 percent of total income. Shiseido is planning to increase its foreign income, which are expected to account for at least 25 percent of net sales in the fiscal year 2003, by expanding foreign operations.

QUESTIONS

1. What are the strengths, weaknesses, opportunities, and threats for Shiseido?
2. Do you think there is potential in the men's market? Considering the current infrastructure/platforms that Shiseido has, what product, and what is the best way to sell it in Japanese market?
3. Does Shiseido need to shift distribution away from its affiliated mom and pop store (beauty stores) toward department stores and supermarkets? Consider the opportunity and cost involved.
4. Is there any possible problem that could arise from Shiseido's policy to classify its customer based on age? If yes, why? If no, why not?
5. What can Shiseido do to maintain its competency against global competition?

REFERENCES

"High Inventory and Low Earnings Force Shiseido to Streamline," *Japan Economic Journal*, Tokyo (April 23, 1988) p. 5.

Nancy Jeffries, "From Tokyo's Ginza to Global Enterprise," *Drug and Cosmetic Industry*, (September 1998).

David Kilburn, "Shiseido Blooms Anew; Fukuhara Expands the Vision of Japanese Giant," *Advertising Age* (October 3, 1988), p. 12.

"Shiseido," *Forbes* (January 13, 1997).

Shiseido Home Page <http://www.shiseido.co.ip/>.

"Shiseido and Johnson & Johnson Form Strategic Alliance," *Mainichi Press Release Service* (January 20, 1999).

CASE 6

TEXAS INSTRUMENTS: GLOBAL PRICING IN THE SEMICONDUCTOR INDUSTRY

Mr. John Szczsponik, Director of North American Distribution for Texas Instruments' Semiconductor Group, placed the phone back on its cradle after a long and gruelling conversation with his key contact at Arrow, the largest distributor of Texas Instruments' semiconductors. With a market-leading 21.5 percent share of total U.S. electronic component distributor sales in 1994, Arrow was the most powerful distribution channel through which Texas Instruments' important semiconductor products flowed. It was also one of only two major American distributors active in the global distribution market.

Arrow's expanding international activities had made it increasingly interested in negotiating with its vendors a common global price for the semiconductors it sold around the world. In the past, semiconductors had been bought and sold at different price levels in different countries to reflect the various cost structures of the countries in which they were produced. Semiconductors made in European countries, for example, were usually more expensive than those made in Asia or North America, simply because it cost manufacturers more to operate in Europe than in the other two regions. Despite these differences, large distributors and some original equipment manufacturers were becoming insistent on buying their semiconductors at one worldwide price, and were pressuring vendors to negotiate global pricing terms. Szczsponik's telephone conversation with Arrow

had been the third in the past month in which the distributor had pushed for price concessions based on international semiconductor rates:

> Yesterday they discovered that we're offering a lower price for a chip we make and sell in Singapore than for the same chip we manufacture here in Dallas for the North American market. They want us to give them the Singapore price on our American chips, even though they know our manufacturing costs are higher here than in the Far East. We can't give them that price without losing money!

In anticipation of increased pressure from Arrow and other large distributors, Szczsponik had organized a meeting with Mr. Kevin McGarity, senior vice president in the Semiconductor Group and manager of Worldwide Marketing, to begin developing a cohesive pricing strategy. They were both to meet with Arrow executives in four days, on February 4, 1995, to discuss the establishment of common global pricing for the distributor.

Szczsponik knew that he needed to answer some basic questions before meeting with Arrow:

> Global pricing might make Arrow's job of planning and budgeting a lot easier, but our different cost structures in each region make it difficult for us to offer one price worldwide. How do we tell Arrow, our largest distributor, that we aren't prepared to negotiate global pricing? Alternatively, how can we reorganize ourselves to make global pricing a realistic option? And what implications will a global pricing strategy have in relationship to other international customers?

With only two hours to go before his meeting with McGarity, Szczsponik wondered how they could respond to Arrow's request.

This case was developed by Profs. Per V. Jenster, CIMID, B. Jaworski, USC, and Michael Stanford as a basis for classroom discussion rather than to highlight effective or ineffective management of an administrative situation.

THE SEMICONDUCTOR INDUSTRY

Semiconductors were silicon chips which transmitted heat, light and electrical charge and performed critical functions in virtually all electronic devices. They were a core technology in industrial robots, computers, office equipment, consumer electronics, the aerospace industry, telecommunications, the military and the automobile industry. The majority of semiconductors consisted of integrated circuits made from monocrystalline silicon imprinted with complex electronic components and their interconnections (refer to Exhibit 1 for the key categories of semiconductors). The remainder of semiconductors were simpler discrete components that performed single functions.

The pervasiveness of semiconductors in electronics resulted in rapidly growing sales and intense competition in the semiconductor industry. Market share in the industry had been fiercely contested since the early 1980s, when the once-dominant U.S. semiconductor industry lost its leadership position to Japanese manufacturers. There followed a series of trade battles in which American manufacturers charged their Japanese competitors with dumping, and accused foreign markets of excessive protectionism. By 1994, after investing heavily in the semiconductor industry and embarking on programs to increase manufacturing efficiency and decrease production costs, American companies once again captured a dominant share of the market (refer to Exhibit 2 for the Top Ten Semiconductor Manufacturers).

In 1994, total shipments of semiconductors reached $99.9 billion, with market share divided among North America (33%), Japan (30%), Europe (18%) and Asia/Pacific (18%). The industry was expected to reach sales of $130 billion in 1995, and $200 billion by the year 2000. To capture growing demand in the industry, many semiconductor manufacturers were investing heavily in

EXHIBIT 1
KEY SEMICONDUCTOR CATEGORIES

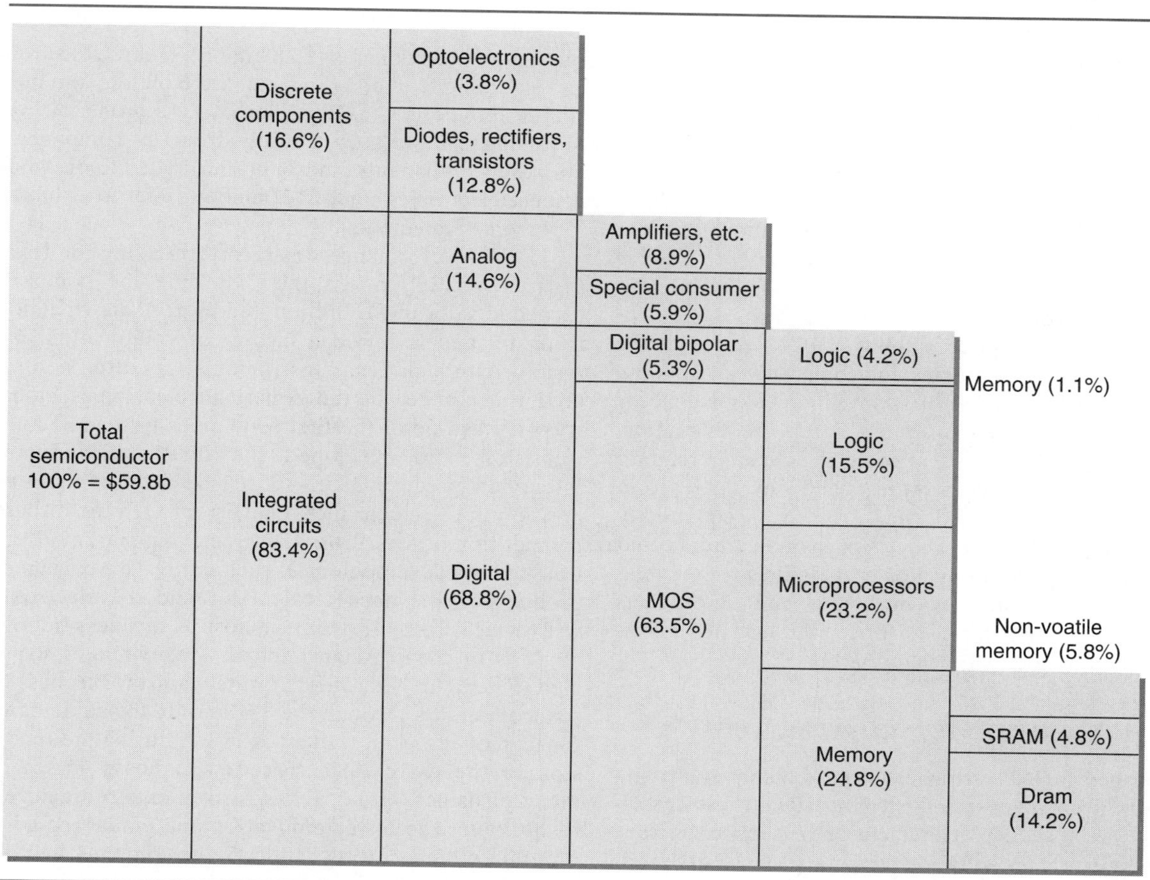

Source: Analysts' reports.

EXHIBIT 2
TOP TEN SEMICONDUCTOR MANUFACTURERS

	1980		1985		1990		1992	
	Company	*Sales $*	*Company*	*Sales $*	*Company*	*Sales $*	*Company*	*Sales $*
1.	Texas Instruments	1,453	NEC	1,800	NEC	4,700	Intel	5,091
2.	Motorola	1,130	Motorola	1,667	Toshiba	4,150	NEC	4,700
3.	Philips	845	Texas Instruments	1,661	Motorola	3,433	Toshiba	4,550
4.	NEC	800	Hitachi	1,560	Hitachi	3,400	Motorola	4,475
5.	National	745	National	1,435	Intel	3,171	Hitachi	3,600
6.	Intel	630	Toshiba	1,400	Texas Instruments	2,518	Texas Instruments	3,105
7.	Hitachi	620	Philips	1,080	Fujitsu	2,300	Fujitsu	2,250
8.	Fairchild	570	Intel	1,020	Mitsubishi	1,920	Mitsubishi	2,200
9.	Toshiba	533	Fujitsu	800	Philips	1,883	Philips	2,041
10.	Siemens	525	Advanced Micro Devices	795	National	1,730	Matsushita	1,900

Source: Analysts' reports.

increased manufacturing capacity, although most industry analysts expected expanding capacity to reach rather than surpass demand. Combined with record low inventories in the industry and reduced cycle times and lead times, a balancing of supply and demand was causing semiconductor prices to be uncharacteristically stable. The last three quarters of 1994 had brought fewer fluctuations and less volatility in the prices of semiconductors (refer to Exhibit 3 for a History of Semiconductor Price Stability) despite their history of dramatic price variations.

Regardless of price stability, most semiconductor manufacturers were looking for competitive advantage in further cost reduction programs, in developing closer relationships with their customers, and in creating differentiated semiconductors that could be sold at a premium price. Integrated circuits were readily available from suppliers worldwide, and were treated as commodity products by most buyers. Any steps manufacturers could take to reduce their production costs, build stronger relationships with customers, or create unique products could protect them from the price wars usually associated with commodity merchandise.

TEXAS INSTRUMENTS INCORPORATED

Established in 1951 as an electronics company serving the American defense industry, by 1995 Texas Instruments was a leading manufacturer of semiconductors, defense electronics, software, personal productivity products and materials and controls. Its 1994 sales of $10.3 billion, a 21 percent increase from the previous year, was

split among components ($6.8 billion), defense electronics ($1.7 billion), digital products ($1.66 billion) and metallurgical materials ($177 million). 1994's profits of over $1 billion came almost entirely from its components business. Components made a profit of $1.1 billion, while defense electronics made $172 million (refer to Exhibit 4 for Income Statements).

1994's performance was record-breaking for Texas Instruments. It marked the first time the company exceeded sales of $10 billion and more than $1 billion in profit, and followed a history of volatile financial results. Although Texas Instruments was often considered the pioneer of the American electronics industry—it was one of the first companies to manufacture transistors and developed the first semiconductor integrated circuit in 1958—it struggled to maintain its position in the electronics industry through the intense competition of the 1980s. After receiving market attention with its development of such innovative consumer products as the pocket calculator and the electronic wrist watch, Texas Instruments lost its business in both markets to cheap Asian imports. Meanwhile, it struggled to keep up with orders for its mainstay business in semiconductors through the 1970s, only to see demand for its pioneer semiconductors shrink during the recession of the early 1980s. Faced with heavy losses in many of its core areas, Texas Instruments reorganized its businesses to foster innovation and embarked on a program of cost-cutting. By 1985, the company had refocused its efforts on its strengths in semiconductors, relinquishing market dominance in favor of greater

EXHIBIT 3
HISTORY OF SEMICONDUCTOR STABILITY

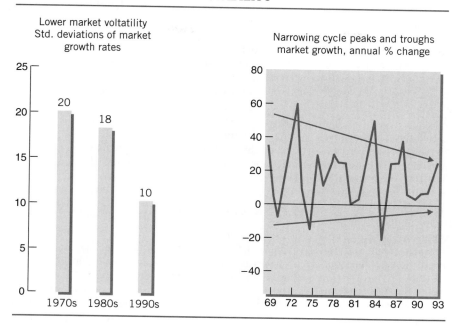

margins. While the company continued to grow its technological leadership, it also sought to build stronger relationships with its customers.

By 1995, Texas Instruments had developed a strong position in the electronics industry, despite its reputation as a technological leader rather than a skilled marketer of its products. The company continued to remain powerful in the semiconductor industry, in part because it was the only American company that continued to manufacture dynamic random access memory chips in the face of fierce Japanese competition in the 1980s. The company had manufacturing sites spread throughout North America, Asia and Europe, and was pursuing its

strategy of increasing manufacturing capacity and developing manufacturing excellence.

The Semiconductor Group

In 1958, Texas Instruments engineer Jack Kilby developed the first integrated circuit, a pivotal innovation in the electronics industry. Made of a single semiconductor material, the integrated circuit eliminated the need to solder circuit components together. Without wiring and soldering, components could be miniaturized and crowded together on a single chip. Only a few years after Kilby's invention, electronics manufacturers were

EXHIBIT 4
INCOME STATEMENTS

	Texas Instruments Key Financial Numbers				
	1994	1993	1992	1991	1990
Sales ($M)	10,200	8,523	7,049	6,628	6,395
Operating Margin (%)	17.5	16.8	9.1	5.0	0.7
Net Profit ($M)	715	459	254	169	0.7
Working Capital ($M)	1,800	1,313	961	813	826
Long-Term Debt ($M)	800	694	909	896	715
Net Worth ($M)	2,975	2,315	1,947	1,955	2,358

demanding these integrated circuits, or chips, in smaller sizes and at lower costs, a move that led to unprecedented innovation in the electronics industry. Soon chips became a commodity, and chip manufacturers relied on high-volume, low-cost production of reliable chips for success. Only a few manufacturers had strong positions in the production of differentiated semiconductors.

Forty years after its discovery, Texas Instruments still remained dependent on its semiconductor sales, which fell primarily in integrated circuits. The Semiconductor Group, a part of the Components Division, had total sales of $2 billion in 1994, the third consecutive year in which Texas Instruments' semiconductor revenues grew faster than the industry. The company's return to financial success in the early 1990s was based on its strong performance in semiconductor sales and profits, both of which were at record levels in 1994. Management in the company expected semiconductor sales to continue to grow strongly, and were planning heavy capital expenditures on new or expanded plants in the United States, Malaysia and Italy to increase the company's capacity.

The Semiconductor Group divided its business into two segments: standard products and differentiated products. Standard semiconductors, which accounted for 90 percent of the Group's sales, included products which could be substituted by competitors. Standard semiconductors performed in the market much like other products for which substitutes were readily available. Texas Instruments, like its competitors, competed for market share in these commodity products based primarily on the price it offered to original equipment manufacturers

and distributors. The remaining 10% of the company's semiconductor business came from differentiated products, of which Texas Instruments was the sole supplier. Because substitutes for these products were not available on the marketplace, differentiated products commanded higher margins than their standard counterparts and were receiving greater strategic emphasis on the part of Group management. While the company continued to hold a strong position in standard semiconductors, it was searching for a strategy that would allow it to achieve a higher return on development and manufacturing investments. Managers at Texas Instruments believed that higher returns were possible only by developing more successful differentiated semiconductors.

ELECTRONICS DISTRIBUTION MARKET

Texas Instruments sold its semiconductors through two channels: directly to original equipment manufacturers or through a network of electronics distributors. Szczsponik estimated that 70 percent of the Group's U.S. customers dealt directly with Texas Instruments. The remainder bought their semiconductors through one or more of the seven major semiconductor distributors that served the North American market (refer to Exhibit 5 for information on the Top Electronics Distributors). Whether an original equipment manufacturer dealt directly with Texas Instruments or bought from a distributor depended on the manufacturer's size. The largest original equipment manufacturers were able to negotiate better prices from semiconductor manufacturers than were the distributors and

EXHIBIT 5
TOP ELECTRONICS DISTRIBUTORS

Company		1994	1993	1992	1991	1990
Arrow Electronics	Sales ($b)	3.973	2.536	1.622	1.044	.971
	Share(%)	21.5	17.4	14.8	11.0	10.2
Avnet	Sales($b)	3.350	2.537	1.690	1.400	1.429
	Share(%)	18.1	17.4	15.4	14.8	15.0
Marshall Industries	Sales($b)	.899	.747	.605	.563	.582
	Share(%)	4.8	5.1	5.5	6.0	6.1
Wyle Laboratories	Sales($b)	.773	.606	.447	.360	.359
	Share(%)	4.2	4.2	4.1	3.8	3.8
Pioneer Standard	Sales($b)	.747	.540	.405	.360	.343
	Share(%)	4.0	3.7	3.7	3.8	3.6
Anthem	Sales($b)	.507	.663	.538	.420	.408
	Share(%)	2.7	4.6	4.9	4.4	4.3
Bell Industries	Sales($b)	.395	.308	.282	.257	.239
	Share(%)	2.1	2.1	2.6	2.7	2.5

Source: Lehman Brothers, "Electronic Distribution Market," December 22, 1994.

therefore bought directly from the manufacturers. Because mid-sized and small original equipment manufacturers were fragmented, and thus more difficult to serve, these customers were served more efficiently through the distribution channel. Szczsponik explained:

> The semiconductor market can be divided into three tiers. Fifty % of our sales in semiconductors go to the top tier of perhaps 100 large electronics manufacturers who deal with us directly. The next 46% of sales come from 1,400 medium-sized companies at the next level, half of whom deal directly with us and half of whom buy through distributors. The remaining 4% of sales are to 150,000 smaller companies at the bottom tier in the market, who deal only through distributors. Distributors have a clearly defined role in servicing mid-sized and small buyers.

Distributors were considered to be clearinghouses for the semiconductor industry. Each distributor dealt with products from all the major semiconductor manufacturers. For example, Arrow Electronics sold semiconductors manufactured by Motorola and Intel as well as those made by Texas Instruments. The distributors specialized in handling logistics, material flows, sales and servicing for electronics manufacturers who were either too small to negotiate directly with the major semiconductor manufacturers or lacked sufficient expertise in logistics management. In addition, the distributors sometimes kitted packages of different products together for the smaller original electronics manufacturers as an added service. Some also performed varying scales of assembly operation.

The electronics distribution network had originally consisted of a large group of smaller companies. By 1995, however, industry consolidation had left almost 40% of the distribution market in the hands of its two largest competitors, Arrow Electronics and Avnet. The seven largest distributors captured 58% of sales in the market (refer to Exhibit 6 for the Sales and Market Shares of the Top Distributors). This trend toward consolidation had a major impact on the nature of the relationships among semiconductor manufacturers and the distributors through which they sold their products. According to Szczsponik:

> Fifteen years ago, 30 distributors were active in the industry and it was clear that the semiconductor manufacturers controlled the distribution network. With the consolidation of the distribution network into only 7 or 8 powerful players, however, power is shifting. It's hard to say if we are more important to them or they are more important to us.

Price Negotiations and Global Pricing Issues

Since the vast majority of semiconductors were considered commodity products, the buying decisions of distributors were based almost entirely on price. Distributors forecasted the demand for the various semiconductor products they carried and negotiated with vendors for their prices. Since semiconductor prices were notoriously volatile, the price levels negotiated between manufacturers and distributors played a vital role in the distributors' profitability. The Semiconductor Group at Texas Instruments combined the practices of forward pricing and continuous price negotiations to set prices with its distributors.

Forward Pricing. The cost of semiconductor manufacturing followed a generally predictable learning curve. When a manufacturer first began producing a new type of chip, it could expect only a small percentage of the chips it produced to function properly. As the manufacturer increased the volume of its production, it both decreased the costs of production and increased the percentage of functioning chips it could produce. This percentage, termed *yield* in the industry, and the standard learning curve of semiconductor manufacturing together had a large impact on the prices semiconductor manufacturers set for their products (refer to Exhibit 7 for the Price Curve of Semiconductor Products). This yield was

EXHIBIT 6
TOTAL SALES AND MARKET SHARE OF TOP DISTRIBUTORS

		1994	1993	1992	1991	1990
Industry Total	Sales($b)	16.22	12.95	10.18	9.06	9.17
Top 25	Sales($b)	13.41	10.69	8.11	7.10	7.20
	Share(%)	82.7	82.5	79.7	78.4	78.5
Top 7	Sales($b)	10.75	8.42	6.36	5.05	5.00
	Share(%)	58.0	57.9	57.9	53.5	52.5
Top 2	Sales($b)	7.32	5.07	3.31	2.44	2.40
	Share(%)	39.6	34.8	30.2	25.8	25.2

Source: Lehman Brothers, "Electronic Distribution Market," December 22, 1994.

EXHIBIT 7
FORWARD PRICING CURVE

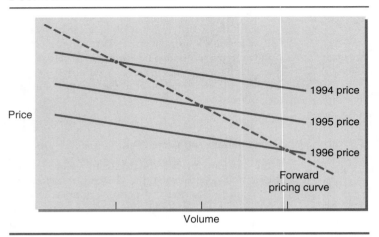

important to TI; a 7 percent increase in overall yield was equivalent to the production of an entire Wafer Fab, an investment of $500 million.

According to Jim Huffhines, Manager of DSP Business Development in the Semiconductor Group, managers could predict with considerable accuracy the production cost decreases and yield improvements they would experience as their production volumes increased:

> We know the manufacturing costs for any given volume of production. We also know that these costs will decrease a certain percentage and our yields will increase a certain percentage each year. These predictions are the basis of the forward prices we set with both original equipment manufacturers and distributors.

Continuous Price Adjustments. Production costs and yield rates were not the only contributing factors to price levels for standard semiconductors: market supply and demand also played a powerful role in establishing prices. As a result of volatile prices caused by shifts in supply and demand, distributors often held inventories of semiconductors that did not accurately reflect current market rates. To protect distributors from price fluctuations, most semiconductor manufacturers offered to reimburse distributors for their overvalued inventories. Szczsponik explained:

> Semiconductor prices have fallen by 15% over the past 9 months. If Arrow bought semiconductors from me for $1.00, 9 months ago, they are worth only 85¢ now. Arrow is carrying a 15% "phantom" inventory. If Arrow sells those semiconductors now, we give it price protection by agreeing to reimburse it the 15¢ it has lost per semiconductor over the past three quarters.

At the same time, distributors had at their disposal sophisticated systems for monitoring semiconductor prices from each of the major manufacturers, and were constantly in search of price adjustments from vendors when placing their orders. Szczsponik continued:

> Distributors have access to the prices of products from all the semiconductor manufacturers at any given time, and some anywhere in the world. The largest distributors have a staff of 20 to 30 people shopping around continuously for the best prices available for different types of semiconductors, add to this group a staff of accountants managing the price adjustment transactions. For example, they may call us to say that Motorola has quoted them a certain price for a semiconductor, and ask us if we can beat their price. In total, we get close to 150,000 of these calls requesting adjustments from distributors a year, and do over 10% of our sales through price adjustments. I have 10 people on my staff who negotiate price adjustments for distributors: 5 answer their calls, and 5 work with our product managers to make pricing decisions. These decisions are critical: if we make a mistake in our pricing, we lose market share in a day that can take us 3 months to recapture. At the same time, through our negotiations with distributors, we capture masses of data regarding the pricing levels of our competitors and the market performance of our different products. This data is critical to our ability to set prices.

As the distribution network consolidated into a small number of powerful companies, Szczsponik had begun to notice that his price negotiations were increasingly focused not only on beating the competition in North America, but on beating prices available around the world, including those of TI in other regions. With distributors becoming more active in the global market, they were more often exposed to semiconductor price levels from Europe and Asia. Industry analysts expected North American distributors to become more active in global markets as they pursued aggressive expansion campaigns in Europe and Asia. Although Texas Instruments' current contracts with its distributors prevented them from selling semiconductors outside of the region in which they were purchased, distributors were becoming insistent on access to freer global supplies and markets. While the concept may have appeared reasonable to the distributors, it was somewhat more complicated for Texas Instruments. Kevin McGarity elaborated:

> Because business is different everywhere in the world, our international distribution channels have evolved independently. They aren't subjected to the same costs, and don't operate under the same methods and calculation models. In the United States, for example, we offer a 30-day payment schedule for our customers. If they don't pay us within 30 days, we cut off their supply, no matter who they are. Italy operates under a 60-day schedule. Europeans include freight in their prices; we don't in North America. Finally, the cost of producing semiconductors varies by country. Europe tends to be more expensive than North America or Asia, simply because their infrastructure is more costly. So when one of our large distributors phones with the Singapore price for semiconductors manufactured in Düsseldorf, he is crossing boundaries that may be invisible to him but are very real to us.

Preparing for the Meeting with Arrow

With sales of almost $4 billion in 1994, Arrow Electronics was the largest semiconductor distributor in North America, of which TI products accounted for approximately 14

percent. Its aggressive growth had taken the company into global markets, and had given it increased exposure to fluctuating price and exchange levels in different international markets. Seeking to minimize its costs, Arrow had begun to pressure semiconductor manufacturers to set standard global prices for each of their products. Motorola, one of Texas Instruments, largest competitors in the semiconductor industry, was rumored to be preparing for global pricing. Management at Texas Instruments, however, was unsure of the wisdom of moving toward global pricing. According to Szczsponik, the pros and cons to global pricing seem unevenly balanced:

> The large distributors want global pricing to reduce their costs and simplify their planning. But does it make sense for us? Right now our organization, calculation systems and costs in each country are too different for us to offer standard global prices. There are other things to consider as well. If we set global prices, we will no longer continue our price adjustment negotiations with the distributors. This may save us the cost of staffing our negotiations team, but it also takes away from us a powerful tool for gathering information on our customers' prices and our product performance. As soon as we stop negotiating price adjustments, we lose our visibility into the market.

To prepare for his discussion with McGarity and forthcoming meeting with Arrow Electronics. Szczsponik knew TI had to make some fundamental decisions regarding global pricing. Who held the power in the relationships Texas Instruments had with its distributors? What was the source of the negotiating strength each party would bring to the meeting? Finally, what position should the Semiconductor Group take with its distributors regarding global pricing? And what organizational implications would such a decision imply?

CASE 7

MARKETING SMS (SHARED MEDICAL SYSTEMS) PACS TO U.S. AND WORLDWIDE AUDIENCES THROUGH A EUROPEAN TESTIMONY

INTRODUCTION

Health care organizations have grown in size and configuration over the last fifteen years. The paradigm of the

This case was prepared by Pat Rocchi of the Fox School of Business and Management at Temple University under the supervision of Professor Masaaki Kotabe for class discussion rather than to illustrate either effective or ineffective management of a situation described (June 1999).

local community hospital has been replaced with the health care network, which consists of connected health-care-providing organizations. Additionally, a vast array of **health care information** products, systems, and applications have been created to meet those needs.

This health care information technology industry began in the late 1960s to help physicians deal with their Medicare reimbursements. Today, the industry is much more complex: Several companies provide a wide range of *information solutions* (including clinical, financial, administrative, ambulatory care, managed care, decision support, and electronic data interchange systems for both the public and private health sectors) to an equally wide variety of *health care providers* (including integrated health networks, multientity health corporations, and community health information networks, and even payers and physician groups).

It is one matter to provide financial information, which is dry in its content and factual in its nature. But many of these providers also provide *clinical* information, such as that found in radiology departments, hospital pharmacies, and clinical laboratories. This information is naturally considered to be of a higher order, as it deals with the critical area of patient health. One distinct segment of clinical systems is the rapidly growing area of Picture and Archiving Communication Systems (PACS) —filmless systems that acquire, move, display, store, and digitally process radiological images.

This case describes Shared Medical Systems' (SMS) most recent attempts to raise its profile in this highly competitive market. The case shows how SMS has progressed toward this goal by expounding a unifying message, which was gleaned through a single videotape that was produced in a foreign company. This case also describes both the logistics of producing a video overseas and the international regulatory considerations behind marketing PACS.

SMS AS A LEADER IN THE HEALTH CARE INFORMATION INDUSTRY

Information is a vital strategic asset for contemporary health systems, and for this reason, the health care information industry has thrived since its inception in the late 1960s. To accommodate the ever-increasing demands for information to unite, manage, and support their networks of provider entities, and to continue to provide the highest possible standards of care, health systems require fully integrated information solutions that create a seamless continuum of information. This information continuum, in turn, enables effective decision making on every level of the organization because all users have all the information they need at their fingertips—whatever they need, wherever and whenever they need it, and in whatever format is most useful to them. They must accommodate changes in policy, evaluate clinical protocols, achieve their business standards, improve their business processes, establish and track health status, and continue to improve quality. Patients themselves need informa-

This case was prepared by Pat Rocchi of the Fox School of Business and Management at Temple University under the supervision of Professor Masaaki Kotabe for class discussion rather than to illustrate either effective or ineffective management of a situation described (June 1999).

tion, such as eligibility status, co-pay amounts, appointments, referrals, discharge summaries, and statements.

In particular, care providers need immediate access to up-to-date individual and global information in order to make informed, effective *clinical* decisions. Patient data must be current, comprehensive, integrated, and cumulative, even though it may have been collected at multiple locations over multiple episodes of care.

SMS has more than 6,000 employees worldwide. There are 5,000 employees in Chester County, Pennsylvania, alone. Additionally, SMS is located in more than fifty offices around the globe, more overseas offices than their competitors *combined*. SMS was founded in 1969, and its original charter was to assist hospitals in their Medicare reimbursements. The company expanded its operations to Europe in 1981, and has grown since then to provide a full range of information solutions, both financial and clinical.

SMS supplies more information solutions to customers in more locations around the world than does any other health care information systems (HIS) supplier. Whether one considers types of customers, customer retention, number of countries served, number of systems installed and operational, integrated technologies, revenues, sales, or revenue backlog, SMS is the recognized leader.

Industry analysts have identified SMS as the company offering the *broadest array* of integrated information solutions in the HIS industry. SMS has more than 3,000 worldwide customers, which includes hospitals, physicians' offices, clinics, and major health provider networks and organization in twenty countries and territories in North America, Europe, and Asia Pacific. SMS solutions include applications and services for clinical results, orders, laboratory, radiology, pharmacy, nursing, patient registration, medical and document imaging, scheduling, physicians' offices, payroll and HR, billing and receivables, managed care, outcomes management, and financial reporting.

SMS solutions also include a broad array of professional (consulting) services critical to the successful design and management of our customers' strategic information systems. These professional services include system installation, support, and education. In addition, SMS provides specialized consulting services for the design and integration of software and networks, for facilities management, for information systems planning, and for system-related process reengineering.

SMS bases its business on building long-term partnerships in the health industry, helping customers improve their quality of care and financial performance, and enhancing their clients' strategic positions by providing superior, cost-effective solutions based on information systems and services.

Other major HIS technology providers include **HBOC** (which is currently in the process of being acquired by pharmaceutical provider McKesson), **Cerner**, and **Meditech**. However, none of these companies offers PACS as SMS does; to do that, they must partner with other companies. The leading PACS vendors are listed later.

AN OVERVIEW OF THE PACS PRODUCT LINE

As defined previously, a PACS (Picture and Archiving Communication Systems) is a computer system that enables digital management of diagnostic imaging and related records to acquire, transmit, store, and display diagnostic images. PACS had historically been relegated to government and academic settings, especially in U.S. Veterans' Administration hospitals. It is now available to organizations as an emerging technology.

PACS are designed to eliminate X-ray film, which, in turn, increases the efficiency of radiology department operations while saving film costs. PACS growth has also escalated due to the recognition of its strategic importance, the development of communications standards, the decrease in communications costs, the decrease in hardware costs, and the fact that there are now open platforms (i.e., that they can interface with a variety of computer systems).

PACS technology can improve the management and distribution of image information across an entire enterprise. PACS technology can break down the traditional and physical barriers associated with image retrieval, dissemination, and display.

Capabilities of PACS in the Current Healthcare Environment

PACS have existed since about 1982. Modality manufacturers—the companies that make radiology equipment—began PACS as a logical extension of the then-burgeoning digital technology (as compared to the more conventional film-based technology). Images could be created digitally and then sent to a work station, enabling radiologists to work with them right on the spot, rather then wait for the film to be delivered to them for viewing over flourescent lights. That image could also be stored in a computerized archive system for instant access, rather than waiting for it to be delivered from a film storage room.

Back in 1982, this technology was seen first as a way to offset the expenses associated with film. A reasonably sized hospital—275 beds and up—could conceivably spend more than a million dollars a year in film. Physicians also realized later that, by virtue of having immediate access to the images, they could save time, both in viewing and delivery.

As cost effectiveness becomes of utmost importance in the health care setting, medical facilities have looked to technology to squeeze the inefficiencies out of their processes. With PACS technology, a group of fifty radiologists might cover five to seven hospitals; travel time is one of the inefficiencies plaguing that setup. With teleradiology equipment, one or two radiologists headquartered in a central receiving center can cover the same hospitals with greater efficiency and at far less expense. They can even use the technology to view images after hours in the comfort of their homes.

Storage, or the lack of it, also became a benefit to PACS users. If films no longer needed to be placed in a folder and the folders kept in a dedicated space, then hospitals would no longer need file rooms. And if file rooms were no longer needed, that space could be put to use generating revenues for the hospital.

Although PACS once may have seemed like science fiction, it is now reality. According to the research group MarketLine International, about 17 percent of U.S. hospitals currently own a full PACS or some *component* of a PACS. Over the next five years, this figure is projected to rise to as much as 68 percent, and like most technology, it has become more and more affordable in recent years. (Due to economics, the penetration overseas is much lower.)

According to MarketLine International, the PACS market value is expected to continue strong double-digit growth due to the ongoing conversion of single, community hospitals to IDSs, or integrated delivery systems (i.e., health "networks," such as the national chains of Columbia and Tenet, or seen locally as Jefferson Health System and Main Line Health System). IDSs, by their very nature, created the need for the wider distribution of information, and that has increased demands on already strained resources. For example, the American Hospital Radiology Association tells us that 65 percent of radiology department managers are managing *multiple* radiology departments, which puts new strain on radiology professionals.

In light of this changing health care environment, PACS is becoming increasingly recognized as a valuable tool, both in the *provision* of health care, and the *management* of health care. The health care industry has become increasingly cost-conscious in a more highly competitive market. More than ever, these organizations are scrutinizing attendant costs, such as numbers of full-time employees (FTEs), resource utilization, and productivity. Many physicians are also using technology to improve their productivity by accessing clinical information in a variety of locations around the clock.

Hospital radiology departments are more focused on *service* to their physician customers. This includes improving how timely images are read, how quickly reports are written, and the amount of consultative time that is available. This is important because physicians *may decide to take their business to other hospitals to get the service they need.*

The Measurable Value of PACS

There is compelling data to support the claim that PACS improve both operational efficiencies and cost improvements to health care imaging facilities. One SMS customer who has been live on the company's PACS system since January 1996 is saving $80,000 a year on film. Another SMS customer has estimated a two-year ROI of $2.5 million on the SMS PACS, including hardware.

According to *Diagnostic Imaging* magazine, the Veterans' Administration Hospital (VA) in Bethesda, Maryland, has shown measurable benefits from going filmless:

- The VA standard is an 8.8-year depreciation schedule, and based on that standard, the PACS began to save money at a volume of just under 37,000 studies a year. There were also measurable results at a five-year depreciation schedule, for which the break-even point was about 57,000 studies per year. When they reached the break-even point, the hospital's costs dropped $12 per exam.

- Labor costs went down, which tends to happen in a filmless environment. The hospital also held their staffing levels constant between (years) 1993 and 1995. This happened in spite of a 42 percent increase in study volume and a 68 percent increase in weighted work units.

- PACS helped physicians save about 12 minutes each day on procedures. This happened while throughput in the emergency room and clinics increased.

- After converting to filmless imaging, the hospital had a 22 percent net increase in the total number of their exams, but it only had a 13 percent increase in the number of technologists. This represents a 40 percent overall increase in technologist productivity.

In summary, the benefits of a PACS include the following:

1. Quick access to information about patients, both onsite and off-site.

2. The archiving of information, for both immediate access and future reference.

3. The ability to extend the scope of operations to imaging centers that are geographically distant from the radiologists. This is particularly important in a multi-entity environment (IDSs).

4. Long-term cost benefits, as shown above.

5. Improved efficiencies in productivity and resource utilization, including faster action and *re*action by physicians. This speed leads to reduced lengths of stay (LOS), which can, in turn, reduce costs. Lower lengths of stay have other benefits: improved utilization of resources and improved patient satisfaction. All of these improvements can translate to increased revenues through a higher throughput of examinations without increased operating costs. And as you deliver quicker, higher-quality, less-expensive radiology services, you can attract more referrals.

6. The development of the computer-based patient record (CPR), which is a goal of the health care industry. A CPR gathers clinical information from the hospital's central information systems; it includes additional information for other sources such as lab, pharmacy, radiology, and home health systems. That information can also be combined with multimedia objects, such as images, voice, and video.

An Analysis of Competition in the PACS Market

The leading vendors in PACS technology are:

- **AGFA Division-Bayer Corporation (www.agfa.com)** — AGFA-Gevaert is an international chemical and pharmaceutical corporation headquartered in Belgium. (In the United States, AGFA is a subsidiary of the Bayer Group, the company most associated with aspirin.) PACS image management and dry imaging fall under AGFA's Medical Systems Division. AGFA's presence in PACS is considered to be very formidable by SMS. For example, AGFA has the first and only full-scale PACS in Oregon, and one of the largest in the northwestern United States, at Doernbecher Children's Hospital in Portland.

- **Eastman Kodak Company (www.Kodak.com)** — The Kodak Medical Imaging Systems Division offers products for remote diagnosis, critical care, ultrasound, digital modalities, and fully digital solutions. At the 1998 HIMSS, the industry convention devoted to health care information, Kodak and Perot Systems announced a joint vendor agreement that will allow customers to contract with Kodak to meet both their PACS and system integration requirements. Additionally, Kodak announced on August 3, 1998, that it had acquired Imation, another leading Medical Imaging business. Imation already has 130 installed PACS sites, so Kodak's saturation improved overnight.

- **Raytheon E-Systems Medical Electronics (EMED) (www.esys.com)** — Raytheon is the third-largest aerospace and defense company, following Boeing and Lockheed Martin. It has three main segments — electronics, aircraft, and engineering and construction — with electronics the largest. Raytheon EMED's PACS customers include the U.S. military and prisons, for whom the PACS reduces the costs and risks associated with transporting patients to off-site facilities.

- **Fuji Medical Systems (www.Fujifilm.com)** — Fuji Photo Film is Japan's number-one photographic film producer and is engaged in a competitive market against rival Eastman Kodak for the world lead. Although photo-based business accounts for the majority of sales, Fuji also makes information systems equipment such as data storage items for computers, electronic filing systems, and microfilming products. Fuji Medical Systems' entry into PACS serves as a filmless alternative to more traditional radiology.

- **GE Medical Systems (www.ge.com)** — The 800-pound gorilla that can sit wherever it wants, GE Medical Systems (GEMS) is the major competitor worldwide for all radiology systems. GE states that its objective is to provide its customers with products that deliver excellence in clinical performance and economical value. This single GE business recorded sales of more than $4 billion in 1997 (compared to $1.2 billion *for all of SMS*). GE reports that its new product introductions, growing services offerings, information technology, and remote diagnostics serve as its foundation for the next century.

- **Siemens (usa.siemens.com)** — Siemens Corporation is a multinational, diversified company with a scope that encompasses energy, industry automation, telecommunications, information systems, transportation and other industries. Just as noted in the introduction section of this case, Siemens cites the shift of the health care industry toward managed care and integration as its reason for evolving its business strategies to emphasize PACS more. Siemens has established new priorities in dealing with its customers. It claims to serve its customers "as business partners and not merely as technology partners." Its PACS product serves a variety of hospital departments with online access to patient diagnostic images. This system is used throughout the United States.

- **SMS (www.SMED.com)** — While SMS is the recognized leader in health care information, that leadership has not transferred into the PACS product line. While SMS has high top-of-the-line recall for both patient-accounting systems and clinical systems (including lab, radiology, and pharmacy), the company is not well known as a PACS vendor. As already shown in the descriptions of SMS' PACS competitors, it is able to point to many installations in its marketing communications. Conversely, SMS had very little to which it could refer. SMS set out to change that by setting a 1998 goal to start increasing its number of PACS "requests for proposals" (RFPs). This goal precipitated the push to use SMS's leading PACS customer in Germany as a proof statement for the company's PACS capabilities.

MEETING SMS'S CHALLENGES IN PACS COMPETITION

Regulatory Issues

One issue facing all PACS vendors in the United States is regulation by the Federal Drug Administration (FDA). As a medical device (i.e., one that can be used for the diagnosis of disease or other medical conditions), all PACS are regulated by the FDA. In order for any medical device to be cleared as one used for diagnostic purposes, one must first obtain approval by filing FDA form *510k*.

SMS currently has approval to use its PACS for review purposes only. This means that physicians can use the SMS system only to get a general look at the situation and make some preliminary notes. The SMS PACS cannot currently be used to make diagnoses; to do that, the clinician must use either traditional X-ray film or a PACS that was approved for diagnoses through form 510k.

SMS is currently filing a 510k (a laborious process) so that its PACS may be used for diagnostic purposes. SMS expects to have the approval in 2000. Until then, SMS must be very careful with the language SMS use in its marketing materials:

- SMS cannot claim that its PACS is usable in diagnoses.
- SMS must avoid using the word *integrate*, as in "*The SMS PACS integrates its images with clinical data.*" To do so *implies* medical use and violates the FDA regulations.

Note: Due to fact that regulatory permits are on file with the FDA and not accessible in a public forum, we cannot state whether SMS's competitors have filed 501ks. There is no evidence that they did, although many of them imply the ability to diagnose. 501k information would be helpful to any PACS vendor, as it would enable a company to challenge its competitors' claims. If a PACS provider has not received 510k approval for its PACS to be used as a medical device, then it cannot claim so. If it does so wrongly, the FDA could launch a full-scale investigation of its entire product line. This, in turn, could conceivably result in all its products in that line being pulled from the market.

Usin1g Video to Meet SMS's Marketing Challenges

In order to meet the challenge that SMS faces in marketing its PACS both in the United States and in Europe, the company sent a video producer to a client's site in Germany. The Kreis Krankenhauser health system in the town of Sonneberg (in eastern Germany) faces needs similar to those expressed throughout this case, as such requirements are not unique to the U.S. health care industry. (It was important to include this information on the video so that the worldwide health care audience could immediately identify with the testifying customers and not merely discount them as irrelevant.)

1. *Why SMS used a German customer in its video*—Kreis Krankenhauser had classic health care challenges that made them suitable subjects for this video. This is a system that consists of two hospitals separated by 25 km (20 miles) of mountain road. They could not afford to send film back and forth between the two sites, so the electronic transmission of images is beneficial to them. Kreis Krankenhauser also knew they could save money by eliminating other attendant film costs. Also important, they needed a system that compared in quality to conventional film.

   While there are one or two U.S. customers who faced the same challenges and had similar results, SMS chose to shoot the video at Kreis Krankenhauser in Germany rather than with a U.S. customer for the most banal of reasons: Kreis Krankenhauser was using the SMS system to its fullest capabilities, and no U.S. customer compared in its use of its SMS PACS.

2. *Technical and cost considerations (video)*—German video is in the PAL format, which runs a picture at more than 625 lines. U.S. and Japanese video runs at NTSC, which is 525 lines. Therefore, SMS had to consider whether to use a German crew shooting in the PAL format and transfer the video later, or take over a U.S. crew.

   SMS management decided to hold the line on costs by limiting costs to those of one SMS communicator. Instead, SMS used a German crew (obtained by the local SMS office) and transferred the tapes to NTSC upon return to the United States. That actually turned out to be a sound managerial decision, as it only cost just $900 to transfer the video, compared to the cost of transporting and housing an entire video crew.

3. *Language and culture*—Another question SMS faced was deciding the *language* in which to shoot the video. As advised by both SMS International and the customers at Kreis Krankenhauser themselves, SMS shot the video in English, which is spoken and read fluently not only by SMS's customers in Germany, but throughout all of Europe and Asia. (Remember that SMS's target market, which consists primarily of clinicians, comprises a highly educated audience that speaks and writes English as a matter of course.) This is evidenced by the overall grasp of English among the people who were interviewed.

   The German *culture* that was exhibited in these customer testimonials was noteworthy. While the subjects were gracious and very happy to give their time to help SMS with the project, it was not in their nature to wax enthusiastic over the product. In fact, it was quite common for the interview subjects to give a long list of capabilities of the system and then conclude by saying it was "OK." Obviously, this was not sufficient for the video, as one wants customers to say that your product is *more* than OK.

   The behavior of these customers is evidence of Germany as a "low-context" culture; that is, Germans rely on the explicit and literal. Therefore, there is little body language or other expressions that show their contentment with the system. What they feel is expressed through their *oral* testimony. On the other hand, what they actually end up saying on tape is extremely valuable because it is distinct, exacting, and measurable (e.g., a precise accounting of the amount of money saved, definite and unequivocal reasons for their contentment with the system).

   (*Note:* These cultural differences did not become obvious until SMS was close to editing the final production. Because there was no footage of anyone saying that they were enthused about the SMS product, there was no concluding testimonial statement that could tie the production together. Therefore, SMS made an eleventh-hour decision to add a *narrator* whose words could provide the missing pieces together and wrap up the video with an appropriate marketing pitch.)

   The customers' willingness to work with us was fairly consistent with their egalitarian culture, and this was reflected in the generous giving of their time and effort toward this project.

   The *individualism* of the German culture is evidenced by the users' varied personal responses to the efficacy of the SMS system. Each respondent describes the efficacy of the system in terms of his/her own position in the organization: The controller speaks only in terms of money saved, the chief of staff of the satellite hospital speaks in terms of his own convenience, the chief of radiology speaks only in terms of the clarity of the image, and so on. There is very little mention of the convenience to co-workers, or even to *patients*.

4. *Regulatory issues in the production of the video*—In producing this video, attention had to be paid to relevant international law. In terms of FDA regulations, all PACS are subject to the international FDA agreement titled "CONFORMITY ASSESSMENT—SECTORAL ANNEX ON MEDICAL DEVICES," which is part of the harmonization that is currently in progress in European trade. This preamble of this document states that "carrying out the provisions of this Annex will further public health protection, will be an important means of facilitating commerce in medical devices, and will lead to reduced costs for regulators and manufacturers of both Parties, because they are medical devices."

   Furthermore, the Sectoral Annex states that its purpose is "to specify the conditions under which a

Party will accept the results of quality system-related evaluations and inspections and pre-market evaluations of the other Party . . . as conducted by listed conformity assessment bodies (CABs) and to provide for other related cooperative activities." The Annex applies to exchange and possible endorsement of certain types of reports from equivalent CABs. These reports include surveillance/post-market and initial/pre-approval inspection reports, pre-market product evaluation reports, quality system evaluation reports, and examination and verification reports (as referred to in the EC).

The medical device Annex is based on the concept of *equivalence*, defined as follows:

- "CABs in the EC are capable of conducting product and quality systems evaluations against U.S. regulatory requirements in a manner equivalent to those conducted by FDA;

- and CABs in the United States are capable of conducting product and quality systems evaluations against EC regulatory requirements in a manner equivalent to those conducted by EC CABs."

Stated in language that is more familiar to laypeople:

- Under the terms of the Sectoral Annex, SMS was not permitted to portray its medical device as one used for diagnostic purposes in the Europe *because it is not cleared for diagnostic purposes in the United States.*

Because the video does not show the SMS PACS being used for diagnoses in Germany—only reviews—SMS may show the video in the United States without violating FDA law.

Initially, the SMS sales team was thrilled that SMS was going to Europe to shoot this video: They advised the producer to show the German physicians using the SMS PACS for diagnostic purposes. They reasoned that, while U.S. doctors may not use the SMS system as a diagnostic tool, German physicians have no such restrictions; therefore, the diagnostic capabilities of the SMS could be shown in use in Germany. This was incorrect, given the terms of the Sectoral Annex as stated above, and SMS did not show its PACS used for diagnoses in the final production.

To overcome this problem, some customer interviews were shot twice: One take would conform to SMS's current status with the FDA, and a second take in which the diagnostic capabilities are touted—which SMS hopes to have in the future. Thus, if SMS files a 510k in the future to have diagnostic capabilities, the company will be able to revise the video with the more appropriate, more timely testimony.

RESULTS OF THIS MARKETING EFFORT

As of this writing, which is less than two months after the release of the video, it is somewhat premature to assess its ultimate success. However, certain promising trends can be noted:

1. *Credibility*—By focusing on a true and verifiable success with Kreis Krankenhauser, *the video gives SMS the opportunity to promote its ability to deliver a successful PACS*; before the testimony, that ability was only theoretical. The video has already been used to kick off marketing presentations, and it reportedly has helped set a positive tone that SMS has been able to follow up.

2. *Message Clarification—SMS's PACS marketers are better able to promulgate the company's ability to deliver the PACS.* These benefits include access to clinical data, archiving, geographical extension, and a host of cost benefits. This improvement can be measured by the additional number of leads generated and the higher level of interest in RFPs from SMS. (One notable example of this improvement: At a recent convention of the Radiological Society of North America—the largest convention or radiology professionals in the world—the producer of the video took the themes expressed therein and turned them into a stand-up presentation that was given every half hour for four days straight. As a result, SMS finished the convention with *double* the number of actionable leads over the previous year.)

3. *International Presence*—SMs can add to its image as a strong international health care technology provider by being able to claim rightfully that it is also a strong PACS provider. (In fact, people who have used the video in presentations have pointed out in their oral presentations that SMS beat the German technology giant, Siemans, in their own backyard!)

4. *Progress In Overseas Video Production*—Finally, this "project turned out to be somewhat different than "line 'em up and shoot" testimonial video for SMS. It was essential that the producer understood the ramifications of international trade law throughout this process, first in order to avoid the unnecessary shooting of video overseas (a potential waste of time and effort), and also to avoid trade regulation violations (market implications for SMS). *This finished production should also serve to make future SMS video producers and other marketing communicators cognizant of the cultural peculiarities of the company's overseas customers.* This heightened awareness will help the communicators predict how the customers will respond to questions and otherwise participate in testimonials.

EXHIBIT 1
THE GROWTH OF PACS

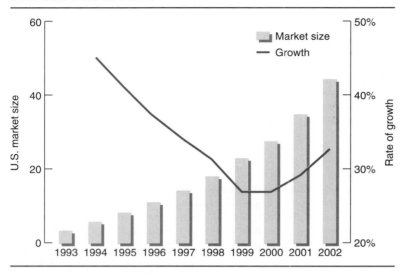

Source: Marketline International, PACS.

Discussion Questions

1. Discuss the capabilities of a PACS and the ways it can contribute to the operations of a health care institution.

2. Discuss SMS's organizational structure and its ability to conduct business internationally.

3. Did cultural differences play a role in SMS's process of recording testimony among the company's German customers? If so, then what was done to adjust?

4. Discuss the regulatory concerns that had to be addressed as they pertained to SMS's PACS as a medical device.

5. Discuss SMS's future plans to take on similar projects in other customer countries in the future. How useful will this experience be in the future?

CASE 8

TILTING WINDMILLS: SANEX TRIES TO CONQUER EUROPE

The message that rolled off the fax machine on August 3, 1993, in the office of Mr. Martin Muñoz, president of the Southern European division of the Household and

This case was prepared by T. V. Krishnan and Chet Borucki of Nijenrode University, The Netherlands. *Copyright 1996 by Nijenrode University, The Netherlands Business School.*

Body Care H&BC business unit of the Dutch-based international company Sara Lee/DE was depressing: "The liquid soap you conceived and successfully commercialised in Spain seven years ago has failed to make any inroads in the UK market. Sorry." To his secretary's utter surprise and shock, Martin Muñoz simply smiled.

As he kept staring at the fax message, Martin's thoughts drifted to the heated conversation he had had a couple of years back with Roger,[1] the head of Nicholas Laboratories in the UK, the pharmaceutical company acquired by Sara Lee/DE in the late 1980s. Martin at the time had caught the attention of senior management in the company by engineering the successful launch and diffusion of a new Bath & Shower liquid soap called Sanex in the overcrowded and mature Bath & Shower market. Though initially the underdog in a market dominated by giants such as Henkel and Reckitt & Coleman, Sanex quickly outpaced the competition in Spain thanks to the clear positioning it mustered through its powerfully appealing concept: Healthy Skin. Impressed by this achievement, Sara Lee/DE headquarters had decided to roll out Sanex throughout Europe, and had asked Martin to act as the coordinator for this project. In one of the many meetings that ensued, Roger vehemently opposed introducing the product to English consumers under the Sanex brand name, which he felt had "sanitary" connotations and would be ill-received by English consumers. Roger further argued, and correctly so, that despite their proximity, European countries had vastly different histories and cultures: a strategy that might look appealing in one market might very well look appalling in another country. Martin strongly counter-argued that the success of Sanex in Spain was more due to rational reasons and had nothing to do with any idiosyncratic nature of the Spanish consumer. Martin did not want any of his proven marketing strategies to be disturbed irrespective of where the products were to be marketed. In his role as project coordinator, Martin realized that he lacked the formal authority to challenge the autonomy of a Sara Lee/DE subsidiary and force Roger to accept his line of thinking, although clearly, he felt Roger was wrong. Undeterred, Roger had gone ahead anyway and introduced Sanex in the UK under a different label and with different marketing strategies.

Martin's informal response to Roger's fax message from the UK was akin to saying: "I told you so" and was further confirmation of his faith in and opinion of the Sanex brand. Senior management at Sara Lee/DE headquarters, too, backed Martin. They completely believed in the Sanex concept and came to believe in the merit of having a consistent marketing strategy to support that concept, and they responded formally and immediately. The following week, the chairman of Sara Lee/DE summoned the presidents of the European countries in the H&BC division to his office in Utrecht, the Netherlands, and made it clear that Sanex was to be rolled out across Europe just as it was. In essence, the chairman's decisive move gave Sanex a much needed shot in the arm, and

Martin was given *carte blanche* to roll out the product across Europe.

On the flight back from Amsterdam to Spain, Martin's heart was light, although his newly assigned responsibility for making Sanex a Euro brand weighed heavily in his mind. He was convinced that the recent decision by Sara Lee/DE's chairman would make things much easier for him. The country managers would be more willing to listen to him and appreciate the necessity of maintaining the integrity of the Sanex concept through adopting the strategy he formulated and successfully implemented in Spain: same brand name, same advertising copy, same pricing policy, same level of advertising and distribution support, etc. As he started penning down the factors that had compelled him to believe in a pan-European marketing strategy for Sanex, he caught a glimpse of a huge windmill disappearing in the Dutch horizon. He suddenly felt a shiver running down his spine: "Am I a maverick ready to challenge all those management theories that talk about the importance of cultural differences across countries or simply another Don Quixote attacking windmills? Can I apply the knowledge I gained by making Sanex a winner against all odds in Spain and make it a Euro brand?"

SARA LEE/DE: HISTORY AND STRUCTURE

Sara Lee/DE, which is a part of Sara Lee Corporation, Chicago, USA, is a Dutch-based multinational manufacturer of high-quality branded consumer products with annual sales of around Dfl 10.4 billion and 26,000 employees. The history of Sara Lee/DE can be traced back to 1753 to the founding of a family business—a small domestic grocery shop located in Joure in the north of the Netherlands that basically dealt in coffee, tea and tobacco. Many of its products were obtained from suppliers in the Far East. For seven generations, until 1976, the same family guided the development of the company, which was called Douwe Egberts.[2] In 1930 Douwe Egberts (DE) entered the export market, concentrating first on marketing tobacco products in Belgium and Germany. In the years following WWII, its export business really began to flourish. By 1960, DE accounted for more than half of Dutch tobacco and coffee exports and 39% of tea exports. The international growth of the company, in its true meaning, got its start in 1973 with the opening of its first coffee roasting plant in Brussels.

During the 1970s, the rich potential of DE captured the attention of senior management at Sara Lee Corporation, the Chicago-based consumer goods company, which at the time was trying to consolidate its businesses around

---

[1]The name of this case character has been disguised for confidentiality reasons.

[2]Douwe Egberts was the son of the founder Egbert Douwes.

a limited number of core product divisions. The history of Sara Lee Corporation, compared to that of DE, is rather short, but is more turbulent. Its roots go back to 1939 when Nathan Cummings took over a company in Baltimore that was trading in coffee, tea and sugar and was then operating under a different name. After the second world war, the company activities widened and it diversified through acquisitions primarily in the food business. In 1954, the company was renamed, aptly so, as Consolidated Foods Corporation (CFC). Soon thereafter, CFC moved its headquarters to Chicago. A notable turning point in the company's history occurred when Charles Lubin, who was managing a very successful and reputed bakery business in Chicago, merged his company with CFC. Lubin's leading product was a cheese cake named after his daughter, Sara Lee. From a reputational standpoint, Sara Lee cheese cake stood for consistent quality and had high brand equity. Initially, this merger had little impact on CFC as the growth of the company was almost totally fuelled by acquisitions of various sorts, including business units in non-food industry sectors. By the 1970s, CFC was a huge conglomerate comprised of 80 business units, many with successful brand names. But given the tremendous diversity of its businesses, the company lacked focus.

Things took a turn for the better when John Bryan became CFC's chairman in 1975. He undertook the massive task of refocusing the company around well-defined business units both within and outside of the food industry, and divested those units that did not fit that focus. He hated the name CFC which he felt connoted more an agglomeration of diverse interests rather than a unified company. Though it took nearly a decade, Bryan was able to rename CFC the Sara Lee Corporation (SLC) which he believed sent an appropriate message to all stakeholders about the quality the company sought to ensure in its products. Bryan also did not hesitate to acquire other companies (such as Hanes and Nicholas Kiwi) that he felt would bolster SLC's core business units. He was always looking for products with powerful brand equity. It wasn't long before the Dutch company DE captured his attention due to its strong brand image (the "coffee lady" who first appeared in 1898 is the trademark that decorates its coffee packages today). He started investing in DE in 1975 in a bid to establish a strong international coffee and grocery business. What started as a minority investment by SLC in DE evolved into a complete merger when in 1989, the former assumed complete control of the latter. The name Douwe Egberts Koninklijke Tabaksfabrick-Koffiebranderijen-Theehandel nv was changed to Sara Lee/DE nv when SLC reached a 100% equity interest, 41% in the form of voting shares and 59% in the form of share certificates issued by the independent Stichting Administratiekantoor Douwe Egberts Sara Lee. Consequently, this independent Dutch trust office retained the majority of voting rights in Sara Lee/DE (SL/DE).

SLC focused on five major divisions: Sara Lee Foods, Food Service, Personal Products, Coffee and Tea, Household and Body Care. After it started acquiring DE in the late 1970s, SLC gradually turned over the management of its Coffee and Tea business to SL/DE. With the support of SLC, the Dutch company immediately switched gears and consolidated its position around the globe, rapidly developing a stronghold in Europe. Like its parent, the Dutch company also pursued growth through acquisition. It acquired other European coffee and tobacco business units such as Maison de Cafe (France, 1977), Merrild (Denmark, 1979), Marcilla (Spain, 1980) and Van Nelle (The Netherlands, 1989). As a result, over the period between 1970 and 1990, sales grew from a mere Dfl 570 million to a mammoth Dfl 3.5 billion. As of 1990, the Coffee and Tea division of SL/DE commanded the market leadership position in its home country the Netherlands (72%) and Belgium (55%) and had sizeable market share in Spain (21%), France (16%) and Denmark (30%), as well as in Norway, Hungary, and Australia, amongst others.

Even though it concentrates exclusively on two main businesses, SL/DE still consists of nearly 100 companies, of which a majority are active in Western Europe. For the most part, these companies operate autonomously and many have their own production, marketing and sales departments. Thus, unlike other multinationals such as Procter & Gamble and Philips, SL/DE operates under different names in different countries. As mentioned previously, SL/DE expanded geographically through the acquisition of well-known name brands and companies in other countries.[3] When a firm was acquired, it was generally treated as a wholly-owned, subsidiary: no changes were made in the name of the company and its brands. Characteristically, SL/DE seldom launched a new brand or company offshore from scratch.

The organisational structure of SL/DE is not the same for all operations and products. The retail coffee operations (Douwe Egberts, Merrild, Marcilla among others) are organised by country and are responsible for their own production, marketing and sales. These country organisations report directly to the board of management in the Netherlands. Douwe Egberts Beverage Systems, active in the out-of-home-consumption market divested in 1998 has central production and marketing facilities in the Netherlands. In addition, it has its own sales organizations in a number of other countries. The H&BC division largely consists of regional units (which are comprised of combinations of several countries) and product groups and reports per region to the board of management in the Netherlands.

---

[3]For a complete listing of the various subsidiaries and affiliated companies of SL/DE around the world, go to www.saralee.com/homepage.html.

SL/DE first entered the Household and Body Care market in 1983 through an acquisition. That year, SLC started transferring control of its other business unit, Household and Body Care (H&BC to SL/DE by selling off its interest in the Dutch company Intradal to SL/DE. Intradal was a household name in oral care (e.g., Prodent Zendium) and toiletries in the Netherlands and Belgium. In 1984, SLC acquired the Australian company Nicholas Kiwi, which had operations all over the world with leading brands in the shoe care business. Later in 1988, control of this division also was transferred to SL/DE's H&BC division. The activities of the H&BC division were further widened with the acquisition of the consumer products division of the chemical giant Akzo in 1987. In summary, by the end of the 1980s, SLC wholly transferred control of the HBC division to SL/DE.

SL/DE managed the "Coffee and Tea" and "Household and H&BC Care" product divisions, and direct selling activities of its parent company Sara Lee Corporation from its headquarters in Utrecht, the Netherlands (see Figure 1). As of 1993, these two business units derived the greater percentage of their sales from Europe than the USA, whereas the sales from SLC's other two business units (Sara Lee Foods and Personal Products) came more from the USA than from Europe.

SL/DE's strategy of growth through acquisitions worked quite well. Table 1 illustrates the successful performance of the company from 1984 to 1992, with special focus on its H&BC division.

The H&BC division, which is comprised of several product groups such as detergents (Biotex, Blanc Nuclear, Neutral), cleaners (brands no longer exist White King, Bloo), shoe care (Kiwi shoe polish, spray and cream, Tuxan, Tana), insecticides (Catch, Bloom, Vapona), air-fresheners (Ambi-Pur, Parry's), divested, body care (lotions, liquid soaps and deodorants under the names of Radox, Sanex, Badedas, oral care (Prodent,

Zendium) and baby care (Zwitsal soap, cream and shampoo) had a turnover of 2.475 billion Dfl in 1992–93, approximately one-third of the total company turnover. Although there were many products in its portfolio, from its start, the H&BC division came to be more widely known for its insecticide and shoe care business units than for its body care and baby care units. This is probably because the company was spending all of its efforts to maintain the image of the strong brands it acquired from other companies, such as Kiwi, and many of these well-known brands happened to fall in the shoe care and insecticide sectors.

THE SPANISH H&BC MARKET AND MARTIN MUÑOZ

Cruz Verde-Legrain (CVL), SL/DE's 100%-owned subsidiary in Spain which was acquired in the early 1980s, was where the idea for Sanex originated. Up until the time it was acquired, CVL was primarily known for its insecticide products. The insecticide market periodically experienced erratic and often sizeable seasonal fluctuations as sales turnover was largely affected by varying weather conditions. To buffer CVL from these cyclical fluctuations, Martin Muñoz and the other members of the subsidiary's management team decided to research the possibility of adding other products to their limited portfolio. Martin and his management team agreed on two issues: first, the product should offer consumers some sort of "protection" like their insecticide products; second, the product should make use of the existing technical knowhow within the company. With these two broad objectives in mind, CVL management went on a 'fishing expedition.' They commissioned a firm to conduct semi-structured "focus group" interviews to surface new product ideas. During these interviews, focus group participants discussed several product categories, one of which was bath and

FIGURE 1

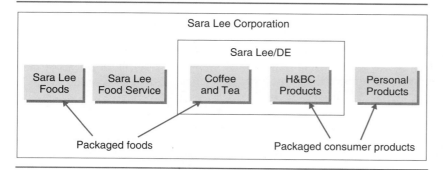

TABLE 1

SALES IN MILLIONS OF US $ OF THE TWO DIVISIONS OF SL/DE[4]

Year	1984	1985	1986	1987	1988	1989	1990	1991	1992
C&T	n.a.	1687	1626	1577	1663	1816	1834	1938	1919
H&BC	643	812	943	983	1104	1281	1196	1319	1227

shower gel. Unexpectedly, the interviewers noted that some of the participants complained bitterly about the irritating skin problems associated with the cosmetic-type liquid soaps available in supermarkets. When probed further, they also complained about the exorbitant prices of the medical-type liquid soaps carried by pharmacists. The "fishing expedition" had yielded promising results. Martin and his management team began to seriously think about the huge potential of a good liquid soap which could simultaneously offer "protection" to the skin and yet be readily available to the general public through supermarket and other retail outlets. Pressing forward, CVL decided to exploit the vacant spot between the cosmetic-type liquid soap and the medical-type liquid soap. It entered the body care market through this "gap."

The Spanish body care market was totally dominated by Henkel (with its FA brand), Beiersdorf (with its Nivea brand), and Gillette (with its Magno brand). CVL was clearly a nonentity. Martin and his management team very well knew that any management guru would advise him against pursuing opportunities that did not fit well with his business's strength or core competency, and would advise him against entering a mature market such as H&BC. But having made the decision to diversify from the volatile insecticide market, he

chose to take the risk. In 1985, against all odds, he entered the market with Sanex,[5] a Bath & Shower liquid soap product. To the whole industry's surprise, the launching of Sanex was not only immensely successful, but also redefined the whole structure of the Spanish H&BC market and was a milestone in CVL's and in Sara Lee/DE's history.

The H&BC Market in Spain

The body care sector of the H&BC market in Spain can be categorised into Bath & Shower Liquid Soap, Bar Soap, Hand Liquid Soap, Hair Shampoo, Deodorant and Body Colognes. The 1990 sales breakdown of this market by these six categories is provided in Table 2. Bath & Shower Liquid Soap leads the pack with annual sales totalling 51.7 million litres followed by Hair Shampoo with annual sales of 38 million litres.

The Bath and Shower Liquid Soap Market

The Bath & Shower liquid soap market experienced unprecedented growth in the 1980s thanks to Sanex. Table 3 illustrates the fantastic growth of this market in the ten year period from 1982 to 1991. From annual sales of 8.8 million litres in 1982, this market virtually exploded to

TABLE 2

1990 SALES BREAK-UP OF BODY CARE MARKET IN SPAIN

Category	1990 Sales in Million Litres	1990 Sales in Million US $
Bath & Shower	51.7	175
Bar Soap	8.7	51
Hand Liquid Soap	1.8	15
Hair Shampoo	38.0	154
Deodorants	34.0	103
Bath Colognes	13.6	54

[4]Toward the end of the 1980s and the early 1990s, the exchange rate between the US $ and the Dutch guilder fluctuated heavily, with Dfl more frequently appreciating against the dollar during this period.

[5]In reviewing the inventory of names CVL had registered that were available for use, Martin and members of his management team immediately chose Sanex due in its close association with the Spanish toast *Salad*, which means "to your health."

TABLE 3

LIQUID SOAP SALES GROWTH

Sales in	1982	1983	1984	1985	1986	1987	1988	1989	1990	1991
million litres	8.73	11.54	14.09	17.97	22.59	32.02	38.61	45.33	51.72	57.40

annual sales of 57.4 million litres in 1991, registering a compounded annual growth of 20.7%.

Much, if not all, of the tremendous sales growth achieved by the Bath & Shower liquid soaps in Spain can be attributed to the successful launching of Sanex in 1985 and to the subsequent frenzy of competitive moves that took place thereafter. Sanex was able to make a big impact in the body care market by the invention of a new dimension in the liquid soap category. The introduction of Sanex gave a vital boost to liquid soap sales, which otherwise were stagnant.

Positioning of Sanex

Prior to the introduction of Sanex in 1985, liquid soap was performing the usual and ubiquitous function of cleansing the body of its tough odors and dirt. Such a perception was reinforced by, for example, incorporating strong perfumes in liquid soaps and making them abrasive. Consumers using such liquid soaps came out of their bathrooms with a strong sense of having a dirt-free, odor-free, scented body. Under Martin's leadership, CVL first thought of viewing liquid soaps as more than a simple dirt and odor remover. CVL introduced properties that widened its scope. From being a mere body cleanser, liquid soap evolved into a dermo-protector (i.e., skin protector) in 1985 thanks to Sanex.

Table 4 identifies the main characteristics of the three key segments in the liquid soap, namely, cosmetics, dermo-protectors, and pharmaceuticals. It should be noted that this type of segmentation in liquid soap came into existence only with the introduction of Sanex. Thus,

with Sanex, CVL could be considered a pioneer in inventing a new dimension (dermo-protection) in the liquid soap category.

The cosmetics-type liquid soaps address, true to their name, only the external effects on the skin, while the dermo-protector seeks to make the skin healthier and more hygienic. CVL differentiated Sanex from the existing cosmetics-type liquid soaps by carefully adopting several unique physical attributes.

While Martin and his management team tried to incorporate the health and hygiene factors into their liquid soap, they did not want Sanex to "degenerate" to the level of an absolute pharmaceutical product (such as Ernopon and Multidermol) which would be a disaster in the mass consumer market. To achieve this goal, Sanex was produced in white color (a non-cosmetic color) to signal its hygienic properties and to differentiate it from the transparent nature of the pharmaceutical gels and the non-white colors of the cosmetics-type liquid soap. CVL made Sanex soft and slightly perfumed, while the cosmetics-type liquid soaps were clearly marked by their abrasive nature and strong perfumes and the pharmaceutical products were odorless. Sanex was also designed to produce foam lather that was to be more than that produced by a pharmaceutical product, but was to be less than that produced by a typical cosmetics-type liquid soap.

Thus, every effort was made to ensure that Sanex had the right combination of the pharmaceutical product and the cosmetic-type liquid soap, but was still well-differentiated from either of them. In this sense, CVL's management "discovered" a void between the cosmetics-type liquid soap which lacked medicinal properties

TABLE 4

THE THREE SEGMENTS OF LIQUID SOAP CATEGORY

Segment	Description	Sales in Million Litres	Stage of PLC
Dermo-protectors	Liquid, low foaming, slightly perfumed, white, soft, protection against bacteria	25.0	Growing
Cosmetics	Fluid, foaming, strongly perfumed, colored, abrasive	23.5	Mature
Pharmaceutical	Non-perfumed, liquid, transparent, low foaming, protective	n.a.	Mature

TABLE 5
SANEX POSITIONING IN THE LIQUID SOAP MARKET

Cosmetics Type	Sanex	Pharmaceutical
Bright colours	White	Transparent
Thick gel	Liquid	Thin Fluid
Strongly perfumed	Slightly perfumed	Non perfumed
Foaming	Low foaming	Non foaming
Abrasive ingredients	PH balanced	Neutral
Nonprotective	Protective	(Over) protection[7]

and the pharmaceutical soaps which lacked mass appeal,[6] and cleverly filled it with Sanex. A detailed list of the two-way differentiating physical characteristics of Sanex is provided in Table 5.

Marketing Mix Elements of Sanex

In 1985, the body care sector of the H&BC market in Spain was populated by about 107 brands managed by many different companies including corporate giants such as Beiersdorf (manufacturer of Nivea), Henkel, Johnson Wax and Revlon. The market was stagnant and very mature, and as such, the competition was severe. Cut-throat pricing was more the norm than the exception. No brand could muster more than a 7 percent market share. New products were being continually tested in the market since it was the only way a company could hope to increase its market share. As a result, the market was saturated with brands. And, it was in such a market Sara Lee/DE (i.e., CVL), an almost non-entity, was trying to launch its new brand, Sanex.

Compared to other me-too new brands in the market, one thing that was different about Sanex was that it had clear and distinctively unique features contributing to healthy skin. What remained to be done was the right marketing of this unique selling point (USP) to the consumer. This was not an easy job by any standard because Sanex's USP had to be conveyed to the consumers with the right message and had to be "sold" to the consumer at the right price. Otherwise, it might not achieve its potential. When interviewed about his role in launching Sanex,

Martin asserted: "If you are convinced about something, defend it with full force, since a half-hearted attempt would not reveal anything."

Advertising: As a first step, as CVL's senior manager, Martin made sure that Sanex maintained strong advertising support year after year, getting the highest share of voice (SOV) of all the liquid soaps (see Table 6).

However, high advertising expenditures were a necessary but insufficient condition. Martin decided that he had to handle the advertising of Sanex adroitly (to get the consumer's attention amidst the existing clatter of advertisement messages and make them *bear* what Sara Lee had to say about Sanex), and credibly (in order to make the consumer *listen* to CVL's claim on the usefulness of Sanex's USPs).

He handed over responsibility for copy creativity to a very young advertising company called Casadevall & Pedreno and asked them to design the message with four specific objectives in mind:

- The message should get the attention of consumers.
- The communication had to be straightforward and clear, focusing on the product.
- The message had to be rational and not emotional.
- The message should concentrate on the main benefit of Sanex, namely, "Sanex for healthy skin."

Casadevall & Pedreno came up with some brilliant advertisement copies. They minimized words (for example, typically the first 15 seconds of the advertising ran

[6]By mentioning that CVL, under Martin's leadership, "discovered" the void, we implicitly assume that there always existed a need for such a product in the market. But one can argue that such a need never existed (i.e., the consumers did not have or know this need), and it was Martin who created this need with Sanex, very similar to what Kellogg did with corn flakes or Compaq did with its portable personal computer. In this sense, the need itself can be said to have been "invented" by Martin.

[7]"Over" protective with respect to the dirt and odour accumulating in a day-to-day life of a typical consumer.

TABLE 6
SHARE OF VOICE OF SANEX AND SOME OF ITS COMPETITORS

SOV of	1987	1988	1989	1990
Sanex	18%	29%	33%	37%
FA	7%	11%	9%	13%
NB	—	—	12%	14%
Lux	—	—	1%	10%

TABLE 7
ADVERTISING MESSAGES

Spot . . .	Year run	Expenditure $	SOV	Objective
Salad	1986–88	1, 2.2, 2.6	na, 18%, 29%	Consumer education, Product description, Brand awareness
Shower	1989–90	3.1, 4.5	30%, 37%	Brand awareness
Pregnant	1991	1.5	35%	Maintenance of awareness, Notoriety

without any sound at all), and used no music for background, but maximized visual impact through slow motion and transition effects. All advertisement copies, however, were subject to the approval of CVL top management.

The initial advertisement that aired in early years clearly supported these objectives. The messages in these advertisements were loud, clear and to-the-point: using Sanex not only results in clear skin, but healthy skin. In the later years, however, as more and more competitive brands moved in, Martin authorised some seemingly unconventional advertising messages. For example, the advertisement titled "Spot Pregnant" was aimed to increase the awareness of healthy skin. To market Sanex deodorant, CVL aired the advertisement called "Spot Kiss" in which a woman was shown (in slow motion) kissing a man's armpit after he used Sanex. These "unconventional" messages were successful in *maintaining* the attention it had received from consumers. Table 7 provides further details on these three advertisements.

Whatever the advertisement message, efforts were undertaken to ensure that the message positioned the brand in the consumer's mind exactly as it was intended to be: the best combination of pharmaceutical and cosmetics-type liquid soaps. Whereas cosmetics-type liquid soaps focused on fantasy presentations and happy themes in their advertising messages and the pharmaceutical gels went for aseptic packaging and technical advertising, Sanex concentrated on informative and serious advertising. Although Sanex's later advertisements were somewhat less conventional, they nevertheless "hit the target" in terms of communicating Sanex's USP: *healthy skin.*

The advertisements were very successful not only for Sanex, but for Casadevall & Pedreno, the young advertising company, too. "The fact that their career success was tied to the success of Sanex," observes Martin, "possibly resulted in some fantastic advertisement copies for Sanex."

Pricing: Since Martin Believed that Sanex provided more benefits than an ordinary liquid soap, he thought it should be priced higher to signal the consumer that he or she was paying a premium to derive its extra utility. Pricing it at par with other liquid soaps and claiming bet-

ter performance would prove to be an oxymoron. Hence, Sanex was launched as a premium priced product and its 1985 shelf price was set at the level of market leader FA, which was at the top end of the market. Table 8 provides pricing information for Sanex and competing brands. Over the years, Sanex's price changed in line with general market trends.

Moreover, the high margin was found to be essential for providing support to the high expenses involved in advertisement and promotions. Of course, to minimize the potential downside of failure, CVL was very careful not to invest in huge manufacturing plants in the uncertain period following the launching of the brand. For the first three or four years, though the formula was created by CVL Laboratories,[8] manufacturing was outsourced. As the product proved itself to be a success, manufacturing was gradually moved in-house. A greenfield plant was built that was dedicated solely to manufacturing current and future Sanex brand products. Thus at the start, CVL tried its best to spend as much as possible solely in marketing the concept.

TABLE 8
PRICING OF SANEX

Price of . . . in Pesetas/Litre[9]	1986	1988	1990
Sanex	437	402	410
FA cosmetic	415	412	378
Nivea cosmetic	405	363	356
Neutrobalance	—	—	417
FA dermo	—	—	413
Nivca dermo	—	—	294

[8]CVL Laboratories was the name that CVL carefully chose to use in their Sanex packaging. The word *Laboratories* was added to signal to the potential buyers that the Sanex product shared only the "medicinal" attributes such as providing healthy skin with their core products (insecticides) and nothing else.

[9]Exchange rate: 1 US $=110 Pesetas.

TABLE 9

ENTRY TIMINGS OF SANEX AND ITS FOLLOWERS

Company	Cosmetic Brands	Dermo Brands	Dermo Launched in
CVL	S3, Moussel	Sanex	1985
Henkel	FA, Shim	Fa dermo, Shim dermo	1989, 1987
Beiersdorf	Nivea gel	Nivea dermo	1990
Colgate-Palmolive	Palmolive	Palmolive dermo	1991
Nobel-Gillette	Tojapin, Magno	Tojadermo	1986
Reckitt & Colman	Nenuco	Nenuco dermo	1989
Johnson & Johnson	—	Johnson's	1991
Bayer	—	Delial	1989
Gal	Nelia	Nelia dermo	1987

The Evolution of the Liquid Soaps Market Segment

Soon after Sanex was launched in 1985, the market signals were very clear that it was likely to be a winner. And as imitation is the sincerest form of flattery, competitors rushed in: Tojadermao (of Nobel-Gillette) in 1986, Nelia Dermo (of Gal) and Shim Dermo (of Henkel) in 1987, Johnson's (of Johnson & Johnson) in 1991, to name a few. Table 9 provides the entry years of some of these followers in the dermo-type liquid soap market.

Almost all of the cosmetics-type liquid soaps extended their lines into the dermo-protective segment by 1991. In 1985, Sanex was the sole market entry in this category, but by 1990, more than 50 different dermo-type liquid soap brands had been introduced in the market place. However, by capitalizing on its pioneering advantage as the first mover and through clever advertising, Sanex was able to maintain and even increase its market share lead over the years (see Table 10).

Partly because of the fact that consumers quickly accepted Sanex and partly because of the intense activity exhibited by all the players in the market place, the dermo segment of the liquid soap grew at an astonishing pace. Starting from virtually nowhere in 1985, within just six years this segment accounted for 50.5% of all the liquid soap sales, thus becoming its largest segment in 1991.

Extension of Sanex Concept to Other Categories

Without question, the success of Sanex created a storm in the highly intense H&BC market, and this storm had started escalating beyond the Spanish borders to cross Europe and even the globe. This was because it was widely becoming known that Sanex was more of a concept than a product, and that this concept of *finding and exploiting a void between two extremes* would soon be applied by its competitors in other categories of the personal care market. Martin decided to move first and fast. Within two years of launching Sanex (rather a short time to come to any conclusion about a product's success), Sanex was launched in the "hand liquid soap" category in 1987. The same name was retained in order to quickly leverage the brand name.[10] The risk paid off. By 1991, Sanex became the second leading brand in the Hand Liquid Soap market, accounting for 25% of its sales.

CVL continued to relentlessly capitalize on the success of the Sanex concept. It entered the deodorant

[10]It may be that he already had the intention to make Sanex an umbrella brand and establish Sanex as the flagship-name of the company across Europe.

TABLE 10

LEADERSHIP POSITION OF SANEX IN THE DERMO AND IN THE WHOLE LIQUID SOAP MARKET

Year	1986		1988		1990	
	Dermo	Liquid	Dermo	Liquid	Dermo	Liquid
Sales in million litres	2.281	22.58	12.585	38.61	25.034	51.72
Share of leader, Sanex	15%	8%	39.5%	12.9%	31.2%	15.1%
Share of first trailer	17.5%	8.6%	14.8%	7.4%	6.6%	7.0%
Share of second trailer	1.1%	4.4%	4.6%	4.2%	5.4%	5.3%

category in 1988 (spray and stick types) and 1989 (roll-on type), in the body milk category in 1990, and in the bath cologne category in 1991 under the Sanex brand. It was a race against time. Nothing else mattered. Table 11 reveals the success story of these launches.

What was remarkable was not just the success of these extensions, but how success was achieved—by carrying over in all details the Sanex concept and the associated marketing philosophy from liquid soap to those categories. The Sanex brand name was used for the products in all of the categories. True to its name, it carried the same USP, too, in all the categories: *Sanex means Healthy Skin*. It was priced at the premium level and positioned similarly in all the categories, and it also had the similar packaging style (blue color, contents conveying healthy skin message, etc.). In short, CVL, under Martin's leadership, made Sanex a concept that was simple, straightforward and could be applied with ease across all the body care products.

FROM SPAIN TO EUROPE

Sanex and SL/DE

For SL/DE, Sanex's performance in Spain was relatively minor compared to the brand equity enjoyed and the sales generated world-wide by its Douwe Egberts coffee and Kiwi shoe polish brands. However, Sanex was a breakthrough for SL/DE in that it represented the first time that the company had launched *a brand new brand,* resulting in the following:

- Until 1983, SL/DE did not exist at all in the H&BC market in Spain, a market that was populated with more than 104 brands, many of which were the likes of FA, Nelia and Nivea. However, thanks to Sanex, by 1990, SL/DE became a powerful force to reckon with in the Spanish H&BC market.

- Until the late 1980s, SL/DE's body care products received less attention than the shoe care and insecticides products. Thanks to Sanex, the company started consolidating its position in the body care market by exerting extra effort to strengthen brands in the UK and by acquiring leading brands in Germany (Duschdas and Badedas) from SmithKline Beecham, and other brands such as Brylcreem and Williams. The acquisition of these brands significantly strengthened the H&BC division.

- Until 1990, the norm for SL/DE was that growth would be achieved primarily through acquiring already established brand names. After 1990, thanks to Sanex, it proved to itself, to its stakeholders and to its parent company SLC that it could build a good brand in-house from scratch.

- Until 1985, since SL/DE's growth for the most part was achieved through acquisitions, its marketing operations were primarily geared towards maintaining and exploiting the acquired brand names. After 1990, thanks to Sanex, it could afford to allocate more resources to developing new brands at home.

The last statement is true not just for SL/DE but for the whole of SLC, because with the exception of the startup brands Douwe Egberts and Sara Lee, most of the leading brands of SLC were acquisitions. This fact was reaffirmed when the tremendous success of brand names like Sanex[11] prompted a change in SLC's mission statement. Formerly, SLC's mission was "to be a premier, global branded consumer packaged goods company." Today Sara Lee Corporation's mission is "to BUILD

---

[11]Another "brand new brand" was the Wonder-bra introduced by SLC in the USA in the early 1990s. Wonder-bra was a highly successful product and was appropriately recognised as such by *Fortune Magazine* in 1994.

TABLE 11
SANEX'S SUCCESS (AS OF 1990) IN EVERY BODY CARE CATEGORY

Category	Sales in m. Litres	Sanex Entered in	Sanex Share	Sanex Position	Main Competing Brands
Liquid soap	51.7	1985	15%	1	FA, Nivea
Hand liquid soap	1.8	1987	25%	2	Tacro, Heno de pravia
Deodorants	34.0	1988/89	7%	3	FA, Rexona
Body milk	2.5	1990	6%	4	Natural honey, Nivea
Bath cologne	13.6	1991	—	—	S3, FA

Leadership Brands in consumer packaged goods markets around the world." This change in the corporate mission statement was probably made to inform stakeholders of SLC's greater orientation toward brand building.

Hence it was no wonder that the management board of SL/DE at Utrecht, the Netherlands, was more than delighted to see an "invented here" brand making strong gains in unfamiliar territory. It also saw what Martin saw in Sanex: "Healthy skin" as a powerfully appealing concept and the tremendous potential to make it a global brand. And because building a global brand an important corporate objective, SL/DE's chairman and vice president of SLC asked Martin to launch Sanex throughout Europe. Martin willingly agreed and in 1988, put forth the following plan.

Martin's Plan to Make Sanex a Euro Brand

The objectives, the product policy, and the marketing policy of introducing Sanex were all identical for all the countries. The plan did not incorporate any modifications that would cater to any idiosyncratic characteristics of a country. What mattered was the integrity of the Sanex concept (whatever the contents, the look, the advertisement, or anything else). The plan was rather sharp (in content) and blunt (in appearance). It read as follows:

1. Global Objective:
   To have the same positioning, concept and product in all countries.
   To have a market share that places Sanex among the first four brands in each country.

2. Philosophy to be adopted:
   What is to be sold is not a product called Sanex, but a concept called Sanex, which simply implies "Healthy Skin."

3. Product Policy:
   Between cosmetic and pharmaceutical.
   Basically for the family.
   Common image for all the product categories.
   Formula is "keep skin healthy."

4. Marketing Policy:
   Premium price.
   Strong advertising that conveys the concept.
   Packaging (color, message etc.) should be same, except, of course, the language.
   Launchings shouldn't be based on promotions, but on the possibility of getting to know the product.
   Massive distribution support to be ensured in a short time.
   Samples should be distributed only after a considerable level of awareness is reached.

5. Formula and specifications of the product to be controlled by R&D centralized in Spain.

6. Manufacturing to be centralized in Barcelona, Spain (IPC, International Production Centre).

7. Status report should go from each country to Spain (i.e., to Martin) every two months.

8. Monthly meeting initially, and quarterly meeting thereafter with the Sanex team in Spain.

9. Any change whatsoever, be it product formula, price, or advertising, to be approved by the IPC.

10. TV creativity in advertisement messages also to be directly managed by IPC.

11. Extensions into other categories:
    Everything remains the same except the pricing factor, which can be reduced if Sanex in that particular product category does not expect to bring any differential benefits to the consumers.

Initial Reaction from SL/DE Headquarters

The management board at SL/DE in the Netherlands, though new to the H&BC market, had nonetheless been overseeing an international company for many years. The international structure of SL/DE, however, is different from that of other multinationals such as Procter & Gamble. SL/DE owns many companies offshore, but they all operate under different names. For the most part, these companies operate autonomously and many have their own production, marketing and sales departments. This is because SL/DE, like its parent, strongly believes in reinforcing and sustaining entrepreneurship qualities, and in fact, this has been one of the main objectives of the company right from the time of DE's merger with SLC.

Although the subsidiaries enjoyed full freedom, the management board in the Netherlands expected little opposition from them in launching Sanex throughout Europe. After all, who would say no to having a proven product with a successful track record like Sanex in his portfolio? Moreover, since SL/DE is new to the H&BC market, it offered no equivalent brand in the H&BC markets of most of these countries that would possibly be cannibalised by introducing Sanex. Hence the chairman of the board was very optimistic that Martin would easily obtain the necessary help to transfer Sanex to other European markets.

Thus, SL/DE headquarters completely agreed with Martin on the importance of maintaining the integrity of the Sanex concept, regardless of the country in which it was to be launched. Such integrity could only be maintained through adopting appropriate advertisement copies, packaging etc. that were consistent with the product image. And, since the set of marketing strategies adopted in Spain had already proven to be one such set of appropriate strategies, the chairman appointed Martin as the Manager of Sanex with the primary responsibility of coordinating the activities concerning the introduction of Sanex in other countries.

For Martin, too, the job seemed straightforward. He had a good product that had already proven its worth in a large country. In his opinion, Sanex helped the consumer satisfy a unique need, and that particular need would be more or less the same irrespective of the country in which the consumer resided. Hence, to introduce it in other European countries, he had to simply talk to his colleagues in these markets and educate them about key success factors, namely, the strategies concerning the positioning of the product and the supporting marketing mix elements, and the rest would take care of itself. However, he wanted to make sure that everything that figured in Sanex's success in Spain should be employed in other countries too without any change. With this idea in mind, the plan was proposed.

To the surprise of SL/DE's chairman and his senior management team at headquarters, the initial reactions from managers from other countries such as Denmark, the Netherlands, France, Belgium, UK, and Greece to the plan were quite unfavorable. Some of them were negative but accommodative, and some were absolutely negative.

Reaction from the Netherlands

The Netherlands was one country that offered considerable support for Sanex, though not initially nor directly. Ironically, the Netherlands was probably the only country that had every reason to abandon Sanex. Almost every member of Intradal, the SL/DE company in the Netherlands (the equivalent of CVL in Spain), had one objection or another to the brand name and product, Recalls Mr.? H. van Doornewaard, Product Manager of the company, "Some objected to its name, some objected to packaging, some to its 'bad' perfume, . . ." Many opposed using the same name Sanex indicating that it implied the sanitary aspects of the product more than anything else. The packaging of Sanex in blue and white looked medicinal to many and signalled a product anything other than a bathroom product. "In fact, it is uniquely ugly with respect to the other bath products in the market such as Nivea" asserts Doornewaard. However, the marketing team understood very well that Sanex, which had been very successful in Spain, deserved more than off-the-cuff comments. In order to do a scientific analysis, the marketing team carried out detailed market research on Sanex in the "as is" condition (i.e., same name, same packaging, etc.)

To everyone's relief in Intradal and to Martin's complete dismay, the market research showed that Sanex would be a disaster in the Dutch market. The survey respondents clearly hated the product. Intradal was

not unfamiliar with market research studies, having carried out many in the past which had predicted actual outcomes remarkably well. In Sanex's case, Intradal would normally have abided by the marketing research results were it not for the assertiveness of its Marketing Director, Mr. Rien van der Veen.[12]

Luckily for Sanex, Rien happened to be an ex-CVL manager who had witnessed first-hand the introduction and growth of Sanex in Spain and who had personally experienced its success. During his stay at CVL, he had come to completely believe in the Sanex concept. As such, he placed less faith in the results of the Dutch market research studies. In the words of Rien, "it is very hard to design questionnaires for new products, especially for those that are radically new such as Sanex, since consumers hardly can tell anything about a new product." To him, it simply sounded foolish to ask the consumers about products that did not exist before. In an after-thought, Doornewaard completely agrees with him, noting the failures of market research studies carried out for New Coke and the Sony Walkman.[13]

Rien overruled the market research results and introduced Sanex in the Dutch market. He adopted the same name Sanex, adopted the same "ugly" packaging, same perfume, same market positioning, same pricing, same advertising, etc. He could not have been more correct. Sanex stormed into the Dutch market like a tornado. The product was so successful that SL/DE's competitors experienced formidable barriers to entering the market with similar products. The few companies who managed to launch their own dermo-protector products did not get to see much daylight, Sanex virtually became a monopoly in the Dutch dermo-protector segment. It ended up receiving many accolades such as "Innovative product of 1991." Sanex Shower, a product extension, also got off to a very good start, capturing around 4 percent of the market within a year of its introduction.

And, the marketing research group at Intradal learned an important lesson.

"Of course we did manage to change one thing," confesses Doornewaard rather proudly. "The Spanish packaging indicates that the product is for both skin and hair,

---

[12]The name of this case character has been disguised for confidentiality reasons.

[13]Coca Cola spent millions of dollars in marketing research in a bid to ensure that New Coke, the replacement for their historically successful 100 year-old mainstay soft drink product, would be very appealing to consumers, but on launch, the widely advertised New Coke failed miserably. On the other hand, market research predicted only a very small market for the Sony Walkman!

while the Dutch packaging stresses only skin and not hair." Mr. Van Bemmelen former President of Intradal, offers an interesting explanation to this: "In Spain, we have a cultural difference. It has become a custom not to treat hair differently from skin, but in the market such as ours, hair is looked at differently from skin." "For example," he continues, "shampoo, the hair-specific product, has never been as important in Spain as it is here."

Sanex was not only successful with its shower gel (liquid soap), but also was very successful with its deodorant and other product extensions. The runaway success of Sanex and its extensions in the Dutch market was partly due to the fact that the marketing team came up with many innovative promotional schemes. For example, door-to-door sampling was done for Sanex liquid soap in more than three waves; in 1991, the third year after Sanex liquid soap got off to a successful start, Sanex deodorant was introduced by giving away free samples to the purchasers of Sanex liquid soap. Thus, the Sanex user base was heavily inundated with product extensions, and before they knew it, had become strong and loyal consumers of Sanex products.

"It is not the Sanex soap or deodorant that our consumers buy," vociferously objects Van Bemmelen, "it is the Health factor that our consumers buy from us through purchasing our Sanex products." The marketing team saw to it that the "Health" concept, and not any specific product of Sanex, got projected in advertisements (they managed to maintain a 30 to 40% SOV in the first two years, which was very high in the Dutch market), packaging, etc. For example, they used the Spot Salad advertisement copy more than any other copy since it was only in that advertisement that the concept "Health," and only the concept "Health," came out. "What other connection could a consumer possibly make between a salad and a shower gel?" quips Van Bemmelen. This may have prompted the company to explore so many successful product extensions[14] around this "Health" concept, and probably may not have happened if they had tried to build those extensions around, say, the Sanex liquid soap product.[15]

However, it became very clear to everyone at SL/DE that the key to Sanex's success in the Dutch market was purely due to its strong and clear positioning strategy and the absolute support it received from the president at Intradal. This victory was crucial for Sanex for many reasons: it was the first success outside Spain, the way success was achieved defied the prevailing rules of the game, and it hinged totally on top management support for the product and the winning Spanish theme.

Reaction from France

The initial reaction from France was similar to that from the Netherlands, but less negative. The management team of Kiwi France (the French subsidiary of SL/DE in the H&BC sector) was appalled by the Sanex brand name and its packaging style. "To the French," asserts Mr. Corinne Oppenheim, the Sanex Product Manager of Kiwi France, "any word that ends with 'ex' sounds 'hard', and in our opinion, the name Sanex did not go well with the mildness (i.e., milder than pharmaceutical equivalent) property it portrayed." All such misgivings Corrine had were shared by everyone on his management team.

Apparently not convinced by Sanex's success story in Spain, Kiwi France carried out a marketing research study on Sanex in the "as is" condition. The study revealed that the French consumers shared the beliefs held by the management team of Kiwi France. Though the results were not as disastrous as those that came out of the Dutch market research study, they did not show any positive support for the Sanex brand name and the packaging style.

However, the research results showed that Sanex could be a strong niche product. Corinne explains: "It addresses shower gel users who want to take care of their skin and all people who take showers and who are attracted by the convenience of gel but refuse existing gels because they are too aggressive and unnatural." The management team totally agreed on the fact that Sanex had a very clear USP in this segment:

Original & new:	Not yet used in France.
Modern:	Compared to present shower gels, the dermo-protector action is "up to date," credible and serious (the pharmaceutical aspects,. i.e., the neutral Ph level, etc., are credible).
Attractive:	For the shower gel users, Sanex is the gel that they have been waiting for that both washes and takes care of the skin, and for soap users, Sanex is attractive because it seems natural and less aggressive than other products.

Hence, the decision was taken to launch the product and Sanex appeared on the French retailers' shelves in January 1991. Kiwi France maintained the Spanish strategy in principle; they favoured the strong and distinctive positioning of Sanex and the pricing strategy (i.e., premium pricing), but were less in favour of the advertising copies. Even in the positioning of the

[14]Since brand extensions needed to be approved by the Sanex co-ordinating team in Spain, the Netherlands team sometimes had to fight with the board for good board extensions.

[15]Mr. Van Bemmelen is rather proud that Intradal was able to successfully market the "Health" concept, which is much broader than the "Healthy Skin" concept marketed by his Spanish predecessor.

brand, Kiwi France made sure that Sanex addressed the needs of a good "shower" gel, and not the "shower & bath" product. "Addressing both bath and shower problems with a single product creates a misunderstanding since the French people use quite different products for bath (which is a leisurely affair) and shower (which is a quick affair)," explains Corrine. The French also prevented Sanex from targeting the hair-care sector, since in their opinion, it was not yet proven.

In the final analysis, Kiwi France maintained the same product, the same packaging (though the market research studies had showed that the French consumers wanted it to be a bit more attractive and lively), same price (i.e., premium price), and same advertising. "The main reason for adopting the same packaging and advertising in spite of lack of support from market reasearch studies," confesses Corinne, "is the fact that they are 'distinct,' serious and clearly understandable, thus satisfying the vital functions of a good communicator." As a result, Sanex started off with a 1.2% share of the market (with sales 5.8 million FF) in 1991, and reached a market share of 2.2% (with sales of 18.6 million FF) the following year. The initial figures showed, in the words of Corinne, "Sanex looks successful in our country."

Reaction from Denmark

The initial reaction from Blumoller, Denmark, (the Danish subsidiary of SL/DE) was very similar to those from the Netherlands and France. It was very negative. The management team and its president, Mr. Vangt Sinius Clausen, both hated the name Sanex and its packaging style, but they were somewhat positive about the perfume. The Danish team also conducted marketing research to test the Sanex name, packaging style, etc. The results showed that the Sanex name would be a disaster in the marketplace and the packaging was found to be unattractive.

However, the fact that Sanex had been hugely successful in Spain and because SL/DE's chairman was interested in furthering its success made Vangt reconsider the issue. To the relief of both Martin and SL/DE senior management, he decided to give it a try. "In fact," Vangt reflected on a similar situation a few years back, "our initial market research about Zendium, our very successful toothpaste, was also equally very negative, but we went ahead with it anyway because we believed in its positioning." In Sanex's case, the management team in Denmark fully agreed that the brand had a fantastic positioning, so it was decided to ignore the market research results and launch Sanex. The initial results indicated that the decision was right. Sanex clearly showed the signs of a very successful launch.

"I firmly believe," asserts Vangt, "that Sanex will eventually get a market share higher than it mustered in Spain in the same time span."

Reaction from the UK

Of all the negative reactions Martin received, probably those from the UK were the most severe. At the time, SL/DE did not have a full-fledged H&BC division in the UK. It intended to use Nicholas Laboratories (acquired for some other purpose) for handling Sanex. The principal manager of the Laboratories was Roger. From the very start, Roger kept raising objections, in a very authoritative tone. He argued that Sanex would imply something similar to sanitary napkins to a typical UK consumer, and hence labeling the liquid soap package as Sanex would be disastrous. Martin, of course, was not pleased as his goal was to make Sanex a Euro brand, and later a highly recognised global brand, similar to brands such as Kiwi, Coca Cola, Douwe Egberts and Sara Lee. Though the name Sanex was derived from the Spanish word 'Sanos' which means "healthy," it had close links to similar sounding words in other languages which had somewhat similar meanings (Table 12). Martin further pointed out that all these different words in different languages were basically rooted in a Latin word which meant health.

"Sanex is not like Nova, the brand name the automobile giant General Motors tried to export to Mexico from the USA,"[16] Martin argued. However, Roger was not about to give up his fight. He countered, "Of course, all these words mean the same in the dictionary, but people in different communities perceive the same word with different implications depending upon the cultural and other influences in the surroundings."

Given SL/DE's policy of subsidiary autonomy, Roger won the battle with Martin. He changed the name Sanex to Sante, altered the marketing strategies accordingly in every aspect, and launched the product in the UK in 1991. But by 1993, the results showed that Roger had lost the war, and lost it heavily. The product failed miserably. The mistake could have been anywhere in the system: the product itself,[17] the new name Roger had adopted, the marketing plan, and/or simply the time of introduction. No one would know for sure what the reasons for failure were.

---

[16]It is rather well known that GM made a big mistake in carrying the car name Nova from the USA to Mexico, because the word Nova in Spanish implies "does not go."

[17]It is worth noting that SL/DE already had a brand called Radox in the UK body care market.

TABLE 12

SANEX IN DIFFERENT LANGUAGES

Language	Closest Word	Meaning
Spanish	Sanos	Healthy
French	Sanitair	Healthy, carrying a medical flavor
English	Sanitary	Healthy, carrying a medical flavor
Dutch	Sanitas	Healthy

The Decisive Role of SL/DE Headquarters

"Without the unequivocal support granted by Headquarters," Martin recollects, "Sanex would have remained confined to Spain."

The board of management in the Netherlands was furious at the way things turned out in the UK. Members of the board had not initially intervened in the conversation between Martin and Roger, and in fact did not intervene in any of the countries' objections to Martin's plan and their marketing research. The board reasoned that the arguments would eventually result in a good plan for each country. That proved to be a mistake—a big and costly mistake.

SL/DE's CEO had a dilemma. Either he had to let things be as they were ("status quo," thus maintaining the subsidiaries' autonomy over the internationalisation plan), or he had to initiate changes in policies and procedures and let them be dictated as far as Sanex was concerned (thus restricting the autonomy of the subsidiaries to a certain extent). He was sure of one thing, however. In his view, the potential success of the Sanex concept throughout Europe was dependent on maintaining its integrity. Moreover, the initial positive signals he had been receiving from Denmark and France, and especially what he saw in the Netherlands where Sanex succeeded in the "as is" condition thanks to the unequivocal support from the president, greatly influenced his ultimate decision to award full authority to pursuing a pan-European strategy based on the original Spanish strategy. Further, he personally believed that an effective implementation of this strategy to make Sanex a Euro brand would need

* a strong strategic consensus among all the country managers,

* a greater centralization of authority for setting policies and allocating resources, at least in the starting phase of Sanex, and

* outright support from the top management of SL/DE.

On the other hand, creating a new line of authority at the product level would certainly cause confusion and escalate organizational control problems. "Since SL/DE has so far been very successful thanks to the autonomy enjoyed by its subsidiaries," the board argued, "changing it for the sake of Sanex could prove to be a disaster."

After carefully weighing the pros and cons of these two options, the CEO and the board decided to retain Martin as project coordinator (i.e., a staff function and not a line function). However, they also took steps to ensure that all the country managers understood that the Sanex concept received the full support of top management. Thus, in the second week of August 1993, SL/DE's CEO called in all the country managers in the H&BC division, and directly informed them of his decision: Sanex was to be introduced in every country, Martin was the coordinating manager for Sanex across Europe empowered with decision-making responsibility such that anything to do with Sanex was subject to his approval, and that Martin should expect full support from each country.

MARTIN'S RATIONALE FOR THE PAN-EUROPEAN STRATEGY

Martin was in good spirits on his return flight to Spain. He had already made up his mind that Sanex had to be introduced in other European countries in the same fashion as was done in Spain and he was pleased that the board and the CEO, in particular, supported his position on the matter. He reclined fully in his seat, and slowly went over the arguments he put forth the day before to the CEO:

1. Having a single product with the same name and a similar packaging for all countries would enable mass production in the International Production Centre at Barcelona for the whole European market.

   Mass production ensures consistent image and quality across countries (which is an attractive feature in itself since people travel a lot these days, especially across Europe, and many of them look for—if not search for—the familiar brand wherever they travel). In addition, mass production results in huge economics of scale through centralized purchasing and logistics design, and it results in rapidly lowering operating costs thanks to a faster learning curve (the phenomenon of gradual reduction in the unit cost of production with experience). The cash saved from production could, if needed, be applied to improving the effectiveness of marketing, through ensuring that Sanex obtains the maximum SOV and distribution support in each country it is entering, which are very important for the brand's success in any overcrowded market.

2. Thanks to the policies adopted by the EU in the past four decades, the Western European countries tend to converge in terms of people's buying power, consumption patterns (for example, more out-of-home consumption), standard of living, general economy of the countries such as per capita income and inflation, consumers' attitude toward maintaining good health and environment, interest and involvement in sports and cultural activities, and their readiness to support products with good value (for example, private label products).

3. In the case of durable goods, where word-of mouth plays a significant role, and in the case of groceries such as cereal or beverages, where the consumption pattern is affected by the particular upbringing in a family and a society, there is a valid reason to believe that differences in the societal behaviour between two countries might influence sales. However, in the case of Sanex, which appeals explicitly to the rational part of the consumers' purchasing process, it can hardly be expected that there will be any significant differences between consumers of two different countries.

4. Though Sanex addresses the whole market, it specifically appeals to those who care more about their health. These consumers tend to have similar lifestyle and purchasing behavior patterns (as far as buying products like Sanex is concerned) regardless of the nation or culture they belong to, just like the jazz lovers and pizza lovers across the world.

5. The marketing conditions, such as the consumers' familiarity with various marketing tools and strategies, and their familiarity with brand proliferation and brand images do not look different from one country to another.

6. Retail and distribution sectors of all the key European countries look alike, with the result that consumers in various European countries are affected (in their purchasing intention and behaviour) in a more or less similar manner to the marketing mix activities such as end-aisle displays in the supermarkets, promotions, price discounts, and media advertising.

7. The market structure of the body care industry in terms of its key competitors and intracompetitive activities is not very different from one country to another.

8. Sanex is positioned in a global body care sector, whether we like it or not, and thus it faces competition mainly from other multinationals and not locals. Hence, a global strategy is needed to wage an international competition.

9. Last, but the most important of all the reasons, is the fact that the integrity of the Sanex concept should not be sacrificed for the sake of a country's idiosyncratic attributes. Moreover, its positioning is very strong and unique and cuts across all borders, whether national or cultural. And, we have a winning theme. Why disturb it?

Martin paused to reflect for a moment. However convincing his arguments were in favour of a concept-consistent pan-European strategy for Sanex, however strong the SL/DE board was in favor of it, and however convincing the success of Sanex in the Netherlands, Martin could not avoid thinking about the possibility of a failure of his strategy in one country or another. After all, the marketing research studies in the Dutch, the French and the Danish markets had initially rejected the product. "Moreover," he could not help continuing in that line of thinking, "though the results I have been receiving from these three markets signal that Sanex is currently performing well, still I cannot overlook the fact that these early sales are only signals, and perhaps unreliable ones at that."

As he adjusted his seat to the upright position in preparation for landing, his thoughts drifted back to the dancing shadows of the blades of the Dutch windmill which he noticed shortly after his plane departed from Schiphol Airport a scant few hours ago. Immediately, the image of Cervantes' hero Don Quixote attempting to tilt windmills came to mind. The recognition of the similarity of his situation to this fictional Spanish *cabellero* initially made him laugh but then caused him to wonder: Was he not also a modern-day Don Quixote challenging dominant paradigms and market research? Was he seeing things clearly, and were his instincts correct? Would his strategy to make Sanex a Euro brand succeed?

POSTSCRIPT 2000

The Sanex brand is currently marketed in more than twenty countries—primarily in Europe, but also in Asia and Africa. Nowadays, Sanex features a wide range of products, including bath and shower gels, deodorants, body care, shaving and hair care products. Sara Lee/DE plans further expansion in the Sanex product line and in the territories within which Sanex is marketed. In just fifteen years Sanex has developed from a local, Spanish brand into a successful Euro brand and is now on the threshold of becoming a true worldwide brand.

The Sanex concept still is healthy skin, the basic positioning still "Keeps Skin Healthy." Due to its healthy skin concept, Sanex is inherently linked to sports. This sports/ health relationship has been successfully developed in many Sanex countries where consumers perceive the brand and its high-quality products as a complement to their daily healthy routine and lifestyle. Since 1997, Sanex has been involved in professional women's tennis. Initially it did this through the sponsorship of young, local tennis talents. In 2000 it was the title sponsor of the Sanex WTA Tour, the premier women's sport Circuit in the world.

◆ ◆

CASE 9

ANHEUSER-BUSCH INTERNATIONAL, INC.: MAKING INROADS INTO BRAZIL AND MEXICO

HISTORY

In 1852 George Schneider started a small brewery in St. Louis. Five years later the brewery faced insolvency. Several St. Louis businessmen purchased the brewery, launching an expansion largely financed by a loan from Eberhard Anheuser. By 1860 the enterprise had run into trouble again. Anheuser, with money already earned from a successful soap-manufacturing business, bought up the interest of minority creditors and became a brewery owner. In 1864 he joined forces with his new son-in-law, Adolphus Busch, a brewery supplier, and eventually Busch became president of the company. Busch is credited with transforming it into a giant industry and is therefore considered the founder of the company.

Busch wanted to break the barriers of all local beers and breweries, so he created a network of railside icehouses to cool cars of beer being shipped long distances. This moved the company that much closer to becoming one of the first national beers.

In the late 1870s, Busch launched the industry's first fleet of refrigerated cars, but they needed more to ensure the beer's freshness over long distances. In response, Busch pioneered the use of a new pasteurization process.

In 1876 Busch created Budweiser, and today they brew Bud the same way as in 1876. In 1896 the company introduced Michelob as its first premium beer. By 1879 annual sales rose to more than 105,000 barrels and in 1901 the company reached the one-million barrel mark.

In 1913, after his father's death, August A. Busch, Sr., took charge of the company. It was a rocky time for the industry, however, with World War I, Prohibition, and the Great Depression. To keep the company running,

Anheuser-Busch switched its emphasis to the production of corn products, baker's yeast, ice cream, soft drinks, commercial refrigeration units, and truck bodies. They stopped most of these activities when Prohibition ended. However, the yeast production was kept and even expanded, to the point that Anheuser-Busch became the nation's leading producer of compressed baker's yeast through the encouragement of the company's new president in 1934, Adolphus Busch III.

August A. Busch, Jr., succeeded his brother as president in 1946 and served as the company's CEO until 1975. During this time eight branch breweries were constructed and annual sales increased from three million barrels in 1946 to more than 34 million in 1974. The company was extended to include family entertainment, real estate, can manufacturing, transportation, and major-league baseball.

August A. Busch III became president in 1974 and was named CEO in 1975. From that time to the present, the company opened three new breweries and acquired one. Other acquisitions included the nation's second-largest baking company and Sea World. The company also increased vertical integration capabilities with the addition of new can manufacturing and malt production facilities, container recovery, metalized label printing, snack foods, and international marketing and creative services.

CORPORATE MISSION STATEMENT

Anheuser-Busch's corporate mission statement provides the foundation for strategic planning for the company's businesses:

> The fundamental premise of the mission statement is that beer is and always will be Anheuser-Busch's core business. In the brewing industry, Anheuser-Busch's goals are to extend its position as the world's leading brewer of quality

This case was prepared by Professor Masaaki Kotabe with the assistance of John Graham of Temple University (1999).

products; increase its share of the domestic beer market 50% by the late 1990s; and extend its presence in the international beer market. In non-beer areas, Anheuser-Busch's existing food products, packaging, and entertainment will continue to be developed.

The mission statement also sets forth Anheuser-Busch's belief that the cornerstones of its success are a commitment to quality and maintaining the highest standards of honesty and integrity in its dealings with all stakeholders.

BEER AND BEER-RELATED OPERATIONS

Anheuser-Busch ranks as the world's largest brewer and has held the position of industry leader in the United States since 1957. More than four out of every ten beers sold in the United States are Anheuser-Busch products.

The company's principal product is beer, produced and distributed by its subsidiary, Anheuser-Busch, Inc. (ABI), in a variety of containers primarily under the brand names Budweiser, Bud Light, Bud Dry Draft, Michelob, Michelob Light, Michelob Dry, Michelob Golden Draft, Michelob Gold, Draft Light, Busch Light, Natural Light, and King Cobra, to name just a few. In 1993 Anheuser-Busch introduced a new brand, Ice Draft from Budweiser, which is marketed in the United States and abroad as the preferred beer because it is lighter and less bitter than beer produced in foreign countries. Bud Draft from Budweiser was first introduced in the United States in late 1993 in fourteen states, with a full national rollout in 1994 in the United States and abroad.

SALES

Anheuser-Busch's sales grew slowly after a sales decline in 1994. The company's principal product, beer, produced and distributed by its subsidiary, ABI, sold 96.6 million barrels of beer in 1997, an increase of 1.05 percent compared to 1996 beer volume of 95.1 million barrels. The gross sales for Anheuser-Busch Companies, Inc., during 1997 were $12.83 billion, an increase of $820 million over 1995 gross sales of $12.01 billion. Net sales for 1997 were $11.07 billion, lower than a record net sales of $11.51 billion in 1993.

ANHEUSER-BUSCH INTERNATIONAL, INC.

Anheuser-Busch International, Inc. (A-BII), was formed in 1981 to explore and develop the international beer market. A-BII is responsible for the company foreign beer operations and for exploring and developing beer markets outside the United States. Its activities include contract and license brewing, export sales, marketing and distribution of the company's beer in foreign markets, and equity partnerships with foreign brewers.

A-BII has a two-pronged strategy: (1) Build Budweiser into an international brand and (2) build an international business through equity investments or leading foreign brewers. In seeking growth, Anheuser-Busch International emphasizes part ownership in foreign brewers, joint ventures, and contract-brewing arrangements. These give the company opportunities to use its marketing expertise and its management practices in foreign markets. The success of these growth opportunities depends largely on finding the right partnerships that create a net gain for both companies. Other options for international expansion include license-brewing arrangements and exporting.

A-BII is currently pursuing the dual objectives of building Budweiser's worldwide presence and establishing a significant international business operation through joint ventures and equity investments in foreign brewers. Anheuser-Busch brands are exported to more than sixty countries and brewed under Anheuser-Busch's supervision in five countries. A-BII has experienced international growth in all operating regions with a 9 percent market share worldwide and has the largest export volume of any U.S. brewer. Anheuser-Busch had more than 45 percent of all U.S. beer exports and exported a record volume of more than 3.4 million barrels of beer in 1998.

Market Share

The top ten beer brands worldwide for 1998 in worldwide market share are as shown in Table I. Most recently, Anheuser-Busch has announced several agreements with other leading brewers around the world, including Modelo in Mexico, Antarctica in Brazil, and Tsingtao Brewery in China. These agreements are part of A-BII's two-pronged strategy of investing internationally through both brand and partnership development. Through partnerships A-BII will continue to identify, execute, and manage significant brewing acquisitions and joint ventures, partnering with the number-one or number-two brewers in growing markets. This strategy will allow A-BII to participate in beer industries around the world by investing in leading foreign brands, such as Corona in Mexico through Modelo. A-BII's goal is to share the best practices with its partners, allowing an open interchange of ideas that will benefit both partners.

Latin America

The development of Budweiser in Latin America is one of the keys to long-term growth in the international beer business as it is one of the world's fastest-growing beer markets. Anheuser-Busch products are sold in eleven Latin American countries—Argentina, Belize, Brazil, Chile, Ecuador, Mexico, Nicaragua, Panama, Paraguay,

TABLE 1
TOP TEN BEER BRANDS, 1998

Brand	Company	Share of World Beer Market
Budweiser	ABI	4.4%
Miller Lite	Miller Brewing Co.	1.7%
Kirin Lager	Kirin Brewery	1.7%
Bud Light	ABI	1.5%
Brahma Chopp	Companhia Cervejaria	1.4%
Coors Light	Coors Brewing Co.	1.4%
Heineken	Heineken NV	1.3%
Antarctica	Antarctica Paulista	1.3%
Polar	Cerveceria Polar SA	1.2%
Asahi Super Dry	Asahi Breweries	1.2%

Uruguay, and Venezuela—with a total population of over 350 million consumers. Particularly, the three countries showing the fastest growth in total beer consumption in the 1980–1999 period are Brazil (+200%), Colombia (130%), and Mexico (+100%). See also the Latin American countries' per capita GDP (Exhibit 1 at the end of the case).

Brazil. Anheuser-Busch International recently made an initial investment of 10 percent in a new Antarctica subsidiary in Brazil that consolidates all of Antarctica's holdings in affiliated companies and controls 75 percent of Antarctica's operations. Anheuser-Busch will have an option to increase its investment to approximately 30 percent in the new company in the future. The amount of the initial investment was approximately $105 million. The investment has established partnership that gives Antarctica a seat on the board of Anheuser-Busch, Inc. and gives Anheuser-Busch International proportionate representation on the board of the new Antarctica subsidiary. The two brewers will also explore joint distribution opportunities in the fast-growing South American beer market.

According to Scott Bussen (South American representative for A-BII), A-BII is currently in the process of signing a deal that calls for an establishment of an Anheuser-Busch–controlled marketing and distribution agreement between the two brewers to support sales of Budweiser in Brazil.

The deal makes Anheuser-Busch the first American brewer to hold an equity stake in the Brazilian beer market, which is the largest in Latin America and the sixth-largest in the world. Last year the Brazilian beer market grew by more than 15 percent. Its potential for future growth markets is one of the most important global beer markets.

The second component of the partnership will be a licensing agreement in which Antarctica will brew Budweiser in Brazil. The joint venture will be 51 percent owned and controlled by Anheuser-Busch, 49 percent by Antarctica. Antarctica's production plants will produce Budweiser according to the brand's quality requirements. Local sourcing of Budweiser will allow more competitive pricing and increased sales of the brand in Brazil. The agreement is expected to be signed sometime before the end of summer.

Antarctica, based in São Paulo, controls 35 percent of the Brazilian beer market. Its annual production in 1998 was about 20 million barrels of beer. Antarctica has a network of close to 1,000 Brazilian wholesalers. Prior to its investment in Antarctica, Budweiser had achieved a distribution foothold in the Brazilian beer market over in cooperation with its distributor, Arisco. Brazil has a population of 161 million people with per capita beer consumption in Brazil estimated to be 40 liters per year. With Brazil's population growing by 1.7 percent a year, reduced import duties, and free market reforms, Anheuser-Busch is expected to do well over the next decade in the Brazilian market.

The combined strengths of Anheuser-Busch and Antarctica in the booming Brazilian environment will lead to increased sales for both companies' products, resulting in a more competitive beer market, which benefits consumers, suppliers, and distribution in Brazil over the long term.

Mexico. In a further move to strengthen its international capabilities, Anheuser-Busch Companies purchased a 37 percent direct and indirect equity interest for $980 million in Grupo Modelo (located in Mexico City) and its subsidiaries, which thus far are privately held. Modelo is Mexico's largest brewer and the producer of Corona, that country's best-selling beer. The brewer has a 51 percent market share and exports to 56 countries. In connection with the purchases, three Anheuser-Busch representatives have been elected to the Modelo board, and a Modelo representative has been elected to serve on the Anheuser-Busch board.

Additionally the agreement includes the planned implementation of a program for the exchange of executives and management personnel between Modelo and Anheuser-Busch in key areas, including accounting/auditing, marketing, operations, planning, and finance. Modelo will remain Mexico's exclusive importer and distributor of Budweiser and other Anheuser-Busch brands, which have achieved a leadership position in imported beers sold in Mexico. These brands will continue to be brewed exclusively by Anheuser-Busch breweries in the United States. Currently Anheuser-Busch brews beer for Mexico at their Houston and Los Angeles breweries, which are not very far away but add to the markup of A-BII brands.

All of Modelo's brands will continue to be brewed exclusively in its seven existing Mexican breweries and a new brewery in North Central Mexico. U.S. distribution rights for the Modelo products are not involved in the arrangement. Corona and other Modelo brands will continue to be imported into the United States by Barton Beers and Gambrinus Company and distributed by those importers to beer wholesalers.

Modelo is the world's tenth-largest brewer and, through sales of Corona Modelo Especial, Pacifico, Negra Modelo and other regional brands, it holds more than 51 percent of the Mexican beer market. Its beer exports to 56 countries in North and South America, Asia, Australia, Europe, and Africa account for more than 69 percent of Mexico's total beer exports.

Modelo is one of several companies that distribute Budweiser besides Antarctica in Brazil and other local import-export companies in other Latin American countries. Modelo is the exclusive importer and distributor of Anheuser-Busch beers in Mexico. The newest brand, Ice Draft, will be the fourth ABI brand distributed in Mexico by Modelo, joining Budweiser, Bud Light, and O'Douls.

The Modelo agreement is significant because beer consumption has grown 6.5 percent annually in Mexico in the past few years. Mexico's beer consumption is the eighth-largest in the world but still only half of U.S. consumption. The per capita beer consumption rate in Mexico is estimated at 44 liters, compared to 87 liters per person in the United States, which is high given that Mexico's per capita income is one-tenth that of the United States. The Mexican market is expected to grow at a rapid rate.

Anheuser-Busch does not have control over pricing. The local wholesalers and retailers set prices for Budweiser. A-BII also does not have plans to set up a full-scale production facility in Mexico at this time.

Right now Budweiser is imported, which makes it two to three times higher in price than local beers. So it is largely an upscale, niche market brand at this time. An equity arrangement in another brewery or an agreement with Modelo could lead to local production and make A-BII brands more competitive with the local beer brands.

Besides the eleven Latin American countries mentioned, Anheuser-Busch has signed agreements with the largest brewers in Costa Rica, El Salvador, Guatemala, and Honduras to distribute and market Budweiser in their respective countries. Local breweries (Cervecerma Costa Rica in Costa Rica, La Constancia in El Salvador, Cervecerma Centroamericans in Guatemala, and Cervecerma Hondureqa in Honduras) distribute Budweiser in the 12-ounce bottles and 12-ounce aluminum cans.

These distribution agreements will allow Budweiser to expand its distribution throughout the rest of Central America. These countries have an extensive national distribution network and, more important, have local market expertise to develop Budweiser throughout the region.

Under the agreements, the Central American brewers will import Budweiser from Anheuser-Busch plants in Houston, Texas, and Williamsburg, Virginia. Anheuser-Busch will share responsibility for Budweiser's marketing with each of its Central American partners, supported by nationwide advertising and promotional campaigns.

ADVERTISING

Event Sponsorship

Given Budweiser's advertising approach traditionally built around sports, the decision to hold the 1994 World Cup tournament in the United States gave A-BII a perfect venue to pitch Budweiser to Latin Americans. The company signed a multimillion-dollar sponsorship deal with the World Cup Organizing Committee, making Budweiser the only beer authorized to use the World Cup logo. "The World Cup has become a vehicle for us to reach Latin America," said Charlie Acevedo, director of Latin American marketing for Anheuser-Busch International.

For ten months, soccer fans in South America saw the Bud logo on everything from soccer balls to beer glasses. Soccer fans collected a World Cup bumper sticker when they purchased a 12-pack of Bud. When they watched the game on television, they saw Budweiser signs decorating the stadiums and a glimpse of the Bud blimp hovering overhead. According to Charlie Acevedo, the goal is to make Budweiser a global icon, like McDonald's golden arches or Coca-Cola.

Anheuser-Busch just signed its second two-year agreement with ESPN Latin America. "Being able to buy on a regional basis gives a consistent message that is very reasonable in terms of cost," said Steve Burrows, A-BII's executive vice president of marketing.

Latin America offers promise with its youthful population and rising personal income. Half of Mexico's population is under 21, and other Latin American countries have similar profiles, offering opportunities for advertisers to reach the region's 450 million population.

The biggest new advertising opportunities in the Latin American market are Fox Latin America, MTV Latino, Cinemax Ole (a premium channel venture with Caracas cable operator Omnivision Latin American Entertainment), USA Network, and Telemundo (a 24-hour Spanish-language news channel). Marketers will have yet another panregional advertising option. Hughes (the U.S. aerospace company) and three Latin American partners—Multivision in Mexico, Televisao Abril in Brazil, and the Cisneros Group in Venezuela—launched a $700 million satellite that will beam programs in Spanish and Portuguese into homes across the continent. The service is called Direct TV. Because of this satellite, Central and South America have added 24 new channels. With digital compression technology, its capability could reach 144 cable channels.

In the past Anheuser-Busch used CNN international as its only ad vehicle, but with all the new opportunities, "the company will begin adding a local media presence throughout Latin America," said Robert Gunthner, A-BII's vice president of the Americas region. (See Table 2)

Anheuser-Busch will be using ads originally aimed at U.S. Hispanics, most of which were created by Carter Advertising of New York. A-BII will let the local agencies pick its messages, customize advertising, and do local media planning. In the past, there has been much criticism toward ABI's ethnocentric approach toward marketing Budweiser; however, because of the world obsession with American pop culture, they feel they don't need to tone down their American image. In Costa Rica, A-BII will use JBQ, San Jose; in El Salvador, Apex/BBDO, San Salvador; in Guatemala, Cerveceria's in-house media department; and in Honduras, McCann-Erickson Centroamericana, San Pedro.

Imported beers cost two or three times as much as locally brewed beers in South America, but thanks to cable television and product positioning in U.S. movies, Budweiser was already a well-known brand in South America when the company began exporting to the continent.

Strategy

According to Charlie Acevedo, Anheuser-Busch has seen double-digit increases in Latin American sales in the past five years. The gains came from both an increase in disposable income and increasingly favorable attitude toward U.S. products, especially in Argentina, Brazil, Chile, and Venezuela. Because Latin America has a very young population, Anheuser-Busch expects this market to grow at 4 percent annually. Furthermore, with NAFTA and a free trade zone, the company expects to see a significant rise in personal income in Latin American countries, which translates to great growth potential for Anheuser-Busch brands.

TABLE 2
PENETRATION OF PAID CABLE TV CHANNELS

Location	TV households (in millions)	Paid subscribers	Penetration rate
Brazil	30.0	3,300,000	15%
Mexico	14.0	1,700,000	12
Argentina	9.0	4,300,000	47
Chile	3.4	200,000	6
Venezuela	3.3	90,000	3
Uruguay	0.7	35,000	5
Ecuador	0.5	25,000	5
Paraguay	0.5	45,000	9

North American products and lifestyles are very much accepted in South America, but beer consumption still lags far behind U.S. levels. Argentines consume about 30 liters annually per capita. Brazilians 40 liters, Chileans 50 liters, and Venezuelans 65 liters, compared to 90 liters per person annually in the United States.

"The international focus will be almost completely on Budweiser because there is a worldwide trend toward less-heavy, less-bitter beers," and Jack Purnell, chair and chief executive officer of Anheuser-Busch International. They're counting on the American image to carry their beer, therefore opting for a universal campaign with American themes as opposed to tailoring Budweiser's image for local markets.

In the past ABI has tinkered with its formula and marketed Budweiser under different names to give a local flavor to their beer but had absolutely no success. Purnell said, "What the market does not need is an American brewery trying to make up from scratch, new European-style beers. Bud should be Bud wherever you get it."

OPPORTUNITIES

Mexico offers the U.S. exporter a variety of opportunities encompassing most product categories. Mexico is continuing to open its borders to imported products.

Mexico's population of approximately 92 million is the eleventh-largest in the world and the third largest in Latin America (after Brazil and Argentina). Mexico is a young country, with 69 percent of its population under thirty years of age. In addition the Mexican government has adopted new privitization policies decreasing its involvement in the country's economy. As a result private resources, both local and foreign, are playing a greater role in all areas of the Mexican economy.

Mexico's overall population in 1998 was estimated at 92.7 million people. Based on 1998 statistics, the age breakdown is as follows: under 15, 38 percent; 15–29, 29 percent; 30–44, 17 percent; 45–59, 9 percent; 60–74, 5 percent; 75 and over, 2 percent. The average age of the Mexican population was 23.3 years.

Between 1970 and 1990 the ratio of the population living in localities with between 100,000 and 500,000 inhabitants grew from 12 to 22 percent. This was largely due to rural–urban migration. More than 71 percent of the population lives in urban areas of Mexico. In 1990, 22 percent of the national population lived in Mexico City and the State of Mexico. The Mexican population is expected to rise to 112 million in the year 2010.

NAFTA, which aims to eliminate all tariffs on goods originating from Canada and the United States, is expected to create a massive market with more than 360 million people and $6 trillion in annual output.

EXHIBIT 1
GDP PER CAPITA IN SELECTED LATIN AMERICAN COUNTRIES

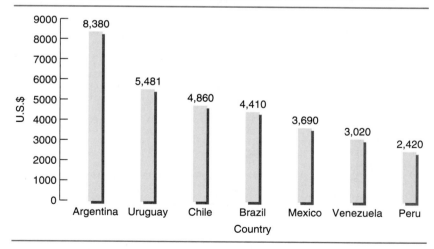

CASE 10

AOL GOES FAR EAST

On an uncharacteristically warm day in Tokyo in December 1999, John Barber, a managing director of AOL Japan, absentmindedly glanced out the window focusing on the sunlight gleaming off a nearby skyscraper. This was his third marketing meeting today, and he had the same sinking feeling about this one that he had about the other two and the hundreds before them. Like 90 percent of the other material that came from the marketing department, this one would flop. The local marketing staff was just not up to speed, and a great deal of resources were being wasted on this exercise in futility.

John had been in his current position since AOL Japan was established in 1997, and he was starting to get impatient. The company was not too far off on its subscription targets and the company was inching towards profitability; however, John was not satisfied. John felt that the company was not living up to the potential that one would expect of a JV between the largest Internet service provider in the world and one of Japan's largest companies.

Some critics complained that AOL entered the Japanese market too late. When AOL Japan started service in April 1997, Niftyserve and BigGlobe already had a large stable of dedicated users. However John dismissed this as being a major factor in the current difficulties. After all, when AOL Inc. registered its first online subscriber, CompuServe had been in business for more than eighteen years. Whatever the case, John was determined to find a way to catapult the company into the leading ISP position in Japan.

THE PARENT: AMERICA ONLINE INC.

America Online Inc. had a modest beginning. Founded in 1985 as Quantum computers, the company began by offering online services for Commodore Business Machines. By the time the World Wide Web came along almost twelve years later, AOL was well positioned to take advantage of it. The company grew at a steady pace for most of its history, but within the past two years, its revenue shot skyward as if gravity had suddenly dissolved. The company grew internally as well as acquiring many promising businesses. Exhibit 1 shows some of the major units of AOL Inc. in 1999.

Finances

America Online Inc. is currently on firm financial footing. The company brings in revenue from three sources: subscription fees, advertising, and the enterprise solutions group.

In 1999, 69 percent of total revenue came from the 20 million paying subscribers to AOL and CompuServe services. Due to the dangers of relying heavily on subscription fees in such a competitive market, the company has clearly stated that it intends to move away from subscriptions and rely more heavily on advertising. Therefore, it should not be a surprise that the fastest-growing segment of revenue comes from the "advertising, commerce and other" category. This category includes online advertising fees, sales of merchandise, as well as other revenues. In 1999, the "advertising, commerce and other" segment accounted for 21 percent of total revenue, as compared to 14 percent of total revenue in 1997. The Enterprise Solutions generates revenue from licensing fees, technical support, consulting, and training services. This segment continues to decrease in importance. In 1997, this segment provided 16.9 percent of total revenue. This figure declined to 10 percent in 1999. The financial information shows that 1999 was AOL's best year ever. Exhibit 2 shows operating income and net income from 1997 to date as well as the cash held in 1999.

International Expansion

AOL's 1999 Annual Report states, "The Company's international strategy is to provide consumers with local services in key international markets featuring local language, content, marketing, and community." AOL started its international expansion in Germany almost five years ago. Since that time, the company has expanded into Australia, Brazil, Canada, France, Japan, United Kingdom, Sweden, and Hong Kong. Jack Davies, vice president of International Operations, led the expansion.

All the Joint Ventures have been undertaken with a partner in the local market. In Germany, AOL chose Bertelsmann AG (Multimedia Company), and in Latin

This case was prepared by Bill Baker, Steven Engen, and Trevor Nelson of Temple University Japan under the supervision of Professor Masaaki Kotabe for class discussion, rather than to illustrate either effective or ineffective management of a situation described (February 2000).

EXHIBIT 1

DIVISIONS OF AMERICA ONLINE INC.

Business Unit	Type of Business	Members	Access	Acquired or Developed
AOL	Internet online service	19,000,000	Subscription	Developed
CompuServe	Internet online service	2,000,000	Subscription	Acquired
Netscape Netcenter	Internet portal	17,000,000	Free	Acquired
AOL Instant Messenger	Web-based communication service	25,000,000	Free	Developed
ICQ	Web-based communication service	50,000,000	Free	Acquired
Digital City	Local online content provider	4,300,000 core	Free	Partnership
AOL MovieFone	Movie guide and ticketing service	150,000,000 hits in 1998	Free	Acquired
Spinner Networks	Internet music provider	2,000,000 core	Free	Acquired

Source: America Online Inc. 1999 Annual Report.

America, it joined with Cisneros (media, entertainment, and telecommunications company). However, in Japan, AOL chose Mitsui & Co., one of Japan's largest and oldest general trading companies.

Mitsui & Co.

Mitsui & Company was founded in 1941. The company was originally part of the Mitsui *zaibatsu* that was bro-

ken up after the end of World War II. Mitsui has more than 11,000 employees in sixty countries, and in 1998 had capital of US$1.9B. Mitsui is known as one of the most traditional trading companies in Japan. Exhibit 3 shows a list of products they are most familiar with. Like most "general" trading companies in Japan, Mitsui's real strength is in facilitating large transactions for commodity-type products. Its core competency, if any, is in import, export, and financing.

EXHIBIT 2

OPERATING INCOME AND NET INCOME: 1997–99

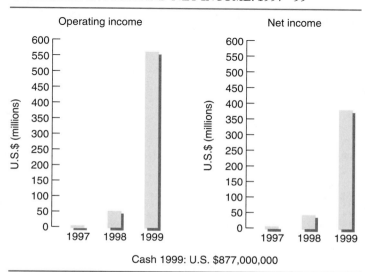

Cash 1999: U.S. $877,000,000

EXHIBIT 3
SAMPLE OF MITSUI PRODUCT PORTFOLIO

Iron and Steel	Energy
Non-Ferrous Metals	Foods
Property Development	Textiles
Machinery	General Merchandise
Electronics	Chemicals

Source: Mitsui & Co. Web Site: http://www.mitsui.co.jp/tk-abz/english/iandpp/index.htm

Mitsui certainly has all the connections and money that are required to succeed in the Japanese "general products" market, but it had very little experience with anything concerning the Internet, especially in 1995 when the discussions with AOL began.

OVERVIEW: INTERNET IN JAPAN

Japan, although catching up, is still lagging behind the United States in terms of connectivity. There are an estimated 46 million households in Japan, of which 33 percent (15 million) have a PC. In addition, only 18 percent of households (8 million) are connected online. Nevertheless, the number of online households is expected to grow significantly, fueled by several factors. First, the number of PC shipments domestically reached 10 million by 2000 (a 12 percent increase from 1999). This would mark the third straight year of double-digit PC growth. In addition, there are clear trends toward lower connection costs for end users. The high cost of connecting to the Internet has been recognized as a primary barrier restricting the percent of Japanese going online. Lower access charges are expected to reduce this barrier and get more consumers connected.

There are five primary ISPs in Japan fighting for market share. The largest is Niftyserve (19%), followed by BigGlobe (7%), DTI (7%), AOL Japan (3%), and CompuServe (1%). A plethora of small-to-midsize ISP companies make up the remaining 63 percent market share.

AOL JAPAN

AOL Japan was established in February 1996 and rolled out its services on April 15, 1997, amid much excitement, as people familiar with the "AOL success story" in the United States held high expectations for AOL's entry into the second-largest economy. *Wired* magazine hailed AOL's entry into Japan, stating, "AOL's Japanese service is certain to cause waves in a nation unaccustomed to competitive pricing for Net access." In an interview at this time, Jack Davies, then AOL's president of new market development, stated, "Our focus is going to be in the consumer market. We think that is going to be the major growth area in the Japanese market over the next five years." Indeed, AOL had hopes for its Japan operations to become its second-largest subscriber base.

Setting up the Business

AOL decided on a joint venture collaboration with local partners as its entry into the Japan market. AOL Japan was established as a joint venture between AOL (50%), Mitsui & Co. (40%) and Nihon Keizai Shinbun ("Nikkei") (10%). According to AOL management, the collaboration with two well-established Japanese companies was an essential component to its strategy; AOL "wouldn't think about going into a major international market without partners. AOL's relationship with Mitsui dated back to the early 1990s, at which time Mitsui USA began researching Internet service providers and was attracted by the potential of AOL. Mitsui USA research on AOL led eventually to meetings with AOL in 1994 to explore entering the Japanese online service market. In late 1995, Mitsui and AOL agreed on the structure of the JV. Mitsui believed it was crucial to have fresh, Japanese content provided to consumers, and therefore introduced Nikkei to AOL, who later agreed on Nikkei becoming a partner in the business. At the onset, Nikkei and Mitsui provided the necessary capital and invested a combined $50 million to get the Japanese business up and operational. For its part, AOL provided value to the collaboration in the form of its technology, know-how, and brand name.

Management Structure

The board of directors of AOL Japan is comprised of seven people, including three non-Japanese people from the U.S. AOL operations. Only one of these non-Japanese board members, Mr. John Barber, lives in Japan and participates in day-to-day operations. The current president of AOL Japan is Kozuo Hiramatsu, who joined the company in July 1999 after serving eight years as president of IDG Corporation. The following five groups report to the president:

- Member Services
- General Affairs
- Marketing
- Content
- Technology

Recruiting responsibilities have rested almost entirely with Mitsui. This includes hiring of top management, although AOL has the ultimate power to approve or reject the nomination. Initially, AOL Japan was staffed primarily with Mitsui employees. In 1997, the company had 120 employees. This number had grown to 230 in 1999.

Management Difficulties

Two years after launching its services in Japan, AOL Japan has clearly not succeeded in meeting initial expectations. The subscriber base, although growing steadily each year, only totals approximately 400,000, a number that is dwarfed by Niftyserve's subscriber base of more than 2.5 million. In the two years since its inception, AOL Japan has experienced a number of difficulties with management. In particular, the company is currently on its third president (Mr. Hiramatsu). The first two presidents, selected by Mitsui, were determined to be unable to take AOL Japan to the next level. After two such failures, AOL decided that it would be responsible for searching and hiring the next president. After a long search, the company hired Mr. Hiramatsu, who is still trying to convince insiders and outsiders alike that he has the "right stuff."

According to John Barber, the difficulty lies in finding top local people who have the necessary managing experience and who have the essential marketing savvy to compete in the world of "Internet time." Such a person has become somewhat of a *Holy Grail*, according to Mr. Barber. The problem is that in Japan, most managers do not reach their position until after the age of forty. This would not be a problem, except that most people over forty lack the leadership and vision necessary to run an Internet ISP. The jury apparently is still out on Mr. Hiramatsu.

AOL certainly has not helped this situation by placing only one non-Japanese AOL person on the ground in Japan. Many of the challenges facing the Japanese corporation are similar to those faced by the U.S. business. One has to believe that AOL Japan would benefit by more experienced AOL non-Japanese participating in the daily operations and management of AOL Japan.

Marketing Organization at AOL Japan

The staffing for the marketing organization in Japan is the responsibility of the Mitsui team. Mitsui has hired all local employees in the marketing department. The marketing organization is one of the five groups that report directly to the president of AOL Japan. The marketing organization is also responsible for the MIS system used to drive their marketing decisions.

The marketing strategy initially employed was based on the strategy that was successful for AOL in the United States. The marketing group in Japan, however, does try its own strategies in addition to those recommended from the United States.

The initial and primary strategy consisted of three main approaches to capturing market share in Japan.

The first is referred to as bundling. The second is the use of magazine inserts. The third approach is the use of direct mail solicitations. A fourth, newer strategy is called *Take-ones*.

Bundling. Bundling is the process by which a PC maker includes AOL software preinstalled on each PC. In this case, when the customer boots the machine, the AOL icon is visible on the desktop. The customer also receives AOL documentation in the box. AOL usually has an offer of X free hours at no risk to the customer for trial usage. If the customer decides to join AOL, it can be done easily just by clicking the AOL icon on the desktop.

Another method of bundling is to have an agreement with the operating system (OS) manufacturer—in this case, Microsoft. By bundling with Microsoft, AOL can ensure that it has a copy of its software on each PC—whether or not AOL has an agreement with the PC manufacturer. The only issue with the installation in the OS is that it is buried within a folder in the OS files so it is not easily accessible to the casual user.

Bundling in the United States has been very successful for America Online. This promotion was responsible for more than 30 percent of the users in the United States (somewhere around 6 million customers). The U.S. manufacturers such as Compaq, Dell, and Gateway, as well as many smaller manufacturers, initially were not interested in the ISP business, so the relationship with AOL was symbiotic with the PC manufacturer because Internet access was an application that drove customers to upgrade their PCs. The consumer received some benefit from having the ISP sign-up form easily accessible from the desktop. In addition, the PC manufacturers received some commission based on the number of customers that signed up for the service.

AOL Japan has also used bundling as the primary mechanism of signing up new users. They have been able to sign contracts with twelve to fifteen PC manufacturers in Japan (including U.S. manufacturers active in the Japanese market). The PC manufacturers in Japan, contrary to the U.S. manufacturers are much more active in the ISP business. Fujitsu, which is one of the top three PC makers in Japan, also owns the largest ISP in Japan, Nifty-Serve. NEC, the largest PC manufacturer in Japan, also owns an ISP. The ISP is BigGlobe, and it is the second largest ISP in Japan. Sony also owns Soo-net, an ISP in Japan. The relationship between the ISPs and the PC manufacturers in Japan is more complicated than in the United States because of the tendencies of the PC manufacturers to be ISP providers as well.

Magazine Inserts. Another successful marketing technique for AOL in America is the use of magazine inserts to deliver the AOL software via CDs inserted into the magazine. One way of doing this was to shrink-wrap each magazine with a CD placed within the shrink-wrap. Another, but more expensive, technique is to actually have the CD attached to a page within the magazine itself. The magazine insert techniques were responsible for initial enrollment of about 30 percent (around 6 million users) of the AOL U.S. customers.

AOL Japan's results with magazine inserts have been disappointing. One of the issues is that the magazine companies, in general, have been tough to do business with. In addition, the shrink-wrapping of magazines is not as prevalent in Japan. AOL Japan has been able to do some magazine inserts, but they have also gone a step further in a couple of marketing promotions. AOL Japan has created its own magazine, which is issued when there is a major software upgrade. It is sold on the newsstands like a normal magazine. Overall, however, the customer hit-rate per yen for magazine insert promotions has been lower than the results obtained via bundling.

Direct Mail.   Direct mail has also been responsible for initial sign-up of about 30 percent of the U.S. AOL customers. However, in Japan, this approach has not been particularly successful. According to John Barber, there are two fundamental issues. The first is the lack of available mailing lists that accurately pinpoint the desired customer base. The second is the fact that the mailing costs in Japan are much higher. The combination of these two points causes the number of new subscribers/yen to be much lower for direct-mail marketing in Japan than in the United States.

Take-Ones.   Another marketing technique for finding new subscribers is called Take-ones. This is where the AOL software CD is prepackaged in a small, thin, package and then put on display in places where potential customers might congregate. One natural place is computer stores, such as SoftMap, where one can find a stack of AOL Take-ones next to the cash register. If the customer is interested in connecting to the Web, he or she would "take one" home. According to John Barber, the Take-ones have been reasonably successful in Japan. The hit-rate for Take-ones is much higher than direct mail or magazine inserts because those who take one home have a much higher level of interest in signing up with an ISP than the reader of a magazine or someone who receives an unsolicited mail offer. In addition, AOL Japan usually combines the Take-ones with another promotion—such as Pokemon or a movie, like *Tarzan*—to increase the hit rate of the Take-ones. The cross promotion with Pokemon had one unexpected drawback—the parents of the children swamped the AOL User Support Line with orders for Pokemon cards!

Moving Forward

AOL Japan's share of the Japan market has grown from nothing to about 3 percent over the past three years. Other ISPs have been relatively flat. In addition, AOL Japan has been capturing 10 to 15 percent of the new subscribers to the Internet in Japan over the past two years. Although other ISPs might be satisfied with this progress, AOL has about a 50 percent market share in the United States and will not be happy with such a small share of the market in Japan.

According to John Barber, AOL Japan looks at three different ways to grow its market share:

- *Increase marketing efficiency*—If AOL Japan can lower the amount of yen it takes to capture a subscriber, then it can capture a higher percentage of new users to the Internet.

- *Take advantage of watershed events*—As technology changes the nature of the Internet or creates new ways to the Internet, there will be opportunities to capture new users through support of these technologies. If AOL anticipates these changes better than other ISPs, it has the opportunity to capture more market share. One example is Internet access via mobile phones. In less than one year, NTT Docomo, with its Imode Internet Access service via the displays on portable phones, went from 0 to 3 million subscribers. This is despite the fact that the services via the portable phone are very limited.

- *Buy other ISPs*—There are many thousands of ISPs in Japan. Many of them are very small and are potential takeover candidates.

QUESTIONS TO CONSIDER

1. Was Mitsui the best partner for AOL to enter the Japanese market? If so, why? If not, what kind of company would make a better partner? Why?

2. What do you think John Barber should recommend to AOL to gain a more stable JV management team?

3. Do you think the current JV structure should continue into the foreseeable future?

4. What structural impediments did AOL face in the Japanese market that do not exist in the U.S. market? What actions should AOL take to overcome these obstacles?

5. Make specific recommendations as to what you think AOL should do to capture additional market share in each of the three areas mentioned: Lower the cost of ¥/new subscriber; capitalize on watershed events; buy other ISPs.

SUBJECT INDEX

Page references in *italic* type indicate illustrations. Page references followed by italic *t* indicate material in tables; italic *n* indicates footnotes. **715**

AUTHOR INDEX

COMPANY INDEX

PHOTO CREDITS